PHILIP'S

STREET ATLAS
West Sussex

First published in 1998 by

Philip's, a division of
Octopus Publishing Group Ltd
2–4 Heron Quays, London E14 4JP

Second colour edition 2001
Second impression 2003

ISBN 0-540-08019-5 (hardback)
ISBN 0-540-08020-9 (spiral)

Printed and bound in Spain
by Cayfosa-Quebecor

Contents

III **Key to map symbols**

IV **Key to map pages**

VI **Route planning**

VIII **Administrative and Postcode boundaries**

1 **Street maps** at 3½ inches to 1 mile

207 **Street map of Brighton city centre** at 7 inches to 1 mile

208 **Town maps of** Eastbourne, Hastings, Lewes and Royal Tunbridge Wells

210 **Index** of towns and villages

211 **Index** of streets, hospitals, industrial estates, railway stations, schools, shopping centres and universities

Digital Data

The exceptionally high-quality mapping found in this atlas is available as digital data in TIFF format, which is easily convertible to other bitmapped (raster) image formats.

The index is also available in digital form as a standard database table. It contains all the details found in the printed index together with the National Grid reference for the map square in which each entry is named.

For further information and to discuss your requirements, please contact Philip's on 020 7531 8439 or ruth.king@philips-maps.co.uk

22a	**Motorway** with junction number
	Primary route – dual/single carriageway
	A road – dual/single carriageway
	B road – dual/single carriageway
	Minor road – dual/single carriageway
	Other minor road – dual/single carriageway
	Road under construction
	Pedestrianised area
DY7	**Postcode boundaries**
	County and unitary authority boundaries
	Railway
	Tramway, miniature railway
	Rural track, private road or narrow road in urban area
	Gate or obstruction to traffic (restrictions may not apply at all times or to all vehicles)
	Path, bridleway, byway open to all traffic, road used as a public path
	The representation in this atlas of a road, track or path is no evidence of the existence right of way
199 156	**Adjoining page indicators**
207	**The map area within the pink band is shown at a larger scale on the page indicated by the red block and arrow**

Abbreviation	Meaning	Abbreviation	Meaning
Allot Gdns	**Allotments**	Meml	**Memorial**
Acad	**Academy**	Mon	**Monument**
Cemy	**Cemetery**	Mus	**Museum**
C Ctr	**Civic Centre**	Obsy	**Observatory**
CH	**Club House**	Pal	**Royal Palace**
Coll	**College**	PH	**Public House**
Crem	**Crematorium**	Recn Gd	**Recreation Ground**
Ent	**Enterprise**	Resr	**Reservoir**
Ex H	**Exhibition Hall**	Ret Pk	**Retail Park**
Ind Est	**Industrial Estate**	Sch	**School**
Inst	**Institute**	Sh Ctr	**Shopping Centre**
Ct	**Law Court**	TH	**Town Hall/House**
L Ctr	**Leisure Centre**	Trad Est	**Trading Estate**
LC	**Level Crossing**	Univ	**University**
Liby	**Library**	Wks	**Works**
Mkt	**Market**	YH	**Youth Hostel**

Walsall	**Railway station**
	Private railway station
	Bus, coach station
	Ambulance station
	Coastguard station
	Fire station
	Police station
	Accident and Emergency entrance to hospital
H	**Hospital**
	Place of worship
i	**Information Centre** (open all year)
P	**Parking**
P&R	**Park and Ride**
PO	**Post Office**
	Camping site
	Caravan site
	Golf course
	Picnic site
Prim Sch	**Important buildings, schools, colleges, universities and hospitals**
River Medway	**Water name**
	Stream
	River or canal – minor and major
	Water
	Tidal water
	Woods
	Houses
House	**Non-Roman antiquity**
VILLA	**Roman antiquity**

■ The dark grey border on the inside edge of some pages indicates that the mapping does not continue onto the adjacent page

■ The small numbers around the edges of the maps identify the 1 kilometre National Grid lines

The scale of the maps is 5.52 cm to 1 km $3\frac{1}{2}$ inches to 1 mile 1: 18103

0 – 1/4 – 1/2 – 3/4 – 1 mile
0 – 250 m – 500 m – 750 m – 1 kilometre

The scale of the maps on pages numbered in red is 11.04 cm to 1 km 7 inches to 1 mile 1: 9051.4

0 – 220 yards – 440 yards – 660 yards – 1/2 mile
0 – 125 m – 250 m – 375 m – 1/2 kilometre

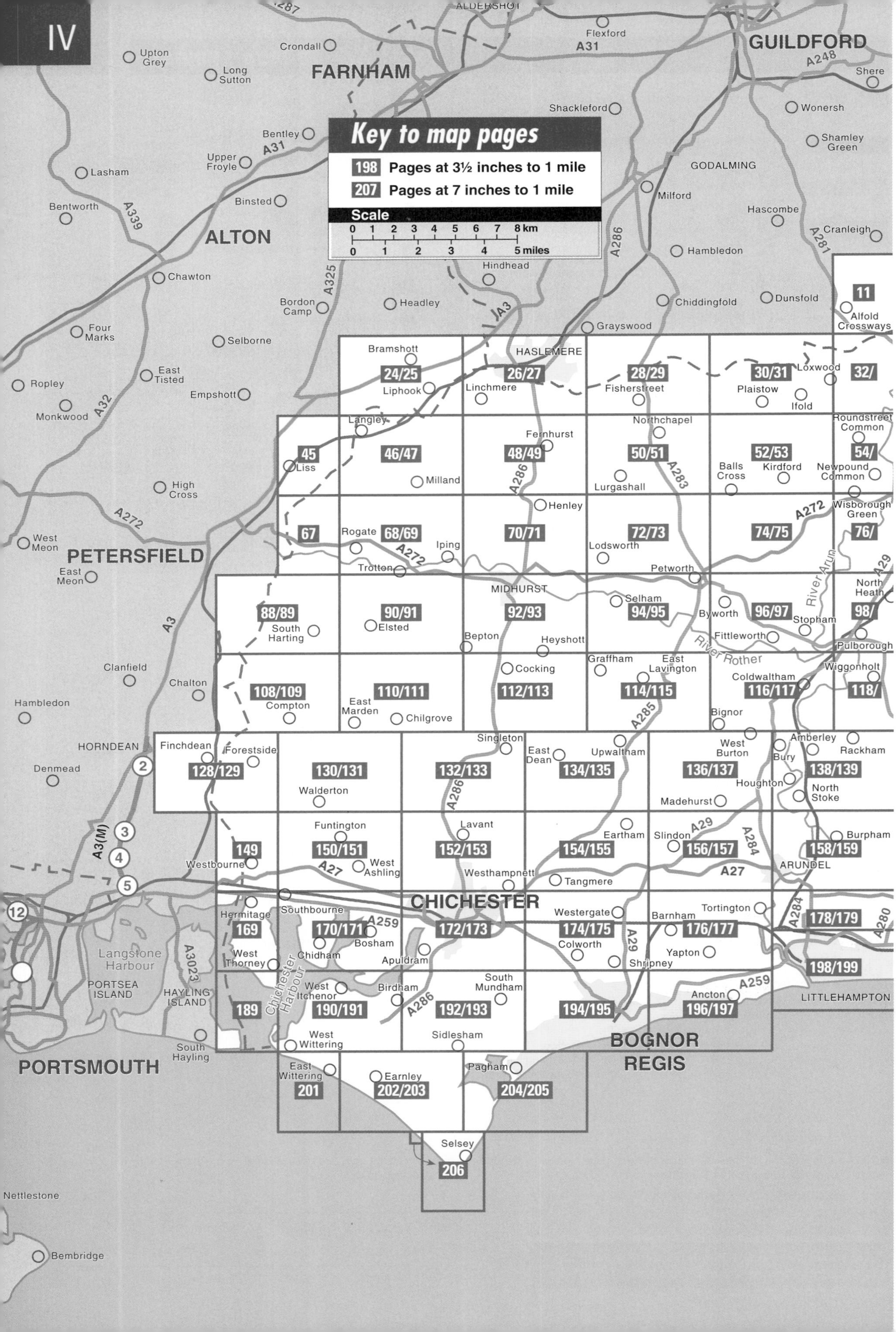
Key to map pages
198 Pages at 3½ inches to 1 mile
207 Pages at 7 inches to 1 mile
Scale
0 1 2 3 4 5 6 7 8 km
0 1 2 3 4 5 miles
ALDERSHOT
Flexford
A31
GUILDFORD
A248
Shere
Upton Grey
Crondall
Long Sutton
FARNHAM
Shackleford
Wonersh
Shamley Green
Bentley
A31
Upper Froyle
Lasham
GODALMING
Milford
Bentworth
A339
Binsted
ALTON
Hascombe
Cranleigh
A281
A286
Hambledon
Chawton
A325
Hindhead
Bordon Camp
Headley
A3
Chiddingfold
Dunsfold
11
Alfold Crossways
Four Marks
Selborne
Grayswood
Bramshott
HASLEMERE
24/25
26/27
28/29
30/31
32/
Loxwood
East Tisted
Ropley
Empshott
Liphook
Linchmere
Fisherstreet
Plaistow
Ifold
Monkwood
A32
Langley
Northchapel
Roundstreet Common
Fernhurst
45
46/47
48/49
50/51
52/53
54/
Liss
Milland
A286
A283
Balls Cross
Kirdford
Newpound Common
Lurgashall
High Cross
A272
Henley
Wisborough Green
A272
West Meon
67
Rogate
68/69
70/71
72/73
74/75
76/
Iping
Lodsworth
PETERSFIELD
A272
Trotton
Petworth
East Meon
River Arun
A29
MIDHURST
North Heath
88/89
90/91
92/93
Selham
94/95
Byworth
96/97
98/
South Harting
Elsted
Stopham
A3
Bepton
Heyshott
Fittleworth
Pulborough
River Rother
Clanfield
Graffham
East Lavington
Wiggonholt
Cocking
Coldwaltham
Chalton
108/109
110/111
112/113
114/115
116/117
118/
Hambledon
Compton
East Marden
Chilgrove
A285
Bignor
HORNDEAN
Singleton
West Burton
Amberley
Rackham
Finchdean
Forestside
East Dean
Upwaltham
Bury
Denmead
128/129
130/131
132/133
134/135
136/137
138/139
Houghton
North Stoke
Walderton
A286
Madehurst
Funtington
Lavant
Eartham
Slindon
A29
Burpham
A3(M)
149
150/151
152/153
154/155
156/157
158/159
West Ashling
A284
Westbourne
A27
Westhampnett
A27
ARUNDEL
Tangmere
Southbourne
CHICHESTER
Hermitage
A259
Westergate
Tortington
169
170/171
172/173
174/175
176/177
178/179
Barnham
A284
A280
Bosham
Colworth
A29
Langstone Harbour
A3023
West Thorney
Chidham
Apuldram
Yapton
Shripney
198/199
PORTSEA ISLAND
HAYLING ISLAND
Chichester Harbour
West Itchenor
Birdham
South Mundham
A259
Ancton
189
190/191
192/193
194/195
196/197
A286
LITTLEHAMPTON
West Wittering
Sidlesham
BOGNOR REGIS
South Hayling
PORTSMOUTH
East Wittering
Earnley
Pagham
201
202/203
204/205
Selsey
206
Nettlestone
Bembridge
2
3
4
5
12

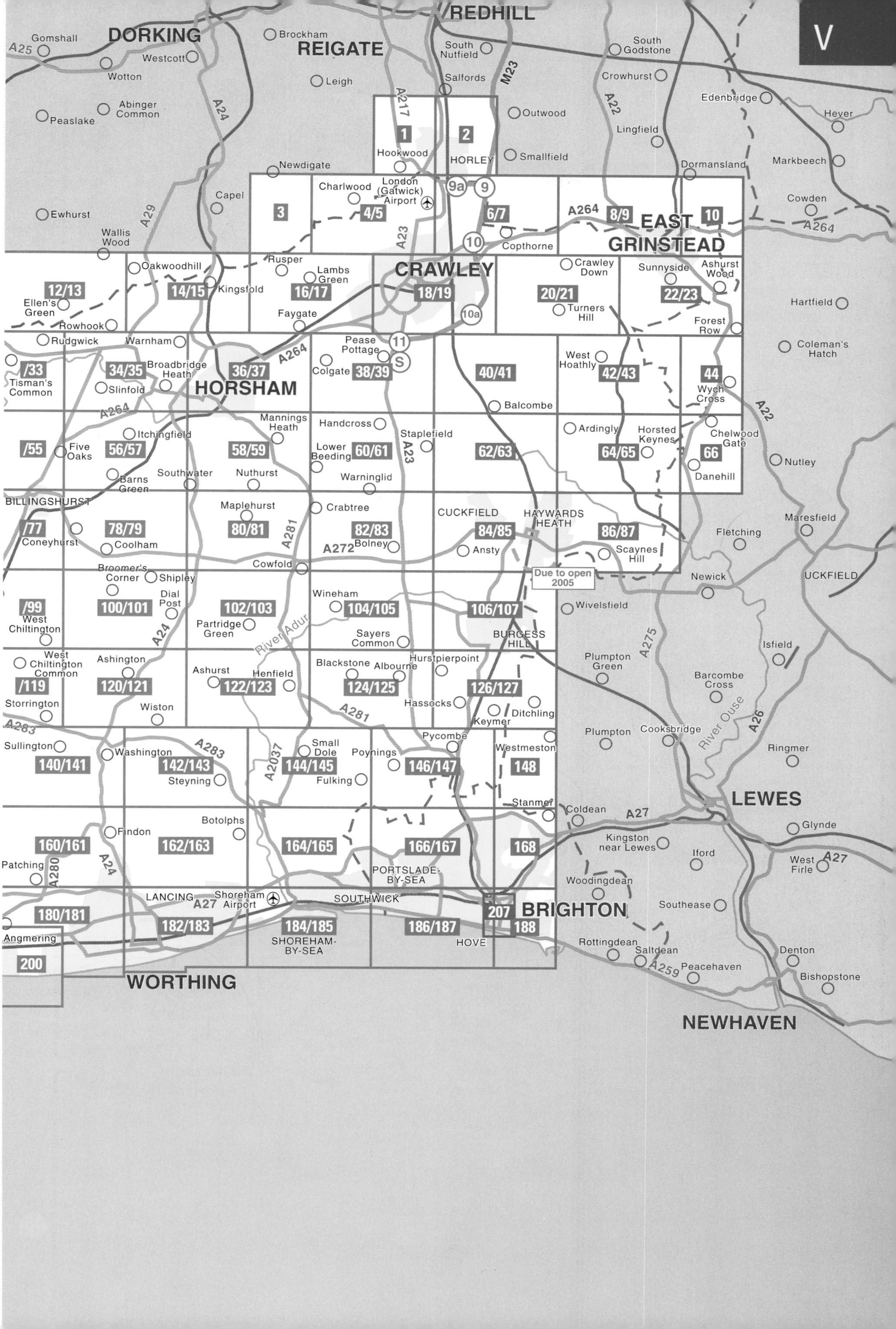

REDHILL
DORKING
Gomshall
A25
Westcott
Wotton
Brockham
REIGATE
South Nutfield
South Godstone
Leigh
Salfords
M23
Crowhurst
Peaslake
Abinger Common
A24
A217
Outwood
A22
Edenbridge
Heyer
1
2
Lingfield
Hookwood
HORLEY
Smallfield
Markbeech
Newdigate
Dormansland
Capel
Charlwood
London (Gatwick) Airport
9a
9
Cowden
3
4/5
6/7
A264
8/9
EAST GRINSTEAD
10
Ewhurst
A29
A23
10
Copthorne
A264
Walls Wood
Rusper
CRAWLEY
Crawley Down
Sunnyside
Ashurst Wood
Oakwoodhill
Lambs Green
12/13
14/15
Kingsfold
16/17
18/19
20/21
22/23
Hartfield
Ellen's Green
Faygate
10a
Turners Hill
Forest Row
Rowhook
Rudgwick
Warnham
Pease Pottage
11
Coleman's Hatch
A264
S
West Hoathly
/33
34/35
Broadbridge Heath
36/37
Colgate
38/39
40/41
42/43
44
Tisman's Common
Slinfold
HORSHAM
Wych Cross
Balcombe
A264
A22
Mannings Heath
Handcross
Staplefield
Ardingly
Horsted Keynes
Chelwood Gate
Itchingfield
/55
Five Oaks
56/57
58/59
Lower Beeding
60/61
A23
62/63
64/65
66
Nutley
Barns Green
Southwater
Nuthurst
Warninglid
Danehill
BILLINGSHURST
Maplehurst
Crabtree
CUCKFIELD
HAYWARDS HEATH
Maresfield
/77
78/79
80/81
A281
82/83
84/85
86/87
Fletching
Coneyhurst
Coolham
A272
Bolney
Ansty
Scaynes Hill
Cowfold
Broomer's Corner
Shipley
Due to open 2005
Newick
UCKFIELD
Dial Post
Wineham
/99
100/101
102/103
104/105
106/107
Wivelsfield
West Chiltington
Partridge Green
A24
River Adur
Sayers Common
BURGESS HILL
A275
Isfield
West Chiltington Common
Ashington
Hurstpierpoint
Plumpton Green
Ashurst
Henfield
Blackstone
Albourne
/119
120/121
122/123
124/125
126/127
Barcombe Cross
Storrington
Wiston
A281
Hassocks
Ditchling
Keymer
A283
A26
River Ouse
Sullington
Washington
A283
A2037
Small Dole
Poynings
Pycombe
Westmeston
Plumpton
Cooksbridge
Ringmer
140/141
142/143
144/145
146/147
148
Steyning
Fulking
Stanmer
LEWES
Coldean
A27
Botolphs
Findon
Glynde
Kingston near Lewes
160/161
162/163
164/165
166/167
168
Iford
West Firle
A27
Patching
A280
A24
PORTSLADE-BY-SEA
Woodingdean
LANCING
Shoreham Airport
A27
SOUTHWICK
207
BRIGHTON
Southease
180/181
182/183
184/185
186/187
188
Angmering
SHOREHAM-BY-SEA
HOVE
Rottingdean
Saltdean
Denton
A259
Peacehaven
200
Bishopstone
WORTHING
NEWHAVEN

Route planning
Scale
0 1 2 3 4 5 6 7 8 km
0 1 2 3 4 5 miles
Crookham
Crookham Village
Up Nately
North Warnborough
Greywell
Odiham
ALDERSHOT
Normandy
Wood Street
Stoughton
Burpham
Ash
Heath End
Mill Lane
Ewshot
Crondall
Hale
Flexford
Onslow Village
GUILDFORD
Tonghams
Puttenham
Hog's Back
Tunworth
Upton Grey
Long Sutton
FARNHAM
Winslade
Herriard
Weston Patrick
South Warnborough
Well
Dippenhall
Runfold
Seale
Compton
Shalford
Albury
Chilworth
Blackheath
Wonersh
Farncombe
Shackleford
Ellisfield
Southrope
Bentley
Waverley Abbey
Tilford
Peper Harow
Elstead
GODALMING
Bramley
Shamley Green
Golden Pot
Lasham
Shalden
Bradley
Lower Wield
Bentworth
Holybourne
Milford
Wheelerstreet
Busbridge
Thorncombe Street
Hydestile
Rowly
Rushmoor
Thursley
Witley
Hascombe
Thedden Grange
ALTON
Wyck
East Worldham
Kingsley
Churt
Bowlhead Green
Brook
Hambledon
Loxhill
Medstead
Beech
West Worldham
Sleaford
Lindford
Bordon Camp
Hindhead
Gibbet Hill
Chiddingfold
Dunsfold
Alfold Crossways
Chawton
Lower Farringdon
Upper Farringdon
Oakhanger
Selborne
Whitehill
Headley
Standford
Grayshott
Grayswood
Four Marks
North Street
Kitwood
Blackmoor
BORDON
Shottermill
HASLEMERE
Tisman's Common
Ropley
Newton Valence
Longmoor Camp
Bramshott
Liphook
Camelsdale
Kingsley Green
Fisherstreet
Plaistow
Ifold
Loxwood
Monkwood
East Tisted
Empshott
Greatham
Liss Forest
Linchmere
Hawkley
Langley
LOW
West Tisted
Liss
East Liss
Fernhurst
Northchapel
Rake
Milland
Lurgashall
Kirdford
Privett
High Cross
Steep
Hill Brow
Henley
Lickfold
Balls Cross
Wisborough Green
Froxfield Green
Sheet
Stroud
Langrish
Ramsdean
Weston
PETERSFIELD
Rogate
Chithurst
Trotton
Iping
Woolbeding
Stedham
Easebourne
Lodsworth
Upperton
Petworth House
Petworth
North Heath
East Meon
Butser Hill
Old Winchester Hill
Nursted
East Harting
Nyewood
Elsted
MIDHURST
West Lavington
South Ambersham
Selham
Tillington
R Rother
Byworth
Fittleworth
Buriton
South Harting
War Down
Treyford
Bepton
Heyshott
Graffham
Stopham
Hardham
Pulborough
Wiggonholt
Greatham
Waterfield
Chidden
Clanfield
Chalton
Uppark
North Marden
Cocking
SOUTH DOWNS
Duncton
Barlavington
Coldwaltham
East Lavington
Sutton
Hambledon
Catherington
Chilgrove
Compton
East Marden
West Marden
Singleton
Charlton
East Dean
Upwaltham
Bignor
West Burton
Rackham
Bury
Amberley
Anthill Common
HORNDEAN
Blendworth
Finchdean
Rowlands Castle
Denmead
Cowplain
FOREST OF BERE
Forestside
Stoughton
West Dean
The Trundle
Houghton
North Stoke
South Stoke
Waterlooville
A3(M)
Walderton
Madehurst
Eartham
Slindon
Arundel Park
Purbrook
HAVANT
Westbourne
Funtington
Woodmancote
Woodend
West Stoke
Lavant
Goodwood House
Halnaker
Fontwell
Burpham
Bedhampton
East Ashling
West Ashling
Strettington
Boxgrove
ARUNDEL
Hambrook
Westhampnett
Tangmere
Norton
Nyton
Walberton
Wymering
Drayton
Cosham
Langstone
EMSWORTH
Hermitage
Southbourne
Broadbridge
Fishbourne
Aldingbourne
Oving
Westergate
Eastergate
Barnham
Tortington
Lyminster
Poling
Hilsea
North Hayling
Thorney Island
Chidham
Bosham
Apuldram
CHICHESTER
Merston
Woodgate
Colworth
Shripney
Yapton
Ford
Wick
North End
Langstone Harbour
Stoke
West Thorney
Chichester Harbour
Emsworth Channel
Donnington
North Mundham
Runcton
Flansham
Climping
Rustington
PORTSEA ISLAND
HAYLING ISLAND
West Itchenor
Hunston
Bersted
Ancton
LITTLEHAMPTON
Fratton
South Hayling
Shipton Green
Birdham
South Mundham
Felpham
Middleton-on-Sea
Eastney
Street End
Nyetimber
Aldwick
BOGNOR REGIS
PORTSMOUTH
Hayling Bay
West Wittering
Somerley
Sidlesham
Pagham
Highleigh
Pagham Harbour
East Wittering
Earnley
Church Norton
Spitbank Fort
Horse Sand Fort
No Man's land Fort
Bracklesham Bay
Selsey
SELSEY BILL
Nettlestone Point
Seaview
Nettlestone
The Priory
St Helen's Fort
Bembridge Point
Bembridge
FORELAND
Whitecliff
M3
M275
A3
A31
A272
A27
A29
A285
A286
A283
A281
A32
A3100
A259
A288
A3023
B3000
B3006
B3004
B2070
B2146
B2145
B2131
B2130
B2133
B2166
B2233
B2198
B3395

East Clandon
Westhumble
Hermitage
Buckland
Godstone
Limpsfield
Oxted
Crockham Hill
DORKING
REDHILL
Nutfield
Bletchingley
Tandridge
Hurst Green
Brockham
Betchworth
REIGATE
South Nutfield
Godstone Sta
South Godstone
Gomshall
Westcott
Wotton
Shere
Abinger Hammer
Sutton Abinger
Marlpit Hill
Four Elms
North Holmwood
Leigh
Salfords
Crowhurst
Blindley Heath
Edenbridge
Bough Beech
Farley Green
Abinger Common
Holmbury St Mary
Peaslake
Hurt Wood
South Holmwood
Anstiebury
Coldharbour
Leith Hill
Holmwood Sta
Beare Green
Parkgate
Norwood Hill
Outwood
Horne
Lingfield
Marsh Green
Hever
Newdigate
Hookwood
HORLEY
Smallfield
Newchapel
Dormansland
Markbeech
Cowden Sta
Burstow
Forest Green
Jayes Park
Ewhurst
Capel
Charlwood
London (Gatwick) Airport
Felcourt
Cowden
Ockley
Cranleigh
Wallis Wood
CRAWLEY
Pound Hill
Copthorne
Crawley Down
Felbridge
EAST GRINSTEAD
Blackham
Oakwoodhill
Rusper
Ifield
Lambs Green
Three Bridges
Ashurst Wood
Kingsfold
Ellen's Green
Worth
Turners Hill
Sunnyside
Saint Hill
Forest Row
Hartfield
Withyham
Faygate
Broadfield
Selsfield Common
Weir Wood Resr
Upper Hartfield
Rudgwick
Rowhook
Worth Abbey
Coleman's Hatch
Bucks Green
Warnham
Roffey
Colgate
Pease Pottage
West Hoathly
Sharpthorne
Slinfold
Broadbridge Heath
HORSHAM
ST LEONARD'S FOREST
Wych Cross
WEALD
Handcross
Balcombe
Highbrook
ASHDOWN FOREST
Itchingfield
Mannings Heath
Ardingly
Horsted Keynes
Chelwood Gate
Five Oaks
Barns Green
Christ's Hospital
Staplefield
Ardingly Resr
Newpound Common
Slaugham
Danehill
Nutley
Southwater
Lower Beeding
Whitemans Green
Fairwarp
Nuthurst
Warninglid
BILLINGSHURST
Crabtree
Copsale
Brooks Green
Cuckfield
Lindfield
HAYWARDS HEATH
Maresfield
Coneyhurst
Maplehurst
Fletching
Coolham
Shipley
Bolney
Ansty
Scayne's Hill
Sheffield Park Sta
Buxted
Gay Street
Cowfold
Newick
Littleworth
Monastery
Broomer's Corner
West Grinstead
Wineham
Wivelsfield
Dial Post
Nutbourne
West Chiltington
Twineham
Wivelsfield Sta
Wivelsfield Green
Chailey
Ridgewood
Partridge Green
Sayers Common
River Adur
BURGESS HILL
LOW WEALD
South Street
Spithurst
Thakeham
Henfield
Blackstone
Albourne
Hurstpierpoint
Little Horsted
Ashurst
Ashington
Ditchling
Plumpton Green
Isfield
Barcombe Cross
Shortgate
Storrington
Hassocks
Keymer
Streat
East Chiltington
Woodmancote
Clayton
Westmeston
Barcombe
Wiston
Plumpton
Cooksbridge
Hamsey
Kithurst Hill
Sullington
Washington
Small Dole
Edburton
Poynings
Pyecombe
Ditchling Beacon
Mount Harry
Offham
Ringmer
Bramber
Steyning
Upper Beeding
Fulking
Devil's Dyke
South Malling
Cliffe Hill
Glyndebourne
Harrow Hill
Castle
LEWES
Stanmer
North End
Findon
Patcham
Coldean
Mount Caburn
Glynde
Botolphs
River Adur
Falmer
Kingston near Lewes
Cissbury Ring
Coombes
SHOREHAM-BY-SEA
West Blatchington
SOUTH DOWNS
Moulsecoomb
Iford
Beddingham
West Firle
North Lancing
Shoreham Airport
Preston
Rodmell
Firle Beacon
Patching
Clapham
High Salvington
Kingston by Sea
Portslade
SOUTHWICK
Bevendean
Durrington
Sompting
Woodingdean
Southease
Angmering
Broadwater
Kemp Town
Tarring Neville
PORTSLADE-BY-SEA
HOVE
Ovingdean
Telscombe
South Lancing
BRIGHTON
Saltdean
Piddinghoe
South Heighton
Denton
East Preston
Ferring
WORTHING
Rottingdean
Bishopstone
Goring-by-Sea
Peacehaven
East Blatchington
NEWHAVEN
SEAFORD
M23
A23
A22
A24
A264
A272
A27
A29
A281
A283
A280
A259
A26
A2037
A2300
A217
A25
A242
A270
A275
B2110
B2116
B2028
B2036
B2112
B2126
B2127
B2128
B2133
B2135
B2139
B2026
B2027
B2028
B2029
B2188
B2192
B2123
B2124
B2114
B2115
9
9a
10
10a
11
ENGLISH CHANNEL

Major administrative and Postcode boundaries

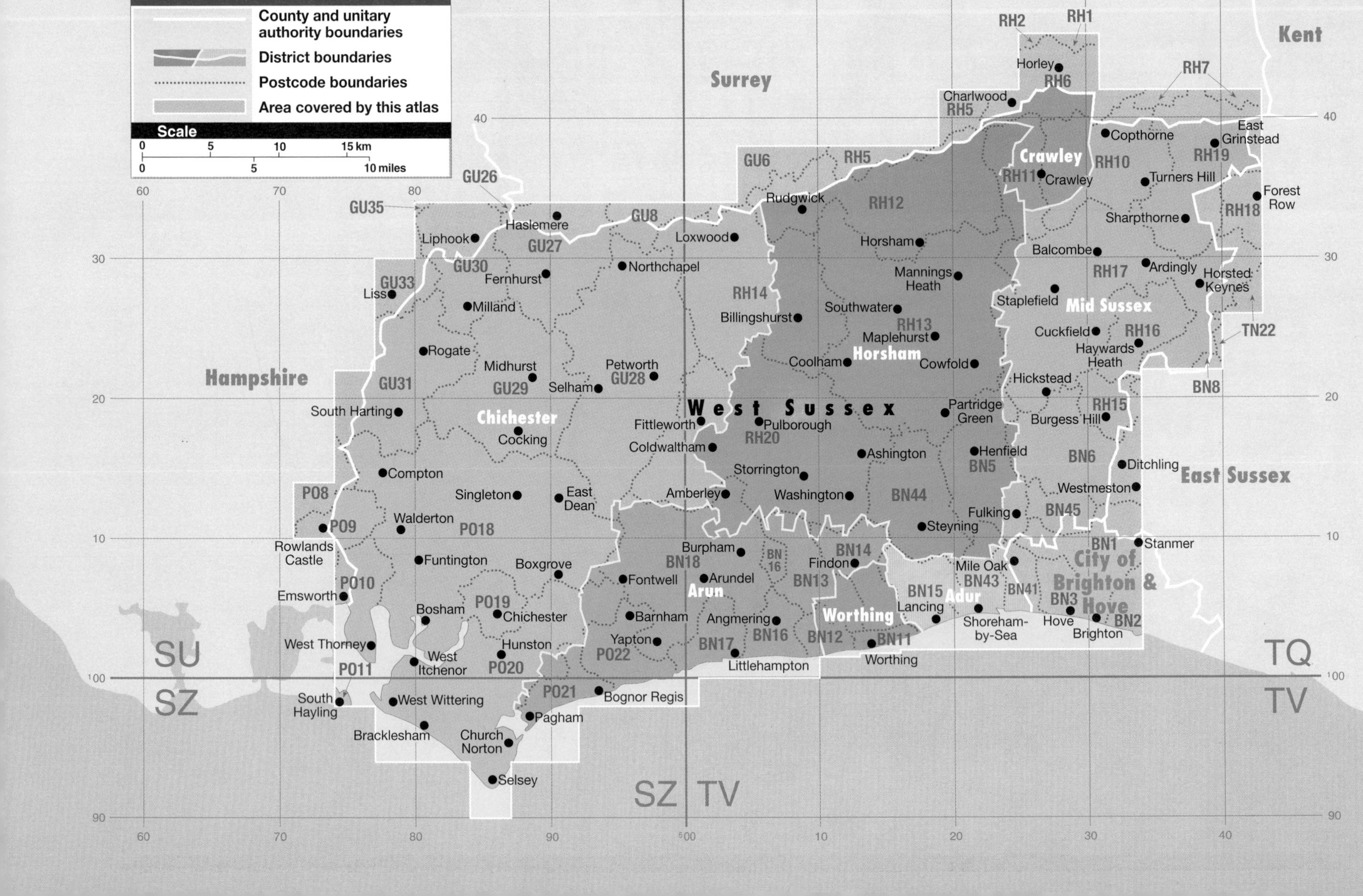
County and unitary authority boundaries
District boundaries
Postcode boundaries
Area covered by this atlas
Scale
0 5 10 15 km
0 5 10 miles
SU TQ
SZ TV
SU
SZ
TQ
TV
Surrey
Kent
Hampshire
East Sussex
West Sussex
Chichester
Horsham
Crawley
Mid Sussex
Arun
Worthing
Adur
City of Brighton & Hove
RH1
RH2
RH5
RH6
RH7
RH10
RH11
RH12
RH13
RH14
RH15
RH16
RH17
RH18
RH19
RH20
TN22
BN1
BN2
BN3
BN5
BN6
BN8
BN11
BN12
BN13
BN14
BN15
BN16
BN17
BN18
BN41
BN43
BN44
BN45
GU6
GU8
GU26
GU27
GU28
GU29
GU30
GU31
GU33
GU35
PO8
PO9
PO10
PO11
PO18
PO19
PO20
PO21
PO22
Horley
Charlwood
Copthorne
East Grinstead
Crawley
Turners Hill
Forest Row
Sharpthorne
Rudgwick
Horsham
Balcombe
Ardingly
Horsted Keynes
Staplefield
Mannings Heath
Southwater
Billingshurst
Cuckfield
Haywards Heath
Maplehurst
Coolham
Cowfold
Hickstead
Partridge Green
Burgess Hill
Henfield
Ditchling
Westmeston
Fulking
Stanmer
Steyning
Mile Oak
Shoreham-by-Sea
Hove
Brighton
Lancing
Worthing
Findon
Washington
Storrington
Ashington
Pulborough
Fittleworth
Coldwaltham
Amberley
Burpham
Arundel
Angmering
Littlehampton
Fontwell
Barnham
Yapton
Bognor Regis
Pagham
Selsey
Church Norton
Bracklesham
West Wittering
South Hayling
West Itchenor
Hunston
Chichester
Bosham
West Thorney
Emsworth
Rowlands Castle
Funtington
Boxgrove
Walderton
Singleton
East Dean
Compton
Cocking
South Harting
Rogate
Midhurst
Selham
Petworth
Milland
Fernhurst
Liss
Liphook
Haslemere
Northchapel
Loxwood
60
70
80
90
500
10
20
30
40
50
100

2

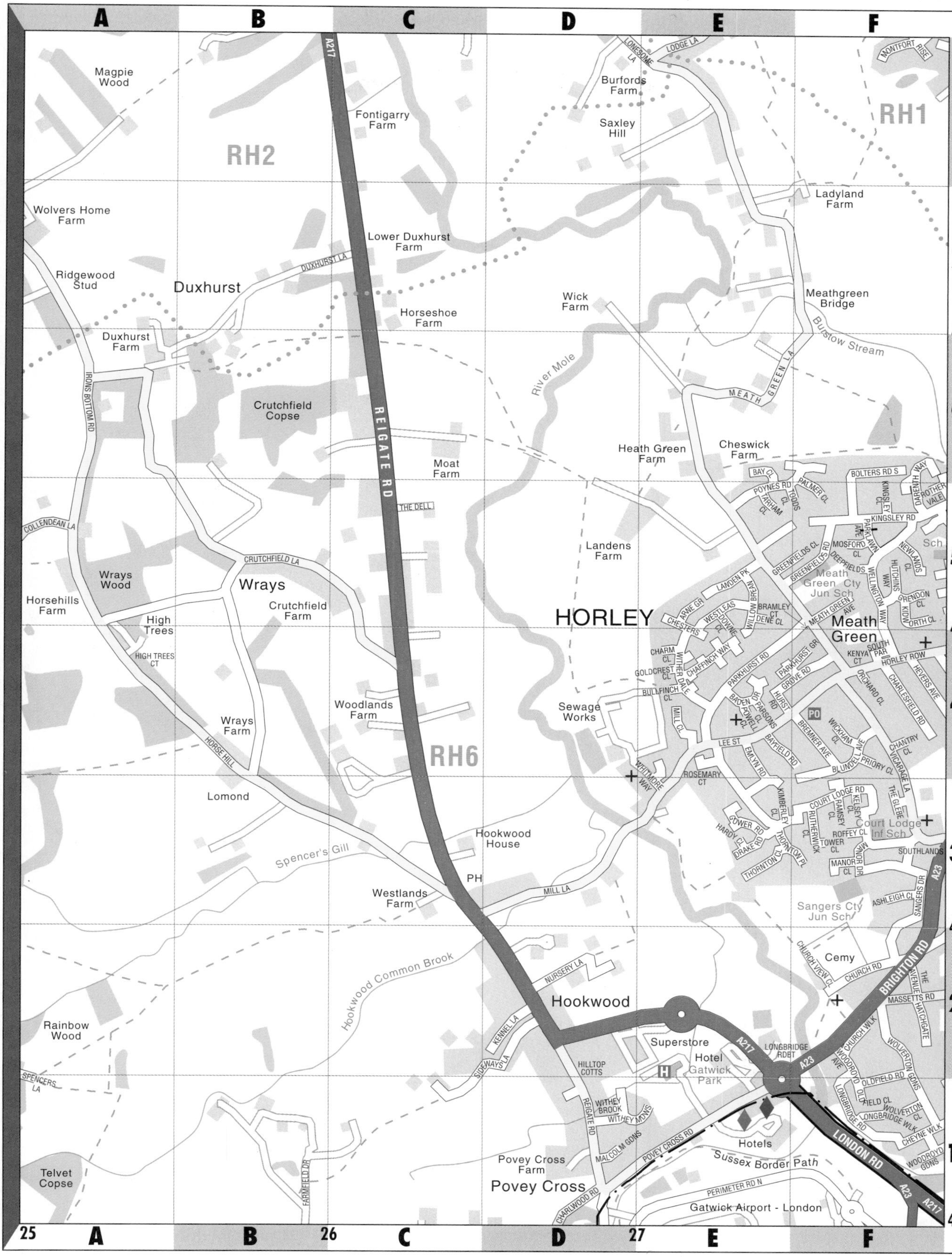
A
B
C
D
E
F
Magpie Wood
RH2
A217
Fontigarry Farm
Burfords Farm
Saxley Hill
LONESOME LA
LODGE LA
MONTFORT RISE
RH1
Wolvers Home Farm
Lower Duxhurst Farm
Ladyland Farm
Ridgewood Stud
Duxhurst
DUXHURST LA
Horseshoe Farm
Wick Farm
Meathgreen Bridge
Burstow Stream
Duxhurst Farm
IRONS BOTTOM RD
River Mole
MEATH GREEN LA
Crutchfield Copse
REIGATE RD
Moat Farm
Heath Green Farm
Cheswick Farm
THE DELL
COLLENDEAN LA
Landens Farm
CRUTCHFIELD LA
Wrays Wood
Wrays
Crutchfield Farm
HORLEY
Meath Green
Horsehills Farm
High Trees
HIGH TREES CT
Sewage Works
Woodlands Farm
Wrays Farm
HORSE HILL
RH6
Lomond
WHITMORE WAY
ROSEMARY CT
Hookwood House
Spencer's Gill
PH
Westlands Farm
MILL LA
Sangers Cty Jun Sch
Cemy
Hookwood Common Brook
NURSERY LA
Hookwood
Rainbow Wood
KENNEL LA
Superstore
Hotel Gatwick Park
LONGBRIDGE RDBT
SIDEWAYS LA
HILLTOP COTTS
SPENCERS LA
WITHEY BROOK
WITHEY MDWS
REIGATE RD
Hotels
MALCOLM GDNS
POVEY CROSS RD
Povey Cross Farm
Sussex Border Path
Telvet Copse
Povey Cross
FARMFIELD DR
PERIMETER RD N
CHARLWOOD RD
Gatwick Airport - London
LONDON RD
BRIGHTON RD
A23
Meath Green Cty Jun Sch
Court Lodge Inf Sch
Sch
PO
H
8
7
45
6
5
44
4
3
43
2
1
42
25
26
27

5

2

1

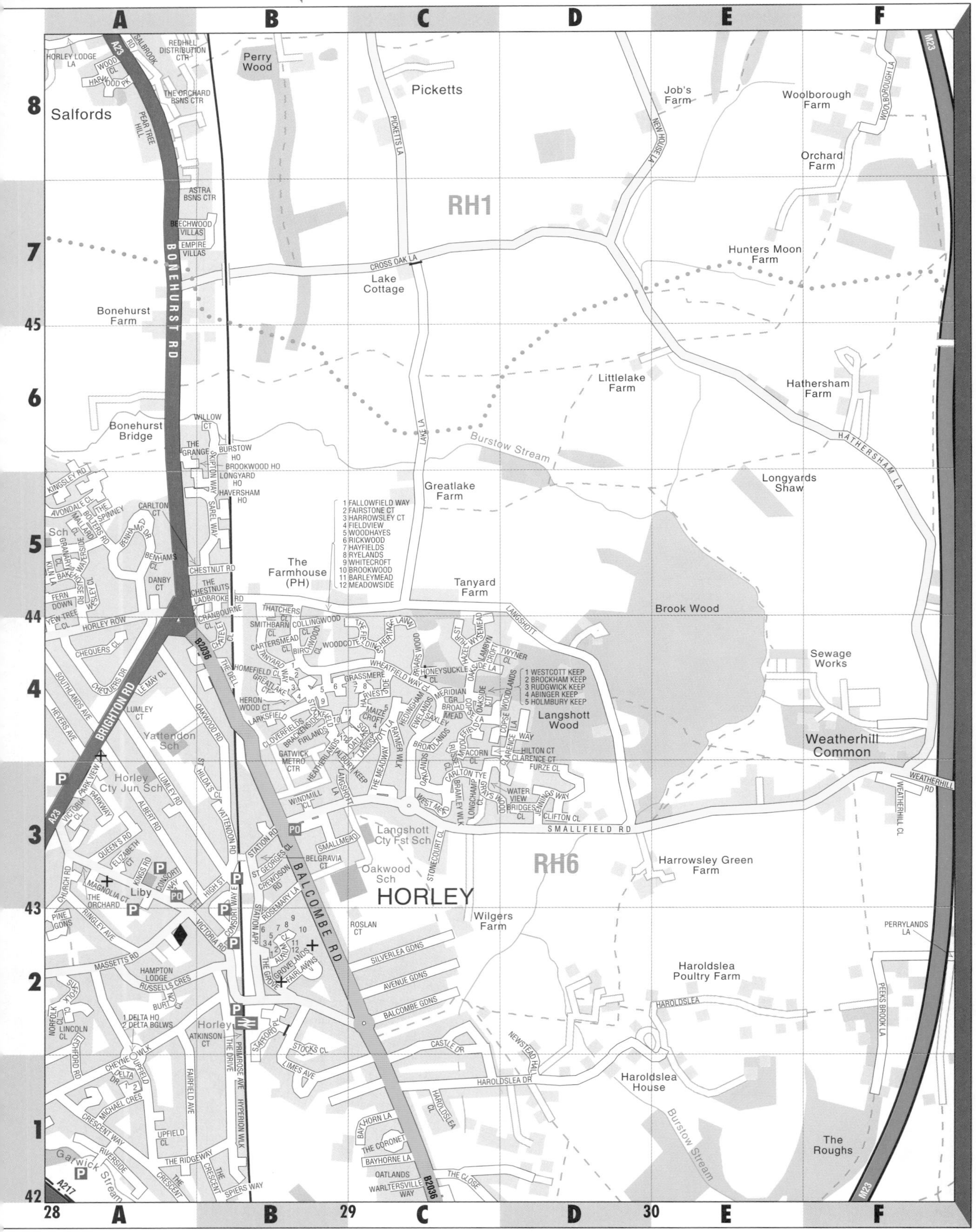
A B C D E F
8 7 6 5 4 3 2 1
45 44 43 42
28 29 30
Salfords
Perry Wood
Picketts
Job's Farm
Woolborough Farm
Orchard Farm
RH1
Hunters Moon Farm
Lake Cottage
CROSS OAK LA
Bonehurst Farm
BONEHURST RD
Littlelake Farm
Hathersham Farm
HATHERSHAM LA
Bonehurst Bridge
Burstow Stream
Greatlake Farm
Longyards Shaw
1 FALLOWFIELD WAY
2 FAIRSTONE CT
3 HARROWSLEY CT
4 FIELDVIEW
5 WOODHAYES
6 RICKWOOD
7 HAYFIELDS
8 RYELANDS
9 WHITECROFT
10 BROOKWOOD
11 BARLEYMEAD
12 MEADOWSIDE
The Farmhouse (PH)
Tanyard Farm
Brook Wood
Sewage Works
1 WESTCOTT KEEP
2 BROCKHAM KEEP
3 RUDGWICK KEEP
4 ABINGER KEEP
5 HOLMBURY KEEP
Langshott Wood
Weatherhill Common
WEATHERHILL RD
Yattendon Sch
Horley Cty Jun Sch
BRIGHTON RD
A23
B2036
BALCOMBE RD
Langshott Cty Fst Sch
Oakwood Sch
HORLEY
RH6
SMALLFIELD RD
Harrowsley Green Farm
Wilgers Farm
Liby
Haroldslea Poultry Farm
Horley
Haroldslea House
HAROLDSLEA DR
The Roughs
Garwick Stream
A217
M23

B2
1 DEEPDALE
2 WENTWORTH
3 MOORPARK
4 ST ANDREWS
5 CHERRY LODGE
6 ROSLAN CT
7 TROON
8 LYTHAM
9 ST GEORGES
10 MUIRFIELD
11 GLEN EAGLES
12 SUNNINGDALE

1

6

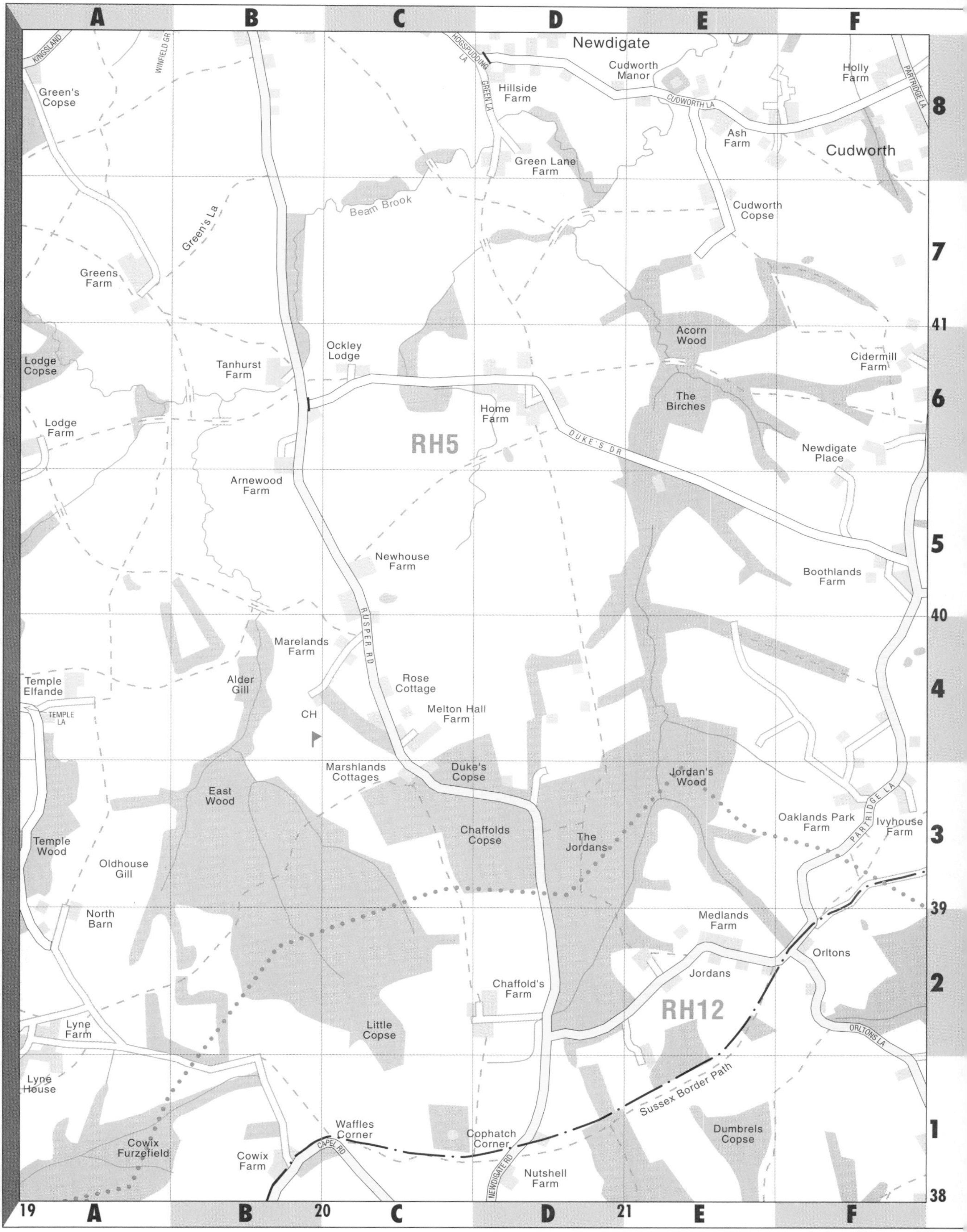
4
A
B
C
D
E
F
Newdigate
Cudworth Manor
Holly Farm
Green's Copse
Hillside Farm
Ash Farm
Cudworth
Green Lane Farm
Beam Brook
Green's La
Cudworth Copse
Greens Farm
Acorn Wood
Ockley Lodge
Tanhurst Farm
Lodge Copse
Cidermill Farm
The Birches
Home Farm
Lodge Farm
RH5
Newdigate Place
Arnewood Farm
Newhouse Farm
Boothlands Farm
Marelands Farm
Temple Elfande
Alder Gill
Rose Cottage
Melton Hall Farm
CH
Marshlands Cottages
Duke's Copse
Jordan's Wood
East Wood
Oaklands Park Farm
Ivyhouse Farm
Chaffolds Copse
The Jordans
Temple Wood
Oldhouse Gill
North Barn
Medlands Farm
Orltons
Jordans
Chaffold's Farm
RH12
Lyne Farm
Little Copse
Lyne House
Sussex Border Path
Waffles Corner
Cophatch Corner
Dumbrels Copse
Cowix Furzefield
Cowix Farm
Nutshell Farm
KINGSLAND
WINFIELD GR
HOGSPUDDING LA
GREEN LA
CUDWORTH LA
PARTRIDGE LA
DUKE'S DR
RUSPER RD
TEMPLE LA
ORLTONS LA
CAPEL RD
NEWDIGATE RD
8
7
41
6
5
40
4
3
39
2
1
38
19
20
21
16

3

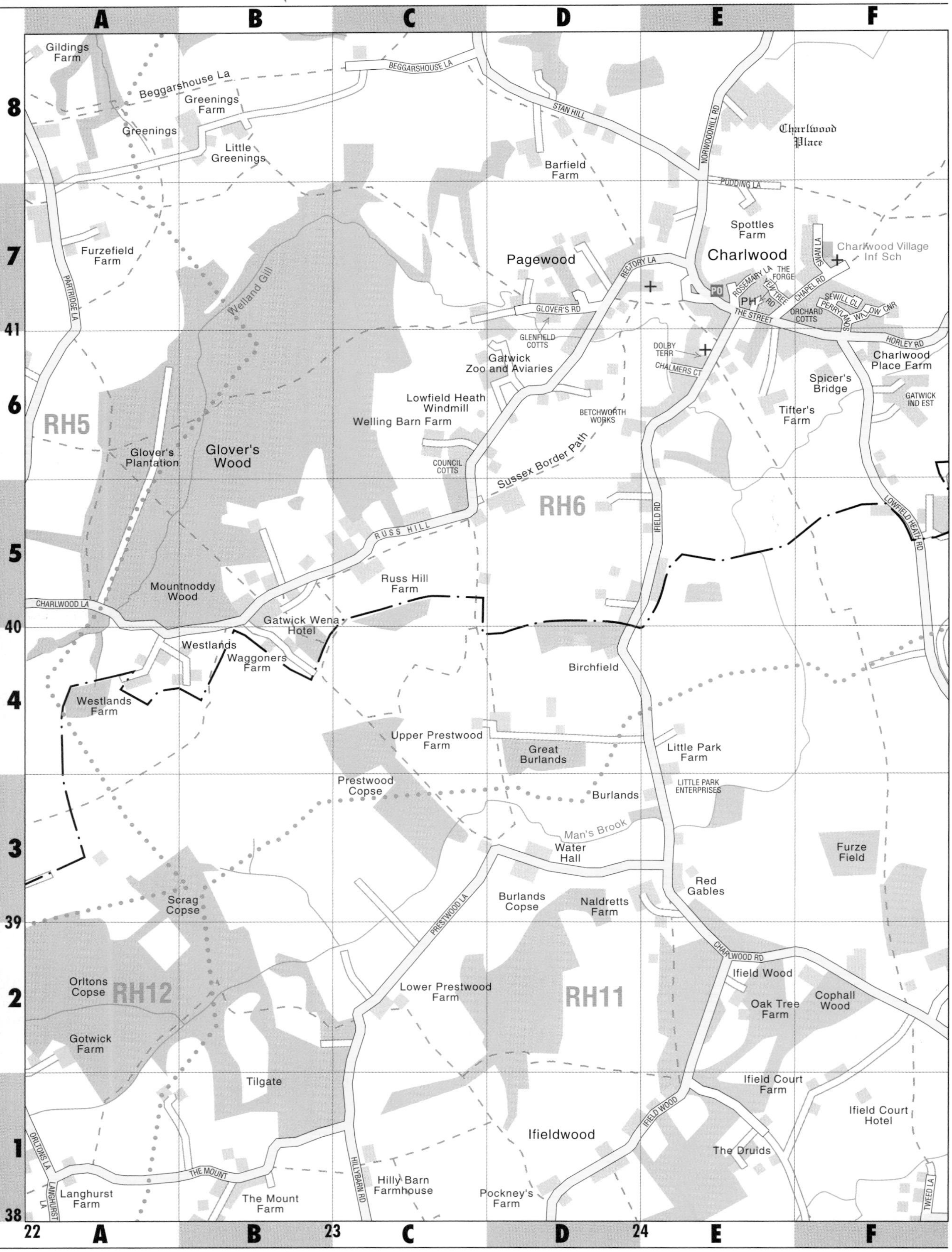
A
B
C
D
E
F
8
7
41
6
5
40
4
3
39
2
1
38
22
23
24
Gildings Farm
Beggarshouse La
BEGGARSHOUSE LA
Greenings Farm
Greenings
Little Greenings
STAN HILL
Barfield Farm
NORWOODHILL RD
Charlwood Place
PUDDING LA
Spottles Farm
Charlwood
Charlwood Village Inf Sch
SWAN LA
Furzefield Farm
PARTRIDGE LA
Welland Gill
Pagewood
RECTORY LA
GLOVER'S RD
GLENFIELD COTTS
PO
PH
ROSEMARY LA
THE FORGE
YEW TREE RD
CHAPEL RD
SEWILL CL
PERRYLANDS
WILLOW CNR
ORCHARD COTTS
THE STREET
HORLEY RD
DOLBY TERR
CHALMERS CT
Gatwick Zoo and Aviaries
Charlwood Place Farm
Spicer's Bridge
GATWICK IND EST
Lowfield Heath Windmill
Welling Barn Farm
BETCHWORTH WORKS
Tifter's Farm
RH5
Glover's Plantation
Glover's Wood
COUNCIL COTTS
Sussex Border Path
RH6
LOWFIELD HEATH RD
RUSS HILL
IFIELD RD
Russ Hill Farm
Mountnoddy Wood
CHARLWOOD LA
Gatwick Wena Hotel
Westlands
Waggoners Farm
Birchfield
Westlands Farm
Upper Prestwood Farm
Great Burlands
Little Park Farm
LITTLE PARK ENTERPRISES
Prestwood Copse
Burlands
Man's Brook
Water Hall
Furze Field
Red Gables
Scrag Copse
Burlands Copse
Naldretts Farm
PRESTWOOD LA
CHARLWOOD RD
Ifield Wood
Orltons Copse
RH12
Lower Prestwood Farm
RH11
Oak Tree Farm
Cophall Wood
Gotwick Farm
Tilgate
Ifield Court Farm
Ifield Court Hotel
IFIELD WOOD
Ifieldwood
The Druids
ORLTONS LA
THE MOUNT
HILLYBARN RD
LANGHURST LA
Langhurst Farm
The Mount Farm
Hilly Barn Farmhouse
Pockney's Farm
TWEED LA

3

17

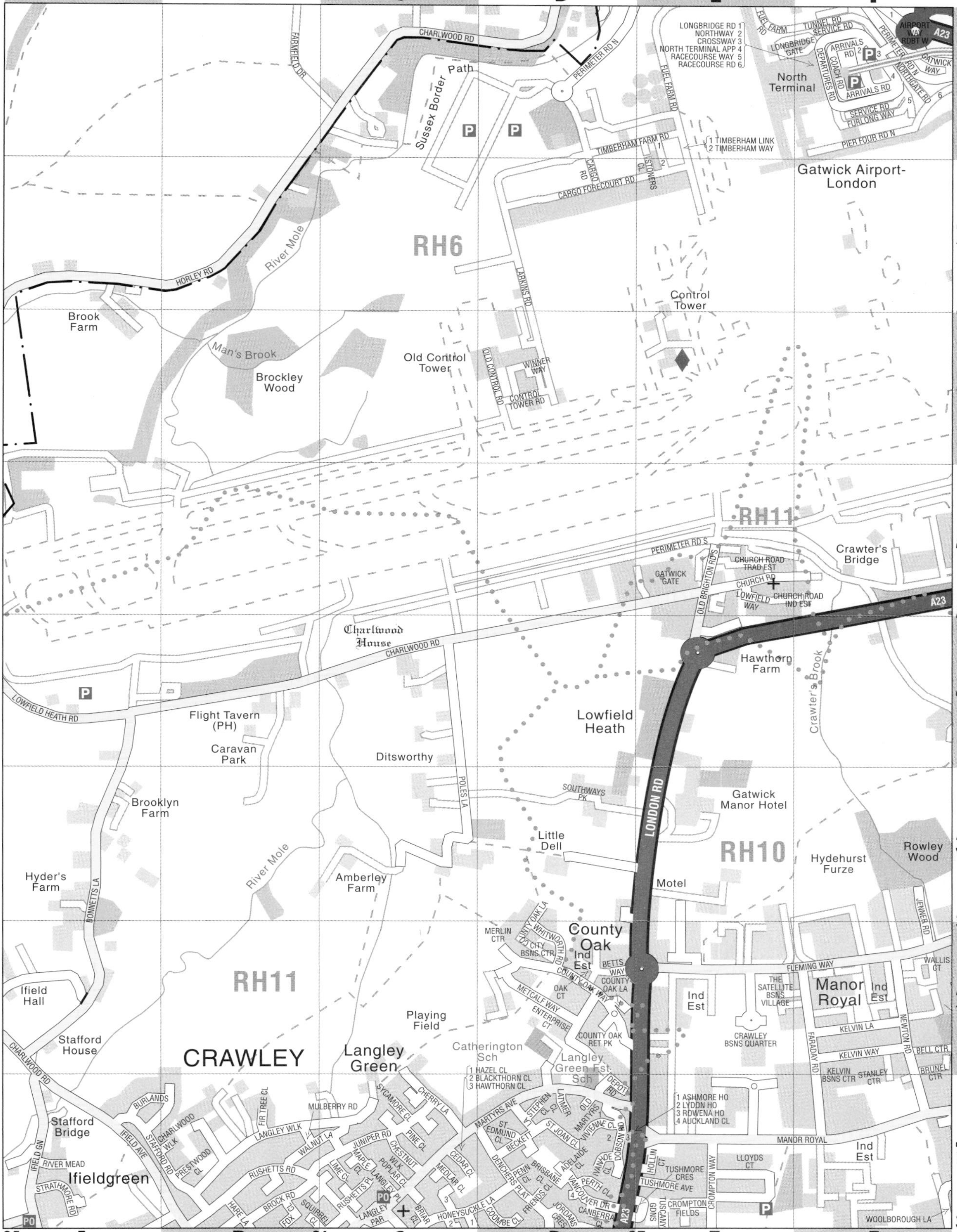
1
6

A B C D E F

8 7 41 6 5 40 4 3 39 2 1 38

LONGBRIDGE RD 1
NORTHWAY 2
CROSSWAY 3
NORTH TERMINAL APP 4
RACECOURSE WAY 5
RACECOURSE RD 6

AIRPORT WAY RDBT W
A23
FUEL FARM RD
TUNNEL RD
SERVICE RD
LONGBRIDGE GATE
ARRIVALS RD
COACH RD
DEPARTURES RD
PERIMETER RD N
GATWICK WAY
NORTHGATE RD
North Terminal
ARRIVALS RD
SERVICE RD
FURLONG WAY
PIER FOUR RD N
CHARLWOOD RD
FARMFIELD DR
Path
Sussex Border Path
PERIMETER RD N
FUEL FARM RD
TIMBERHAM FARM RD
1 TIMBERHAM LINK
2 TIMBERHAM WAY
CARGO RD
STONERS CL
CARGO FORECOURT RD
Gatwick Airport-London
RH6
HORLEY RD
River Mole
LARKINS RD
Control Tower
Brook Farm
Man's Brook
Brockley Wood
Old Control Tower
OLD CONTROL RD
WINNER WAY
CONTROL TOWER RD
RH11
PERIMETER RD S
OLD BRIGHTON RD S
CHURCH ROAD TRAD EST
Crawter's Bridge
GATWICK GATE
CHURCH RD
LOWFIELD WAY
CHURCH ROAD IND EST
A23
Charlwood House
CHARLWOOD RD
Hawthorn Farm
Crawter's Brook
LOWFIELD HEATH RD
Flight Tavern (PH)
Lowfield Heath
Caravan Park
Ditsworthy
POLES LA
SOUTHWAYS PK
LONDON RD
Gatwick Manor Hotel
Brooklyn Farm
Little Dell
RH10
Rowley Wood
Hydehurst Furze
River Mole
Hyder's Farm
Amberley Farm
Motel
BONNETTS LA
JENNER RD
MERLIN CTR
UNITY OAK LA
WHITWORTH RD
CITY BSNS CTR
County Oak Ind Est
BETTS WAY
COUNTY OAK WAY
COUNTY OAK LA
FLEMING WAY
WALLIS CT
Ifield Hall
RH11
OAK CT
METCALFE WAY
Ind Est
THE SATELLITE BSNS VILLAGE
Manor Royal
Ind Est
Playing Field
ENTERPRISE CT
COUNTY OAK RET PK
CRAWLEY BSNS QUARTER
KELVIN LA
NEWTON RD
Stafford House
CRAWLEY
Langley Green
Catherington Sch
Langley Green Fst Sch
KELVIN WAY
BELL CTR
FARADAY RD
KELVIN BSNS CTR
STANLEY CTR
BRUNEL CTR
CHARLWOOD RD
1 HAZEL CL
2 BLACKTHORN CL
3 HAWTHORN CL
DEPOT RD
BURLANDS
MULBERRY RD
CHERRY LA
SYCAMORE CL
FIR TREE CL
1 ASHMORE HO
2 LYDON HO
3 ROWENA HO
4 AUCKLAND CL
Stafford Bridge
CHARLWOOD WLK
STAFFORD RD
LANGLEY WLK
WALNUT LA
MARTYRS AVE
STEPHEN CL
LATIMER CL
OLD MARTYRS
ST EDMUND CL
BECKET
ST JOAN CL
VIVIENNE CL
DOBSON RD
MANOR ROYAL
IFIELD GN
IFIELD AVE
PRESTWOOD CL
JUNIPER RD
CHESTNUT WLK
PINE CL
CEDAR CL
DENCHERS PLAT
PENN CL
BRISBANE CL
ADELAIDE CL
WAKEHOE CL
HOLLIN CT
TUSHMORE CRES
CROMPTON WAY
LLOYDS CT
Ind Est
RIVER MEAD
RUSHETTS RD
LIME CL
MAPLE CL
POPLAR CL
MEDLAR CL
TUSHMORE AVE
Ifieldgreen
STRATHMORE RD
BROCK RD
RUSHETTS PL
LANGLEY PL
PERTH CL
VANCOUVER DR
CROMPTON FIELDS
FOX CL
HARE LA
SQUIRREL CL
LANGLEY PAR
BRIAR CL
HONEYSUCKLE LA
COOMBE CL
FRIENDS CL
JORDANS CRES
CANBERRA CL
A23
GDNS
TUSCANY
WOOLBOROUGH LA
PO
P

25 A B 26 C D 27 E F

5
2
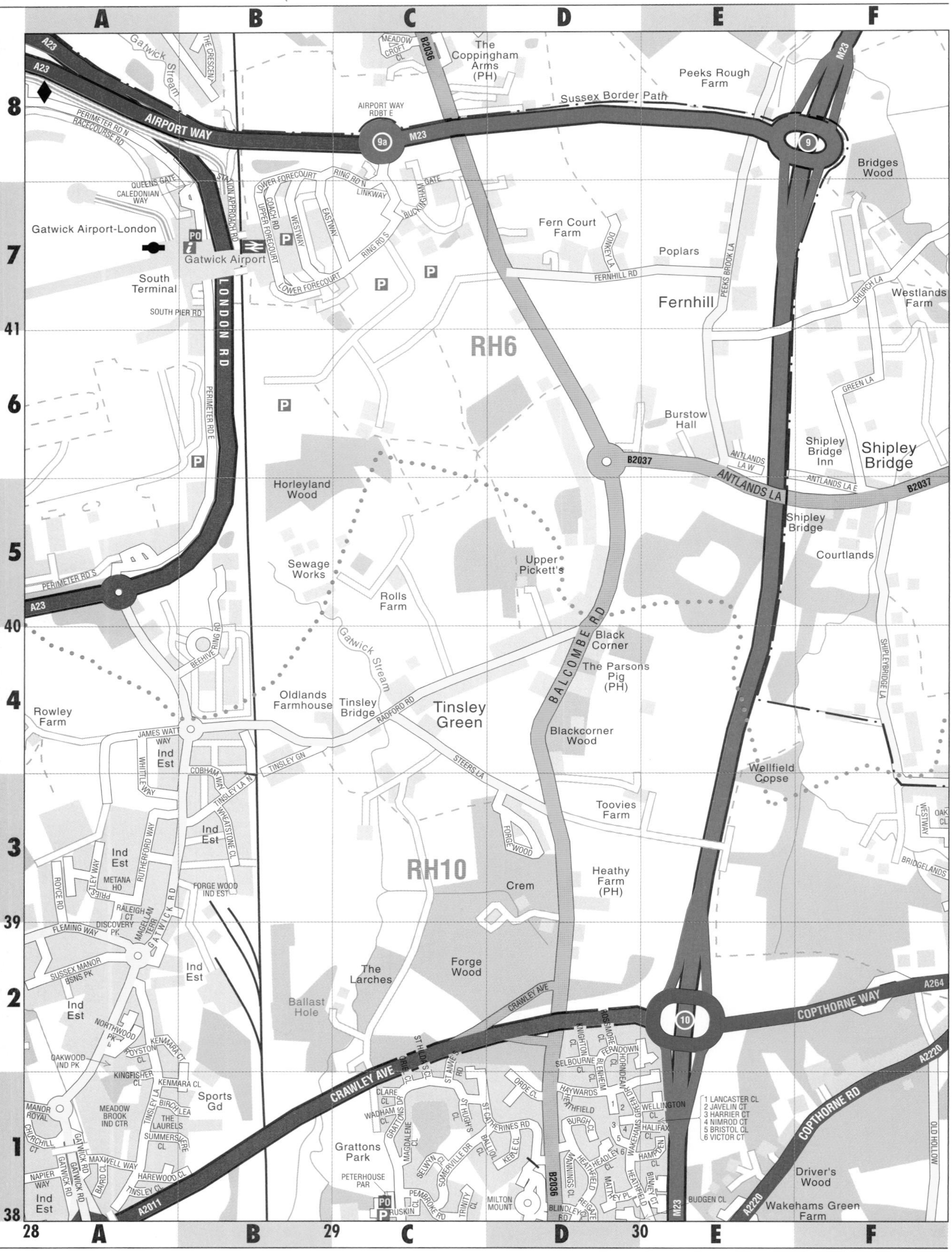
A
B
C
D
E
F
8
7
41
6
5
40
4
3
39
2
1
38
28
29
30
A23
Gatwick Stream
THE CRESCENT
MEADOW CROFT CL
B2036
The Coppingham Arms (PH)
Peeks Rough Farm
M23
Sussex Border Path
AIRPORT WAY
AIRPORT WAY RDBT E
9a
9
PERIMETER RD N
RACECOURSE RD
Bridges Wood
QUEENS GATE
CALEDONIAN WAY
STATION APPROACH RD
LOWER FORECOURT
RING RD N
LINKWAY
BUCKINGHAM GATE
UPPER FORECOURT
COACH RD
WESTWAY
EASTWAY
RING RD S
Gatwick Airport-London
PO
Gatwick Airport
Fern Court Farm
DONKEY LA
Poplars
PEEKS BROOK LA
FERNHILL RD
South Terminal
LONDON RD
Fernhill
CHURCH LA
Westlands Farm
SOUTH PIER RD
RH6
GREEN LA
PERIMETER RD E
Burstow Hall
Shipley Bridge Inn
Shipley Bridge
B2037
ANTLANDS LA W
ANTLANDS LA
ANTLANDS LA E
Horleyland Wood
Shipley Bridge
Courtlands
Sewage Works
Upper Pickett's
PERIMETER RD S
Rolls Farm
BALCOMBE RD
Black Corner
BEEHIVE RING RD
Gatwick Stream
The Parsons Pig (PH)
SHIPLEYBRIDGE LA
Rowley Farm
Oldlands Farmhouse
Tinsley Bridge
RADFORD RD
Tinsley Green
JAMES WATT WAY
Ind Est
Blackcorner Wood
WHITTLE WAY
COBHAM WAY
TINSLEY GN
TINSLEY LA N
STEERS LA
Wellfield Copse
WESTWAY
OAK CL
Ind Est
WHEATSTONE CL
Toovies Farm
FORGE WOOD
Ind Est
RUTHERFORD WAY
PRIESTLEY WAY
METANA HO
RH10
Heathy Farm (PH)
BRIDGELANDS
ROYCE RD
FORGE WOOD IND EST
Crem
GATWICK RD
RALEIGH CT
MAGELLAN TERR
DISCOVERY PK
FLEMING WAY
SUSSEX MANOR BSNS PK
Ind Est
The Larches
Forge Wood
A264
CRAWLEY AVE
Ind Est
Ballast Hole
ROSSMORE CL
COPTHORNE WAY
10
NORTHWOOD PK
KENMARA CT
ROYSTON CL
OAKWOOD IND PK
ST HILDA'S CL
ORDE CL
ST ANNE'S RD
KNIGHTON CL
FERNDOWN
SELBOURNE CL
BLENHEIM CL
HORNDEAN CL
A2220
KINGFISHER CL
CRAWLEY AVE
KENMARA CL
CLARE CL
ORDE CL
HAYWARDS
Sports Gd
BIRCH LEA
MANOR ROYAL
MEADOW BROOK IND CTR
WADHAM CL
GRATTONS DR
ST HUGHS CL
ST CATHERINES RD
HEATHFIELD
WELLINGTON CL
1 LANCASTER CL
2 JAVELIN CT
3 HARRIER CT
4 NIMROD CT
5 BRISTOL CL
6 VICTOR CT
COPTHORNE RD
THE LAURELS
BURGH CL
HALIFAX CL
CHURCHILL CT
SUMMERSVERE CL
MAGDALENE CL
WAKEHAMS GREEN DR
OLD HOLLOW
Grattons Park
SELWYN CL
SOMERVILLE DR
BALLIOL CL
KEBLE CL
MANNINGS CL
HEADLEY
HAMPDEN CL
MAXWELL WAY
TINSLEY LA
BAIRD CL
GATWICK RD
NAPIER WAY
HAREWOOD CL
PETERHOUSE PAR
HEATHFIELD
MATHEY PL
BINNEY CT
Driver's Wood
Ind Est
TINSLEY CL
PEMBROKE RD
TRINITY CL
MILTON MOUNT
B2036
REIGATE RD
BUDGEN CL
M23
Wakehams Green Farm
A2011
RUSKIN
BLINDLEY RD
5
19

8

A
B
C
D
E
F
8
7
6
5
4
3
2
1
41
40
39
38
31
32
33
Bellhatch Wood
Dowlands Farm
CROSS LA
BROADBRIDGE LA
REDEHALL RD
Redeham Hall
Rainscombe Farm
Rede Hall
Redeham Hall Farm
CHURCH LA
CHURCH RD
RH6
DOWLANDS LA
CHITHURST LA
RH7
Burstow
FIRBANK COTTS
HAWTHORNE COTTS
Keeper's Corner
Keepers Farm
Brick Barns Farm
Palmers Farm
ANTLANDS LA
Downswood Cottage
Kerlyn Farm
Perry Farm
B2028
Kiln Heath
EFFINGHAM RD
EAST HILL LA
Beechfield
The Hedgehog Inn
Newhouse Farm
Roseleigh Farm
Sussex Border Path
Allingham Farm
Moorland Farm
ROWLAND CL
WEST PARK RD
Burstow Park Farm
Heatherley Cheshire Home
SNOWHILL LA
SNOW HILL
COPTHORNE BANK
The Cherry Tree Inn (PH)
EFFINGHAM LA
B2037
CLAY HALL LA
Effingham Park
CHAPEL LA
Stonelands Farm
Hunters Moon
RH10
Copthorne CE Jun Sch
SHIPLEYBRIDGE LA
ELGER WAY
BOFFEY'S CL
ST FRANCIS GDNS
MAYNARD CL
BORDERS CL
BORERS YARD IND EST
GREEN LA
THE GLEBE
CHURCH RD
BORERS ARMS RD
LASHMERE
MILL LA
A264
OAK CL
MEADOW APP
MEADOW CL
THE GREEN
THE LINDENS
LIME CL
BEECHEY WAY
BEECHEY CL
KNOWLE DR
KNOWLE CL
SPRING COPSE
SPRING GDNS
CH
THE DRIVE
ABERGAVENNY GDNS
Copthorne Sch Trust Ltd
NEWLANDS PK
WESTWAY
THE MEADOW
BROOKSIDE
PO
BROOKVIEW
AKEHURST CL
PINETREES CL
Copthorne
COPTHORNE COMMON RD
SOUTH VIEW CL
BRIDGELANDS
Copthorne Fairway Inf Sch
NEW TOWN
PO
The Dukes Head (PH)
CALLUNA DR
BROOKHILL RD
BROOKHILL CL
CHURCH LA
P
THE GABLES
PEMBLEY GN
COTTAGE PL
Firs Farm
ERICA WAY
KITSMEAD
BRACKEN CL
BRAMBLE CL
FAIRWAY
HEATHER CL
COPTHORNE COMMON RD
FAIRWAY CL
GORSE CL
Haynes Farm
COPTHORNE WAY
BORDER CHASE
Copthorne Common
Chart's Plain
TURNERS HILL RD
Shepherds Farm
COPTHORNE RD
A2220
Hotel
Woodmans Farm
Bashfords Wood
Westlands Wood
Pot Common
Keeper's Cottage
Coombers Wood
Copthorne Wood
Birchen Wood
Wins Wood
B2028

20

8

7

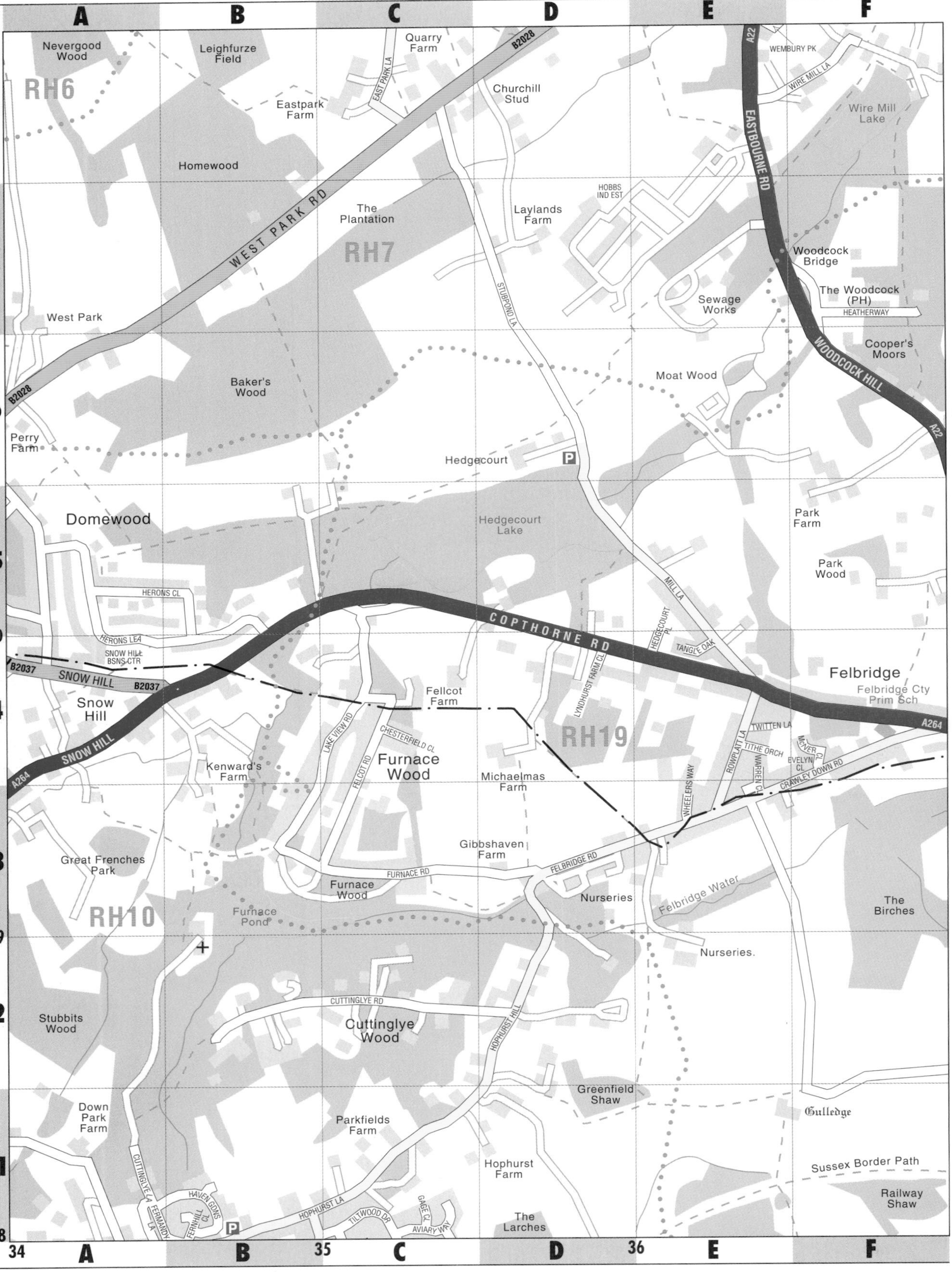
A
B
C
D
E
F
8
7
41
6
5
40
4
3
39
2
1
38
34
35
36
Nevergood Wood
Leighfurze Field
Quarry Farm
RH6
Eastpark Farm
EAST PARK LA
B2028
Churchill Stud
WEMBURY PK
WIRE MILL LA
Wire Mill Lake
A22
EASTBOURNE RD
Homewood
WEST PARK RD
The Plantation
RH7
HOBBS IND EST
Laylands Farm
Woodcock Bridge
The Woodcock (PH)
HEATHERWAY
Sewage Works
STUBPOND LA
West Park
Cooper's Moors
WOODCOCK HILL
Moat Wood
Baker's Wood
Perry Farm
Hedgecourt
P
Domewood
Hedgecourt Lake
Park Farm
Park Wood
HERONS CL
HERONS LEA
MILL LA
COPTHORNE RD
HEDGECOURT PL
TANGLE OAK
SNOW HILL BSNS CTR
B2037
SNOW HILL
Snow Hill
Fellcot Farm
Felbridge
Felbridge Cty Prim Sch
A264
LYNDHURST FARM CL
RH19
TWITTEN LA
TITHE ORCH
MCIVER CL
EVELYN CL
CRAWLEY DOWN RD
LAKE VIEW RD
CHESTERFIELD CL
FELLCOT RD
Furnace Wood
Kenward's Farm
Michaelmas Farm
WHEELERS WAY
ROWPLATT LA
WARREN CL
Gibbshaven Farm
Great Frenches Park
FURNACE RD
FELBRIDGE RD
Nurseries
Felbridge Water
The Birches
RH10
Furnace Wood
Furnace Pond
Nurseries.
CUTTINGLYE RD
HOPHURST HILL
Stubbits Wood
Cuttinglye Wood
Greenfield Shaw
Down Park Farm
Parkfields Farm
Gulledge
Hophurst Farm
Sussex Border Path
CUTTINGLYE LA
HAVEN GDNS
FERNHILL CL
FERMANDY LA
HOPHURST LA
TILTWOOD DR
GAGE CL
AVIARY WAY
Railway Shaw
The Larches

7
21

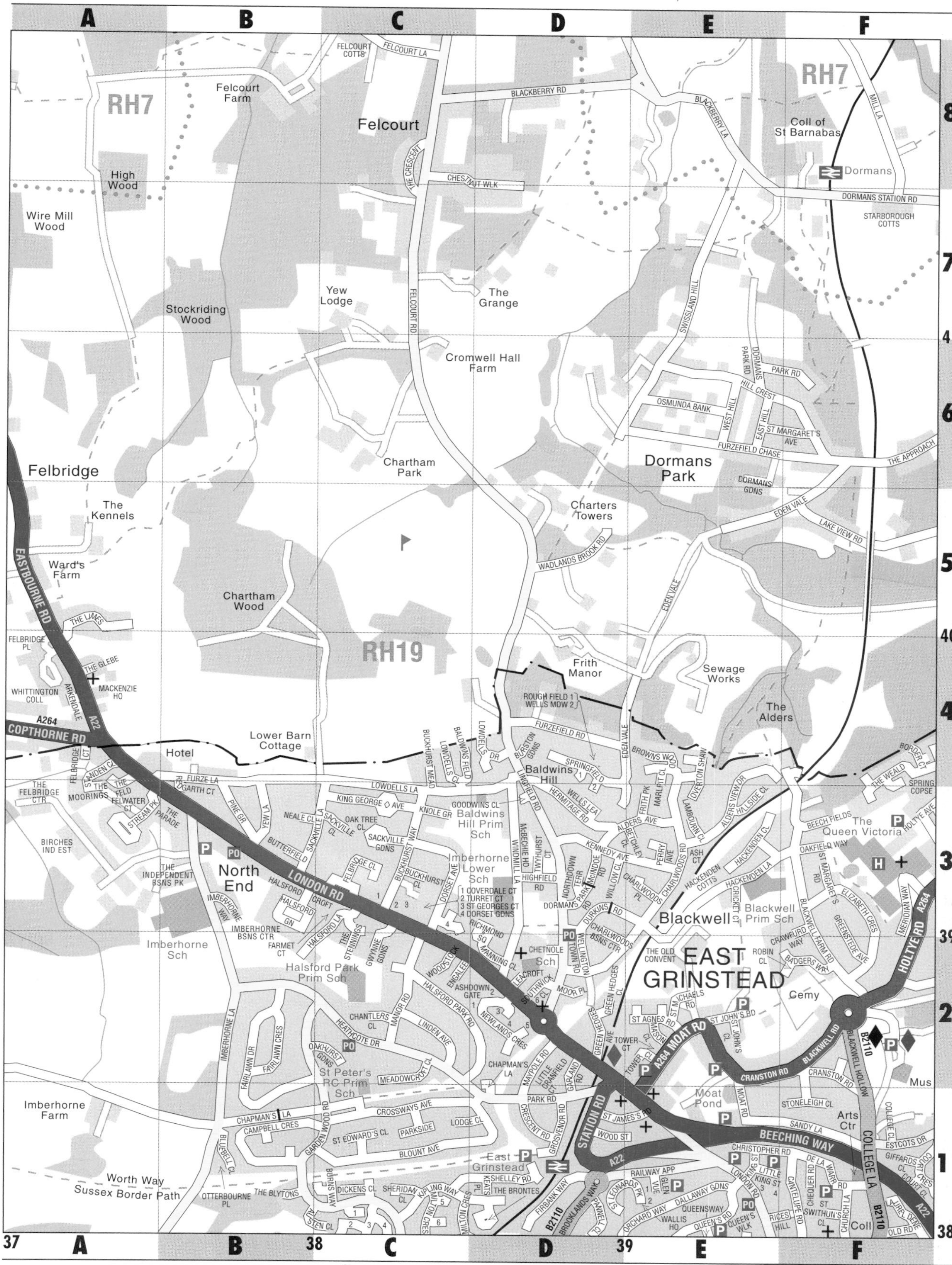

C1
1 THE BROWNINGS
2 BYRON GR
3 CHAUCER AVE
4 TENNYSON RISE
5 THE SAYERS
6 WORDSWORTH RISE

D2
1 YEW CT
2 BIRCH HO
3 BEECH CL
4 ELM CT
5 FERNSIDE
6 SOUTHWICK HO

E1
1 GLENSIDE
2 GREGORY CT
3 WHITEHALL PAR
4 CANTELUPE MEWS

9

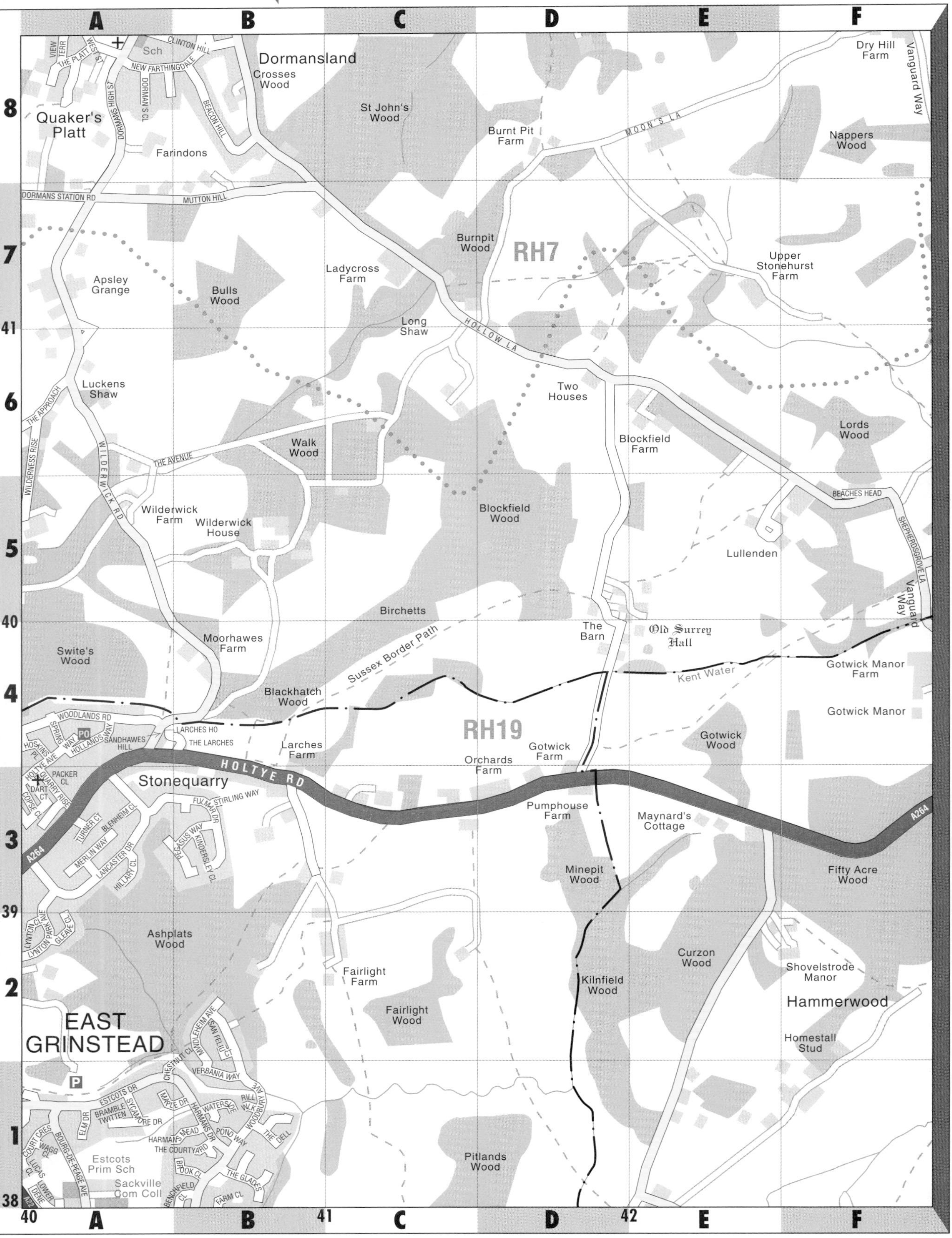
A
B
C
D
E
F
8
7
41
6
5
40
4
3
39
2
1
38
40
41
42
Dormansland
Crosses Wood
Quaker's Platt
Sch
CLINTON HILL
NEW FARTHINGDALE
DORMANS HIGH ST
DORMAN'S CL
BEACON HILL
VIEW TERR
THE PLATT
WEST ST
Farindons
St John's Wood
Burnt Pit Farm
MOON'S LA
Dry Hill Farm
Vanguard Way
Nappers Wood
DORMANS STATION RD
MUTTON HILL
Burnpit Wood
RH7
Ladycross Farm
Apsley Grange
Bulls Wood
Upper Stonehurst Farm
Long Shaw
HOLLOW LA
Luckens Shaw
THE APPROACH
Two Houses
WILDERNESS RISE
WILDERWICK RD
THE AVENUE
Walk Wood
Blockfield Farm
Lords Wood
BEACHES HEAD
Wilderwick Farm
Wilderwick House
Blockfield Wood
SHEPHERDSGROVE LA
Lullenden
Birchetts
Vanguard Way
Switе's Wood
Moorhawes Farm
Sussex Border Path
The Barn
Old Surrey Hall
Kent Water
Gotwick Manor Farm
Blackhatch Wood
Gotwick Manor
WOODLANDS RD
PO
HOSKINS PL
SPRING WAY
HOLLANDS WAY
SANDHAWES HILL
LARCHES HO
THE LARCHES
Larches Farm
RH19
Gotwick Farm
Gotwick Wood
Orchards Farm
HOLTYE RD
Stonequarry
PACKER CL
DART CT
COPSE CL
QUARRY RISE
HOLTYE AVE
FULMAR DR
STIRLING WAY
Pumphouse Farm
Maynard's Cottage
A264
BLENHEIM CL
TURNER CT
MERLIN WAY
LANCASTER DR
HILLARY CL
PEGASUS WAY
KINDERSLEY CL
Minepit Wood
Fifty Acre Wood
LYNTON PARK AVE
GLEAVE CL
Ashplats Wood
Curzon Wood
Shovelstrode Manor
Fairlight Farm
Kilnfield Wood
Hammerwood
EAST GRINSTEAD
Fairlight Wood
Homestall Stud
WOODHEIM AVE
SAN FELIU CT
CHESTNUT CL
VERBANIA WAY
P
ESTCOTS DR
BRAMBLE TWITTEN
SYCAMORE DR
MAPLE DR
HARMANS DR
WATERSIDE
RILL WK
WOODBURY AVE
ELM DR
COURT CRES
WAGG CL
BOURG-DE-PEAGE AVE
HARMANS MEAD
THE COURTYARD
POND WAY
THE DELL
LUCAS CL
Estcots Prim Sch
BROOK CL
THE GLADES
Pitlands Wood
Sackville Com Coll
LOWER DENE
BENCHFIELD CL
FARM CL
A22

9
23

12

A
B
C
D
E
F
Cranleigh
Highpark
B2128
Sparrow Copse
Bushy Copse
Garson Copse
Little Garson
8
Holdhurst Farm
White Meads Copse
Great Garson
Boy & Donkey (PH)
Snoxhall Farm
Wey-South Path
ALFOLD RD
VACHERY LA
Thornhurst Brook
Vachery Pond
7
Lion's La
Wey & Arun Junction Canal (dis)
37
Water Bridge
Flash Bridge
Hammer Farm
A281
Waterland Farm
Waterbridge Farm
Downs Link
6
Bridge Farm
Newhouse Farm
Bookers Lee
GU6
Little Withybush
Birch Copse
ALFOLD BY-PASS
5
WILDWOOD LA
KNOWLE LA
36
HAZELWOOD COTTS
Little Wildwood Farm
Lodge Copse
4
Butcherhouse Farm
Works
CROSSWAYS COTTS
Pickenswood Copse
Alfold Crossways
LOXWOOD RD
CH
Wildwood Copse
3
B2133
STONE HATCH
HATCH CL
Shrubs Copse
CLAPPERS MEADOW
35
Ivelle Farm
2
Furzefield Wood
Aldermoor Copse
Pallinghurst Farm
HORSHAM RD
BAYNARDS RD
Hazel Copse
Highfield Copse
RH12
White Lea
Little Birchett
Alfold Farm
Hook St
1
HILLHOUSE LA
Sussex Border Path
White's Copse
A281
GUILDFORD RD
Males Farm
Lower Hill House
COOKS HILL
34
04
05
06

32

12

11

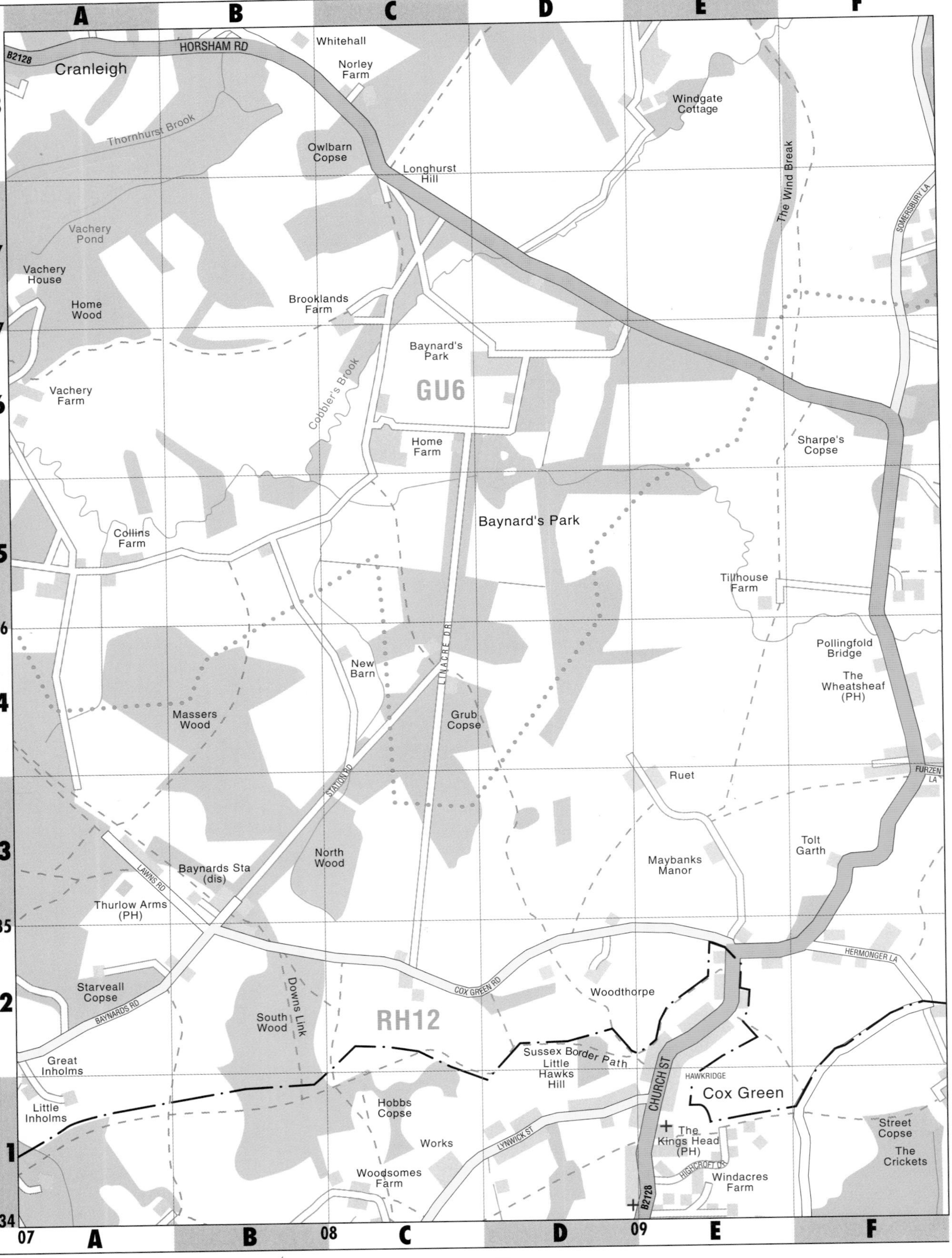
A
B
C
D
E
F
8
7
37
6
5
36
4
3
35
2
1
34
07
08
09
B2128
HORSHAM RD
Cranleigh
Whitehall
Norley
Farm
Thornhurst Brook
Owlbarn
Copse
Longhurst
Hill
Windgate
Cottage
The Wind Break
SOMERSBURY LA
Vachery
Pond
Vachery
House
Home
Wood
Brooklands
Farm
Baynard's
Park
GU6
Cobbler's Brook
Vachery
Farm
Home
Farm
Sharpe's
Copse
Baynard's Park
Collins
Farm
Tillhouse
Farm
New
Barn
LINACRE DR
Pollingfold
Bridge
The
Wheatsheaf
(PH)
Massers
Wood
Grub
Copse
STATION RD
Ruet
FURZEN
LA
Tolt
Garth
North
Wood
Maybanks
Manor
Baynards Sta
(dis)
LAWNS RD
Thurlow Arms
(PH)
HERMONGER LA
COX GREEN RD
Woodthorpe
Starveall
Copse
BAYNARDS RD
Downs Link
South
Wood
RH12
Sussex Border Path
Little
Hawks
Hill
Great
Inholms
CHURCH ST
HAWKRIDGE
Cox Green
Little
Inholms
Hobbs
Copse
The
Kings Head
(PH)
Street
Copse
Works
LYNWICK ST
The
Crickets
HIGHCROFT DR
Woodsomes
Farm
Windacres
Farm
B2128

11

33

14

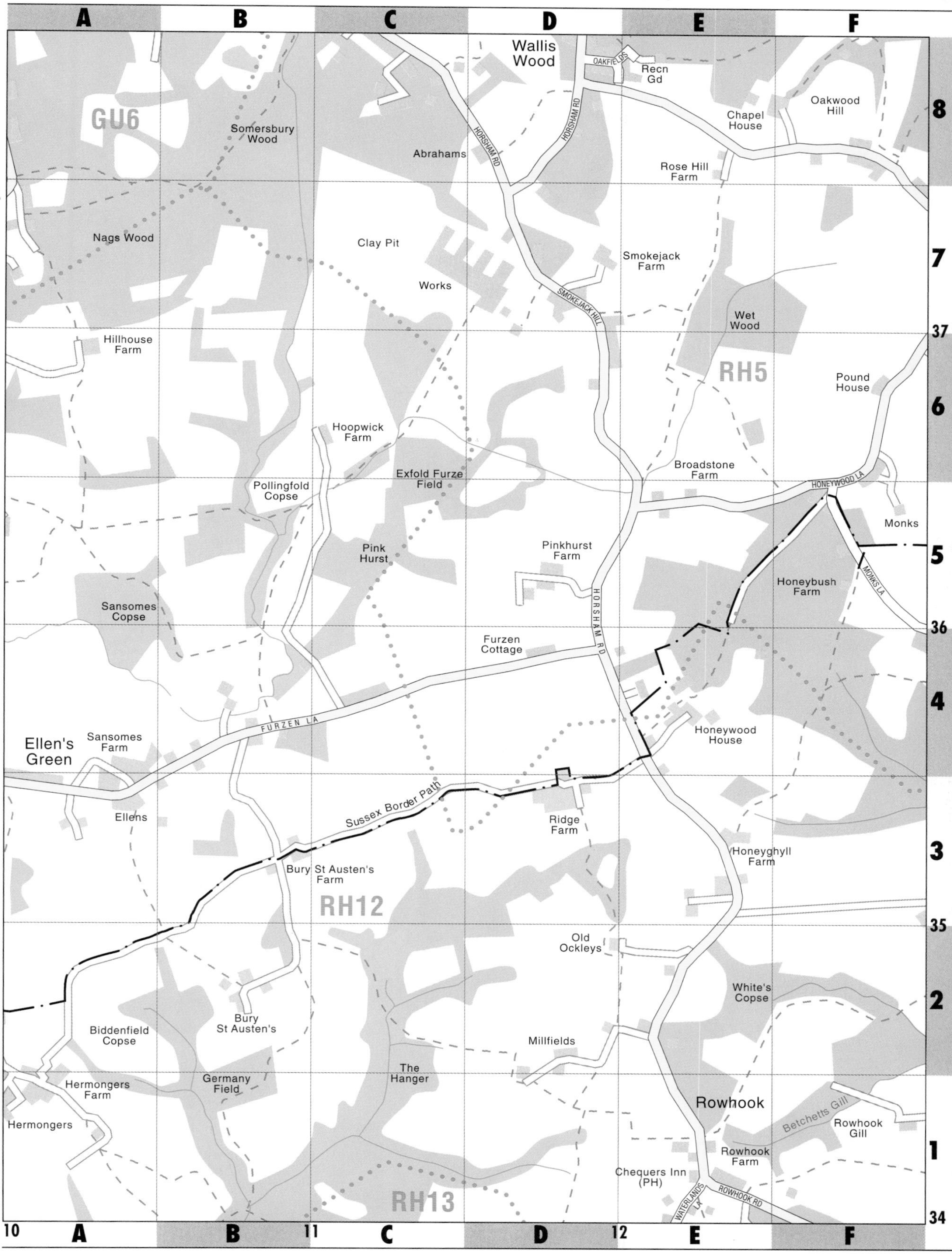

A
B
C
D
E
F
Wallis Wood
OAKFIELDS
Recn Gd
GU6
Somersbury Wood
Abrahams
HORSHAM RD
Chapel House
Oakwood Hill
Rose Hill Farm
Nags Wood
Clay Pit
Works
Smokejack Farm
SMOKEJACK HILL
Wet Wood
Hillhouse Farm
RH5
Pound House
Hoopwick Farm
Broadstone Farm
Exfold Furze Field
Pollingfold Copse
HONEYWOOD LA
Monks
Pink Hurst
Pinkhurst Farm
MONKS LA
Honeybush Farm
Sansomes Copse
Furzen Cottage
FURZEN LA
Ellen's Green
Sansomes Farm
Honeywood House
Sussex Border Path
Ellens
Ridge Farm
Honeyghyll Farm
Bury St Austen's Farm
RH12
Old Ockleys
White's Copse
Biddenfield Copse
Bury St Austen's
Millfields
Hermongers Farm
Germany Field
The Hanger
Rowhook
Hermongers
Betchetts Gill
Rowhook Gill
Rowhook Farm
Chequers Inn (PH)
WATERLANDS LA
ROWHOOK RD
RH13
8
7
37
6
5
36
4
3
35
2
1
34
10
11
12

13

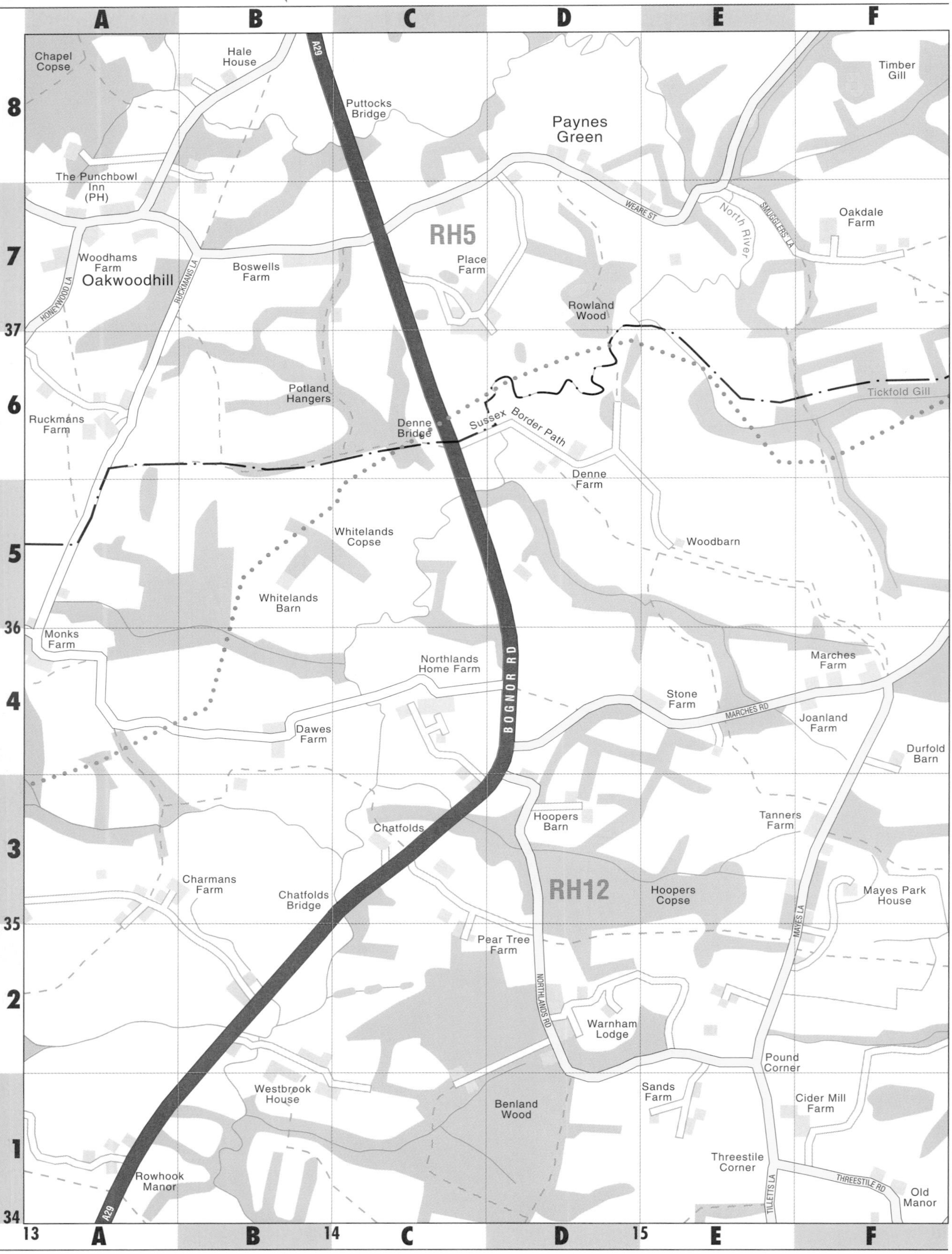
A
B
C
D
E
F
8
7
37
6
5
36
4
3
35
2
1
34
13
14
15
A29
Chapel Copse
Hale House
Puttocks Bridge
Paynes Green
Timber Gill
The Punchbowl Inn (PH)
WEARE ST
North River
SMUGGLERS LA
Oakdale Farm
RH5
Woodhams Farm
Oakwoodhill
HONEYWOOD LA
RUCKMANS LA
Boswells Farm
Place Farm
Rowland Wood
Potland Hangers
Tickfold Gill
Ruckmans Farm
Denne Bridge
Sussex Border Path
Denne Farm
Whitelands Copse
Woodbarn
Whitelands Barn
Monks Farm
BOGNOR RD
Northlands Home Farm
Marches Farm
Stone Farm
MARCHES RD
Joanland Farm
Dawes Farm
Durfold Barn
Hoopers Barn
Tanners Farm
Chatfolds
RH12
Charmans Farm
Chatfolds Bridge
Hoopers Copse
Mayes Park House
MAYES LA
Pear Tree Farm
NORTHLANDS RD
Warnham Lodge
Pound Corner
Westbrook House
Sands Farm
Benland Wood
Cider Mill Farm
Threestile Corner
Rowhook Manor
TILLETTS LA
THREESTILE RD
Old Manor

13

35

16

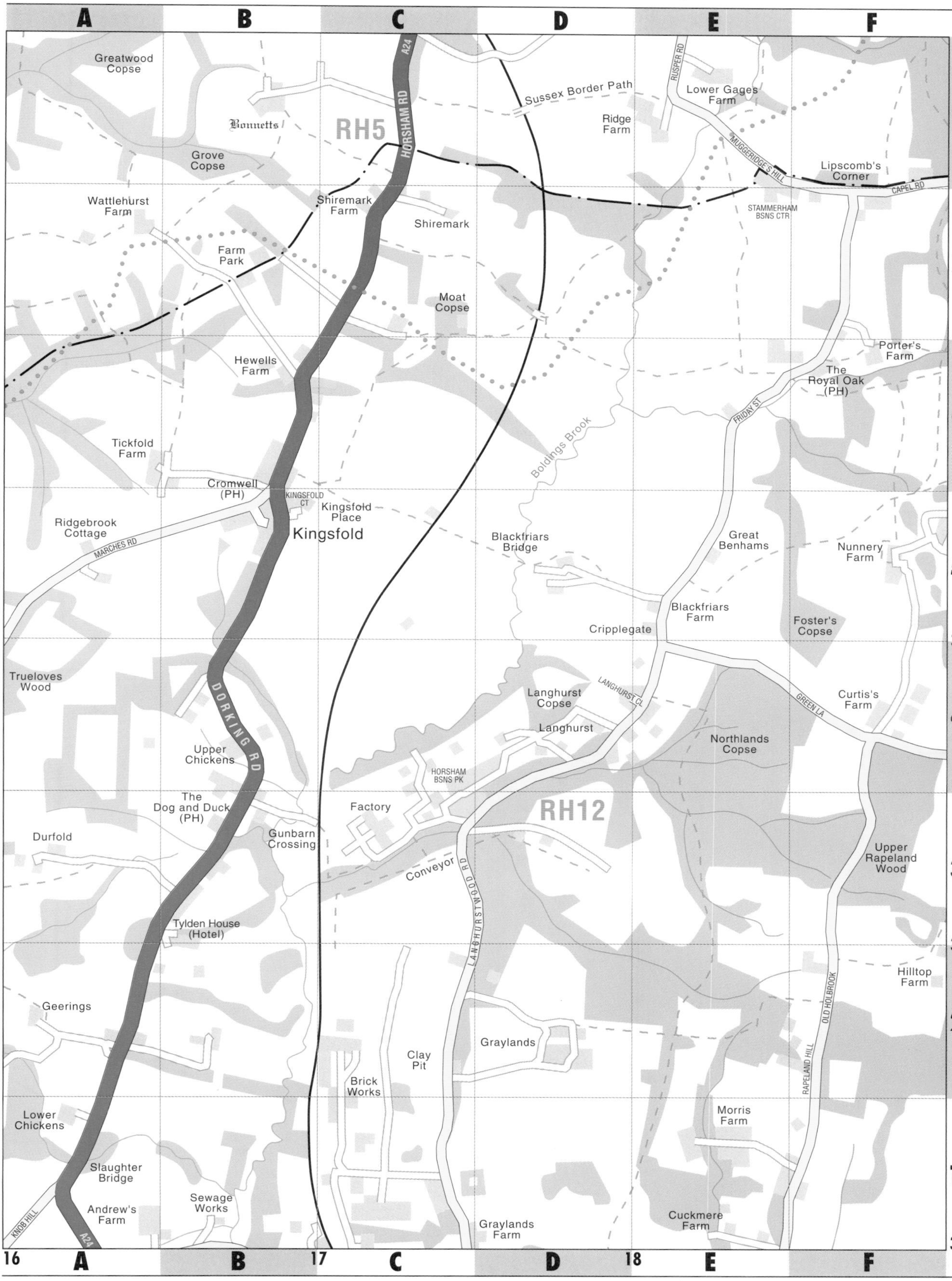
A
B
C
D
E
F
8
7
37
6
5
36
4
3
35
2
1
34
16
17
18
Greatwood Copse
Bonnetts
RH5
HORSHAM RD
A24
Sussex Border Path
RUSPER RD
Lower Gages Farm
Ridge Farm
Grove Copse
MUGGERIDGE'S HILL
Lipscomb's Corner
CAPEL RD
Wattlehurst Farm
Shiremark Farm
Shiremark
STAMMERHAM BSNS CTR
Farm Park
Moat Copse
Porter's Farm
Hewells Farm
The Royal Oak (PH)
FRIDAY ST
Tickfold Farm
Boldings Brook
Cromwell (PH)
KINGSFOLD CT
Kingsfold Place
Ridgebrook Cottage
Kingsfold
MARCHES RD
Blackfriars Bridge
Great Benhams
Nunnery Farm
Blackfriars Farm
Cripplegate
Foster's Copse
Trueloves Wood
LANGHURST CL
Langhurst Copse
Langhurst
GREEN LA
Curtis's Farm
DORKING RD
Northlands Copse
Upper Chickens
HORSHAM BSNS PK
The Dog and Duck (PH)
Factory
RH12
Durfold
Gunbarn Crossing
Upper Rapeland Wood
Conveyor
LANGHURSTWOOD RD
Tylden House (Hotel)
Hilltop Farm
OLD HOLBROOK
Geerings
Graylands
Clay Pit
Brick Works
RAPELAND HILL
Lower Chickens
Morris Farm
Slaughter Bridge
Sewage Works
Andrew's Farm
KNOB HILL
Cuckmere Farm
Graylands Farm

36
16

15
3

A
B
C
D
E
F
8
7
37
6
5
36
4
3
35
2
1
34
19
20
21
Rome Wood
CAPEL RD
New Barn Farm
Highams
CAPEL RD
NEWDIGATE RD
Yew Tree Cott
Furzefield Wood
Rusper House
Venters Farm
Venters
Ghyll Manor (Hotel)
Sussex Border Path
HIGH ST
Rusper
EAST ST
Chowles
PO
PH
Rusper Prim Sch
COOKS MEAD
COOKS MEADOW
Millfields Farm
Normans
Cobnor
Horsegills Wood
ST PETERS HILL
ASHMORE LA
Pucks Croft
Lambs Green
CANONBURY COTTS
LAMBS GREEN RD
PH
Dialpost Farm
GARDENERS GN
Baldhorns Copse
Kiln Copse
Ashfolds
Sewage Farm
Nurseries
Axmas Farm
Rusper Court Farm
Cow Wood
Nuns Wood
Rusper Court House
Rusper Nunnery
Manns Farm
Baldhorns Park Farm
Saykers
HORSHAM RD
River Mole
Baldhorns Park
Old Park
Seers Croft
Fay Cottages
The Lodge
WIMLAND RD
FAYGATE LA
Caryll's Farm
Furze Field
GREEN LA
RH12
Faygate Wood Farm
Sloughbrook Gill
Carylls Lodge
Coombers Farm
Rusper Copse
North Grange Farm
KILNWOOD LA
Holming Wood
WIMLANDS LA
Allingham Wood
Culross
Breakey Gill
Caryll's Lea Farm
Wimland Farm
WIMLAND HILL
Hurst Wood
Hurst Hill
Bakehouse Copse
Durrants Copse
Bush Copse
FAYGATE BSNS CTR
OAK WLK
RUSPER RD
Durrants
Holmbush Inn (PH)
Faygate
Budd's Farm
Hawkesbourne Farm
Benson's Cottage
WIMLAND RD
Faygate
PARK RD
The Castle
BENSON'S LA
CLOVERS COTTS
CARYLLS COTTS
CRAWLEY RD
A264

15
37

4
18

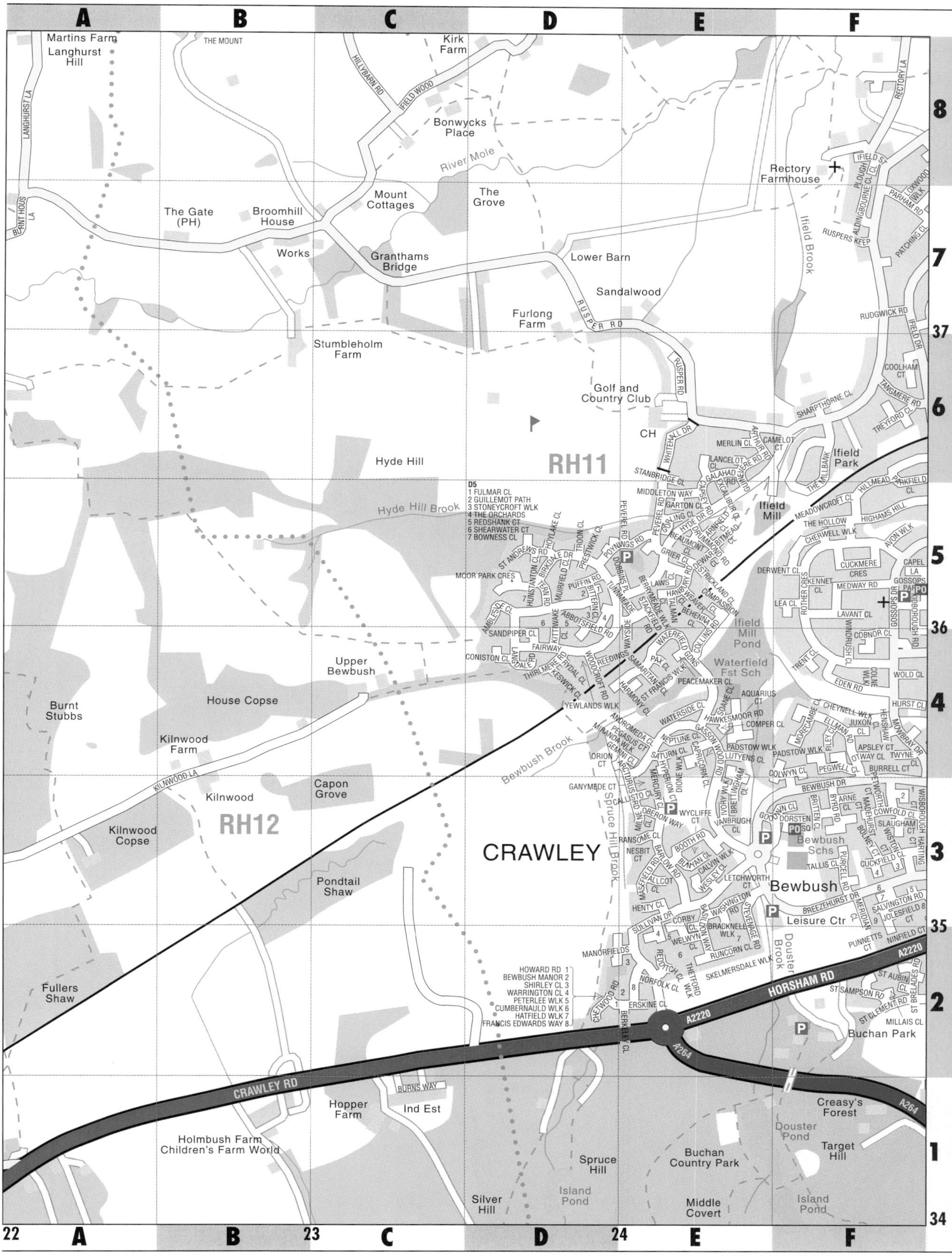

38
18

F3
1 BERSTEAD WLK
2 DONNINGTON CT
3 HASSOCKS CT
4 PYECOMBE CT
5 TELHAM CT
6 WARBLETON HO
7 CALDBECK HO
8 HALNAKER WLK
9 ICKLESHAM HO

17

5

D5
1 THE COURTYARD
2 WALSTEAD HO
3 RAVENDENE CT
4 WILLOWFIELD
5 ASHWOOD
6 PARISH HO
7 PERRYFIELD HO
8 HANDSWORTH HO
9 GLENDON HO
10 ALEXANDRA CT

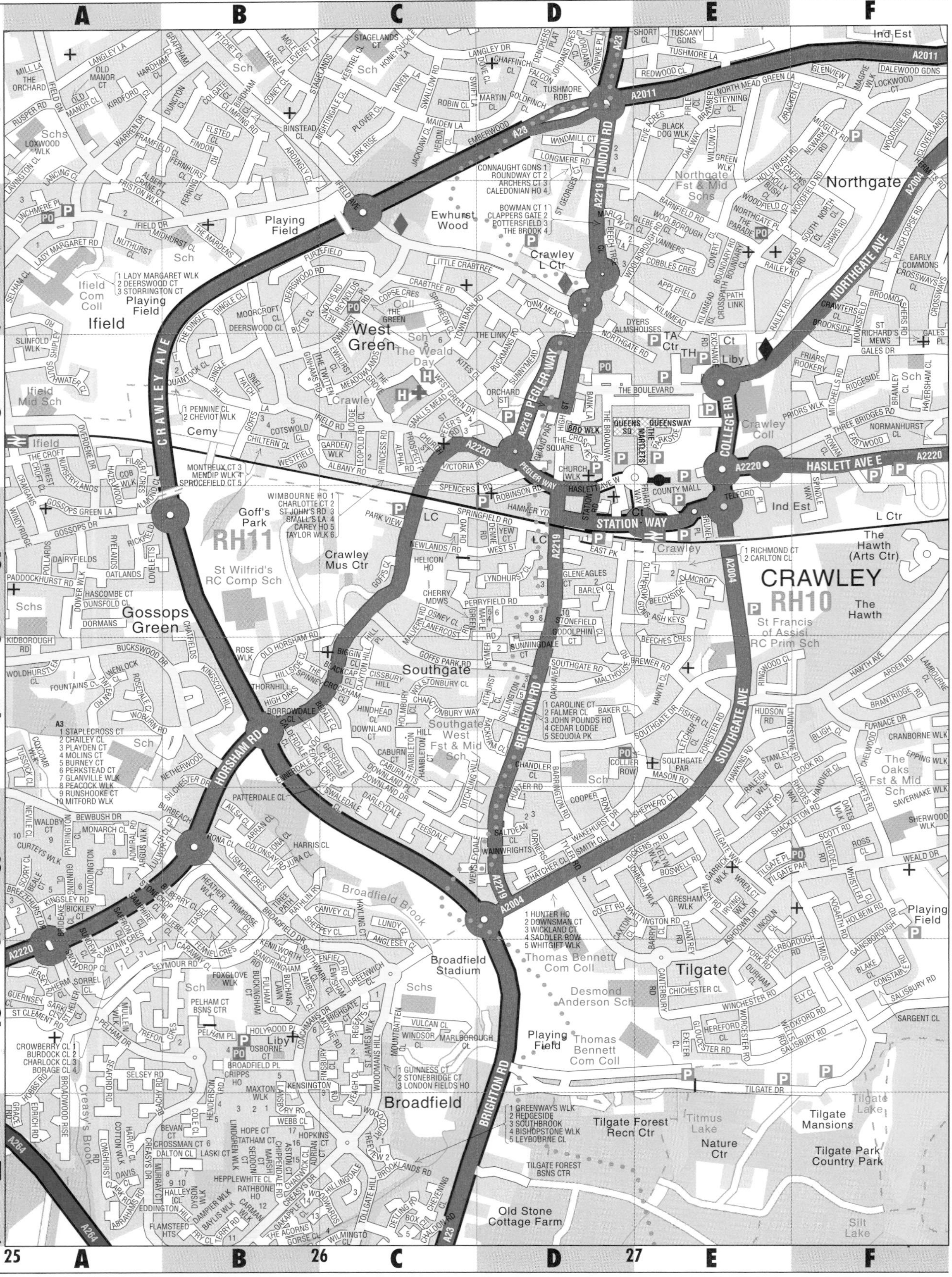

B1
1 STRACHEY CT
2 GREENWOOD CT
3 SHINWELL WLK
4 WILKINSON CT
5 MORRISON CT
6 ADAMSON CT
7 KEIR HARDIE HO
8 SILKIN WLK
9 HERSCHEL WLK
10 JEANS CT
11 PANKHURST CT
12 SHERATON WLK
13 TIMBERLANDS
14 WOODING GR
15 THOMPSON CT
16 RICHARDSON CT
17 RAMSEY CT

17

39

B2
1 CELANDINE CL
2 HENBANE CT
3 SELSEY CT
4 BROADFIELD BARTON
5 ATTLEE HO
6 BALMORAL CT
7 LAMBETH WLK

6
20

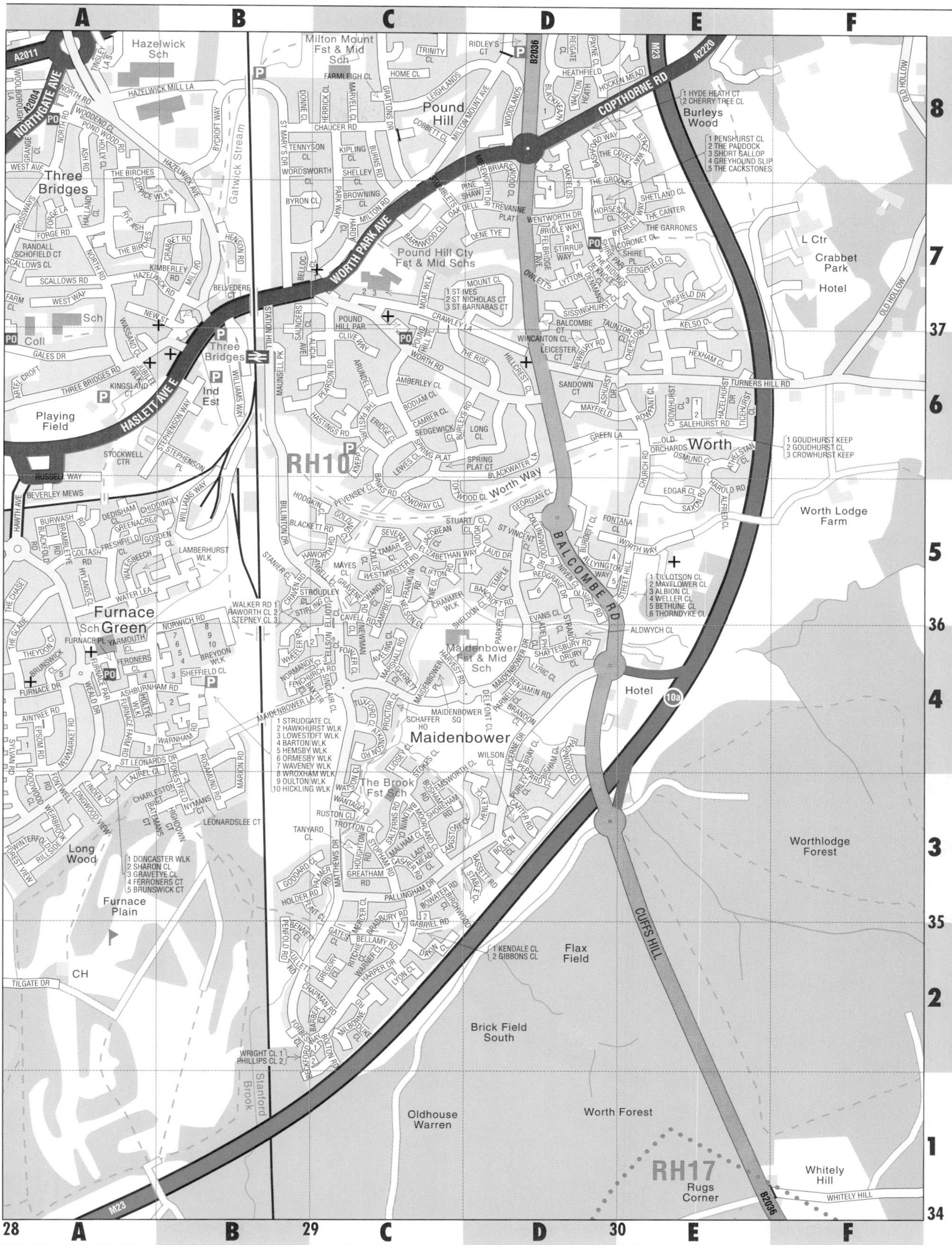

A
B
C
D
E
F
8
7
37
6
5
36
4
3
35
2
1
34
28
29
30
Hazelwick Sch
Milton Mount Fst & Mid Sch
Pound Hill
Burleys Wood
Three Bridges
Pound Hill Cty Fst & Mid Schs
L Ctr
Crabbet Park
Hotel
Coll
Sch
Three Bridges
Ind Est
Playing Field
RH10
Worth
Worth Lodge Farm
Worth Way
Furnace Green
Maidenbower Fst & Mid Sch
Maidenbower
The Brook Fst Sch
Long Wood
Furnace Plain
CH
Worthlodge Forest
Flax Field
Brick Field South
Oldhouse Warren
Worth Forest
RH17
Rugs Corner
Whitely Hill
Gatwick Stream
Stanford Brook
NORTHGATE AVE
HASLETT AVE E
WORTH PARK AVE
COPTHORNE RD
BALCOMBE RD
CUFFS HILL
CRAWLEY LA
TURNERS HILL RD
GREEN LA
WORTH RD
M23
A2011
A2004
A2220
B2036
TILGATE DR
WHITELY HILL
OLD HOLLOW
1 HYDE HEATH CT
2 CHERRY TREE CL
1 PENSHURST CL
2 THE PADDOCK
3 SHORT GALLOP
4 GREYHOUND SLIP
5 THE CACKSTONES
1 GOUDHURST KEEP
2 GOUDHURST CL
3 CROWHURST KEEP
1 TILLOTSON CL
2 MAYFLOWER CL
3 ALBION CL
4 WELLER CL
5 BETHUNE CL
6 THORNDYKE CL
1 ST IVES
2 ST NICHOLAS CT
3 ST BARNABAS CT
WALKER RD 1
RAWORTH CL 2
STEPNEY CL 3
1 STRUDGATE CL
2 HAWKHURST WLK
3 LOWESTOFT WLK
4 BARTON WLK
5 HEMSBY WLK
6 ORMESBY WLK
7 WAVENEY WLK
8 WROXHAM WLK
9 OULTON WLK
10 HICKLING WLK
1 DONCASTER WLK
2 SHARON CL
3 GRAVETYE CL
4 FERRONERS CT
5 BRUNSWICK CT
1 KENDALE CL
2 GIBBONS CL
WRIGHT CL 1
PHILLIPS CL 2

40
20

19
7

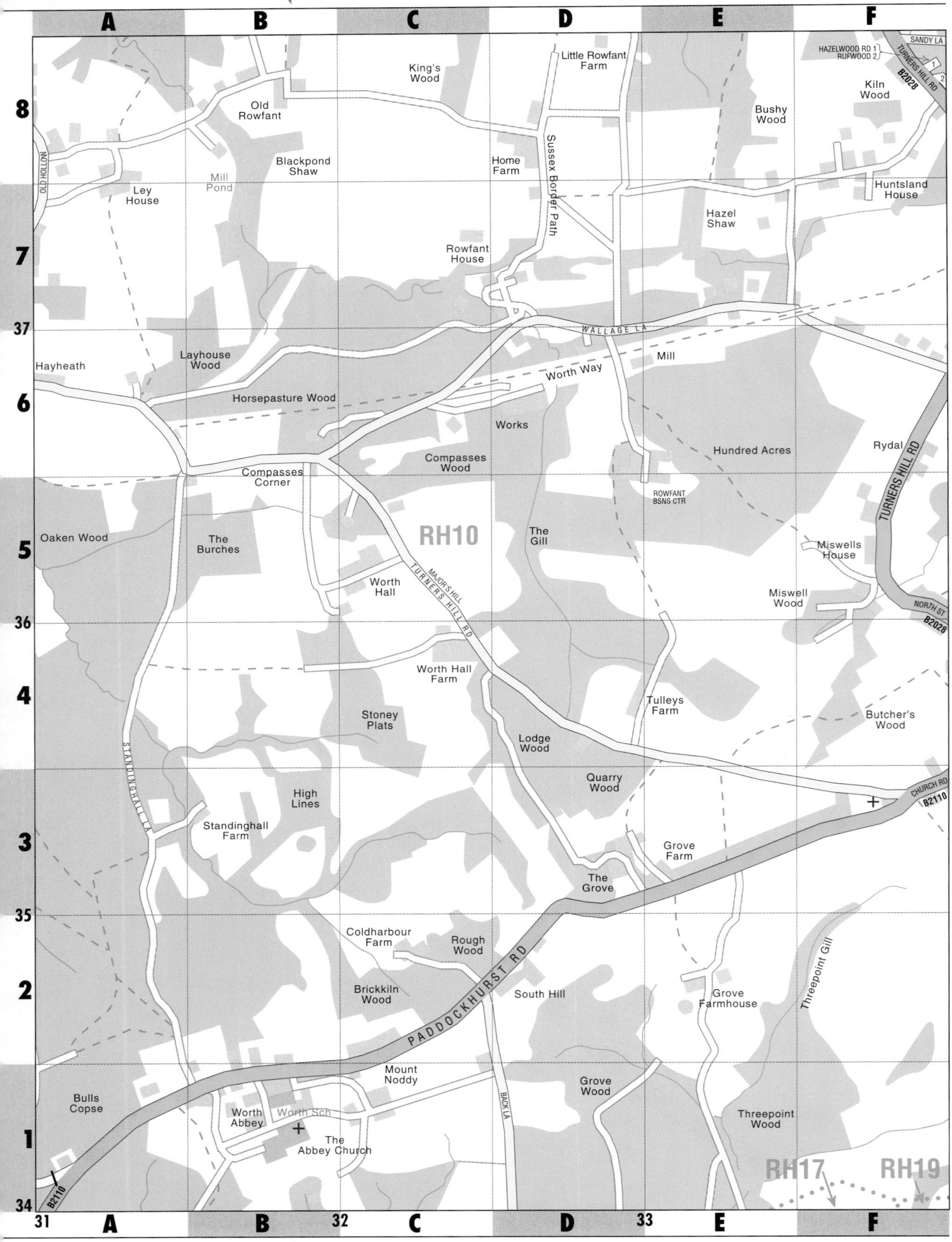
A
B
C
D
E
F
8
7
37
6
5
36
4
3
35
2
1
34
31
32
33
OLD HOLLOW
Old Rowfant
King's Wood
Little Rowfant Farm
SANDY LA
HAZELWOOD RD 1
RUFWOOD 2
TURNERS HILL RD
B2028
Kiln Wood
Bushy Wood
Blackpond Shaw
Mill Pond
Ley House
Home Farm
Sussex Border Path
Huntsland House
Hazel Shaw
Rowfant House
WALLAGE LA
Hayheath
Layhouse Wood
Mill
Worth Way
Horsepasture Wood
Works
Rydal
Hundred Acres
Compasses Wood
Compasses Corner
ROWFANT BSNS CTR
TURNERS HILL RD
Oaken Wood
The Burches
RH10
The Gill
Miswells House
MAJOR'S HILL
TURNERS HILL RD
Worth Hall
Miswell Wood
NORTH ST
B2028
Worth Hall Farm
Tulleys Farm
Stoney Plats
Butcher's Wood
Lodge Wood
STANDINGHALL LA
Quarry Wood
CHURCH RD
B2110
High Lines
Standinghall Farm
Grove Farm
The Grove
Coldharbour Farm
Rough Wood
PADDOCKHURST RD
Threepoint Gill
Brickkiln Wood
South Hill
Grove Farmhouse
Mount Noddy
Bulls Copse
BACK LA
Grove Wood
Worth Abbey
Worth Sch
The Abbey Church
Threepoint Wood
RH17
RH19
B2110

19
41

8
22

A
B
C
D
E
F
8
7
37
6
5
36
4
3
35
2
1
34
34
35
36
SANDY LA
SUNNYHILL CL
HOPHURST CL
HOPHURST DR
THE COPPICE
HILLSIDE
HARWARDEN CL
ASH CL
GRANSTON WAY
THE MARTINS
HAWMEAD
TILTWOOD DR
HALLSLAND
RUFWOOD
GARDNER LA
LONG ACRE
BUCKLEY PL
Schs
UNDERWOOD CL
BURLEIGH WAY
BURLEIGH CL
LARCHES WAY
SPINNEY CL
SQUARES CL
WYNLEA CL
VICARAGE RD
BOWERS PL
STATION RD
FOREST CL
ALDER CL
BIRCH CL
HAZEL WAY
HAZEL CL
COB CL
Worth Way
Rushetts Wood
Gulledge Wood
French Wood
SUNNY AVE
Front Wood
BEECH GDNS
BEECH HOLME
BRICKYARD LA
COPSE CL
WOODLAND DR
PO
SCHOLARS CT
FELBELANDS
OLD STATION CL
KILN RD
BRICKLANDS
WOODLANDS CL
Crawley Down
GRANGE RD
GRANGE CRES
Worth Way
TURNERS HILL RD
SUNNYMEAD 1
RIDGEDALE 2
AUCHINLECK CT 3
ROYAL OAK HO 4
BURLEIGH LA
SANDHILL LA
Sussex Border Path
Tilkhurst Farm
Burleigh House Farm
Grange Farm
The Grange
B2110
Sandhill
Rainbow Shaw
RH10
Little Nobs
Warren Wood
Fen Place Mill
River Medway
Peartree Shaw
Burleigh Oaks Farm
Burleigh Arches Wood
Home Wood
Moat Shaw
Hurley Farm
Mill Wood
MILLWOOD
Ash Leigh Farm
TURNER'S HILL RD
Furze Field
MEDWAY
Burleigh Oaks House
Alexander House
HILL HOUSE CL
B2110
EAST ST
Furzewood Farm
Castle Shaw
NORTH ST
Turners Hill
Target Shaw
LION LA
NOAH'S CT
MOUNT LA
NEW COTTS
PO
Burleigh Farm
Tickeridge Farm
B2110
CHURCH RD
The Crown (PH)
Kingscote
WILLOW RIDGE
WITHYPITTS E
Sch
WITHYPITTS
Spring Wood
Tickeridge Shaw
Rashes Farm
Holstein Wood
South Wood
Rookery Wood
Bluebell Rly
Stone Wood
Withypitts
Coomberdean Wood
Vowels Forest Walk
Withy Pitts Farm
Great Wildgoose Wood
VOWELS LA
P
Minepit Wood
The Punch Bowl (PH)
Thornhill Cottages
Vowels Gill
Mill Place Wood
RH19
SELSFIELD RD
Selsfield Common
Selsfield Place
Drive Shaw
Bushy Wood
Bramblehill
Moatlands
Home Farm
Selsfield Common
Warren's Wood
Ducknell's Wood
Pine Wood
Selsfield House
Hastings Wood
B2028
Gravetye Manor (Hotel)
Lower Lake

42
22

21
9

F8
1 MIDDLE ROW
2 FOREST LODGE
3 SACKVILLE CT
4 GREAT HOUSE CT
5 PORTLAND HO
6 CORNWALL GDNS
7 NORMANDY CL
8 WILLOW MEAD
9 KINGS COPSE
10 REGAL DR
11 BECKETT WAY

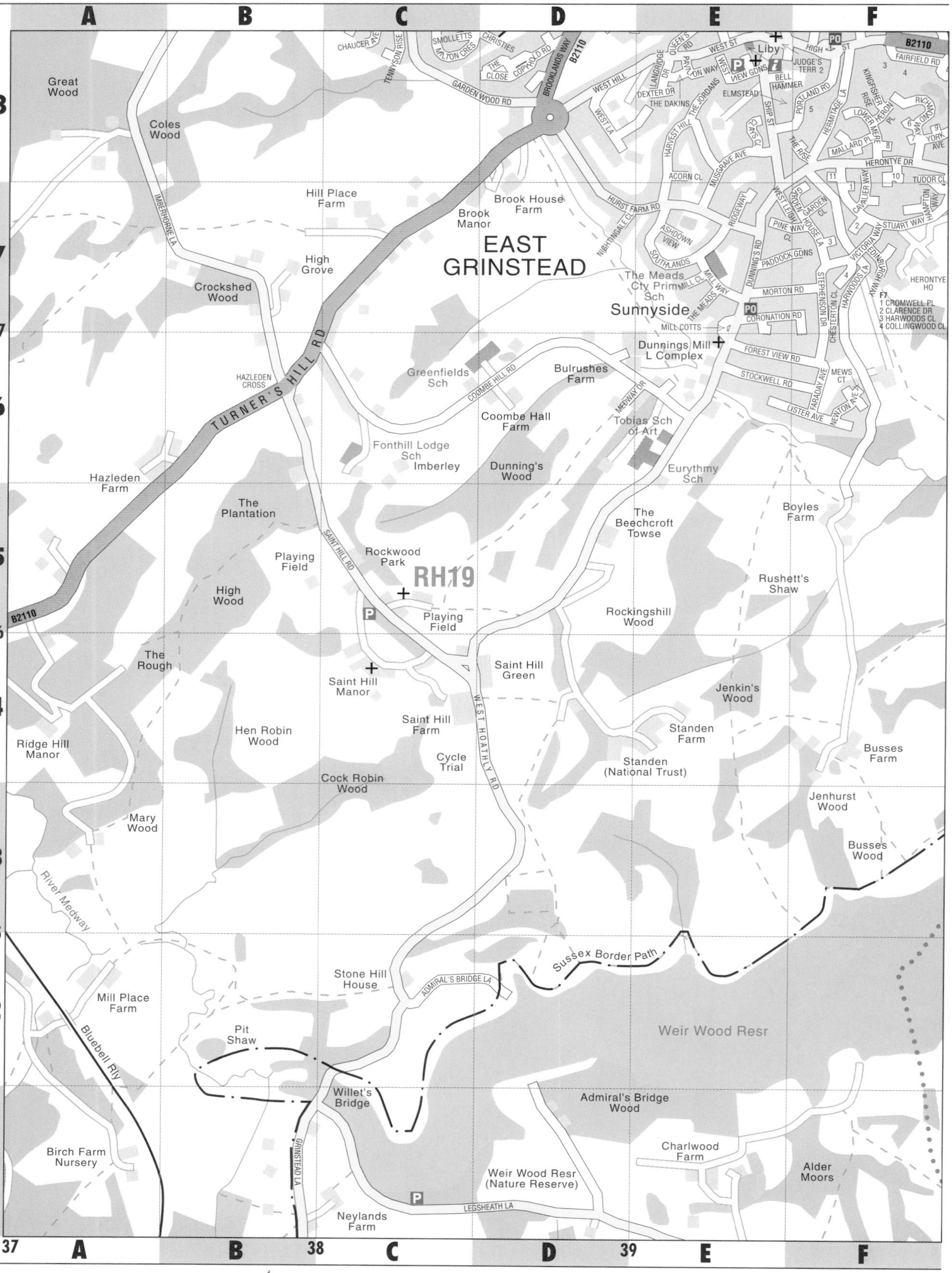

21
43

10

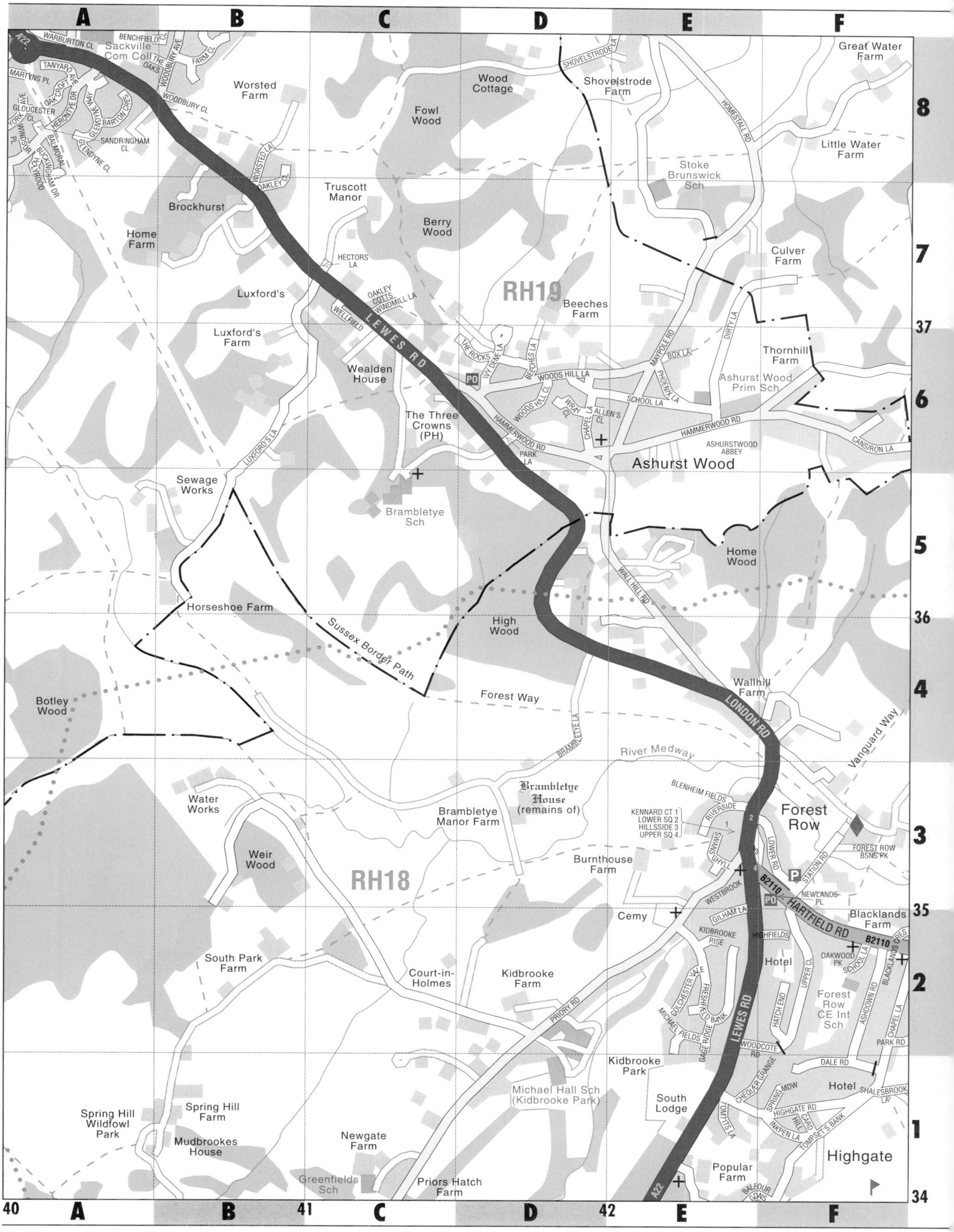
A
B
C
D
E
F
8
7
37
6
5
36
4
3
35
2
1
34
40
41
42
A22
WARBURTON CL
BENCHFIELD CL
Sackville Com Coll
THE OAKS
WOODBURY AVE
FARM CL
TANYARD AVE
MARTYNS PL
OAK CROFT
HERONTYE DR
GLENDYNE WAY
BARTON CRES
GLOUCESTER CL
YORK AVE
WINDSOR PL
BALMORAL
BUCKINGHAM DR
HOLYROOD
SANDRINGHAM CL
GLENDYNE CL
WOODBURY CL
Worsted Farm
Wood Cottage
Fowl Wood
Shovelstrode Farm
SHOVELSTRODE LA
HOMESTALL RD
Great Water Farm
Little Water Farm
Stoke Brunswick Sch
WORSTED LA
OAKLEY CL
Brockhurst
Truscott Manor
Berry Wood
Home Farm
HECTORS LA
Culver Farm
Luxford's
OAKLEY COTTS
WINDMILL LA
RH19
Beeches Farm
WELLFIELD
LEWES RD
Luxford's Farm
THE ROCKS
IVY DENE LA
BEECHES LA
MAYPOLE RD
DIRTY LA
BOX LA
Thornhill Farm
Wealden House
PO
WOODS HILL LA
PHOENIX LA
Ashurst Wood Prim Sch
WOODS HILL CL
WRAY CL
CHAPEL LA
ALLEN'S CL
SCHOOL LA
The Three Crowns (PH)
HAMMERWOOD RD
CANSIRON LA
LUXFORD'S LA
PARK LA
ASHURSTWOOD ABBEY
Ashurst Wood
Sewage Works
Brambletye Sch
Home Wood
WALL HILL RD
Horseshoe Farm
High Wood
Sussex Border Path
Forest Way
Wallhill Farm
Botley Wood
LONDON RD
Vanguard Way
BRAMBLETYE LA
River Medway
Brambletye House (remains of)
BLENHEIM FIELDS
Water Works
Brambletye Manor Farm
RIVERSIDE
KENNARD CT 1
LOWER SQ 2
HILLSIDE 3
UPPER SQ 4
Forest Row
Weir Wood
Burnthouse Farm
SWANS GHYLL
LOWER RD
STATION RD
FOREST ROW BSNS PK
RH18
P
WESTBROOK
B2110
NEWLANDS PL
PO
HARTFIELD RD
Blacklands Farm
Cemy
GILHAM LA
KIDBROOKE RISE
HIGHFIELDS
B2110
BLACKLANDS CRES
South Park Farm
OAKWOOD PK
SCHOOL LA
Hotel
Court-in-Holmes
Kidbrooke Farm
COLCHESTER VALE
FRESHFIELD BANK
UPPER CL
Forest Row CE Inf Sch
ASHDOWN RD
HATCH END
CHAPEL LA
PRIORY RD
MICHAEL FIELDS
GAGE RIDGE
WOODCOTE RD
PARK RD
DALE RD
Kidbrooke Park
CHEQUER GRANGE
Hotel
SHALESBROOK LA
Michael Hall Sch (Kidbrooke Park)
South Lodge
SPRING MDW
HIGHGATE RD
Spring Hill Wildfowl Park
Spring Hill Farm
TOMTITS LA
HILL CARD
INKPEN LA
TOMPSET'S BANK
Mudbrookes House
Newgate Farm
Highgate
Popular Farm
Greenfields Sch
Priors Hatch Farm
BALFOUR GDNS

44

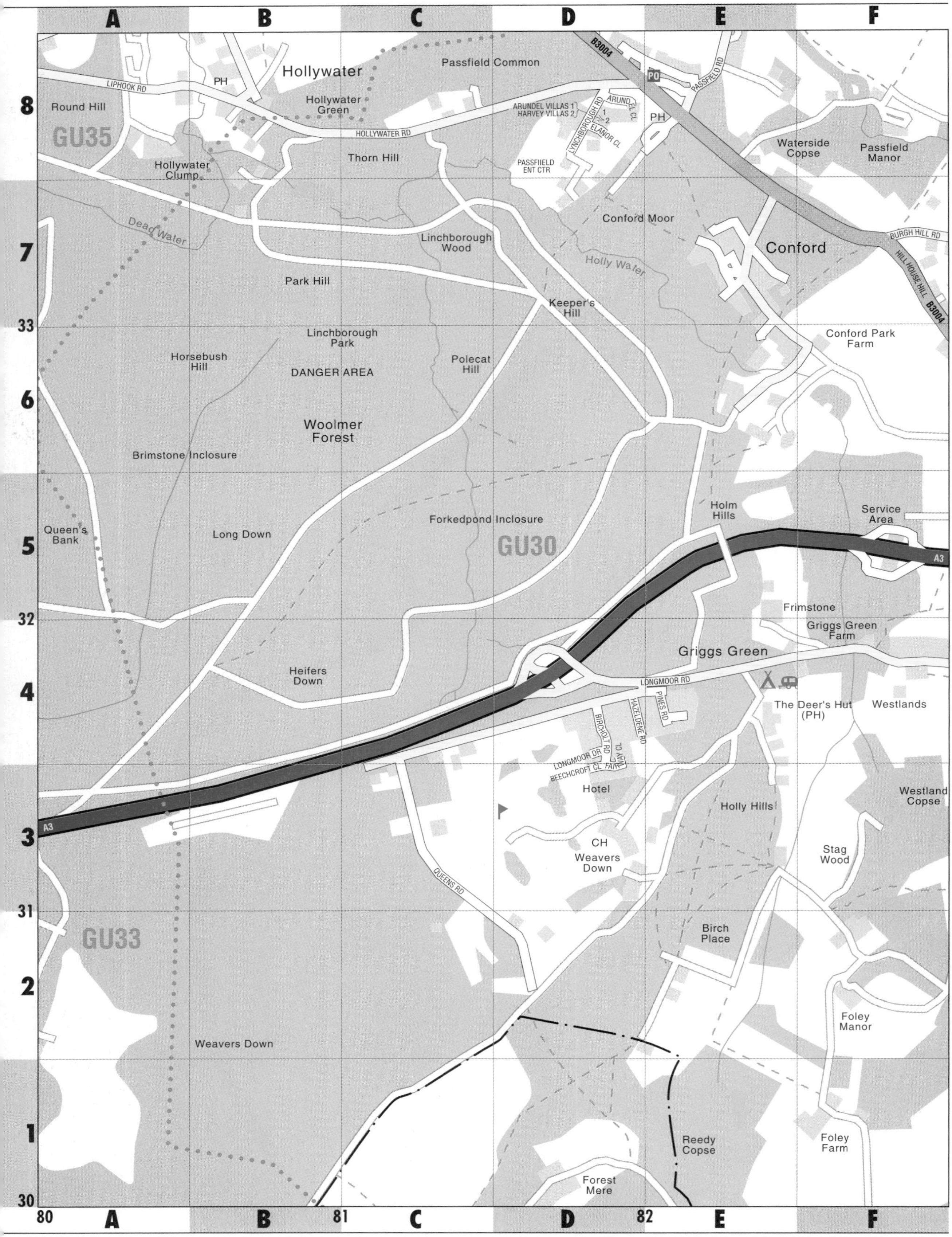

A
B
C
D
E
F
8
7
33
6
5
32
4
3
31
2
1
30
80
81
82
Round Hill
GU35
PH
Hollywater
LIPHOOK RD
Hollywater Green
Passfield Common
B3004
PO
PASSFIELD RD
ARUNDEL VILLAS 1
HARVEY VILLAS 2
ARUNDEL CL
LYNCHBOROUGH RD
ELANOR CL
PH
HOLLYWATER RD
Thorn Hill
Hollywater Clump
PASSFIELD ENT CTR
Waterside Copse
Passfield Manor
Dead Water
Conford Moor
Linchborough Wood
Holly Water
Conford
BURGH HILL RD
HILL HOUSE HILL
B3004
Park Hill
Keeper's Hill
Linchborough Park
Horsebush Hill
DANGER AREA
Polecat Hill
Conford Park Farm
Woolmer Forest
Brimstone Inclosure
Holm Hills
Service Area
Queen's Bank
Long Down
Forkedpond Inclosure
GU30
A3
Frimstone
Griggs Green Farm
Griggs Green
Heifers Down
LONGMOOR RD
PINES RD
HAZELDENE RD
BIRCHOLT RD
FAIRWAY CL
LONGMOOR DR
BEECHCROFT CL
The Deer's Hut (PH)
Westlands
Hotel
Holly Hills
Westland Copse
A3
CH
Weavers Down
Stag Wood
QUEENS RD
GU33
Birch Place
Foley Manor
Weavers Down
Reedy Copse
Foley Farm
Forest Mere

A
B
C
D
E
F
8
7
6
5
4
3
2
1
33
32
31
30
83
84
85
The Hanger
Coach House Copse
Kent's Hill
GU26
Bramshott Court
Oaklea Farm
Spring Pond Hanger
Downlands Farm
Spring Pond
Cooper's Stream
Coopers Bridge
Camp Site (disused)
Cooper's Bridge Farm
Glebe House Farm
BURGH HILL RD
RECTORY LA
Elm Grove Farm
LIMES CL
A3
HAMPSHIRE HO
CHURCH LA
Bramshott
Bramshott Vale
CHURCH RD
TUNBRIDGE LA
PORTSMOUTH RD
HILL HOUSE HILL
Bramshott Vale Farm
Conford Park Gate
Woodlands
B2171
Cold Ash Hill
LONDON RD
Old Barn Farm
DRYDEN WAY
Penally Farm
Hewshott Farm
HEADLEY RD
HUNTERS CHASE
TYLSTON MEADOW
ALLEE DR
VALLEY SIDE
TUNBRIDGE CRES
PADDOCK WAY
WEYLAND CL
GREENFIELD CL
HEWSHOTT GR
HEWSHOTT LA
Lowsley Farm
THE MEAD
MEADOW END
Hewshott Lodge
TREGENNA HO
LARK RISE
HANOVER CT
MEADOW WAY
GU30
HURST CL
YEOMANS LA
THE AVENUE
TOWER RD
FOREST LANE CL
CHALCRAFT CL
AVENUE CL
TOWER CL
MEADOW CL
CALVECROFT
WEY LODGE CL
LOCKE RD
STONEHOUSE RD
Schs
Liphook
THE GROVE
HAWKSHAW CL
LONGMOOR RD
CANDLEFORD GATE
CHILDERSTONE CL
MALTHOUSE MDWS
WYCH WOOD
THE MALTINGS
COLLYERS CRES
MALTHOUSE CT
ERLES RD
HASLEMERE RD
Bridge
GILHAM'S LA
B3004
Liby
LINCOLN CT
CHAPPELL CL
GRENVILLE CL
CHILTLEE CL
MANOR FIELDS
HAZELBANK CL
Bridge Lodge
B2131
LIPHOOK RD
Bohunt Com Sch
B2070
CHILTLEE MANOR
ONTARIO WAY
HURON DR
DEVILS LA
PO
SHIPLEY CT
Superstore
WILLOW CL
ASH GR
LARCH CL
COURT CL
THE FIRS
FIRVIEW 1
CHURCHFIELD CT 2
MONTREAL WLK
CANADA WAY
WILLOW GDNS
CHESTNUT CL
Lower Brookham
FIELD PL
WINNIPEG CL
SHEPHERDS WAY
GOLDENFIELDS CL
FLETCHERS HO 1
GOOSERYE CT 2
FLETCHERS FIELD
Brookham Plantation
NEWTOWN RD
BEAVER IND EST
HIGHFIELD LA
Bohunt
HARRIS CT
REDHOUSE MEWS
MIDHURST RD
CHILTLEY LA
Brookham Sch
STATION RD
Newtown
Liphook
Highfield Sch
GU27
Bohunt Manor Garden
The Links Hotel
BLEACH'S YARD IND EST
THE CLOSE
GUNNS FARM
CHILTLEY WAY
Littlefield Sch
ADMERS CRES
HOLLYCOMBE CL
SOUTH RD
Stanley Common
NORTH LODGE IND PK

25

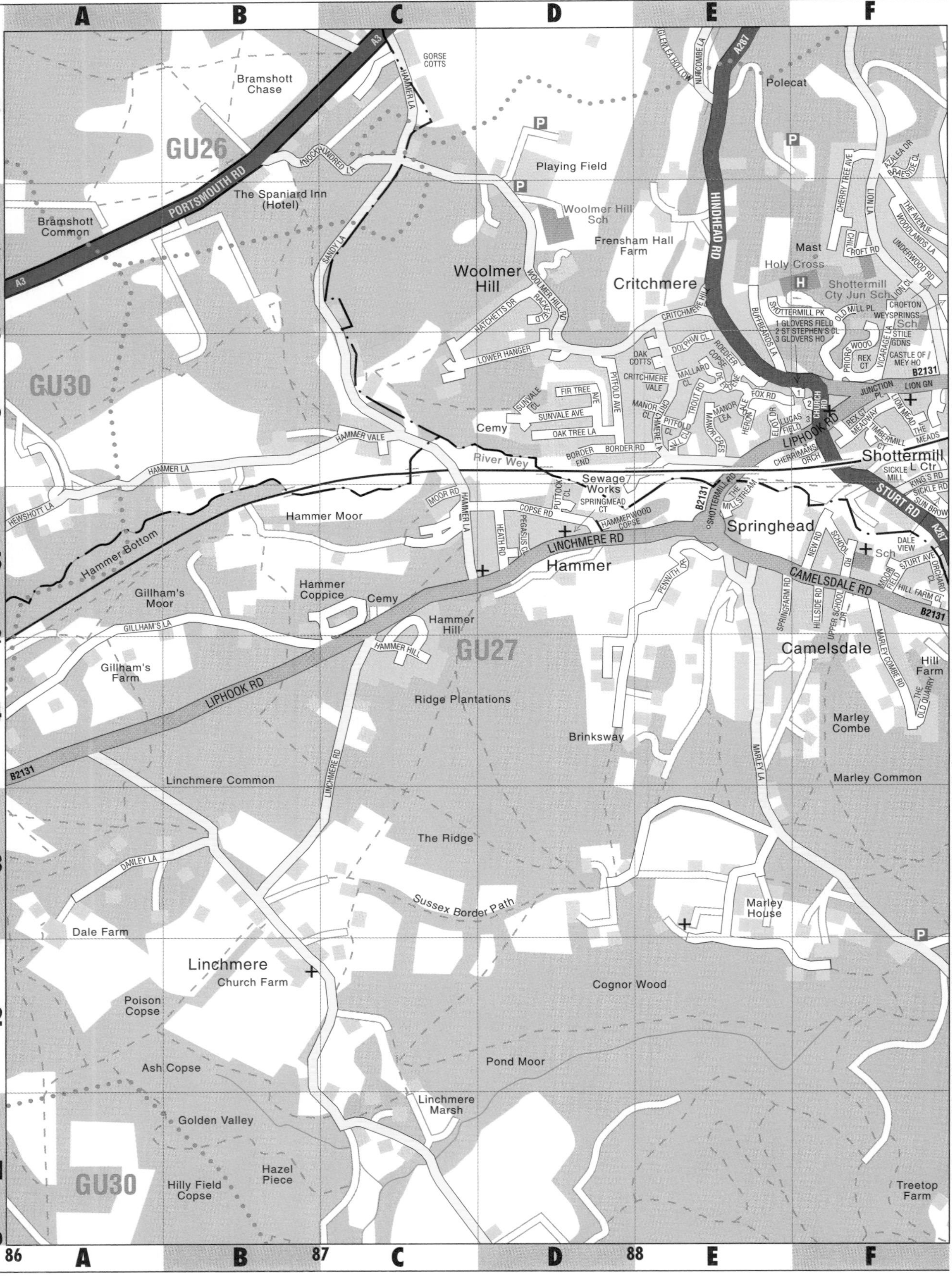
A
B
C
D
E
F
8
7
33
6
5
32
4
3
31
2
1
30
86
87
88
A3
GORSE COTTS
HAMMER LA
Bramshott Chase
GU26
KNOCKHUNDRED LA
PORTSMOUTH RD
The Spaniard Inn (Hotel)
Bramshott Common
SANDY LA
Playing Field
Woolmer Hill Sch
Frensham Hall Farm
Woolmer Hill
WOOLMER HILL RD
HATCHETTS DR
LOWER HANGER
Critchmere
CRITCHMERE HILL
GLEN LEA HOLLOW
NUTCOMBE LA
A287
HINDHEAD RD
Polecat
Mast
Holy Cross
H
Shottermill Cty Jun Sch
CHERRY TREE AVE
LION LA
AZALEA DR
BRAESIDE CL
THE AVENUE
WOODLANDS LA
UNDERWOOD RD
ROFT RD
LION CL
CROFTON
WEYSPRINGS
Sch
STILE GDNS
CASTLE OF MEY HO
SHOTTERMILL PK
OLD MILL PL
1 GLOVERS FIELD
2 ST STEPHEN'S CL
3 GLOVERS HO
BUFFBEARDS LA
PRIORS WOOD
REX CT
VICARAGE LA
B2131
JUNCTION PL
LION GN
LION MEAD
THE MEADS
DOLPHIN CL
ROEDEER COPSE
OAK COTTS
CRITCHMERE VALE
MALLARD CL
MANOR CL
FIR TREE AVE
SUNVALE CL
SUNVALE AVE
OAK TREE LA
PITFOLD AVE
PITFOLD CL
TROUT RD
MANOR LEA
MANOR CRES
HERONS
FOX RD
ELIOT DR
LUCAS FIELD
CHURCH LA
LIPHOOK RD
CHERRIMANS ORCH
REX CT
MEADWAY
TIMBERMILL CT
Shottermill
SICKLE MILL
L Ctr
KING'S RD
SICKLE RD
SUN BROW
STURT RD
GU30
Cemy
HAMMER VALE
River Wey
BORDER END
BORDER RD
Sewage Works
HAMMER LA
HEWSHOTT LA
Hammer Bottom
MOOR RD
Hammer Moor
COPSE RD
PUTTOCK CL
SPRINGMEAD CT
HAMMERWOOD COPSE
SHOTTERMILL RD
THE MAULSTREAM
Springhead
HEATH RD
PEGASUS CL
LINCHMERE RD
Hammer
NEW RD
SCHOOL RD
DALE VIEW
Sch
STURT AVE
ORCHARD CL
MOOR FIELD
HILL FARM CL
CAMELSDALE RD
Gillham's Moor
Hammer Coppice
Cemy
PENWITH DR
SPRINGFARM RD
HILLSIDE RD
UPPER SCHOOL DR
GILLHAM'S LA
Hammer Hill
HAMMER HILL
GU27
Camelsdale
MARLEY COMBE RD
Hill Farm
Gillham's Farm
LIPHOOK RD
THE OLD QUARRY
Ridge Plantations
Brinksway
Marley Combe
B2131
Linchmere Common
LINCHMERE RD
MARLEY LA
Marley Common
The Ridge
DANLEY LA
Sussex Border Path
Marley House
P
Dale Farm
Linchmere
Church Farm
Cognor Wood
Poison Copse
Pond Moor
Ash Copse
Linchmere Marsh
Golden Valley
GU30
Hazel Piece
Hilly Field Copse
Treetop Farm

25

48

28

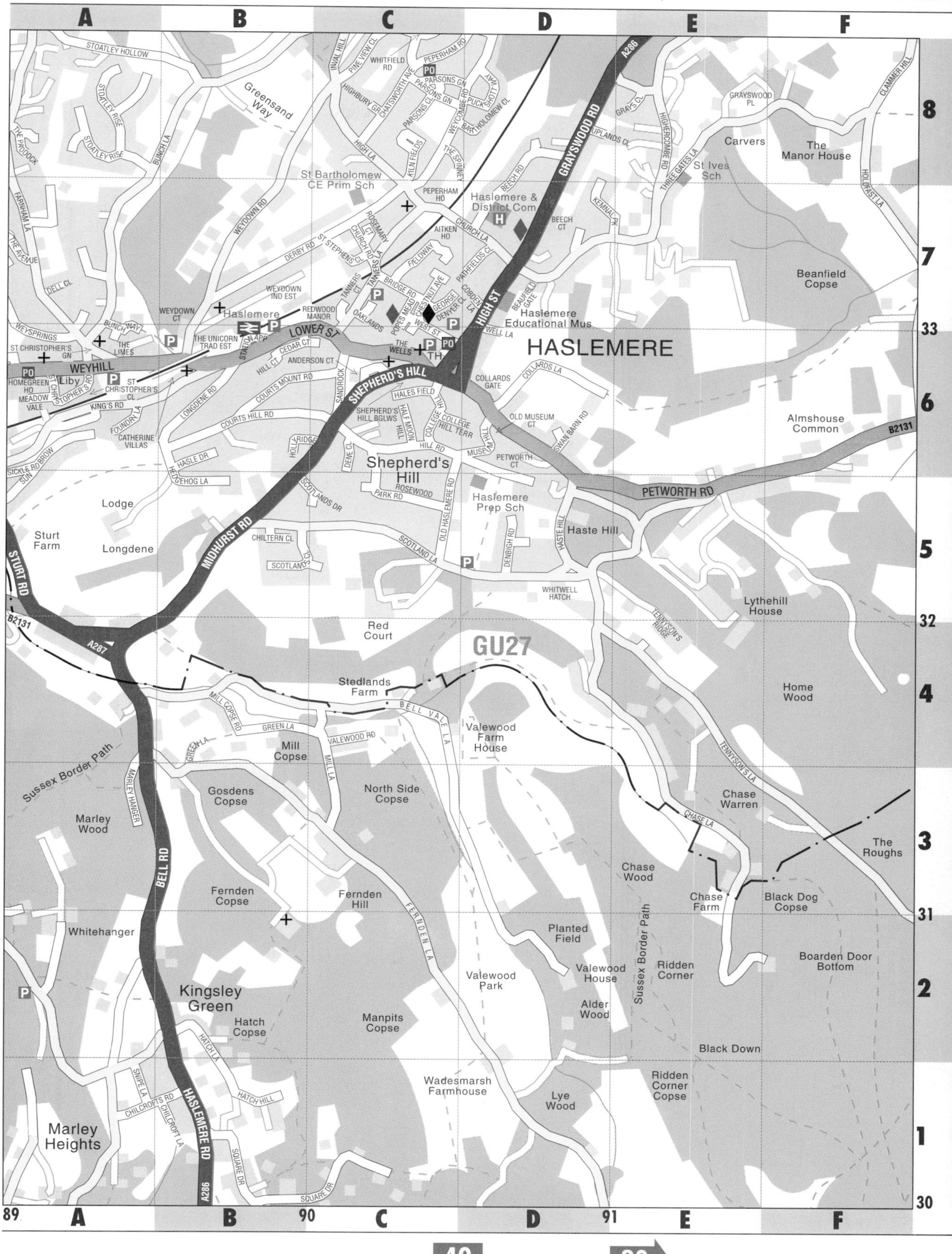
A
B
C
D
E
F
HASLEMERE
GU27
Shepherd's Hill
STOATLEY HOLLOW
STOATLEY RISE
Greensand Way
BUNCH LA
THE PADDOCK
FARNHAM LA
THE AVENUE
DELL CL
WEYDOWN RD
St Bartholomew CE Prim Sch
INVAL HILL
PINE VIEW CL
WHITFIELD RD
PEPERHAM RD
PARSONS GN
HIGHBURY GR
CHATSWORTH AVE
PARSONS CL
WEYCOMBE RD
PUCKSHOTT WAY
BARTHOLOMEW CL
HIGH LA
KILN FIELDS
THE SPINNEY
PEPERHAM HO
Haslemere & District Com
BEECH RD
GRAYSWOOD RD
GRAYS CL
UPLANDS CL
HIGHERCOMBE RD
THREE GATES LA
GRAYSWOOD PL
CLAMMER HILL
Carvers
The Manor House
St Ives Sch
KEMNAL PK
HOLDFAST LA
BEECH CT
AITKEN HO
CHURCH LA
ROSEMARY CT
CHURCH RD
ST STEPHENS CL
DERBY RD
TANNERS LA
FIELDWAY
PATHFIELDS CL
Beanfield Copse
WEYDOWN IND EST
TANNERS CT
BRIDGE RD
CHESTNUT AVE
GEORGE RD
COBDEN LA
BEAUFIELD GATE
HIGH ST
Haslemere Educational Mus
WEYDOWN CT
Haslemere
REDWOOD MANOR
OAKLANDS
POPES MEAD
DENYER CL
WEST ST
WELL LA
WEYSPRINGS
BUNCH WAY
THE LIMES
THE UNICORN TRAD EST
STATION APP
LOWER ST
ST CHRISTOPHER'S GN
WEYHILL
HOMEGREEN HO
MEADOW VALE
Liby
ST CHRISTOPHER'S RD
ST CHRISTOPHER'S CL
KING'S RD
HILL CT
CEDAR CT
ANDERSON CT
THE WELLS
TH
COLLARDS GATE
COLLARDS LA
FOUNDRY LA
LONGDENE RD
COURTS MOUNT RD
SANDROCK
SHEPHERD'S HILL
HALES FIELD
OLD MUSEUM CT
SWAN BARN RD
Almshouse Common
B2131
CATHERINE VILLAS
COURTS HILL RD
SHEPHERD'S HILL BGLWS
HALF MOON HILL
COLLEGE HILL
COLLEGE HILL TERR
HILL RD
MUSEUM HILL
SICKLE RD
SUN BROW
HOLLY RIDGE
HASLE DR
DEME CL
PETWORTH CT
PETWORTH RD
HEDGEHOG LA
ROSEWOOD
PARK RD
SCOTLANDS DR
OLD HASLEMERE RD
Haslemere Prep Sch
Lodge
Sturt Farm
Longdene
MIDHURST RD
CHILTERN CL
SCOTLAND LA
SCOTLANDS CL
DENBIGH RD
HASTE HILL
Haste Hill
STURT RD
WHITWELL HATCH
Lythehill House
TENNYSON'S RIDGE
Red Court
A287
A286
Stedlands Farm
BELL VALE LA
Home Wood
MILL COPSE RD
GREEN LA
VALEWOOD RD
Valewood Farm House
Mill Copse
MILL LA
Sussex Border Path
MARLEY HANGER
Gosdens Copse
North Side Copse
TENNYSON'S LA
Chase Warren
Marley Wood
CHASE LA
The Roughs
BELL RD
Chase Wood
Fernden Copse
Fernden Hill
FERNDEN LA
Chase Farm
Black Dog Copse
Whitehanger
Planted Field
Valewood House
Ridden Corner
Boarden Door Bottom
Valewood Park
Kingsley Green
Hatch Copse
Manpits Copse
Alder Wood
Black Down
HATCH LA
SNIPE LA
HATCH HILL
Wadesmarsh Farmhouse
Lye Wood
Ridden Corner Copse
CHILCROFTS RD
CHILCROFT LA
HASLEMERE RD
Marley Heights
SQUARE DR
8
7
33
6
5
32
4
3
31
2
1
30
89
90
91

49

28

27

A
B
C
D
E
F
8
7
33
6
5
32
4
3
31
2
1
30
92
93
94
Imbhams Farm
Newhouse Great Copse
WEST END LA
Hollis's Hanger
GU8
KILLINGHURST LA
Ramster
Hovell Copse
Killinghurst
Furnace Moor
HOLDFAST LA
Holdfast House
Furnace Place
Killinghurst Great Copse
Chaleshurst Copse
Verney Copse
Chaleshurst
A283
PH
Knobby Copse
B2131
Lytho Hill
PETWORTH RD
Benham Stud
CRIPPLECRUTCH HILL
B2131
Lythe Hill Hotel
Ansteadbrook
RODGATE LA
Dickhurst House
Dencher Copse
Home Wood
GU27
East Broadlands
Anstead Brook Stud
Dickhurst Farm
GU8
High Barn Farm
Barfold Copse
Hearne Copse
Boxalland Farm
Gospel Green
Barfold Firs
Boxalland Copse
A283
Owlden
Sussex Border Path
Fisherstreet
JAY'S LA
Breachhurst Copse
Barfold
Jay's Farm
Fisherstreet Farm
TENNYSON'S LA
Blanshotts Copse
GU28
Aldworth House
Hovel Copse
Jay's Copse
Moorland Copse
JOBSON'S LA
P
P
Upper Roundhurst Farm
Roundhurst Common
Fisherstreet Copse
Lower Roundhurst
Greenland Copse
Copygrove Copse
Greenland Farm
Wateredge Copse

27

50

30

A
B
C
D
E
F
8
7
33
6
5
32
4
3
31
2
1
30
95
96
97
A283
Windmill Copse
Great Copse
Chiddingfold
Tugley Farm
Hungry Corner
Sparkes Copse
PICKHURST RD
Rovehurst Wood
Fisherlane Hanger
Griggs Bottom
Gostrode Farm
Fisher Lane Nursery
Little Tugley
Surrey Copse
Robins Farm
FISHER LA
Sussex Border Path
GODSTRODE LA
Ramsnest Common
White's Hill
Redlands Farm
Works
Surrey Belt
CH
Furze Field
PLAISTOW RD
Surrey Rough
Big Copse
Potlane Farm
Downlands
Walk Copse
Shillinglee Park
Upper North Pond
GU8
Downlands Wood
Parkgate
Lower North Pond
Shillinglee Home Farm
Manorhill Copse
Stilland Farm
SHILLINGLEE RD
Gaston's Farm
Newhouse Farm
Turnour's Wood
Deer Tower
New Copse
Nine Acre Rew
Beanfield Copse
Little Hayman's Farm
Eastland Farm
Haymans Farm
Twenty Four Acres
China Bridge
The Lake
RH14
GU28
Mill Copse
Park Mill Farm
Frith Lodge
The Plantation
Frith Wood
Frith Hill
Dale's Farm Hanger
Dale's Farm

51

30

A
B
C
D
E
F
8
7
33
6
5
32
4
3
31
2
1
30
98
99
00
Oaken Wood
Canterbury Copse
Ireland
Hurlands Copse
Burntwood Kennels
Old Lands
Peartree Hanger
PLAISTOW RD
Oak Wood
The Hatchetts
Tugley Wood
GU8
Upper Ifold
Inside Copse
Tidy's Copse
Durfold Hall Farm
Durfold Hatch Cottage
Birch Copse
FISHER LA
Dungate Farm
Woodland Walks
Oakhurst Farm
Upper Ifold Wood
Sussex Border Path
Fisherlane Wood
Durfold Wood
Weald Barkfold Copse
DURFOLD WOOD
Shortland Copse
Downlands Wood
DUNSFOLD RD
Barkfold Hanger
Wilkins Wood Farm
Ashpark Wood
Weald Barkfold
RH14
Short's Farm
Works
Oakhurst
SHILLINGLEE RD
Highbridge House
Lyon's Farm
COUNCIL COTTS
Kingspark Wood
Plaistow Inf Sch
PH
PO
NELL BALL
OAKFIELD
THE STREET
ASHFIELD
BACK LA
LOXWOOD RD
Ifold Copse
Plaistow
Beggars Copse
BUSHFIELD
Birchfold Copse
RICKMAN'S LA
GU28
Sparrwood Hangar
Rumbold Wood
Rumbolds Farm
Chilsfold Farm

32

A
B
C
D
E
F
Old Knightons
Upper Ifold Farm
GU8
Old Lock House
Glasshouse Copse
Priorswood
Alfold
B2133
ROSEMARY LA
Turtles Farm
LOXWOOD RD
High Bridge
Sydney Wood Cott
GU6
Westland Copse
Sir Roger Tichbourne (PH)
Alfold Bars
PIGBUSH LA
THE WALLED GARDEN
Loxwood Hall
Gennets Wood
OAKHURST LA
Oakhurst Farm
Tokens Farm
Thirds Copse
Sydney Farm
Lee House Farm
Gennets Wood
The Rookery
Barberry Furze
Sussex Border Path
Barberry Bridge
Wey-South Path
Gennets Furze
Pawlies Farm
Hog Wood
Oxoncroft Copse
Pond Copse
POND COPSE LA
Hog Copse
Gennets Farm
Furzen Wood
IFOLD BRIDGE LA
POUND CL
Loxwood
POND CL
THE LANE
Hogwood Farm
Barn Wood
RH14
NICHOLSFIELD
GLEBELANDS
PO
STATION RD
THISTLEDOWN VALE
HOGWOOD RD
Loxwood Place Farm
Devil's Hole
B2133
POUNDFIELD LA
Ifold
CHALK RD
WYCHWOOD
WILDACRE CL
THE CLOSE
Loxwoodhills Pond
LOXWOOD RD
THE RIDE
Charleshurst
THE DRIVE
Quennells Farm
Spring Copse
IFOLDHURST
Headfoldswood Farm
Corner Copse
PLAISTOW RD
Flitchings Farm
LAKERS LEA
RICKMAN'S LA
FOXBRIDGE LA
Foxbridge Hanger
Little Headfoldswood Copse
Foxbridge Farm
Woodlands Farm
CH
8
7
33
6
5
32
4
3
31
2
1
30
01
02
03

53

32

31
11

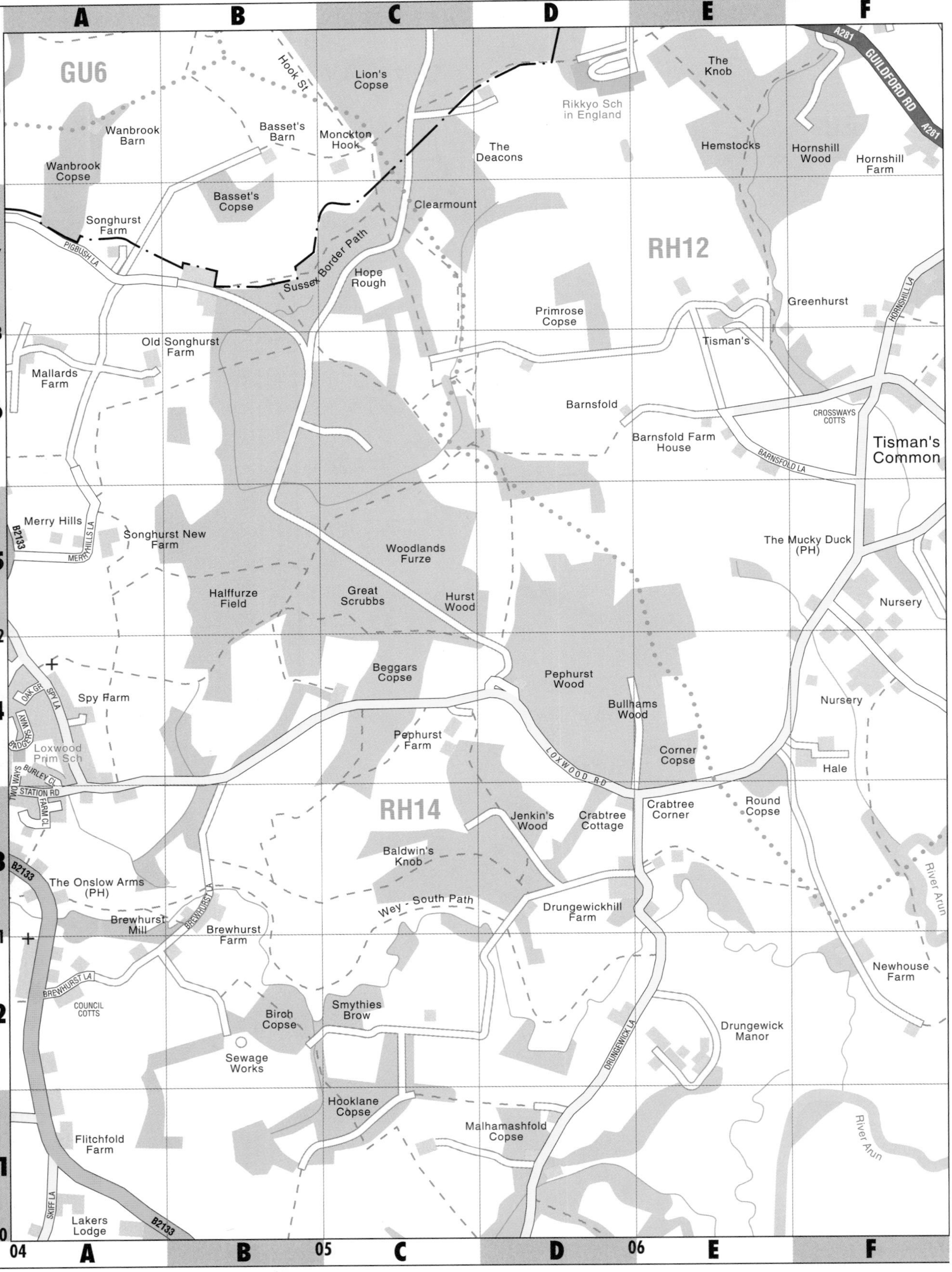
A
B
C
D
E
F
GU6
Hook St
Lion's Copse
Rikkyo Sch in England
The Knob
A281
GUILDFORD RD
Wanbrook Barn
Wanbrook Copse
Basset's Barn
Monckton Hook
The Deacons
Hemstocks
Hornshill Wood
Hornshill Farm
Basset's Copse
Clearmount
Songhurst Farm
PIGBUSH LA
Sussex Border Path
RH12
Hope Rough
Primrose Copse
Greenhurst
HORNSHILL LA
Old Songhurst Farm
Tisman's
Mallards Farm
Barnsfold
CROSSWAYS COTTS
Barnsfold Farm House
Tisman's Common
BARNSFOLD LA
Merry Hills
B2133
MERRYHILLS LA
Songhurst New Farm
Woodlands Furze
The Mucky Duck (PH)
Halffurze Field
Great Scrubbs
Hurst Wood
Nursery
Beggars Copse
Pephurst Wood
Spy Farm
OAK GR
SPY LA
Bullhams Wood
Nursery
BADGERS WAY
Loxwood Prim Sch
Pephurst Farm
Corner Copse
Hale
LOXWOOD RD
TWO WAYS
BURLEY CL
STATION RD
FARM CL
RH14
Jenkin's Wood
Crabtree Cottage
Crabtree Corner
Round Copse
Baldwin's Knob
River Arun
The Onslow Arms (PH)
BREWHURST LA
Wey - South Path
Brewhurst Mill
Brewhurst Farm
Drungewickhill Farm
Newhouse Farm
BREWHURST LA
COUNCIL COTTS
Smythies Brow
Birch Copse
Drungewick Manor
DRUNGEWICK LA
Sewage Works
Hooklane Copse
Malhamashfold Copse
River Arun
Flitchfold Farm
SKIFF LA
Lakers Lodge
B2133
8
7
33
6
5
32
4
3
31
2
1
30
04
05
06

31
54

12
34

A
B
C
D
E
F
8
7
33
6
5
32
4
3
31
2
1
30
07
08
09
Godley's Copse
Greathouse Farm
Lynwick Hanger
Well Grove
COOKS HILL
LYNWICK ST
Tip Pond
BUCKHURST COTTS
FURZE RD
CHURCH ST
THE RIDGE
B2128
FRESHWOODS
KILNFIELD RD
PONDFIELD RD
JUBILEE RD
WOODFIELD RD
FOXHOLES
MARTLET CNR
PO
STATION RD
THE SIDINGS
THURNE WAY
BRIDGE RD
GASKYNS CL
THE MARTS
Gravatt's Farm
Bowcroft La
Rudgwick
Pennthorpe Sch
PRINCESS MARGARET RD
Rudgwick Prim Sch
HORNSHILL LA
RH12
Smithers Farm
Weyhurst Copse
Weyhurst Farm
ORCHARD HILL
QUEEN ELIZABETH RD
TATE'S WAY
PATHFIELD CL
PATHFIELD RD
CAGE COPSE
PRINCESS ANNE RD
Swaynes Farm
SMITHERS COTTS
A281
PH
Watts Corner
GUILDFORD RD
Smithers Rough
Woodfalls Manor
THE RIDDENS
Bucks Green
Downs Link
River Arun
LOXWOOD RD
Wanford Bridges
RH13
Exfold Farm
MILL COTTS
Warhams
ROUNDABOUT COTTS
Upper Barn
Pensfold Farm
Rolls Farm
Chephurst Farm
NALDRETTS LA
Naldretts Farm
PENSFOLD LA
Morelands
Pensfold La
Sewage Works
Chephurst Copse
Pensfold Furzefield
Colin's Cross
Rudgwick Grange
Howick Farm
Smithwood Copse
Howick Copse
HAVEN RD
RH13
Tittlesfold Copse
Park Farm
Tittlesfold Farm
RH14
Mill House
Garlands
Havenhurst Farm
Gibbons Mill Farm
Gibbons Mill
River Arun
The Haven
PH
Lower Lodge Farm
Morgan's Green
Marshall's Farm
Smerrick's Copse
OKEHURST RD
MARLES LA
Heathers Copse
Cousins Farm
Heathers Farm

55
34

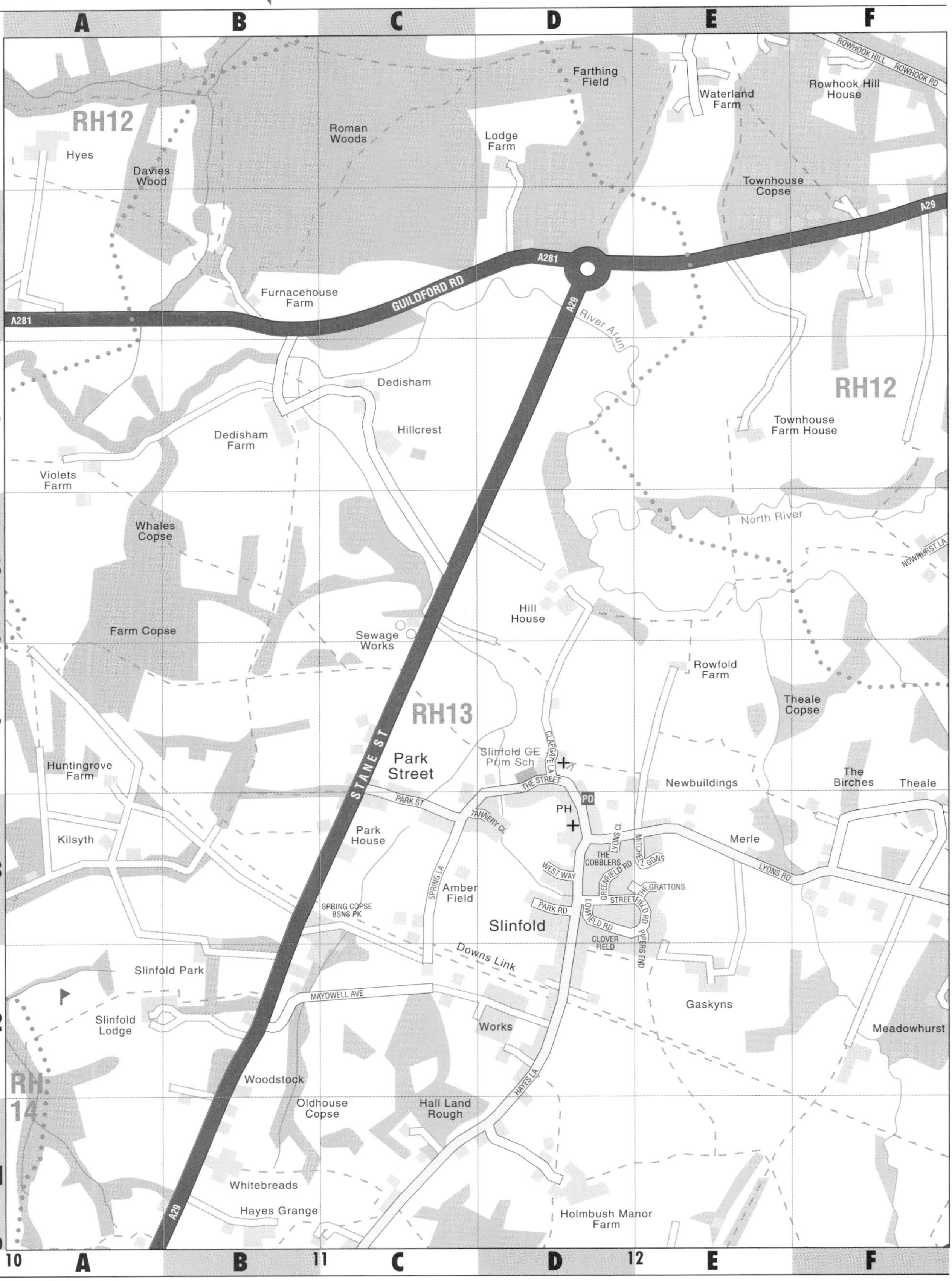
A
B
C
D
E
F
8
7
33
6
5
32
4
3
31
2
1
30
10
11
12
RH12
Hyes
Davies Wood
Roman Woods
Lodge Farm
Farthing Field
Waterland Farm
Rowhook Hill House
ROWHOOK HILL
ROWHOOK RD
Townhouse Copse
A29
A281
GUILDFORD RD
Furnacehouse Farm
River Arun
Dedisham
Hillcrest
Dedisham Farm
Violets Farm
Townhouse Farm House
North River
NOWHURST LA
Whales Copse
Farm Copse
Sewage Works
Hill House
Rowfold Farm
Theale Copse
RH13
STANE ST
Park Street
Slinfold CE Prim Sch
CLAPGATE LA
THE STREET
PO
PH
Huntingrove Farm
PARK ST
TANNERY CL
Newbuildings
The Birches
Theale
Kilsyth
Park House
Merle
LYONS CL
MITCHELL GDNS
THE COBBLERS
GREENFIELD RD
LYONS RD
WEST WAY
THE GRATTONS
SPRING LA
Amber Field
STREET
SPRING COPSE BSNS PK
PARK RD
LOWFIELD RD
THE FIELD RD
Slinfold
CLOVER FIELD
PIPERS END
Downs Link
Slinfold Park
MAYDWELL AVE
Gaskyns
Slinfold Lodge
Works
Meadowhurst
RH14
Woodstock
Oldhouse Copse
Hall Land Rough
HAYES LA
Whitebreads
Hayes Grange
Holmbush Manor Farm

14
36

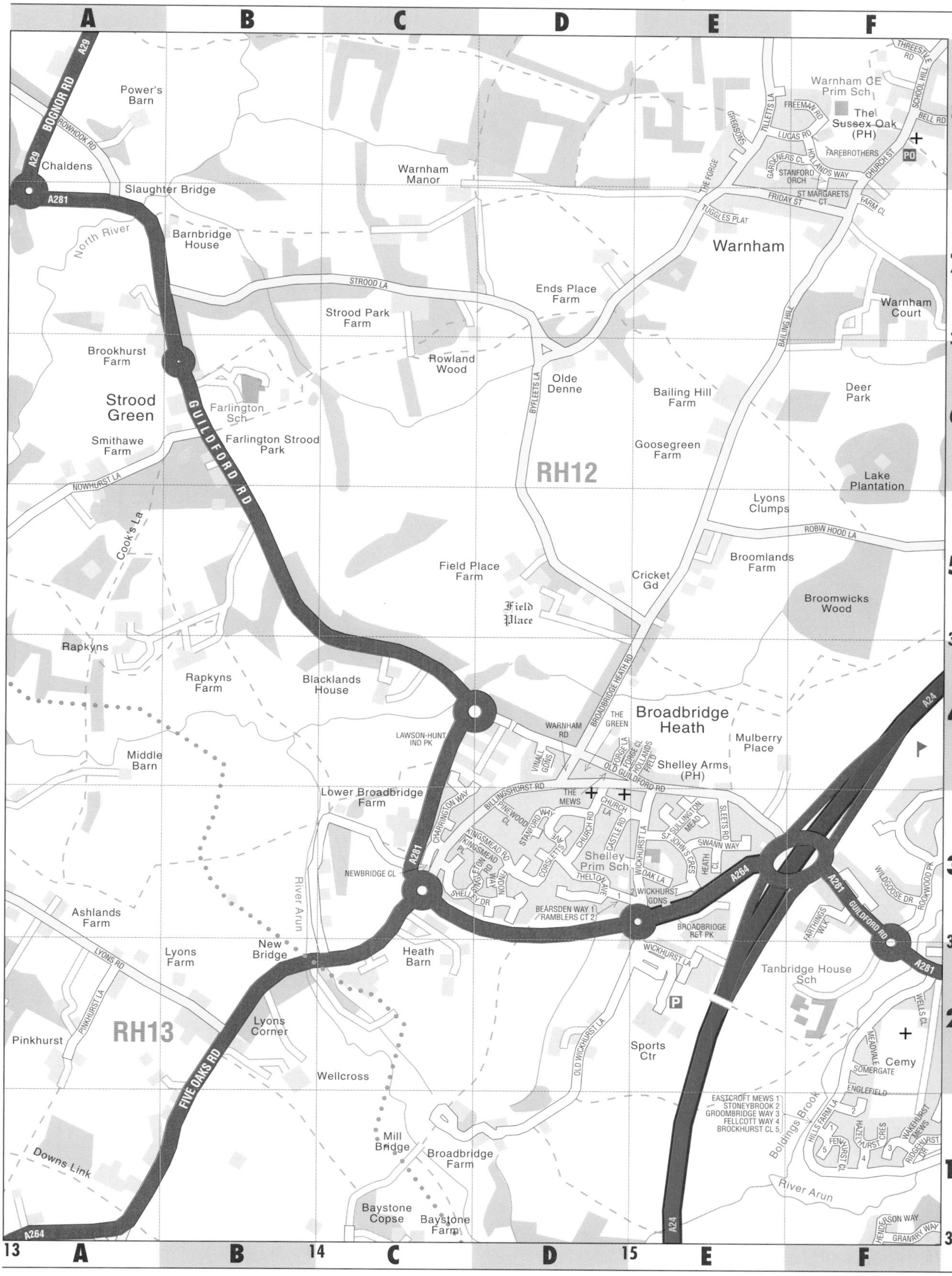
A
B
C
D
E
F
8
7
6
5
4
3
2
1
33
32
31
30
13
14
15
A29
BOGNOR RD
ROWHOOK RD
Power's Barn
Chaldens
A281
Slaughter Bridge
North River
Barnbridge House
Warnham Manor
STROOD LA
Strood Park Farm
Ends Place Farm
Brookhurst Farm
Strood Green
GUILDFORD RD
Farlington Sch
Farlington Strood Park
Smithawe Farm
NOWHURST LA
Cook's La
Rowland Wood
Olde Denne
BYFLEETS LA
RH12
Bailing Hill Farm
Goosegreen Farm
BAILING HILL
Warnham
Warnham CE Prim Sch
The Sussex Oak (PH)
PO
THREESTILE RD
SCHOOL HILL
BELL RD
GREGSONS
TILLETTS LA
FREEMAN RD
LUCAS RD
FAREBROTHERS
HOLLANDS WAY
GARDENERS CL
STANFORD ORCH
CHURCH ST
THE FORGE
ST MARGARETS CT
FRIDAY ST
FARM CL
TUGGLES PLAT
Warnham Court
Deer Park
Lake Plantation
Lyons Clumps
ROBIN HOOD LA
Broomlands Farm
Broomwicks Wood
Field Place Farm
Field Place
Cricket Gd
Rapkyns
Rapkyns Farm
Blacklands House
BROADBRIDGE HEATH RD
WARNHAM RD
THE GREEN
Broadbridge Heath
Mulberry Place
LAWSON-HUNT IND PK
VINALL GDNS
FORGE LA
FORGE CL
HOLLANDS FIELD
OLD GUILDFORD RD
Shelley Arms (PH)
Middle Barn
Lower Broadbridge Farm
BILLINGSHURST RD
THE MEWS
CHARRINGTON WAY
PINEWOOD CL
STANFORD WAY
CHURCH RD
CHURCH LA
CASTLE RD
KINGSMEAD PL
KINGSMEAD RD
SINGLETON RD
CORSLETTS AVE
Shelley Prim Sch
WICKHURST LA
SULLINGTON MEAD
ST JOHN'S CRES
SWANN WAY
SLEETS RD
HEATH CL
OAK LA
THELTON AVE
WICKHURST GDNS
SHELLEY DR
NEWBRIDGE CL
A281
River Arun
BEARSDEN WAY 1
RAMBLERS CT 2
BROADBRIDGE RET PK
A264
A24
A281
GUILDFORD RD
WILDGOOSE DR
ROOKWOOD PK
FARTHINGS WLK
Ashlands Farm
LYONS RD
Lyons Farm
New Bridge
Heath Barn
WICKHURST LA
Tanbridge House Sch
PINKHURST LA
RH13
Pinkhurst
Lyons Corner
FIVE OAKS RD
P
OLD WICKHURST LA
Sports Ctr
WELLS CL
MEADVALE
SOMERGATE
Cemy
ENGLEFIELD
EASTCROFT MEWS 1
STONEYBROOK 2
GROOMBRIDGE WAY 3
FELLCOTT WAY 4
BROCKHURST CL 5
Boldings Brook
HILLS FARM LA
HAZELHURST CRES
FENHURST CL
WAKEHURST MEWS
RIDGEHURST DR
Wellcross
Mill Bridge
Broadbridge Farm
Downs Link
River Arun
Baystone Copse
Baystone Farm
A264
HENDERSON WAY
GRANARY WAY

57
36

35
15

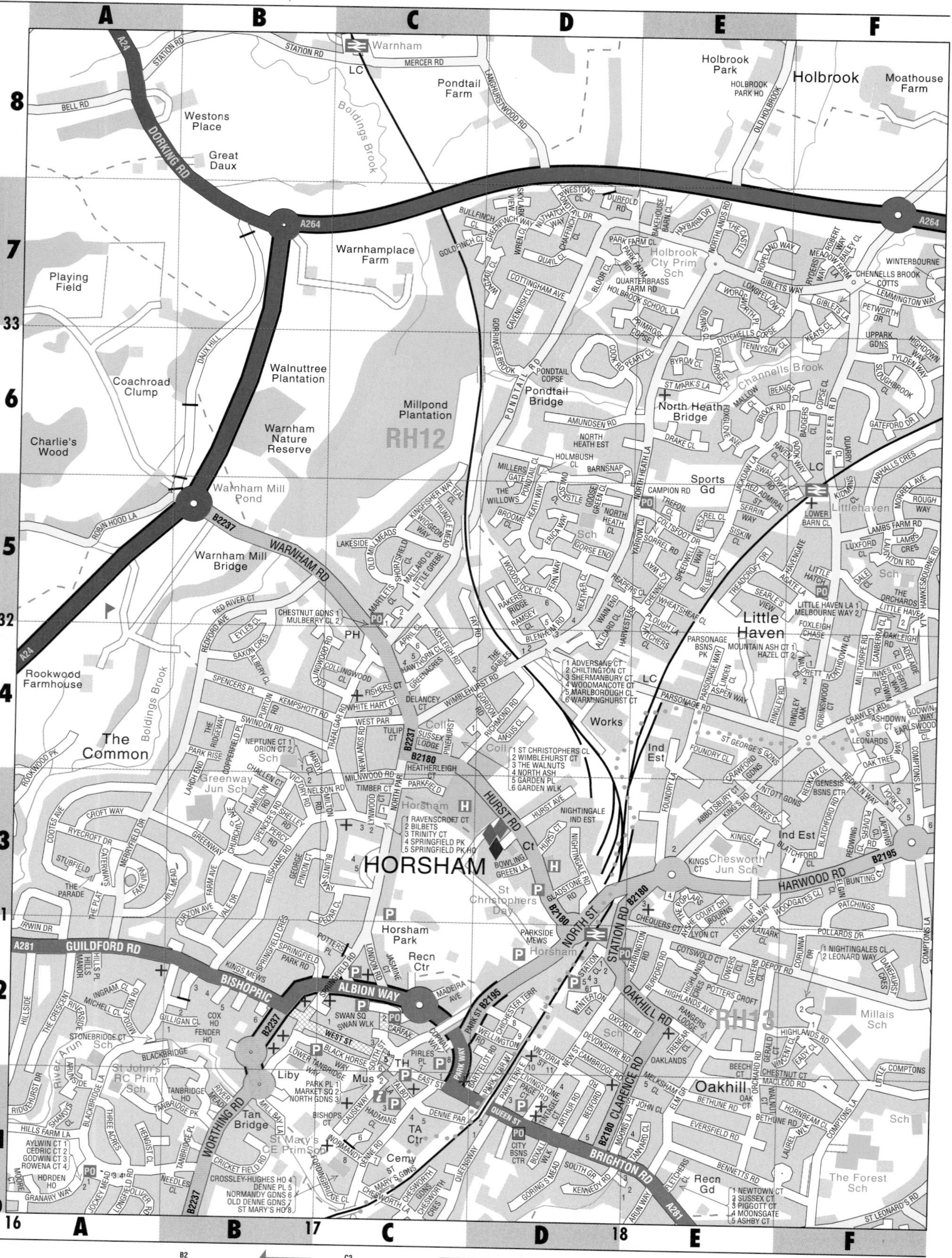

B2
1 ARRANCOURT
2 LANGRIDGE HO
3 TANFIELD CT
4 PELHAM CT
5 WAVERLEY CT
6 BISHOPRIC CT

35

C2
1 SPRINGFIELD CT
2 MEDWYN WLK
3 STERLING BLDGS
4 COLLETS ALLEY
5 MIDDLE ST
6 GLYNDE PL
7 STAN'S WAY
8 BURTONS CT

58

D1
1 QUEENS CT
2 QUEEN PAR
3 BURNHAM PL
4 GARDENERS CT
5 CHERRY CT
D2
1 LANE HO
2 HAMPERS CT
3 HAMPSHIRE CT
4 SURREY CT
5 KENT CT
6 DORSET CT
7 BARRINGTON GATE
8 NORFOLK RD
9 NORFOLK TERR
10 STANLEY WLK
11 VICTORIA CT

E3
1 TYMPERLEY CT
2 WESTLANDS
3 KARENZA CT
4 BOOTH WAY
5 WATERFIELD CL

F3
1 HANOVER CT
2 STUART HO
3 COMPTONS CT
4 TUDOR HO
5 WINDSOR CT
6 COMPTONS EA

16
38

A
B
C
D
E
F
8
7
6
5
4
3
2
1
33
32
31
30
19
20
21
Benson's Farm
Castle Copse
Cow Barn
Owlscastle Farm
Bush La
Channells Brook
The Cherry Tree (PH)
Dobsongill Pond
Tower Rd
A264
Rookfield Pond
Beechwood
Middle Hill
Dobson Gill
Faygate Forest
Rusper Rd
Wimland Rd
Brook La
LC
Crawley Rd
Clovers Way
Roffey Park
Roffey Place (Christian Training Ctr)
Newhouse Farm
Old Crawley Rd
Winterbourne
RH12
Moorhead Farm
B2195
1 Buttermere Cl
2 Grasmere Gdns
Cherry Tree Wlk
The Birches
New Moorhead Dr
High Wood
Beedingwood Dr
Beedingwood
Roffey Park Management Coll
Roffey Hurst
Forest Rd
Woodside Farm
Stonelodge Plain
Highbirch Hill
Knights Strength
Roffey
Cemy
Sch
Kaithewood HO
Pinetops
Roffey Cnr
The Orchard
The Courtyard
Owlbeech Wood
Playing Fields
Whitevane Hill
Whitevane Pond
Race Hill
Harwood Rd
Leechpool & Owlbeech Wood Nature Reserve
Dogkennel Pond
Greenbroom Hill
Leechpool Wood
Townhouse Copse
St Leonard's Park
St Leonard's Park HO
Home Farm
RH13
1 Oakhurst Mews
2 Forest Oaks
3 Gillett HO
Hamper's La
High Weald Landscape Trail
Sandpit Clump
Stew Pond
Dry Pond
Turf Plain
Lily Beds
Scragged Oak Hill
Mick's Cross
Sheepwash Wood
Sheepwash Gill
Scragged Oak
Inholme Gill
Greenslade Wood
Heron Way Prim Sch
Heron Way
The Glen
Sunoak Plantation
Bens Acre
Grebe Cres
St Leonard's Rd
Brambling Rd
Doomsday Gdn

59
38

37
17

A
B
C
D
E
F
8
7
33
6
5
32
4
3
31
2
1
30
22
23
24
Holmbush
Hooks Copse
Foxhole Pond
Buchan Hill Forest
Sch
House Pond
CH
Shepherdsfield Farm
TOWER RD
Holmbush Forest
RH12
Dobson Gill
Beacon Hill
Black Hill Stud
Water Tower
FOREST RD
Black Hill
RH11
Sand Plat
Road Farm
The Dragon Inn (PH)
Rookfield Farm
Colgate Prim Sch
Black Hill Wood
Colgate
Combe Wood
Shelley Cottages
BLACKHOUSE RD
Colgate Lodge
Blackhouse Farm
Colegate Hill
Combe Bottom Wood
Forest Heights Farm
Pearl Cottage
Shelley Farm
SPRINGFIELD LA
New Barn Farm
Combe Bottom
Blindman's Wood
RH13
Shelley Middle Gill
St Leonard's Forest
Springfield Farm
Pyefall Gill
Spring Farm
Newstead Ghyll
GROUSE RD
WOODLAND LA
The Larches
Old Springfield Stud
Barnsnap
Stone Edge Nursery
Newstead Gill
Elenge Plat Farm
Barnsnap Wood
Newstead Farm
Old Copse
Lower Grouse Farm
RH17
Grouselands
Frenchbridge Gill
Forest Lodge
Hyde Gill
Grouselands Farm
Mount Noddy
The Hyde
Old Copse

37
60

18
40

A
B
C
D
E
F
8
7
6
5
4
3
2
1
33
32
31
30
25
26
27
CREASYS DR
HOLMAN CL 1
RAMBLERS WAY 2
WILBERFORCE CL 3
FAULKNER CL 4
JACKSON RD
MORTON RD
RUMMER CL
LOWE CL
JARVIS CL
WILLIAM MORRIS WAY
HAMMOND RD
HOLLINGBOURNE CRES
OTFORD CL
RANMORE CL
TOLLGATE HILL
KELMSCOTT RISE
MERTON RD
LINNELL CL
HYNDMAN CL
MANN CL
FARNHAM CL
WYE CL
NETLEY CL
BRIGHTON RD (PEASE POTTAGE HILL)
1 HILLVIEW GDNS
2 SURRENDEN RISE
3 KINGSWOOD CL
4 WESTCOTT CL
A264
A23
M23
Pease Pottage Forest
STABLE COTTS
STABLE FLATS
Creasy's Brook
Stanford (Scout Camp Site)
Cottesmore Sch
Keepers
Cherrytree Plantation
Tilgate Forest
11
BRIGHTON RD
BRIGHTON ROAD (NORTH)
Hardriding
The James King (PH)
Wr Twr
Horsham Corner
RH11
BLACK SWAN CL
OLD BRIGHTON ROAD (NORTH)
BARN CL
Pease Pottage Service Area
New Pond
CH
HORSHAM RD
COTSFORD
FOREST RD
South Lodge
PARISH LA
Pease Pottage
THE PAVILIONS
GROUSE RD
Finches Field (Sports Gd)
Starvemouse Farm
Benson's Hill
New Buildings Farm
RH10
Finches Shaw
OLD BRIGHTON ROAD (SOUTH)
Crawley Forest House
Bensonshill Wood
TILGATE FOREST ROW
Stanford Brook
Woodhurst
Furze Field
The Home Farm
BRIGHTON RD
Shelley Plain Farm
Tilgate Forest Lodge
Home Wood
B2114
Hungry Down
Highbeeches Forest
Yewtree Cottages
Hyde Gill
Woodhurst Plantation
High Wood
Hydehill Wood
COOPERS WOOD
Oak Cottages
RH17
HIGH BEECHES COTTS
B2110
Nashlands Farm
High Beeches Gardens
HIGH BEECHES LA
Holkham's Corner
Dencombe Wood
Handcross Park Prep Sch
HEADLANDS COTTS
Hoadlands Farm
Handcross Prim Sch
Dencombe House
Bunnyland
Darkalley Gill
GRAVELPIT CNR
Harry's Wood
Blackfold Wood
The Square
Mast
P
B2110 HIGH ST
Carroty Wood
PH
CHADDS COTTS

61
40

39
19

A
B
C
D
E
F
8
7
33
6
5
32
4
3
31
2
1
30
28
29
30
M23
Oldhouse Warren
Bennetts Rough
B2036
BALCOMBE RD
PADDOCKHURST RD
Denches Copse
PH
B2110
Burnt Place
Cowdray Forest
PARISH LA
RH10
Forest House
B2110
LONDON RD
Mount Pleasant Farm
Sherlocks
Greentrees Farm
Monks Forest Cott
B2036
Stanford Brook
Monks Forest
HIGH ST
Forest Lodge
Kings Farm
Balcombe Forest
Brantridge Forest
RH17
Sedgy Gill
Burnt Field
Highley Manor (Hotel)
CRAWLEY LA
Brantridge Forest
Lodgelands
Scott's Gill
Kelsey House
B2036
Hourglass Wood
Brantridge Forest Farm
Works
BOUNDARY RD
HANDCROSS RD
Wellgrove Wood
B2110
HIGH BEECHES LA
New England Cottages
Water Tower
Knoll Wood
Great Cooper's Corner Farm
Red Bridge
Balcombe House
LONDON RD
Balcombe
Half Moon Inn
Brantridge Wood
HAYWARDS HEATH RD
Pond Wood
Casteye Wood
Brantridge Park Farm
BRANTRIDGE LA
Alder Wood
Balcombe CE Prim Sch
BRAMBLE HILL
PO
WESTUP RD
MEAD
Ashen Wood
BRAMBLE
Banks Wood
Long Shaw
ROCKS LA
Brantridge Park
Westup Farm
Balcombe
NEWLANDS
JOBS
Peter's Wood
B2036

39
62

20
42

A
B
C
D
E
F
B2110
Cricket Field
Downside Wood
Paddockhurst Park
Park House
RH10
Great Strudgate Farm
Green Wood
Kiln Wood
Monks
Home Wood
BACK LA
Newhouse Farm
Bushycroft Wood
LONDON RD
Balcombe Lane
The Warren
Little Strudgate Farm
Marchants Banks Show
Long Wood
STONEY LA
Fire Wood
Littlebushy Wood
Bloomer's Valley
Bethlehem Wood
Yewtree Farm
BOUNDARY RD
Upperstaff Wood
RH17
Square Wood
Millennium Seedbank
Forest Farm
The Oaks
Horsebridge Wood
Chestnut Wood
Ardingly Brook
Wakehurst Place (Royal Bot Gdn)
Woodward's Farm
PADDOCKHURST LA
Balcombe Lake
Southfield Grove
Tilgate Wood
Westwood Valley
Walk Wood
P
Southfield Gill
Tillinghurst Farm
TILLINGHURST LA
Alder Wood
Flatfield Wood
1 ST JAMES COTTS
2 COUNCIL COTTS
HAYWARDS HEATH RD
MEADOW TERR
STOCKCROFT RD
WILTON VILLAS
MEADOW CL
TROYMEDE
West Hill
Edmond's Farm
Balcombe Mill (dis)
Lullings
Great Racks Wood
VICTORIA RD
DEANLAND RD
COOMBERS
BARN MDW
MILL LA
Ardingly Resr
WEST HILL
FOXWELLS
GLEBE VIEW
OLDLANDS AVE
STUMBLEMEAD
Great Burrow Wood
SHELL LA
Westhill Place
Bushy Wood
8
7
33
6
5
32
4
3
31
2
1
30
31
32
33

63
42

41
21

A
B
C
D
E
F
8
7
33
6
5
32
4
3
31
2
1
30
34
35
36
B2028
Duckyls
Bird's Eye Wood
Square Wood
Old House Farm
Wayside
Duckyls Farm
Giffard's Wood
Rocks Wood
Old House
Whitestone Wood
SELSFIELD RD
Longwood Slip
Stonelands
The White Hart (PH)
CHAPEL ROW
BROADFIELD
Shagswell Wood
THE BEACON
RIDLEYS
PO
Chiddinglye Farm
West Hoathly CE Prim Sch
HILLTOP RD
Pearcelands
Chiddinglye
West Hoathly
COOMBE COTTS
THE HOLLOW
MELCHBOURNE VILLAS
SANDY LA
RH19
NORTH LA
Cat Inn (PH)
Lower Barn
P
CHURCH RD
BAYHAMS FIELD
Sheepwash Wood
GARDEN HEAD
VINOLS CROSS
TOP RD
The Priest House (Mus)
BULLDOGS BANK
HOATHLY HILL
PHILPOTS LA
Chiddinglye Wood
Pearcelands Wood
Philpots Manor Sch
Philpots
Ashurst Wood
SELSFIELD RD
Langridge Farm House
ASHURST COTTS
Philpots Farm
Boundary Wood
Langridge Wood
Coneyburrow Wood
Courtland Wood
P
Stonehurst
HOOK LA
Grovelands Farm
South Wood
Hook Farm
East Wood
Cob Brook
Barnland Wood
West Wood
Newlands Cotts
HAMMINGDEN LA
Fulling Mill Farm
Ludwell Farm
Hoathly Shaw
TILLINGHURST LA
Whitestone
RH17
NEWCROFT COTTS
Scott's Wood
Gardeners Arms (PH)
Little London
Horncombe
HOOK LA
Whitestone Wood
Furtherhouse Wood
COB LA
Holly Farm
Pickeridge Farm
The Showground
Long Shaw
WATNEY COTTS
Highbrook
Hudds Wood
Moorlands Wood
B2028

41
64

22
44

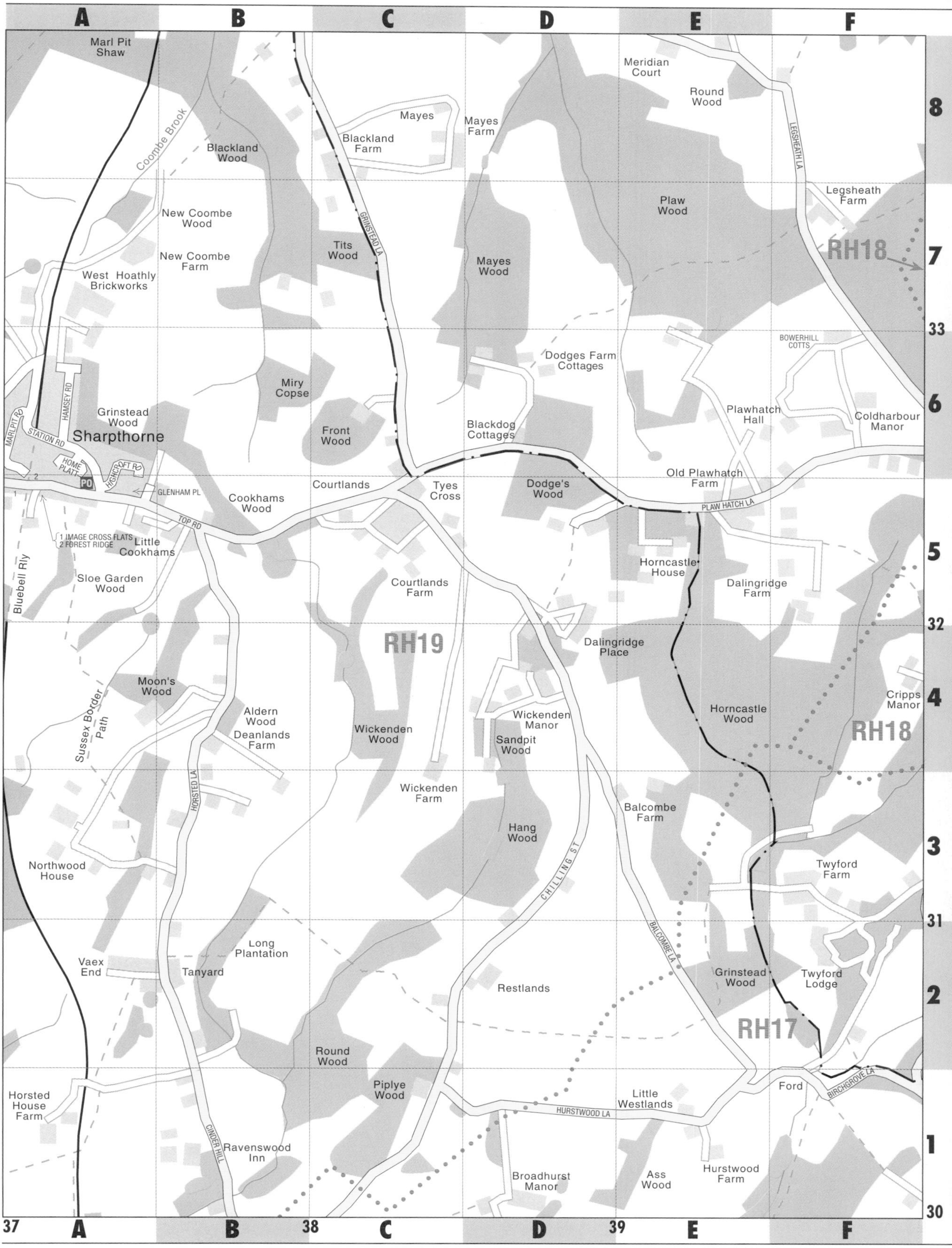
A
B
C
D
E
F
8
7
6
5
4
3
2
1
33
32
31
30
37
38
39
Marl Pit Shaw
Coombe Brook
Blackland Wood
Mayes
Blackland Farm
Mayes Farm
Meridian Court
Round Wood
LEGSHEATH LA
Legsheath Farm
Plaw Wood
RH18
New Coombe Wood
New Coombe Farm
West Hoathly Brickworks
Tits Wood
GRINSTEAD LA
Mayes Wood
BOWERHILL COTTS
Dodges Farm Cottages
HAMSEY RD
Miry Copse
MARLPIT RD
Grinstead Wood
Sharpthorne
STATION RD
HOME PLATT
PO
HIGHCROFT RD
Front Wood
Blackdog Cottages
Plawhatch Hall
Coldharbour Manor
GLENHAM PL
Cookhams Wood
Courtlands
Tyes Cross
Dodge's Wood
Old Plawhatch Farm
PLAW HATCH LA
TOP RD
1 IMAGE CROSS FLATS
2 FOREST RIDGE
Little Cookhams
Horncastle House
Courtlands Farm
Dalingridge Farm
Sloe Garden Wood
Bluebell Rly
RH19
Dalingridge Place
Moon's Wood
Aldern Wood
Deanlands Farm
Sussex Border Path
Wickenden Wood
Wickenden Manor
Sandpit Wood
Horncastle Wood
Cripps Manor
RH18
HORSTED LA
Wickenden Farm
Balcombe Farm
Hang Wood
Northwood House
CHILLING ST
Twyford Farm
BALCOMBE LA
Long Plantation
Vaex End
Tanyard
Restlands
Grinstead Wood
Twyford Lodge
RH17
Round Wood
Piplye Wood
Ford
BIRCHGROVE LA
Horsted House Farm
Little Westlands
HURSTWOOD LA
CINDER HILL
Ravenswood Inn
Broadhurst Manor
Ass Wood
Hurstwood Farm

65
44

43
23

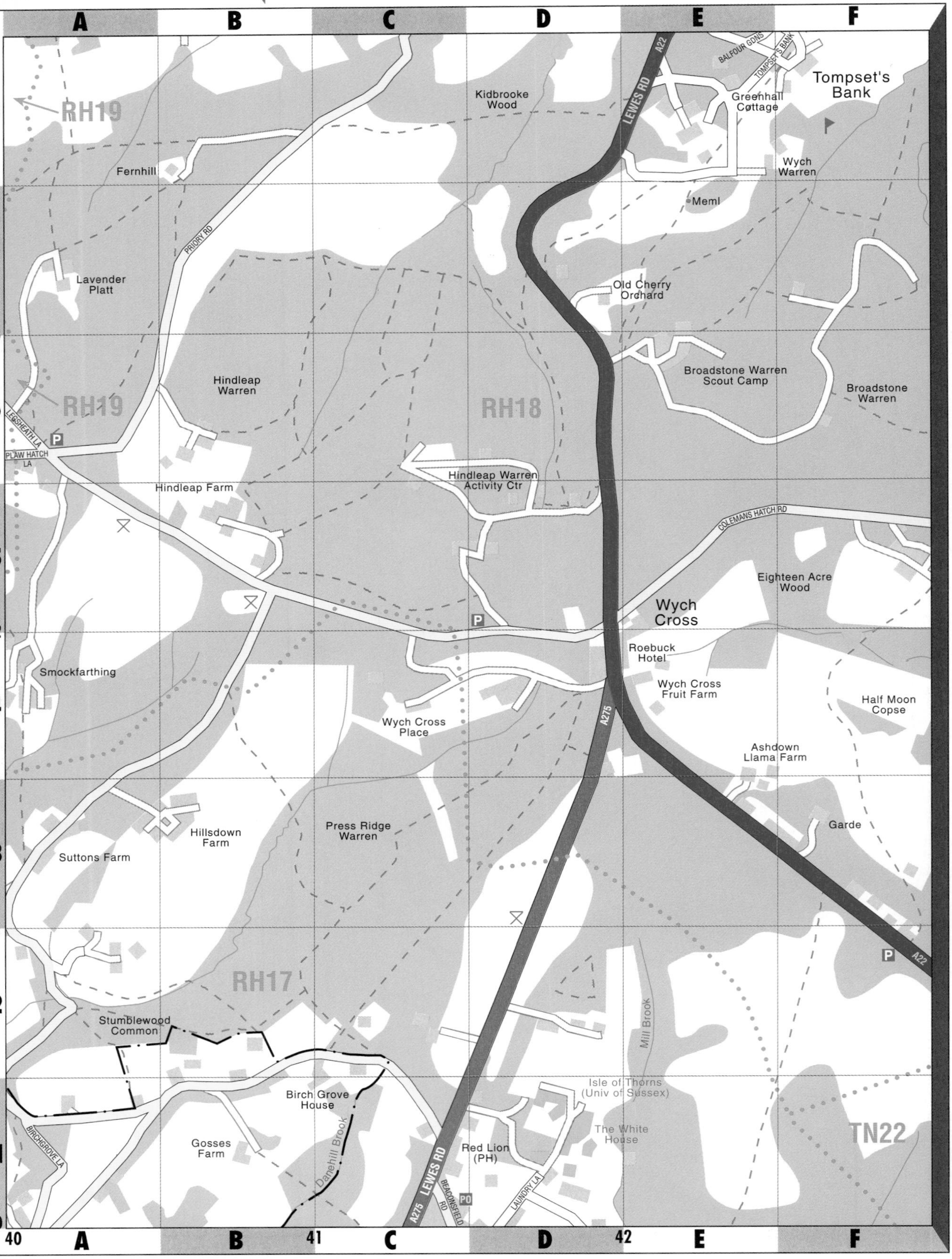
A
B
C
D
E
F
8
7
33
6
5
32
4
3
31
2
1
30
40
41
42
RH19
RH19
RH18
RH17
TN22
Kidbrooke Wood
LEWES RD
A22
BALFOUR GDNS
TOMPSET'S BANK
Tompset's Bank
Greenhall Cottage
Fernhill
Wych Warren
Meml
PRIORY RD
Lavender Platt
Old Cherry Orchard
Broadstone Warren Scout Camp
Broadstone Warren
Hindleap Warren
LEGSHEATH LA
PLAW HATCH LA
Hindleap Warren Activity Ctr
Hindleap Farm
COLEMANS HATCH RD
Eighteen Acre Wood
Wych Cross
Roebuck Hotel
Smockfarthing
Wych Cross Fruit Farm
Half Moon Copse
A275
Wych Cross Place
Ashdown Llama Farm
Hillsdown Farm
Press Ridge Warren
Garde
Suttons Farm
Stumblewood Common
Mill Brook
Isle of Thorns (Univ of Sussex)
Birch Grove House
BIRCHGROVE LA
Gosses Farm
Danehill Brook
The White House
Red Lion (PH)
LAUNDRY LA
BEACONSFIELD RD
PO
P

43
66

46

A
B
C
D
E
F
8
7
29
6
5
28
4
3
27
2
1
26
77
78
79
Goleigh Farm House
Ham Barn Farm
Moor Park Farm
Works
Longmoor Inclosure
Little Dean Bottom
Warren Hill
The Wylds
Wylds Farm
The Lake
Westfork
Greatham Bridge
Burgates Farm
Kippences
PH
ELM TERR
HOMEFIELD COTTS
Upper Green
The Blue Bell (PH)
West Liss
River Rother
The Temple Inn (PH)
Liss Forest
The Mint
Mangers
Reeds
Whangarei Nursery
Palmers Farm
Home Farm
Palmers
GU33
LC
Wyld Green Farm
Ciddy Hall
ROCKPIT COTTS
East Liss
St Patrick's Copse
Brows Farm
Fieldview
Liss
High Firs House
Highfield Wood
Sewage Works
Liss Cty Inf & Jun Schs
East Hill
Hill Side
Andlers Ash Farm
Prince's Marsh
Black Pond
Rake Common
Rake Hanger
Hill Brow
Farther Commons
Hambledon Piece
Pruetts
Stodham Park
Clayton Court
GU31
Combe Hill
Sussex Border Path
A3
B3006
B2070
CHURCH ST
HAWKLEY RD
FARNHAM RD
KILN FIELD
HAWKS MEAD
THE GREEN
BISHEARNE GDNS
STATION RD
ST MARY'S RD
WESTERN RD
YORKWOOD
CHILMARK CT
BALFOUR DR
RIVERSIDE CL
BRIDGE MDWS
LONGMEAD
LINDEN DR
RUSHFIELD RD
BARNSIDE WAY
UPPER MOUNT
NURSERY FIELD
ANDLERS ASH RD
FOREST RD
FOREST CNR
PINE COTTS
BRIAR WOOD
BERRYLANDS
SHERWOOD CL
NEWFIELD RD
BEECHWOOD CT
PINE WLK
TEMPLE RD
ROTHERBANK FARM LA
FOREST RISE
WARREN RD
MINT RD
REEDS LA
DUCKMEAD LA
DUDLEY TERR
WYLD GREEN LA
ST PATRICK'S LA
PRIMROSE LA
WOODBOURNE CL
THE ROUN
ABOUTS
KELSEY CL
MILLBROOK CL
MILL RD
SILVER BIRCH CL
PATRICK'S COPSE RD
BIRCH CL
THE OVAL
SYERS CL
SYERS RD
SHOTTERFIELD TERR
LIMES CL
THE MEAD
SCHOOL LA
OAK TREE DR
MIDDLE MDW
GREENFIELDS
MEADOW WLK
ROWAN TREE CL
COPSE CL
POTTERS FIELD
YEW TREE PL
PATRICK'S CL
LONGACRE CL
RAKE RD
LITTLE BARN PL
HIGHFIELD GDNS
THE RIDINGS
HATCH LA
SPRINGFIELD
MOSS CL
CHASE RD
CHASE CL
WILLOW RD
PORTLAND SQ
OLD SCHOOL RD
INWOOD RD
VINSON RD
ROTHER HO
1 TEACHERS TERR
2 SUMMERSFIELD
3 COLLARD WAY
CARDEW RD
DENNIS WAY
LAMBS LEASE
EAST HILL DR
HUNTSBOTTOM LA
WOODLANDS LA
HILL BROW RD
EDGEWOOD CT
MALVERN RD
PLANTATION RD
COMBE RD
STODHAM LA
PRUETTS LA
TANKERDALE LA
LONDON RD
KNOWLES MEADOW
PO
P

67
46

45 24

A
B
C
D
E
F
8
7
29
6
5
28
4
3
27
2
1
26
80
81
82
The Broom
Folly Pond
Hilly Fields Copse
Heath Patch
Horse Trials Show Gd
Ram's Horn Copse
Sussex Border Path
Home Park
Langley
The Vineyard
Hutfield Copse
Ripsley Farm
Fox Copse
Bishop's Copse
Ripsley House
PH
B2070
Langley Bridge Farm
Langley Court
Broad Copse
Heath Patch
REEDS LA
Brewells Farm
Little Langley Farm
Langley Wood
GU33
Chapel Common
Great Hanger
BREWELLS LA
Rake Firs
Newlands
Rock Field Firs
Maysleith
Rake CE Fst Inf Sch
ST PATRICK'S LA
RAKE BSNS PK
Maysleith Hanger
GU30
The Flying Bull (PH)
Rake
Coldharbour Park Farm
Maysleith Wood
PO
Sun Inn
FIR TREE COTTS
BULL HILL
SANDY LA
Coldharbour Wood
Hulls Copse
Coldharbour Wood
Canhouse Copse
Pot Well
Combeland Farm
CANHOUSE LA
Combe Pond
Canhouse Cottage
Great Trippetts Farm
Goldring
GU31
Lower Common Wood
RAKE RD
Combe Lodge Farm
Marsh Wood
Harting Combe
New Barn Farm

45 68

25
48

A
B
C
D
E
F
8
7
29
6
5
28
4
3
27
2
1
26
83
84
85
B2070
Wheatsheaf Enclosure
Sussex Border Path
CH
Wheatsheaf Common
Hatch Birch Piece
Hatch Fir
Hatch Farm
Shufflesheeps
Lower End Plantation
Iron Hill
VICTORIA PL
Hollycombe Steam Collection
Hollycombe
Hillands Plantations
Hollycombe Hanger
Hirtwell
Tank Copse
Wardley Hanger
Wardley Moor
Upper Wardley
Home Farm
Milland House
Milland Place (Hotel)
Hatch Hanger
GU30
Becksfield Farm
Ford
MILLAND LA
Elmers Copse
Wardley
WARDLEY COTTS
Wardley Marsh
Hollycombe Prim Sch
Wardley Farm
Crockers Wood
Bembrook
Northend Farm
Northend Copse
Hammer Stream
Mill Farm
FERNHURST RD
Old Moor Copse
Slathurst Pond
Alfords Farm
Square Copse
Martin's Copse
MILL VALE MDWS
STRETTONS COPSE
CARTERSLAND
Cartersland
The Rising Sun (PH)
Milland Marsh
DRAKELEYS FIELD
PENNELS CL
WEST MEADE
Slathurst Farm
LAMBOURNE LA
Milland
Hurst Farm
Chorley Common
RAKE RD
Waldergrove Farm
IPING RD
Churchfield Row
Lambourne Copse
Inholms Copse
Cook's Pond
COOK'S POND RD
GU29
Weston's Farm
Lyford Farm

69
48

47
26

A
B
C
D
E
F
8
7
29
6
5
28
4
3
27
2
1
26
86
87
88
Stanley Farm
The Leithe
Newlands Cottage
The Moor
Shulbrede Priory
Well Copse
West Leithe
Greenhill Wood
Parkgate Copse
Green Hill
Parkgate Rough
Bird Piece
Greenhill House
Oakreeds Wood
Lower Lodge Farm
Highbuilding Farm
GU30
Elmers Marsh
Hawksfold Farm
HAWKSFOLD LA
Minepit Copse
Furnace Pond
GU27
Hartley Green Copse
Luckin's Copse
Lower Hawksfold
Taylors Copse
Upper North Park Farm
Heathfield Rough
Lower North Park Farm
Amon's Copse
Whites Lane Gully
Ward Copse
Woodmansgreen
Butler's Rough
Turner's Copse
WHITES LA
Peckham's Copse
Whitter's Copse
Footway Copse
Cavalry Quarters
LINCH RD
Older Hill Copse
Older Hill
West Copse
Birchhill Copse
Pondfield Copse
Upper Lodge
Redford Farm
Telegraph Hill
Hookland
A286
Redford
GU29
Pine Hill House
Northpark Copse
Henley Common
PO
P

47
70

27
50

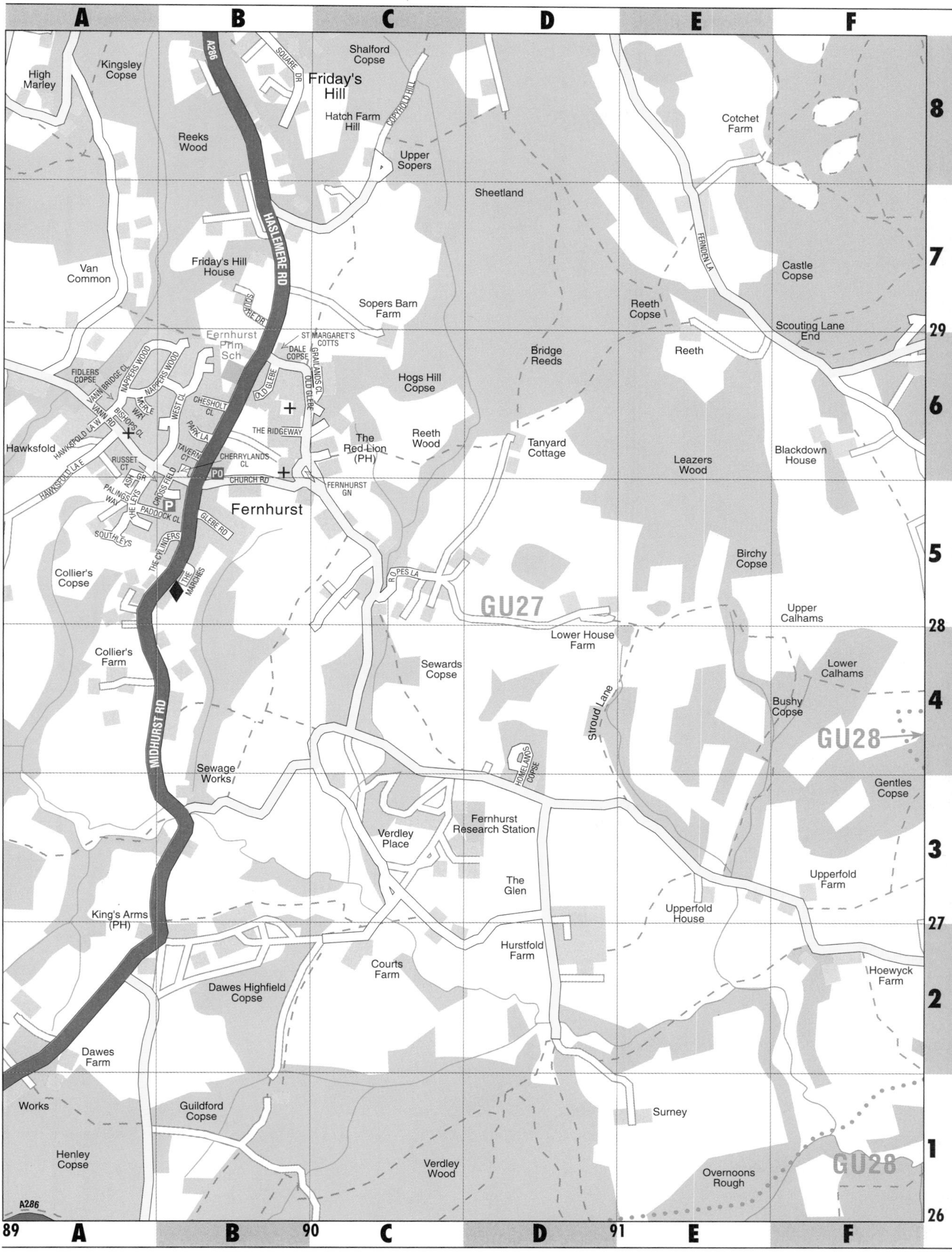
A
B
C
D
E
F
High Marley
Kingsley Copse
A286
Shalford Copse
Friday's Hill
SQUARE DR
Hatch Farm Hill
COPYHOLD HILL
Cotchet Farm
Reeks Wood
Upper Sopers
Sheetland
HASLEMERE RD
FERNDEN LA
Van Common
Friday's Hill House
Castle Copse
Sopers Barn Farm
SQUARE DR
Reeth Copse
Scouting Lane End
Fernhurst Prim Sch
ST MARGARET'S COTTS
DALE COPSE
GRAILANDS CL
Bridge Reeds
Reeth
FIDLERS COPSE
VANN BRIDGE CL
NAPPERS WOOD
NAPPERS WOOD
OLD GLEBE
OLD GLEBE
Hogs Hill Copse
MERLE WAY
WEST CL
CHESHOLT CL
VANN RD
BISHOPS CL
HAWKSFOLD LA W
PARK LA
THE RIDGEWAY
Hawksfold
The Red Lion (PH)
Reeth Wood
Tanyard Cottage
Leazers Wood
Blackdown House
TAVERN CT
CHERRYLANDS CL
RUSSET CT
ASH GR
CROSS FIELD
PO
CHURCH RD
FERNHURST GN
HAWKSFOLD LA E
PALINGS WAY
THE LEYS
P
Fernhurst
PADDOCK CL
GLEBE RD
SOUTHLEYS
THE CYLINDERS
Birchy Copse
Collier's Copse
THE MARCHES
ROPES LA
GU27
Upper Calhams
Lower House Farm
Collier's Farm
Sewards Copse
Lower Calhams
MIDHURST RD
Stroud Lane
Bushy Copse
GU28
Sewage Works
HOMELANDS COPSE
Gentles Copse
Verdley Place
Fernhurst Research Station
The Glen
Upperfold Farm
King's Arms (PH)
Upperfold House
Hurstfold Farm
Courts Farm
Hoewyck Farm
Dawes Highfield Copse
Dawes Farm
Works
Guildford Copse
Surney
Henley Copse
Verdley Wood
Overnoons Rough
GU28
A286
8
7
29
6
5
28
4
3
27
2
1
26
89
90
91

71
50

49
28

A
B
C
D
E
F
8
7
29
6
5
28
4
3
7
2
92
93
94
Rickfield Copse
Abesters Copse
Upper Diddlesford Farm
Fulwick's Copse
Chapel Copse
Abesters
Ramsfold Wood
Ramsfold House
JOBSON'S LA
Bullocks La
New Copse
Diddlesford Manor Farm
Temple of the Winds
FERNDEN LA
GU27
Quellwood Common
Shopp Hill Farm
Hookhams Farm
Hillgrove
Blackdown Farm
Hobstevens
Tanland Copse
Upper Barn Hanger
Upper Barn Park Farm
Windfall Wood
Sybs Farm
Navant Hill
Coochway Ground
Mire Hanger
Windfallwood Common
High La
Spring Coppice
Park Farm
GU28
Screechhouse Copse
CROSSWAYS
Little Brockhurst
Great Brockhurst Farm
Northurst Farm
Dial Green
The Noah's Ark (PH)
Gatehouse Farm
Goffs Copse
Gentilshurst Farm
Lurgashall
PO
GU27
Greengates Farmhouse
GREENGATES
Benefold Copse
Ragham Lodge
Bishop's Hanger
Woodfield Row
Lower Gentilshurst Farm
HIGHSTEAD LA
High Hampstead Farm
Sods Farm
Lickfold Bridge
The Hanger
Chillinghurst Copse
The Lickford Inn (PH)
Shotter's Farm
Mill Pond
Old Mill Farm

49
72

29
52

A
B
C
D
E
F
8
7
29
6
5
28
4
3
27
2
1
26
95
96
97
A283
Mitchell Park Farm
Hammer Cottages
VALENTINES LEA
PH
PIPERS LA
PH
Northchapel Com Prim Sch
ST MICHAELS CL
LUFFS MDW
Northchapel
PO
SANDROCK COTTS
Hortons Farm
Garlands
Peacock's Farm
Beacon
Piper's Copse
Freehold Copse
Little Wood
Kiln Copse
Wet Wood
Burrell's Wood
Freehold Farmhouse
Mercers Copse
Mercers Furze
Goff's Farm
Pheasant Court Farm
Chafold Copse
Ebernoe House
STREEL'S LA
Old School House
GU28
Ashfold Copse
Colhook Farm
Ebernoe
Furnace Pond
School House Farm
Swedes Copse
Willand Wood
Kentfield's Lodge
Copsegreen
Little London
Sibland Farm
Blind La
Ebernoe Common
Lodgefield Copse
Colhook Common
Blackwool Farm
Hook Copse
Greyhound Plantation
Palfrey Copse
Birch Copse
COLHOOK IND PK
Chillinghurst Plantations
Chillinghurst
Redhill House

73
52

51
30

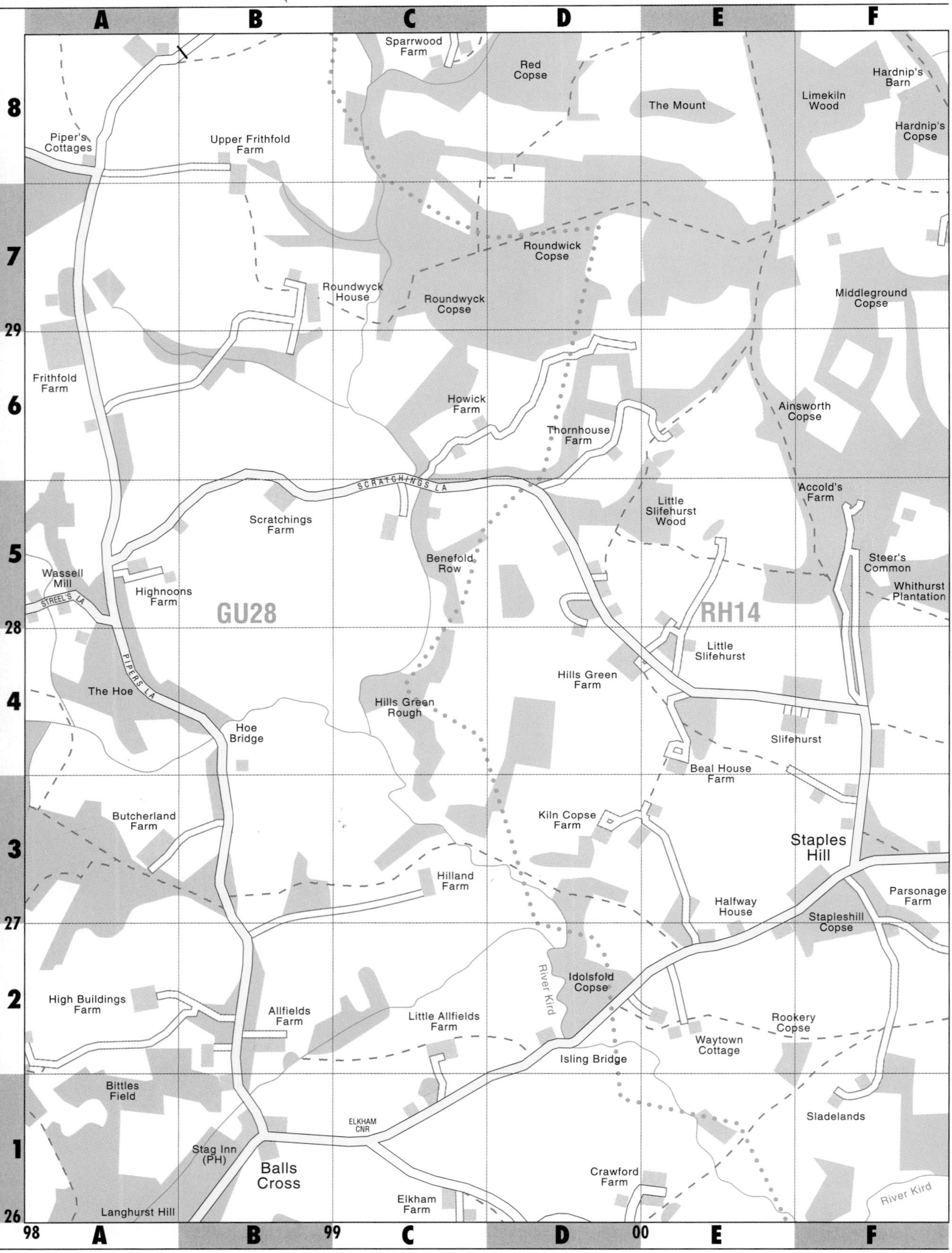
A
B
C
D
E
F
8
7
29
6
5
28
4
3
27
2
1
26
98
99
00
Sparrwood Farm
Red Copse
The Mount
Limekiln Wood
Hardnip's Barn
Hardnip's Copse
Piper's Cottages
Upper Frithfold Farm
Roundwick Copse
Roundwyck House
Roundwyck Copse
Middleground Copse
Frithfold Farm
Howick Farm
Ainsworth Copse
Thornhouse Farm
SCRATCHINGS LA
Accold's Farm
Scratchings Farm
Little Slifehurst Wood
Benefold Row
Steer's Common
Wassell Mill
Highnoons Farm
Whithurst Plantation
STREEL'S LA
GU28
RH14
Little Slifehurst
PIPERS LA
Hills Green Farm
The Hoe
Hills Green Rough
Hoe Bridge
Slifehurst
Beal House Farm
Butcherland Farm
Kiln Copse Farm
Staples Hill
Hilland Farm
Parsonage Farm
Halfway House
Stapleshill Copse
River Kird
Idolsfold Copse
High Buildings Farm
Allfields Farm
Little Allfields Farm
Rookery Copse
Waytown Cottage
Isling Bridge
Bittles Field
Sladelands
ELKHAM CNR
Stag Inn (PH)
Balls Cross
Crawford Farm
River Kird
Elkham Farm
Langhurst Hill

51
74

31
54

A
B
C
D
E
F
8
7
29
6
5
28
4
3
27
2
1
26
01
02
03
Streeter's Farm
RICKMAN'S LA
FOXBRIDGE LA
Wephurst Wood
Orchard Cottage
Pond Field Plantation
Furze Field
Old Furze Field
Crouchland
Broad Field
Costrong Copse
Beldhamland Copse
Walthurst Copse
Costrong Farm
Wephurst Park
Laneland
Spitwick Barn
Wephurst Park Farm
Walthurst Farm
Gunshot Farm
Wephurst Furze
Oakley Grange
Whithurst Copse
Crabfield Copse
SKIFF LA
Mackaralls
Mackerel's Common
PLAISTOW RD
Holland's Heath Farm
Holland's Heath Copse
RH14
Dounhurst Farm
Lakelands Farm
Fountain's Farm
Belchamber's Farm
Great Common
Chandler's Barn
Hookhurst Farm
Boxalland Farm
Barkfold Rough
Dunhurst Copse
Pound Common
Herons Farm
Boxal Brook
NEW BARN
HERONS CL
Oliver's Copse
The Foresters Arms (PH)
Boxalland Copse
Kiln Copse
Boxal Bridge
TOWNFIELD
PO
Kirdford
Kirdford Jun Sch
Half Moon (PH)
Fordland Copse
Barkfold Manor
Hayling Green
Bridgefoot
Jacksland Copse
River Kird
Churchland Copse
River Kird
Great Cavis

75
54

53
32
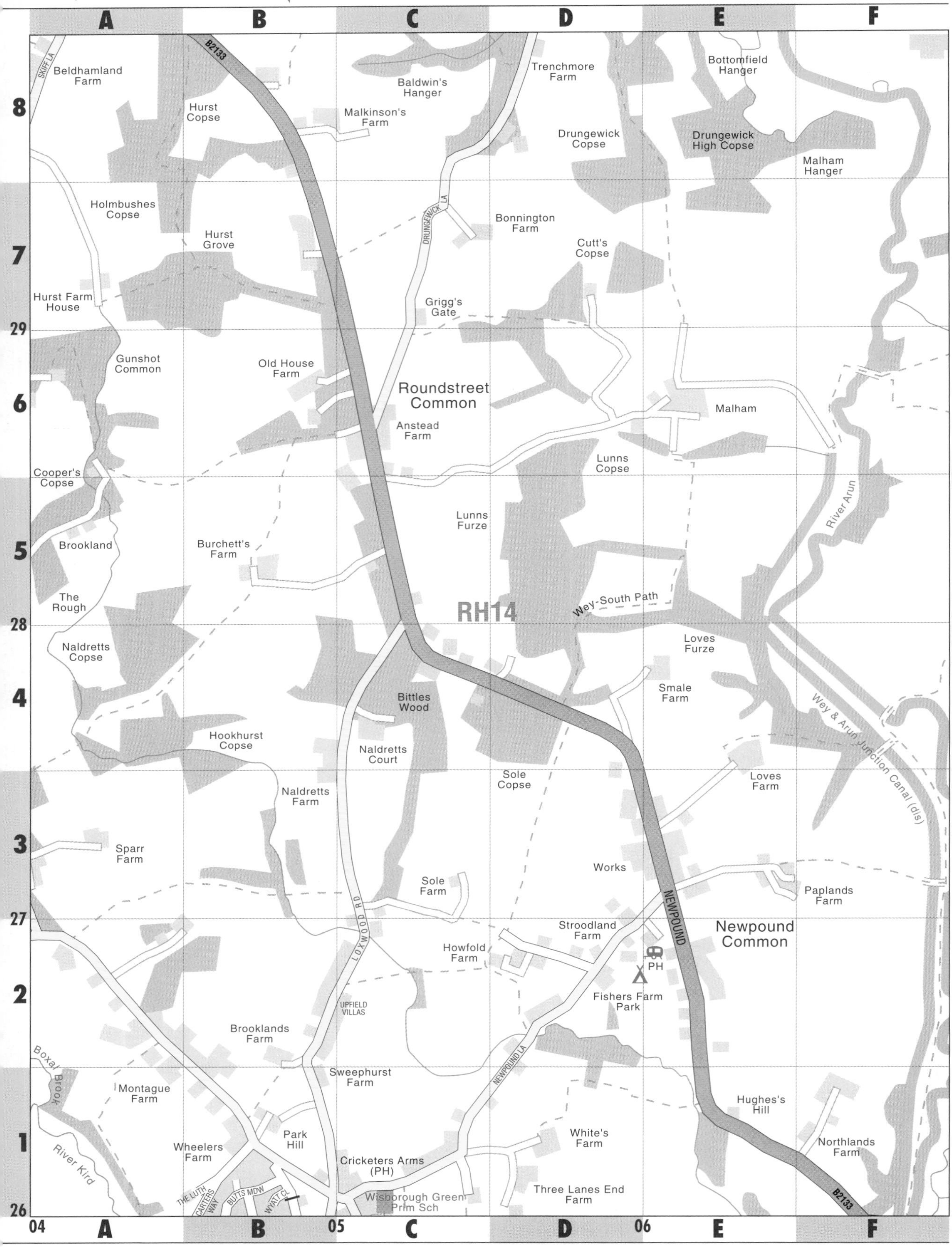
A
B
C
D
E
F
8
7
29
6
5
28
4
3
27
2
1
26
04
05
06
SKIFF LA
Beldhamland Farm
B2133
Hurst Copse
Baldwin's Hanger
Malkinson's Farm
Trenchmore Farm
Bottomfield Hanger
Drungewick Copse
Drungewick High Copse
Malham Hanger
Holmbushes Copse
Hurst Grove
DRUNGEWICK LA
Bonnington Farm
Cutt's Copse
Hurst Farm House
Grigg's Gate
Gunshot Common
Old House Farm
Roundstreet Common
Anstead Farm
Malham
Cooper's Copse
Lunns Copse
Lunns Furze
River Arun
Brookland
Burchett's Farm
The Rough
RH14
Wey-South Path
Naldretts Copse
Loves Furze
Smale Farm
Bittles Wood
Wey & Arun Junction Canal (dis)
Hookhurst Copse
Naldretts Court
Sole Copse
Loves Farm
Naldretts Farm
Sparr Farm
Works
Sole Farm
Paplands Farm
LOXWOOD RD
NEWPOUND
Stroodland Farm
Newpound Common
Howfold Farm
PH
Fishers Farm Park
UPFIELD VILLAS
Brooklands Farm
NEWPOUND LA
Boxal Brook
Sweephurst Farm
Montague Farm
Hughes's Hill
Park Hill
White's Farm
Northlands Farm
Wheelers Farm
River Kird
Cricketers Arms (PH)
THE LUTH
CARTERS WAY
BUTTS MDW
WYATT CL
Wisborough Green Prim Sch
Three Lanes End Farm
B2133
53
76

33 56

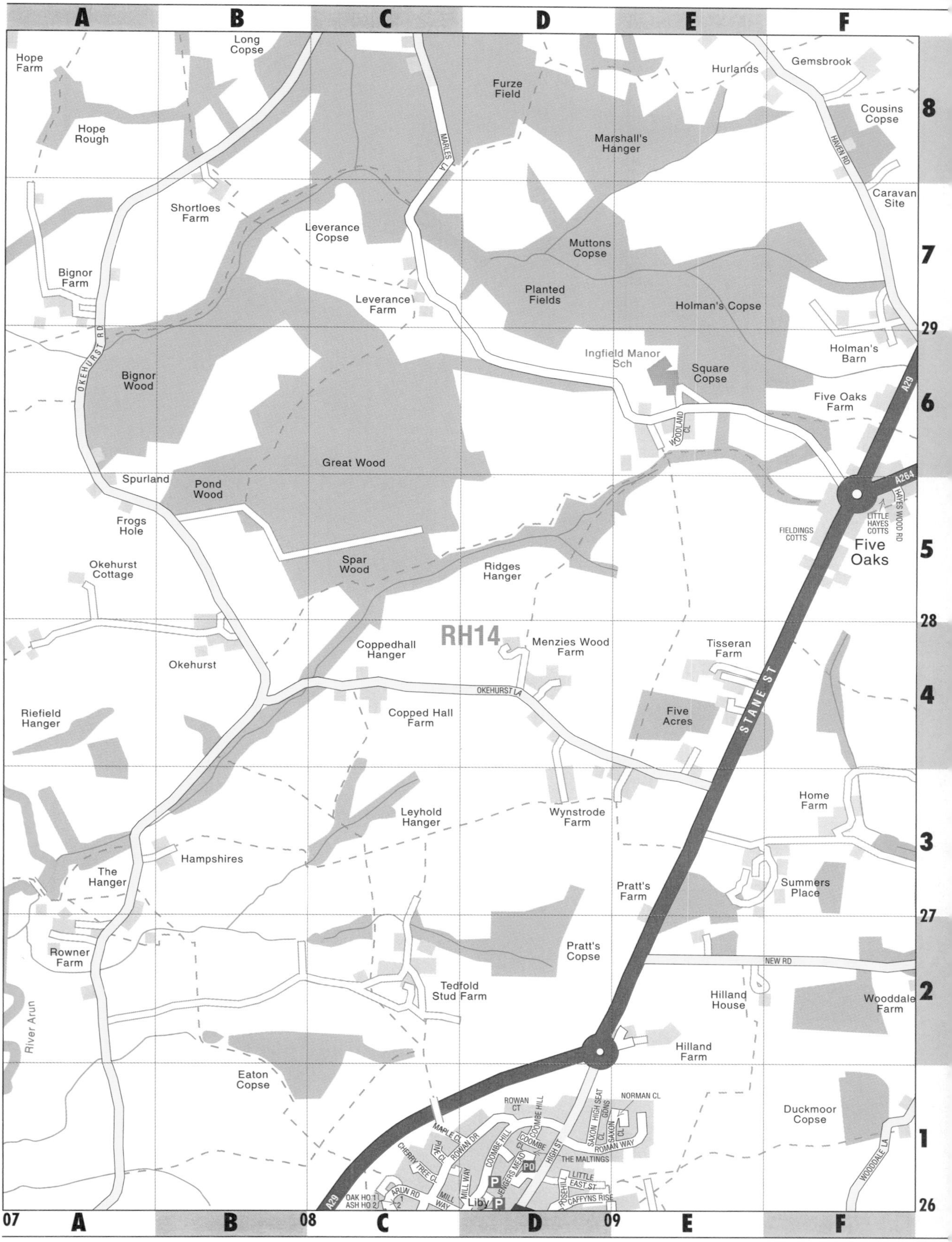

A B C D E F
8 7 29 6 5 28 4 3 27 2 1 26
07 08 09
Hope Farm
Long Copse
Furze Field
Hurlands
Gemsbrook
Cousins Copse
Hope Rough
Marshall's Hanger
MARLES LA
HAVEN RD
Caravan Site
Shortloes Farm
Leverance Copse
Muttons Copse
Bignor Farm
Planted Fields
Leverance Farm
Holman's Copse
Holman's Barn
OKEHURST RD
Bignor Wood
Ingfield Manor Sch
Square Copse
A29
Five Oaks Farm
WOODLAND CL
Great Wood
Spurland
Pond Wood
A264
HAYES WOOD RD
LITTLE HAYES COTTS
FIELDINGS COTTS
Frogs Hole
Five Oaks
Spar Wood
Ridges Hanger
Okehurst Cottage
RH14
Coppedhall Hanger
Menzies Wood Farm
Tisseran Farm
Okehurst
OKEHURST LA
Riefield Hanger
Copped Hall Farm
Five Acres
STANE ST
Home Farm
Leyhold Hanger
Wynstrode Farm
Hampshires
The Hanger
Pratt's Farm
Summers Place
Rowner Farm
Pratt's Copse
NEW RD
Tedfold Stud Farm
Hilland House
Wooddale Farm
River Arun
Hilland Farm
Eaton Copse
Duckmoor Copse
ROWAN CT
COOMBE HILL
HIGH SEAT GDNS
NORMAN CL
SAXON CL
SAXON CL
ROMAN WAY
MAPLE CL
ROWAN DR
CHERRY TREE CL
PINE CL
COOMBE HILL
COOMBE CL
HIGH ST
THE MALTINGS
JEWGERS MEAD
MILL WAY
PO
P
LITTLE EAST ST
POSEHILL
CAFFYNS RISE
ARUN RD
MILL WAY
OAK HO 1
ASH HO 2
Liby
P
WOODDALE LA

77 56

55
34

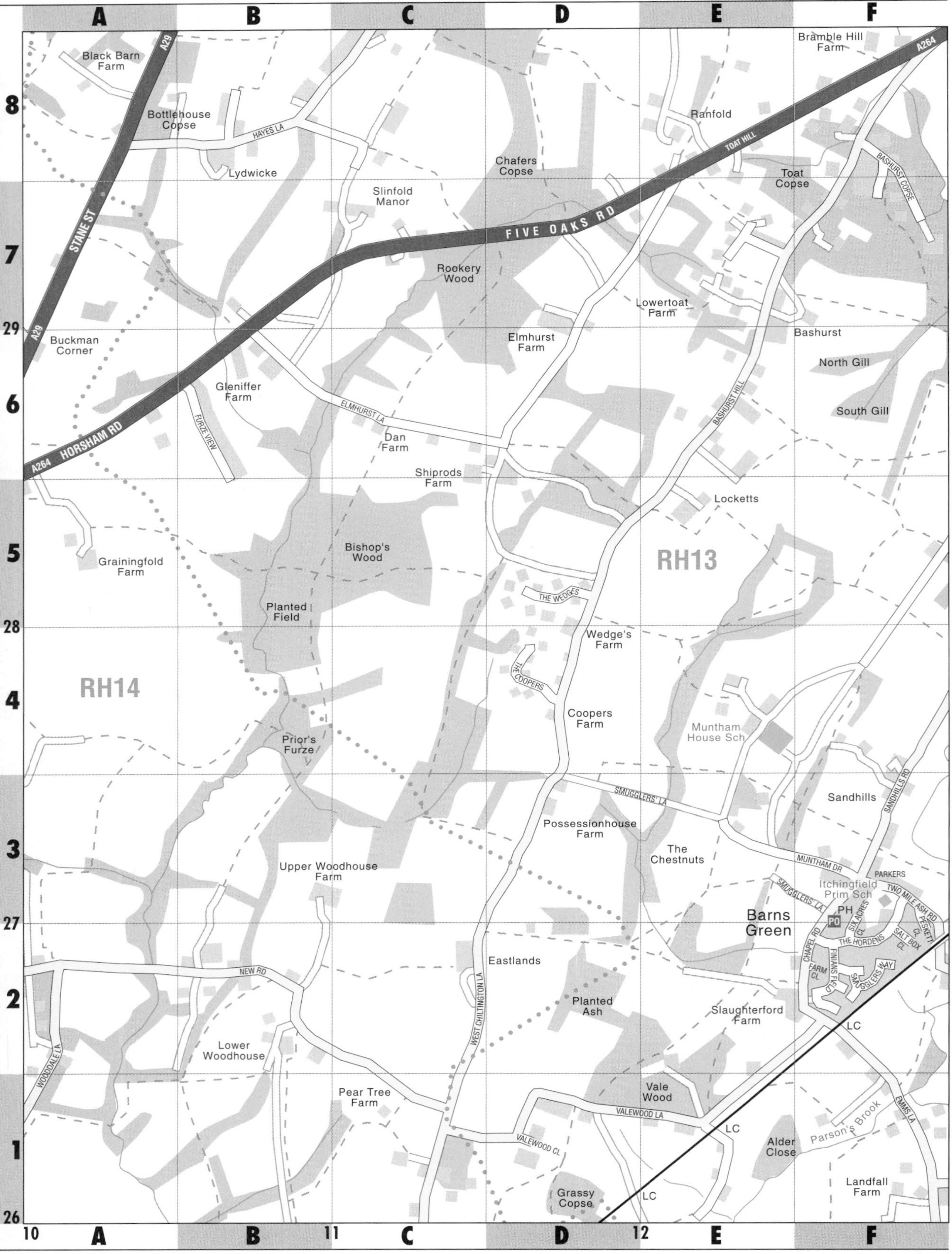
A
B
C
D
E
F
8
7
29
6
5
28
4
3
27
2
1
26
10
11
12
Black Barn Farm
A29
Bottlehouse Copse
HAYES LA
Lydwicke
STANE ST
Slinfold Manor
Chafers Copse
Bramble Hill Farm
A264
Ranfold
TOAT HILL
Toat Copse
BASHURST COPSE
FIVE OAKS RD
Rookery Wood
Lowertoat Farm
Bashurst
North Gill
South Gill
Buckman Corner
Elmhurst Farm
Gleniffer Farm
FURZE VIEW
ELMHURST LA
BASHURST HILL
HORSHAM RD
Dan Farm
Shiprods Farm
Locketts
Grainingfold Farm
Bishop's Wood
RH13
THE WEDGES
Planted Field
Wedge's Farm
RH14
THE COOPERS
Coopers Farm
Muntham House Sch
Prior's Furze
SMUGGLERS' LA
Sandhills
SANDHILLS RD
Possessionhouse Farm
The Chestnuts
MUNTHAM DR
PARKERS
Upper Woodhouse Farm
Itchingfield Prim Sch
SMUGGLERS' LA
TWO MILE ASH RD
PH
PO
SIX ACRES CL
PESKETT CL
Barns Green
THE HORDENS
SALT BOX CL
CHAPEL RD
FINIANS FD
FARM CL
SMUGGLERS WAY
Eastlands
NEW RD
Planted Ash
WEST CHILTINGTON LA
Slaughterford Farm
LC
Lower Woodhouse
WOODDALE LA
Pear Tree Farm
Vale Wood
VALEWOOD LA
LC
EMMS LA
Parson's Brook
Alder Close
VALEWOOD CL
Landfall Farm
Grassy Copse
LC

55
78

35
58

A
B
C
D
E
F
A264
Downs Link
High Wood
RH12
A24
WINDRUM CL
HENDERSON WAY
PARSONS WLK
PARSONS WLK
ALDER COPSE
RH12
8
PARTHINGS LA
Parthings
Fulfords Farm
River Arun
Sewage Works
FULFORDS HILL
Christ's Hospital (West Horsham)
STATION COTTS
7
Grigg's Farm
Church Farm
Weston's Farm
Butler's Gill
Lower Barn
STATION RD
29
Itchingfield
KING EDWARD CL
KING EDWARD RD
BLUECOAT POND
CHRIST'S HOSPITAL RD
CHRIST'S HOSPITAL RD
Itchingfield Prim Sch
6
WESTONS HILL
Shelley's Wood
Sports Ctr
INFIRMARY DR
Pilfolds
A24
THE AVENUE
THE AVENUE
WEST GUN COPSE RD
EAST GUN COPSE RD
PLUMTREE CROSS
5
PLUMTREE CROSS LA
Sharpenhurst Hill
Christ's Hospital (Sch)
Lanaways Farm
28
RH13
NEW RD
Marlands
Downs Link
4
Bodimans
Hen & Chicken (PH)
Sharpenhurst Farm
Newlands
NETHERTON CL
ROBERTS CL
Sayers Farm
Butts Pond
Watlings Meathouse
SOUTHWATER ST
ALLENDALE
Little Stammerham Farm
TWO MILE ASH RD
WARREN DR
FLETCHERS
Two Mile Ash
Courtland Wood
BLAKES FARM RD
3
Rye Farm Gill
POND FARM CL
The Bax Castle (PH)
Caravan Park
Rye Farm
GREEN CL
THE OAKS
THE LAURELS
27
Lawson's Farm
Great House Farm
THE COPSE
GRANGE WAY
RYE FARM LA
MAPLEDOWN CL
Richmond Farm
CEDAR DR
WORTHING RD
Southwater Jun Sch
2
College Farm
WOODHATCH
Melrose Farm
Southwater Inf Sch
TIMBER MILL
DOVER CL
QUARRY WAY
MARLPOST RD
GHYLL CT
ANVIL CL
PEVENSEY RD
Marlpost Farm
CHURCH LA
Southwater
PIPERS
PO
THE FORGE
TROUT LA
Trading Est
The Vicarage
WOODFIELD CL
STATION RD
Cemy
LITTLE BRIDGES CL
1
P
OAK RD
PH
ANDREW'S LA
Madgeland Farm
FLETCHER HO 1
GARDENER HO 2
BAKERS CL
SOUTHWATER BSNS PK
CROSS LA
SHAW'S LA
IVY CL
Chase Farm
ASH RD
COLLEGE RD
AMBER GLADE
P
26
13
A
B
14
C
D
15
E
F

79
58

57
36

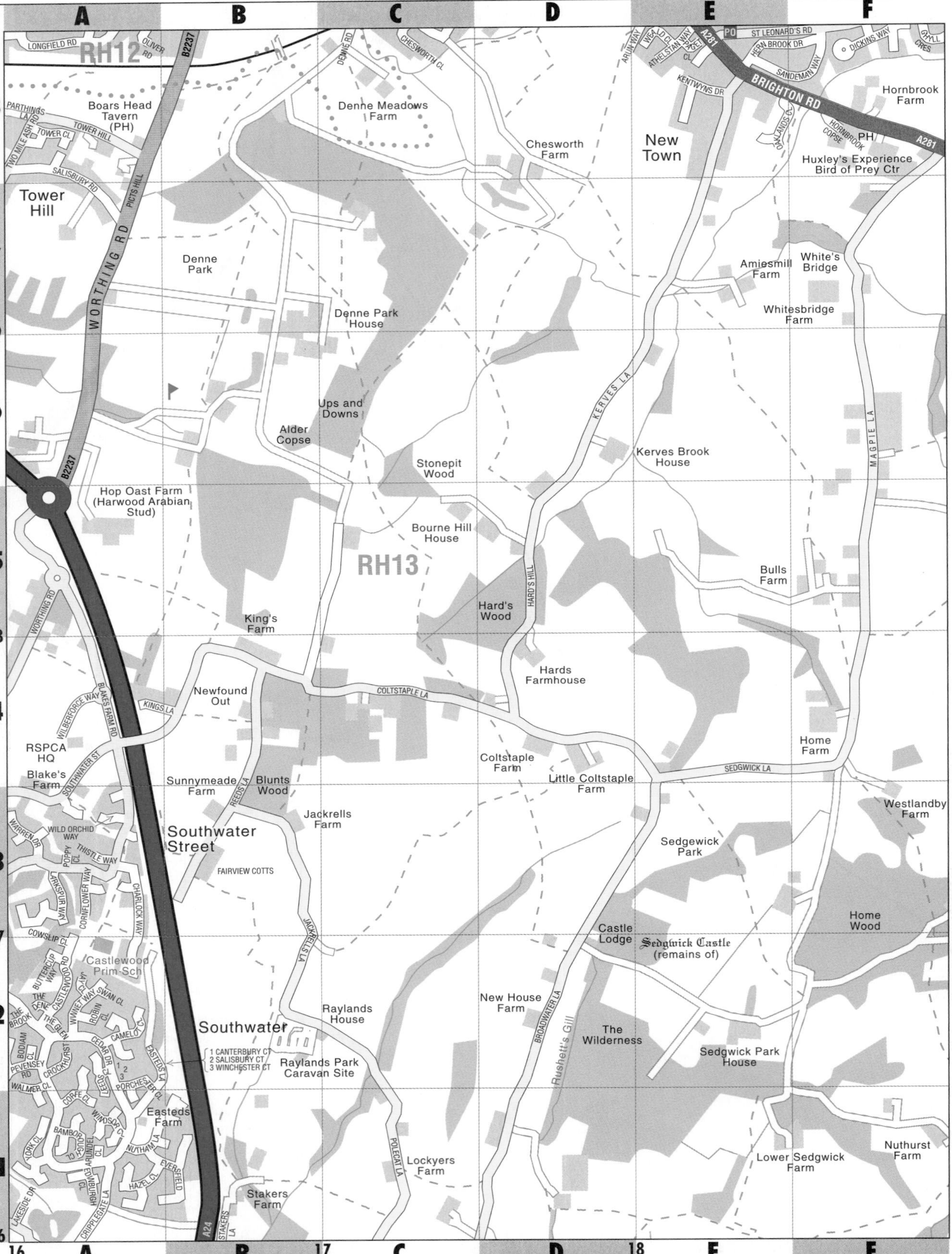
A
B
C
D
E
F
8
7
29
6
5
28
4
3
27
2
1
26
16
17
18
RH12
RH13
LONGFIELD RD
OLIVER RD
B2237
PARTHINGS LA
Boars Head Tavern (PH)
TOWER HILL
TOWER CL
TWO MILE ASH RD
SALISBURY RD
PICTS HILL
Tower Hill
WORTHING RD
Denne Park
DENNE RD
CHESWORTH CL
Denne Meadows Farm
Chesworth Farm
ARUN WAY
WEALD CL
ATHELSTAN WAY
A281
PO
ST LEONARD'S RD
HERN BROOK DR
DICKINS WAY
GHYLL CRES
SANDEMAN WAY
KENTWYNS DR
BRIGHTON RD
OAKLANDS CL
HORNBROOK COPSE
Hornbrook Farm
PH
New Town
Huxley's Experience Bird of Prey Ctr
Amiesmill Farm
White's Bridge
Whitesbridge Farm
Denne Park House
Ups and Downs
Alder Copse
Stonepit Wood
KERVES LA
Kerves Brook House
MAGPIE LA
Hop Oast Farm (Harwood Arabian Stud)
Bourne Hill House
HARD'S HILL
Hard's Wood
Bulls Farm
WORTHING RD
King's Farm
Hards Farmhouse
COLTSTAPLE LA
KINGS LA
BLAKES FARM RD
WILBERFORCE WAY
Newfound Out
RSPCA HQ
Blake's Farm
SOUTHWATER ST
Coltstaple Farm
Little Coltstaple Farm
SEDGWICK LA
Home Farm
Westlandby Farm
Sunnymeade Farm
REEDS LA
Blunts Wood
Jackrells Farm
WARREN DR
WILD ORCHID WAY
THISTLE WAY
POPPY CL
Southwater Street
FAIRVIEW COTTS
Sedgewick Park
LARKSPUR WAY
CORNFLOWER WAY
CHARLOCK WAY
COWSLIP CL
JACKRELLS LA
Castle Lodge
Sedgwick Castle (remains of)
Home Wood
Castlewood Prim Sch
BUTTERCUP WAY
CASTLEWOOD RD
SWAN CL
THE DENE
THE BROOK
THE GLEN
ROBIN CL
CAMELOT CL
Raylands House
New House Farm
BROADWATER LA
The Wilderness
Southwater
BODIAM CL
PEVENSEY RD
CROCKHURST
CEDAR DR
EASTEDS LA
1 CANTERBURY CT
2 SALISBURY CT
3 WINCHESTER CT
Raylands Park Caravan Site
Rushett's Gill
Sedgwick Park House
WALMER CL
CORFE CL
PORCHESTER CL
WINDSOR CL
Easteds Farm
BAMBOROUGH CL
YORK CL
ARUNDEL CL
NUTHAM LA
EVERSFIELD
HAZEL CL
EDINBURGH CL
POLECAT LA
Lockyers Farm
Lower Sedgwick Farm
Nuthurst Farm
Stakers Farm
LAKESIDE DR
CRIPPLEGATE LA
A24
STAKERS LA

57
80

37
60

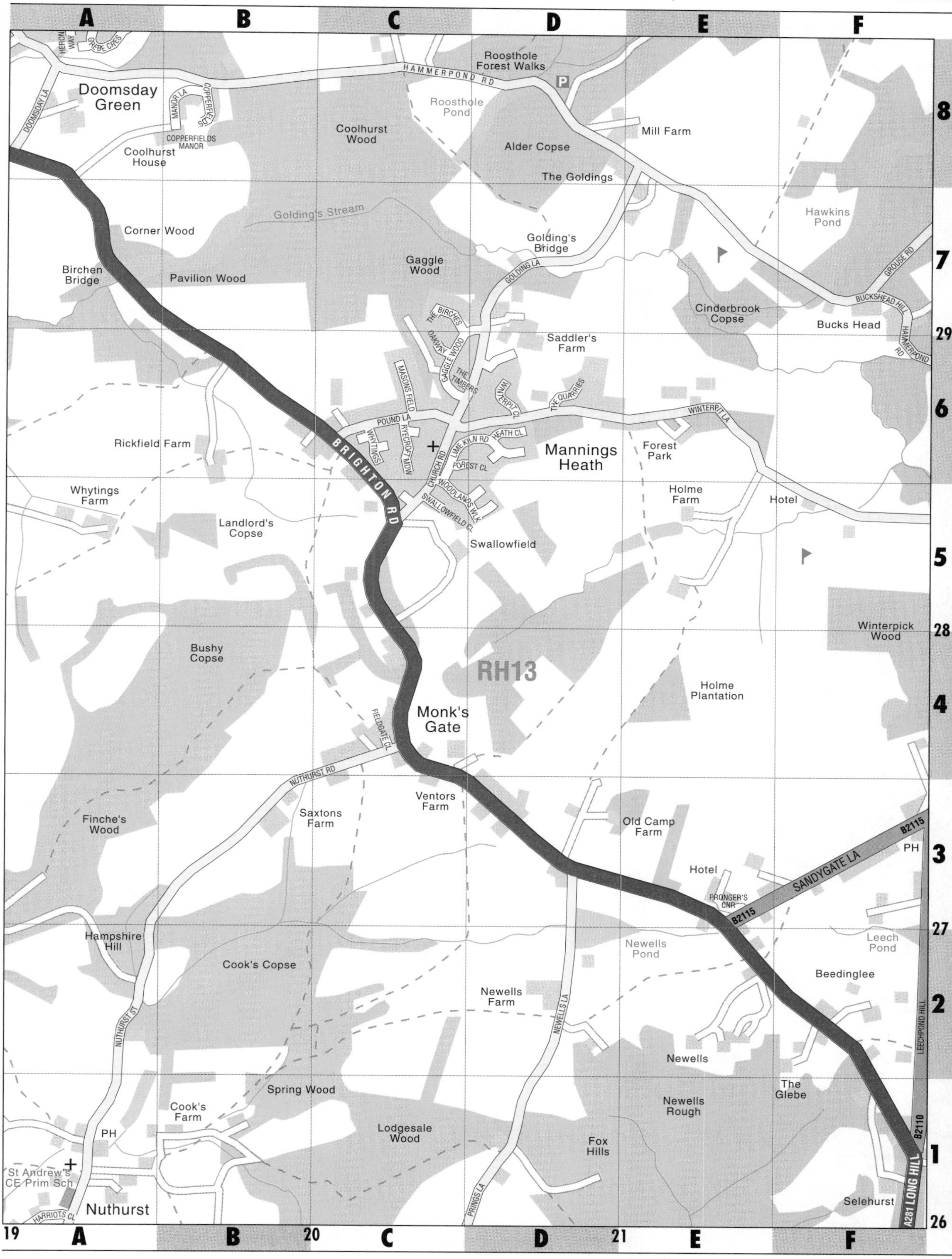
A
B
C
D
E
F
8
7
29
6
5
28
4
3
27
2
1
26
19
20
21
Heron Way
Glebe Cres
Doomsday La
Doomsday Green
Manor La
Copperfields
Copperfields Manor
Coolhurst House
Hammerpond Rd
Roosthole Forest Walks
P
Roosthole Pond
Coolhurst Wood
Alder Copse
Mill Farm
The Goldings
Golding's Stream
Corner Wood
Birchen Bridge
Pavilion Wood
Gaggle Wood
Golding's Bridge
Golding La
Hawkins Pond
Grouse Rd
Buckshead Hill
Cinderbrook Copse
Bucks Head
Hammerpond Rd
The Birches
Oakway
Gaggle Wood
The Timbers
Saddler's Farm
Masons Field
Winterpit Cl
The Quarries
Winterpit La
Pound La
Whytings
Ryecroft Mdw
Church Rd
Lime Kiln Rd
Heath Cl
Forest Cl
Woodlands Walk
Swallowfield Cl
Brighton Rd
Rickfield Farm
Mannings Heath
Forest Park
Whytings Farm
Holme Farm
Hotel
Landlord's Copse
Swallowfield
Winterpick Wood
Bushy Copse
RH13
Holme Plantation
Monk's Gate
Fieldgate Cl
Nuthurst Rd
Ventors Farm
Saxtons Farm
Finche's Wood
Old Camp Farm
B2115
PH
Sandygate La
Hotel
Pronger's Cnr
Hampshire Hill
Newells Pond
Leech Pond
Cook's Copse
Beedinglee
Newells Farm
Nuthurst St
Newells La
Leechpond Hill
Newells
The Glebe
Spring Wood
Newells Rough
Cook's Farm
PH
Lodgesale Wood
Fox Hills
B2110
St Andrew's CE Prim Sch
Prings La
Selehurst
A281 Long Hill
Harriots Cl
Nuthurst

81
60

59
38

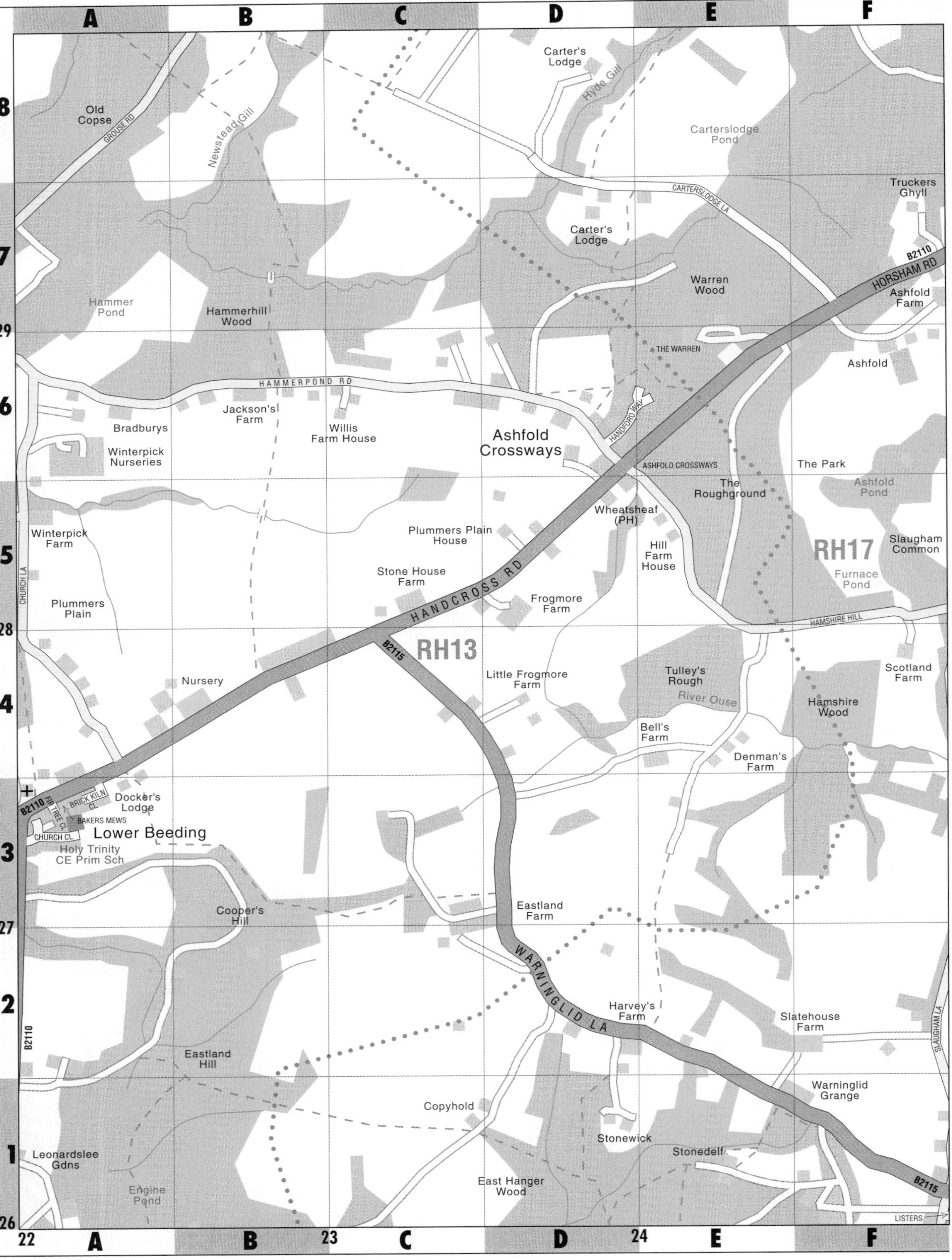
A
B
C
D
E
F
8
7
29
6
5
28
4
3
27
2
1
26
22
23
24
Old Copse
GROUSE RD
Newstead Gill
Carter's Lodge
Hyde Gill
Carterslodge Pond
CARTERSLODGE LA
Truckers Ghyll
Carter's Lodge
B2110
HORSHAM RD
Warren Wood
Ashfold Farm
Hammer Pond
Hammerhill Wood
THE WARREN
Ashfold
HAMMERPOND RD
Jackson's Farm
Bradburys
Willis Farm House
HANDFORD WAY
Ashfold Crossways
Winterpick Nurseries
ASHFOLD CROSSWAYS
The Park
The Roughground
Ashfold Pond
Wheatsheaf (PH)
Winterpick Farm
Plummers Plain House
Hill Farm House
RH17
Slaugham Common
Furnace Pond
Stone House Farm
HANDCROSS RD
CHURCH LA
Plummers Plain
Frogmore Farm
HAMSHIRE HILL
B2115
RH13
Nursery
Little Frogmore Farm
Tulley's Rough
Scotland Farm
River Ouse
Hamshire Wood
Bell's Farm
Denman's Farm
B2110
FIR TREE CL
BRICK KILN CL
Docker's Lodge
BAKERS MEWS
CHURCH CL
Lower Beeding
Holy Trinity CE Prim Sch
Cooper's Hill
Eastland Farm
WARNINGLID LA
Harvey's Farm
Slatehouse Farm
SLAUGHAM LA
B2110
Eastland Hill
Warninglid Grange
Copyhold
Stonewick
Stonedelf
Leonardslee Gdns
East Hanger Wood
Engine Pond
B2115
LISTERS

59
82

39
62

A
B
C
D
E
F
A23
Chodd's Farm
Hoadlands Wood
HIGH ST B2110
OAKLEY COTTS
PO
PH
1 THE FORGE
2 THE PLATT
3 WINDMILL PLATT
4 SMUGGLERS END
TRUGGERS
B2110
WARREN COTTS
HIGHBURY COTTS
B2114
Handcross
Cow Wood
8
HORSHAM RD
COVERT MEAD
OLD RD
WEST PARK
ST MARTIN CL
BRIGHTON RD
NYMANS COTTS
Sewage Works
Nymans Gardens
Dillion's Farm
Oldhouse
7
Farthings
29
West Park Farm
COOS LA
Hill House Farm
Tanyard Wood
Homestead Wood
East Park Cottages
East Park
6
Slaugham Park
Orange Gill
Tanyard Cottages
The Jolly Tanners (PH)
Staplefield Court
TANNERS MEAD
St Mark's CE Prim Sch
The Chequers Inn (PH)
Slaugham
Slaugham Common
5
Brantridge Sch
BRANTRIDGE LA
Staplefield
STAPLEFIELD RD
Home Farm
28
CUCKFIELD RD
B2114
RH17
Slaugham Place (remains of)
River Ouse
4
Pond Tail Farmhouse
Slaugham Manor
Little Ashfold
STAPLEFIELD RD
Slaughamplace Farm
Stanbridge House
3
Old Park Farm
Old Park House
Stanbridge Grange Farm
North Hall
SLAUGHAM LA
Warninglid Prim Sch
27
2
MALLION'S LA
Mallion's Farm
Upper Barn
Beacon Hall
Warninglid
Anne's Wood
1
White House Farm
CUCKFIELD LA
PH
SLOUGHGREEN LA
Portways Farm
B2115
B2115
B2115
26
25
26
27

61
40

A
B
C
D
E
F
8
7
29
6
5
28
4
3
27
2
1
26
Bury Wood
Northland Wood
Brook Wood
WESTUP RD
B2036
Kemps House
LONDON RD
Jarretts Farm
Northlands Farm
Norfolk Cottage
Kemps Farm
Allen's Farm
Soles Coppice
Seyron Wood
Rowhill Wood
Long Wood
Washlands Farm
ROW HILL LA
Pilstye Wood
Furze Wood
Brownings
Little Sion Wood
BRANTRIDGE LA
Brightwell Farm
WHITETHROAT LA
Upper Pilstye Cottages
White House
Court Farm
Spicer's Farm
Old Hall
Pilstye Farm
CHERRY LA
STONECOURT COTTS
Tyes Place
ROSE COTTAGE LA
Upper Staplefield Common
Hillside
River Ouse
RH17
Sidnye Cottages
Chiffley Grange
B2114
The Old Kennels
Sidnye Farm
Hammerhill Bridge
HAMMER HILL
Toll Shaw
Barrack Cottages
Collin's Farm
Hammer Hill
Bigges Farm
Hammerhill Copse
CUCKFIELD RD
Holmsted Manor
SPARK'S LA
Cleaver's Cottages
Mizbrook's Farm
Lower Spark's Farm
BROOK ST
CLEAVER'S LA
Holmsted Farm
HOLMSTED HILL
Tanyard Farm
High Weald Landscape Trail
Brook Street
BROOK GN
Little Mizbrooks
Slough Green
Slough Place Farm
Slough Place
Taylors Barn
B2115
28
29
30

61
84

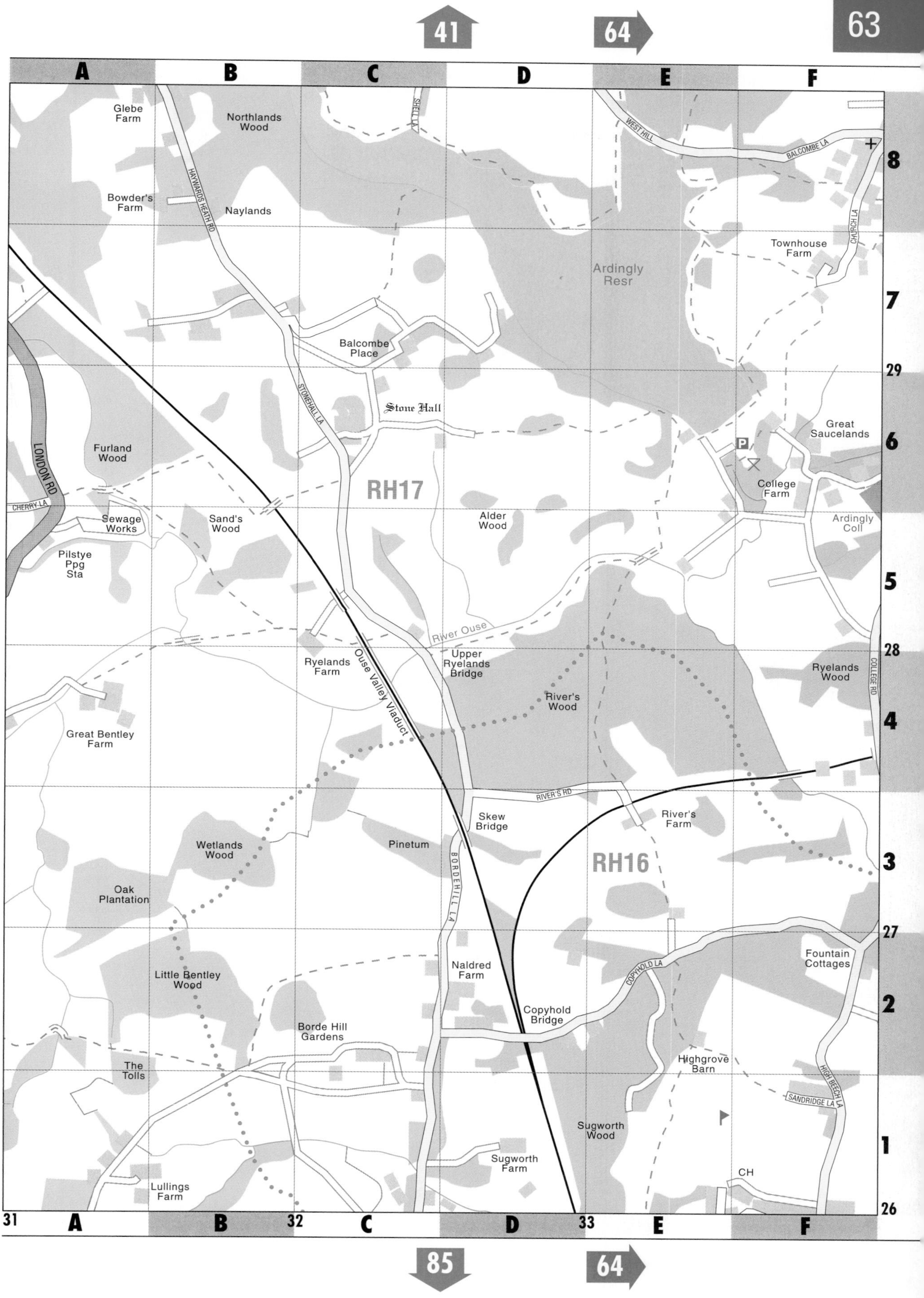
41
64
A
B
C
D
E
F
Glebe Farm
Northlands Wood
SHELL LA
WEST HILL
BALCOMBE LA
HAYWARDS HEATH RD
Bowder's Farm
Naylands
CHURCH LA
Townhouse Farm
Ardingly Resr
Balcombe Place
STONEHALL LA
Stone Hall
Great Saucelands
LONDON RD
Furland Wood
RH17
College Farm
CHERRY LA
Sewage Works
Sand's Wood
Alder Wood
Ardingly Coll
Pilstye Ppg Sta
River Ouse
Ryelands Farm
Ouse Valley Viaduct
Upper Ryelands Bridge
Ryelands Wood
COLLEGE RD
River's Wood
Great Bentley Farm
RIVER'S RD
Skew Bridge
River's Farm
Wetlands Wood
Pinetum
BORDEHILL LA
RH16
Oak Plantation
Naldred Farm
Fountain Cottages
COPYHOLD LA
Little Bentley Wood
Copyhold Bridge
Borde Hill Gardens
The Tolls
Highgrove Barn
SANDRIDGE LA
HIGH BEECH LA
Sugworth Wood
Sugworth Farm
CH
Lullings Farm
8
7
29
6
5
28
4
3
27
2
1
26
31
32
33
85
64

63
42

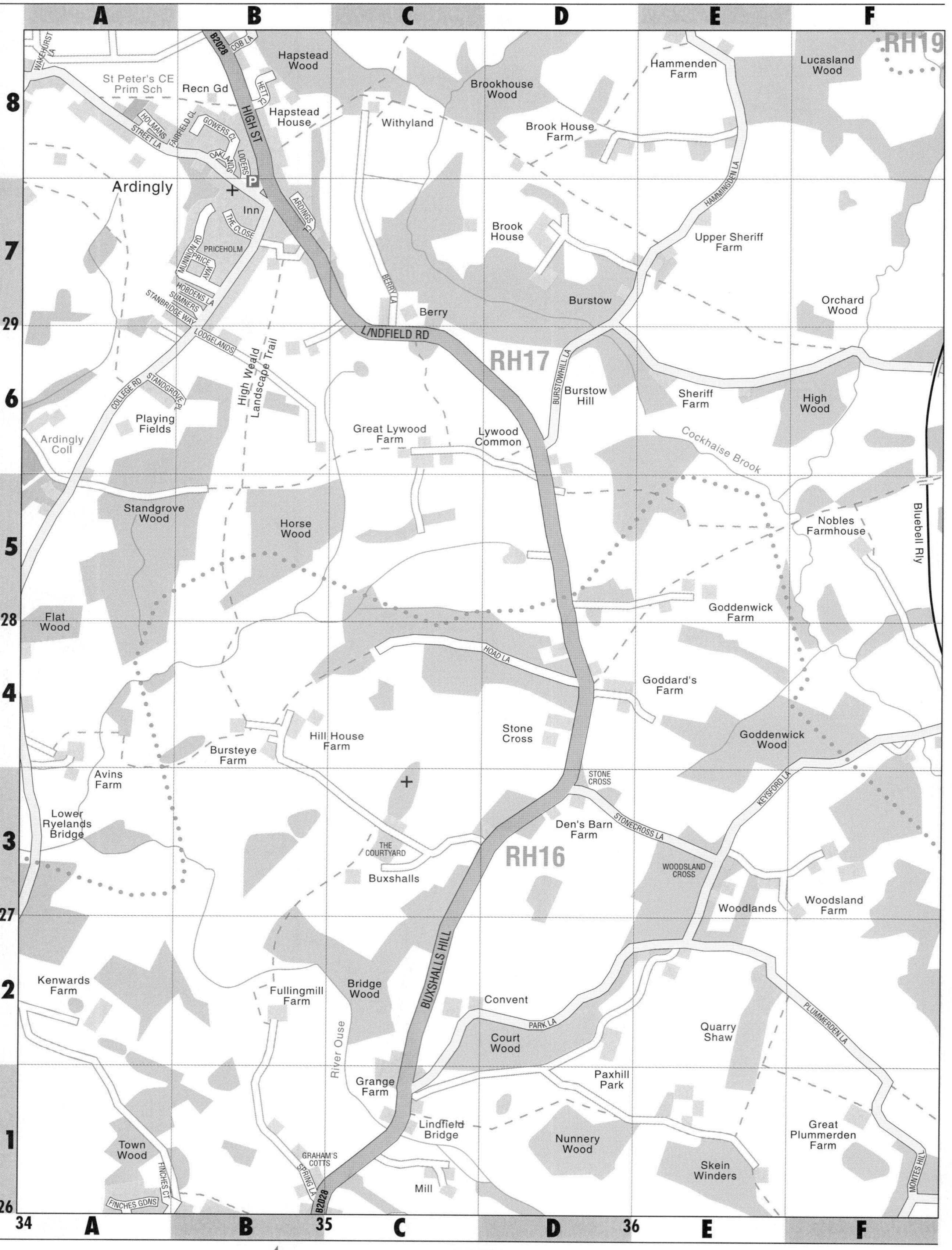
A
B
C
D
E
F
8
7
29
6
5
28
4
3
27
2
1
26
34
35
36
RH19
RH17
RH16
B2028
COB LA
HETTY CL
HIGH ST
WAKEHURST LA
St Peter's CE
Prim Sch
Recn Gd
Hapstead
Wood
Hapstead
House
Brookhouse
Wood
Withyland
Brook House
Farm
Hammenden
Farm
Lucasland
Wood
HOLMANS
STREET LA
FAIRFIELD CL
GOWERS CL
OAKLANDS
LODERS
Ardingly
Inn
ARDINGS CL
THE CLOSE
PRICEHOLM
MUNNION RD
PRICE WAY
HOBDENS LA
SUMNERS
STANBRIDGE WAY
LODGELANDS
BERRY LA
Berry
Brook
House
Burstow
HAMMINGDEN LA
Upper Sheriff
Farm
Orchard
Wood
LINDFIELD RD
High Weald
Landscape Trail
COLLEGE RD
STANDGROVE PL
Playing
Fields
Ardingly
Coll
Great Lywood
Farm
Lywood
Common
BURSTOWHILL LA
Burstow
Hill
Sheriff
Farm
High
Wood
Cockhaise Brook
Standgrove
Wood
Horse
Wood
Nobles
Farmhouse
Bluebell Rly
Flat
Wood
Goddenwick
Farm
HOAD LA
Goddard's
Farm
Hill House
Farm
Stone
Cross
Bursteye
Farm
Goddenwick
Wood
Avins
Farm
STONE
CROSS
KEYSFORD LA
Lower
Ryelands
Bridge
Den's Barn
Farm
STONECROSS LA
THE
COURTYARD
Buxshalls
WOODSLAND
CROSS
Woodlands
Woodsland
Farm
Kenwards
Farm
Fullingmill
Farm
Bridge
Wood
BUXSHALLS HILL
Convent
PARK LA
Court
Wood
Quarry
Shaw
PLUMMERDEN LA
River Ouse
Grange
Farm
Paxhill
Park
Lindfield
Bridge
Nunnery
Wood
Great
Plummerden
Farm
Town
Wood
FINCHES CT
GRAHAM'S
COTTS
SPRING LA
Skein
Winders
MONTES HILL
Mill
FINCHES GDNS

63
86

43
66

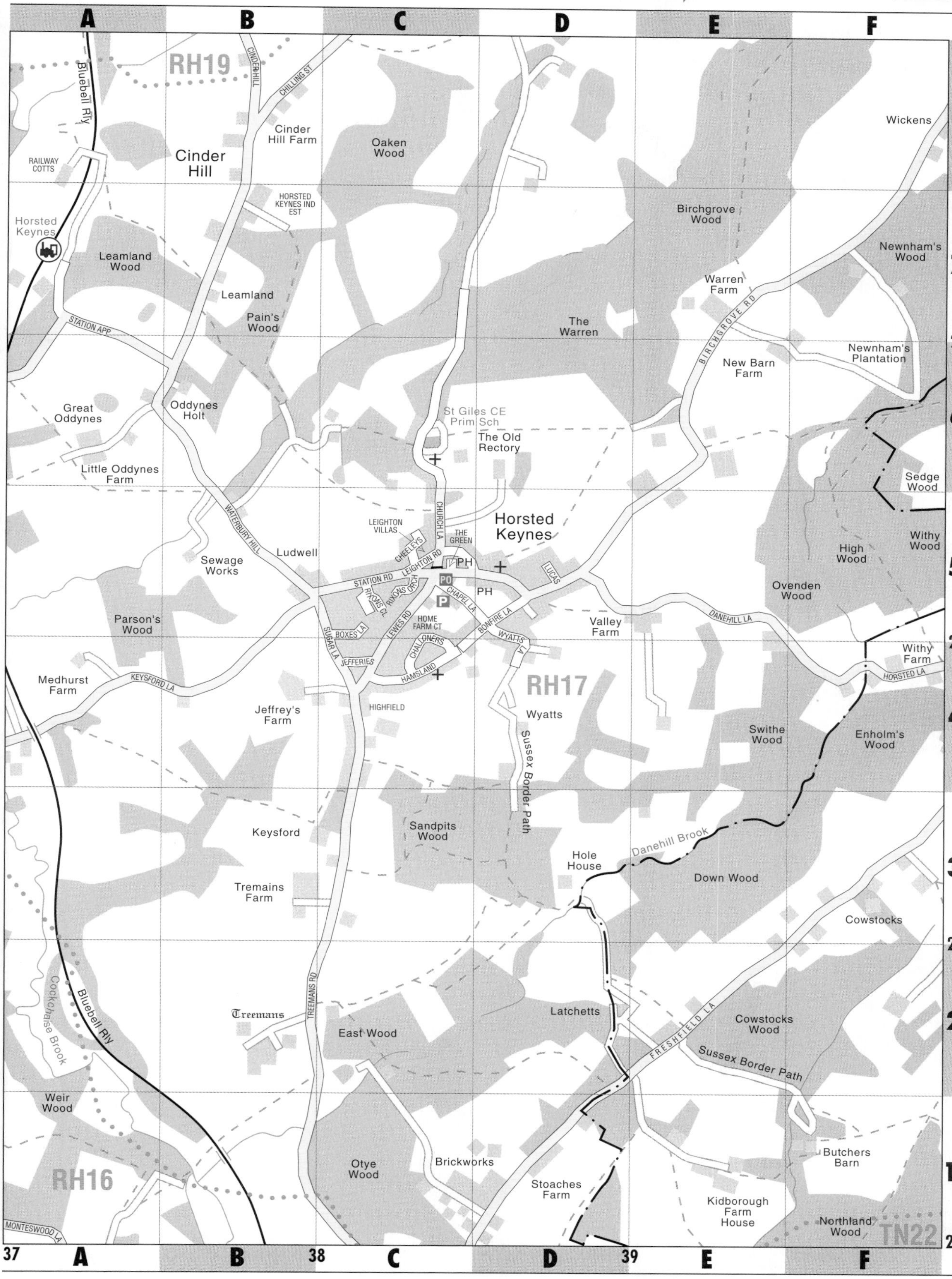
A
B
C
D
E
F
RH19
Bluebell Rly
CINDER HILL
CHILLING ST
Cinder Hill Farm
Cinder Hill
Oaken Wood
Wickens
8
RAILWAY COTTS
HORSTED KEYNES IND EST
Horsted Keynes
Birchgrove Wood
Leamland Wood
Newnham's Wood
7
Warren Farm
Leamland
Pain's Wood
The Warren
STATION APP
BIRCHGROVE RD
Newnham's Plantation
29
New Barn Farm
Great Oddynes
Oddynes Holt
St Giles CE Prim Sch
6
The Old Rectory
Little Oddynes Farm
Sedge Wood
WATERBURY HILL
CHURCH LA
Horsted Keynes
LEIGHTON VILLAS
THE GREEN
Withy Wood
High Wood
Sewage Works
Ludwell
CHEELEYS
LEIGHTON RD
PH
5
LUCAS
STATION RD
PO
P
PH
Ovenden Wood
RIXONS CL
RIXONS ORCH
CHAPEL LA
Parson's Wood
HOME FARM CT
LEWES RD
BONFIRE LA
Valley Farm
DANEHILL LA
SUGAR LA
BOXES LA
WYATTS LA
28
CHALLONERS
Withy Farm
JEFFERIES
HAMSLAND
RH17
HORSTED LA
Medhurst Farm
KEYSFORD LA
HIGHFIELD
Jeffrey's Farm
Wyatts
4
Swithe Wood
Enholm's Wood
Sussex Border Path
Sandpits Wood
Keysford
Danehill Brook
Hole House
3
Down Wood
Tremains Farm
Cowstocks
27
Cockchaise Brook
Bluebell Rly
TREEMANS RD
Treemans
Latchetts
Cowstocks Wood
2
FRESHFIELD LA
East Wood
Sussex Border Path
Weir Wood
Butchers Barn
Otye Wood
Brickworks
1
RH16
Stoaches Farm
Kidborough Farm House
Northland Wood
TN22
MONTESWOOD LA
26
37
A
B
38
C
D
39
E
F

87
66

65
44

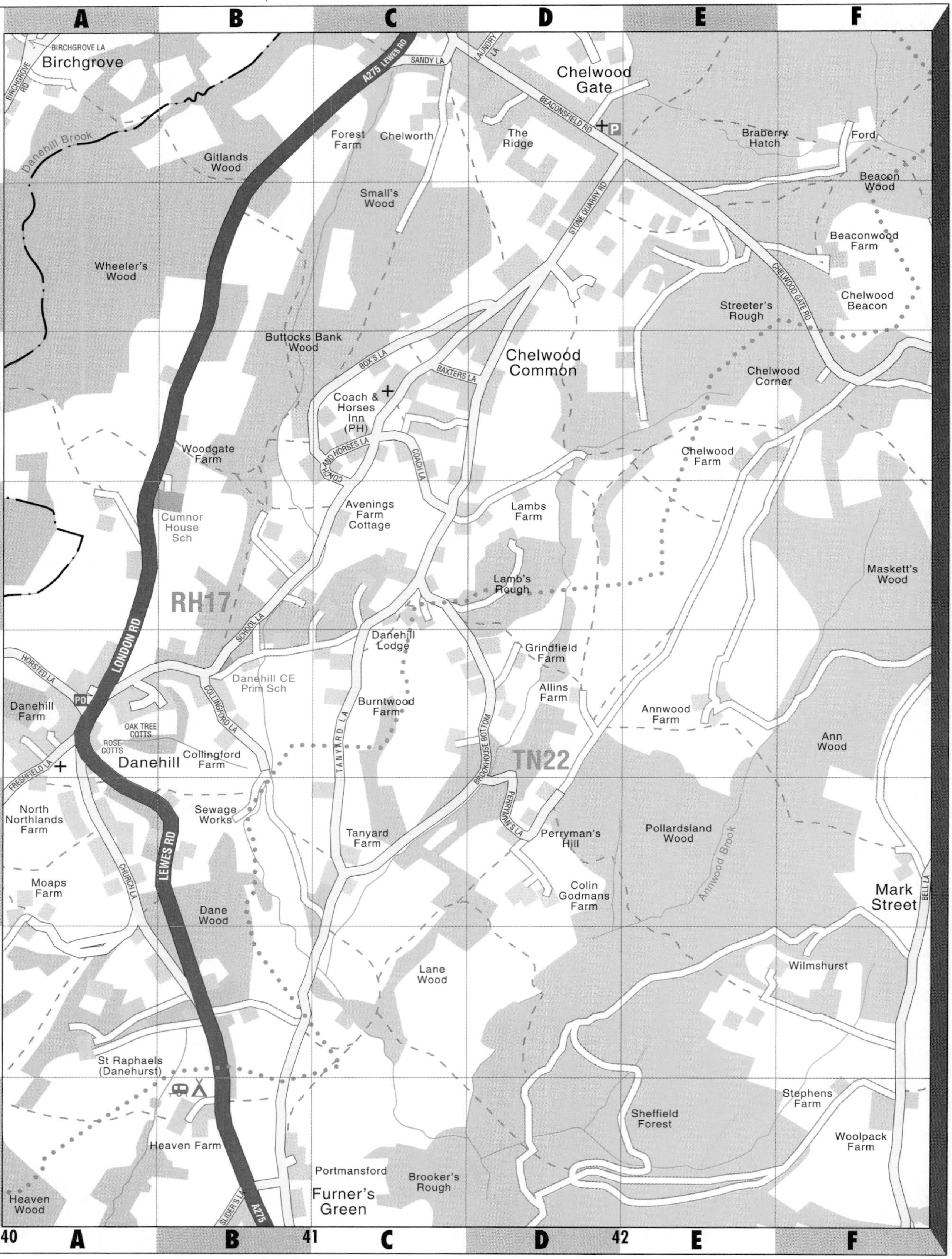
A
B
C
D
E
F
8
7
29
6
5
28
4
3
27
2
1
26
40
41
42
BIRCHGROVE LA
Birchgrove
BIRCHGROVE RD
A275 LEWES RD
SANDY LA
LAUNDRY LA
Chelwood Gate
BEACONSFIELD RD
Danehill Brook
Gitlands Wood
Forest Farm
Chelworth
The Ridge
Braberry Hatch
Ford
Beacon Wood
Small's Wood
STONE QUARRY RD
Beaconwood Farm
Wheeler's Wood
CHELWOOD GATE RD
Chelwood Beacon
Streeter's Rough
Buttocks Bank Wood
BOX'S LA
Chelwood Common
BAXTERS LA
Chelwood Corner
Coach & Horses Inn (PH)
COACH AND HORSES LA
COACH LA
Woodgate Farm
Chelwood Farm
Cumnor House Sch
Avenings Farm Cottage
Lambs Farm
Maskett's Wood
Lamb's Rough
RH17
SCHOOL LA
Danehill Lodge
Grindfield Farm
HORSTED LA
LONDON RD
Danehill CE Prim Sch
COLLINGFORD LA
Allins Farm
Danehill Farm
PO
Burntwood Farm
Annwood Farm
OAK TREE COTTS
ROSE COTTS
Collingford Farm
Danehill
TANYARD LA
BROOKHOUSE BOTTOM
TN22
Ann Wood
FRESHFIELD LA
North Northlands Farm
Sewage Works
PERRYMAN'S LA
Tanyard Farm
Perryman's Hill
Pollardsland Wood
Annwood Brook
LEWES RD
Moaps Farm
CHURCH LA
Colin Godmans Farm
Mark Street
BELL LA
Dane Wood
Lane Wood
Wilmshurst
St Raphaels (Danehurst)
Stephens Farm
Sheffield Forest
Heaven Farm
Woolpack Farm
Portmansford
Brooker's Rough
Heaven Wood
SLIDER'S LA
A275
Furner's Green

65

45
68

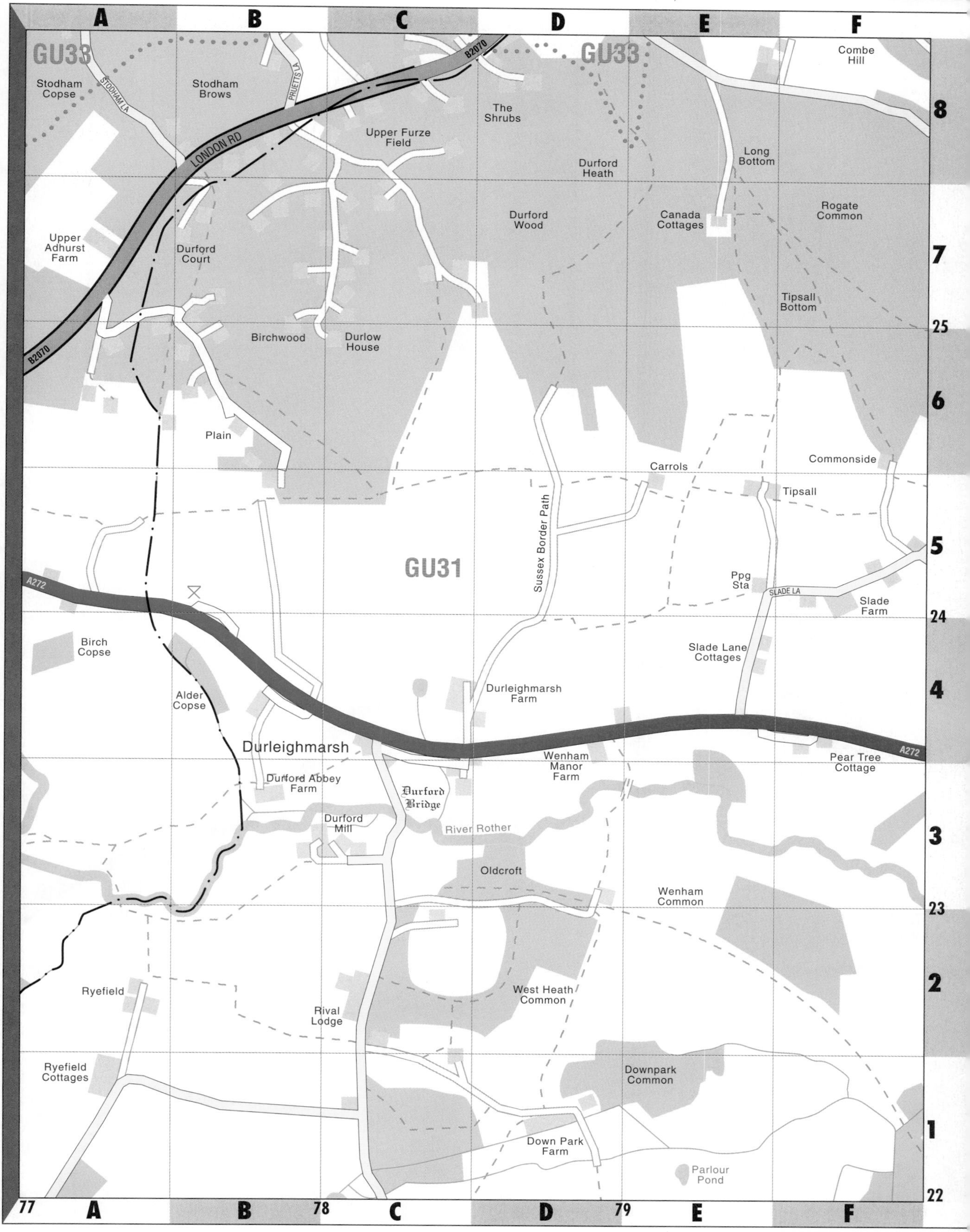
A
B
C
D
E
F
GU33
GU33
Stodham Copse
STODHAM LA
Stodham Brows
PRUETTS LA
B2070
LONDON RD
The Shrubs
Upper Furze Field
Combe Hill
Durford Heath
Long Bottom
Upper Adhurst Farm
Durford Court
Durford Wood
Canada Cottages
Rogate Common
Tipsall Bottom
Birchwood
Durlow House
Plain
Carrols
Commonside
Tipsall
GU31
Sussex Border Path
A272
Ppg Sta
SLADE LA
Slade Farm
Birch Copse
Slade Lane Cottages
Alder Copse
Durleighmarsh Farm
Durleighmarsh
Wenham Manor Farm
Pear Tree Cottage
Durford Abbey Farm
Durford Bridge
Durford Mill
River Rother
Oldcroft
Wenham Common
Ryefield
West Heath Common
Rival Lodge
Ryefield Cottages
Downpark Common
Down Park Farm
Parlour Pond
8
7
25
6
5
24
4
3
23
2
1
22
77
78
79

89
68

67
46
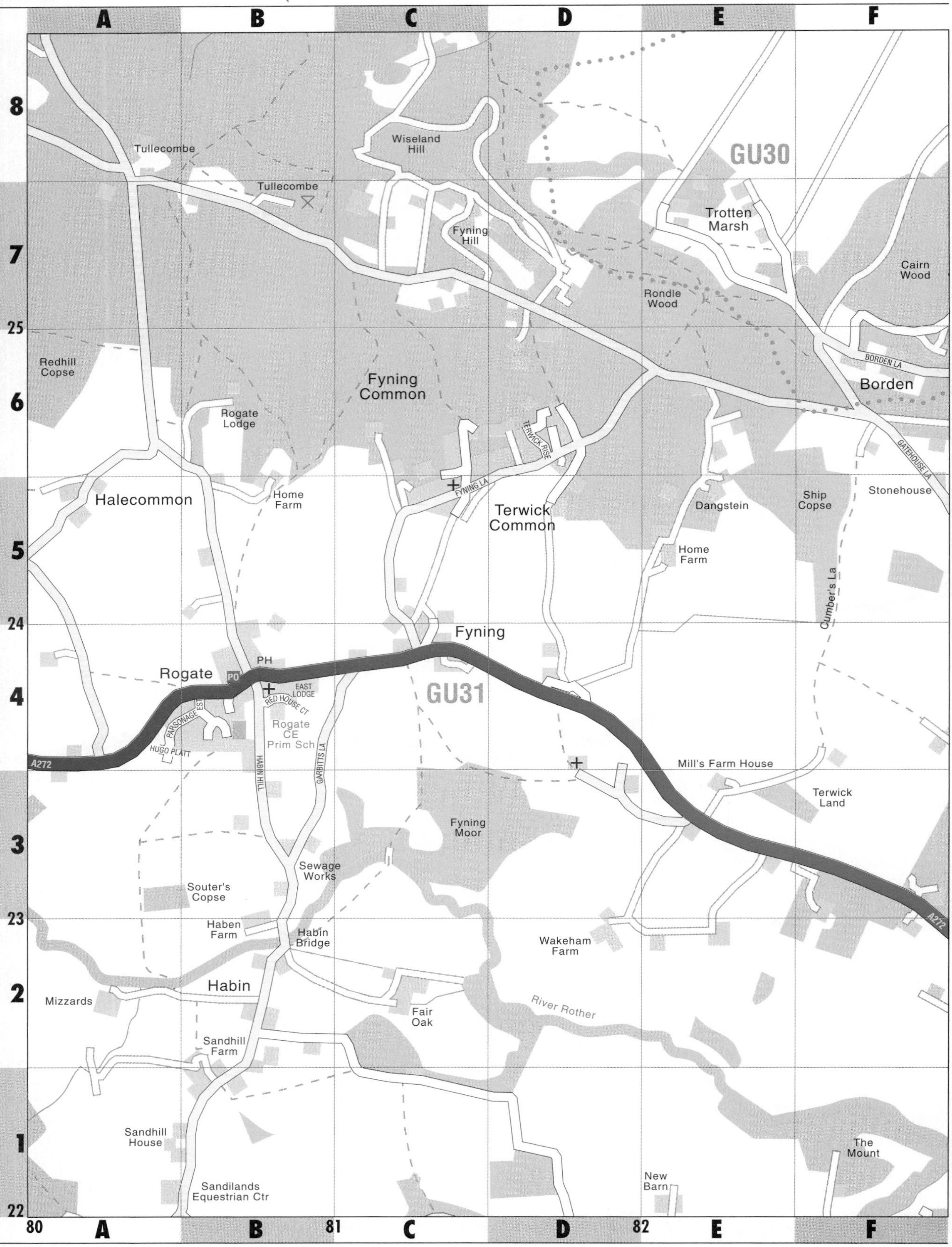
A
B
C
D
E
F
8
7
25
6
5
24
4
3
23
2
1
22
80
81
82
Tullecombe
Tullecombe
Wiseland Hill
GU30
Trotten Marsh
Fyning Hill
Cairn Wood
Rondle Wood
Redhill Copse
Fyning Common
BORDEN LA
Borden
Rogate Lodge
TERWICK RISE
GATEHOUSE LA
Halecommon
Home Farm
FYNING LA
Terwick Common
Dangstein
Ship Copse
Stonehouse
Home Farm
Cumber's La
Fyning
PH
Rogate
PO
EAST LODGE
RED HOUSE CT
GU31
PARSONAGE EST
Rogate CE Prim Sch
HUGO PLATT
A272
HABIN HILL
GARBITTS LA
Mill's Farm House
Terwick Land
Fyning Moor
Sewage Works
Souter's Copse
A272
Haben Farm
Habin Bridge
Wakeham Farm
Habin
Mizzards
River Rother
Fair Oak
Sandhill Farm
Sandhill House
The Mount
New Barn
Sandilands Equestrian Ctr
67
90

47
70

A
B
C
D
E
F
Bobbolds Farm
Lyford Copse
Lower Bowley Copse
Titty Hill
LAMBOURNE LA
IPING RD
Three Ponds Wood
COOK'S POND RD
Queen's Corner
Stedham Marsh
Iping Marsh
Kingsham Wood
GU30
Cemy
Dunner Hill
Upper Bowley Copse
Borden Wood
Hammer Stream
Robins Farm
Wispers Copse
ROBINS LA
Bowley Farm
Jungle Wood
BORDEN LA
MOORHOUSE LA
Stubbs Farm House
Stubb Hill
Kingsham Farm
Holm Wood
Pond Copse
Stubb Hill Farm
Oakham Common
Wick Wood
Tentworth
New Bridge
Coopers Heath
Hammer Wood
Ash House
GU29
Gatehouse Farm
GATEHOUSE LA
CHITHURST LA
Hammer Pond
GU31
Cumber's Farm
Horn Hill
HAMMER LA
IPING LA
STANWATER LA
Hammerwood House
Crouchhouse Farm
Hammer Hanger
Cumberspark Wood
Chithurst Manor
Chithurst
Ambletts
River Rother
Iping
Trotton Farm
Rotherhill House
Trotton
ROTHER LA
Trotton Bridge
Crowshole Farm
The Keepers Arms (PH)
Nurseries
COMMON VIEW
HAMILTON CL
PH
SCHOOL LA
Black Pond
Trotton Common
Stedham Prim Sch
Terwick Mill
MILL LA
TERWICK LA
ELSTED RD
A272
8
7
25
6
5
24
4
3
23
2
1
22
83
84
85

91
70

69
48

A
B
C
D
E
F
8
7
25
6
5
24
4
3
3
2
1
86
87
88
A286
GU27
Scotland Farmhouse
Woolbeding Common
Little Common
West Heath
Madam's Farm
Linch Old Rectory
The Lair
Lord's Common
KINGS DR
LINCH RD
Woolhouse Farm
Pound Farm
King Edward VII
H
Great Common
St Cuthman's Sch
Tote Hill
Pound Common
Eastshaw Farm
Hollist Common
Woodgate Farm
Chapelland Copse
TOTE LA
Old School
Paylins Copse
Chapelland Buildings
GU29
Cherryorchard Cottage
Lock's Cottages
WOOLBEDING LA
EASTSHAW LA
Whitters Farm
Farthings
STEDHAM LA
OLD BUDDINGTON LA
Old Buddington
Brambling Farm
Hurst Hills
BUDDINGTON LA
Stedham Mill
BRAMBLING LA
Buddington Farm
UPPERFIELD
Woolbeding
HOLLIST LA
River Rother
Hollist House
MILL LA
Bridgefoot
WEAVERS CL
Stedham Bridge
Stedham Hall
Woolbeding House
Sewage Works
QUEENS ST
DODSLEY GR
THE ALLEY
Midhurst Cottage
COMMON VIEW
Stedham
SCHOOL LA
THE STREET
STRATHMOOR GDNS
DODSLEY LA
Great House Farm
Woolbeding Bridge
Midhurst Gram Sch
NORTH ST
A272

69
92

49
72

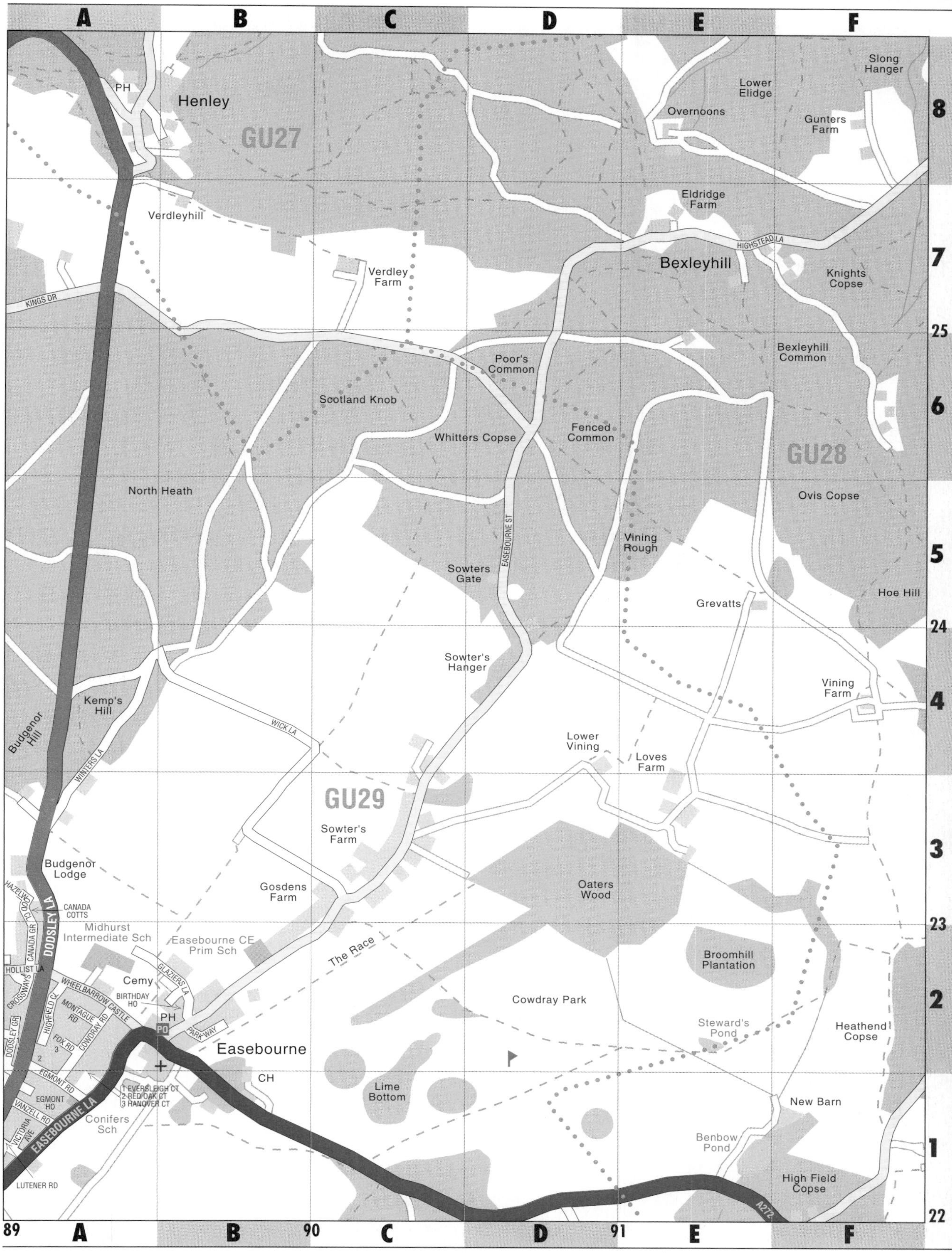
A
B
C
D
E
F
8
7
25
6
5
24
4
3
23
2
1
22
89
90
91
Henley
PH
GU27
Verdleyhill
Verdley Farm
KINGS DR
Overnoons
Lower Elidge
Slong Hanger
Gunters Farm
Eldridge Farm
HIGHSTEAD LA
Bexleyhill
Knights Copse
Bexleyhill Common
Poor's Common
Scotland Knob
Whitters Copse
Fenced Common
GU28
Ovis Copse
North Heath
EASEBOURNE ST
Vining Rough
Sowters Gate
Grevatts
Hoe Hill
Sowter's Hanger
Vining Farm
Kemp's Hill
Budgenor Hill
WICK LA
WINTERS LA
Lower Vining
Loves Farm
GU29
Sowter's Farm
Budgenor Lodge
Gosdens Farm
Oaters Wood
HAZELWAY
CANADA COTTS
CANADA GR
DODSLEY LA
Midhurst Intermediate Sch
Easebourne CE Prim Sch
The Race
Broomhill Plantation
HOLLIST LA
CROSSWAYS
Cemy
GLAZIERS LA
WHEELBARROW CASTLE
BIRTHDAY HO
Cowdray Park
HIGHFIELD CL
MONTAGUE RD
COWDRAY RD
PH
PO
PARK WAY
Steward's Pond
Heathend Copse
DODSLEY GR
FOX RD
Easebourne
EGMONT RD
CH
Lime Bottom
1 EVERSLEIGH CT
2 RED OAK CT
3 HANOVER CT
EGMONT HO
VANZELL RD
EASEBOURNE LA
New Barn
VICTORIA AVE
Conifers Sch
Benbow Pond
High Field Copse
A272
LUTENER RD

93
72

71
50

A
B
C
D
E
F
8
7
25
6
5
24
4
3
23
2
1
22
92
93
94
Slong Farm
Lickfold
HIGHSTEAD LA
Cobden Farm
Mill Pond
Mill Farm
The Plash
COLLYERS COTTS
Wadlington
Close Copse
Dirty Bridge Barn
Dirty Bridge Field
White's Green
Jacksonslake Copse
Captains
River Park Farm
Furze Field
Outtens Copse
Lodsworth Common
GU28
Lord's Wood
Snapelands Copse
Snapelands
Redens
Limekiln Rough
Lodge Farm
Leggatt Hill
Redlands Farm
Leggatt Hill Farm
Leggatt Hill
Kimbers Cottage
WESTLAND'S COPSE LA
Smithbrook
Vining Copse
SCHOOL LA
Salmonsbridge Farm
River Common
BEECHFIELD COTTS
SHEPHERDS LA
Lodsworth
Oldpark Copse
Roundabouts Farm
OAKFIELD
THE CROFT
Hollist Arms (PH)
River
RIVER LA
JAMES LA
Eel Bridge
Twr
Pitshill
BROOKFIELD LA
VICARAGE LA
Lodsworth House
CHURCH LA
River Nursery
Heathend Copse
River Wood
Standlands
Brookfield Cottage
Gosdens Heath
Langham Stables
BROOKFIELD LA
Gosdensheath Copse
Boughton Dairy Farm
Gosdensheath Farm
Path Field
Beggars' Corner
A272

71
94

51
74

A
B
C
D
E
F
8
7
25
6
5
24
4
3
23
2
1
22
95
96
97
Glasshouse Pond Plantation
Dry Pond
Stagpark Farm
Hoads Common
Palfrey Farm
Pug's Bottom Roughs
A283
Spring Pond Rough
Jacksonslake Plantation
Great Spring Pond
CH
Osiers Farm
Kiln Copse
Pheasantcopse Lodge
Little Spring Pond
W Twr
W Twr
Burrell's Cottage
Parkhurst Farm
Raffling Wood
Limbo
Limbo Farm
Pheasant Copse
Westlands Copse
Adelaide Lodge
Keyfox Farm
WESTLAND'S COPSE LA
P
Halfmoon Furze
Ratford Farm
Shepherds Cottage
GU28
Guntersbridge Farm
Upper Copse
Nithurst Farm
Gunter's Bridge
Upperton Common
Mon
Lower Pond
Upper Lodge
HAMPERS GN
Cemy
Upperton
Kennels
Westbrook House
Hampers Common
Petworth Park Deer Park
HAMPERS COMMON IND EST
NEW RD
P
Dene Dip
UPPERTON RD
NORTH END CL
NORTHMEAD
A283
Cemy
PH
HORSHAM RD A272
Upperton Farm
Boat House
NORTH ST A272
DEAN LA
THOMPSON'S HOSPITAL
GLEBE VILLAS
The Manor of Dean
PARK TERR
LINTON HO
Horse Guards Inn (PH)
Upper Pond
CEMETERY LA

95
74

73
52

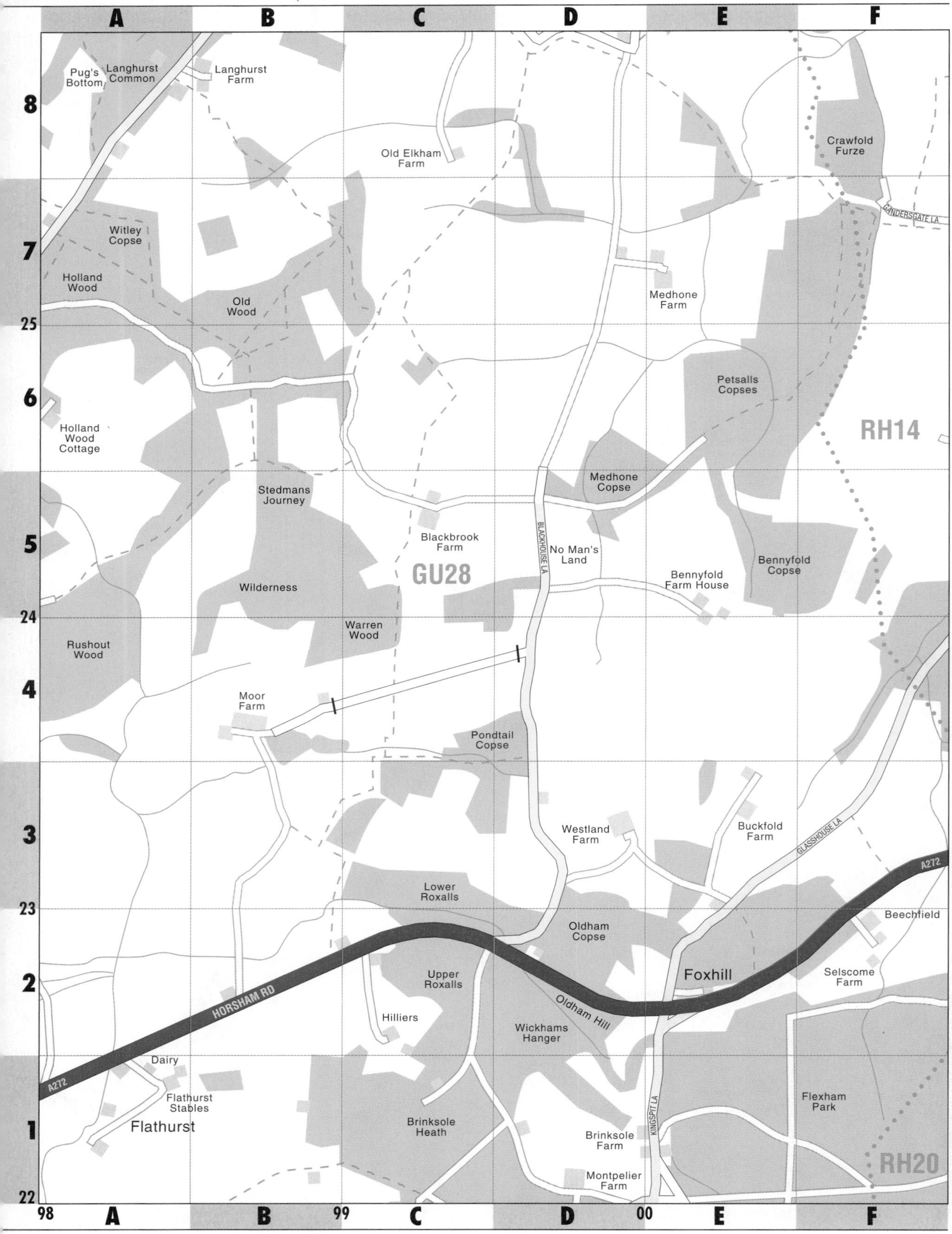
A
B
C
D
E
F
8
7
25
6
5
24
4
3
23
2
1
22
98
99
00
Pug's Bottom
Langhurst Common
Langhurst Farm
Old Elkham Farm
Crawfold Furze
GANDERSGATE LA
Witley Copse
Holland Wood
Old Wood
Medhone Farm
Petsalls Copses
Holland Wood Cottage
RH14
Stedmans Journey
Medhone Copse
Blackbrook Farm
BLACKHOUSE LA
No Man's Land
Bennyfold Copse
Bennyfold Farm House
GU28
Wilderness
Warren Wood
Rushout Wood
Moor Farm
Pondtail Copse
Westland Farm
Buckfold Farm
GLASSHOUSE LA
A272
Lower Roxalls
Beechfield
Oldham Copse
Foxhill
Selscome Farm
Upper Roxalls
HORSHAM RD
Oldham Hill
Hilliers
Wickhams Hanger
Dairy
A272
Flathurst Stables
Flathurst
Flexham Park
Brinksole Heath
Brinksole Farm
KINGSPIT LA
RH20
Montpelier Farm

73
96

53
76

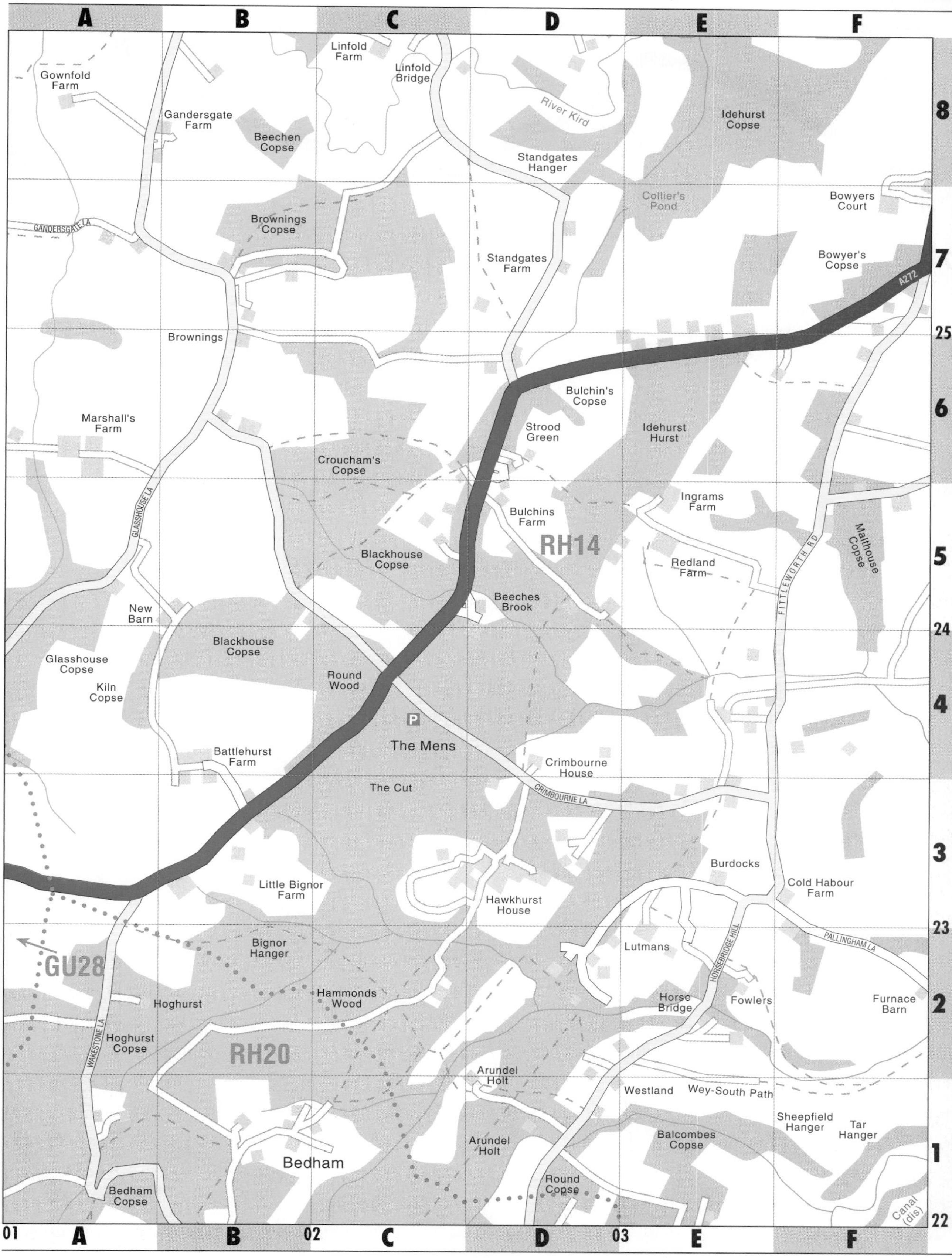
A
B
C
D
E
F
8
7
25
6
5
24
4
3
23
2
1
22
01
02
03
Gownfold Farm
Gandersgate Farm
Linfold Farm
Linfold Bridge
Beechen Copse
River Kird
Idehurst Copse
Standgates Hanger
Collier's Pond
Bowyers Court
GANDERSGATE LA
Brownings Copse
Standgates Farm
Bowyer's Copse
A272
Brownings
Bulchin's Copse
Marshall's Farm
Strood Green
Idehurst Hurst
Croucham's Copse
Ingrams Farm
GLASSHOUSE LA
Bulchins Farm
RH14
Blackhouse Copse
Redland Farm
Malthouse Copse
FITTLEWORTH RD
New Barn
Beeches Brook
Blackhouse Copse
Glasshouse Copse
Kiln Copse
Round Wood
P
The Mens
Battlehurst Farm
Crimbourne House
The Cut
CRIMBOURNE LA
Burdocks
Little Bignor Farm
Cold Habour Farm
Hawkhurst House
Bignor Hanger
Lutmans
PALLINGHAM LA
GU28
HORSEBRIDGE HILL
Hoghurst
Hammonds Wood
Horse Bridge
Fowlers
Furnace Barn
Hoghurst Copse
WAKESTONE LA
RH20
Arundel Holt
Westland
Wey-South Path
Sheepfield Hanger
Tar Hanger
Balcombes Copse
Arundel Holt
Bedham
Round Copse
Bedham Copse
Canal (dis)

97
76

75
54

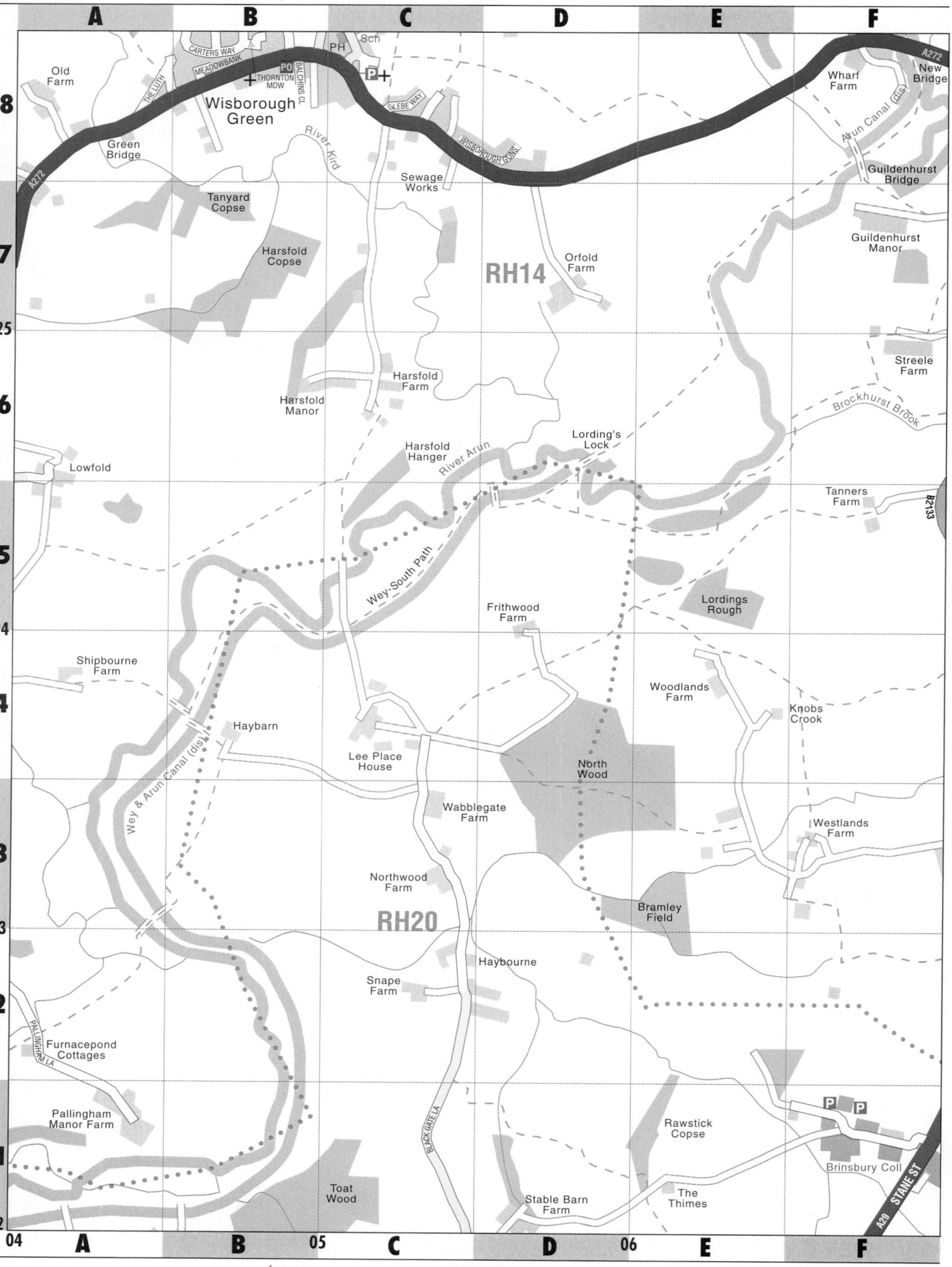
A
B
C
D
E
F
8
7
25
6
5
24
4
3
23
2
1
22
04
05
06
Old Farm
CARTERS WAY
MEADOWBANK
THE LUTH
PO
THORNTON MDW
BALCHINS CL
Wisborough Green
PH
Sch
P
GLEBE WAY
A272
Green Bridge
River Kird
Sewage Works
WISBOROUGH GDNS
Wharf Farm
New Bridge
Arun Canal (dis)
Guildenhurst Bridge
Tanyard Copse
Harsfold Copse
RH14
Orfold Farm
Guildenhurst Manor
Streele Farm
Harsfold Farm
Harsfold Manor
Brockhurst Brook
Lording's Lock
Harsfold Hanger
River Arun
Lowfold
Tanners Farm
B2133
Wey-South Path
Lordings Rough
Frithwood Farm
Shipbourne Farm
Woodlands Farm
Knobs Crook
Haybarn
Lee Place House
North Wood
Wey & Arun Canal (dis)
Wabblegate Farm
Westlands Farm
Northwood Farm
RH20
Bramley Field
Haybourne
Snape Farm
PALLINGHAM LA
Furnacepond Cottages
Pallingham Manor Farm
BLACK GATE LA
Rawstick Copse
Brinsbury Coll
STANE ST
A29
Toat Wood
Stable Barn Farm
The Thimes

75
98

55
78

A
B
C
D
E
F
8
7
25
6
5
24
4
3
23
2
1
22
07
08
09
Newbridge Farm
NEWBRIDGE RD
B2133
Bridgewaters Farm
The Limeburners (PH)
Hammonds
A272
EAST ST
WEST ST
HIGH ST
PO
CONEYHURST RD
WOODDALE LA
ELM HO 1
BEECH HO 2
ARUN RD
POND CL
PLATTS MDW
NEWBRIDGE RD
FRENCHES MEAD
LAKERS MDW
GRATWICKE CL
DELL LA
NIGHTINGALE WLK
EASTON CRES
ST GABRIELS RD
GORSELANDS
CLEVELANDS
WILLOW DR
BROOMFIELD DR
DOWNSVIEW COTTS
ANVIL CL
FORGE WAY
CEDARS FM CL
STEMP DR
WICKS RD
TRENTON CL
THE WADEYS
BELINUS DR
ALICKS HILL
CARPENTERS
CLEVE WAY
SILVER LA
OSTLERS VIEW
FARRIERS CL
FREEMANS CL
Schs
OAKLANDS
STATION RD
MAPLE RD
BIRCH DR
Billingshurst
Little Daux Farm
Parbrook
MORRIS DR
BERRALL WAY
LUXFORD WAY
BARROW CL
TURNER AVE
HURSTLANDS
The Weald Sch
SAVILLE GDNS
SAVILLE CT
BROOKER'S RD
WEALD CT
EAGLE EST
HUFFWOOD TRAD EST
MYRTLE LA
Billingshurst
ROSIER COMMERCIAL CTR
LC
DAUX RD
Ind Est
CHESTNUT RD
BROOKFIELD WAY
LOWER STATION RD
DAUX WAY
DAUX AVE
AUXWOOD CL
WATTS LA
CRANHAM AVE
GROOMSLAND DR
GILLMANS IND EST
WOODLANDS WAY
ROSIER WAY
A272
Par Brook
Brockhurst Brook
Sewage Works
BRIDGEWATER CL
LORDINGS RD
Great Lordings Wood
Rosier Gate
Rosier Wood
Beck Copse
KINGSFOLD CL
Little Gillmans Farm
Kingsfold
Andrew's Hill
Denham's Farm
RH14
Lordings Farm
Stonepits Rough
Kingslea Farm
MARRINGDEAN RD
Lordings Cottages
Providence Cottage
STANE ST
LC
Oakdene
Marringdean Farmhouse
Hadfold Farm
Marringdean Wood
Southlands Farm
South House Farm
Hadfold Wood
Adversane
B2133
Blacksmiths Arms (PH)
WALNUT TREE COTTS
LC
Coombland Farm
Jackmans Farm
ADVERSANE LA
Steepwood Copse
Highfure
WEST CHILTINGTON LA
Brookdale Farm
Steepwood Farm
Wood Barn Farm
Todhurst Farm (Brinsbury Coll annexe)
RH20
B2133

99
78

77
56

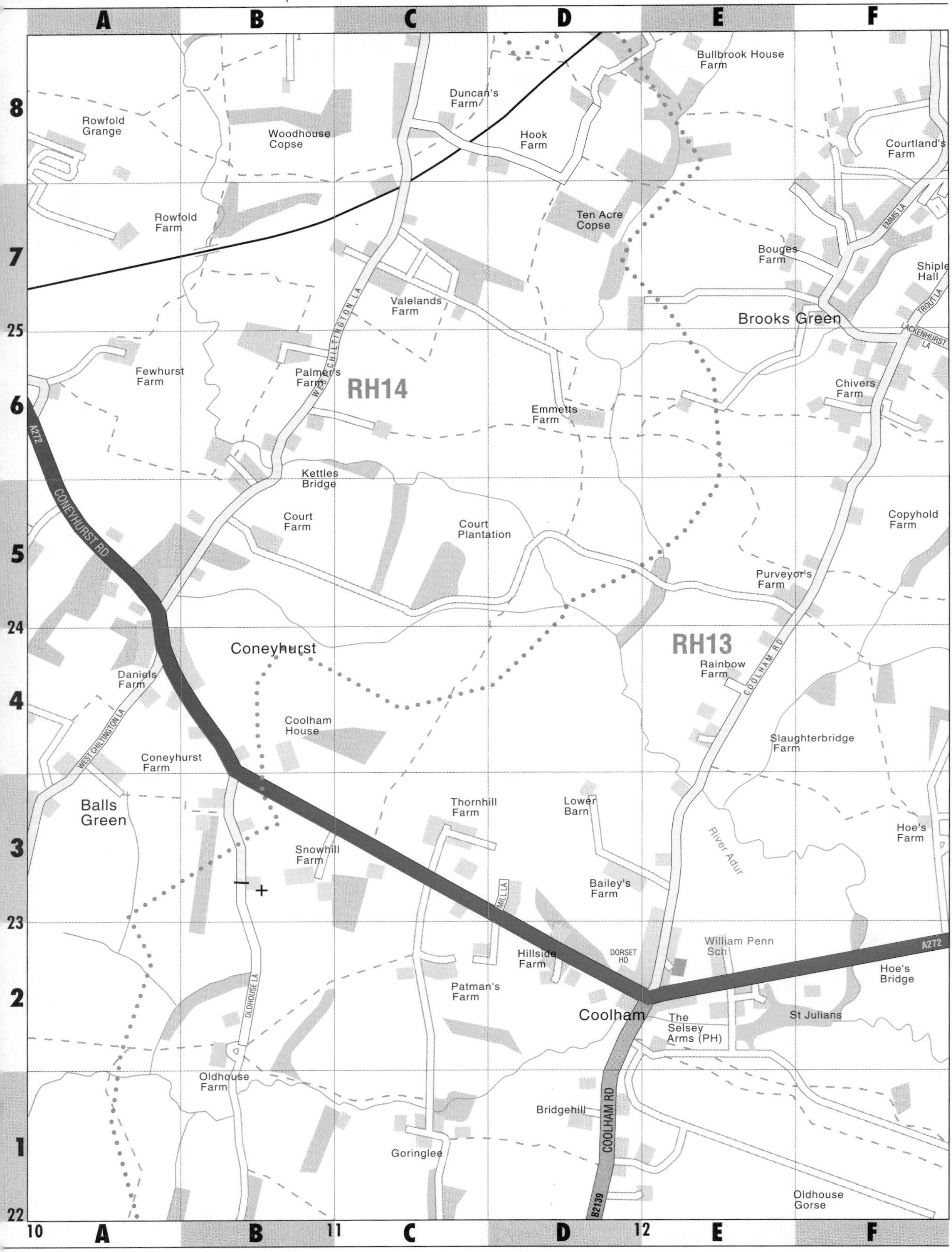
A
B
C
D
E
F
8
7
25
6
5
24
4
3
23
2
1
22
10
11
12
Rowfold Grange
Woodhouse Copse
Duncan's Farm
Hook Farm
Bullbrook House Farm
Courtland's Farm
Rowfold Farm
Ten Acre Copse
Bouges Farm
EMMS LA
Shiple Hall
TROUT LA
LACKENHURST LA
Valelands Farm
WEST CHILTINGTON LA
Brooks Green
Fewhurst Farm
Palmer's Farm
RH14
Chivers Farm
Emmetts Farm
A272
Kettles Bridge
CONEYHURST RD
Court Farm
Court Plantation
Copyhold Farm
Purveyor's Farm
Coneyhurst
RH13
Rainbow Farm
COOLHAM RD
Daniels Farm
Coolham House
Slaughterbridge Farm
WEST CHILTINGTON LA
Coneyhurst Farm
Balls Green
Thornhill Farm
Lower Barn
Hoe's Farm
River Adur
Snowhill Farm
MILL LA
Bailey's Farm
William Penn Sch
A272
DORSET HO
Hillside Farm
Hoe's Bridge
Patman's Farm
OLDHOUSE LA
Coolham
The Selsey Arms (PH)
St Julians
Oldhouse Farm
Bridgehill
COOLHAM RD
Goringlee
B2139
Oldhouse Gorse

77
100

57
80

A
B
C
D
E
F
Crookhorn Farm
Chase Farm
ASH RD
COLLEGE RD
WORTHING RD
Southwater County Park
Madgeland Wood
SHAW'S LA
WOODLANDS WAY
BEECHWOOD
Birch Wood
Birchwood Farm
Marlpost Wood
THE GABLES
MILL STRAIGHT
WEALDEN CL
TROUT LA
MARLPOST RD
FOXES CL
St Johns Farm
Blinks Wood
TREETOPS
ANDREWS RD
LITTLE CT
FOXFIELD COTTS
OAK CL
THE FIELDINGS
Middle Wood
RASCALS CL
The Gill
Rascals Farm
Netherwood
Lackenhurst Furzefield
COUNCIL COTTS 1
INGLENOOK 2
ANDREWS COTTS 3
Woodfords
NETHERWOODS RD
LACKENHURST LA
Northlands Wood
Trawler's Farm
Woodgetters
The Delph
Newbuildings Plantation
Newbuildings Place
DRAGONS GREEN RD
Abraham's Plantation
Brick Kiln Farm
SHIPLEY RD
The Plantation
BAKER'S LA
Goffsland Farm
Baker's Farm
RH13
Hoe's Wood
Shepherd's Farm
Hartsgravel Bridge
Old Keepers Cott
Renche's Cott
DRAGONS LA
Dragons Green
Cock's Hill
Hoe's Wood
The George and Dragon (PH)
Renche's Wood
Hoe's Farm
DRAGONS GREEN COUNCIL COTTS
Oakleigh Farm
SCOLLIERS CROSSWAYS
Great Cockshill Wood
Cuckoo Barn
Green Street
Shipley Paygate
A272
Butterstocks Farm
Greenstreet Farm
North Lodge
Lodge Farm
Perrets
SMITHERS HILL LA
POUND LA
Jackie's Copse
Merrik Wood
Greenstreet Furzeland
Spring Wood
Ashbrook Bridge
SCHOOL LA
Knepp Park
Church Farm North
RED LA
Knight's Farm
Shipley CE Prim Sch
8
7
25
6
5
24
4
3
23
2
1
22
13
14
15

101
80

79 58

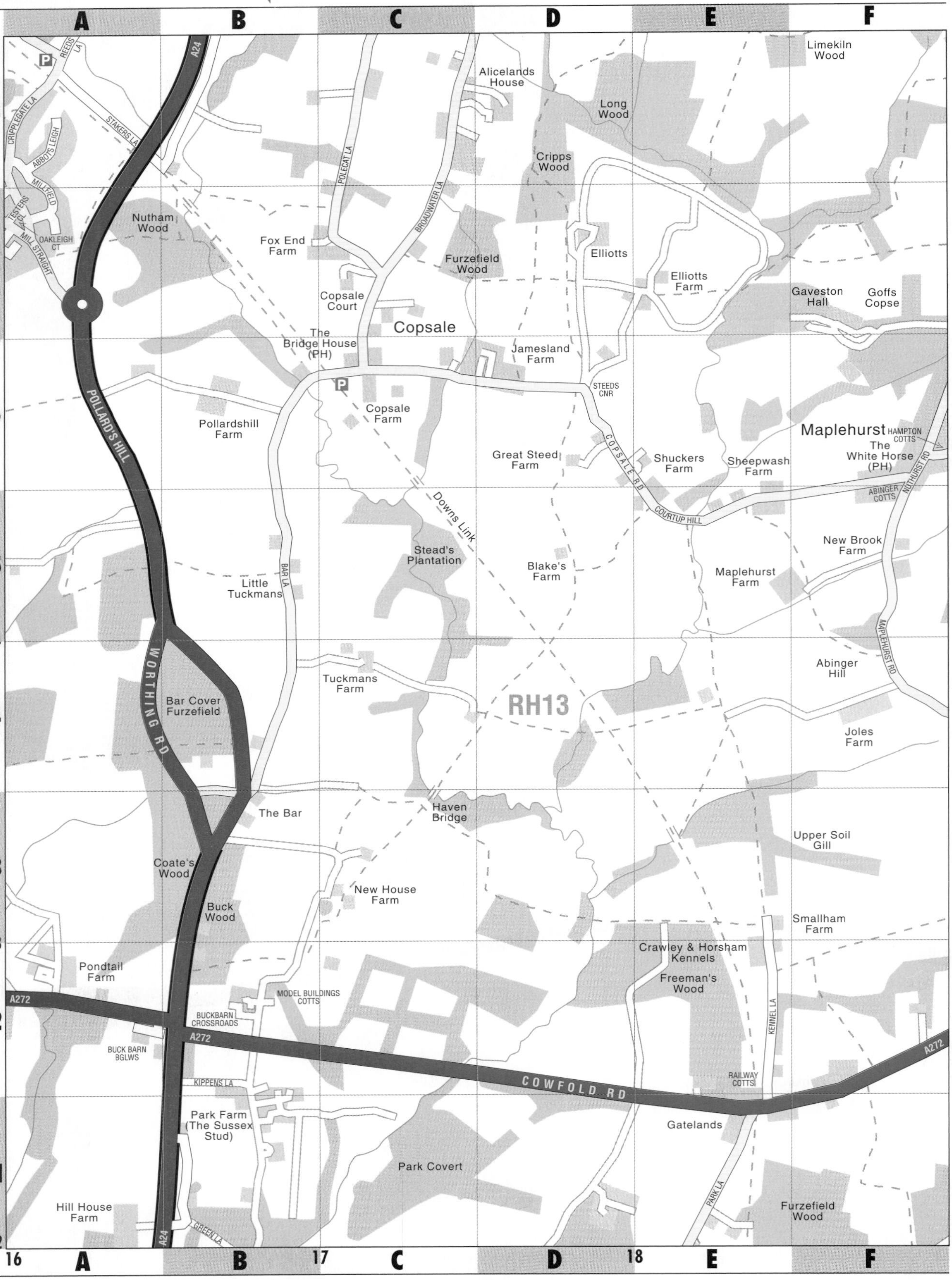

A B C D E F
8 7 25 6 5 24 4 3 23 2 1 22
16 17 18
Limekiln Wood
Alicelands House
Long Wood
Cripps Wood
REEDS LA
STAKERS LA
CRIPPLEGATE LA
ABBOT'S LEIGH
MILLFIELD
TESTERS CL
OAKLEIGH CT
MILL STRAIGHT
A24
POLECAT LA
BROADWATER LA
Nutham Wood
Fox End Farm
Furzefield Wood
Elliotts
Elliotts Farm
Gaveston Hall
Goffs Copse
Copsale Court
Copsale
The Bridge House (PH)
Jamesland Farm
STEEDS CNR
POLLARD'S HILL
Pollardshill Farm
Copsale Farm
Maplehurst
HAMPTON COTTS
The White Horse (PH)
Great Steed Farm
COPSALE RD
Shuckers Farm
Sheepwash Farm
ABINGER COTTS
NUTHURST RD
COURTUP HILL
Downs Link
New Brook Farm
Stead's Plantation
Blake's Farm
Maplehurst Farm
BAR LA
Little Tuckmans
MAPLEHURST RD
Abinger Hill
WORTHING RD
Tuckmans Farm
RH13
Bar Cover Furzefield
Joles Farm
The Bar
Haven Bridge
Upper Soil Gill
Coate's Wood
Buck Wood
New House Farm
Smallham Farm
Crawley & Horsham Kennels
Freeman's Wood
Pondtail Farm
A272
MODEL BUILDINGS COTTS
BUCKBARN CROSSROADS
KENNEL LA
BUCK BARN BGLWS
COWFOLD RD
RAILWAY COTTS
KIPPENS LA
Park Farm (The Sussex Stud)
Gatelands
Park Covert
PARK LA
Hill House Farm
Furzefield Wood
GREEN LA

79 102

59
82

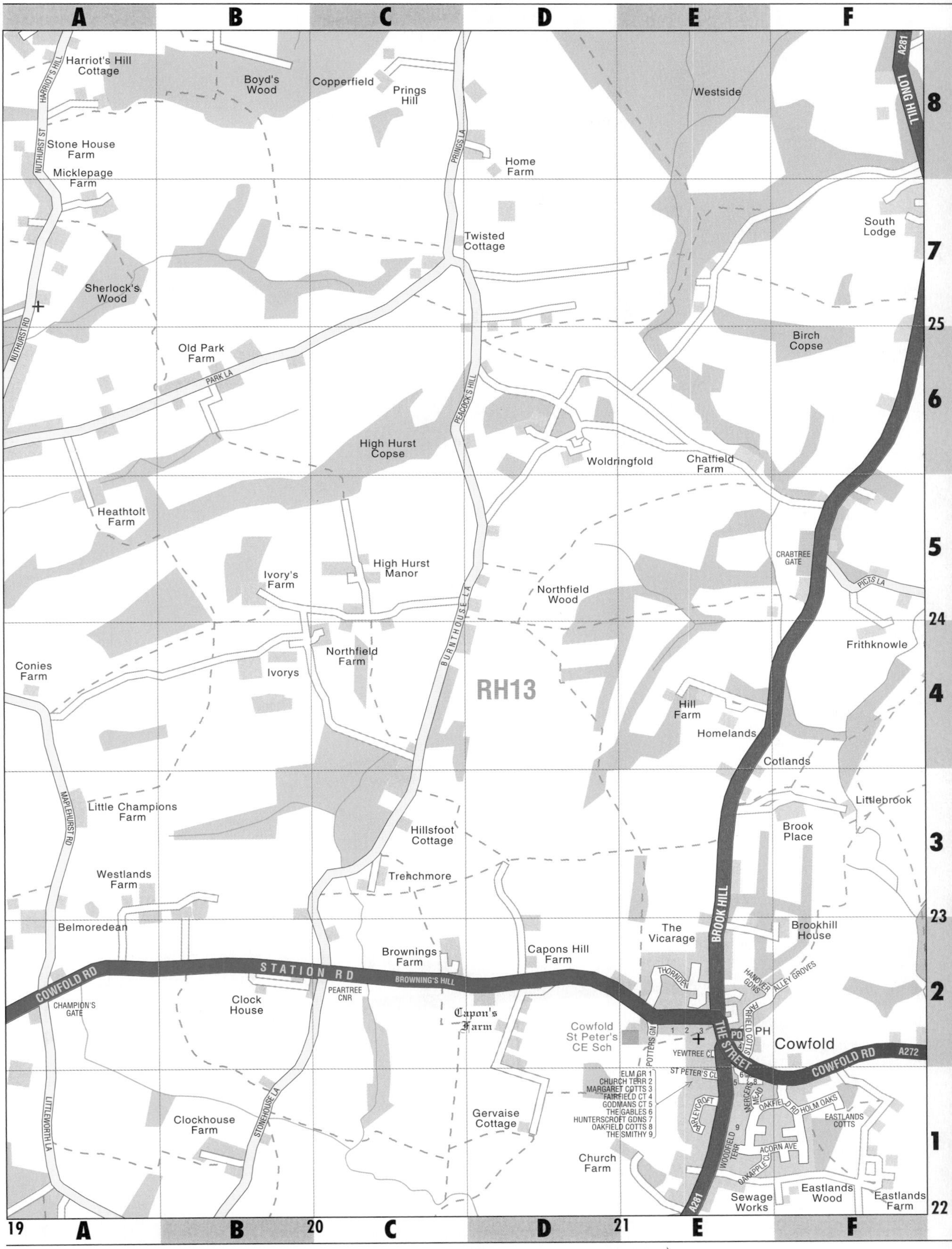
A
B
C
D
E
F
8
7
6
5
4
3
2
1
25
24
23
22
19
20
21
Harriot's Hill Cottage
HARRIOT'S HILL
Boyd's Wood
Copperfield
Prings Hill
Westside
A281
LONG HILL
NUTHURST ST
Stone House Farm
Micklepage Farm
PRINGS LA
Home Farm
South Lodge
Twisted Cottage
Sherlock's Wood
NUTHURST RD
Birch Copse
Old Park Farm
PARK LA
PEACOCK'S HILL
High Hurst Copse
Woldringfold
Chatfield Farm
Heathtolt Farm
CRABTREE GATE
High Hurst Manor
Ivory's Farm
Northfield Wood
PICTS LA
Frithknowle
Northfield Farm
Conies Farm
Ivorys
BURNTHOUSE LA
RH13
Hill Farm
Homelands
Cotlands
MAPLEHURST RD
Little Champions Farm
Littlebrook
Brook Place
Hillsfoot Cottage
Westlands Farm
Trenchmore
BROOK HILL
Belmoredean
The Vicarage
Brookhill House
Brownings Farm
Capons Hill Farm
STATION RD
BROWNING'S HILL
COWFOLD RD
CHAMPION'S GATE
PEARTREE CNR
Clock House
Capon's Farm
THORNDEN
HANOVER GDNS
ALLEY GROVES
FAIRFIELD COTTS
Cowfold St Peter's CE Sch
POTTERS GN
PO
PH
THE STREET
Cowfold
YEWTREE CL
COWFOLD RD
A272
ST PETER'S CL
ELM GR 1
CHURCH TERR 2
MARGARET COTTS 3
FAIRFIELD CT 4
GODMANS CT 5
THE GABLES 6
HUNTERSCROFT GDNS 7
OAKFIELD COTTS 8
THE SMITHY 9
MERCERS MEAD
OAKFIELD RD
HOLM OAKS
EASTLANDS COTTS
BARLEYCROFT
LITTLEWORTH LA
Clockhouse Farm
STONEHOUSE LA
Gervaise Cottage
WOODFIELD TERR
ACORN AVE
Church Farm
OAKAPPLE CL
Eastlands Wood
Eastlands Farm
Sewage Works
A281

103
82

81
60

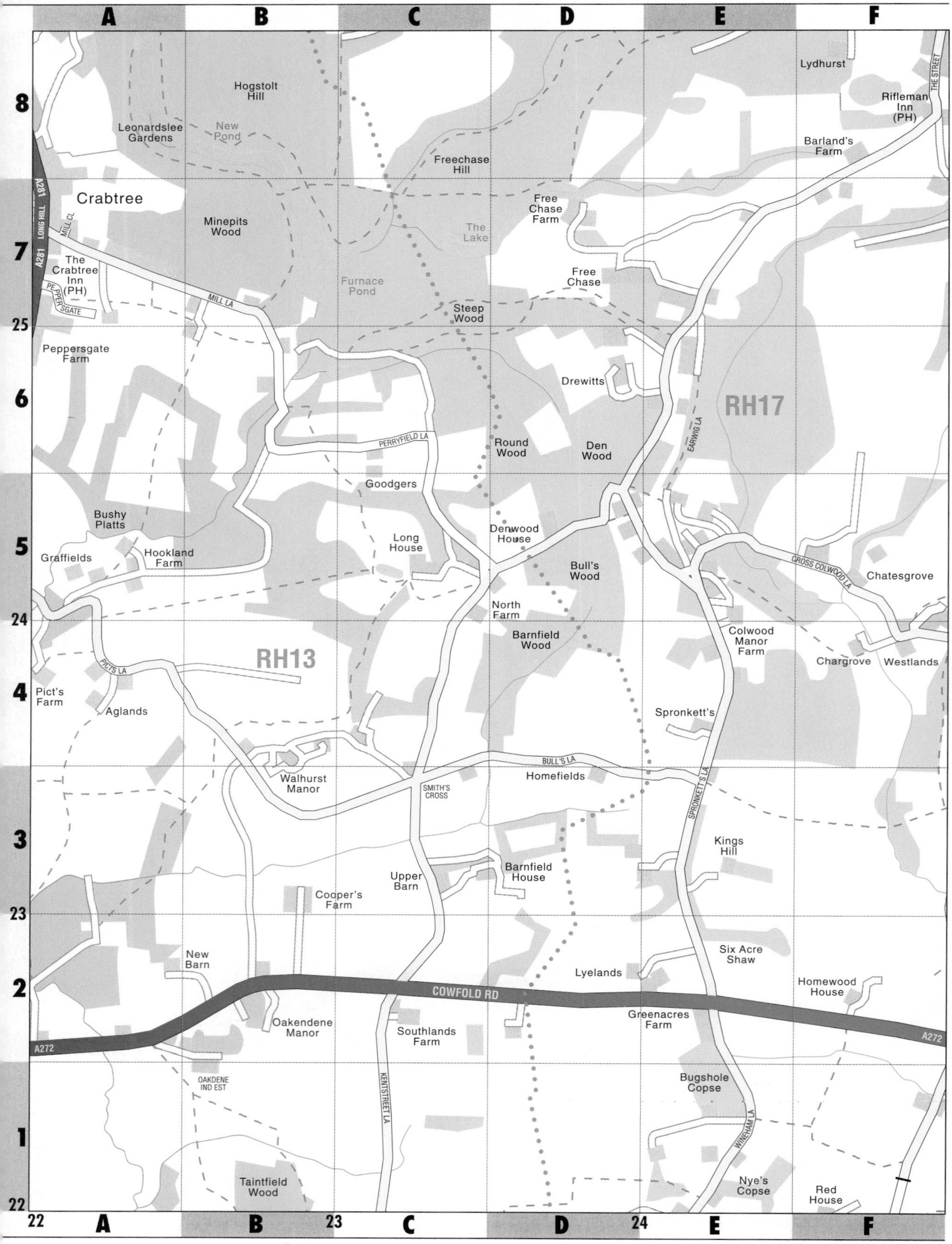
A
B
C
D
E
F
8
7
6
5
4
3
2
1
25
24
23
22
Hogstolt Hill
Leonardslee Gardens
New Pond
Freechase Hill
Lydhurst
Rifleman Inn (PH)
THE STREET
Barland's Farm
A281
LONG HILL
Crabtree
MILL CL
Minepits Wood
Free Chase Farm
The Lake
The Crabtree Inn (PH)
PEPPERSGATE
MILL LA
Furnace Pond
Free Chase
Steep Wood
Peppersgate Farm
Drewitts
RH17
EARWIG LA
PERRYFIELD LA
Round Wood
Den Wood
Goodgers
Bushy Platts
Long House
Denwood House
CROSS COLWOOD LA
Graffields
Hookland Farm
Bull's Wood
Chatesgrove
North Farm
Colwood Manor Farm
Barnfield Wood
RH13
PICTS LA
Chargrove
Westlands
Pict's Farm
Aglands
Spronkett's
BULL'S LA
Homefields
Walhurst Manor
SMITH'S CROSS
SPRONKETT'S LA
Kings Hill
Upper Barn
Barnfield House
Cooper's Farm
New Barn
Six Acre Shaw
Lyelands
COWFOLD RD
Homewood House
Greenacres Farm
Oakendene Manor
Southlands Farm
A272
A272
OAKDENE IND EST
KENTSTREET LA
Bugshole Copse
WINGHAM LA
Taintfield Wood
Nye's Copse
Red House
22
A
B
23
C
D
24
E
F

81
104

61
84
A
B
C
D
E
F
8
7
25
6
5
24
4
3
23
2
1
22
25
26
27
CUCKFIELD LA
A23
B2115
SLOUGHGREEN LA
Paternosters
SLOUGHGREEN LA
B2115
North Gravelies Wood
Great Thorndean Farm
North Gravelies Farm
ORCHARD WAY
Moorfield Farm
THORNDEAN DR
Colwood Hill
BROXMEAD LA
Rout Farm
Colwood Court
Wr Twr
Playdells Farm
COLWOOD LA
Hill House Farm
Wykehurst Corner
JEREMY'S LA
The Hanger
Broxmead
Dan Tree Farm
Broxmead Farm
Wykehurst Park
RH17
Bundys
New Park Farm
Colwood Park
Wykehurst Park
BROXMEAD LA
Long Wood
BROXMEAD LA
PH
CROSS COLWOOD LA
Horsmanshoad
PICKWELL LA
Black Forest
Oakview Farm
SPRINGFIELD COTTS
SPRINGFIELD CL
Bolney Wood
Buncton Court
Nailard's Wood
TOP ST
MAYFIELDS
TYTHE BARN
BOLNEY LODGE LA
CHERRY LA
BENNETTS
Woodland Farm
Ragget's Wood
RYECROFT RD
Dalton's Farm
Bolney
BUNCTON LA
Pickwell
Bookers Farm
BOLNEY ST
DROVERS
PAYNESFIELD
Old Highlands
Highlands
FOXHOLE LA
BANKSIDE
Bolney CE Prim Sch
Foxhole
Ormonde Hall
Hanger Wood
P
PO
Eight Bells Inn (PH)
Farney Close Sch
Bolney Court
North Wood
A272
CROSSWAYS
BOLNEY RD
COWFOLD RD
Purvey's Cottages
Foxashes
DIAMOND COTTS
Crosspost
CROSSPOST IND PK
CROSSPOST
BOLNEY CROSSWAYS
Lovell's Farm
STAIRBRIDGE LA
BOLNEY CHAPEL RD
COUNCIL COTTS
Little Gravenhurst
A23
105
84

83
62

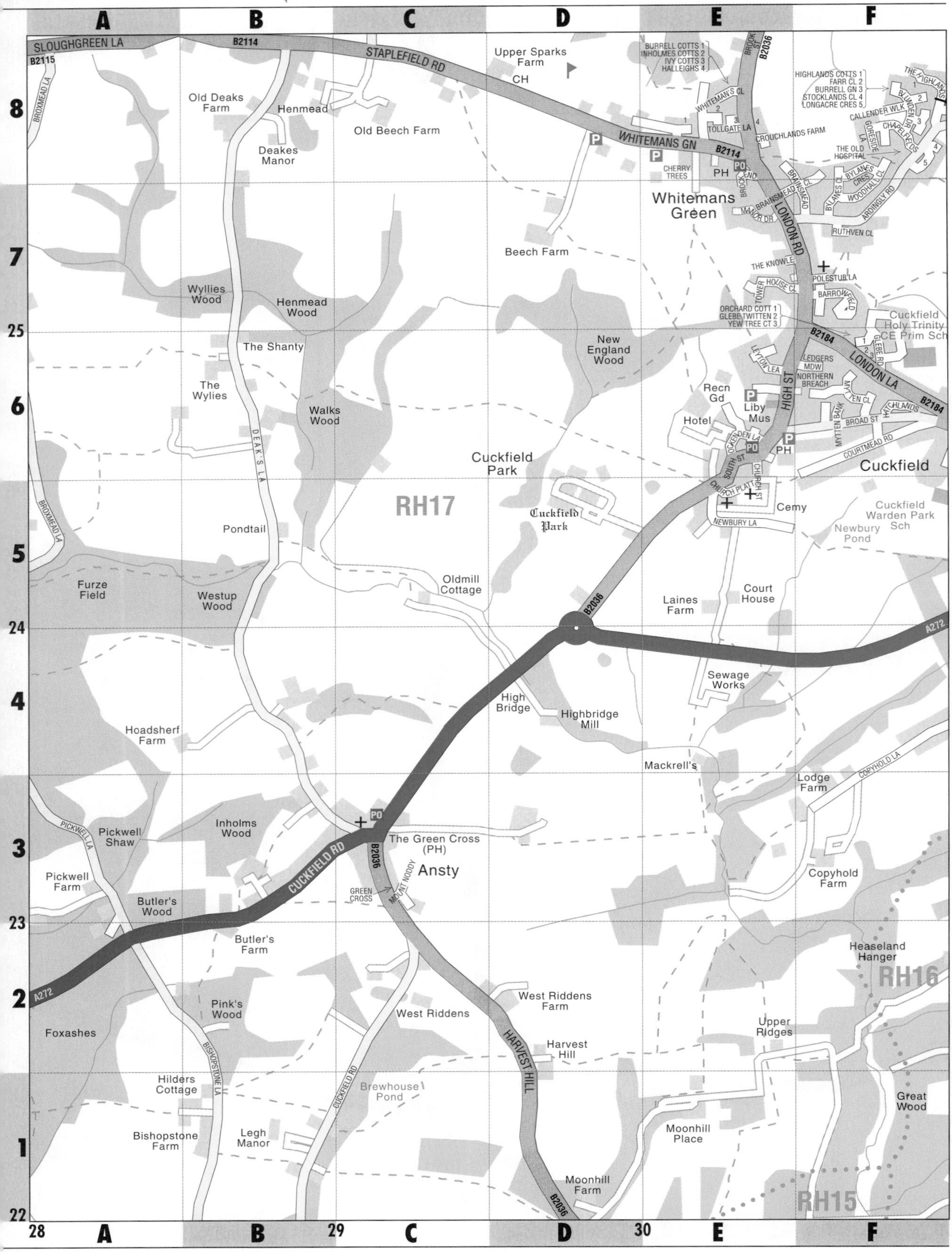
A
B
C
D
E
F
8
7
25
6
5
24
4
3
23
2
1
22
28
29
30
SLOUGHGREEN LA
B2115
B2114
STAPLEFIELD RD
BROXMEAD LA
Upper Sparks Farm
CH
BURRELL COTTS 1
INHOLMES COTTS 2
IVY COTTS 3
HALLEIGHS 4
BROOK ST
B2036
HIGHLANDS COTTS 1
FARR CL 2
BURRELL GN 3
STOCKLANDS CL 4
LONGACRE CRES 5
Old Deaks Farm
Henmead
Old Beech Farm
Deakes Manor
WHITEMANS GN
WHITEMAN'S CL
TOLLGATE LA
CROUCHLANDS FARM
CALLENDER WLK
GORESIDE LA
CHAPELFIELDS
THE OLD HOSPITAL
CHERRY TREES
PH
PO
BROOK END
BRAINSMEAD
BRAINSMEAD CL
MANOR DR
BYLANES CL
BYLANES CRES
WOODHALL CL
ARDINGLY RD
Whitemans Green
LONDON RD
RUTHVEN CL
Beech Farm
THE KNOWLE
POLESTUB LA
TOWER HOUSE CL
BARROWFIELD
Wyllies Wood
Henmead Wood
ORCHARD COTT 1
GLEBE TWITTEN 2
YEW TREE CT 3
Cuckfield Holy Trinity CE Prim Sch
B2184
GLEBE RD
LONDON LA
The Shanty
New England Wood
LEYTON LEA
LEDGERS MDW
NORTHERN BREACH
HIGH ST
The Wylies
Walks Wood
Recn Gd
Liby
Mus
MYTTEN CL
HATCHLANDS
MYTTEN BANK
BROAD ST
Hotel
DEAK'S LA
OCKENDEN LA
COURTMEAD RD
Cuckfield Park
SOUTH ST
CHURCH ST
Cuckfield
CHURCH PLATT
RH17
Cemy
Cuckfield Warden Park Sch
Cuckfield Park
NEWBURY LA
Newbury Pond
Pondtail
Oldmill Cottage
Court House
Furze Field
Westup Wood
Laines Farm
A272
Sewage Works
High Bridge
Highbridge Mill
Hoadsherf Farm
Mackrell's
COPYHOLD LA
Lodge Farm
Inholms Wood
PICKWELL LA
Pickwell Shaw
The Green Cross (PH)
Ansty
Copyhold Farm
Pickwell Farm
CUCKFIELD RD
GREEN CROSS
MOUNT NODDY
Butler's Wood
Butler's Farm
Heaseland Hanger
RH16
Pink's Wood
West Riddens Farm
Foxashes
West Riddens
HARVEST HILL
Upper Ridges
Harvest Hill
BISHOPSTONE LA
Hilders Cottage
Brewhouse Pond
Great Wood
Bishopstone Farm
Legh Manor
Moonhill Place
Moonhill Farm
RH15

83
106

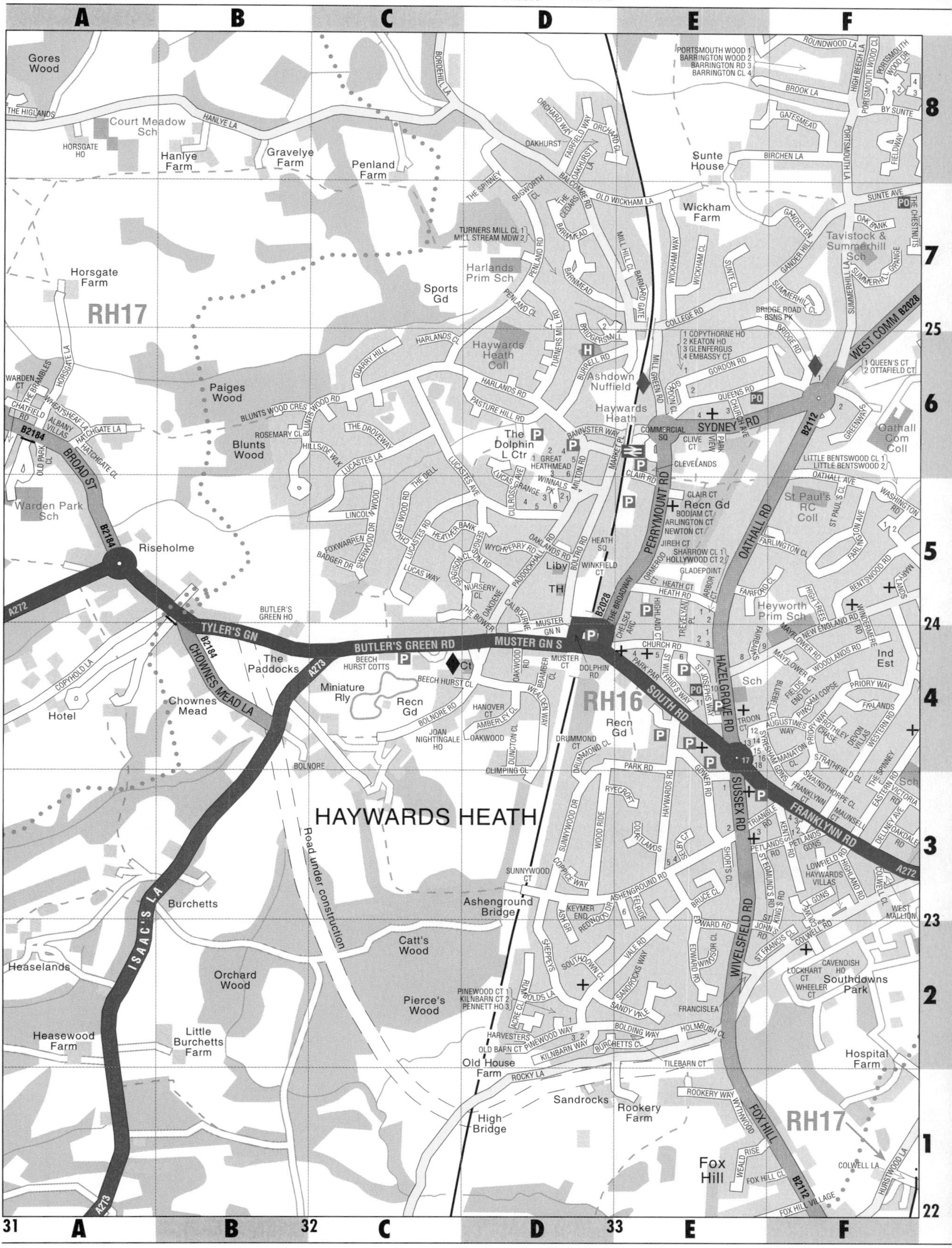
A
B
C
D
E
F
Gores Wood
THE HIGLANDS
Court Meadow Sch
HANLYE LA
HORSGATE HO
Hanlye Farm
Gravelye Farm
Penland Farm
BORDEHILL LA
Horsgate Farm
RH17
Sports Gd
Harlands Prim Sch
Haywards Heath Coll
Paiges Wood
Blunts Wood
Warden Park Sch
Riseholme
B2184
BROAD ST
A272
TYLER'S GN
CHOWNES MEAD LA
BUTLER'S GREEN RD
MUSTER GN S
BUTLER'S GREEN HO
The Paddocks
Miniature Rly
Recn Gd
Chownes Mead
Hotel
A273
BOLNORE
HAYWARDS HEATH
Road under construction
ISAAC'S LA
Burchetts
Heaselands
Orchard Wood
Catt's Wood
Pierce's Wood
Ashenground Bridge
Heasewood Farm
Little Burchetts Farm
Old House Farm
ROCKY LA
High Bridge
Sandrocks
Rookery Farm
Fox Hill
FOX HILL
B2112
RH17
Hospital Farm
COLWELL LA
HURSTWOOD LA
FOX HILL VILLAGE
Sunte House
Wickham Farm
Tavistock & Summerhill Sch
WEST COMM
B2028
Ashdown Nuffield
Haywards Heath
The Dolphin L Ctr
COMMERCIAL SQ
SYDNEY RD
PERRYMOUNT RD
OATHALL RD
Oathall Com Coll
St Paul's RC Coll
Heyworth Prim Sch
Ind Est
Liby
TH
RH16
SOUTH RD
HAZELGROVE RD
SUSSEX RD
FRANKLYNN RD
WIVELSFIELD RD
Recn Gd
Southdowns Park
West Mallion
8
7
6
5
4
3
2
1
25
24
23
22
31
32
33

85
64

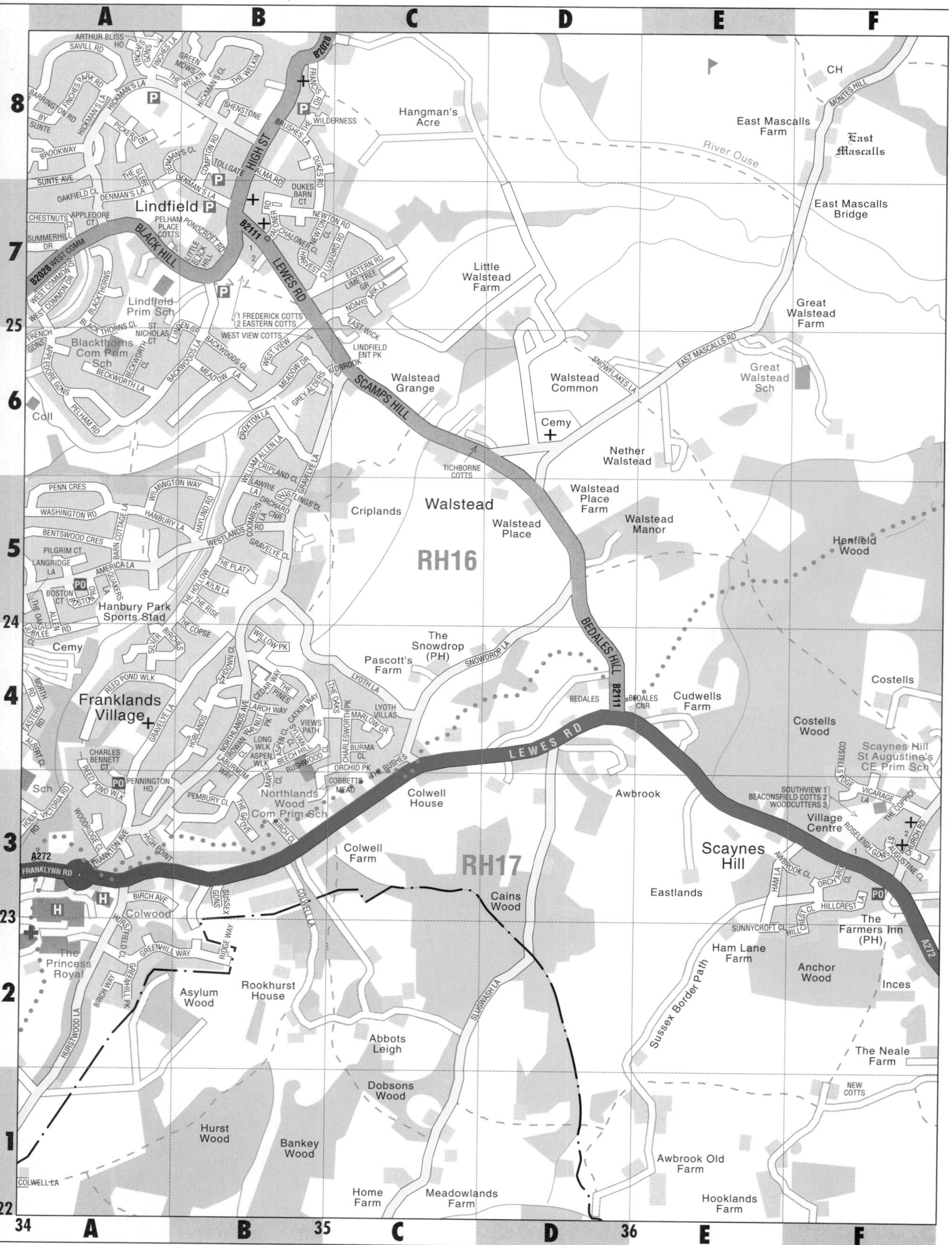
A
B
C
D
E
F
8
7
25
6
5
24
4
3
23
2
1
22
34
35
36
Lindfield
Hangman's Acre
East Mascalls Farm
East Mascalls
River Ouse
East Mascalls Bridge
Little Walstead Farm
Great Walstead Farm
Lindfield Prim Sch
Blackthorns Com Prim Sch
Walstead Grange
Walstead Common
Great Walstead Sch
Cemy
Nether Walstead
Criplands
Walstead
Walstead Place
Walstead Place Farm
Walstead Manor
Henfield Wood
RH16
Hanbury Park Sports Stad
The Snowdrop (PH)
Pascott's Farm
Costells
Frankland's Village
Cudwells Farm
Costells Wood
Scaynes Hill St Augustine's CE Prim Sch
Colwell House
Awbrook
Village Centre
Northlands Wood Com Prim Sch
Colwell Farm
Scaynes Hill
RH17
Cains Wood
Eastlands
Colwood
The Farmers Inn (PH)
Ham Lane Farm
The Princess Royal
Anchor Wood
Inces
Asylum Wood
Rookhurst House
Sussex Border Path
Abbots Leigh
The Neale Farm
Dobsons Wood
Hurst Wood
Bankey Wood
Awbrook Old Farm
Home Farm
Meadowlands Farm
Hooklands Farm
HIGH ST
LEWES RD
SCAMPS HILL
BEDALES HILL
BLACK HILL
EAST MASCALLS RD
SNOWDROP LA
SLUGWASH LA
COLWELL LA
HURSTWOOD LA
FRANKLYNN RD
A272
B2028
B2111

85

65

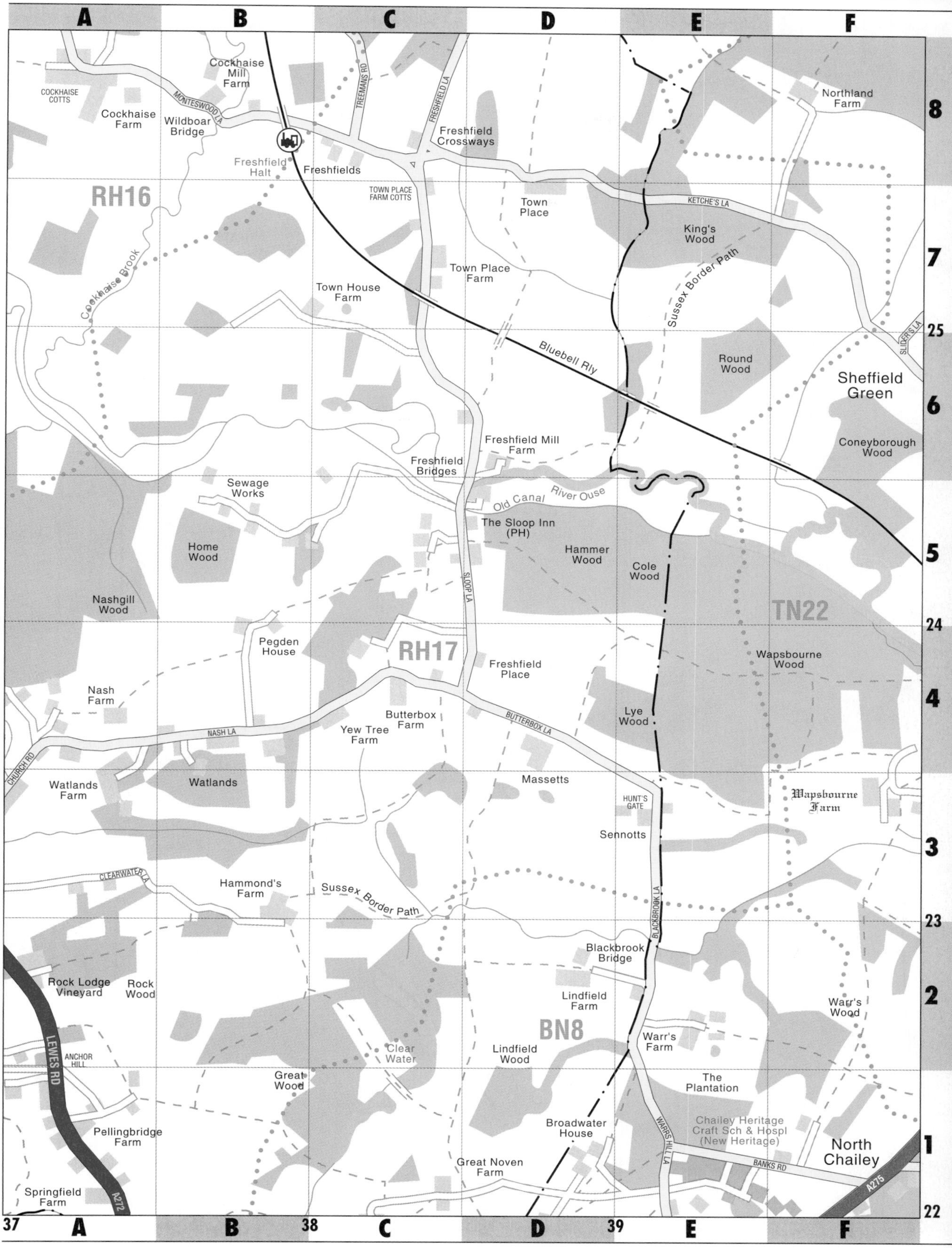

A
B
C
D
E
F
8
7
6
5
4
3
2
1
25
24
23
22
37
38
39
COCKHAISE COTTS
Cockhaise Farm
Cockhaise Mill Farm
MONTESWOOD LA
Wildboar Bridge
TREEMANS RD
FRESHFIELD LA
Freshfield Crossways
Northland Farm
Freshfield Halt
Freshfields
TOWN PLACE FARM COTTS
RH16
Town Place
KETCHE'S LA
King's Wood
Sussex Border Path
Cockhaise Brook
Town Place Farm
Town House Farm
SLIDER'S LA
Bluebell Rly
Round Wood
Sheffield Green
Coneyborough Wood
Freshfield Mill Farm
Freshfield Bridges
Sewage Works
Old Canal
River Ouse
The Sloop Inn (PH)
Home Wood
Hammer Wood
Cole Wood
SLOOP LA
Nashgill Wood
TN22
Pegden House
RH17
Freshfield Place
Wapsbourne Wood
Nash Farm
Butterbox Farm
BUTTERBOX LA
Yew Tree Farm
NASH LA
Lye Wood
CHURCH RD
Watlands Farm
Watlands
Massetts
HUNT'S GATE
Wapsbourne Farm
Sennotts
CLEARWATER LA
Hammond's Farm
Sussex Border Path
BLACKBROOK LA
Blackbrook Bridge
Rock Lodge Vineyard
Rock Wood
Lindfield Farm
Warr's Wood
BN8
LEWES RD
ANCHOR HILL
Clear Water
Lindfield Wood
Warr's Farm
Great Wood
The Plantation
Pellingbridge Farm
Broadwater House
WARRS HILL LA
Chailey Heritage Craft Sch & Hospl (New Heritage)
North Chailey
BANKS RD
Great Noven Farm
A275
Springfield Farm
A272

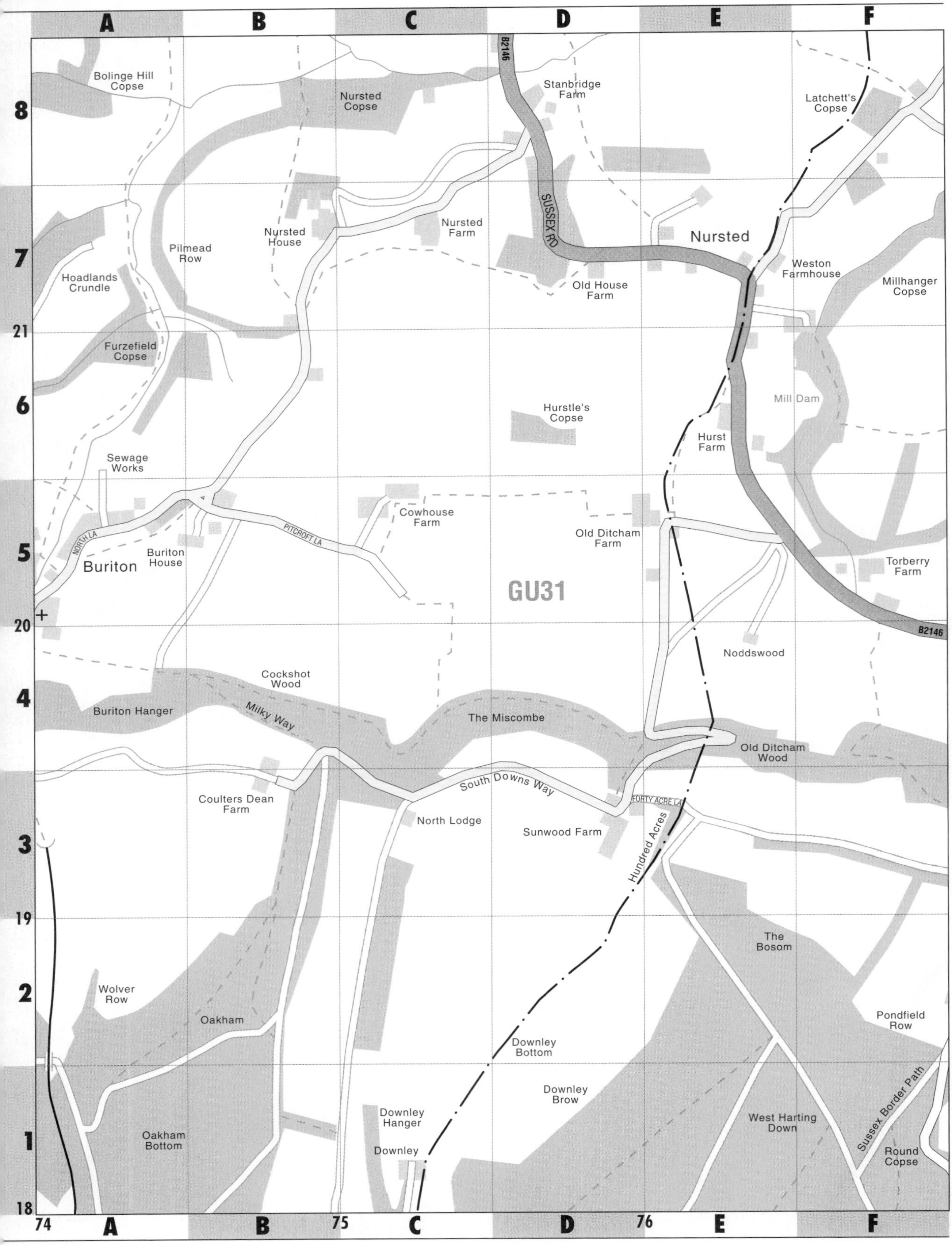
A
B
C
D
E
F
8
7
21
6
5
20
4
3
19
2
1
18
74
75
76
B2146
Bolinge Hill Copse
Nursted Copse
Stanbridge Farm
Latchett's Copse
SUSSEX RD
Nursted House
Nursted Farm
Nursted
Pilmead Row
Hoadlands Crundle
Weston Farmhouse
Millhanger Copse
Old House Farm
Furzefield Copse
Mill Dam
Hurstle's Copse
Hurst Farm
Sewage Works
Cowhouse Farm
Old Ditcham Farm
NORTH LA
PITCROFT LA
Buriton
Buriton House
Torberry Farm
GU31
Noddswood
Cockshot Wood
Buriton Hanger
Milky Way
The Miscombe
Old Ditcham Wood
South Downs Way
Coulters Dean Farm
FORTY ACRE LA
North Lodge
Sunwood Farm
Hundred Acres
The Bosom
Wolver Row
Oakham
Pondfield Row
Downley Bottom
Downley Brow
Sussex Border Path
West Harting Down
Downley Hanger
Oakham Bottom
Round Copse
Downley

108

67
90

A
B
C
D
E
F
Goff's Plantation
Harting Pond
Goose Green
Pondtail Plantation
Tom Rokes Row
Nyewood
Manor Farm
Quebec
COLLINS LA
Hill Ash Farm
Barrows Copse
Severals
West Harting
Upperton
Mellersh's Copse
PUTMANS LA
Putmans
CANADA CNR
Weeks's Common
Torberry Copse
Sussex Border Path
Torberry Hill
GU31
Manor House
Pays Farm
Little Torberry Hill
THE MEADS
NORTH LA
Sewage Works
Hollist Farm
Leith Copse
HOLLIST LA
COW LA
THE SQUARE
PO
PH
MILL LA
Hemner Hill
Horsesnap
EAST HARTING ST
Church Farm
CULVERS
Turkey Island
Sch
PEASE CROFT
TIPPER LA
SOUTH ACRE
THE HOP GARDEN
WARREN SIDE
Old Copse
WELLFIELD COTTS
South Harting
Engine Farm
NEW LA
Foxcombe Cottages
Hampshire Cottage
HILL LA
The Warren
Foxcombe Farm
South Downs Way
B2141
Down Place
Main Down
Harting Downs
The Bosom
Round Down
Tower Hill
Round Copse Row
Two Beach Gate
P
B2146
B2141
Round Down
8
7
21
6
5
20
4
3
19
2
1
18
77
78
79

109
90

89
68

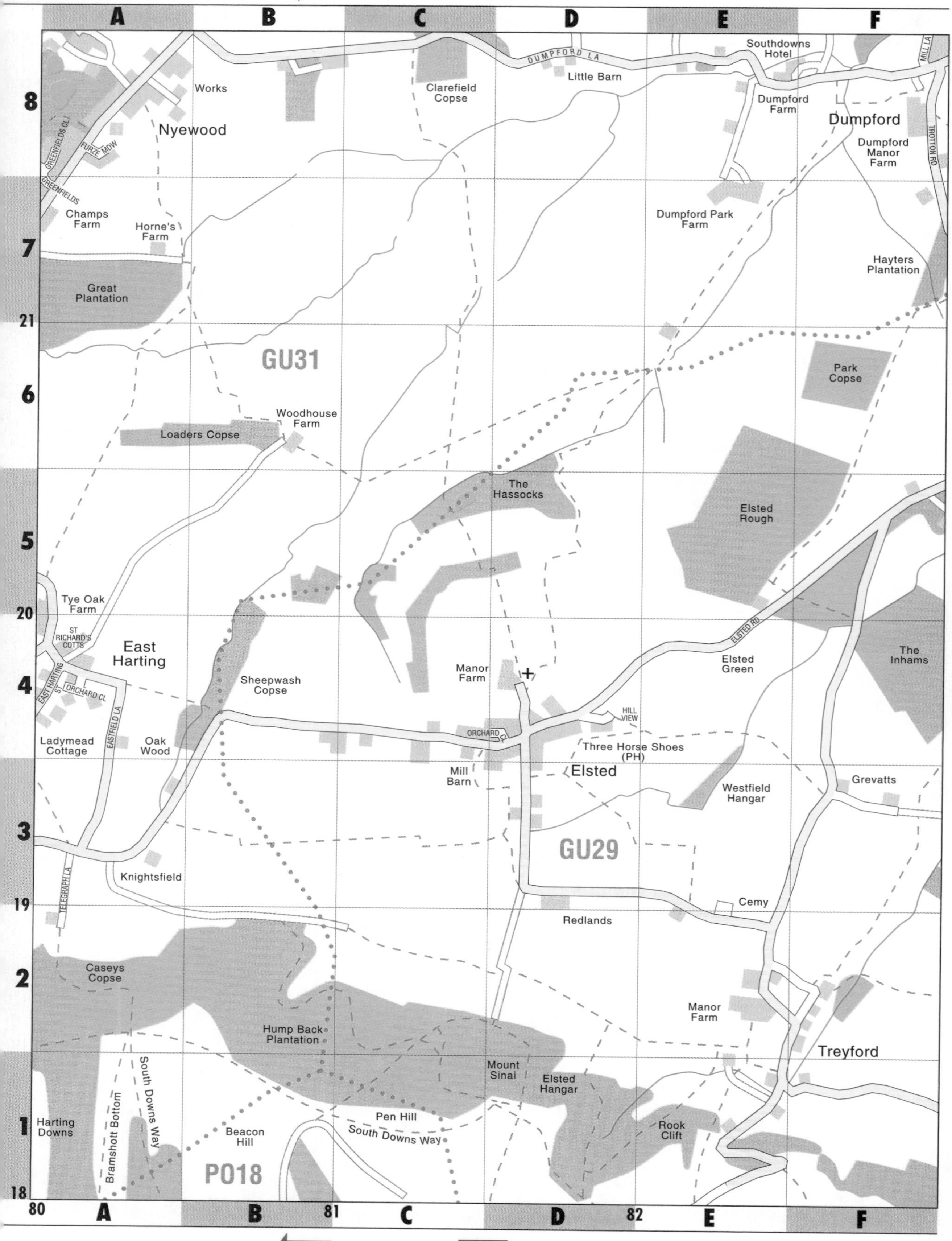
A
B
C
D
E
F
8
7
21
6
5
20
4
3
19
2
1
18
80
81
82
DUMPFORD LA
Southdowns Hotel
Little Barn
Works
Clarefield Copse
Dumpford Farm
Dumpford
Dumpford Manor Farm
MILL LA
TROTTON RD
Nyewood
GREENFIELDS CL
FURZE MDW
GREENFIELDS
Champs Farm
Horne's Farm
Dumpford Park Farm
Hayters Plantation
Great Plantation
GU31
Park Copse
Woodhouse Farm
Loaders Copse
The Hassocks
Elsted Rough
Tye Oak Farm
ST RICHARD'S COTTS
East Harting
EAST HARTING ST
ORCHARD CL
EASTFIELD LA
Sheepwash Copse
Manor Farm
ELSTED RD
Elsted Green
The Inhams
HILL VIEW
ORCHARD CL
Three Horse Shoes (PH)
Ladymead Cottage
Oak Wood
Mill Barn
Elsted
Westfield Hangar
Grevatts
GU29
TELEGRAPH LA
Knightsfield
Cemy
Redlands
Caseys Copse
Manor Farm
Hump Back Plantation
Treyford
South Downs Way
Mount Sinai
Elsted Hangar
Harting Downs
Bramshott Bottom
Beacon Hill
Pen Hill
South Downs Way
Rook Clift
PO18

89
110

69
92

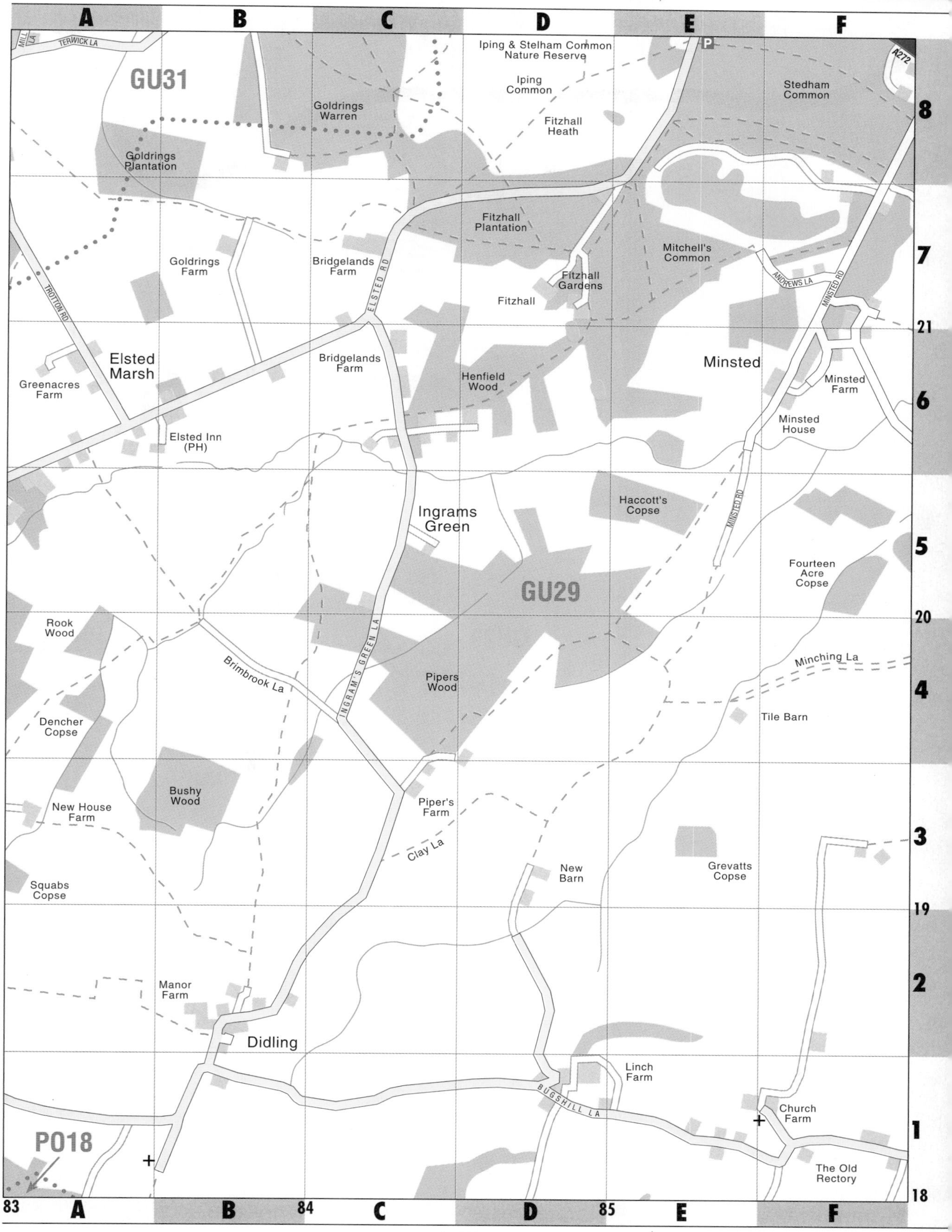
A
B
C
D
E
F
MILL LA
TERWICK LA
GU31
Goldrings Warren
Iping & Stelham Common Nature Reserve
Iping Common
Fitzhall Heath
Stedham Common
A272
P
8
Goldrings Plantation
Fitzhall Plantation
Mitchell's Common
7
Goldrings Farm
Bridgelands Farm
ELSTED RD
Fitzhall Gardens
ANDREWS LA
MINSTED RD
TROTTON RD
Fitzhall
21
Elsted Marsh
Bridgelands Farm
Henfield Wood
Minsted
Minsted Farm
Greenacres Farm
6
Minsted House
Elsted Inn (PH)
Ingrams Green
Haccott's Copse
MINSTED RD
5
Fourteen Acre Copse
GU29
Rook Wood
20
Minching La
Brimbrook La
INGRAM'S GREEN LA
Pipers Wood
4
Tile Barn
Dencher Copse
Bushy Wood
New House Farm
Piper's Farm
3
Clay La
New Barn
Grevatts Copse
Squabs Copse
19
2
Manor Farm
Didling
Linch Farm
BUGSHILL LA
Church Farm
1
PO18
The Old Rectory
18
83
84
85

111
92

91
70

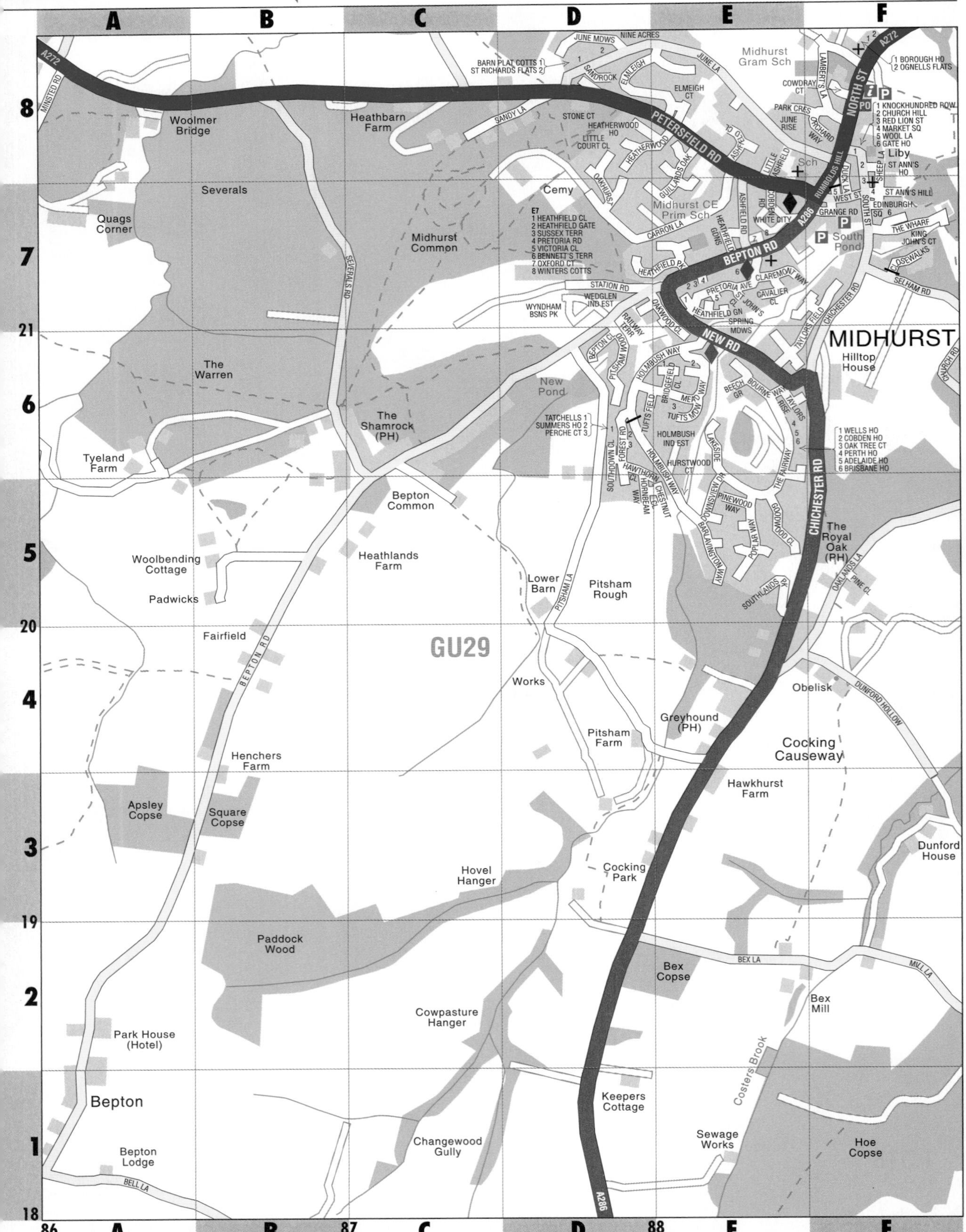
A
B
C
D
E
F
8
7
21
6
5
20
4
3
19
2
1
18
86
87
88
A272
MINSTED RD
Woolmer Bridge
Heathbarn Farm
SANDY LA
Severals
Quags Corner
Midhurst Common
SEVERALS RD
The Warren
The Shamrock (PH)
Tyeland Farm
Bepton Common
Woolbending Cottage
Padwicks
Heathlands Farm
Fairfield
BEPTON RD
GU29
Henchers Farm
Apsley Copse
Square Copse
Hovel Hanger
Paddock Wood
Cowpasture Hanger
Park House (Hotel)
Bepton
Bepton Lodge
BELL LA
Changewood Gully
Keepers Cottage
A286
JUNE MDWS
NINE ACRES
BARN PLAT COTTS 1
ST RICHARDS FLATS 2
SANDROCK
ELMLEIGH
JUNE LA
Midhurst Gram Sch
ELMLEIGH CT
STONE CT
HEATHERWOOD HO
LITTLE COURT CL
PETERSFIELD RD
HEATHERWOOD
GUILLARDS OAK
OAKHURST
Cemy
E7
1 HEATHFIELD CL
2 HEATHFIELD GATE
3 SUSSEX TERR
4 PRETORIA RD
5 VICTORIA CL
6 BENNETT'S TERR
7 OXFORD CT
8 WINTERS COTTS
Midhurst CE Prim Sch
CARRON LA
HEATHFIELD GDNS
ASHFIELD RD
HEATHFIELD PK
BEPTON RD
STATION RD
WEDGLEN IND EST
WYNDHAM BSNS PK
RAILWAY TERR
OAKWOOD CL
PRETORIA AVE
HEATHFIELD GN
SPRING MDWS
CLAREMONT WAY
CAVALIER CL
ST JOHN'S CL
NEW RD
BEPTON CL
PITSHAM WOOD
HOLMBUSH WAY
BRIDGEFIELD CL
MEADOW WAY
TUFTS MDW
TUFTS FIELD
New Pond
TATCHELLS 1
SUMMERS HO 2
PERCHE CT 3
FOREST RD
SOUTHDOWN CL
HOLMBUSH IND EST
HURSTWOOD CT
HAWTHORN CL
HORNBEAM WAY
CHESTNUT CL
LAKESIDE
DOWNSVIEW DR
PINEWOOD WAY
BARLAVINGTON WAY
POPLAR WAY
GOODWOOD CL
SOUTHLANDS PK
BEECH GR
BOURNE WAY
RISE
TAYLORS
THE FAIRWAY
Lower Barn
PITSHAM LA
Pitsham Rough
Works
Pitsham Farm
Greyhound (PH)
Cocking Park
Bex Copse
BEX LA
Costers Brook
Sewage Works
COWDRAY CT
LAMBERT'S LA
PARK CRES
JUNE RISE
ORCHARD WAY
ASHFIELD CL
LITTLE ASHFIELD
Sch
RUMBOLDS HILL
A286
CORDON RD
WHITE CITY
NORTH ST
DUCK LA
WEST ST
SOUTH ST
GRANGE RD
South Pond
SHEEP LA
Liby
PO
1 BOROUGH HO
2 OGNELLS FLATS
1 KNOCKHUNDRED ROW
2 CHURCH HILL
3 RED LION ST
4 MARKET SQ
5 WOOL LA
6 GATE HO
ST ANN'S HO
ST ANN'S HILL
EDINBURGH SQ
THE WHARF
KING JOHN'S CT
CLOSEWALKS
SELHAM RD
CHICHESTER RD
TAYLORS FIELD
MIDHURST
Hilltop House
CHURCH RD
1 WELLS HO
2 COBDEN HO
3 OAK TREE CT
4 PERTH HO
5 ADELAIDE HO
6 BRISBANE HO
CHICHESTER RD
The Royal Oak (PH)
OAKLANDS LA
PINE CL
Obelisk
DUNFORD HOLLOW
Cocking Causeway
Hawkhurst Farm
Dunford House
MILL LA
Bex Mill
Hoe Copse

91
112

71
94

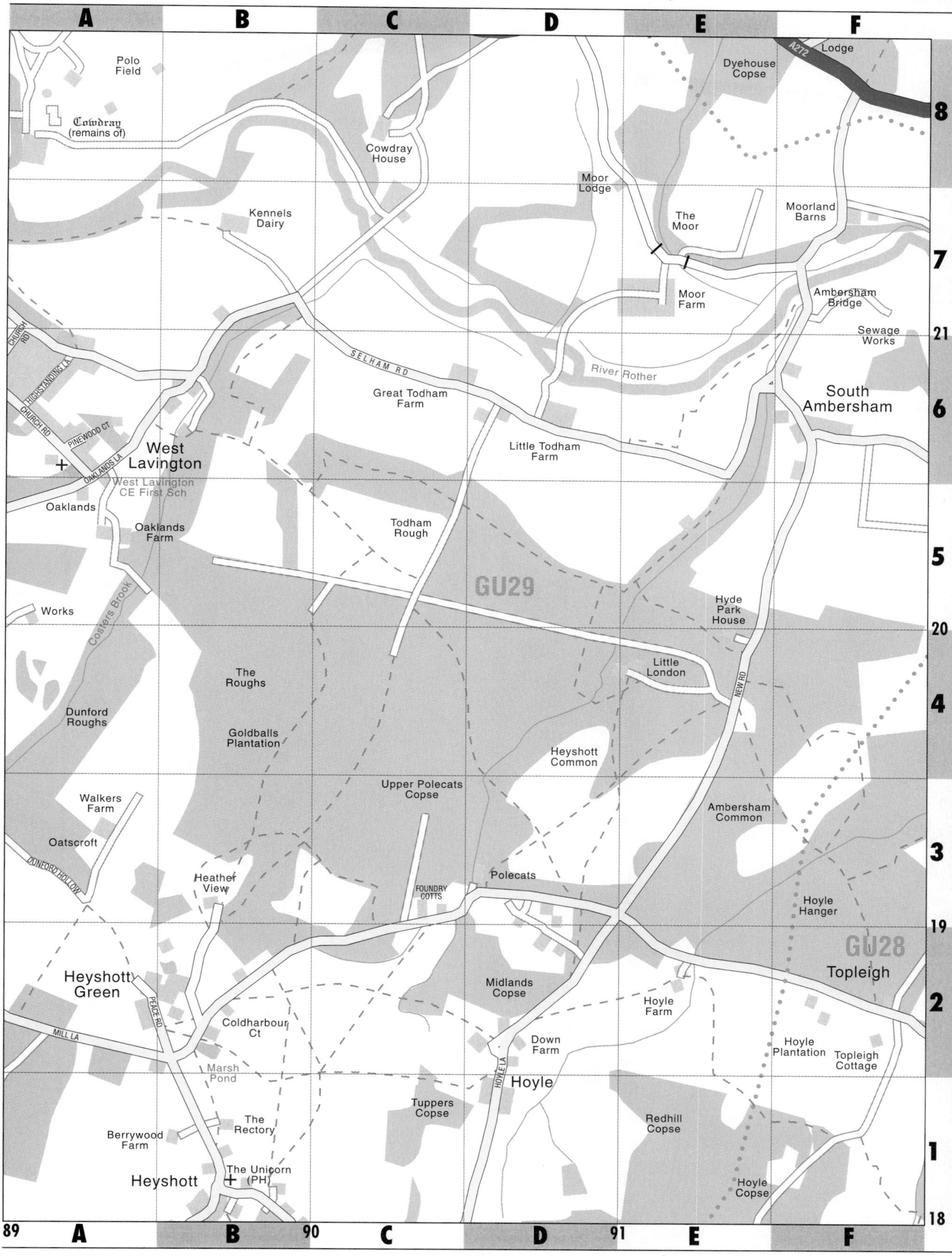
A
B
C
D
E
F
Polo Field
Cowdray (remains of)
Cowdray House
Dyehouse Copse
Lodge
A272
8
Moor Lodge
Kennels Dairy
The Moor
Moorland Barns
7
Moor Farm
Ambersham Bridge
Sewage Works
21
CHURCH RD
HIGHSTANDING LA
SELHAM RD
River Rother
Great Todham Farm
South Ambersham
6
CHURCH RD
PINEWOOD CT
West Lavington
OAKLANDS LA
Little Todham Farm
West Lavington CE First Sch
Oaklands
Todham Rough
Oaklands Farm
5
GU29
Works
Costers Brook
Hyde Park House
20
The Roughs
Little London
NEW RD
Dunford Roughs
4
Goldballs Plantation
Heyshott Common
Upper Polecats Copse
Walkers Farm
Ambersham Common
Oatscroft
DUNFORD HOLLOW
3
Heather View
Polecats
FOUNDRY COTTS
Hoyle Hanger
19
GU28
Heyshott Green
Topleigh
Midlands Copse
Hoyle Farm
2
PEACE RD
MILL LA
Coldharbour Ct
Down Farm
Hoyle Plantation
Topleigh Cottage
Marsh Pond
HOYLE LA
Hoyle
Tuppers Copse
The Rectory
Redhill Copse
Berrywood Farm
1
The Unicorn (PH)
Heyshott
Hoyle Copse
18
89
90
91

113
94

93
72

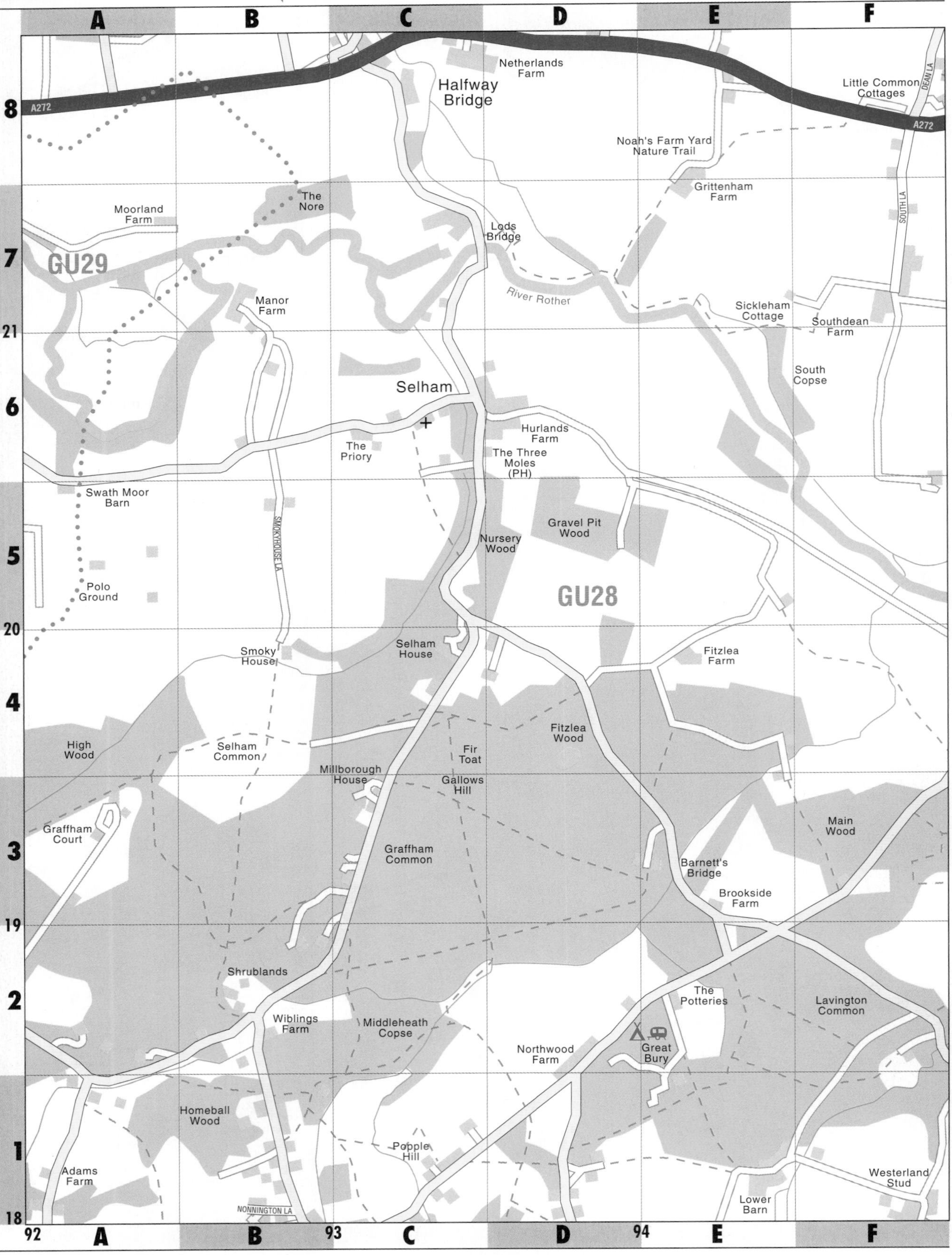
A
B
C
D
E
F
8
7
21
6
5
20
4
3
19
2
1
18
92
93
94
A272
Netherlands Farm
Halfway Bridge
Little Common Cottages
DEAN LA
Noah's Farm Yard Nature Trail
The Nore
Moorland Farm
Grittenham Farm
SOUTH LA
Lods Bridge
GU29
River Rother
Manor Farm
Sickleham Cottage
Southdean Farm
South Copse
Selham
Hurlands Farm
The Priory
The Three Moles (PH)
Swath Moor Barn
Gravel Pit Wood
SMOKYHOUSE LA
Nursery Wood
GU28
Polo Ground
Selham House
Smoky House
Fitzlea Farm
Fitzlea Wood
High Wood
Selham Common
Fir Toat
Millborough House
Gallows Hill
Main Wood
Graffham Court
Graffham Common
Barnett's Bridge
Brookside Farm
Shrublands
The Potteries
Lavington Common
Wiblings Farm
Middleheath Copse
Northwood Farm
Great Bury
Homeball Wood
Popple Hill
Adams Farm
Westerland Stud
Lower Barn
NONNINGTON LA

93
114

73
96

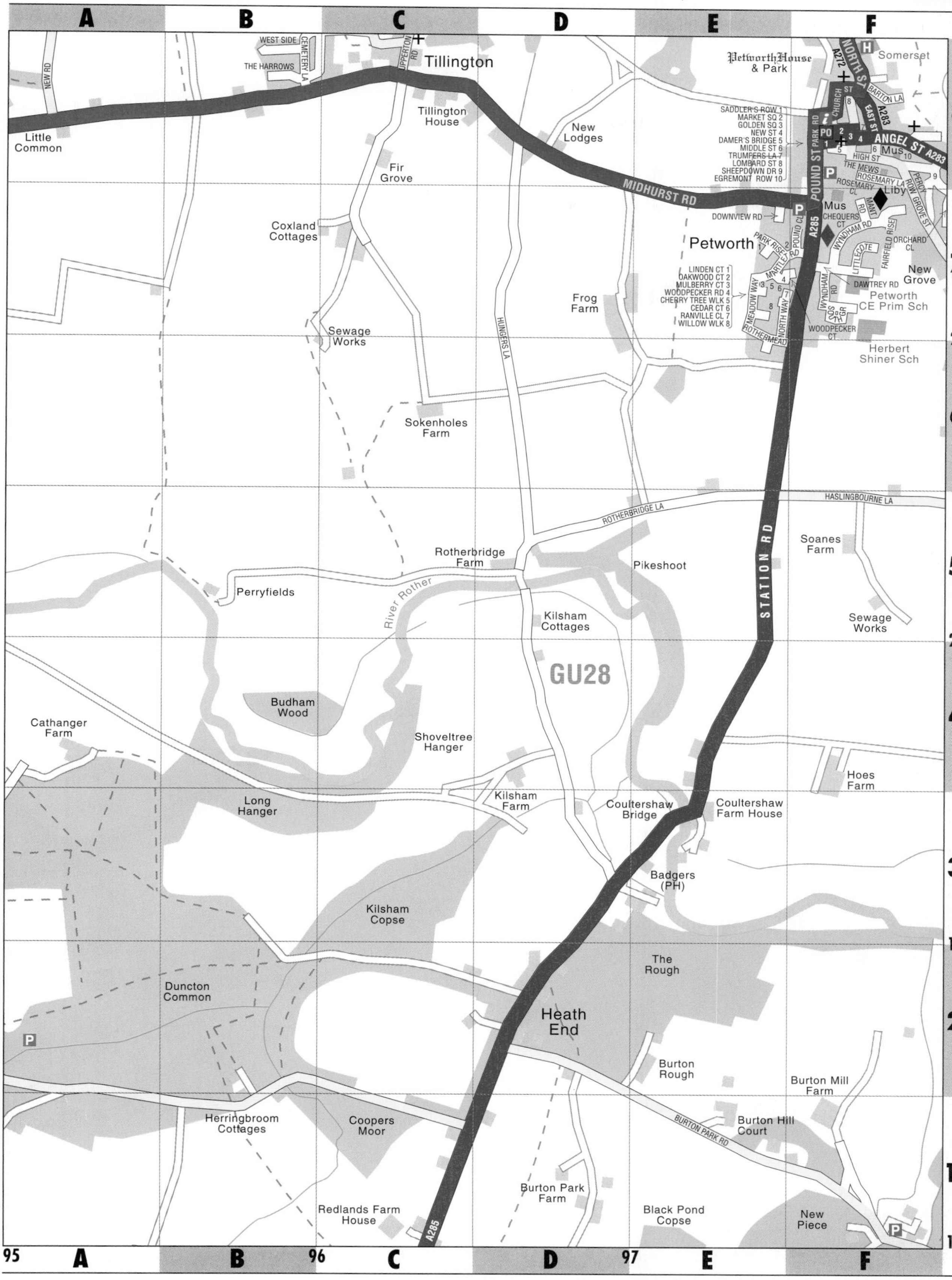
A
B
C
D
E
F
Tillington
WEST SIDE
THE HARROWS
CEMETERY LA
UPPERTON RD
NEW RD
Little Common
Tillington House
New Lodges
Petworth House & Park
Somerset
NORTH ST
A272
CHURCH ST
EAST ST
BARTON LA
A283
ANGEL ST
A283
PO
Mus
HIGH ST
THE MEWS
ROSEMARY LA
ROSEMARY CL
PERCY ROW
GROVE ST
Liby
SADDLER'S ROW 1
MARKET SQ 2
GOLDEN SQ 3
NEW ST 4
DAMER'S BRIDGE 5
MIDDLE ST 6
TRUMPERS LA 7
LOMBARD ST 8
SHEEPDOWN DR 9
EGREMONT ROW 10
Fir Grove
MIDHURST RD
DOWNVIEW RD
POUND ST
PARK RD
A285
Mus
CHEQUERS CT
MANT RD
WYNDHAM RD
FAIRFIELD RISE
ORCHARD CL
New Grove
Coxland Cottages
Petworth
PARK RISE
POUND CL
MARTLET RD
LINDEN CT 1
OAKWOOD CT 2
MULBERRY CT 3
WOODPECKER RD 4
CHERRY TREE WLK 5
CEDAR CT 6
RANVILLE CL 7
WILLOW WLK 8
MEADOW WAY
NORTH WAY
ROTHERMEAD
LITTLECOTE
DAWTREY RD
WYNDHAM RD
Petworth CE Prim Sch
WOODPECKER CT
Frog Farm
Sewage Works
HUNGERS LA
Herbert Shiner Sch
Sokenholes Farm
ROTHERBRIDGE LA
HASLINGBOURNE LA
STATION RD
Soanes Farm
Rotherbridge Farm
Pikeshoot
Perryfields
River Rother
Kilsham Cottages
Sewage Works
GU28
Budham Wood
Cathanger Farm
Shoveltree Hanger
Hoes Farm
Long Hanger
Kilsham Farm
Coultershaw Bridge
Coultershaw Farm House
Badgers (PH)
Kilsham Copse
The Rough
Duncton Common
Heath End
P
Burton Rough
Burton Mill Farm
Herringbroom Cottages
Coopers Moor
Burton Hill Court
BURTON PARK RD
Burton Park Farm
Redlands Farm House
Black Pond Copse
New Piece
A285
8
7
21
6
5
20
4
3
19
2
1
18
95
96
97

115
96

95
74

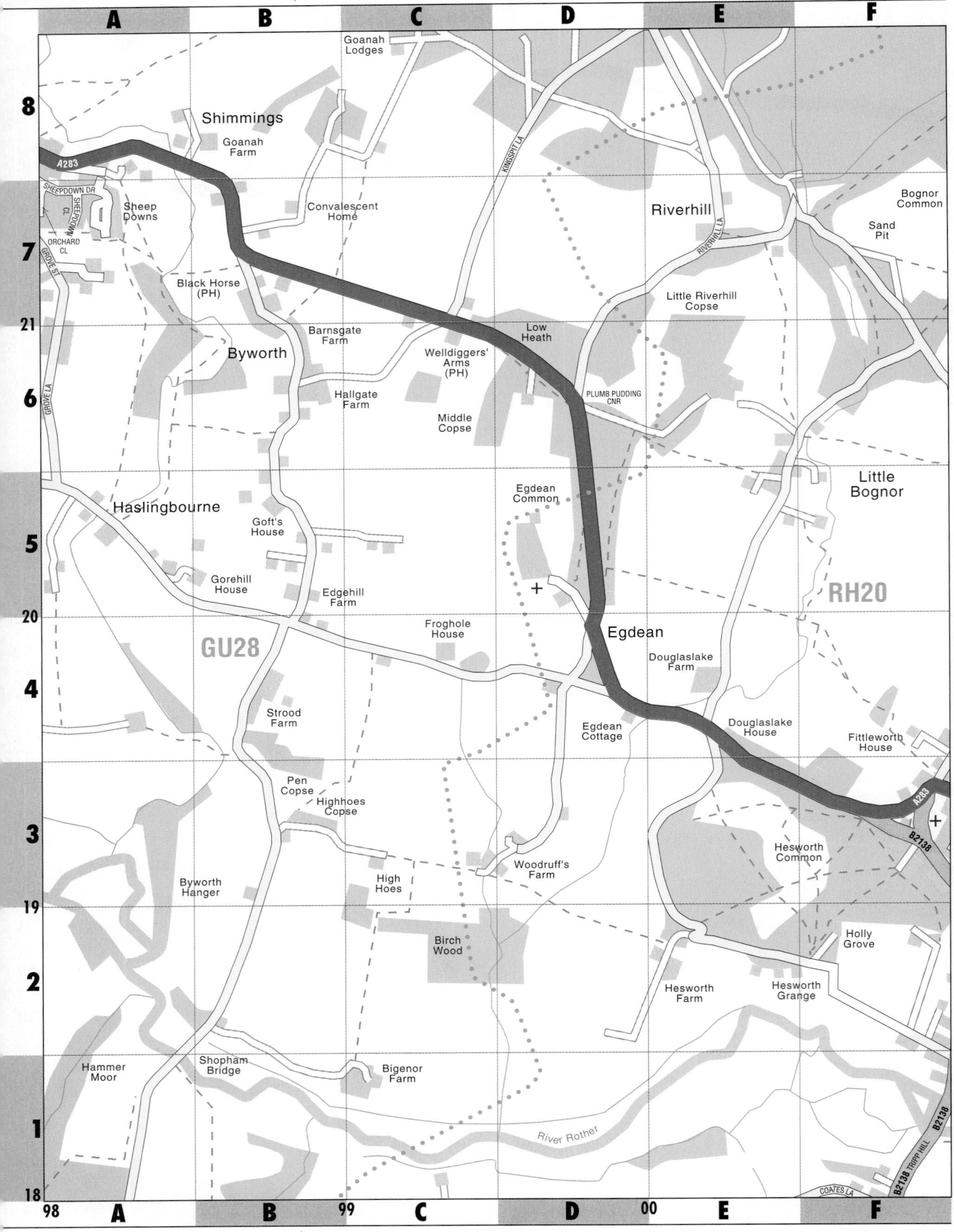
A
B
C
D
E
F
8
7
21
6
5
20
4
3
19
2
1
18
98
99
00
Goanah
Lodges
Shimmings
Goanah
Farm
A283
SHEEPDOWN DR
SHEEPDOWN
CL
Sheep
Downs
ORCHARD
CL
GROVE ST
Convalescent
Home
KINGSPIT LA
Riverhill
RIVERHILL LA
Bognor
Common
Sand
Pit
Black Horse
(PH)
Little Riverhill
Copse
Barnsgate
Farm
Byworth
Welldiggers'
Arms
(PH)
Low
Heath
PLUMB PUDDING
CNR
GROVE LA
Hallgate
Farm
Middle
Copse
Little
Bognor
Egdean
Common
Haslingbourne
Goft's
House
RH20
Gorehill
House
Edgehill
Farm
Froghole
House
Egdean
GU28
Douglaslake
Farm
Strood
Farm
Egdean
Cottage
Douglaslake
House
Fittleworth
House
Pen
Copse
Highhoes
Copse
B2138
Hesworth
Common
Woodruff's
Farm
Byworth
Hanger
High
Hoes
Birch
Wood
Holly
Grove
Hesworth
Farm
Hesworth
Grange
Hammer
Moor
Shopham
Bridge
Bigenor
Farm
River Rother
B2138 TRIPP HILL
COATES LA

95
116

75
98

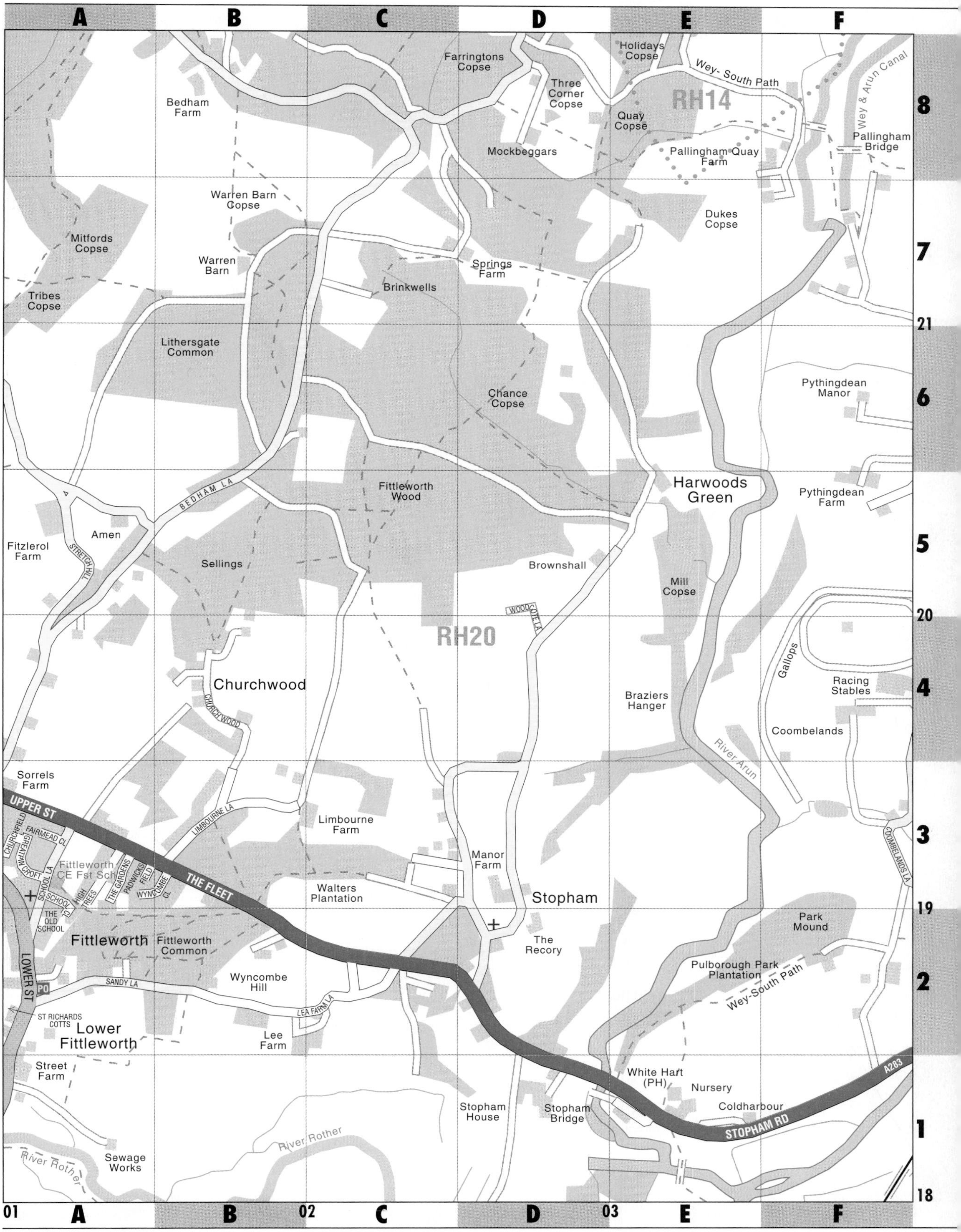
A
B
C
D
E
F
8
7
21
6
5
20
4
3
19
2
1
18
01
02
03
Farringtons Copse
Holidays Copse
Wey- South Path
Wey & Arun Canal
RH14
Bedham Farm
Three Corner Copse
Quay Copse
Pallingham Bridge
Mockbeggars
Pallingham Quay Farm
Warren Barn Copse
Dukes Copse
Mitfords Copse
Warren Barn
Springs Farm
Brinkwells
Tribes Copse
Lithersgate Common
Pythingdean Manor
Chance Copse
Harwoods Green
Fittleworth Wood
Pythingdean Farm
BEDHAM LA
Amen
Fitzlerol Farm
STRETCH HILL
Sellings
Brownshall
Mill Copse
WOODCOTE LA
RH20
Gallops
Churchwood
Racing Stables
Braziers Hanger
CHURCHWOOD
Coombelands
River Arun
Sorrels Farm
UPPER ST
LIMBOURNE LA
Limbourne Farm
CHURCHFIELD
FAIRMEAD CL
GREATPIN CROFT
Fittleworth CE Fst Sch
SCHOOL LA
SCHOOL CL
HIGH TREES
THE GARDENS
PADWICKS FIELD
WYNCOMBE CL
THE FLEET
Manor Farm
COOMBELANDS LA
Walters Plantation
Stopham
THE OLD SCHOOL
Park Mound
Fittleworth
Fittleworth Common
The Recory
LOWER ST
Pulborough Park Plantation
Wey-South Path
Wyncombe Hill
PO
SANDY LA
LEA FARM LA
ST RICHARDS COTTS
Lower Fittleworth
Lee Farm
Street Farm
White Hart (PH)
Nursery
A283
Coldharbour
Stopham House
Stopham Bridge
STOPHAM RD
River Rother
Sewage Works
River Rother

117
98

97
76

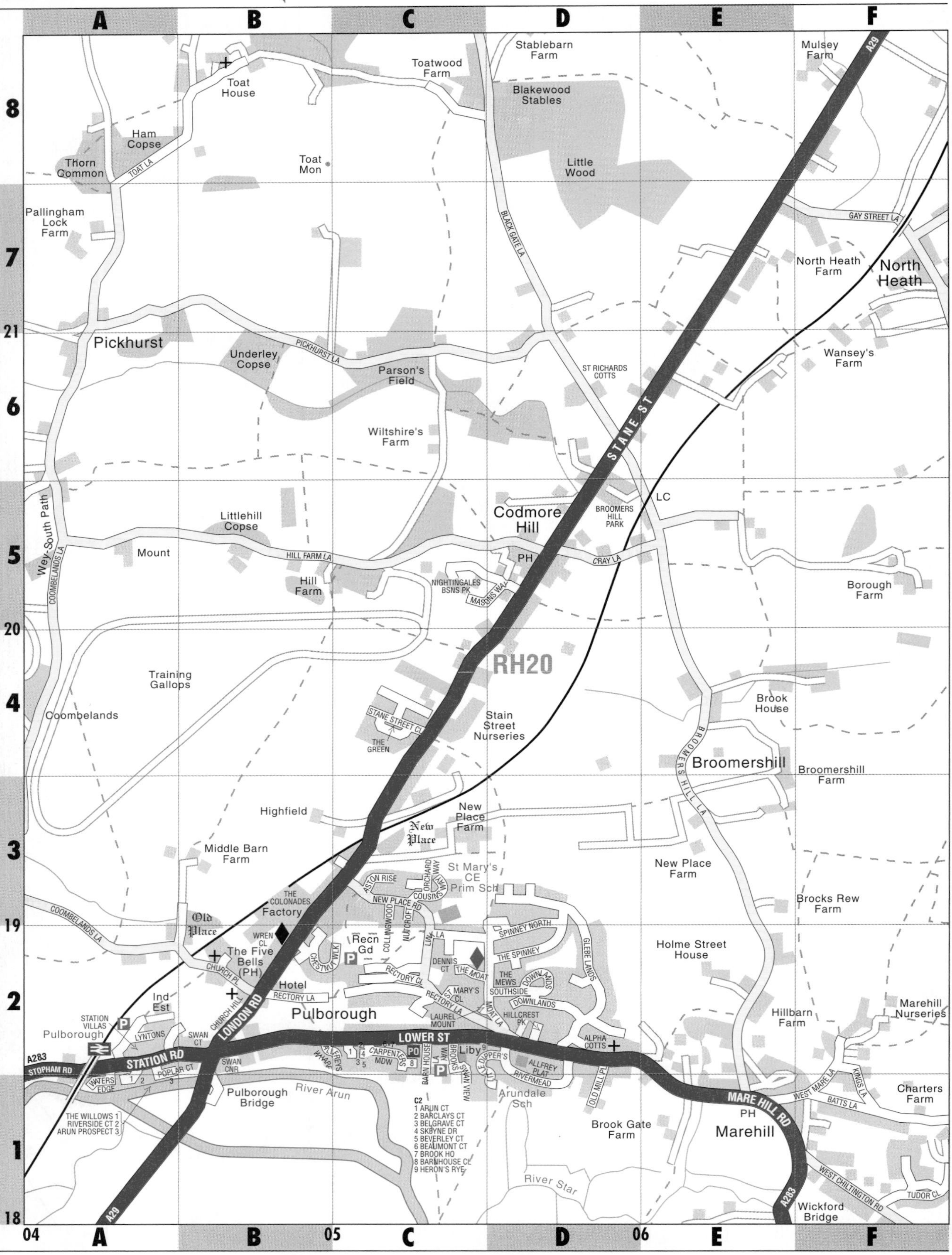
A
B
C
D
E
F
8
7
21
6
5
20
4
3
19
2
1
18
04
05
06
Stablebarn Farm
Mulsey Farm
A29
Toat House
Toatwood Farm
Blakewood Stables
Ham Copse
Thorn Common
TOAT LA
Toat Mon
Little Wood
Pallingham Lock Farm
GAY STREET LA
BLACK GATE LA
North Heath Farm
North Heath
Pickhurst
PICKHURST LA
Underley Copse
Parson's Field
ST RICHARDS COTTS
Wansey's Farm
Wiltshire's Farm
STANE ST
Wey-South Path
COOMBELANDS LA
Littlehill Copse
Codmore Hill
BROOMERS HILL PARK
LC
Mount
HILL FARM LA
PH
CRAY LA
Hill Farm
NIGHTINGALES BSNS PK
MASONS WAY
Borough Farm
RH20
Training Gallops
Coombelands
STANE STREET CL
THE GREEN
Stain Street Nurseries
Brook House
BROOMERS HILL LA
Broomershill
Broomershill Farm
Highfield
New Place Farm
New Place
Middle Barn Farm
New Place Farm
ASTON RISE
NEW PLACE RD
ORCHARD WAY
COUSINS WAY
St Mary's CE Prim Sch
Brocks Rew Farm
THE COLONADES
Factory
Old Place
COOMBELANDS LA
WREN CL
CHESTNUT WLK
COLLINGWOOD
NUTCROFT
LINK LA
SPINNEY NORTH
THE SPINNEY
GLEBE LANDS
Recn Gd
Holme Street House
The Five Bells (PH)
CHURCH PL
DENNIS CT
THE MOAT
THE MEWS
DOWNLANDS
RECTORY CL
SOUTHSIDE
Hotel
RECTORY LA
MARY'S CL
Ind Est
CHURCH HILL
LONDON RD
Pulborough
RECTORY LA
LAUREL MOUNT
MOAT LA
HILLCREST PK
Marehill Nurseries
Hillbarn Farm
STATION VILLAS
Pulborough
LYNTONS
SWAN CT
LOWER ST
ALPHA COTTS
A283
STOPHAM RD
STATION RD
POPLAR CT
SWAN CNR
ALLFREYS WHARF
CARPENTERS MDW
PO
BARN HOUSE LA
BROOKS WAY
SWAN VIEW
Liby
ALLFREY PLAT
RIVERMEAD
OLD MILL PL
WEST MARE LA
KINGS LA
BATTS LA
Charters Farm
WATERS EDGE
Pulborough Bridge
River Arun
Arundale Sch
MARE HILL RD
PH
Marehill
Brook Gate Farm
THE WILLOWS 1
RIVERSIDE CT 2
ARUN PROSPECT 3
C2
1 ARUN CT
2 BARCLAYS CT
3 BELGRAVE CT
4 SKEYNE DR
5 BEVERLEY CT
6 BEAUMONT CT
7 BROOK HO
8 BARNHOUSE CL
9 HERON'S RYE
River Stor
WEST CHILTINGTON RD
TUDOR CL
A283
Wickford Bridge
A29

97
118

77
100

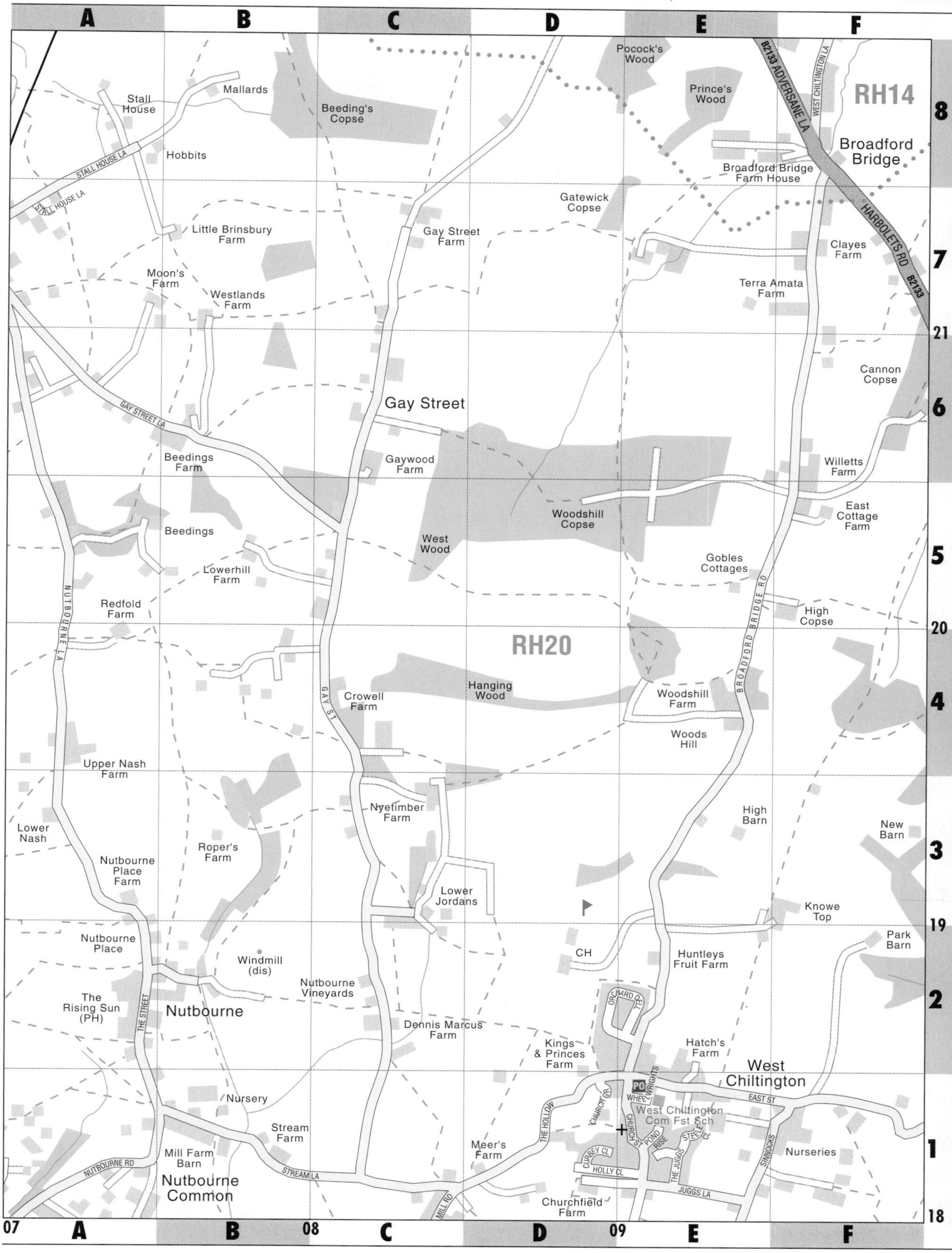
A
B
C
D
E
F
8
7
21
6
5
20
4
3
19
2
1
18
07
08
09
Stall House
Mallards
Beeding's Copse
Pocock's Wood
Prince's Wood
B2133 ADVERSANE LA
WEST CHILTINGTON LA
RH14
Broadford Bridge
Broadford Bridge Farm House
Hobbits
STALL HOUSE LA
Gatewick Copse
HARBOLETS RD
B2133
Little Brinsbury Farm
Gay Street Farm
Clayes Farm
Moon's Farm
Westlands Farm
Terra Amata Farm
Cannon Copse
Gay Street
GAY STREET LA
Beedings Farm
Gaywood Farm
Willetts Farm
Beedings
Woodshill Copse
East Cottage Farm
West Wood
Lowerhill Farm
Gobles Cottages
NUTBOURNE LA
Redfold Farm
BROADFORD BRIDGE RD
High Copse
RH20
GAY ST
Crowell Farm
Hanging Wood
Woodshill Farm
Woods Hill
Upper Nash Farm
Nyetimber Farm
High Barn
Lower Nash
New Barn
Roper's Farm
Nutbourne Place Farm
Lower Jordans
Knowe Top
Nutbourne Place
CH
Park Barn
Windmill (dis)
Huntleys Fruit Farm
Nutbourne Vineyards
ORCHARD DELL
The Rising Sun (PH)
Nutbourne
THE STREET
Dennis Marcus Farm
Kings & Princes Farm
Hatch's Farm
West Chiltington
PO
WHEELWRIGHTS
EAST ST
Nursery
CHURCH GR
West Chiltington Com Fst Sch
Stream Farm
THE HOLLOW
CHURCH ST
POND RISE
STEELE CL
SINNOCKS
Nurseries
Mill Farm Barn
Meer's Farm
CURBEY CL
THE JUGGS
HOLLY CL
NUTBOURNE RD
STREAM LA
Nutbourne Common
MILL RD
JUGGS LA
Churchfield Farm

119
100

99
78

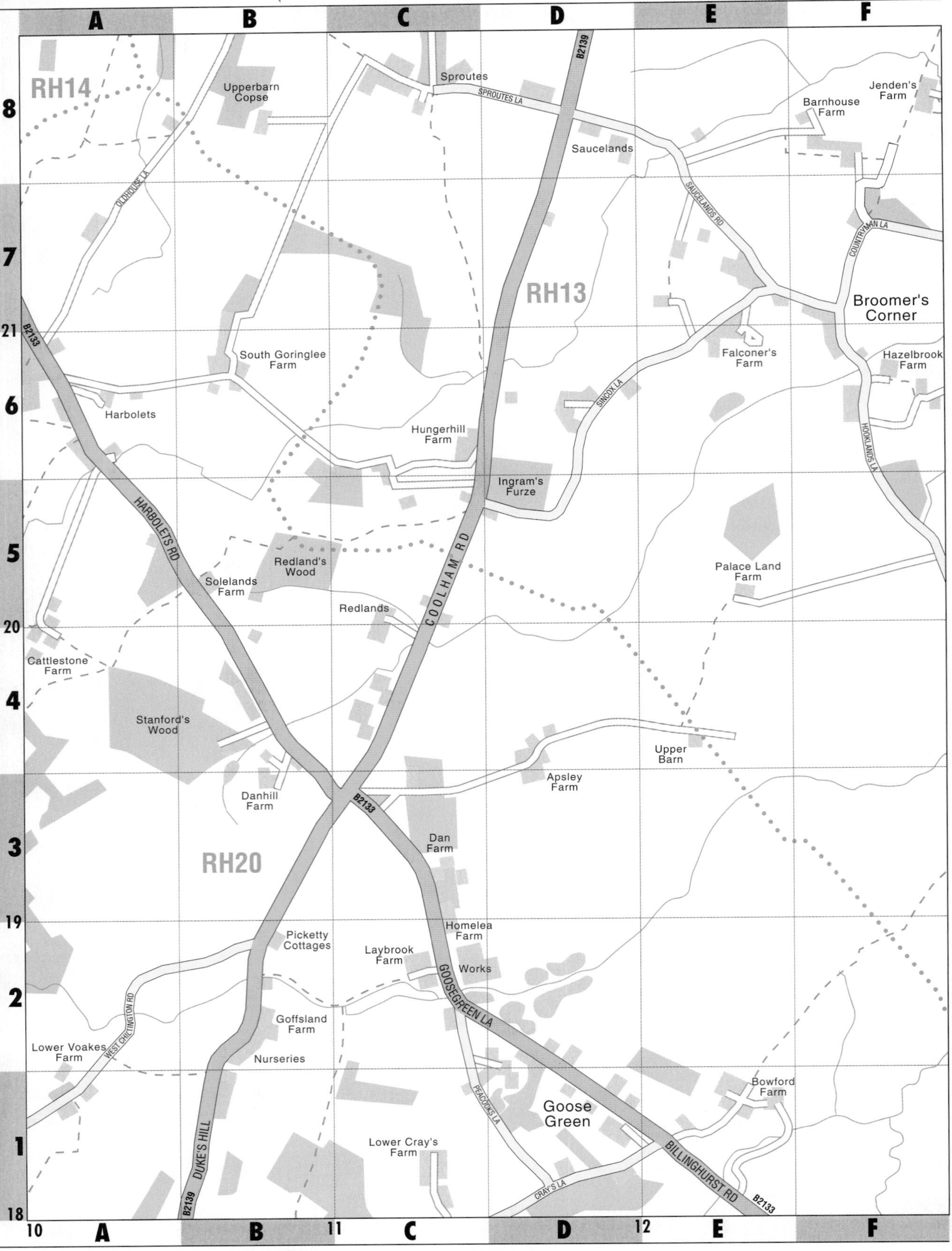
A
B
C
D
E
F
RH14
Upperbarn Copse
Sproutes
SPROUTES LA
B2139
Jenden's Farm
Barnhouse Farm
Saucelands
OLDHOUSE LA
SAUCELANDS RD
COUNTRYMAN LA
RH13
Broomer's Corner
B2133
South Goringlee Farm
Falconer's Farm
Hazelbrook Farm
Harbolets
SINCOX LA
Hungerhill Farm
HOOKLANDS LA
Ingram's Furze
HARBOLETS RD
Redland's Wood
COOLHAM RD
Palace Land Farm
Solelands Farm
Redlands
Cattlestone Farm
Stanford's Wood
Upper Barn
Danhill Farm
Apsley Farm
RH20
Dan Farm
Picketty Cottages
Homelea Farm
Laybrook Farm
Works
GOOSEGREEN LA
WEST CHILTINGTON RD
Goffsland Farm
Lower Voakes Farm
Nurseries
Bowford Farm
PEACOCKS LA
Goose Green
Lower Cray's Farm
DUKE'S HILL
BILLINGHURST RD
CRAY'S LA
8
7
21
6
5
20
4
3
19
2
1
18
10
11
12

99
120

79
102

A
B
C
D
E
F
8
7
21
6
5
20
4
3
19
2
1
18
13
14
15
School La
Red La
Kings Platt
Church Cl
King's Windmill
Shipley
Capp's Bridge
Smithers Hill La
Pound La
Church Farm South
Knepp Castle
Kneppmill Pond
New Lodge
Whitehall
Hampshires Farm
Countryman La
Pound Cnr
Pound Farm
The Countryman (PH)
Smoke House Farm
Tenchford
Charlwood Barn
Castle La
Hammer Farm
River Adur
Hammer Pond
Pen Bridge
Lower Barn
Honeypools Barn
Swallows La
Jackson's Wood
New Barn Farm
Lancing Brook
RH13
Swallows Farm
Brookhouse Farm
A24
Worthing Rd
Bentons Place Farm
Tory Copse
Dial Post
Sewage Works
The Green
Worthing Rd
Bentons La
Crown Inn (PH)
Hooklands La
Blonks Farm
Oakwood Farm Cottages
Woodmans Stud
Thistleworth Farm
Oakwood
Bottomhole Copse
Perryland Farm
Furzefield Wood
Hookland Wood
Grinder's La
Honeybridge Poultry Farm
Honeybridge La
Grinder's Wood
Honeybride Pk
Basing Hill
A24
Honeybridge La
Round Wood
RH20
Oxcopse Barn

121
102

101
80

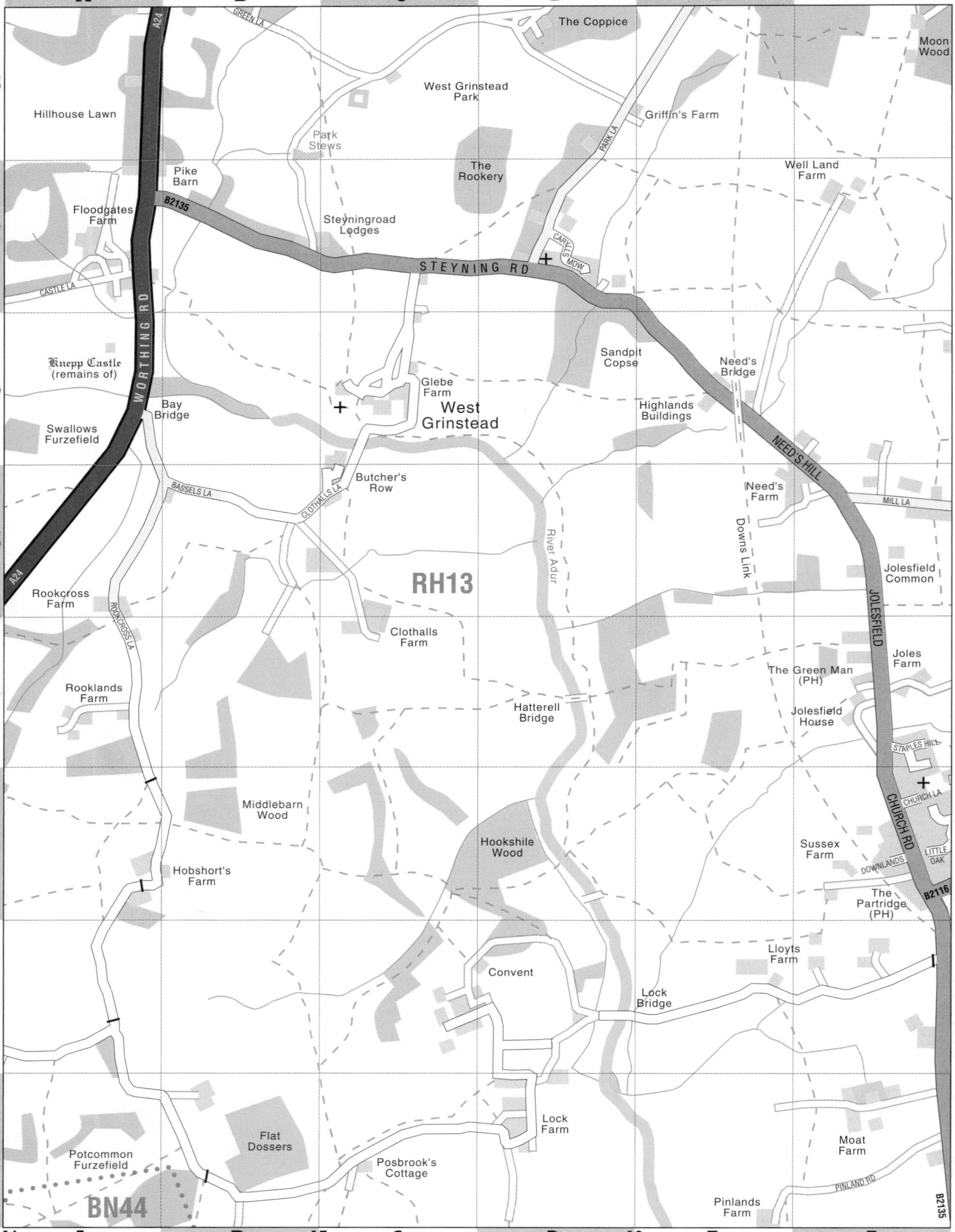
A
B
C
D
E
F
8
7
21
6
5
20
4
3
19
2
1
18
16
17
18
A24
GREEN LA
The Coppice
Moon Wood
West Grinstead Park
Hillhouse Lawn
Park Stews
Griffin's Farm
PARK LA
The Rookery
Pike Barn
Well Land Farm
Floodgates Farm
B2135
Steyningroad Lodges
CARYLLS MDW
STEYNING RD
CASTLE LA
WORTHING RD
Sandpit Copse
Knepp Castle (remains of)
Need's Bridge
Glebe Farm
West Grinstead
Highlands Buildings
Bay Bridge
Swallows Furzefield
NEED'S HILL
Butcher's Row
Need's Farm
BASSELS LA
CLOTHALLS LA
MILL LA
Downs Link
River Adur
Jolesfield Common
RH13
Rookcross Farm
JOLESFIELD
ROOKCROSS LA
Clothalls Farm
Joles Farm
The Green Man (PH)
Rooklands Farm
Hatterell Bridge
Jolesfield House
STAPLES HILL
Middlebarn Wood
CHURCH LA
CHURCH RD
Hookshile Wood
Sussex Farm
LITTLE OAK
DOWNLANDS
Hobshort's Farm
B2116
The Partridge (PH)
Lloyts Farm
Convent
Lock Bridge
Lock Farm
Flat Dossers
Moat Farm
Potcommon Furzefield
Posbrook's Cottage
PINLAND RD
BN44
Pinlands Farm
B2135

101
122

81
104

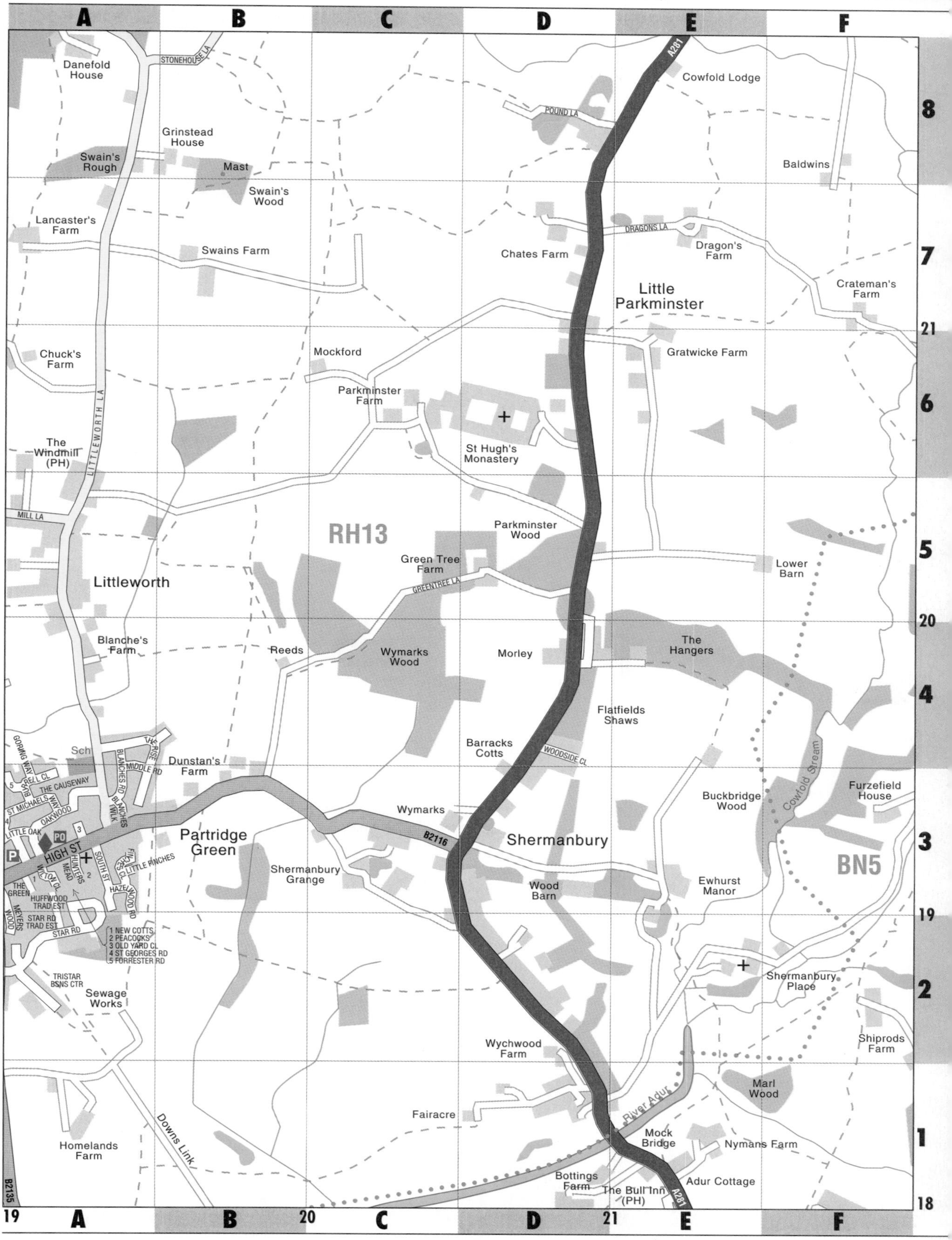
A
B
C
D
E
F
Danefold House
STONEHOUSE LA
Cowfold Lodge
POUND LA
Grinstead House
Swain's Rough
Mast
Swain's Wood
Baldwins
Lancaster's Farm
DRAGONS LA
Dragon's Farm
Chates Farm
Swains Farm
Little Parkminster
Crateman's Farm
Chuck's Farm
Mockford
Gratwicke Farm
Parkminster Farm
LITTLEWORTH LA
St Hugh's Monastery
The Windmill (PH)
MILL LA
RH13
Parkminster Wood
Green Tree Farm
GREENTREE LA
Lower Barn
Littleworth
Blanche's Farm
Reeds
Wymarks Wood
Morley
The Hangers
Flatfields Shaws
Barracks Cotts
WOODSIDE CL
Sch
Dunstan's Farm
Cowfold Stream
Furzefield House
Buckbridge Wood
Wymarks
Partridge Green
HIGH ST
B2116
Shermanbury
BN5
Shermanbury Grange
Wood Barn
Ewhurst Manor
HUFFWOOD TRAD EST
STAR RD TRAD EST
STAR RD
1 NEW COTTS
2 PEACOCKS
3 OLD YARD CL
4 ST GEORGES RD
5 FORRESTER RD
TRISTAR BSNS CTR
Sewage Works
Shermanbury Place
Shiprods Farm
Wychwood Farm
Marl Wood
River Adur
Fairacre
Mock Bridge
Nymans Farm
Homelands Farm
Downs Link
Bottings Farm
Adur Cottage
The Bull Inn (PH)
A281
B2135
8
7
21
6
5
20
4
3
19
2
1
18
19
20
21

123
104

103
82

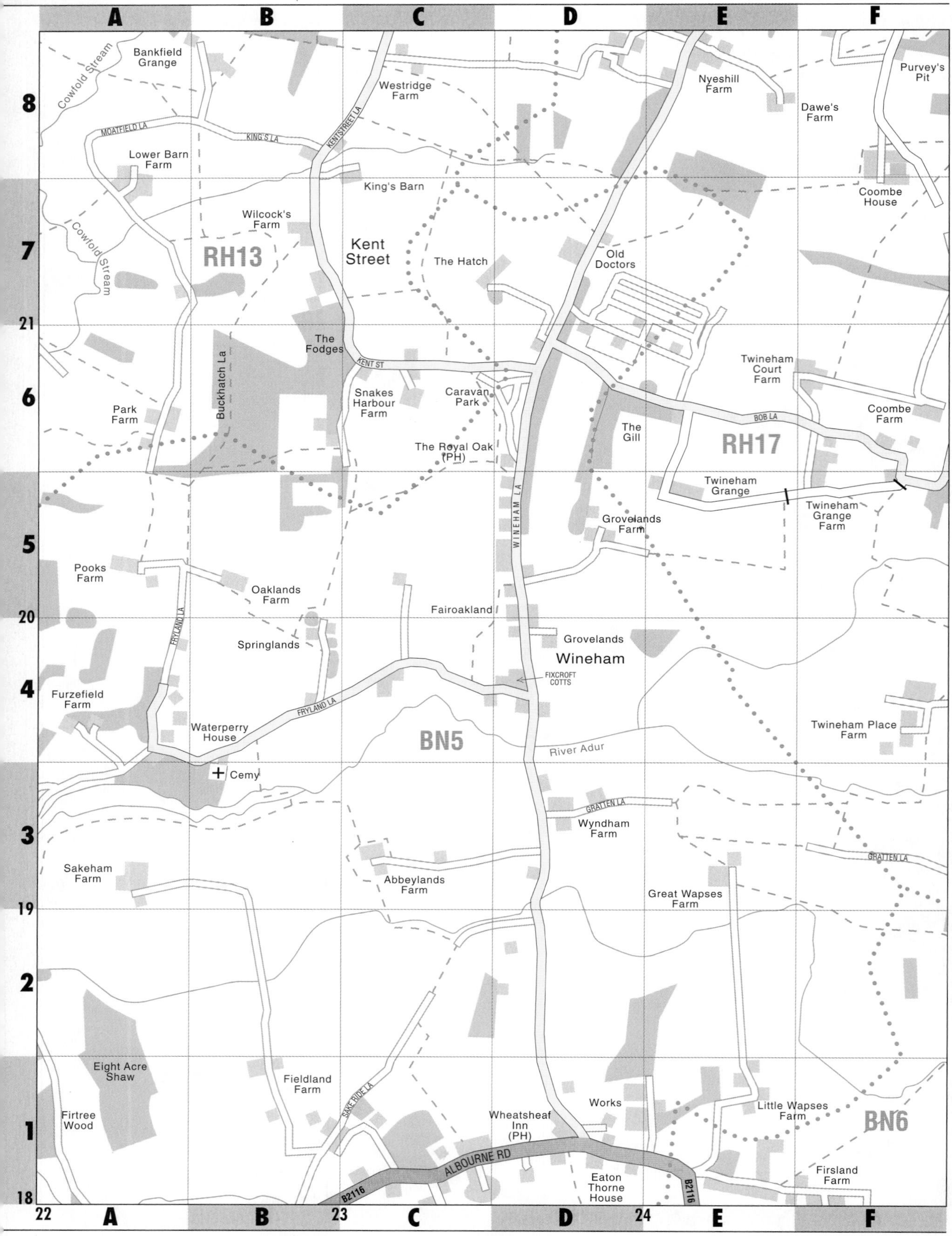
A B C D E F
8 7 21 6 5 20 4 3 19 2 1 18
22 23 24
Bankfield Grange
Cowfold Stream
Westridge Farm
Nyeshill Farm
Purvey's Pit
Dawe's Farm
MOATFIELD LA
KING'S LA
KENTSTREET LA
Lower Barn Farm
King's Barn
Coombe House
Wilcock's Farm
RH13
Kent Street
The Hatch
Old Doctors
The Fodges
KENT ST
Buckhatch La
Twineham Court Farm
Snakes Harbour Farm
Caravan Park
Park Farm
Coombe Farm
BOB LA
The Gill
RH17
The Royal Oak (PH)
Twineham Grange
WINEHAM LA
Grovelands Farm
Pooks Farm
Oaklands Farm
Fairoakland
FRYLAND LA
Springlands
Grovelands
Wineham
FIXCROFT COTTS
Furzefield Farm
Waterperry House
BN5
Twineham Place Farm
River Adur
Cemy
GRATTEN LA
Wyndham Farm
Sakeham Farm
Abbeylands Farm
Great Wapses Farm
Eight Acre Shaw
Fieldland Farm
Works
Firtree Wood
SAKE RIDE LA
Wheatsheaf Inn (PH)
Little Wapses Farm
BN6
ALBOURNE RD
B2116
Eaton Thorne House
Firsland Farm

103
124

83
106

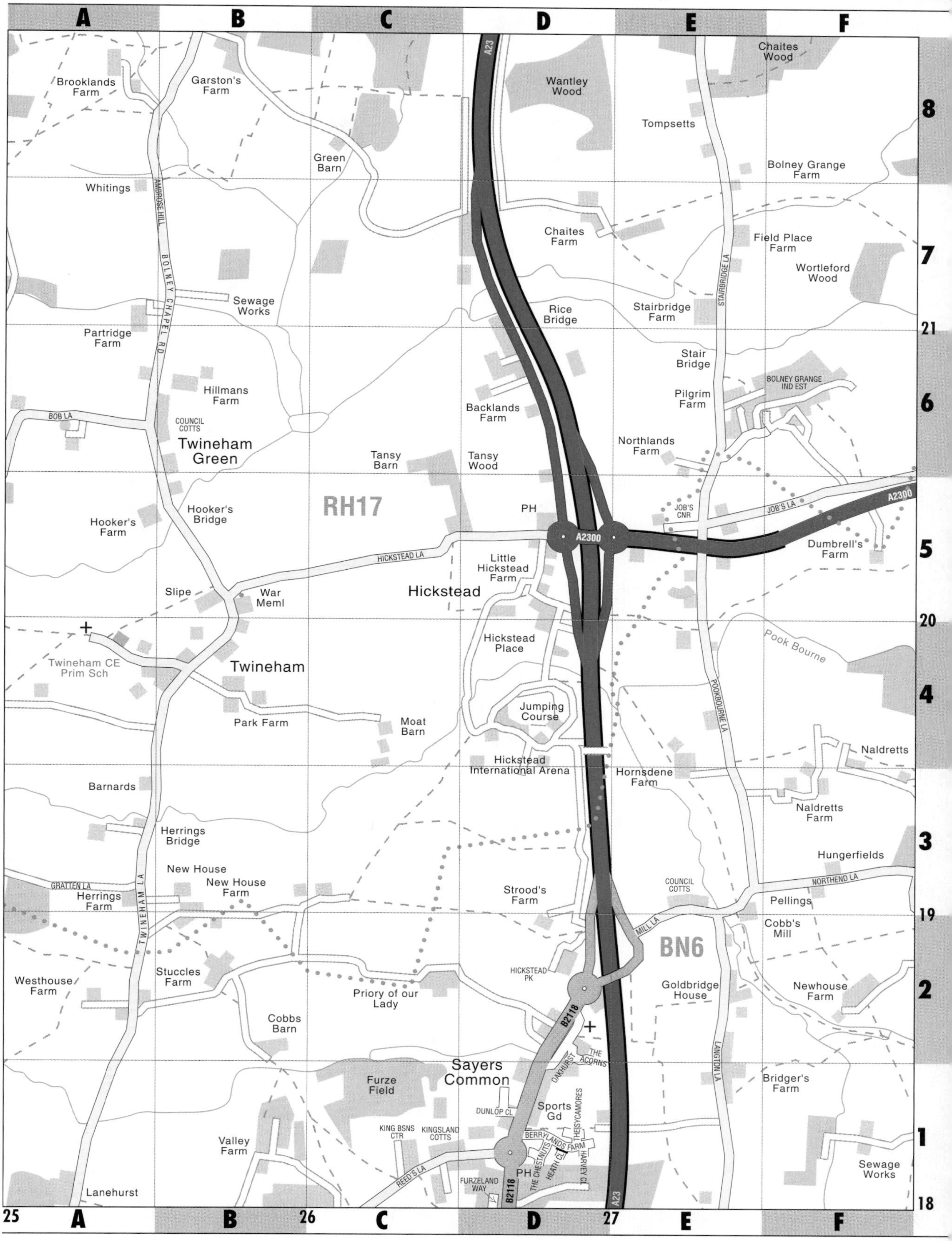
A
B
C
D
E
F
8
7
21
6
5
20
4
3
19
2
1
18
25
26
27
Brooklands Farm
Garston's Farm
Green Barn
Wantley Wood
Chaites Wood
Tompsetts
Bolney Grange Farm
Whitings
AMBROSE HILL
BOLNEY CHAPEL RD
Chaites Farm
Field Place Farm
Wortleford Wood
Sewage Works
Rice Bridge
Stairbridge Farm
STAIRBRIDGE LA
Partridge Farm
Stair Bridge
BOLNEY GRANGE IND EST
Hillmans Farm
Pilgrim Farm
BOB LA
COUNCIL COTTS
Backlands Farm
Twineham Green
Tansy Barn
Tansy Wood
Northlands Farm
RH17
JOB'S CNR
JOB'S LA
A2300
Hooker's Farm
Hooker's Bridge
PH
Dumbrell's Farm
HICKSTEAD LA
Little Hickstead Farm
Slipe
War Meml
Hickstead
Twineham CE Prim Sch
Hickstead Place
Pook Bourne
Twineham
Jumping Course
POOKBOURNE LA
Park Farm
Moat Barn
Naldretts
Hickstead International Arena
Hornsdene Farm
Barnards
Naldretts Farm
Herrings Bridge
Hungerfields
New House
New House Farm
Strood's Farm
COUNCIL COTTS
NORTHEND LA
GRATTEN LA
Herrings Farm
Pellings
TWINEHAM LA
MILL LA
Cobb's Mill
BN6
Stuccles Farm
HICKSTEAD PK
Westhouse Farm
Goldbridge House
Newhouse Farm
Priory of our Lady
B2118
Cobbs Barn
THE ACORNS
OAKHURST
LANGTON LA
Sayers Common
Furze Field
Bridger's Farm
Sports Gd
DUNLOP CL
THE SYCAMORES
KING BSNS CTR
KINGSLAND COTTS
BERRYLANDS FARM
Valley Farm
THE CHESTNUTS
HEATH CL
HARVEY CL
REED'S LA
PH
Sewage Works
FURZELAND WAY
B2118
A23
Lanehurst

125
106

105
84

105
126

85

A
B
C
D
E
F
Holmbush Wood
Brooklands Farm
Folly Farm
Kiln Wood
Fox & Hounds (PH)
FOX HILL VILLAGE
SCRACE HILL TERR
RH17
Cleavewaters Farm
A273
ISAAC'S LA
Holmbush Farm
Holmbush Cottages
RH16
ROCKY LA
CLEARWATERS LA
Clearwaters Farm
Roger's Farm
FOX HILL
LUNCE'S HILL
B2112
Lunce's Common
JESTERS
Vale Bridge
Goose Pit
Tilebarn Wood
Brook Lodge
Big Wood
Bedelands Farm Local Nature Reserve
Bedelands Farm
HOMESTEAD LA
VALEBRIDGE RD
THEOBALDS RD
Antye Farm
Lunces Hall
Wivelsfield Cty Prim Sch
CHURCH LA
Wivelsfield
Theobalds
VALEBRIDGE CL
Lowlands Farm
RH17
Works
FREEK'S LA
CHICHESTER WAY
CHARLWOOD RD
DOWNSCROFT
HAWTHORN CL
SPRINGFIELDS FARM IND EST
Great Ote Hall
Works
1 OAKENFIELD
2 SHEDDINGDEAN NEIGHBOURHOOD CTR
MARCHANTS WAY
COOPERS CL
THE WILLOWS
MAPLE CL
THE BLACKTHORNS
GRANGE CL
CHARLWOOD GDNS
LAUREL CL
OAKROYD CL
JAMES CL
LADYMEAD
Recn Gd
Great Otehall Wood
FAULKNERS WAY
BERRY CL
THE HAWTHORNS
CEDAR CL
CHESTNUT CL
BEDELANDS CL
LEYLANDS PK
MAPLE DR
DUMBRILLS CL
LOWLANDS RD
THE SPINNEY
GANDER CL
AMBERLEY CL
PETWORTH DR
BRAMBER WAY
SHEDDINGDEAN CL
3 CHELWOOD CT
4 FORGE WAY
MARLE AVE
LEYLANDS RD
NOEL GN
Wivelsfield
Manor Field Prim Sch
GLADSTONE RD
GORDON RD
GORDON HO
FARNLEA
BARKDALE
HUNTINGDON WAY
ROMAINE CL
WELBECK DR
WELBECK CL
JANES LA
Ote Hall Farm
The Royal Oak (PH)
MILLBANK
RIDGEWAY
THE TWITTEN
NOEL RISE
BLACKHOUSE LA
JUNCTION CL
STIRLING CT
STIRLING CL
COURT RD
MANOR RD
World's End
Bankside Farm
HIGHLANDS DR
WINDMILL DR
FIELD COTTS
WOODLEIGH RD
ADUR RD
THE CLOSE
NORTHWAY
MANOR CL
EASTDALE RD
WYBERLYE RD
UPPER ST JOHNS RD
ST PETERS RD
MILLERS WAY
SPANISH CT
MIDFIELDS WLK
THE DRIVE
ST WILFREDS RD
WOODLAND AVE
THE NURSERY
THE HALLANDS
ST ANDREWS RD
PRESCOTT GDNS
MILL PK
MIDFIELDS CL
MIDFIELDS DR
WOODLAND CRES
BROOKWAY
CANTS CL
THE KILN
MANOR RD
PARK RD
1 ST JOHNS CT
2 WARNER CT
3 ARCHER CT
MILL RD
FIRTOFT CL
LC
NYE RD
CANTS LA
THE VINERIES
SWANN CL
GOLDEN HILL
JOHNSON DR
St George's Retreat
ST JOHNS RD
CHURCH CL
CRESCENT RD
MILL WOOD
JUNCTION RD
RH15
TILERS CL
1 HUMPHREY LODGE
2 KELSEY CT
3 WARE CT
4 SCRASE LODGE
5 BENJAMIN LODGE
6 PAYTON HO
7 WATTS LODGE
LOWER CHURCH RD
ST LUKES CT
CRESCENT
MIDDLE WAY
TURKEY LA
RAVENSWOOD RD
Works
Clay Pit
QUARRY CL
COPESTAKE DR
TINDAL CL
MANSION CL
ROLFE DR
EGERTON CL
NORMAN RD
CHURCH WLK
CRESCENT WAY
FOUNDRY CT
CYPRUS RD
CYPRUS MEWS
GROVE RD
KNIVETON CT
MAYFIELD CT
MANSELL CT
AVONHURST
1 YEW TREE COTTS
2 OAK TREE COTTS
3 WOODLAND CT
4 WRENTHAM HO
Hope Farm
CIVIC WAY
THE BROW
THE MARTLETS
INHOLMES PARK RD
INHOLMES CL
Liby
MARKET PL
CHURCH RD
BARONS CT
OAKWOOD RD
CHURCHILL WAY
MARLBOROUGH DR
St Mary's House
Mkt
CLEVELAND GDNS
OAKWOOD RD
ROSARY CT
DALEWOOD GDNS
ALEXANDRA RD
QUEEN ELIZABETH AVE
STATION RD
DOUBLEDAYS
BURGESS HILL
LONGHURST
KINGS WAY
STATION RD
MEEDS RD
ASHWAY
QUEENS CRES
TOWER HO
SILVERDALE RD
KEYMER PAR
KEYMER CT
Stubs Copse
WOLSTONBURY CT 1
WOLSTONBURY WAY 2
Burgess Hill
WYNNSTAY
GLENDALE RD
BROAD GREEN AVE
WYKEHAM WAY
BADGERS WLK
Freckborough Manor
Oakmeeds Com Coll
Burgess Hill Sch
FERNDALE RD
LURGASHALL
THE HOLT
RUSPERS
COLDWALTHAM LA
Ditchling Common
KEYMER RD
THE RIDINGS
DROVERS WAY
London Meed Com Prim Sch
OAK HALL PK
Sch
BIRCHWOOD GROVE RD
BURDOCKS DR
KINGS RIDE
SAWYERS CL
BURNERS CL
WEAVERS CL
Pollards Farm
BN6
Newick House Sch
THE WARREN
KILNFORD CL
THATCHERS CL
WHEELWRIGHT LA
Ditchling Common Country Park
HOLMESDALE RD
CHANCTONBURY RD
PINEHURST
HAZEL GR
BOUGH BEECHES
BARNSIDE AVE
FARM WAY
WINKHURST WAY
TITCHFIELD CL
Ind Est
WOODCREST RD
PRIORY RD
BEECHWOODS
KEYMER RD
CHILCOMB
SINGLETON WAY
PENDEAN
HAMBROOK
ROSEBARN CL
FOLDERS CL
SADDLERS CL
Folders Farm
FRANKLANDS CL
KEYMER GDNS
WOODWARDS CL
FOLDERS LA
B2113
B2112
8
7
21
6
5
20
4
3
19
2
1
18
31
32
33
A
B
C
D
E
F

88

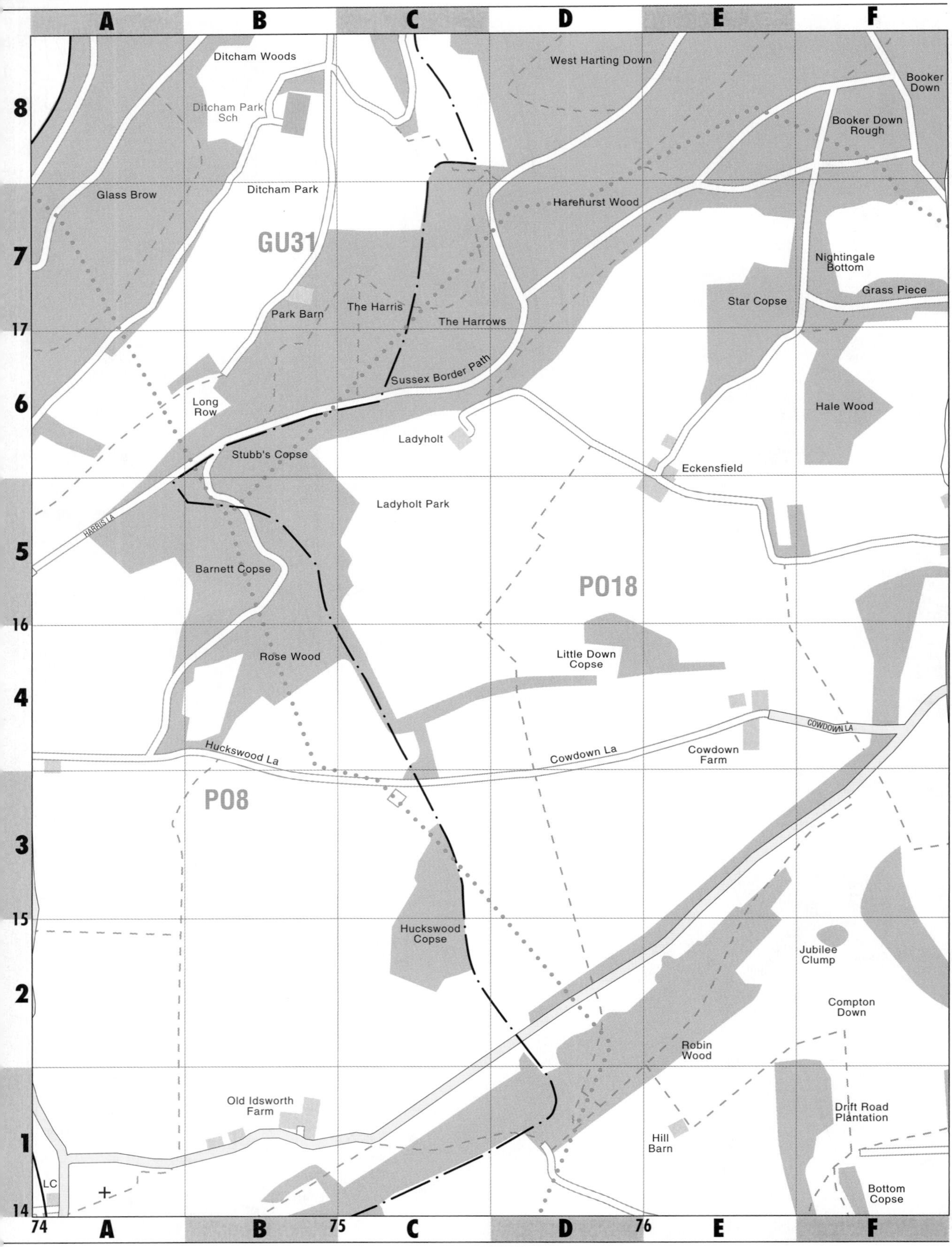
A
B
C
D
E
F
Ditcham Woods
West Harting Down
Booker Down
Ditcham Park Sch
Booker Down Rough
8
Glass Brow
Ditcham Park
Harehurst Wood
GU31
7
Nightingale Bottom
Grass Piece
Star Copse
The Harris
Park Barn
The Harrows
17
Sussex Border Path
Long Row
6
Hale Wood
Ladyholt
Stubb's Copse
Eckensfield
Ladyholt Park
HARRIS LA
5
Barnett Copse
PO18
16
Rose Wood
Little Down Copse
4
COWDOWN LA
Cowdown Farm
Hucksword La
Cowdown La
PO8
3
15
Huckswood Copse
Jubilee Clump
2
Compton Down
Robin Wood
Old Idsworth Farm
Drift Road Plantation
Hill Barn
1
LC
Bottom Copse
14
74
75
76

89
110

A
B
C
D
E
F
8
7
17
6
5
16
4
3
15
2
1
14
77
78
79
Round Down
B2146
Garden Wood
B2141
Harting Hill
Whitcombe Bottom
Upper West Wood
Uppark
Stony Wood
Two Beech Bottom
The Belt
Hudsons Copse
Icehouse Bottom
Bell Vue Hill
Lower West Wood
Deer Barn Bottom
Belt Plain
Kill Devil Copse
Lawn Bottom
Up Park
Padswood Bottom
Park Copse
GU31
Sixteen Acre Plain
The Forest
Killing Wood
Pads Wood
Bushy Piece
Hucksholt Farm
Wills Wood
Littlegreen Wood
Edgar Plantation
Compton Corner
Fernbeds Down
Littlegreen Sch
Handle Down
Compton Park
Chalkpit Plantation
Hundred Acre Farm
Fernbeds Farm
Bevis's Thumb
Gold Mine Plantation
LONG LA
PO18
Apple Down
Telegraph Hill
Compton Farm
PO
CHURCH
BGLWS
Compton
SCHOOL LA
PH
East Hanger
Battines Hill Wood
Compton & Up Marden CE Prim Sch
West Hanger
Up Marden Farm
Up Marden

130
110

109
90

A
B
C
D
E
F
8
7
17
6
5
16
4
3
15
2
1
14
80
81
82
South Downs Way
Bramshott Bottom
Little Round Down
Harting Downs Nature Reserve
Telegraph House
Millpond Bottom
Buriton Farm
Treyford Hill
GU29
Devil's Jumps
South Downs Way
Buriton Hanger
GU31
Philliswood Down
Monkton Copse
North Marden Down
Germanleith Copse
Bushy Piece
Philliswood Farm
Gutteridge Row
Monkton Farm
B2141
North Marden
Royal Oak (PH)
Hooksway
Meredon Farm
Hill Lands Farm
Phillis Wood
PO18
Stubbs Copse
Batten Hanger
LONG LA
Fourways
Newbuildings
PHILLISWOOD LA
Upton Farm
Manor Place
The Glebe House
East Marden
East Marden Farm
HILLSIDE COTTS
The White Horse (PH)
Bow Hill Farm
Chilgrove Hill
Smithy
B2141
Chilgrove
East Marden Down
Faraway
Hill Barn
Whitelands Copse

109
131

91
112

A
B
C
D
E
F
8
7
17
6
5
16
4
3
15
2
1
14
Didling Hanger
Linch Down
Didling Hill
Monkton House
South Downs Way
Linch Ball
Bepton Down
GU29
Newfarm Plantation
Monkton Wood
Linchball Wood
Winden Wood
Bepton Wood
Winden Field
Several Beeches
Venus Wood
Slippers Row
PO18
Westdean Woods
Yewtree Cottage
Keeper's Cottage
Brooms Farm
Staple Ash Farm
Rabbit Warren
Colworth Down
Colworth Barn
Stapleash Down
Chilgrove House
HYLTERS'S LA
Hylter's Farm
Colworth Farm
B2141
Ham Wood
83
84
85

132
112

111
92

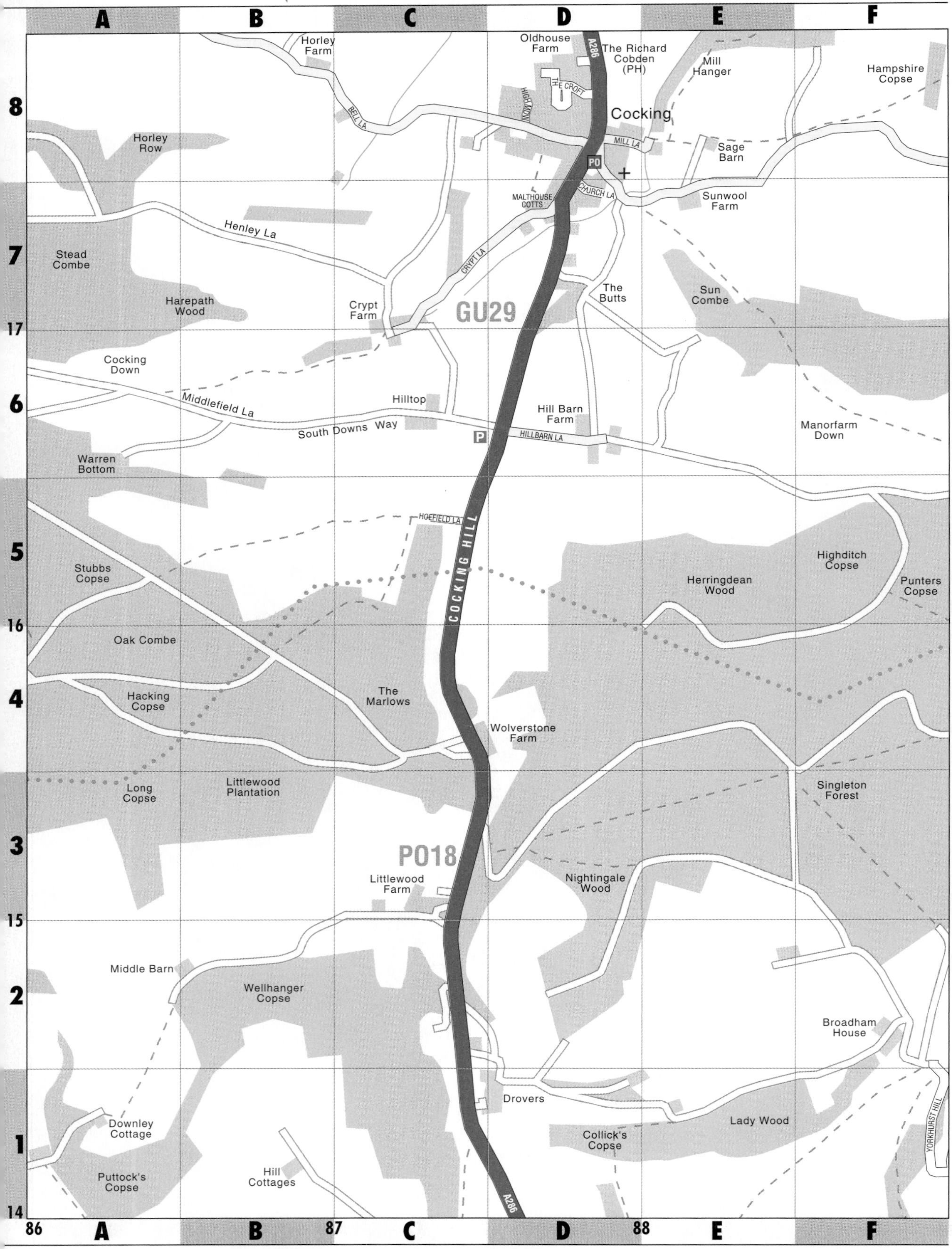
A
B
C
D
E
F
8
7
17
6
5
16
4
3
15
2
1
14
86
87
88
Horley Farm
Oldhouse Farm
A286
The Richard Cobden (PH)
Mill Hanger
Hampshire Copse
THE CROFT
HIGH MDW
BELL LA
Cocking
MILL LA
Horley Row
Sage Barn
PO
MALTHOUSE COTTS
CHURCH LA
Sunwool Farm
Henley La
Stead Combe
CRYPT LA
The Butts
Sun Combe
Harepath Wood
Crypt Farm
GU29
Cocking Down
Hilltop
Middlefield La
Hill Barn Farm
South Downs Way
P
HILLBARN LA
Manorfarm Down
Warren Bottom
HOEFIELD LA
COCKING HILL
Highditch Copse
Stubbs Copse
Herringdean Wood
Punters Copse
Oak Combe
The Marlows
Hacking Copse
Wolverstone Farm
Long Copse
Littlewood Plantation
Singleton Forest
PO18
Littlewood Farm
Nightingale Wood
Middle Barn
Wellhanger Copse
Broadham House
Drovers
Lady Wood
Downley Cottage
Collick's Copse
YORKHURST HILL
Puttock's Copse
Hill Cottages

111
133

93
114

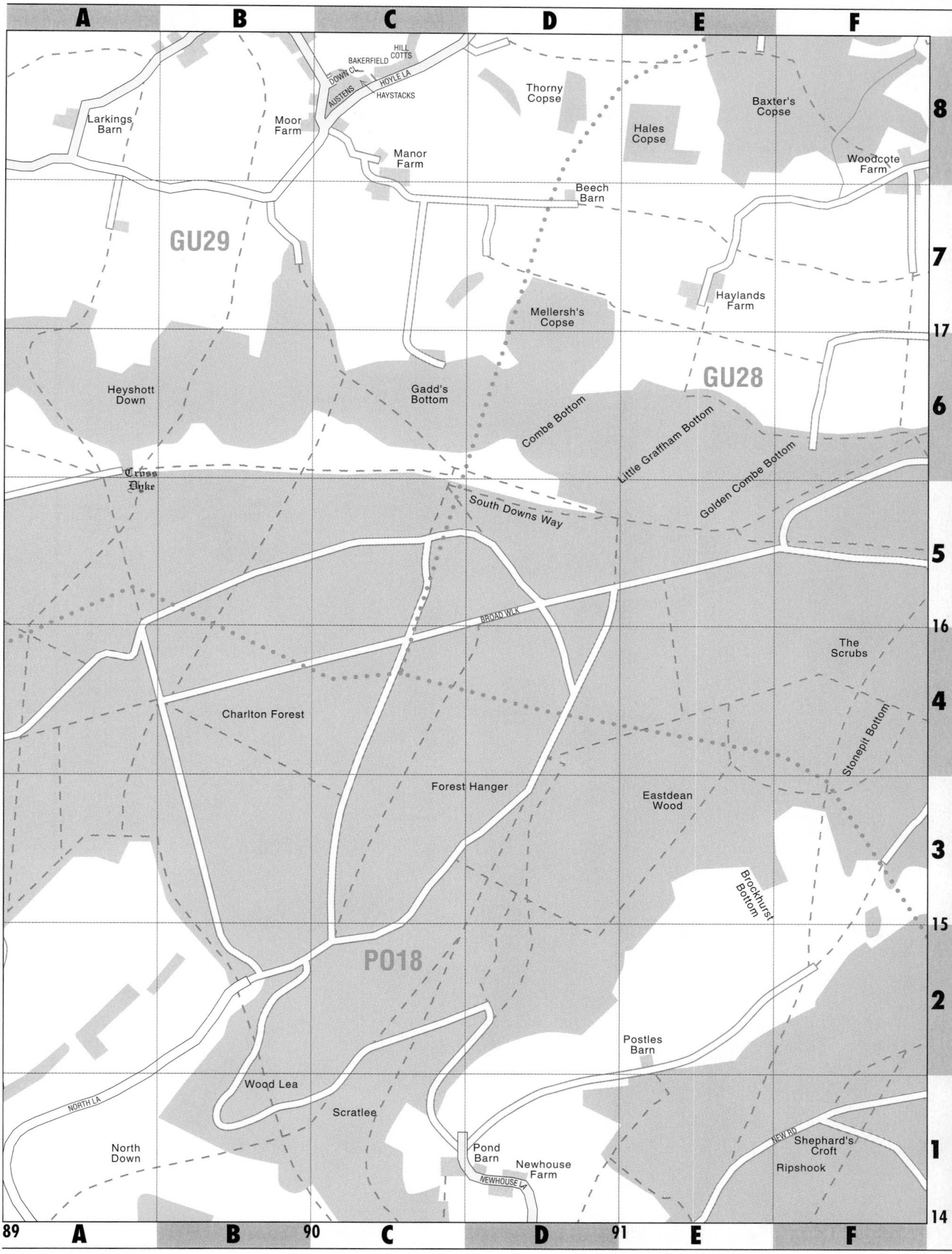
A
B
C
D
E
F
HILL COTTS
BAKERFIELD
DOWN CL
HOYLE LA
AUSTENS
HAYSTACKS
Thorny Copse
Baxter's Copse
Larkings Barn
Moor Farm
Hales Copse
Manor Farm
Woodcote Farm
Beech Barn
GU29
Haylands Farm
Mellersh's Copse
GU28
Heyshott Down
Gadd's Bottom
Combe Bottom
Little Graffham Bottom
Golden Combe Bottom
Cross Dyke
South Downs Way
BROAD WLK
The Scrubs
Charlton Forest
Stonepit Bottom
Forest Hanger
Eastdean Wood
Brockhurst Bottom
PO18
Postles Barn
Wood Lea
NORTH LA
Scratlee
North Down
Pond Barn
Newhouse Farm
NEWHOUSE LA
NEW RD
Shephard's Croft
Ripshook
8
7
17
6
5
16
4
3
15
2
1
14
89
90
91

134
114

113
94

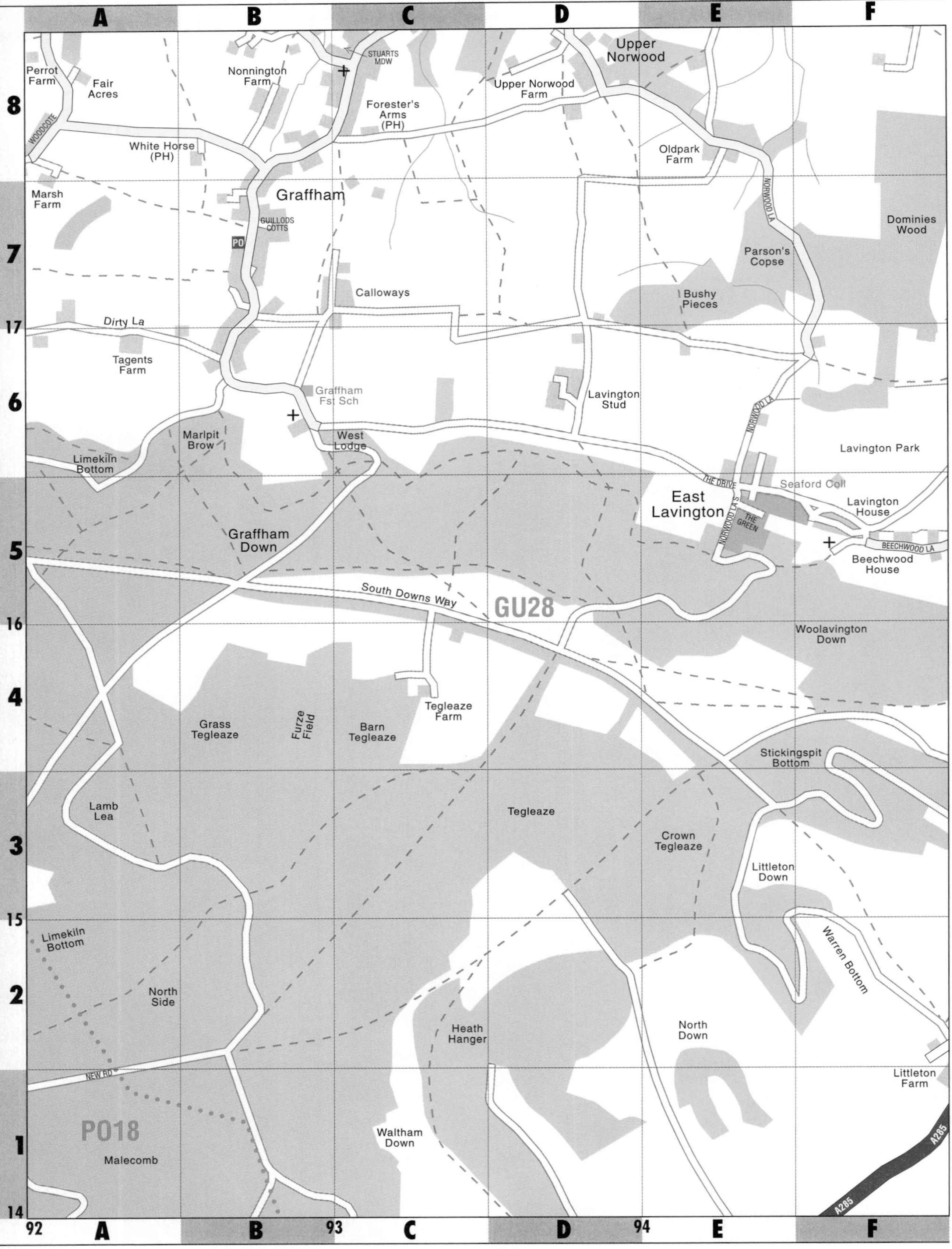
A
B
C
D
E
F
8
7
17
6
5
16
4
3
15
2
1
14
92
93
94
Perrot Farm
Fair Acres
WOODCOTE
Nonnington Farm
STUARTS MDW
Forester's Arms (PH)
Upper Norwood
Upper Norwood Farm
White Horse (PH)
Oldpark Farm
Marsh Farm
Graffham
GUILLODS COTTS
PO
NORWOOD LA
Dominies Wood
Parson's Copse
Bushy Pieces
Calloways
Dirty La
Tagents Farm
Graffham Fst Sch
Lavington Stud
NORWOOD LA
Marlpit Brow
West Lodge
Lavington Park
Limekiln Bottom
THE DRIVE
Seaford Coll
East Lavington
Lavington House
NORWOOD LA S
THE GREEN
Graffham Down
BEECHWOOD LA
Beechwood House
South Downs Way
GU28
Woolavington Down
Tegleaze Farm
Grass Tegleaze
Furze Field
Barn Tegleaze
Stickingspit Bottom
Lamb Lea
Tegleaze
Crown Tegleaze
Littleton Down
Limekiln Bottom
Warren Bottom
North Side
Heath Hanger
North Down
NEW RD
Littleton Farm
PO18
Malecomb
Waltham Down
A285
A285

113
135

95
116

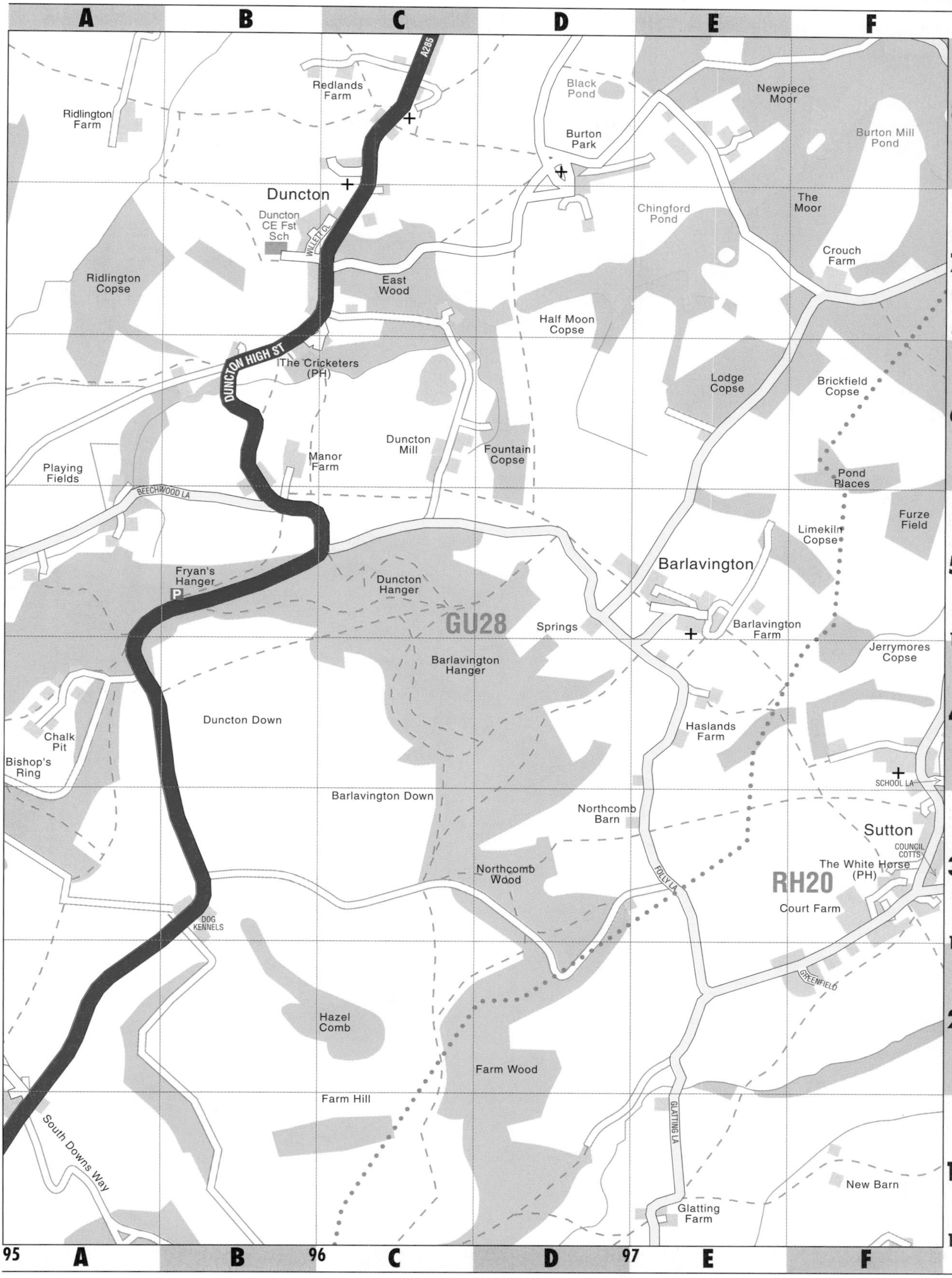
A
B
C
D
E
F
8
7
17
6
5
16
4
3
15
2
1
14
95
96
97
A285
Redlands Farm
Ridlington Farm
Black Pond
Newpiece Moor
Burton Mill Pond
Burton Park
Duncton
Duncton CE Fst Sch
WILLETT CL
Chingford Pond
The Moor
Crouch Farm
Ridlington Copse
East Wood
Half Moon Copse
DUNCTON HIGH ST
The Cricketers (PH)
Lodge Copse
Brickfield Copse
Duncton Mill
Manor Farm
Fountain Copse
Playing Fields
BEECHWOOD LA
Pond Places
Furze Field
Limekiln Copse
Barlavington
Fryan's Hanger
P
Duncton Hanger
GU28
Springs
Barlavington Farm
Barlavington Hanger
Jerrymores Copse
Duncton Down
Haslands Farm
Chalk Pit
Bishop's Ring
SCHOOL LA
Barlavington Down
Northcomb Barn
Sutton
COUNCIL COTTS
Northcomb Wood
The White Horse (PH)
RH20
FOLLY LA
Court Farm
DOG KENNELS
GREENFIELD
Hazel Comb
Farm Wood
Farm Hill
GLATTING LA
South Downs Way
New Barn
Glatting Farm

136
116

115 96

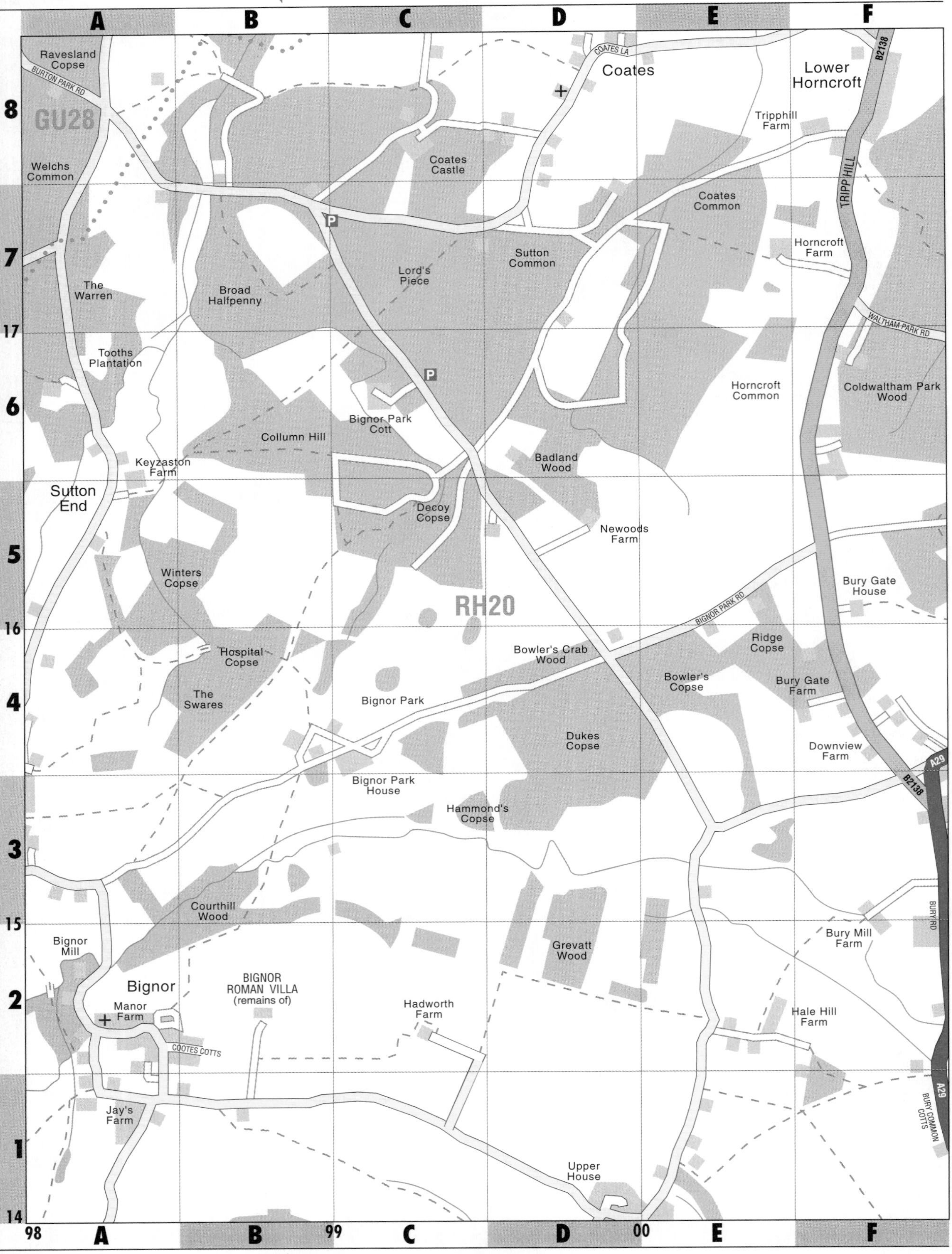
A
B
C
D
E
F
8
7
17
6
5
16
4
3
15
2
1
14
98
99
00
Ravesland Copse
BURTON PARK RD
GU28
Welchs Common
The Warren
Broad Halfpenny
Tooths Plantation
Keyzaston Farm
Sutton End
Collumn Hill
Winters Copse
Hospital Copse
The Swares
COATES LA
Coates
Coates Castle
Lord's Piece
Sutton Common
Bignor Park Cott
Decoy Copse
Badland Wood
Newoods Farm
RH20
Lower Horncroft
Tripphill Farm
Coates Common
Horncroft Farm
B2138
TRIPP HILL
WALTHAM PARK RD
Horncroft Common
Coldwaltham Park Wood
Bury Gate House
BIGNOR PARK RD
Ridge Copse
Bowler's Crab Wood
Bowler's Copse
Bury Gate Farm
Bignor Park
Dukes Copse
Downview Farm
A29
Bignor Park House
Hammond's Copse
BURY RD
Courthill Wood
Bignor Mill
Bignor
Manor Farm
BIGNOR ROMAN VILLA (remains of)
COOTES COTTS
Grevatt Wood
Bury Mill Farm
Hadworth Farm
Hale Hill Farm
Jay's Farm
Upper House
BURY COMMON COTTS

115 137

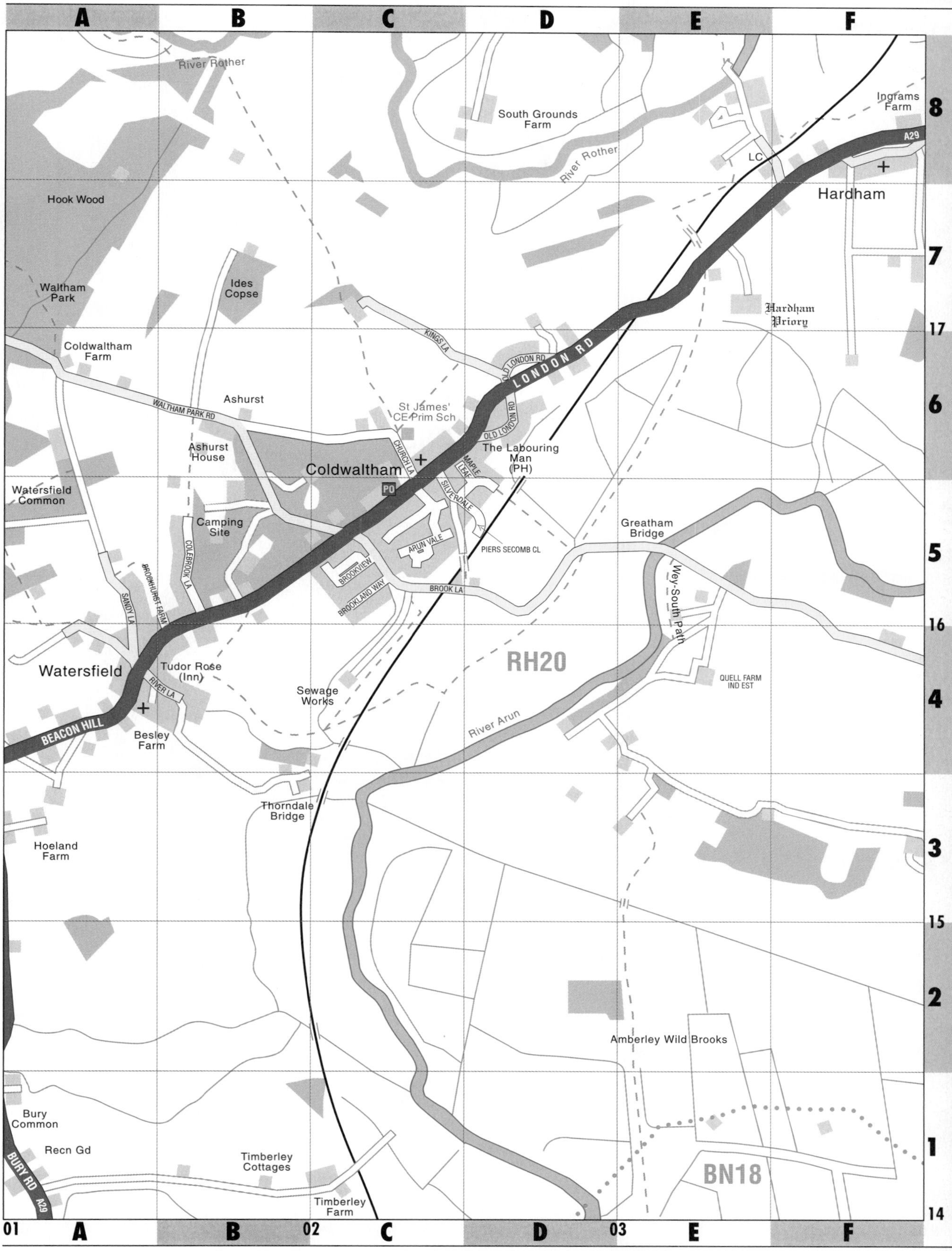
97
118
A
B
C
D
E
F
River Rother
South Grounds Farm
Ingrams Farm
A29
LC
Hardham
Hook Wood
Waltham Park
Ides Copse
Hardham Priory
Coldwaltham Farm
KINGS LA
OLD LONDON RD
LONDON RD
Ashurst
WALTHAM PARK RD
St James' CE Prim Sch
Ashurst House
CHURCH LA
Coldwaltham
PO
MAPLE LEAF
The Labouring Man (PH)
Watersfield Common
SILVERDALE
Camping Site
ARUN VALE
PIERS SECOMB CL
Greatham Bridge
COLEBROOK LA
BROOKHURST FARM
SANDY LA
BROOKVIEW
BROOKLAND WAY
BROOK LA
Wey-South Path
RH20
Watersfield
Tudor Rose (Inn)
RIVER LA
Sewage Works
QUELL FARM IND EST
BEACON HILL
Besley Farm
River Arun
Thorndale Bridge
Hoeland Farm
Amberley Wild Brooks
Bury Common
Recn Gd
BURY RD
A29
Timberley Cottages
Timberley Farm
BN18
8
7
17
6
5
16
4
3
15
2
1
14
01
02
03
138
118

117
98

A
B
C
D
E
F
8
7
17
6
5
16
4
3
15
2
1
14
04
05
06
A29
LONDON RD
A283
Sewage
Works
Winterfields
Farm
River Chilt
Banks
Cottage
Lickfold
Farm
GOLF CLUB LA
River Arun
Wiggonholt
Farm
River Stor
RH20
Wiggonholt
Upperton's Barn
Visitors Ctr
Rush
Brook
Pulborough Brooks
Nature Reserve
P
Wiggonholt
Common
Redford
House
Manor
Farm
Greatham
Wassel Pond
Washingham
Northpark
Wood
Bog
Common
Greatham
Common
Sparrite
Farm
Sparrite
Common
HURSTON LA
Glebe
Farm
The
Sawyard
Bog
Common
Cottages
Rackham
Common
Parham
Farm
Lillywhites
Field
Fangrove
Hill
Rackham
Plantation
Sparrite
Farm
West
Lodges
Limekiln
Plat
Douglas's
Lodge
Parham Park
(Deer Park)
West Plain
Parham House
& Gardens
Windmill
Hill
BN18
Rackham Mill
(disused)
RACKHAM ST
Rackham
House

117
139

99
120

A
B
C
D
E
F
Recn Gd
Nutbourne Common
Heath Mill
WEST CHILTINGTON RD
HARBOROUGH MDW
HARBOROUGH GORSE
NEW BARN LA
HARBOROUGH DR
OLD BOUNDARY LA
FINCHES LA
MILL RD
MILL LA
FOXFIELDS
LITTLE HILL
HARBOROUGH HILL
HARBOROUGH CL
THE COMMON
THE BIRCHES
HEATHFIELD COPSE
MILL END
MARTLETS
OAK END
BIRCH END
LARCH END
HAGLANDS COPSE
HAGLANDS LA
CASTLEGATE
KINGSWOOD
BARKWORTH WAY
MORRIS WAY
OAKVALE
KENSINGTON CL
NIGHTINGALES
HINDLE CL
SILVERWOOD COPSE
SILVERWOOD
NYETIMBER LA
NYETIMBER COPSE
CHESTNUT BRIDGE
West Chiltington Common
CROSSWAYS PK
CROSSWAYS
CHILTINGTON CL
GARDEN WOOD CL
COMMON HILL
RAMBLEDOWN LA
BROOK CHASE
FIR TREE CL
FIR TREE LA
WYNDHAM LEA
MONKMEAD LA
MONKMEAD COPSE
HEATHER LA
WESTWARD LA
SUNSET LA
SPINNEY LA
Perrett's Copse
BIRCH GR
ROUNDABOUT LA
BOWER LA
BIRCH TREE LA
SILVER GLADE
BADGERS WOOD
GROVE LA
THREALS COPSE
HIGH SPINNEY
ROUNDABOUT COPSE
Roundabout Farm
WILLOW CL
LORDINGS LA
THE HAWTHORNS
SMOCK ALLEY
Smock Alley
Nestledown Nursery
Whale's Farm
SOUTHLANDS LA
Southlands Farm
Sewage Works
Rushfield Nurseries
HIGH BAR LA
LINFIELD COPSE
FURZE COMMON RD
Highbar Copse
THREAL'S LA
Champions Farm
Threal's Farm
River Chilt
Hurston Warren
CH
GOLF CLUB LA
Hurston Place Farm
Hurston Place
WEST CHILTINGTON RD
GREENHURST LA
Hareswith Pond
RH20
Hurston Street Farm
Poultry Farm
NORTHLANDS LA
Northlands
HURSTON LA
River Stor
Sewage Works
Freeland
Fryern Home Farm
East Wantley
WATER LANE IND EST
FRYERN RD
MELTON DR
MELTON AVE
ALDERMOOR AVE
MELTON CL
BANNISTER GDNS
BOBELL WAY
BROOK CL
SOUTHDOWN WAY
ROTHER CL
CONCORDE CL
JUBILEE WAY
RAINBOW WAY
SNAPES RD
BEECH GR
THE GREEN
Parham Airfield
HURSTON GR
FAITHFULL CRES
DEAN WAY
RAPLEY AVE
HORMARE CRES
CROWHURST CRES
BRAMBER AVE
LONGLAND AVE
STEYNING CRES
Storrington
MERRYFIELD WAY
FRENCHES
LOBS WOOD LA
GREENFIELD WAY
DOWNSVIEW AVE
DENSHIRE DR
SULLINGTON COPSE
ROWAN CL
BANKS CROFT
OAK END
OAK CL
KINGSLAND CL
B2139
THAKEHAM RD
Rydon Com Coll
WATER LA
Southdown Gliding Club
Cootham
Charity Farm
DUKES ROW
PH
COOTHAM GN
TRITTON PL
TANSY MEAD
TURNERS MEAD
SHERMANBURY DR
FRYERN CL
SPIERBRIDGE RD
MERRYFIELD RD
GARDEN CL
LIME CHASE
WINDMILL COPSE
SHERSTON CL
FIELD END
MEAD LA
WOODSIDE RD
MARLEY WAY
MARLEY CL
PALMER CL
HEATHERLANDS
WANTLEY LA
KINGSFIELD
Sch
FLETCHER'S CROFT
L Ctr
Recn Gd
SWAN CL
REED CL
HOLLY CT
LOVE LA
HOLLY CL
FRAZIER HO
RYECROFT LA
NORTH ST
SUNNYSIDE COTTS
STOR MDW
HAWTHORN WAY
RIVERSIDE
MILL LA
SCHOOL HILL
TIMBERLANDS
PUTTICK CL
NIGHTINGALE CL
NIGHTINGALE PK
Sullington Warren
PULBOROUGH RD
THE CRESCENT
CHAPEL LA
ST RICHARDS COTTS
WARREN CROFT
CASSIDY PL
THE PLANTATION
BROW CL
COOTHAM BROW
GREENACRE CL
FOXDELL
THE BRACKENS
PLANTATION WAY
AMBERLEY CL
B2139
WEST ST
Liby
PO
BREWERS YD
OLD MILL DR
OLD MILL SQ
B2139
WISBOROUGH LA
BYNE CL
NIGHTINGALE LA
WOODPECKER LA
HEATHER WAY
NEW TOWN RD
FOX CT
1 SPRING COTTS
2 THE WILLOWS
MONASTERY LA
RECTORY RD
RECTORY CL
RECTORY WLK
THE SQUARE
HIGH ST
MANLEY'S HILL
HANOVER WLK
MEADOWSIDE
ROSEMARY CL
MEADOWSIDE
CHANTRY LA
WASHINGTON RD
A283
E1
1 BERKELEY LODGE
2 CHANTRY CL
3 WIMROD HO
4 VULCAN HO
5 STANMORE HO
6 HARRIER HO
7 LYSANDER HO
AMBERLEY RD
FERN RD
DOWNLANDS
LINK HILL
Monastery
SCHOOL LA
CHURCH ST
MANOR CL
BROWN'S LA
AMBERLEY GATE
KITHURST PK
KITHURST LA
CLAY LA
07
08
09
8
7
17
6
5
16
4
3
15
2
1
14

D1
1 RECTORY COTTS
2 WHITE HORSE CT
3 HAMMOND PL
4 MALDEN PL
5 LANGTON PL
6 LINDALE PL
7 MANOR CT
8 CHANCTONBURY WLK

140
120

119
100

A B C D E F

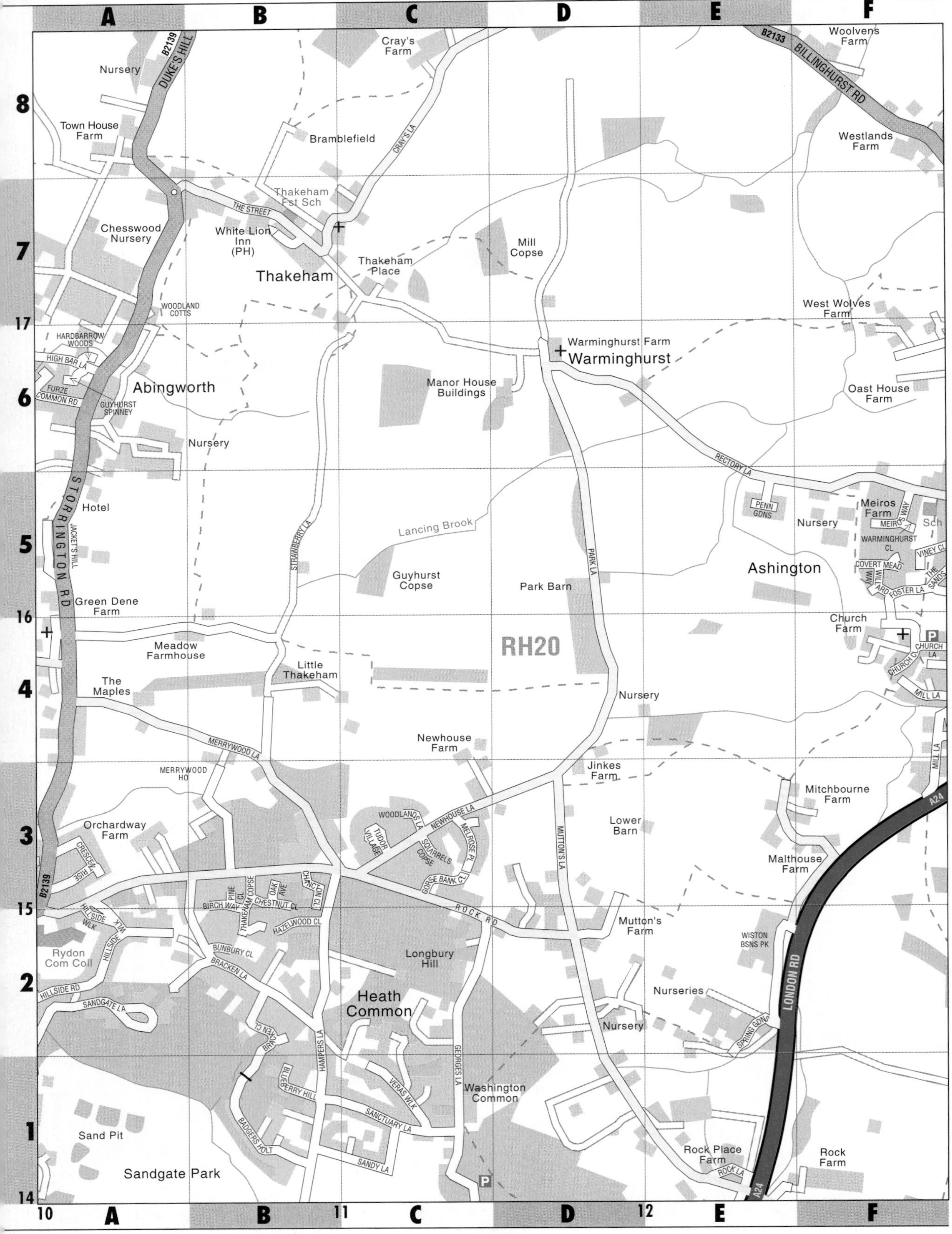
8
7
17
6
5
16
4
3
15
2
1
14
10
11
12
Cray's Farm
Woolvens Farm
B2133 BILLINGHURST RD
Nursery
B2139 DUKE'S HILL
Town House Farm
Bramblefield
CRAY'S LA
Westlands Farm
Thakeham Fst Sch
THE STREET
Chesswood Nursery
White Lion Inn (PH)
Mill Copse
Thakeham Place
Thakeham
WOODLAND COTTS
West Wolves Farm
HARDBARROW WOODS
HIGH BAR LA
Warminghurst Farm
Warminghurst
FURZE COMMON RD
Abingworth
GUYHURST SPINNEY
Manor House Buildings
Oast House Farm
Nursery
RECTORY LA
STORRINGTON RD
Hotel
PENN GDNS
Meiros Farm
MEIROS WAY
Sch
Nursery
WARMINGHURST CL
VINEY CL
Lancing Brook
JACKET'S HILL
STRAWBERRY LA
PARK LA
COVERT MEAD
THE SANDS
Ashington
WILLARD WAY
FOSTER LA
Guyhurst Copse
Park Barn
Green Dene Farm
Church Farm
CHURCH LA
CHURCH CL
Meadow Farmhouse
RH20
Little Thakeham
MILL LA
The Maples
Nursery
Newhouse Farm
MERRYWOOD LA
Jinkes Farm
MERRYWOOD HO
MILL LA
Mitchbourne Farm
A24
Orchardway Farm
WOODLANDS LA
NEWHOUSE LA
Lower Barn
TUDOR VILLAGE
MELROSE PL
MUTTON'S LA
CRESCENT RISE
SQUIRRELS COPSE
Malthouse Farm
CHANCTONBURY CL
GORSE BANK CL
B2139
PINE CL
OAK AVE
THAKEHAM COPSE
BIRCH WAY
CHESTNUT CL
ROCK RD
HILLSIDE WLK
HAZELWOOD CL
Mutton's Farm
WISTON BSNS PK
Rydon Com Coll
BUNBURY CL
HILLSIDE WLK
Longbury Hill
LONDON RD
BRACKEN LA
HILLSIDE RD
Nurseries
Heath Common
SANDGATE LA
Nursery
BRACKEN CL
SPRING GDNS
HAMPERS LA
BILBERRY HILL
GEORGES LA
VERAS WLK
Washington Common
SANCTUARY LA
BADGERS HOLT
Sand Pit
Rock Place Farm
Rock Farm
ROCK LA
SANDY LA
Sandgate Park
P
A24

A B C D E F

119
141

101
122

142
122

121
102

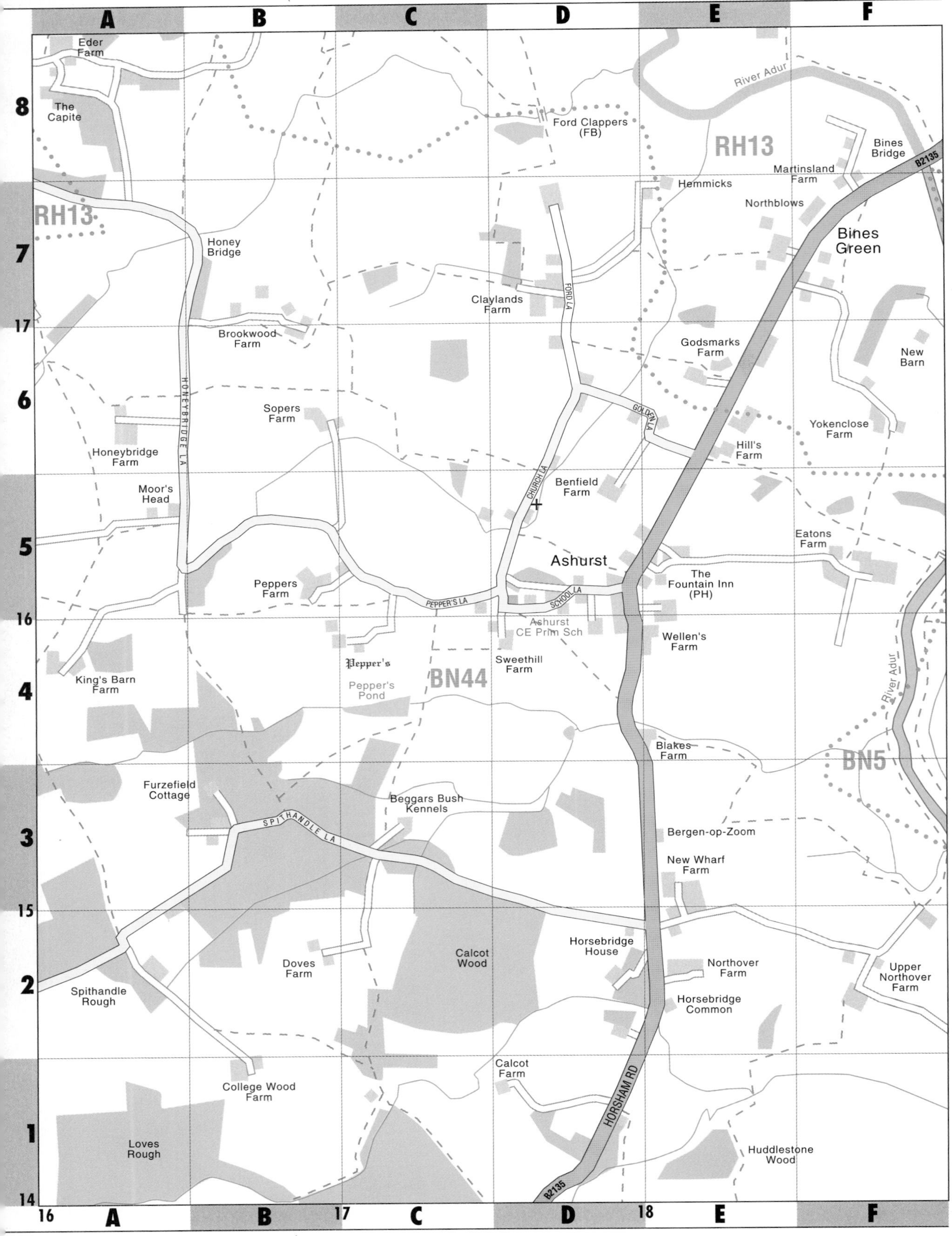
A
B
C
D
E
F
8
7
17
6
5
16
4
3
15
2
1
14
16
17
18
Eder Farm
The Capite
River Adur
Ford Clappers (FB)
RH13
Bines Bridge
B2135
Martinsland Farm
Hemmicks
Northblows
Bines Green
Honey Bridge
Claylands Farm
FORD LA
Brookwood Farm
Godsmarks Farm
New Barn
HONEYBRIDGE LA
Sopers Farm
GOLDEN LA
Yokenclose Farm
Hill's Farm
Honeybridge Farm
Benfield Farm
CHURCH LA
Moor's Head
Eatons Farm
Ashurst
The Fountain Inn (PH)
Peppers Farm
PEPPER'S LA
SCHOOL LA
Ashurst CE Prim Sch
Wellen's Farm
Pepper's
Sweethill Farm
King's Barn Farm
Pepper's Pond
BN44
Blakes Farm
BN5
Furzefield Cottage
Beggars Bush Kennels
SPITHANDLE LA
Bergen-op-Zoom
New Wharf Farm
Horsebridge House
Calcot Wood
Doves Farm
Northover Farm
Upper Northover Farm
Spithandle Rough
Horsebridge Common
Calcot Farm
College Wood Farm
HORSHAM RD
Loves Rough
Huddlestone Wood

121
143

103
124

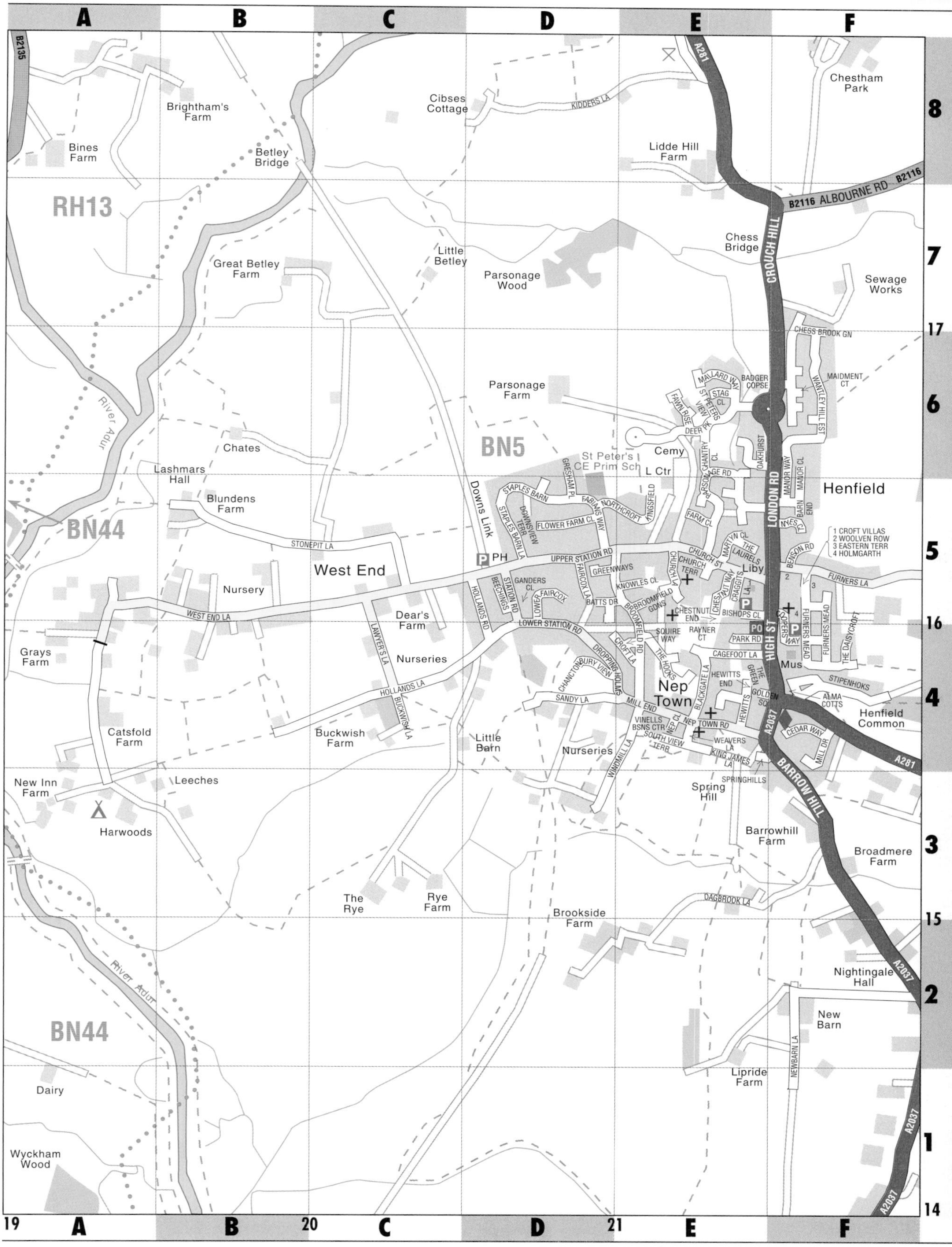
A
B
C
D
E
F
B2135
A281
Brightham's Farm
Bines Farm
Betley Bridge
Cibses Cottage
KIDDERS LA
Lidde Hill Farm
Chestham Park
B2116 ALBOURNE RD B2116
8
RH13
Great Betley Farm
Little Betley
Parsonage Wood
Chess Bridge
CROUCH HILL
Sewage Works
7
17
CHESS BROOK GN
MAIDMENT CT
WANTLEY HILL EST
MALLARD WAY
BADGER COPSE
STAG CL
ST PETERS VIEW
FAWN RISE
DEER PK
Parsonage Farm
River Adur
6
BN5
Chates
St Peter's CE Prim Sch
Cemy
L Ctr
CHANTRY CL
OAKHURST
MANOR WAY
MANOR CL
Lashmars Hall
Blundens Farm
Downs Link
GRESHAM PL
STAPLES BARN
STAPLES BARN LA
DOWNSVIEW TERR
FLOWER FARM CL
FABIANS WAY
NORTHCROFT
KINGSFIELD
FARM CL
LONDON RD
BARN END
NYES CL
Henfield
BN44
STONEPIT LA
PH
1 CROFT VILLAS
2 WOOLVEN ROW
3 EASTERN TERR
4 HOLMGARTH
5
West End
UPPER STATION RD
CHURCH LA
CHURCH TERR
CHURCH ST
MARTYN CL
THE LAURELS
BENSON RD
Liby
FURNERS LA
Nursery
GANDERS CL
FAIRCOX LA
GREENWAYS
KNOWLES CL
HOLLANDS RD
BEECHINGS
STATION RD
LOWER FAIRCOX
BATTS DR
BROOMFIELD GDNS
CHESTNUT END
CHESTNUT WAY
CRAGGITS LA
BISHOPS CL
COOPERS WAY
FURNERS MEAD
THE DAISYCROFT
WEST END LA
Dear's Farm
LOWER STATION RD
SQUIRE WAY
RAYNER CT
BROOMFIELD RD
PO
PARK RD
16
Grays Farm
LAWYER'S LA
Nurseries
CROFT LA
DROPPING HOLMS
THE HOOKS
CAGEFOOT LA
HIGH ST
Mus
CHANCTONBURY VIEW
HEWITTS END
THE GREEN
HEWITTS
STIPENHOKS
HOLLANDS LA
SANDY LA
Nep Town
BLACKGATE LA
GOLDEN SQ
ALMA COTTS
Henfield Common
4
Catsfold Farm
BUCKWISH LA
Buckwish Farm
Little Barn
MILL END
VINELLS BSNS CTR
NEP CL
NEP TOWN RD
SOUTH VIEW TERR
WEAVERS LA
A2037
CEDAR WAY
MILL DR
Nurseries
WINDMILL LA
KING JAMES LA
BARROW HILL
A281
New Inn Farm
Leeches
SPRINGHILLS
Spring Hill
Harwoods
Barrowhill Farm
3
Broadmere Farm
The Rye
Rye Farm
OAGBROOK LA
Brookside Farm
15
A2037
Nightingale Hall
2
New Barn
BN44
NEWBARN LA
Lipride Farm
Dairy
A2037
Wyckham Wood
1
A2037
14
19
20
21

144
124

123
104

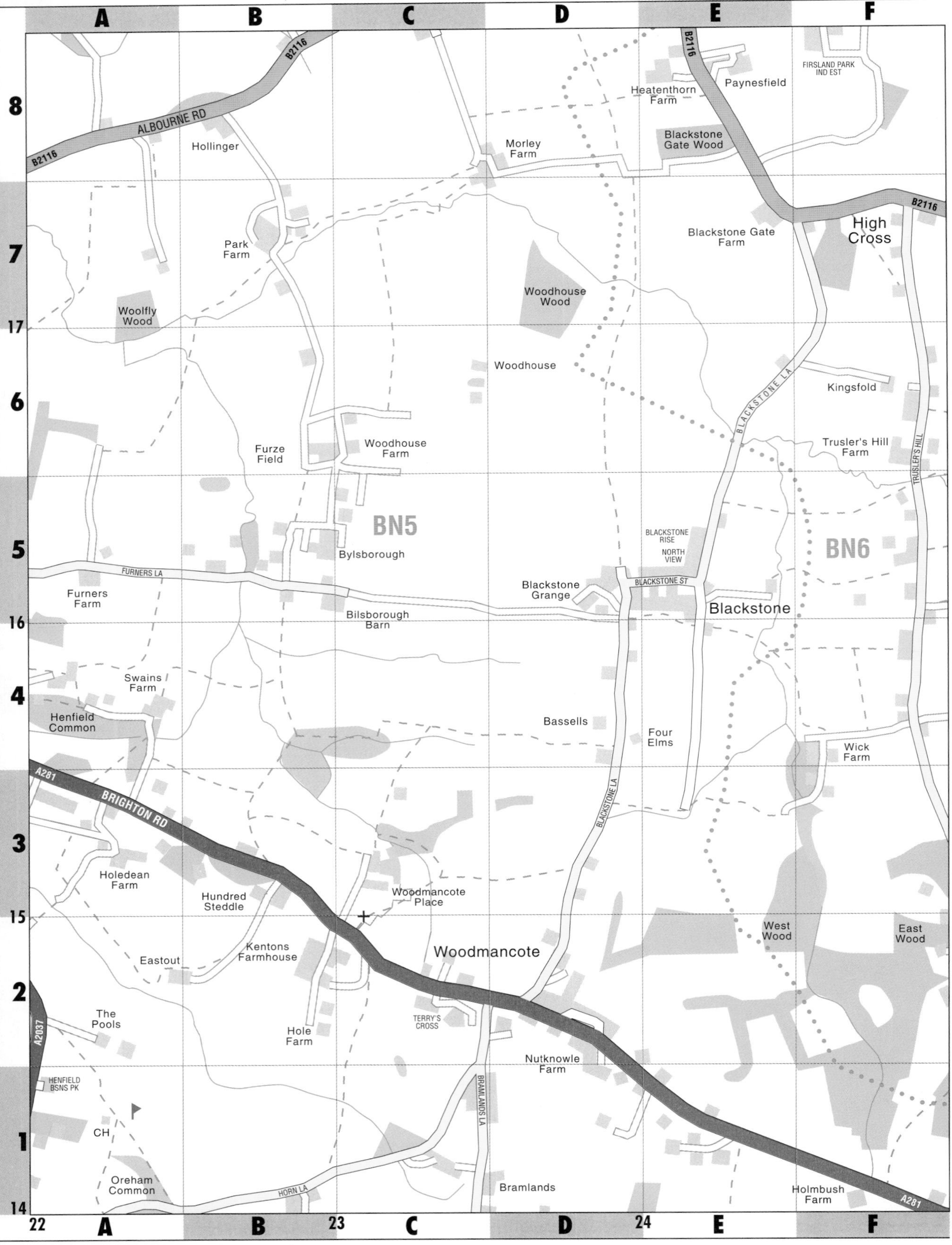
A
B
C
D
E
F
8
7
17
6
5
16
4
3
15
2
1
14
22
23
24
B2116
ALBOURNE RD
Hollinger
Morley Farm
Heatenthorn Farm
Paynesfield
FIRSLAND PARK IND EST
Blackstone Gate Wood
Park Farm
Blackstone Gate Farm
High Cross
Woolfly Wood
Woodhouse Wood
Woodhouse
Kingsfold
BLACKSTONE LA
Furze Field
Woodhouse Farm
Trusler's Hill Farm
TRUSLER'S HILL
BN5
BN6
Bylsborough
BLACKSTONE RISE
NORTH VIEW
FURNERS LA
Furners Farm
Blackstone Grange
BLACKSTONE ST
Blackstone
Bilsborough Barn
Swains Farm
Henfield Common
Bassells
Four Elms
Wick Farm
A281
BRIGHTON RD
Holedean Farm
Hundred Steddle
Woodmancote Place
West Wood
East Wood
Kentons Farmhouse
Eastout
Woodmancote
The Pools
A2037
Hole Farm
TERRY'S CROSS
Nutknowle Farm
HENFIELD BSNS PK
BRAMLANDS LA
CH
Oreham Common
HORN LA
Bramlands
Holmbush Farm

123
145

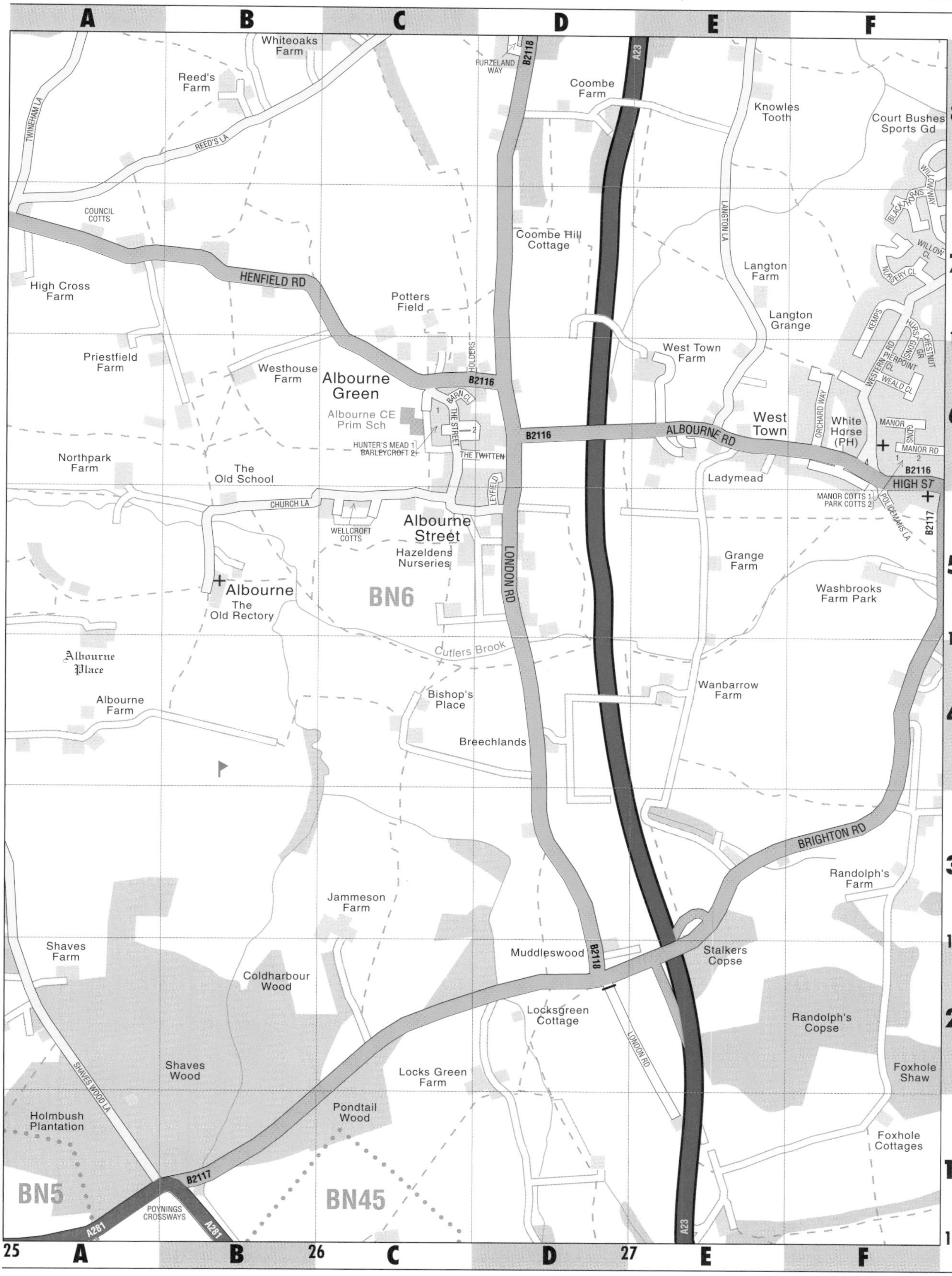
A
B
C
D
E
F
Whiteoaks Farm
Reed's Farm
FURZELAND WAY
B2118
A23
Coombe Farm
Knowles Tooth
Court Bushes Sports Gd
TWINEHAM LA
REED'S LA
COUNCIL COTTS
LANGTON LA
WILLOW WAY
BLACKTHORNS
WILLOW CL
NURSERY CL
Coombe Hill Cottage
HENFIELD RD
High Cross Farm
Potters Field
Langton Farm
Langton Grange
KEMPS
HURST GDNS
HURST GR
CHESTNUT
Priestfield Farm
HOLDERS
West Town Farm
Westhouse Farm
Albourne Green
B2116
BARN CL
ORCHARD WAY
WESTERN RD
PIERPOINT CL
WEALD CL
Albourne CE Prim Sch
THE STREET
West Town
White Horse (PH)
MANOR GDNS
MANOR RD
ALBOURNE RD
HUNTER'S MEAD 1
BARLEYCROFT 2
Northpark Farm
The Old School
THE TWITTEN
Ladymead
HIGH ST
LEYFIELD
CHURCH LA
MANOR COTTS 1
PARK COTTS 2
POLICEMANS LA
B2117
Albourne Street
WELLCROFT COTTS
Hazeldens Nurseries
LONDON RD
Grange Farm
Albourne
The Old Rectory
BN6
Washbrooks Farm Park
Cutlers Brook
Albourne Place
Wanbarrow Farm
Albourne Farm
Bishop's Place
Breechlands
BRIGHTON RD
Randolph's Farm
Jammeson Farm
Shaves Farm
Muddleswood
Stalkers Copse
Coldharbour Wood
Locksgreen Cottage
Randolph's Copse
Shaves Wood
SHAVES WOOD LA
Locks Green Farm
Foxhole Shaw
Holmbush Plantation
Pondtail Wood
Foxhole Cottages
BN5
BN45
A281
POYNINGS CROSSWAYS
8
7
17
6
5
16
4
3
15
2
1
14
25
26
27

125
106

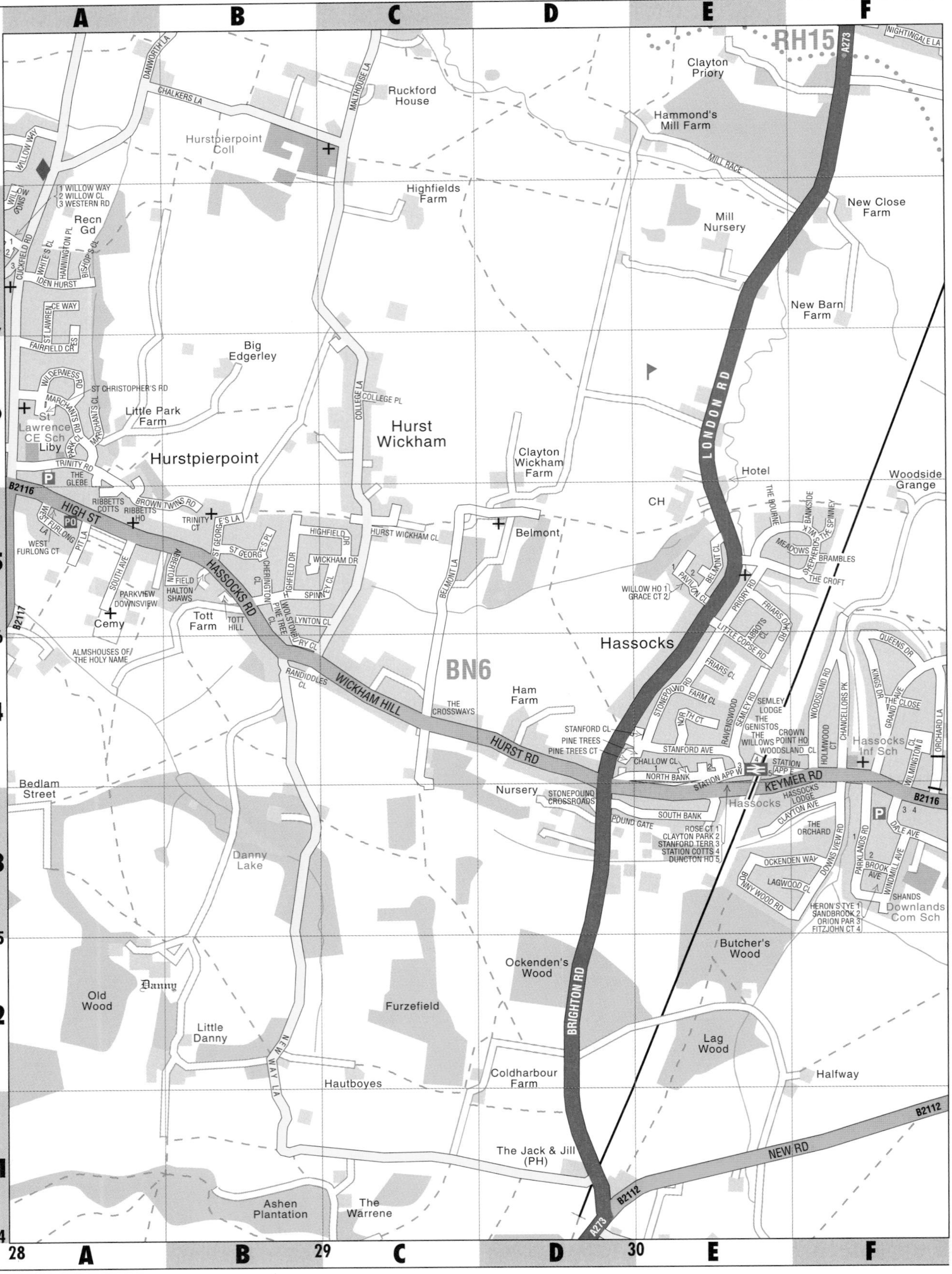
A B C D E F
8 7 17 6 5 16 4 3 15 2 1 14
28 29 30
RH15
A273
NIGHTINGALE LA
Clayton Priory
Ruckford House
DANWORTH LA
CHALKERS LA
MALTHOUSE LA
Hurstpierpoint Coll
Hammond's Mill Farm
MILL RACE
WILLOW WAY
1 WILLOW WAY
2 WILLOW CL
3 WESTERN RD
Highfields Farm
New Close Farm
Mill Nursery
Recn Gd
CUCKFIELD RD
WHITE'S CL
HANNINGTON PL
BISHOP'S CL
IDEN HURST
New Barn Farm
ST LAWRENCE WAY
FAIRFIELD CRES
Big Edgerley
WILDERNESS RD
ST CHRISTOPHER'S RD
COLLEGE LA
COLLEGE PL
St Lawrence CE Sch
Liby
Little Park Farm
Hurst Wickham
Clayton Wickham Farm
LONDON RD
Hurstpierpoint
TRINITY RD
THE GLEBE
Hotel
Woodside Grange
B2116
HIGH ST
RIBBETTS COTTS
RIBBETTS HO
BROWN TWINS RD
TRINITY CT
CH
THE BOURNE
BANKSIDE
THE SPINNEY
WEST FURLONG LA
WEST FURLONG CT
PIT LA
ST GEORGE'S LA
ST GEORGE'S PL
HIGHFIELD DR
WICKHAM DR
HURST WICKHAM CL
Belmont
MEADOWS
SHEPHERDS WALK
BRAMBLES
THE CROFT
SOUTH AVE
ABBERTON FIELD
HALTON SHAWS
PARKVIEW
DOWNSVIEW
CHERINGTON CL
HIGHFIELD DR
SPINNEY CL
HASSOCKS RD
BELMONT LA
PAVILION CL
BELMONT CL
WILLOW HO 1
GRACE CT 2
PRIORY RD
FRIARS OAK RD
Cemy
Tott Farm
TOTT HILL
PINE TREE CL
WOLSTONBURY CL
LYNTON CL
LITTLE COPSE RD
ABBOTS CL
B2117
Hassocks
ALMSHOUSES OF THE HOLY NAME
RANDIDDLES CL
WICKHAM HILL
BN6
FRIARS CL
QUEENS DR
Ham Farm
STONEPOUND RD
FARM CL
NORTH CT
WOODSLAND RD
CHANCELLORS PK
KINGS DR
THE CLOSE
GRAND AVE
ORCHARD LA
THE CROSSWAYS
RAVENSWOOD
SEMLEY RD
SEMLEY LODGE
THE GENISTOS
THE WILLOWS
CROWN POINT HO
HOLMWOOD CT
STANFORD CL
PINE TREES
PINE TREES CT
HURST RD
STANFORD AVE
WOODSLAND CL
Hassocks Inf Sch
WILMINGTON CL
CHALLOW CL
STATION APP E
NORTH BANK
STATION APP W
KEYMER RD
Bedlam Street
Nursery
STONEPOUND CROSSROADS
HASSOCKS LODGE
CLAYTON AVE
B2116
SOUTH BANK
POUND GATE
THE ORCHARD
PARKLANDS RD
DALE AVE
ROSE CT 1
CLAYTON PARK 2
STANFORD TERR 3
STATION COTTS 4
DUNCTON HO 5
DOWNS VIEW RD
Danny Lake
OCKENDEN WAY
LAGWOOD CL
BONNY WOOD RD
BROOK AVE
WINDMILL AVE
SHANDS
HERON'S TYE 1
SANDBROOK 2
ORION PAR 3
FITZJOHN CT 4
Downlands Com Sch
Butcher's Wood
Ockenden's Wood
Old Wood
Danny
BRIGHTON RD
Furzefield
Little Danny
NEW WAY LA
Lag Wood
Hautboyes
Coldharbour Farm
Halfway
B2112
NEW RD
The Jack & Jill (PH)
Ashen Plantation
The Warrene
A273
B2112

125
147

107

High Chimneys
Water Twr
The Blenheims
Wellhouse Farm
WELLHOUSE LA
Upper Furzefield
Fragbarrow Farm
Hopkin's Crank
Clearview Farm
RH15
The Oaks Poultry Farm
Ockley Wood
The Tole
Broadhill Farm
Townmead
Swansyard Farm
COMMON LA
COTTAGE HOMES
SOUTH VIEW
Ockley Manor Farm
Ockley Manor
Court Gardens Farm
Windmill
Oldland
BN6
Oaktree Farm
Stocks Farm
Sussex Border Path
ORCHARD LA
Keymer
DUMBRELLS COURT RD
DUMBRELLS CT
Lodge Hill
North End Farm
Newtons Farm
NORTH END
Ditchling
Stoneywish Country Park
Sewage Farm
Spatham Gardens Nursery
Ditchling Mus
HIGH ST
WEST ST
KEYMER RD
Prim Sch
East End
Cemy
BARNFIELD GDNS
Windmills Jun Sch
1 THE MINNELS
2 WILLOWBROOK WAY
3 THE POPLARS
4 ST ANNE'S GDNS
PARK AVE
CLAYTON RD
Lodge Farm
LEWES RD
NEVILL COTTS
NEW RD
The Nye
Bungalow Farm
Molehilly Shaw
Jointer Copse
Blackdog Hill
Millbrook Shaw
Ditchling Nurseries
Park Barn Farm
Wellcroft Shaw
Westminster Priory
NIGHTINGALE LA
GREENLANDS CL
GREENLANDS DR
1 FRANKLANDS WAY
2 FRANKLANDS GDNS
KEYMER RD
BROADLANDS
OCKLEY LA
OCKLEY HILL
MACKIE AVE
ANN CL
FARNHAM AVE
SWEETLANDS
MANOR AVE
OCKLEY WAY
BROMLEY CL
GRAND AVE
ADASTRA AVE
OLDLANDS AVE
DAMIAN WAY
NEWLANDS CL
CHURCH MEAD
F Ed Ctr
Liby
PH
PO
THE CRESCENT
SILVERDALE
HIGHLANDS CL
STAFFORD WAY
DALE AVE
KEYMER PK
BEACON HURST
LODGE HILL LA
BODDINGTONS LA
CHURCH LA
EAST GDNS
DYMOCK'S
THE MULBERRY LA
THE TWITTEN
EASTEND LA
FIELDWAY
FARM LA
SOUTH ST
CHARLTON GDNS
LONG PARK CNR
BEACON RD
NYE LA
SHIRLEYS
SPATHAM LA
B2112
B2116
LODGE LA
A B C D E F
8 7 17 6 5 16 4 3 15 2 1 14
31 32 33

148

A
B
C
D
E
F
8
7
13
6
5
12
4
3
11
2
1
10
71
72
73
Blendworth House
CRABDEN LA
Blendworth Farm
BLENDWORTH LA
Rectory
Blendworth Fst Sch
Blendworth
St Giles Farm
Cadlington House
Nobles Farm
Wick Farm
Wick Hanger
Oxleys Copse
Murrants Copse
Idsworth House
Idsworth Park
WOODHOUSE LA
ASHCROFT LA
Finchdean
The George (PH)
Finchdean Farm
IDSWORTH CL
ROWLANDS CASTLE RD
Eastlands
Woodhouse
Treadwheel Farm
TREADWHEEL RD
PO8
Pyle Farm
Motleys Copse
MAGPIE RD
DEAN LA
B2149
Calf Dell
MAGPIE COTTS
Sussex Border Path
The Holt
Monarch's Way
Cherry Row
Woodhouse Ashes Farm
Great Wellsworth
Stein Wood
PO9
WELLSWORTH LA
WELLSWOOD GDNS
MEADOWLANDS
HOLT GDNS
BOWES HILL
FINCHDEAN RD
GREATFIELD WAY
THE PEAK
BROAD CROFT
UPLANDS RD
LINKS LA
Horsefoot Hill
Rowlands Castle
The Sling
Recn Gd
Havant Thicket
THE FAIRWAY
PO
PH
Long Wood
CH
THE GREEN
Staunton Country Park
The Forest
Rowland's Castle
PO7
KINGS CL
CASTLE RD
LINKS CL
STANSTEAD CL
GLEN DALE
WOODBERRY LA
MANOR LODGE RD
KINGS WAY
ROYAL GDNS
NIGHTINGALE CL
KINGFISHER
DUNNOCK CL
Red Hill
REDHILL RD
YARDLEA CL
COLLEGE CL
Furzy Plain
BLACKCAP CL
THE DRIFT
MALLARD RD
Red Hill Farm
BRAMBLING RD 1
NUTHATCH CL 2
HILL BROW CL
Nightingale Bottom
HAZELDEAN DR
Upper Lake

108 130

A B C D E F
8 7 13 6 5 12 4 3 11 2 1 10
74 75 76
PO8
PO18
PO9
PO10
Manor Copse
Markwells Wood
Old Idsworth Garden
Lostlabour Copse
Horsley Farm
West Marden Hall
High Copse
Grub Copse
South Holt Farm
OLDHOUSE LA
Shortleys Copse
Adam's Copse
Northwood Farm
Bottom Copse
Lodge Farm
FOOTE LA
Forestside
Woods Copse
Forestside Farm
Deanlane End
Warren Down
Firtree Piece
Batty's Park
Wythy Piece
Drews Farm
Rosamond's Hill
Long Copse
Stanstead Forest
Forest Hanger
Lumley Seat
Hare Warren
Lumley Wood
North Coopers Wood
Stansted Park
Orange Grove
The Avenue
Monarch's Way
Horsepasture Farm
Lyels Wood
The Slip
South Coopers Wood
Stansted House
Sussex Border Path
Saw Mill

149 130

129
109

A B C D E F

8 7 13 6 5 12 4 3 11 2 1 10

DOWN COTTS
B2146
PH
NORE DOWN WAY
West Marden
Sewage Works
Wheatcroft
Nore Down
OLDHOUSE LA
Cabragh House
Busto Copse
Watergate Hanger
PO9
Broadreed Farm
Oak Copse
WOODLANDS LA
Woodlands Cottages
Park Slip
Locksash Farm
Malthouse Copse
LOCKSASH LA
Fanny's Row
Birchin Copse
Watergate Farm
Watergate Park
Monarch's Way
Lordington Copse
River Ems
Grevitts Copse
Dolly's Hanger
Lyecommon
Warren Copse
Haslett Copse
Woodbarn
PO18
Piglegged Row
Manor Farm
COOKS LA
The BarleyMow (PH)
BROOKLANDS COTTS
Walderton
Walderton Hill Plantation
Hill Farm
Blinkard Copse
Lower Farm
Lowerfarm Copse
Pitlands Farm
Holmes Row
Inholmes Wood
Dundarroch
Mitchamer Farm
MITCHAMER COTTS
Walderton Down

77 A B 78 C D 79 E F

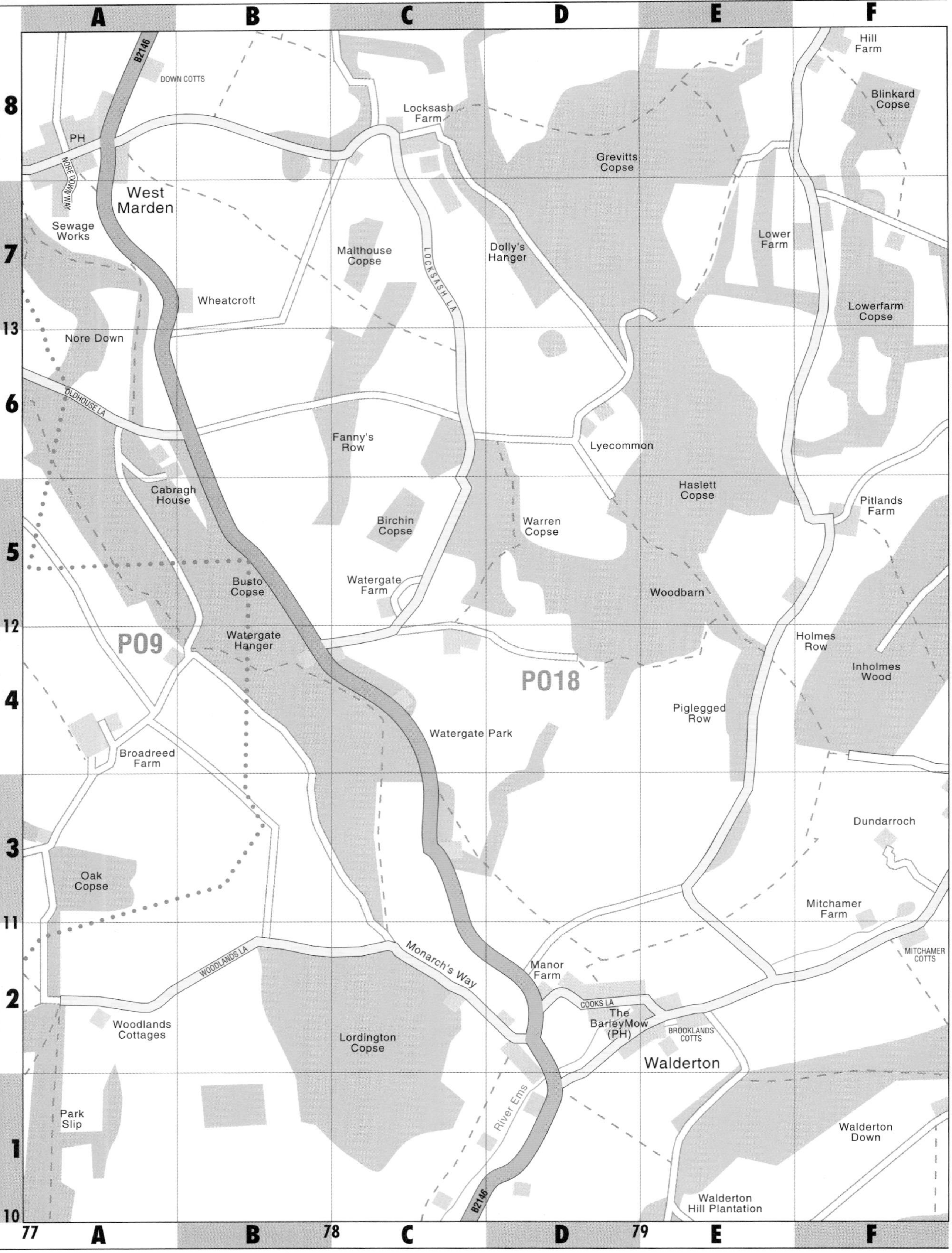

129
150

110
132

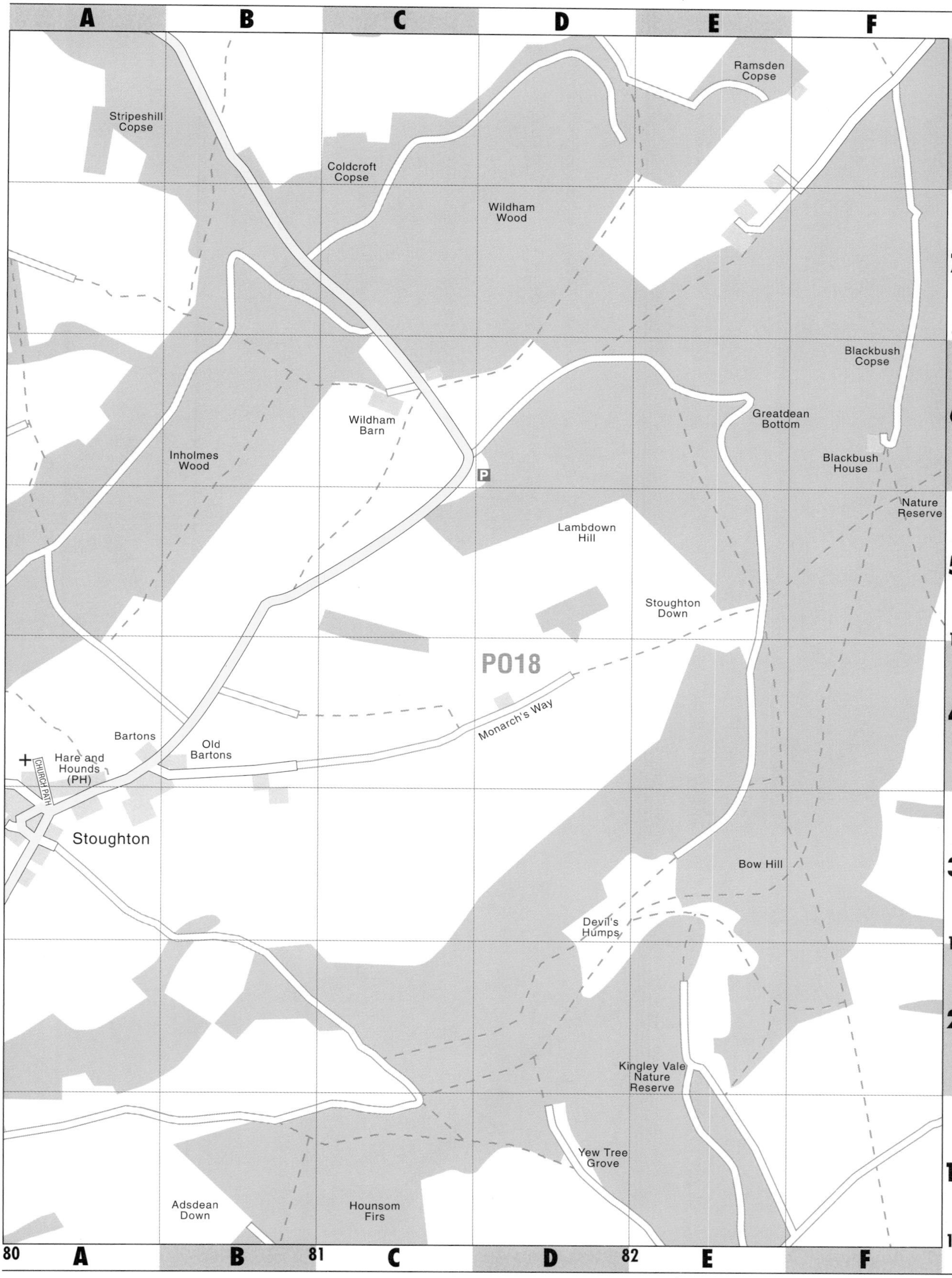
A
B
C
D
E
F
8
7
13
6
5
12
4
3
11
2
1
10
80
81
82
Stripeshill Copse
Coldcroft Copse
Wildham Wood
Ramsden Copse
Blackbush Copse
Greatdean Bottom
Blackbush House
Nature Reserve
Wildham Barn
Inholmes Wood
P
Lambdown Hill
Stoughton Down
PO18
Monarch's Way
Bartons
Old Bartons
Hare and Hounds (PH)
CHURCH PATH
Stoughton
Bow Hill
Devil's Humps
Kingley Vale Nature Reserve
Yew Tree Grove
Adsdean Down
Hounsom Firs

151
132

131
111

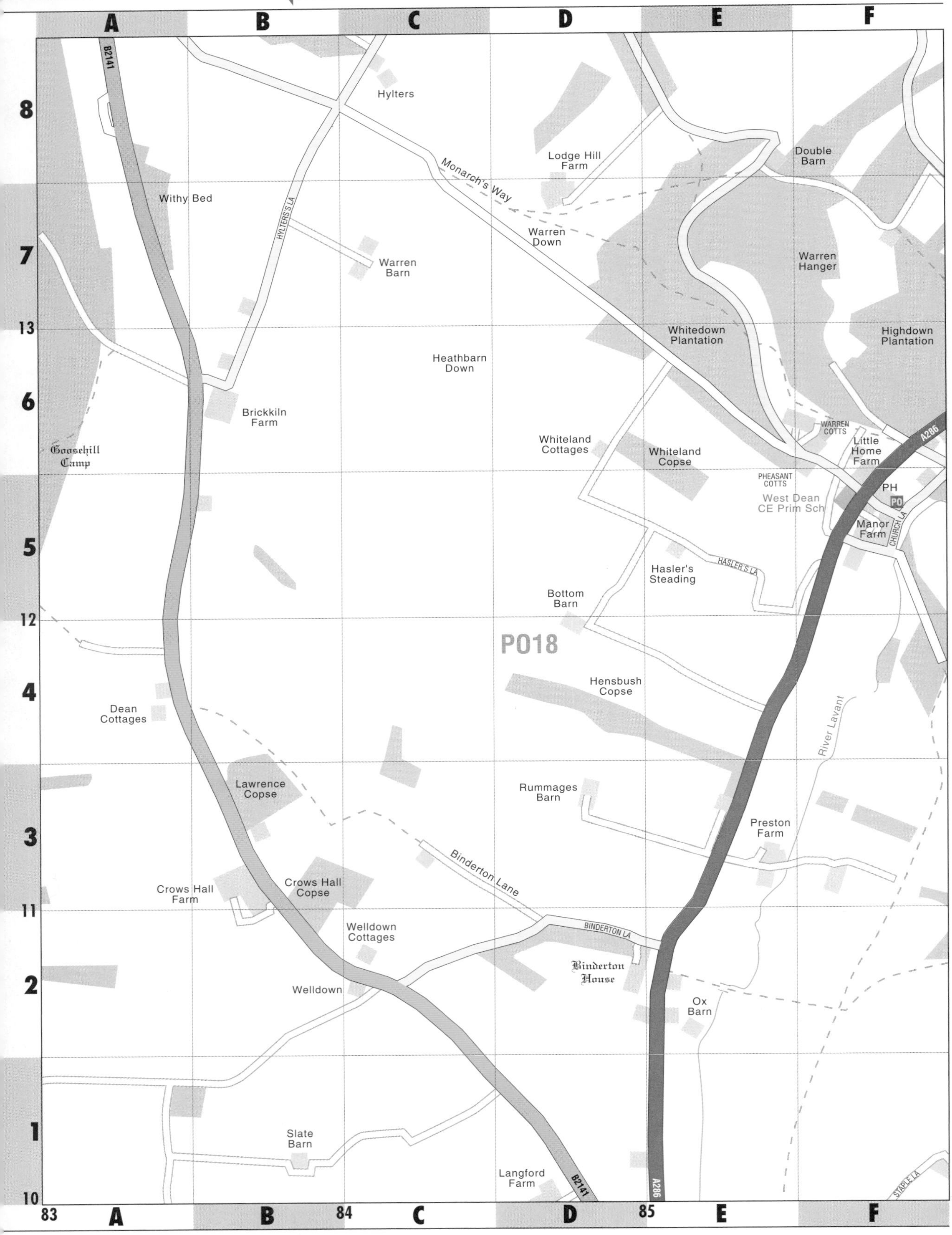
A
B
C
D
E
F
8
7
13
6
5
12
4
3
11
2
1
10
83
84
85
B2141
A286
Hylters
HYLTERS'S LA
Lodge Hill
Farm
Monarch's Way
Double
Barn
Withy Bed
Warren
Down
Warren
Barn
Warren
Hanger
Whitedown
Plantation
Highdown
Plantation
Heathbarn
Down
Brickkiln
Farm
WARREN
COTTS
Little
Home
Farm
Goosehill
Camp
Whiteland
Cottages
Whiteland
Copse
PHEASANT
COTTS
PH
PO
West Dean
CE Prim Sch
Manor
Farm
CHURCH LA
HASLER'S LA
Hasler's
Steading
Bottom
Barn
PO18
Hensbush
Copse
Dean
Cottages
River Lavant
Lawrence
Copse
Rummages
Barn
Preston
Farm
Binderton Lane
Crows Hall
Farm
Crows Hall
Copse
BINDERTON LA
Welldown
Cottages
Binderton
House
Welldown
Ox
Barn
Slate
Barn
Langford
Farm
STAPLE LA

131
152

112
134

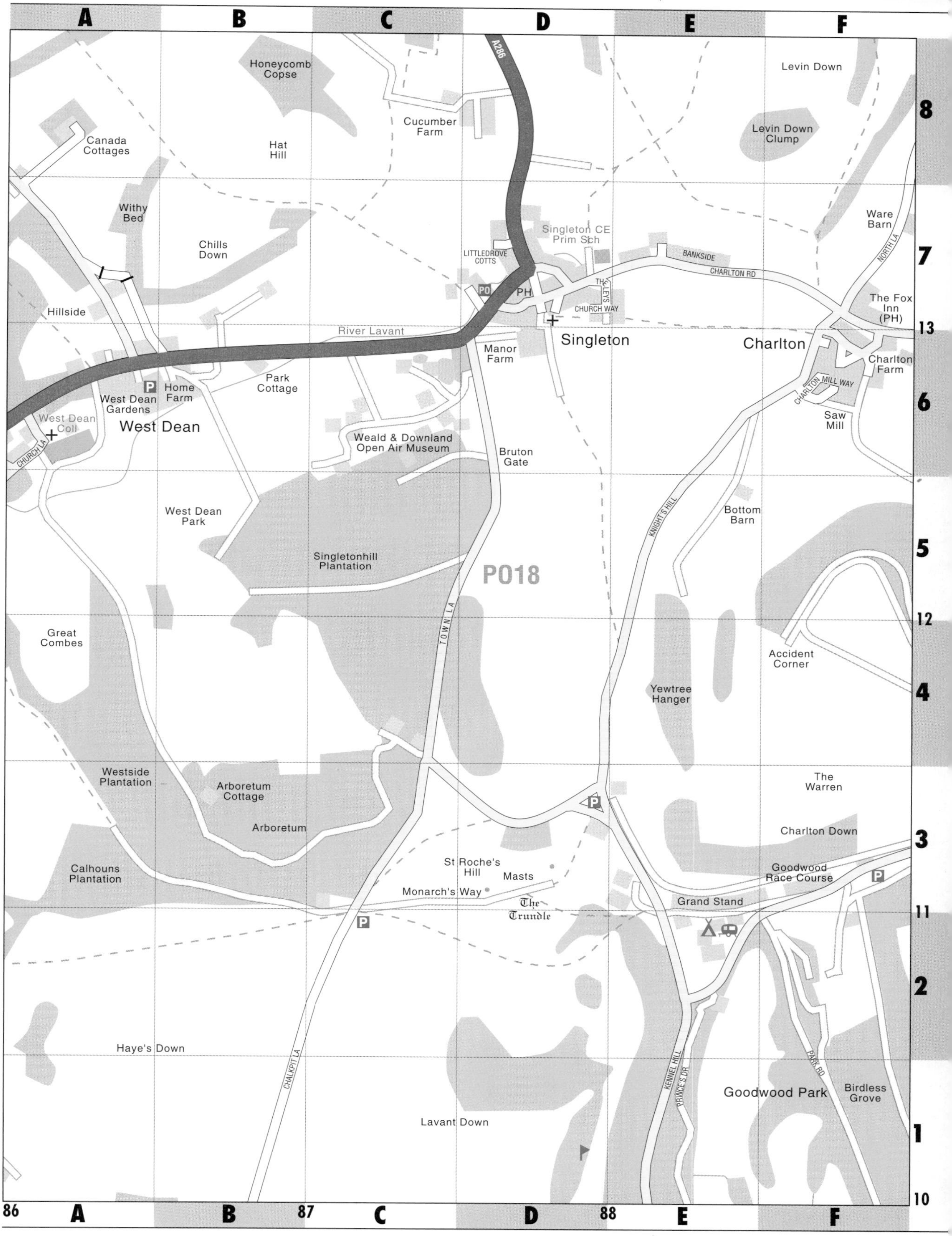
A
B
C
D
E
F
A286
Honeycomb
Copse
Levin Down
Canada
Cottages
Cucumber
Farm
Hat
Hill
Levin Down
Clump
Withy
Bed
Ware
Barn
Chills
Down
Singleton CE
Prim Sch
LITTLEDROVE
COTTS
BANKSIDE
CHARLTON RD
NORTH LA
THE LEYS
CHURCH WAY
PO
PH
The Fox
Inn
(PH)
Hillside
River Lavant
Singleton
Charlton
Manor
Farm
Charlton
Farm
CHARLTON MILL WAY
Park
Cottage
Home
Farm
West Dean
Gardens
West Dean
Coll
West Dean
CHURCH LA
Saw
Mill
Weald & Downland
Open Air Museum
Bruton
Gate
KNIGHT'S HILL
West Dean
Park
Bottom
Barn
Singletonhill
Plantation
PO18
TOWN LA
Great
Combes
Accident
Corner
Yewtree
Hanger
Westside
Plantation
Arboretum
Cottage
The
Warren
Arboretum
Charlton Down
Calhouns
Plantation
St Roche's
Hill
Masts
Goodwood
Race Course
Monarch's Way
The
Trundle
Grand Stand
Haye's Down
CHALKPIT LA
KENNEL HILL
PRINCE'S DR
PARK RD
Goodwood Park
Birdless
Grove
Lavant Down
8
7
13
6
5
12
4
3
11
2
1
10
86
87
88

153
134

133
113

Court Hill
Halfmoon Piece
Green Hill
New Barn
Highdown Croft
High Down
NORTH LA
COURTYARD LA
NEWHOUSE LA
NEW RD
PH
Ide's Barn
CHARLTON RD
DROKE LA
MAIN RD
PO
CHAPEL ROW
Manor Farm
East Dean
Wallerdean Hill
Bubholts
Shotter's Ground
EASTDEAN HILL
Chiseldown
Potcomb
Charlton Park
Park Hill
PO18
Monarch's Way
Eastdean Park
Eastdean Hill
Goodwood Country Park
SELHURSTPARK RD
CHALK RD
Pilleygreen Lodges
P
Open Winkins
Appletree Bottom
The Plantation
Red Copse
Molecomb Peak
Little Copse
MOLECOMB BROADWALK
Halnaker Gallop
Ladys Winkins
Halnaker Park
Hat Hill
Denge Bottom
Molecomb
A
B
C
D
E
F
8
7
13
6
5
12
4
3
11
2
1
10
89
90
91

133
154

114
136
A
B
C
D
E
F
Heath Hill
A285
Malecomb
Upwaltham
Upwaltham Farm
Oxen Down
Lambdown Bottom
Shepherd's Copse
Deep Coombe
DROKE LA
Droke
Bonney's Hanger
GU28
Upwaltham Hill
Droke Hanger
Astead Down
Benges Wood
Stubbs Wood
Selhurstpark Hill
North Wood
Selhurst Forest Walk
SELHURSTPARK RD
St Mary's Farm
Selhurst Park
PO18
Eartham Wood
Ide's Common
St Mary's Wood
Selhurst Park Farm
Jackdine Farm
Eartham Trail
Monarch's Way
Middle Barn
The Rough
Wood Cottage
North Barn Farm
Bushy Copse
Nore Hill Plantation
A285
8
7
13
6
5
12
4
3
11
2
1
10
92
93
94
155
136

135
115

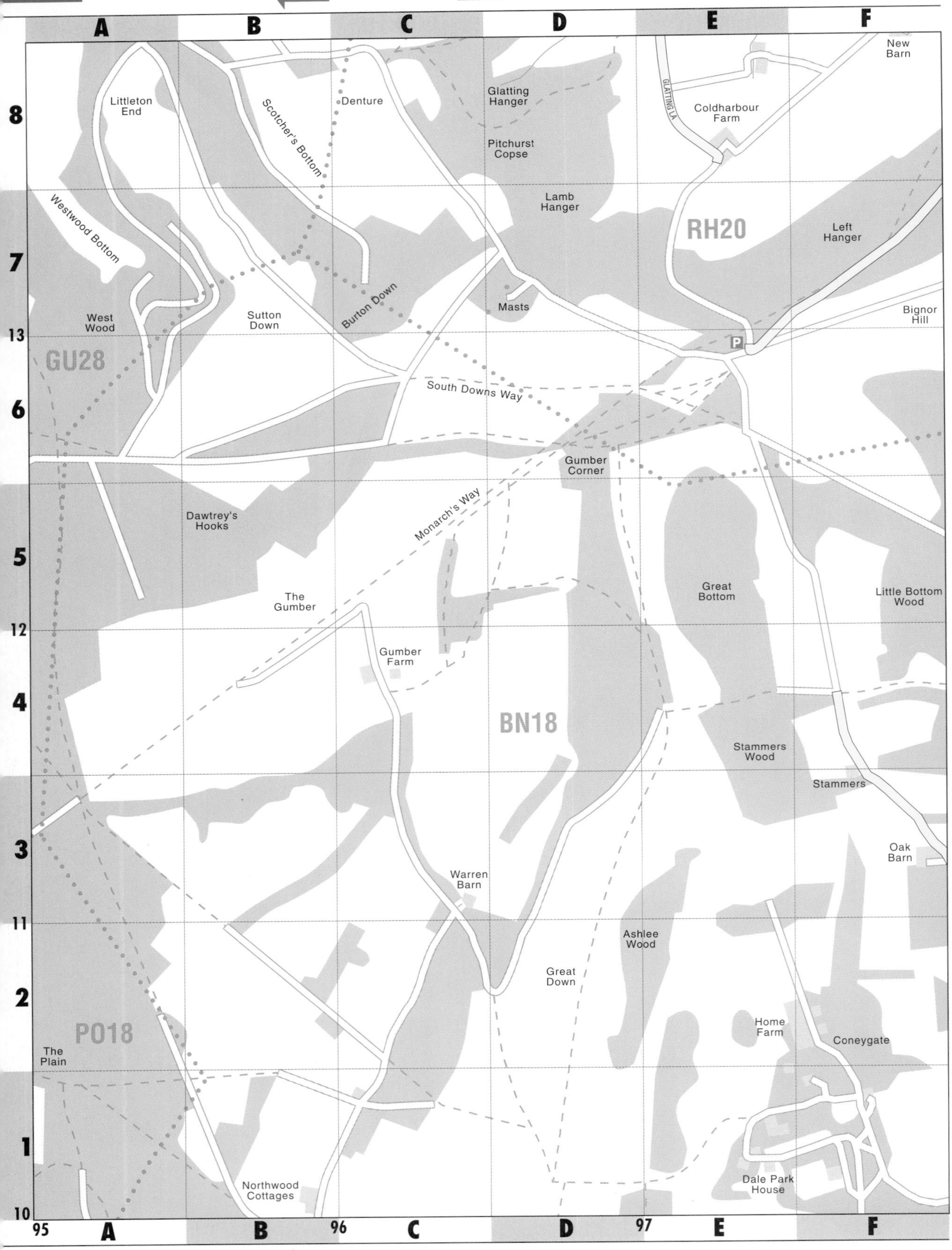
A
B
C
D
E
F
8
7
13
6
5
12
4
3
11
2
1
10
95
96
97
Littleton End
Denture
Glatting Hanger
Scotcher's Bottom
GLATTING LA
Coldharbour Farm
New Barn
Pitchurst Copse
Lamb Hanger
Westwood Bottom
RH20
Left Hanger
Burton Down
Masts
West Wood
Sutton Down
Bignor Hill
GU28
South Downs Way
Gumber Corner
Dawtrey's Hooks
Monarch's Way
Great Bottom
Little Bottom Wood
The Gumber
Gumber Farm
BN18
Stammers Wood
Stammers
Oak Barn
Warren Barn
Ashlee Wood
Great Down
Home Farm
Coneygate
PO18
The Plain
Northwood Cottages
Dale Park House

135
156

116
138

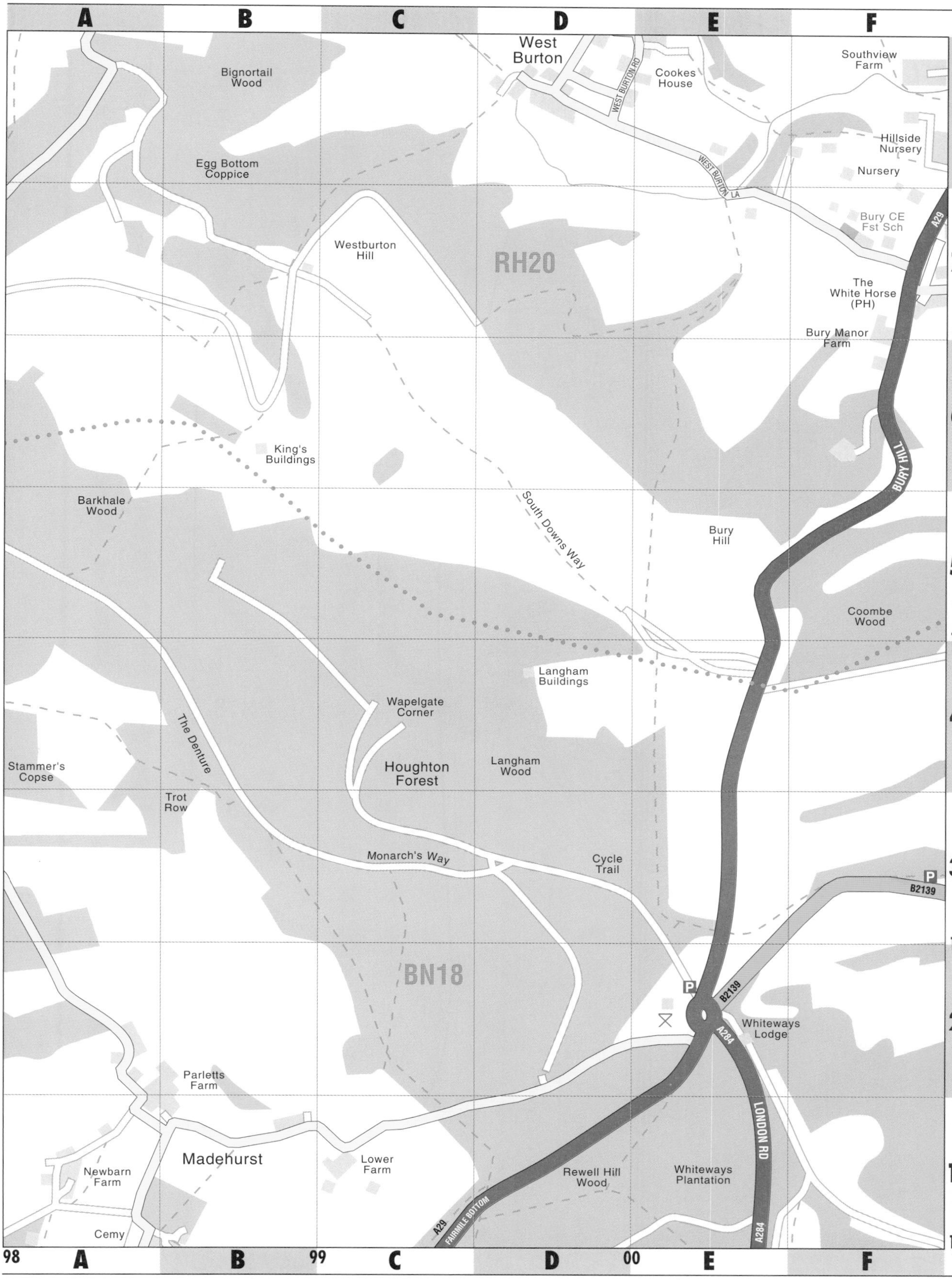
A
B
C
D
E
F
West Burton
Bignortail Wood
Cookes House
WEST BURTON RD
Southview Farm
8
Hillside Nursery
Nursery
Egg Bottom Coppice
WEST BURTON LA
Bury CE Fst Sch
A29
Westburton Hill
RH20
7
The White Horse (PH)
Bury Manor Farm
13
6
King's Buildings
BURY HILL
Barkhale Wood
South Downs Way
Bury Hill
5
Coombe Wood
12
Langham Buildings
Wapelgate Corner
4
The Denture
Stammer's Copse
Houghton Forest
Langham Wood
Trot Row
Monarch's Way
Cycle Trail
3
P
B2139
11
BN18
P
B2139
2
Whiteways Lodge
A284
Parletts Farm
LONDON RD
Madehurst
Lower Farm
Newbarn Farm
Rewell Hill Wood
Whiteways Plantation
1
A29
FAIRMILE BOTTOM
A284
Cemy
10
98
A
B
99
C
D
00
E
F

157
138

137
117

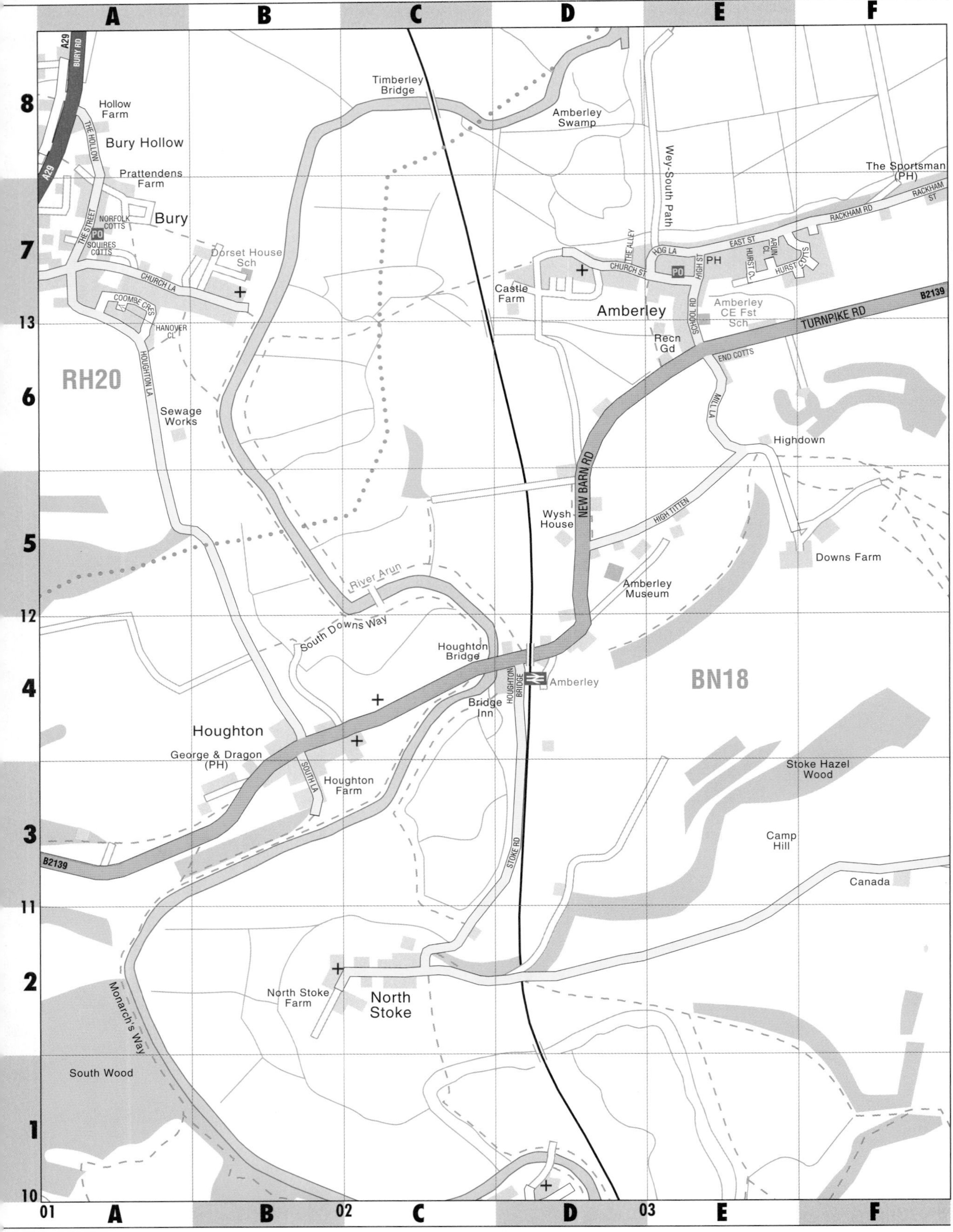
Hollow Farm
Bury Hollow
Prattendens Farm
Bury
Dorset House Sch
Timberley Bridge
Amberley Swamp
Wey-South Path
The Sportsman (PH)
RACKHAM RD
RACKHAM ST
Castle Farm
Amberley
Amberley CE Fst Sch
Recn Gd
TURNPIKE RD
B2139
END COTTS
MILL LA
Highdown
RH20
Sewage Works
NEW BARN RD
Wysh House
HIGH TITTEN
Downs Farm
River Arun
Amberley Museum
South Downs Way
Houghton Bridge
Amberley
BN18
Bridge Inn
Houghton
George & Dragon (PH)
Houghton Farm
Stoke Hazel Wood
Camp Hill
Canada
STOKE RD
North Stoke Farm
North Stoke
Monarch's Way
South Wood
THE HOLLOW
THE STREET
NORFOLK COTTS
SQUIRES COTTS
CHURCH LA
COOMBE CRES
HANOVER CL
HOUGHTON LA
SOUTH LA
HOUGHTON BRIDGE
CHURCH ST
HOG LA
THE ALLEY
HIGH ST
SCHOOL RD
EAST ST
HURST CL
ARUN CL
HURST COTTS
BURY RD
A29
PO
PH

137
158

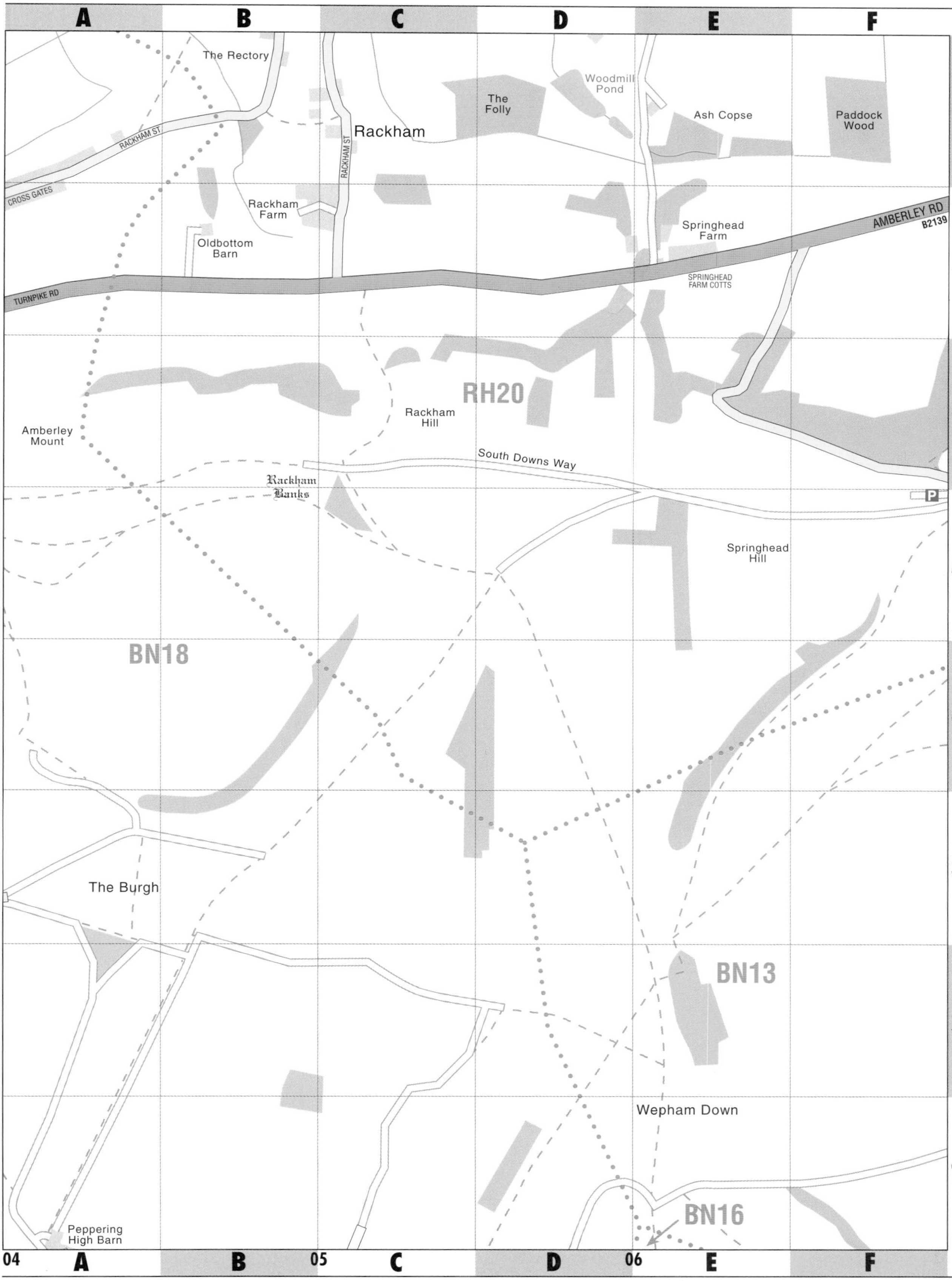
A
B
C
D
E
F
The Rectory
Woodmill Pond
The Folly
Ash Copse
Paddock Wood
Rackham
RACKHAM ST
RACKHAM ST
CROSS GATES
Rackham Farm
Oldbottom Barn
Springhead Farm
AMBERLEY RD
B2139
TURNPIKE RD
SPRINGHEAD FARM COTTS
RH20
Rackham Hill
Amberley Mount
South Downs Way
Rackham Banks
P
Springhead Hill
BN18
The Burgh
BN13
Wepham Down
BN16
Peppering High Barn
8
7
13
6
5
12
4
3
11
2
1
10
04
05
06

139
119

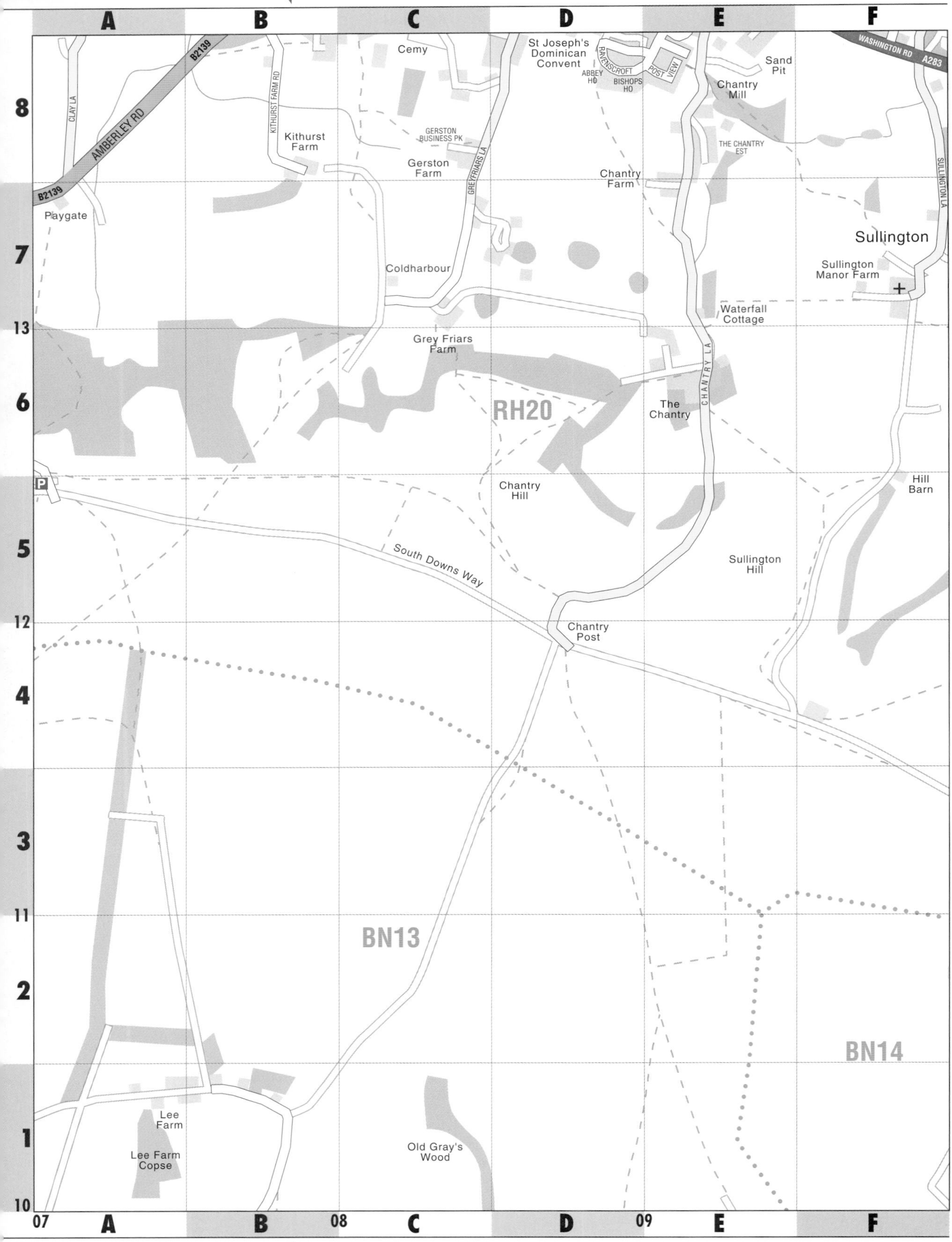
A
B
C
D
E
F
Cemy
St Joseph's Dominican Convent
RAVENSCROFT
POST VIEW
ABBEY HO
BISHOPS HO
Sand Pit
WASHINGTON RD
A283
Chantry Mill
B2139
CLAY LA
AMBERLEY RD
KITHURST FARM RD
Kithurst Farm
GERSTON BUSINESS PK
Gerston Farm
GREYFRIARS LA
THE CHANTRY EST
Chantry Farm
SULLINGTON LA
B2139
Paygate
Sullington
Coldharbour
Sullington Manor Farm
Waterfall Cottage
Grey Friars Farm
CHANTRY LA
RH20
The Chantry
P
Chantry Hill
Hill Barn
South Downs Way
Sullington Hill
Chantry Post
BN13
BN14
Lee Farm
Lee Farm Copse
Old Gray's Wood
8
7
13
6
5
12
4
3
11
2
1
10
07
08
09

139
160

120
142

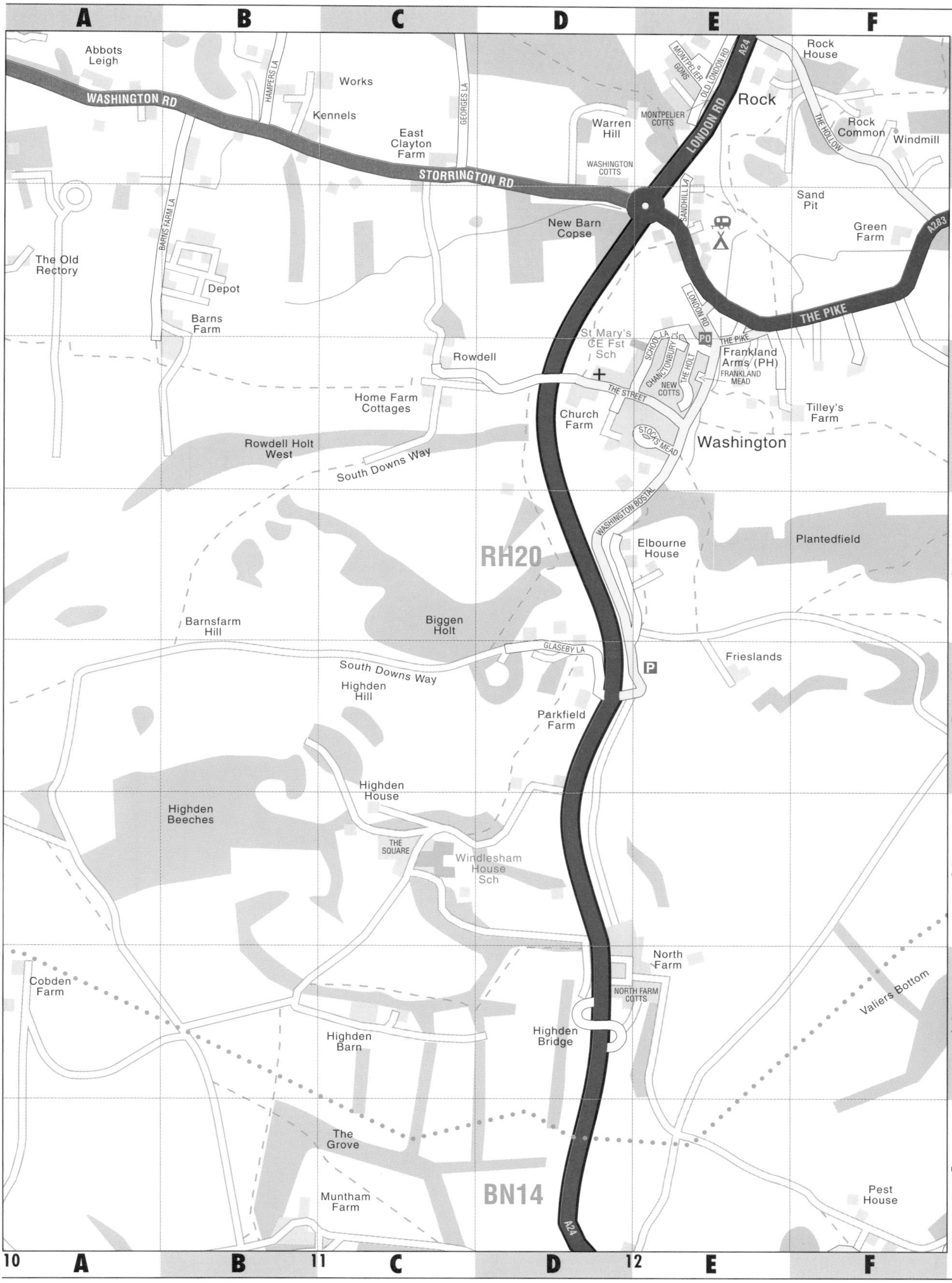
A
B
C
D
E
F
Abbots Leigh
WASHINGTON RD
HAMPERS LA
Works
Kennels
GEORGES LA
East Clayton Farm
STORRINGTON RD
Warren Hill
MONTPELIER COTTS
WASHINGTON COTTS
MONTPELIER GDNS
OLD LONDON RD
A24
LONDON RD
Rock
Rock House
THE HOLLOW
Rock Common
Windmill
Sand Pit
Green Farm
A283
SANDHILL LA
New Barn Copse
BARNS FARM LA
The Old Rectory
Depot
Barns Farm
St Mary's CE Fst Sch
SCHOOL LA
CHANCTONBURY CL
THE HOLT
NEW COTTS
FRANKLAND MEAD
THE PIKE
Frankland Arms (PH)
Tilley's Farm
Rowdell
Home Farm Cottages
THE STREET
Church Farm
STOCKS MEAD
Washington
Rowdell Holt West
South Downs Way
WASHINGTON BOSTAL
Elbourne House
Plantedfield
RH20
Barnsfarm Hill
Biggen Holt
GLASEBY LA
Frieslands
Highden Hill
Parkfield Farm
Highden House
Highden Beeches
THE SQUARE
Windlesham House Sch
North Farm
NORTH FARM COTTS
Cobden Farm
Highden Barn
Highden Bridge
Valiers Bottom
The Grove
Muntham Farm
BN14
Pest House
8
7
13
6
5
12
4
3
11
2
1
10
10
11
12

161
142

141
121

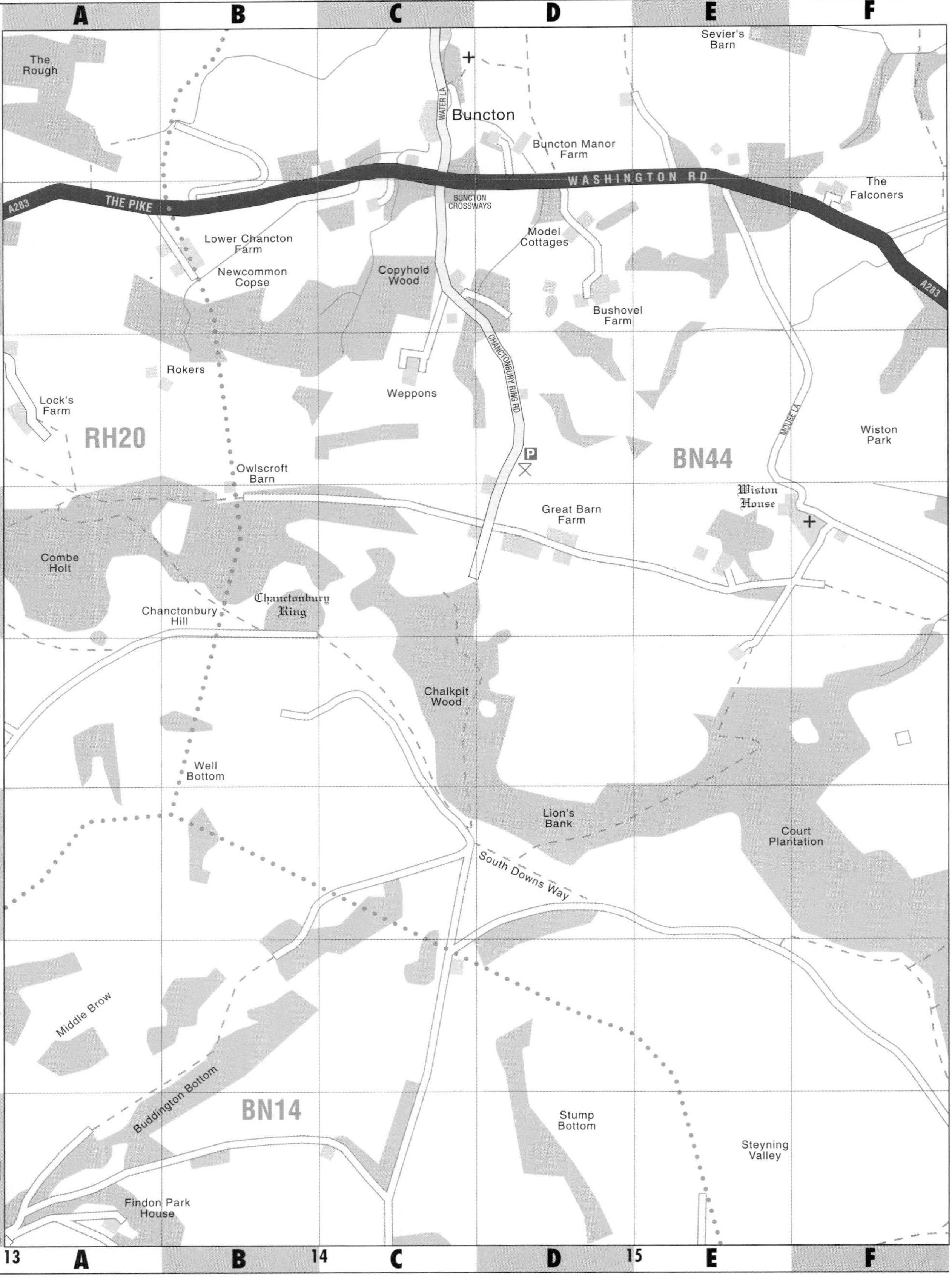
A
B
C
D
E
F
8
7
13
6
5
12
4
3
11
2
1
10
14
15
The Rough
Sevier's Barn
Buncton
WATER LA
Buncton Manor Farm
WASHINGTON RD
The Falconers
A283
THE PIKE
BUNCTON CROSSWAYS
Lower Chancton Farm
Newcommon Copse
Copyhold Wood
Model Cottages
Bushovel Farm
CHANCTONBURY RING RD
Rokers
Lock's Farm
Weppons
RH20
MOUSE LA
Wiston Park
BN44
Owlscroft Barn
Great Barn Farm
Wiston House
Combe Holt
Chanctonbury Hill
Chanctonbury Ring
Chalkpit Wood
Well Bottom
Lion's Bank
Court Plantation
South Downs Way
Middle Brow
Buddington Bottom
BN14
Stump Bottom
Steyning Valley
Findon Park House

141
162

122 144

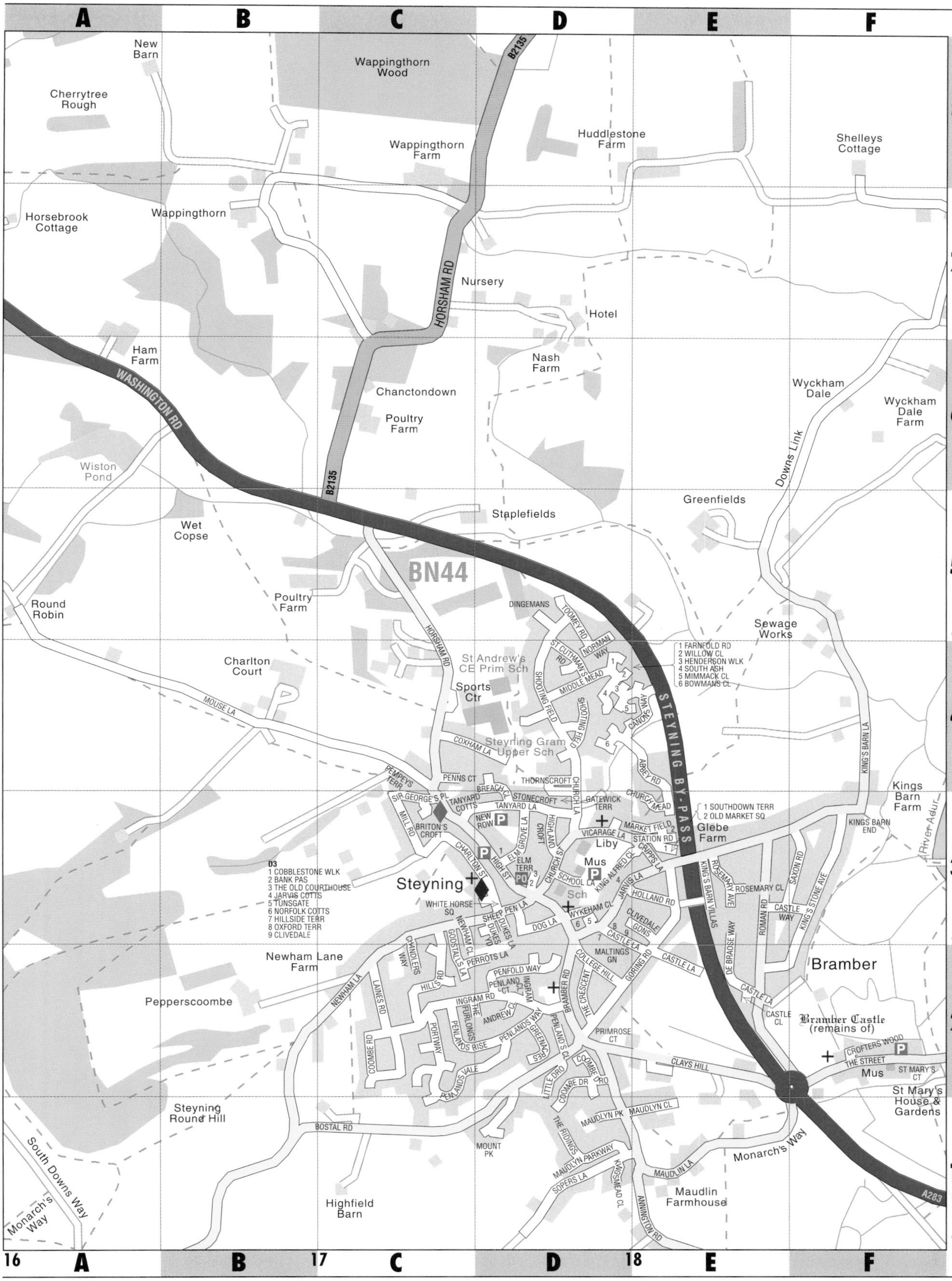

A B C D E F
8 7 6 5 4 3 2 1
13 12 11 10
16 17 18
New Barn
Cherrytree Rough
Wappingthorn Wood
B2135
Wappingthorn Farm
Huddlestone Farm
Shelleys Cottage
Horsebrook Cottage
Wappingthorn
HORSHAM RD
Nursery
Hotel
Ham Farm
Nash Farm
WASHINGTON RD
Chanctondown
Poultry Farm
Wyckham Dale
Wyckham Dale Farm
Downs Link
Wiston Pond
Greenfields
Staplefields
Wet Copse
BN44
Round Robin
Poultry Farm
DINGEMANS
Sewage Works
Charlton Court
St Andrew's CE Prim Sch
Sports Ctr
MOUSE LA
Steyning Gram Upper Sch
STEYNING BY-PASS
1 FARNFOLD RD
2 WILLOW CL
3 HENDERSON WLK
4 SOUTH ASH
5 MIMMACK CL
6 BOWMANS CL
KING'S BARN LA
Kings Barn Farm
1 SOUTHDOWN TERR
2 OLD MARKET SQ
Glebe Farm
KINGS BARN END
River Adur
D3
1 COBBLESTONE WLK
2 BANK PAS
3 THE OLD COURTHOUSE
4 JARVIS COTTS
5 TUNSGATE
6 NORFOLK COTTS
7 HILLSIDE TERR
8 OXFORD TERR
9 CLIVEDALE
Steyning
Liby
Mus
Sch
Newham Lane Farm
Bramber
Pepperscoombe
Bramber Castle (remains of)
Mus
St Mary's House & Gardens
Steyning Round Hill
BOSTAL RD
MOUNT PK
Monarch's Way
South Downs Way
Maudlin Farmhouse
Highfield Barn
A283

163 144

143
123

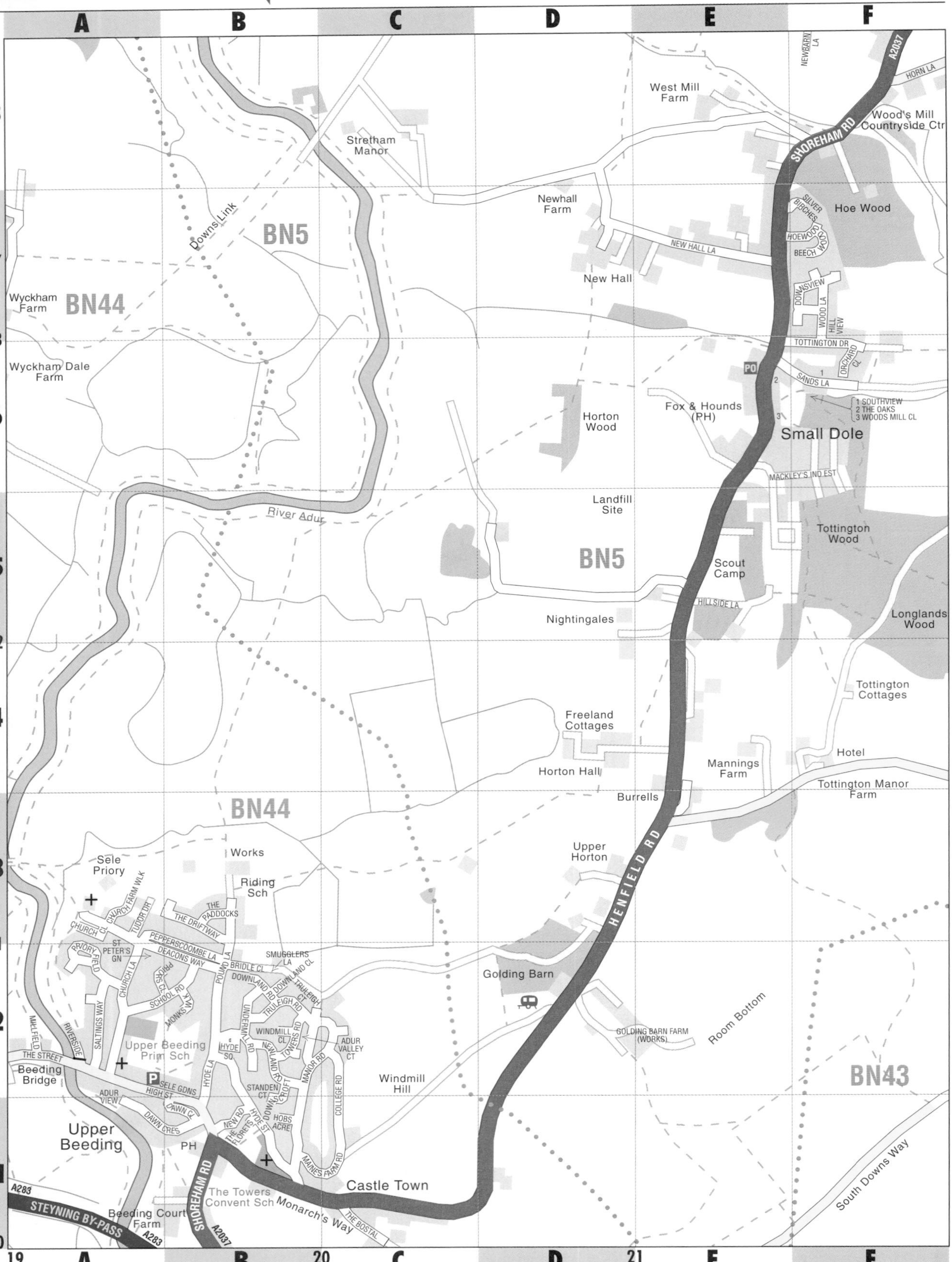
A
B
C
D
E
F
8
7
13
6
5
12
4
3
11
2
1
10
19
20
21
West Mill Farm
Wood's Mill Countryside Ctr
Stretham Manor
NEWBARN LA
A2037
HORN LA
SHOREHAM RD
Newhall Farm
Hoe Wood
SILVER BIRCHES
HOEWOOD
WOOD
BEECH
NEW HALL LA
Downs Link
BN5
New Hall
Wyckham Farm
BN44
DOWNSVIEW
WOOD LA
HILL VIEW
TOTTINGTON DR
ORCHARD CL
Wyckham Dale Farm
PO
SANDS LA
1 SOUTHVIEW
2 THE OAKS
3 WOODS MILL CL
Horton Wood
Fox & Hounds (PH)
Small Dole
MACKLEY'S IND EST
Landfill Site
River Adur
Tottington Wood
BN5
Scout Camp
HILLSIDE LA
Nightingales
Longlands Wood
Tottington Cottages
Freeland Cottages
Hotel
Mannings Farm
Horton Hall
Tottington Manor Farm
Burrells
BN44
Upper Horton
Works
Sele Priory
Riding Sch
HENFIELD RD
CHURCH FARM WLK
TUDOR DR
THE PADDOCKS
THE DRIFTWAY
CHURCH CL
PRIORY FIELD
ST PETER'S GN
PEPPERSCOOMBE LA
DEACONS WAY
CHURCH LA
PRIORS CL
SCHOOL RD
MONKS WALK
POUND LA
BRIDLE CL
SMUGGLERS LA
DOWNLAND CL
DOWNLAND RD
TRULEIGH CT
TRULEIGH RD
UNDERMILL RD
WINDMILL CL
NEWLAND RD
TOWERS RD
ADUR VALLEY CT
MANOR RD
Golding Barn
GOLDING BARN FARM (WORKS)
Room Bottom
MILLFIELD
RIVERSIDE
SALTINGS WAY
Upper Beeding Prim Sch
HYDE SQ
HYDE LA
THE STREET
Beeding Bridge
P
SELE GDNS
HIGH ST
ADUR VIEW
STANDEN CT
CROFT
DOWN
COLLEGE RD
Windmill Hill
BN43
DAWN CL
DAWN CRES
NEW RD
THE FLORETS
HYDE ST
HOBS ACRE
MAINES FARM RD
Upper Beeding
PH
A283
STEYNING BY-PASS
SHOREHAM RD
The Towers Convent Sch
Castle Town
Monarch's Way
Beeding Court Farm
A283
A2037
THE BOSTAL
South Downs Way

143
164

124
146
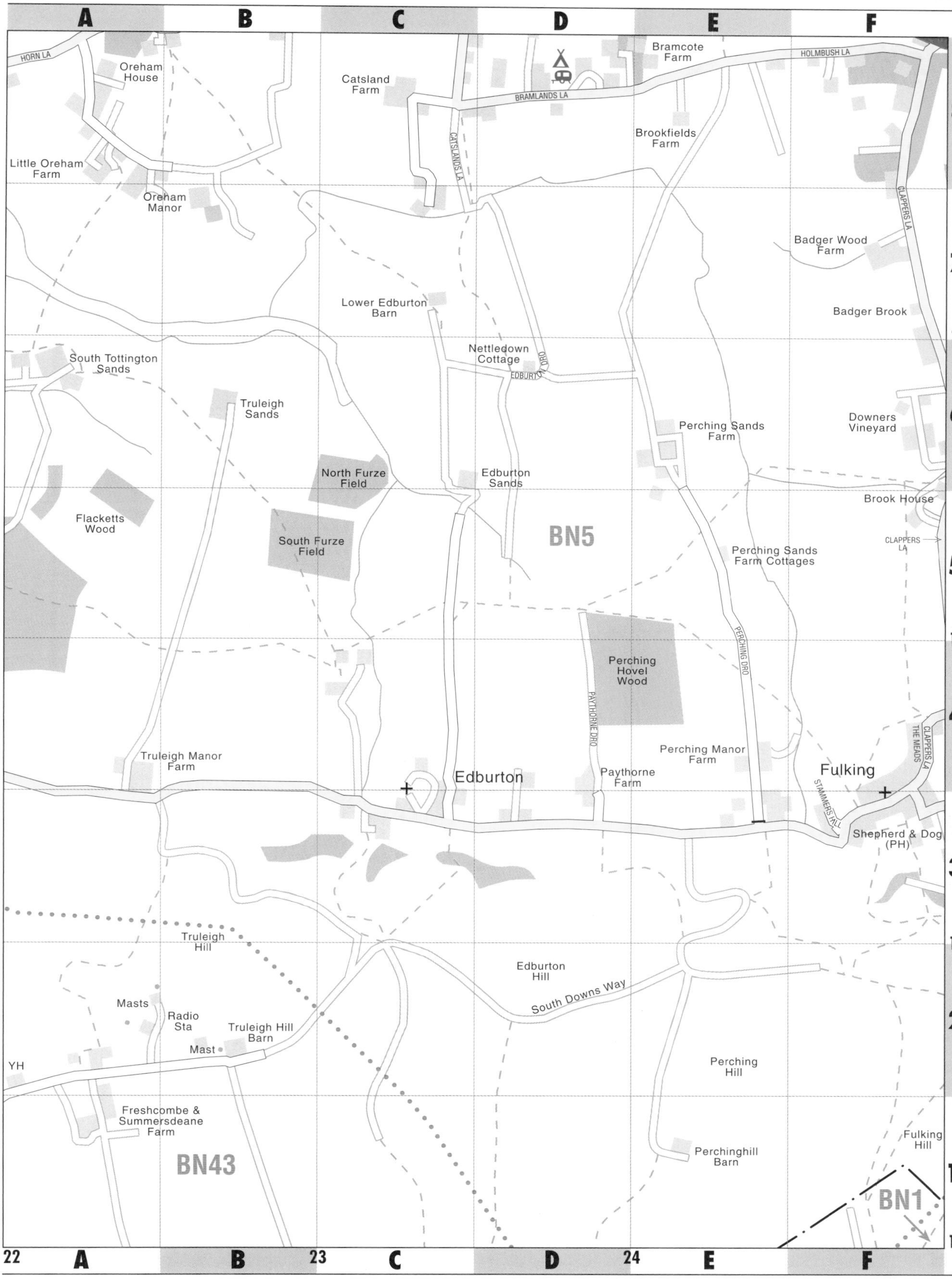
A
B
C
D
E
F
HORN LA
Oreham House
Catsland Farm
Bramcote Farm
HOLMBUSH LA
BRAMLANDS LA
8
CATSLANDS LA
Brookfields Farm
Little Oreham Farm
Oreham Manor
CLAPPERS LA
Badger Wood Farm
7
Lower Edburton Barn
Badger Brook
13
Nettledown Cottage
EDBURTON DRO
South Tottington Sands
Truleigh Sands
Perching Sands Farm
Downers Vineyard
6
North Furze Field
Edburton Sands
Brook House
Flacketts Wood
South Furze Field
BN5
CLAPPERS LA
Perching Sands Farm Cottages
5
12
PERCHING DRO
Perching Hovel Wood
PAYTHORNE DRO
4
THE MEADS
CLAPPERS LA
Perching Manor Farm
Truleigh Manor Farm
Edburton
Fulking
Paythorne Farm
STAMMERS HILL
Shepherd & Dog (PH)
3
Truleigh Hill
11
Edburton Hill
South Downs Way
Masts
Radio Sta
2
Truleigh Hill Barn
Mast
YH
Perching Hill
Freshcombe & Summersdeane Farm
Fulking Hill
BN43
Perchinghill Barn
1
BN1
10
22
23
24
165
146

145 125

A B C D E F
8 7 13 6 5 12 4 3 11 2 1 10
25 26 27
A281
A23
Park Cottages
Stonestaples Wood
Park Wood
Newtimber Place
Old Rectory
Round Hill
Newtimber Wood
BN6
CHURCH LA
LONDON RD
Redhouse Farm
Poynings Grange Farm
WEST RD
Cobsham Rough
Grange Lodge Cottages
CROSSWAYS COTTS
CLAPPERS LA
Newtimber Holt
High Beeches
BEGGAR'S LA
Newtimber Hill
MILL CT
MILL CL
MILL LA
Poynings
BN5
BN45
North Hill
ROYAL OAK COTTS
DYKE CL
THE STREET
PH
PO
Cemy
West Hill
Wickhurst Barns
East Hill
Saddlescombe
Devil's Dyke
P
Devil's Dyke Hotel
Sussex Border Path
South Downs Way
Summer Down
BN1
Ewe Bottom
CH
Pond Brow
DEVIL'S DYKE RD
Devil's Dyke Farm

145 166

126
148
A
B
C
D
E
F
Wolstonbury
Wolstonbury Hill
Wellcombe Bottom
A273
Clayton
SPRING LA
UNDERHILL LA
8
Clayton Holt
Clayton Windmills
Jill
Jack
Rockrose
CLAYTON HILL
MILL LA
Chantry
7
Clayton Tunnel
BN6
13
A23
DALE HILL
PYECOMBE ST
A281
WEST RD
South Downs Way
New Barn Farm
Pyecombe
CH
6
Wayfield Farm
THE WYSHE
SCHOOL LA
CHURCH HILL
CHURCH LA
PH
Rag Bottom
Riding School
Cow Down
Haresdean
A273
5
Middle Brow
12
BN45
LONDON RD
4
Pangdean Farm
Holt Bottom
Pangdean Holt
3
South Hill
Sussex Border Path
War Meml
BN1
11
South Hill Cottages
South Hill Farm
Poor Brow
2
Deep Bottom
The Pylons
Hogtrough Bottom
Sussex Border Path
Scare Hill
1
Varncombe Hill
Ewebottom Hill
Ewe Bottom
A23
10
28
29
30
167
148

147
127

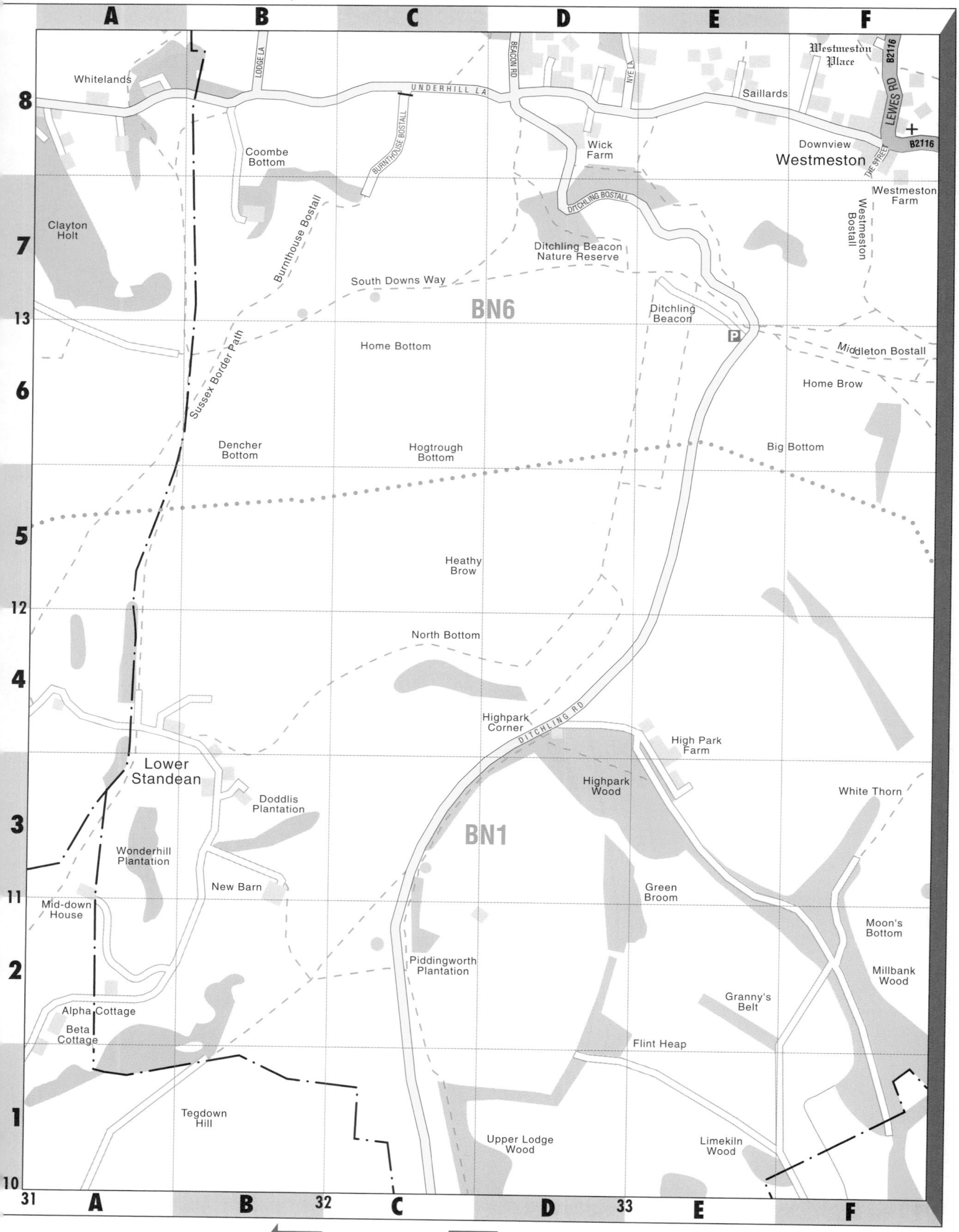
A
B
C
D
E
F
Whitelands
LODGE LA
BEACON RD
NYE LA
UNDERHILL LA
Westmeston Place
B2116
LEWES RD
Saillards
Downview
Westmeston
THE STREET
Westmeston Farm
Westmeston Bostall
Coombe Bottom
BURNTHOUSE BOSTALL
Wick Farm
DITCHLING BOSTALL
Clayton Holt
Burnthouse Bostall
Ditchling Beacon Nature Reserve
South Downs Way
BN6
Ditchling Beacon
P
Home Bottom
Middleton Bostall
Home Brow
Sussex Border Path
Dencher Bottom
Hogtrough Bottom
Big Bottom
Heathy Brow
North Bottom
Highpark Corner
DITCHLING RD
High Park Farm
Lower Standean
Highpark Wood
Doddlis Plantation
White Thorn
BN1
Wonderhill Plantation
New Barn
Green Broom
Mid-down House
Moon's Bottom
Piddingworth Plantation
Millbank Wood
Granny's Belt
Alpha Cottage
Beta Cottage
Flint Heap
Tegdown Hill
Upper Lodge Wood
Limekiln Wood
8
7
13
6
5
12
4
3
11
2
1
10
31
32
33

147
168

129
150
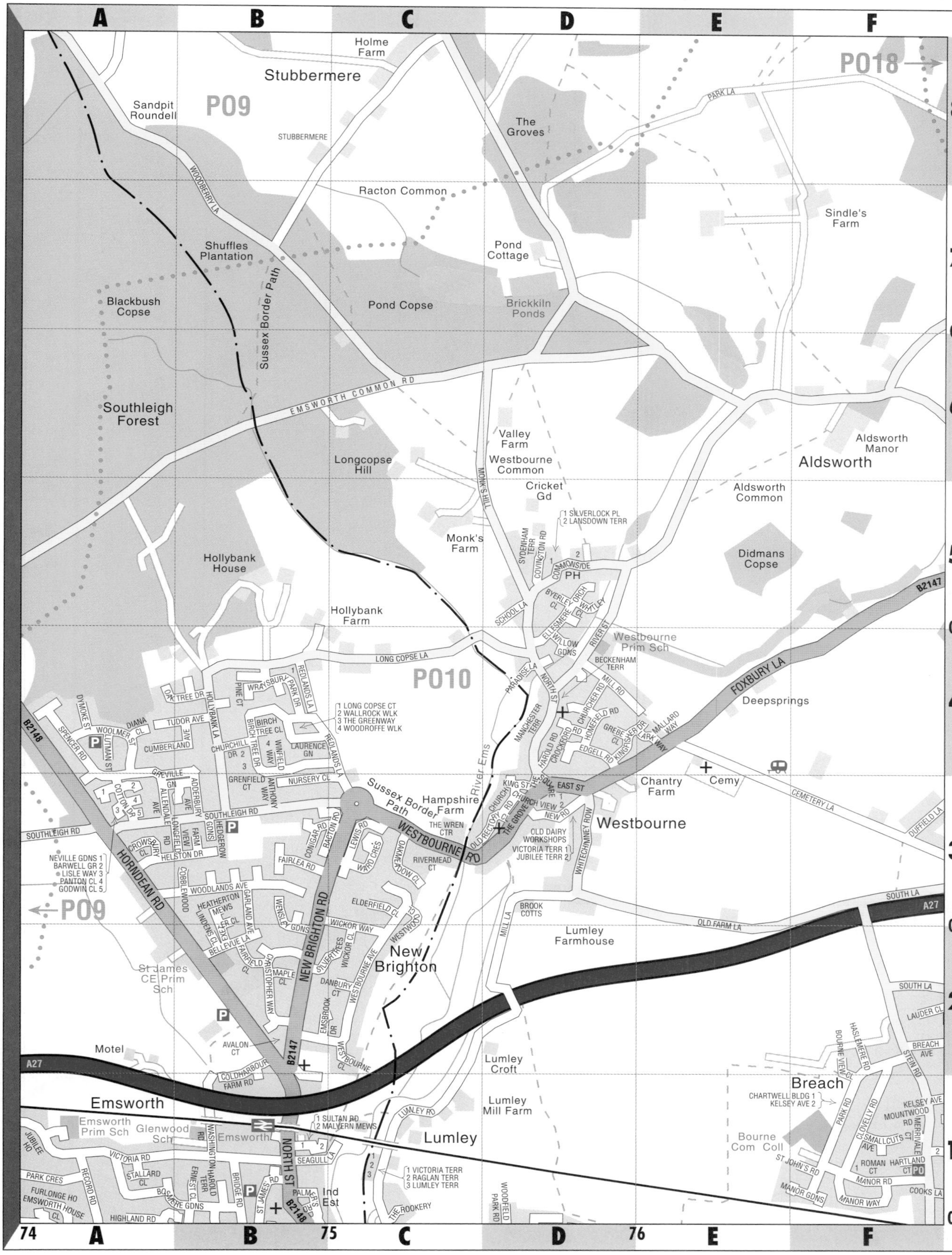
A
B
C
D
E
F
Holme Farm
Stubbermere
PO9
PO18
Sandpit Roundell
STUBBERMERE
The Groves
PARK LA
WOODBERRY LA
Racton Common
Sindle's Farm
Shuffles Plantation
Sussex Border Path
Pond Cottage
Blackbush Copse
Pond Copse
Brickkiln Ponds
EMSWORTH COMMON RD
Southleigh Forest
Valley Farm
Westbourne Common
Aldsworth Manor
Aldsworth
Longcopse Hill
MONK'S HILL
Cricket Gd
Aldsworth Common
1 SILVERLOCK PL
2 LANSDOWN TERR
Monk's Farm
SYDENHAM TERR
COVINGTON RD
COMMONSIDE
PH
Didmans Copse
Hollybank House
B2147
BYERLEY CL
ORCHARD
WHITLEY CL
SCHOOL LA
ELLESMERE
WILLOW GDNS
RIVER ST
Hollybank Farm
Westbourne Prim Sch
LONG COPSE LA
BECKENHAM TERR
PO10
PARADISE LA
NORTH ST
MILL RD
FOXBURY LA
OAK TREE DR
HOLLYBANK LA
PINE CT
WRAYSBURY PARK DR
REDLANDS LA
1 LONG COPSE CT
2 WALLROCK WLK
3 THE GREENWAY
4 WOODROFFE WLK
MANCHESTER TERR
CHURCHER RD
HOMEFIELD RD
Deepsprings
DYMOKE ST
TUDOR AVE
DIANA CL
BIRCH TREE CL
WOOLMER ST
SPENCER RD
LITMAN ST
CUMBERLAND
CHURCHILL DR
BIRCH TREE DR
WINFIELD WAY
LAURENCE GN
HAROLD RD
CROCKFORD RD
GREBE CL
KINGSHER DR
LARK WAY
MALLARD WAY
EDGELL RD
B2148
GREVILLE GN
ALLENDALE AVE
ADDERBURY AVE
GRENFIELD CT
ANTHONY WAY
NURSERY CL
River Ems
KING ST
CHURCH RD
THE SQUARE
EAST ST
Chantry Farm
Cemy
COTTON DR
Sussex Border Path
Hampshire Farm
CHURCH VIEW
CEMETERY LA
SOUTHLEIGH RD
LONGFIELD RD
FARM VIEW
HEDGEROW GDNS
CONIGAR RD
BACTON RD
LEWIS RD
THE WREN CTR
OLD RECTORY RD
THE GROVE
NEW RD
WHITECHIMNEY ROW
Westbourne
DUFFIELD LA
CROWSBURY CL
HELSTON DR
WARD CRES
OAKMEADOW CL
RIVERMEAD CT
OLD DAIRY WORKSHOPS
VICTORIA TERR 1
JUBILEE TERR 2
WESTBOURNE RD
NEVILLE GDNS 1
BARWELL GR 2
LISLE WAY 3
PANTON CL 4
GODWIN CL 5
HORNDEAN RD
FAIRLEA RD
COBBLEWOOD
WOODLANDS AVE
HEATHERTON MEWS
GARLAND AVE
NEW BRIGHTON RD
ELDERFIELD CL
WESTWOOD CL
LINDENS CL
BELLEVUE LA
FAIRFIELD CL
WENSLEY GDNS
WICKOR WAY
WICKOR CL
SILVERTREES
WESTBOURNE AVE
SOUTH LA
A27
OLD FARM LA
BROOK COTTS
MILL LA
Lumley Farmhouse
St James CE Prim Sch
CHRISTOPHER WAY
MAPLE CL
New Brighton
DANBURY CT
EMSBROOK DR
SOUTH LA
LAUDER CL
Motel
AVALON CT
BOURNE VIEW CL
HASLEMERE RD
BREACH AVE
STEIN RD
WESTBOURNE CL
COLDHARBOUR FARM RD
Lumley Croft
Breach
Emsworth
Lumley Mill Farm
CHARTWELL BLDG 1
KELSEY AVE 2
KELSEY AVE
MOUNTWOOD RD
PARK RD
CLOVELLY RD
MERRIVALE CT
Emsworth Prim Sch
Glenwood Sch
Emsworth
1 SULTAN RD
2 MALVERN MEWS
LUMLEY RD
Lumley
Bourne Com Coll
SMALLCUTS AVE
JUBILEE HO
VICTORIA RD
WASHINGTON RD
HAROLD TERR
SEAGULL LA
1 VICTORIA TERR
2 RAGLAN TERR
3 LUMLEY TERR
ST JOHN'S RD
ROMAN CT
HARTLAND CT
PO
PARK CRES
RECORD RD
STALLARD CL
ERNEST CL
BRIDGE RD
ST JAMES RD
NORTH ST
PALMER'S RD
Ind Est
MANOR RD
FURLONGE HO
EMSWORTH HOUSE CL
BOSMERE GDNS
HIGHLAND RD
THE ROOKERY
WOODFIELD PARK RD
MANOR GDNS
MANOR WAY
COOKS LA
8
7
09
6
5
08
4
3
07
2
1
06
74
75
76
169
150

149
130

Lordington House
New Barn Cottage
Lordington
Racton Mon
Down Copse
Adsdean Park
Adsdean House
Adsdean Farm
Racton Park Farm
Ellbridge Buildings
Ell Bridge
River Ems
Ractonpark Wood
Stanes Farm
Hambrook Buildings
PO18
Research Establishment
Hambrook Grange
Woodmancote
Bishopbarn Farm
The Grange
PO10
Manor House
Balsam's Farm
South Lane Farm
Devils Copse
Little Court Farm
Hambrook House
Wintons Farm
Ridge Farm
North Lodge
Spring Gardens
Watercress Beds
Hambrook
Priors Leaze Farm
Loveders Farm
Brook Farm
Inlands Farm
Flat Farm
HARES LA
COMMON RD
WOODMANCOTE LA
FOXBURY LA
WEST ASHLING RD
A27

149
170

131
152

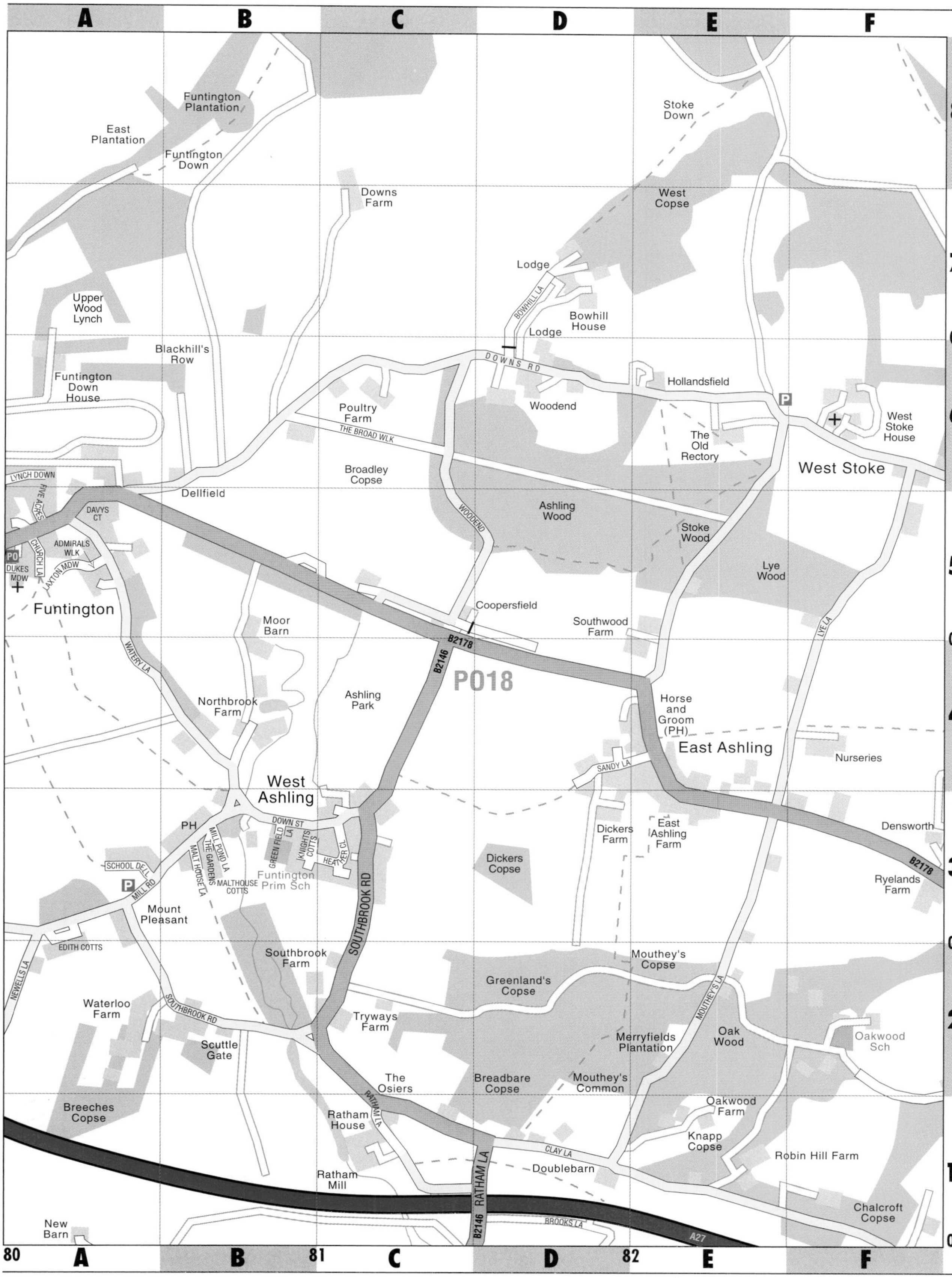
Funtington Plantation
East Plantation
Funtington Down
Downs Farm
Stoke Down
West Copse
Lodge
Upper Wood Lynch
Bowhill House
Lodge
Blackhill's Row
Funtington Down House
DOWNS RD
Hollandsfield
Poultry Farm
Woodend
The Old Rectory
West Stoke House
THE BROAD WLK
West Stoke
Broadley Copse
LYNCH DOWN
Dellfield
Ashling Wood
DAVYS CT
Stoke Wood
ADMIRALS WLK
Lye Wood
Funtington
Coopersfield
Southwood Farm
Moor Barn
B2178
B2146
PO18
Northbrook Farm
Ashling Park
Horse and Groom (PH)
East Ashling
Nurseries
SANDY LA
West Ashling
PH
DOWN ST
Dickers Farm
East Ashling Farm
Densworth
Dickers Copse
SCHOOL DELL
Funtington Prim Sch
Ryelands Farm
Mount Pleasant
SOUTHBROOK RD
EDITH COTTS
Mouthey's Copse
Southbrook Farm
Greenland's Copse
Waterloo Farm
Tryways Farm
Scuttle Gate
Merryfields Plantation
Oak Wood
Oakwood Sch
The Osiers
Breadbare Copse
Mouthey's Common
Breeches Copse
Ratham House
Oakwood Farm
Knapp Copse
Robin Hill Farm
CLAY LA
Doublebarn
Ratham Mill
RATHAM LA
Chalcroft Copse
New Barn
BROOKS LA
A27
A B C D E F
8 7 09 6 5 08 4 3 07 2 1 06
80 81 82

171
152

151
132

A
B
C
D
E
F
8
7
09
6
5
08
4
3
07
2
1
06
83
84
85
B2141
A286
Langford Farm
STAPLE LA
Stoke Clump
PATNORE
LAVANT DOWN RD
River Lavant
YARBROOK
GASTON WAY
HERON CL
ST MARY'S CL
HAYES CL
EAST VIEW CL
ST ROCHE'S CL
EASTMEAD IND EST
MIDHURST RD
NORTHSIDE
SPRINGFIELD CL
TRUNDLE CL
DOWNVIEW CL
ST NICHOLAS RD
CHURCHMEAD CL
WARBLE HEATH CL
MARSH LA
TWO BARNS LA
PO18
Trumley Copse
PH
West Stoke Farm
Trumley
Lavant CE Prim Sch
DOWNS RD
HILLSIDE COTTS
West Lavant Farm
Mid Lavant
PO
SHEEPWASH LA
Lavant House (Rosemead Sch)
Fletchers
THE CLOSE
OLDWICK MDWS
POOK LA
Little Tomlins Copse
RAUGHMERE DR
RAUGHMERE CT
Little Oldwick House
Densworth Copse
Well House
Oldwick Farm
HUNTERS RACE
Densworth Farm
CHAPEL LA
Oldwick Copse
WEST STOKE RD
Huntersrace Farm
Centurion Way
LAVANT RD
REW LA
KEEPERS WOOD
THE DRIVE
STANTON DR
B2178
Sennicotts
SUMMERSDALE CT
HUNTERS WAY
STAVELY GDNS
CHESTNUT AVE
WINSTON CT
BAYTREE CL
LARCH CL
GARDEN HO
PLAINWOOD CL
THE AVENUE
Marldell Copse
West Broyle House
PO19
THE BARN
HERONDEAN
WARREN FARM LA
CHICHESTER
TUDOR CL
Lodge
OLD BROYLE RD
BRANDY HOLE LA
East Broyle Copse
HIGHLAND RD
Oakwood Park
WEST BROYLE DR
WEST WAY
PINE GR
BRISTOL GDNS
WORCESTER RD
DONEGAL RD
Mus
BROYLE RD
A286
NORTHLANDS
Fairyhill
YORK CHASE
HEREFORD CL
SPRINGBANK CL
Little Cotfield Plantation
SALTHILL RD
SALISBURY WAY
DURHAM GDNS
ROCHESTER CL
BROYLE CL
LINCOLN GN
TRURO CL
Salthill Park
GLOUCESTER WAY
The Sherburne
Stocker's Copse
Salthill House
The Barracks
Upper Rouse Copse
ST PAUL'S RD
EXETER RD
WELLS CRES
NORWICH RD
H
CARLISLE GDNS
LITTLE BREACH

151
172

133
154

A
B
C
D
E
F
Racklands
Bexley Bushes
Bexley Plantation
Reservoir Clump
PARK RD
Carne's Seat
KENNEL HILL
PRINCE'S DR
The Gallop
Chalkpit Plantation
CHALKPIT LA
MIDDLEFIELD LA
Kennel Lodges
Pheasantry
Goodwood Park
CH
High Wood
Hound Lodge
The Valdoe
Goodwood House
STAPLE LA
PARKER'S COTTS
PO18
The Cottage
Emperors Brow
DAME SCHOOL CT
PH
Manor Farm
POOK LA
SHOP LA
LOWER RD
Grub Ground
The Goldings
East Lavant
Church Farm
FORDWATER RD
South Lodges
Valdoe Yard
NEW RD
FORDWATER RD
Woodcote House
Ford Water
WOODLAND PL
REW LA
1 DUNSTAN CL
2 MARCH SQ
3 MARCHWOOD GATE
4 COMPTON CL
Westerton
RICHMOND RD
Chichester (Goodwood) Airfield
Westerton Farm
River Lavant
STOCKS LA
HARE CRES
THE DRIVE
MARCHWOOD
SELHAM CL
GRAFFHAM CL
STANTON DR
FERNDALE RD
MAPLEHURST RD
CHESTNUT AVE
WYBERTON HO
FORDWATER LA
THE AVENUE
Summersdale
Goodwood Motor Circuit
CLAYPIT LA
TREGARTH RD
THE LANE
CROFT MEAD
THE COPSE
Summersdale Copse
HIGHLAND RD
A2
1 MYTCHETT HO
2 CASSSELLS RD
3 DEMPSEY RD
4 YOUNG ST
5 AUGUSTA CT
PO19
GRAYLINGWELL COTTS
WINTERBOURNE RD
THE BROADWAY
OTWAY RD
SUMMERSDALE RD
ANSWORTH CL
PINEWOOD HO
PH
OLD ARUNDEL RD
RICHMOND AVE
NAUNTON RD
MARCHWELL IND UNIT
Maudlin
Rousillon Barracks
BLOMFIELD DR
Fordwater Sch
The March CE Prim Sch
MADGWICK LA
WHISTLER AVE
STANE ST
JEFFREYS AVE
Graylingwell
OSBORN CRES
CRESSEY WAY
DAIRY LA
SMEE LA
Westhampnett
BROYLE RD A286
HAVENSTOKE CL
PALMERS FIELD AVE
MANSBERGH RD
CARSE RD
KIDD RD
PEACOCK CL
COACH RD
Maudlin Farm
WELLINGTON RD
COLLEGE LA
Martin's Farm
Westhampnett Mill
THE SADLERS
A27
8
7
09
6
5
08
4
3
07
2
1
06
86
87
88

173
154

153
134

A
B
C
D
E
F
8
7
09
6
5
08
4
3
07
2
1
06
89
90
92
Sculpture at Goodwood
Halnaker Park
Denge Barn
Halnaker Hill
Bushey Clump
Hathill Copse West
Denge Bottom
Rook Wood
PARK RD
NEW BARN HILL
Halnaker Park
The Cockpit
Little Halnaker
Stone Dell
Seeley Copse
Home Farm
Stud Farm
Halnaker House (remains of)
Warehead Farm
A285
Warehead House
Goodwood Park
Home Farm Dairy
PO18
Ounces Barn
Sandpit Copse
Redvins Copse West
Redvin's Copse
PARK LA
The Folly
Boxgrove Common
Hotel
Waterbeach
Halnaker
TINWOOD LA
The Anglesey Arms (PH)
Inkpen Furze
Redvin's Shaw
Redvin's Barn
Keeper's House
The Old Granary
Boxgrove CE Prim Sch
NEW RD
THE ALMSHOUSES
ST MARY'S RD
ST BLAISES RD
KIRKBY CL
THE STREET
Priory Farm
Strettington
CROUCH CROSS LA
CHURCH LA
STANE ST
THE CLOSE
PO
Boxgrove
STRETTINGTON LA
BARN ELM
PRIORY CL
Temple Bar
Strettington Farm
PRIORS ACRE
BOXGROVE HO
ABBOTTS CL
A27
GARLAND SQ
Pear Tree Knap
A285
EDWARDS AVE
GIBSON RD
BISHOPS RD
Tangmere Prim Sch
East Hampnett
EAST HAMPNETT LA
MEADOWSIDE WLK
CITY FIELDS WAY
CITY FIELDS
NETTLETON AVE
MIDDLETON GDNS
HAMPDEN PL
MEADOW WAY
OAKWOOD CL
SUNDERLAND CL
Chestnut Farm
The Bader Arms (PH)
JERRARD RD
SPITFIRE CT
CANBERRA PL
Sewage Works
MARSH LA
MALCOLM RD
TAMAR WAY
NELSON CL
DERWENT CL
CHURCHWOOD DR
FULMAR WAY
CAMPBELL RD
MALCOLM RD
CHESHIRE CRES
CAEDWALLA DR
CHESTNUT WLK
TANGMERE RD
WOODFIELD
WINDMILL CT
LYSANDER WAY
WYVERN CL
MANNOCK RD
COPPER BEECH DR
OLD COTTAGE CL
CHESTER DR
WHITEBEAM WAY
1 BARNCROFT CL
2 THE GLEBE
BAYLEY RD
ST ANDREWS LA
HAVEBRIDGE WLK
Church Farm House
CHURCH LA
Tangmere
PO20
HEARN CL
3 HARESFIELD TERR
4 GAMECOCK TERR
SAXON MDW
Tangmere Military Aviation Mus
Nursery

153
174

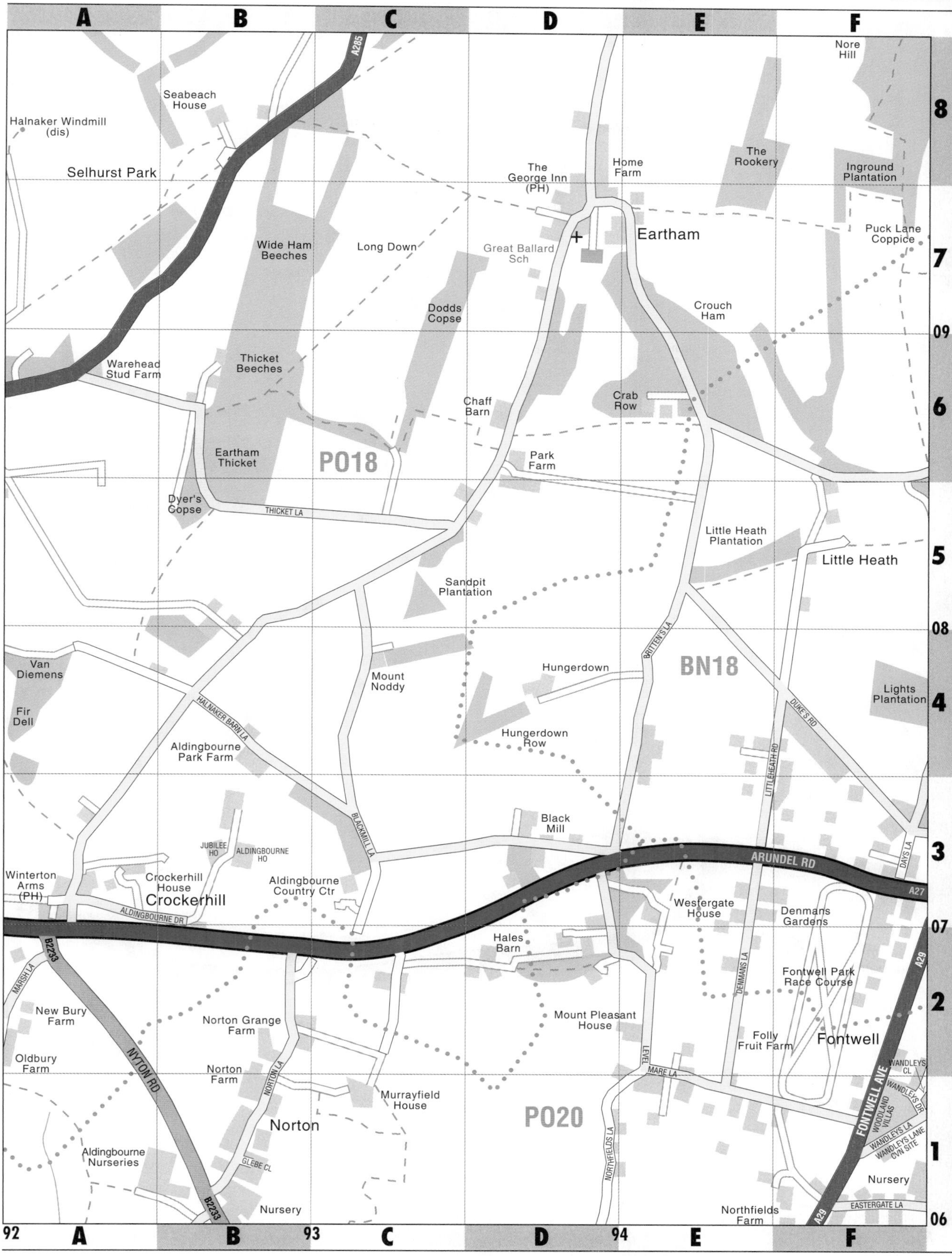
A
B
C
D
E
F
8
7
09
6
5
08
4
3
07
2
1
06
92
93
94
A285
Nore Hill
Seabeach House
Halnaker Windmill (dis)
Selhurst Park
The George Inn (PH)
Home Farm
The Rookery
Inground Plantation
Eartham
Great Ballard Sch
Puck Lane Coppice
Wide Ham Beeches
Long Down
Dodds Copse
Crouch Ham
Warehead Stud Farm
Thicket Beeches
Chaff Barn
Crab Row
Eartham Thicket
PO18
Park Farm
Dyer's Copse
THICKET LA
Little Heath Plantation
Little Heath
Sandpit Plantation
BRITTEN'S LA
BN18
Van Diemens
Mount Noddy
Hungerdown
Lights Plantation
Fir Dell
HALNAKER BARN LA
DUKE'S RD
Aldingbourne Park Farm
Hungerdown Row
LITTLEHEATH RD
Black Mill
BLACKMILL LA
JUBILEE HO
ALDINGBOURNE HO
DAYS LA
ARUNDEL RD
Winterton Arms (PH)
Crockerhill House
Crockerhill
Aldingbourne Country Ctr
ALDINGBOURNE DR
A27
Westergate House
Denmans Gardens
B2233
Hales Barn
MARSH LA
DENMANS LA
Fontwell Park Race Course
A29
New Bury Farm
Norton Grange Farm
Mount Pleasant House
Oldbury Farm
Folly Fruit Farm
Fontwell
NYTON RD
Norton Farm
NORTON LA
LEVEL
MARE LA
WANDLEYS CL
WANDLEYS DR
Murrayfield House
FONTWELL AVE
WOODLAND VILLAS
Norton
PO20
WANDLEYS LA
WANDLEYS LANE CVN SITE
Aldingbourne Nurseries
NORTHFIELDS LA
GLEBE CL
Nursery
B2233
Nursery
Northfields Farm
EASTERGATE LA

155
136

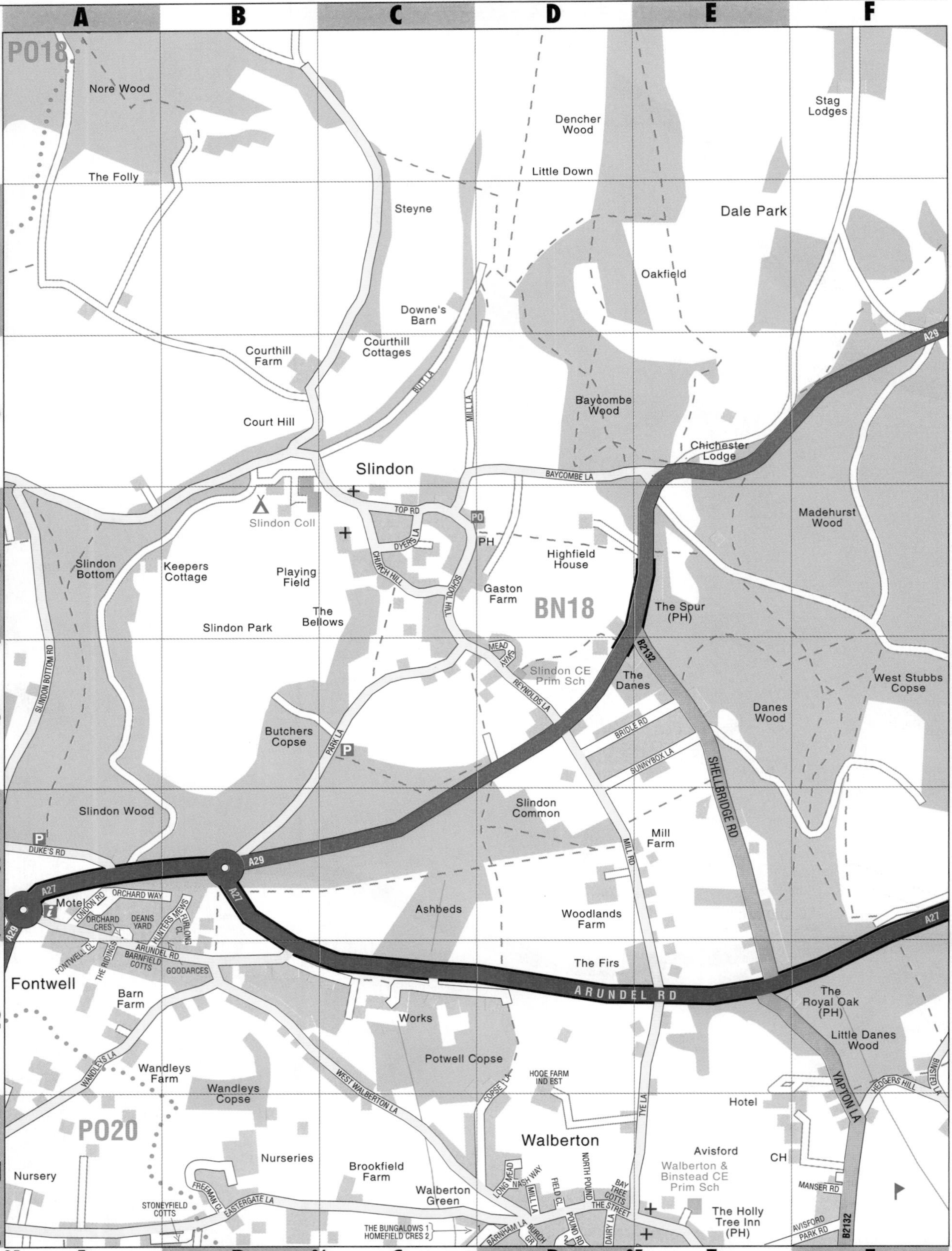
A B C D E F
8 7 09 6 5 08 4 3 07 2 1 06
95 96 97
PO18
Nore Wood
The Folly
Dencher Wood
Little Down
Stag Lodges
Steyne
Dale Park
Oakfield
Downe's Barn
Courthill Farm
Courthill Cottages
Court Hill
BUTT LA
MILL LA
Baycombe Wood
Chichester Lodge
A29
Slindon
BAYCOMBE LA
Slindon Coll
TOP RD
PO
PH
DYERS LA
CHURCH HILL
SCHOOL HILL
Highfield House
Madehurst Wood
Slindon Bottom
Keepers Cottage
Playing Field
Gaston Farm
BN18
The Spur (PH)
Slindon Park
The Bellows
MEAD WAYS
B2132
Slindon CE Prim Sch
The Danes
West Stubbs Copse
SLINDON BOTTOM RD
REYNOLDS LA
Danes Wood
Butchers Copse
PARK LA
BRIDLE RD
SUNNYBOX LA
SHELLBRIDGE RD
Slindon Wood
Slindon Common
Mill Farm
DUKE'S RD
MILL RD
A27
Motel
ORCHARD WAY
LONDON RD
ORCHARD CRES
DEANS YARD
HUNTERS MEWS
FURLONG CL
Ashbeds
Woodlands Farm
FONTWELL CL
THE RIDINGS
ARUNDEL RD
BARNFIELD COTTS
GOODACRES
The Firs
Fontwell
Barn Farm
The Royal Oak (PH)
Works
Little Danes Wood
WANDLEYS LA
Wandleys Farm
Potwell Copse
HOOE FARM IND EST
BINSTED LA
HEDGERS HILL
Wandleys Copse
WEST WALBERTON LA
COPSE LA
TYE LA
YAPTON LA
Hotel
PO20
Walberton
Nurseries
Avisford
CH
Nursery
Brookfield Farm
Walberton & Binstead CE Prim Sch
Walberton Green
LONG MEAD
NASH WAY
MILL LA
FIELD CL
NORTH POUND
BAY TREE COTTS
THE STREET
MANSER RD
FREEMAN CL
EASTERGATE LA
STONEYFIELD COTTS
THE BUNGALOWS 1
HOMEFIELD CRES 2
BARNHAM LA
BURCH GR
POUND RD
DAIRY LA
The Holly Tree Inn (PH)
AVISFORD PARK RD
B2132

155
176

137
158

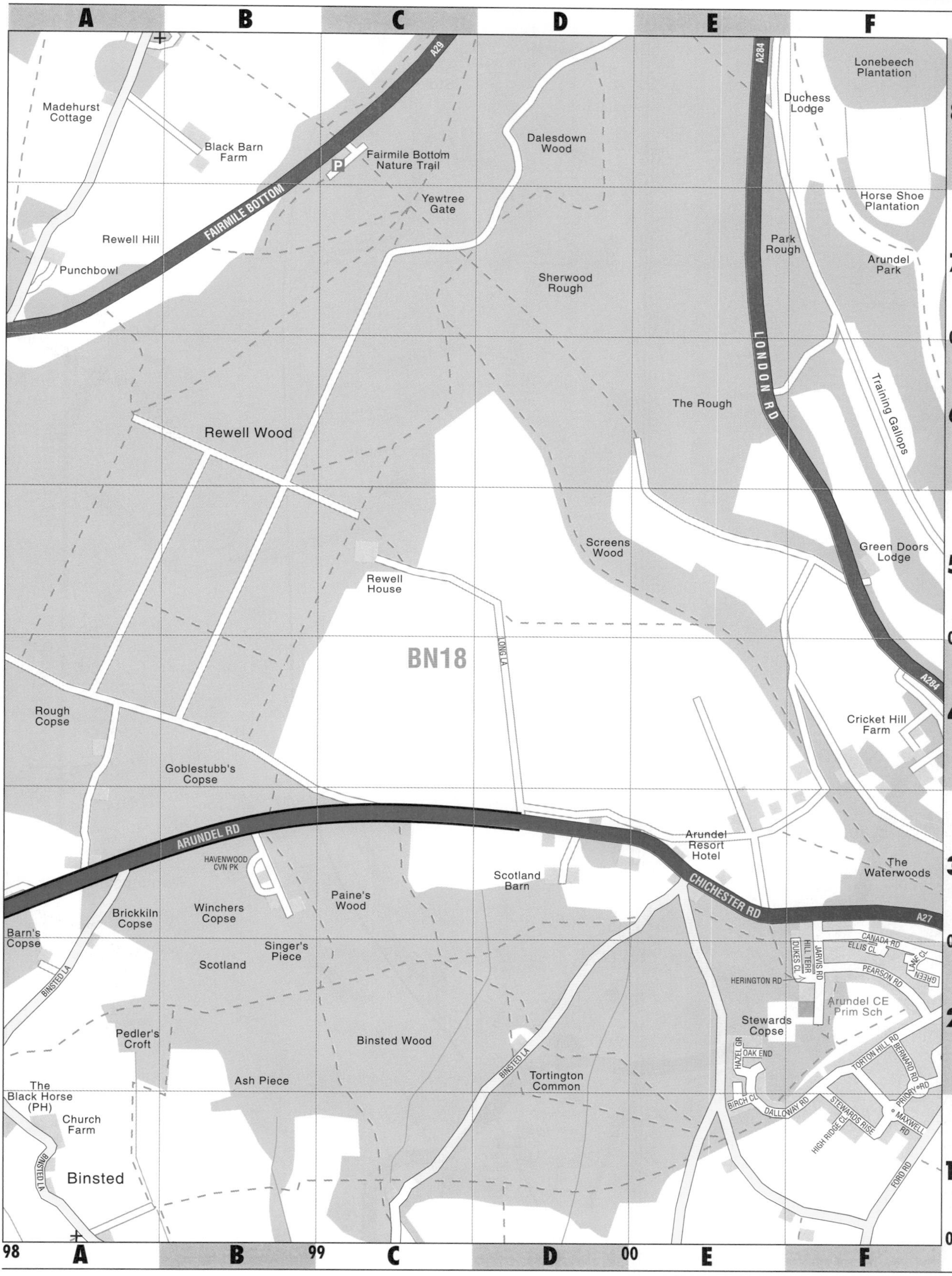
A
B
C
D
E
F
8
7
09
6
5
08
4
3
07
2
1
06
98
99
00
A29
A284
Lonebeech Plantation
Duchess Lodge
Madehurst Cottage
Black Barn Farm
Fairmile Bottom Nature Trail
Dalesdown Wood
Horse Shoe Plantation
Yewtree Gate
FAIRMILE BOTTOM
Rewell Hill
Punchbowl
Park Rough
Arundel Park
Sherwood Rough
LONDON RD
Training Gallops
The Rough
Rewell Wood
Screens Wood
Green Doors Lodge
Rewell House
LONG LA
BN18
A284
Rough Copse
Cricket Hill Farm
Goblestubb's Copse
ARUNDEL RD
Arundel Resort Hotel
HAVENWOOD CVN PK
Scotland Barn
The Waterwoods
CHICHESTER RD
A27
Brickkiln Copse
Winchers Copse
Paine's Wood
Barn's Copse
Singer's Piece
Scotland
CANADA RD
ELLIS CL
DUKES CL
HILL TERR
JARVIS RD
PEARSON RD
LANE CL
GREEN
HERINGTON RD
BINSTED LA
Arundel CE Prim Sch
Stewards Copse
Pedler's Croft
Binsted Wood
HAZEL GR
OAK END
TORTON HILL RD
BERNARD RD
BINSTED LA
Tortington Common
Ash Piece
PRIORY RD
The Black Horse (PH)
BIRCH CL
DALLOWAY RD
STEWARDS RISE
MAXWELL RD
Church Farm
HIGH RIDGE CL
BINSTED LA
Binsted
FORD RD

177
158

157 138

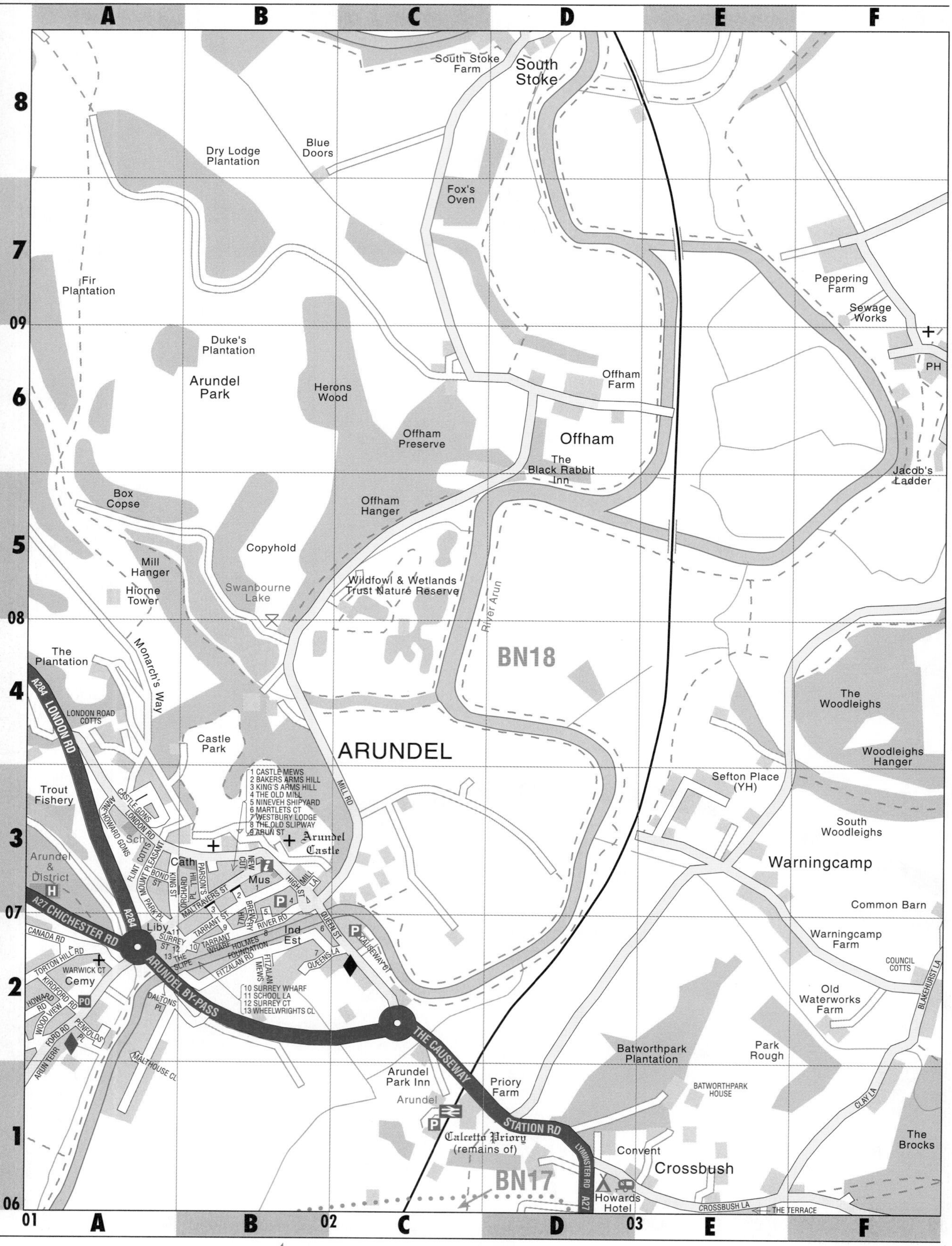
A
B
C
D
E
F
8
7
6
5
4
3
2
1
09
08
07
06
01
02
03
South Stoke Farm
South Stoke
Dry Lodge Plantation
Blue Doors
Fox's Oven
Peppering Farm
Sewage Works
Fir Plantation
Duke's Plantation
Arundel Park
Herons Wood
Offham Farm
PH
Offham Preserve
Offham
The Black Rabbit Inn
Jacob's Ladder
Box Copse
Offham Hanger
Copyhold
Mill Hanger
Hiorne Tower
Swanbourne Lake
Wildfowl & Wetlands Trust Nature Reserve
River Arun
BN18
The Plantation
Monarch's Way
A284 LONDON RD
LONDON ROAD COTTS
Castle Park
ARUNDEL
The Woodleighs
Woodleighs Hanger
Sefton Place (YH)
Trout Fishery
1 CASTLE MEWS
2 BAKERS ARMS HILL
3 KING'S ARMS HILL
4 THE OLD MILL
5 NINEVEH SHIPYARD
6 MARTLETS CT
7 WESTBURY LODGE
8 THE OLD SLIPWAY
9 ARUN ST
MILL RD
South Woodleighs
Arundel Castle
Warningcamp
Arundel & District
Sch
Cath
Mus
CASTLE GDNS
LONDON RD
ANNE HOWARD GDNS
FLINT COTTS
MOUNT PLEASANT
BOND ST
KING ST
ORCHARD PL
PARSON'S HILL
NEW CUT
HIGH ST
MILL LA
MALTRAVERS ST
PARK PL
BREWERY HILL
TARRANT ST
RIVER RD
QUEEN ST
CAUSEWAY CT
Common Barn
A27 CHICHESTER RD
A284
Liby
SURREY ST
THE SLIPE
TARRANT WHARF
HOLMES FOUNDATION
FITZALAN RD
FITZALAN MEWS
Ind Est
QUEENS LA
Warningcamp Farm
CANADA RD
TORTON HILL RD
WARWICK CT
Cemy
COUNCIL COTTS
BLAKEHURST LA
ARUNDEL BY-PASS
DALTONS PL
10 SURREY WHARF
11 SCHOOL LA
12 SURREY CT
13 WHEELWRIGHTS CL
Old Waterworks Farm
HOWARD RD
KIRDFORD RD
WOOD VIEW
FORD RD
PENFOLDS PL
PO
ARUN TERR
MALTHOUSE CL
THE CAUSEWAY
Arundel Park Inn
Priory Farm
Batworthpark Plantation
Park Rough
BATWORTHPARK HOUSE
CLAY LA
Arundel
STATION RD
Calcetto Priory (remains of)
LYMINSTER RD
A27
Convent
Crossbush
The Brocks
BN17
Howards Hotel
CROSSBUSH LA
THE TERRACE

157 178

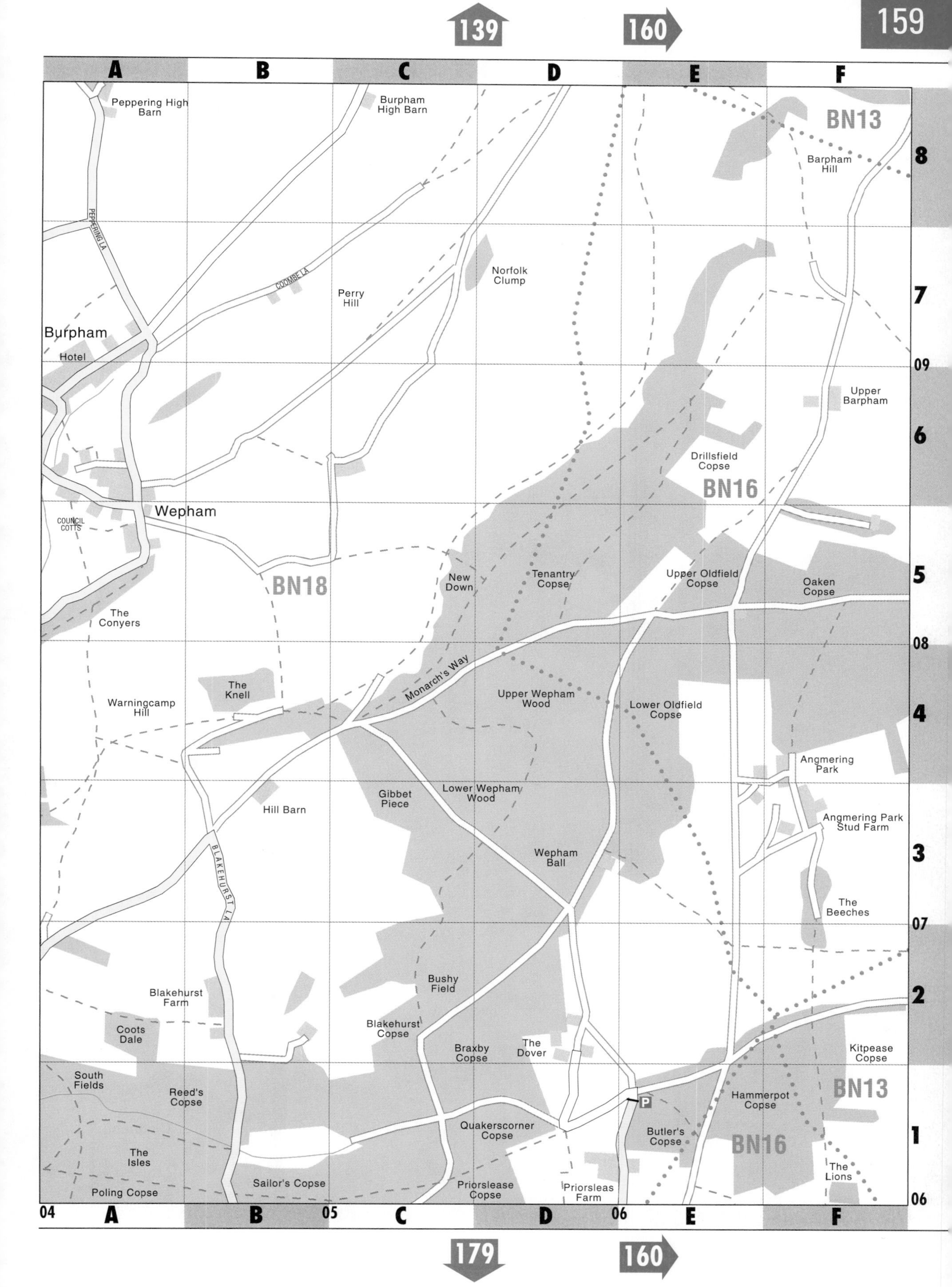
139
160
A
B
C
D
E
F
Peppering High Barn
Burpham High Barn
BN13
Barpham Hill
8
PEPPERING LA
COOMBE LA
Norfolk Clump
Perry Hill
7
Burpham
Hotel
09
Upper Barpham
6
Drillsfield Copse
BN16
Wepham
COUNCIL COTTS
New Down
Tenantry Copse
Upper Oldfield Copse
Oaken Copse
5
BN18
The Conyers
08
Monarch's Way
The Knell
Warningcamp Hill
Upper Wepham Wood
Lower Oldfield Copse
4
Angmering Park
Gibbet Piece
Lower Wepham Wood
Hill Barn
Angmering Park Stud Farm
BLAKEHURST LA
Wepham Ball
3
The Beeches
07
Bushy Field
Blakehurst Farm
2
Coots Dale
Blakehurst Copse
Braxby Copse
The Dover
Kitpease Copse
South Fields
Reed's Copse
Hammerpot Copse
BN13
P
Quakerscorner Copse
Butler's Copse
1
BN16
The Isles
The Lions
Sailor's Copse
Priorslease Copse
Priorsleas Farm
Poling Copse
06
04
05
06
179
160

159 140

A B C D E F
8 7 09 6 5 08 4 3 07 2 1 06
07 08 09
BN14
BN16
BN13
Harrow Hill
Blackpatch Hill
Lower Barpham
Beech Copse
Michelgrove House
MICHELGROVE COTTS
Monarch's Way
Myrtle Grove Farm
Michelgrove Park
LONGFURLONG LA
Michelgrove Park Lodges
Stables
Longfurlong Barn
A280
Barnstake Copse
The Buckmans
Patching Rough
Patching Hill
LONG FURLONG
Stonyland Copse
Surgeon's Fields
Selden Fields
Church Copse
Olivers Copse
Patching Copse
THE STREET
Patching
Clapham Farm
Parham Fields
Patching Farm
HILLSIDE COTTS
COUNCIL COTTS
CHURCH CL
WOOD
DLANDS CL
COLDHARBOUR LA
COUNCIL COTTS
THE STREET
Norfolk House
Selden Farm
Clapham & Patching CE Prim Sch
PO
CLAPHAM CL
Clapham
Jewshead Wood
SWILLAGE LA
SELDEN LA
FRANCE LA
A280
Wyatt's Copse
The Harehams

159 180

141
162

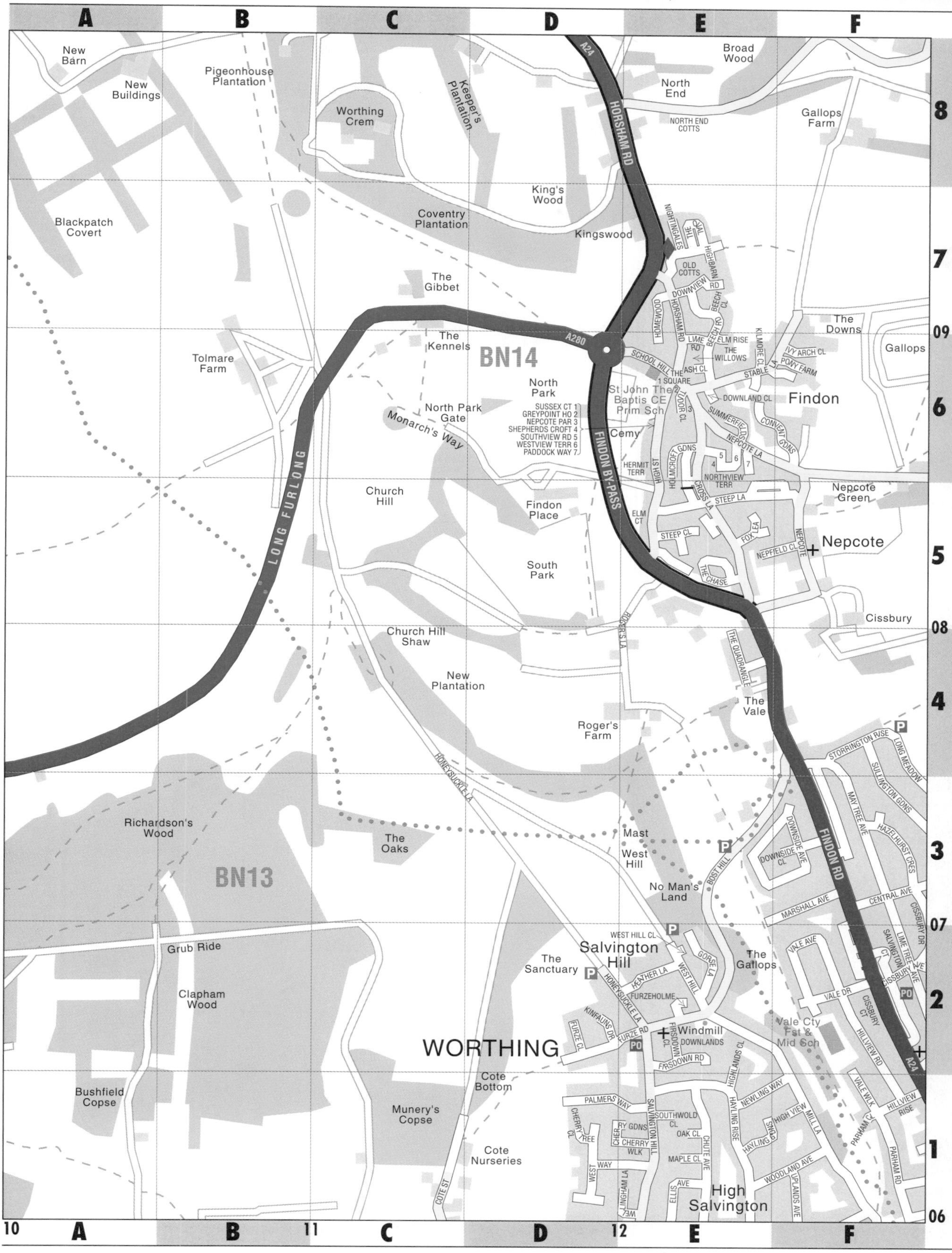

181
162

161
142
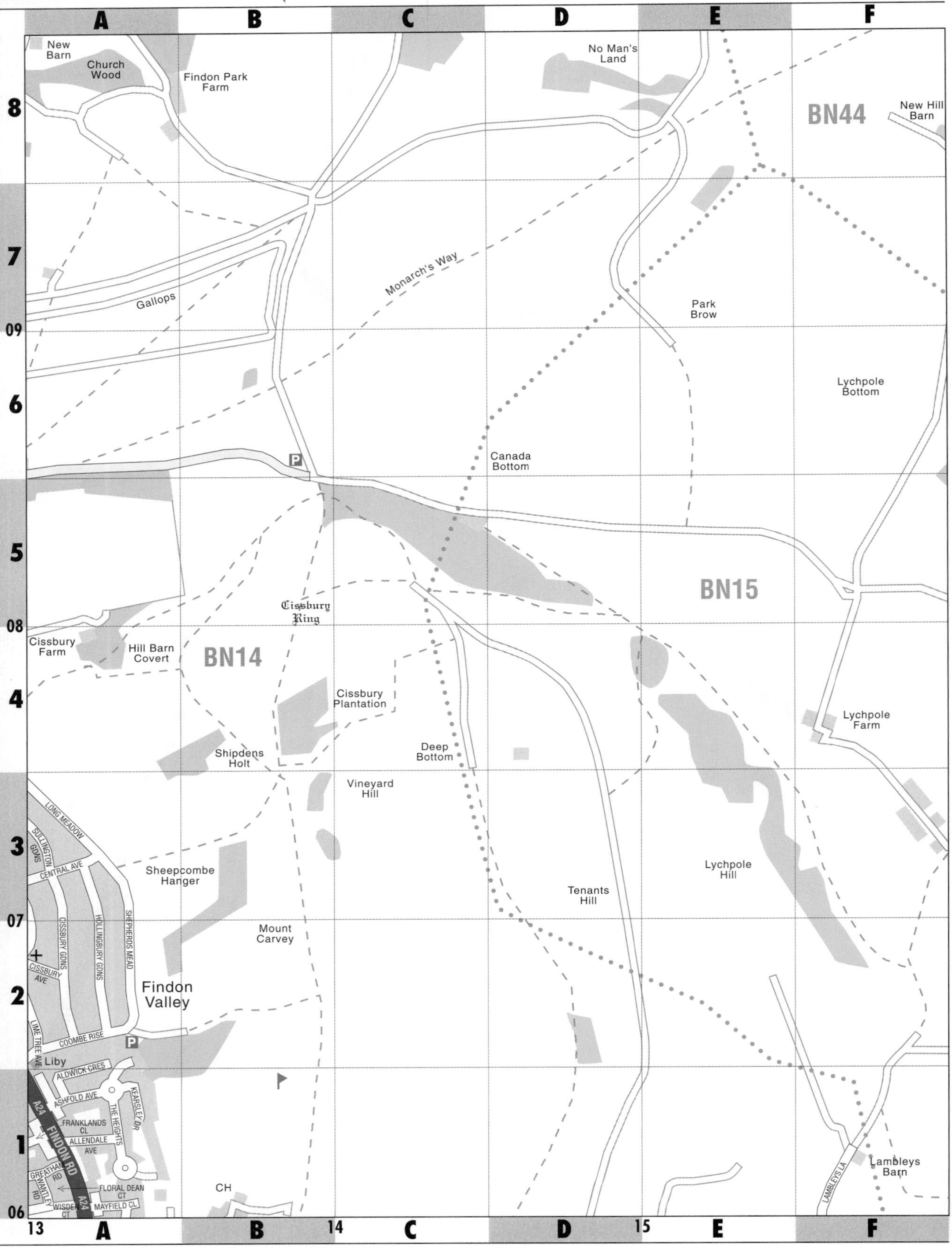
A
B
C
D
E
F
8
7
09
6
5
08
4
3
07
2
1
06
13
14
15
New Barn
Church Wood
Findon Park Farm
No Man's Land
BN44
New Hill Barn
Gallops
Monarch's Way
Park Brow
Lychpole Bottom
Canada Bottom
P
BN15
Cissbury Ring
Cissbury Farm
Hill Barn Covert
BN14
Cissbury Plantation
Lychpole Farm
Shipdens Holt
Deep Bottom
Vineyard Hill
LONG MEADOW
SULLINGTON GDNS
CENTRAL AVE
Sheepcombe Hanger
Lychpole Hill
Tenants Hill
CISSBURY GDNS
HOLLINGBURY GDNS
SHEPHERDS MEAD
Mount Carvey
CISSBURY AVE
Findon Valley
LIME TREE AVE
COOMBE RISE
Liby
ALDWICK CRES
ASHFOLD AVE
KEARSLEY DR
THE HEIGHTS
FRANKLANDS CL
ALLENDALE AVE
A24
FINDON RD
GREATHAM RD
WANTLEY RD
FLORAL DEAN CT
MAYFIELD CL
WISDEN CT
CH
LAMBLEYS LA
Lambleys Barn
161
182

143
164

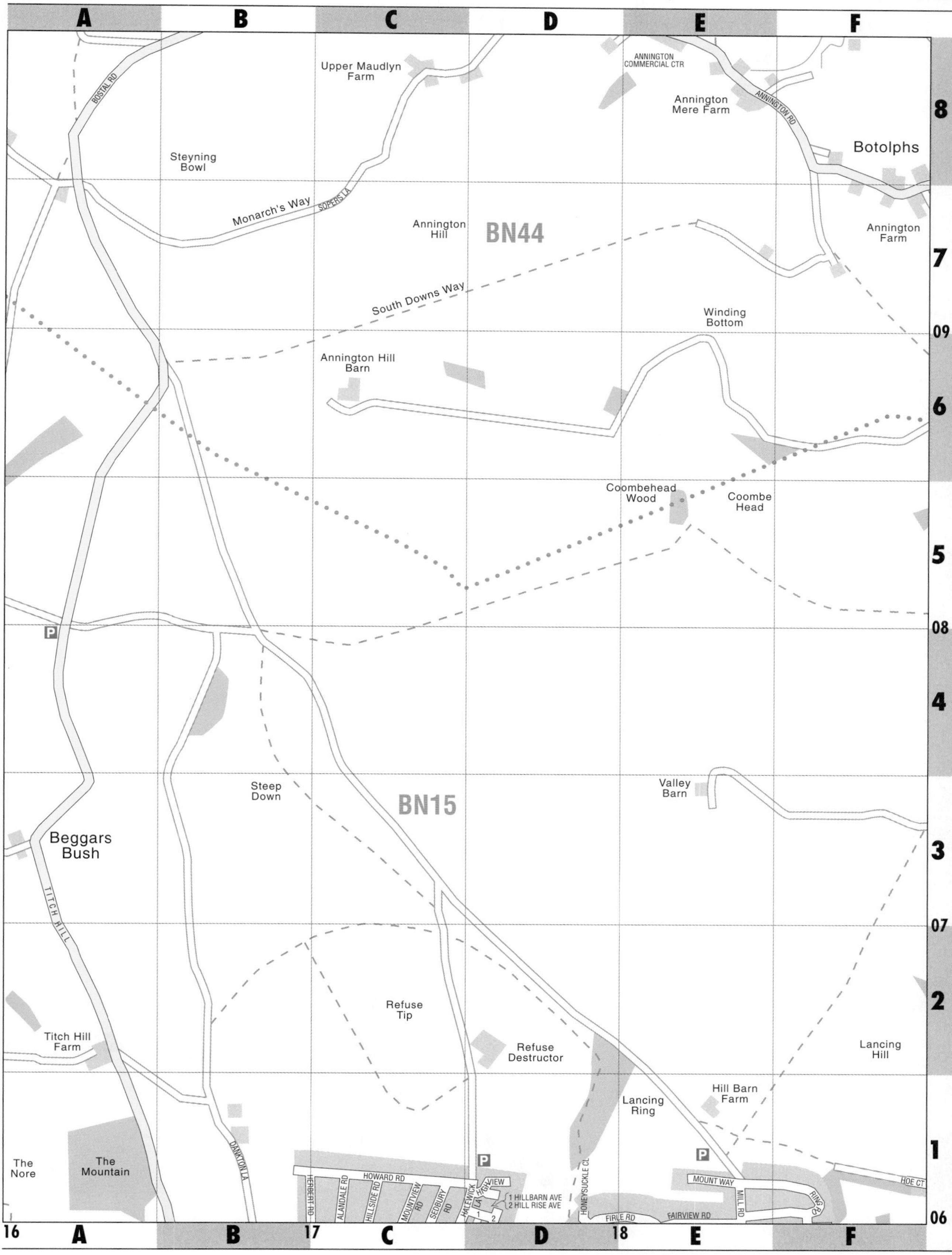
A
B
C
D
E
F
Upper Maudlyn Farm
ANNINGTON COMMERCIAL CTR
Annington Mere Farm
ANNINGTON RD
Botolphs
BOSTAL RD
8
Steyning Bowl
Monarch's Way
SOPERS LA
Annington Hill
BN44
Annington Farm
7
South Downs Way
Winding Bottom
09
Annington Hill Barn
6
Coombehead Wood
Coombe Head
5
08
4
Steep Down
Valley Barn
BN15
Beggars Bush
3
TITCH HILL
07
Refuse Tip
2
Lancing Hill
Titch Hill Farm
Refuse Destructor
Lancing Ring
Hill Barn Farm
1
The Nore
The Mountain
DANKTON LA
HOWARD RD
HERBERT RD
ALANDALE RD
HILLSIDE RD
MOUNTVIEW RD
SEDBURY RD
HALEWICK LA
HIGH VIEW
1 HILLBARN AVE
2 HILL RISE AVE
HONEYSUCKLE CL
FIRLE RD
FAIRVIEW RD
MOUNT WAY
MILL RD
RING RD
HOE CT
06
16
17
18

183
164

163
144

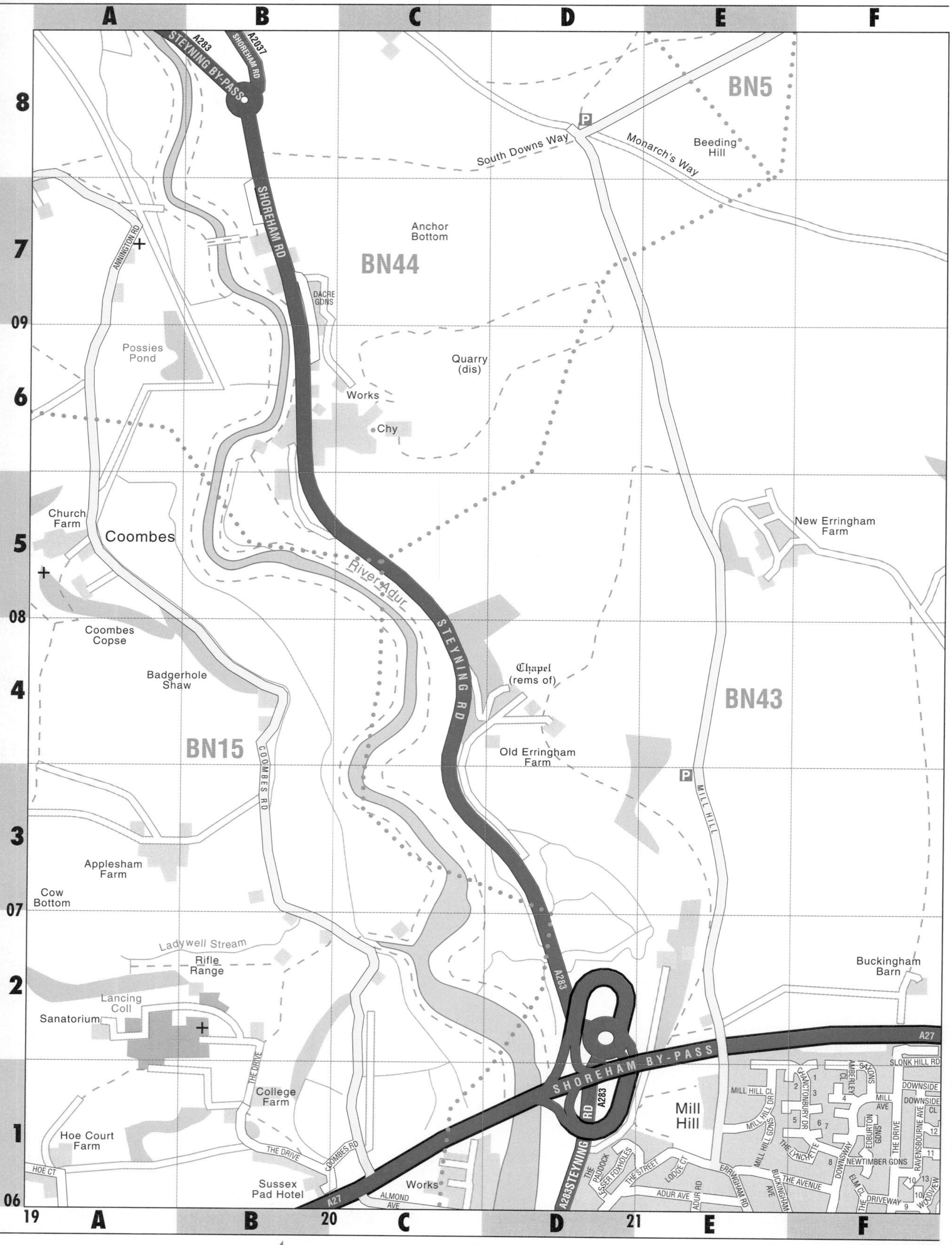
A
B
C
D
E
F
8
7
09
6
5
08
4
3
07
2
1
06
19
20
21
A283
STEYNING BY-PASS
A2037
SHOREHAM RD
BN5
Beeding Hill
South Downs Way
Monarch's Way
ANNINGTON RD
SHOREHAM RD
Anchor Bottom
BN44
DACRE GDNS
Possies Pond
Quarry (dis)
Works
Chy
Church Farm
Coombes
New Erringham Farm
River Adur
Coombes Copse
STEYNING RD
Chapel (rems of)
Badgerhole Shaw
BN43
BN15
COOMBES RD
Old Erringham Farm
MILL HILL
Applesham Farm
Cow Bottom
Ladywell Stream
Rifle Range
A283
Buckingham Barn
Lancing Coll
Sanatorium
A27
SHOREHAM BY-PASS
SLONK HILL RD
THE DRIVE
College Farm
MILL HILL CL
CHANCTONBURY DR
AMBERLEY CL
SAXONS
DOWNSIDE
MILL AVE
RD
A283
Mill Hill
MILL HILL DR
MILL HILL GDNS
THE LYNCHETTE
DOWNSWAY
EDBURTON GDNS
THE DRIVE
RAVENSBOURNE AVE
Hoe Court Farm
THE DRIVE
COOMBES RD
NEWTIMBER GDNS
HOE CT
Sussex Pad Hotel
Works
A27
ALMOND AVE
A283 STEYNING
THE PADDOCK
LESSER FOXHOLES
THE STREET
LODGE CT
ADUR AVE
ADUR RD
ERRINGHAM RD
BUCKINGHAM AVE
THE AVENUE
ELM CL
THE DRIVEWAY
WOODVIEW

163
184

F1
1 WESSEX WLK
2 WESTMORLAND WLK
3 WARWICK WLK
4 ANNINGTON GDNS
5 CISSBURY WAY
6 BLACKPATCH GR
7 WOLSTONBURY WLK
8 NOMANSCOURT
9 NORMAN CRES
10 BUCKINGHAM MEWS
11 RAVENSBOURNE CL
12 CYPRESS CL
13 WOODVIEW CT

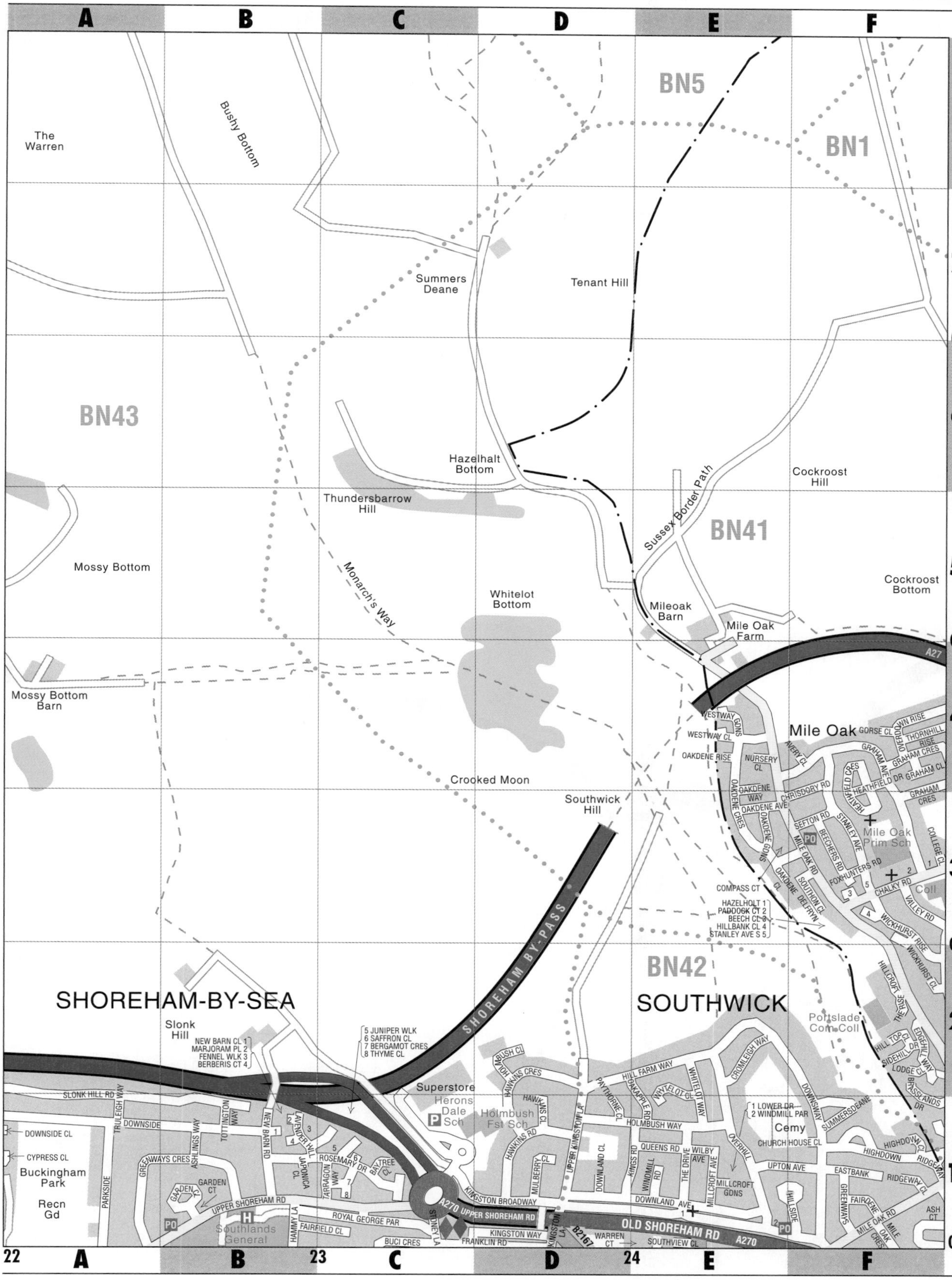
145
166
The Warren
Bushy Bottom
BN5
BN1
Summers Deane
Tenant Hill
BN43
Hazelhalt Bottom
Thundersbarrow Hill
Cockroost Hill
Sussex Border Path
BN41
Mossy Bottom
Monarch's Way
Whitelot Bottom
Mileoak Barn
Mile Oak Farm
Cockroost Bottom
Mossy Bottom Barn
Mile Oak
Crooked Moon
Southwick Hill
Mile Oak Prim Sch
Coll
BN42
SHOREHAM-BY-SEA
SOUTHWICK
Portslade Com Coll
Slonk Hill
SHOREHAM BY-PASS
Superstore
Herons Dale Sch
Holmbush Fst Sch
Cemy
Buckingham Park
Recn Gd
Southlands General
OLD SHOREHAM RD
UPPER SHOREHAM RD
KINGSTON BROADWAY
A27
A270
B2167
185
166

165
146

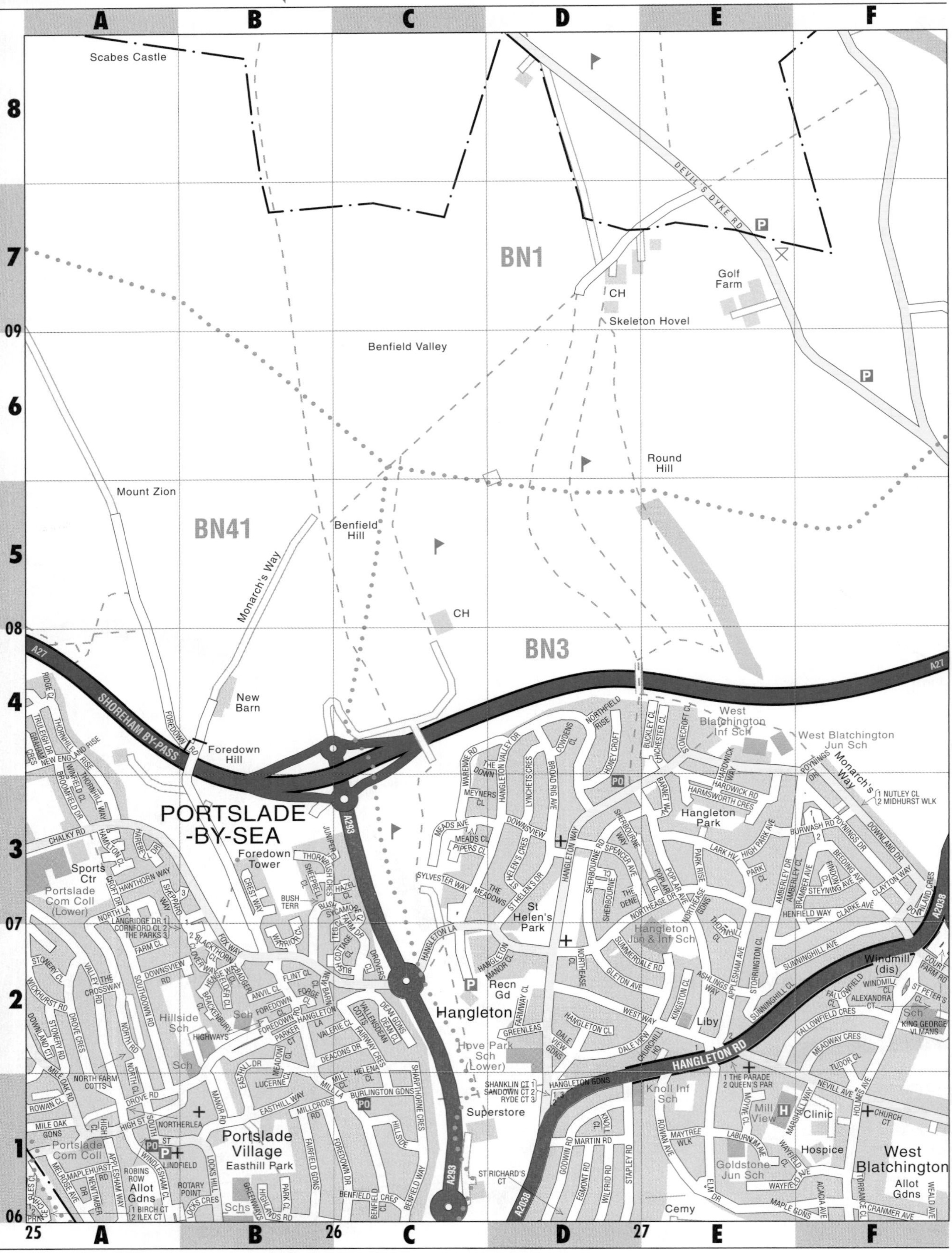
A
B
C
D
E
F
8
7
09
6
5
08
4
3
07
2
1
06
25
26
27
Scabes Castle
BN1
CH
Golf Farm
Skeleton Hovel
DEVIL'S DYKE RD
Benfield Valley
Round Hill
Mount Zion
BN41
Benfield Hill
Monarch's Way
CH
BN3
A27
SHOREHAM BY-PASS
New Barn
Foredown Hill
FOREDOWN RD
PORTSLADE -BY-SEA
Foredown Tower
A293
West Blatchington Inf Sch
West Blatchington Jun Sch
Monarch's Way
1 NUTLEY CL
2 MIDHURST WLK
Hangleton Park
Sports Ctr
Portslade Com Coll (Lower)
St Helen's Park
Hangleton Jun & Inf Sch
Windmill (dis)
A2038
Recn Gd
Hangleton
Hillside Sch
Sch
Liby
HANGLETON RD
Hove Park Sch (Lower)
Superstore
Knoll Inf Sch
Mill View
Clinic
Hospice
West Blatchington
Portslade Com Coll
Portslade Village
Easthill Park
Allot Gdns
Goldstone Jun Sch
Cemy
Allot Gdns
1 THE PARADE
2 QUEEN'S PAR
SHANKLIN CT
SANDOWN CT
RYDE CT
ST RICHARD'S CT
1 BIRCH CT
2 ILEX CT
LANGRIDGE DR
CORNFORD CL
THE PARKS
KING GEORGE VI MANS

147 168

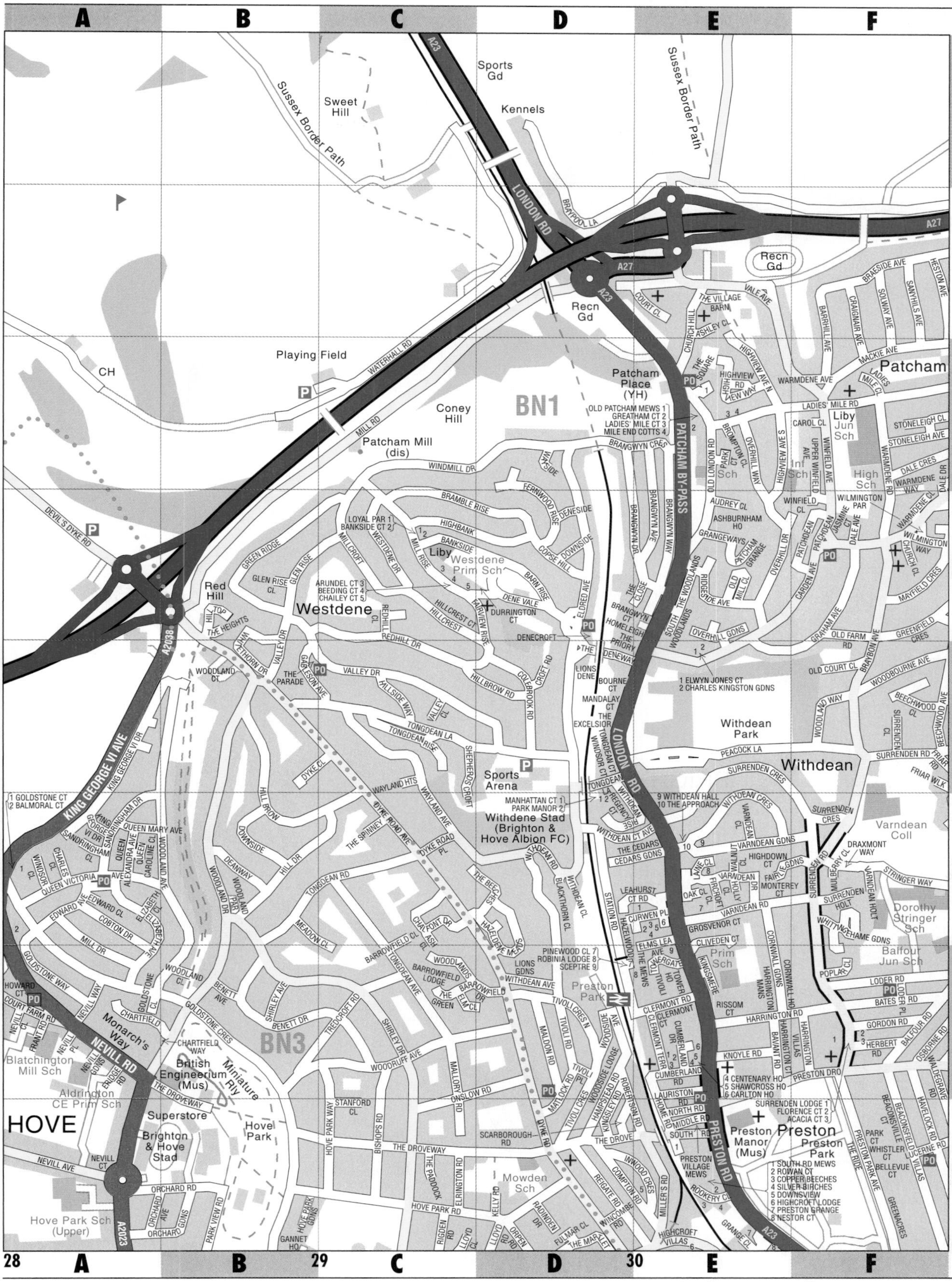

E2
1 LYNDEN CT
2 STAMFORD LODGE
3 CUMBERLAND LODGE

E3
1 LEAHURST CT
2 CHERRYWOOD
3 CEDARWOOD
4 MAPLEWOOD
5 PINEWOOD
6 BEECHWOOD
7 WITHDEAN CT
8 WELLINGTONIA CL

187 168

167
148

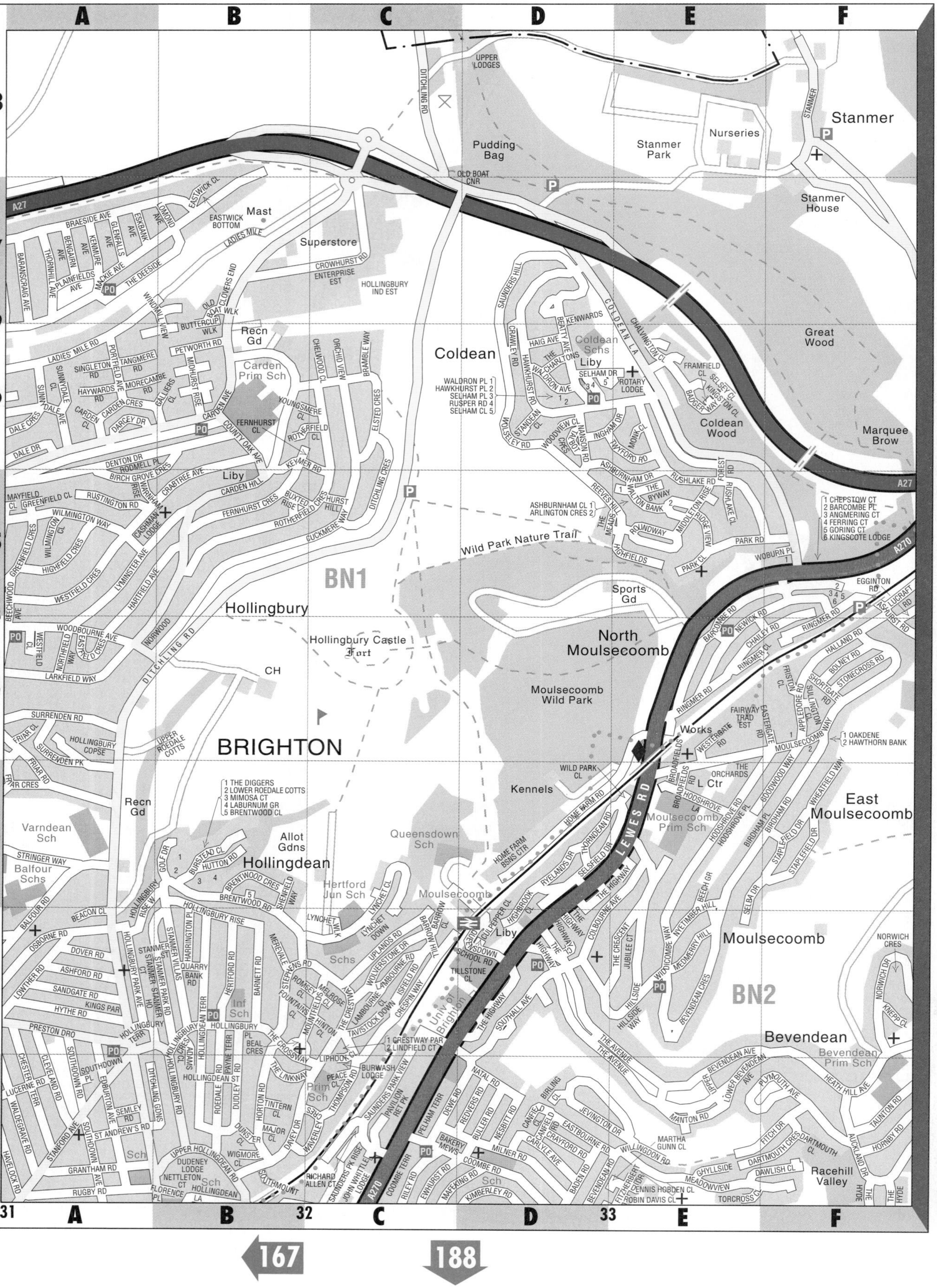
A
B
C
D
E
F
8
7
09
6
5
08
4
3
07
2
1
06
31
32
33
A27
A270
UPPER LODGES
DITCHLING RD
Pudding Bag
OLD BOAT CNR
Stanmer Park
Nurseries
Stanmer
STANMER
Stanmer House
Great Wood
Marquee Brow
EASTWICK CL
EASTWICK BOTTOM
Mast
LADIES MILE
BRAESIDE AVE
BARONSCRAIG AVE
THORNHILL AVE
BENGAIRN AVE
KENMURE AVE
GLENFALLS AVE
ESKBANK AVE
LOMOND AVE
MACKIE AVE
PLAINFIELDS AVE
THE DEESIDE
Superstore
CROWHURST RD
ENTERPRISE EST
HOLLINGBURY IND EST
CLOVERS END
OLD BOAT WLK
BUTTERCUP WLK
WINDMILL VIEW
Recn Gd
LADIES MILE RD
PORTFIELD AVE
TANGMERE RD
PETWORTH RD
MIDHURST RISE
SINGLETON RD
SUNNYDALE CL
HAYWARDS RD
MORECAMBE RD
GALLIERS CL
Carden Prim Sch
CARDEN AVE
CARDEN CRES
DARCEY DR
DALE CRES
DALE DR
FERNHURST CL
COUNTY OAK AVE
YOUNGSMERE CL
ROTHERFIELD CL
CHELWOOD CL
ORCHID VIEW
BRAMBLE WAY
ELSTED CRES
DENTON DR
RODMELL PL
BIRCH GROVE CRES
CRABTREE AVE
Liby
CARDEN HILL
KEYMER RD
MAYFIELD CL
GREENFIELD CL
RUSTINGTON RD
WARNHAM RISE
CASHMAN LODGE
FERNHURST CRES
BUXTED RISE
ROTHERFIELD CRES
HURST HILL
DITCHLING CRES
CUCKMERE WAY
WILMINGTON WAY
WILMINGTON CL
GREENFIELD CRES
HIGHFIELD CRES
LYMINSTER AVE
HARTFIELD AVE
WESTFIELD CRES
BEECHWOOD AVE
BN1
Hollingbury
Hollingbury Castle Fort
WOODBOURNE AVE
WESTFIELD CL
NORTHFIELD WAY
EASTFIELD CRES
NORWOOD
DITCHLING RD
LARKFIELD WAY
CH
SURRENDEN RD
FRIAR CL
HOLLINGBURY COPSE
SURRENDEN PK
UPPER ROEDALE COTTS
BRIGHTON
FRIAR RD
FRIAR CRES
Recn Gd
Varndean Sch
1 THE DIGGERS
2 LOWER ROEDALE COTTS
3 MIMOSA CT
4 LABURNUM GR
5 BRENTWOOD CL
Allot Gdns
Queensdown Sch
STRINGER WAY
Balfour Schs
GOLF DR
BURSTEAD CL
HUTTON RD
Hollingdean
BRENTWOOD CRES
BRENTWOOD RD
SHENFIELD WAY
Hertford Jun Sch
LYNCHET CL
LYNCHET WLK
LYNCHET DOWN
Moulsecoomb
BALFOUR RD
BEACON CL
OSBORNE RD
HOLLINGBURY RISE W
HOLLINGBURY RISE
DOVER RD
ASHFORD RD
SANDGATE RD
HYTHE RD
KINGS PAR
LOWTHER RD
STANMER ST
STANMER VILLAS
STANMER PARK RD
HARRINGTON PL
QUARRY BANK RD
HERTFORD RD
BARNETT RD
MEREVALE
STEPHENS RD
ROMSEY CL
FOUNTAINS CL
MOUNTFIELDS
HINTON CL
MELROSE CL
THE CRESTWAY
UPLANDS RD
WOLVERSTONE DR
LAMBOURNE RD
LAMBOURNE CL
TAVISTOCK DOWN
ISFIELD RD
CRESPIN WAY
BARROW HILL
BARROW CL
Schs
Inf Sch
HOLLINGBURY PARK AVE
HOLLINGBURY TERR
HOLLINGDEAN TERR
PRESTON DRO
SOUTHDOWN PL
SOUTHDOWN RD
CLEVELAND RD
CHESTER TERR
LUCERNE RD
WALDEGRAVE RD
HAVELOCK RD
STANFORD AVE
EDBURTON AVE
SEMLEY RD
ST ANDREW'S RD
SOUTHDOWN AVE
GRANTHAM RD
RUGBY RD
DITCHLING GDNS
HOLLINGBURY RD
ADAMS CL
HOLLINGDEAN ST
ROEDALE RD
PAYNE TERR
DUDLEY RD
BEAL CRES
THE CROSSWAY
THE LINKWAY
HORTON RD
TINTERN CL
MAJOR CL
DAVEY DR
DUNSTER CL
WIGMORE CL
UPPER HOLLINGDEAN RD
DUDENEY LODGE
NETTLETON CT
FLORENCE PL
HOLLINGDEAN LA
Sch
SOUTHMOUNT
RICHARD ALLEN CT
LIPHOOK CL
PEACE CL
Prim Sch
BURWASH LODGE
THOMPSON RD
WAVERLEY CRES
SAUNDERS PARK VIEW
SAUNDERS PK RISE
JOHN WHITTLE LODGE
PAVILION RET PK
1 CRESTWAY PAR
2 LINDFIELD CT
Univ of Brighton
Coldean
SAUNDERS HILL
CRAWLEY RD
HAWKHURST RD
HAIG AVE
THE CHARLTONS
BEATTY AVE
KENWARDS
Coldean Schs
WALDRON AVE
SELHAM DR
ROTARY LODGE
WALDRON PL 1
HAWKHURST PL 2
SELHAM PL 3
RUSPER RD 4
SELHAM CL 5
STANDEAN CL
WOLSELEY RD
WOODVIEW CL
NANSON RD
TALBOT CRES
INGHAM DR
MONK CL
TWYFORD RD
COLDEAN LA
CHALVINGTON CL
FRAMFIELD CL
SELSFIELD CL
KINGSTON CL
BADGERS WAY
Coldean Wood
ASHBURNHAM DR
THE BYWAY
WALTON BANK
RUSHLAKE RD
FOREST RD
RUSHLAKE CL
REEVES HILL
ASHBURNHAM CL 1
ARLINGTON CRES 2
THE MEADS
ROUNDWAY
MIDDLETON RISE
RIDGE VIEW
Wild Park Nature Trail
HIGHFIELDS
PARK RD
PARK CL
WOBURN PL
1 CHEPSTOW CT
2 BARCOMBE PL
3 ANGMERING CT
4 FERRING CT
5 GORING CT
6 KINGSCOTE LODGE
Sports Gd
North Moulsecoomb
EGGINTON RD
BARCOMBE RD
NEWICK RD
CHAILEY RD
RINGMER RD
LUCRAFT RD
ASHURST RD
HALLAND RD
BOLNEY RD
STONECROSS RD
Moulsecoomb Wild Park
FRISTON CL
SULLINGTON CL
SHORTGATE RD
APPLEDORE RD
FAIRWAY TRAD EST
EASTERGATE RD
Works
WESTERGATE RD
MOULSECOOMB WAY
1 OAKDENE
2 HAWTHORN BANK
WILD PARK CL
Kennels
BROADFIELDS RD
THE ORCHARDS
L Ctr
HOME FARM RD
HOME FARM BSNS CTR
LEWES RD
THORNDEAN RD
HODSHROVE LA
HODSHROVE RD
HODSHROVE PL
Moulsecoomb Prim Sch
BIRDHAM PL
BIRDHAM RD
BODDINGWOOD WAY
WHEATFIELD WAY
East Moulsecoomb
STAPLEFIELD DR
RYELANDS DR
SELSFIELD DR
THE HIGHWAY
COLBOURNE AVE
THE CRESCENT
JUBILEE CT
WIDDICOMBE WAY
NYETIMBER HILL
BEECH GR
SELBA DR
Moulsecoomb
NORWICH CRES
NORWICH DR
KNEPP CL
BN2
HIGHBROOK CL
CULPEPPER CL
SCHOOL RD
TILLSTONE CL
SOUTHALL AVE
HILLSIDE
HILLSIDE WAY
MCWHIRTER CL
BEVENDEAN CRES
Bevendean
Bevendean Prim Sch
THE AVENUE
UPPER BEVENDEAN AVE
LOWER BEVENDEAN AVE
PLYMOUTH AVE
HEATH HILL AVE
NATAL RD
DEWE RD
REDVERS RD
BULLER RD
NESBITT RD
PELHAM TERR
BAKERY MEWS
MILNER RD
COOMBE RD
COOMBE TERR
RILEY RD
EWHURST RD
MAFEKING RD
KIMBERLEY RD
Sch
BIRLING CL
CANFIELD CL
CANFIELD RD
CRAYFORD RD
CARLYLE AVE
EASTBOURNE RD
JEVINGTON DR
BADEN RD
BEVENDEAN RD
WILLINGDON RD
MARTHA GUNN CL
FITZHERBERT DR
DENNIS HOBDEN CL
ROBIN DAVIS CL
MEADOWVIEW
GHYLLSIDE
TORCROSS CL
MANTON RD
FITCH DR
DARTMOUTH CRES
DARTMOUTH CL
DAWLISH CL
Racehill Valley
TAUNTON RD
HORNBY RD
AUCKLAND DR
HYDE
THE HYDE

167
188

B8
1 WHITTINGTON CT
2 ST JAMES' RD
3 CHURCH PATH
4 MEADOW CT
5 WARWICK CT
6 KING'S TERR
7 OYSTER MEWS
8 FROBISHER GDNS
9 ST PETER'S SQ
10 WESTGROVE GDNS

C8
1 ST PETERS CT
2 FRANKLAND TERR

149
170

189
170

169 150

A B C D E F
8 7 05 6 5 04 4 3 03 2 1 02
77 78 79
Southbourne
LODGEBURY CL
Southbourne Jun & Inf Sch
Southbourne
NEW RD
GOODWOOD CT
MOSDELL RD
A259
LC
INLANDS RD
Ham Brook
PO10
SCHOOL LA
BELL CT
FARM LA
PO
MAIN RD
Nutbourne
Nursery
Marsh Farm
Works
Nutbourne
LC
FLATT RD
BROAD RD
POTTERY LA
BROAD MDW
MANSFIELD COTTS
MAYBUSH DR
PH
IVYDENE CRES
Flat Farm
Longacres
DRIFT LA
LC
GREEN LA
LC
The Bosham Inn (PH)
A259
HAMSTEAD MDW
Chidham Prim Sch
COT LA
CHIDHAM LA
Eastfield Farm
STEELS LA
PO18
Chidham Point
Middleton Farm
HARBOUR WAY
Landing Stages
Old House at Home (PH)
MARSH LA
Easton Farm
Chidham
Hard
Hovel Barn
Chidmere Pond
Thorney Channel
Cobnor Farm
New Barn
Cullimer's Pond
Bosham Channel
Hard
Cobnor Hard
Cobnor House

169 190

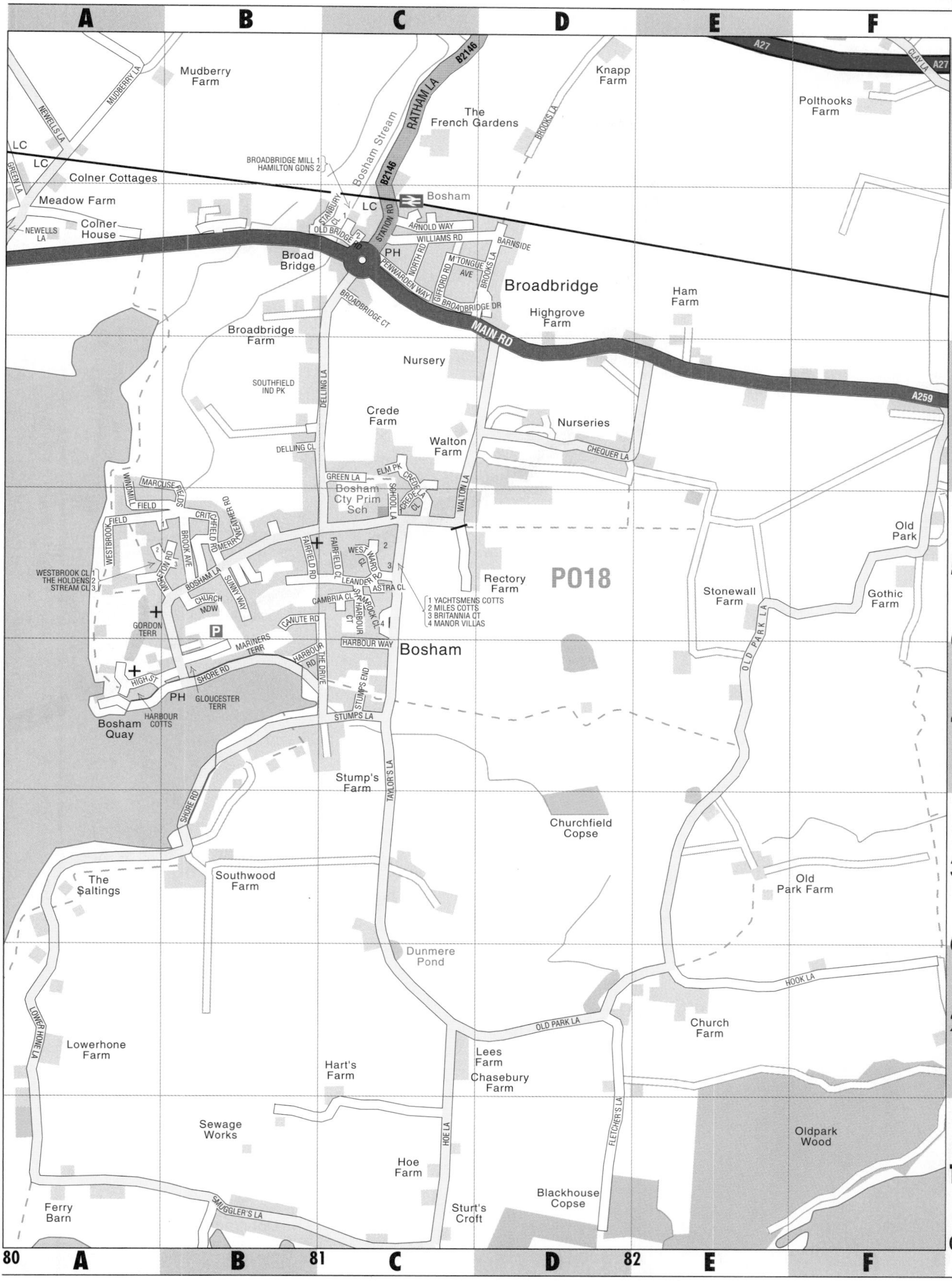
151
172
A
B
C
D
E
F
8
7
05
6
5
04
4
3
03
2
1
02
80
81
82
Mudberry Farm
Knapp Farm
Polthooks Farm
The French Gardens
Colner Cottages
Meadow Farm
Colner House
Bosham
Broad Bridge
Broadbridge
Ham Farm
Highgrove Farm
Broadbridge Farm
Nursery
SOUTHFIELD IND PK
Crede Farm
Nurseries
Walton Farm
Bosham Cty Prim Sch
Old Park
Rectory Farm
PO18
Stonewall Farm
Gothic Farm
1 YACHTSMENS COTTS
2 MILES COTTS
3 BRITANNIA CT
4 MANOR VILLAS
WESTBROOK CL 1
THE HOLDENS 2
STREAM CL 3
BROADBRIDGE MILL 1
HAMILTON GDNS 2
Bosham Quay
HARBOUR COTTS
GLOUCESTER TERR
GORDON TERR
Stump's Farm
Churchfield Copse
The Saltings
Southwood Farm
Old Park Farm
Dunmere Pond
Church Farm
Lowerhone Farm
Hart's Farm
Lees Farm
Chasebury Farm
Sewage Works
Oldpark Wood
Hoe Farm
Blackhouse Copse
Ferry Barn
Sturt's Croft
A27
A259
B2146
MAIN RD
RATHAM LA
STATION RD
DELLING LA
TAYLOR'S LA
OLD PARK LA
HOOK LA
LOWER HONE LA
SMUGGLER'S LA
HOE LA
FLETCHER'S LA
SHORE RD
CHEQUER LA
WALTON LA
BROOKS LA
191
172

171
152

F7
1 PAULUS CT
2 PASCOE CT
3 DENISON CT
4 LANCASTRIAN GRANGE
5 THE PROVIDENCE
6 PROVIDENCE PL

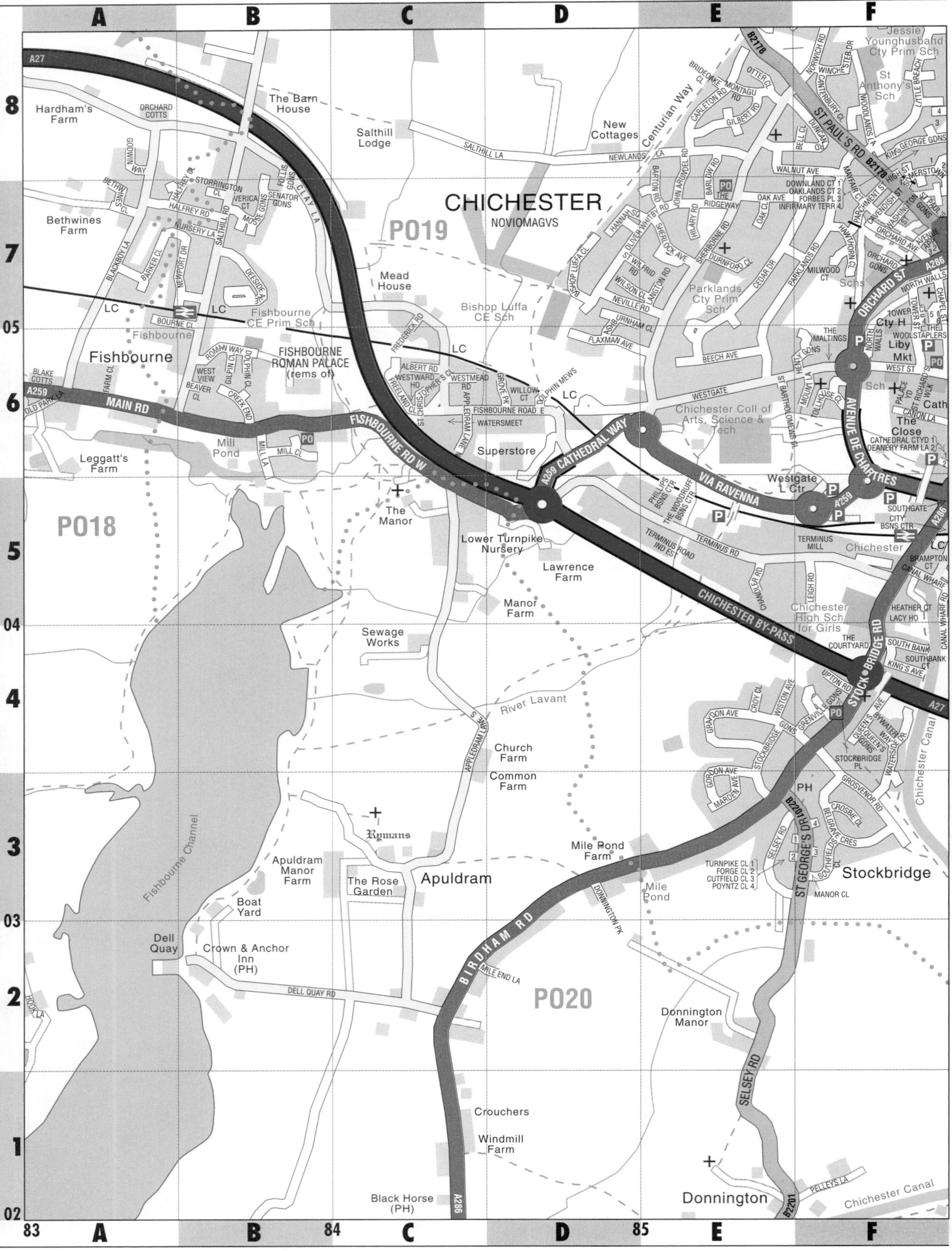

171
192

A6
1 ST MARY'S LODGE
2 EAST WALLS CL
3 EAST ROW MEWS
4 SADLERS WLK
5 LITTLE LONDON MEWS
6 JAY WLK
7 BAFFINS CT
8 VICARS CL
9 THEATRE PL
10 OLD MARKET AVE
11 NEW TOWN

153
174

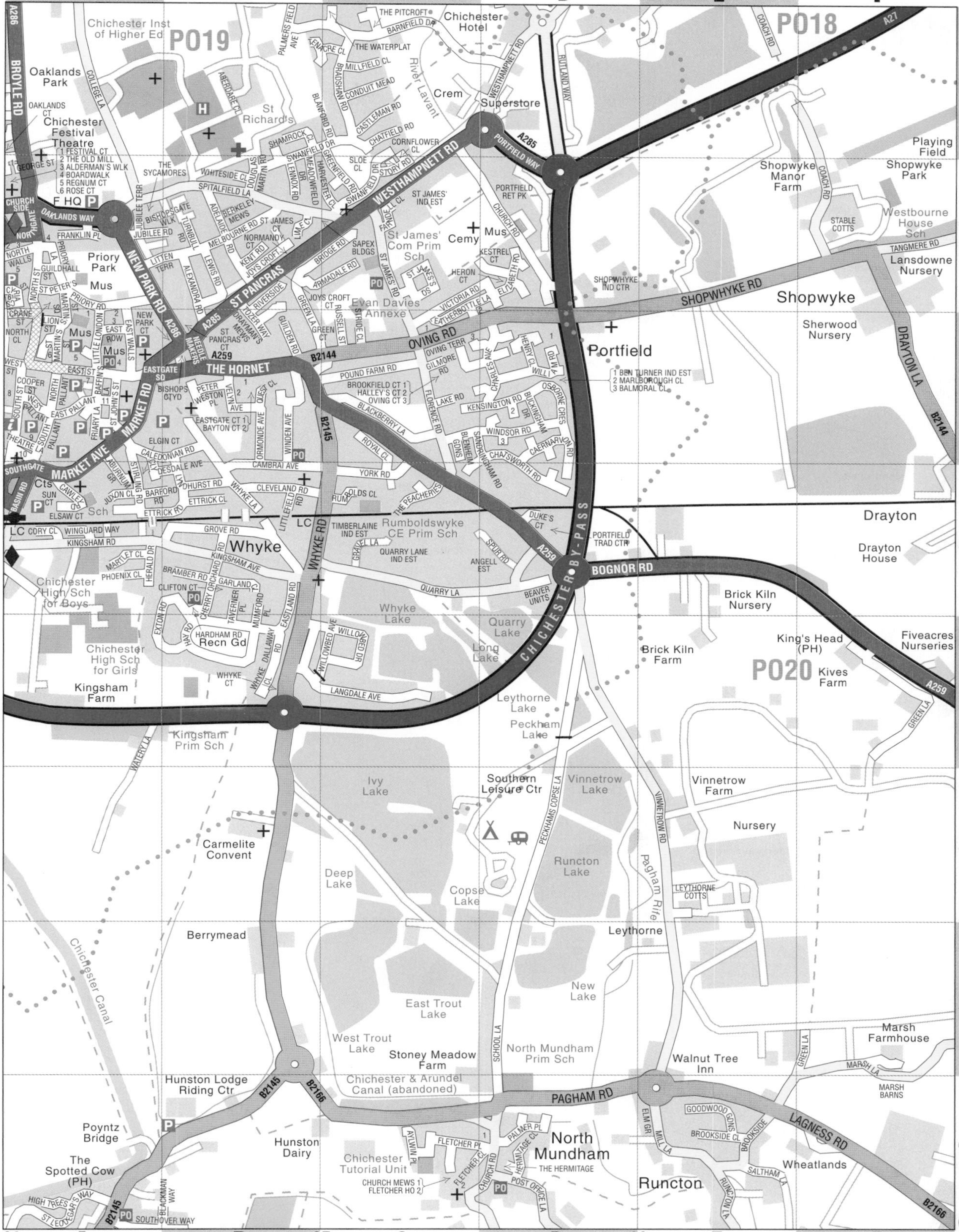

193
174

173
154

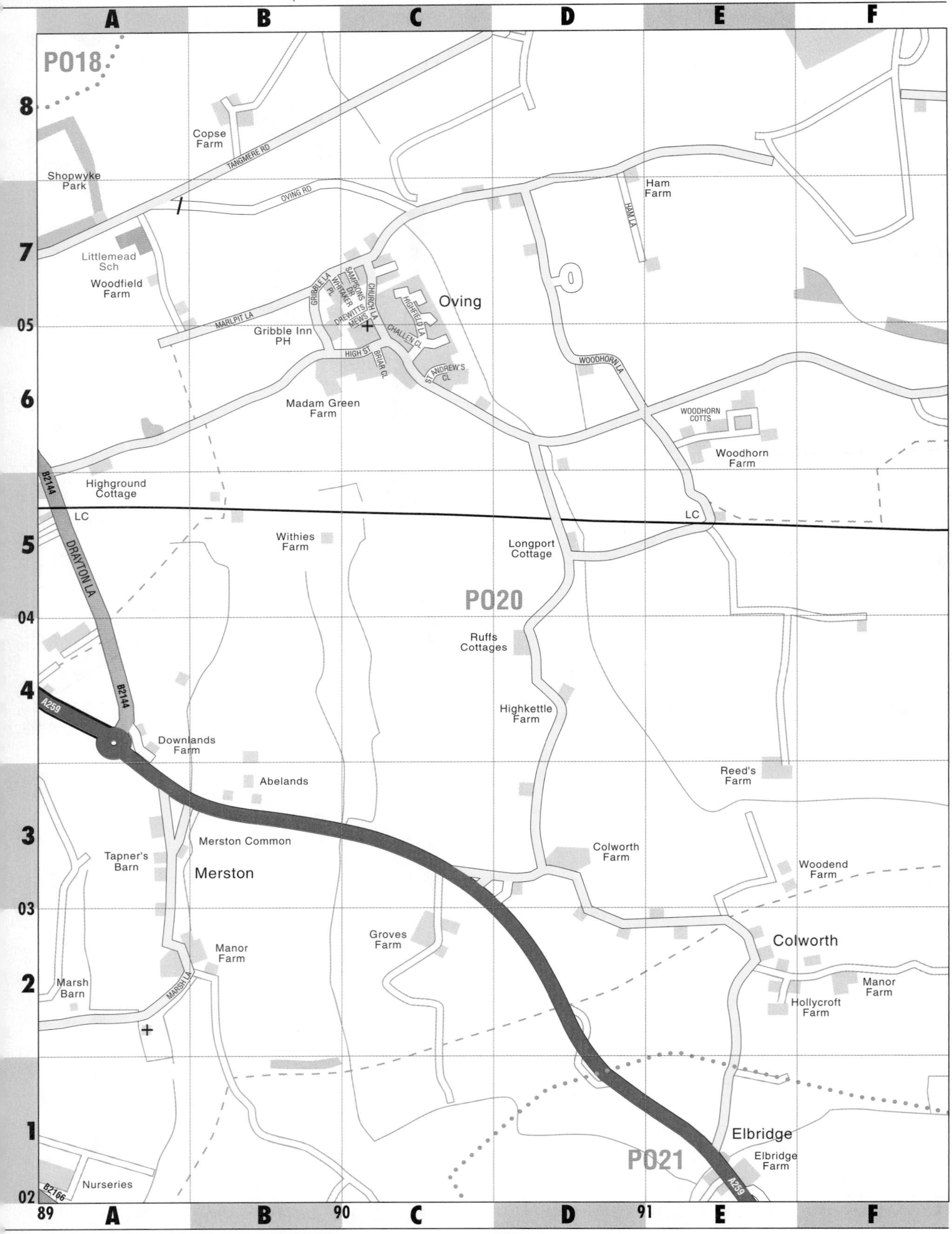
A
B
C
D
E
F
PO18
Copse Farm
TANGMERE RD
Shopwyke Park
OVING RD
Ham Farm
HAM LA
Littlemead Sch
Woodfield Farm
GRIBBLE LA
WHITAKER PL
SAMPSONS DR
CHURCH LA
DREWITTS MEWS
HIGHFIELD LA
CHALLEN CL
Oving
MARLPIT LA
Gribble Inn PH
HIGH ST
BRIAR CL
ST ANDREW'S CL
WOODHORN LA
Madam Green Farm
WOODHORN COTTS
Woodhorn Farm
B2144
Highground Cottage
LC
Withies Farm
Longport Cottage
DRAYTON LA
PO20
Ruffs Cottages
A259
Highkettle Farm
Downlands Farm
Abelands
Reed's Farm
Merston Common
Tapner's Barn
Merston
Colworth Farm
Woodend Farm
Groves Farm
Colworth
Manor Farm
Marsh Barn
MARSH LA
Hollycroft Farm
Elbridge
PO21
Elbridge Farm
Nurseries
B2166
8
7
05
6
5
04
4
3
03
2
1
02
89
90
91

173
194

155
176

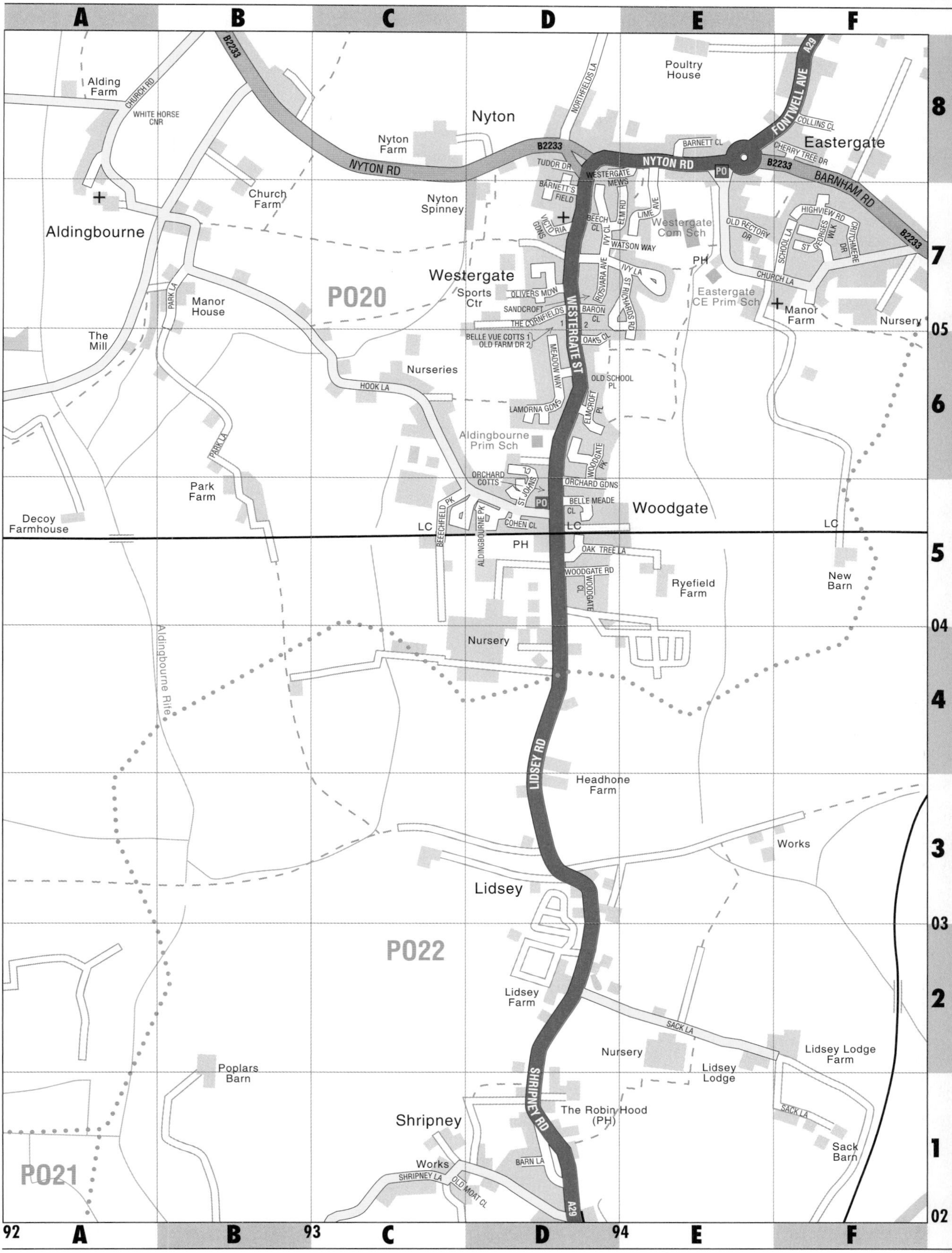
A
B
C
D
E
F
Alding Farm
WHITE HORSE CNR
CHURCH RD
Aldingbourne
Church Farm
Nyton
Nyton Farm
NYTON RD
B2233
Nyton Spinney
Poultry House
NORTHFIELDS LA
Eastergate
FONTWELL AVE
A29
COLLINS CL
CHERRY TREE DR
BARNETT CL
NYTON RD
PO
BARNHAM RD
WESTERGATE MEWS
TUDOR DR
BARNETT'S FIELD
Westergate Com Sch
Westergate
Sports Ctr
OLIVERS MDW
SANDCROFT
THE CORNFIELDS
BELLE VUE COTTS
OLD FARM DR
WESTERGATE ST
PO20
Manor House
PARK LA
The Mill
Nurseries
HOOK LA
MEADOW WAY
LAMORNA GDNS
OLD SCHOOL PL
ELMCROFT PL
Aldingbourne Prim Sch
WOODGATE PK
ORCHARD COTTS
ORCHARD GDNS
BELLE MEADE CL
Woodgate
Park Farm
Decoy Farmhouse
LC
BEECHFIELD PK
ALDINGBOURNE PK
COHEN CL
PH
OAK TREE LA
WOODGATE RD
Ryefield Farm
Eastergate CE Prim Sch
Manor Farm
Nursery
OLD RECTORY DR
SCHOOL LA
HIGHVIEW RD
CRITCHMERE DR
CHURCH LA
New Barn
Nursery
Aldingbourne Rife
LIDSEY RD
Headhone Farm
Works
Lidsey
PO22
Lidsey Farm
SACK LA
Nursery
Lidsey Lodge Farm
Lidsey Lodge
Poplars Barn
SHRIPNEY RD
The Robin Hood (PH)
Shripney
Works
SHRIPNEY LA
OLD MOAT CL
BARN LA
Sack Barn
PO21
8
7
05
6
5
04
4
3
03
2
1
02
92
93
94

195
176

175
156

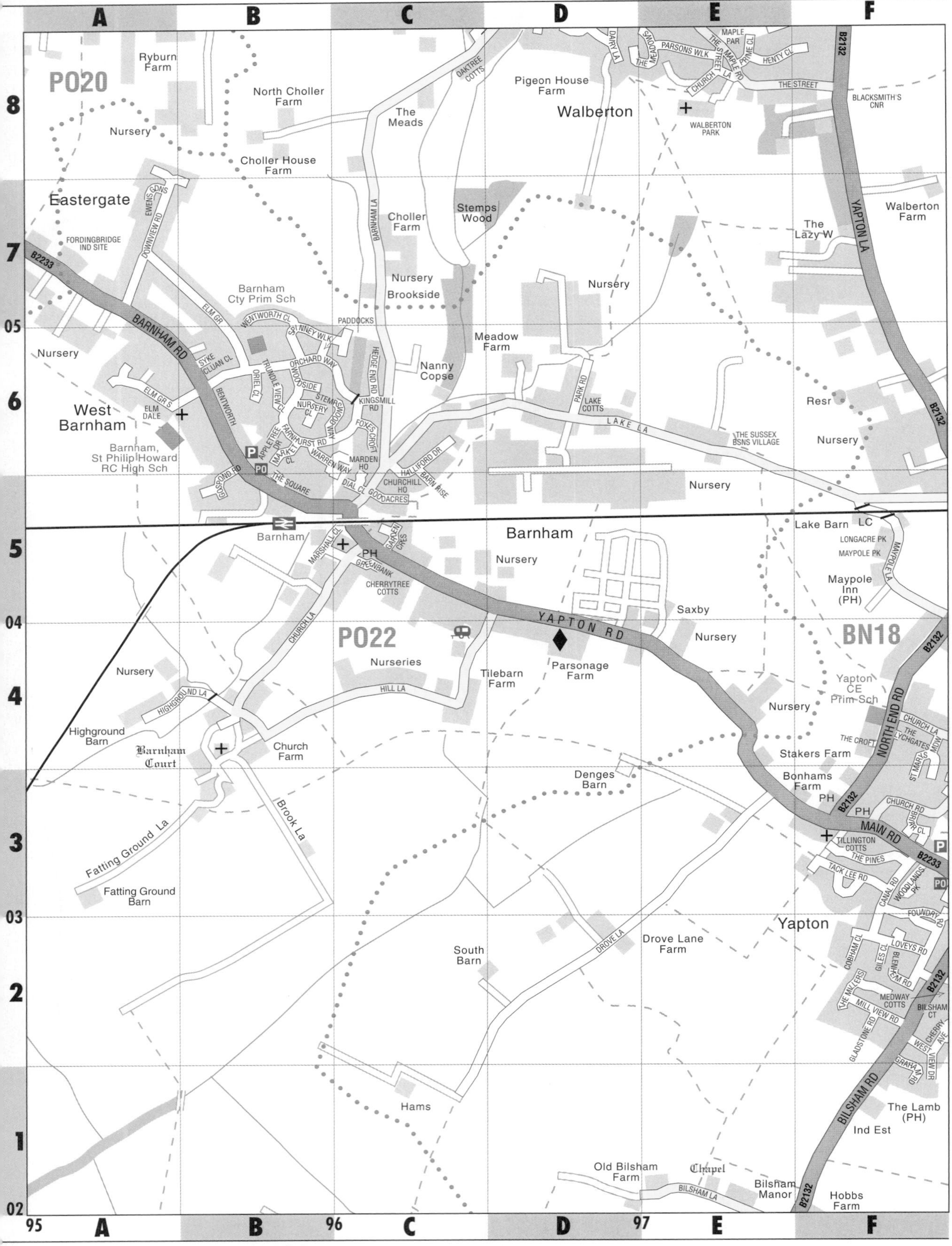
A
B
C
D
E
F
8
7
05
6
5
04
4
3
03
2
1
02
95
96
97
PO20
PO22
BN18
Ryburn Farm
North Choller Farm
Nursery
Choller House Farm
Eastergate
FORDINGBRIDGE IND SITE
EWENS GDNS
DOWNVIEW RD
B2233
BARNHAM RD
Barnham Cty Prim Sch
ELM GR
WENTWORTH CL
SPINNEY WLK
PADDOCKS
ORCHARD WAY
SYKE CLUAN CL
ORIEL CL
TRUNDLE VIEW CL
WOODSIDE
NURSERY CL
STEMPS
ELM GR S
ELM DALE
West Barnham
BENTWORTH
Barnham, St Philip Howard RC High Sch
APPLETREE DR
MARKET CL
FARNHURST RD
WARREN WAY
MARDEN HO
KINGSMILL RD
FOXES CROFT
HEDGE END RD
BARNHAM LA
CHURCHILL HO
DIAL CL
GOODACRES
HALLIFORD DR
BARN RISE
GOSPORD RD
THE SQUARE
P
PO
The Meads
Choller Farm
Nursery
Brookside
OAKTREE COTTS
Stemps Wood
Nanny Copse
Meadow Farm
Pigeon House Farm
Walberton
DARY LA
THE MEADOWS
PARSONS WLK
THE STREET
CHURCH LA
MAPLE PAR
MAPLE RD
PRIME CL
HENTY CL
THE STREET
WALBERTON PARK
BLACKSMITH'S CNR
B2132
YAPTON LA
Walberton Farm
The Lazy W
Nursery
PARK RD
LAKE COTTS
LAKE LA
THE SUSSEX BSNS VILLAGE
Resr
Nursery
Nursery
Barnham
MARSHALL CL
GARDEN CRES
PH
GREENBANK
CHERRYTREE COTTS
Nursery
YAPTON RD
Saxby
Nursery
Lake Barn
LC
LONGACRE PK
MAYPOLE PK
MAYPOLE LA
Maypole Inn (PH)
CHURCH LA
Nursery
HIGHGROUND LA
Nurseries
HILL LA
Tilebarn Farm
Parsonage Farm
Yapton CE Prim Sch
Nursery
Highground Barn
Barnham Court
Church Farm
Denges Barn
Stakers Farm
Bonhams Farm
PH
PH
NORTH END RD
CHURCH LA
THE LYCHGATES
THE CROFT
ST MARYS MW
CHURCH RD
BRIAR CL
MAIN RD
TILLINGTON COTTS
THE PINES
TACK LEE RD
CANAL RD
WOODLANDS PK
FOUNDRY RD
Brook La
Fatting Ground La
Fatting Ground Barn
Yapton
South Barn
DROVE LA
Drove Lane Farm
COBHAM CL
GILES CL
BLENHEIM RD
LOVEYS RD
THE MILLERS
MILL VIEW RD
MEDWAY COTTS
BILSHAM CT
GLADSTONE RD
WEST VIEW DR
CHERRY AVE
GRAHAM RD
BILSHAM RD
Hams
The Lamb (PH)
Ind Est
Old Bilsham Farm
Chapel
BILSHAM LA
Bilsham Manor
Hobbs Farm

175
196

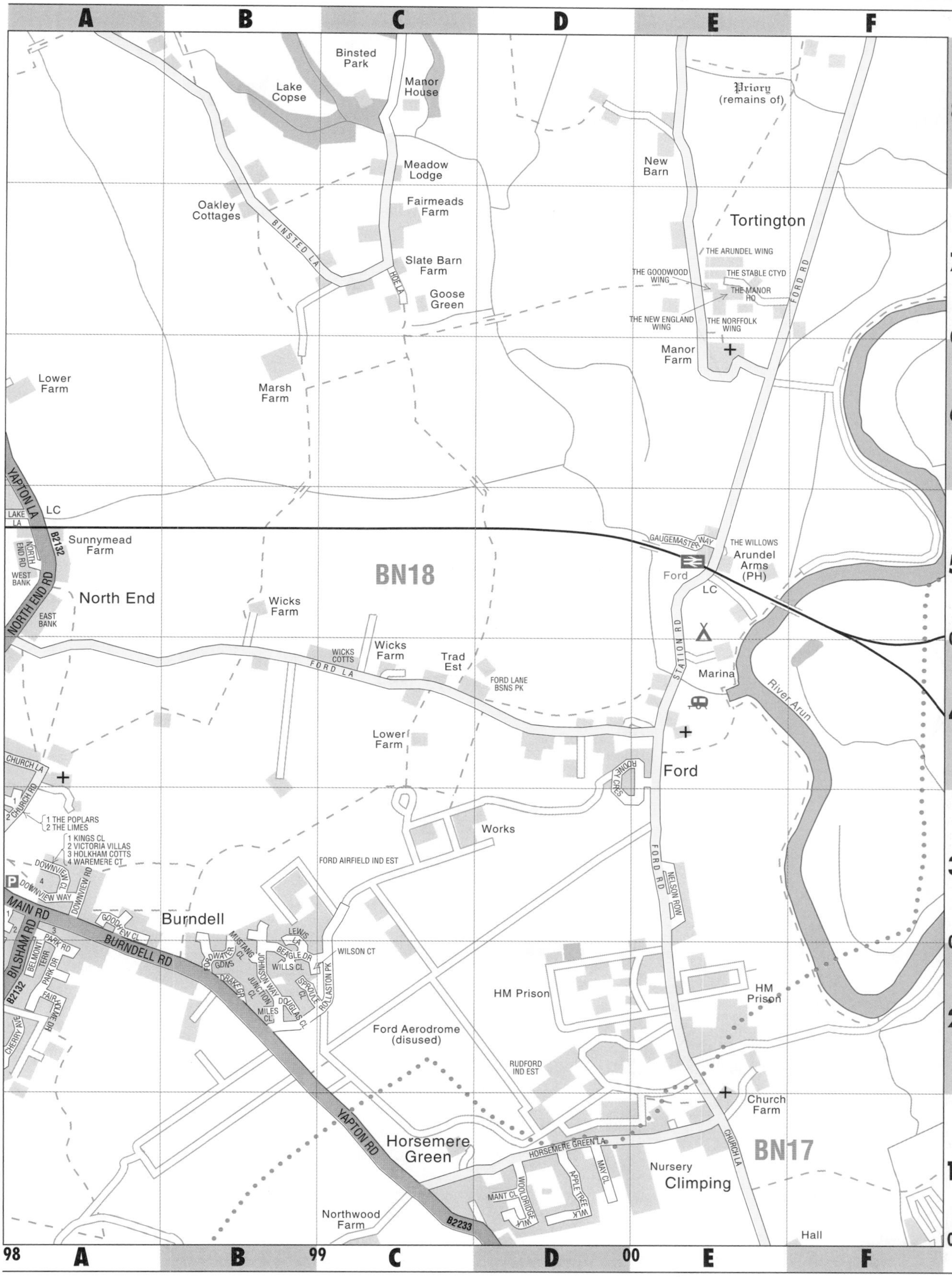
157
178
197
178
Binsted Park
Lake Copse
Manor House
Priory (remains of)
New Barn
Meadow Lodge
Oakley Cottages
Fairmeads Farm
Tortington
BINSTED LA
Slate Barn Farm
HOE LA
Goose Green
THE ARUNDEL WING
THE GOODWOOD WING
THE STABLE CTYD
THE MANOR HO
THE NEW ENGLAND WING
THE NORFOLK WING
FORD RD
Manor Farm
Lower Farm
Marsh Farm
YAPTON LA
LAKE LA
LC
Sunnymead Farm
B2132
NORTH END RD
WEST BANK
EAST BANK
North End
BN18
Wicks Farm
GAUGEMASTER WAY
THE WILLOWS
Arundel Arms (PH)
Ford
LC
STATION RD
Marina
River Arun
WICKS COTTS
FORD LA
Wicks Farm
Trad Est
FORD LANE BSNS PK
Lower Farm
Ford
ROONEY CRS
CHURCH LA
CHURCH RD
1 THE POPLARS
2 THE LIMES
1 KINGS CL
2 VICTORIA VILLAS
3 HOLKHAM COTTS
4 WAREMERE CT
DOWNVIEW CL
DOWNVIEW WAY
DOWNVIEW RD
Works
FORD AIRFIELD IND EST
MAIN RD
Burndell
GOODVIEW CL
BURNDELL RD
BILSHAM RD
BELMONT TERR
PARK RD
PARK DR
FAIRVIEW
LEWIS LA
MUSTANG CL
BEAGLE DR
WILSON CT
FORDWATER GDNS
JOHNSON WAY
WILLS CL
DRAKE GR
JUNCTION CL
SPROULE CL
ROLLASTON PK
MILES CL
DOUGLAS CL
CHERRY AVE
NELSON ROW
HM Prison
HM Prison
Ford Aerodrome (disused)
RUDFORD IND EST
YAPTON RD
Church Farm
Horsemere Green
HORSEMERE GREEN LA
CHURCH LA
BN17
Nursery
Climping
MAY CL
MANT CL
WOOLDRIDGE WLK
APPLE TREE WLK
Northwood Farm
B2233
Hall
A
B
C
D
E
F
8
7
05
6
5
04
4
3
03
2
1
02
98
99
00

177
158

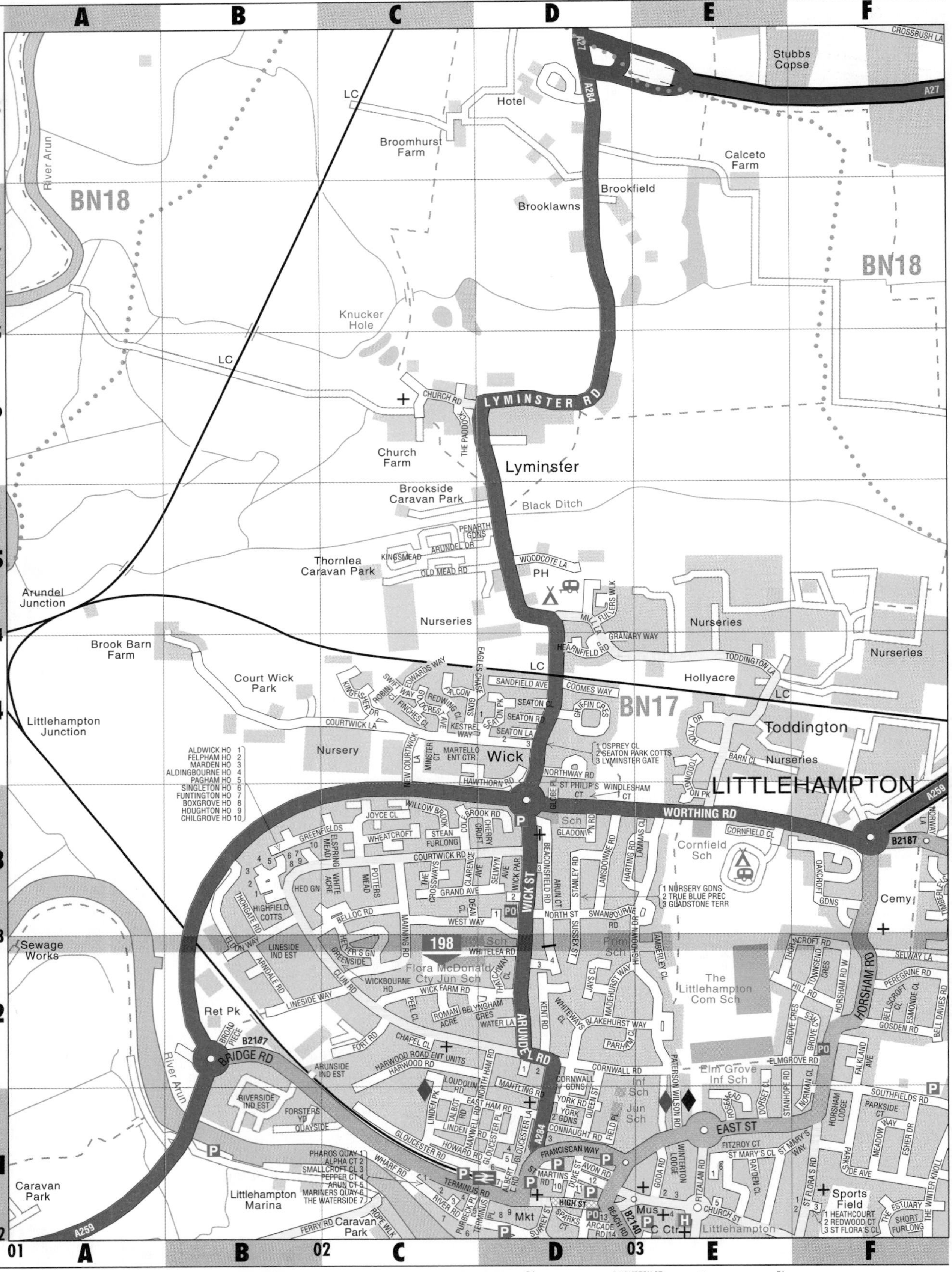

177
198

D1
1 SCOTT LODGE
2 THATCHERS LODGE
3 DEVON CT
4 WYCHCROFT
5 HOWARD PL
6 MADEHURST CT
7 ROSE CT
8 HAMPTON CT
9 ANTONIA CT
10 ST MARTIN'S LA
11 DUKE'S CT
12 ANCHOR SPRINGS
13 THE ARCADE
14 EVANS GDNS

D2
1 MERTON DR
2 QUANTOCKS
3 MALTHOUSE PAS
4 HAMPTON FIELDS

E1
1 ST MARY'S GDNS
2 TEMPLE CT
3 AMENIC CT
4 WHITE LODGE
5 SUMMERLEA GDNS
6 ST MARY'S CT

159
180

A
B
C
D
E
F
BN13
Hammerpot
The Woodman Arms (PH)
Charloe Copse
Poling Corner
Westlands Copse
St John's Priory (remains of)
The Nurseries
ARUNDEL RD
A27
Newplace Farm
B2225
Perry Barn
Orchard Rough
Poling Furzefields
BN18
POLING ST
Steyne Wood
St Margaret's CE Prim Sch
Decoy Pond
Peckhams
Decoy Wood
Poling
ARUNDEL RD
Manor Farm
Black Ditch
New Barn
LONGBACK COTTS 1
ST MARGARET'S CT 2
LANSDOWNE CL 3
HUDDLESTONES 4
St Wilfrid's Catholic Prim Sch
Old Place Farm
RECTORY LA
Liby
A280
WATER LA
HIGH ST
THE THATCHWAY
Angmering
CHAPEL WLK 1
CHURCH RD 2
HILLSIDE CRES 3
CUMBERLAND CRES 4
BN16
MILL RD
THE COTTRELLS
STATION RD
NORTH DR
Littlefield Farm
CH
BADGERS WLK 1
LIME GR 2
BLUE CEDARS CL
HAM MANOR WAY
Old Brook Barn
LC
HAM MANOR FARM COTTS
Golf Ctr
BN17
WEST DR
EAST DR
GOLFERS LA
The Angmering Sch
1 DREWETTS CL
2 BLENHEIM CL
CONISTON WAY 1
ULLSWATER DR 2
NEW RD
A259
ROUNDSTONE BY-PASS RD
WORTHING RD
Superstore
Superstore
HEATHFIELD AVE
DOWNS WAY
BROOKSIDE IND EST
MILL LA
B2187
199
Angmering
WORTHING RD
B2140
Recn Gd
Sch
Prim Sch
B2140
STATION RD
Recn Gd
BEAUMONT CT 1
FARM ACRE 2
FLINT CL 3
VICARAGE LA
BARN ROW 1
BAY TREE GDN 2
BAY TREES CL 3
WEST PRESTON MEWS
WEST PRESTON MANOR
THE STREET
CHURCHILL PAR
Rustington
Zachary Merton Com
SEA LA
CUDLOW AVE
CUDLOW GDN
Liby
04
05
06
8
7
05
6
5
04
4
3
03
2
1
02

A2
1 TIMBERLEYS
2 BERMUDA CT
3 SCHOONER CT
4 BEAUFORT CT
5 THE MOORINGS
6 SEXTANT CT
7 MOUNTBATTEN CT

B1
1 HIGHFIELD GDNS
2 CLARE LODGE
3 RICHMOND CT

C1
1 ROWAN HO
2 WINDERMERE
3 STERLING PAR
4 BROADMARK PAR
5 CHURCHILL CT
6 BROADMARK HO
7 WHITECROFT
8 EASTERGATE GN
9 FITTLEWORTH GDN
10 SILVERWOOD CT
11 CHICHESTER CT
12 ARUNDEL GDN

C2
1 MENDIP CT
2 DONNINGTON PL
3 TRAFALGAR CT

199

D2
1 ST ANTHONY'S WAY
2 HERNE CT
3 SHIRLANDS CT

180

E2
1 RICHMOND CL
2 THORNTON CT
3 MUNMERE WAY
4 COPPER HALL CL
5 CRUNDENS CNR
6 STATION PAR

179
160

A
B
C
D
E
F
8
7
05
6
5
04
4
3
03
2
1
02
07
08
09
Fox Rough
Merrivale Farm
The Fox (PH)
Selden
France Cottages
Patching Pond
Clapham Common
Cottage Rough
Horse & Groom (PH)
A27
Mast
ARUNDEL RD
Ecclesden Common
Poling Furzefields
Oak Tree Farm
WATER LA
Potlands Copse
Northdown Farm Buildings
BN13
Herons Farm
Motor Racing Circuit
Groom's Copse
Northdown Copse
Woodlands Stables
Titnore Wood
Nurseries
Miles's Copse
Ecclesden Farm
Highdown Copse
Goring Wood
Avenals Farm
Ham Spinney
The Spotted Cow (PH)
Ecclesden Manor
The Mill House
Highdown Hill
Highdown Tower
Nurseries
Hill Barn
Highdown Gardens
BN16
Road under construction
South Ecclesden Farm
Hill View Farm
Hangleton
Hangleton Farm
BN12
Nurseries
Nurseries
LITTLEHAMPTON RD
Roundstone Farm
ROUNDSTONE BY-PASS RD
A259
OLD WORTHING RD
LC
Caravan Park
Ferring
East Preston
Schs
Liby
Park Barn
Ferring Rife
Caravan Park
Kingston Manor
East Kingston
Sch
200

161
182

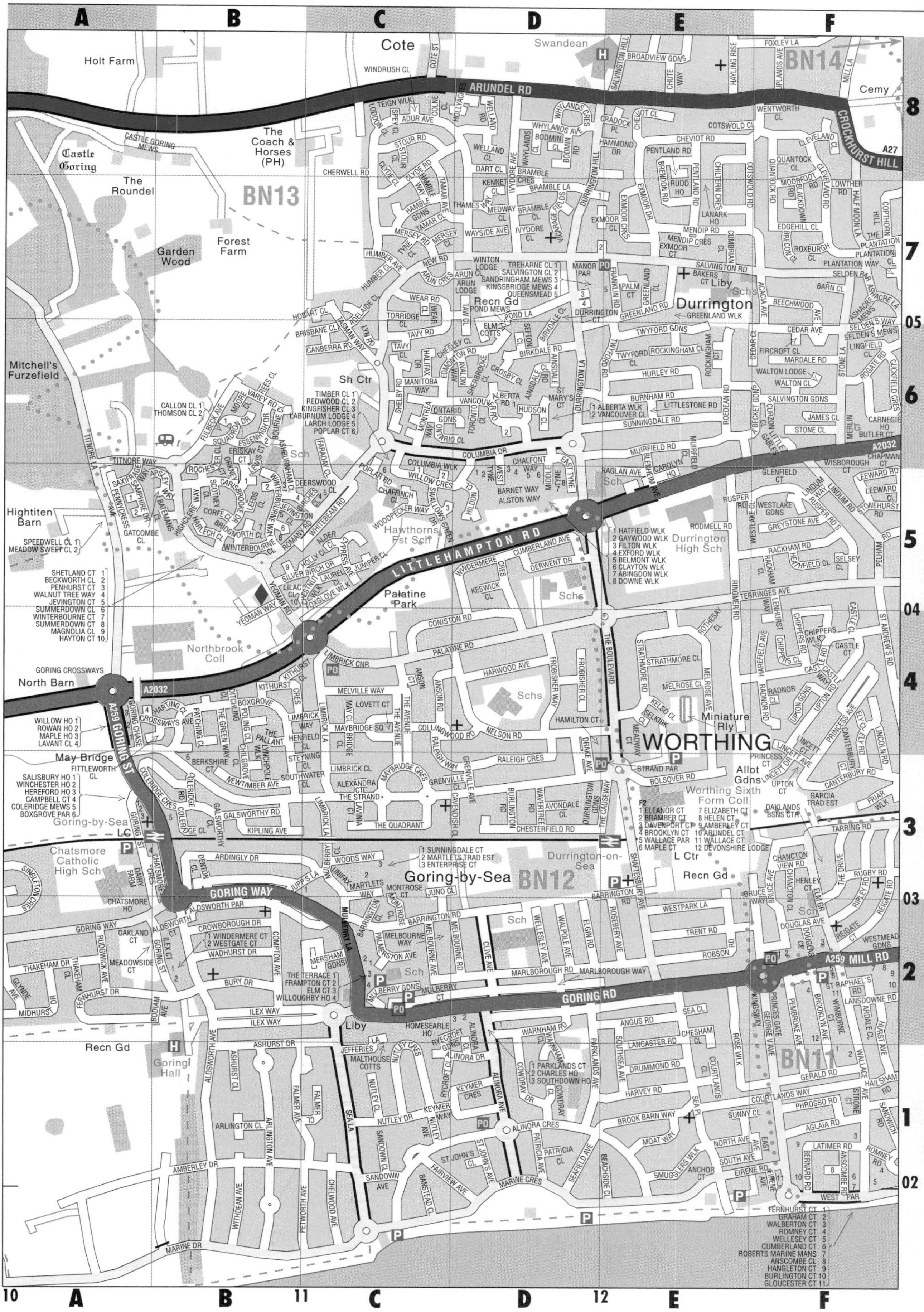
A
B
C
D
E
F
10
11
12
8
7
05
6
5
04
4
3
03
2
1
02
Cote
Swandean
Holt Farm
BN14
Cemy
ARUNDEL RD
CROCKHURST HILL
A27
Castle Goring
The Coach & Horses (PH)
The Roundel
BN13
Garden Wood
Forest Farm
Durrington
Recn Gd
Sh Ctr
Mitchell's Furzefield
Hightiten Barn
LITTLEHAMPTON RD
A2032
Hawthorns Fst Sch
Durrington High Sch
Palatine Park
Northbrook Coll
North Barn
GORING CROSSWAYS
May Bridge
GORING ST
A259
Miniature Rly
WORTHING
Allot Gdns
Worthing Sixth Form Coll
Goring-by-Sea
Chatsmore Catholic High Sch
Durrington-on-Sea
Goring-by-Sea
BN12
L Ctr
Recn Gd
GORING WAY
GORING RD
A259 MILL RD
BN11
Liby
Recn Gd
Goring Hall
MARINE DR
WEST PAR
SALVINGTON RD
SALVINGTON GDNS
COLUMBIA DR
PALATINE RD
THE BOULEVARD
STRAND PAR
THE STRAND
MULBERRY LA
SEA LA
ALINORA CRES
MARINE CRES
COURTLANDS WAY
BROOK BARN WAY
TARRING RD
TERRINGES AVE
FERNHURST CT 1
GRAHAM CT 2
WALBERTON CT 3
ROMNEY CT 4
WELLESEY CT 5
CUMBERLAND CT 6
ROBERTS MARINE MANS 7
ANSCOMBE CT 8
HANGLETON CT 9
BURLINGTON CT 10
GLOUCESTER CT 11

A1
1 CHICHESTER CT
2 EXETER CT
3 LICHFIELD CT
4 CARDINAL CT
5 WINDLESHAM CT
6 BELMER CT
7 DOWNVIEW CT
8 WINCHELSEA CT
9 HASTINGS CT
10 SUN CT
11 DAVIES CT
12 DOLPHIN LODGE
13 MARINE POINT

181

A2
1 WELLINGTON CT
2 CHESTER LODGE
3 CHARLWOOD LODGE
4 LANCASTER HO
5 RAGLAN CT
6 PARHAM CT

162

7 LANGHAM CT
A3
1 STATION PAR
2 WESTDOWN CT
3 RUGBY CT
4 CAMARGUE CT
5 QUEENSBOROUGH CT

A5
1 RECTORY MEWS
2 ELIZABETH HO
3 TRENT HO
4 FAIROAK CT
5 DORSET PL
6 PELHAM CT

7 BELLVIEW CT
B1
1 FULMER CT
2 WILLMINGTON CT
3 BEVERLEY CT
4 SEAVIEW CT
5 UNITA HO

6 SHREWSBURY CT
7 WAVERLEY CT
8 CAVERSHAM CT
9 NORMANDY CT
10 QUINTA CARMEN
11 SEABRIGHT
12 SHERATON CT

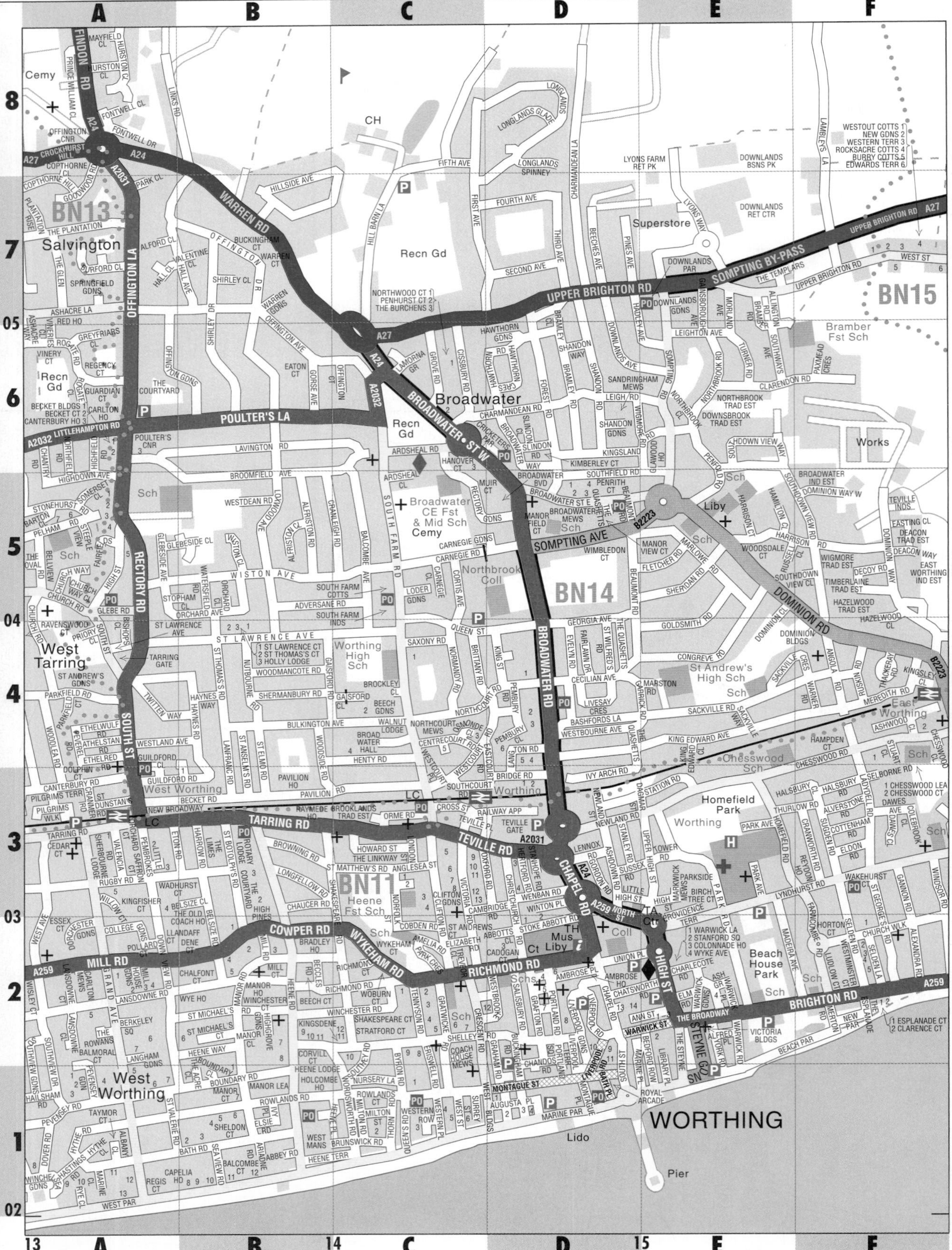

B2
1 REDCOTTS
2 CHAPPELL CROFT
3 THE MANOR
4 WESTBURY CT
5 GREENTREES
6 HARLEY CT
7 HOMEPIER HO
8 AIRDALE CT
9 WEST VIEW CT

10 LINCOLN HO
11 MORA SOOMAREE
B3
1 PILGRIMS CL
2 ST BOTOLPHS CT
3 WHITWORTH HO
C1
1 SANDOWN CT
2 MILTON CT
3 EDINBURGH COTTS

4 BURLEIGH CT
5 BELMAINE CT
6 WYVERN CT
C2
1 BEECHWOOD CT
2 WESSEX CT
3 HARDWICK LODGE
4 TENNYSON HO
5 OAKLAND CT
6 AVILA HO

181

7 CAMBOURNE CT
8 GREENA CT
9 CRANLEIGH CT
10 HOPEDENE CT
11 PEGASUS CT
12 SHAKESPEARE HO
C3
1 NORFOLK CT
2 VICTORIA PARK GDNS
3 VICTORIA CT

4 CLIFTON CT
5 PIGGOTT'S BSNS PK
6 CHARLES CT
7 VICTORIA LODGE
8 DAWSON CT
9 CHESTNUT CT
10 VICTORIA CT
11 YORK LODGE
12 BARONS CT
13 FENNERS CT

C4
1 GAINSBOROUGH LODGE
2 LOXLEY GDNS
3 OSMONDE CT
4 HENTY CL
5 CENTRECOURT CL
D1
1 CALEDONIAN PL
2 NEW ST
3 PROSPECT PL

4 AUGUSTA HO
D2
1 EAST HILL CT
2 STOKE ABBOTT CT
3 NORTH LODGE MANS
4 GROSVENOR RD
5 HUMPHRYS RD
6 GROSVENOR HO
7 GRAFTON PL
8 FIELD ROW

9 LIVERPOOL BLDGS
10 MONTAGUE CTR
11 BANK PAS
12 WESTBROOKE CT
13 MARKET ST
14 THE GUILDBOURNE CTR
D3
1 FORDYCE CT
2 CARLYLE HO
3 HERTFORD CT

4 CHRISTCHURCH HO
D4
1 LOURIER CT
2 FAIRFIELDS
3 HOMESTEYNE HO
4 CAXTON CT
5 CHALEFORD CT
6 LANGTON CT
D5
1 STEYNING HO

2 ALFRISTON HO
3 BURY HO
4 ASHINGTON CT
F2
1 ST GEORG'S GDNS
2 CHURCH COTTS
3 SELDEN MEWS
4 EASTFIELD HO
5 MARIK MEWS

C7
1 BALL TREE CROFT
2 WESTERN LODGE
3 SOUTH LODGE
4 INGLECROFT CT

D5
1 LOXWOOD
2 STEYNING
3 BRAMBER
4 ARUNDEL
5 SOMPTING LODGE
6 TOWER RD FLATS
7 ST MICHAEL'S CT
8 FAIRLANDS

163

D6
1 CHERRY TREE LODGE
2 CRABTREE LODGE
3 ST NICHOLAS' CT
4 ST DAVID'S GATE
5 ST JOHN'S CT

184

E5
1 ST ROBERT'S LODGE
2 STATION PAR
3 FRESHBROOK CT
4 THE WILLOWS
5 RUSSELL CT
6 BEVERLEY HO

F5
1 COWLEY DR
2 OAKLANDS
3 HAZELWOOD LODGE
4 PENHILL CT
5 SANDRINGHAM CT
6 KENWOOD QUAY

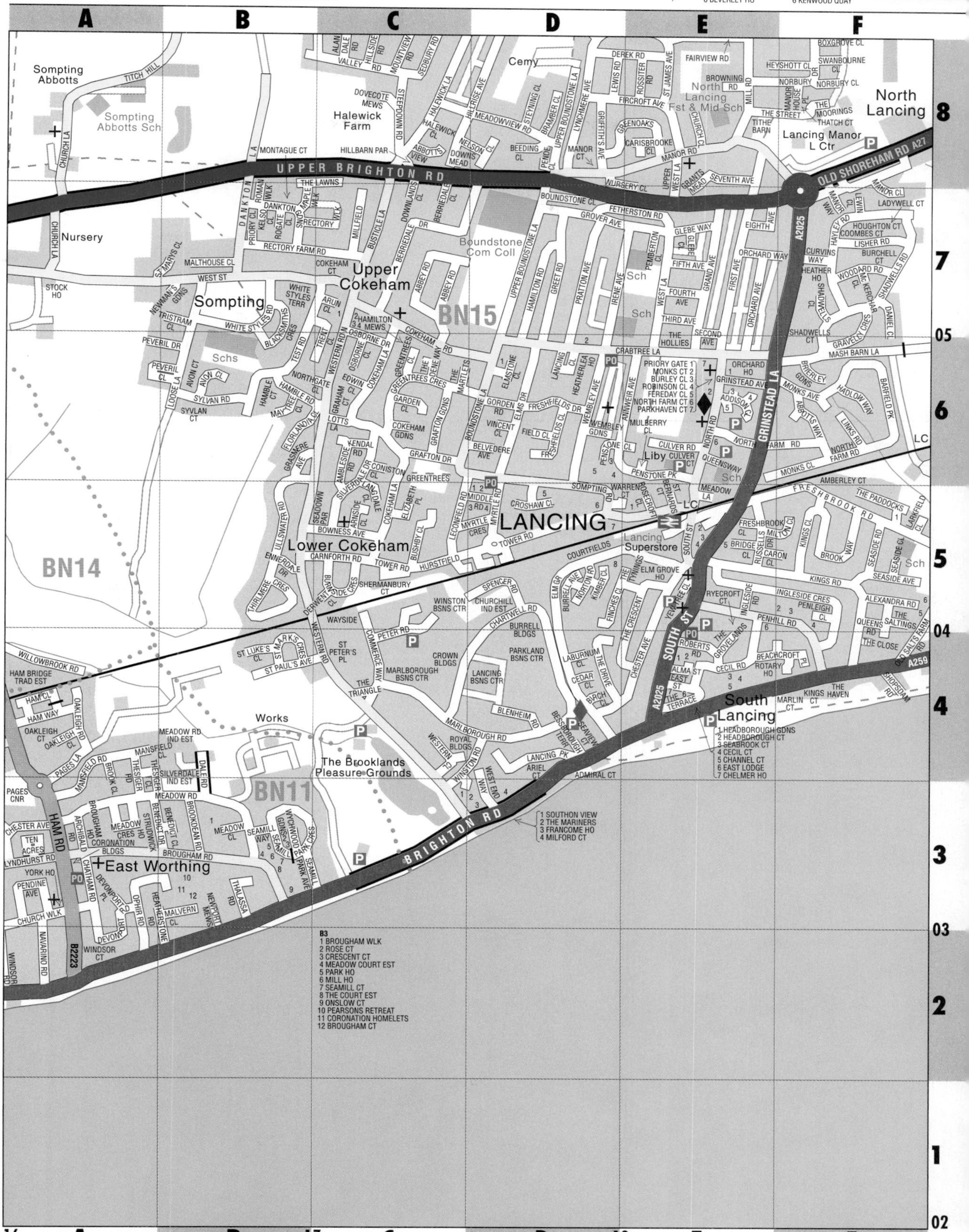

184

183
164

F7
1 CLEMENT'S CT
2 WEPPONS
3 CECIL NORRIS HO
4 NORMANHURST
5 OAKLAND CT
6 TINTAGEL CT
7 SWANBOROUGH CT
8 MANNINGS
9 GLYNDEBOURNE CT
10 PASHLEY CT
11 RIVERSIDE BSNS CTR

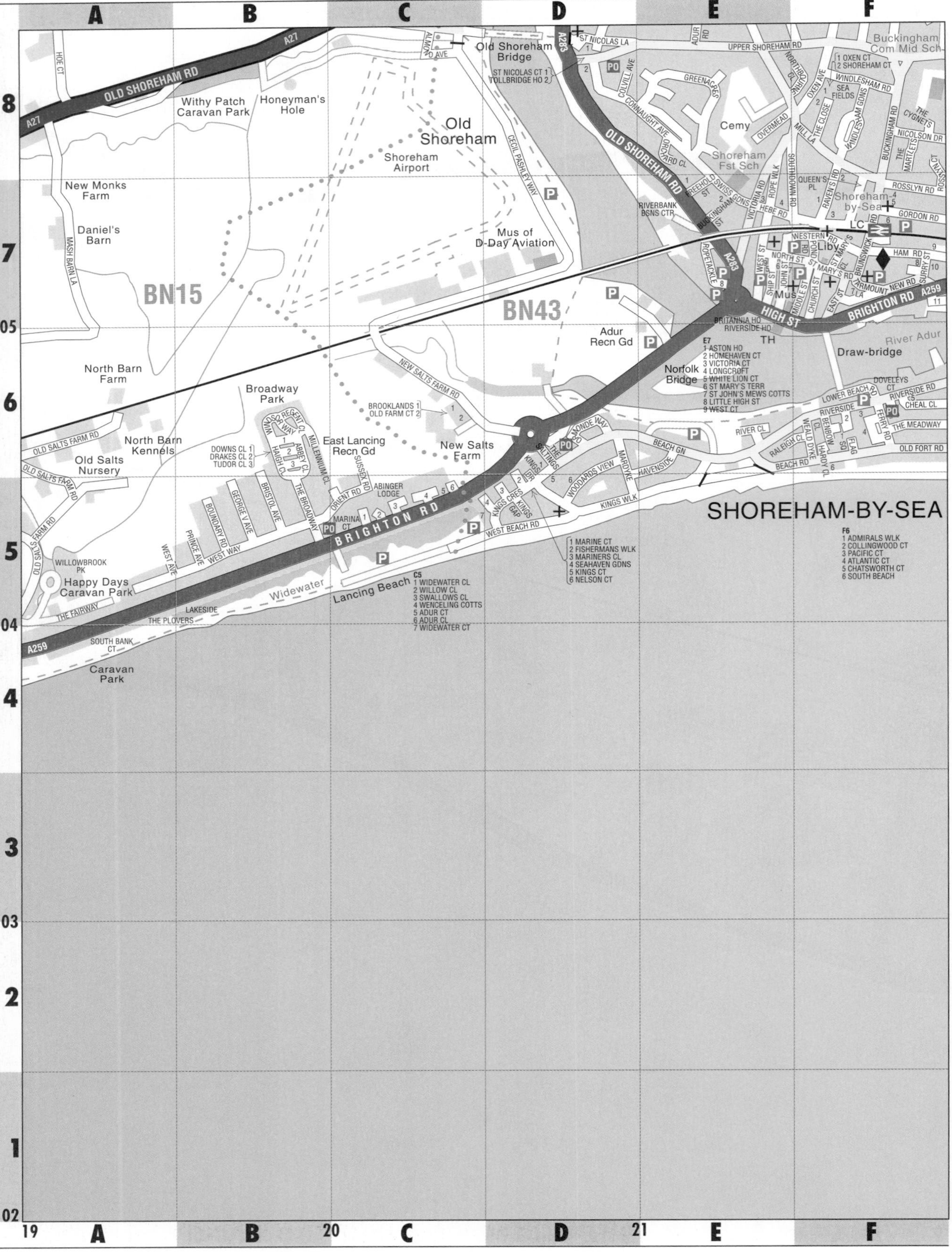

183

C8
1 LONEY CT
2 FRASER CT
3 MILWARD CT
4 PENSTONE CT
5 JULIAN CT
6 WILMOT CT
7 OSBORNE CT
8 HOLMBUSH CT
9 DOWNES CT
10 ADUR CT
11 BROADWAY CT
12 WISTON CT
13 ARUN CT

165

C8
14 ARUNDEL CT
15 RECTORY CT
16 CAIUS CT
17 KINGSTON CT

186

E7
1 SCHOOL CL
2 TWITTEN CL
3 GREEN CT
4 GREEN CL
5 WATLING CL
6 SPRING GDNS
7 STATION RD
8 WATLING CT
9 GRANGE CT
10 LOCKS CT
11 COATES CT
12 ROCK CL
13 CHANNEL VIEW
14 SEA HO

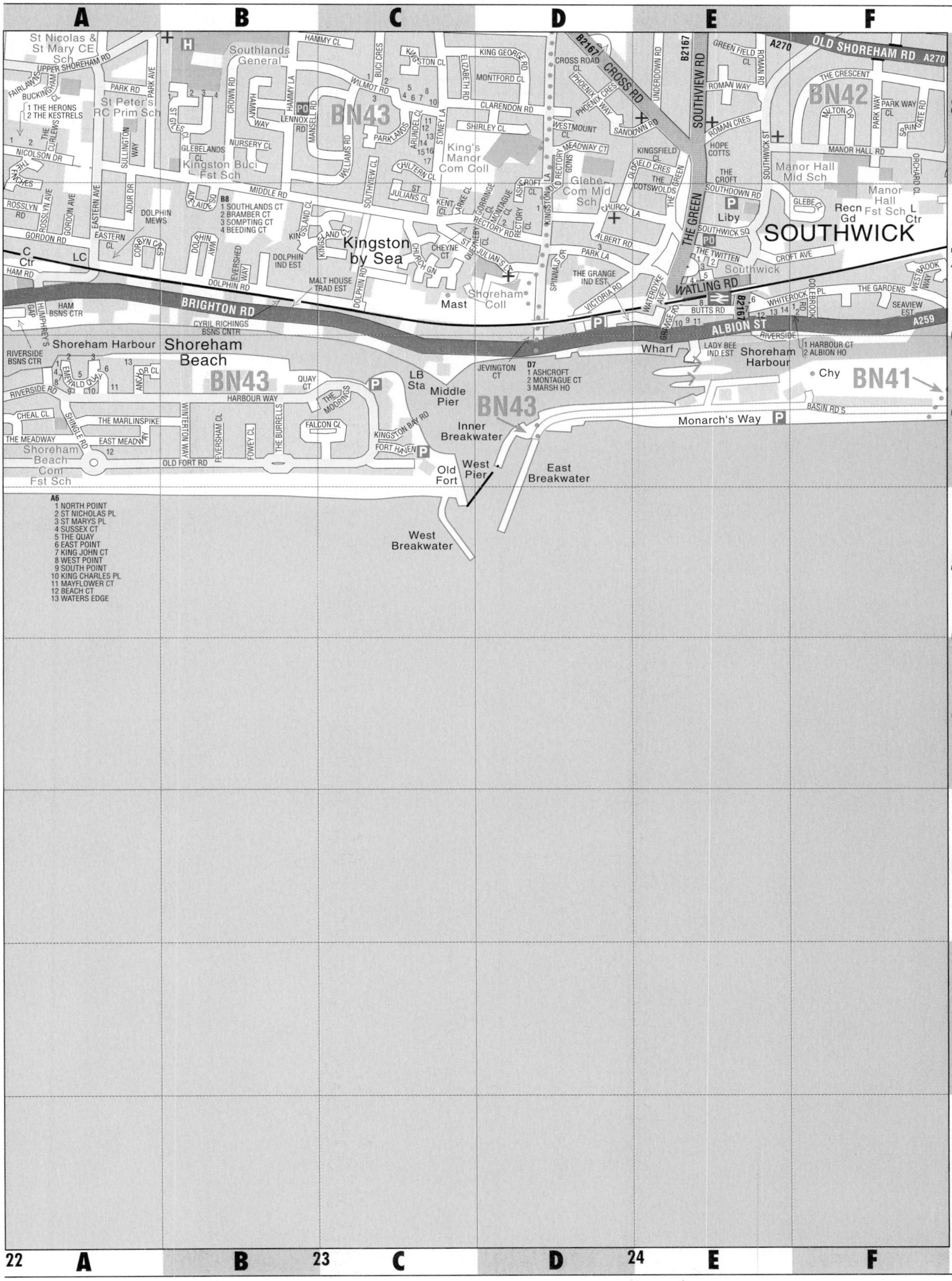

186

185
166

D7
1 BEVERLEY CT
2 CRANLEY CT
3 BRITTANY CT
4 MORNINGTON MANS
5 BEACON HO
6 ERROLL MANS

F7
1 MAINSTONE RD
2 EVEREST HO
3 ST PHILIPS MEWS
4 LION MEWS
5 RICHARDSON CT
6 STRATTON CT

185

B7
1 CONWAY CT
2 CLARENDON HO
3 ELLEN HO
4 GOLDSTONE HO
5 LIVINGSTONE HO
6 CLIFTONVILLE CT
7 STEYNING CT
8 BRAMBER CT
9 EATON CT
10 GRANVILLE CT
11 HADDINGTON ST
12 MALVERN ST
13 MONMOUTH ST

C7
1 DEVONSHIRE CT
2 CORNWALL CT
3 SOMERSET CT
4 JANESTON CT
5 STIRLING CT
6 BRECON CT
7 ELIZABETH CT
8 PHILIP CT
9 BALTIMORE CT
10 DRIVE LODGE
11 EATON MANOR
12 VERIC
13 VALVERDE HO
14 VALENTINE CT
15 HEREFORD CT
16 GAINSBOROUGH HO
17 EATON GATE
18 CHARIS CT
19 EATON HALL
20 EATON GDNS MANS

167

C7
21 VANBRUGH CT

D7
1 COWDRAY CT
2 GOODWOOD CT
3 CROMWELL CT
4 WILLOW CT

188

D7
5 KINSALE CT
6 PALMEIRA HO
7 BELL MEAD
8 AMBER CT
9 CONISTON CT
10 SOMERHILL CT
11 CHIDDINGLY HO
12 BERESFORD CT
13 PARHAM HO
14 PETWORTH HO
15 BODIHAM HO

A6
1 BLENHEIM CT
2 PEMBROKE CT
3 WENDOVER GRANGE
4 AYMER HO
5 DOLPHIN CT
6 PRINCES CT
7 VALLANCE CT
8 HOVE MANOR
9 FAIRLAWNS
10 VICEROY LODGE
11 BLUEBIRD CT
12 LANCASTER CT
13 ST AUBYN'S GDNS

B5
1 VICTORIA TERR
2 VICTORIA COTTS
3 BENHAM CT
4 SPA CT
5 THE PRIORY
6 ST CATHERINE'S TERR
7 COURTENAY TERR
8 HAMILTON MANS
9 OLIVER HO

B6
1 GROSVENOR MANS
2 LORRAINE CT
3 PARNELL CT
4 DURHAM CT
5 WINDSOR LODGE

C6
1 MARLBOROUGH CT
2 COPTHORNE CT
3 NORMANDY HO
4 GRAND AVENUE MANS
5 COOMBE LEA
6 VICTORIA CT
7 VICTORIA GR
8 HAREWODD CT
9 WILBURY GRANGE
10 THE AMBASSADORS
11 BOWEN CT
12 GROVE CT
13 WILBURY LODGE
14 ASHDOWN
15 SUSSEX CT
16 THE ATHENAEUM
17 SANDRINGHAM LODGE
18 HATFIELD CT
19 AMBER CT
20 AVENUE CT
21 PALMEIRA MANS
22 ST JOHN'S PL

D5
1 LANSDOWNE SQ
2 ALICE CL
3 BRUNSWICK MEWS
4 DONKEY MEWS
5 UPPER MARKET ST
6 LOWER MARKET ST
7 KERRISON MEWS
8 CHAPEL MEWS
9 WATERLOO HO
10 EMBASSY CT
11 GOLDEN LA
12 CAVANDISH MEWS
13 IVY MEWS
14 CROSS ST
15 FARMAN ST

D6
1 CROWN CL
2 PALM CT
3 GWYDYR MANS
4 ROCHESTER CT
5 ROCHESTER CL
6 ST ANNES WELL HO
7 LANSDOWNE MEWS
8 THE COURTYARD

E5
1 LITTLE WESTERN ST
2 DORCHESTER CT
3 NORFOLK PL
4 NORFOLK CT
5 NORFOLK BLDGS
6 NORFOLK MEWS
7 KINGSLEY CT
8 CAVENDISH HO
9 BEDFORD TWRS
10 ASTRA HO
11 ABBOTTS
12 METROPOLE CT
13 SUSSEX HTS
13 SUSSEX HTS
14 RUSSELL MEWS
15 REGENCY MEWS
16 FRED EMERY CT
17 SILWOOD PL
18 OSPREY HO
19 SILLWOOD CT
20 SILLWOOD HALL
21 WESTERN TERR
22 SILLWOOD TERR
23 MITRE HO
24 HAMPTON ST

E6
1 WORCESTER CT
2 KENYA CT
3 VERNON CT
4 VERNON GDNS
5 BELVEDERE TERR
6 VICTORIA PL
7 HAMPTON TERR
8 HEATHER CT
9 MONTPELLIER LODGE
10 BOUNDARY PAS
11 BRAEMAR HO

E7
1 WESTCOMBE
2 PRESTONVILLE CT
3 CADOGAN CT
4 BELMONT CT
5 ST ANNS MANS
6 BERKELEY CT
7 DERBY CT
8 WARWICK CT
9 RICHMOND CT
10 MARSTON CT
11 LORRAINE CT
12 CHESTER CT
13 YORK CT
14 WINDLESHAM CT
15 PAVILION CT
16 WESTMORLAND CT

188

For full street detail of the highlighted area see page 207.

B8
1 ST SAVIOURS CT
2 ROUND HILL RD
3 ROUND HILL ST
4 DITCHLING CT
5 MAYO CT
6 CENTENARY IND EST
7 ASHDOWN RD
8 EDINBURGH RD

C5
1 LAKE VIEW
2 HILARY LODGE
3 THE GRAPERIES
4 SLOANE CT

187

C5
5 PATCHING LODGE
6 JACQUELINE DU PRE CT
7 EVELYN GLENNIE CT
8 CELLO CT

C6
1 FINSBURY LODGE

168

C6
2 HIGHDEN
3 WESTMOUNT
4 CROWN HILL
5 SYDNEY TIDY HO
6 ATTREE CT
7 CARN CT
8 BARN FIELD GDNS
9 WINDERMERE CT
10 STONEHURST CT

C8
1 FREEHOLD TERR
2 SAUNDERS PARK HO
3 STANLEY CT
4 INVERNESS RD
5 ABERDEEN RD
6 LEWIS CT
7 PEVENSEY RD
8 FAIRLIGHT PL
9 ST LEONARD'S RD
10 OLD VIADUCT CT
11 SHANKLIN CT
12 NEWMARKET TERR

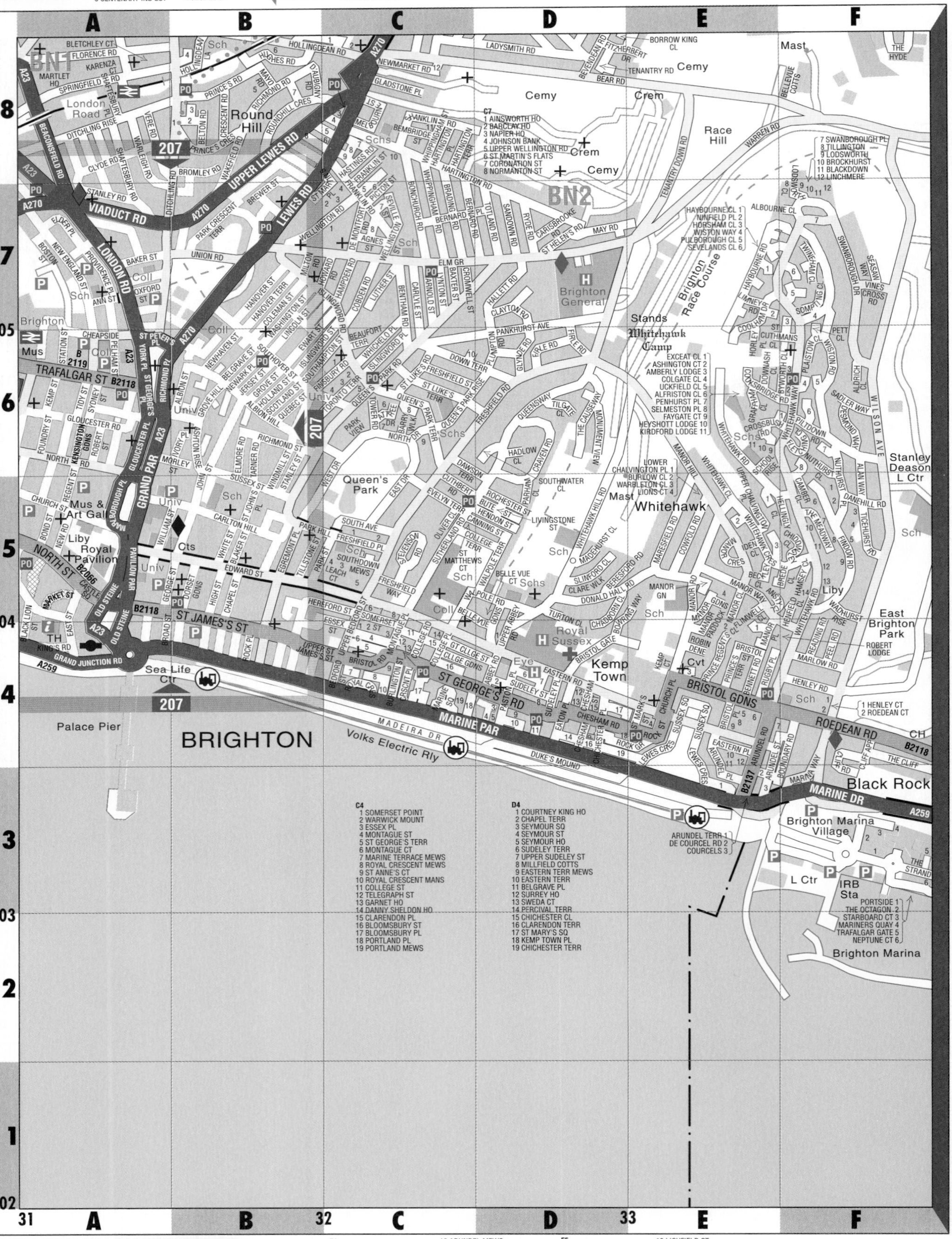

For full street detail of the highlighted area see page 207.

187

E4
1 PLAYDEN CL
2 PRINCE REGENT'S CT
3 BRISTOL MEWS
4 SUSSEX MEWS
5 RUGBY CT
6 ARUNDEL CT
7 BELL TOWER IND EST
8 HOLLINGBOURNE CT
9 LANGHURST
10 ARUNDEL MEWS
11 KEMPTOWN MEWS
12 LEWES MEWS

F5
1 SANDERSTEAD
2 KINGSFOLD
3 BYLANDS
4 GRINSTEAD MOUNT
5 LANCING CT
6 HURSTWOOD
7 COTSWOLD PL
8 WELLSBOURNE
9 SOUTH LODGE
10 LICHFIELD CT
11 FRAMFIELD
12 RYECROFT
13 WESTHAM
14 WALTER MAY HO

169
190

A
B
C
D
E
F
8
7
01
6
5
00
4
3
99
2
1
98
74
75
76
Sussex Border Path
PO10
Longmere Point
Pilsey Sand
Pilsey Island
Chichester Harbour
Stocker's Lake
East Head
Black Point
Marina
HAYLING ISLAND
The Spit
Lifeboat Station
PO20
P
FISHERMANS WLK
WITTERING RD
EARNLEY RD
SELSEY CL
EASTOKE AVE
HASLEMERE GDNS
SIDLESHAM CL
ITCHENOR RD
PAGHAM GDNS
BRACKLESHAM RD
SEAFARERS WLK
BIRDHAM RD
HAVEN RD
BOSMERE RD
NUTBOURNE RD
SANDY POINT RD
TRELOAR RD
WHEATLANDS CRES
CORONATION RD
South Hayling
PO11
WHEATLANDS AVE
SOUTHWOOD RD
SANDY BEACH EST
Eastoke Point

190

189
170

A
B
C
D
E
F
8
7
01
6
5
00
4
3
99
2
1
98
77
78
79
Cobnor Point
Chichester Harbour
Chichester Channel
Thorney Channel
Ferry P
Chalkdock Point
Ship Inn (PH)
THE STREET
Itchenor Park
West Itchenor
FARM COTTS
Itchenor House
ITCHENOR RD
Pilsey Island
PO20
ROOKWOOD LA
Rookwood House
Rookwood Lane House
Redlands
SHEEPWASH LA
Ella Nore
Lane End House
Wicks Farm
Tara
REDLANDS LA
B2179
Walnut Tree House
Gate Lodge
MALTHOUSE COTTS
ELLANORE LA
ACRE ST
CHAPEL LA
Mast
Nunnington Farm
ROOKWOOD RD
Holmes Farm
ROMAN LANDING
SUMMERFIELD RD
Snow Hill
LOCKSASH CL
CUNLIFFE CL
ELMSTEAD GDNS
ELMSTEAD PARK RD
ELMS WAY
MEADOW LA
Speedscroft
COASTGUARDS COTTS
COASTGUARD LA
West Wittering Parochial CE Sch
POUND RD
PH
ROYCE CL
ELMS RIDE
ELMS LA
THE WAD
MIDDLEFIELD
ELMWOOD CL
ROYCE WAY
West Wittering
Home Farm
PIGGERY HALL LA
SEAWARD DR
THE BYEWAY
CAKEHAM RD
WELLSFIELD
BRIAR AVE
FURZEFIELD

189
201

171
192

202
192

191
172

A
B
C
D
E
F
8
7
01
6
5
00
4
3
99
2
1
98
83
84
85
A286
Crouchers Bottom (Hotel)
New Barn
Crosbie Bridge
B2201
Bridge Courtyard
Chichester Canal
The Blacksmith's Arms (PH)
TRAMWAY CL
HIGH BANK
B2145
Salterns Copse
Pump Bottom Farm
OAK VIEW
Nurseries
Chichester Yacht Basin
P
Cutfield Bridge
BIRDHAM RD
Price's Cottage
SELSEY RD
Sussex Falconry Ctr
Manhood End Farm
WOPHAMS LA
Tennessee Farm
Kipson Bank
Nursery
Kipson Bank Farm
Coombers Barn Farm
Southend Farm
GREEN LA
SELSEY RD
ALLMAN BSNS PK
White Walls
Harding's Farm
Birdham Farm
Chichester Golf Ctr
Cowdray Farm
PO20
Jury Farm
Driving Range
Hunston Common
Sidlesham Common
JURY LA
CHICHESTER RD
The Piggeries
B2201
Jury Cottage
GORSE TERR
BRIMFAST LA
SIDLESHAM LA
Marblebridge Farm
Nurseries
COLLINS'S LA
LOCKGATE RD
Fletchers
Street End
Nurseries
Woodhorn Farm
Lockgate Cottage
FLETCHERS LA
BOXHAM LA
STREET END RD
STREET END LA
Hillands Farm
Nurseries
CHALDER LA
MAPSONS LA
Mapsons Farm
ROTTEN ROW
CHURCH LA
PH
FLETCHERS EST
BATCHMERE RD
CHURCHFARM LA
Church Farm
PO
HIGHLEIGH RD
Highleigh Farm
SELSEY RD
Nurseries
Keynor Rife
Haise Farm
Highleigh
Sidlesham
CRITCHEL'S LA
Littleton Barn
GREEN LA
Nurseries
Willow Glen
ROOKERY LA
B2145

191
203

173
194

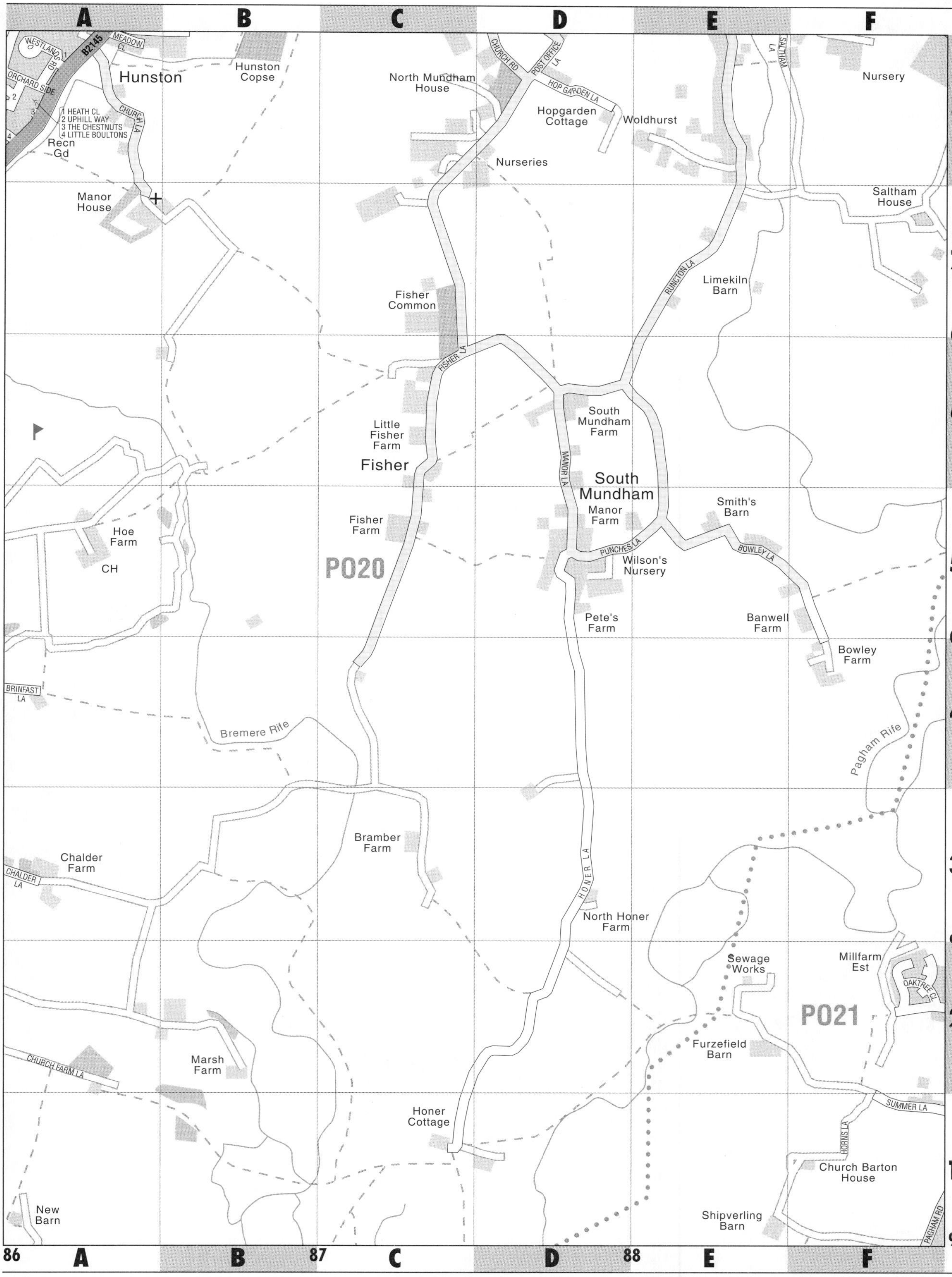

A
B
C
D
E
F
Hunston
Hunston Copse
North Mundham House
Hopgarden Cottage
Woldhurst
Nursery
Nurseries
Manor House
Recn Gd
Saltham House
Limekiln Barn
Fisher Common
South Mundham Farm
Little Fisher Farm
Fisher
South Mundham
Manor Farm
Smith's Barn
Fisher Farm
Hoe Farm
CH
PO20
Wilson's Nursery
Pete's Farm
Banwell Farm
Bowley Farm
Bremere Rife
Pagham Rife
Bramber Farm
Chalder Farm
North Honer Farm
Sewage Works
Millfarm Est
PO21
Furzefield Barn
Marsh Farm
Honer Cottage
Church Barton House
New Barn
Shipverling Barn
WESTLAND RD
MEADOW CL
B2145
ORCHARD SIDE
CHURCH LA
1 HEATH CL
2 UPHILL WAY
3 THE CHESTNUTS
4 LITTLE BOULTONS
CHURCH RD
POST OFFICE LA
HOP GARDEN LA
SALTHAM LA
RUNCTON LA
FISHER LA
MANOR LA
PUNCHES LA
BOWLEY LA
BRINFAST LA
CHALDER LA
HONER LA
OAKTREE CL
SUMMER LA
HORNS LA
CHURCH FARM LA
PAGHAM RD
8
7
01
6
5
00
4
3
99
2
1
98
86
87
88

204
194

193 174

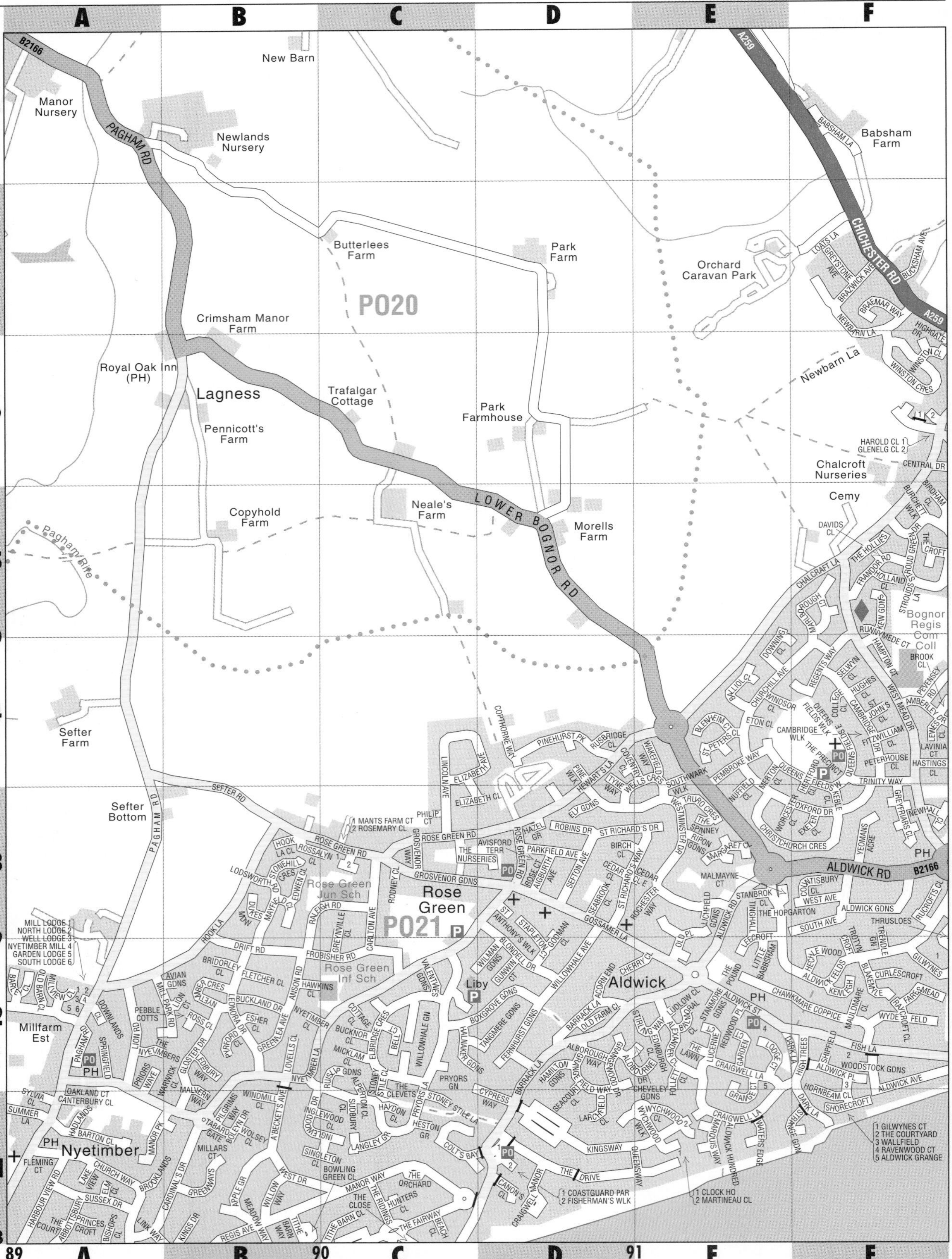
A B C D E F
8
7
01
6
5
00
4
3
99
2
1
98
89 90 91
New Barn
Manor Nursery
Newlands Nursery
Babsham Farm
Butterlees Farm
Park Farm
Orchard Caravan Park
PO20
Crimsham Manor Farm
Royal Oak Inn (PH)
Lagness
Trafalgar Cottage
Park Farmhouse
Pennicott's Farm
Chalcroft Nurseries
Cemy
Copyhold Farm
Neale's Farm
Morells Farm
LOWER BOGNOR RD
PAGHAM RD
CHICHESTER RD
Newbarn La
Bognor Regis Com Coll
Sefter Farm
Sefter Bottom
Rose Green
PO21
Rose Green Jun Sch
Rose Green Inf Sch
Aldwick
ALDWICK RD
Millfarm Est
Nyetimber
Liby

193 205

175
196

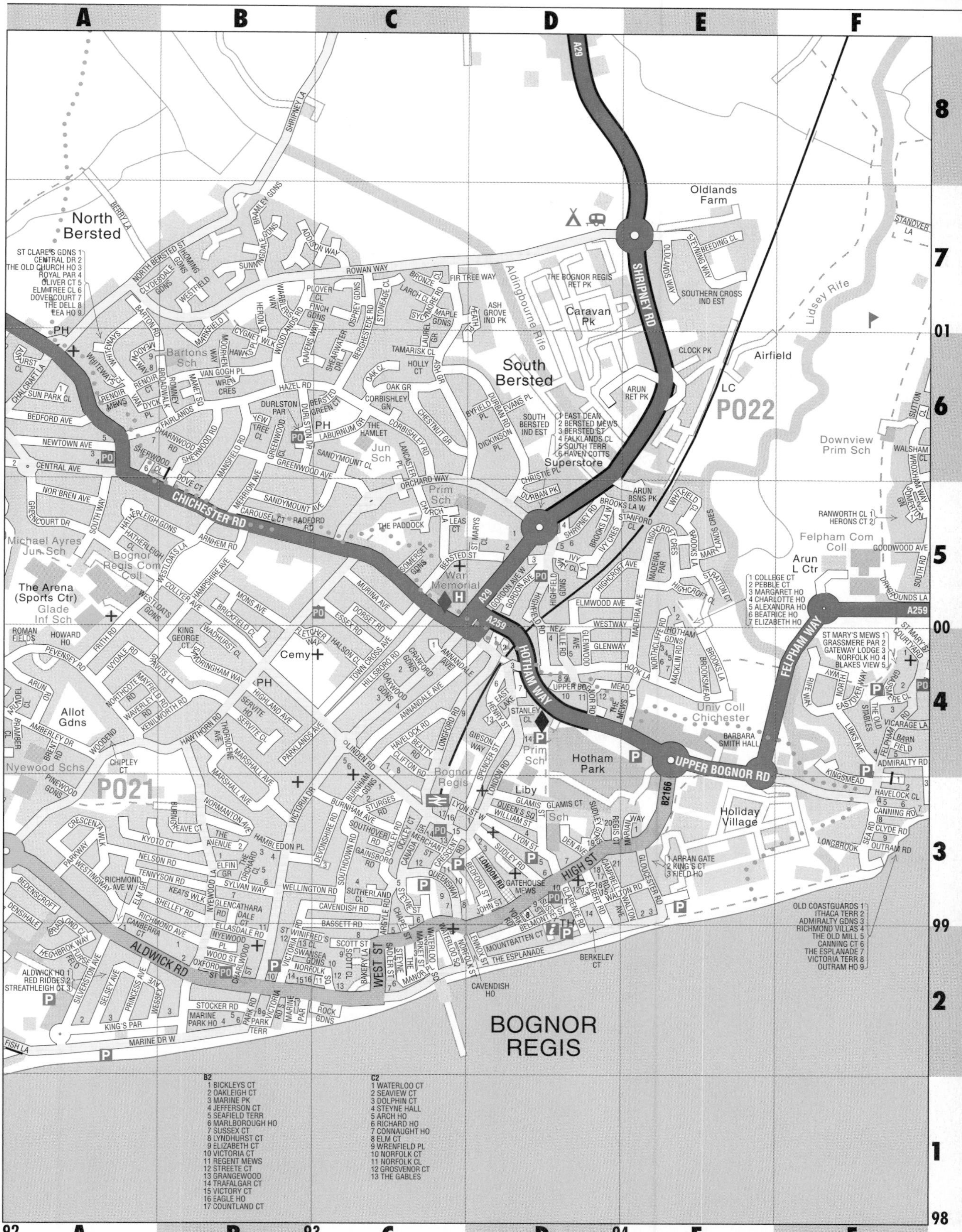

B3
1 ELFIN MEWS
2 NYEWOOD GDNS
3 THE MAPLES
4 COURTFIELD HO
5 HOMECROFT HO
6 DANEHURST
7 WIDWORTHY MEWS

C3
1 LINDEN CT
2 BERNARD DEEGAN HO
3 DEVONSHIRE PL
4 SUTHERLAND CT
5 ARGYLE CIR
6 SEAWARD CT
7 QUEENSWAY HO
8 GORDON HO
9 FITZLEET HO
10 KINRARA HO
11 RICHMOND HO
12 SEYMORE PL
13 SIMON CT
14 THE MEWS
15 STATION RD
16 RICHMOND RD
17 REGIS HO

C4
1 CARLINGFORD CT
2 HOLLY HO
3 OAKWOOD CT
4 MOORE PL
5 THE WILLOWS
6 THE HAWTHORNS
7 DEANE CT
8 SAFFRON CT
9 AUSTEN CT

D3
1 LYON CT
2 CENTRAL BLDGS
3 WATER TOWER BLDGS
4 PRINCE WILLIAM CT
5 ASTON CT
6 HARFIELD CT
7 RUSSELL PL
8 THE ARCADE
9 CLOCK WLK
10 CLARENCE GATE
11 ELIZABETH HO
12 BENIZI CT
13 HISLOP WLK
14 ALEXANDRA TERR
15 ALLESTREE CT
16 SABEY CT
17 PRIORY CT
18 CLAREMONT CT
19 FRASER CT
20 PRINCESS HO
21 SOVEREIGN CT

196

D4
1 GORDON AVE
2 BANKVIEW CL
3 UPPER BOGNOR RD
4 THE BEECHES
5 LEVINE CT
6 RICHMOND RD N
7 BERRYMILL CL
8 WOODBINE CT
9 WOOD ACRE CT
10 PARKSIDE
11 TUDOR CT
12 MELANIE'S GDNS
13 CHESHIRE CL
14 SIR ROBERT PEEL CT

195
176

A
B
C
D
E
F
8
7
01
6
5
00
4
3
99
2
1
98
95
96
97
Bilsham
BILSHAM LA
B2132
BILSHAM RD
BILSHAM CNR
GREVATT'S LA W
Weststone Bridge
Ryebank Rife
BN18
White Rails
Hoe Farm
Flansham
Poultry Houses
HOE LA
STANOVER LA
GREVATT'S LA
A259
WORMS LA
Sheepwash Barn
YAPTON RD
Guernsey Farm
BOGNOR REGIS
PO22
FLANSHAM LA
GOLF LINKS RD
CH
1 ULLSWATER GR
2 DERWENT GR
3 OUTERWYKE GDNS
4 AMBLESIDE CL
1 SATINWOOD CL
2 LAVENDER CL
3 WHITEBEAM WAY
4 MARLOWE CL
MIDDLETON BSNS PK
ANCTON LA
WROXHAM WAY
WHITELANDS
WALSHAM CL
SHIRLEY DR
STALHAM WAY
PULBOROUGH WAY
DITCHFIELD CL
COMPTON DR
BYRON CL
CHAUCER WAY
BURNS
PRIESTLEY WAY
MEADOW CT
TUDOR CL
THE BYWAY
MIDDLETON RD
MIDDLETON PL
SUNDALE LA
MORAUNT DR
SILVER BIRCH DR
KINGFISHER CT
NIGHTINGALE CT
ELMER RD
CROSSWAYS
LEAMAN CL
TUSCAN AVE
GREEN WAY
FLANSHAM MEWS
Schs
PENNYFIELDS
GUERNSEY FARM LA
1 NORTHWYKE CL
2 NORWOOD CT
B2132
FELPHAM WAY
GEORGE IV WLK
GOODWOOD AVE
FERRING GDNS
BURSLEDON CL
OLD SCHOOL MEWS
MONTEREY PINES
MANOR CL
GROVE
OVERDOWN RD
1 CLOVELLY AVE
2 FELPHAM GDNS
3 OLD MANOR HOUSE GDNS
4 INNERWYKE MANOR
Felpham
1 SUMMERLEY CNR
2 ATHRINGTON CT
MERRY END
SOUTH WLK
Middleton-on -Sea
SEA WAY
OLD POINT
Middleton Point
F5
1 SHAW CL
2 ROSE AVE
3 MAIN DR
4 DOUGLAS CL
5 ST NICHOLAS LA
6 MIDDLETON CT
7 GRANGE CT
8 ST NICHOLAS CT
9 SOUTHDEAN CL
SEA DR
THE LOOP
STRAND WAY
WEST CL
MINTON RD
DAVENPORT RD
CULVER RD
BEREWEEKE RD
BLAKES RD
1 OAKLAND CT
2 THE OLD RECTORY
3 OLD RECTORY FLATS
4 TURRET HO
5 CHURCH HOUSE MEWS

A
B
C
D
E
F
A259
B2233
YAPTON RD
CROOKTHORN LA
GREVATT'S LA
GREVATT'S LA W
BN18
BN17
PO22
St Mary's CE Sch
CROOKTHORN LA
BROOKPITS LA
Hobb's Farm
Kent's Farm
LANGMEAD CL
Sewage Works
Climping Camp Site
Hobbs' New Barn
Ryebank Rife
Grevatt's Bridge
Ryebank House
The Black Horse (PH)
CLIMPING ST
New Barn
Nature Trail
BREAD LA
Atherington
Ancton
Bailiffscourt Hotel
Cudlow Barn
Elmer
Poole Place
ANCTON LA
KINGSMEAD GDNS
ANCTON DR
KINGSMEAD RD
SUMMYMEAD CL
ANCTON WAY
LODGE CL
MEADOW WLK
ANCTON LODGE LA
WILLOW BROOK
FARM CNR
LANE END RD
THE CLOSE
THE LAYNE
ARUNDEL WAY
FARM CL
NORFOLK WAY
ELM DR
STABLE FIELD
ALLEYNE WAY
ELMER CL
SEA WAY
THE HARD
ELMER CT
1 NORTH AVE E
2 NORTH AVE S
ELMER RD
TEMPLESHEEN RD
MANOR WAY
WEST DR
CENTRAL DR
EAST DR
DEEPDENE CL
VILLA PLAGE
THE JETTY
1 SUSSEX CT
2 SUSSEX VILLAGE
3 MANOR CT
8
7
01
6
5
00
4
3
99
2
1
98
98
99
00

177
178

A
B
C
D
E
F
8
7
6
5
4
3
2
1
03
02
01
00
Brook Barn Farm
Court Wick Park
Littlehampton Junction
Nursery
Wick
Toddington
Hollyacre
Nurseries
LC
Cornfield Sch
Cemy
Sewage Works
Ret Pk
BN17
BN16
Caravan Park
Littlehampton Marina
River Arun
Wickbourne Sch
Flora McDonald Cty Jun Sch
Prim Sch
The Littlehampton Com Sch
Elm Grove Inf Sch
Inf Sch
Jun Sch
Sports Field
Mkt
IRB Sta
Mus
C Ctr
Liby
Littlehampton
Ferry P
CH
The Green
East Pier
The Mill
Ryebank Rife
LITTLEHAMPTON
A259
A284
B2187
B2140
LYMINSTER RD
WORTHING RD
WICK ST
ARUNDEL RD
BRIDGE RD
EAST ST
HORSHAM RD
BEACH RD
SOUTH TERR
SEA RD
HIGH ST
TERMINUS RD
FERRY RD
RIVERSIDE
THE PROMENADE
COURTWICK LA
GRANARY WAY
TODDINGTON LA
ALDWICK HO 1
FELPHAM HO 2
MARDEN HO 3
ALDINGBOURNE HO 4
PAGHAM HO 5
SINGLETON HO 6
FUNTINGTON HO 7
BOXGROVE HO 8
HOUGHTON HO 9
CHILGROVE HO 10
1 OSPREY CL
2 SEATON PARK COTTS
3 LYMINSTER GATE
1 NURSERY GDNS
2 TRUE BLUE PREC
3 GLADSTONE TERR
PHAROS QUAY 1
ALPHA CT 2
SMALLCROFT CL 3
PEPPER CT 4
ARUN CT 5
MARINERS QUAY 6
THE WATERSIDE 7
CHURCH HO 1
THE SWALLOWS 2
FLOYDS COTTS 3
ST CATHERINES CT 4
1 HEATHCOURT
2 REDWOOD CT
3 ST FLORA'S CL
D5
1 SCOTT LODGE
2 THATCHERS LODGE
3 DEVON CT
4 WYCHCROFT
5 HOWARD PL
6 MADEHURST CT
7 ROSE CT
8 HAMPTON CT
9 ANTONIA CT
10 ST MARTIN'S LA
11 DUKE'S CT
12 ANCHOR SPRINGS
13 THE ARCADE
14 EVANS GDNS
D6
1 MERTON DR
2 QUANTOCKS
3 MALTHOUSE PAS
4 HAMPTON FIELDS
E5
1 ST MARY'S GDNS
2 TEMPLE CT
3 AMENIC CT
4 WHITE LODGE
5 SUMMERLEA GDNS
6 ST MARY'S CT
E4
1 CHURCH APP
2 MALTRAVERS CT
3 FITZALAN CT
4 LEEMARK HO
5 CLARE CT
6 WOODSIDE CT
7 OAKLAND CT
8 WELLESLEY CT
9 BERKELEY CT
10 KINGMERE
11 CHANNEL KEEP
12 ST AUGUSTINE RD
13 BUSHBY TERR
14 SOUTHLANDS CT
15 NORTH PL
16 GLENMORE CT
F4
1 WESTFIELD CT
2 AMSTEL CT
3 BEACH MEWS
4 NORFOLK PL
5 SURREY COTT
6 NORFOLK MEWS
7 THE WHAPPLE
8 MIDDLE MEAD
9 STARBOARD WLK
01
02
03

197

179
200

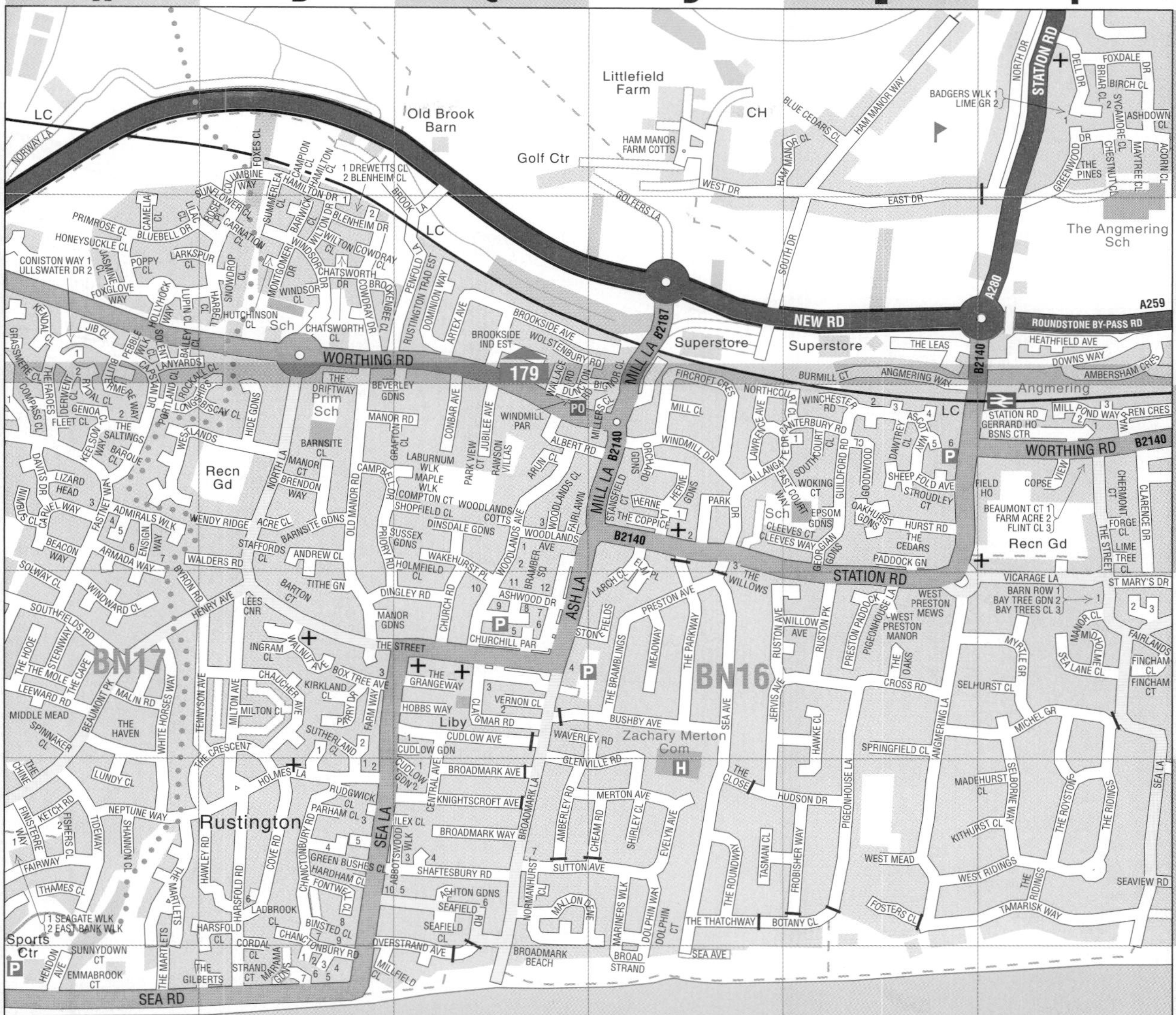

A6	B3		C4		C6	E6
1 TIMBERLEYS	1 ALDWICK CL	4 KIRDFORD CL	1 ILEX HO	4 BROADMARK PAR	1 MENDIP CT	1 RICHMOND CL
2 BERMUDA CT	2 CLIMPING CT	5 KNIGHTSCROFT CL	2 FLINT HO	5 CHURCHILL CT	2 DONNINGTON PL	2 THORNTON CT
3 SCHOONER CT	3 RACKHAM RD	6 BEACH CT	3 HERON'S COURT CL	6 BROADMARK HO	3 TRAFALGAR CT	3 MUNMERE WAY
4 BEAUFORT CT	4 FITZALAN CT	7 SELSEY CT	4 SHAFTESBURY CT	7 WHITECROFT	**D6**	4 COPPER HALL CL
5 THE MOORINGS	5 PETWORTH CT	8 COPPETS WOOD	5 SEAVIEW GDNS	8 EASTERGATE GN	1 ST ANTHONY'S WAY	5 CRUNDENS CNR
6 SEXTANT CT	6 DOWNSIDE CT	9 NORFOLK CT	6 HAWTHORN CL	9 FITTLEWORTH GDN	2 HERNE CT	6 STATION PAR
7 MOUNTBATTEN CT	7 HOWARDS WAY	10 RAWSON CT	7 RAVENS CROFT	10 SILVERWOOD C	3 SHIRLANDS CT	
	B4	**B5**	**C5**	11 CHICHESTER CT		
	1 NORDSETER LODGE	1 HIGHFIELD GDNS	1 ROWAN HO	12 ARUNDEL GDN		
	2 MARIGOLDS LODGE	2 CLARE LODGE	2 WINDERMERE			
	3 KNIGHTSCROFT HO	3 RICHMOND CT	3 STERLING PAR			

200

199
180

A
B
C
D
E
F
8
7
03
6
5
02
4
3
01
2
1
00
07
08
09
Hill View Farm
Nurseries
Road under construction
South Ecclesden Farm
Hangleton
Hangleton Farm
Nurseries
ROUNDSTONE LA
LITTLEHAMPTON RD
A259
Roundstone Farm
HAILSHAM CL 1
BURWASH CL 2
THAKEHAM CL 3
MAYFLOWER WAY
B2225
ROUNDSTONE BY-PASS RD
MAYFIELD
ARLINGTON CRES
LOXWOOD
DOWNS WAY
B2140
OLD WORTHING RD B2140
CROSSWAYS
SAXON CL
ASHURST WAY
180
HANGLETON LA
BROOKSIDE CL
HIGHDOWN CL
DOWNVIEW AVE
FERRING LA
RIFESIDE GDNS
HIGHDOWN WAY
ORCHARD CL
LANGBURY CL
HANGLETON GRANGE
CISSBURY RD
HERMIONE CL
MIDDLE ONSLOW CL
GREEN PK
GLENBARRIE WAY
LANGBURY LA
SINGLETON CL
LC
WEST ONSLOW CL
EAST ONSLOW CL
EASTERGATE CL
WESTERGATE CL
ANCREN CL
ELM PK
SINGLETON CRES
ONSLOW DR
Caravan Park
WARREN CRES
LC
EASTERN CL
RUSSELL'S CL
1 BOUNDARY WAY
2 AMADEUS HO
B2140 WORTHING RD
ROUNDSTONE CRES
SOMERSET RD
BN12
MEADOW WAY
ST MAURS RD
ST ANDREW'S CL
FERRING ST
PO
Ferring
GORING WAY
ROUNDSTONE DR
MENDIP CL
HILLVIEW CRES
CHEVIOT CL
East Preston
RIFE WAY
Liby
SEA LANE CL
Sch
CHILTERN CL
COTSWOLD WAY
ORCHARD RD
BN16
ST OSMUND RD
COLINDALE RD N
GREYSTOKE MEWS
GREYSTOKE RD
REGENCY CT
PARK DR
MIDHURST CL
GLYNDE CL
Schs
LASHMAR RD
THE MEADOWS
WINDLESHAM GDNS
PINEWOOD CL
NORTH LA
Park Barn
Ferring Rife
COLINDALE RD
MULBERRY CL
GROVE CL
CHURCH LA
GLEN GDNS
FERRING GRANGE FLATS
HOMESTEAD COTTS
MIDHURST DR
Caravan Park
BROOK LA
FERRING GRANGE GDNS
SEA LA
ST MARY'S DR
ELM AVE
KINGSTON LA
WESTLANDS
GRANGE CL
EAST MEAD
Liby
BEECHLANDS CT
MONTPELIER RD
THE STREET
MEADOW PK
GOLDEN AVE
POLPERRO CL
ANSISTERS RD
BARBARY LA
GRANGE PARK
GREENWAYS CRES
KENHURST
BEECHLANDS CL
LAVINIA WAY
BROU CL
CLOVER LA
CEDAR CL
LABURNUM CL
ARUN CT
FAIRLANDS
MALCOLM CL 1
FERRINGHAM CT 2
FERRINGHAM LA
LANE GDNS
CHESTNUT CT
VERMONT DR
THE PLANTATION
HAZELMEAD DR
THE CROFT
THE FRAMPTONS
DRAYCLIFF
FOAMCOURT WAYE
LITTLE PADDOCKS
MEASHAM CL
SEA RD
Kingston Manor
THE PANTILES
UPPER WEST DR
LITTLE DR
CORNER GARTH
THE HOMESTEAD
WOODBRIDGE PK
SEAWAVES CL
East Kingston
BEEHIVE LA
BEEHIVE CL
OAKLEY GDNS
VERMONT DR
VICEROY CT
LETCHWORTH CL
TAMARISK WAY
THE NOOKERY
SARK GDNS
NORMANDY DR
NURSERY CL
THE SPINNEY
SOUTH VIEW
HOMELANDS AVE
VERONICA CL
APPLETREES
UPPER DR
OCEAN PAR
CHALET CL
HENTY RD
SOMERSET RD
NORMANDY LA
MANOR RD
THE CRESCENT
GOLDEN AVENUE CL
FERRINGHAM WAY
PH
THE POPLARS
APRIL CL
OCEAN DR
CHALET RD
TELGARTH RD
JERSEY RD
GUERNSEY RD
WILLOWHAYNE AVE
Kingston Gorse
OVAL WAYE
WEST DR
ALDERNEY RD
ST HELIER RD
PO
WESTFIELD AVE
SEAVIEW AVE
THE CIRCLE
THE WAY
THE DRIVE
GOLDEN ACRE
SEA LA
PEAK LA
INGLE GREEN CL
OCEAN CL
CHALET GDNS
FLORIDA RD
HERM RD
ST MALO CL
SEAVIEW RD
SOUTH STRAND
MIDDLE WAY
DOWNSVIEW RD
BROOKSIDE RD
FERRING CL
SOUTH DR
THE WARREN
THE MAPLES
FERRING MARINE
ARUNDEL CT
SEA DR
SEAFIELD RD
PH
COASTAL RD
SEAVIEW AVE
THE STRAND
FLORIDA CL
LAMORNA GDNS
THE LAWNS
CLUB WLK
West Kingston
GORSE AVE
A4
1 WENTWORTH CT
2 CROWN PL
3 CROWN CT
4 WILLOWHAYNE CL
5 WILLOWHAYNE CRES
6 SOUTH STRAND PAR
7 THE PARADE
8 PARADE MANS
9 WILLOWHAYNE CT
10 COASTGUARD COTTS
11 STRAND CT
12 PALM COURT COTTS
F4
1 ST AUBINS CT
2 ST HELIER CT
3 ST AUBINS RD
4 ST MALO CT
5 ELVERLANDS CL
6 DOONE END
7 MILBURY CL
8 FLORIDA GDNS

199

190
202

A
B
C
D
E
F
P
WEST STRAND
BERRYBARN LA
EAST STRAND
B2179
PO20
Cakeham Manor House
Webb's Farm House
CAKEHAM RD
PIGGERY HALL LA
Thatched Tavern (PH)
1 KINGFISHER PAR
2 ADMIRALTY CT
3 ADMIRALTY ROW
4 GREEN CT
5 SEAWOOD HO
6 ST ANNE'S CT
CHARTERHOUSE MEWS
ASCOT CL
ETON DR
ELY CL
CAMBRIDGE AVE
RUSSELL RD
CHAUCER DR
CHURCH RD
OXFORD CL
BENNETTS CL
HARROW
MILL GDNS
CAKEHAM WAY
WINDSOR
FOXWARREN CL
WINDMILL CT
TOWER PL
NORTHERN CRES
Windmill (dis)
HOWARD AVE
SUNNINGDALE GDNS
JOLLIFFE RD
ELLA CL
CULIMORE
SOUTHCOTE AVE
THE CRES
CRES CENT
NEW PAR
CAKEHAM RD THE PARADE
HAVEN CT
Sch
MARINE DR W
OWERS WAY
CULIMORE RD
Liby
WYATT CT
STOCKS LA B2179
BAWI RD
LANKA CT
SHORE RD
OAKFIELD RD
OAKFIELD AVE
MARINE DR
MARINE CL
SHORESIDE WLK
SOLENT RD
CONEY CL
CONEY RD
SEAGATE CT
LONGLANDS RD
WATERSEDGE GDNS
BARN WLK
NAB WLK
SHINGLE WLK
CONEY SIX
CHARLMEAD
TAMARISK WLK
East Wittering
8
7
97
6
5
96
4
3
95
2
1
94
77
78
79

202

201
191

A
B
C
D
E
F
8
7
97
6
5
96
4
3
95
2
1
94
80
81
82
Mus
CHURCH FARM LA
CHURCH FARM CT
HILTON PK
EAST WITTERING BSNS CTR
Stubcroft Farm
B2198
Cherry Tree Farm
BOOKERS LA
SOMERLEY LA
THIRD AVE
Batchmere Estate
Almodington
Somerley Farm
ALMODINGTON LA
MANHOOD COTTS
EASTON LA
CLAYTON LA
STUBCROFT LA
BRACKLESHAM LA
FIELD RD
MEADOWS RD
WESSEX AVE
Holiday Centre
Earnley Grange
Grange Farm
EARNLEY MANOR CL
SOUTHDOWN CT
DOWNVIEW CL
B2179
STOCKS LA
Camping Site
BRACKLESHAM CT
BARTON WAY
CLAPPERS LA
CHURCH COTTS
Manor Farm
Earnley
PO20
SEAFIELD CL
SEAFIELD WAY
KIMBRIDGE PK
PEERLEY RD
PEERLEY CL
LEGION WAY
KESTREL CL
PLOVER CL
MIDDLETON CL
HALE CL
GRAYSWOOD AVE
ELM CL
GARDEN AVE
BEECH AVE
Bracklesham
Grange Rife
CORMORANT WAY
SANDPIPER CT
WEST BRACKLESHAM DR
BOURNE CT
BRACKLESHAM CL
ROSTOCK CT
POND RD
SANDRINGHAM CL
HARMONY DR
PO
WOODBOROUGH CL
ELCOMBE CL
SHALBOURNE CRES
AXFORD CL
WESTERLEY GDNS 1
AZARA PAR 2
ELMDENE CT
ARMADA CT
FIRST AVE
SECOND AVE
FARM RD
WILTON CL
MANTON CL
AVEBURY CL
Marsh Barn
P
OLD FARM CL
THIRD AVE
LACOCK CL
EAST BRACKLESHAM DR
MARINESIDE
SUSSEX GR
WALMSLEYS WAY
DROVE LA
Marsh Farm
SEAFIELDS
SILVER WAY
Sussex Beach Holiday Village
STONES LA
LEIGH CT
BYWAVES
Bracklesham Bay

201

192
204

A
B
C
D
E
F
8
7
97
6
5
96
4
3
95
2
1
94
83
84
85
Oldhouse Farm Cottages
OLDHOUSE LA
Sheepwash Cottage
Easton Cottages
Easton Farm
EASTON LA
The Elms
Veriwell
HAM RD
Oakhurst Farm
Greenwood Farm
Easton Rife
PO20
Porthole Farm
Littleham Farm
Great Ham Farm
Broad Rife
GREEN LA
HIGHLEIGH RD
CYMENS ORA
KEYNOR LA
Sidlesham Prim Sch
Keynor House
COW LA
Wildlife Hospl
Keynor Copse
Keynor Estate
CHALK LA
Keynor Rife
Bakers Farm
Mast
Sewage Works
MAY CL
B2145
SHOTFORD
ROOKERY LA
MANHOOD LA
THE TERRACE
MILL LA
SELSEY RD
Visitors Ctr
Ferry Farm House
Works
B2145
Ferry Farm
Bailey Cottages
Farm Ctr
CH
Northcommon Farm
GOLF LINKS LA
UPWAYS CL
CHICHESTER RD
B2145
The Elms
Green Lawns Caravan Park
PADDOCK LA
Warners Farm
SEAGULL CL
CHAINBRIDGE LA
NAB TOWER LA

206
204

203
193

A
B
C
D
E
F
8
7
97
6
5
96
4
3
95
2
1
94
86
87
88
PO20
Rookery Farm
ROOKERY LA
Halsey's Farm
Caravan Site
Cumbers
MILL LA
Crab & Lobster (PH)
Pagham Wall
Little Welbourne
Pagham
CHURCH LA
CHURCH CL
VENUS LA
Becket's Barn
Church Farm Holiday Village
PAGHAM RD
QUEENSMEAD
SEA WAY
SAXON CL
ST THOMAS DR
JUNE CL
MARTLET WAY
SEA LA
HERON MEAD
SWAN DENE
MALLARD CRES
KESTREL CT
WELL RD
WYTHERING CL
LAGOON RD
WEST FRONT RD
HARBOUR RD
PO21
Pagham Lagoon
Pagham Harbour
(Nature Reserve)
Pagham Beach Estate
P
B2145
Home Farm
Norton
Church Norton
Norton Priory
RECTORY LA
GRANGE LA
Pigeonhouse Farm
PO20
Lydiate
Greenlease Farm
Coles Farm
CHICHESTER RD
The Grange
Bird Reserve
Four Ways
Park Farm
PARK LA
East Beach
PARK COPSE
EAST BEACH RD
MANOR LA
DRIFT RD

203
206

194

A
B
C
D
E
F
THE CRESCENT
BISHOPS CL
PAYNE CL
LINK WAY
PRIORY CL
MEADOW WAY
THE CLOSE
THE BYEWAY
BAY WLK
THE DUNES
ABBOTTSBURY
BARONS MEAD
GOLDEN ACRE
CHURCH WAY
EAST MEAD
KINGS DR
REGIS AVE
THE FAIRWAY
ARUN WAY
TITHE BARN CT 1
BAY CT 2
Aldwick Bay Estate
HARBOUR VIEW RD
THE VIEW
THE GREEN
THE GLADE
SHIRLEY CL
THE CAUSEWAY
LEDRA DR
VISCOUNT DR
WV8
CHANNEL VIEW
DURHAM CL
ELLIS WAY
CONWAY DR
SILVERDALE CL
ST THOMAS DR
THE PARADE
ASHCROFT WAY
WEBB CL
WOODFIELD CL
SANDY RD
EAST FRONT RD
BEACH RD
WEST FRONT RD
BOGNOR REGIS
1 ST THOMAS CT
2 CHURCHILL WLK
3 MULBERRY CT
8
7
97
6
5
96
4
3
95
2
1
94
89
90
91

203

204

B
C
D
E
F
G
8
7
93
6
5
92
4
3
2
91
1
90
84
85
86
East Beach
Caravan Parks
Manhood Com Col
Liby
THE LONDERRY IND EST
Medmerry Prim Sch
Selsey
Seal Prim Sch
West Sands Caravan Park
Mill House Windmill (dis)
PO20
Crablands Farm
CHICHESTER RD B2145
HIGH ST
HILLFIELD RD
B2145
EAST ST
WEST ST
MANOR RD
NORTH RD
MANOR LA
CHURCH RD
SCHOOL LA
MILL LA
MEDMERRY
WEST SANDS LA
CRABLANDS
ORCHARD PAR
Lifeboat Mus
IRB Sta
LB Sta
Selsey Bill
1 COXSWAIN WAY
2 DOMEHOUSE CL
3 CANADIAN CRES
4 BARNES CL
DONALDSON CL 1
BLACKBERRY LA 2
HONEYSUCKLE LA 3
A
PETER'S PL
PETER'S LA
DEER PARK LA
NAB TOWER LA
MEDMERRY
8
93
84

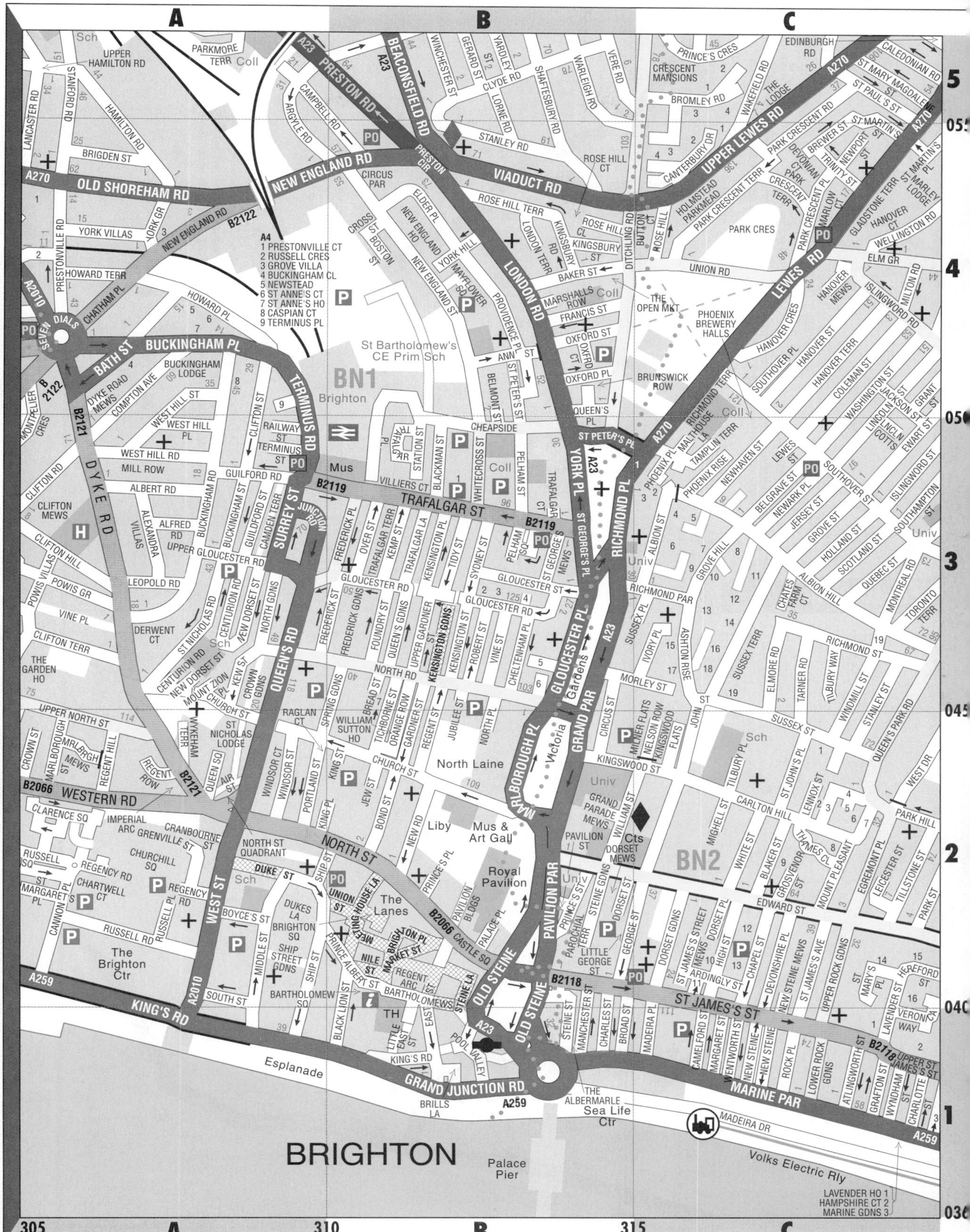
A
B
C
BRIGHTON
BN1
BN2
Brighton
A4
1 PRESTONVILLE CT
2 RUSSELL CRES
3 GROVE VILLA
4 BUCKINGHAM CL
5 NEWSTEAD
6 ST ANNE'S CT
7 ST ANNE'S HO
8 CASPIAN CT
9 TERMINUS PL
OLD SHOREHAM RD
NEW ENGLAND RD
PRESTON RD
BEACONSFIELD RD
VIADUCT RD
UPPER LEWES RD
LEWES RD
LONDON RD
BUCKINGHAM PL
TERMINUS RD
DYKE RD
SURREY ST
QUEEN'S RD
WEST ST
TRAFALGAR ST
NORTH ST
WESTERN RD
KING'S RD
GRAND JUNCTION RD
MARINE PAR
ST JAMES'S ST
OLD STEINE
GRAND PAR
RICHMOND PL
YORK PL
GLOUCESTER PL
PAVILION PAR
MARLBOROUGH PL
CASTLE SQ
SEVEN DIALS
St Bartholomew's CE Prim Sch
North Laine
The Lanes
Royal Pavilion
Mus & Art Gall
The Brighton Ctr
Victoria Gardens
Sea Life Ctr
Palace Pier
Esplanade
Volks Electric Rly
MADEIRA DR
THE ALBEMARLE
LAVENDER HO 1
HAMPSHIRE CT 2
MARINE GDNS 3
5
4
3
2
1
055
050
045
040
036
305
310
315

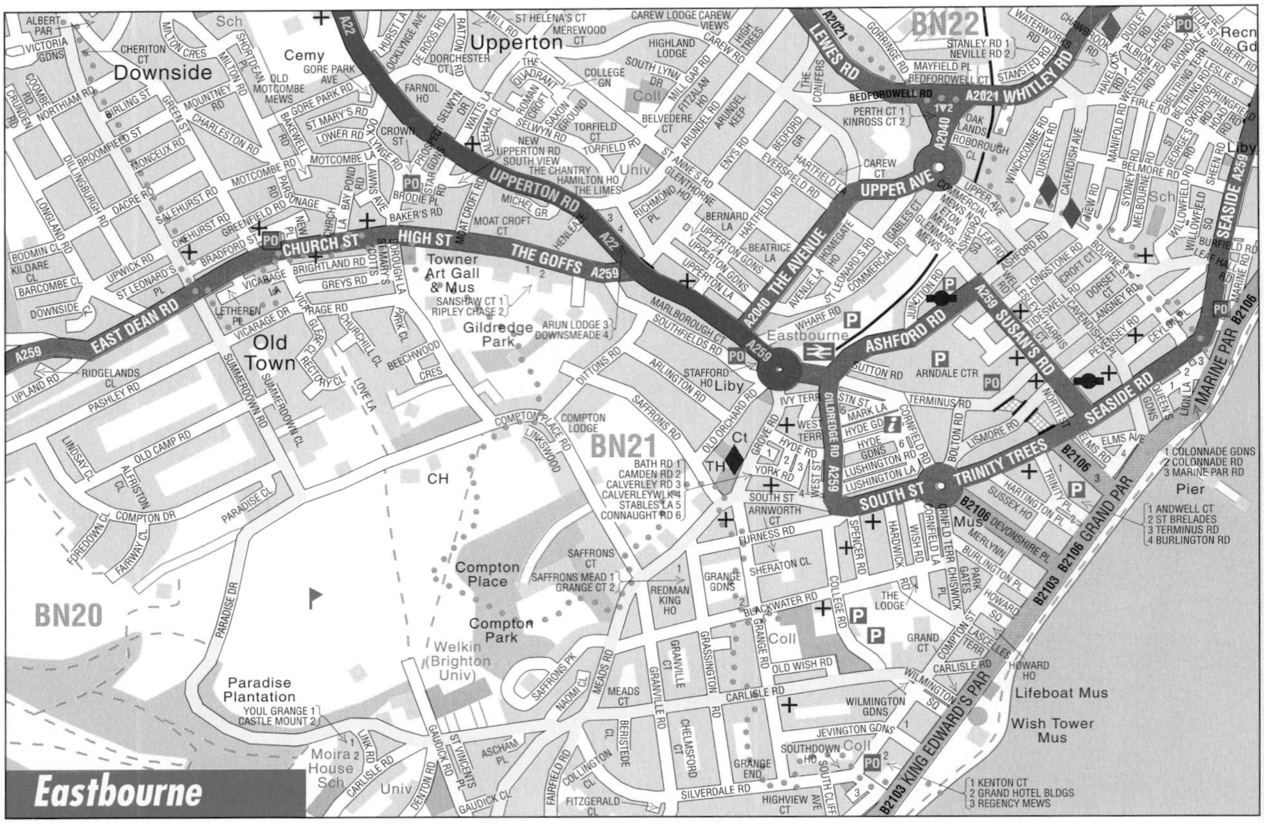
Eastbourne
Downside
Upperton
BN22
BN21
BN20
Old Town
Cemy
Towner Art Gall & Mus
Gildredge Park
Eastbourne
Compton Place
Compton Park
Welkin (Brighton Univ)
Paradise Plantation
Moira House Sch
Univ
CH
Coll
Liby
Ct
TH
Mus
Pier
Lifeboat Mus
Wish Tower Mus
Recn Gd
ARNDALE CTR
CHURCH ST
HIGH ST
THE GOFFS
EAST DEAN RD
UPPERTON RD
THE AVENUE
UPPER AVE
LEWES RD
WHITLEY RD
BEDFORDWELL RD
ASHFORD RD
SUSAN'S RD
SEASIDE RD
SEASIDE
TRINITY TREES
SOUTH ST
GILDREDGE RD
GRAND PAR
MARINE PAR
KING EDWARD'S PAR
DEVONSHIRE PL
SAFFRONS RD
MEADS RD
CARLISLE RD
COMPTON PLACE RD
PARADISE DR
SUMMERDOWN RD
UPLAND RD
SILVERDALE RD
GAUDICK RD
DENTON RD
UPWICK RD
BROOMFIELD ST
DILLINGBURGH RD
SALEHURST RD
MOTCOMBE RD
VICARAGE DR
RIDGELANDS CL
PASHLEY RD
OLD CAMP RD
COMPTON DR
GRANGE RD
COLLEGE RD
BLACKWATER RD
FURNESS RD
HARTFIELD RD
ARUNDEL RD
SAFFRONS MEAD 1
GRANGE CT 2
BATH RD 1
CAMDEN RD 2
CALVERLEY RD 3
CALVERLEYWLK 4
STABLES LA 5
CONNAUGHT RD 6
SANSHAW CT 1
RIPLEY CHASE 2
ARUN LODGE 3
DOWNSMEADE 4
YOUL GRANGE 1
CASTLE MOUNT 2
STANLEY RD 1
NEVILLE RD 2
PERTH CT 1
KINROSS CT 2
1 COLONNADE GDNS
2 COLONNADE RD
3 MARINE PAR RD
1 ANDWELL CT
2 ST BRELADES
3 TERMINUS RD
4 BURLINGTON RD
1 KENTON CT
2 GRAND HOTEL BLDGS
3 REGENCY MEWS
A22
A259
A2021
A2040
B2106
B2103

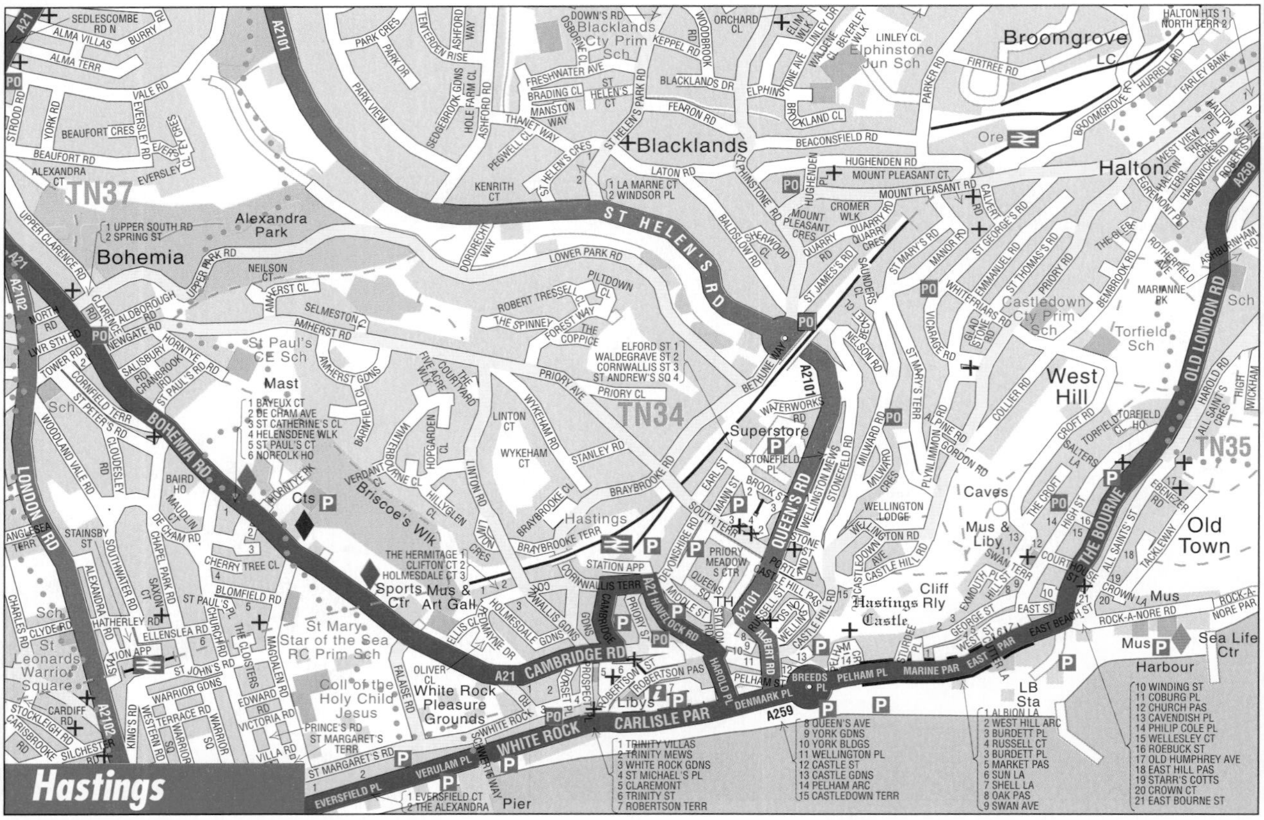
Hastings
Broomgrove
Blacklands
Blacklands Cty Prim Sch
Elphinstone Jun Sch
Ore
Halton
Alexandra Park
Bohemia
TN37
TN34
TN35
St Paul's CE Sch
Mast
Superstore
Cts
Briscoe's Wlk
Hastings
Sports Ctr
Mus & Art Gall
St Mary Star of the Sea RC Prim Sch
St Leonards Warrior Square
Coll of the Holy Child Jesus
White Rock Pleasure Grounds
Libys
TH
Pier
Castledown Cty Prim Sch
Torfield Sch
West Hill
Caves
Mus & Liby
Cliff
Hastings Castle
Old Town
LB Sta
Harbour
Sea Life Ctr
Sch
ST HELEN'S RD
QUEEN'S RD
BOHEMIA RD
LONDON RD
CAMBRIDGE RD
CARLISLE PAR
WHITE ROCK
VERULAM PL
EVERSFIELD PL
PELHAM PL
MARINE PAR
EAST PAR
ROCK-A-NORE RD
THE BOURNE
OLD LONDON RD
ALBERT RD
BREEDS PL
HAVELOCK RD
STATION APP
BEACONSFIELD RD
MOUNT PLEASANT RD
LOWER PARK RD
AMHERST RD
PRIORY AVE
BRAYBROOKE RD
ELFORD ST 1
WALDEGRAVE ST 2
CORNWALLIS ST 3
ST ANDREW'S SQ 4
1 LA MARNE CT
2 WINDSOR PL
1 UPPER SOUTH RD
2 SPRING ST
1 BAYEUX CT
2 DE CHAM AVE
3 ST CATHERINE'S CL
4 HELENSDENE WLK
5 ST PAUL'S CT
6 NORFOLK HO
THE HERMITAGE 1
CLIFTON CT 2
HOLMESDALE CT 3
HALTON HTS 1
NORTH TERR 2
1 TRINITY VILLAS
2 TRINITY MEWS
3 WHITE ROCK GDNS
4 ST MICHAEL'S PL
5 CLAREMONT
6 TRINITY ST
7 ROBERTSON TERR
8 QUEEN'S AVE
9 YORK GDNS
10 YORK BLDGS
11 WELLINGTON PL
12 CASTLE ST
13 CASTLE GDNS
14 PELHAM ARC
15 CASTLEDOWN TERR
1 ALBION LA
2 WEST HILL ARC
3 BURDETT PL
4 RUSSELL CT
5 MARKET PAS
6 SUN LA
7 SHELL LA
8 OAK PAS
9 SWAN AVE
10 WINDING ST
11 COBURG PL
12 CHURCH PAS
13 CAVENDISH PL
14 PHILIP COLE PL
15 WELLESLEY CT
16 ROEBUCK ST
17 OLD HUMPHREY AVE
18 EAST HILL PAS
19 STARR'S COTTS
20 CROWN CT
21 EAST BOURNE ST
1 EVERSFIELD CT
2 THE ALEXANDRA
A21
A259
A2101
A2102

Lewes

Landport
South Malling
The Brooks
Wallands Park
Pells
Cliffe
Cuilfail
St Anne's
Southover
BN7
BN8
Southerham Farm
Rise Farm
The Cockshut
Obelisk
Lewes Tertiery Coll
Priory Sch
Sewage Works

ST JOHN'S HILL 1
ST JOHN'S TERR 2
ST JOHN ST 3
EDWARD ST 4
EARLS GDN 5
WELLINGTON ST 6
WATERLOO PL 7

8 MALLING ST
9 RUSBRIDGE LA
10 SOUTH CLIFFE
11 SOUTH CT
12 FARNCOMBE RD
13 THE MOORINGS

MOUNT PL 1
CASTLE BANKS 2
CASTLE RISE 3
CASTLE PREC 4
CASTLE GATE 5
PIPE PAS 6

14 FULLER'S PAS
15 BROOMAN'S LA
16 CHURCH TWITTEN
17 WALWERS LA
18 ST NICHOLAS LA

1 CLEVEDOWN
2 BARONS WLK

DUMBRELL CT 1
GREENE CT 2
BARBER CT 3
THE COURSE 4
CLEVE TERR 5

1 PRIORY HO
2 PRIORY CT
3 ROYAL SUSSEX CT

BULL LA 1
STEWARDS INN LA 2
ST SWITHUN'S LA 3
ST SWITHUN'S TERR 4
ST MARTIN'S LA 5
ST ANDREW'S LA 6
TANNERS' BROOK 7
DORSET RD 8

ANNE'S PATH 6
VERRALL'S WLK 7
MONKS LA 8

Royal Tunbridge Wells

Denny Bottom
Mount Ephraim
Bishop's Down
Tunbridge Wells Golf Club
Nevill Park
Mount Sion
Tunbridge Wells Common
Hungershall Park
Calverley Park
Camden Park
Banner Farm
Madeira Park
Hawkenbury
Chilston House
Nuffield
TN1
TN2
TN4

1 DUDLEY LODGE
2 NEVILL LODGE
3 LADYFERN CT
4 OSMUNDA CT
5 LOMARIA CT

1 GROVER ST
2 SPENCER'S MEWS

1 BISHOPS CT
2 CEDAR LODGE
3 CHANCELLOR HO
4 SOUTHGATE

CHRIST CHURCH AVE 1
WARWICK RD 2
SPENCER MEWS 3
BERKELEY RD 4
CHAPEL PL 5
BEDFORD TERR 6
CUMBERLAND YD 7
CUMBERLAND MEWS 8
MARKET ST 9
SUSSEX MEWS 10
THE PANTILES 11
UNION SQ 12

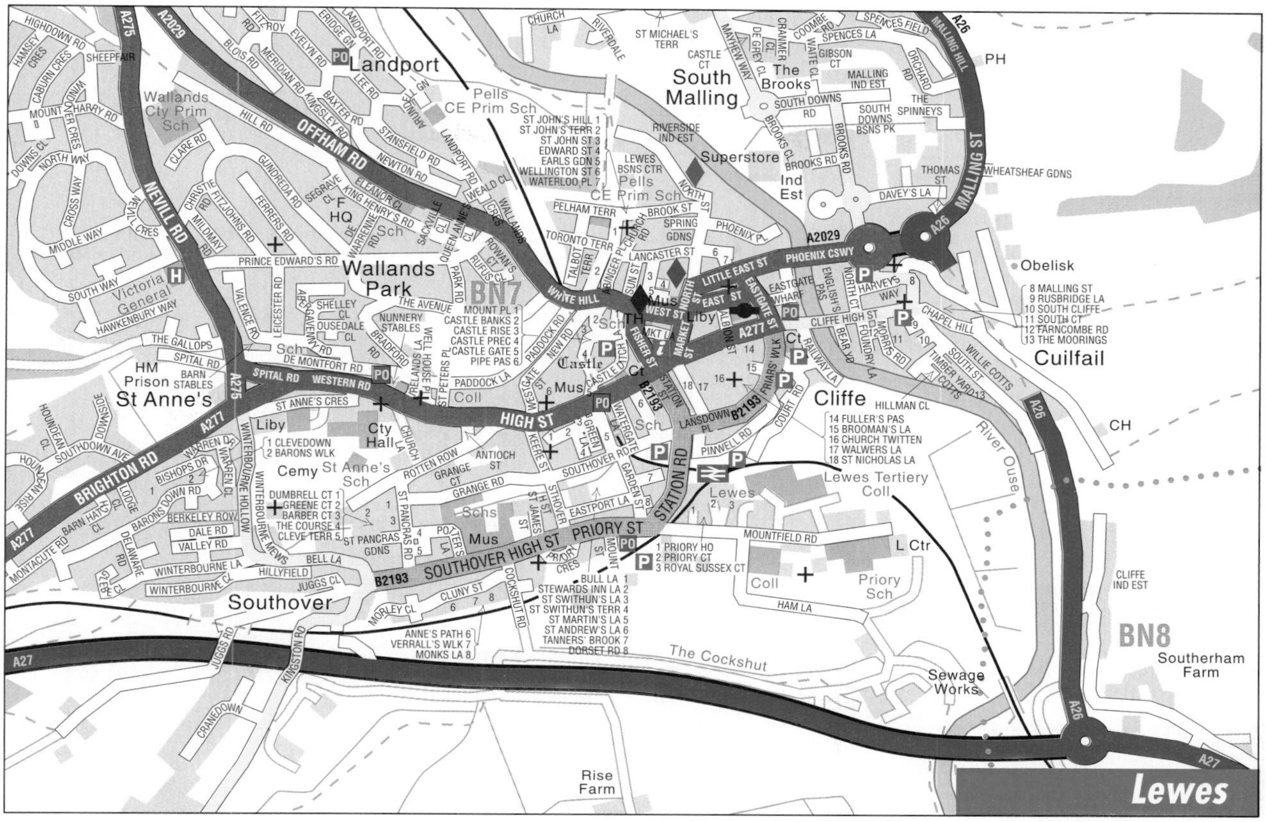

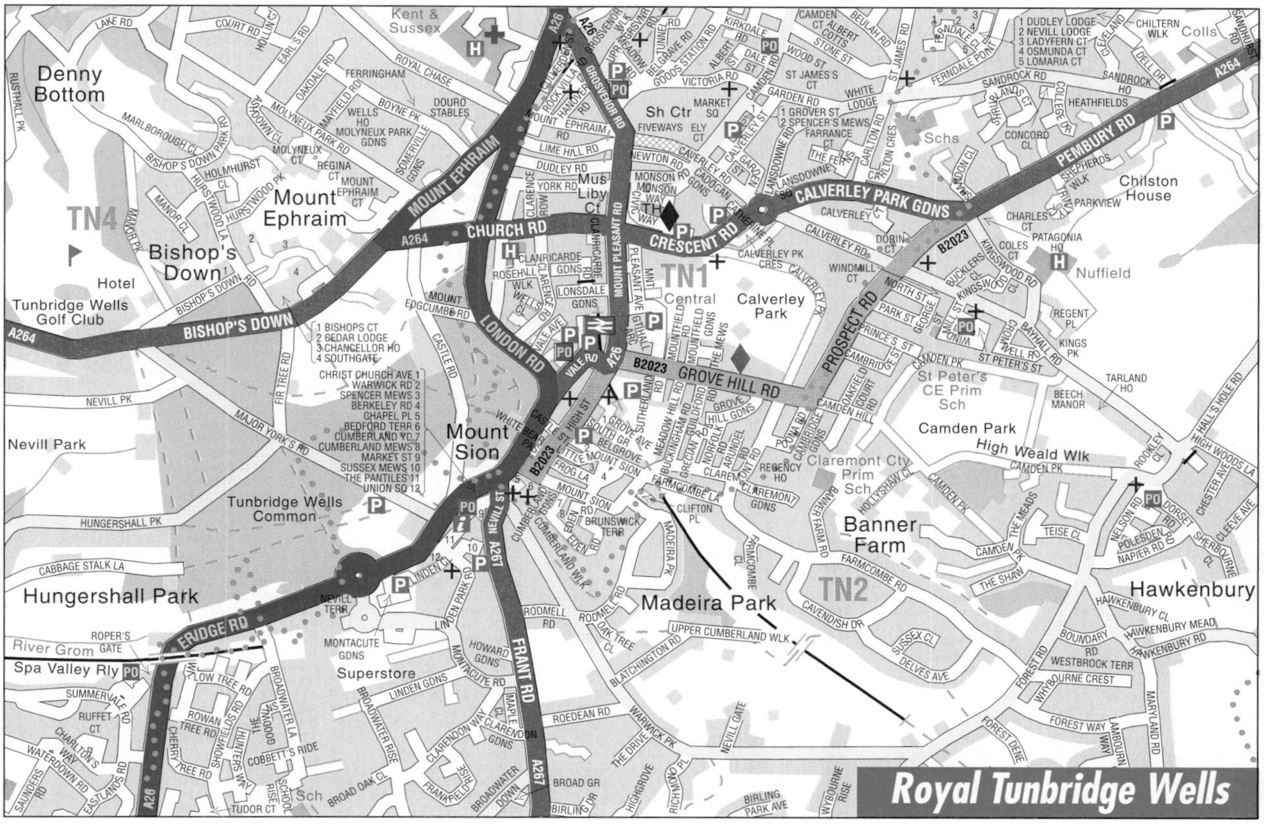

Index

Street names are listed alphabetically and show the locality, the Postcode District, the page number and a reference to the square in which the name falls on the map page

Arundel Ct **6** Brighton BN2..............**188** E4

Full street name
This may have been abbreviated on the map

Location number
If present, this indicates the street's position on a congested area of the map instead of the name

Town, village or locality in which the street falls.

Postcode District for the street name

Page number of the map on which the street name appears

Grid square in which the centre of the street falls

Schools, hospitals, sports centres, railway stations, shopping centres, industrial estates, public amenities and other places of interest are also listed. These are highlighted in magenta

Abbreviations used in the index

App	Approach	Cl	Close	Espl	Esplanade	N	North	S	South
Arc	Arcade	Comm	Common	Est	Estate	Orch	Orchard	Sq	Square
Ave	Avenue	Cnr	Corner	Gdns	Gardens	Par	Parade	Strs	Stairs
Bvd	Boulevard	Cotts	Cottages	Gn	Green	Pk	Park	Stps	Steps
Bldgs	Buildings	Ct	Court	Gr	Grove	Pas	Passage	St	Street, Saint
Bsns Pk	Business Park	Ctyd	Courtyard	Hts	Heights	Pl	Place	Terr	Terrace
Bsns Ctr	Business Centre	Cres	Crescent	Ind Est	Industrial Estate	Prec	Precinct	Trad	Trading Est
Bglws	Bungalows	Dr	Drive	Intc	Interchange	Prom	Promenade	Wlk	Walk
Cswy	Causeway	Dro	Drove	Junc	Junction	Ret Pk	Retail Park	W	West
Ctr	Centre	E	East	La	Lane	Rd	Road	Yd	Yard
Cir	Circus	Emb	Embankment			Rdbt	Roundabout		

Town and village index

Albourne 125 B5
Albourne Green 125 C6
Aldingbourne 175 A7
Aldsworth 149 F6
Alfold 31 F8
Alfold Crossways 11 A3
Almodington 202 F8
Amberley 138 D7
Angmering 179 E5
Ansteadbrook 28 C5
Ansty 84 C3
Apuldram 172 C3
Ardingly 64 A7
Arundel 158 C4
Ashington 121 B5
Ashurst 122 D5
Ashurst Wood 23 E6
Atherington 197 F6
Balcombe 40 F2
Balcombe Lane 40 A6
Balls Cross 52 B1
Balls Green 78 A3
Barlavington 115 E5
Barnham 176 D5
Barns Green 56 E3
Barnsnap 38 B3
Bepton 92 A1
Bignor 116 A2
Billingshurst 77 E7
Birdham 191 E5
Blackstone 124 E5
Blendworth 128 A7
Bognor Regis 195 D2
Bolney 83 C3
Bosham 171 C4
Bosham Hoe 191 C8
Botolphs 163 F8
Boxgrove 154 D3
Bracklesham 202 B6
Bramber 143 F2
Bramshott 25 C6
Breach 149 F1
Brighton 188 B4
Brighton 207 A4
Broadbridge 171 D7
Broadford Bridge 99 F8
Broadridge Heath 35 E4
Brook Street 62 F1
Broomer's Corner 100 F7
Bucks Green 33 B6
Buncton 142 C8
Burgess Hill 107 D2
Buriton 88 A5
Burndell 177 B3
Burpham 159 A7
Burstow 7 A7
Bury 138 A7
Byworth 96 B6
Camelsdale 26 F4
Charlton 133 F6
Charlwood 4 E7
Chelwood Common 66 D6
Chelwood Gate 66 D8
Chichester 172 D7
Chiddingfold 29 E8
Chidham 170 F4
Chilgrove 110 F1
Chithurst 69 C3
Church Norton 204 B4
Cinder Hill 65 B8
Clapham 160 F1
Clayton 147 E8
Climping 177 E1
Cocking 112 D8
Codmore Hill 98 D5
Coldwaltham 117 C6
Colgate 38 C6
Colworth 174 E2
Compton 109 A2
Coneyhurst 78 B4
Conford 24 E7
Coolham 78 D2
Coombes 164 A5
Cootham 119 B2
Copsale 80 C7
Copthorne 7 C3
Cowfold 81 F2
Cox Green 12 E1
Crabtree 82 A7
Cranleigh 12 A8
Crawley 18 F5
Crawley Down 21 C7
Crockerhill 155 B3
Crossbush 158 E1
Crosspost 83 B1
Cuckfield 84 F5
Cudworth 3 F8
Danehill 66 A4
Dial Post 101 E4
Ditchling 127 D3
Domewood 8 A5
Donnington 172 E1
Doomsday Green 59 A8
Dormans Park 9 E6
Dormansland 10 B8
Dragons Green 79 C3
Dumpford 90 F8
Duncton 115 B7
Earnley 202 D6
Eartham 155 E7
Easebourne 71 B2
East Ashling 151 E4
East Beach 206 F8
East Dean 134 C6
East Grinstead 9 E2
East Harting 90 A4
East Lavant 153 A5
East Lavington 114 E5
East Liss 45 C4
East Marden 110 B2
East Preston 200 B6
East Wittering 201 E6
Eastergate 175 F8
Ebernoe 51 E4
Edburton 145 C4
Ellen's Green 13 A4
Elmer 197 A6
Elsted 90 D3
Emsworth 149 A1
Faygate 16 F1
Felbridge 8 F4
Felcourt 9 C8
Fernhill 6 E7
Fernhurst 49 B5
Ferring 200 F6
Finchdean 128 F6
Findon 161 F6
Fishbourne 172 A6
Fisherstreet 28 F3
Fittleworth 97 A2
Five Oaks 55 F5
Flansham 196 C7
Fontwell 156 A2
Ford 177 E4
Forest Row 23 F3
Forestside 129 D6
Foxhill 74 E2
Fulking 145 F4
Funtington 151 A5
Furnace Wood 8 C4
Furner's Green 66 C1
Goddards' Green 106 A5
Goodwood Park 153 F7
Graffham 114 B7
Greatham 118 A4
Halnaker 154 E5
Hambrook 150 C2
Hammer 26 D5
Hammerpot 179 F8
Handcross 61 C8
Hangleton 180 D4
Hardham 117 F7
Harwoods Green 97 E5
Haslemere 27 D6
Hassocks 126 D4
Haywards Heath 85 C3
Heath Common 120 C2
Henfield 123 F5
Henley 71 B8
Hermitage 169 D8
Heyshott 93 B1
Heyshott Green 93 A2
Hickstead 105 C5
High Cross 124 F7
Highbrook 42 E1
Highleigh 192 C1
Hill Brow 45 D2
Hill Side 45 D3
Hollywater 24 B8
Hookwood 1 D2
Horley 2 C3
Horsemere Green 177 C1
Horsham 36 C3
Horsted Keynes 65 D5
Houghton 138 B4
Hove 187 B5
Hunston 193 A8
Hurst Wickham 126 C6
Hurstpierpoint 126 B6
Ifold 31 D3
Iping 69 E2
Itchingfield 57 A6
Keymer 127 B4
Kingsfold 15 B5
Kingsley Green 27 B2
Kingston Gorse 200 D4
Kirdford 53 B2
Lambs Green 16 F6
Lancing 183 D5
Lickfold 72 A8
Linchmere 26 B2
Lindfield 86 A7
Liphook 25 C3
Liss 45 A4
Liss Forest 45 C6
Little London 42 A2
Little Parkminster 103 E7
Littlehampton 198 E3
Littleworth 103 A5
Lodsworth 72 A3
Lower Beeding 60 A3
Lower Fittleworth 97 A2
Loxwood 31 F4
Lumley 149 C1
Lurgashall 50 C3
Lyminster 178 D6
Madehurst 137 B1
Mannings Heath 59 D6
Maplehurst 80 F6
Marehill 98 E1
Mark Street 66 F3
Marley Heights 27 A1
Maudlin 153 F1
Merston 174 B3
Mid Lavant 152 E5
Middleton-on-Sea 196 E4
Midhurst 92 F6
Milland 47 B2
Monk's Gate 59 C4
Navant Hill 50 E5
Nep Town 123 E4
Nepcote 161 F5
New Brighton 149 C2
Newdigate 3 D8
Newpound Common 54 E2
North Chailey 87 F1
North End 177 A5
North Heath 98 F7
North Lancing 183 F8
North Marden 110 B5
North Mundham 173 D1
North Stoke 138 C2
Northchapel 51 A7
Norton 155 B1
Nursted 88 E7
Nutbourne Common 99 B1
Nutbourne (Emsworth) .170 C7
Nutbourne (Pulborough) .99 B2
Nuthurst 59 A1
Nyewood 90 A8
Nyton 175 D8
Oakwoodhill 14 A7
Oving 174 C7
Pagham 204 E8
Park Street 34 C4
Partridge Green 103 B3
Patching 160 D2
Paynes Green 14 D8
Pease Pottage 39 B6
Petworth 95 E7
Plaistow 30 F2
Poling 179 B6
Portslade Village 166 B1
Portslade-by-Sea 186 B5
Poynings 146 C5
Prince's Marsh 45 A2
Prinsted 169 F7
Pulborough 98 D1
Pyecombe 147 B6
Rackham 139 C8
Rake 46 B4
Ramsnest Common 29 A6
Red Hill 128 D1
River 72 D3
Rogate 68 B4
Roundstreet Common ...54 C6
Rowhook 13 E1
Rowland's Castle 128 F2
Rudgwick 33 C7
Runcton 173 E1
Rusper 16 D7
Rustington 199 B4
Salfords 2 A8
Sayers Common 105 D1
Scaynes Hill 86 E3
Selden 180 C8
Selham 94 C6
Selsey 206 D7
Sharpthorne 43 A6
Sheffield Green 87 F6
Shermanbury 103 D3
Shipley 101 D8
Shipton Green 191 A4
Shopwyke 173 F7
Shoreham-by-Sea 184 E5
Shottermill 26 F6
Shripney 175 C1
Sidlesham 192 F1
Singleton 133 D6
Slaugham 61 B5
Slindon 156 C6
Slinfold 34 D3
Slough Green 62 A1
Small Dole 144 F6
Somerley 191 D2
Sompting 183 B7
South Ambersham 93 F6
South Harting 89 D3
South Hayling 189 B1
South Mundham 193 D5
South Stoke 158 D8
Southbourne 170 A8
Southwater 57 E1
Southwater Street 58 A3
Southwick 185 F7
St John's Common 106 E4
Staplefield 61 F5
Stedham 70 A1
Steyning 143 C3
Stockbridge 172 F3
Stopham 97 D3
Storrington 119 D2
Stoughton 131 A3
Street End 192 D4
Strettington 154 A3
Strood Green 35 A6
Stubbermere 149 B8
Sullington 140 F7
Sutton 115 F3
Tangmere 154 D1
Terwick Common 68 D5
Thakeham 120 B7
Thorney Island 169 D4
Tillington 95 C8
Tinsley Green 6 C4
Tisman's Common 32 F6
Toddington 178 E4
Tortington 177 E7
Tower Hill 58 A7
Treyford 90 F2
Trotton 69 A1
Turners Hill 21 A4
Twineham 105 B4
Twineham Green 105 B6
Upper Beeding 144 A1
Upperton 73 B2
Upwaltham 135 E8
Walberton 156 D1
Walderton 130 E2
Wallis Wood 13 D8
Warminghurst 120 D6
Warnham 35 E7
Warningcamp 158 F3
Warninglid 61 A1
Washington 141 E6
Watersfield 117 A4
Wepham 159 A5
West Ashling 151 B3
West Barnham 176 A6
West Burton 137 D8
West Chiltington 99 E1
West Chiltington Common 119 C7
West Dean 133 A6
West Grinstead 102 C6
West Harting 89 D7
West Hoathly 42 E6
West Itchenor 190 F7
West Kingston 200 B4
West Lavington 93 A6
West Liss 45 B5
West Marden 130 A7
West Stoke 151 F6
West Thorney 169 F1
West Wittering 190 C1
Westbourne 149 D3
Westergate 175 D7
Westerton 153 F3
Westhampnett 153 E1
Westlands 191 E6
Westmeston 148 F8
Whitemans Green 84 E7
Wick 178 D4
Wiggonholt 118 E6
Wineham 104 D4
Wisborough Green 76 B8
Wiston 121 D1
Woodgate 175 E5
Woodmancote (Emsworth) 150 A4
Woodmancote (Henfield) 124 C2
Woolbeding 70 C2
Worthing 182 E1
Wrays 1 B5
Yapton 176 F2

A

A'becket Gdns BN13 .....181 F6
A'becket's Ave PO21 .....194 B1
Abberton Field BN6 .....126 B5
Abbey Cl BN15 ....184 B6
Abbey Ho RH20 ....140 D8
Abbey Rd Brighton BN2 ...188 D4
Lancing BN15 ....183 C7
Steyning BN44 ....143 E4
Worthing BN11 ....182 B1
Abbots Cl BN6 ....126 E4
Abbots Leigh RH13 ....80 A8
Abbotsbury Ct RH12 ......36 E3
Abbotsfield Rd RH11 .....17 D4
Abbotsford
Com Specl Sch RH15 ...106 E6
Abbotswood Wlk BN16 ..199 C4
Abbotts 11 BN1 ....187 E5
Abbotts Cl Boxgrove PO18 154 D3
Worthing BN11 ....182 D2
Abbotts View BN15 ......183 C8
Abbotts Way BN15 ......183 F6
Abbottsbury PO21 ....205 A8
Aberdeen Rd 5 BN2 ....188 C8
Abergavenny Gdns RH10 ..7 D3
Abigail Ho 10 RH16 ....85 E4
Abingdon Wlk BN13 .....181 D5
Abinger Cotts RH13 ....80 F5
Abinger Keep RH6 ....2 C4
Abinger Lodge BN15 ....184 C5
Abinger Rd BN41 ....186 B8
Abrahams Rd RH11 ....18 A1
Acacia Ave Hove BN3 .....166 F1
Worthing BN13 ....181 F7
Acacia Ct BN1 ....167 F2
Acorn Ave RH13 ....81 F1
Acorn Cl Angmering BN16 .179 F4
East Grinstead RH19 ....22 E8
Horley RH6 ....2 C4
Selsey PO20 ....206 D8
Acorn End PO21 ....194 D2
Acorns RH13 ....37 A4
Acorns The
Burgess Hill RH15 ....106 D4
Crawley RH11 ....18 B1
Sayers Common BN6 .....105 D2
Acre Cl
Haywards Heath RH16 .....85 D2
Rustington BN16 ....199 B6
Acre Cl The BN11 ....182 B1
Acre St PO20 ....190 F2
Adams Cl BN1 ....168 B2
Adamson Ct 6 RH11 ......18 B1
Adastra Ave BN6 ....127 A4
Adderbury Ave PO10 ....149 B3
Addison Cl BN15 ....183 E6
Addison Rd BN1, BN3 ....187 E7
Addison Way PO22 ......195 C7
Adelaide Cl Crawley RH11 ...5 D1
Horsham RH12 ....36 F4
Worthing BN13 ....181 C7
Adelaide Cres BN3 ......187 C5
Adelaide Ho GU29 ....92 E6
Adelaide Rd PO19 ......173 B7
Adelaide Sq BN43 ......185 B7
Adelphi Cl RH10 ....19 D4
Admers Cres GU30 ....25 C2
Admiral Ct BN15 ....183 D4
Admiral Rd RH11 ....18 A3
Admiral's Bridge La RH19 .22 C2
Admirals Wlk
Funtington PO18 ....151 A5
Littlehampton BN17 ....199 A6
1 Shoreham-by-Sea BN43 .184 F6
Admiralty Ct PO20 ....201 F7
Admiralty Gdns PO22 ....195 F3
Admiralty Rd PO22 ......195 F4
Admiralty Row PO20 .....201 F7
Adrian Ct RH11 ....18 B1
Adur Ave
Shoreham-by-Sea BN43 ....164 E1
Worthing BN13 ....181 C8
Adur Cl 6 BN15 ....184 C5
Adur Ct
5 Shoreham-by-Sea BN15 .184 C5
10 Shoreham-by-Sea BN43 .185 C8
Adur Dr BN43 ....185 A7
Adur Rd Burgess Hill RH15 107 C4
Shoreham-by-Sea BN43 ...184 E8
Adur Valley Ct BN44 .....144 B2
Adur View BN44 ....144 B2
Adversane Ct RH12 ....36 D4
Adversane La RH14 ....77 D2
Adversane Rd BN14 .....182 B5
Agate La RH12 ....36 F5
Aglaia Rd BN11 ....181 F1
Agnes St BN2 ....188 C7
Aigburth Ave PO21 ......194 D3
Ailsa Cl RH11 ....18 B3
Ainsdale Cl BN13 ....181 D6
Ainsdale Rd BN13 ....181 D6
Ainsworth Ho 1 BN2 ....188 C7
Aintree Rd RH10 ....19 A4
Air St BN1 ....207 A2
Airedale Ct 8 BN11 .....182 B2
Airport Way RH6 ....6 B8
Airport Way Rdbt E RH6 ...6 C8
Airport Way Rdbt W RH6 ...5 F8
Aitken Ho GU27 ....27 C7
Ajax Pl PO22 ....196 C5
Akehurst Cl RH10 ....7 B3
Alan Way BN2 ....188 F5
Alandale Rd Birdham PO20 191 F4
Sompting BN15 ....163 C1
Albany Cl BN11 ....182 A1
Albany Mews BN3 ....187 B6
Albany Rd RH11 ....18 C6
Albany Villas
Cuckfield RH17 ....85 A6
Hove BN3 ....187 B6
Albermarle The BN2 .....207 B1
Albert Cl RH16 ....86 A4
Albert Crane Ct RH11 .....18 A8
Albert Dr RH15 ....106 E2
Albert Mews BN3 ....187 C6
Albert Rd
Bognor Regis PO21 ....195 D3
Brighton BN1 ....207 A3
Fishbourne PO19 ....172 C6
Horley RH6 ....2 A3
Littlehampton BN17 ....198 D5
Rustington BN16 ....199 C6
Southwick BN42 ....185 D7
Alberta Rd BN13 ....181 D6
Alberta Wlk BN13 ....181 D6
Albery Cl RH12 ....36 B4
Albion Cl RH10 ....19 D5
Albion Ct RH15 ....106 F2
Albion Hill BN2 ....207 C3
Albion Ho 4 Brighton BN2 207 C3
Southwick BN42 ....185 F7
Albion Rd PO20 ....206 F6
Albion St Brighton BN2 ...207 C3
Portslade-by-Sea BN41,BN42
BN41,BN42 ....186 B7
Southwick BN42 ....185 E7
Albion Way RH12 ....36 C2
Alborough Way PO21 ....194 D2
Albourne CE Prim Sch
BN6 ....125 C6
Albourne Cl BN2 ....188 F7
Albourne Rd Henfield BN5 124 A8
Hurstpierpoint BN6 ....125 E6
Albury Keep RH6 ....2 B4
Aldbourne Dr PO21 ......194 D2
Alder Cl Crawley Down RH10 21 B8
Worthing BN13 ....181 C5
Alder Copse RH12 ....57 F8
Alder Way PO22 ....196 E6
Alderman's Wlk PO19 ...173 A7
Aldermoor Ave RH20 .....119 E3
Alderney Rd BN12 ....200 F4
Alders Ave RH19 ....9 E3
Alders View Dr RH19 ......9 E3
Aldingbourne Cl RH11 ....17 F7
Aldingbourne Ctry Ctr
PO18 ....155 C3
Aldingbourne Dr PO18 ..155 B3
Aldingbourne Ho
Crockerhill PO18 ....155 B3
Littlehampton BN17 ....178 B3
Aldingbourne Pk PO20 ..175 D5
Aldingbourne Prim Sch
PO20 ....175 D6
Aldrich Cl BN2 ....188 F6
Aldrington Ave BN3 .....187 A8
Aldrington CE Prim Sch
BN3 ....167 A2
Aldrington Cl BN3 ......186 D7
Aldrington House Hospl
BN3 ....186 F6
Aldrington Pl BN3 ......186 D8
Aldrington Sta BN3 ......187 A8
Aldsworth Ave BN12 .....181 B1
Aldsworth Ct BN12 ......181 B2
Aldsworth Par BN12 .....181 B2
Aldwick Ave PO21 ....194 F2
Aldwick Cl 1 BN16 .....199 B3
Aldwick Cres BN14 ......162 A1
Aldwick Felds PO21 .....194 F2
Aldwick Gdns PO21 .....194 F3
Aldwick Grange PO21 ...194 E2
Aldwick Ho
Bognor Regis PO21 ....195 A2
Littlehampton BN17 ....178 B3
Aldwick Hundred PO21 ..194 E1
Aldwick Pl PO21 ....194 F2
Aldwick Rd PO21 ....195 B2
Aldwick St PO21 ....194 E2
Aldwych Cl RH10 ....19 D4
Alexander Cl PO21 ......194 E2
Alexandra Ct
10 Crawley RH10 ....18 D5
Hove BN3 ....166 F2
Worthing BN12 ....181 C3
Alexandra Ho PO22 .....195 E4
Alexandra Rd
Burgess Hill RH15 ....107 C2
Chichester PO19 ....173 B7
Lancing BN15 ....183 F5
Worthing BN11 ....182 F2
Alexandra Terr 14 PO21 ..195 D3
Alexandra Villas BN1 ....207 A3
Alfold By-Pass GU6 ......11 A5
Alfold La GU6 ....11 A7
Alfold Rd GU6 ....11 B7
Alford Cl BN14 ....182 A7
Alfred Cl
Bognor Regis PO22 ....196 F5
Crawley RH10 ....19 E5
Alfred Pl BN11 ....182 E2
Alfred Rd BN1 ....207 A3
Alfrey Cl PO10 ....169 E8
Alfriston Cl
Bognor Regis PO22 ....196 C6
Brighton BN2 ....188 F6
Worthing BN14 ....182 B5
Alfriston Ho 2 BN14 ....182 D5
Alfriston Rd BN14 ......182 B5
Alice Cl 2 BN3 ....187 D5
Alice St BN3 ....187 D5
Alicia Ave Ashington RH20 .121 A5
Crawley RH10 ....19 C6
Alicks Hill RH14 ....77 D8
Alinora BN17 ....198 E4
Alinora Ave BN12 ....181 D1
Alinora Cl BN12 ....181 D1
Alinora Cres BN12 ......181 D1
Alinora Dr BN12 ....181 D1
Allandale Cl PO20 ......206 F8
Allangate Dr BN16 ......199 D6
Allcard Cl RH12 ....36 D4
Allcot Cl RH11 ....17 E3
Allee Dr GU30 ....25 B5
Allen Rd RH16 ....86 A4
Allen's Cl RH19 ....23 D6
Allendale RH13 ....57 F3
Allendale Ave
New Brighton PO10 ....149 A3
Worthing BN14 ....162 A1
Allestree Ct 15 PO21 ....195 D3
Alley Groves RH13 ....81 F2
Alley The Amberley BN18 ..138 D7
Stedham GU29 ....70 A1
Alleyne Way PO22 ......197 B5
Allfrey Plat RH20 ....98 D2
Allfreys Wharf RH20 .....98 B2
Allingham Gdns RH12 ....37 B5
Allington Rd BN14 ......182 E7
Allman Bsns Pk PO20 ...192 B6
Allyington Way RH10 .....19 F4
Alma Cotts BN5 ....123 F4
Alma Rd RH16 ....86 B8
Alma St BN15 ....183 E4
Almodington La PO20 ...202 E7
Almond Ave BN15,BN43 .164 C1
Almond Cl RH11 ....18 A5
Almshouses of
The Holy Name BN6 ...126 A4
Almshouses The PO18 ..154 D4
Alperton Cl PO21 ....194 C1
Alpha Cotts RH20 ....98 D2
Alpha Ct BN17 ....198 C5
Alpha Rd RH11 ....18 C6
Alpine Rd BN3 ....186 F8
Alston Way BN13 ....181 D5
Alverstone Rd BN11 .....182 F3
Amadeus Ho BN16 ......200 B6
Ambassadors The 10
BN3 ....187 C6
Amber Ct 13 Hove BN3 ...187 C6
8 Hove BN3 ....187 D7
Amber Glade RH13 ....57 F1
Amberley CE Fst Sch
BN18 ....138 E7
Amberley Cl
Burgess Hill RH15 ....107 A4
Crawley RH10 ....19 C6
Haywards Heath RH16 .....85 D4
Horsham RH12 ....37 A6
Hove BN3 ....166 E3
Littlehampton BN17 ....198 E6
Shoreham-by-Sea BN43 ...164 F1
Storrington RH20 ....119 C1
Amberley Ct Lancing BN15 183 F6
9 Worthing BN11 ....181 F2
Amberley Dr
Bognor Regis PO21 ....195 A4
Hove BN3 ....166 E3
Worthing BN12 ....181 B1
Amberley Gate RH20 ....119 B1
Amberley Lodge BN2 ....207 B4
Amberley Mus BN18 ....138 D5
Amberley Rd
Horsham RH12 ....37 A6
Littlehampton BN16 ....199 C4
Storrington RH20 ....140 A8
Amberley Sta BN18 .....138 D4
Amberly Lodge BN2 .....188 F6
Ambersham Cres BN16 ..179 F3
Ambleside Cl
Bognor Regis PO22 ....196 B6
Crawley RH11 ....17 D5
Ambleside Rd BN15 .....183 C6
Ambrose Hill RH17 ......105 B7
Ambrose Ho BN11 ......182 D2
Ambrose Pl BN11 ....182 D2
Amelia Rd BN11 ....182 C2
Amenic Ct 3 BN17 ......198 E5
America La RH16 ....86 A5
Amesbury Cres BN3 .....186 E7
Amherst Cres BN3 ......186 F8
Amstel Ct 2 BN17 ......198 F4
Amundsen Rd RH12 ....36 D6
Anchor Cl BN43 ....185 A6
Anchor Ct BN12 ....181 E1
Anchor Hill RH17 ....87 A2
Anchor Springs 12 BN17 .198 D5
Ancren Cl BN12 ....180 F3
Ancton Cl PO22 ....196 F5
Ancton Dr PO22 ....197 A6
Ancton La PO22 ....196 F6
Ancton Lodge La PO22 ..197 A5
Ancton Way PO22 ....197 B5
Anderson Ct GU27 ....27 C6
Andlers Ash Rd GU33 ....45 A3
Andrew Ave PO22 ....196 C5
Andrew Cl
Rustington BN16 ....199 B6
Steyning BN44 ....143 D2
Andrew's La RH13 ....57 F1
Andrews Cotts RH13 .....79 F7
Andrews La GU29 ....91 F7
Andrews Rd RH13 ....79 F7
Andromeda Cl RH11 .....17 E4
Angel St GU28 ....95 F8
Angell Cl RH10 ....19 C5
Angell Est PO19 ....173 D5
Anglesea St BN11 ......182 C3
Anglesey Cl RH11 ....18 C2
Angmering Ct BN1 ......168 F5
Angmering La BN16 .....199 E4
Angmering Sch The
BN16 ....179 F3
Angmering Sta BN16 ....199 F6
Angmering Way BN16 ...179 E3
Angola Rd BN14 ....182 F4
Angus Cl RH12 ....36 D4
Angus Rd BN12 ....181 E2
Ann Cl BN6 ....127 A5
Ann St Brighton BN1 .....207 B4
Worthing BN11 ....182 E2
Annandale Ave PO21 ....195 C4
Anne Howard Gdns
BN18 ....158 A3
Annington
Commercial Ctr BN44 ..163 E8
Annington Gdns 4 BN43 .164 F1
Annington Rd BN44,BN15 .163 F8
Annweir Ave BN15 ......183 E6
Anscombe Cl BN11 .....181 F1
Anscombe Rd BN11 .....181 F1
Anscome 5 RH16 ....85 D6
Ansisters Rd BN12 ......200 E5
Anson Ct BN12 ....181 C4
Anson Rd
Bognor Regis PO21 ....194 B2
Worthing BN12 ....181 C4
Ansty Cl BN2 ....188 E5
Answorth Cl PO19 ......153 B1
Anthony Way PO10 .....149 B3
Antlands La RH6 ....7 B6
Antlands La E RH6 ....6 F5
Antlands La W RH6 ....6 E6
Antonia Ct 9 BN17 ......198 D5
Anvil Cl Billingshurst RH14 ..77 C8
Portslade-by-Sea BN41 ....166 B2
Southwater RH13 ....57 F1
Apple Gr
Bognor Regis PO21 ....194 B1
Hermitage PO10 ....169 D8
Apple Tree Wlk BN17 ...177 D1
Appledore Ct RH16 ....86 A7
Appledore Gdns RH16 ....86 A6
Appledore Rd BN2 ......168 F4
Appledram La N PO19 ...172 C6
Appledram La S PO20 ...172 C4
Applefield RH10 ....18 E7
Applesham Ave BN3 .....166 E2
Applesham Way BN41 ...166 A1
Appletree Dr PO22 ......176 B6
Appletrees BN16 ....200 B4
Approach The
Brighton BN1 ....167 E3
Dormans Park RH19 ....9 F6
April Cl Horsham RH12 .....36 C4
Kingston Gorse BN12 .....200 E4
Apsley Ct RH11 ....17 F4
Apsley Way BN13 ....181 B5
Aquarius Ct RH11 ....17 E4
Arbor Ct RH16 ....85 E5
Arcade Rd BN17 ....198 D5
Arcade The
8 Bognor Regis PO21 ....195 D3
13 Littlehampton BN17 ...198 D5
Arch Ho 5 PO21 ....195 C2
Archer Ct RH15 ....107 A3
Archers Ct RH10 ....18 D8
Archibald Rd BN11 .....183 A3
Arcturus Rd RH11 ....17 E3
Ardale Cl BN11 ....181 F2
Arden Rd RH10 ....18 F4
Ardingly Cl RH11 ....18 B8
Ardingly Coll RH17 ......64 A6
Ardingly Ct 10 BN2 .....207 C2
Ardingly Dr BN12 ....181 B3
Ardingly Rd RH17 ....84 F7
Ardingly St BN2 ....207 C2
Ardings Cl RH17 ....64 B7
Ardmore Sch BN11 .....182 D2
Ardsheal Cl BN14 ......182 C5
Ardsheal Rd BN14 ......182 C6
Argus Wlk RH11 ....18 A3
Argyle Cir 5 PO21 ......195 C3
Argyle Rd
Bognor Regis PO21 ....195 C3
Brighton BN1 ....207 A5
Ariadne Rd BN11 ....182 B1
Ariel Ct BN15 ....183 D4
Arkendale RH19 ....9 A4
Arlington Ave BN12 .....181 B1
Arlington Cl BN12 ......181 B1
Arlington Cres
Brighton BN1 ....168 E5
East Preston BN16 ....180 B3
Arlington Ct RH16 ....85 E5
Armada Ct PO20 ....202 B5
Armada Way BN17 ......199 A6
Armadale Rd PO19 ......173 C7
Arndale Rd BN17 ....198 B6
Arne Cl RH11 ....17 F3
Arne Gr RH6 ....1 E5
Arnell Ave PO20 ....206 E7
Arnfield Cl RH11 ....17 E5
Arnhem Rd PO21 ....195 B5
Arnold St BN2 ....188 C7
Arnold Way PO18 ....171 C7
Arnside Cl BN15 ....183 C5
Arran Cl RH11 ....18 B3
Arran Gate PO21 ....195 E3
Arrancourt 1 RH12 ......36 B2
Arrivals Rd RH6 ....5 F8
Artel Croft RH10 ....19 A6
Artex Ave BN16 ....179 C3
Arthur Bliss Ho RH16 ....86 A8
Arthur Rd Crawley RH11 ...17 E6
Horsham RH13 ....36 D1
Arthur St BN3 ....187 A8
Arun Bsns Pk PO22 .....195 E5
Arun Cl Amberley BN18 ...138 E7
Arun Cl *continued*
Lancing BN15 ....183 C7
Rustington BN16 ....199 C6
Worthing BN13 ....181 D7
Arun Cres BN13 ....181 C7
Arun Ct East Preston BN16 200 A5
Littlehampton BN17 ....198 C5
Littlehampton, Wick BN17 ..178 D3
1 Pulborough RH20 ....98 C2
13 Shoreham-by-Sea BN43 .185 C8
Arun L Ctr PO22 ....195 F5
Arun Lodge BN13 ....181 D7
Arun Par BN17 ....198 D3
Arun Prospect RH20 .....98 A1
Arun Rd Billingshurst RH14 .55 C1
Bognor Regis PO21 ....195 A4
Arun Ret Pk PO22 ......195 E6
Arun St BN18 ....158 B2
Arun Terr BN18 ....158 A2
Arun Vale RH20 ....117 C5
Arun Vale Cty Inf Sch
BN17 ....198 D5
Arun Way
Bognor Regis PO21 ....205 B8
Horsham RH13 ....36 E1
Arundale Sch RH20 ......98 D2
Arundel 4 BN15 ....183 D5
Arundel & District Hospl
BN18 ....158 A3
Arundel By-Pass BN18 ..158 B2
Arundel Castle BN18 ...158 B3
Arundel CE Prim Sch
BN18 ....157 F2
Arundel Cl
Bognor Regis PO21 ....195 A4
Conford GU30 ....24 D8
Crawley RH10 ....19 C6
Shoreham-by-Sea BN43 ...185 C8
Southwater RH13 ....58 A1
Arundel Ct
6 Brighton BN2 ....188 E4
Burgess Hill RH15 ....106 F4
Ferring BN12 ....200 F4
Hove BN1 ....167 C5
14 Shoreham-by-Sea BN43 .185 C8
10 Worthing BN11 ....181 F2
Arundel Dr BN17 ....178 C5
Arundel Gdn 12 BN16 ...199 C5
Arundel Mews 10 BN2 ...188 E4
Arundel Mus
& Heritage Ctr BN18 ..158 B3
Arundel Pl BN2 ....188 E3
Arundel RC Cathedral
BN18 ....158 B3
Arundel Rd
Angmering BN16 ....179 F6
Brighton BN2 ....188 E4
Fontwell BN18 ....155 F3
Littlehampton BN17 ......198 D6
Selden BN16,BN13 ....180 C8
Walberton BN18 ....156 D2
Worthing BN13 ....181 D8
Arundel St BN2 ....188 E3
Arundel Sta BN18 ......158 C1
Arundel Terr BN2 ....188 E3
Arundel Villas GU30 .....24 D8
Arundel Way PO22 ......197 B5
Arundel Wing The BN18 .177 E7
Arunside RH12 ....36 A1
Arunside Cty Prim Sch
RH12 ....36 A2
Arunside Ind Est BN17 ..198 C6
Ascot Cl PO20 ....201 F8
Ascot Way BN16 ....199 E6
Ash Cl Crawley Down RH10 ..21 C8
Findon BN14 ....161 E6
Hove BN3 ....167 C3
Ash Ct East Grinstead RH19 ..9 E3
Southwick BN42 ....165 F1
Ash Gr Bognor Regis PO22 .195 C6
Fernhurst GU27 ....49 A6
Haywards Heath RH16 .....85 D2
Liphook GU30 ....25 D3
Worthing BN11 ....182 E2
Ash Grove Ind Pk PO22 ..195 D7
Ash Ho RH14 ....55 C1
Ash Keys RH10 ....18 E5
Ash La BN16 ....199 C5
Ash Rd Crawley RH10 ......19 A8
Southwater RH13 ....57 E1
Ashacre La BN13 ....182 A7
Ashacre Mews BN13 ....181 F7
Ashacre Way BN13 .....182 A6
Ashburnham Cl
Brighton BN1 ....168 E5
Chichester PO19 ....172 D7
Worthing BN13 ....181 B5
Ashburnham Dr BN1 ....168 E5
Ashburnham Ho BN1 ....167 E5
Ashburnham Rd RH10 ....19 A4
Ashby Ct RH13 ....36 E1
Ashcroft 1 BN43 ....185 D7
Ashcroft Cl BN43 ......185 D8
Ashcroft La PO8 ....128 F6
Ashcroft Way PO21 .....205 A8
Ashdene Gdns RH20 ....121 A4
Ashdown 14 BN3 ....187 C6
Ashdown Cl
Angmering BN16 ....179 F4
Haywards Heath RH16 .....86 B4
Ashdown Ct RH13 ....36 F4
Ashdown Dr RH10 ....18 E3
Ashdown Gate RH19 ......9 D2
Ashdown Llama Farm
RH18 ....44 E4

Ashdown Nuffield Hospl RH16 85 D6
Ashdown Rd
7 Brighton BN2 188 B8
Forest Row RH18 23 F2
Worthing BN11 182 D3
Ashdown View RH19 22 E7
Ashenground Cl 6 RH16 85 E3
Ashenground Rd RH16 85 E3
Ashfield RH14 30 E2
Ashfield Cl GU29 92 E8
Ashfield Rd GU29 92 E7
Ashfold Ave BN14 162 A1
Ashfold Crossways RH13 60 E6
Ashford Rd BN1 168 A2
Ashington CE Fst Sch RH20 120 F5
Ashington Ct
Brighton BN2 188 F6
4 Worthing BN14 182 D5
Ashleigh Cl
Angmering BN16 180 A6
Horley RH6 1 F3
Ashleigh Rd RH12 36 C4
Ashley Cl BN1 167 E7
Ashley Ct BN3 187 C5
Ashlings Way Hove BN3 166 E2
Shoreham-by-Sea BN43 165 B1
Ashmere Gdns PO22 196 D5
Ashmere La PO22 196 D5
Ashmore Ho RH11 5 D1
Ashmore La RH12 16 C6
Ashton Gdns BN16 199 C4
Ashton Lodge 15 BN2 207 C3
Ashton Rise BN2 207 C3
Ashurst CE Prim Sch BN44 122 D5
Ashurst Cl
Bognor Regis PO21 195 A6
Horsham RH12 37 A5
Worthing BN12 181 B1
Ashurst Cotts RH19 42 F4
Ashurst Dr Crawley RH10 19 D6
Worthing BN12 181 B1
Ashurst Rd BN2 168 F5
Ashurst Way BN16 180 A3
Ashurst Wood Prim Sch RH19 23 E6
Ashurstwood Abbey RH19 23 E6
Ashway RH15 107 A2
Ashwood 5 RH11 18 D5
Ashwood Cl BN11 182 F4
Ashwood Dr BN16 199 C5
Ashwyn Bsns Ctr RH15 106 F5
Aspen Cl RH16 86 B4
Aspen Way Horsham RH12 36 E4
Middleton-on-Sea PO22 196 E6
Aspen Wlk RH16 86 B4
Aston Ct
5 Bognor Regis PO21 195 D3
Crawley RH11 18 B1
Aston Ho 1 BN43 184 E7
Aston Rise RH20 98 C3
Astra Bsns Ctr RH1 2 A7
Astra Cl PO18 171 C5
Astra Ho 10 BN1 187 E5
Athelstan Cl RH10 19 E6
Athelstan Rd BN14 182 A4
Athelstan Way RH13 58 E8
Athenaeum The 16 BN3 187 C6
Athrington Ct PO22 196 B4
Atkinson Ct RH6 2 B2
Atkinson Rd RH10 19 C4
Atlantic Ct 4 BN43 184 F6
Atlingworth St BN2 207 C1
Attlee Ho 5 RH11 18 B2
Attree Ct 6 BN2 188 C6
Attree Dr BN2 188 C6
Auchinleck Ct RH10 21 B7
Auckland Cl RH11 5 D1
Auckland Dr BN2 168 F1
Audrey Cl BN1 167 E5
Augusta Ct 5 PO19 153 A2
Augusta Ho 4 BN11 182 D1
Augusta Pl BN11 182 D1
Augustines Way RH16 85 F4
Aurum Cl RH6 2 B2
Austen Cl RH19 9 B1
Austen Ct 9 PO21 195 C4
Austens GU29 113 C8
Avalon Ct PO10 149 B2
Avalon Way BN13 181 D6
Avebury Cl
Bracklesham PO20 202 C5
Horsham RH12 37 A7
Aveling Cl RH10 19 C4
Avenals The BN16 180 A5
Avenue App PO19 172 F7
Avenue Cl GU30 25 B4
Avenue Ct 20 BN3 187 C6
Avenue De Chartres PO19 172 F6
Avenue Gdns RH6 2 C2
Avenue The
Bognor Regis PO21 195 B3
Brighton BN2 168 E1
Chichester PO19 153 A2
Dormansland RH19 10 B6
Funtington PO18 150 F2
Hambrook PO18 150 D1
Haslemere GU27 26 F7
Horley RH6 1 F2
Horsham RH13 57 D5
Liphook GU30 25 B4
Shoreham-by-Sea BN43 164 F1
Avenue The *continued*
Worthing BN12 181 C4
Avery Cl BN41 165 F4
Avian Gdns PO21 194 B2
Aviary Cl PO18 150 D2
Aviary Way RH10 8 C1
Avila Ho 6 BN11 182 C2
Avisford Park Rd BN18 156 F1
Avisford Terr PO21 194 D3
Avocet Quay PO10 169 C7
Avocet Trad Est RH15 106 F2
Avon Cl Bognor Regis PO22 196 D5
Lancing BN15 183 B6
Avon Ct BN15 183 B6
Avon Rd BN17 198 D5
Avon Wlk RH11 17 F5
Avondale Cl Horley RH6 2 A5
Worthing BN12 181 D3
Avondale Rd BN3 187 D7
Avonhurst RH15 107 B3
Awbrook Cl RH17 86 F3
Axford Cl PO20 202 C5
Aylesbury BN3 187 E6
Aylwin Ct RH12 36 A1
Aylwin Pl PO20 173 C1
Aymer Ho 4 BN3 187 A6
Aymer Rd BN3 187 A6
Aynsley Ct BN3 187 C8
Ayshe Court Dr RH12 36 E3
Azalea Dr GU27 26 F8
Azara Par PO20 202 B6

B

Babsham La PO21 194 F8
Back La
Balcombe Lane RH10, RH17 41 C7
Plaistow RH14 30 E2
Backwoods Cl RH16 86 B6
Backwoods La RH16 86 B6
Baden Dr RH6 1 E4
Baden Rd BN2 168 D1
Badger Cl BN41 166 B2
Badger Copse BN5 123 E6
Badger Dr RH16 85 C5
Badger Way BN1 168 E6
Badgers Cl RH12 36 F6
Badgers Holt RH20 120 B1
Badgers Way
East Grinstead RH19 9 F2
Loxwood RH14 32 A4
Badgers Wlk
Angmering BN16 179 F4
Burgess Hill RH15 107 D2
Badgers Wood RH20 119 D6
Baffin's La PO19 173 A6
Baffins Ct 7 PO19 173 A6
Bailey Cl Horsham RH12 36 F7
Littlehampton BN17 179 A3
Bailing Hill RH12 35 E7
Baird Cl RH10 6 A1
Bakehouse Barn Cl RH12 36 E7
Bakehouse Rd RH6 2 A5
Baker Cl RH10 18 D4
Baker St BN1, BN2 207 B4
Baker's La RH13 79 B4
Bakerfield GU29 113 C8
Bakers Arms Hill BN18 158 B3
Bakers Cl RH13 57 F1
Bakers Ct BN13 181 E7
Bakers Mews RH13 60 A3
Bakery La PO21 195 C2
Bakery Mews BN1 168 C1
Bala Cres PO22 196 B6
Balchins Cl RH14 76 B8
Balcombe Ave BN14 182 C5
Balcombe CE Prim Sch RH17 40 F2
Balcombe Ct Crawley RH10 19 D7
Worthing BN11 182 B1
Balcombe Gdns RH6 2 C2
Balcombe La Ardingly RH17 63 F8
Sharpthorne RH17, RH19 43 E2
Balcombe Rd
Balcombe Lane RH17 40 F8
Crawley RH10 19 D5
Haywards Heath RH16 85 D7
Horley RH6 2 B2
Tinsley Green RH10, RH6 6 D4
Balcombe Sta RH17 40 F1
Baldwin Cl Crawley RH10 19 C3
Middleton-on-Sea PO22 196 D6
Baldwins Field RH19 9 C4
Baldwins Hill Prim Sch RH19 9 D3
Balfour Dr GU33 45 B4
Balfour Gdns RH18 23 E1
Balfour Inf Sch BN1 168 A3
Balfour Jun Sch BN1 168 A3
Balfour Rd BN1 168 A2
Ball Tree Croft 1 BN15 183 C7
Balliol Cl
Bognor Regis PO21 194 E4
Crawley RH10 6 D1
Balmoral RH19 23 A8
Balmoral Cl
Bognor Regis PO21 194 E2
Chichester PO19 173 D6
Balmoral Ct
6 Crawley RH11 18 B2
Hove BN3 167 A3
Worthing BN11 182 A2
Baltimore Ct 9 BN3 187 C7
Bamborough Cl RH13 58 A1
Bampfield St BN41 186 B8
Bancroft Rd RH10 19 D5
Banjo Rd BN17 198 E3
Bank La RH11 18 D6
Bank Pas
2 Steyning BN44 143 D3
11 Worthing BN11 182 D2
Banks Croft RH20 119 E2
Banks Rd Crawley RH10 19 C5
North Chailey BN8 87 F1
Bankside
Bognor Regis PO22 196 E5
Bolney RH17 83 C2
Brighton BN1 167 C5
Hassocks BN6 126 F5
Singleton PO18 133 E7
Bankside Ct BN1 167 C5
Bankview Cl 2 PO22 195 D4
Bannister Gdns RH20 119 E3
Bannister Way RH16 85 D6
Banstead Cl BN12 181 C1
Bar La RH13 80 B5
Baranscraig Ave BN1 168 A7
Barbara Smith Hall PO21 195 E4
Barbary La BN12 200 E5
Barber Cl RH10 19 C2
Barclay Ho 2 BN2 188 C7
Barclays Ct 2 RH20 98 C2
Barcombe Pl BN1 168 F5
Barcombe Rd BN1 168 E4
Barfield Pk BN15 183 F6
Barford Rd PO19 173 A5
Barkdale RH15 107 D5
Barker Cl PO18 172 A7
Barkworth Way RH20 119 C7
Barlavington Way GU29 92 E5
Barley Cl
Bognor Regis PO21 194 A2
Crawley RH10 18 D5
Barley Dr RH15 106 D4
Barleycroft
Albourne Green BN6 125 C6
Cowfold RH13 81 E1
Barleymead RH6 2 B4
Barlow Rd
Chichester PO19 172 E8
Crawley RH11 17 E3
Barn Cl
Albourne Green BN6 125 C6
Littlehampton BN17 178 E4
Pease Pottage RH11 39 B7
Worthing BN13 181 F7
Barn Cottage La RH16 86 A5
Barn Elm PO18 154 D3
Barn End BN5 123 F5
Barn Field PO22 195 F4
Barn Field Gdns 8 BN2 188 C6
Barn House La RH20 98 C2
Barn La PO22 175 D1
Barn Mdw RH17 41 A1
Barn Plat Cotts GU29 92 D8
Barn Rd PO20 201 F7
Barn Rise Barnham PO22 176 C5
Brighton BN1 167 D5
Barn The PO19 152 F2
Barn Wlk PO20 201 F6
Barnard Gate RH16 85 E7
Barncroft Cl PO20 154 C1
Barnes Cl PO20 206 E5
Barnes Rd BN41 186 B8
Barnet Way Hove BN3 166 E3
Worthing BN13 181 D5
Barnett Cl PO20 175 E8
Barnett Rd BN1 168 B2
Barnett's Field PO20 175 D7
Barnfield Cl PO10 150 A1
Barnfield Cotts BN18 156 A2
Barnfield Dr PO19 173 C8
Barnfield Gdns BN6 127 E3
Barnfield Rd RH10 18 E7
Barnham Cty Prim Sch PO22 176 B6
Barnham La BN18, PO22 176 C7
Barnham Rd PO20, PO22 176 A6
Barnham Sta PO22 176 B5
Barnham, St Philip Howard RC High Sch PO22 176 A6
Barnhouse Cl 8 RH20 98 C2
Barnmead RH16 85 D7
Barns Farm La RH20 141 B7
Barnsfold La RH12 32 E6
Barnside PO18 171 D7
Barnside Ave RH15 107 D1
Barnside Way GU33 45 B3
Barnsite Cl BN16 199 B6
Barnsite Gdns BN16 199 B6
Barnsnap Cl RH12 36 D6
Barnwood Cl RH10 19 C7
Baron Cl PO20 175 D7
Barons Ct
Burgess Hill RH15 107 B2
12 Worthing BN11 182 C3
Barons Mead PO21 205 A8
Barque Cl BN17 199 A6
Barrack La PO21 194 D2
Barrhill Ave BN1 167 F7
Barrington Cl
Lindfield RH16 85 F8
Worthing BN12 181 C2
Barrington Gate 7 RH12 36 D2
Barrington Rd
Crawley RH10 18 D3
Horsham RH13 36 E2
Lindfield RH16 86 A8
Worthing BN12 181 C2
Worthing BN12 181 C3
Barrington Wood RH16 85 F8
Barrow Cl
Billingshurst RH14 77 C7
Brighton BN1 168 C2
Barrow Hill Brighton BN1 168 C2
Henfield BN5 123 F3
Barrowfield RH17 84 F7
Barrowfield Cl BN3 167 C3
Barrowfield Dr BN3 167 D2
Barrowfield Lodge BN3 167 C2
Barry Cl RH10 18 E3
Barry Wlk BN2 188 C6
Bartholomew Cl GU27 27 D8
Bartholomew Sq BN1 207 B2
Bartholomew Way RH12 37 A7
Bartholomews BN1 207 B2
Barton Cl
Bognor Regis PO21 194 A1
Worthing BN13 182 A5
Barton Cres RH19 23 A8
Barton Ct BN16 199 B5
Barton La GU28 95 F8
Barton Rd
Bognor Regis PO22 195 A7
Chichester PO19 172 E7
Barton Way PO20 202 B6
Barton Wlk RH10 19 B4
Bartons Inf Sch PO22 195 B6
Barttelot Rd RH12 36 D2
Barwell Gr PO10 149 A3
Barwick Cl BN16 179 B3
Bashford Way RH10 19 D8
Bashfords La BN14 182 D4
Bashurst Copse RH13 56 F8
Bashurst Hill RH13 56 E6
Basildon Way RH11 17 E2
Basin Rd PO19 173 A5
Basin Rd N BN41 186 B6
Basin Rd S BN3, BN41 186 B6
Basing Hill RH20,RH13 121 C7
Bassels La RH13 102 B5
Bassett Rd
Bognor Regis PO21 195 C3
Crawley RH10 19 D3
Batchmere Est PO20 191 F1
Batchmere Rd PO20 192 A2
Batemans Cl BN13 181 B5
Batemans Ct RH10 19 A3
Bates Rd BN1 167 F2
Bath Ct BN3 187 A5
Bath Pl BN11 182 D1
Bath Rd Emsworth PO10 169 B8
Worthing BN11 182 B1
Bath St BN1 207 A4
Batts Dr BN5 123 D5
Batts La RH20 98 F1
Batworthpark Ho BN18 158 E1
Bavant Rd BN1 167 E2
Baxter Cl RH10 19 B4
Baxter St BN2 188 C7
Baxters La RH17 66 C6
Bay Cl RH6 1 E6
Bay Ct PO21 205 B8
Bay Tree Cl BN43 165 C1
Bay Tree Cotts BN18 156 D1
Bay Tree Gdn BN16 199 F5
Bay Trees Cl BN16 199 F5
Bay Wlk PO21 205 C8
Baycombe La BN18 156 D6
Bayfield Rd RH6 1 E4
Bayford Rd BN17 198 D4
Bayhams Field RH19 42 F6
Bayhorne La RH6 2 C1
Bayley Rd PO20 154 C1
Baylis Cres RH15 106 D4
Baylis Wlk RH11 18 B1
Baynards Rd RH12 12 A2
Bayton Ct PO19 173 B6
Baytree Cl PO19 152 F3
Beach Cl PO21 194 C1
Beach Cres BN17 198 E3
Beach Ct
Littlehampton BN17 198 E4
6 Rustington BN16 199 B4
12 Shoreham-by-Sea BN43 185 A6
Beach Gdns PO20 206 D5
Beach Gn BN43 184 E6
Beach Mews 3 BN17 198 F4
Beach Par BN11 182 F2
Beach Rd
Bognor Regis PO21 205 A7
Emsworth PO10 169 A8
Littlehampton BN17 198 E4
Selsey PO20 206 F8
Shoreham-by-Sea BN43 184 E6
Beachcroft Pl BN15 183 F4
Beachside Cl BN12 181 E1
Beachy Rd RH11 18 A1
Beacon Cl BN1 168 A2
Beacon Ct RH13 37 A4
Beacon Dr PO20 206 E6
Beacon Hill
Dormansland RH7 10 B8
Watersfield RH20 117 A4
Beacon Ho 5 BN3 186 D7
Beacon Hurst BN6 127 B3
Beacon Rd BN6 127 D2
Beacon Sq PO10 169 A7
Beacon The RH19 42 E7
Beacon Way BN17 199 A6
Beaconsfield Cl PO22 196 E5
Beaconsfield Cotts RH17 86 F3
Beaconsfield Rd
Brighton BN1 188 A8
Chelwood Gate RH17 66 D8
Littlehampton BN17 178 D3
Portslade-by-Sea BN41 186 B8
Beaconsfield Villas BN1 167 F1
Beaconsville Ct BN1 167 F1
Beagle Dr BN18 177 B2
Beal Cres BN1 168 B2
Beale Ct RH11 18 A3
Beale St RH15 106 F1
Bear Rd BN2 188 D8
Bearsden Way RH12 35 D3
Beatrice Ho PO22 195 E4
Beatty Ave BN1 168 D6
Beatty Rd PO21 195 C4
Beaufield Cl PO20 206 D5
Beaufield Gate GU27 27 D7
Beaufort Ct 4 BN17 199 A6
Beaufort Terr BN2 188 C6
Beaumont Cl RH11 17 E5
Beaumont Ct
East Preston BN16 199 F6
6 Pulborough RH20 98 C2
Beaumont Pk BN17 199 A5
Beaumont Rd BN14 182 D5
Beaver Cl Fishbourne PO19 172 B6
Horsham RH12 36 F6
Beaver Ind Est GU30 25 C3
Beaver Units PO19 173 D5
Beccles Rd BN11 182 B2
Beckenham Terr PO10 149 D4
Becket Bldgs BN14 182 A6
Becket Rd BN14 182 B3
Beckett La RH11 5 D1
Beckett Way 11 RH19 22 F8
Beckford Way RH10 19 B2
Beckley Cl BN2 188 E5
Beckworth Cl
Lindfield RH16 86 A6
Worthing BN13 181 B5
Beckworth La RH16 86 A6
Bedale Cl RH11 18 C4
Bedales RH17 86 D4
Bedales Cnr RH17 86 D4
Bedales Hill RH16,RH17 86 D4
Bedelands Cl RH15 107 B5
Bedenscroft PO21 195 A3
Bedford Ave PO21 195 A6
Bedford Pl BN1 187 E5
Bedford Rd RH13 36 D1
Bedford Row BN11 182 E2
Bedford Sq BN1 187 E5
Bedford St
Bognor Regis PO21 195 D3
Brighton BN2 188 C4
Bedford Twrs 9 BN1 187 E5
Bedham La RH20 97 B5
Beech Ave
Bracklesham PO20 202 B6
Chichester PO19 172 E6
Beech Cl
3 East Grinstead RH19 9 D2
Findon BN14 161 E7
Portslade-by-Sea BN41 165 F3
Westergate PO20 175 D7
Beech Ct Haslemere GU27 27 D7
Horsham RH13 36 E2
Worthing BN11 182 B2
Beech Fields RH19 9 F3
Beech Gdns
Crawley Down RH10 21 A8
Worthing BN14 182 C4
Beech Gr Brighton BN2 168 E3
Midhurst GU29 92 E6
Storrington RH20 119 F3
Beech Hill RH16 86 B4
Beech Ho RH14 77 C8
Beech Holme RH10 21 B8
Beech Hurst Cl RH16 85 C4
Beech Hurst Cotts RH16 85 C4
Beech Rd Findon BN14 161 E7
Haslemere GU27 27 D8
Horsham RH12 37 B5
Beech Tree Cl RH10 18 D7
Beech View BN16 180 A6
Beech Wood BN5 144 F7
Beechcroft Cl GU30 24 D3
Beechers Rd BN41 165 F3
Beeches Ave BN14 182 D7
Beeches Cres RH10 18 E4
Beeches Head RH19 10 F5
Beeches La RH19 23 D6
Beeches The
4 Bognor Regis PO22 195 D4
Brighton BN1 167 D3
Beechey Cl RH10 7 B3
Beechey Way RH10 7 B3
Beechfield Cotts GU28 72 B3
Beeching Way RH19 9 E1
Beechings BN5 123 D5
Beechlands Cl BN16 200 A5
Beechlands Ct BN16 200 A5
Beechside RH10 18 E5
Beechwood
6 Brighton BN1 167 E3
Southwater RH13 79 F8
Beechwood Ave
Brighton BN1 167 F4
Worthing BN13 181 F7
Beechwood Cl BN1 167 F4
Beechwood Ct
Liss Forest GU33 45 C6
1 Worthing BN11 182 C2
Beechwood La GU28 115 B5
Beechwood Villas RH1 2 A7
Beechwoods RH15 107 A1
Beeding Ave BN3 166 F3
Beeding Cl
Bognor Regis PO22 195 E7
Horsham RH12 37 A5
Lancing BN15 183 D8
Beeding Ct Hove BN1 167 C5
4 Shoreham-by-Sea BN43 185 B8
Beedingwood Dr RH12 37 F6
Beechfield Pk PO20 175 C5
Beehive Cl BN12 200 F5
Beehive La BN12 200 F5

Beehive Ring Rd RH6 ...6 B4
Beggar's La BN45 ...146 D6
Beggarshouse La RH6 ...4 C8
Behenna Cl RH11 ...17 E5
Belbourne Ct 7 BN1 ...207 B3
Belfast St BN3 ...187 B7
Belgrave Cres PO19 ...172 F3
Belgrave Ct 3 RH20 ...98 C2
Belgrave Pl 11 BN2 ...188 D4
Belgrave St BN2 ...207 C3
Belgravia Ct RH6 ...2 B3
Belinus Dr RH14 ...77 C8
Bell Cl PO19 ...172 F8
Bell Ct Bognor Regis PO21 .194 C2
Nutbourne PO18 ...170 B7
Bell Ctr RH10 ...5 F2
Bell Davies Rd BN17 ...198 F6
Bell Hammer RH19 ...22 E8
Bell La Cocking GU29 ...112 C8
Mark Street TN22 ...66 F3
Somerley PO20 ...191 D2
Bell Mead 7 BN3 ...187 D7
Bell Rd Kingsley Green GU27 27 B3
Warnham RH12 ...36 A8
Bell Tower Ind Est 7
BN2 ...188 E4
Bell Vale La GU27 ...27 C4
Bellamy Rd RH10 ...19 C2
Belle Meade Cl PO20 ...175 D5
Belle Vue Cotts PO20 ...175 D7
Belle Vue Ct BN2 ...188 D5
Bellevue Cotts BN2 ...188 F8
Bellevue Ct BN1 ...167 F1
Bellevue Gdns BN2 ...188 D4
Bellevue La PO10 ...149 B2
Bellingham Cres BN3 ...186 D8
Belloc Cl RH10 ...19 C7
Belloc Ct RH13 ...37 A3
Belloc Rd BN17 ...178 C3
Bellscroft Cl BN17 ...198 F6
Bellview Ct 7 BN13 ...182 A5
Bellview Rd BN13 ...182 A5
Belmaine Ct 5 BN11 ...182 C1
Belmer Ct 6 BN11 ...182 A1
Belmont BN1, BN3 ...187 E7
Belmont Cl BN6 ...126 E5
Belmont Ct 4 BN1 ...187 E7
Belmont La BN6 ...126 C5
Belmont St
Bognor Regis PO21 ...195 D3
Brighton BN1 ...207 B3
Belmont Terr BN18 ...177 A2
Belmont Wlk BN13 ...181 D5
Belsize Cl BN11 ...182 B3
Belsize Rd BN11 ...182 B2
Belton Rd BN2 ...188 B8
Belvedere Ave BN15 ...183 D6
Belvedere Ct RH10 ...19 B7
Belvedere Terr 5 BN1 ...187 E6
Belyngham Cres BN17 ...198 D6
Bembridge St BN2 ...188 C8
Ben Turner Ind Est PO19 .173 D6
Benbow Cl BN43 ...184 F6
Benchfield Cl RH19 ...10 B1
Benedict Cl BN11 ...183 B3
Benedict Dr BN11 ...183 A3
Benett Ave BN3 ...167 B2
Benett Dr BN3 ...167 B2
Benfield Cl BN41 ...166 C1
Benfield Cres BN41 ...166 C1
Benfield Ct BN41 ...186 C8
Benfield Jun Sch BN41 .186 C8
Benfield Way BN41 ...166 C1
Bengairn Ave BN1 ...168 A7
Benham Ct 3 BN3 ...187 B5
Benhams Cl RH6 ...2 A5
Benhams Dr RH6 ...2 A5
Benizi Ct 12 PO21 ...195 D3
Benjamin Lodge RH15 ...107 D3
Benjamin Rd RH10 ...19 D4
Bennett Cl RH10 ...19 B2
Bennett Rd BN2 ...188 E4
Bennett's Terr 6 GU29 ...92 E7
Bennetts RH17 ...83 C3
Bennetts Cl PO20 ...201 F7
Bennetts Rd RH13 ...36 E1
Bens Acre RH13 ...37 A2
Benson Ct BN3 ...186 E7
Benson Rd BN5 ...123 F5
Benson's La RH12 ...16 C1
Bentham Rd BN2 ...188 C7
Bentons La RH13 ...101 E3
Bentswood Cres RH16 ...86 A5
Bentswood Rd RH16 ...85 F5
Bentworth PO22 ...176 B6
Bepton Cl GU29 ...92 D6
Bepton Rd GU29 ...92 B4
Berberis Ct BN43 ...165 B1
Beresford Ct 12 BN3 ...187 D7
Beresford Rd BN2 ...188 D5
Bereweeke Rd PO22 ...196 A4
Bergamot Cres BN43 ...165 C1
Berghestede Rd PO22 ...195 C6
Berkeley Cl RH11 ...17 E2
Berkeley Ct
Bognor Regis PO21 ...195 D2
6 Hove BN3 ...187 E7
9 Littlehampton BN17 ...198 E4
Berkeley Lodge 1 RH20 ...119 E1
Berkeley Mews PO19 ...173 B7
Berkeley Sq BN11 ...182 A2
Berkshire Ct BN12 ...181 B3
Bermuda Ct 2 BN17 ...199 A6
Bernard Deegan Ho 2
PO21 ...195 C3
Bernard Pl BN2 ...188 C7
Bernard Rd Arundel BN18 .157 F2
Brighton BN2 ...188 C7
Bernard Rd *continued*
Worthing BN11 ...181 F1
Berrall Way RH14 ...77 C7
Berriedale Ave BN3 ...186 E6
Berriedale Cl BN15 ...183 C7
Berriedale Dr BN15 ...183 C7
Berriedale Ho BN3 ...186 E6
Berry Cl RH15 ...107 A5
Berry La Ardingly RH17 ...64 C7
Bognor Regis PO22 ...195 A7
Littlehampton BN17 ...198 F4
Berrybarn La PO20 ...201 B8
Berrylands GU33 ...45 C7
Berrylands Farm BN6 ...105 D1
Berrymeade Wlk RH11 ...17 E5
Berrymill Cl 7 PO21 ...195 D4
Berstead Wlk 1 RH11 ...17 F3
Bersted Green Ct PO22 ...195 C6
Bersted Mews PO22 ...195 D5
Bersted St
Bognor Regis PO22 ...195 C5
Bognor Regis PO22 ...195 D5
Bessborough Terr BN15 .183 D4
Betchley Cl RH19 ...9 E3
Betchworth Works RH6 ...4 D6
Bethune Cl RH10 ...19 D5
Bethune Rd RH13 ...36 E1
Bethwines Cl PO18 ...172 A7
Betts Way RH11 ...5 D2
Bevan Ct RH11 ...18 B1
Bevendean Cres BN2 ...168 E2
Bevendean Prim Sch
BN2 ...168 F1
Bevendean Rd BN2 ...168 D1
Beverley Cl PO20 ...206 F7
Beverley Ct 1 Hove BN3 .186 D7
5 Pulborough RH20 ...98 C2
3 Worthing BN11 ...182 B1
Beverley Gdns BN16 ...179 C3
Beverley Ho 6 BN15 ...183 E5
Beverley Mews RH10 ...19 A5
Bewbush Comm Mid Sch
RH11 ...17 F3
Bewbush Dr RH11 ...17 F3
Bewbush Fst Sch RH11 ...17 F3
Bewbush Manor RH11 ...17 E2
Bewley Rd BN16 ...179 F6
Bex La GU29 ...92 E2
Bickley Ct RH11 ...18 A3
Bickleys Ct 1 PO21 ...195 B2
Biggin Cl RH11 ...18 C4
Bignor Cl Horsham RH12 ...37 A7
Rustington BN16 ...199 D6
Bignor Park Rd RH20 ...116 E5
Bignor Roman Villa
(remains of) RH20 ...116 B2
Bigwood Ave BN3 ...187 D8
Bilberry Cl RH11 ...18 B3
Bilbets RH12 ...36 C3
Billinghurst Rd RH20 ...120 F8
Billingshurst Inf Sch
RH14 ...77 B7
Billingshurst Jun Sch
RH14 ...77 D7
Billingshurst Rd RH12 ...35 D3
Billingshurst Sta RH14 ...77 D7
Billinton Dr RH10 ...19 B5
Bilsham Cnr BN18 ...196 F8
Bilsham Ct BN18 ...176 F2
Bilsham La BN18 ...176 E1
Bilsham Rd BN18 ...176 F1
Binderton La PO18 ...132 D2
Binney Ct RH10 ...6 E1
Binstead Ave PO22 ...196 A5
Binstead Cl RH11 ...18 B8
Binsted Cl BN16 ...199 B4
Binsted La BN18 ...177 B7
Birch Ave RH17 ...86 A3
Birch Cl Angmering BN16 ..179 F4
Arundel BN18 ...157 E1
Bognor Regis PO21 ...194 D3
Crawley Down RH10 ...21 C8
Haywards Heath RH17 ...86 B3
Lancing BN15 ...183 D4
Liss GU33 ...45 C4
Birch Ct BN42 ...166 A1
Birch Dr RH14 ...77 D7
Birch End RH20 ...119 D7
Birch Gr RH20 ...119 D5
Birch Grove Cres BN1 ...168 A5
Birch Ho 2 RH19 ...9 D2
Birch Lea RH10 ...6 A1
Birch Tree Cl PO10 ...149 B4
Birch Tree Ct BN11 ...182 E3
Birch Tree Dr PO10 ...149 B4
Birch Tree La RH20 ...119 E6
Birch Way
Haywards Heath RH17 ...86 A2
Heath Common RH20 ...120 B3
Birchen La RH16 ...85 F8
Birches Cl Selsey PO20 ...206 C7
Worthing BN13 ...181 C5
Birches Ind Est RH19 ...9 A3
Birches Rd RH12 ...37 B5
Birches The Crawley RH10 ..19 A7
Mannings Heath RH13 ...59 C7
West Chiltington
Common RH20 ...119 C8
Birchgrove La RH17 ...44 A1
Birchgrove Rd RH17 ...65 E7
Bircholt Rd GU30 ...24 D4
Birchwood Cl
Crawley RH10 ...19 C3
Horley RH6 ...2 B4
Birchwood Grove
Com Prim Sch RH15 ...107 C1
Birchwood Grove Rd
RH15 ...107 C1
Birdham CE Prim Sch
PO20 ...191 E5
Birdham Cl
Bognor Regis PO21 ...194 F5
Crawley RH11 ...18 B8
Birdham Pl BN2 ...168 E3
Birdham Rd
Apuldram PO19, PO20 ...172 D2
Brighton BN2 ...168 F3
South Hayling PO11 ...189 A2
Birkdale Cl BN13 ...181 D6
Birkdale Dr RH11 ...17 D5
Birkdale Rd BN13 ...181 D6
Birling Cl BN2 ...168 D1
Birthday Ho GU29 ...71 B2
Biscay Cl BN16 ...199 B6
Bisham Cl RH10 ...19 D3
Bishearne Gdns GU33 ...45 A5
Bishop Luffa CE Sch
PO19 ...172 D7
Bishop Luffa Cl PO19 ...172 D7
Bishop Tufnell
CE Inf Sch PO22 ...196 C5
Bishop Tufnell
CE Jun Sch PO22 ...196 C5
Bishop's Cl BN6 ...126 A7
Bishopric RH12 ...36 B2
Bishopric Ct 6 RH12 ...36 B2
Bishops Cl
Bognor Regis PO21 ...205 A8
Fernhurst GU27 ...49 A6
Henfield BN5 ...123 E5
Worthing BN13 ...182 A4
Bishops Ct RH12 ...36 C1
Bishops Ctyd PO19 ...173 B6
Bishops Ho RH20 ...140 D8
Bishops Rd Hove BN3 ...167 C1
Tangmere PO20 ...154 D2
Bishopsgate Wlk PO19 ...173 B7
Bishopstone La BN6,RH17 106 A7
Bishopstone Wlk RH11 ...18 C1
Bitmead Cl RH11 ...17 E5
Bittern Cl RH11 ...17 D5
Black Dog Wlk RH10 ...18 E8
Black Gate La RH20 ...98 D7
Black Hill RH16 ...86 A7
Black Horse Way RH12 ...36 C2
Black Lion St BN1 ...207 B1
Black Swan Cl RH11 ...39 B7
Blackberry La
Chichester PO19 ...173 C6
Dormans Park RH7 ...9 E8
Selsey PO20 ...206 C7
Blackberry Rd RH19, RH7 ...9 D8
Blackbird Cl RH15 ...106 D3
Blackboy La PO18 ...172 A7
Blackbridge Ct RH12 ...36 B2
Blackbridge La RH12 ...36 A1
Blackbrook La BN8,RH17 ...87 E2
Blackcap Cl Crawley RH11 .18 C4
Red Hill PO9 ...128 C1
Blackdown BN2 ...188 F7
Blackdown Rd BN13 ...181 F7
Blackett Rd RH10 ...19 C5
Blackfold Rd RH10 ...19 A5
Blackgate La BN5 ...123 E4
Blackheath RH10 ...19 D8
Blackhouse La
Burgess Hill RH15 ...107 B4
Foxhill GU28 ...74 D5
Blackhouse Rd RH13 ...38 D5
Blacklands Cres RH18 ...23 F2
Blackman St BN1 ...207 B3
Blackman Way PO20 ...173 B1
Blackmill La PO18 ...155 C3
Blackpatch Gr 6 BN43 ...164 F1
Blacksmith's Cnr BN18 ...176 F8
Blacksmiths Cl RH20 ...121 A4
Blacksmiths Cres BN15 ...183 B6
Blackstone La
Blackstone BN5,BN6 ...124 E6
Woodmancote BN5 ...124 D3
Blackstone Rise BN5 ...124 E5
Blackstone St BN5 ...124 E5
Blackstone Way RH15 ...107 A5
Blackthorn Cl
Brighton BN1 ...167 D3
Crawley RH11 ...5 C1
Horsham RH13 ...37 A2
Portslade-by-Sea BN41 ...166 B2
Blackthorns
Hurstpierpoint BN6 ...125 F7
Lindfield RH16 ...86 A7
Blackthorns Cl RH16 ...86 A6
Blackthorns
Com Prim Sch RH16 ...86 A6
Blackthorns The RH15 ...107 B5
Blackwater La RH10 ...19 D6
Blackwell Farm Rd RH19 ...9 F3
Blackwell Hollow RH19 ...9 F2
Blackwell Prim Sch RH19 ...9 E3
Blackwell Rd RH19 ...9 F2
Blake Cl RH10 ...18 F2
Blake Cotts PO18 ...172 A6
Blake Ct 3 BN2 ...207 C3
Blakehurst La BN18 ...159 B3
Blakehurst Way BN17 ...198 D6
Blakemyle PO21 ...194 F2
Blaker St BN2 ...207 C2
Blakes Farm Rd RH13 ...58 A3
Blakes Rd PO22 ...196 A4
Blakes View PO22 ...195 F4
Blanches Rd RH13 ...103 A3
Blanches Wlk RH13 ...103 A3
Blanford Rd PO19 ...173 C8
Blatchen The BN17 ...198 F4
Blatchford Cl RH13 ...36 F3
Blatchford Rd RH13 ...36 F3
Blatchington Mill Sch
BN3 ...166 F2
Blatchington Rd BN3 ...187 B7
Bleach's Yard Ind Est
GU30 ...25 B2
Blendworth CE Inf Sch
PO8 ...128 A7
Blendworth Fst Sch PO8 .128 A8
Blendworth La PO8 ...128 A7
Blenheim Ave BN13 ...181 E5
Blenheim Cl Crawley RH10 ..6 D1
East Grinstead RH19 ...10 A3
Littlehampton BN16 ...179 B3
Blenheim Ct
Bognor Regis PO21 ...194 E4
1 Hove BN3 ...187 A6
Blenheim Dr BN16 ...179 B3
Blenheim Fields RH18 ...23 E3
Blenheim Gdns PO19 ...173 C6
Blenheim Pl 5 BN1 ...207 B3
Blenheim Rd
Horsham RH12 ...36 D4
Lancing BN15 ...183 D4
Yapton BN18 ...176 F2
Bletchley Ct BN1 ...188 A8
Bligh Cl RH10 ...18 F4
Blindley Rd RH10 ...6 D1
Blomfield Dr PO19 ...153 A1
Blondell Dr PO21 ...194 D2
Bloomsbury Pl 17 BN2 ...188 C4
Bloomsbury St 16 BN2 ...188 C4
Bloor Cl RH12 ...36 D7
Blount Ave RH19 ...9 C1
Blue Cedars Cl BN16 ...179 E4
Bluebell Cl Crawley RH11 ..18 B3
East Grinstead RH19 ...9 B1
Haywards Heath RH16 ...85 F4
Horsham RH12 ...36 E5
Bluebell Dr BN17 ...179 A3
Bluebell Rly
RH17, RH19, TN22 ...43 A5
Bluebell Way RH15 ...106 D4
Blueberry Hill RH20 ...120 B1
Bluebird Ct 11 BN3 ...187 A6
Bluecoat Pond RH13 ...57 D6
Blundell Ave RH6 ...1 F4
Blunden Dr RH17 ...84 F8
Blunts Way RH12 ...36 C3
Blunts Wood Cres RH16 ...85 B6
Blunts Wood Rd RH16 ...85 C6
Blytons The RH19 ...9 B1
Boardwalk PO19 ...173 A7
Bob La BN5,RH17 ...104 E6
Boddingtons La BN6 ...127 D3
Bodiam Ave BN12 ...181 B2
Bodiam Cl Crawley RH10 ...19 C6
Southwater RH13 ...58 A2
Bodiam Ct RH16 ...85 E5
Bodiham Ho 15 BN3 ...187 D7
Bodmin Cl BN13 ...181 D8
Bodmin Rd BN13 ...181 D8
Bognor Rd
Chichester PO19, PO20 ...173 D5
Warnham RH12, RH5 ...14 D4
Bognor Regis Com Coll
Bognor Regis PO21 ...194 F4
Bognor Regis PO21 ...195 A5
Bognor Regis Ret Pk
The PO22 ...195 D7
Bognor Regis Sta PO21 ..195 C3
Bohunt Com Sch GU30 ...25 B4
Bohunt Manor Gdn GU30 .25 A2
Bolding Way RH16 ...85 E2
Boleyn Cl RH10 ...19 D3
Boleyn Dr PO21 ...194 B1
Bolney CE Prim Sch RH17 83 C2
Bolney Chapel Rd RH17 .105 B7
Bolney Crossways RH17 ...83 D1
Bolney Ct RH11 ...17 F3
Bolney Grange Ind Est
RH17 ...105 F6
Bolney Lodge La RH17 ...83 B3
Bolney Rd Bolney RH17 ...83 E2
Brighton BN2 ...168 F4
Bolney St RH17 ...83 C3
Bolnore RH16 ...85 B4
Bolnore Rd RH16 ...85 C4
Bolsover Rd Hove BN3 ...186 E8
Worthing BN13 ...181 E3
Bolters Rd RH6 ...2 A5
Bolters Rd S RH6 ...1 F6
Bolton Rd RH10 ...19 C2
Boltro Rd RH16 ...85 D5
Bonchurch Rd BN2 ...188 C7
Bond St Arundel BN18 ...158 A3
Brighton BN1 ...207 B2
Bonehurst Rd RH1, RH6 ...2 A7
Bonfire La RH17 ...65 D5
Bonnar Cl PO20 ...206 D6
Bonnar Rd PO20 ...206 D6
Bonnetts La RH11 ...5 A3
Bonny Wood Rd BN6 ...126 E3
Bookers La PO20 ...202 C8
Booth Mus
of Natural History BN1 .187 E8
Booth Rd RH11 ...17 E3
Booth Way 4 RH12 ...36 E3
Borage Cl RH11 ...18 A3
Borde Hill Gdns RH16 ...63 C2
Bordehill La RH16,RH17 ...63 D3
Borden La GU30 ...69 A6
Border Chase RH10 ...7 A2
Border Ct RH19 ...9 F4
Border End GU27 ...26 D6
Border Rd GU27 ...26 D6
Borders Cl RH10 ...7 C4
Borers Arms Rd RH10 ...7 C3
Borers Yard Ind Est RH10 ...7 C3
Borough Ho GU29 ...92 F8
Borough St BN1 ...187 E6
Borrow King Cl BN2 ...188 D8
Borrowdale Cl RH11 ...18 B4
Bosham Cty Prim Sch
PO18 ...171 C5
Bosham La PO18 ...171 B5
Bosham Rd RH10 ...19 C3
Bosham Sta PO18 ...171 C7
Bosmere Gdns PO10 ...149 B1
Bosmere Rd PO11 ...189 A2
Bost Hill BN13, BN14 ...161 E3
Bostal Rd BN44 ...143 C1
Bostal The BN44 ...144 C1
Bostock Ave RH12 ...37 A5
Boston Ct RH16 ...86 A5
Boston Rd RH16 ...86 A5
Boston St BN1 ...207 B4
Boswell Rd RH10 ...18 E3
Botany Cl BN16 ...199 E4
Bough Beeches RH15 ...107 C1
Boulevard The
Crawley RH10 ...18 E6
Worthing BN12, BN13 ...181 E4
Boundary Cl Crawley RH10 .18 E7
Worthing BN11 ...182 B1
Boundary Pas 10 BN3 ...187 E6
Boundary Rd
Balcombe RH17 ...41 B4
Brighton BN2 ...188 F4
Crawley RH10 ...18 E7
Portslade-by-Sea
BN3, BN41 ...186 C7
Shoreham-by-Sea BN15 ...184 B5
Worthing BN11 ...182 B1
Boundary Way BN16 ...200 B6
Boundstone Cl BN15 ...183 D7
Boundstone Com Coll
BN15 ...183 D7
Boundstone La BN15 ...183 D6
Bourg-de-Peage Ave
RH19 ...10 A1
Bourne Cl
Fishbourne PO19 ...172 A7
Worthing BN13 ...181 B6
Bourne Com Coll PO10 ...149 F1
Bourne Ct
Bracklesham PO20 ...202 A6
Brighton BN1 ...167 D4
Bourne The BN6 ...126 E5
Bourne View Cl PO10 ...149 F2
Bourne Way GU29 ...92 E6
Bourns Ct RH12 ...36 E3
Bowater Rd RH10 ...19 C3
Bowen Ct 11 BN3 ...187 C6
Bower La RH20 ...119 D6
Bower The RH16 ...85 D5
Bowerhill Cotts RH19 ...43 F6
Bowers Pl RH10 ...21 B8
Bowes Cl RH13 ...36 E3
Bowes Hill PO9 ...128 E3
Bowhill La PO18 ...151 D7
Bowley La PO20 ...193 E5
Bowling Green Cl PO21 ...194 B1
Bowling Green La RH12 ...36 D3
Bowman Ct RH10 ...18 D7
Bowmans Cl BN44 ...143 D4
Bowness Ave BN15 ...183 C5
Bowness Cl 7 RH11 ...17 D5
Bowring Way BN2 ...188 D4
Box Cl RH11 ...18 C1
Box La RH19 ...23 E6
Box Tree Ave BN16 ...199 B5
Box's La RH17 ...66 C6
Boxall Wlk RH13 ...36 D1
Boxes La RH17 ...65 C5
Boxgrove BN12 ...181 B4
Boxgrove CE Prim Sch
PO18 ...154 D4
Boxgrove Cl BN15 ...183 F8
Boxgrove Gdns PO21 ...194 D2
Boxgrove Ho
Boxgrove PO18 ...154 D3
Littlehampton BN17 ...178 B3
Boxgrove Par BN12 ...181 B3
Boxham La PO20 ...192 D3
Boyce's St BN1 ...207 A2
Bracken Cl Copthorne RH10 ..7 B2
Crawley RH10 ...18 F8
Heath Common RH20 ...120 B2
Bracken Gr RH12 ...37 B5
Bracken La RH20 ...120 B2
Brackenbury Cl BN41 ...166 B2
Brackens The RH20 ...119 B1
Brackenside RH6 ...2 B4
Bracklesham Cl PO20 ...202 B6
Bracklesham Ct PO20 ...202 B6
Bracklesham La PO20 ...202 B7
Bracklesham Rd PO11 ...189 B2
Bracknell Wlk RH11 ...17 E3
Bradbury Rd RH10 ...19 C3
Brading Rd BN2 ...188 C7
Bradley Ho BN11 ...182 B2
Bradlond Cl PO21 ...195 A3
Bradshaw Rd PO19 ...173 C8
Braemar Ho 11 BN1 ...187 E6
Braemar Way PO21 ...194 F7
Braemore Ct BN3 ...186 E6
Braemore Rd BN3 ...186 E6
Braeside Ave BN1 ...168 A7
Braeside Cl GU27 ...26 F8
Brainsmead RH17 ...84 F7
Brainsmead Cl RH17 ...84 F7
Bramber 3 BN15 ...183 D5
Bramber Ave Hove BN3 ...166 F3

Bramber Ave *continued*
Storrington RH20 119 C2
Bramber Castle BN44 143 F2
Bramber Cl
Bognor Regis PO21 195 A4
Crawley RH10 18 E8
Haywards Heath RH16 85 D4
Horsham RH12 37 B5
Lancing BN15 183 D8
Bramber Ct 8 Hove BN3 187 B7
2 Shoreham-by-Sea BN43 185 B8
2 Worthing BN11 181 F2
Bramber Fst Sch BN14 182 F6
Bramber Rd
Chichester PO19 173 B5
Steyning BN44 143 D2
Worthing BN14 182 E6
Bramber Sq BN16 199 C6
Bramber Way RH15 107 A4
Bramble Cl
Copthorne RH10 7 B3
Worthing BN13 181 D7
Bramble Cres BN13 181 D8
Bramble Gdns RH15 106 D4
Bramble Hill RH17 40 F2
Bramble La BN13 181 D7
Bramble Mead RH17 40 F1
Bramble Rise BN1 167 C5
Bramble Twitten RH19 10 A1
Bramble Way BN1 168 C6
Brambledean Rd BN41 186 B7
Brambles BN6 126 F5
Brambles The RH17 85 A6
Brambletye La RH18 23 D4
Brambletye Rd RH10 19 A5
Brambletye Sch RH19 23 C5
Brambletyne Cl BN16 180 A6
Brambling Cl RH13 37 A1
Brambling La GU29 70 C3
Brambling Rd
Horsham RH13 37 A1
Red Hill PO9 128 D1
Bramblings The BN16 199 D5
Bramfield Rd PO22 196 C4
Bramlands La BN5 145 D8
Bramley Cl Crawley RH10 18 F6
Worthing BN14 182 D6
Bramley Ct RH6 1 F5
Bramley Gdns
Bognor Regis PO22 195 B7
Hermitage PO10 169 D8
Bramley Rd BN14 182 D6
Bramley Wlk RH6 2 C3
Brampton Cl PO20 206 D7
Brampton Ct PO19 172 F5
Brandy Hole La PO19 152 E2
Brangwyn Ave BN1 167 E5
Brangwyn Cres BN1 167 E6
Brangwyn Ct BN1 167 E5
Brangwyn Dr BN1 167 E5
Brangwyn Way BN1 167 E5
Brantridge La RH17 62 B6
Brantridge Rd RH10 18 F4
Brantridge Sch RH17 61 E5
Brasslands Dr BN41 165 F1
Bray Cl RH10 19 C4
Braybon Ave BN1 167 F4
Braybon Bsns Pk RH15 106 E2
Braypool La BN1 167 D7
Brazwick Ave PO21 194 F7
Breach Ave PO10 150 A2
Breach Cl BN44 143 D4
Bread La BN17 197 F6
Bread St BN1 207 B3
Bream Cl PO20 206 B8
Brecon Cl BN13 181 F7
Brecon Ct 6 BN3 187 C7
Brede Cl BN2 188 F5
Breezehurst Dr RH11 17 E3
Bremner Ave RH6 1 F4
Brendon Rd BN13 181 E7
Brendon Way BN16 199 B6
Brent Ct PO10 169 A8
Brent Rd PO21 195 A4
Brentwood Cl BN1 168 B3
Brentwood Cres BN1 168 B3
Brentwood Rd BN1 168 B3
Brettingham Cl RH11 17 E3
Bretton RH15 106 E5
Brewells La GU33 46 A5
Brewer Rd RH10 18 E4
Brewer St BN2 207 C4
Brewers Yd RH20 119 D1
Brewery Hill BN18 158 B2
Brewhurst La RH14 32 A2
Breydon Wlk RH10 19 B4
Briar Ave PO20 190 F1
Briar Cl Angmering BN16 179 F4
Crawley RH11 5 C1
Oving PO20 174 C6
Yapton BN18 176 F3
Briar Wood GU33 45 C7
Briars Wood RH6 2 C4
Briarswood Cl RH10 19 D8
Brick Kiln Cl RH13 60 A3
Brickfield Cl PO21 195 B5
Bricklands RH10 21 B7
Brickyard La RH10 21 B8
Brideake Cl RH11 18 A3
Brideoake Cl PO19 172 E8
Bridge Cl
Burgess Hill RH15 106 F4
Lancing BN15 183 E5
Worthing BN12 181 C4
Bridge Mdws GU33 45 B4
Bridge Rd
Chichester PO19 173 C7
Emsworth PO10 149 B1
Haslemere GU27 27 C7
Haywards Heath RH16 85 F6
Littlehampton BN17 198 B6
Rudgwick RH12 33 D7
Worthing BN14 182 D3
Bridge Road Bsns Pk RH16 85 F7
Bridgefield Cl GU29 92 E6
Bridgefoot Path PO10 169 B8
Bridgelands RH10 7 A3
Bridgersmill RH16 85 D6
Bridges Cl RH6 2 D3
Bridges Ct RH12 37 A5
Bridgewater Cl RH14 77 C6
Bridgeway The PO20 206 D6
Bridgnorth Cl BN13 181 B5
Bridle Cl BN44 144 B2
Bridle Rd BN18 156 D4
Bridle Way RH10 19 D7
Bridle Way The PO20 206 D7
Bridorley Cl PO21 194 B2
Brierley Gdns BN15 183 F6
Brigden St BN1 207 A4
Brigham Pl PO22 196 D4
Brighton & Hove High Sch for Girls BN3 187 E6
Brighton & Hove Stad BN3 167 B1
Brighton Coll BN2 188 C5
Brighton Coll of Tech
Brighton BN1 207 A5
Brighton BN1 207 B3
Brighton BN2 207 C4
Brighton College Pre-Prep Sch BN2 188 C5
Brighton General Hospl BN2 188 D7
Brighton Information Ctr BN1 207 B2
Brighton Marina BN2 188 F2
Brighton Marina Village BN2 188 F3
Brighton Mus & Art Gall BN1 207 B2
Brighton Pl BN1 207 B2
Brighton Rd
Crawley RH10, RH11 18 D4
Handcross RH17 61 C8
Hassocks BN6 126 D2
Horley RH6 1 F2
Hurstpierpoint BN6 125 F3
Mannings Heath RH13 59 C6
Pease Pottage RH11 39 B4
Shoreham-by-Sea BN43 185 B7
Woodmancote BN5 124 A3
Worthing BN11,BN15,BN43 183 C3
Brighton Rd (Pease Pottage Hill) RH11 39 C8
Brighton Road Hornbrook Hill RH13 58 F8
Brighton Sea Life Ctr BN1 207 B1
Brighton Sq BN1 207 B2
Brighton Sta BN1 207 B3
Brighton Steiner Sch (John Howard Ho) BN2 188 F4
Brighton, Hove & Sussex Sixth Form Coll BN3 187 E8
Brills La BN1, BN2 207 B1
Brimfast La PO20 192 F4
Brinsbury Coll RH20 76 F1
Brisbane Cl Crawley RH11 5 D1
Worthing BN13 181 C6
Brisbane Ho GU29 92 E6
Bristol Ave BN15 184 B5
Bristol Cl RH10 6 D1
Bristol Gate BN2 188 D4
Bristol Gdns Brighton BN2 188 E4
Chichester PO19 152 F2
Bristol Mews 3 BN2 188 E4
Bristol Pl BN2 188 E4
Bristol Rd BN2 188 C4
Bristol St BN2 188 E4
Britannia Ct PO18 171 C5
Britannia Ho BN43 184 E7
British Engineerium (Mus) BN3 167 B2
Briton's Croft BN44 143 C3
Brittany Ct 3 BN3 186 D7
Brittany Rd Hove BN3 186 D6
Worthing BN14 182 C4
Britten Cl Crawley RH11 17 F3
Horsham RH13 37 B4
Britten's La BN18 155 E4
Broad Croft PO9 128 E3
Broad Green Ave RH15 107 C2
Broad Mdw PO18 170 D8
Broad Piece BN17 198 B6
Broad Rd PO18 150 D2
Broad Rig Ave BN3 166 D3
Broad St Brighton BN2 207 B1
Cuckfield RH17 85 A6
Broad Strand BN16 199 D3
Broad View PO20 206 F7
Broad Wlk Crawley RH10 18 D6
Heyshott GU28,GU28,PO18 113 D5
Broad Wlk The PO18 151 C6
Broadbridge Cotts RH20 121 A4
Broadbridge Ct PO18 171 C7
Broadbridge Dr PO18 171 C7
Broadbridge Heath Rd RH12 35 D4
Broadbridge La RH6 7 B8
Broadbridge Mill PO18 171 C7
Broadbridge Ret Pk RH12 35 E3
Broadfield RH19 42 E7
Broadfield Barton 4 RH11 18 B2
Broadfield Dr RH11 18 B3
Broadfield East Fst Sch RH11 18 C2
Broadfield East Mid Sch RH11 18 C2
Broadfield North Cty Fst & Mid Sch RH11 18 B2
Broadfield Pl RH11 18 B2
Broadfields BN2 168 E3
Broadfields Rd BN2 168 E3
Broadford Bridge Rd RH20, RH14 99 E4
Broadlands
Burgess Hill RH15 127 B8
Horley RH6 2 C4
Broadmark Ave BN16 199 C4
Broadmark Beach BN16 199 C3
Broadmark Ho 6 BN16 199 C5
Broadmark La BN16 199 C4
Broadmark Par 4 BN16 199 C5
Broadmark Way BN16 199 C4
Broadmead RH6 2 C4
Broadview Gdns BN13 181 E8
Broadwater Bvd BN14 182 D5
Broadwater CE Fst & Mid Sch BN14 182 C5
Broadwater Hall BN14 182 C4
Broadwater Ind Est BN14 182 F5
Broadwater La RH13 58 D2
Broadwater Manor Sch BN14 182 D5
Broadwater Mews BN14 182 D5
Broadwater Rd BN11, BN14 182 D4
Broadwater St E BN14 182 D5
Broadwater St W BN14 182 C6
Broadwater Way BN14 182 D6
Broadway PO20 206 C8
Broadway Ct 11 BN43 185 C8
Broadway The
Chichester PO19 153 A2
Crawley RH10 18 D6
Haywards Heath RH16 85 E5
Shoreham-by-Sea BN15 184 B5
Worthing BN11 182 E2
Broadwood Cl RH12 37 A5
Broadwood Rise RH11 18 A2
Brock End RH17 84 E8
Brock Rd RH11 5 B1
Brockham Keep RH6 2 C4
Brockhurst BN2 188 F7
Brockhurst Cl RH12 35 F1
Brockhurst Farm RH20 117 B5
Brockley Cl BN14 182 C4
Bromley Cl BN6 127 A4
Bromley Rd BN2 207 C5
Brompton Cl BN1 167 E6
Brontes The RH19 9 D1
Bronze Cl PO22 195 C7
Brook Ave Bosham PO18 171 B5
Hassocks BN6 126 F3
Brook Barn Way BN12 181 E1
Brook Cl
Bognor Regis PO21 194 F4
East Grinstead RH19 10 B1
Storrington RH20 119 F3
Worthing BN11 183 A4
Brook Cotts PO10 149 D3
Brook Fst Sch The RH10 19 C3
Brook Gdns PO10 169 A8
Brook Gn RH17 62 E1
Brook Hill RH13 81 E3
Brook Ho 7 RH20 98 C2
Brook La
Coldwaltham RH20 117 C5
Faygate RH12 37 C8
Ferring BN12 200 E6
Lindfield RH16 85 F8
Rustington BN16 179 C3
Brook Rd RH12 36 E6
Brook St RH17 62 F2
Brook The Crawley RH10 18 D7
Southwater RH13 58 A2
Brook Way BN15 183 F5
Brookdean Rd BN11 183 B3
Brookenbee Cl BN16 179 B3
Brooker Pl BN3 187 A7
Brooker St BN3 187 A7
Brooker's Rd RH14 77 D7
Brookfield Ct PO19 173 C6
Brookfield La River GU28 72 D1
Upperton GU28 72 F2
Brookfield Way RH14 77 D6
Brookham Sch GU30 25 E2
Brookhill Cl RH10 7 A3
Brookhill Rd RH10 7 A3
Brookhouse Bottom TN22 66 D4
Brookland Way RH20 117 C5
Brooklands
Bognor Regis PO21 194 A1
Shoreham-by-Sea BN43 184 C6
Brooklands Cotts PO18 130 E2
Brooklands Rd RH11 18 C1
Brooklands Trad Est BN14 182 C3
Brooklands Way RH19 22 D8
Brooklyn Ave BN11 181 F2
Brooklyn Ct 4 BN11 181 F2
Brookpits La BN17 197 F8
Brooks La
Bognor Regis PO22 195 E4
Bognor Regis PO22 195 E5
Broadbridge PO18 171 D7
Brooks La W PO22 195 D5
Brooks The RH15 106 E5
Brooks Way RH20 98 C2
Brookside Ashington RH20 121 A4
Copthorne RH10 7 A3
Crawley RH10 18 F7
Runcton PO20 173 E1
Brookside Ave BN16 179 C3
Brookside Cl Ferring BN12 180 E3
Runcton PO20 173 E1
Brookside Ind Est BN16 179 F3
Brookside Rd BN16 200 D4
Brooksmead PO22 195 E4
Brookview
Coldwaltham RH20 117 C5
Copthorne RH10 7 A3
Brookway
Burgess Hill RH15 107 C3
Lindfield RH16 86 A8
Brookwood RH6 2 B4
Brookwood Ho RH6 2 B6
Broomcroft Rd PO22 196 C4
Broomdashers Rd RH10 18 F7
Broome Cl RH12 36 D5
Broomers Hill La RH20 98 E4
Broomers Hill Pk RH20 98 D5
Broomfield Ave BN14 182 B5
Broomfield Dr
Billingshurst RH14 77 E8
Portslade-by-Sea BN41 166 A3
Broomfield Gdns BN5 123 E5
Broomfield Rd
Henfield BN5 123 E5
Selsey PO20 206 F8
Brou Cl BN16 200 B5
Brougham Ct 12 BN11 183 B3
Brougham Ho BN11 183 A3
Brougham Rd BN11 183 B3
Brougham Wlk 1 BN11 183 B3
Brow Cl RH20 119 B1
Brow The RH15 107 A2
Brown Twins Rd BN6 126 B5
Brown's La RH20 119 D1
Browning Cl RH10 19 C7
Browning Rd
Lancing BN15 183 E8
Worthing BN11 182 B3
Browning's Hill RH13 81 C2
Brownings The 1 RH19 9 C1
Browns Wood RH19 9 E4
Broxmead La Bolney RH17 83 D4
Slough Green RH17 84 A5
Broyle Cl PO19 152 F1
Broyle Rd PO19 173 A8
Bruce Ave BN11 181 F3
Bruce Cl RH16 85 E3
Bruce Way BN11 181 F3
Brunel Ctr RH10 5 F2
Brunel Pl RH10 18 E5
Brunswick Cl
Bognor Regis PO22 196 A5
Crawley RH10 19 A4
Brunswick Ct RH10 19 A4
Brunswick Mews 3 BN3 187 D5
Brunswick Pl BN3 187 D6
Brunswick Rd Hove BN3 187 D6
Shoreham-by-Sea BN43 184 F7
Worthing BN11 182 C1
Brunswick Row BN1 207 B4
Brunswick Sq BN3 187 D5
Brunswick St E BN3 187 D5
Brunswick St W BN3 187 D5
Brunswick Terr BN1, BN3 187 D5
Brushes La RH16 86 B8
Brushwood Rd RH12 37 B6
Bryce Cl RH12 37 A5
Buchans Lawn RH11 18 B2
Buci Cres BN43 165 C1
Buck Barn Bglws RH13 80 A2
Buckbarn Crossroads RH13 80 B2
Buckhurst Cl RH19 9 C3
Buckhurst Cotts RH12 33 D8
Buckhurst Mead RH19 9 C4
Buckhurst Way RH19 9 C3
Buckingham Ave BN43 164 E1
Buckingham Cl
4 Brighton BN1 207 A4
Shoreham-by-Sea BN43 185 A8
Buckingham Com Mid Sch BN43 184 F8
Buckingham Ct
Crawley RH11 18 B2
Worthing BN14 182 B7
Buckingham Dr
Chichester PO19 173 D6
East Grinstead RH19 23 A8
Buckingham Gate RH6 6 C7
Buckingham Lodge BN1 207 A4
Buckingham Mews 10 BN43 164 F1
Buckingham Pl BN1 207 A4
Buckingham Rd
Brighton BN1 207 A3
Shoreham-by-Sea BN43 184 F8
Worthing BN11 182 D2
Buckingham St
Brighton BN1 207 A3
Shoreham-by-Sea BN43 184 E7
Buckland Dr PO21 194 B2
Buckler St BN41 186 B8
Buckley Cl BN3 166 E4
Buckley Pl RH10 21 A8
Buckmans Rd RH11 18 D6
Bucknor Cl PO21 194 C2
Bucks Green Sch RH12 33 B7
Bucksham Ave PO21 194 F7
Buckshead Hill RH13 59 F7
Buckswood Dr RH11 18 A4
Buckwish La BN5 123 C4
Buddington La GU29 70 F3
Budgen Cl RH10 6 D1
Buffbeards La GU27 26 E6
Bugshill La GU29 91 D1
Bulbeck Cl RH15 106 E1
Bulkington Ave BN14 182 B4
Bull Hill GU33 46 A4
Bull's La RH13, RH17 82 D4
Bulldogs Bank RH19 42 F5
Buller Rd BN2 168 D1
Bullfinch Cl Horley RH6 1 E4
Horsham RH12 36 C7
Bunbury Cl RH20 120 B2
Bunch La GU27 27 B8
Bunch Way GU27 27 A6
Buncton Crossways BN44 142 C7
Buncton La RH17 83 E3
Bungalows The BN18 156 D1
Bunting Cl RH13 36 F3
Bunyan Cl RH11 17 E3
Burbeach Cl RH11 18 B3
Burch Gr BN18 156 D1
Burchell Ct BN15 183 F7
Burchens The BN14 182 C6
Burchett Wlk PO21 194 F5
Burchetts Cl RH16 85 E2
Burdett Cl RH10 19 D5
Burdock Cl RH11 18 A2
Burdocks Dr RH15 107 D1
Burford Cl BN14 182 A7
Burford Rd RH13 36 E2
Burgess Hill Sch RH15 107 B2
Burgess Hill Sta RH15 107 B2
Burgh Cl RH10 6 D1
Burgh Hill Rd GU30 25 A7
Burlands RH11 5 A1
Burleigh Cl RH10 21 B8
Burleigh Ct 4 BN11 182 C1
Burleigh Inf Sch RH10 21 B8
Burleigh La RH10 21 C7
Burleigh Way RH10 21 B8
Burley Cl Lancing BN15 183 E6
Loxwood RH14 32 A4
Burley Rd PO22 196 D4
Burleys Rd RH10 19 C6
Burlington Ct BN11 181 F1
Burlington Gdns
Portslade-by-Sea BN41 166 C1
Selsey PO20 206 F6
Burlington Rd BN12 181 D3
Burlington St BN2 188 C4
Burlow Cl Birdham PO20 191 D4
Brighton BN2 188 E5
Burma Cl RH16 86 C4
Burmill Ct BN16 179 E3
Burndell Rd BN18 177 A2
Burners Cl RH15 107 D1
Burney Ct 5 RH11 18 A3
Burngreave Ct PO21 195 B3
Burnham Ave PO21 195 C3
Burnham Gdns PO21 195 C3
Burnham Pl 3 RH13 36 D1
Burnham Rd BN13 181 E6
Burns Cl RH12 36 E7
Burns Gdns PO22 196 D6
Burns Rd RH10 19 C8
Burns Way Crawley RH12 17 C1
East Grinstead RH19 9 C1
Burnside Cres BN15 183 C5
Burnt House La RH12 17 A7
Burnthouse Bostall BN6 148 C8
Burnthouse La RH13 81 C4
Burrell Ave BN15 183 D5
Burrell Bldgs BN15 183 D5
Burrell Cl RH13 103 A3
Burrell Cotts RH17 84 E8
Burrell Ct RH11 17 F4
Burrell Gn RH17 84 F8
Burrell Rd RH16 85 D6
Burrells The BN43 185 B6
Burry Cotts BN15 182 F7
Bursledon Cl PO22 196 A5
Burstead Cl BN1 168 B3
Burston Gdns RH19 9 D4
Burstow Ho RH6 2 B6
Burstowhill La RH17 64 D6
Burton Cl RH6 2 A2
Burton Park Rd GU28 95 E1
Burton Villas BN3 187 D8
Burtons Ct 8 RH12 36 C2
Burwash Cl BN16 180 B3
Burwash Lodge BN1 168 C1
Burwash Rd Crawley RH10 19 A5
Hove BN3 166 F3
Bury CE Fst Sch RH20 137 F7
Bury Common Cotts RH20 116 F1
Bury Dr BN12 181 B2
Bury Hill BN18, RH20 137 F6
Bury Ho 3 BN14 182 D5
Bury Rd RH20 116 F3
Bush Cottage Cl BN41 166 C2
Bush Farm Dr BN41 166 C3
Bush Terr BN41 166 B3
Bushby Ave BN16 199 D5
Bushby Cl BN15 183 C5
Bushby Terr 13 BN17 198 E4
Bushfield RH14 30 F2
Busticle La BN15 183 C7
Bute St BN2 188 D5
Butler's Green Ho RH16 85 B5
Butler's Green Rd RH16 85 C4
Butlers Rd RH13 37 B4
Butt La BN18 156 C6
Butterbox La RH17 87 D4
Buttercup Way RH13 58 A2

Buttercup Wlk BN1 ......168 B7
Butterfield RH19 ....9 B3
Buttermere Cl RH12 ......37 B6
Buttermere Way BN17 ...179 A3
Button Ct BN2 ....207 C4
Butts Cl RH11 ....18 B7
Butts Mdw RH14 ....54 B1
Butts Rd BN42 ....185 E7
Buxshalls Hill RH16 ....64 C2
Buxted Rise BN1 ....168 B5
Buxton Rd BN1 ....187 E7
By Sunte RH16 ....85 F8
Bycroft Way RH10 ....19 B8
Byerley Cl PO10 ....149 D5
Byerley Way RH10 ....19 E7
Byeway The
Bognor Regis PO21 ....205 C8
West Wittering PO20 .....190 C1
Byfield Pl PO22 ....195 D6
Byfleets La RH12 ....35 D6
Bylands 3 BN2 ....188 F5
Bylanes Cl RH17 ....84 F7
Bylanes Cres RH17 ....84 F8
Byne Cl RH20 ....119 E1
Byrd Rd RH11 ....17 F3
Byron Cl
Bognor Regis PO22 ....196 D6
Crawley RH10 ....19 B7
Horsham RH12 ....36 E6
Byron Ct 1 RH16 ....85 D5
Byron Gr 2 RH19 ....9 C1
Byron Rd
Littlehampton BN16 ....199 A5
Worthing BN11 ....182 C1
Byron St BN3 ....187 A7
Bywater Way PO19 ......172 F4
Bywaves PO20 ....202 C4
Byway The Brighton BN1 ..168 E5
Middleton-on-Sea PO22 ....196 E5
Byways PO20 ....206 E5
Byworth Cl BN2 ....188 F6

C

Caburn Ct RH11 ....18 C4
Caburn Hts RH11 ....18 C4
Caburn Rd BN3 ....187 E7
Cackstones The RH10 .....19 D7
Cadogan Ct
Worthing BN11 ....182 D2
3 Brighton BN1 ....187 E7
Caedwalla Dr PO20 ......154 C2
Caernarvon Rd PO19 ....173 D6
Caffins Cl RH10 ....18 E8
Caffyns Rise RH14 ....55 D1
Cagefoot La BN5 ....123 E4
Caister's Cl BN3 ....187 C8
Caius Ct 16 BN43 ....185 C8
Cakeham Rd PO20 ....201 D8
Cakeham Way PO20 .....201 E7
Calbourne RH16 ....85 D5
Caldbeck Ho 7 RH11 .....17 F3
Calderdale Cl RH11 ....18 B4
Caledon Ave PO22 ......196 D5
Caledonian Ho RH10 .....18 D8
Caledonian Pl 1 BN11 ...182 D1
Caledonian Rd
Brighton BN2 ....207 C5
Chichester PO19 ....173 B6
Caledonian Way RH6 ......6 B8
Callender Wlk RH17 ......84 F8
Callisto Cl RH11 ....17 E3
Callon Cl BN13 ....181 B6
Calluna Dr RH10 ....7 A3
Calvecroft GU30 ....25 C4
Calvin Wlk RH11 ....17 E3
Camargue Ct 4 BN11 ...182 A3
Camber Cl Brighton BN2 ..188 F5
Crawley RH10 ....19 C6
Cambourne Ct 7 BN11 ..182 C2
Cambrai Ave PO19 ......173 B5
Cambria Cl PO18 ....171 C5
Cambridge Ave PO20 ....201 E8
Cambridge Dr PO21 .....194 F4
Cambridge Gr BN3 ......187 C7
Cambridge Rd
Horsham RH13 ....36 D2
Hove BN3 ....187 D6
Worthing BN11 ....182 D3
Cambridge Wlk PO21 ....194 F4
Camden St BN41 ....186 C6
Camden Terr BN1 ....207 A3
Camelford St BN2 ....207 C1
Camelia Cl BN17 ....179 A3
Camelot Cl RH13 ....58 A2
Camelot Ct RH11 ....17 E6
Camelsdale Cty Fst Sch
GU27 ....26 F5
Camelsdale Rd GU27 .....26 F5
Campbell Cres RH19 ....9 B1
Campbell Ct BN12 ....181 A3
Campbell Dr BN16 ......199 B6
Campbell Rd
Bognor Regis PO21 ....195 D3
Brighton BN1 ....207 A5
Crawley RH10 ....19 C5
Tangmere PO20 ....154 B1
Campion Cl BN16 ....179 B4
Campion Rd RH12 ....36 E5
Canada Cnr GU31 ....89 B6
Canada Cotts GU29 ....71 A3
Canada Gr
Bognor Regis PO21 ......195 C3
Easebourne GU29 ....71 A2
Canada Rd BN18 ....157 F3
Canada Way GU30 ....25 C3
Canadian Cres PO20 .....206 E5
Canal Rd BN18 ....176 F3
Canal Wharf PO19 ....172 F5
Canal Wharf Rd PO19 ...172 F5
Canberra Cl Crawley RH11 ..5 D1
Horsham RH12 ....36 F4
Canberra Ct PO21 ....195 A2
Canberra Pl Horsham RH12 .36 F5
Tangmere PO20 ....154 D2
Canberra Rd
Thorney Island PO10 .....169 C3
Worthing BN13 ....181 C6
Candleford Gate GU30 ....25 C4
Canfield Cl BN2 ....168 D1
Canfield Rd BN2 ....168 D1
Canhouse La GU31, GU33 ..46 C3
Canning Ct PO22 ....195 F3
Canning Rd PO22 ....195 F3
Canning St BN2 ....188 D5
Cannon Pl BN1 ....207 A2
Canon La PO19 ....172 F6
Canon's Cl PO21 ....194 D1
Canonbury Cotts RH12 ....16 F6
Canons Way BN44 ....143 E4
Cansiron La RH19 ....23 F6
Cantelupe Mews 4 RH19 ...9 E1
Cantelupe Rd RH19 ....9 F1
Canter The RH10 ....19 E7
Canterbury Cl
Bognor Regis PO21 ....194 A1
Chichester PO19 ....172 F8
Canterbury Ct
Southwater RH13 ....58 A2
Worthing BN13 ....181 F3
Canterbury Dr 5 BN2 ...207 C4
Canterbury Rd
Crawley RH10 ....18 E2
Rustington BN16 ....199 E6
Worthing BN13 ....182 A3
Canton 3 RH16 ....85 D6
Cants Cl RH15 ....107 C3
Cants La RH15 ....107 C3
Canute Rd PO18 ....171 B5
Canvey Cl RH11 ....18 C3
Cape Copse RH12 ....33 D7
Cape The BN17 ....199 A5
Capel La RH11 ....17 F5
Capel Rd RH12 ....16 A8
Capelia Ho BN11 ....182 A1
Capenors RH15 ....106 F1
Capricorn Cl RH11 ....17 E4
Capsey Rd RH11 ....17 E6
Capstan Dr BN17 ....179 A3
Caraway Cl RH11 ....18 B2
Card Hill RH18 ....23 F1
Carden Ave BN1 ....168 B6
Carden Cl BN1 ....168 A6
Carden Cres BN1 ....168 A6
Carden Hill BN1 ....168 B5
Carden Prim Sch BN1 ...168 B6
Cardew Rd GU33 ....45 C3
Cardinal Ct 4 BN11 .....182 A1
Cardinal Newman Sch
BN3 ....187 D8
Cardinal's Dr PO21 .....194 B1
Carey Ho RH11 ....18 C6
Carfax RH12 ....36 C2
Cargo Forecourt Rd RH6 ...5 D7
Cargo Rd RH6 ....5 D7
Carisbrooke Cl BN15 ....183 E8
Carisbrooke Dr BN13 ...181 B5
Carisbrooke Rd BN2 ....188 D7
Carleton Rd PO19 ......172 E8
Carlingford Ct 1 PO21 ..195 C4
Carlisle Gdns PO19 .....152 F1
Carlisle Rd BN3 ....186 F6
Carlton Ave PO21 ......194 C3
Carlton Cl RH10 ....18 E5
Carlton Ct Horley RH6 ......2 A5
Portslade-by-Sea BN41 ...186 C8
Carlton Hill BN2 ....207 C2
Carlton Hill
Cty Prim Sch BN2 ......207 C2
Carlton Ho Brighton BN1 ..167 E2
Worthing BN13 ....182 A6
Carlton Mews BN11 .....182 A2
Carlton Pl 5 BN2 ....207 C2
Carlton Terr BN3,BN41 ...186 C8
Carlton Tye RH6 ....2 C3
Carlyle Ave BN2 ....168 D1
Carlyle Ho 2 BN14 .....182 D3
Carlyle St BN2 ....188 C7
Carman Wlk RH11 ....18 B1
Carn Ct 7 BN2 ....188 C6
Carnation Cl BN17 ......179 B3
Carnegie Cl BN14 ......182 C5
Carnegie Gdns BN14 ....182 D5
Carnegie Ho BN13 ......181 F6
Carnegie Rd BN14 ......182 C5
Carnforth Rd BN15 .....183 C5
Carnoustie Ct 18 RH16 ...85 E4
Carol Cl BN1 ....167 F6
Caroline Ct RH11 ....18 D4
Carolyn Ho BN13 ....181 E5
Caron Cl BN15 ....183 E5
Carousel Ct PO21,PO22 ..195 B5
Carpenters RH14 ....77 D8
Carpenters Mdw RH20 ....98 C2
Carron La GU29 ....92 E7
Carse Rd PO19 ....153 C1
Carter Rd RH10 ....19 D3
Carters Way RH14 ....76 B8
Cartersland GU30 ....47 B3
Carterslodge La RH17 ....60 E7
Cartersmead Cl RH6 ......2 B4
Carvel Way BN17 ......199 A6
Carylls Cotts RH12 ......16 F1
Carylls Mdw RH13 .....102 D7
Casher Rd RH10 ....19 C3
Cashman Lodge BN1 ....168 A5
Caspian Ct 8 BN1 ......207 A4
Cassells Rd 2 PO19 .....153 A2
Cassidy Pl RH20 ....119 B1
Castle Cl Bramber BN44 ...143 E2
Worthing BN13 ....181 F4
Castle Ct BN13 ....181 F4
Castle Dr RH6 ....2 C2
Castle Gdns BN18 ......158 A3
Castle Goring Mews
BN13 ....181 A8
Castle La Bramber BN44 ..143 E2
West Grinstead RH13 ....101 F7
Castle Mews BN18 .....158 B3
Castle Of Mey Ho GU27 ...26 F6
Castle Rd
Broadridge Heath RH12 ....35 D3
Red Hill PO9 ....128 D1
Worthing BN13 ....181 F4
Castle Sq BN1 ....207 B2
Castle St BN1 ....187 E5
Castle The RH12 ....36 E7
Castle Way Bramber BN44 .143 E3
Worthing BN13 ....181 F4
Castledean Sch BN1 ....168 C2
Castlegate RH20 ....119 B7
Castleman Rd PO19 .....173 C8
Castlereagh Gn PO22 ....196 A5
Castlewood Prim Sch
RH13 ....58 A2
Castlewood Rd RH13 .....58 A2
Caterways RH12 ....36 A3
Cathedral Ctyd PO19 ....172 F6
Cathedral Way PO19 ....172 D6
Catherine Villas GU27 ....27 B6
Catherington Sch RH11 .....5 D2
Catkin Way RH16 ....86 B4
Catslands La BN5 ......145 C8
Causeway RH12 ....36 C1
Causeway Ct BN18 .....158 C2
Causeway The
Arundel BN18 ....158 C2
Bognor Regis PO21 ......205 A8
Brighton BN2 ....188 D6
Partridge Green RH13 ....103 A3
Selsey PO20 ....206 C8
Westlands PO20 ....191 F6
Worthing BN12 ....181 E3
Cavalier Cl GU29 ....92 E7
Cavalier Way RH19 ......22 F7
Cavandish Mews 12 BN1 .187 D5
Cavell Rd RH10 ....19 C5
Cavendish Cl
Horsham RH12 ....36 D7
Worthing BN12 ....181 D3
Cavendish Ho
Bognor Regis PO21 ......195 D2
8 Brighton BN1 ....187 E5
Haywards Heath RH16 ....85 F2
Cavendish Pl BN1 ......187 E5
Cavendish Rd PO21 ....195 C3
Cavendish St
11 Brighton BN2 ....207 C2
Chichester PO19 ....172 F7
Caversham Ct 8 BN11 ..182 B1
Cawley Rd PO19 ....173 A5
Caxton Cl RH10 ....18 E3
Caxton Ct 4 BN14 ......182 D4
Caxton Way 15 RH16 .....85 E4
Cecil Ct BN15 ....183 E4
Cecil Norris Ho 3 BN43 ..184 F7
Cecil Pashley Way BN43 .184 D8
Cecil Rd BN15 ....183 E4
Cecilian Ave BN14 .....182 D4
Cedar Ave BN13 ....181 F6
Cedar Cl
Bognor Regis PO21 .....194 D3
Burgess Hill RH15 ......107 B5
Crawley RH11 ....5 C1
Ferring BN12 ....200 E5
Horsham RH12 ....36 C3
Lancing BN15 ....183 D4
Worthing BN13 ....181 F6
Cedar Cl E PO21 ......194 D3
Cedar Ct Haslemere GU27 ..27 B6
Petworth GU28 ....95 E7
Worthing BN11 ....182 A3
Cedar Dr Chichester PO19 .172 E7
Southwater RH13 ....58 A1
Cedar Lodge RH11 ....18 D4
Cedar Way
Haywards Heath RH16 ....86 B4
Henfield BN5 ....123 F4
Cedars Farm Cl RH14 ....77 C8
Cedars Gdns BN1 ......167 E3
Cedars The
1 Brighton BN2 ....207 C5
Brighton, Withdean BN1 ..167 E3
Haywards Heath RH16 ....85 D7
Rustington BN16 ....199 E6
Cedarwood 3 BN1 ......167 E3
Cedric Ct RH12 ....36 A1
Celandine Cl 1 RH11 ....18 B2
Cello Ct 8 BN2 ....188 C5
Cemetery La
Tillington GU28 ....73 C1
Westbourne PO10 ......149 F3
Centenary Ho BN1 .....167 E2
Centenary Ind Est 6
BN2 ....188 B8
Central Ave
Bognor Regis PO21 .....195 A6
Littlehampton BN16 .....199 C4
Worthing BN14 ....161 F3
Central Bldgs 2 PO21 ...195 D3
Central CE Jun Sch PO19 172 F7
Central Dr
Bognor Regis PO21 .....195 A6
Central Dr *continued*
Middleton-on-Sea PO22 ...197 A5
Centrecourt Cl 5 BN14 ..182 C4
Centrecourt Rd BN14 ....182 C4
Centurion Rd BN1 ......207 A3
Ceres Pl PO22 ....196 D4
Chadborn Cl BN2 ....188 D5
Chadds Cotts RH17 ......39 C1
Chadwick Cl RH11 ....18 B1
Chaffer La PO20 ....191 D4
Chaffinch Cl
Burgess Hill RH15 ......106 D4
Crawley RH11 ....18 D8
Horsham RH12 ....36 D7
Worthing BN13 ....181 C5
Chaffinch Way RH6 ....1 E4
Chailey Cl 2 RH11 ....18 A3
Chailey Ct
2 Haywards Heath RH16 ...85 F3
Hove BN1 ....167 C5
Chailey Heritage
Craft Sch & Hospl
(New Heritage) BN8 ......87 E1
Chailey Rd BN1 ....168 E4
Chainbridge La PO20 ....203 C1
Chalcraft Cl GU30 ....25 A4
Chalcraft La PO21 ......194 F5
Chalder La PO20 ....192 F3
Chaldon Rd RH11 ....18 C1
Chaleford Ct 5 BN14 ....182 D4
Chalet Cl BN12 ....200 E4
Chalet Gdns BN12 ......200 F4
Chalet Rd BN12 ....200 E4
Chalfont Cl PO22 ......196 E5
Chalfont Ct BN11 ......182 B2
Chalfont Dr BN3 ....167 C3
Chalfont Way BN13 ....181 D6
Chalk La PO20 ....203 E7
Chalk Rd
Goodwood Park PO18 ....134 A4
Ifold RH14 ....31 C3
Chalkdock La PO20 .....191 A5
Chalkers La BN6 ....126 B8
Chalkpit La PO18 ....153 B7
Chalky Rd BN41 ....166 A3
Challen Cl PO20 ....174 C6
Challen Ct RH12 ....36 B3
Challoners RH17 ....65 C4
Challow Cl BN6 ....126 E4
Chalmers Ct RH6 ....4 E6
Chaloner Cl RH16 ....86 B7
Chaloner Rd RH16 ......86 B7
Chalvington Cl BN1 ....168 E6
Champion's Gate RH13 ...81 A2
Champions Row BN3 ....187 C8
Chancellors Pk BN6 ....126 F4
Chancton Cl
Heath Common RH20 ....120 B3
Worthing BN11 ....181 F3
Chancton View Rd BN11 .181 F3
Chanctonbury RH20 .....121 A4
Chanctonbury Cl RH20 ..141 E6
Chanctonbury Dr BN43 ..164 F1
Chanctonbury Rd
Burgess Hill RH15 ......107 A1
Hove BN3 ....187 E7
Littlehampton BN16 .....199 B4
Chanctonbury Ring Rd
BN44 ....142 D6
Chanctonbury View BN5 .123 D4
Chanctonbury Way RH11 ..18 C4
Chanctonbury Wlk 8
RH20 ....119 D1
Chandler Cl RH10 ....18 D4
Chandler Rd PO19 ......172 E5
Chandlers Reach PO20 ..191 A7
Chandlers Way BN44 ....143 C2
Chandos Rd BN11 ......182 D2
Channel Ct BN15 ......183 E4
Channel Keep 11 BN17 ..198 E4
Channel View
Bognor Regis PO21 .....205 A8
13 Southwick BN42 .....185 E7
Chantlers Cl RH19 ....9 C2
Chantrey Rd RH10 ....18 E3
Chantry Cl Henfield BN5 ..123 E6
Horley RH6 ....1 F4
Storrington RH20 ....119 E1
Chantry Est The RH20 ....140 E8
Chantry La RH20 ......140 E6
Chantry Rd BN13 ......182 A6
Chantryfield Rd BN16 ...179 F6
Chapel Cl
Burgess Hill RH15 ......106 F4
Littlehampton BN17 .....198 C6
Chapel La
Ashurst Wood RH19 ......23 D6
Cootham RH20 ....119 A1
Copthorne RH10 ....7 F4
East Ashling PO18 ......152 A3
Forest Row RH18 ....23 F2
Horsted Keynes RH17 ....65 C5
West Wittering PO20 ....190 F2
Chapel Mews 8 BN3 ....187 D5
Chapel Pl BN41 ....186 B7
Chapel Rd
Barns Green RH13 ....56 F2
Charlwood RH6 ....4 F7
Southwick BN41 ....186 A7
Worthing BN11 ....182 D3
Chapel Row
East Dean PO18 ....134 C6
West Hoathly RH19 ......42 E7
Chapel St
Bognor Regis PO21 .....195 C2
Brighton BN2 ....207 C2
Chichester PO19 ....172 F6
Chapel Terr 2 BN2 .....188 D4
Chapel Wlk BN16 ......179 F5
Chapelfields RH17 ....84 F8
Chapman Ct BN13 ......181 F6
Chapman Rd RH10 ....19 C2
Chapman's La
East Grinstead RH19 ....9 B1
East Grinstead RH19 ....9 D1
Chappell Cl GU30 ....25 C4
Chappell Croft 2 BN11 ..182 B2
Charis Ct 18 BN3 ....187 C7
Charlecote Rd BN11 ....182 E2
Charles Ave
Burgess Hill RH15 ......106 D2
Chichester PO19 ....173 D6
Charles Bennett Ct RH16 .86 A4
Charles Cl BN3 ....167 A3
Charles Ct 6 BN11 .....182 C3
Charles Ho BN12 ......181 D2
Charles Kingston Gdns
BN1 ....167 E4
Charles St BN2 ....207 B1
Charlesfield Rd RH6 ......1 F4
Charleston Ct RH10 .....19 B3
Charlesworth Pk RH16 ...86 C4
Charlmead PO20 ....201 F6
Charlock Cl RH11 ....18 A2
Charlock Way RH13 .....58 A3
Charlotte Ct RH11 ......18 C6
Charlotte Ho PO22 .....195 E4
Charlotte St BN2 ......207 C1
Charlton Gdns BN6 ....127 D3
Charlton Mill Way PO18 .133 F6
Charlton Rd PO18 .....134 B6
Charlton St BN44 ......143 C3
Charltons The BN1 ....168 D6
Charlwood Gdns RH15 ..107 C5
Charlwood La RH5 ....4 A5
Charlwood Lodge 3
BN11 ....182 A2
Charlwood Rd
Burgess Hill RH15 ......107 D6
Charlwood RH11, RH6 .....4 E2
Crawley RH6,RH11 ....5 C4
Hookwood RH6 ....5 C8
Charlwood St PO21 ....195 B2
Charlwood Village
Inf Sch RH6 ....4 F7
Charlwood Wlk RH11 .....5 B1
Charlwoods Bsns Ctr RH19 .9 D2
Charlwoods Pl RH19 ......9 E3
Charlwoods Rd RH19 .....9 E3
Charm Cl RH6 ....1 E4
Charmandean La BN14 ..182 D8
Charmandean Rd BN14 ..182 D6
Charmans Cl RH12 ......37 B5
Charnwood Rd PO22 ...195 B6
Charrington Way RH12 ...35 C3
Charterhouse Mews
PO20 ....201 F8
Chartfield BN3 ....167 A2
Chartfield Way BN3 ....167 B2
Chartwell Bldg PO10 ...149 F1
Chartwell Ct BN1 ......207 A2
Chartwell Rd BN15 ....183 D5
Chase Cl GU33 ....45 C4
Chase La GU27 ....27 E3
Chase Rd GU33 ....45 C4
Chase The Crawley RH10 ..19 A5
Nepcote BN14 ....161 E5
Chatelet Cl RH6 ....2 B4
Chates Farm Ct BN2 ...207 C3
Chatfield Rd
Chichester PO19 ....173 C8
Cuckfield RH17 ....85 A6
Chatfields RH11 ....18 B4
Chatham Pl BN1 ......207 A4
Chatham Rd BN11 .....183 A3
Chatsmore Cath
High Sch BN12 ....181 A3
Chatsmore Cres BN12 ..181 B3
Chatsmore Ho BN12 ....181 A2
Chatsworth Ave GU27 ....27 C8
Chatsworth Cl BN16 ...179 B3
Chatsworth Ct
Brighton BN1 ....187 E8
5 Shoreham-by-Sea BN43 .184 F6
Chatsworth Dr BN16 ...179 B3
Chatsworth Rd
Brighton BN1 ....187 E8
Chichester PO19 ....173 D6
Hove BN3 ....187 D7
Worthing BN11 ....182 D2
Chaucer Ave 3 RH19 .....9 C1
Chaucer Ct 2 RH16 ......85 D5
Chaucer Dr PO20 ......201 F8
Chaucer Rd Crawley RH10 .19 C8
Worthing BN11 ....182 B3
Chaucer Way PO22 .....196 D6
Chaucher Ave BN16 ....199 B5
Chawkmare
Coppice PO21 ....194 F2
Chayle Gdns PO20 .....206 E6
Cheal Cl BN43 ....184 F6
Cheam Rd BN16 ....199 D4
Cheapside BN1 ....207 B3
Cheeleys RH17 ....65 C5
Cheesemans La PO18 ...150 E4
Chelmer Ho BN15 ......183 E4
Chelsea Arc RH16 ......85 E4
Chelston Ave BN3 .....186 D7
Cheltenham Pl BN1 ....207 B3
Chelwood Ave BN12 ...181 C1
Chelwood Cl
Brighton BN1 ....168 C6
Crawley RH10 ....18 F4

Chelwood Ct RH15 107 A4
Chelwood Gate Rd
RH17,TN22 66 F7
Chennells Brook Cotts
RH12 36 F7
Chennells Way RH12 36 E5
Chepstow Cl RH10 19 E6
Chepstow Ct BN1 168 F5
Chequer Grange RH18 23 E1
Chequer La PO18 171 D6
Chequer Mead Arts Ctr
RH19 9 F1
Chequer Rd RH19 9 F1
Chequers Cl RH6 2 A4
Chequers Ct Horsham RH13 36 E2
Petworth GU28 95 F7
Chequers Dr RH6 2 A4
Chequers Quay PO10 169 C8
Cherington Cl BN6 126 B5
Chermont Ct BN16 199 F6
Cherrimans Orch GU27 26 F6
Cherry Ave BN18 177 A2
Cherry Cl
Bognor Regis PO21 194 E2
Burgess Hill RH15 106 E3
Cherry Croft BN17 178 D3
Cherry Ct [5] RH13 36 D1
Cherry Gdns Selsey PO20 206 D5
Worthing BN13 161 D1
Cherry La Birdham PO20 191 F5
Bolney RH17 83 C3
Brook Street RH17 62 F5
Crawley RH11 5 C1
Cherry Lodge [5] RH6 2 B2
Cherry Mdws RH11 18 C5
Cherry Orchard Rd PO19 173 B5
Cherry Tree Ave GU27 26 F7
Cherry Tree Cl
Billingshurst RH14 55 C1
Crawley RH10 19 D8
Worthing BN13 161 D1
Cherry Tree Dr PO20 175 F8
Cherry Tree Lodge [1]
BN15 183 D6
Cherry Tree Wlk
Horsham RH12 37 B6
Petworth GU28 95 E7
Cherry Trees RH17 84 E8
Cherry Wlk BN13 161 E1
Cherrylands Cl GU27 49 B6
Cherrytree Cotts PO22 176 C5
Cherrywood [2] BN1 167 E3
Cherwell Rd BN13 181 C8
Cherwell Wlk RH11 17 F5
Chesham Cl BN12 181 E2
Chesham Pl BN2 188 D4
Chesham Rd BN2 188 D4
Chesham St BN2 188 D4
Cheshire Cl [13] PO21 195 D4
Cheshire Cres PO20 154 C1
Cheshire Way PO10 150 A2
Chesholt Cl GU27 49 B6
Chesley Cl BN13 181 C6
Chess Brook Gn BN5 123 F7
Chesswood Ave PO22 196 C6
Chesswood Cl BN11 182 F4
Chesswood Ct BN11 182 F4
Chesswood Lea BN11 182 F4
Chesswood Mid Sch
BN11 182 E4
Chesswood Rd BN11 182 F4
Chester Ave Lancing BN15 183 E4
Worthing BN11 183 A3
Chester Ct [12] BN3 187 E7
Chester Lodge [2] BN11 182 A2
Chester Terr BN1 168 A1
Chesterfield Cl RH10 8 C4
Chesterfield Rd BN12 181 D3
Chesters RH6 1 E5
Chesterton Cl RH19 22 F7
Chesterton Ct RH13 37 A4
Chestnut Ave
Chichester PO19 152 F3
Haslemere GU27 27 C7
Chestnut Bridge RH20 119 C7
Chestnut Cl
Angmering BN16 179 F4
Burgess Hill RH15 107 B5
East Grinstead RH19 10 A1
Heath Common RH20 120 B3
Liphook GU30 25 D3
Midhurst GU29 92 E5
Chestnut Ct
East Preston BN16 200 A5
Horsham RH13 36 E2
[9] Worthing BN11 182 C3
Chestnut End BN5 123 E5
Chestnut Gdns RH12 36 C5
Chestnut Gr
Bognor Regis PO22 195 C6
Hurstpierpoint BN6 125 F7
Chestnut Rd
Billingshurst RH14 77 D7
Horley RH6 2 B5
Chestnut Way BN5 123 E5
Chestnut Wlk Crawley RH11 5 C1
Felcourt RH19 9 C8
Pulborough RH20 98 B2
Tangmere PO20 154 C1
Worthing BN13 181 C5
Chestnuts Cl RH16 86 A7
Chestnuts The Horley RH6 2 A5
Hunston PO20 193 A8
Lindfield RH16 85 F7
Sayers Common BN6 105 D1
Chesworth Cl RH13 58 C8
Chesworth Cres RH13 36 C1
Chesworth Gdns RH13 36 C1
Chesworth Jun Sch RH12 36 E3
Chesworth La RH12, RH13 36 C1
Chet Nole RH19 9 D2
Chetwood Rd RH11 17 D2
Cheveley Gdns PO21 194 E2
Chevening Cl RH11 18 C1
Cheviot Cl
East Preston BN16 200 A6
Worthing BN13 181 E8
Cheviot Rd BN13 181 E8
Cheviot Wlk RH11 18 B6
Cheyne Ct BN43 185 C7
Cheyne Wlk RH6 2 A1
Cheynell Wlk RH11 17 F4
Chichester By-Pass
Chichester PO20 173 D5
Stockbridge PO19 172 F4
Chichester Cath PO19 172 F6
Chichester Cl
[15] Brighton BN2 188 D4
Crawley RH10 18 E2
Hove BN3 166 E4
Chichester Coll of Arts,
Science & Tech PO19 172 E6
Chichester Ct
[11] Rustington BN16 199 C5
[1] Worthing BN11 182 A1
Chichester District Mus
PO19 173 A6
Chichester Dr PO20 154 D1
Chichester
Festival Theatre PO19 173 A8
Chichester High Sch
for Boys PO19 173 A5
Chichester High Sch
for Girls PO19 172 F5
Chichester Inst
of Higher Ed PO19 173 A8
Chichester Pl BN2 188 D4
Chichester Rd
Arundel BN18 157 E3
Bognor Regis PO21,PO22 195 B5
East Beach PO20 203 F1
Midhurst GU29 92 F5
Selsey PO20 206 E8
Street End PO20 192 E5
Chichester Sta PO19 172 F5
Chichester Terr
[19] Brighton BN2 188 D4
Horsham RH12 36 D2
Chichester Tutorial Unit
PO20 173 C1
Chichester Way
Burgess Hill RH15 107 C5
Selsey PO20 206 G8
Chiddingley Cl BN2 188 F5
Chiddingly Cl RH10 19 B5
Chiddingly Ho [11] BN3 187 D7
Chidham La PO18 170 E6
Chidham Prim Sch PO18 170 E6
Chilcomb RH15 107 C1
Chilcroft La GU27 27 B1
Chilcroft Rd GU27 26 F7
Chilcrofts Rd GU27 27 A1
Childerstone Cl GU30 25 B4
Chilgrove Cl BN12 181 B3
Chilgrove Ho BN17 178 B3
Chilling St RH19 43 D3
Chillis Wood Rd RH16 85 C5
Chilmark Ct GU33 45 B4
Chiltern Cl Crawley RH11 18 B6
East Preston BN16 200 A6
Haslemere GU27 27 B5
Shoreham-by-Sea BN43 185 C8
Chiltern Cres BN13 181 E7
Chiltington Cl
Burgess Hill RH15 106 F5
West Chiltington
Common RH20 119 C7
Chiltington Ct RH12 36 D4
Chiltlee Cl GU30 25 C4
Chiltlee Manor GU30 25 C3
Chiltley La GU30 25 D2
Chiltley Way GU30 25 C2
Chine The BN17 199 A4
Chipley Ct PO21 195 A4
Chippendale Rd RH11 18 B1
Chippers Cl BN13 181 F4
Chippers Rd BN13 181 F4
Chippers Wlk BN13 181 F4
Chithurst La
Chithurst GU31,GU30 69 C4
Domewood RH6, RH7, RH10 7 F7
Chownes Mead La RH16 85 B4
Chrisdory Rd BN41 165 F3
Christ's Hospital (Sch)
RH13 57 D5
Christ's Hospital Rd
Horsham RH13 57 E6
Itchingfield RH13 57 C6
Christ's Hospital Sta
(West Horsham) RH13 57 D7
Christchurch Cres PO21 194 E3
Christchurch Ho [4] BN11 182 D3
Christchurch Rd BN11 182 D3
Christie Pl PO22 195 D6
Christies RH19 22 D8
Christopher Rd RH19 9 E1
Christopher Way PO10 149 B2
Church App [1] BN17 198 E4
Church Ave RH16 85 E6
Church Bglws PO18 109 B2
Church Cl Ashington RH20 120 F4
Brighton BN1 167 F5
Burgess Hill RH15 107 A3
Church Cl *continued*
Clapham BN13 160 F1
Lancing BN15 183 E8
Lower Beeding RH13 60 A3
Pagham PO21 204 E7
Shipley RH13 101 D8
Upper Beeding BN44 144 A3
Church Cotts
Earnley PO20 202 D6
[2] Worthing BN11 182 F2
Church Ct
[3] Haywards Heath RH16 85 E4
Hove BN3 166 F1
Church Farm Ct PO20 202 A8
Church Farm La PO20 202 A8
Church Farm Wlk BN44 144 A3
Church Gn BN43 185 C7
Church Gr RH20 99 D1
Church Hill Brighton BN1 167 E7
Midhurst GU29 92 F8
Pulborough RH20 98 B2
Pyecombe BN45 147 C6
Slindon BN18 156 C5
Church Ho BN17 198 D4
Church House Cl BN42 165 F1
Church House Mews
PO22 196 A4
Church La Albourne BN6 125 B5
Ardingly RH17 63 F8
Ashington RH20 121 A4
Ashurst BN44 122 D5
Barnham PO22 176 B4
Birdham PO20 191 E5
Bognor Regis PO22 195 C5
Boxgrove PO18 154 D3
Bramshott GU30 25 C6
Broadridge Heath RH12 35 D3
Burgess Hill RH17 107 F6
Burstow RH6 6 F7
Bury RH20 138 A7
Climping BN17,BN18 177 E1
Cocking GU29 112 D7
Coldwaltham RH20 117 C6
Copthorne RH10 7 B3
Danehill RH17 66 A3
Ditchling BN6 127 D3
East Grinstead RH19 9 F1
Eastergate PO20 175 E8
Ferring BN12 200 E6
Funtington PO18 151 A5
Haslemere GU27 27 D7
Henfield BN5 123 E5
Horsted Keynes RH17 65 C5
Hunston PO20 193 A8
Lancing BN15 183 A8
Lodsworth GU28 72 C2
Lower Beeding RH13 60 A5
Oving PO20 174 C7
Pagham PO21 204 E8
Partridge Green RH13 102 F3
Poynings BN45, BN6 146 E7
Pyecombe BN45 147 C6
Southwater RH13 57 E1
Southwick BN42 185 D7
Steyning BN44 143 D4
Street End PO20 192 E3
Tangmere PO20 154 C1
Upper Beeding BN44 144 A2
Walberton BN18 176 E8
West Dean PO18 132 F5
Yapton BN18 176 F4
Church Mdw PO18 171 B5
Church Mead Keymer BN6 127 B3
Steyning BN44 143 E3
Church Mews PO20 173 D1
Church Path
[3] Emsworth PO10 169 B8
Stoughton PO18 131 A4
Church Pl Brighton BN2 188 E4
Pulborough RH20 98 B2
Church Platt RH17 84 E5
Church Rd
Aldingbourne PO20 175 A8
Angmering BN16 179 F5
Bramshott GU30 25 C6
Broadridge Heath RH12 35 D3
Burgess Hill RH15 107 A3
Burstow RH6 7 A7
Chichester PO19 173 D7
Copthorne RH10 7 B3
Crawley RH11 5 E5
Crawley, Worth RH10 19 E6
East Wittering PO20 201 F8
Fernhurst GU27 49 B5
Haslemere GU27 27 C7
Haslemere, Shottermill GU27 26 F6
Haywards Heath RH16 85 E4
Horley RH6 1 F2
Horley RH6 2 A3
Horsham RH12 37 B5
Hove BN3 187 B6
Littlehampton BN17 178 C6
Mannings Heath RH13 59 C6
North Mundham PO20 173 D1
Partridge Green RH13 102 F3
Portslade-by-Sea BN41 186 B7
Rustington BN16 199 C5
Scaynes Hill RH17 86 F3
Selsey PO20 206 E8
Southbourne PO10 169 F8
Turners Hill RH10 21 A3
West Hoathly RH19 42 F6
West Lavington GU29 93 A6
West Thorney PO10 169 F1
Westbourne PO10 149 D3
Worthing BN13 182 A4
Yapton BN18 176 F3
Church Road Ind Est RH11 5 E5
Church Road Trad Est
RH11 5 E5
Church St Amberley BN18 138 D7
Brighton BN1 207 B2
Cox Green RH12 12 E1
Crawley RH11 18 C6
Cuckfield RH17 84 E6
Henfield BN5 123 E5
Liss GU33 45 A6
Littlehampton BN17 198 E5
Petworth GU28 95 F8
Portslade-by-Sea BN41 186 B7
Rudgwick RH12 33 E8
Shoreham-by-Sea BN43 184 F7
Steyning BN44 143 D3
Storrington RH20 119 D1
Warnham RH12 35 F8
West Chiltington RH20 99 E1
Church Terr Cowfold RH13 81 E2
Henfield BN5 123 E5
Church View PO10 149 D3
Church View Cl RH6 1 F2
Church Way
Bognor Regis PO21 194 A1
[6] Brighton BN2 207 C3
Singleton PO18 133 D7
Worthing BN13 182 A5
Church Way Cl BN13 182 A5
Church Wlk
Burgess Hill RH15 107 A3
Crawley RH10 18 D6
Horley RH6 1 F2
Worthing BN11 182 F2
Church Wood RH20 97 B4
Churcher Rd PO10 149 D4
Churchfarm La PO20 192 F2
Churchfield RH20 97 A3
Churchfield Ct GU30 25 B3
Churchill Ave
Bognor Regis PO21 194 E4
Horsham RH12 36 B3
Churchill Ct Crawley RH10 6 A1
[5] Rustington BN16 199 C5
Churchill Dr PO10 149 B4
Churchill Ho
Barnham PO22 176 C5
Hove BN3 166 E2
Churchill Ind Est BN15 183 D5
Churchill Par BN16 199 C5
Churchill Sq BN1 207 A2
Churchill Way RH15 107 C2
Churchill Wlk PO21 205 A8
Churchmead Cl PO18 152 F6
Churchside PO19 173 A7
Churchwood Dr PO20 154 D1
Chute Ave BN13 161 E1
Chute Way BN13 181 E8
Cinder Hill RH19 43 B1
Circle The BN16 200 A4
Circus Par BN1 207 B4
Circus St BN2 207 B2
Cissbury Ave BN14 161 F2
Cissbury Cl RH12 37 A6
Cissbury Ct BN14 161 F2
Cissbury Dr BN14 161 F3
Cissbury Gdns BN14 162 A2
Cissbury Hill RH11 18 C4
Cissbury Rd
Burgess Hill RH15 106 E4
Ferring BN12 180 E3
Hove BN3 187 E7
Worthing BN14 182 C6
Cissbury Ring BN14 162 B5
Cissbury Way [5] BN43 164 F1
City Bsns Ctr
Chichester PO19 172 F5
Crawley RH11 5 D2
Horsham RH13 36 D1
City Fields PO20 154 D2
City Fields Way PO20 154 D2
Civic Way RH15 107 A3
Claigmar Rd BN16 199 C5
Clair Ct RH16 85 E5
Clair Rd RH16 85 E5
Clammer Hill GU27 27 F8
Clapgate La RH13 34 D4
Clapham & Patching
CE Prim Sch BN13 160 E1
Clapham Cl BN13 160 F1
Clapham Comm BN13 180 E8
Clappers Gate RH10 18 D7
Clappers La
Bracklesham PO20 202 C6
Fulking BN5 145 F5
Clappers Meadow GU6 11 A3
Clare Cl RH10 6 C1
Clare Ct [5] BN17 198 E4
Clare Lodge [2] BN16 199 B5
Clare Wlk BN2 188 D5
Claremont Ct [18] PO21 195 D3
Claremont Way GU29 92 E7
Clarence Ave BN17 178 C3
Clarence Ct Horley RH6 2 D4
Worthing BN11 182 F2
Clarence Dr
[2] East Grinstead RH19 22 F7
East Preston BN16 199 F6
Clarence Gate [10] PO21 195 D3
Clarence Rd
Bognor Regis PO21 195 D3
Horsham RH13 36 E1
Clarence Sq BN1 207 A2
Clarence Way RH6 2 D4
Clarendon Ho [2] BN3 187 B7
Clarendon Pl
[15] Brighton BN2 188 C4
Portslade-by-Sea BN41 186 C6
Clarendon Rd Hove BN3 187 B7
Clarendon Rd *continued*
Shoreham-by-Sea
BN42, BN43 185 D8
Worthing BN14 182 E6
Clarendon Terr [16] BN2 188 D4
Clarendon Villas BN3 187 B7
Clark Rd RH11 18 A1
Clarke Ave BN3 166 F3
Clarke Ct BN3 186 F6
Clarks Ind Est BN3 187 B8
Clay Hall La RH10 7 C4
Clay La Crossbush BN18 158 F1
Fishbourne PO18, PO19 172 B7
Storrington RH20 119 A1
West Ashling PO18 151 D1
Claypit La PO18 153 D2
Clays Cl RH19 22 E8
Clays Hill BN44 143 E2
Clayton Ave BN6 126 F3
Clayton Ct PO20 206 C6
Clayton Dr RH15 106 F1
Clayton Hill
Clayton BN6,BN45 147 D7
Crawley RH11 18 C4
Clayton La PO20 202 B7
Clayton Pk BN6 126 E4
Clayton Rd Brighton BN2 188 D7
Ditchling BN6 127 C3
Selsey PO20 206 C6
Clayton Way BN3 166 F3
Clayton Windmills BN6 147 E7
Clayton Wlk BN13 181 D5
Claytons Cnr PO20 191 E5
Clearwater La RH17 87 A3
Clearwaters La RH16 107 D8
Cleaver's La RH17 62 B2
Cleeves Ct BN16 199 E6
Cleeves Way BN16 199 E6
Clement's Ct [1] BN43 184 F7
Clerks Acre BN6 127 A4
Clermont Ct BN1 167 E2
Clermont Rd BN1 167 E2
Clermont Terr BN1 167 E2
Cleve Way RH14 77 D8
Cleveland Cl BN13 181 F8
Cleveland Gdns RH15 107 B2
Cleveland Rd
Brighton BN1 168 A1
Chichester PO19 173 B5
Worthing BN13 181 F7
Clevelands
Billingshurst RH14 77 D8
Haywards Heath RH16 85 E6
Clevets The PO21 194 C1
Cliff App BN2 188 F4
Cliff Rd BN2 188 F4
Cliff The BN2 188 F4
Clifton Cl RH6 2 D3
Clifton Ct Chichester PO19 173 B5
[4] Worthing BN11 182 C3
Clifton Gdns BN11 182 C3
Clifton Hill BN1 207 A3
Clifton Mews BN1 207 A3
Clifton Pl BN1 187 E6
Clifton Rd
Bognor Regis PO21 195 C4
Brighton BN1 207 A3
Burgess Hill RH15 106 D5
Crawley RH10 19 C5
Littlehampton BN17 198 D4
Worthing BN11 182 C3
Clifton St BN1 207 A4
Clifton Terr BN1 207 A3
Cliftonville Ct [6] BN3 187 B7
Climping & West Beach
Nature Trail BN17 197 F7
Climping Cl RH16 85 D3
Climping Ct [2] BN16 199 B3
Climping Rd RH11 18 B8
Climping St BN17 197 E7
Clinton Hill RH7 10 A8
Clitherow Gdns RH10 18 E5
Clive Ave BN12 181 D2
Clive Way RH10 19 C6
Clivedale [9] BN44 143 D3
Clivedale Gdns BN44 143 E3
Cliveden Ct BN1 167 E3
Clock Ho PO21 194 E1
Clock Pk PO22 195 E6
Clock Wlk [9] PO21 195 D3
Cloisters The BN17 198 F4
Close The Ardingly RH17 64 B7
Ashington RH20 121 A5
Bognor Regis PO21 194 C1
Boxgrove PO18 154 D3
Brighton BN1 167 E5
Burgess Hill RH15 107 C4
East Grinstead RH19 22 D8
Hassocks BN6 126 F4
Horley RH6 2 C1
Ifold RH14 31 D3
Lancing BN15 183 F4
Liphook GU30 25 C2
Littlehampton BN16 199 D4
Mid Lavant PO18 152 F5
Middleton-on-Sea PO22 197 A5
Selsey PO20 206 G8
Shoreham-by-Sea BN43 184 F8
Closewalks GU29 92 F7
Clothalls La RH13 102 B5
Clovelly Ave PO22 196 B5
Clovelly Rd Breach PO10 149 F1
Emsworth PO10 169 A8
Clover Ct [2] RH16 85 E4
Clover Field RH12 34 D4
Clover La BN12 200 E5
Clover Way BN41 166 B2
Cloverfields RH6 2 B4

Cloverlands RH10 18 F8
Clovers Cotts RH12 16 F1
Clovers End Brighton BN1 168 B7
Horsham RH12 37 A5
Clovers Way RH12 37 D7
Club Wlk BN16 200 A4
Clun Rd BN17 198 C6
Clyde Cl BN13 181 C8
Clyde Rd
Bognor Regis PO22 195 F3
Brighton BN1 207 B5
Worthing BN13 181 C8
Clydesdale Ave PO19 173 B5
Clydesdale Gdns PO22 195 A7
Coach & Horses La RH17 66 C6
Coach House Cl PO20 206 E7
Coach House Mews
BN11 182 C2
Coach La RH17 66 C6
Coach Rd Gatwick Airport,
North Terminal RH6 5 F8
Gatwick Airport, South
Terminal RH6 6 B7
Shopwyke PO20 173 F7
Westhampnett PO18 153 E1
Coachmans Dr RH11 18 B2
Coastal Counties Ho [19]
BN2 207 C3
Coastal Rd BN16 200 C4
Coastguard Cotts [10]
BN16 200 A4
Coastguard La PO20 190 A1
Coastguard Par PO21 194 D1
Coastguard Rd BN17 198 D3
Coastguards Cotts PO20 190 A1
Coates Ct [11] BN42 185 E7
Coates La RH20 116 D8
Cob Cl RH10 21 C8
Cob La RH17 42 B1
Cob Wlk RH11 18 A6
Cobbett Cl RH10 19 C8
Cobbetts Mead RH16 86 B3
Cobblers RH12 34 D4
Cobbles Cres RH10 18 E7
Cobblestone Wlk [1]
BN44 143 D3
Cobblewood PO10 149 B3
Cobden Ho GU29 92 E6
Cobden La GU27 27 D7
Cobden Rd Brighton BN2 188 C7
Midhurst GU29 92 E7
Worthing BN11 182 C2
Cobham Cl BN18 176 F2
Cobham Way RH10 6 B4
Cobnor Cl RH11 17 F4
Cobton Dr BN3 167 A3
Cockhaise Cotts RH16 87 A8
Cocking Hill GU29, PO18 112 C5
Cohen Cl PO20 175 D5
Cokeham Ct BN15 183 C7
Cokeham Gdns BN15 183 C6
Cokeham La BN15 183 C5
Cokeham Rd BN15 183 C6
Colbourne Ave BN2 168 D2
Colbourne Rd BN3 187 E7
Colchester Vale RH18 23 E2
Colchins RH15 106 F1
Coldean Inf Sch BN1 168 D6
Coldean Jun Sch BN1 168 D6
Coldean La BN1 168 E6
Coldharbour Farm Rd
PO10 149 B2
Coldharbour La BN13 160 D1
Coldwaltham La RH15 107 D2
Cole Cl RH11 18 B1
Colebrook Cl BN11 182 F3
Colebrook La RH20 117 B5
Colebrook Rd
Brighton BN1 167 D4
Littlehampton BN17 178 C3
Southwick BN42 185 F7
Coleman Ave BN3 186 E7
Coleman St BN2 207 C4
Colemans Hatch Rd RH18 44 E5
Coleridge Cl Horsham RH12 36 E6
Worthing BN12 181 B3
Coleridge Cres BN12 181 A3
Coleridge Mews BN12 181 B3
Coleridge Rd BN12 181 B3
Coleridge St BN3 187 A8
Colet Rd RH10 18 D3
Colgate Cl Brighton BN2 188 F6
Crawley RH11 18 B8
Colgate Prim Sch RH13 38 C6
Colhook Ind Pk GU28 51 D1
Colindale Rd BN12 200 E6
Colindale Rd N BN12 200 E6
Coll of Richard Collyer
RH12 36 D4
Collard Way GU33 45 B4
Collards Gate GU27 27 D6
Collards La GU27 27 D6
College Cl
Bognor Regis PO21 194 F4
East Grinstead RH19 9 F1
Portslade-by-Sea BN41 165 F3
Red Hill PO9 128 E1
College Ct PO22 195 E5
College Gdns
Brighton BN2 188 C4
Worthing BN11 182 A2
College Hill
Haslemere GU27 27 C6
Steyning BN44 143 D2
College Hill Terr GU27 27 C6
College La
Chichester PO19 173 A8
East Grinstead RH19 9 F1
College La *continued*
Hurst Wickham BN6 126 C6
College Pl Brighton BN2 188 C4
Hurst Wickham BN6 126 C6
College Rd
Ardingly RH16, RH17 64 A5
Brighton BN2 188 C4
Crawley RH10 18 E6
Haywards Heath RH16 85 E7
Southwater RH13 57 E1
Upper Beeding BN44 144 C1
College St [11] BN2 188 C4
College Terr BN2 188 D5
Collendean La RH6 1 A5
Collets Alley [4] RH12 36 C2
Collier Row RH10 18 D4
Collingford La RH17 66 B4
Collingwood RH20 98 C3
Collingwood Cl
[4] East Grinstead RH19 22 F7
Horley RH6 2 B4
Horsham RH12 36 C4
Collingwood Ct [2] BN43 184 F6
Collingwood Rd
Crawley RH10 19 D5
Horsham RH12 36 B4
Worthing BN12 181 C4
Collins Cl PO20 175 F8
Collins La GU31 89 C7
Collins Rd RH11 17 E4
Collins's La PO20 192 C4
Collyer Ave PO21 195 B5
Collyers Cotts GU28 72 B7
Collyers Cres GU30 25 E4
Colmer Ct RH15 106 E3
Colmer Pl RH15 106 E3
Colne Cl BN13 181 C8
Colne Wlk RH11 17 F5
Colonades The RH20 98 B3
Colonnade Ho BN11 182 E2
Colonsay Rd RH11 18 B3
Colt St PO20 206 D8
Colt's Bay PO21 194 C1
Coltash Rd RH10 19 A5
Coltsfoot Dr RH12 36 E5
Coltstaple La RH13 58 C4
Columbia Dr BN13 181 D6
Columbia Wlk BN13 181 C6
Columbine Way BN17 179 B4
Colvill Ave BN43 184 D8
Colwell Cl RH16 85 F3
Colwell Gdns RH16 85 F3
Colwell La
Haywards Heath RH17 86 B3
Haywards Heath, Fox
Hill RH17 85 F1
Colwell Rd RH16 85 F2
Colwood Hospl RH17 86 A3
Colwood La RH17 83 B6
Colwyn Cl RH11 17 F4
Combe Rd GU33 45 E1
Commerce Way BN15 183 C4
Commercial Rd RH15 106 F3
Commercial Sq RH16 85 E6
Common Hill RH20 119 D6
Common La BN6 127 D6
Common Rd PO10, PO18 150 D5
Common The RH20 119 C8
Common View GU29 69 F1
Commonside PO10 149 D5
Compass Cl BN17 199 A6
Compass Ct BN41 165 E3
Compassion Cl RH11 17 E5
Comper Cl RH11 17 E4
Compton & Up Marden
CE Prim Sch PO18 109 B2
Compton Ave
Brighton BN1 207 A4
Worthing BN12 181 B2
Compton Cl PO19 153 A3
Compton Ct BN16 199 C6
Compton Dr PO22 196 D6
Compton Rd Brighton BN1 167 D1
Lindfield RH16 86 B8
Comptons Brow La RH13 37 A3
Comptons Ct [3] RH12 36 F3
Comptons La RH13 36 F3
Comptons Lea [6] RH12 36 F3
Conbar Ave BN16 199 C6
Concorde Cl RH20 119 F3
Condor Way RH15 106 E3
Conduit Mead PO19 173 C8
Coney Cl Crawley RH11 18 B8
East Wittering PO20 201 F6
Coney Croft RH12 37 B5
Coney Rd PO20 201 F6
Coney Six PO20 201 F6
Coneyhurst Rd RH14 77 F8
Congreve Rd BN14 182 E4
Conifer Dr PO18 150 E2
Conifers Cl RH12 37 B6
Conifers Sch GU29 71 A1
Conigar Rd PO10 149 B3
Coniston Cl
Bognor Regis PO22 196 B6
Crawley RH11 17 D4
Horsham RH12 37 B6
Lancing BN15 183 C6
Coniston Ct [9] BN3 187 D7
Coniston Rd BN12 181 C4
Coniston Way BN17 179 A3
Connaught Ave BN43 184 E8
Connaught Ctr
Brighton Coll
of Tech & F Ed BN3 187 A6
Connaught Cty Jun Sch
BN17 198 D5
Connaught Gdns RH10 18 D8
Connaught Ho [7] PO21 195 C2
Connaught Rd Hove BN3 187 A6
Littlehampton BN17 198 D5
Connaught Terr BN3 187 B7
Consort Way
Burgess Hill RH15 106 E2
Horley RH6 2 A3
Consort Way E RH6 2 B2
Constable Dr PO20 206 F7
Constable Rd RH10 18 F2
Control Tower Rd RH6 5 D6
Convent Cl PO10 169 A8
Convent Gdns BN14 161 F6
Convent La PO10 169 B8
Conway Ct [1] BN3 187 B7
Conway Dr PO21 205 A8
Conway Pl BN3 187 A8
Conway St BN3 187 B8
Cook Rd Crawley RH10 18 F4
Horsham RH12 36 D6
Cook's Pond Rd GU30 69 A7
Cooks Hill RH12 33 A8
Cooks La
Breach PO10, PO18 150 A1
Walderton PO18 130 D2
Cooks Mead RH12 16 D7
Cooks Meadow RH12 16 D7
Cooksbridge Rd BN2 188 E6
Coolham Ct RH11 17 F6
Coolham Dr BN2 188 E7
Coolham Rd RH13, RH20 100 C5
Coolhurst La RH13 37 A1
Coombe Cl
Billingshurst RH14 55 D1
Crawley RH11 5 D1
Coombe Cotts RH19 42 F6
Coombe Cres RH20 138 A7
Coombe Dr BN44 143 D2
Coombe Dro BN44 143 D2
Coombe Hill RH14 55 D1
Coombe Hill Rd RH19 22 D6
Coombe La BN18 159 B7
Coombe Lea [5] BN3 187 C6
Coombe Rd Brighton BN2 168 D1
Steyning BN44 143 C2
Coombe Rise BN14 162 A2
Coombe Road Prim Sch
BN2 168 D1
Coombe Terr BN2 168 C1
Coombelands La RH20 98 A5
Coombers RH17 41 A1
Coombers La RH16 86 B5
Coombes Ct BN15 183 F7
Coombes Rd BN15 164 B3
Coomes Way BN17 178 D4
Cooper Row RH10 18 D3
Cooper St PO19 173 A6
Coopers Cl RH15 107 B5
Coopers The RH13 56 D4
Coopers Way BN5 123 F4
Coopers Wood RH17 39 C3
Coos La RH17 61 A6
Cootes Ave RH12 36 A3
Cootes Cotts RH20 116 B2
Cootes La PO22 196 F5
Cootham Brow RH20 119 B1
Cootham Gn RH20 119 B2
Copeland Rd PO22 196 B4
Copestake Dr RH15 107 D3
Copnall Way RH12 36 C2
Copper Beech Dr PO20 154 C1
Copper Beeches BN1 167 E1
Copper Cl RH15 106 C4
Copper Hall Cl [4] BN16 199 E6
Copperfield Pl RH12 36 B4
Copperfields RH13 59 B8
Copperfields Manor RH13 59 B8
Coppets Wood [8] BN16 199 B4
Coppice La PO20 206 D8
Coppice Rd RH12 37 A5
Coppice The
Crawley Down RH10 21 B8
Rustington BN16 199 D6
Scaynes Hill RH17 86 F3
Coppice Way RH16 85 D3
Coppice Wlk RH10 19 A7
Coppins Ct PO22 196 D5
Copsale Rd RH13 80 D6
Copse Cl
Crawley Down RH10 21 B8
East Grinstead RH19 10 A3
East Liss GU33 45 C4
Horsham RH12 36 F6
Copse Cres RH11 18 C7
Copse Hill BN1 167 D5
Copse La Horley RH6 2 C3
Walberton BN18 156 D2
Copse Rd GU27 26 D5
Copse The
Chichester PO19 153 B2
Haywards Heath RH16 86 B5
Southwater RH13 57 F2
Copse View BN16 199 B3
Copthorne Bank RH10, RH6 7 C4
Copthorne CE Jun Sch
RH10 7 B3
Copthorne Cl BN13 182 A8
Copthorne Common Rd
RH10 7 C3
Copthorne Ct [2] BN3 187 C6
Copthorne Fairway
Inf Sch RH10 7 B3
Copthorne Hill BN13 181 F7
Copthorne Rd
Copthorne RH10 6 F1
Felbridge RH10, RH19 8 D4
Copthorne Sch Trust Ltd
RH10 7 E3
Copthorne Way
Bognor Regis PO21 194 D4
Copthorne RH10 6 F2
Copyhold Hill GU27 49 C8
Copyhold La Cuckfield RH17 85 A4
Haywards Heath RH16 63 E2
Copyhold Rd RH19 22 D8
Copythorne Ho RH16 85 E6
Coral Cl PO20 206 B8
Coral La PO20 206 B8
Corbishley Gn PO22 195 C6
Corbishley Rd PO22 195 C6
Corby Cl RH11 17 E3
Corbyn Cres BN43 185 A7
Cordal Cl BN16 199 B4
Corfe Cl Southwater RH13 58 A1
Worthing BN13 181 B5
Cormorant Way PO20 202 A6
Corner Garth BN12 200 F5
Cornfield Cl BN17 178 E3
Cornfield Sch BN17 178 E3
Cornfields The PO20 175 D7
Cornflower Cl PO19 173 C8
Cornflower Way RH13 58 A3
Cornford Cl
Burgess Hill RH15 106 E5
Portslade-by-Sea BN41 166 B2
Cornwall Ct [2] BN3 187 C7
Cornwall Gdns
Brighton BN1 167 E2
[6] East Grinstead RH19 22 F8
Littlehampton BN17 198 D6
Cornwall Ho BN1 167 E2
Cornwall Rd BN17 198 D6
Coronation Bldgs BN11 183 A3
Coronation
Homelets BN11 183 B3
Coronation Rd
East Grinstead RH19 22 E7
South Hayling PO11 189 A1
Coronation St [7] BN2 188 C7
Coronet Cl RH10 19 E7
Coronet The RH6 2 C1
Corsletts Ave RH12 35 D3
Cortis Ave BN14 182 C5
Corunna Dr RH13 36 F2
Corvill Ct BN11 182 B2
Cory Cl PO19 173 A5
Costells Edge RH17 86 F3
Cot La PO18 170 D6
Cote St BN13 161 C1
Cotland Rd PO20 206 F6
Cotsford RH11 39 B7
Cotswold Cl Crawley RH11 18 B6
Worthing BN13 181 E8
Cotswold Ct RH13 36 E2
Cotswold Pl [7] BN2 188 F5
Cotswold Rd BN13 181 E7
Cotswold Way BN16 200 A6
Cotswolds The BN42 185 E7
Cottage Cl
Bognor Regis PO21 194 C2
Horsham RH12 37 B6
Cottage Homes BN6 127 E6
Cottage Pl RH10 7 E3
Cottenham Rd BN11 182 F3
Cottesmore Sch RH11 39 A8
Cottesmore St Mary's
RC Prim Sch BN3 187 D8
Cottingham Ave RH12 36 D7
Cotton Dr PO10 149 A3
Cotton Wlk RH11 18 A1
Cottrells The BN16 179 F5
Coulstock Rd RH15 106 C3
Council Cotts
Balcombe RH17 41 A1
Charlwood RH6 4 C6
Clapham BN13 160 E1
Crosspost RH17 83 B1
High Cross BN6 125 A7
Loxwood RH14 32 A2
Plaistow RH14 30 D3
Sayers Common BN6 105 E3
Southwater RH13 79 F7
Sutton RH20 115 F3
Twineham Green RH17 105 B6
Warningcamp BN18 158 F2
Wepham BN18 159 A5
Countisbury Cl PO21 194 F3
Countland Ct [17] PO21 195 B2
Countryman La RH13 101 B7
County Mall RH10 18 E5
County Oak Ave BN1 168 B6
County Oak La RH11 5 D3
County Oak Ret Pk RH11 5 D2
County Oak Way RH11 5 D2
Courcels BN2 188 E3
Court Barn La PO20 191 E6
Court Cl Brighton BN1 167 E7
East Grinstead RH19 9 F1
Liphook GU30 25 B3
Court Cres RH19 9 F1
Court Est The [8] BN11 183 B3
Court Farm Rd BN3 167 A2
Court Lodge Inf Sch RH6 1 F3
Court Lodge Rd RH6 1 F3
Court Meadow Sch RH17 85 A8
Court The PO21 194 A1
Courtenay Terr [7] BN3 187 B5
Courtfield Ho [4] PO21 195 B3
Courtfields BN15 183 D5
Courtlands
[13] Brighton BN2 207 C3
Haywards Heath RH16 85 E3
Courtlands Cl BN12 181 E1
Courtlands Way
Bognor Regis PO22 196 C6
Worthing BN11, BN12 181 F1
Courtmead Rd RH17 84 F6
Courtney Gate BN3 187 B5
Courtney King Ho [1]
BN2 188 D4
Courts Hill Rd GU27 27 B6
Courts Mount Rd GU27 27 B6
Courtup Hill RH13 80 E6
Courtwick La BN17 178 C4
Courtwick Rd BN17 178 C3
Courtyard La PO18 134 C7
Courtyard The
Bognor Regis PO21 194 F2
Chichester PO19 172 F4
[1] Crawley RH10 18 D5
Crawley RH13 37 E4
East Grinstead RH19 10 B1
Haywards Heath RH16 64 C3
[8] Hove BN3 187 D6
Worthing BN11 182 B3
Worthing, Salvington BN14 182 A6
Cousins Way RH20 98 C3
Cove Rd BN16 199 B4
Coventry Cl PO21 194 D4
Coventry St BN1 187 E8
Coverdale Ct RH19 9 C3
Covert Cl RH10 18 E7
Covert Mead
Ashington RH20 120 F5
Handcross RH17 61 B7
Covey The RH10 19 E8
Covington Rd PO10 149 D5
Cow La Sidlesham PO20 203 D7
South Harting GU31 89 C4
Cowdens Cl BN3 166 D4
Cowdown La PO18 108 F4
Cowdray GU29 93 A8
Cowdray Cl Crawley RH10 19 C5
Rustington BN16 179 B3
Worthing BN12 181 D1
Cowdray Ct [1] Hove BN3 187 D7
Midhurst GU29 92 F8
Cowdray Dr
Rustington BN16 179 B3
Worthing BN12 181 D1
Cowdray Rd GU29 71 A2
Cowfold Cl RH11 17 F3
Cowfold Rd Brighton BN2 188 E5
Cowfold RH13 80 D2
Crosspost RH13, RH17 82 C2
Cowfold St Peter's CE Sch
RH13 81 E2
Cowley Dr [1] BN15 183 F5
Cowper Rd BN11 182 B2
Cowper St BN3 187 A7
Cowslip Cl RH13 58 A2
Cox Gr RH15 106 E5
Cox Green Rd RH12 12 C2
Cox Ho RH12 36 B2
Coxcomb Wlk RH11 18 A4
Coxes Rd PO20 206 D6
Coxham La BN44 143 C4
Coxswain Way PO20 206 E5
Crabbet Rd RH10 19 B7
Crabden La PO8 128 A8
Crablands PO20 206 D7
Crablands Cl PO20 206 C7
Crabtree Ave BN1 168 B5
Crabtree Gate RH13 81 F5
Crabtree La BN15 183 E6
Crabtree Lodge [2] BN15 183 D6
Crabtree Rd RH11 18 C7
Cradock Pl BN13 181 E8
Craggits La BN5 123 E5
Craigans RH11 18 A5
Craignair Ave BN1 167 F7
Craigweil La PO21 194 E2
Craigwell La PO21 194 E2
Craigwell Manor PO21 194 D1
Cranborne Wlk RH10 18 F4
Cranbourne Cl RH6 2 B5
Cranbourne St BN1 207 A2
Cranbrook [14] BN2 207 C3
Crane St PO19 173 A6
Cranford Gdns PO21 195 C4
Cranham Ave RH14 77 C6
Cranleigh Ct [9] BN11 182 C2
Cranleigh Rd BN14 182 C5
Cranley Ct [2] BN3 186 D7
Cranmer Ave BN3 166 F1
Cranmer Rd BN13 182 A3
Cranmer Wlk RH10 19 C5
Cranston Rd RH19 9 F2
Cranworth Rd BN11 182 F3
Craven Rd Brighton BN2 188 D6
Crawley RH10 19 B5
Crawford Gdns RH13 36 E4
Crawfurd Way RH19 9 F3
Crawley Ave
Crawley, Ifield RH10, RH11 18 A6
Crawley, Three Bridges RH10 6 C1
Crawley Bsns Quarter RH10 5 E2
Crawley Coll RH10 18 E6
Crawley Coll (West Green
Annexe) RH11 18 C7
Crawley Coll
Three Bridges Ctr RH10 19 A7
Crawley Down
CE Jun Sch RH10 21 B8
Crawley Down Rd RH19 8 F4
Crawley Hospl RH11 18 C6
Crawley La Balcombe RH17 40 E4
Crawley RH10 19 C7
Crawley Mus Ctr RH11 18 C5
Crawley Rd Brighton BN1 168 D6
Crawley RH12 17 B1

Crawley Rd *continued*
Horsham RH12 .37 B5
Crawley Sta RH10 .18 E5
Crawters Cl RH10 .18 F7
Cray La RH20 .98 D5
Cray's La RH20 .120 C8
Crayford Rd BN2 .168 D1
Creasys Dr RH11 .18 B1
Crede Cl PO18 .171 C5
Crede La PO18 .171 C5
Creek End Emsworth PO10 169 B7
Fishbourne PO19 .172 B6
Crescent Cl RH15 .107 B3
Crescent Ct 3 BN11 .183 B3
Crescent Mans BN2 .207 C5
Crescent Pl BN2 .188 C4
Crescent Rd
Bognor Regis PO21 .195 C3
Brighton BN2 .188 B8
Burgess Hill RH15 .107 A3
East Grinstead RH19 .9 D1
Worthing BN11 .182 C2
Crescent Rise RH20 .120 A3
Crescent The Bognor Regis, Felpham PO22 .196 A4
Bognor Regis, Pagham PO21 .205 A8
Brighton BN2 .168 E2
Cootham RH20 .119 A2
East Wittering PO20 .201 E7
Felcourt RH19 .9 C8
Horley RH6 .6 B8
Horsham RH12 .36 A2
Keymer BN6 .127 B3
Lancing BN15 .183 E5
Littlehampton BN17 .199 A4
Southbourne PO10 .169 F8
Southwick BN42 .185 F8
Steyning BN44 .143 D2
West Kingston BN16 .200 A4
Crescent Way
Burgess Hill RH15 .107 A3
Horley RH6 .2 A1
Crescenta Wlk PO21 .195 A3
Crespin Way BN1 .168 C2
Cressey Way PO19 .153 A1
Crest Way BN41 .166 B3
Crestway Par BN1 .168 C2
Crestway The BN1 .168 C2
Crewdson Rd RH6 .2 B3
Cricket Ct RH19 .9 E3
Cricket Field Rd RH12 .36 B1
Cricketers Cl RH20 .121 A4
Cricketers Par BN14 .182 D6
Crimbourne La RH14 .75 D3
Cripland Cl RH16 .86 B6
Cripplecrutch Hill GU8, GU27 .28 F5
Cripplegate La RH13 .80 A8
Cripps Ho RH11 .18 B2
Cripps La BN44 .143 E3
Critchel's La PO20 .192 C1
Critchfield Rd PO18 .171 B5
Critchmere Dr PO20 .175 F7
Critchmere Hill GU27 .26 E7
Critchmere La GU27 .26 E6
Critchmere Vale GU27 .26 E6
Crockford Rd PO10 .149 D4
Crockham Cl RH11 .18 C4
Crockhurst RH13 .58 A2
Crockhurst Hill BN13 .181 F8
Croft Ave BN42 .185 F7
Croft Dr BN41 .166 A3
Croft La BN5 .123 E4
Croft Mead PO19 .153 A2
Croft Rd Brighton BN1 .167 D4
Selsey PO20 .206 D7
Croft The
Bognor Regis PO21 .194 F5
Cocking GU29 .112 D8
Crawley RH11 .18 A6
East Preston BN16 .200 A5
Hassocks BN6 .126 F5
Lodsworth GU28 .72 B3
Southwick BN42 .185 E8
Yapton BN18 .176 F4
Croft Villas BN5 .123 E5
Croft Way
Bognor Regis PO22 .196 C6
Horsham RH12 .36 A3
Selsey PO20 .206 D7
Crofters Wood BN44 .143 F2
Cromleigh Way BN42 .165 E2
Crompton Fields RH10 .5 E1
Crompton Way RH10 .5 E1
Cromwell Ct 3 BN3 .187 D7
Cromwell Pl 1 RH19 .22 F7
Cromwell Rd
Burgess Hill RH15 .106 F3
Hove BN3 .187 C7
Cromwell St BN2 .188 C7
Crooked La PO20 .191 E4
Crookthorn La BN17 .197 E8
Crosbie Cl PO19 .172 F3
Crosby Cl BN13 .181 D6
Croshaw Cl BN15 .183 D5
Cross Colwood La RH17 .82 F5
Cross Gates BN18 .139 A7
Cross Keys RH10 .18 D6
Cross La Barns Green RH13 .57 A1
Burstow RH6 .7 C8
Findon BN14 .161 E5
Cross Oak La RH1, RH6 .2 C7
Cross Rd Rustington BN16 .199 E5
Shoreham-by-Sea BN42 .185 D8
Cross St Brighton BN1 .207 B4
14 Hove BN1, BN3 .187 D5
Worthing BN11 .182 C3
Crossbush La BN18 .158 E1
Crossbush Rd
Bognor Regis PO22 .196 C4
Brighton BN2 .188 E6
Crossfield GU27 .49 B5
Crossley-Hughes Ho RH12 .36 C1
Crossman Ct RH11 .18 B1
Crosspath RH10 .18 E7
Crosspost RH17 .83 B1
Crosspost Ind Pk RH17 .83 B1
Crossroad Cl BN42 .185 D8
Crossway RH6 .5 F8
Crossway The
Brighton BN1 .168 B2
Portslade-by-Sea BN41 .166 A2
Crossways Bolney RH17 .83 D2
Crawley RH10 .19 A7
Easebourne GU29 .71 A2
East Preston BN16 .180 B3
Middleton-on-Sea PO22 .196 F5
Navant Hill GU28 .50 E4
West Chiltington Common RH20 .119 D7
Crossways Ave
East Grinstead RH19 .9 C1
Worthing BN12 .181 B4
Crossways Cl RH10 .18 F7
Crossways Cotts
Alfold Crossways GU6 .11 A3
Poynings BN45 .146 C6
Tisman's Common RH12 .32 F6
Crossways Pk RH20 .119 D7
Crossways The
Hassocks BN6 .126 C4
Littlehampton BN17 .178 C3
Crouch Cross La PO18 .154 D3
Crouch Hill BN5 .123 F7
Crouchlands Farm RH17 .84 E8
Crowberry Cl RH11 .18 A2
Crowborough Dr BN12 .181 B2
Crowhurst Cl RH10 .19 E6
Crowhurst Cres RH20 .119 C2
Crowhurst Keep RH10 .19 E6
Crowhurst Rd BN1 .168 C7
Crown Bldgs BN15 .183 C4
Crown Cl 1 BN3 .187 D6
Crown Ct 3 BN16 .200 A4
Crown Gdns BN1 .207 A2
Crown Hill 4 BN2 .188 C6
Crown Pl 2 BN16 .200 A4
Crown Point Ho BN6 .126 F4
Crown Rd
Portslade-by-Sea BN41 .186 A8
Shoreham-by-Sea BN43 .185 B8
Crown St BN1 .207 A2
Crowsbury Cl PO10 .149 A3
Croxton La RH16 .86 B6
Croy Cl PO19 .172 E4
Crundens Cnr 5 BN16 .199 E6
Crutchfield La RH6 .1 B5
Crypt La GU29 .112 C7
Cuckfield Cl RH11 .17 F4
Cuckfield Cres BN13 .181 F6
Cuckfield Holy Trinity CE Prim Sch RH17 .84 F6
Cuckfield La RH17 .61 B1
Cuckfield Mus RH17 .84 E6
Cuckfield Rd
Burgess Hill RH15 .106 E7
Goddards' Green BN6,RH17 106 A4
Slough Green RH17 .62 A2
Cuckmere Cres RH11 .17 F5
Cuckmere Way BN1 .168 C5
Cudlow Ave BN16 .199 C5
Cudlow Gdn
Littlehampton BN16 .199 C4
Littlehampton BN16 .199 C5
Cudworth La RH5 .3 E8
Cuffs Hill RH10 .19 E2
Culimore Cl PO20 .201 E7
Culimore Rd PO20 .201 E7
Culpepper RH15 .106 E4
Culpepper Cl BN2 .168 D2
Culross Ave RH16 .85 D5
Culver Ct BN15 .183 E6
Culver Rd
Bognor Regis PO22 .196 A4
Lancing BN15 .183 E6
Culvers GU31 .89 D3
Cumberland Ave
New Brighton PO10 .149 B4
Worthing BN12 .181 D5
Cumberland Cl BN16 .180 A5
Cumberland Cres BN16 .179 F5
Cumberland Ct BN11 .181 F1
Cumberland Dr BN1 .167 E2
Cumberland Lodge 3 BN1 .167 E2
Cumberland Rd
Angmering BN16 .180 A6
Brighton BN1 .167 E2
Cumbernauld Wlk RH11 .17 E2
Cumbrian Cl BN13 .181 E7
Cumnor House Sch RH17 .66 B5
Cunliffe Cl PO20 .190 C2
Cunningham Gdns PO22 .196 C5
Curbey Cl RH20 .99 D1
Curlescroft PO21 .194 F2
Curlew Cl PO10 .169 A7
Curlews The BN43 .185 A8
Curteys Wlk RH11 .18 A3
Curvins Way BN15 .183 F7
Curwen Pl BN1 .167 E3
Curzon Ave RH12 .36 B3
Curzon Cl BN13 .181 F6
Cutfield Cl PO19 .172 F3
Cuthbert Rd BN2 .188 C5
Cuttinglye La RH10 .8 A1
Cuttinglye Rd RH10 .8 C2
Cygnet Wlk PO22 .195 B6
Cygnets The BN43 .184 F8
Cylinders The GU27 .49 B5
Cymens Ora PO20 .203 D8
Cypress Ave BN13 .181 C5
Cypress Cl 12 BN43 .164 F1
Cypress Way PO21 .194 D1
Cyprus Mews RH15 .107 B3
Cyprus Rd RH15 .107 A3
Cyril Richings Bsns Cntr BN43 .185 B7

D

D'aubigny Rd BN2 .188 B8
Dacre Gdns BN44 .164 B7
Dagbrook La BN5 .123 E3
Dagmar St BN11 .182 E3
Dairy Farm BN12 .181 A3
Dairy La Maudlin PO18 .153 F1
Walberton BN18 .156 D1
Dairyfields RH11 .18 A5
Daisycroft The BN5 .123 F4
Dakin Cl RH10 .19 C2
Dakins The RH19 .22 E8
Dale Ave Brighton BN1 .167 F5
Keymer BN6 .127 A3
Dale Cl RH12 .36 F5
Dale Copse GU27 .49 B6
Dale Cres BN1 .167 F6
Dale Ct PO21 .195 B3
Dale Dr BN1 .168 A6
Dale Hill BN45 .147 A6
Dale Rd Forest Row RH18 .23 F1
Worthing BN11 .183 B4
Dale View Camelsdale GU27 .26 F5
Hove BN3 .166 D2
Dale View Gdns BN3 .166 D2
Dalewood Gdns
Burgess Hill RH15 .107 C2
Crawley RH10 .18 F8
Dallaway Gdns RH19 .9 E1
Dallaway Rd PO19 .173 B4
Dallington Rd BN3 .186 F8
Dalloway Rd BN18 .157 F1
Dalton Cl RH11 .18 B1
Daltons Pl BN18 .158 A2
Dame School Ct PO18 .153 A5
Damer's Bridge GU28 .95 F8
Damian Way BN6 .127 B4
Dampier Wlk RH11 .18 B1
Danbury Ct PO10 .149 C2
Danby Ct RH6 .2 A5
Danefield Rd PO20 .206 C6
Danehill CE Prim Sch RH17 .66 B4
Danehill La RH17 .65 E5
Danehill Rd BN2 .188 F5
Danehurst 6 PO21 .195 B3
Danehurst Cres RH13 .36 F2
Daniel Cl BN15 .183 F7
Dankton Gdns BN15 .183 B7
Dankton La BN15 .183 B7
Danley La GU27 .26 A3
Danny Sheldon Ho 14 BN2 .188 C4
Danworth La BN6 .106 B2
Dapper's La BN16 .180 A7
Darcey Dr BN1 .168 A6
Darenth Way RH6 .1 F6
Dark La PO21 .194 F1
Darleydale RH11 .18 C3
Dart Cl BN13 .181 D8
Dart Ct RH19 .10 A3
Dartmouth Cl BN2 .168 F1
Dartmouth Cres BN2 .168 F1
Darwin Cl RH12 .36 F4
Daux Ave RH14 .77 D6
Daux Hill RH12 .36 B6
Daux Rd RH14 .77 D7
Daux Way RH14 .77 D6
Dauxwood Cl RH14 .77 D6
Davenport Ct 3 BN11 .181 F2
Davenport Rd PO22 .196 B4
Davey Dr BN1 .168 B1
Davids Cl PO21 .194 F5
Davies Ct 11 BN11 .182 A1
Davigdor Cty Inf Sch BN3 .187 D6
Davigdor Rd BN3 .187 E7
Davis Cl RH11 .18 A1
Davison CE Girls' High Sch BN11 .182 F4
Davits Dr BN17 .199 A6
Davys Ct PO18 .151 A5
Dawes Ave BN11 .182 F3
Dawes Cl BN11 .182 F3
Dawlish Cl BN2 .168 F1
Dawn Cl BN44 .144 B1
Dawn Cres BN44 .144 A1
Dawson Ct 8 BN11 .182 C3
Dawson Terr BN2 .188 C6
Dawtrey Cl BN16 .199 E6
Dawtrey Rd GU28 .95 F7
Daynes Way RH15 .106 E1
Days La PO18 .155 F3
De Braose Way BN44 .143 E2
De Courcel Rd BN2 .188 E3
De La Warr Rd RH19 .9 F1
De Montfort Rd BN2 .188 C7
Deacon Trad Est BN14 .182 F5
Deacon Way BN14 .182 F5
Deacons Dr BN41 .166 C2
Deacons Way BN44 .144 B2
Deak's La RH17 .84 B6
Dean Cl
Littlehampton BN17 .178 C3
Portslade-by-Sea BN41 .166 C2
Dean Gdns BN41 .166 C2
Dean La
Finchdean PO8, PO9 .128 F5
Upperton GU28 .73 A1
Dean St BN1 .187 E5
Dean Way RH20 .119 C2
Deane Ct 7 PO21 .195 C4
Deanery Farm La PO19 .172 F6
Deanland Rd RH17 .41 A1
Deans Yd BN18 .156 A3
Deanway BN3 .167 B3
Decoy Dr BN16 .179 F7
Decoy Rd BN14 .182 F5
Dedisham Cl RH10 .19 A5
Deepdale 1 RH6 .2 B2
Deepdene GU27 .26 E6
Deepdene Cl PO22 .197 A5
Deepdene Sch BN3 .186 D7
Deepfields RH6 .1 F5
Deer Park Cl PO20 .206 B8
Deer Park Dr PO20 .206 B8
Deer Park La PO20 .206 B8
Deer Pk BN5 .123 E6
Deerswood Cl
Crawley RH11 .18 B7
Worthing BN13 .181 B5
Deerswood Ct RH11 .18 A7
Deerswood Lower Sch RH11 .18 A8
Deerswood Rd RH11 .18 B7
Deerswood Upper Sch RH11 .18 A8
Deeside Ave PO19 .172 B7
Deeside The BN1 .168 A7
Defiance Pl PO22 .196 C4
Delancey Ct RH12 .36 C4
Delfont Cl RH10 .19 C4
Delfryn BN41 .165 F3
Delius Gdns RH13 .37 B4
Dell Cl GU27 .27 A7
Dell Dr BN16 .179 F4
Dell La RH14 .77 D8
Dell Quay Rd PO20 .172 B2
Dell The
Bognor Regis PO22 .195 A6
East Grinstead RH19 .10 B1
Haywards Heath RH16 .85 C5
Horley RH6 .2 B4
Wrays RH6 .1 C5
Delling Cl PO18 .171 B6
Delling La PO18 .171 C6
Dellney Ave RH16 .85 F3
Delta Bglws RH6 .2 A1
Delta Dr RH6 .2 A1
Delta Ho RH6 .2 A1
Dempsey Rd 3 PO19 .153 A2
Den Ave PO21 .195 D3
Denbigh Rd GU27 .27 D5
Denchers Plat RH11 .5 D1
Dene Cl Haslemere GU27 .27 C6
Horley RH6 .1 E5
Dene Ct BN11 .182 B2
Dene The Hove BN3 .166 D3
Southwater RH13 .58 A2
Dene Tye RH10 .19 D7
Dene Vale BN1 .167 D5
Denecroft BN1 .167 D5
Deneside BN1 .167 D5
Deneway The
Brighton BN1 .167 D4
Lancing BN15 .183 C6
Denham Cl PO22 .196 E5
Denham Ct RH15 .106 D3
Denham Rd RH15 .106 D3
Denison Ct 3 PO19 .172 F7
Denman's Cl RH16 .86 A8
Denman's La RH16 .86 A7
Denmans RH10 .19 D7
Denmans Gardens BN18, .155 F3
Denmans La BN18,PO20 .155 E2
Denmark Rd BN41 .186 C7
Denmark Terr BN1 .187 E6
Denmark Villas BN3 .187 B7
Denne Par RH12 .36 C1
Denne Pl RH12 .36 C1
Denne Rd Crawley RH11 .18 D5
Horsham RH12 .36 C1
Dennis Ct RH20 .98 C2
Dennis Hobden Cl BN2 .168 E1
Dennis Way GU33 .45 C3
Denny's Cl PO20 .206 E7
Denshare Rd PO20 .206 E8
Denshire Dr RH20 .119 E2
Densihale PO21 .195 A3
Denton Cl BN12 .181 B3
Denton Dr BN1 .168 A6
Departures Rd RH6 .5 F8
Depot Rd Crawley RH11 .5 D1
Horsham RH13 .36 E2
Derby Ct 7 BN3 .187 E7
Derby Pl 6 BN2 .207 C2
Derby Rd GU27 .27 B7
Derek Ave BN3 .186 D6
Derek Ho BN3 .186 F6
Derek Rd BN15 .183 E8
Dervia Ho BN3 .187 C7
Derwent Cl Crawley RH11 .17 F5
Horsham RH12 .37 B6
Lancing BN15 .183 C5
Littlehampton BN17 .179 A3
Tangmere PO20 .154 D2
Derwent Ct BN1 .207 A3
Derwent Dr BN12, BN13 .181 D5
Derwent Gr PO22 .196 B6
Desmond Anderson Sch RH10 .18 E2
Desmond Way BN2 .188 F6
Detling Rd RH11 .18 C1
Devil's Dyke BN1, BN45 .146 C3
Devil's Dyke Rd BN1,BN3 .166 E7
Devils La GU30 .25 E3
Devon Ct 3 BN17 .198 D5
Devon Villas RH16 .85 F4
Devonian Ct BN2 .207 C4
Devonport Pl BN11 .183 A3
Devonport Rd BN11 .183 A2
Devonshire Ct 1 BN3 .187 C7
Devonshire Lodge 12 BN11 .181 F2
Devonshire Pl
3 Bognor Regis PO21 .195 C3
Brighton BN2 .207 C2
Devonshire Rd
Bognor Regis PO21 .195 C3
Horsham RH13 .36 D2
Dewar Cl RH11 .17 E5
Dewe Rd BN2 .168 C1
Dexter Dr RH19 .22 E8
Dial Cl PO22 .176 C5
Diamond Cotts RH17 .83 B1
Diana Cl PO10 .149 A4
Dickens Cl RH19 .9 C1
Dickens Rd RH10 .18 E3
Dickins Way RH13 .58 F8
Dickinson Pl PO22 .195 D6
Diggers The BN1 .168 B3
Dinapore Ho 11 BN2 .207 C3
Dingemans BN44 .143 D5
Dingle Cl RH11 .18 B7
Dingle The RH11 .18 B6
Dingley Rd BN16 .199 C5
Dinsdale Gdns BN16 .199 C6
Dione Wlk RH11 .17 E4
Dirty La RH19 .23 E7
Discovery Pk RH10 .6 A2
Ditcham Park Sch GU31 .108 B8
Ditchfield Cl PO22 .196 D6
Ditchling Beacon Nature Reserve BN6 .148 D7
Ditchling Bostall BN6 .148 D7
Ditchling Cl BN12 .181 B4
Ditchling Common Ctry Pk BN6 .107 F1
Ditchling Cres BN1 .168 C5
Ditchling Ct 4 BN1 .188 B8
Ditchling Gdns BN1 .168 B1
Ditchling Hill RH11 .18 C4
Ditchling Mus BN6 .127 C3
Ditchling Rd
Brighton BN1, BN2 .168 B4
Westmeston BN1,BN6 .148 D4
Ditchling Rise BN1 .188 A8
Ditchling St Margarets Prim Sch BN6 .127 D3
Dobbins Pl RH11 .17 E5
Dobson Rd RH11 .5 D1
Dodsley Gr GU29 .70 F2
Dodsley La GU29 .71 A2
Dog Kennels GU28 .115 B3
Dog La BN44 .143 D3
Dolby Terr RH6 .4 E6
Doll Mus The GU28 .95 F7
Dollis Cl RH10 .19 C5
Dolphin Cl
Fishbourne PO19 .172 B6
Haslemere GU27 .26 E6
Dolphin Ct
3 Bognor Regis PO21 .195 C2
5 Hove BN3 .187 A6
Rustington BN16 .199 D4
Worthing BN13 .182 A3
Dolphin Ind Est BN43 .185 B7
Dolphin L Ctr The RH16 .85 D6
Dolphin Lodge 12 BN11 .182 A1
Dolphin Mews
Chichester PO19 .172 D6
Shoreham-by-Sea BN43 .185 A7
Dolphin Rd
Haywards Heath RH16 .85 D4
Shoreham-by-Sea BN43 .185 B7
Dolphin Way
Littlehampton BN16 .199 D4
Shoreham-by-Sea BN43 .185 B7
Domehouse Cl PO20 .206 E5
Dominion Bldgs BN14 .182 F4
Dominion Cl BN14 .182 E5
Dominion Rd BN14 .182 F5
Dominion Way
Rustington BN16 .179 C3
Worthing BN14 .182 F5
Dominion Way W BN14 .182 F5
Donald Hall Rd BN2 .188 D5
Donaldson Cl PO20 .206 C8
Doncaster Wlk RH10 .19 A4
Donegal Rd PO19 .152 F1
Donkey La RH6 .6 D7
Donkey Mews 4 BN3 .187 D5
Donne Cl RH10 .19 B8
Donnington Ct 2 RH11 .17 F3
Donnington Pk PO20 .172 D3
Donnington Pl 2 BN16 .199 C6
Doomsday Gdn RH13 .37 A1
Doomsday La RH13 .59 A8
Doone End 6 BN12 .200 F4
Dorchester Ct 2 BN1 .187 E5
Dorchester Gdns BN11 .182 A2
Dorking Rd RH12, RH5 .15 B4
Dorman's Cl RH7 .10 A8
Dormans RH11 .18 A5
Dormans Gdns RH19 .9 E6

Dormans High St RH7 . . . .10 A8
Dormans Park Rd
Dormans Park RH19 . . . . .9 E6
East Grinstead RH19 . . . . .9 D3
Dormans Sta RH7 . . . . .9 F8
Dormans Station Rd RH7 . . .9 F7
Dormansland Prim Sch
RH7 .10 A8
Dorothy Rd BN3 . . . . .186 D8
Dorothy Stringer Sch
BN1 . . . . .167 F3
Dorset Ave RH19 . . . . .9 C3
Dorset Cl BN17 . . . . .198 E5
Dorset Ct 6 Horsham RH13 36 D2
Hove BN3 . . . . .186 F6
Dorset Gdns Brighton BN2 207 C2
East Grinstead RH19 . . . . .9 C3
Dorset Ho RH13 . . . . .78 D2
Dorset House Sch RH20 .138 B7
Dorset Mews BN2 . . . . . . .207 B2
Dorset Pl Brighton BN2 . . .207 C2
5 Worthing BN14 . . . . .182 A5
Dorset Rd PO21 . . . . .195 C5
Dorset St BN2 . . . . .207 B2
Dorsten Sq RH11 . . . . .17 F2
Doubledays RH15 . . . . . . .107 B2
Douglas Ave BN11 . . . . . . .181 F2
Douglas Cl
4 Bognor Regis PO22 . . . . .196 F5
Burndell BN18 . . . . .177 B2
Worthing BN11 . . . . .181 F2
Douglas Martin Rd PO19 .173 B7
Dove Cl RH11 . . . . .18 D8
Dove Ct PO22 . . . . .195 B5
Dovecote Mews BN15 . . .183 C8
Dovedale Cres RH11 . . . . . .18 B4
Doveleys Ct BN43 . . . . . . .184 F6
Dover Cl RH13 . . . . .57 F2
Dover Rd Brighton BN1 . . .168 A2
Worthing BN11 . . . . .182 A1
Dovercourt PO22 . . . . .195 A6
Dower Wlk RH11 . . . . .18 A5
Dowlands La RH10, RH6 . . . .7 D7
Down Cl GU29 . . . . .113 C8
Down Cotts PO18 . . . . . . .130 A8
Down St PO18 . . . . .151 B3
Down Terr BN2 . . . . .188 C6
Down The BN3 . . . . .166 D4
Down View Rd BN11 . . . . .182 A2
Downash Cl BN2 . . . . .188 E6
Downe Cl RH6 . . . . .1 E5
Downe Wlk BN13 . . . . . . .181 D5
Downes Ct 9 BN43 . . . . . .185 C8
Downing Cl PO21 . . . . . . .194 E4
Downland Ave BN42 . . . . .165 E1
Downland Cl Findon BN14 161 E6
Southwick BN42 . . . . .165 D1
Upper Beeding BN44 . . . . . .144 B2
Downland Cres BN3 . . . . .166 F3
Downland Ct
Chichester PO19 . . . . .172 F8
Crawley RH11 . . . . .18 C4
Portslade-by-Sea BN41 . . . .166 A2
Downland Dr Crawley RH11 18 C3
Hove BN3 . . . . .166 F3
Downland Pl RH11 . . . . . . .18 C4
Downland Rd BN44 . . . . . .144 B2
Downlands Cootham RH20 119 B1
Partridge Green RH13 . . . . .102 F3
Pulborough RH20 . . . . .98 D2
Worthing BN13 . . . . .161 E2
Downlands Ave BN14 . . . .182 D6
Downlands Bsns Pk
BN14 . . . . .182 E8
Downlands Cl
Bognor Regis PO21 . . . . . . .194 A2
Lancing BN15 . . . . .183 C7
Downlands Com Sch
BN6 . . . . .126 F3
Downlands Gdns BN14 . .182 E7
Downlands Par BN14 . . . .182 E7
Downlands Ret Ctr BN14 182 E7
Downs Cl BN15 . . . . .184 B6
Downs Inf Sch BN1 . . . . . .188 B8
Downs Jun Sch BN1 . . . . . .168 A1
Downs Mead BN15 . . . . . .183 C8
Downs Park Sch BN41 . . .166 B2
Downs Rd
Burgess Hill RH15 . . . . .106 E4
West Stoke PO18 . . . . .151 D6
Downs View Rd BN6 . . . . .126 F3
Downs Way BN16 . . . . . . .179 F3
Downsbrook Mid Sch
BN14 . . . . .182 E5
Downsbrook Trad Est
BN14 . . . . .182 E6
Downscroft
Burgess Hill RH15 . . . . .107 D6
Upper Beeding BN44 . . . . . .144 B1
Downside Brighton BN1 . . .167 D5
Hove BN3 . . . . .167 B3
Shoreham-by-Sea BN43 . . .165 A1
Downside Ave BN14 . . . . .161 F3
Downside Cl
Shoreham-by-Sea BN43 . . . .164 F1
Worthing BN14 . . . . .161 F3
Downside Ct 6 BN16 . . . .199 B3
Downsman Ct RH10 . . . . . . .18 D3
Downsview Brighton BN1 .167 E1
Hove BN3 . . . . .166 D3
Hurstpierpoint BN6 . . . . . . .126 A5
Small Dole BN5 . . . . .144 F7
Downsview Ave RH20 . . . .119 E2
Downsview Cotts RH14 . . .77 C8
Downsview Dr GU29 . . . . . .92 E5
Downsview Rd
Horsham RH12 . . . . .37 B6
Kingston Gorse BN16 . . . . .200 D4
Downsview Rd *continued*
Portslade-by-Sea BN41 . . . .166 A2
Downsview Terr BN5 . . . . .123 D5
Downsway
Shoreham-by-Sea BN43 . . . .164 F1
Southwick BN42 . . . . .165 F1
Downview Ave BN12 . . . . .180 E3
Downview Cl
Burndell BN18 . . . . .177 A3
East Wittering PO20 . . . . . .202 A6
Mid Lavant PO18 . . . . .152 E6
Downview Ct 7 BN11 . . . .182 A1
Downview Prim Sch
PO22 . . . . .195 F6
Downview Rd
Bognor Regis PO22 . . . . . . .196 A5
Burndell BN18 . . . . .177 A3
Ferring BN12 . . . . .180 E3
Findon BN14 . . . . .161 E7
Petworth GU28 . . . . .95 E7
West Barnham PO22 . . . . . .176 A7
Downview Way BN18 . . . .177 A3
Dragons Green Council Cotts RH13 . . . . . .79 C3
Dragons Green Rd RH13 . .79 C5
Dragons La
Dragons Green RH13 . . . . . . .79 C3
Little Parkminster RH13 . . .103 E7
Drake Ave BN12 . . . . .181 D4
Drake Cl RH12 . . . . .36 E6
Drake Gr BN18 . . . . .177 B2
Drake Pk PO22 . . . . .196 C5
Drake Rd Crawley RH10 . . . .18 E3
Horley RH6 . . . . .1 E3
Drakeleys Field GU30 . . . . .47 B2
Drakes Cl BN15 . . . . .184 B6
Draxmont Way BN1 . . . . . .167 F3
Draycliff Cl BN12 . . . . . . .200 E5
Drayman's Mews PO19 . . .173 B6
Drayton La PO20 . . . . .174 A5
Drewetts Cl BN16 . . . . . . .179 B3
Drewitts Mews PO20 . . . .174 C7
Drift La Nutbourne PO18 . .170 E8
Selsey PO20 . . . . .206 C7
Drift Rd Bognor Regis PO21 194 B2
Selsey PO20 . . . . .206 G8
Drift The PO9 . . . . .128 D1
Driftway The
Rustington BN16 . . . . .179 B3
Upper Beeding BN44 . . . . . .144 B3
Drive Lodge 10 BN3 . . . . .187 C7
Drive The
Bognor Regis PO21 . . . . . . .194 D1
Bosham PO18 . . . . .171 C4
Burgess Hill RH15 . . . . .107 B4
Chichester PO19 . . . . .153 A3
Copthorne RH10 . . . . .7 C3
East Lavington GU28 . . . . . .114 E5
Horley RH6 . . . . .2 B1
Hove BN3 . . . . .187 C7
Ifold RH14 . . . . .31 D2
Lancing BN15 . . . . .183 D4
North Lancing BN15 . . . . . .164 B1
Shoreham-by-Sea BN43 . . . .164 F1
Southbourne PO10 . . . . . . .169 F8
Southwick BN42 . . . . .165 E1
West Kingston BN16 . . . . . .200 B4
Worthing BN11 . . . . .181 F3
Driveway The BN43 . . . . . .164 F1
Droke La PO18 . . . . .134 E6
Dropping Holms BN5 . . . .123 D4
Drove Cres BN41 . . . . .166 A2
Drove La Earnley PO20 . . .202 D5
Yapton BN18 . . . . .176 D2
Drove Rd BN41 . . . . .166 A1
Drove The BN1 . . . . .167 D1
Drovers RH17 . . . . .83 C3
Drovers Cl BN41 . . . . .166 C2
Drovers Way RH15 . . . . . .107 C1
Droveway The
Haywards Heath RH16 . . . . .85 C6
Hove BN3 . . . . .167 C1
Drummond Cl RH16 . . . . . .85 D4
Drummond Ct RH16 . . . . . .85 D4
Drummond Rd
Crawley RH11 . . . . .17 E5
Worthing BN12 . . . . .181 E1
Drungewick La RH14 . . . . .32 D2
Drury Cl RH10 . . . . .19 D4
Dryad Way PO22 . . . . .196 D4
Dryad Wlk PO22 . . . . .196 D4
Dryden Way GU30 . . . . .25 A5
Drygrounds La PO22 . . . . .195 F5
Duck La Midhurst GU29 . . . .92 F7
Selsey PO20 . . . . .206 B8
Duckmead La GU33 . . . . . .45 D5
Dudeney Lodge BN1 . . . . .168 B1
Dudley Rd BN1 . . . . .168 B1
Dudley Terr GU33 . . . . .45 C5
Duffield La PO10 . . . . . . .150 A3
Duke Cl RH10 . . . . .19 C2
Duke St Brighton BN1 . . . . .207 A2
Littlehampton BN17 . . . . . .198 D5
Duke's Ct Chichester PO19 173 D5
11 Littlehampton BN17 . . . .198 D5
Duke's Dr RH5 . . . . .3 D6
Duke's Hill RH20 . . . . .120 A8
Duke's Mound BN2 . . . . . .188 D4
Duke's Rd BN18 . . . . .155 F4
Dukes Barn Ct RH16 . . . . . .86 B7
Dukes Cl BN18 . . . . .157 F2
Dukes La Brighton BN1 . . .207 A2
Steyning BN44 . . . . .143 D3
Dukes Mdw
Bognor Regis PO21 . . . . . . .194 B3
Funtington PO18 . . . . .150 F5
Dukes Rd RH16 . . . . .86 B8
Dukes Row RH20 . . . . .119 A2
Dukes Yd BN44 . . . . .143 D3
Dumbrells Court Rd BN6 127 D4
Dumbrells Ct BN6 . . . . . . .127 D4
Dumbrills Cl RH15 . . . . . .107 A5
Dumpford La GU31 . . . . . . .90 D8
Duncan Rd PO19 . . . . .172 F8
Duncton CE Fst Sch
GU28 . . . . .115 B7
Duncton Cl
Bognor Regis PO22 . . . . . . .196 B4
Crawley RH11 . . . . .18 B8
Haywards Heath RH16 . . . . .85 D4
Duncton High St GU28 . .115 B6
Duncton Ho BN6 . . . . .126 E4
Duncton Rd BN16 . . . . . . .199 C6
Dunes The PO21 . . . . .205 C8
Dunford Hollow GU29 . . . .93 A3
Dunlop Cl BN6 . . . . .105 D1
Dunning's Rd RH19 . . . . . . .22 E7
Dunnings Mill L Complex
RH19 . . . . .22 E6
Dunnock Cl PO9 . . . . .128 D1
Dunsfold Cl RH11 . . . . .18 A5
Dunsfold Rd GU8, RH14 . . .30 D4
Dunstall Ave RH15 . . . . . .106 E4
Dunstall Farm Rd RH15 . .106 F4
Dunstan Cl PO19 . . . . .153 A3
Dunster Cl BN1 . . . . .168 B1
Durban Pk PO22 . . . . .195 D5
Durban Rd PO22 . . . . .195 D6
Durfold Rd RH12 . . . . .36 D7
Durfold Wood RH14 . . . . . .30 D5
Durfold Wood Woodland Walks GU8,RH14 . . . . .30 C6
Durham Cl
Bognor Regis PO21 . . . . . . .205 A8
Crawley RH10 . . . . .18 E2
Durham Ct 4 BN3 . . . . . . .187 B6
Durham Gdns PO19 . . . . . .152 F1
Durkins Rd RH19 . . . . .9 D3
Durlston Dr PO22 . . . . . . .195 B6
Durlston Par PO22 . . . . . .195 B6
Durnford Cl PO19 . . . . . . .172 E7
Durrington Ct Hove BN1 .167 D5
Worthing BN13 . . . . .181 D7
Durrington Cty Mid Sch
BN13 . . . . .181 E7
Durrington Fst Sch BN13 181 E7
Durrington Gdns BN12 . .181 D3
Durrington High Sch
BN13 . . . . .181 E5
Durrington Hill BN13 . . . .181 D7
Durrington La BN13 . . . . .181 D6
Durrington-on-Sea Sta
BN12 . . . . .181 E3
Dutchells Copse RH12 . . . .36 E7
Duxhurst La RH2 . . . . .1 B7
Dyall Cl RH15 . . . . .106 E4
Dyers Almshouses RH10 . .18 D7
Dyers La BN18 . . . . .156 C5
Dyke Cl Hove BN3 . . . . . . .167 B4
Poynings BN45 . . . . .146 C4
Dyke Rd BN1, BN3 . . . . . . .187 E7
Dyke Road Ave BN1, BN3 .167 C3
Dyke Road Dr BN1 . . . . . .187 F8
Dyke Road Mews BN1 . . .207 A4
Dyke Road Pl BN1 . . . . . .167 C3
Dymock's The BN6 . . . . . .127 D3
Dymoke St PO10 . . . . .149 A4
Dyson Wlk RH11 . . . . .18 B1

E

Eady Cl RH13 . . . . .36 F2
Eagle Est RH14 . . . . .77 D7
Eagle Ho 16 PO21 . . . . . . .195 B2
Eagles Chase BN17 . . . . . .178 D4
Earles Mdw RH12 . . . . .37 B6
Earlswood Cl RH13 . . . . . . .37 A4
Early Commons RH10 . . . . .18 F7
Earnley Manor Cl PO20 . .202 D7
Earnley Rd PO11 . . . . .189 B2
Eartham Trail PO18 . . . . . .135 D2
Earwig La RH17 . . . . .82 E6
Easebourne CE Prim Sch
GU29 . . . . .71 B2
Easebourne La GU29 . . . . . .71 A1
Easebourne St GU28, GU29 71 D5
East Ave
Middleton-on-Sea PO22 . . . .196 F6
Worthing BN12 . . . . .181 F1
East Bank North End BN18 177 A5
Selsey PO20 . . . . .206 F7
East Bank Wlk BN17 . . . . .199 A4
East Beach Rd PO20 . . . . .206 G8
East Bracklesham Dr
PO20 . . . . .202 B5
East Brighton Coll of Media Arts (Sch) BN2 . .188 F5
East Cl PO22 . . . . .196 E5
East Court Way BN16 . . . .199 E6
East Dean PO22 . . . . .195 D5
East Dr Angmering BN16 . .179 E3
Brighton BN2 . . . . .188 C5
Middleton-on-Sea PO22 . . . .197 A5
East Field Cl PO10 . . . . . .150 A1
East Front Rd PO21 . . . . .205 A7
East Gdns BN6 . . . . .127 D3
East Grinstead Sta RH19 . . .9 D1
East Grinstead Town Mus
RH19 .9 F2
East Gun Copse Rd RH13 .57 D5
East Ham Rd BN17 . . . . . .198 D5
East Hampnett La PO18 . .154 F2
East Harting St GU31 . . . . .89 F3
East Hill RH19 . . . . .9 E6
East Hill Ct 1 BN11 . . . . .182 D2
East Hill Dr GU33 . . . . .45 C3
East Hill La RH10 . . . . .7 D5
East Lake PO21 . . . . .195 D4
East Lodge Lancing BN15 .183 E4
Rogate GU31 . . . . .68 B4
East Mascalls Rd RH16 . . .86 E6
East Mead
Bognor Regis PO21 . . . . . . .205 A8
Ferring BN12 . . . . .200 F5
East Meadway BN43 . . . . .185 A6
East Onslow Cl BN12 . . . .200 E6
East Pallant PO19 . . . . . .173 A6
East Park La RH7 . . . . .8 C8
East Pk RH10 . . . . .18 D5
East Point 6 BN43 . . . . . .185 A6
East Preston Inf Sch
BN16 . . . . .200 A6
East Preston Jun Sch
BN16 . . . . .200 A6
East Row PO19 . . . . .173 A6
East Row Mews 3 PO19 .173 A6
East St Amberley BN18 . . . .138 E7
Billingshurst RH14 . . . . .77 D8
Brighton BN1 . . . . .207 B1
Chichester PO19 . . . . .173 A6
Horsham RH12 . . . . .36 C1
Lancing BN15 . . . . .183 E4
Littlehampton BN17 . . . . . .198 E5
Petworth GU28 . . . . .95 F8
Portslade-by-Sea BN41 . . . .186 C7
Rusper RH12 . . . . .16 E7
Selsey PO20 . . . . .206 E7
Shoreham-by-Sea BN43 . . . .184 F7
Turners Hill RH10, RH19 . . . .21 C4
West Chiltington RH20 . . . . .99 E1
Westbourne PO10 . . . . .149 D3
East Strand PO20 . . . . . . .201 C8
East Tyne BN13 . . . . .181 D6
East View Cl PO18 . . . . . .152 F7
East Walls PO19 . . . . .173 A6
East Walls Cl 2 PO19 . . . .173 A6
East Way PO20 . . . . .206 F7
East Wick RH16 . . . . .86 C7
East Wittering Bsns Ctr
PO20 . . . . .202 A8
East Wittering Com Prim Sch PO20 . . . .201 F7
East Worthing Ind Est
BN14 . . . . .182 F5
East Worthing Sta BN11 .182 F4
Eastbank BN42 . . . . .165 F1
Eastbourne Rd
Brighton BN2 . . . . .168 D1
Felbridge RH7 . . . . .8 E8
Eastbrook Rd BN41 . . . . . .186 B7
Eastbrook Way BN42 . . . . .186 A7
Eastcourt Rd BN14 . . . . . .182 D4
Eastcroft Mews RH12 . . . . .35 F1
Eastdale Rd RH15 . . . . . . .107 D4
Eastdean Hill PO18 . . . . . .134 C5
Easteds La RH13 . . . . .58 A2
Eastend La BN6 . . . . .127 D3
Eastergate CE Prim Sch
PO20 . . . . .175 E7
Eastergate Cl BN12 . . . . . .180 F3
Eastergate Gn 8 BN16 . . .199 C5
Eastergate La BN18,PO20 .156 B1
Eastergate Rd BN2 . . . . . .168 F4
Eastern Ave BN43 . . . . . . .185 A7
Eastern Cl
East Preston BN16 . . . . . . .200 B6
Shoreham-by-Sea BN43 . . .185 A7
Eastern Cotts RH16 . . . . . .86 B7
Eastern Pl BN2 . . . . .188 E4
Eastern Rd Brighton BN2 .188 D4
Haywards Heath RH16 . . . . . .85 F3
Lindfield RH16 . . . . .86 C7
Eastern Terr 10 BN2 . . . . .188 D4
Eastern Terrace Mews
BN2 . . . . .188 D4
Eastfield Cres BN1 . . . . . .168 A4
Eastfield Ho 4 BN11 . . . . .182 F2
Eastfield La GU31 . . . . . . .90 A4
Eastgate Ct PO19 . . . . . . .173 B6
Eastgate Sq PO19 . . . . . . .173 A6
Easthill Dr BN41 . . . . .166 B2
Easthill Way BN41 . . . . . .166 B1
Easting Cl BN14 . . . . .182 F5
Eastland Rd PO19 . . . . . . .173 B5
Eastlands Cotts RH13 . . . . .81 F1
Eastmead Ind Est PO18 . .152 E7
Eastoke Ave PO11 . . . . . . .189 A2
Easton Cres RH14 . . . . . . .77 E8
Easton La PO20 . . . . .203 A6
Eastover Way PO22 . . . . . .195 F4
Eastshaw La GU29 . . . . . . .70 C4
Eastway RH6 . . . . .6 B7
Eastwick Bottom BN1 . . .168 B7
Eastwick Cl BN1 . . . . .168 B7
Eastwood RH10 . . . . .18 F6
Eaton Ct 9 Hove BN3 . . . .187 B7
Worthing BN14 . . . . .182 B6
Eaton Gardens Mans
20 BN3 . . . . .187 C7
Eaton Gate 17 BN3 . . . . . .187 C7
Eaton Gdns BN3 . . . . .187 C7
Eaton Gr BN3 . . . . .187 C7
Eaton Hall 19 BN3 . . . . . .187 C7
Eaton Manor 11 BN3 . . . . .187 C7
Eaton Pl BN2 . . . . .188 D4
Eaton Rd BN3 . . . . .187 C7
Eaton Villas BN3 . . . . .187 B7
Ecclesden 7 BN2 . . . . . . .207 C3
Edburton Ave BN1 . . . . . .168 A1
Edburton Dro BN5 . . . . . .145 D6
Edburton Gdns BN43 . . . .164 F1
Eddington Hill RH11 . . . . . .18 B1
Eden Rd RH11 . . . . .17 F4
Eden Vale
Dormans Park RH19 . . . . .9 F5
East Grinstead RH19 . . . . .9 D4
Edgar Cl RH10 . . . . .19 E5
Edgehill Cl BN13 . . . . .181 F7
Edgehill Way BN41 . . . . . .165 F2
Edgell Rd PO10 . . . . .149 D4
Edgewood Ct GU33 . . . . . . .45 D2
Edinburgh Cl
Bognor Regis PO21 . . . . . . .194 E2
Southwater RH13 . . . . .58 A1
Edinburgh Cotts 3 BN11 .182 C1
Edinburgh Rd 8 BN2 . . . .188 B8
Edinburgh Sq GU29 . . . . . . .92 F7
Edinburgh Way RH19 . . . . .22 F7
Edith Cotts PO18 . . . . .151 A2
Edmonton Rd BN13 . . . . . .181 D6
Edrich Rd RH11 . . . . .18 A1
Edward Ave BN3 . . . . .167 A3
Edward Bryant Prim Sch
PO21 . . . . .195 D4
Edward Cl BN3 . . . . .167 A3
Edward Ho BN3 . . . . .186 F6
Edward Rd RH16 . . . . .85 E2
Edward St BN2 . . . . .207 C2
Edward Way RH15 . . . . . . .106 D2
Edwards Ave PO20 . . . . . . .154 C2
Edwards Terr BN15 . . . . . .182 F7
Edwards Way BN17 . . . . . .178 C4
Edwen Cl PO21 . . . . .194 B3
Edwin Cl BN15 . . . . .183 C6
Eels Cross PO20 . . . . .206 B8
Effingham La RH10 . . . . .7 E4
Effingham Rd RH10, RH6 . . .7 D6
Egginton Rd BN2 . . . . .168 F5
Egmont Ho GU29 . . . . .71 A1
Egmont Rd
Easebourne GU29 . . . . .71 A1
Hove BN3 . . . . .166 D1
Egremont Pl BN2 . . . . . . .207 C2
Egremont Row GU28 . . . . . .95 F8
Eighth Ave BN15 . . . . .183 E7
Eirene Ave BN12 . . . . .181 F1
Eirene Rd BN11, BN12 . . . .181 F1
Elanor Cl GU30 . . . . .24 D8
Elbridge Cres PO21 . . . . . .194 C2
Elcombe Cl PO20 . . . . . . .202 C5
Elder Cl BN41 . . . . .166 B2
Elder Pl BN1 . . . . .207 B4
Elderfield Cl PO10 . . . . . .149 C3
Eldon Rd BN11 . . . . .182 F3
Eldon Way BN17 . . . . .198 B6
Eldred Ave BN1 . . . . .167 D5
Eleanor Ct 1 BN11 . . . . . .181 F2
Eleanor Gdns PO22 . . . . . .196 D5
Elfin Gr PO21 . . . . .195 B3
Elfin Mews 1 PO21 . . . . . .195 B3
Elgar Way RH13 . . . . .37 B4
Elger Way RH10 . . . . .7 A4
Elgin Cl RH13 . . . . .36 F3
Elgin Ct PO19 . . . . .173 A5
Elgin Rd BN12 . . . . .181 D2
Eliot Dr GU27 . . . . .26 E6
Eliot Ho 5 RH16 . . . . .85 E3
Elizabeth Ave
Bognor Regis PO21 . . . . . . .194 D4
Hove BN3 . . . . .167 A3
Elizabeth Cl
Bognor Regis PO21 . . . . . . .194 C3
Hove BN3 . . . . .167 A3
Elizabeth Cres RH19 . . . . . .9 F3
Elizabeth Ct
9 Bognor Regis PO21 . . . . .195 B2
Horley RH6 . . . . .2 A3
7 Hove BN3 . . . . .187 C7
7 Worthing BN11 . . . . .181 F2
Elizabeth Ho
11 Bognor Regis PO21 . . . .195 D3
Bognor Regis PO22 . . . . . . .195 E4
2 Worthing BN13 . . . . .182 A5
Elizabeth Pl BN15 . . . . . . .183 C5
Elizabeth Rd
Chichester PO19 . . . . .173 D7
Shoreham-by-Sea BN43 . . .185 C8
Worthing BN11 . . . . .182 C2
Elizabethan Way RH10 . . . .19 C5
Elkham Cnr GU28 . . . . .52 C1
Ella Cl PO20 . . . . .201 E7
Ellanore La PO20 . . . . . . .190 B2
Ellasdale Rd PO21 . . . . . .195 B2
Ellen Ho 3 BN3 . . . . .187 B7
Ellen St Hove BN3 . . . . . . .187 B7
Portslade-by-Sea BN41 . . . .186 C7
Ellesmere Orch PO10 . . . .149 D5
Elliot Cl RH10 . . . . .19 C4
Ellis Ave BN13 . . . . .161 E1
Ellis Cl BN18 . . . . .157 F2
Ellis Way PO21 . . . . .205 A8
Ellman Rd RH11 . . . . .17 F4
Ellson Cl RH10 . . . . .19 C4
Elm Ave BN16 . . . . .200 B6
Elm Cl Bognor Regis PO21 .194 A1
Bracklesham PO20 . . . . . . .202 B6
Hove BN3 . . . . .167 C2
Shoreham-by-Sea BN43 . . . .164 F1
Elm Ct
8 Bognor Regis PO21 . . . . .195 C2
Brighton BN1 . . . . .187 E8
4 East Grinstead RH19 . . . . .9 D2
Findon BN14 . . . . .161 E5
Portslade-by-Sea BN41 . . . .186 B8
Worthing BN12 . . . . .181 C2
Elm Dale PO22 . . . . .176 A6
Elm Dr East Grinstead RH19 .10 A1
Hove BN3 . . . . .166 E1

Elm Dr continued
Middleton-on-Sea PO22 197 B5
Elm Gr Bognor Regis PO21 195 A3
Brighton BN2 188 C7
Cowfold RH13 81 E2
Horsham RH13 36 E1
Lancing BN15 183 D5
Runcton PO20 173 E1
Selsey PO20 206 D7
West Barnham PO22 176 B7
Worthing BN11 181 F2
Elm Gr S PO22 176 A6
Elm Grove Fst Sch BN11 181 F2
Elm Grove Ho BN15 183 E5
Elm Grove Inf Sch BN17 198 E6
Elm Grove La BN44 143 D3
Elm Grove Prim Sch BN2 188 C7
Elm Ho RH14 77 C8
Elm Pk Bosham PO18 171 C6
Ferring BN12 180 F3
Elm Pl BN16 199 D6
Elm Rd
Portslade-by-Sea BN41 186 B8
Westergate PO20 175 E7
Worthing BN11 182 E2
Elm Rise BN14 161 E6
Elm Terr Liss GU33 45 A5
Steyning BN44 143 D3
Elm Tree Cl
Bognor Regis PO21 195 A6
Selsey PO20 206 E8
Elmcroft Pl PO20 175 D6
Elmdene Ct PO20 202 B5
Elmeigh Ct GU29 92 E8
Elmer Cl PO22 197 B5
Elmer Ct PO22 197 C5
Elmer Rd PO22 196 F5
Elmgrove Rd BN17 198 F6
Elmhurst Cl BN16 180 A6
Elmhurst La RH13 56 C6
Elmleigh GU29 92 D8
Elmore Rd BN2 207 C3
Elms Dr BN15 183 D6
Elms La PO20 190 D1
Elms Lea Ave BN1 167 E3
Elms Ride PO20 190 C1
Elms Way PO20 190 C2
Elmsfield PO20 206 E7
Elmstead RH19 22 E8
Elmstead Gdns PO20 190 C2
Elmstead Park Rd PO20 190 C2
Elmstone Cl BN15 183 D6
Elmwood Ave PO22 195 D5
Elrington Rd BN3 167 C1
Elsaw Ct PO19 173 A5
Elsie Rd BN11 182 B1
Elspring Mead BN17 178 C3
Elsted Cl RH11 18 B8
Elsted Cres BN1 168 C6
Elsted Rd GU29 91 C7
Elverlands Cl 5 BN12 200 F4
Elwood Cl RH15 106 F1
Elwyn Jones Ct BN1 167 E4
Ely Cl Crawley RH10 18 F2
East Wittering PO20 201 F8
Worthing BN13 181 F4
Ely Gdns PO21 194 D3
Ely Rd BN13 181 F4
Embassy Ct
10 Brighton BN1 187 D5
Haywards Heath RH16 85 E6
Emberwood RH11 18 D8
Emerald Quay BN43 185 A6
Emlyn Rd RH6 1 E4
Emmabrook Ct BN16 199 A3
Emms La RH13 78 F7
Empire Villas RH1 2 B7
Emsbrook Dr PO10 149 B2
Emsworth Cl RH10 19 C3
Emsworth Common Rd
PO10, PO9 149 C6
Emsworth House Cl
PO10 149 A1
Emsworth Mus PO10 169 B8
Emsworth Prim Sch
PO10 149 A1
Emsworth Rd PO10 169 D2
Emsworth Sta PO10 149 B1
End Cotts BN18 138 E6
End La BN5 123 A5
Enfield Rd RH11 18 C2
Engalee RH19 9 C2
Englefield RH12 35 F2
English Cl BN3 186 E8
English Martyrs
RC Prim Sch BN12 181 D5
Ennerdale Cl RH11 18 B4
Ennerdale Dr BN15 183 B5
Ensign Way BN17 199 A6
Enterprise Ct Crawley RH11 5 D2
Worthing BN12 181 C3
Enterprise Est BN1 168 C7
Epping Wlk RH10 18 F4
Epsom Gdns BN16 199 E6
Epsom Rd RH10 19 A4
Erica Way Copthorne RH10 7 A2
Horsham RH12 36 D5
Ericsson Way RH15 106 D2
Eridge Cl RH10 19 C6
Eridge Rd BN3 167 A2
Erin Way RH15 106 E3
Eriskay Ct BN13 181 B6
Eriswell Rd BN11 182 C1
Erles Rd GU30 25 C4
Ernest Cl PO10 149 B1
Erringham Rd BN43 164 E1
Erroll Mans 6 BN3 186 D7
Erroll Rd BN3 186 C6
Erskine Cl RH11 17 E2
Esher Cl PO21 194 B2
Esher Dr BN17 198 F5
Eskbank Ave BN1 168 A7
Esmond Cl PO10 169 B8
Esmonde Cl BN17 198 F6
Esplanade Ct BN11 182 F2
Esplanade The
Bognor Regis PO21 195 D2
Bognor Regis,
Felpham PO22 195 F3
Worthing BN11 182 F2
Essenhigh Dr BN13 181 B6
Essex Ct BN11 182 A2
Essex Pl 3 BN2 188 C4
Essex Rd PO21 195 C5
Essex St BN2 188 C4
Estcots Dr RH19 10 A1
Estcots Prim Sch RH19 10 A1
Estuary The BN17 198 F5
Ethel St BN3 187 B7
Ethelred Rd BN14 182 A4
Ethelwulf Rd BN14 182 A4
Eton Cl PO21 194 E4
Eton Dr PO20 201 F8
Eton Rd BN11 182 A3
Ettrick Cl PO19 173 B5
Ettrick Rd PO19 173 B5
Eurythmy Sch RH19 22 E6
Evans Cl RH10 19 D5
Evans Gdns 14 BN17 198 D5
Evans Pl PO22 195 D6
Evelyn Ave BN16 199 D4
Evelyn Cl RH19 8 F4
Evelyn Ct BN41 186 A8
Evelyn Glennie Ct 7
BN2 188 C5
Evelyn Rd BN14 182 D4
Evelyn Terr BN2 188 C5
Evelyn Wlk RH10 18 E3
Everest Ho 2 BN3 186 F7
Eversfield RH13 58 B1
Eversfield Rd RH13 36 E1
Evershed Way BN43 185 B7
Eversleigh Ct GU29 71 A2
Ewart St BN2 207 C3
Ewbank Ho BN3 187 D7
Ewelands RH6 2 C4
Ewens Gdns PO22 176 A7
Ewhurst Cl RH11 18 C6
Ewhurst Rd Brighton BN2 168 C1
Crawley RH11 18 C7
Excalibur Cl RH11 17 E5
Excelsior The BN1 167 D4
Exchange Rd RH10 18 E6
Exeat Cl BN2 188 E6
Exeter Cl
Bognor Regis PO21 194 F3
Crawley RH10 18 E2
New Brighton PO10 149 B2
Exeter Ct 2 BN11 182 A1
Exeter Rd PO19 152 E1
Exeter St BN1 187 E8
Exford Wlk BN13 181 D5
Exmoor Cl BN13 181 E7
Exmoor Cres BN13 181 E7
Exmoor Ct BN13 181 E7
Exmoor Dr BN13 181 E7
Exton Rd PO19 173 A4
Eyles Cl RH12 36 B4

F

Fabians Way BN5 123 D5
Fair View RH12 36 A3
Fairbanks RH16 85 E4
Fairbridge Way RH15 106 F5
Faircox La BN5 123 D5
Fairdene BN42 165 F1
Fairfield Ave RH6 2 A1
Fairfield Cl Ardingly RH17 64 A8
Bosham PO18 171 C5
Burgess Hill RH15 106 F4
New Brighton PO10 149 B2
Shoreham-by-Sea BN43 165 C1
Fairfield Cotts RH13 81 E2
Fairfield Cres BN6 126 A6
Fairfield Ct RH13 81 E2
Fairfield Gdns
Burgess Hill RH15 106 F4
Portslade-by-Sea BN41 166 B1
Fairfield Rd
Ashington RH20 121 A4
Bosham PO18 171 B5
Burgess Hill RH15 106 F4
East Grinstead RH19 22 F8
Fairfield Rise GU28 95 F7
Fairfield Way
Ashington RH20 121 A4
Haywards Heath RH16 85 D8
Fairfields
2 Worthing BN14 182 D4
Worthing, West
Tarring BN14 182 A5
Fairford Cl RH16 85 E5
Fairholme Dr BN18 177 A2
Fairlands
Bognor Regis PO22 195 B6
East Preston BN16 200 A5
8 Lancing BN15 183 D5
Fairlawn
1 Haywards Heath RH16 85 E4
Rustington BN16 199 C6
Fairlawn Cres RH19 9 B2
Fairlawn Dr
East Grinstead RH19 9 B2
Worthing BN14 182 D4
Fairlawns Horley RH6 2 B2
9 Hove BN3 187 A6
Shoreham-by-Sea BN43 185 A8
Fairlea Cl RH15 106 F4
Fairlea Rd PO10 149 B3
Fairlead BN17 198 F4
Fairlie Gdns BN1 167 E3
Fairlight Pl 8 BN2 188 C8
Fairlight Prim Sch BN2 188 C8
Fairmead Cl RH20 97 A3
Fairmile Bottom BN18 157 B7
Fairmile Bottom
Nature Trail BN18 157 C8
Fairoak Ct 4 BN13 182 A5
Fairstone Ct RH6 2 B4
Fairview Ave BN12 181 C1
Fairview Cotts RH13 58 B3
Fairview Rd BN15 183 E8
Fairview Rise BN1 167 D5
Fairway Copthorne RH10 7 B2
Crawley RH11 17 D4
Littlehampton BN17 199 A4
Fairway Cl Copthorne RH10 7 A2
Liphook GU30 24 D3
Fairway Cres BN41 166 C2
Fairway The
Bognor Regis PO21 205 B8
Midhurst GU29 92 E6
Rowland's Castle PO9 128 E2
Shoreham-by-Sea BN15 184 A5
Fairway Trad Est BN2 168 E4
Fairways BN1 187 E8
Faithfull Cres RH20 119 B2
Falcon Cl Crawley RH11 18 D8
Shoreham-by-Sea BN43 185 C6
Falcon Gdns BN17 178 C4
Falkland Ave BN17 198 F6
Falklands Cl PO22 195 D5
Falklands Dr RH13 37 B4
Fallow Deer Cl RH13 37 B4
Fallowfield Cl BN3 166 F2
Fallowfield Cres BN3 166 F2
Fallowfield Way RH6 2 B4
Falmer Ave BN12 181 B1
Falmer Cl Crawley RH11 18 D4
Worthing BN12 181 C1
Faraday Ave RH19 22 F6
Faraday Cl BN13 181 C5
Faraday Rd RH10 5 F2
Farebrothers RH12 35 F8
Faresmead PO21 194 F2
Farhalls Cres RH12 36 F6
Farlington Ave RH16 85 F5
Farlington Cl RH16 85 F5
Farlington Sch RH12 35 B6
Farm Acre BN16 199 F6
Farm Ave RH12 36 B3
Farm Cl Barns Green RH13 56 F2
Crawley RH10 19 A7
East Grinstead RH19 23 B8
Fishbourne PO18 172 A6
Hassocks BN6 126 E4
Henfield BN5 123 E5
Loxwood RH14 32 A3
Middleton-on-Sea PO22 197 B5
Portslade-by-Sea BN41 166 A2
Warnham RH12 35 F7
Farm Cnr PO22 197 A5
Farm Cotts PO20 190 F6
Farm La Ditchling BN6 127 E3
Nutbourne PO18 170 B7
Farm Mews BN3 187 D6
Farm Rd
Bracklesham PO20 202 B5
Hove BN3 187 D6
Farm View PO10 149 B3
Farm Way
Burgess Hill RH15 107 D1
Rustington BN16 199 B5
Southwick BN42 186 A7
Farman St 15 BN3 187 D5
Farmet Ct RH19 9 C3
Farmfield Dr RH6 5 B8
Farmfield Hospl RH6 1 B1
Farmleigh Cl RH10 19 C8
Farmway Cl BN3 166 D2
Farncombe Rd BN11 182 F2
Farndell Cl PO19 173 C7
Farne Cl PO20 191 E4
Farne La PO20 191 E4
Farney Close Sch RH17 83 D2
Farnfold Rd BN44 143 D4
Farnham Ave BN6 127 A5
Farnham Cl RH11 39 C8
Farnham La GU27 27 A7
Farnham Rd GU33 45 A4
Farnhurst Rd PO22 176 B6
Farnlea RH15 107 D5
Faroes The BN17 199 A6
Farr Cl RH17 84 F8
Farriers Cl RH14 77 C7
Farthings Wlk RH12 35 F3
Fastnet Way BN17 199 A6
Faulkner Cl RH11 39 C8
Faulkners Way RH15 107 A5
Fawn Rise BN5 123 E6
Fay Rd RH12 36 C5
Faygate Bsns Ctr RH12 16 F1
Faygate Ct BN2 188 E6
Faygate La RH12 16 F4
Faygate Sta RH12 16 F1
Felbridge Ave RH10 19 D7
Felbridge Cl RH19 9 C3
Felbridge Ct RH19 9 A4
Felbridge Ctr The RH19 9 A3
Felbridge Cty Prim
Sch RH19 8 F4
Felbridge Pl RH19 9 A4
Felbridge Rd RH19 8 D3
Felcot Rd RH10 8 C4
Felcourt Cotts RH19 9 C8
Felcourt La RH19, RH7 9 C8
Felcourt Rd RH19, RH7 9 C7
Feld The RH19 9 A3
Fellcott Way RH12 35 F1
Felpham Com Coll PO22 195 F5
Felpham Gdns PO22 196 B5
Felpham Ho BN17 178 B3
Felpham Rd PO22 195 F4
Felpham Way PO22 196 A5
Felride RH16 85 E3
Felwater Ct RH19 9 A3
Fenby Cl RH13 37 B4
Fenchurch Rd RH10 19 B4
Fender Ho RH12 36 B2
Fenhurst Cl RH12 35 F1
Fennel Cres RH11 18 B2
Fennel Wlk BN43 165 B1
Fenners Ct 13 BN11 182 C3
Fereday Cl BN15 183 E6
Fermandy La RH10 8 A1
Fern Rd RH20 119 C1
Fern Way RH12 36 D5
Ferndale Rd
Burgess Hill RH15 107 C2
Chichester PO19 153 A3
Hove BN3 187 D7
Ferndale Wlk BN16 180 A6
Fernden La GU27 27 C2
Ferndown Crawley RH10 6 D2
Horley RH6 2 A5
Ferndown Gdns PO22 196 A5
Fernhill Cl RH10 8 B1
Fernhill Rd RH6 6 D7
Fernhurst Cl Brighton BN1 168 B6
Crawley RH11 18 B8
Fernhurst Cres BN1 168 B5
Fernhurst Ct BN11 181 F1
Fernhurst Dr BN12 181 A2
Fernhurst Gdns PO21 194 D2
Fernhurst Gn GU27 49 B6
Fernhurst Prim Sch GU27 49 B6
Fernhurst Rd GU30 47 C3
Fernside 5 RH19 9 D2
Fernwood Rise BN1 167 D5
Feroners Cl RH10 19 A4
Ferring CE Prim Sch
BN12 200 F6
Ferring Cl Crawley RH11 18 B8
Ferring BN12 200 E4
Ferring Ct BN1 168 F5
Ferring Gdns PO22 196 A5
Ferring Grange Flats
BN12 200 E6
Ferring Grange Gdns
BN12 200 E6
Ferring La BN12 180 F3
Ferring Marine BN12 200 F4
Ferring St BN12 200 E6
Ferringham Ct BN12 200 E5
Ferringham La BN12 200 E5
Ferringham Way BN12 200 E4
Ferroners Ct RH10 19 A4
Ferry Rd
Littlehampton BN17 198 B4
Shoreham-by-Sea BN43 184 F6
Festival Ct PO19 173 A7
Fetherston Rd BN15 183 E7
Feversham Cl BN43 185 B6
Fidlers Copse GU27 49 A6
Field Cl Burgess Hill RH15 106 E4
Lancing BN15 183 D6
Walberton BN18 156 D1
Field Cotts RH15 107 B4
Field End RH20 119 E2
Field Ho
Bognor Regis PO21 195 E3
East Preston BN16 199 F6
Field Pl Liphook GU30 25 C3
Littlehampton BN17 198 D5
Field Place Fst Sch BN12 181 D4
Field Rd PO20 202 A7
Field Row 8 BN11 182 D2
Fieldend RH12 37 B5
Fieldgate Cl RH13 59 C4
Fieldings Cotts RH14 55 F5
Fieldings The Horley RH6 2 C4
Southwater RH13 79 F7
Fields End Cl RH16 85 F4
Fieldview RH6 2 B4
Fieldway Ditchling BN6 127 D3
Haslemere GU27 27 C7
Lindfield RH16 85 F8
Fifth Ave Lancing BN15 183 E7
Worthing BN14 182 C8
Filbert Cres RH11 18 A6
Filey Cl RH11 17 F4
Filton Wlk BN13 181 D6
Finch Gdns PO22 195 B7
Fincham Cl BN16 199 F5
Fincham Ct BN16 199 F5
Finchdean Rd PO9 128 F3
Finches Cl Lancing BN15 183 D5
Littlehampton BN17 178 C4
Partridge Green RH13 103 A3
Finches Ct RH16 64 A1
Finches Gdns RH16 86 A8
Finches La Lindfield RH16 86 A8
West Chiltington
Common RH20 119 C8
Finches Park Rd RH16 86 A8
Finches The BN43 185 A8
Findon By-Pass BN14 161 D6
Findon Cl BN3 166 F3
Findon Dr PO22 196 D6
Findon Rd Brighton BN2 188 F5
Crawley RH11 18 B8
Worthing BN14 161 F3
Findon Way RH12 35 D3
Finians Field RH13 56 F2
Finisterre Way BN17 199 A4
Finsbury Cl RH11 18 C2
Finsbury Lodge 1 BN2 188 C6
Finsbury Rd BN2 188 C6
Fir Tree Ave GU27 26 D6
Fir Tree Cl Crawley RH11 5 B1
Lower Beeding RH13 60 A3
West Chiltington
Common RH20 119 D6
Fir Tree Cotts GU33 46 A4
Fir Tree La RH20 119 D6
Fir Tree Way
Bognor Regis PO22 195 C7
Keymer BN6 127 A4
Firbank Cotts RH6 7 C7
Fircroft Ave BN15 183 E8
Fircroft Cl Brighton BN1 167 E3
Worthing BN13 181 F6
Fircroft Cres BN16 179 D3
Firlands
Haywards Heath RH16 85 F4
Horley RH6 2 B4
Firle Cl RH10 18 E8
Firle Rd Brighton BN2 188 D6
North Lancing BN15 163 E1
Firs Ave PO22 196 B5
Firs Ave W PO22 196 B5
Firs The GU30 25 B3
Firsdown Cl BN13 161 E2
Firsdown Rd BN13 161 E2
Firsland Park Ind Est
BN6 124 F8
First Ave
Almodington PO20 191 F2
Bognor Regis PO22 196 B4
Bracklesham PO20 202 B5
Hove BN3 187 C6
Lancing BN15 183 E7
Middleton-on-Sea PO22 196 F6
Southbourne PO10 169 F8
Worthing BN14 182 C7
Firtoft Cl RH15 107 B3
Firview GU30 25 B3
Fish La
Bognor Regis PO21 194 F2
Selsey PO20 206 B8
Fishbourne CE Prim Sch
PO19 172 B6
Fishbourne Rd E PO19 172 D6
Fishbourne Rd
W PO19, PO20 172 C6
Fishbourne Roman Pal
PO19 172 B6
Fishbourne Sta PO19 172 B7
Fisher Cl RH10 18 E4
Fisher La Plaistow GU8 30 B7
South Mundham PO20 193 C6
Fisherman's Wlk
Bognor Regis PO21 194 D1
Selsey PO20 206 F7
Fishermans The PO10 169 C8
Fishermans Wlk
Shoreham-by-Sea BN43 184 D5
South Hayling PO11 189 A2
Fishers Cl BN17 199 A4
Fishers Ct RH12 36 C4
Fishers Farm Pk RH14 54 D2
Fishersgate Cl BN41 186 A7
Fishersgate Com Fst Sch
BN41 186 A7
Fishersgate Sta BN41 186 B7
Fishersgate Terr BN41 186 A7
Fitch Dr BN2 168 F1
Fitchet Cl RH11 18 B8
Fittleworth CE Fst Sch
RH20 97 A3
Fittleworth Cl BN12 181 B4
Fittleworth Dr PO22 196 C7
Fittleworth Gdn 9 BN16 199 C5
Fittleworth Rd RH14 75 F5
Fitzalan Ct
3 Littlehampton BN17 198 E4
4 Rustington BN16 199 B3
Fitzalan Mews BN18 158 B2
Fitzalan Rd Arundel BN18 158 B2
Horsham RH12, RH13 37 A4
Littlehampton BN17 198 E4
Fitzhall Gdns GU29 91 D7
Fitzherbert Dr BN2 188 D8
Fitzjohn Ct BN6 126 F3
Fitzleet Ho 9 PO21 195 C3
Fitzroy Ct BN17 198 E5
Fitzwilliam Cl PO21 194 F4
Five Acres Crawley RH10 18 E8
Funtington PO18 151 A5
Five Oaks Rd RH13 56 D7
Fixcroft Cotts BN5 104 D4
Flag Ct BN3 187 B5
Flag Sq BN43 184 F6
Flamsteed Hts RH11 18 B1
Flansham La PO22 196 C6
Flansham Mews PO22 196 C6
Flansham Pk PO22 196 D6
Flatt Rd PO18 170 D8
Flax Mean PO22 196 B5
Flax Mean Ho PO22 196 B5
Flaxman Ave PO19 172 D6
Fleet Cl BN17 199 A6
Fleet The RH20 97 B3
Fleming Ct PO21 194 A1
Fleming Way RH10, RH11 5 F2

Fletcher Cl
Bognor Regis PO21 ....194 B2
Crawley RH10 ....18 E4
North Mundham PO20 .....173 D1
Fletcher Ho
North Mundham PO20 .....173 C1
Southwater RH13 ....57 E1
Fletcher Pl PO20 ....173 C1
Fletcher Rd BN14 ....182 E5
Fletcher Way
Angmering BN16 ....179 F6
Bognor Regis PO21 ....195 B4
Fletcher's Croft RH20 ...119 D2
Fletcher's La PO18 ......171 D1
Fletchers RH13 ....57 F3
Fletchers Cl RH13 ....36 E1
Fletchers Est PO20 ....192 D2
Fletchers Field GU30 .....25 C3
Fletchers Ho GU30 ....25 B3
Fletchers La PO20 ....192 D3
Fletching Cl BN2 ....188 F6
Flimwell Cl BN2 ....188 E5
Flint Cl Crawley RH10 ......19 B3
Portslade-by-Sea BN41 ....166 B2
Rustington BN16 ....199 F6
Flint Cotts BN18 ....158 A3
Flint Ho 2 BN16 ....199 C4
Flora McDonald
Cty Jun Sch BN17 ......198 C6
Floral Dean Ct BN14 .....162 A1
Florence Ave BN3 ....186 D8
Florence Cl PO20 ....191 D4
Florence Ct BN1 ....167 F2
Florence Pl BN1 ....168 B1
Florence Rd Brighton BN1 188 A8
Chichester PO19 ....173 C6
Florets The BN44 ....144 B1
Florida Cl BN12 ....200 F4
Florida Gdns 8 BN12 .....200 F4
Florida Rd BN12 ....200 F4
Florlandia Cl BN15 ....183 B6
Flower Farm Cl BN5 .....123 D5
Floyds Cotts BN17 ....198 D4
Foamcourt Waye BN12 ..200 E5
Fold Sch The BN3 ....186 D7
Folders Cl RH15 ....107 D1
Folders La RH15 ....107 D1
Follett Cl PO21 ....194 E2
Follis Gdns PO19 ....172 B8
Folly La GU28, RH20 ......115 E3
Fontana Cl RH10 ....19 E5
Fonthill Lodge Sch RH19 .22 C6
Fonthill Rd BN3 ....187 B8
Fontwell Ave BN18,PO20 ..155 F1
Fontwell Cl Fontwell BN18 156 A2
Littlehampton BN16 ....199 B4
Worthing BN14 ....182 A8
Fontwell Dr BN14 ....182 A8
Fontwell Park
Race Course BN18 .....155 F2
Fontwell Rd Crawley RH10 .19 A3
East Beach PO20 ....206 G8
Forbes Cl RH10 ....19 B2
Forbes Pl PO19 ....172 F8
Ford Airfield Ind Est
BN18 ....177 C3
Ford La Ashurst BN44 ....122 D7
Ford BN18 ....177 C4
Ford Lane Bsns Pk BN18 177 D4
Ford Rd Arundel BN18 ....158 A2
Ford BN18 ....177 E3
Tortington BN18 ....177 F7
Ford Sta BN18 ....177 E5
Fordingbridge Cl RH12 ....36 C1
Fordingbridge Ind Site
PO22 ....176 A7
Fordwater Gdns BN18 ...177 B2
Fordwater La PO19 ......153 A2
Fordwater Rd
Chichester PO18, PO19 ....153 A3
East Lavant PO18 ....153 A5
Fordwater Sch PO19 .....153 A1
Fordyce Ct 1 BN14 .....182 D3
Foredown Cl BN41 ....166 B2
Foredown Dr BN41 ....166 C1
Foredown Rd
Portslade Village BN41 ....166 B4
Portslade-by-Sea BN41 ....166 B2
Foredown Twr BN41 .....166 B3
Forest Cl
Crawley Down RH10 ....21 B8
Horsham RH12 ....37 B4
Mannings Heath RH13 ......59 C6
Forest Cnr GU33 ....45 C7
Forest Lane Cl GU30 ......25 A4
Forest Lodge 2 RH19 .....22 F8
Forest Oaks RH13 ....37 B4
Forest Rd Brighton BN1 ...168 E6
Colgate RH11,RH12,RH13 ...38 D6
Liss Forest GU33 ....45 C7
Midhurst GU29 ....92 D6
Worthing BN14 ....182 D6
Forest Ridge RH19 ....43 A5
Forest Rise GU33 ....45 C6
Forest Row Bsns Pk RH18 .23 F4
Forest Row CE Inf Sch
RH18 ....23 F2
Forest Sch The RH13 .....36 F1
Forest View RH10 ....19 A3
Forest View Rd RH19 .....22 E6
Forester Rd RH10 ....18 E4
Forestfield Crawley RH10 ..19 B3
Horsham RH13 ....37 A3
Forge Cl
Broadbridge Heath RH12 ...35 D4
East Preston BN16 ....199 F6
Portslade-by-Sea BN41 ....166 B2
Stockbridge PO19 ....172 F3
Forge La
Broadridge Heath RH12 ....35 D4
Crawley RH10 ....19 A7
Forge Rd RH10 ....19 A7
Forge The Charlwood RH6 ...4 E7
Handcross RH17 ....61 C8
Selsey PO20 ....206 D7
Southwater RH13 ....57 F1
Warnham RH12 ....35 E7
Forge Way
Billingshurst RH14 ....77 C8
Burgess Hill RH15 ....107 A4
Forge Wood RH10 ....6 D3
Forge Wood Ind Est RH10 ..6 B3
Forrester Rd RH13 ....103 A3
Forsters Yd BN17 ....198 B5
Fort Haven BN43 ....185 C6
Fort Rd BN17 ....198 C6
Forty Acre La GU31 ....88 E3
Foster Ct BN3 ....187 E6
Foster La RH20 ....120 F5
Fosters Cl BN16 ....199 E4
Foundry Cl RH13 ....36 E4
Foundry Cotts GU29 ......93 C3
Foundry Ct RH15 ....107 B3
Foundry La
Haslemere GU27 ....27 A6
Horsham RH13 ....36 E3
Foundry St BN1 ....207 B3
Fountains Cl Brighton BN1 168 B2
Crawley RH11 ....18 A4
Fourth Ave
Bognor Regis PO22 ....196 C4
Hove BN3 ....187 B6
Lancing BN15 ....183 E7
Worthing BN14 ....182 D7
Fowey Cl BN43 ....185 B6
Fowler Cl RH10 ....19 C4
Fox Cl Burgess Hill RH15 ..106 F1
Crawley RH11 ....5 B1
Fox Ct RH20 ....119 B1
Fox Dell RH20 ....119 B1
Fox Hill RH16 ....85 E1
Fox Hill Cl RH16 ....85 F1
Fox Hill Village RH16 .....85 F1
Fox Lea BN14 ....161 E5
Fox Rd Easebourne GU29 ...71 A2
Haslemere GU27 ....26 E6
Fox Way BN41 ....166 B2
Foxbridge La RH14 ....31 C1
Foxbury La PO10 ....149 E4
Foxdale Dr BN16 ....179 F4
Foxes Cl Rustington BN16 .179 B4
Southwater RH13 ....79 F7
Foxes Croft PO22 ....176 C6
Foxfield Cotts RH13 ......79 F7
Foxfields RH20 ....119 C8
Foxglove Ave RH12 ....36 E6
Foxglove Cl RH15 ....106 D4
Foxglove Way BN17 .....179 A3
Foxglove Wlk
Crawley RH11 ....18 B3
Worthing BN13 ....181 C5
Foxhill Ct 3 RH16 ....85 E3
Foxhole La RH17 ....83 B2
Foxholes RH12 ....33 D8
Foxhunters Rd BN41 .....165 F3
Foxleigh Chase RH12 .....36 F5
Foxley La BN13 ....181 F8
Foxwarren RH16 ....85 C5
Foxwarren Cl PO20 ......201 F7
Foxwells RH17 ....41 A1
Framfield 11 BN2 ....188 F5
Framfield Cl Brighton BN1 168 E6
Crawley RH11 ....18 A8
Framnaes BN3 ....186 D7
Frampton Ct BN12 ....181 C2
Framptons The BN16 .....200 B5
France La BN13 ....160 D1
Francis Edwards Way
RH11 ....17 E2
Francis Rd RH16 ....86 B8
Francis St BN1, BN2 .....207 B4
Franciscan Way BN17 ...198 D5
Francislea RH16 ....85 E2
Francome Ho BN15 ......183 D3
Frandor Rd PO21 ....194 F5
Frankland Mead RH20 ...141 E6
Frankland Terr 2 PO10 ..169 C8
Franklands Cl
Burgess Hill RH15 ....107 B1
Worthing BN14 ....162 A1
Franklands Gdns RH15 ..127 A8
Franklands Way RH15 ..127 A8
Franklin Pl PO19 ....173 A7
Franklin Rd Brighton BN2 .188 C7
Crawley RH10 ....19 C5
Portslade-by-Sea BN41 ....186 C7
Shoreham-by-Sea BN43 ...165 D1
Worthing BN13 ....181 E7
Franklin St BN2 ....188 C8
Franklynn Ct RH16 ....85 F3
Franklynn Rd RH16 ....85 F3
Frankton Ave RH16 ......86 A3
Frant Rd BN3 ....167 A2
Frarydene PO10 ....169 F8
Fraser Cl PO20 ....206 F6
Fraser Ct
19 Bognor Regis PO21 ....195 D3
2 Shoreham-by-Sea BN43 .185 C8
Fraser Gdns PO10 ....150 A2
Frazier Ho RH20 ....119 D1
Fred Emery Ct 16 BN1 ...187 E5
Frederick Cotts RH16 .....86 B7
Frederick Gdns BN1 .....207 B3
Frederick Pl BN1 ....207 B3
Frederick Rd PO19 ....172 C7
Frederick St BN1 ....207 B3
Freehold St BN43 ....184 E7
Freehold Terr 1 BN2 ....188 C8
Freek's La RH15 ....107 A5
Freeland Cl PO19 ....172 C6
Freeman Cl BN18 ....156 B1
Freeman Rd RH12 ....35 F8
Freemans Cl RH14 ....77 C8
Freemans Rd BN41 ......186 A8
Freeways PO20 ....206 C8
French Gdns RH16 ....86 A6
Frenches RH20 ....119 D2
Frenches Mead RH14 .....77 C8
Freshbrook Cl BN15 .....183 E5
Freshbrook Ct 3 BN15 ..183 E5
Freshbrook Fst Sch
BN15 ....183 E6
Freshbrook Rd BN15 ....183 F5
Freshfield Bank RH18 .....23 E2
Freshfield Cl RH10 ....19 A5
Freshfield Halt RH17 .....87 B8
Freshfield La RH17 ....65 E2
Freshfield Pl BN2 ....188 C5
Freshfield Rd BN2 ......188 D6
Freshfield St BN2 ....188 C6
Freshfield Way BN2 .....188 C5
Freshfields Cl BN15 .....183 D6
Freshfields Dr BN15 .....183 D6
Freshwoods RH12 ....33 D8
Friar Cl BN1 ....168 A4
Friar Cres BN1 ....168 A3
Friar Rd BN1 ....168 A3
Friar Wlk Brighton BN1 ...167 F4
Worthing BN13 ....181 F3
Friars Cl BN6 ....126 E4
Friars Oak Rd BN6 ......126 E5
Friars Rookery RH10 ......18 F6
Friary Cl PO22 ....196 E5
Friary La PO19 ....173 A6
Friary Way RH10 ....18 E5
Friday St Faygate RH12 ....15 E6
Warnham RH12 ....35 E7
Friends Cl RH11 ....5 D1
Friston Cl BN2 ....168 F4
Friston Wlk RH11 ....18 A7
Frith Pk RH19 ....9 E3
Frith Rd
Bognor Regis PO21 ....195 A4
Hove BN3 ....187 A8
Frobisher Cl BN12 ......181 D4
Frobisher Gdns 8 PO10 .169 B8
Frobisher Rd PO21 ......194 C2
Frobisher Way
Littlehampton BN16 ....199 E4
Worthing BN12 ....181 D4
Fry Cl RH11 ....18 B1
Fry Cres RH15 ....106 E5
Fryern Cl RH20 ....119 C2
Fryern Rd RH20 ....119 D3
Fryland La BN5 ....104 B4
Fuel Farm Rd RH6 ....5 E8
Fulbeck Ave BN13 ....181 B6
Fulfords Hill RH13 ....57 A7
Fulham Cl RH11 ....18 B2
Fullers Wlk BN17 ....178 D5
Fulmar Cl Brighton BN3 ..167 D1
1 Crawley RH11 ....17 D5
Fulmar Dr RH19 ....10 B3
Fulmar Way PO20 ....154 E1
Fulmer Ct 1 BN11 ......182 B1
Funtington Ho BN17 .....178 B3
Funtington Prim Sch
PO18 ....151 B3
Furlong Cl BN18 ....156 B3
Furlong Way RH6 ....5 B8
Furlonge Ho PO10 ......149 A1
Furlongs The BN44 ......143 D2
Furnace Dr RH10 ....18 F4
Furnace Farm Rd RH10 ...19 A4
Furnace Par RH10 ....19 A4
Furnace Pl RH10 ....19 A4
Furnace Rd RH10, RH19 ....8 C3
Furners La BN5 ....124 A5
Furners Mead BN5 ......123 F4
Furnston Gr PO10 ....150 A1
Furse Feld PO21 ....195 A2
Furze Cl Horley RH6 ....2 D3
Worthing BN13 ....161 D2
Furze Common Rd RH20 .120 A6
Furze Croft BN3 ....187 D6
Furze Hill BN3 ....187 D6
Furze Hill Ct BN3 ....187 E6
Furze Hill Ho BN3 ....187 E6
Furze La RH19 ....9 B4
Furze Mdw GU31 ....90 A8
Furze Rd Rudgwick RH12 ..33 D8
Worthing BN13 ....161 E2
Furze View RH13 ....56 B6
Furzedene BN3 ....187 D6
Furzedown BN17 ....198 E4
Furzefield Crawley RH11 ..18 C7
East Wittering PO20 ......190 F1
Furzefield Chase RH19 ....9 E6
Furzefield Cl BN16 ......179 F7
Furzefield Rd
East Grinstead RH19 ....9 D4
Horsham RH12 ....37 B5
Furzeholme BN13 ....161 E2
Furzeland Way BN6 .....125 D8
Furzen La RH12, RH5 .....13 B4
Fyning La GU31 ....68 C5

G

Gables The
13 Bognor Regis PO21 ....195 C2
Copthorne RH10 ....7 B3
Cowfold RH13 ....81 E1
Gables The *continued*
Horsham RH12 ....36 D4
Southwater RH13 ....79 F8
Gableson Ave BN1 ....167 B4
Gabriel Rd RH10 ....19 C2
Gage Cl RH10 ....8 C1
Gage Ridge RH18 ....23 E2
Gaggle Wood RH13 ....59 C6
Gainsboro Rd PO21 .....195 C3
Gainsborough Ave BN14 .182 E7
Gainsborough Dr PO20 ..206 F7
Gainsborough Ho 16
BN3 ....187 C7
Gainsborough Lodge 1
BN14 ....182 C4
Gainsborough Rd RH10 ...18 F3
Gaisford Cl BN14 ....182 C4
Gaisford Rd BN14 ....182 B4
Galahad Rd RH11 ....17 E6
Gales Dr RH10 ....18 F6
Gales Pl RH10 ....18 F6
Galliers Cl BN1 ....168 B6
Galsworthy Cl BN12 .....181 B3
Galsworthy Rd BN12 .....181 B3
Gamecock Terr PO20 ....154 D1
Gander Cl RH15 ....107 A5
Gander Gn RH16 ....85 F7
Gander Hill RH16 ....85 F7
Ganders Cl BN5 ....123 D5
Gandersgate La RH14 ....75 A7
Gannet Ho BN3 ....167 B1
Gannon Rd BN11 ....182 F3
Ganymede Ct RH11 ......17 E3
Garbitts La GU31 ....68 B4
Garcia Trad Est BN13 ....181 F3
Garden Ave PO20 ....202 B6
Garden Cl
Angmering BN16 ....180 A7
East Grinstead RH19 ....22 F7
Lancing BN15 ....183 C6
Portslade-by-Sea BN41 ....186 C8
Shoreham-by-Sea BN43 ...165 B1
Storrington RH20 ....119 D2
Garden Cres PO22 ......176 C5
Garden Ct
Bogner Regis PO21 ....194 E2
Shoreham-by-Sea BN43 ...165 B1
Garden Head RH19 ....42 E6
Garden Ho PO19 ....152 F2
Garden Ho The BN1 .....207 A3
Garden House La RH19 ...22 F7
Garden Lodge PO21 .....194 A2
Garden Pl RH12 ....36 C4
Garden Wlk Crawley RH11 .18 C6
Horsham RH12 ....36 C4
Garden Wood Cl RH20 ...119 D6
Garden Wood Rd RH19 ...22 C8
Gardener Ho RH13 ....57 E1
Gardener St BN41 ....186 B8
Gardeners Cl RH12 ....35 E8
Gardeners Ct 4 RH13 ....36 D1
Gardeners Gn RH12 ......16 C6
Gardens The
Fittleworth RH20 ....97 A3
Southwick BN42 ....185 F7
West Ashling PO18 ....151 B3
Gardner La RH10 ....21 A8
Gardner Rd BN41 ....186 A7
Gardner St BN1 ....207 B2
Garland Ave PO10 ....149 B3
Garland Cl PO19 ....173 B5
Garland Rd RH19 ....9 D2
Garland Sq PO20 ....154 D2
Garnet Ho 13 BN2 ....188 C4
Garrett Cl RH10 ....19 C4
Garrick Rd BN14 ....182 E4
Garrick Wlk RH10 ....18 E3
Garrones The RH10 ....19 E7
Garsons Rd PO10 ....169 F8
Garton Cl RH11 ....17 E5
Gaskyns Cl RH12 ....33 D7
Gasson Wood Rd RH11 ...17 E4
Gaston Way PO18 ....152 E7
Gatcombe Cl BN13 ......181 B5
Gate Ho GU29 ....92 F7
Gateford Dr RH12 ....36 F6
Gatehouse La
Burgess Hill BN6,RH15 ....106 C4
Trotton GU31 ....69 A4
Gatehouse Mews PO21 ..195 D3
Gates Cl RH10 ....19 C2
Gatesmead RH16 ....85 F8
Gateway Lodge PO22 ....195 F4
Gatewick Terr BN44 .....143 D3
Gattons Inf Sch The
RH15 ....106 E3
Gattons The RH15 ......106 E3
Gatwick Airport Sta RH6 ...6 B7
Gatwick Airport-London
RH6 ....5 F7
Gatwick Gate RH6,RH11 ....5 E5
Gatwick Ind Est RH6 ....4 F6
Gatwick Metro Ctr RH6 ....2 B4
Gatwick Park Hospl RH6 ...1 E2
Gatwick Rd RH10, RH6 .....6 A3
Gatwick Way RH6 ....5 F8
Gatwick Zoo & Aviaries
RH6 ....4 D6
Gaugemaster Way BN18 .177 E5
Gay St RH20 ....99 C4
Gay Street La RH20 ......99 A6
Gaywood Wlk BN13 .....181 D5
Gemini Cl RH11 ....17 E4
Genesis Bsns Ctr RH13 ...36 F3
Genistos The BN6 ....126 E4
Genoa Cl BN17 ....199 A6
George Denyer Cl GU27 ..27 C7
George IV Wlk PO22 ....196 A5
George Pinion Ct RH12 ...36 B3
George St Brighton BN2 ..207 B2
Chichester PO19 ....173 A7
Hove BN3 ....187 B6
Portslade-by-Sea BN41 ....186 C7
Southwick BN41 ....186 A7
George V Ave
Shoreham-by-Sea BN15 ....184 B5
Worthing BN11 ....181 F2
Georges La RH20 ....120 C1
Georgia Ave BN14 ....182 D4
Georgian Cl RH10 ....19 D5
Georgian Gardens
Com Prim Sch BN16 ....199 E6
Georgian Gdns BN16 ....199 E6
Gerald Cl RH15 ....107 D3
Gerald Ct RH13 ....36 E2
Gerald Rd BN11 ....181 F1
Gerard St BN1 ....207 B5
Gerrard House Bsns Ctr
BN16 ....199 F6
Gerston Bsns Pk
RH20 ....140 C8
Ghyll Cres RH13 ....58 F8
Ghyll Ct RH13 ....57 F1
Ghyllside BN2 ....168 E1
Gibbons Cl RH10 ....19 C3
Giblets La RH12 ....36 F7
Giblets Way RH12 ....36 E7
Gibson Rd PO20 ....154 C2
Gibson Way PO21 ....195 D4
Giffards Cl RH19 ....9 F1
Gifford Rd PO18 ....171 C7
Gilbert Rd PO19 ....172 E8
Gilberts The BN16 ......199 B3
Giles Cl BN18 ....176 F2
Gilham La RH18 ....23 E2
Gillett Ct RH13 ....37 B4
Gillett Ho RH13 ....37 B4
Gillham's La GU27 ....26 A5
Gilligan Cl RH12 ....36 B2
Gillmans The RH15 .....106 F5
Gillmans Ind Est RH14 ....77 D6
Gillway PO20 ....206 G8
Gilmore Rd PO19 ....173 C6
Gilpin Cl PO19 ....172 B6
Gilwynes PO21 ....194 F2
Gilwynes Ct PO21 ......194 F2
Ginhams Rd RH11 ....18 B6
Girton Ho BN3 ....186 F6
Glade Inf Sch PO21 .....195 A5
Glade The
Bognor Regis PO21 ....205 A8
Crawley RH10 ....19 A4
Horsham RH13 ....37 A3
Gladepoint RH16 ....85 E5
Glades The RH19 ....10 B1
Gladonian Rd BN17 .....178 D3
Gladstone Pl BN2 ......188 C8
Gladstone Rd
Burgess Hill RH15 ....107 C4
Horsham RH12 ....36 D3
Portslade-by-Sea BN41 ....186 B7
Yapton BN18 ....176 F2
Gladstone Terr
Brighton BN2 ....207 C4
Littlehampton BN17 ......178 D3
Gladys Rd BN3 ....186 D8
Glamis Ct PO21 ....195 D3
Glamis St PO21 ....195 D3
Glanville Wlk 7 RH11 ....18 A3
Glaseby La RH20 ....141 D4
Glasshouse La GU28, RH14 .74 F3
Glastonbury Rd BN3 ....186 D6
Glatting La RH20 ....115 E1
Glawood Ho BN14 ......182 E6
Glaziers La GU29 ....71 B2
Gleave Cl RH19 ....10 A2
Glebe Cl Crawley RH10 ....18 E7
Lancing BN15 ....183 E7
Norton PO20 ....155 B1
Southwick BN42 ....185 F7
Glebe Com Mid Sch
BN42 ....185 D8
Glebe Field Rd PO20 ....191 A5
Glebe Lands RH20 ....98 D2
Glebe Rd Cuckfield RH17 ...84 F6
Fernhurst GU27 ....49 B5
Worthing BN14 ....182 A5
Glebe The Copthorne RH10 ...7 B3
Felbridge RH19 ....9 A4
Horley RH6 ....1 F3
Hurstpierpoint BN6 ....126 A6
Lindfield RH16 ....86 A8
Tangmere PO20 ....154 C1
Glebe Twitten RH17 ......84 F6
Glebe View RH17 ....41 A1
Glebe Villas Petworth GU28 .73 F1
Portslade-by-Sea BN3 .....186 D7
Glebe Way Lancing BN15 ..183 E7
Wisborough Green RH14 ....76 C8
Glebelands
Crawley Down RH10 ....21 A7
Loxwood RH14 ....31 F4
Glebelands Cl BN43 .....185 B8
Glebeside Ave BN14 ....182 A5
Glebeside Cl BN14 .....182 B5
Glen Cres PO20 ....206 E7
Glen Dale PO9 ....128 E1
Glen Eagles 11 RH6 ....2 B2
Glen Gdns BN12 ....200 F6
Glen Rise BN1 ....167 B5
Glen Rise Cl BN1 ....167 B5
Glen The Southwater RH13 ..58 A2
Worthing BN13 ....182 A7

Glen Vue RH19 .... 9 E1
Glenbarrie Way BN12 .... 180 E3
Glencathara Rd PO21 .... 195 B3
Glendale Cl RH12 .... 37 A6
Glendale Rd
Burgess Hill RH15 .... 107 B2
Hove BN3 .... 187 D7
Glendon Ho 9 RH11 .... 18 D5
Glendor Rd BN3 .... 186 E6
Glendyne Cl RH19 .... 23 A8
Glendyne Way RH19 .... 23 A8
Gleneagles Ct
Crawley RH10 .... 18 D5
13 Haywards Heath RH16 .... 85 E4
Glenelg Cl PO21 .... 194 F6
Glenfalls Ave BN1 .... 168 A7
Glenfergus RH16 .... 85 E6
Glenfield Cotts RH6 .... 4 D7
Glenham Pl RH19 .... 43 A5
Glenlea Hollow
GU26, GU27 .... 26 E8
Glenmore Ct 16 BN17 .... 198 E4
Glenside 1 RH19 .... 9 E1
Glenview Cl RH10 .... 18 F8
Glenville Rd BN16 .... 199 D4
Glenway PO22 .... 195 D4
Glenwood Ave PO22 .... 195 D4
Glenwood Rd PO10 .... 150 A1
Glenwood Sch PO10 .... 149 B1
Gleton Ave BN3 .... 166 D2
Globe Pl BN17 .... 178 D3
Gloster Dr PO21 .... 194 B2
Gloucester Cl RH19 .... 23 A8
Gloucester Ct BN12 .... 181 F1
Gloucester La BN17 .... 198 D5
Gloucester Mews 2 BN1 .... 207 B3
Gloucester Pas 4 BN1 .... 207 B3
Gloucester Pl
Brighton BN1, BN2 .... 207 B3
Littlehampton BN17 .... 198 D5
Gloucester Rd
Bognor Regis PO21 .... 195 E3
Brighton BN1 .... 207 B3
Burgess Hill RH15 .... 106 F3
Crawley RH10 .... 18 E2
Littlehampton BN17 .... 198 C5
Gloucester St BN1, BN2 .... 207 B3
Gloucester Terr PO18 .... 171 B4
Gloucester Way PO19 .... 152 F1
Gloucester Yd 3 BN1 .... 207 B3
Glover's Rd RH6 .... 4 D7
Glovers Field GU27 .... 26 F6
Glovers Ho GU27 .... 26 F6
Glynde Ave BN12 .... 181 A2
Glynde Cl BN12 .... 200 F6
Glynde Cres PO22 .... 196 A5
Glynde Ho BN3 .... 187 D6
Glynde Pl 6 RH12 .... 36 C2
Glynde Rd BN2 .... 188 D6
Glyndebourne Ct 9
BN43 .... 184 F7
Glynleigh 18 BN2 .... 207 C3
Goda Rd BN17 .... 198 E5
Goddard Cl RH10 .... 19 B3
Godman Cl PO21 .... 194 D2
Godmans Ct RH13 .... 81 E1
Godolphin Ct RH10 .... 18 D5
Godstalls La BN44 .... 143 C2
Godstrode La GU8 .... 29 A6
Godwin Cl PO10 .... 149 A3
Godwin Ct RH12 .... 36 A1
Godwin Rd BN3 .... 166 D1
Godwin Way
Fishbourne PO18 .... 172 A8
Horsham RH13 .... 37 A4
Goffs Cl RH11 .... 18 C5
Goffs La RH11 .... 18 B6
Goffs Park Rd RH11 .... 18 C4
Goldcrest Ave BN17 .... 178 C4
Goldcrest Cl RH6 .... 1 E4
Golden Acre
Bognor Regis PO21 .... 205 A8
West Kingston BN16 .... 200 B4
Golden Ave BN16 .... 200 B5
Golden Avenue Cl BN16 .... 200 B4
Golden Hill RH15 .... 107 D3
Golden La Ashurst BN44 .... 122 E6
11 Hove BN1 .... 187 D5
Golden Sq Henfield BN5 .... 123 E4
Petworth GU28 .... 95 F8
Goldenfields GU30 .... 25 D3
Goldenfields Cl GU30 .... 25 D3
Goldfinch Cl Crawley RH11 .... 18 D8
Horsham RH12 .... 36 C7
Golding Barn Farm
(Works) BN5 .... 144 E2
Golding Cl RH10 .... 19 C5
Golding La RH13 .... 59 D7
Goldsmid Rd BN1, BN3 .... 187 E7
Goldsmith Rd BN14 .... 182 E4
Goldstone Cl BN3 .... 167 A2
Goldstone Cres BN3 .... 167 B2
Goldstone Ct BN3 .... 167 A3
Goldstone Ho 4 BN3 .... 187 B7
Goldstone Jun Sch BN3 .... 166 E1
Goldstone La BN3 .... 187 B8
Goldstone Rd BN3 .... 187 B7
Goldstone Ret Pk BN3 .... 187 B8
Goldstone St BN3 .... 187 B7
Goldstone Villas BN3 .... 187 B7
Goldstone Way BN3 .... 167 A2
Golf Club La RH20 .... 118 F7
Golf Dr BN1 .... 168 B3
Golf Links La PO20 .... 203 E1
Golf Links Rd PO22 .... 196 A6
Golfers La BN16 .... 179 D3
Goodacres Barnham PO22 .... 176 C5
Fontwell BN18 .... 156 B2
Goodhew Cl BN18 .... 177 A3
Goodwin Cl RH11 .... 17 F3
Goodwins Cl RH19 .... 9 D3
Goodwood Ave PO22 .... 195 F5
Goodwood Cl
Crawley RH10 .... 19 A3
Midhurst GU29 .... 92 E5
Rustington BN16 .... 199 E6
Goodwood Ct
2 Hove BN3 .... 187 D7
Selsey PO20 .... 206 E8
Southbourne PO10 .... 170 A8
Goodwood Ctry Pk PO18 .... 134 A4
Goodwood Gdns PO20 .... 173 E1
Goodwood Ho PO18 .... 153 F6
Goodwood Rd BN13 .... 182 A7
Goodwood Way BN2 .... 168 F3
Goodwood Wing The
BN18 .... 177 E7
Goose Green Cl RH12 .... 36 D5
Goosegreen La RH20 .... 100 C2
Gooserye Ct GU30 .... 25 B3
Gorden Rd BN15 .... 183 D6
Gordon Ave
Bognor Regis PO22 .... 195 D5
Shoreham-by-Sea BN43 .... 185 A7
Stockbridge PO19 .... 172 E3
Gordon Ave W PO22 .... 195 D5
Gordon Cl RH16 .... 85 E6
Gordon Ho
8 Bognor Regis PO21 .... 195 C3
Burgess Hill RH15 .... 107 C4
Gordon Rd Brighton BN1 .... 167 F2
Burgess Hill RH15 .... 107 C4
Haywards Heath RH16 .... 85 E6
Hermitage PO10 .... 169 D8
Horsham RH12 .... 36 D4
Portslade-by-Sea BN41 .... 186 C7
Shoreham-by-Sea BN43 .... 185 A7
Southwick BN41 .... 186 A7
Worthing BN11 .... 182 D3
Gordon Terr PO18 .... 171 A5
Goreside La RH17 .... 84 F8
Goring Chase BN12 .... 181 A4
Goring Crossways BN12 .... 181 A4
Goring Ct BN1 .... 168 F5
Goring Hall Hospl
(Private) BN12 .... 181 B1
Goring Rd Steyning BN44 .... 143 E2
Worthing BN12 .... 181 D2
Goring St BN12 .... 181 A3
Goring Way
Partridge Green RH13 .... 103 A3
Worthing BN12 .... 181 A2
Goring's Mead RH13 .... 36 D1
Goring-by-Sea
CE Fst Sch BN12 .... 181 C2
Goring-by-Sea Sta BN12 .... 181 A3
Gorling Cl RH11 .... 17 E5
Gorringe Cl BN43 .... 185 D7
Gorringes Brook RH12 .... 36 D6
Gorse Ave
Bognor Regis PO22 .... 196 D6
Kingston Gorse BN16 .... 200 D4
Worthing BN14 .... 182 B6
Gorse Bank Cl RH20 .... 120 C3
Gorse Cl Copthorne RH10 .... 7 B2
Crawley RH11 .... 18 B1
Portslade-by-Sea BN41 .... 165 F4
Gorse Cotts GU26 .... 26 C8
Gorse End RH12 .... 36 D5
Gorse La BN13 .... 161 E2
Gorse Terr PO20 .... 192 D4
Gorselands RH14 .... 77 E8
Gosden Cl RH10 .... 19 A5
Gosden Rd BN17 .... 198 F6
Gospond Rd PO22 .... 176 B5
Gossamer La PO21 .... 194 D3
Gossops Dr RH11 .... 18 A5
Gossops Green
Com Fst Sch RH11 .... 18 A5
Gossops Green
Com Mid Sch RH11 .... 18 A5
Gossops Green La RH11 .... 18 A5
Gossops Par RH11 .... 17 F5
Goudhurst Cl RH10 .... 19 E6
Goudhurst Keep RH10 .... 19 E6
Gower Rd
Haywards Heath RH16 .... 85 E3
Horley RH6 .... 1 E3
Gowers Cl RH17 .... 64 B8
Grace Ct BN6 .... 126 E5
Grace Rd RH11 .... 18 A1
Graffham Cl Brighton BN2 .... 188 E6
Chichester PO19 .... 153 A3
Crawley RH11 .... 18 B8
Graffham Fst Sch GU28 .... 114 B6
Grafton Ave PO22 .... 196 C6
Grafton Cl BN16 .... 199 C6
Grafton Ct PO20 .... 206 E6
Grafton Dr BN15 .... 183 C6
Grafton Gdns BN15 .... 183 C6
Grafton Pl 7 BN11 .... 182 D2
Grafton Rd Selsey PO20 .... 206 E6
Worthing BN11 .... 182 D2
Grafton St BN2 .... 207 C1
Graham Ave Brighton BN1 .... 167 F5
Portslade-by-Sea BN41 .... 165 F4
Graham Cl BN41 .... 165 F4
Graham Cres BN41 .... 165 F4
Graham Ct Lancing BN15 .... 183 C6
Worthing BN11 .... 181 F1
Graham Rd
Worthing BN11 .... 182 D2
Yapton BN18 .... 176 F1
Graham's Cotts RH16 .... 64 B1
Grailands Cl GU27 .... 49 C6
Granary Cl RH6 .... 2 A5
Granary La PO20 .... 206 D8
Granary Way
Horsham RH12 .... 36 A1
Littlehampton BN17 .... 178 D4
Grand Ave Hassocks BN6 .... 126 F4
Hove BN3 .... 187 C6
Lancing BN15 .... 183 E7
Littlehampton BN17 .... 178 C3
Worthing BN11 .... 182 A2
Grand Avenue Mans 4
BN3 .... 187 C6
Grand Junction Rd
BN1, BN2 .... 207 B1
Grand Par Brighton BN2 .... 207 B2
Crawley RH10 .... 18 D6
Grand Parade Mews BN2 .... 207 B2
Grange Cl Brighton BN1 .... 167 E1
Burgess Hill RH15 .... 107 C5
Crawley RH10 .... 19 A8
Worthing BN12 .... 200 E5
Grange Cres RH10 .... 21 B7
Grange Ct
Bognor Regis PO21 .... 194 E1
7 Middleton-on-Sea PO22 .... 196 F5
9 Southwick BN42 .... 185 E7
Grange Field Way PO21 .... 194 D2
Grange Ind Est The
BN42 .... 185 D7
Grange La PO20 .... 204 B2
Grange Park BN12 .... 200 E5
Grange Rd
Crawley Down RH10 .... 21 A7
Hove BN3 .... 186 E8
Midhurst GU29 .... 92 F7
Southwick BN42 .... 185 E7
Grange The RH6 .... 2 A6
Grange Way RH13 .... 57 F2
Grangeway The BN16 .... 199 C5
Grangeways BN1 .... 167 E5
Grangewood 13 PO21 .... 195 B2
Grangewood Dr PO21 .... 194 D2
Granston Way RH10 .... 21 C8
Grant Cl PO20 .... 206 D7
Grant St BN2 .... 207 C4
Grantham Rd BN1 .... 168 A1
Grantsmead BN15 .... 183 E8
Granville Ct 10 BN3 .... 187 B7
Granville Rd Hove BN3 .... 187 E7
Littlehampton BN17 .... 198 E4
Graperies The 3 BN2 .... 188 C5
Grasmere Ave BN15 .... 183 B6
Grasmere Gdns RH12 .... 37 B6
Grassmere RH6 .... 2 C4
Grassmere Cl
Bognor Regis PO22 .... 195 F4
Littlehampton BN17 .... 179 A3
Grassmere Par PO22 .... 195 F4
Gratten La BN5,RH17 .... 104 D3
Grattons Dr RH10 .... 6 C1
Grattons The RH13 .... 34 E3
Gratwicke Cl RH14 .... 77 D8
Gratwicke Rd BN11 .... 182 C2
Gravel La PO19 .... 173 C5
Gravelly Cres BN15 .... 183 F6
Gravelpit Cnr RH17 .... 39 C1
Gravelye Cl RH16 .... 86 B5
Gravelye La Haywards
Heath, Franklands
Village RH16 .... 86 A4
Lindfield RH16 .... 86 B6
Graveney Rd RH10 .... 19 C5
Gravett Ct RH15 .... 106 F2
Gravetye Cl RH10 .... 19 A4
Gravits La PO21 .... 195 B4
Graydon Ave PO19 .... 172 E4
Graylingwell Cotts PO19 .... 153 A2
Graylingwell Hospl PO19 .... 153 B1
Grays Cl GU27 .... 27 E8
Grays Wood RH6 .... 2 C3
Grayswood Ave PO20 .... 202 B6
Grayswood Pl GU27 .... 27 E8
Grayswood Rd GU27 .... 27 D8
Great Ballard Sch PO18 .... 155 D7
Great College St BN2 .... 188 C4
Great Heathmead RH16 .... 85 D6
Great House Ct 4 RH19 .... 22 F8
Great Walstead Sch RH16 .... 86 F6
Greatfield Way PO9 .... 128 D3
Greatham Ct BN1 .... 167 E6
Greatham Rd Crawley RH10 .... 19 C3
Worthing BN14 .... 162 A1
Greatlake Ct RH6 .... 2 B4
Greatpin Croft RH20 .... 97 A3
Grebe Cl PO10 .... 149 D4
Grebe Cres RH13 .... 37 A1
Green Bushes Cl BN16 .... 199 B4
Green Cl Southwater RH13 .... 57 F3
4 Southwick BN42 .... 185 E7
Green Cross RH17 .... 84 C3
Green Ct Chichester PO19 .... 173 C6
East Wittering PO20 .... 201 F7
3 Southwick BN42 .... 185 E7
Green Field Cl BN42 .... 185 E8
Green Field La PO18 .... 151 B3
Green Hedges Ave RH19 .... 9 D2
Green Hedges Cl RH19 .... 9 D2
Green La Bosham PO18 .... 171 C6
Broadbridge PO18 .... 171 A8
Burstow RH6 .... 6 F6
Chichester PO19 .... 173 B6
Copthorne RH10 .... 7 F4
Crawley RH10 .... 18 E8
Crawley, Worth RH10 .... 19 D6
Faygate RH12 .... 15 F4
Fernhurst GU27 .... 27 B4
Green La *continued*
Merston PO20 .... 173 F4
Newdigate RH5 .... 3 D8
Runcton PO20 .... 173 F2
Selsey PO20 .... 206 D6
Sidlesham PO20 .... 203 C8
Street End PO20 .... 192 E6
West Grinstead RH13 .... 102 B8
Green Lane Cl BN18 .... 157 F2
Green Mdws RH16 .... 86 B8
Green Pk BN12 .... 180 F3
Green Ridge BN1 .... 167 B5
Green The
Bognor Regis PO21 .... 205 A8
Broadridge Heath RH12 .... 35 D4
Copthorne RH10 .... 7 B3
Crawley RH11 .... 18 C7
Dial Post RH13 .... 101 E3
East Lavington GU28 .... 114 E5
Henfield BN5 .... 123 E4
Horsted Keynes RH17 .... 65 C5
Hove BN3 .... 167 C2
Liss GU33 .... 45 A5
Partridge Green RH13 .... 103 A3
Pulborough RH20 .... 98 C4
Rowland's Castle PO9 .... 128 E2
Southwick BN42 .... 185 E7
Storrington RH20 .... 119 F2
Green View RH15 .... 106 E3
Green Way PO22 .... 196 F5
Green Way The BN12 .... 181 B4
Green Wlk RH10 .... 18 E8
Greena Ct 8 BN11 .... 182 C2
Greenacre Cl RH20 .... 119 B1
Greenacres
Ashington RH20 .... 121 A6
Brighton BN1 .... 167 F1
Crawley RH10 .... 19 A5
Horsham RH12 .... 36 C4
Shoreham-by-Sea BN43 .... 184 E8
Steyning BN44 .... 143 D2
Westlands PO20 .... 191 D6
Greenacres Ring BN16 .... 180 A6
Greenbank PO22 .... 176 C5
Greencourt Dr PO21 .... 195 A5
Greenfield RH20 .... 115 F2
Greenfield Cl
Brighton BN1 .... 168 A5
Liphook GU30 .... 25 C5
Greenfield Cres BN1 .... 167 F5
Greenfield Rd
Chichester PO19 .... 173 C7
Slinfold RH13 .... 34 D3
Greenfield Way RH20 .... 119 E2
Greenfields Liss GU33 .... 45 C4
Littlehampton BN17 .... 178 B3
Nyewood GU31 .... 90 A7
Greenfields Cl Horley RH6 .... 1 E5
Horsham RH12 .... 37 A6
Nyewood GU31 .... 90 A8
Greenfields Rd Horley RH6 .... 1 F5
Horsham RH12 .... 37 A5
Greenfields Sch
East Grinstead RH19 .... 22 D6
Forest Row RH18 .... 23 C1
Greenfields Way RH12 .... 37 A6
Greenfinch Way RH12 .... 36 D7
Greengates GU28 .... 50 D2
Greenhill Pk RH17 .... 86 A2
Greenhill Way RH17 .... 86 A2
Greenhurst La RH20 .... 119 E4
Greenland Cl BN13 .... 181 E7
Greenland Rd BN13 .... 181 E7
Greenland Wlk BN13 .... 181 E7
Greenlands Cl RH15 .... 127 B8
Greenlands Dr RH15 .... 127 B8
Greenlea Ave PO21 .... 194 B2
Greenleas BN3 .... 166 D2
Greenoaks BN15 .... 183 E8
Greenside BN17 .... 198 C6
Greenstede Ave RH19 .... 9 F2
Greentree La RH13 .... 103 C5
Greentrees
Lancing BN15 .... 183 C6
5 Worthing BN11 .... 182 B2
Greentrees Cl BN15 .... 183 C6
Greentrees Cres BN15 .... 183 C6
Greenway RH12 .... 36 B3
Greenway Jun Sch RH12 .... 36 B3
Greenway The PO10 .... 149 B4
Greenways
Bognor Regis PO21 .... 194 B1
Haywards Heath RH16 .... 85 F6
Henfield BN5 .... 123 D5
Portslade-by-Sea BN41 .... 166 B1
Southwick BN42 .... 165 F1
Greenways Cres
Ferring BN12 .... 200 F5
Shoreham-by-Sea BN43 .... 165 A1
Greenways Wlk RH11 .... 18 C1
Greenwich Cl RH11 .... 18 C2
Greenwood Ave PO22 .... 195 B6
Greenwood Cl PO22 .... 195 B6
Greenwood Ct 2 RH11 .... 18 B1
Greenwood Dr BN16 .... 179 F4
Greet Rd BN15 .... 183 D7
Gregory Cl RH10 .... 19 C2
Gregory Ct 2 RH19 .... 9 E1
Gregsons RH12 .... 35 E8
Grendon Cl RH6 .... 1 F5
Grenfield Ct PO10 .... 149 B3
Grenville Ave BN12 .... 181 D3
Grenville Cl Liphook GU30 .... 25 C4
Worthing BN12 .... 181 D3
Grenville Gdns PO19 .... 172 F4
Grenville St BN1 .... 207 A2
Gresham Pl BN5 .... 123 D5
Gresham Wlk RH10 .... 18 E3
Grevatt's La
BN17,BN18,PO22 .... 197 B8
Grevatt's La W BN18 .... 196 F8
Greville Gn PO10 .... 149 A3
Grey Alders RH16 .... 86 B6
Greyfriars BN3 .... 187 D8
Greyfriars Cl
Bognor Regis PO21 .... 194 F3
Worthing BN13 .... 182 A6
Greyfriars La RH20 .... 140 C8
Greyhound Slip RH10 .... 19 D7
Greynville Cl PO21 .... 194 C2
Greypoint Ho BN14 .... 161 E6
Greystoke Mews BN12 .... 200 E6
Greystoke Rd BN12 .... 200 E6
Greystone Ave
Bognor Regis PO21 .... 194 F7
Worthing BN13 .... 181 F5
Gribble La PO20 .... 174 B7
Grier Cl RH11 .... 17 E5
Griffin Cres BN17 .... 178 D4
Griffith's Ave BN15 .... 183 D8
Grinder's La RH13 .... 101 E2
Grinstead Ave BN15 .... 183 E6
Grinstead La
Lancing BN15 .... 183 E6
Sharpthorne RH19 .... 43 C7
Grinstead Mount 4 BN2 .... 188 F5
Grisedale Cl RH11 .... 18 C4
Groombridge Way RH12 .... 35 F1
Grooms The RH10 .... 19 D8
Groomsland Dr RH14 .... 77 C6
Grosvenor Ct
12 Bognor Regis PO21 .... 195 C2
Brighton BN1 .... 167 E3
Grosvenor Gdns PO21 .... 194 C3
Grosvenor Ho 6 BN11 .... 182 D2
Grosvenor Mans 1 BN3 .... 187 B6
Grosvenor Rd
East Grinstead RH19 .... 9 D1
Stockbridge PO19 .... 172 F3
4 Worthing BN11 .... 182 D2
Grosvenor St BN2 .... 207 C2
Grosvenor Way PO21 .... 194 C3
Grouse Rd
Barnsnap RH11, RH13 .... 38 D3
Mannings Heath RH13 .... 59 F7
Grove Bank 9 BN2 .... 207 C3
Grove Cres BN17 .... 198 F6
Grove Ct 12 BN3 .... 187 C6
Grove Hill BN2 .... 207 C3
Grove La Petworth GU28 .... 96 A6
West Chiltington
Common RH20 .... 119 E5
Grove Pk PO19 .... 172 D6
Grove Rd
Burgess Hill RH15 .... 107 B3
Chichester PO19 .... 173 B5
Horley RH6 .... 1 F4
Selsey PO20 .... 206 E6
Worthing BN14 .... 182 C6
Grove St Brighton BN2 .... 207 C3
Petworth GU28 .... 95 F7
Grove The
Bognor Regis PO22 .... 196 A4
Crawley RH11 .... 18 C6
Ferring BN12 .... 200 E6
Haywards Heath RH16 .... 86 B3
Horley RH6 .... 2 B2
Liphook GU30 .... 25 B4
Westbourne PO10 .... 149 D3
Grove Villa 3 BN1 .... 207 A4
Grovelands RH6 .... 2 B2
Grovelands Cl RH15 .... 106 F1
Grovelands The BN15 .... 183 E4
Grover Ave BN15 .... 183 D7
Guardian Ct BN13 .... 182 A6
Guernsey Cl RH11 .... 18 A2
Guernsey Farm La PO22 .... 196 D5
Guernsey Rd BN12 .... 200 F4
Guildbourne Ctr The 14
BN11 .... 182 D2
Guilden Rd PO19 .... 173 B6
Guildford Cl Breach PO10 .... 150 A1
Worthing BN14 .... 182 A3
Guildford Pl PO19 .... 152 F1
Guildford Rd
Horsham RH12 .... 36 A2
Rowhook RH12 .... 34 C7
Rudgwick RH12 .... 33 C6
Rustington BN16 .... 199 E6
Strood Green RH12 .... 35 B6
Worthing BN14 .... 182 A3
Guildford St BN1 .... 207 A3
Guildhall St PO19 .... 173 A7
Guilford Rd BN1 .... 207 A3
Guillards Oak GU29 .... 92 E7
Guillemot Path 2 RH11 .... 17 D5
Guillods Cotts GU28 .... 114 B7
Guinevere Rd RH11 .... 17 E6
Guinness Ct RH11 .... 18 C2
Gunning Cl RH11 .... 18 A3
Gunns Farm GU30 .... 25 C2
Gunwin Ct PO21 .... 194 D2
Guyhurst Spinney RH20 .... 120 A6
Gwydyr Mans 3 BN3 .... 187 D6
Gwynne Gdns RH19 .... 9 C2

H

Habin Hill GU31 .... 68 B3
Hackenden Cl RH19 .... 9 E3
Hackenden Cotts RH19 .... 9 E3
Hackenden La RH19 .... 9 E3
Haddington Cl BN3 .... 187 B6
Haddington St 11 BN3 .... 187 B7
Hadlands PO21 .... 194 A1

Hadley Ave BN14 ....182 D6
Hadley Cl PO22 ....196 E6
Hadlow Cl BN2 ....188 D6
Hadlow Way BN15 ....183 F6
Hadmans Cl RH12 ....36 C1
Hadrian Ave BN42 ....186 A8
Haglands Copse RH20 ....119 D7
Haglands La RH20 ....119 D7
Haig Ave BN1 ....168 D6
Haigh Cl BN15 ....184 B6
Hailsham Cl BN16 ....180 B3
Hailsham Rd BN11 ....181 F1
Hale Cl PO20 ....202 B6
Hales Field GU27 ....27 C6
Halewick Cl BN15 ....183 C8
Halewick La BN15 ....183 C8
Haleybridge Wlk PO20 ....154 D1
Half Moon Hill GU27 ....27 C6
Half Moon La BN13 ....181 F7
Halfrey Cl PO18 ....172 A7
Halfrey Rd PO18, PO19 ....172 B7
Halifax Cl RH10 ....6 E1
Halifax Dr BN13 ....181 C6
Hall Ave BN14 ....182 B7
Hall Cl BN14 ....182 A7
Halland Cl RH10 ....19 A7
Halland Rd BN2 ....168 F4
Hallands The RH15 ....107 C4
Halleighs RH17 ....84 E8
Hallett Rd BN2 ....188 D7
Halley Cl RH11 ....18 B1
Halley's Ct PO19 ....173 C6
Halliford Dr PO22 ....176 C6
Halliwick Gdns PO22 ....196 B4
Hallsland RH10 ....21 C8
Hallyburton Rd BN3 ....186 D8
Halnaker Barn La PO18 ....155 B4
Halnaker Gdns PO21 ....194 C2
Halnaker Wlk 8 RH11 ....17 F3
Halsbury Cl BN11 ....182 F3
Halsbury Rd BN11 ....182 F3
Halsford Croft RH19 ....9 B3
Halsford Gn RH19 ....9 B3
Halsford La RH19 ....9 C3
Halsford Park Prim Sch RH19 ....9 C2
Halsford Park Rd RH19 ....9 C2
Halson Cl PO21 ....195 C4
Halton Shaws BN6 ....126 B5
Ham Bridge Trad Est BN14 ....183 A4
Ham Bsns Ctr BN43 ....185 A7
Ham Cl BN11 ....183 A4
Ham La Oving PO20 ....174 D7
 Prinsted PO10 ....169 F7
 Scaynes Hill RH17 ....86 E3
Ham Manor Cl BN16 ....179 E4
Ham Manor Farm Cotts BN16 ....179 D4
Ham Manor Way BN16 ....179 E4
Ham Rd
 Shoreham-by-Sea BN43 ....184 F7
 Sidlesham PO20 ....203 C5
 Worthing BN11,BN14 ....183 A3
Ham Way BN11 ....183 A4
Hamble Ct BN15 ....183 B6
Hamble Gdns BN13 ....181 C7
Hamble Rd BN15 ....183 B6
Hamble Way BN13 ....181 C7
Hambledon Pl PO21 ....195 B3
Hambleton Ct RH11 ....18 C4
Hambleton Hill RH11 ....18 C4
Hambrook RH15 ....107 C1
Hambrook Bsns Ctr PO18 ....150 D4
Hambrook Hill N PO18 ....150 D3
Hambrook Hill S PO18 ....150 D2
Hamilton Cl
 Portslade-by-Sea BN41 ....166 A3
 Rustington BN16 ....179 B4
 Stedham GU29 ....69 F1
 Worthing BN14 ....182 E5
Hamilton Ct BN12 ....181 D4
Hamilton Dr BN16 ....179 B4
Hamilton Gdns
 Bognor Regis PO21 ....194 D2
 Broadbridge PO18 ....171 C7
Hamilton Lodge Sch BN2 ....188 D5
Hamilton Mans 8 BN3 ....187 B5
Hamilton Mews BN15 ....183 C6
Hamilton Rd Brighton BN1 207 A4
 Horsham RH12 ....36 B3
 Lancing BN15 ....183 D7
Hamlet The PO22 ....195 C6
Hamlin's Cnr BN6 ....106 A6
Hammer Hill Hammer GU27 26 C4
 Staplefield RH17 ....62 A3
Hammer La Chithurst GU29 .69 D4
 Hammer GU26 ....26 C5
 Hammer GU27, GU30 ....26 B6
 Haslemere GU26 ....26 C8
Hammer Vale GU27 ....26 C6
Hammer Yd RH11 ....18 D5
Hammerpond Rd
 Ashfold Crossways RH13 ....60 B6
 Doomsday Green RH13 ....59 C8
Hammerwood Copse GU27 ....26 D5
Hammerwood Rd RH19 ....23 E6
Hammingden La RH17, RH19 ....42 E3
Hammond Dr BN13 ....181 E8
Hammond Pl 3 RH20 ....119 D1
Hammond Rd RH11 ....39 B8
Hammonds Gardens RH15 ....106 F1
Hammonds Ridge RH15 ....106 F1
Hammy Cl BN43 ....185 C8
Hammy La BN43 ....185 B8
Hammy Way BN43 ....185 B8
Hampden Cl Crawley RH10 ..6 E1
 Middleton-on-Sea PO22 ....196 F5
Hampden Ct BN11 ....182 F4
Hampden Pl PO20 ....154 D2
Hampden Rd BN2 ....188 C7
Hamper's La RH13 ....37 A2
Hampers Common Ind Est GU28 ....73 F2
Hampers Ct 2 RH13 ....36 D2
Hampers Gn GU28 ....73 E2
Hampers La RH20 ....120 B2
Hampshire Ave PO21 ....195 B5
Hampshire Ct
 Brighton BN2 ....207 C1
 3 Horsham RH13 ....36 D2
Hampshire Ho GU30 ....25 B7
Hampstead Rd BN1 ....167 D1
Hampton Cotts RH13 ....80 F6
Hampton Ct
 Bognor Regis PO21 ....194 F4
 8 Littlehampton BN17 ....198 D5
Hampton Fields 4 BN17 .198 D6
Hampton Lodge RH6 ....2 A2
Hampton Pl BN1 ....187 E5
Hampton St 24 BN1 ....187 E5
Hampton Terr 7 BN1 ....187 E6
Hampton Way RH19 ....22 F7
Hamsey Cl BN2 ....188 F5
Hamsey Rd RH19 ....43 A6
Hamshire Hill RH17 ....60 F5
Hamsland RH17 ....65 C4
Hamstead Mdw PO18 ....170 E7
Hanbury La RH16 ....86 A5
Hanbury Rd RH11 ....17 E5
Handcross Park Prep Sch RH17 ....39 C2
Handcross Prim Sch RH17 39 C2
Handcross Rd
 Balcombe RH17 ....40 D3
 Lower Beeding RH13,RH17 ..60 C5
Handford Way RH13 ....60 D6
Handsworth Ho 8 RH11 ..18 D5
Hangleton Cl BN3 ....166 D2
Hangleton Ct BN11 ....181 F1
Hangleton Gdns BN3 ....166 D1
Hangleton Grange BN12 .180 E3
Hangleton Inf Sch BN3 ..166 E2
Hangleton Jun Sch BN3 .166 E2
Hangleton La
 Hangleton BN12 ....180 D4
 Hove BN3, BN41 ....166 C2
 Portslade-by-Sea BN41 ....166 B2
Hangleton Manor Cl BN3 ....166 D2
Hangleton Rd BN3 ....166 E2
Hangleton Valley Dr BN3 ....166 D4
Hangleton Way BN3 ....166 D3
Hanlye La RH17 ....85 B8
Hannah Sq PO19 ....172 D7
Hannington Pl BN6 ....126 A7
Hanover Cl Bury RH20 ....138 A7
 Crawley RH10 ....18 F3
 Selsey PO20 ....206 F7
Hanover Cres BN2 ....207 C4
Hanover Ct Brighton BN2 .207 C4
 Easebourne GU29 ....71 A2
 Haywards Heath RH16 ....85 D4
 1 Horsham RH13 ....36 F3
 Liphook GU30 ....25 B5
 Worthing BN14 ....182 C6
Hanover Gdns RH13 ....81 E2
Hanover Mews BN2 ....207 C4
Hanover St BN2 ....207 C4
Hanover Terr BN2 ....207 C4
Hanover Wlk RH20 ....119 D1
Harbell Cl BN17 ....179 B3
Harberton Cres PO19 ....153 A3
Harbolets Rd RH14, RH20 .100 A5
Harborough Cl RH20 ....119 B8
Harborough Dr RH20 ....119 B8
Harborough Gorse RH20 .119 B8
Harborough Hill RH20 ....119 B8
Harborough Mdw RH20 ..119 B8
Harbour Cotts PO18 ....171 A4
Harbour Ct Bosham PO18 .171 C5
 Southwick BN42 ....185 F7
Harbour Rd
 Bognor Regis PO21 ....204 F6
 Bosham PO18 ....171 B4
Harbour View Rd PO21 ..205 A8
Harbour Way
 Bosham PO18 ....171 C4
 Chidham PO18 ....170 F5
 Emsworth PO10 ....169 C8
 Shoreham-by-Sea BN43 ....185 B6
Harcourt Way PO20 ....206 F8
Hard The PO22 ....197 C5
Hard's Hill RH13 ....58 D5
Hardbarrow Woods RH20 ....120 A6
Hardham Cl Crawley RH11 ..18 A8
 Rustington BN16 ....199 B4
Hardham Rd PO19 ....173 B5
Hardwick Lodge 8 BN11 182 C2
Hardwick Rd BN3 ....166 E3
Hardwick Way BN3 ....166 E3
Hardy Cl
 Bognor Regis PO22 ....196 D5
 Crawley RH10 ....19 C7
 Horley RH6 ....1 E3
 Horsham RH12 ....36 B4
 Shoreham-by-Sea BN43 ....184 F6
Hare La Crawley RH11 ....18 B8
 Selsey PO20 ....206 B8
Harebell Dr BN41 ....166 A3
Harefield Ave BN13 ....181 F4
Harefield Gdns PO22 ....196 F5
Harefield Rd PO22 ....196 F6
Hares La PO18 ....150 E6
Haresfield Terr PO20 ....154 D1
Haresfoot Cl PO18 ....150 F5
Harewood Cl RH10 ....6 A1
Harewood Ct 8 BN3 ....187 C6
Harfield Ct 6 PO21 ....195 D3
Harlands Cl RH16 ....85 C6
Harlands Prim Sch RH16 .85 D7
Harlands Rd RH16 ....85 D6
Harlech Cl BN13 ....181 B5
Harley Ct 6 BN11 ....182 B2
Harmans Dr RH19 ....10 B1
Harmans Mead RH19 ....10 B1
Harmony Cl RH11 ....17 E4
Harmony Dr PO20 ....202 B5
Harmsworth Cres BN3 ....166 E3
Harold Cl PO21 ....194 F6
Harold Rd Crawley RH10 ..19 E5
 Westbourne PO10 ....149 D4
Harold Terr PO10 ....149 B1
Haroldslea RH6 ....2 E2
Haroldslea Cl RH6 ....2 C1
Haroldslea Dr RH6 ....2 D1
Harper Dr RH10 ....19 C2
Harrier Ct RH10 ....6 D1
Harrier Ho 6 RH20 ....119 E1
Harrington Ct BN1 ....167 E2
Harrington Mans BN1 ....167 E2
Harrington Pl BN1 ....168 B2
Harrington Rd BN1 ....167 E2
Harrington Villas BN1 ....167 F2
Harriot's Hill RH13 ....81 A8
Harriots Cl RH13 ....59 A1
Harris Cl RH11 ....18 B3
Harris Ct GU30 ....25 B2
Harris La PO8 ....108 A5
Harrison Ct BN14 ....182 E5
Harrison Rd BN14 ....182 F5
Harrow Dr PO20 ....201 F7
Harrow Rd BN11 ....182 B3
Harrows The GU28 ....95 B8
Harrowsley Ct RH6 ....2 B4
Harsfold Cl BN16 ....199 B4
Harsfold Rd BN16 ....199 B4
Hartfield Ave BN1 ....168 A5
Harting Cl BN12 ....181 B4
Harting Ct RH11 ....17 F3
Harting Downs Nature Reserve PO18 ....110 A7
Harting Rd BN17 ....178 D3
Hartings The PO22 ....196 D6
Hartington Pl BN2 ....188 C8
Hartington Rd BN2 ....188 C8
Hartington Terr BN2 ....188 C8
Hartington Villas BN3 ....187 B8
Hartland Ct PO10 ....149 F1
Harvest Cl RH16 ....86 B7
Harvest Hill Ansty RH17 ....84 D2
 East Grinstead RH19 ....22 E8
Harvest Rd RH10 ....19 C4
Harvester Cl PO19 ....173 C7
Harvesters
 Haywards Heath RH16 ....85 D2
 Horsham RH12 ....36 D5
Harvestside RH6 ....2 C4
Harvey Cl Crawley RH11 ....18 A1
 Sayers Common BN6 ....105 D1
Harvey Rd BN12 ....181 E1
Harvey Villas GU30 ....24 D8
Harwarden Cl RH10 ....21 C8
Harwood Ave BN12 ....181 D4
Harwood Pk RH1 ....2 A8
Harwood Rd
 Horsham RH12, RH13 ....37 A3
 Littlehampton BN17 ....198 C6
Harwood Road Ent Units BN17 ....198 C6
Harwoods Cl 3 RH19 ....22 F7
Harwoods La RH19 ....22 F7
Hascombe Ct RH11 ....18 A5
Hasle Dr GU27 ....27 B6
Haslemere & District Com Hospl GU27 ....27 D7
Haslemere Educational Mus GU27 ..27 D7
Haslemere Gdns PO11 ....189 B2
Haslemere Prep Sch GU27 ....27 D5
Haslemere Rd
 Breach PO10 ....149 F2
 Fernhurst GU27 ....49 B7
 Liphook GU30 ....25 D4
Haslemere Sta GU27 ....27 B6
Hasler's La PO18 ....132 E5
Haslett Ave E RH10 ....19 A6
Haslett Ave W RH10 ....18 D5
Haslingbourne La GU28 ....95 F5
Hassocks Ct 3 RH11 ....17 F3
Hassocks Inf Sch BN6 ....126 F4
Hassocks Lodge BN6 ....126 F3
Hassocks Rd BN6 ....126 B5
Hassocks Sta BN6 ....126 E4
Haste Hill GU27 ....27 D5
Hastings Cl PO21 ....194 F4
Hastings Ct 9 BN11 ....182 A1
Hastings Rd Brighton BN2 .188 C8
 Crawley RH10 ....19 C6
 Worthing BN11 ....182 A1
Hatch Cl GU6 ....11 A3
Hatch End RH18 ....23 F2
Hatch Hill GU27 ....27 B1
Hatch La East Liss GU33 ....45 E4
 Kingsley Green GU27 ....27 B2
Hatchetts Dr GU27 ....26 D7
Hatchgate RH6 ....1 F2
Hatchgate Cl RH17 ....85 A6
Hatchgate La RH17 ....85 A6
Hatchlands Cuckfield RH17 .84 F6
 Horsham RH12 ....37 A7
Hatfield Ct 18 BN3 ....187 C6
Hatfield Wlk Crawley RH11 .17 E2
 Worthing BN13 ....181 D5
Hatherleigh Cl PO21 ....195 A5
Hatherleigh Gdns PO21 ....195 A5
Hathersham La RH1, RH6 ....2 F6
Havant Rd PO10 ....169 A8
Havelock Cl PO22 ....195 F3
Havelock Rd
 Bognor Regis PO21 ....195 C4
 Brighton BN1 ....167 F1
Haven Cotts PO22 ....195 D5
Haven Ct PO20 ....201 F7
Haven Gdns RH10 ....8 B1
Haven Rd
 Rudgwick RH12, RH14 ....33 D3
 South Hayling PO11 ....189 A1
Haven The Lancing BN15 .183 F4
 Rustington BN17 ....199 A5
Havengate RH12 ....36 F5
Havenside BN43 ....184 E6
Havenstoke Cl PO19 ....153 A1
Havenwood Cvn Pk BN18 157 B3
Haversham Cl RH10 ....18 F6
Haversham Ho RH6 ....2 B5
Hawke Cl BN16 ....199 E5
Hawkesbourne Rd RH12 ....36 F5
Hawkesmoor Rd RH11 ....17 E4
Hawkhurst Pl BN1 ....168 D6
Hawkhurst Rd BN1 ....168 D6
Hawkhurst Wlk RH10 ....19 B4
Hawkins Cl
 Bognor Regis PO21 ....194 B2
 Shoreham-by-Sea BN43 ....165 D1
Hawkins Cres BN43 ....165 D2
Hawkins Rd Crawley RH10 .18 E4
 Shoreham-by-Sea BN43 ....165 D1
Hawkley Rd GU33 ....45 A5
Hawkridge RH12 ....12 E1
Hawks Mead GU33 ....45 A5
Hawks Pl PO22 ....195 B6
Hawksfold La E GU27 ....49 A6
Hawksfold La W GU27 ....49 A6
Hawkshaw Cl GU30 ....25 D4
Hawley Rd BN16 ....199 B4
Hawmead RH10 ....21 C8
Haworth Rd RH10 ....19 C5
Hawth Ave RH10 ....18 F4
Hawth Cl RH10 ....18 E4
Hawthorn Bank BN2 ....168 F4
Hawthorn Cl
 Burgess Hill RH15 ....107 D5
 Chichester PO19 ....172 F7
 Crawley RH11 ....5 C1
 Horsham RH12 ....36 C4
 Midhurst GU29 ....92 D6
 6 Rustington BN16 ....199 C4
Hawthorn Cres BN14 ....182 D6
Hawthorn Gdns BN14 ....182 D6
Hawthorn Rd
 Bognor Regis PO21,PO22 .195 B4
 Littlehampton BN17 ....178 D3
 Worthing BN14 ....182 D6
Hawthorn Way
 Portslade-by-Sea BN41 ....166 A3
 Storrington RH20 ....119 D2
Hawthorne Cotts RH6 ....7 C7
Hawthorns Fst Sch BN13 181 C5
Hawthorns The
 6 Bognor Regis PO21 ....195 C4
 Burgess Hill RH15 ....107 A5
 West Chiltington Common RH20 ....119 E7
Hay Rd PO19 ....173 B4
Haybarn Dr RH12 ....36 E7
Haybourne Cl BN2 ....188 E7
Haybourne Rd BN2 ....188 E7
Haydon Cl PO21 ....194 C1
Hayes Cl Mid Lavant PO18 .152 E7
 Portslade-by-Sea BN41 ....186 C8
Hayes La RH13 ....34 D2
Hayes Wood Rd RH14 ....55 F5
Hayfields RH6 ....2 C4
Hayley Rd BN15 ....183 F7
Hayley's Gdns PO22 ....196 A4
Haylind Rd RH16 ....86 B5
Hayling Ct RH11 ....18 C3
Hayling Gdns BN13 ....161 E1
Hayling Rise BN13 ....161 E1
Haynes Rd BN14 ....182 B4
Haynes Way BN14 ....182 B4
Haystacks GU29 ....113 C8
Hayton Ct BN13 ....181 B5
Haywards RH10 ....6 D1
Haywards Cl PO22 ....196 B5
Haywards Heath Coll RH16 ....85 D6
Haywards Heath Rd RH17 .41 A1
Haywards Heath Sta RH16 85 E6
Haywards Rd
 Brighton BN1 ....168 A6
 Haywards Heath RH16 ....85 E3
Haywards Villas RH16 ....85 F3
Hazel Bank 3 BN2 ....207 C4
Hazel Cl Crawley RH11 ....5 C1
 Crawley Down RH10 ....21 C8
 Portslade-by-Sea BN41 ....166 C3
 Southwater RH13 ....58 A1
Hazel Ct RH12 ....36 F4
Hazel Gr Arundel BN18 ....157 E2
 Bognor Regis PO21 ....194 D3
 Burgess Hill RH15 ....107 B1
Hazel Rd PO22 ....195 B6
Hazel Way RH10 ....21 C8
Hazelbank Cl GU30 ....25 D4
Hazeldean Dr PO9 ....128 D1
Hazeldene Meads BN1 ....167 D3
Hazeldene Rd GU30 ....24 D4
Hazelgrove Gdns 8 RH16 .85 E4
Hazelgrove Rd RH16 ....85 E4
Hazelholt BN41 ....165 F3
Hazelhurst RH6 ....2 C4
Hazelhurst Cres
 Horsham RH12 ....35 F1
 Worthing BN14 ....161 F3
Hazelhurst Dr RH10 ....19 E6
Hazelmead Dr BN16 ....200 A5
Hazelwick Ave RH10 ....19 B8
Hazelwick Mill La RH10 ....19 A8
Hazelwick Rd RH10 ....19 A7
Hazelwick Sch RH10 ....19 A8
Hazelwood Brighton BN1 .167 D3
 Crawley RH11 ....18 A5
Hazelwood Cl
 Crawley RH10 ....20 F8
 Easebourne GU29 ....71 A3
 Heath Common RH20 ....120 B2
 Worthing BN14 ....182 F4
Hazelwood Cotts GU6 ....11 D4
Hazelwood Lodge 3 BN15 ....183 F5
Hazelwood Rd RH13 ....103 A3
Hazelwood Trad Est BN14 ....182 F5
Hazleden Cross RH19 ....22 B6
Headborough Ct BN15 ....183 E4
Headborough Gdns BN15 ....183 E4
Headlands Cotts RH17 ....39 C2
Headley Cl RH10 ....6 D1
Headley Rd GU30 ....25 B5
Hearn Cl PO20 ....154 C1
Hearnfield Rd BN17 ....178 D4
Heath Cl
 Broadridge Heath RH12 ....35 E3
 9 Haywards Heath RH16 ....85 E4
 Hunston PO20 ....193 A8
 Mannings Heath RH13 ....59 D6
 Sayers Common BN6 ....105 D1
Heath Ct RH16 ....85 E5
Heath Hill Ave BN2 ....168 F1
Heath Pl PO22 ....195 D7
Heath Rd Hammer GU27 ....26 D5
 Haywards Heath RH16 ....85 E5
Heath Sq RH16 ....85 D5
Heath Way RH12 ....36 D5
Heathcote Dr RH19 ....9 C2
Heathcourt BN17 ....198 F5
Heather Bank RH16 ....85 C5
Heather Cl Copthorne RH10 ..7 B2
 Horsham RH12 ....36 D5
 West Ashling PO18 ....151 C3
Heather Ct
 8 Brighton BN1 ....187 E6
 Chichester PO19 ....172 F5
Heather Ho BN15 ....183 F7
Heather La West Chiltington Common RH20 ..119 C6
 Worthing BN13 ....161 E2
Heather Way RH20 ....119 F1
Heather Wlk RH11 ....18 B3
Heatherlands Horley RH6 ..2 B4
 Storrington RH20 ....119 F2
Heatherlea Ho BN15 ....183 D6
Heatherleigh Ct RH12 ....36 C4
Heathers The BN16 ....179 F6
Heatherstone Rd BN11 ....183 B2
Heatherton Mews PO10 .149 B3
Heatherway RH19, RH7 ....8 F7
Heatherwood GU29 ....92 D8
Heatherwood Ho GU29 ....92 D8
Heathfield RH10 ....19 D8
Heathfield Ave BN16 ....179 F3
Heathfield Cl
 1 Midhurst GU29 ....92 E7
 Worthing BN13 ....181 F5
Heathfield Copse RH20 ....119 C7
Heathfield Cres BN41 ....165 F3
Heathfield Dr BN41 ....165 F4
Heathfield Gate 2 GU29 ....92 E7
Heathfield Gdns GU29 ....92 E7
Heathfield Gn GU29 ....92 E7
Heathfield Pk GU29 ....92 E7
Heaven Farm RH17 ....66 B1
Hebe Rd BN43 ....184 D7
Hechle Wood PO21 ....194 F2
Hectors La RH19 ....23 C7
Hedge End Rd PO22 ....176 C6
Hedgecourt Pl RH19 ....8 E4
Hedgehog La GU27 ....27 B5
Hedgerow Gdns PO10 ....149 B3
Hedgers Hill BN18 ....156 F2
Hedgeside RH11 ....18 C1
Hedgeway PO22 ....196 D5
Hedingham Cl RH6 ....2 C4
Heene CE Fst Sch BN11 .182 C3
Heene Lodge BN11 ....182 B1
Heene Pl BN11 ....182 C1
Heene Rd BN11 ....182 B2
Heene Terr BN11 ....182 B1
Heene Way BN11 ....182 B2
Heghbrok Way PO21 ....195 A2
Heights The Brighton BN1 .167 B5
 6 Haywards Heath RH16 ....85 E4
 Worthing BN14 ....162 A1
Helen Ct 8 BN11 ....181 F2
Helena Cl BN41 ....166 C2
Helicon Ho RH11 ....18 C5

Hellingly Cl BN2 . . . . .188 F5
Helston Dr PO10 . . . . .149 B3
Helyer's Gn BN17 . . . . . . .198 C6
Hemsby Wlk RH10 . . . . .19 B4
Henbane Ct 2 RH11 . . . . . .18 B2
Henderson Rd RH11 . . . . . .18 B1
Henderson Way RH12 . . . . .57 F8
Henderson Wlk BN44 . . .143 D4
Hendon Ave BN16 . . . . . . .199 A3
Hendon St BN2 . . . . .188 D5
Henfield Bsns Pk BN5 . . .124 A1
Henfield Cl Brighton BN2 . .188 F5
Worthing BN12 . . . . .181 B4
Henfield Mus BN5 . . . . . . .123 F4
Henfield Rd
Albourne Green BN6 . . . . . .125 B7
Upper Beeding BN44,BN5 . .144 D3
Henfield Way
Bognor Regis PO22 . . . . . . .196 D6
Hove BN3 . . . . .166 F3
Henge Way BN41 . . . . .166 B2
Hengist Cl RH12 . . . . .36 A1
Henley Cl RH10 . . . . .19 D3
Henley Ct Brighton BN2 . . .188 F4
Worthing BN11 . . . . .181 F3
Henley Rd BN2 . . . . .188 F4
Henry Ave BN16 . . . . .199 B5
Henry Burt Way RH15 . . .106 E1
Henry Cl PO19 . . . . .173 D6
Henry St PO21 . . . . .195 D4
Henshaw Cl RH11 . . . . .17 F4
Henson Rd RH10 . . . . .19 B7
Henty Cl Crawley RH11 . . . . .17 E3
Walberton BN18 . . . . .176 E8
4 Worthing BN14 . . . . .182 C4
Henty Gdns PO19 . . . . . . .172 F6
Henty Rd Ferring BN12 . . . .200 F4
Worthing BN14 . . . . .182 C4
Heo Gn BN17 . . . . .178 B3
Hepplewhite Cl RH11 . . . . .18 B2
Herald Dr PO19 . . . . .173 A5
Herbert Rd Brighton BN1 . .167 F2
North Lancing BN15 . . . . . .163 B1
Herbert Shiner Sch GU28 . .95 F7
Hercules Pl PO22 . . . . . . .196 D5
Hereford Cl
Chichester PO19 . . . . .152 F1
Crawley RH10 . . . . .18 E2
Hereford Ct
15 Brighton BN2 . . . . .207 C2
15 Hove BN3 . . . . .187 C7
Hereford Ho BN12 . . . . . . .181 A3
Hereford St BN2 . . . . .188 C5
Herington Rd BN18 . . . . . .157 F2
Heritage Lawn RH6 . . . . .2 C4
Herm Cl RH11 . . . . .18 A2
Herm Rd BN12 . . . . .200 F4
Hermione Cl BN12 . . . . . . .180 E3
Hermit Terr BN14 . . . . . . .161 E6
Hermitage Cl PO20 . . . . . .173 D1
Hermitage La RH19 . . . . . . .22 F8
Hermitage Rd RH19 . . . . . . .9 D3
Hermitage The PO20 . . . . .173 D1
Hermits Rd RH10 . . . . .18 F7
Hermonger La RH12 . . . . . .12 F2
Hernbrook Dr RH13 . . . . . .58 E8
Herne Ct 2 BN16 . . . . . . .199 D6
Herne Gdns BN16 . . . . . . .199 D6
Herne La BN16 . . . . .199 D6
Heron Cl
Bognor Regis PO22 . . . . . . .195 B7
Crawley RH11 . . . . .18 C8
Mid Lavant PO18 . . . . .152 E7
Heron Ct PO19 . . . . .173 D7
Heron La PO20 . . . . .206 B8
Heron Mead PO21 . . . . . . .204 F7
Heron Pl RH19 . . . . .22 F8
Heron Quay PO10 . . . . . . .169 C7
Heron Way RH13 . . . . .37 A1
Heron Way Prim Sch
RH13 . . . . .37 A1
Heron's Ct Cl 3 BN16 . . . .199 C4
Heron's Rye 9 RH20 . . . . . .98 C2
Heron's Tye BN6 . . . . .126 F3
Herondale GU27 . . . . .26 E6
Herondean PO19 . . . . .152 F2
Herons Cl Domewood RH10 . .8 B5
Kirdford RH14 . . . . .53 B2
Herons Ct PO22 . . . . .195 F5
Herons Dale Sch BN43 . . .165 C1
Herons Lea RH10 . . . . .8 A4
Herons The Selsey PO20 . .206 D7
Shoreham-by-Sea BN43 . . .185 A8
Herons Wood Ct RH6 . . . . . .2 B4
Herontye Dr RH19 . . . . .23 A8
Herontye Ho RH19 . . . . .22 F7
Herrick Cl RH10 . . . . .19 C8
Herschel Wlk 9 RH11 . . . .18 B1
Hersee Way PO20 . . . . . . .206 C7
Hertford Cl PO21 . . . . . . .194 F3
Hertford Ct 3 BN11 . . . . .182 D3
Hertford Inf Sch BN1 . . . .168 B2
Hertford Jun Sch BN1 . . .168 C2
Hertford Rd Brighton BN1 .168 B2
Worthing BN11 . . . . .182 D3
Heston Ave BN1 . . . . .167 F7
Heston Gr PO21 . . . . .194 C1
Hett Cl RH17 . . . . .64 B8
Hevers Ave RH6 . . . . .2 A4
Hewart's La PO21 . . . . . . .194 D4
Hewitts BN5 . . . . .123 E4
Hewitts End BN5 . . . . .123 E4
Hewshott Gr GU30 . . . . . . .25 E5
Hewshott La GU30 . . . . . . .25 E5
Hexham Cl RH10 . . . . .19 E6
Heyshott Cl BN15 . . . . . . .183 F8
Heyworth Prim Sch RH16 .85 F4
Hickling Wlk RH10 . . . . . . .19 B4
Hickman's Cl RH16 . . . . . . .86 B8
Hickman's La RH16 . . . . . . .86 A8
Hickstead Int Arena
RH17 . . . . .105 D4
Hickstead La RH17 . . . . . .105 C5
Hickstead Pk BN6 . . . . . . .105 D2
Hide Gdns BN16 . . . . .199 B6
High Bank PO20 . . . . .192 F8
High Bar La RH20 . . . . . . .120 A6
High Beech La RH16 . . . . . .63 F1
High Beeches Cotts RH17 .39 E2
High Beeches Gdns RH17 .39 F2
High Beeches La RH17 . . . .39 E2
High Cl BN41 . . . . .166 A1
High Heath La BN6 . . . . . .106 B4
High La GU27 . . . . .27 C8
High Mdw GU29 . . . . .112 D8
High Oaks RH11 . . . . .18 B4
High Park Ave BN3 . . . . . .166 E3
High Pines BN11 . . . . .182 B2
High Point RH16 . . . . .86 A3
High Ridge Cl BN18 . . . . .157 F1
High Salvington Windmill
BN13 . . . . .161 E2
High Seat Gdns RH14 . . . . .55 D1
High Spinney RH20 . . . . . .119 E5
High St Amberley BN18 . . .138 E7
Angmering BN16 . . . . .180 A5
Ardingly RH17 . . . . .64 B8
Arundel BN18 . . . . .158 B3
Balcombe RH17 . . . . .40 C5
Billingshurst RH14 . . . . .55 D1
Bognor Regis PO21 . . . . . . .195 D3
Bosham PO18 . . . . .171 A4
Brighton BN2 . . . . .207 C2
Chichester PO19 . . . . .172 F7
Crawley RH10 . . . . .18 D6
Cuckfield RH17 . . . . .84 E6
Ditchling BN6 . . . . .127 D3
East Grinstead RH19 . . . . . .22 F8
Emsworth PO10 . . . . .169 B8
Findon BN14 . . . . .161 E6
Handcross RH17 . . . . .61 C8
Haslemere GU27 . . . . .27 D7
Henfield BN5 . . . . .123 F4
Horley RH6 . . . . .2 B3
Hurstpierpoint BN6 . . . . . .126 A5
Lindfield RH16 . . . . .86 B8
Littlehampton BN17 . . . . . .198 D5
Oving PO20 . . . . .174 C6
Partridge Green RH13 . . . .103 A3
Petworth GU28 . . . . .95 F8
Portslade-by-Sea BN41 . . . .166 A1
Rusper RH12 . . . . .16 D7
Selsey PO20 . . . . .206 D7
Shoreham-by-Sea BN43 . . . .184 E7
Steyning BN44 . . . . .143 D3
Storrington RH20 . . . . .119 D1
Upper Beeding BN44 . . . . . .144 A2
Worthing BN11 . . . . .182 E2
Worthing BN11 . . . . .182 E3
Worthing, West
Tarring BN14 . . . . .182 A5
High Titten BN18 . . . . .138 E5
High Trees
Bognor Regis PO21 . . . . . . .194 F2
Fittleworth RH20 . . . . .97 A3
Haywards Heath RH16 . . . . . .85 F5
Hunston PO20 . . . . .173 A1
High Trees Ct RH6 . . . . .1 A4
High View BN13 . . . . .161 F1
Highams Hill RH11 . . . . . . .17 F5
Highbank BN1 . . . . .167 C5
Highbarn BN14 . . . . .161 E7
Highbirch Cl RH12 . . . . . . .37 B5
Highbrook Cl BN2 . . . . . . .168 D3
Highbury Cotts RH17 . . . . .61 B8
Highbury Gr GU27 . . . . .27 C8
Highclere Way BN13 . . . .181 B5
Highcroft Ave PO22 . . . . .195 D5
Highcroft Cl PO22 . . . . . .195 E5
Highcroft Cres PO22 . . . .195 E5
Highcroft Dr RH12 . . . . . . .12 E1
Highcroft Lodge BN1 . . . .187 E8
Highcroft Rd RH19 . . . . . . .43 A6
Highcroft Villas BN1, BN3 .187 E8
Highden 2 BN2 . . . . .188 C6
Highdown BN41, BN42 . . . .165 F1
Highdown Ave BN13 . . . . .182 A5
Highdown Cl
Ferring BN12 . . . . .180 E3
Southwick BN42 . . . . .165 F1
Highdown Ct
Brighton BN1 . . . . .167 E3
Crawley RH10 . . . . .19 B3
Highdown Dr BN17 . . . . . .198 D6
Highdown Rd BN1, BN3 . .187 E7
Highdown Sch BN13 . . . . .181 D5
Highdown Way
Ferring BN12 . . . . .180 E3
Horsham RH12 . . . . .36 F6
Highercombe Rd GU27 . . . .27 E8
Highfield RH17 . . . . .65 C4
Highfield Cl
Angmering BN16 . . . . .180 A5
Easebourne GU29 . . . . .71 A2
Highfield Cotts BN17 . . . .178 B3
Highfield Cres BN1 . . . . . .168 A5
Highfield Ct 7 RH16 . . . . . .85 E4
Highfield Dr BN6 . . . . .126 C5
Highfield Gdns
Bognor Regis PO22 . . . . . . .195 D5
Liss GU33 . . . . .45 D4
1 Rustington BN16 . . . . . . .199 B5
Highfield La Liphook GU30 .25 E3
Highfield La continued
Oving PO20 . . . . .174 C7
Highfield Rd
Bognor Regis PO22 . . . . . . .195 D5
East Grinstead RH19 . . . . . . .9 D3
Worthing BN13 . . . . .182 A6
Highfield Sch GU30 . . . . . . .25 E2
Highfields Brighton BN1 . .168 E5
Forest Row RH18 . . . . .23 F2
Highgate Ct RH11 . . . . .18 C2
Highgate Dr PO21 . . . . . . .194 F6
Highgate Rd RH18 . . . . .23 F1
Highground La PO22 . . . . .176 B4
Highgrove Gdns BN11 . . . .182 B2
Highland Ave PO21 . . . . . .195 B4
Highland Cl PO10 . . . . . . .169 A8
Highland Croft BN44 . . . .143 D3
Highland Ct RH16 . . . . .85 E4
Highland Rd
Chichester PO19 . . . . .153 A2
Emsworth PO10 . . . . .149 A1
Haywards Heath RH16 . . . . . .85 F3
Highlands Ave RH13 . . . . . .36 F2
Highlands Cl Keymer BN6 .127 A3
Worthing BN13 . . . . .161 E1
Highlands Cotts RH17 . . . .84 F8
Highlands Cres RH13 . . . . .36 E2
Highlands Dr RH15 . . . . . .107 A4
Highlands Rd
Horsham RH13 . . . . .36 F2
Portslade-by-Sea BN41 . . . .166 B1
Highlands The RH17 . . . . . .84 F8
Highleigh 8 BN2 . . . . .207 C3
Highleigh Rd PO20 . . . . . .192 C2
Highstanding La GU29 . . . .93 A6
Highstead La GU28 . . . . . . .72 A8
Highview BN15 . . . . .163 D1
Highview Ave N BN1 . . . . .167 E6
Highview Ave S BN1 . . . . .167 E6
Highview Rd Brighton BN1 167 E6
Eastergate PO20 . . . . .175 F7
Highview Way BN1 . . . . . .167 E6
Highway Cl BN2 . . . . .168 D2
Highway The BN2 . . . . . . .168 D3
Highways BN41 . . . . .166 B2
Hilary Lodge 2 BN2 . . . . .188 C5
Hilary Rd PO19 . . . . .172 E7
Hildon Cl BN13 . . . . .181 D5
Hill Barn La BN14 . . . . . . .182 C7
Hill Brow BN3 . . . . .167 B3
Hill Brow Cl PO9 . . . . .128 D1
Hill Brow Rd GU33 . . . . . . .45 C3
Hill Cotts GU29 . . . . .113 C8
Hill Crest RH19 . . . . .9 E6
Hill Ct GU27 . . . . .27 B6
Hill Dr BN3 . . . . .167 B3
Hill Farm Cl GU27 . . . . .26 F5
Hill Farm La RH20 . . . . . . .98 B5
Hill Farm Way
BN42, BN43 . . . . .165 E2
Hill House Cl RH10 . . . . . . .21 A5
Hill House Hill GU30 . . . . .25 A6
Hill La Barnham PO22 . . . . .176 C4
South Harting GU31 . . . . . . .89 E2
Hill Mead RH12 . . . . .36 B3
Hill Pl RH11 . . . . .18 C5
Hill Rd Haslemere GU27 . . . .27 C6
Littlehampton BN17 . . . . . .198 F6
Hill Top BN1 . . . . .167 B5
Hill Top Cl BN41 . . . . .165 F2
Hill View Elsted GU29 . . . . .90 D4
Small Dole BN5 . . . . .144 F7
Hillary Cl RH19 . . . . .10 A3
Hillbank Cl BN41 . . . . .165 F3
Hillbarn Ave BN15 . . . . . .163 D1
Hillbarn La GU29 . . . . .112 D6
Hillbarn Par BN15 . . . . . . .183 C8
Hillbrow Rd BN1 . . . . .167 D4
Hillcrest BN1 . . . . .167 C5
Hillcrest Cl
Ashington RH20 . . . . .121 A5
Crawley RH10 . . . . .19 D6
Scaynes Hill RH17 . . . . .86 F3
Hillcrest Ct BN1 . . . . .167 C5
Hillcrest Dr RH20 . . . . . . .121 A5
Hillcrest La RH17 . . . . .86 F3
Hillcrest Pk RH20 . . . . .98 D2
Hillcroft BN41 . . . . .165 F2
Hillfield Rd PO20 . . . . . . .206 D6
Hillhouse La RH12 . . . . .11 F1
Hillingdale RH11 . . . . .18 C1
Hillmead RH11 . . . . .17 F6
Hillrise Ave BN15 . . . . . . .183 D8
Hills Farm La RH12 . . . . . . .35 F1
Hills Manor RH12 . . . . .36 A2
Hills Pl RH12 . . . . .36 A2
Hills Rd BN44 . . . . .143 C2
Hillsboro Rd PO21 . . . . . .195 C4
Hillside Brighton BN2 . . . .168 E2
Crawley Down RH10 . . . . . . .21 B8
Forest Row RH18 . . . . .23 E3
Horsham RH12 . . . . .36 A2
Portslade-by-Sea BN41 . . . .166 C1
Southwick BN42 . . . . .165 F1
Hillside Ave BN14 . . . . . . .182 B7
Hillside Cl Crawley RH11 . .18 B4
East Grinstead RH19 . . . . . . .9 E3
Hillside Cotts
Clapham BN13 . . . . .160 E1
East Marden PO18 . . . . . . .110 B1
West Stoke PO18 . . . . .152 A5
Hillside Cres BN16 . . . . . .180 A5
Hillside La BN5 . . . . .144 E5
Hillside Rd
Camelsdale GU27 . . . . .26 F5
Heath Common RH20 . . . . . .120 A2
Sompting BN15 . . . . .163 C1
Hillside Sch BN41 . . . . . . .166 B2
Hillside Terr 7 BN44 . . . .143 D3
Hillside Way Brighton,
Moulsecoomb BN2 . . . . . . .168 E2
Brighton, Westdene BN1 . . .167 C4
Hillside Wlk
Haywards Heath RH16 . . . . .85 C6
Heath Common RH20 . . . . .120 A2
Hilltop Cotts RH6 . . . . .1 D2
Hilltop Rd RH19 . . . . .42 E6
Hillview Cres BN16 . . . . . .200 A6
Hillview Gdns RH11 . . . . . .39 C8
Hillview Rd BN14 . . . . . . .161 F2
Hillview Rise BN14 . . . . . .161 F1
Hillybarn Rd RH11 . . . . .4 C1
Hilton Ct RH6 . . . . .2 C4
Hilton Pk PO20 . . . . .202 A8
Hinde Rd PO22 . . . . .196 C4
Hindhead Cl RH11 . . . . .18 C4
Hindhead Rd GU26, GU27 . .26 E7
Hindle Cl RH20 . . . . .119 D7
Hindleap Warren
Activity Ctr RH18 . . . . .44 D5
Hinton Cl BN1 . . . . .168 C2
Hislop Wlk 13 PO21 . . . . .195 D3
Hither Gn PO10 . . . . .150 A2
Hoad La RH16 . . . . .64 D4
Hoathly Hill RH19 . . . . .42 F5
Hobart Cl BN13 . . . . .181 C7
Hobbs Ind Est RH7 . . . . .8 D7
Hobbs Rd RH11 . . . . .18 A2
Hobbs Way BN16 . . . . .199 C5
Hobdens La RH17 . . . . .64 B7
Hoblands RH16 . . . . .86 B4
Hobs Acre BN44 . . . . .144 B1
Hocken Mead RH10 . . . . . . .19 D8
Hodgkin Cl RH10 . . . . .19 C5
Hodshrove La BN2 . . . . . .168 E3
Hodshrove Pl BN2 . . . . . . .168 E3
Hodshrove Rd BN2 . . . . . .168 E3
Hoe Ct North Lancing BN15 163 F1
Shoreham-by-Sea BN15 . . . .184 A8
Hoe La Bosham PO18 . . . . .171 C1
Flansham PO22 . . . . .196 B7
Walberton BN18 . . . . .177 C7
Hoefield La GU29 . . . . . . .112 C5
Hoewood BN5 . . . . .144 F7
Hog La BN18 . . . . .138 E7
Hogarth Rd Crawley RH10 . .18 F3
Hove BN3 . . . . .186 F7
Hogspudding La RH5 . . . . . .3 C8
Hogwood Rd RH14 . . . . . . .31 C3
Holbein Rd RH10 . . . . .18 F3
Holbrook Cty Prim Sch
RH12 . . . . .36 E7
Holbrook Park Ho RH12 . .36 E8
Holbrook School La RH12 .36 E7
Holcombe Ho BN11 . . . . .182 B1
Holdens The PO18 . . . . . .171 A5
Holder Rd RH10 . . . . .19 B3
Holders BN6 . . . . .125 C6
Holdfast La GU27 . . . . .27 F8
Hole St BN44,RH20 . . . . . .121 B2
Holford Gn PO20 . . . . . . .206 F8
Holkham Cotts BN18 . . . . .177 A3
Holland Cl PO21 . . . . .194 F5
Holland Mews BN3 . . . . . .187 D5
Holland Rd Hove BN3 . . . .187 D6
Steyning BN44 . . . . .143 E3
Holland St BN2 . . . . .207 C3
Hollands Field RH12 . . . . . .35 E4
Hollands La BN5 . . . . .123 C4
Hollands Rd BN5 . . . . .123 D5
Hollands Way
East Grinstead RH19 . . . . . .10 A4
Warnham RH12 . . . . .35 F8
Hollies The
Bognor Regis PO21 . . . . . . .194 F5
Lancing BN15 . . . . .183 E6
Hollin Ct RH10 . . . . .5 E1
Hollingbourne Cres RH11 .39 C8
Hollingbourne Ct 8 BN2 .188 E4
Hollingbury Copse BN1 . .168 A4
Hollingbury Cres BN1 . . .168 B2
Hollingbury Gdns BN14 . .162 A2
Hollingbury Ind Est BN1 .168 C7
Hollingbury Park Ave
BN1 . . . . .168 A2
Hollingbury Pl BN1 . . . . .168 B2
Hollingbury Rd BN1 . . . . .168 B1
Hollingbury Rise BN1 . . . .168 B2
Hollingbury Rise W BN1 .168 A3
Hollingbury Terr BN1 . . . .168 A2
Hollingdean La BN1 . . . . .188 B8
Hollingdean Rd BN2 . . . . .188 B8
Hollingdean St BN1 . . . . .168 B1
Hollingdean Terr BN1 . . . .168 B2
Hollist La Easebourne GU29 .70 E2
South Harting GU31 . . . . . . .89 F4
Hollow La RH19, RH7 . . . . .10 D6
Hollow The Bury RH20 . . .138 A8
Crawley RH11 . . . . .17 F5
Lindfield RH16 . . . . .86 B5
Washington RH20 . . . . .141 F8
West Chiltington RH20 . . . . .99 D1
West Hoathly RH19 . . . . .42 F6
Holly Bank 3 BN2 . . . . . .207 C5
Holly Cl Brighton BN1 . . . .167 E3
Crawley RH10 . . . . .19 A8
Horsham RH12 . . . . .37 B5
Storrington RH20 . . . . .119 C1
West Chiltington RH20 . . . . .99 D1
Worthing BN13 . . . . .181 C5
Holly Ct
Bognor Regis PO22 . . . . . . .195 C6
Storrington RH20 . . . . .119 C2
Holly Dr BN17 . . . . .178 E4
Holly Ho 2 PO21 . . . . . . .195 C4
Holly Lodge BN14 . . . . . . .182 B4
Holly Rd RH16 . . . . .86 A3
Hollyacres BN13 . . . . .181 D8
Hollybank La PO10 . . . . . .149 B4
Hollybush Cl RH10 . . . . . . .18 E7
Hollybush Rd RH10 . . . . . . .18 E8
Hollycombe Cl GU30 . . . . .25 C2
Hollycombe Prim Sch
GU30 . . . . .47 D4
Hollycombe
Steam Collection GU30 . .47 E7
Hollyhock Way BN17 . . . .179 A3
Hollyridge GU27 . . . . .27 B6
Hollywater Rd GU30, GU35 .24 C8
Hollywood Ct RH16 . . . . . . .85 E5
Holm Oaks RH13 . . . . .81 F1
Holman Cl RH11 . . . . .39 B8
Holmans RH17 . . . . .64 A8
Holmbury Cl RH11 . . . . . . .18 C4
Holmbury Keep RH6 . . . . . . .2 C4
Holmbush Cl
Haywards Heath RH16 . . . . .85 E2
Horsham RH12 . . . . .36 D6
Shoreham-by-Sea BN43 . . .165 D2
Holmbush Ct 8 BN43 . . . .185 C8
Holmbush Farm
Children's Farm World
RH12 . . . . .17 B1
Holmbush Fst Sch BN43 .165 D1
Holmbush Ind Est GU29 . . .92 E6
Holmbush La BN5 . . . . . . .145 F8
Holmbush Way
Midhurst GU29 . . . . .92 E6
Southwick BN42, BN43 . . . .165 E1
Holmcroft RH10 . . . . .18 E5
Holmcroft Gdns BN14 . . .161 E6
Holmes Ave BN3 . . . . .166 F1
Holmes Foundation
BN18 . . . . .158 B2
Holmes La BN16 . . . . .199 B4
Holmesdale Rd RH15 . . . .107 A1
Holmfield Cl BN16 . . . . . .199 B6
Holmgarth BN5 . . . . .123 F5
Holming End RH12 . . . . . . .37 B5
Holmstead BN2 . . . . .207 C4
Holmsted Hill RH17 . . . . . .62 A1
Holmwood Cl PO20 . . . . . .190 C1
Holmwood Ct BN6 . . . . . . .126 F4
Holt Gdns PO9 . . . . .128 D3
Holt Lodge 1 BN2 . . . . . .207 C4
Holt The Burgess Hill RH15 107 C2
Washington RH20 . . . . .141 E6
Holtye Ave RH19 . . . . .10 A3
Holtye Rd RH19 . . . . .10 B3
Holtye Wlk RH10 . . . . .19 A4
Holy Cross Hospl GU27 . . .26 F7
Holy Trinity CE Prim Sch
RH13 . . . . .60 A3
Holy Trinity CE Sec Sch
The RH11 . . . . .18 A4
Holyrood RH19 . . . . .23 A8
Holyrood Pl RH11 . . . . .18 B2
Home Cl RH10 . . . . .19 C8
Home Farm Bsns Ctr
BN1 . . . . .168 D3
Home Farm Ct RH17 . . . . . .65 C5
Home Farm Rd BN1 BN2 .168 D3
Home Platt RH19 . . . . .43 A6
Home Rd BN1 . . . . .167 E1
Homecroft Ho 5 PO21 . . .195 B3
Homedrive Ho BN3 . . . . . .187 C8
Homefield Ave PO22 . . . . .196 C6
Homefield Cl RH6 . . . . .2 B4
Homefield Cotts GU33 . . . .45 A5
Homefield Cres BN18 . . .156 D1
Homefield Rd
Westbourne PO10 . . . . .149 D4
Worthing BN11 . . . . .182 E3
Homegreen Ho GU27 . . . . .27 A6
Homehaven Ct 2 BN43 . . .184 E7
Homelands Ave BN16 . . . .200 A4
Homelands Copse GU27 . .49 D4
Homeleigh BN1 . . . . .167 E5
Homepier Ho 7 BN11 . . .182 B2
Homesearle Ho BN12 . . . .181 C2
Homestall Rd RH19 . . . . . .23 E8
Homestead Cotts BN12 . .200 F6
Homestead La RH15 . . . . .107 C6
Homestead The BN16 . . . .200 A5
Homesteyne Ho 3 BN14 .182 D4
Homewood BN14 . . . . .161 E7
Homing Gdns PO22 . . . . . .195 B7
Honer La PO20 . . . . .193 D3
Honey Croft BN3 . . . . . . .166 D4
Honey La BN16 . . . . .180 A5
Honeybridge La
Ashurst BN44,RH13 . . . . . .122 A6
Dial Post RH13 . . . . .101 E1
Honeysuckle Cl Horley RH6 .2 C4
North Lancing BN15 . . . . . .163 D1
Rustington BN17 . . . . .179 A3
Honeysuckle La
Crawley RH11 . . . . .5 C1
Selsey PO20 . . . . .206 C8
Worthing BN13, BN14 . . . . .161 C3
Honeysuckle Wlk RH12 . . .37 A5
Honeywood La RH5 . . . . . . .13 F5
Honeywood Rd RH13 . . . . .37 A4
Hooe Farm Ind Est BN18 156 D2
Hooe The BN17 . . . . .199 A5
Hook La
Bognor Regis PO22 . . . . . . .195 E4
Bosham PO18 . . . . .171 F2
West Hoathly RH17, RH19 . . .42 D4
Woodgate PO20 . . . . .175 C6
Hook La Cl PO21 . . . . .194 B3
Hooklands La RH13 . . . . .101 B3
Hooks The BN5 . . . . .123 E4
Hop Garden La PO20 . . . .193 D8

Hop Garden The GU31 89 D3
Hope Cotts BN42 185 E8
Hope Ct RH11 18 B1
Hopedene Ct 10 BN11 182 C2
Hopgarton The PO21 194 E3
Hophurst Cl RH10 21 B8
Hophurst Dr RH10 21 B8
Hophurst Hill RH10, RH19 8 D2
Hophurst La RH10 8 B1
Hopkins Ct RH11 18 B1
Horden Ho RH12 36 A1
Hordens The RH13 56 F2
Horley Cty Jun Sch RH6 2 A3
Horley Lodge La RH1 2 A8
Horley Pl BN2 188 E6
Horley Rd RH6 5 B7
Horley Row RH6 2 A4
Horley Sta RH6 2 B2
Hormare Cres RH20 119 C2
Horn La BN5 124 B1
Hornbeam Cl
Bognor Regis PO21 194 F1
Horsham RH13 36 F1
Hornbeam Way GU29 92 D5
Hornbeams The RH15 106 D4
Hornbrook Copse RH13 58 F8
Hornby Rd BN2 168 F1
Horndean Cl RH10 6 D2
Horndean Rd PO10 149 A3
Hornet Ent Ctr PO19 173 B6
Hornet Rd PO10 169 C3
Hornet The PO19 173 B6
Horns La PO21 193 F1
Hornshill La RH12 32 F7
Horse Hill RH6 1 B4
Horse Shoe The PO20 206 D7
Horsebridge Hill RH14 75 E2
Horsefield Rd PO20 206 D8
Horsemere Green La
BN17 177 D1
Horseshoe Cl RH10 19 D7
Horsgate Ho RH17 85 A8
Horsgate La RH17 85 A6
Horsham Bsns Pk RH12 15 C4
Horsham Cl BN2 188 F6
Horsham Hospl RH12 36 C3
Horsham Lodge BN17 198 F5
Horsham Mus RH12 36 C1
Horsham Rd
Alfold Crossways GU6, RH12 11 C1
Ashurst BN44 143 C7
Cranleigh GU6 12 B8
Crawley RH11 18 B4
Findon BN14 161 D8
Five Oaks RH13, RH14 56 A6
Handcross RH17 61 B7
Kingsfold RH5 15 C8
Littlehampton BN17 198 F6
Pease Pottage RH11 39 B6
Petworth GU28 74 B2
Rowhook RH5, RH12 13 D5
Rusper RH12 16 B5
Steyning BN44 143 C4
Wallis Wood RH5 13 D8
Horsham Rd W BN17 198 F6
Horsham Sta RH13 36 D2
Horsted Ho 1 RH16 85 F3
Horsted Keynes Ind Est
RH17 65 B7
Horsted Keynes Sta RH17 65 A7
Horsted La Danehill RH17 66 A4
Sharpthorne RH19 43 B3
Horton Ct BN11 182 F2
Horton Rd BN1 168 B1
Hoskins Pl RH19 10 A4
Hotham Gdns PO22 195 E4
Hotham Way PO21,PO22 195 D4
Houghton Bridge BN18 138 D4
Houghton Ct BN15 183 F7
Houghton Ho BN17 178 B3
Houghton La RH20 138 A6
Houghton Rd RH10 19 C3
Hova Villas BN3 187 B6
Hove Bsns Ctr BN3 187 B8
Hove Ent Ctr BN41 186 C6
Hove General Hospl BN3 187 A7
Hove Manor 8 BN3 187 A6
Hove Mus & Art Gall
BN3 187 A6
Hove Nuffield Hospl BN3 186 F7
Hove Park Gdns
Hove BN3 167 B1
Hove BN3 187 B8
Hove Park Rd BN3 167 C1
Hove Park Sch (Lower)
BN3 166 D2
Hove Park Sch (Upper)
BN3 167 A1
Hove Park Villas BN3 187 B8
Hove Park Way BN3 167 C1
Hove Pl BN3 187 B5
Hove St BN3 187 A6
Hove Sta BN3 187 B8
Hovedene BN3 187 C7
Howard Ave
Burgess Hill RH15 106 E4
East Wittering PO20 201 D7
Howard Ct BN3 167 A2
Howard Ho PO21 195 A4
Howard Pl Brighton BN1 207 A4
5 Littlehampton BN17 198 D5
Howard Rd Arundel BN18 158 A2
Brighton BN2 188 C7
Crawley RH11 17 D2
Horsham RH13 37 A4
Littlehampton BN17 198 C5
Sompting BN15 163 C1
Howard St BN11 182 C3
Howard Terr BN1 207 A4
Howards Way BN16 199 B3
Hoylake Cl RH11 17 D5
Hoyle La GU29 93 D2
Huddlestones BN16 179 F6
Hudson Cl BN13 181 D6
Hudson Dr BN16 199 E4
Hudson Rd RH10 18 E4
Huffwood Trad Est
Billingshurst RH14 77 D7
Partridge Green RH13 103 A3
Hughes Cl PO21 194 F4
Hughes Rd BN2 188 B8
Hugo Platt GU31 68 A4
Humber Ave BN13 181 C7
Humber Cl
Littlehampton BN17 198 F4
Worthing BN13 181 C7
Humphrey Lodge RH15 107 D3
Humphrey's Gap BN43 185 A7
Humphrys Rd 5 BN11 182 D2
Hundredsteddle La PO20 191 D2
Hungers La GU28 95 D6
Hunstanton Cl RH11 17 D5
Hunt's Gate RH17 87 E3
Hunter Ho RH10 18 D3
Hunter Rd Crawley RH10 18 D4
Thorney Island PO10 169 C3
Hunter's Mead BN6 125 C6
Hunters Chase GU30 25 B5
Hunters Cl PO21 194 C1
Hunters Mead RH13 103 A3
Hunters Mews BN18 156 B3
Hunters Race PO19 152 E3
Hunters Way PO19 152 F3
Hunterscroft Gdns RH13 81 E1
Huntingdon Way RH15 107 D5
Huntsbottom La GU33 45 D3
Hurley Rd BN13 181 E6
Huron Dr GU30 25 D3
Hurst Ave Horsham RH12 36 D3
Worthing BN11 181 F2
Hurst Cl Amberley BN18 138 E7
Crawley RH11 17 F4
Liphook GU30 25 A5
Hurst Cotts BN18 138 E7
Hurst Cres BN41 186 B8
Hurst Ct RH12 36 D3
Hurst Farm Rd RH19 22 D7
Hurst Gdns BN6 125 F7
Hurst Hill BN1 168 C5
Hurst Rd Hassocks BN6 126 D4
Horley RH6 1 E4
Horsham RH12 36 D3
Rustington BN16 199 E6
Hurst Wickham Cl BN6 126 C5
Hurstfield BN15 183 D5
Hurstfield Cl RH17 86 A2
Hurstlands RH14 77 C7
Hurston Cl BN14 182 A8
Hurston Gr RH20 119 B3
Hurston La RH20 119 B3
Hurstpierpoint Coll BN6 126 B8
Hurstwood 6 BN2 188 F5
Hurstwood Ave PO10 150 A1
Hurstwood Ct GU29 92 E5
Hurstwood La
Haywards Heath RH17 86 A2
Sharpthorne RH17, RH19 43 D1
Hutchins Way RH6 1 F5
Hutchinson Cl BN16 179 B3
Hutton Rd BN1 168 B3
Huxley's Experience
Bird of Prey Ctr RH13 58 F8
Hyde Dr RH11 17 E5
Hyde Heath Ct RH10 19 D8
Hyde La BN44 144 B2
Hyde Sq BN44 144 B2
Hyde St BN44 144 B1
Hyde The BN2 188 F8
Hylands Cl RH10 19 A5
Hylters's La PO18 132 B7
Hyndman Cl RH11 39 B8
Hyperion Ct RH11 17 E4
Hyperion Wlk RH6 2 B1
Hythe Cl BN11 182 A1
Hythe Rd Brighton BN1 168 A2
Worthing BN11 182 A1

I

Icarus Way PO22 196 C5
Icklesham Ho 9 RH11 17 F3
Iden Cl BN2 188 E5
Iden Hurst BN6 126 A7
Idsworth Cl PO8 128 A6
Ifield Ave RH11 18 C7
Ifield Com Sch RH11 18 A7
Ifield Dr RH11 18 A7
Ifield Fst Sch RH11 18 A8
Ifield Gn RH11 5 A1
Ifield Mid Sch RH11 18 A6
Ifield Rd Charlwood RH6 4 E5
Crawley RH11 18 C6
Ifield St RH11 17 F8
Ifield Sta RH11 18 A6
Ifield Wood RH11 4 E1
Ifold Bridge La RH14 31 D4
Ifoldhurst RH14 31 C2
Ilex Cl BN16 199 C4
Ilex Ct
Portslade-by-Sea BN42 166 A1
Worthing BN12 181 B2
Ilex Ho 1 BN16 199 C4
Ilex Way
Middleton-on-Sea PO22 196 E6
Worthing BN12 181 B2
Image Cross Flats RH19 43 A5
Imberhorne Bsns Ctr RH19 9 B3
Imberhorne La RH19 9 B2
Imberhorne Lower Sch
RH19 9 D3
Imberhorne Sch RH19 9 B3
Imberhorne Way RH19 9 B3
Imperial Arc BN1 207 A2
Independent Bsns Pk
The RH19 9 B3
Infirmary Dr RH13 57 E6
Infirmary Terr PO19 172 F8
Ingfield Manor Sch RH14 55 E6
Ingham Dr BN1 168 D6
Ingle Green Cl BN12 200 E4
Inglecroft Ct 4 BN15 183 C7
Inglenook RH13 79 F7
Ingleside Cres BN15 183 F5
Ingleside Rd BN15 183 E5
Inglewood Cl PO21 194 C1
Inglewood Dr PO21 194 B1
Ingram Cl Horsham RH12 36 A2
Rustington BN16 199 B5
Steyning BN44 143 D2
Ingram Cres E BN3 186 E8
Ingram Cres W BN3 186 E8
Ingram Ct BN3 186 E7
Ingram Rd BN44 143 D2
Ingram's Green La GU29 91 C4
Ingrams Ho 4 RH16 85 E3
Inholmes Cl RH15 107 C3
Inholmes Cotts RH17 84 E8
Inholmes Park Rd RH15 107 B3
Inkpen La RH18 23 F1
Inlands Rd PO18 170 B8
Innerwyke Cl PO22 196 B5
Innerwyke Manor PO22 196 B5
Innes Rd RH12 36 F4
Innovation Dr RH15 106 D2
Inval Hill GU27 27 C8
Inverness Rd 4 BN2 188 C8
Inwood Cres BN1 167 E1
Inwood Rd GU33 45 C3
Iona Cl RH11 18 B3
Iona Way 12 RH16 85 E4
Iping & Stelham Common
Nature Reserve
GU29 91 D8
Iping La GU29,GU30 69 E4
Iping Rd GU30, GU29 47 C2
Irene Ave BN15 183 D7
Irons Bottom Rd RH2, RH6 1 A6
Irvine Rd BN17 198 E4
Irving Wlk RH10 18 E3
Irwin Dr RH12 36 A2
Isaac's La RH16, RH15 85 A2
Isabel Cres BN3 186 E8
Isfield Rd BN1 168 C2
Island La PO20 206 B8
Island Loop PO20 206 B8
Isle of Thorns
(Univ of Sussex) RH17 44 D1
Islingword Pl BN2 188 C6
Islingword Rd BN2 188 C7
Islingword St BN2 207 C3
Itchenor Rd
Shipton Green PO20 191 A5
South Hayling PO11 189 B2
Itchingfield Prim Sch
Barns Green RH13 56 F3
Itchingfield RH13 57 A6
Ithaca Terr PO22 195 F3
Ivanhoe Cl RH11 5 D1
Ivanhoe Pl PO22 196 C5
Iveagh Cl RH11 18 C1
Ivory Pl BN2 207 C3
Ivory Wlk RH11 17 E3
Ivy Arch Cl BN14 161 F6
Ivy Arch Rd BN14 182 D3
Ivy Cl Ashington RH20 121 A5
Southwater RH13 57 F1
Westergate PO20 175 D7
Ivy Cotts RH17 84 E8
Ivy Cres PO22 195 D5
Ivy Dene La RH19 23 D6
Ivy La Ashington RH20 121 A6
Bognor Regis PO22 195 D5
Westergate PO20 175 E7
Ivy Mews 13 BN3 187 D5
Ivy Pl Hove BN1, BN3 187 D5
Worthing BN11 182 B1
Ivydale Rd PO21 195 A4
Ivydene Cres PO18 170 D7
Ivydore Ave BN13 181 D8
Ivydore Cl BN13 181 D7

J

Jackdaw Cl RH11 18 C8
Jackdaw La RH12 36 E6
Jacken Cl PO22 196 C4
Jacket's Hill RH20 120 A5
Jackrells La RH13 58 B2
Jackson Rd RH11 39 B8
Jackson St BN2 207 C4
Jacobean Cl RH10 19 C5
Jacqueline Du Pre Ct
BN2 188 C5
James Cl BN13 181 F6
James St PO20 206 E6
James Watt Way RH10 6 A4
Jane Murray Way
BN6,RH15 106 C3
Janes Cl RH15 107 C5
Janes La
Burgess Hill RH15 107 D4
River GU28 72 E3
Janeston Ct 4 BN3 187 C7
Japonica Cl BN43 165 B1
Jarvis Cl RH11 39 B8
Jarvis Cotts 4 BN44 143 D3
Jarvis La BN44 143 D3
Jarvis Rd BN18 157 F2
Jasmine Cl BN17 179 A3
Jasmine Ct Brighton BN1 167 F5
Horsham RH12 36 C2
Hove BN3 187 D7
Javelin Ct RH10 6 D1
Javelin Rd PO10 169 C3
Jay Cl RH13 58 A2
Jay's La GU27 28 C3
Jays Cl BN17 198 D6
Jays The RH15 106 E4
Jeans Ct 10 RH11 18 B1
Jefferies RH17 65 C4
Jefferies La BN12 181 C1
Jefferson Ct 4 PO21 195 B2
Jeffreys Ave PO19 153 A1
Jengers Mead RH14 55 D1
Jenner Rd RH10 5 F3
Jennings Way RH6 2 D3
Jeremy's La RH17 83 C6
Jerrard Rd PO20 154 D2
Jersey Rd Crawley RH11 18 A2
Ferring BN12 200 F4
Jersey St BN2 207 C3
Jervis Ave BN16 199 D5
Jesmond Cl BN3 186 E7
Jesmond Rd BN3 186 E7
Jessie Younghusband
Cty Prim Sch PO19 172 F8
Jesters RH16 107 C7
Jetty The PO22 197 A5
Jevington Cl BN13 181 B5
Jevington Ct
Southwick BN43 185 D6
Worthing BN13 181 B5
Jevington Dr BN2 168 D1
Jew St BN1 207 B2
Jib Cl BN17 179 A3
Jireh Ct RH16 85 E5
Joan Nightingale Ho
RH16 85 C4
Job's Cnr BN6 105 E5
Job's La BN6, RH17 105 F5
Jobes RH17 40 F1
Jobson's La GU27 28 D2
Jockey Mead RH12 36 A1
John Arundel Rd PO19 172 E7
John Horniman Sch
BN11 182 E2
John King Shipyard
PO10 169 C8
John Pounds Ho RH11 18 D4
John St Bognor Regis PO21 195 D3
Brighton BN2 207 C3
Shoreham-by-Sea BN43 184 E7
John Whittle Lodge BN2 168 C1
Johnson Bank 4 BN2 188 C7
Johnson Dr RH15 107 D3
Johnson Way BN18 177 B2
Johnson Wlk RH10 18 E3
Jolesfield Crawley RH11 17 F3
Partridge Green RH13 102 F4
Jolesfield CE Prim Sch
RH13 103 A4
Jolliffe Rd PO20 201 D7
Jones Sq PO20 206 E6
Jordan Ct BN3 186 E8
Jordans Cl RH11 18 D8
Jordans Cres RH11 5 D1
Jordans The RH19 22 E8
Joy Wlk 6 PO19 173 A6
Joyce Cl BN17 178 C3
Joys Croft PO19 173 B7
Joys Croft Ct PO19 173 B7
Jubilee Ave BN16 199 C6
Jubilee Cl RH16 86 A4
Jubilee Ct BN2 168 E2
Jubilee Ho
Crockerhill PO18 155 B3
Emsworth PO10 149 A1
Jubilee Rd
Burgess Hill RH15 106 E2
Chichester PO19 173 A7
Portslade-by-Sea BN41 186 A8
Rudgwick RH12 33 D8
Jubilee St BN1 207 B3
Jubilee Terr
Chichester PO19 173 A7
Westbourne PO10 149 D3
Jubilee Way RH20 119 F3
Jubilee Wlk RH10 19 A6
Judge's Terr RH19 22 E8
Juggs La RH20 99 E1
Juggs The RH20 99 E1
Julian Ct 5 BN43 185 C8
Julian Rd BN3 187 E7
Junction Cl
Burgess Hill RH15 107 C4
Burndell BN18 177 B2
Junction Pl GU27 26 F6
Junction Rd Brighton BN1 207 A3
Burgess Hill RH15 107 B3
June Cl PO21 204 F8
June La GU29 92 E8
June Mdws GU29 92 D8
June Rise GU29 92 E8
Juniper Cl
Middleton-on-Sea PO22 196 E6
Portslade-by-Sea BN41 166 B3
Worthing BN13 181 C5
Juniper Rd RH11 5 C1
Juniper Wlk BN43 165 C1
Juno Cl BN12 181 C2
Jupp's La BN12 181 C3
Jura Cl RH11 18 B3
Jury La PO20 192 D5
Juxon Cl Chichester PO19 173 A5
Crawley RH11 17 F4

K

Kaithwood Ho RH12 37 B5
Karenza Ct Brighton BN1 188 A8
3 Horsham RH12 36 E3
Kearsley Dr BN14 162 A1
Keaton Ho RH16 85 E6
Keats Cl RH12 36 F7
Keats Pl RH19 9 D1
Keats Wlk PO21 195 B3
Kebbell Lodge 12 BN2 207 C2
Keble Cl
Bognor Regis PO21 194 F3
Crawley RH10 6 D1
Keelson Way BN17 199 A6
Keepers Wood PO19 152 F3
Keir Hardie Ho 7 RH11 18 B1
Kelly Rd BN3 167 D1
Kelmscott Rise RH11 39 B8
Kelsey Ave PO10 150 A1
Kelsey Cl East Liss GU33 45 C5
Horley RH6 1 F3
Kelsey Ct RH15 107 D3
Kelso Cl Crawley RH10 19 E7
Lancing BN15 183 B7
Worthing BN13 181 E4
Kelvin Bsns Ctr RH10 5 F2
Kelvin La RH10 5 F2
Kelvin Way RH10 5 F2
Kemnal Pk GU27 27 D7
Kemp Ct BN2 188 E4
Kemp St BN1 207 B3
Kemp Town Pl 18 BN2 188 D4
Kemps BN6 125 F7
Kempshott Rd RH12 36 B4
Kemptown Mews 11 BN2 188 E4
Kendal Cl BN17 179 A3
Kendal Rd Hove BN3 186 F8
Lancing BN15 183 C6
Kendale Cl RH10 19 C2
Kenhurst BN16 200 A5
Kenilworth Cl RH11 18 B2
Kenilworth Rd PO21 195 B4
Kenlegh PO21 194 F2
Kenmara Cl RH10 6 A1
Kenmara Ct RH10 6 A2
Kenmure Ave BN1 168 A7
Kennard Ct RH18 23 E3
Kennedy Ave RH19 9 D3
Kennedy Rd RH13 36 D1
Kennel Hill PO18 133 E1
Kennel La Hookwood RH6 1 D2
Maplehurst RH13 80 E2
Kennet Cl Crawley RH11 17 F5
Worthing BN13 181 D7
Kensett's Cnr RH20 121 A3
Kensington Cl RH20 119 C7
Kensington Gdns BN1 207 B3
Kensington Pl BN1 207 B3
Kensington Rd
Chichester PO19 173 D6
Crawley RH11 18 C2
Kensington St BN1 207 B3
Kent Cl BN43 185 C7
Kent Ct 5 RH13 36 D2
Kent Rd Chichester PO19 173 B7
Littlehampton BN17 198 D6
Kent St BN5,BN13 104 C6
Kenton Rd BN3 186 D7
Kents Rd RH16 85 F3
Kentstreet La RH13 82 C1
Kentwyns Dr RH13 58 E8
Kenwards BN1 168 D7
Kenwood Quay 6 BN15 183 F5
Kenya Ct 2 Brighton BN1 187 E6
Horley RH6 1 F4
Kerrison Mews 7 BN3 187 D5
Kerves La RH13 58 D6
Kestrel Cl
Bracklesham PO20 202 A6
Crawley RH11 18 C8
Horsham RH12 36 E5
Hove BN3 187 D8
Kestrel Ct
Bognor Regis PO21 204 F7
Chichester PO19 173 D7
Kestrel Way BN17 178 C4
Kestrels The BN43 185 A8
Keswick Cl Crawley RH11 17 D4
Worthing BN12 181 D5
Ketch Rd BN17 199 A4
Ketche's La RH17,TN22 87 E7
Kew Gdns PO21 194 F5
Kew St BN1 207 A3
Kewell's Cnr PO20 191 E5
Keymer Cres BN12 181 D1
Keymer Ct RH15 107 B2
Keymer End RH16 85 D3
Keymer Gdns RH15 107 B1
Keymer Par RH15 107 B2
Keymer Pk BN6 127 B3
Keymer Rd Brighton BN1 168 B6
Burgess Hill RH15 127 B8
Crawley RH11 18 D4
Hassocks BN6 126 F3
Keymer Way BN12 181 C1
Keynor La PO20 203 E8
Keysford La RH16, RH17 64 E3

Kidborough Rd RH11 .....17 F4
Kidbrook RH16 ....86 B6
Kidbrooke Rise RH18 .....23 E2
Kidd Rd PO19 ....153 B1
Kidders La BN5 ....123 D8
Kidmans Cl RH12 ....36 F5
Kidworth Cl RH6 ....1 F5
Killinghurst La GU27 .....28 D8
Kilmore Cl BN14 ....161 E6
Kiln Field GU33 ....45 A5
Kiln Fields GU27 ....27 C8
Kiln La Horley RH6 ....2 A5
Lindfield RH16 ....86 B5
Kiln Rd RH10 ....21 B7
Kiln The RH15 ....107 C3
Kilnbarn Ct RH16 ....85 D2
Kilnbarn Way RH16 ....85 D2
Kilnfield Rd RH12 ....33 D8
Kilnmead RH10 ....18 E7
Kilnmead Cl RH10 ....18 E7
Kilnwood Cl PO20 ....206 F7
Kilnwood La RH12 ....17 B3
Kilwich Cl PO22 ....196 D6
Kimber Cl BN15 ....183 D5
Kimberley Cl RH6 ....1 E3
Kimberley Ct BN14 ......182 D6
Kimberley Rd
Brighton BN2 ....168 D1
Crawley RH10 ....19 B7
Kimbridge Pk PO20 .....202 A6
Kimbridge Rd PO20 .....202 A6
Kindersley Cl RH19 ....10 B3
Kinfauns Dr BN13 ....161 D2
King Alfred (Swimming Pool & Sports Ctr) BN3 187 A5
King Alfred Cl BN44 .....143 D3
King Bsns Ctr BN6 ......105 C1
King Charles Pl 10 BN43 .185 A6
King Edward Ave BN14 ..182 E4
King Edward Cl
Horsham RH13 ....57 D6
Worthing BN14 ....182 E4
King Edward Rd RH13 ....57 D6
King Edward VII Hospl GU29 ....70 E6
King George Ave RH19 .....9 C3
King George Ct PO21 ....195 B4
King George Gdns PO19 .172 F8
King George Rd BN43 ...185 D8
King George VI Ave BN1, BN3 ....167 A3
King George VI Dr BN3 ..167 A4
King George VI Mans BN3 ....166 F2
King James La BN5 ......123 E4
King John Ct 7 BN43 ...185 A6
King John's Ct GU29 ......92 F7
King Pl BN1 ....207 A2
King St Arundel BN18 .....158 A3
Brighton BN1 ....207 B2
East Grinstead RH19 ....9 E1
Emsworth PO10 ....169 C8
Westbourne PO10 ....149 D3
Worthing BN14 ....182 D4
King's Arms Hill BN18 ...158 B3
King's Ave PO19 ....172 F4
King's Barn La BN44 .....143 F4
King's Barn Villas BN44 .143 E3
King's Ct PO21 ....195 E3
King's Espl BN3 ....187 A5
King's Gdns BN3 ....187 B5
King's La RH13 ....104 B8
King's Manor Com Coll BN43 ....185 D8
King's Par PO21 ....195 A2
King's Rd
Brighton BN1, BN3 ....187 E5
Emsworth PO10 ....169 A8
Haslemere GU27 ....27 A6
Haywards Heath RH16 .....85 F3
Horsham RH12 ....36 E3
King's Stone Ave BN44 ..143 F3
King's Terr 6 PO10 ......169 B8
Kingfisher Cl Crawley RH10 .6 A1
Rowland's Castle PO9 .....128 D1
Worthing BN13 ....181 C5
Kingfisher Ct
Bognor Regis PO22 ....196 F5
Worthing BN11 ....182 A3
Kingfisher Dr
Littlehampton BN17 ......178 C4
Westbourne PO10 ....149 D4
Kingfisher Par PO20 .....201 F7
Kingfisher Rise RH19 .....22 F8
Kingfisher Way RH12 .....36 C5
Kingley Vale Nature Reserve PO18 ...131 E2
Kingmere 10 BN17 ....198 E4
Kings Barn End BN44 ....143 F3
Kings Cl Burndell BN18 ...177 A3
Lancing BN15 ....183 F5
Red Hill PO9 ....128 C1
Kings Copse 9 RH19 .....22 F8
Kings Cres BN43 ....184 D5
Kings Ct Horsham RH12 ...36 E3
Lancing BN15 ....183 F4
Selsey PO20 ....206 E8
Shoreham-by-Sea BN43 ...184 D5
Kings Dr
Bognor Regis PO21 ......205 B8
Hassocks BN6 ....126 F4
Midhurst GU29 ....70 E7
Shoreham-by-Sea BN43 ...184 D5
Kings Gap BN43 ....184 D5
Kings Gate BN3 ....187 C8
Kings La
Coldwaltham RH20 ....117 C6
Marehill RH20 ....98 F1
Southwater Street RH13 ....58 A4
Kings Mdw PO18 ....150 D1
Kings Mews Horsham RH12 36 B2
Hove BN3 ....187 B6
Kings Par BN1 ....168 A2
Kings Platt RH13 ....101 D8
Kings Rd Horley RH6 ....2 A3
Lancing BN15 ....183 F5
Southwick BN42 ....185 E1
Kings Ride RH15 ....107 D1
Kings Way
Burgess Hill RH15 ....107 D2
Red Hill PO9 ....128 C1
Kings Wlk BN43 ....184 D5
Kingsbridge Mews BN13 181 D7
Kingsbury Rd BN1 ....207 B4
Kingsbury St BN1, BN2 ...207 B4
Kingscote Hill RH11 ......18 B4
Kingscote Lodge BN1 ....168 F5
Kingscote Sta RH19 ......21 F4
Kingsdene BN11 ....182 B2
Kingsey Ave PO10 ....169 A8
Kingsfield Henfield BN5 ..123 E5
Storrington RH20 ....119 E2
Kingsfield Cl BN42 ......185 E8
Kingsfold 2 BN2 ....188 F5
Kingsfold Cl RH14 ....77 D6
Kingsfold Ct RH12 ....15 B5
Kingsham Ave PO19 .....173 B5
Kingsham Prim Sch PO19 ....173 B4
Kingsham Rd PO19 ......173 A5
Kingsland RH5 ....3 A8
Kingsland Cl
Shoreham-by-Sea BN43 ...185 C7
Storrington RH20 ....119 E2
Kingsland Cotts BN6 ....105 C1
Kingsland Ct RH10 ....19 A6
Kingsland Rd BN14 ......182 D6
Kingslea RH12 ....36 E3
Kingsley Cl Horley RH6 ......1 F5
Worthing BN14 ....182 F4
Kingsley Ct 7 BN1 ....187 E5
Kingsley Rd Brighton BN1 .167 D1
Crawley RH11 ....18 A3
Horley RH6 ....1 F5
Kingsmead
Bognor Regis PO22 ....195 F3
Littlehampton BN17 ......178 C5
Kingsmead Cl
Horsham RH12 ....37 B6
Steyning BN44 ....143 D1
Kingsmead Gdns PO22 ..197 A6
Kingsmead Pl RH12 ....35 C3
Kingsmead Rd
Ancton PO22 ....197 A5
Broadridge Heath RH12 ....35 D3
Kingsmere BN1 ....167 E2
Kingsmill Rd PO22 ......176 C6
Kingspit La GU28 ....96 D8
Kingsthorpe Rd BN3 .....186 F8
Kingston Bay Rd BN43 ...185 C6
Kingston Broadway BN42, BN43 ....165 D1
Kingston Buci Fst Sch BN43 ....185 B8
Kingston Cl Brighton BN1 .168 E6
Hove BN3 ....166 E2
Shoreham-by-Sea BN43 ...185 C8
Kingston Ct 17 BN43 .....185 C8
Kingston La
East Preston BN16 ....200 B5
Southwick BN42,BN43 ....185 D7
Kingston Way BN42, BN43 ....165 D1
Kingsway
Bognor Regis PO21 ......194 D1
Hove BN3, BN41 ....187 B5
Selsey PO20 ....206 F6
Worthing BN12 ....181 F2
Kingsway Ct BN3 ....187 C5
Kingswood RH20 ....119 C7
Kingswood Cl RH11 ....39 C8
Kingswood Flats BN2 ....207 C2
Kingswood St BN2 ......207 B2
Kinnell Cl PO10 ....169 B8
Kinrara Ho 10 PO21 .....195 C3
Kinsale Ct 5 BN3 ....187 D7
Kipling Ave BN12 ....181 B3
Kipling Cl RH10 ....19 C8
Kipling Ct
3 Haywards Heath RH16 ...85 D5
Horsham RH13 ....37 A4
Kipling Way RH19 ....9 C1
Kippens La RH13 ....80 B2
Kirdford Cl
Burgess Hill RH15 ....107 C1
Crawley RH11 ....18 A8
4 Littlehampton BN16 ....199 B4
Kirdford Jun Sch RH14 ....53 B2
Kirdford Rd BN18 ....158 A2
Kirkby Cl PO18 ....154 D3
Kirkland Cl BN16 ....199 B5
Kites Cl RH11 ....18 C6
Kithurst Cl Crawley RH11 ..18 D4
Littlehampton BN16 ......199 F4
Worthing BN12 ....181 B4
Kithurst Cres BN12 ......181 B4
Kithurst Farm Rd RH20 ..140 B8
Kithurst La RH20 ....119 C1
Kithurst Pk RH20 ....119 B1
Kitilear Ct BN3 ....187 D6
Kitsmead RH10 ....7 A2
Kittiwake Cl RH11 ....17 D4
Knap La PO20 ....206 D7
Knepp Cl Brighton BN2 ...168 F2
Crawley RH10 ....19 C6
Knight's Hill PO18 ....133 E5
Knighton Cl RH10 ....6 D2
Knights Cotts PO18 ......151 B3
Knightscroft Ave BN16 ..199 C4
Knightscroft Cl 5 BN16 ..199 B4
Knightscroft Ho 3 BN16 .199 B4
Knob Hill RH12 ....15 A1
Knockhundred La GU26 ...26 C8
Knockhundred Row GU29 .92 F8
Knole Cl RH10 ....19 D7
Knole Gr RH19 ....9 C3
Knoll Bsns Ctr The BN3 ..186 D8
Knoll Cl BN3 ....166 D1
Knoll Inf Sch BN3 ....166 D1
Knowle Cl RH10 ....7 C3
Knowle Dr RH10 ....7 B3
Knowle La GU6, RH12 .....11 D4
Knowle The RH17 ....84 E7
Knowles Cl BN5 ....123 E5
Knowles Meadow GU33 ...45 D1
Knoyle Rd BN1 ....167 E2
Knyveton Ct RH15 ....107 B3
Kymer Gdns BN6 ....127 A3
Kynon Gdns PO22 ....196 D6
Kyoto Ct PO21 ....195 B3

L

Laburnum Ave BN3 ......166 E1
Laburnum Cl Ferring BN12 200 F5
Lancing BN15 ....183 D4
Laburnum Gr
Bognor Regis PO22 ....195 C6
Brighton BN1 ....168 B3
Chichester PO19 ....173 A5
Laburnum Grove Jun Sch PO22 ....195 C6
Laburnum Lodge BN13 ..181 C5
Laburnum Way RH16 .....86 B4
Laburnum Wlk BN16 .....199 C6
Lackenhurst La RH13 .....79 A6
Lacock Cl PO20 ....202 C5
Lacy Ho PO19 ....172 F5
Ladbroke Rd RH6 ....2 B5
Ladbrook Cl BN16 ....199 B4
Ladies Mile BN1 ....168 B7
Ladies Mile Cl BN1 ......167 F6
Ladies' Mile Ct BN1 .....167 E6
Ladies' Mile Rd BN1 .....167 F6
Lady Bee Ind Est BN42 ..185 E6
Lady Margaret Rd RH11 ..18 A7
Lady Margaret Wlk RH11 .18 A7
Ladydell Rd BN11 ....182 F3
Ladymead RH15 ....107 C5
Ladymead Cl RH10 ....19 C3
Ladysmith Rd BN2 ......188 D8
Ladywell Ct BN15 ....183 F7
Lagness Rd PO20 ....173 F1
Lagoon Rd PO21 ....204 F7
Lagwood Cl BN6 ....126 F3
Laine Cl BN1 ....167 E3
Laines Rd BN44 ....143 C2
Lake Cotts PO22 ....176 D6
Lake La
Barnham BN18, PO22 .....176 D6
Horley RH1, RH6 ....2 C6
Lake Rd PO19 ....173 C6
Lake View
Bognor Regis PO21 ....194 A1
1 Brighton BN2 ....188 C5
Lake View Rd
East Grinstead RH19 ....9 F5
Furnace Wood RH10 ....8 C4
Lakers Lea RH14 ....31 F1
Lakers Mdw RH14 ....77 D8
Lakeside Horsham RH12 ...36 C5
Midhurst GU29 ....92 E6
Shoreham-by-Sea BN15 ...184 B5
Lakeside Dr RH13 ....58 A1
Lamberhurst Wlk RH10 ...19 A5
Lambert's La GU29 ....92 F8
Lambeth Cl RH11 ....18 B2
Lambeth Wlk RH11 ....18 B2
Lambleys La BN14 ......182 F8
Lambourn Cl RH19 ....9 E3
Lambourne Cl
Brighton BN1 ....168 C2
Crawley RH10 ....18 F4
Lambourne La GU29, GU30 .47 E2
Lambourne Rd BN1 .....168 C2
Lambs Cres RH12 ....36 F5
Lambs Farm Cl RH12 .....37 A5
Lambs Farm Rd RH12 .....37 A6
Lambs Green Rd RH12 ....16 F6
Lambs Lease GU33 ....45 D3
Lambyn Croft RH6 ....2 C4
Lammas Cl BN17 ....178 E3
Lamorna Gdns
Ferring BN12 ....200 F4
Westergate PO20 ....175 D6
Lamorna Gr BN14 ....182 C6
Lanark Cl RH13 ....36 E2
Lanark Ho BN13 ....181 E7
Lancaster Cl RH10 ....6 D1
Lancaster Ct 12 BN3 ....187 A6
Lancaster Dr RH19 ....10 A3
Lancaster Ho 4 BN11 ...182 A2
Lancaster Pl PO22 ......195 C6
Lancaster Rd
Brighton BN1 ....207 A4
Worthing BN12 ....181 E2
Lancasterian Grange PO19 ....172 F6
Lancastrian Cty Inf Sch PO19 ....172 F7
Lancastrian Grange 4 PO19 ....172 F7
Lancelot Cl RH11 ....17 E6
Lancing Bsns Ctr BN15 ..183 D4
Lancing Cl Crawley RH11 ..18 A8
Lancing BN15 ....183 D6
Lancing Coll BN15 ......164 A2
Lancing Ct
5 Brighton BN2 ....188 F5
Horsham RH12 ....37 A4
Lancing Pk BN15 ....183 D4
Lancing Sta BN15 ....183 E5
Landen Pk RH6 ....1 E5
Landseer Dr PO20 ......206 F7
Landseer Rd BN3 ....187 A8
Lane End Dr PO10 ......169 B8
Lane End Rd PO22 ......197 A5
Lane Ho 1 RH13 ....36 D2
Lane The Chichester PO19 .153 A2
Ifold RH14 ....31 C4
Lanercost Rd RH11 ....18 C5
Lanfranc Rd BN14 ......182 B4
Langbury Cl BN12 ....180 D3
Langbury La BN12 ......180 E3
Langdale Ave PO19, PO20 173 C4
Langdale Cl BN15 ....183 C5
Langdale Ct BN3 ....186 F6
Langdale Gdns BN3 .....186 F6
Langdale Rd Crawley RH11 .17 D4
Hove BN3 ....186 F6
Langham Ct 7 BN11 ....182 A2
Langham Gdns BN11 ....182 A2
Langhurst 9 BN2 ....188 E4
Langhurst Cl RH12 ....15 E4
Langhurst La RH12 ....17 A8
Langhurstwood Rd RH12 .15 D3
Langley Dr RH11 ....18 D8
Langley Gr PO21 ....194 C1
Langley Green Fst Sch RH11 ....5 D1
Langley Green Mid Sch RH11 ....18 C8
Langley La RH11 ....18 A8
Langley Par RH11 ....5 C1
Langley Pl RH11 ....5 C1
Langley Wlk RH11 ....5 B1
Langmead Cl BN17 ......197 E8
Langridge Dr
East Grinstead RH19 ....22 E8
Portslade-by-Sea BN41 ...166 B3
Langridge Ho 2 RH12 ....36 B2
Langridge La RH16 ....86 A5
Langridge Way RH15 ....106 E5
Langshott RH6 ....2 A7
Langshott Cty Fst Sch RH6 .2 C3
Langshott La RH6 ....2 C4
Langstone Cl RH10 ....19 C3
Langton Cl PO20 ....206 D6
Langton Ct 6 BN14 .....182 D4
Langton La BN6 ....125 E7
Langton Pl 5 RH20 ......119 D1
Langton Rd
Chichester PO19 ....172 E7
Worthing BN14 ....182 D4
Lanka Ct PO20 ....201 E7
Lansbury Rd RH11 ....18 B1
Lansdown Cl RH12 ....37 B6
Lansdown Terr PO10 ....149 D5
Lansdowne Cl
Angmering BN16 ....179 F6
Worthing BN11 ....182 A2
Lansdowne Ct BN11 ....182 A2
Lansdowne Mews 7 BN3 ....187 D6
Lansdowne Pl BN3 ......187 D6
Lansdowne Rd
Angmering BN16 ....179 F6
Hove BN1, BN3 ....187 D6
Littlehampton BN17 ......178 D3
Worthing BN11 ....182 A2
Lansdowne Sq 1 BN3 ...187 D5
Lansdowne St BN3 .....187 D6
Lansdowne Way BN16 ..179 F6
Lanyards BN17 ....179 A3
Lanyon Cl RH12 ....37 A6
Lanyon Mews RH12 ....37 A6
Lapwing Cl RH13 ....36 F3
Larch Cl
Bognor Regis PO22 ....195 C7
Chichester PO19 ....152 F2
Liphook GU30 ....25 B3
Rustington BN16 ....199 D5
Larch End Horsham RH12 ..36 B4
West Chiltington Common RH20 ....119 D7
Larch Lodge BN13 ......181 C5
Larch Way RH16 ....86 B4
Larches Ho RH19 ....10 B4
Larches The
East Grinstead RH19 ....10 B4
Horsham RH12 ....37 C6
Larches Way RH10 ....21 C8
Larchfield Cl PO21 ......194 D1
Large Acres PO20 ....206 D7
Lark Hill BN3 ....166 E3
Lark Rise Crawley RH11 ...18 C8
Liphook GU30 ....25 A5
Lark Way PO10 ....149 E4
Larke Cl BN43 ....185 C7
Larkfield Cl BN15 ....183 F5
Larkfield Way BN1 ......168 A4
Larkins Rd RH6 ....5 D7
Larksfield RH6 ....2 B4
Larkspur Cl BN17 ....179 A3
Larkspur Way RH13 ....58 A3
Lashmar Rd BN16 ....200 A6
Lashmere RH10 ....7 D3
Laski Ct RH11 ....18 B1
Latham Rd PO20 ....206 D6
Latimer Cl RH11 ....5 D1
Latimer Rd BN11 ....181 F1
Laud Dr RH10 ....19 D5
Lauder Cl PO10 ....149 F2
Laughton Rd RH12 ....36 F5
Laundry La RH17 ....44 D1
Laurel 2 RH16 ....85 D6
Laurel Cl
Burgess Hill RH15 ....107 D5
Crawley RH10 ....19 A3
Worthing BN13 ....181 C5
Laurel Dene RH19 ....9 F1
Laurel Gr PO22 ....195 C6
Laurel Mount RH20 ....98 C2
Laurel Wlk RH13 ....36 F1
Laurels Cty Fst Sch The BN13 ....181 B6
Laurels The
4 Brighton BN2 ....207 C5
Crawley RH10 ....6 A1
Henfield BN5 ....123 E5
Southwater RH13 ....57 F2
Laurence Gn PO10 ......149 B4
Lauriston Rd BN1 ....167 E2
Lavant CE Prim Sch PO18 ....152 E6
Lavant Cl Crawley RH11 ...17 F5
Worthing BN12 ....181 A4
Lavant Down Rd PO18 ..152 E7
Lavant Ho (Rosemead Sch) PO18 ..152 E5
Lavant Rd PO18, PO19 ...152 F3
Lavender Cl PO22 ....196 E6
Lavender Hill BN43 .....165 B1
Lavender Ho BN2 ....207 C1
Lavender St BN2 ....207 C1
Lavington Cl RH11 ....18 A8
Lavington Rd BN14 .....182 B6
Lavinia Ct
Bognor Regis PO21 ....194 F4
Worthing BN12 ....181 C3
Lavinia Way BN16 ....200 A5
Lawn The PO21 ....194 E2
Lawns Rd RH12 ....12 A3
Lawns The Lancing BN15 .183 C8
West Kingston BN16 ......200 A4
Lawrence Ave BN16 .....199 D6
Lawrence Cl PO20 ......206 E6
Lawrence Rd BN3 ....186 F7
Lawrie La RH16 ....86 B5
Laws Cl RH11 ....17 E5
Lawson-Hunt Ind Pk RH12 ....35 C4
Lawyer's La BN5 ....123 C4
Laxton Mdw PO18 ....151 A5
Laylands Ct BN41 ....186 A7
Laylands Rd BN41 ......186 A7
Layne The PO22 ....197 A5
Lazy Acre PO10 ....169 F8
Le May Cl RH6 ....2 A4
Lea Cl RH11 ....17 F5
Lea Farm La RH20 ....97 C2
Lea Ho PO22 ....195 A6
Leach Ct BN2 ....188 C5
Leacroft RH19 ....9 D2
Leahurst Court Rd BN1 ..167 E3
Leahurst Ct 1 BN1 ......167 E3
Leaman Cl PO22 ....196 F5
Leander Rd PO18 ....171 C5
Leas Ct PO22 ....195 C5
Leas The Angmering BN16 .179 E3
Burgess Hill RH15 ....106 F4
Leatherbottle La PO19 ...173 C6
Lechford Rd RH6 ....2 A1
Leconfield Rd BN15 .....183 C5
Ledbury Way PO21 ......194 B2
Ledgers Mdw RH17 ....84 F6
Ledra Dr PO21 ....205 B8
Lee St RH6 ....1 E4
Leechpond Hill RH13 .....59 F2
Leechpool La RH12, RH13 .37 A4
Leechpool Prim Sch RH13 37 A4
Leechwood & Owlbeech Wood Nature Reserve RH13 ...37 B3
Leecroft PO21 ....194 E2
Leeds Cl Southwater RH13 ..58 A2
Worthing BN13 ....181 B5
Leemark Ho 4 BN17 .....198 E4
Lees Cnr BN16 ....199 B5
Leeward Cl BN13 ....181 F5
Leeward Rd
Littlehampton BN17 ......199 A5
Worthing BN13 ....181 F5
Legion Way PO20 ....202 A6
Legsheath La RH18, RH19 .43 F8
Leicester Ct RH10 ....19 D6
Leicester St BN2 ....207 C2
Leicester Villas BN3 .....186 D7
Leigh Ct PO20 ....202 C4
Leigh Rd Chichester PO19 .172 F5
Worthing BN14 ....182 D6
Leighlands RH10 ....19 C8
Leighton Ave BN14 .....182 E6
Leighton Rd
Horsted Keynes RH17 .....65 C5
Hove BN3 ....187 A8
Leighton Villas RH17 .....65 C5
Leinster Gdns PO22 .....196 D4
Leith View Rd RH12 ......37 A5
Lemmington Way RH12 ...37 A7
Lenhurst Way BN13 .....181 F4
Lennox Rd
Chichester PO19 ....173 B7
Hove BN3 ....186 F8
Shoreham-by-Sea BN43 ...185 B8
Worthing BN11 ....182 D3

Lennox St
Bognor Regis PO21 ... 195 D2
Brighton BN2 ... 207 C2
Leonard Way RH13 ... 36 F2
Leonardslee Ct RH10 ... 19 B3
Leonardslee Gdns RH13 ... 60 A1
Leonora Dr PO21 ... 194 B2
Leopold Cl PO22 ... 196 A5
Leopold Rd Brighton BN1 ... 207 A3
Crawley RH11 ... 18 C6
Lesser Foxholes BN43 ... 164 D1
Letchworth Cl BN12 ... 200 E5
Letchworth Ct RH11 ... 17 E3
Level Mare La PO20 ... 155 E2
Leveret La RH11 ... 18 B8
Leverton Ave PO22 ... 196 D4
Levine Ct 5 PO22 ... 195 D4
Lewes Cl
Bognor Regis PO21 ... 194 F4
Crawley RH10 ... 19 C6
Lewes Cres BN2 ... 188 E4
Lewes Mews 12 BN2 ... 188 E4
Lewes Rd
Brighton BN1, BN2 ... 168 E3
Chelwood Gate RH17, RH18 ... 44 C1
Danehill RH17 ... 66 B3
Ditchling BN6 ... 127 E2
Forest Row RH18 ... 23 E2
Haywards Heath RH16,RH17 ... 86 D4
Horsted Keynes RH17 ... 65 C5
Lindfield RH16 ... 86 B7
Scaynes Hill RH17 ... 86 D4
Lewes St BN2 ... 207 C3
Lewin Cl BN15 ... 183 F7
Lewis Ct 6 Brighton BN2 ... 188 C8
Worthing BN13 ... 181 B5
Lewis La BN18 ... 177 B2
Lewis Rd Chichester PO19 ... 173 B7
Lancing BN15 ... 183 D8
New Brighton PO10 ... 149 C3
Selsey PO20 ... 206 E7
Lewisham Cl RH11 ... 18 C2
Ley Rd PO22 ... 196 B4
Leybourne Cl RH11 ... 18 C1
Leyfield BN6 ... 125 D5
Leylands Pk RH15 ... 107 B5
Leylands Rd RH15 ... 107 B4
Leys The Fernhurst GU27 ... 49 A5
Singleton PO18 ... 133 D7
Leythorne Cotts PO20 ... 173 E3
Leyton Ct PO22 ... 196 B4
Leyton Lea RH17 ... 84 E6
Library Pl BN11 ... 182 E1
Lichfield Ct
10 Brighton BN2 ... 188 F5
3 Worthing BN11 ... 182 A1
Lichfield Gdns PO21 ... 194 E3
Lidsey Cl RH10 ... 19 C4
Lidsey Rd PO20, PO22 ... 175 D4
Lifeboat Way PO20 ... 206 E5
Lilac Cl
Middleton-on-Sea PO22 ... 196 E6
Rustington BN17 ... 179 A3
Worthing BN13 ... 181 B5
Lillywhite Cl RH15 ... 106 F5
Limbourne La RH20 ... 97 B3
Limbrick Cl BN12 ... 181 C3
Limbrick Cnr BN12 ... 181 C4
Limbrick La BN12 ... 181 C4
Limbrick Way BN12 ... 181 C4
Lime Ave Horsham RH12 ... 37 A4
Woodgate PO20 ... 175 E7
Lime Chase RH20 ... 119 D2
Lime Cl Chichester PO19 ... 173 B7
Copthorne RH10 ... 7 B3
Crawley RH11 ... 5 C1
Lime Gr BN16 ... 179 F4
Lime Kiln Rd RH13 ... 59 D6
Lime Rd BN14 ... 161 E6
Lime Tree Ave BN14 ... 161 F2
Lime Tree Cl BN16 ... 199 F6
Lime Tree Gr RH16 ... 86 C7
Limes Ave RH6 ... 2 B1
Limes Cl Bramshott GU30 ... 25 C7
Liss GU33 ... 45 B4
Limes The
Dormans Park RH19 ... 9 A5
Haslemere GU27 ... 27 A6
Worthing BN11 ... 182 B3
Yapton BN18 ... 177 A3
Limmard Way PO22 ... 196 C4
Limmer La PO22 ... 196 B4
Limney Rd BN2 ... 188 E7
Linacre Dr GU6, RH12 ... 12 C4
Lincett Ave BN13 ... 181 F4
Lincett Ct BN13 ... 181 F4
Lincett Dr BN13 ... 181 F3
Linch Rd GU29 ... 70 B7
Linchmere BN2 ... 188 F7
Linchmere Pl RH11 ... 18 A7
Linchmere Rd
Hammer GU27 ... 26 D5
Linchmere GU27 ... 26 C4
Lincoln Ave PO21 ... 194 C4
Lincoln Cl Crawley RH10 ... 18 E3
Horley RH6 ... 2 A2
Lincoln Cotts BN2 ... 207 C3
Lincoln Ct Hove BN3 ... 187 C8
Liphook GU30 ... 25 C4
Lincoln Gn PO19 ... 152 F1
Lincoln Ho 10 BN11 ... 182 B2
Lincoln Rd
Portslade-by-Sea BN41 ... 186 B7
Worthing BN13 ... 181 F4
Lincoln St BN2 ... 207 C4
Lincoln Wood RH16 ... 85 C5
Lindale Pl 6 RH20 ... 119 D1
Linden Ave RH19 ... 9 C2
Linden Cl Crawley RH10 ... 19 A3
Horsham RH12 ... 36 E4
Linden Ct
1 Bognor Regis PO21 ... 195 C3
Petworth GU28 ... 95 E7
Linden Dr GU33 ... 45 B4
Linden Gr RH16 ... 86 B7
Linden Pk BN17 ... 198 C5
Linden Rd
Bognor Regis PO21 ... 195 C4
Littlehampton BN17 ... 198 C5
Lindens Cl PO10 ... 149 B2
Lindens The
4 Brighton BN2 ... 207 C4
Copthorne RH10 ... 7 B3
Lindfield BN41 ... 166 A1
Lindfield Ct BN1 ... 168 C2
Lindfield Ent Pk RH16 ... 86 C6
Lindfield Prim Sch RH16 ... 86 A7
Lindfield Rd RH17 ... 64 C6
Lindgren Wlk RH11 ... 18 B1
Lindsey Ct PO22 ... 196 A6
Lindum Rd BN13 ... 181 F5
Lindum Way BN13 ... 181 F5
Lineside Ind Est BN17 ... 198 B6
Lineside Way BN17 ... 198 B6
Linfield Copse RH20 ... 119 F6
Lingfield Cl BN13 ... 181 F6
Lingfield Dr RH10 ... 19 E7
Lingfield Rd RH19 ... 9 D3
Lingfield Way PO20 ... 206 F7
Link Hill RH20 ... 119 B1
Link La RH20 ... 98 C2
Link The RH11 ... 18 D6
Link Way PO21 ... 194 A1
Links Ave PO22 ... 195 F4
Links Cl
Portslade-by-Sea BN41 ... 186 C8
Red Hill PO9 ... 128 D1
Links La PO9 ... 128 D2
Links Rd Lancing BN15 ... 183 F6
Portslade-by-Sea BN41 ... 186 C8
Worthing BN14 ... 182 A8
Linkway RH6 ... 6 C7
Linkway The Brighton BN1 ... 168 B1
Worthing BN11 ... 182 C3
Linnell Cl RH11 ... 39 B8
Linton Ho GU28 ... 73 C1
Linton Rd BN3 ... 186 F8
Lintott Gdns RH12 ... 36 E3
Lion Cl GU27 ... 26 F7
Lion Ct PO21 ... 194 B2
Lion Gn GU27 ... 26 F6
Lion La Haslemere GU27 ... 26 F7
Turners Hill RH10 ... 21 A4
Lion Mead GU27 ... 26 F6
Lion Mews 4 BN3 ... 186 F7
Lion Rd PO21 ... 194 A2
Lion St PO19 ... 173 A6
Lionel Ave PO22 ... 196 C6
Lions Ct BN2 ... 188 E5
Lions Dene BN1 ... 167 D4
Lions Gdns BN1 ... 167 D2
Liphook CE Jun Sch GU30 ... 25 B4
Liphook Cl BN1 ... 168 C1
Liphook Inf Sch GU30 ... 25 B4
Liphook Rd
Haslemere GU27 ... 26 F6
Hollywater GU35 ... 24 A8
Linchmere GU27,GU30 ... 26 B4
Liphook Sta GU30 ... 25 C2
Lisher Rd BN15 ... 183 F7
Lisle Way PO10 ... 149 A3
Lismore Cres RH11 ... 18 B3
Liss Cty Inf Sch GU33 ... 45 C3
Liss Cty Jun Sch GU33 ... 45 C3
Liss Sta GU33 ... 45 B4
Lister Ave RH19 ... 22 F6
Listers RH17 ... 60 F1
Litten Terr PO19 ... 173 A7
Little Ashfield GU29 ... 92 E8
Little Babbsham PO21 ... 194 E2
Little Barn Pl GU33 ... 45 D4
Little Bentswood RH16 ... 85 F5
Little Bentswood Cl RH16 ... 85 F5
Little Black Hill RH16 ... 86 B7
Little Boultons PO20 ... 193 A8
Little Breach PO19 ... 172 F8
Little Bridges Cl RH13 ... 57 F1
Little Cl RH13 ... 79 F7
Little Comptons RH13 ... 36 F2
Little Copse Rd BN6 ... 126 E4
Little Court Cl GU29 ... 92 D8
Little Crabtree RH11 ... 18 C7
Little Cranfield Ct RH19 ... 9 D1
Little Dipper's RH20 ... 98 C2
Little Dr BN12 ... 200 E5
Little Dro BN44 ... 143 D2
Little East St
Billingshurst RH14 ... 55 D1
Brighton BN2 ... 207 B1
Little Finches RH13 ... 103 A3
Little Gables BN13 ... 181 F6
Little George St BN2 ... 207 B1
Little Grebe RH12 ... 36 C5
Little Hatch RH12 ... 36 F5
Little Haven La RH12 ... 36 F5
Little Hayes Cotts RH14 ... 55 F5
Little High St
8 Shoreham-by-Sea BN43 ... 184 E7
Worthing BN11 ... 182 D3
Little Hill RH20 ... 119 C8
Little King St RH19 ... 9 E1
Little London PO19 ... 173 A6
Little London Mews 5
PO19 ... 173 A6
Little Oak RH13 ... 103 A3
Little Paddocks BN12 ... 200 E5
Little Paddocks Way
BN12 ... 200 F5
Little Park Enterprises
RH11 ... 4 E3
Little Pembrokes BN11 ... 182 A3
Little Preston St BN1 ... 187 E5
Little Western St 1 BN1 ... 187 E5
Littlecote GU28 ... 95 F7
Littledrove Cotts PO18 ... 133 D7
Littlefield Cl PO20 ... 206 E7
Littlefield Rd PO19 ... 173 B5
Littlefield Sch GU30 ... 25 D2
Littlegreen Sch PO18 ... 109 A4
Littlehampton Com Sch
The BN17 ... 198 E6
Littlehampton Hospl
BN17 ... 198 E5
Littlehampton
Information Ctr BN17 ... 198 D3
Littlehampton Marina
BN17 ... 198 B5
Littlehampton Mus BN17 ... 198 E5
Littlehampton Rd
Ferring BN12 ... 180 D3
Worthing BN12, BN13 ... 181 D5
Littlehampton Sta BN17 ... 198 D5
Littlehaven Inf Sch RH12 ... 36 F5
Littleheath Rd BN18 ... 155 E4
Littlemead Sch PO20 ... 174 A7
Littlestone Rd BN13 ... 181 E6
Littleworth La RH13 ... 103 A6
Liverpool Bldgs 9 BN11 ... 182 D2
Liverpool Gdns BN11 ... 182 D2
Liverpool Rd BN11 ... 182 D2
Liverpool Terr BN11 ... 182 D2
Livesay Cres BN14 ... 182 D4
Livingstone Ho 5 BN3 ... 187 B7
Livingstone Rd
Burgess Hill RH15 ... 106 F3
Crawley RH10 ... 18 E4
Horsham RH13 ... 36 D1
Hove BN3 ... 187 B7
Livingstone St BN2 ... 188 D5
Lizard Head BN17 ... 199 A6
Lloyd Cl BN3 ... 187 C8
Lloyd Goring Cl BN16 ... 179 F6
Lloyd Rd BN3 ... 187 C8
Lloyds Ct RH10 ... 5 E1
Loats La PO21 ... 194 F7
Lobs Wood La RH20 ... 119 D2
Lobster La PO20 ... 206 B8
Lock La PO20 ... 191 F6
Locke Rd GU30 ... 25 D4
Lockgate Rd PO20 ... 192 C4
Lockhart Ct RH16 ... 85 F2
Locks Cres BN41 ... 166 B1
Locks Ct 10 BN42 ... 185 E7
Locks Hill BN41 ... 166 B1
Locksash Cl PO20 ... 190 C2
Locksash La PO18 ... 130 C7
Lockwood Cl RH12 ... 37 A5
Lockwood Ct RH10 ... 18 F8
Loddon Cl BN13 ... 181 C8
Loder Gdns BN14 ... 182 C5
Loder Pl BN1 ... 167 F2
Loder Rd BN1 ... 167 F2
Loders RH17 ... 64 B8
Lodge Cl Crawley RH11 ... 18 C6
East Grinstead RH19 ... 9 D1
Middleton-on-Sea PO22 ... 197 A5
Portslade-by-Sea BN41 ... 165 F2
Lodge Ct
Bognor Regis PO21 ... 194 E2
Shoreham-by-Sea BN43 ... 164 E1
Lodge Hill La BN6 ... 127 C4
Lodge La Forestside PO9 ... 129 F6
Keymer BN6 ... 127 A2
Salfords RH1 ... 1 E8
Lodge The BN2 ... 207 C5
Lodgebury Cl PO10 ... 170 A8
Lodgelands RH17 ... 64 B6
Lodsworth BN2 ... 188 F7
Lodsworth Cl BN2 ... 188 F7
Lodsworth Rd PO21 ... 194 B3
Lombard St GU28 ... 95 F8
Lomond Ave BN1 ... 168 B7
Londerry Ind Est The
PO20 ... 206 D8
London Fields Ho RH11 ... 18 C2
London La RH17 ... 84 F6
London Meed
Com Prim Sch RH15 ... 107 A1
London Rd
Albourne Green BN6 ... 125 D5
Arundel BN18 ... 157 E6
Arundel BN18 ... 158 A3
Ashington RH20 ... 121 A4
Balcombe RH17 ... 40 F2
Bognor Regis PO21 ... 195 D3
Brighton BN1 ... 207 B4
Brighton, Withdene BN1 ... 167 D4
Burgess Hill RH15 ... 106 F5
Coldwaltham RH20 ... 117 D6
Crawley RH11 ... 5 E3
Cuckfield RH17 ... 84 E7
Danehill RH17 ... 66 A4
East Grinstead RH19 ... 9 C3
Fontwell BN18 ... 156 A3
Forest Row RH18 ... 23 E4
Hassocks BN6, RH15 ... 126 E6
Heath Common RH20 ... 120 E2
Henfield BN5 ... 123 F6
Hill Brow GU31,GU33 ... 67 B8
Horsham RH12 ... 36 C2
Hurstpierpoint BN6 ... 125 E2
Liphook GU30 ... 25 C5
Poynings BN45, BN6 ... 146 F7
Pyecombe BN1,BN45 ... 147 C4
London Rd *continued*
Washington RH20 ... 141 E7
London Road Cotts BN18 ... 158 A4
London Road Sta BN1 ... 188 A8
London St BN11 ... 182 C3
London Terr BN1 ... 207 B4
Lonesome La RH2 ... 1 D8
Loney Ct 1 BN43 ... 185 C8
Long Acre
Crawley Down RH10 ... 21 A8
Selsey PO20 ... 206 D6
Long Cl RH10 ... 19 D6
Long Copse Ct PO10 ... 149 B4
Long Copse La PO10 ... 149 C4
Long Furlong BN13, BN14 ... 161 B5
Long Hill RH13 ... 81 F8
Long La Arundel BN18 ... 157 D4
East Marden PO18 ... 110 B3
Long Mead BN18 ... 156 D1
Long Meadow BN14 ... 162 A3
Long Park Cnr BN6 ... 127 D2
Long Wlk RH16 ... 86 B4
Longacre Cl GU33 ... 45 C4
Longacre Cres RH17 ... 84 F8
Longacre La PO20 ... 206 E6
Longacre Pk BN18 ... 176 F5
Longback Cotts BN16 ... 179 F6
Longbridge Gate RH6 ... 5 E8
Longbridge Rd Crawley RH6 ... 5 F8
Horley RH6 ... 1 F1
Longbridge Rdbt RH6 ... 1 E2
Longbridge Wlk RH6 ... 1 F1
Longbrook PO22 ... 195 F3
Longchamp Cl RH6 ... 2 C3
Longcroft 4 BN43 ... 184 E7
Longdene Rd GU27 ... 27 B6
Longfellow Cl RH12 ... 36 E7
Longfellow Rd BN11 ... 182 B3
Longfield Rd
New Brighton PO10 ... 149 B3
Tower Hill RH12 ... 58 A8
Longford Rd PO21 ... 195 C4
Longfurlong La BN13 ... 160 E4
Longhurst RH15 ... 107 D2
Longhurst Rd RH11 ... 18 A1
Longland Ave RH20 ... 119 C2
Longlands BN14 ... 182 D8
Longlands Glade BN14 ... 182 D8
Longlands Rd
East Wittering PO20 ... 201 F6
Southbourne PO10 ... 169 F8
Longlands Spinney BN14 ... 182 D8
Longmead GU33 ... 45 B4
Longmeadow Gdns PO20 ... 191 E4
Longmere Rd RH10 ... 18 D8
Longmoor Dr GU30 ... 24 D4
Longmoor Rd GU30 ... 24 E4
Longport Rd PO22 ... 196 B4
Longships BN17 ... 199 A6
Longwood View RH10 ... 19 A3
Longyard Ho RH6 ... 2 B5
Loop The PO22 ... 196 C4
Loose La BN15 ... 183 B6
Loppets Rd RH10 ... 18 F3
Lordings La RH20 ... 119 D7
Lordings Rd RH14 ... 77 A6
Loriners RH10 ... 18 D3
Loriners Ct BN3 ... 186 D8
Lorna Rd BN3 ... 187 D7
Lorne Rd BN1 ... 207 B5
Lorraine Ct
11 Brighton BN3 ... 187 E7
2 Hove BN3 ... 187 B6
Lotts La BN15 ... 183 C6
Loudoun Rd BN17 ... 198 C5
Lourier Ct 1 BN14 ... 182 D4
Love La RH20 ... 119 D2
Lovegrove Ct BN3 ... 186 E8
Loveletts RH11 ... 18 A5
Lovells Cl PO21 ... 194 B2
Lover's Wlk BN1 ... 187 F8
Lover's Wlk Cotts BN1 ... 187 F8
Lovett Ct BN12 ... 181 C4
Loveys Rd BN18 ... 176 F2
Lowdells Cl RH19 ... 9 C4
Lowdells Dr RH19 ... 9 D4
Lowdells La RH19 ... 9 C3
Lowe Cl RH11 ... 39 B8
Lower Barn Cl RH12 ... 36 F5
Lower Beach Rd BN43 ... 184 F6
Lower Bevendean Ave
BN2 ... 168 E1
Lower Bognor Rd
PO20,PO21 ... 194 D5
Lower Chalvington Pl
BN2 ... 188 E5
Lower Church Rd RH15 ... 106 F3
Lower Dene RH19 ... 10 A1
Lower Dr BN42 ... 165 E1
Lower Faircox BN5 ... 123 D5
Lower Forecourt RH6 ... 6 B7
Lower Hanger GU27 ... 26 D6
Lower Hone La PO18 ... 171 A2
Lower Market St 6 BN3 ... 187 D5
Lower Mere RH19 ... 22 F8
Lower Rd
East Lavant PO18 ... 153 A5
Forest Row RH18 ... 23 F3
Lower Rock Gdns BN2 ... 207 C1
Lower Roedale Cotts
BN1 ... 168 B3
Lower Sq RH18 ... 23 E3
Lower St Fittleworth RH20 ... 97 A2
Haslemere GU27 ... 27 C6
Pulborough RH20 ... 98 C2
Lower Station Rd
Billingshurst RH14 ... 77 D6
Henfield BN5 ... 123 D4
Lower Tanbridge Way
RH12 ... 36 B2
Lowestoft Wlk RH10 ... 19 B4
Lowfield Heath Rd RH5, RH6 ... 4 F5
Lowfield Heath Windmill
RH6 ... 4 C6
Lowfield Rd
Haywards Heath RH16 ... 85 F3
Slinfold RH13 ... 34 D3
Lowfield Way RH11 ... 5 E5
Lowlands Rd RH15 ... 107 B5
Lowther Rd Brighton BN1 ... 168 A2
Worthing BN13 ... 181 F7
Loxdale (The Swedish
Folk High Sch) BN41 ... 166 B1
Loxley Gdns 2 BN14 ... 182 C4
Loxwood
East Preston BN16 ... 180 B3
1 Lancing BN15 ... 183 D5
Loxwood Ave BN14 ... 182 B5
Loxwood Prim Sch RH14 ... 32 A4
Loxwood Rd
Alfold Crossways GU6 ... 11 A3
Bucks Green RH12 ... 33 A6
Ifold RH14 ... 31 A2
Loxwood RH12, RH14 ... 32 D4
Wisborough Green RH14 ... 54 C2
Loxwood Wlk RH11 ... 18 A8
Loyal Par BN1 ... 167 C5
Lucas RH17 ... 65 D5
Lucas Cl RH19 ... 10 A1
Lucas Field GU27 ... 26 E6
Lucas Grange RH16 ... 85 D5
Lucas Rd RH12 ... 35 F8
Lucas Way RH16 ... 85 C5
Lucastes Ave RH16 ... 85 D6
Lucastes La RH16 ... 85 C6
Lucastes Rd RH16 ... 85 C5
Lucerne Cl BN41 ... 166 B1
Lucerne Ct PO21 ... 194 E2
Lucerne Dr RH10 ... 19 D4
Lucerne Rd BN1 ... 168 A1
Lucking La PO22 ... 196 F5
Lucraft Rd BN2 ... 168 F5
Ludlow Cl PO21 ... 194 E2
Ludlow Ct BN11 ... 182 F2
Luffs Mdw GU28 ... 51 A7
Lullington Ave BN3 ... 186 F8
Lulworth Cl RH11 ... 18 A3
Lumley Ct RH6 ... 2 A4
Lumley Gdns PO10 ... 169 C8
Lumley Rd Horley RH6 ... 2 A3
Lumley PO10 ... 149 C1
Lumley Terr PO10 ... 149 C1
Lunce's Hill RH16, RH17 ... 107 F8
Lundy Cl Crawley RH11 ... 18 C3
Littlehampton BN17 ... 199 A4
Lupin Cl BN17 ... 179 A3
Lurgashall RH15 ... 107 C1
Lutener Rd GU29 ... 71 A1
Luth The
Wisborough Green RH14 ... 54 B1
Wisborough Green RH14 ... 76 A8
Luther St BN2 ... 188 C7
Lutman St PO10 ... 149 A4
Lutyens Cl RH11 ... 17 E4
Luxford Cl RH12 ... 36 F5
Luxford Rd RH16 ... 86 B7
Luxford Way RH14 ... 77 C7
Luxford's La RH19 ... 23 B6
Lychgates The BN18 ... 176 F4
Lydon Ho RH11 ... 5 D1
Lye La PO18 ... 151 F5
Lyminster Ave BN1 ... 168 A5
Lyminster Cty Inf Sch
BN17 ... 178 D3
Lyminster Gate BN17 ... 178 D4
Lyminster Rd
Crossbush BN18 ... 158 D1
Littlehampton BN17,BN18 ... 178 D6
Lyn Rd BN13 ... 181 C6
Lynch Down PO18 ... 151 A6
Lynchborough Rd GU30 ... 24 D8
Lynchet Cl BN1 ... 168 C3
Lynchet Down BN1 ... 168 C2
Lynchet Wlk BN1 ... 168 C2
Lynchets Cres BN3 ... 166 D3
Lynchette The BN43 ... 164 F1
Lynchmere Ave BN15 ... 183 D8
Lynchpole Wlk BN12 ... 181 B3
Lynden Ct 1 BN1 ... 167 E2
Lyndhurst Cl RH11 ... 18 D5
Lyndhurst Ct
8 Bognor Regis PO21 ... 195 B2
Hove BN3 ... 187 D7
Lyndhurst Farm Cl RH19 ... 8 D4
Lyndhurst Fst Sch BN11 ... 182 F3
Lyndhurst Rd
Chichester PO19 ... 173 B5
Hove BN3 ... 187 D7
Worthing BN11 ... 182 F3
Lynton Cl
East Grinstead RH19 ... 10 A2
Hurstpierpoint BN6 ... 126 B5
Lynton Park Ave RH19 ... 10 A2
Lynton St BN2 ... 188 C7
Lyntons RH20 ... 98 A2
Lynwick St RH12 ... 33 C8
Lynwood Ct RH12 ... 36 C3
Lyon Cl Crawley RH10 ... 19 C2
Hove BN3 ... 187 D7
Lyon Ct
1 Bognor Regis PO21 ... 195 D3
Horsham RH13 ... 36 E2
Lyon St PO21 ... 195 D3

Lyon St W PO21 . . . . .195 D3
Lyons Cl RH13 . . . . .34 D3
Lyons Farm Ret Pk BN14 182 E8
Lyons Rd RH13 . . . . .34 E3
Lyons Way BN14 . . . . .182 E7
Lyoth La RH16 . . . . .86 C4
Lyoth Villas RH16 . . . . .86 C4
Lyric Cl RH10 . . . . .19 D4
Lysander Ho 7 RH20 . . . .119 E1
Lysander Way PO20 . . . . .154 D1
Lytham 8 RH6 . . . . .2 B2
Lytton Dr RH10 . . . . .19 D7

M

M'tongue Ave PO18 . . . . .171 C7
Mackenzie Ho RH19 . . . . . . .9 A4
Mackerel Cl PO20 . . . . . . .206 B8
Mackie Ave Brighton BN1 .168 A7
Keymer BN6 . . . . .127 A5
Mackley's Ind Est BN5 . . .144 F6
Macklin Rd PO22 . . . . .195 E4
Macleod Rd RH13 . . . . .36 F1
Madehurst Cl
Brighton BN2 . . . . .188 D5
Littlehampton BN16 . . . . . . .199 F4
Madehurst Ct Crawley RH11 17 F3
6 Littlehampton BN17 . . . .198 D5
Madehurst Way BN17 . . .198 D6
Madeira Ave
Bognor Regis PO22 . . . . . .195 E5
Horsham RH12 . . . . .36 C2
Worthing BN11 . . . . .182 E2
Madeira Dr BN2 . . . . .188 C4
Madeira Par PO22 . . . . . . .195 E5
Madeira Pl BN2 . . . . .207 C1
Madgwick La PO18 . . . . . .153 D1
Mafeking Rd BN2 . . . . . . .168 D1
Magdalene Cl RH10 . . . . . . .6 C1
Magellan Terr RH10 . . . . . . .6 A2
Magnolia Cl BN13 . . . . . . .181 B5
Magnolia Ct RH6 . . . . .2 A3
Magpie Cotts PO8 . . . . . . .128 E4
Magpie La Horsham RH13 . .58 F6
Selsey PO20 . . . . .203 C1
Magpie Rd PO8 . . . . .128 E5
Magpie Wlk RH10 . . . . .18 F8
Maiden La RH11 . . . . .18 C8
Maidenbower Dr RH10 . . .19 D4
Maidenbower
Fst & Mid Sch RH10 . . . . .19 C4
Maidenbower La RH10 . . . .19 B4
Maidenbower Pl RH10 . . . .19 C4
Maidenbower Sq RH10 . . .19 C4
Maidment Ct BN5 . . . . . . .123 F6
Main Dr 3 PO22 . . . . .196 F5
Main Rd Birdham PO20 . . .191 E4
Broadbridge PO18 . . . . . . .171 D7
East Dean PO18 . . . . .134 C6
Nutbourne PO10 . . . . .170 C7
Yapton BN18 . . . . .176 F3
Maines Farm Rd BN44 . . .144 C1
Mainstone Rd 1 BN3 . . . .186 F7
Maizecroft RH6 . . . . .2 C4
Major Cl BN1 . . . . .168 B1
Major's Hill RH10 . . . . .20 C5
Malcolm Cl BN12 . . . . .200 E5
Malcolm Gdns RH6 . . . . .1 D1
Malcolm Rd PO20 . . . . . . .154 C2
Malden Pl 4 RH20 . . . . . .119 D1
Malden Way PO20 . . . . . .206 D7
Maldon Rd BN1 . . . . .167 D2
Malham Cl RH10 . . . . .19 C3
Malin Rd BN17 . . . . .199 A5
Mallard Cl Haslemere GU27 .26 E6
Horley RH6 . . . . .2 A5
Horsham RH12 . . . . .36 C5
Mallard Cres PO21 . . . . . .204 F7
Mallard Pl RH19 . . . . .22 F8
Mallard Rd PO9 . . . . .128 D1
Mallard Way Henfield BN5 123 E6
Westbourne PO10 . . . . .149 E4
Mallards La PO20 . . . . . . .206 B8
Mallion's La RH17 . . . . .61 E2
Mallon Dene BN16 . . . . . .199 D4
Mallory Rd BN3 . . . . .167 C2
Mallow Cl RH12 . . . . .36 F6
Malmayne Ct PO21 . . . . . .194 E3
Malt House Trad Est
BN43 . . . . .185 B7
Malthouse Cl
Arundel BN18 . . . . .158 A2
Lancing BN15 . . . . .183 B7
Malthouse Cotts
Cocking GU29 . . . . .112 D7
West Ashling PO18 . . . . . . .151 B3
West Wittering PO20 . . . . . .190 D3
Worthing BN12 . . . . .181 C1
Malthouse Ct
14 Brighton BN2 . . . . .207 C2
Liphook GU30 . . . . .25 C4
Malthouse La
Brighton BN2 . . . . .207 C3
Burgess Hill BN6,RH15 . . . .106 C2
St John's Common RH15 . . .106 D4
West Ashling PO18 . . . . . . .151 B3
Malthouse Mdws GU30 . . .25 C4
Malthouse Pas 3 BN17 . .198 D6
Malthouse Rd
Crawley RH10 . . . . .18 D4
Selsey PO20 . . . . .206 E7
Malthouse Trad Est
BN43 . . . . .185 B7
Maltings Gn BN44 . . . . . . .143 D2
Maltings The
Billingshurst RH14 . . . . .55 D1
Burgess Hill RH15 . . . . .106 D4
Chichester PO19 . . . . .172 F6
Liphook GU30 . . . . .25 D4
Maltravers Ct 2 BN17 . . .198 E4
Maltravers Dr BN17 . . . . .198 E4
Maltravers Rd BN17 . . . . .198 E4
Maltravers St BN18 . . . . . .158 B3
Malvern Cl BN11 . . . . .183 B3
Malvern Mews PO10 . . . . .149 B1
Malvern Rd Crawley RH11 . .18 C5
Hill Brow GU33 . . . . .45 D2
Malvern St 12 BN3 . . . . . . .187 B7
Malvern Way PO21 . . . . . . .194 B1
Manaton Cl RH16 . . . . .85 F4
Manchester St BN2 . . . . . .207 B1
Manchester Terr PO10 . . .149 D4
Mandalay Ct BN1 . . . . . . .167 D4
Manet Sq PO22 . . . . .195 B6
Manhattan Ct BN1 . . . . . .167 D3
Manhood Com Coll
PO20 . . . . .206 D8
Manhood Cotts PO20 . . . .202 F7
Manhood La PO20 . . . . . . .203 F8
Manitoba Way BN13 . . . . .181 C6
Manley's Hill RH20 . . . . . .119 E1
Mann Cl RH11 . . . . .39 B8
Manning Cl RH19 . . . . .9 D2
Manning Rd BN17 . . . . . . .198 C6
Mannings 8 BN43 . . . . . . .184 F7
Mannings Cl RH10 . . . . .6 D1
Mannock Rd PO20 . . . . . . .154 B1
Manor Ave BN6 . . . . .127 A5
Manor Cl
Bognor Regis PO22 . . . . . . .196 A4
Brighton BN2 . . . . .188 E5
Burgess Hill RH15 . . . . .107 D4
East Preston BN16 . . . . . . .199 F5
Haslemere GU27 . . . . .26 E6
Henfield BN5 . . . . .123 F5
Horley RH6 . . . . .1 F3
Lancing BN15 . . . . .183 F7
Southwick BN42 . . . . .186 A8
Stockbridge PO19 . . . . .172 F3
Storrington RH20 . . . . .119 D1
Worthing BN11 . . . . .182 B2
Manor Cotts BN6 . . . . .125 F5
Manor Cres Brighton BN2 .188 E5
Haslemere GU27 . . . . .26 E6
Manor Ct Elmer PO22 . . . .197 B5
Horsham RH12 . . . . .37 A5
North Lancing BN15 . . . . . .183 D8
Rustington BN16 . . . . .199 B6
Southwick BN42 . . . . .186 A7
7 Storrington RH20 . . . . . .119 D1
Worthing BN11 . . . . .182 B1
Manor Dr Cuckfield RH17 . . .84 E7
Horley RH6 . . . . .1 F3
Manor Farm Cl PO20 . . . .206 E8
Manor Farm Ct PO20 . . . .206 E8
Manor Field Ct BN14 . . . .182 D5
Manor Field Prim Sch
RH15 . . . . .107 C4
Manor Fields
Horsham RH12, RH13 . . . . . .37 A4
Liphook GU30 . . . . .25 D4
Manor Gdns Breach PO10 .149 F1
Brighton BN2 . . . . .188 E5
Hurstpierpoint BN6 . . . . . . .125 F6
Rustington BN16 . . . . .199 B5
Manor Gn BN2 . . . . .188 E5
Manor Hall Fst Sch BN42 185 F7
Manor Hall Mid Sch
BN42 . . . . .185 F8
Manor Hall Rd BN42 . . . . .185 F8
Manor Hill BN2 . . . . .188 E6
Manor Ho BN11 . . . . .182 B2
Manor Ho The BN18 . . . . .177 E7
Manor House Pl BN15 . . .183 F8
Manor La
Doomsday Green RH13 . . . . .59 B8
East Beach PO20 . . . . .206 F8
South Mundham PO20 . . . . .193 D6
Manor Lea Haslemere GU27 26 E6
Worthing BN11 . . . . .182 B1
Manor Lodge Rd PO9 . . . .128 C1
Manor Paddock BN2 . . . .188 E4
Manor Par BN13 . . . . .181 D7
Manor Pk PO21 . . . . .194 A1
Manor Pl
Bognor Regis PO21 . . . . . . .195 C2
Brighton BN2 . . . . .188 E4
Manor Rd Breach PO10 . . .149 F1
Brighton BN2 . . . . .188 E5
Burgess Hill RH15 . . . . .107 D3
East Grinstead RH19 . . . . .9 C2
Horsham RH12 . . . . .37 A5
Hurstpierpoint BN6 . . . . . . .125 F6
Lancing BN15 . . . . .183 E8
Portslade-by-Sea BN41 . . . .166 B1
Rustington BN16 . . . . .199 B6
Selsey PO20 . . . . .206 E7
Upper Beeding BN44 . . . . . .144 B2
West Kingston BN16 . . . . . .200 A4
Worthing BN11 . . . . .182 B2
Manor Royal RH10 . . . . .5 E1
Manor The 3 BN11 . . . . . .182 B2
Manor View Ct BN14 . . . .182 D5
Manor Villas PO18 . . . . . .171 C5
Manor Way
Bognor Regis PO21 . . . . . . .194 C1
Breach PO10 . . . . .149 F1
Brighton BN2 . . . . .188 E5
Henfield BN5 . . . . .123 F6
Lancing BN15 . . . . .183 F7
Middleton-on-Sea PO22 . . . .197 B5
Manorfields RH11 . . . . .17 D2
Mansbergh Rd PO19 . . . . .153 B1
Mansell Ct RH15 . . . . .107 B3
Mansell Rd BN43 . . . . .185 B8
Manser Rd BN18 . . . . .156 F1
Mansfield Cl BN11 . . . . . .183 A4
Mansfield Cotts PO18 . . .170 D7
Mansfield Rd
Bognor Regis PO22 . . . . . . .195 B6
Hove BN3 . . . . .186 E7
Worthing BN11 . . . . .183 A4
Mansion Cl RH15 . . . . . . .107 D3
Mant Cl
Horsemere Green BN17 . . .177 D1
Storrington RH20 . . . . .119 D1
Mant Rd GU28 . . . . .95 F7
Mantell Ho 2 BN2 . . . . . .207 C2
Mantling Rd BN17 . . . . . .198 D5
Manton Cl PO20 . . . . .202 C5
Manton Rd BN2 . . . . .168 E1
Mants Farm Ct PO21 . . . .194 C3
Maple Cl Billingshurst RH14 .55 D1
Burgess Hill RH15 . . . . .107 B5
Crawley RH11 . . . . .5 C1
Haywards Heath RH16 . . . . . .86 B3
Horsham RH12 . . . . .37 A5
Middleton-on-Sea PO22 . . . .196 E6
New Brighton PO10 . . . . . . .149 B2
Worthing BN13 . . . . .161 E1
Maple Ct
St John's Common RH15 . . .106 D3
6 Worthing BN11 . . . . .181 F2
Maple Dr
Burgess Hill RH15 . . . . .107 A5
East Grinstead RH19 . . . . . . .10 A1
Maple Gdns
Bognor Regis PO22 . . . . . . .195 C7
Hove BN3 . . . . .166 F1
Maple Ho BN12 . . . . .181 A4
Maple Leaf RH20 . . . . .117 D6
Maple Par BN18 . . . . .176 E8
Maple Rd Billingshurst RH14 77 D7
Walberton BN18 . . . . .176 E8
Maple Wlk Lancing BN15 . .183 B7
Rustington BN16 . . . . .199 C6
Mapledown Cl RH13 . . . . . .57 F2
Maplegreen RH11 . . . . .18 D5
Maplehurst Rd
Chichester PO19 . . . . .153 B2
Maplehurst RH13 . . . . .81 A3
Portslade-by-Sea BN41 . . . .166 A1
Maples The
3 Bognor Regis PO21 . . . . .195 B3
Ferring BN12 . . . . .200 F4
Maplewood 4 BN1 . . . . . .167 E3
Mapsons La PO20 . . . . . . .192 B3
Marama Gdns BN16 . . . . .199 B3
March CE Prim Sch The
PO18 . . . . .153 E1
March Sq PO19 . . . . .153 A3
Marchants Cl BN6 . . . . . . .126 A6
Marchants Rd BN6 . . . . . .126 A6
Marchants Way RH15 . . . .106 F5
Marches Rd RH12 . . . . .14 E4
Marches The GU27 . . . . . . .49 B5
Marchwell Ind Unit PO19 153 B1
Marchwood PO19 . . . . . . .153 A3
Marchwood Gate PO19 . . .153 A3
Marcuse Fields PO18 . . . .171 B6
Mardale Rd BN13 . . . . . . .181 F6
Marden Ave PO19 . . . . . . .172 E3
Marden Ho Barnham PO22 176 C6
Littlehampton BN17 . . . . . . .178 B3
Mardens The RH11 . . . . . . .18 B7
Mardyke BN43 . . . . .184 D6
Mare Hill Rd RH20 . . . . .98 E1
Maresfield Rd BN2 . . . . . .188 E5
Margaret Cl PO21 . . . . . . .194 E3
Margaret Cotts RH13 . . . . . .81 E2
Margaret Ho PO22 . . . . . .195 E4
Margaret St BN2 . . . . .207 C1
Margery Rd BN3 . . . . .186 D8
Marian Way PO21 . . . . . . .195 E3
Marigolds Lodge 2
BN16 . . . . .199 B4
Marik Mews 5 BN11 . . . . .182 F2
Marina Cl PO10 . . . . .169 C7
Marina Ct BN15 . . . . .184 C5
Marina Way BN2 . . . . .188 F3
Marine Ave BN3 . . . . .186 E6
Marine Cl
East Wittering PO20 . . . . . .201 E6
Worthing BN11 . . . . .182 A1
Marine Cres BN12 . . . . . . .181 D1
Marine Ct
Littlehampton BN17 . . . . . . .198 E4
Shoreham-by-Sea BN43 . . . .184 D5
Marine Dr
East Wittering PO20 . . . . . .201 E7
Selsey PO20 . . . . .206 F7
Worthing BN12 . . . . .181 B1
Marine Dr W
Bognor Regis PO21 . . . . . . .195 A2
East Wittering PO20 . . . . . .201 D7
Marine Gdns
Brighton BN2 . . . . .207 C1
Selsey PO20 . . . . .206 D5
Marine Par
Bognor Regis PO21 . . . . . . .195 B2
Brighton BN2 . . . . .188 C4
Worthing BN11 . . . . .182 D1
Marine Park Ho PO21 . . . .195 B2
Marine Pk 3 PO21 . . . . . .195 B2
Marine Pl BN11 . . . . .182 D1
Marine Point 13 BN11 . . . .182 A1
Marine Sq BN2 . . . . .188 C4
Marine Terrace Mews
BN2 . . . . .188 C4
Marine View 3 BN2 . . . . .207 C2
Mariners Cl BN43 . . . . . . .184 D5
Mariners Quay
Brighton BN2 . . . . .188 F3
Littlehampton BN17 . . . . . . .198 C5
Mariners Terr PO18 . . . . . .171 B4
Mariners The BN15 . . . . . .183 D3
Mariners Wlk BN16 . . . . .199 D4
Marineside PO20 . . . . .202 B5
Marion Rd RH10 . . . . .19 B3
Marisfield Pl PO20 . . . . . .206 F8
Marjoram Pl BN43 . . . . . .165 B1
Market Ave PO19 . . . . . . .173 A5
Market Cl PO22 . . . . .176 B6
Market Field BN44 . . . . . .143 E3
Market Pl
Burgess Hill RH15 . . . . .107 A2
Haywards Heath RH16 . . . . . .85 D6
Market Rd PO19 . . . . .173 A6
Market Sq Horsham RH12 . .36 C1
Midhurst GU29 . . . . .92 F7
Petworth GU28 . . . . .95 F8
Market St
Bognor Regis PO21 . . . . . . .195 C2
Brighton BN1 . . . . .207 B2
13 Worthing BN11 . . . . .182 D2
Markfield PO22 . . . . .195 B6
Markwick Mews BN11 . . .182 E3
Marlborough Bsns Ctr
BN15 . . . . .183 C4
Marlborough Cl
Chichester PO19 . . . . .173 D6
Crawley RH11 . . . . .18 C2
Horsham RH12 . . . . .36 D5
Marlborough Ct
Bognor Regis PO21 . . . . . . .194 F5
Burgess Hill RH15 . . . . .106 E3
1 Hove BN3 . . . . .187 C6
Marlborough Dr RH15 . . .107 C2
Marlborough Ho 6 PO21 195 B2
Marlborough Mews BN1 .207 A2
Marlborough Pl 6
BN1, BN2 . . . . .207 B3
Marlborough Rd
Lancing BN15 . . . . .183 D4
Worthing BN12 . . . . .181 D2
Marlborough St BN1 . . . .207 A2
Marlborough Way BN12 .181 D2
Marle Ave RH15 . . . . .107 A4
Marles La RH14 . . . . .55 C8
Marley Combe Rd GU27 . . .26 F4
Marley Hanger GU27 . . . . .27 A3
Marley La GU27 . . . . .26 E4
Marley Lodge BN2 . . . . . .207 C4
Marley Way RH20 . . . . . . .119 E2
Marlin Ct BN15 . . . . .183 F4
Marlinspike The BN43 . . .185 A6
Marlipins Mus BN43 . . . . .184 E7
Marlow Ct Brighton BN2 . .207 C4
Crawley RH10 . . . . .18 D7
Marlow Dr RH16 . . . . .86 C4
Marlow Rd BN2 . . . . .188 F4
Marlowe Cl PO22 . . . . . . .196 D6
Marlowe Rd BN14 . . . . . . .182 E5
Marlpit Cl RH19 . . . . .9 E4
Marlpit La Oving PO20 . . .174 B7
Woodmancote PO10,PO18 .150 C4
Marlpit Rd RH19 . . . . .43 A6
Marlpost Rd RH13 . . . . . . .57 C1
Marmion Rd BN3 . . . . . . .186 F7
Marquis Way PO21 . . . . . .194 E1
Marringdean Rd RH14 . . . .77 E4
Marsh Barns PO20 . . . . . .173 F2
Marsh Ct RH11 . . . . .18 B1
Marsh Ho 3 BN42 . . . . . . .185 D7
Marsh La Chidham PO18 . .170 C4
Crockerhill PO18 . . . . .155 A2
Merston PO20 . . . . .174 A2
Mid Lavant PO18 . . . . .152 F6
Marshall Ave
Bognor Regis PO21 . . . . . . .195 B4
Worthing BN14 . . . . .161 F3
Marshall Cl PO22 . . . . . . .176 B5
Marshall Rd RH10 . . . . .19 C4
Marshall Way BN3 . . . . . . .166 F1
Marshalls Row BN1 . . . . .207 B4
Marston Ct 10 BN3 . . . . . .187 E7
Marston Rd BN14 . . . . . . .182 E4
Martello Ent Ctr BN17 . . .178 C4
Martha Gunn Cl BN2 . . . .168 E1
Martin Cl RH11 . . . . .18 D8
Martin Rd BN3 . . . . .166 D1
Martineau Cl PO21 . . . . . .194 E1
Martins La PO20 . . . . .191 F5
Martins The RH10 . . . . .21 C8
Martlet Cl PO19 . . . . .173 A5
Martlet Cnr RH12 . . . . .33 D7
Martlet Ho BN1 . . . . .188 A8
Martlet Rd GU28 . . . . .95 E7
Martlet The BN3 . . . . .167 D1
Martlet Way PO21 . . . . . .204 F7
Martlets RH20 . . . . .119 D8
Martlets Cl RH12 . . . . .36 C5
Martlets Ct BN18 . . . . . . .158 B2
Martlets The
Burgess Hill RH15 . . . . .107 A3
Crawley RH10 . . . . .18 E6
Lancing BN15 . . . . .183 C6
Littlehampton BN16 . . . . . . .199 A4
Shoreham-by-Sea BN43 . . . .184 F8
Martlets Trad Est BN12 . .181 C3
Martlets Way BN12 . . . . . .181 C3
Marts The RH12 . . . . .33 D7
Martyn Cl BN5 . . . . .123 E5
Martyns Pl RH19 . . . . .23 A8
Martyrs Ave RH11 . . . . .5 D1
Marvell Cl RH10 . . . . .19 C8
Marylands RH16 . . . . .85 F5
Marylands Cres PO22 . . . .195 E5
Masefield Rd RH11 . . . . . . .17 E3
Mash Barn La BN15 . . . . .184 A7
Mason Cl RH19 . . . . .9 E2
Mason Rd RH10 . . . . .18 E4
Masons Field RH13 . . . . . .59 C6
Masons Way RH20 . . . . . . .98 D5
Massetts Rd RH6 . . . . .2 A2
Matlock Rd BN1 . . . . .167 D2
Matthews Dr RH10 . . . . . . .19 C3
Matthey Pl RH10 . . . . .6 D1
Maudlin La BN44 . . . . . . .143 E1
Maudlyn Cl BN44 . . . . . . .143 E1
Maudlyn Parkway BN44 .143 D1
Maudlyn Pk BN44 . . . . . . .143 D1
Mauldmare Cl PO21 . . . . .194 F2
Maunsell Ct RH16 . . . . .85 F3
Maunsell Pk RH10 . . . . . . .19 B6
Maxton Wlk RH11 . . . . .18 B2
Maxwell Rd Arundel BN18 .157 F1
Littlehampton BN17 . . . . . . .198 C5
Maxwell Way RH10 . . . . .6 A1
May Cl Bognor Regis PO22 .195 D5
Horsemere Green BN17 . . .177 D1
Sidlesham PO20 . . . . .203 F8
Worthing BN12 . . . . .181 C4
May Rd BN2 . . . . .188 D7
May Tree Ave BN14 . . . . . .161 F3
Maybridge Cres BN12 . . .181 C3
Maybridge Sq BN12 . . . . .181 C4
Maybush Dr PO18 . . . . . . .170 D7
Maydwell Ave RH13 . . . . . .34 C2
Mayes Cl RH10 . . . . .19 C5
Mayes La RH12 . . . . .14 F3
Mayfair Ct PO19 . . . . .172 F7
Mayfield Crawley RH10 . . . .19 D6
East Preston BN16 . . . . . . .180 B3
Mayfield Cl
Bognor Regis PO21 . . . . . . .194 B3
Brighton BN1 . . . . .168 A5
Worthing BN14 . . . . .162 A1
Mayfield Cres BN1 . . . . . .167 F5
Mayfield Ct RH15 . . . . . . .107 B3
Mayfield Rd PO21 . . . . . . .195 A4
Mayfields RH17 . . . . .83 C4
Mayflower Cl RH10 . . . . . . .19 D5
Mayflower Ct
Haywards Heath RH16 . . . . . .85 F4
11 Shoreham-by-Sea BN43 .185 A6
Mayflower Rd RH16 . . . . . .85 F4
Mayflower Sq BN1 . . . . . .207 B4
Mayflower Way BN16 . . . .180 A3
Mayhouse Rd RH15 . . . . .106 F1
Maynard Cl RH10 . . . . .7 C4
Mayo Ct 5 BN2 . . . . .188 B8
Mayo Rd BN2 . . . . .188 B8
Maypole La BN18 . . . . . . .176 F5
Maypole Pk BN18 . . . . . . .176 F5
Maypole Rd
Ashurst Wood RH19 . . . . .23 E6
East Grinstead RH19 . . . . .9 D2
Mayridge PO20 . . . . .206 B8
Maytree Cl
Angmering BN16 . . . . .179 F4
Lancing BN15 . . . . .183 B6
Maytree Wlk BN3 . . . . . . .166 E1
Mcbechie Ho RH19 . . . . .9 D3
McIndoe Rd RH19 . . . . .9 D3
McIver Cl RH19 . . . . .8 F4
McKerchar Cl BN15 . . . . .183 F7
McNair Cl PO20 . . . . .206 D8
McRae Ct PO20 . . . . .206 D7
Mead La
Bognor Regis PO22 . . . . . . .195 E4
Storrington RH20 . . . . .119 E2
Mead Rd RH10 . . . . .18 F7
Mead Sway BN18 . . . . . . .156 D4
Mead The Liphook GU30 . . . .25 B5
Liss GU33 . . . . .45 B4
Mead Way GU29 . . . . .92 E6
Meadow App RH10 . . . . .7 A3
Meadow Brook Ind Ctr
RH10 .6 A1
Meadow Cl Balcombe RH17 .41 A1
Copthorne RH10 . . . . .7 A3
Horsham RH12 . . . . .37 A5
Hove BN3 . . . . .167 B3
Hunston PO20 . . . . .193 A8
Liphook GU30 . . . . .25 C4
Portslade-by-Sea BN41 . . . .166 B2
Southwick BN42 . . . . .186 A8
Worthing BN11 . . . . .183 B3
Meadow Court Est 4
BN11 . . . . .183 B3
Meadow Cres BN11 . . . . .183 A3
Meadow Croft Cl RH6 . . . . . .6 C8
Meadow Ct
4 Emsworth PO10 . . . . .169 B8
Middleton-on-Sea PO22 . . .196 D6
Meadow Dr RH16 . . . . .86 B6
Meadow End GU30 . . . . . . .25 C5
Meadow Farm La RH12 . . .36 F7
Meadow La
Burgess Hill RH15 . . . . .106 F1
Lancing BN15 . . . . .183 E5
Lindfield RH16 . . . . .86 B6
West Wittering PO20 . . . . . .190 D2
Meadow Pk BN16 . . . . . . .200 B5
Meadow Rd BN11 . . . . . . .183 B3
Meadow Road Ind Est
BN11 . . . . .183 B4
Meadow Sweet Cl BN13 .181 A5
Meadow Terr RH17 . . . . . . .41 A1
Meadow The RH10 . . . . .7 A3
Meadow Vale GU27 . . . . . . .27 A6
Meadow Way Bognor
Regis, North Bersted PO22 .195 A6
Bognor Regis,
Nyetimber PO21 . . . . .194 B1

Meadow Way *continued*
Ferring BN12 200 E6
Liphook GU30 25 C5
Littlehampton BN17 198 F5
Petworth GU28 95 E7
Tangmere PO20 154 D2
Westergate PO20 175 D6
Meadow Wlk Liss GU33 45 B4
Middleton-on-Sea PO22 197 A5
Meadowbank RH14 76 B8
Meadowcroft Cl
Crawley RH11 17 F5
East Grinstead RH19 9 C2
Meadowfield Dr PO19 173 B7
Meadowland PO20 206 D6
Meadowlands
Crawley RH11 18 C6
Rowland's Castle PO9 128 E3
Meadows BN6 126 F5
Meadows Rd PO20 202 A7
Meadows The
East Preston BN16 200 A5
Hove BN3 166 C3
Walberton BN18 176 E8
Meadowside
Angmering BN16 180 A6
Horley RH6 2 B4
Storrington RH20 119 D1
Meadowside Ct BN12 181 A2
Meadowside Wlk PO20 154 D2
Meadowview BN2 168 E1
Meadowview Rd BN15 183 D8
Meads Ave BN3 166 C3
Meads Cl BN3 166 C3
Meads Prim Sch The
RH19 22 E7
Meads The Brighton BN1 168 D5
East Grinstead RH19 22 E7
Fulking BN5 145 F4
Haslemere GU27 26 F6
South Harting GU31 89 D4
Meadvale RH12 35 F2
Meadway Haslemere GU27 26 F6
Rustington BN16 199 D5
Meadway Cres BN3 166 F2
Meadway Ct
Southwick BN42 185 D8
Worthing BN13 181 E4
Meadway The
Brighton BN2 188 F5
Horley RH6 2 C3
Shoreham-by-Sea BN43 185 A6
Measham Cl BN12 200 F5
Meath Green Ave RH6 1 F5
Meath Green Cty Inf Sch
RH6 1 F5
Meath Green Cty Jun Sch
RH6 1 F5
Meath Green La RH1, RH6 1 E6
Mechanical Music
& Dolls Mus PO19 173 D7
Medina Pl BN3 187 B6
Medina Terr BN3 187 B5
Medina Villas BN3 187 B6
Medlar Cl RH11 5 C1
Medmerry PO20 206 A8
Medmerry Hill BN2 168 E2
Medmerry Prim Sch
PO20 206 D7
Medway RH10 21 A5
Medway Cl BN13 181 D7
Medway Cotts BN18 176 F2
Medway Ct RH12 37 B5
Medway Dr RH19 22 D6
Medway Rd RH11 17 F5
Medwyn Wlk 2 RH12 36 C2
Meeds Rd RH15 107 A2
Meeting House La BN1 207 B2
Meiros Way RH20 120 F5
Melanie's Gdns 12 PO21 195 D4
Melbourne Ave BN12 181 C2
Melbourne Rd
Chichester PO19 173 B7
Worthing BN12 181 D2
Melbourne St BN2 188 C8
Melbourne Way
Horsham RH12 36 F5
Worthing BN12 181 C2
Melchbourne Villas RH19 42 E6
Melksham Cl RH13 36 E1
Melrose Ave
Portslade-by-Sea BN41 166 A1
Worthing BN13 181 E4
Melrose Cl Brighton BN1 168 C2
Worthing BN13 181 E4
Melrose Pl RH20 120 C3
Melton Ave RH20 119 D3
Melton Cl RH20 119 E3
Melton Dr RH20 119 E3
Melville Rd BN3 187 E7
Melville Way BN12 181 C4
Mendip Cl BN16 200 A6
Mendip Cres BN13 181 E7
Mendip Ct 1 BN16 199 C6
Mendip Rd BN13 181 E7
Mendip Wlk RH11 18 B6
Mercer Cl RH10 19 C3
Mercer Rd RH12 36 C8
Mercers Mead RH13 81 E1
Merchant St PO21 195 C3
Mercury Cl RH11 17 E3
Meredith Rd BN14 182 F4
Merevale BN1 168 B2
Mereworth Dr RH10 19 D8
Meridian Cl RH11 17 F3
Meridian Gr RH6 2 C4
Meridian Way RH19 9 F3
Merle Way GU27 49 A6
Merlin Cl Crawley RH11 17 E6
Hove BN3 187 D8
Merlin Ct BN13 181 F6
Merlin Ctr RH11 5 D2
Merlin Way
East Grinstead RH19 10 A3
Middleton-on-Sea PO22 196 D6
Merrion Ave PO21,PO22 195 B5
Merrivale Ct PO10 149 F1
Merry End PO22 196 D5
Merryfield Cres BN16 180 A6
Merryfield Dr
Horsham RH12 36 A3
Selsey PO20 206 F7
Merryfield Rd RH20 119 D2
Merryfield Way RH20 119 D2
Merryhills La RH14 32 A5
Merryweather Rd PO18 171 B5
Merrywood Ho RH20 120 B3
Merrywood La RH20 120 B4
Mersey Cl BN13 181 C7
Mersey Rd BN13 181 C7
Mersham Gdns BN12 181 C2
Merton Ave BN16 199 D4
Merton Cl PO21 194 E4
Merton Dr 1 BN17 198 D6
Merton Rd
Pease Pottage RH11 39 B8
Worthing BN11 182 F2
Metana Ho RH10 6 A3
Metcalf Way RH11 5 D2
Meteor Rd PO10 169 C3
Metropole Ct 12 BN1 187 E5
Mews Ct RH19 22 F6
Mews The
14 Bognor Regis PO21 195 C3
Bognor Regis PO22 195 E4
Brighton BN1 167 E2
Broadridge Heath RH12 35 D4
Petworth GU28 95 F8
Pulborough RH20 98 D2
Meyers Wood RH13 103 A2
Meyners Cl BN3 166 C3
Michael Ayres Jun Sch
PO21 195 A5
Michael Cres RH6 2 A1
Michael Fields RH18 23 E2
Michael Hall Sch
(Kidbrooke Park) RH18 23 D1
Michel Gr BN16 199 F5
Michelbourne Cl RH15 106 E1
Michelgrove Cotts BN13 160 C5
Michell Cl RH12 36 A2
Micklam Cl PO21 194 C2
Middle Mdw GU33 45 C4
Middle Mead
Littlehampton BN17 199 A5
Steyning BN44 143 D4
Middle Onslow Cl BN12 180 E3
Middle Rd Brighton BN1 167 E1
Lancing BN15 183 D5
Partridge Green RH13 103 A3
Shoreham-by-Sea BN43 185 B7
Middle Row 1 RH19 22 F8
Middle St Brighton BN1 207 A2
5 Horsham RH12 36 C2
Petworth GU28 95 F8
Portslade-by-Sea BN41 186 B6
Shoreham-by-Sea BN43 184 F7
Middle Street Prim Sch
BN1 207 A2
Middle Tyne BN13 181 D5
Middle Way
Burgess Hill RH15 107 B3
Kingston Gorse BN16 200 D4
Middlefield Horley RH6 2 C4
West Wittering PO20 190 C1
Middlefield La PO18 153 C7
Middleton Ave BN3 186 D6
Middleton Bsns Pk PO22 196 E6
Middleton Cl PO20 202 B6
Middleton Ct 6 PO22 196 F5
Middleton Gdns PO20 154 D2
Middleton Pl PO22 196 E5
Middleton Rd
Horsham RH12 36 A2
Middleton-on-Sea PO22 196 D5
Middleton Rise BN1 168 E5
Middleton Way RH11 17 E5
Midfields Cl RH15 107 B3
Midfields Dr RH15 107 B3
Midfields Wlk RH15 107 B4
Midgley Rd RH10 18 F8
Midholme BN16 199 F5
Midhurst CE Prim Sch
GU29 92 E7
Midhurst Cl Crawley RH11 18 A7
Ferring BN12 200 F6
Midhurst Cottage Hospl
GU29 70 F1
Midhurst Dr BN12 181 A2
Midhurst Gram Sch GU29 92 F8
Midhurst Intermediate Sch
GU29 71 B1
Midhurst Rd
Fernhurst GU27 49 A4
Haslemere GU27 27 B5
Liphook GU30 25 C2
Petworth GU28 95 E7
Midhurst Rise BN1 168 B6
Midhurst Wlk BN3 166 F3
Midway The PO22 196 A4
Mighell St BN2 207 C2
Milborne Rd RH10 19 C2
Milbury Cl 7 BN12 200 F4
Milcote Ave BN3 186 F8
Mile End Cotts BN1 167 E6
Mile End La PO20 172 C2
Mile Oak Cres BN42 165 F1
Mile Oak Gdns BN41 166 A1
Mile Oak Prim Sch BN41 165 F3
Mile Oak Rd
Portslade-by-Sea BN41 165 F3
Southwick BN42 165 F1
Miles Cl BN18 177 B2
Miles Cotts PO18 171 C5
Milford Ct BN15 183 D3
Mill Ave BN43 164 F1
Mill Bay La RH12 36 B1
Mill Cl Crabtree RH13 82 A7
East Grinstead RH19 22 E7
Fishbourne PO19 172 B6
Haslemere GU27 26 E6
Horley RH6 1 E4
Portslade-by-Sea BN41 166 C1
Poynings BN45 146 C5
Rustington BN16 199 D6
Mill Copse Rd GU27 27 B4
Mill Cotts
East Grinstead RH19 22 E7
Rudgwick RH12 33 D5
Mill Ct Poynings BN45 146 C5
Worthing BN11 182 B2
Mill Dr Henfield BN5 123 F4
Hove BN3 167 A3
Mill End Hermitage PO10 169 D8
West Chiltington
Common RH20 119 C8
Mill Farm Rd RH13 37 A4
Mill Gdns PO20 201 F7
Mill Green Rd RH16 85 E6
Mill Hill BN43 164 E3
Mill Hill Cl
Haywards Heath RH16 85 E7
Shoreham-by-Sea BN43 164 E1
Mill Hill Dr BN43 164 E1
Mill Hill Gdns BN43 164 E1
Mill Ho 6 BN11 183 B3
Mill House Gdns BN11 182 A2
Mill La Amberley BN18 138 E6
Arundel BN18 158 B3
Ashington RH20 120 F4
Balcombe RH17 41 C1
Clayton BN6,BN45 147 E7
Cocking GU29 112 D8
Coolham RH13 78 D3
Copthorne RH10 7 E3
Crabtree RH13 82 B7
Crawley RH11 18 A8
Dormans Park RH7 9 F8
Dumpford GU31 90 F8
Felbridge RH19 8 E5
Fernhurst GU27 27 C3
Fishbourne PO19 172 B6
Goddards' Green BN6 106 A3
Heyshott Green GU29 93 A2
Hookwood RH6 1 D3
Littlehampton BN17 178 D5
Littleworth RH13 102 F5
Portslade-by-Sea BN41 166 B1
Poynings BN45 146 C5
Runcton PO20 173 E1
Rustington BN16 179 D3
Sayers Common BN6 105 E2
Selsey PO20 206 C7
Shoreham-by-Sea BN43 184 F8
Sidlesham PO20 203 F7
Slindon BN18 156 C6
South Harting GU31 89 D4
Stedham GU29 70 A2
Storrington RH20 119 D2
Trotton GU31 69 A1
Walberton BN18 156 D1
West Chiltington
Common RH20 119 C8
Westbourne PO10 149 D3
Worthing BN13 161 F1
Mill Lodge PO21 194 A2
Mill Mead RH20 121 A4
Mill Park Rd PO21 194 B2
Mill Pk RH15 107 B3
Mill Pond La PO18 151 B3
Mill Pond Way BN16 199 F6
Mill Quay PO10 169 C7
Mill Race BN6 126 E8
Mill Rd Angmering BN16 179 F5
Arundel BN18 158 C3
Brighton BN1 167 C6
Burgess Hill RH15 107 B3
Crawley RH10 19 B7
Lancing BN15 183 E8
Liss GU33 45 C4
Southwick BN41 186 B7
Steyning BN44 143 C3
Walberton BN18 156 D3
West Ashling PO18 151 A3
West Chiltington
Common RH20 119 C8
Westbourne PO10 149 D4
Worthing BN11 182 A2
Mill Rd Ind Est BN41 186 B7
Mill Rise BN1 167 C5
Mill Road Ave BN16 179 F5
Mill Row BN1 207 A3
Mill Straight RH13 79 F8
Mill Stream Mdw RH16 85 D7
Mill Vale Mdws GU30 47 B3
Mill View Hospl BN3 166 E1
Mill View Rd BN18 176 F2
Mill Way Billingshurst RH14 55 D1
East Grinstead RH19 22 E7
Mill Wood RH15 107 B3
Millais RH13 37 A3
Millais Cl RH11 17 F2
Millais Ct RH13 37 A4
Millais Sch RH13 36 F2
Milland La GU30 47 A5
Millars Ct PO21 194 B1
Millbank RH15 107 B4
Millbank The RH11 17 F6
Millbrook Cl GU33 45 C4
Millcroft BN1 167 C5
Millcroft Ave BN42 165 E1
Millcroft Gdns BN42 165 E1
Millcross Rd BN41 166 B1
Millennium Cl BN15 184 B6
Miller's Rd BN1 167 E1
Millers Cl BN16 199 D6
Millers Gate RH12 36 D6
Millers The BN18 176 F2
Millers Way RH15 107 B4
Millfield Lancing BN15 183 C7
Southwater RH13 80 A7
Upper Beeding BN44 144 A2
Millfield Cl
Chichester PO19 173 C8
Littlehampton BN16 199 B3
Millfield Cotts 8 BN2 188 D4
Millstream The GU27 26 F5
Millthorpe Rd RH12 36 F4
Millview Cl PO21 194 A2
Millwood RH10 21 E5
Milne Cl RH11 17 E3
Milner Flats BN2 207 C2
Milner Rd BN2 168 D1
Milnthorpe Rd BN3 186 F8
Milnwood Rd RH12 36 C3
Milton Ave BN16 199 B5
Milton Cl Lancing BN15 183 F5
Rustington BN16 199 B5
Milton Cres RH19 22 C8
Milton Ct
6 Haywards Heath RH16 85 D5
2 Worthing BN11 182 C1
Milton Dr BN42 185 F8
Milton Mount RH10 6 D1
Milton Mount Ave RH10 19 D8
Milton Mount
Fst & Mid Sch RH10 19 C8
Milton Rd Brighton BN2 207 C4
Crawley RH10 19 C7
Haywards Heath RH16 85 D6
Horsham RH12 36 C3
Worthing BN11 182 C1
Milton St BN11 182 C1
Milward Ct 3 BN43 185 C8
Milwood Ct PO19 172 F7
Mimmack Cl BN44 143 D4
Mimosa Ct BN1 168 B3
Mindleheim Ave RH19 10 B2
Minnels The BN6 127 A3
Minsted Rd GU29 91 F7
Minster Ct BN17 178 C4
Mint Rd GU33 45 D6
Minton Rd PO22 196 B4
Miranda Wlk RH11 17 E4
Mitchamer Cotts PO18 130 F2
Mitchell Gdns RH13 34 E3
Mitchells Rd RH10 18 F6
Mitford Wlk 10 RH11 18 A3
Mitre Ho 23 BN1 187 E5
Mixon Cl PO20 206 E6
Moat La RH20 98 D2
Moat Rd RH19 9 E2
Moat The RH20 98 C2
Moat Way BN12 181 E1
Moat Wlk RH10 19 C7
Moatfield La RH13 104 A8
Mocatta Way RH15 106 D5
Model Buildings Cotts
RH13 80 B2
Modena Rd BN3 186 F7
Mole Cl RH11 18 B8
Mole The BN17 199 A5
Molecomb Broadwalk
PO18 134 A2
Molesworth St BN3 186 F8
Molins Ct 4 RH11 18 A3
Monarch Cl RH11 18 A3
Monastery La RH20 119 C1
Monk Cl BN1 168 E6
Monk's Hill PO10 149 C5
Monkmead Copse RH20 119 C6
Monkmead La RH20 119 B6
Monks Ave BN15 183 F6
Monks Cl BN15 183 F6
Monks Ct BN15 183 E6
Monks La RH5 13 F5
Monks Wlk BN44 144 B2
Monksfield RH10 18 F7
Monmouth St 13 BN3 187 B7
Mons Ave PO21 195 B5
Montagu Rd PO19 172 E8
Montague Cl BN43 185 D7
Montague Ct
6 Brighton BN2 188 C4
Lancing BN15 183 B7
2 Shoreham-by-Sea BN43 185 D7
Montague Ctr 10 BN11 182 D2
Montague Pl
Brighton BN2 188 C4
Worthing BN11 182 D1
Montague Rd GU29 71 A2
Montague St
4 Brighton BN2 188 C4
Worthing BN11 182 D1
Montalan Cres PO20 206 B8
Montefiore Rd BN3 187 E7
Monterey Ct BN1 167 E3
Monterey Pines PO22 196 A5
Montes Hill RH16 86 F8
Monteswood La
RH16,RH17 87 B8
Montford Cl BN43 185 D8
Montfort Rise RH1 1 F8
Montgomeri Dr BN16 179 B3
Montgomery Dr PO22 196 D6
Montgomery St BN3 187 A7
Montpelier Cotts RH20 141 E8
Montpelier Cres BN1 187 E6
Montpelier Gdns RH20 141 E8
Montpelier Lodge 9
BN1 187 E6
Montpelier Rd
Brighton BN1 187 E5
East Preston BN16 200 A5
Montpelier St BN1 187 E6
Montpelier Villas BN1 187 E6
Montreal Rd BN2 207 C3
Montreal Way BN13 181 C6
Montreal Wlk GU30 25 C3
Montreux Ct RH11 18 B6
Montrose Cl BN12 181 C2
Montrose Ct BN12 181 C3
Monument La PO18 150 B7
Monument View BN2 188 D6
Moon's La RH19, RH7, TN8 10 E8
Moons La RH13 36 E1
Moonsgate RH13 36 E1
Moor Park Cres RH11 17 D5
Moor Pl RH19 9 D2
Moor Rd GU27 26 C5
Moorcroft Cl RH11 18 B7
Moore Cl BN13 181 B6
Moore Ct RH12 36 A1
Moore Pl 4 PO21 195 C4
Moorfield GU27 26 F5
Moorfoot Rd BN13 181 F7
Moorhead Rd RH12 37 B5
Moorhen Way PO22 195 B6
Moorhouse La GU29 69 D6
Moorings The
East Grinstead RH19 9 A3
Lancing BN15 183 F8
5 Littlehampton BN17 199 A6
Shoreham-by-Sea BN43 185 C6
Moorland Cl RH10 19 C3
Moorpark 3 RH6 2 B2
Mora Soomaree 11 BN11 182 B2
Moraunt Dr PO22 196 E6
Morecambe Cl RH11 17 F4
Morecambe Rd BN1 168 A6
Moreton Ct BN41 186 B8
Moreton Rd PO18 171 B5
Morland Ave BN14 182 E7
Morley St BN2 207 C3
Morleys RH20 121 A4
Mornington Cres
Bognor Regis PO22 196 A5
Portslade-by-Sea BN3 186 D7
Mornington Mans 4
BN3 186 D7
Morrell Ave RH12 36 F6
Morris Dr RH14 77 C7
Morris Way RH20 119 C7
Morrison Ct 5 RH11 18 B1
Mortimer Rd BN3 187 A8
Morton Cl RH11 39 B8
Morton Rd RH19 22 E7
Mosdell Rd PO10 170 A8
Mosford Cl RH6 1 F5
Moss Cl GU33 45 C4
Mosse Gdns PO19 172 B7
Moulsecoomb Prim Sch
BN2 168 E3
Moulsecoomb Sta BN2 168 D2
Moulsecoomb Way BN2 168 F4
Mount Cl RH10 19 D7
Mount Ct PO20 206 E7
Mount La Chichester PO19 172 F6
Turners Hill RH10 21 A4
Mount Noddy RH17 84 C3
Mount Pk BN44 143 D1
Mount Pleasant
Arundel BN18 158 A3
Brighton BN2 207 C2
Mount The
Lambs Green RH11 17 B8
Rusper RH11, RH12 4 B1
Mount Way BN15 163 E1
Mount Zion Pl BN1 207 A3
Mountain Ash Ct RH12 36 F4
Mountbatten Cl RH11 18 C2
Mountbatten Ct
Bognor Regis PO21 195 D2
Hove BN3 186 E8
7 Littlehampton BN17 199 A6
Mountfields BN1 168 C2
Mountview Rd BN15 163 C1
Mountwood Rd
Breach PO10 149 F1
Selsey PO20 206 F8
Mouse La BN44 142 E6
Mouthey's La PO18 151 E2
Mowbray Dr RH11 17 F4
Mowden Sch BN1 167 D1
Moyne Cl BN3 166 E1
Moyne Rd RH11 18 C2
Mudberry La PO18 171 A8
Muggeridge's Hill
RH12, RH5 15 E8
Muir Ct BN14 182 D5
Muirfield 10 RH6 2 B2
Muirfield Cl Crawley RH11 17 D5
Worthing BN13 181 E6
Muirfield Ct 16 RH16 85 E4
Muirfield Rd BN13 181 E6
Mulberry Cl Brighton BN1 167 F3
Ferring BN12 200 E6

Mulberry Cl *continued*
Horsham RH12 36 C5
Lancing BN15 183 E6
Shoreham-by-Sea BN43 165 D1
Worthing BN12 181 C3
Mulberry Ct
Bognor Regis PO21 205 A7
Petworth GU28 95 E7
Selsey PO20 206 D7
Worthing BN12 181 C2
Mulberry Gdns BN12 181 C2
Mulberry La Ditchling BN6 127 D3
Worthing BN12 181 C2
Mulberry Rd RH11 5 B1
Mullein Wlk RH11 18 A2
Mumford Pl PO19 173 B4
Munmere Way 3 BN16 199 E6
Munnion Rd RH17 64 B7
Munns Dr RH15 107 B4
Muntham Dr RH13 56 F3
Muntham House Sch RH13 56 E4
Murina Ave PO21 195 C5
Murray Ct Crawley RH11 18 A1
Horsham RH13 37 B4
Murray Rd PO20 206 D6
Mus of D-Day Aviation BN43 184 D7
Museum Hill GU27 27 D6
Mus of Royal Military Police PO19 152 F1
Musgrave Ave RH19 22 E8
Mustang Cl BN18 177 B2
Muster Ct RH16 85 D4
Muster Gn N RH16 85 D4
Muster Gn S RH16 85 D4
Mutton Hill RH7 10 B7
Mutton's La RH20 120 D3
Myrtle Cres BN15 183 D5
Myrtle Gr BN16 199 F5
Myrtle La RH14 77 D7
Myrtle Rd BN15 183 D5
Mytchett Ho 1 PO19 153 A2
Mytten Bank RH17 84 F6
Mytten Cl RH17 84 F6

N

Nab Tower La PO20 206 B8
Nab Wlk PO20 201 F6
Nagels Cl PO20 202 A6
Naiad Gdns PO22 196 D5
Naldrett Cl RH12 36 F4
Naldretts La RH12 33 D5
Namrik Mews BN3 187 A6
Nanson Rd BN1 168 D6
Napier Ho 3 BN2 188 C7
Napier Way RH10 6 A1
Nappers Wood GU27 49 A6
Nash La RH17 87 B4
Nash Rd RH10 18 E3
Nash Way BN18 156 D1
Natal Rd BN2 168 D1
Natts La RH14 77 D6
Naunton Rd PO19 153 B1
Navarino Rd BN11 183 A2
Neale Cl RH19 9 B3
Need's Hill RH13 102 F6
Needlemakers PO19 173 B6
Needles Cl RH12 36 B1
Nell Ball RH14 30 E2
Nelson Cl Crawley RH10 19 C5
Lancing BN15 183 D8
Tangmere PO20 154 D2
Nelson Ct BN43 184 D5
Nelson Pl 17 BN2 207 C3
Nelson Rd
Bognor Regis PO21 195 A3
Horsham RH12 36 C3
Worthing BN12 181 D4
Nelson Row Brighton BN2 207 C2
Ford BN18 177 E3
Nep Cl BN5 123 E4
Nep Town Rd BN5 123 E4
Nepcote BN14 161 F5
Nepcote La BN14 161 F5
Nepcote Par BN14 161 E6
Nepfield Cl BN14 161 F5
Neptune Cl RH11 17 E4
Neptune Ct
Bognor Regis PO22 196 D4
Brighton BN2 188 F3
Horsham RH12 36 B4
Neptune Way BN17 199 A4
Nesbit Ct RH11 17 E3
Nesbitt Rd BN2 168 D1
Nestor Ct BN1 187 E8
Netherton Cl Selsey PO20 206 E7
Southwater RH13 57 F4
Netherwood RH11 18 B4
Netherwoods Rd RH13 79 B6
Netley Cl RH11 39 C8
Nettleton Ave PO20 154 C2
Nettleton Ct BN1 168 B1
Nevile Cl RH11 18 A3
Nevill Ave BN3 166 F1
Nevill Cl BN3 167 A2
Nevill Cotts BN6 127 D2
Nevill Ct BN3 167 A1
Nevill Gdns BN3 167 A2
Nevill Pl BN3 167 A2
Nevill Rd BN3 167 A2
Nevill Way BN3 167 A2
Neville Gdns PO10 149 A3
Neville Rd
Bognor Regis PO22 195 D4
Chichester PO19 172 D7
New Barn RH14 53 A2
New Barn Cl
Portslade-by-Sea BN41 166 B2
Shoreham-by-Sea BN43 165 B1
New Barn Hill PO18 154 B7
New Barn La RH20 119 B8
New Barn Rd
Amberley BN18 138 D5
Shoreham-by-Sea BN43 165 B1
New Brighton Rd PO10 149 B2
New Broadway BN14 182 A3
New Church Rd BN3 186 E7
New Cotts
Partridge Green RH13 103 A3
Scaynes Hill RH17 86 F1
Turners Hill RH10 21 A4
Washington RH20 141 E6
New Courtwick La BN17 178 C4
New Cut BN18 158 B3
New Dorset St BN1 207 A3
New England Ho BN1 207 B4
New England Rd
Brighton BN1 207 A4
Haywards Heath RH16 85 F4
New England Rise BN41 166 A4
New England St BN1 207 B4
New England Wing The BN18 177 E7
New Farthingdale RH7 10 B8
New Gdns BN15 182 F7
New Hall La BN5 144 E7
New House La RH1 2 E8
New La GU31 89 D2
New Moorhead Dr RH12 37 C6
New Par
East Wittering PO20 201 E7
Selsey PO20 206 D7
Worthing BN11 182 F2
New Park Ct PO19 173 B6
New Park Rd PO19 173 A7
New Place Rd RH20 98 C3
New Rd Billingshurst RH14 56 B2
Brighton BN1 207 B2
Camelsdale GU27 26 F5
East Dean PO18 134 D8
Keymer BN6 127 B2
Littlehampton BN17 198 D4
Midhurst GU29 92 E6
Rustington BN16 179 E3
Shoreham-by-Sea BN43 184 F7
South Ambersham GU29 93 E4
Southbourne PO10 170 A8
Southwater RH13 57 F4
Upper Beeding BN44 144 B1
Upperton GU28 73 A2
Westbourne PO10 149 D3
Westerton PO18 153 D4
Worthing BN13 181 C7
New Row BN44 143 C3
New Salts Farm Rd BN43 184 C6
New St Crawley RH10 19 A7
Horsham RH13 36 D2
Petworth GU28 95 F8
2 Worthing BN11 182 D1
New Steine BN2 207 C1
New Steine Mews BN2 207 C2
New Sussex Hospl BN3 187 E6
New Town
11 Chichester PO19 173 A6
Copthorne RH10 7 B3
New Town Rd RH20 119 B1
New Way La BN6 126 B2
Newark Pl BN2 207 C3
Newark Rd RH10 18 F8
Newbarn La Bognor Regis, Felpham PO22 196 B6
Bognor Regis, North Bersted PO21 194 F6
Henfield BN5 123 F2
Walderton PO18 150 B8
Newbridge Cl RH12 35 C3
Newbridge Rd RH14 77 B8
Newbury La RH17 84 E5
Newbury Rd RH10 19 D6
Newcroft Cotts RH17 42 A2
Newdigate Rd RH12 16 C8
Newells La
Broadbridge PO18 171 A7
Monk's Gate RH13 59 D2
West Ashling PO18 150 F1
Newfield Rd
Liss Forest GU33 45 C6
Selsey PO20 206 G8
Newhall Cl PO21 194 F3
Newham Cl BN44 143 C3
Newham La BN44 143 C2
Newhaven St BN2 207 C3
Newhouse La
East Dean PO18 134 D8
Heath Common RH20 120 C3
Newick House Sch RH15 107 C1
Newick Rd BN1 168 E4
Newland Rd
Upper Beeding BN44 144 B2
Worthing BN11 182 D3
Newland St BN11 182 D3
Newlands RH17 40 F1
Newlands Cl Horley RH6 1 F5
Keymer BN6 127 B3
Newlands Cres RH19 9 D2
Newlands La PO19 172 D8
Newlands Pk RH10 7 E3
Newlands Pl RH18 23 F3
Newlands Rd Crawley RH11 18 C5
Horsham RH12 36 C4
Newling Way BN13 161 E1
Newman Cl RH10 19 C4
Newman's Gdns BN15 183 B7
Newmarket Rd
Brighton BN2 188 C8
Crawley RH10 19 A4
Newmarket Terr 12 BN2 188 C8
Newport Dr PO19 172 B7
Newport Mews BN11 183 B3
Newport Rd RH15 106 F3
Newport St BN2 207 C4
Newpound RH14 54 E3
Newpound La RH14 54 D1
Newstead 5 BN1 207 A4
Newstead Hall RH6 2 D1
Newtimber Ave BN12 181 B3
Newtimber Dr BN41 166 A1
Newtimber Gdns BN43 164 F1
Newton Ave RH19 22 F6
Newton Cl RH16 86 B7
Newton Ct RH16 85 E5
Newton Rd Crawley RH10 5 F2
Lindfield RH16 86 C7
Newtown Ave PO21 195 A6
Newtown Ct RH13 36 E1
Newtown Rd Hove BN3 187 B8
Liphook GU30 25 C3
Nicholsfield RH14 31 F4
Nicolson Dr BN43 185 A8
Nightingale Cl
Crawley RH11 18 C8
East Grinstead RH19 22 D7
Red Hill PO9 128 C1
Storrington RH20 119 E1
Nightingale Ct PO22 196 F5
Nightingale Ind Est RH12 36 D3
Nightingale La
Burgess Hill RH15 126 F8
Hambrook PO18 150 D3
Storrington RH20 119 E1
Nightingale Pk RH20 119 E1
Nightingale Rd RH12 36 D3
Nightingale Wlk RH14 77 E8
Nightingales Findon BN14 161 E7
West Chiltington Common RH20 119 D7
Nightingales Bsns Pk RH20 98 C5
Nightingales Cl RH13 36 F2
Nile St Brighton BN1 207 B2
Emsworth PO10 169 B8
Nimbus Cl BN17 199 A6
Nimrod Ct RH10 6 D1
Nine Acres GU29 92 D8
Nineveh Shipyard BN18 158 B3
Ninfield Ct RH11 17 F2
Ninfield Pl BN2 188 E7
Niven Cl RH10 19 D5
Nizells Ave BN3 187 E7
Noah's Ct RH10 21 A4
Noah's Farm Yard Nature Trail GU28 94 E8
Noahs Ark La RH16 86 C7
Noble Ct BN3 186 E7
Noel Gn RH15 107 B4
Noel Rise RH15 107 B4
Nonnington La GU28 94 B1
Nookery The BN16 200 A5
Nor'bren Ave PO21 195 A5
Norbury Cl BN15 183 F8
Norbury Dr BN15 183 F8
Nordseter Lodge 1 BN16 199 B4
Nore Down Way PO18 130 A8
Norfolk Wing The BN18 177 E7
Norfolk Bldgs 5 BN1 187 E5
Norfolk Cl
11 Bognor Regis PO21 195 C2
Crawley RH11 17 E2
Horley RH6 2 A2
Norfolk Cotts Bury RH20 138 A7
6 Steyning BN44 143 D3
Norfolk Ct
10 Bognor Regis PO21 195 C2
4 Brighton BN1 187 E5
Horsham RH12 37 B5
9 Rustington BN16 199 B4
1 Worthing BN11 182 C3
Norfolk Gdns BN17 198 F4
Norfolk Ho PO22 195 F4
Norfolk Mews
6 Brighton BN1 187 E5
6 Littlehampton BN17 198 F4
Norfolk Pl
3 Brighton BN1 187 E5
4 Littlehampton BN17 198 F4
Norfolk Rd
8 Horsham RH12 36 D2
Hove BN1 187 E6
Littlehampton BN17 198 F4
Norfolk Sq
Bognor Regis PO21 195 C2
Brighton BN1 187 E5
Norfolk St
Bognor Regis PO21 195 C2
Brighton BN1 187 E5
Worthing BN11 182 C3
Norfolk Terr Brighton BN1 187 E6
9 Horsham RH12 36 D2
Norfolk Way PO22 197 B5
Norman Cl
Billingshurst RH14 55 E1
Littlehampton BN17 198 F5
Norman Cres 9 BN43 164 F1
Norman Rd
Burgess Hill RH15 107 A3
Hove BN3 186 E6
Norman Way
Bognor Regis PO22 196 F5
Steyning BN44 143 D4
Norman's Dr PO22 196 B6
Normandy RH12 36 C1
Normandy Cl Crawley RH10 19 C4
7 East Grinstead RH19 22 F8
Normandy Ct
Chichester PO19 173 B7
9 Worthing BN11 182 B1
Normandy Dr BN16 200 A4
Normandy Gdns RH12 36 C1
Normandy Ho 3 BN3 187 C6
Normandy La BN16 200 A4
Normandy Rd BN14 182 C4
Normanhurst
10 Brighton BN2 207 C3
4 Shoreham-by-Sea BN43 184 F7
Normanhurst Cl
Crawley RH10 18 F6
Rustington BN16 199 C4
Normanscourt 8 BN43 164 F1
Normanton Ave PO21 195 B3
Normanton St 8 BN2 188 C7
North Ash RH12 36 C4
North Ave
Middleton-on-Sea PO22 196 F5
Worthing BN12 181 E1
North Ave E PO22 197 A5
North Ave S PO22 197 A5
North Bank BN6 126 E4
North Bay PO10 169 C3
North Bersted St PO22 195 A7
North Cl Chichester PO19 173 A7
Crawley RH10 18 F7
Portslade-by-Sea BN41 166 A2
North Ct BN6 126 E4
North Dr Angmering BN16 179 F4
Brighton BN2 188 C6
North End BN6 127 D4
North End Cl GU28 73 F1
North End Cotts BN14 161 E8
North End Rd BN18 176 F4
North Farm Cotts
Findon RH20 141 D2
Portslade-by-Sea BN41 166 A2
North Farm Ct BN15 183 E6
North Farm Rd BN15 183 F6
North Gdns Brighton BN1 207 A3
Horsham RH12 36 C1
North Ham Rd BN17 198 D6
North Heath Cl RH12 36 D5
North Heath Com Prim Sch RH12 36 D5
North Heath Est RH12 36 D6
North Heath La RH12 36 E6
North Holmes Cl RH12 37 B5
North La Buriton GU31 88 A5
Charlton PO18 134 A8
East Preston BN16 200 B6
Littlehampton BN16 199 B6
Portslade-by-Sea BN41 166 A3
South Harting GU31 89 D4
West Hoathly RH19 42 E6
Wiston BN44 121 C2
North Lancing Fst & Mid Sch BN15 183 E8
North Lodge PO21 194 A2
North Lodge Ind Pk GU30 25 D1
North Lodge Mans 3 BN11 182 D2
North Mead RH10 18 E8
North Mundham Prim Sch PO20 173 D1
North Pallant PO19 173 A6
North Par RH12 36 C3
North Pl Brighton BN1 207 B2
15 Littlehampton BN17 198 E4
North Point 1 BN43 185 A6
North Pound BN18 156 D1
North Rd Brighton BN1 207 B3
Brighton, Preston BN1 167 E1
Broadbridge PO18 171 C7
Crawley RH10 19 A7
Haywards Heath RH16 86 A4
Lancing BN15 183 E6
Portslade-by-Sea BN41 166 A2
Selsey PO20 206 E7
North St Brighton BN1 207 B2
Chichester PO19 173 A7
Emsworth PO10 149 B1
Horsham RH12, RH13 36 D3
Littlehampton BN17 178 D3
Midhurst GU29 92 F8
Petworth GU28 73 F1
Portslade-by-Sea BN41 186 C7
Shoreham-by-Sea BN43 184 E7
Storrington RH20 119 D1
Turners Hill RH10 21 A4
Westbourne PO10 149 D4
Worthing BN11 182 D3
North Terminal App RH6 5 F8
North View BN5 124 E5
North Walls
Chichester PO19 172 F6
Chichester PO19 172 F7
North Way
Bognor Regis PO22 195 F4
Petworth GU28 95 E7
Northbourne Cl BN43 184 F8
Northbrook Cl BN14 182 E6
Northbrook Coll
Worthing,Goring-by-Sea BN13 181 B4
Worthing,West Worthing BN11 182 D2
Northbrook Coll Design & Tech BN14 182 D5
Northbrook Coll Sussex RH12 36 C4
Northbrook Rd BN14 182 E6
Northbrook Trad Est BN14 182 E6
Northchapel Com Prim Sch GU28 51 A7
Northcliffe Rd PO22 195 E4
Northcote Rd PO21 195 A4
Northcourt Cl BN16 199 E6
Northcourt Mews BN14 182 C4
Northcourt Rd BN14 182 C4
Northcroft BN5 123 E5
Northdown Cl RH12 36 F4
Northdown Terr RH19 9 D3
Northease Cl BN3 166 D2
Northease Dr BN3 166 E3
Northease Gdns BN3 166 E3
Northend La BN6 105 F3
Northerlea BN41 166 A1
Northern Breach RH17 84 F6
Northern Cres PO20 201 F7
Northfield PO20 206 F7
Northfield Rd BN13 182 A6
Northfield Rise BN3 166 D4
Northfield Way BN1 168 A4
Northfields La PO20 155 D1
Northgate PO19 173 A7
Northgate Ave RH10 18 F7
Northgate Cl BN15 183 C6
Northgate Fst Sch RH10 18 E7
Northgate Mid Sch RH10 18 E7
Northgate Pl RH10 18 E7
Northgate Rd
Crawley RH10 18 D6
Gatwick Airport RH6 5 F8
Northlands PO19 152 B1
Northlands Ave RH16 86 B4
Northlands La RH20 119 E4
Northlands Rd
Horsham RH12 36 E7
Warnham RH12 14 D2
Northlands Wood Com Prim Sch RH16 86 B4
Northmead GU28 73 F1
Northolmes Jun Sch RH12 37 A4
Northside PO18 152 E7
Northview Terr BN14 161 E6
Northway
Burgess Hill RH15 107 C4
Gatwick Airport RH6 5 F8
Northway Rd BN17 178 D4
Northwood Ct BN14 182 C6
Northwood Pk RH10 6 A2
Northwyke Cl PO22 196 C5
Northwyke Rd PO22 196 C5
Norton Cl BN3 187 B6
Norton La PO20 155 B1
Norton Rd Hove BN3 187 B6
Lancing BN15 183 D5
Norway La BN17 178 F3
Norway St BN41 186 C7
Norwich Cres BN2 168 F2
Norwich Dr BN2 168 F2
Norwich Rd
Chichester PO19 152 F1
Crawley RH10 19 B5
Norwood BN1 168 A4
Norwood La GU28 114 E8
Norwood La S GU28 114 E5
Norwoodhill Rd RH6 4 E8
Nowhurst La RH12 35 A5
Nuffield Cl PO21 194 E3
Nurseries The PO21 194 C3
Nursery Cl
Haywards Heath RH16 85 D5
Hurstpierpoint BN6 125 F7
Lancing BN15 183 D7
New Brighton PO10 149 B3
Portslade-by-Sea BN41 165 E4
Shoreham-by-Sea BN43 185 B8
West Barnham PO22 176 B6
West Kingston BN16 200 A4
Nursery Field GU33 45 A3
Nursery Gdns BN17 178 D3
Nursery La
Fishbourne PO19 172 B7
Hookwood RH6 1 D2
Worthing BN11 182 C1
Nursery The RH15 107 C4
Nurserylands RH11 18 A6
Nutbourne Halt PO18 170 D8
Nutbourne La RH20 99 A4
Nutbourne Rd
Nutbourne Common RH20 99 A1
South Hayling PO11 189 A1
Worthing BN14 182 B4
Nutbourne Vineyards RH20 99 C2
Nutcombe La GU26, GU27 26 E8
Nutcroft RH20 98 C3
Nutham La RH13 58 A1
Nuthatch Cl PO9 128 D1
Nuthatch Way RH12 36 D7
Nuthurst Cl Brighton BN2 188 F6
Crawley RH11 18 A7
Nuthurst Pl BN2 188 F5
Nuthurst Rd
Maplehurst RH13 80 F6
Monk's Gate RH13 59 B3
Nuthurst St RH13 59 A2
Nutley Ave BN12 181 C1
Nutley Cl Hove BN3 166 F3
Worthing BN12 181 C1
Nutley Cres BN12 181 C1
Nutley Dr BN12 181 C1
Nye La Ditchling BN6 127 D1
Westmeston BN6 148 D8

Nye Rd RH15 107 C3
Nyes Cl BN5 123 F5
Nyes La RH13 57 F3
Nyetimber Cl
Bognor Regis PO21 194 B2
West Chiltington Common RH20 119 C6
Nyetimber Copse RH20 119 C7
Nyetimber Cres PO21 194 B2
Nyetimber Hill BN2 168 E2
Nyetimber La
Bognor Regis PO21 194 B2
West Chiltington Common RH20 119 C7
Nyetimber Mill PO21 194 A2
Nyetimbers The PO21 194 A2
Nyewood CE Inf Sch PO21 195 A4
Nyewood CE Jun Sch PO21 195 A3
Nyewood Gdns [2] PO21 195 B3
Nyewood La PO21 195 B3
Nyewood Pl PO21 195 B2
Nymans Cl RH12 37 A7
Nymans Cotts RH17 61 C7
Nymans Ct RH10 19 B3
Nymans Gardens RH17 61 D7
Nyton Rd PO20 175 C8

O

Oak Ave Chichester PO19 172 E7
Heath Common RH20 120 B3
Oak Bank RH16 85 F7
Oak Cl Bognor Regis PO22 195 C6
Brighton BN1 167 E3
Chichester PO19 172 E7
Copthorne RH10 7 A3
Southwater RH13 79 F7
Storrington RH20 119 F2
Worthing BN13 161 E1
Oak Cotts GU27 26 E6
Oak Croft RH19 23 A8
Oak Ct RH10 5 D2
Oak Dell RH10 19 C7
Oak End Arundel BN18 157 E2
West Chiltington Common RH20 119 D8
Oak Gr Bognor Regis PO22 195 C6
Loxwood RH14 32 A4
Oak Hall Pk RH15 107 B1
Oak Ho RH14 55 C1
Oak La RH12 35 E3
Oak Mdw PO20 191 E5
Oak Rd Crawley RH11 18 C5
Southwater RH13 57 E1
Oak Tree Cl RH19 9 C3
Oak Tree Cotts
Burgess Hill RH15 107 B3
Danehill RH17 66 A4
Oak Tree Ct GU29 92 E6
Oak Tree Dr Liss GU33 45 C4
New Brighton PO10 149 B4
Oak Tree Farm PO18 150 D1
Oak Tree La
Haslemere GU27 26 D6
Woodgate PO20 175 D5
Oak Tree Way RH13 36 F4
Oak View PO20 192 F7
Oak Way RH10 18 E8
Oak Wlk RH12 16 F1
Oakapple Cl Cowfold RH13 81 E1
Crawley RH11 18 B1
Oakapple Rd BN42 165 E1
Oakcroft Gdns BN17 178 F3
Oakdene Brighton BN2 168 F4
Haywards Heath RH16 85 D5
Oakdene Ave BN41 165 E3
Oakdene Cl BN41 165 E3
Oakdene Cres BN41 165 E3
Oakdene Gdns BN41 165 E3
Oakdene Rise BN41 165 E4
Oakdene Way BN41 165 E4
Oakendene Ind Est RH13 82 B1
Oakenfield RH15 107 A5
Oakfield Lodsworth GU28 72 B3
Plaistow RH14 30 E2
Oakfield Ave PO20 201 F7
Oakfield Cl RH16 86 A7
Oakfield Cotts RH13 81 E1
Oakfield Mid Sch BN15 183 E7
Oakfield Rd Cowfold RH13 81 F1
East Wittering PO20 201 F7
Oakfield Way RH19 9 F3
Oakfields Crawley RH10 19 D7
Wallis Wood RH5 13 D8
Oakhaven RH10 18 D4
Oakhill Rd RH13 36 E2
Oakhurst
Haywards Heath RH16 85 D8
Henfield BN5 123 F6
Midhurst GU29 92 D7
Sayers Common BN6 105 D2
Oakhurst Gdns
East Grinstead RH19 9 C2
Rustington BN16 199 E6
Oakhurst La
Haywards Heath RH16 85 D8
Loxwood RH14 31 E7
Oakhurst Mews RH13 37 A4
Oakland Ct
Bognor Regis PO22 196 A4
Bognor Regis, Nyetimber PO21 194 A1
[7] Littlehampton BN17 198 E4
[5] Shoreham-by-Sea BN43 184 F7
Oakland Ct *continued*
Worthing, Goring-by-Sea BN12 181 A2
[5] Worthing, West Worthing BN11 182 C2
Oaklands Ardingly RH17 64 B8
Billingshurst RH14 77 D7
Haslemere GU27 27 C7
Horley RH6 2 C3
Horsham RH13 36 E2
[2] Lancing BN15 183 F5
Oaklands Bsns Ctr BN11 181 F3
Oaklands Cl RH13 58 E8
Oaklands Ct PO19 173 A8
Oaklands La GU29 92 F5
Oaklands Rd RH16 85 D5
Oaklands Way PO19 173 A7
Oakleigh Cl BN11 183 A4
Oakleigh Ct
[2] Bognor Regis PO21 195 B2
Southwater RH13 80 A7
Worthing BN11 183 A4
Oakleigh Rd Horsham RH12 36 F4
Worthing BN11 183 A4
Oakley Cl RH19 23 B7
Oakley Cotts
Ashurst Wood RH19 23 C7
Handcross RH17 61 C8
Oakley Gdns BN16 200 A5
Oakmead Rd RH15 106 F1
Oakmeadow Cl PO10 149 C3
Oakmeeds Com Coll RH15 107 A2
Oakroyd Cl RH15 107 D5
Oaks Cl Horsham RH12 37 B6
Westergate PO20 175 D6
Oaks Fst & Mid Sch The RH10 18 F3
Oaks The
Burgess Hill RH15 106 D4
East Grinstead RH19 23 B8
Haywards Heath RH16 86 A4
Haywards Heath RH16 86 C4
Rustington BN16 199 E5
Small Dole BN5 144 E6
Southwater RH13 57 F2
Oakside Ct RH6 2 C4
Oakside La RH6 2 C4
Oaktree Cl PO21 193 F2
Oaktree Cotts BN18 176 C8
Oakvale RH20 119 C7
Oakway RH13 59 C6
Oakwood
Haywards Heath RH16 85 D4
Partridge Green RH13 103 A3
Oakwood Cl
Burgess Hill RH15 107 B2
Midhurst GU29 92 E7
Tangmere PO20 154 D2
Oakwood Ct
[3] Bognor Regis PO21 195 C4
Petworth GU28 95 F7
Oakwood Gdns PO21 195 C4
Oakwood Ind Pk RH10 6 A2
Oakwood Pk RH18 23 F2
Oakwood Rd
Burgess Hill RH15 107 B2
Haywards Heath RH16 85 D4
Horley RH6 2 B4
Oakwood Sch
East Ashling PO18 151 F2
Horley RH6 2 C3
Oates Wlk RH10 18 F3
Oathall Ave RH16 85 F6
Oathall Com Coll RH16 85 F6
Oathall Rd RH16 85 E5
Oatlands Crawley RH11 18 A5
Horley RH6 2 C1
Horley RH6 2 C4
Oberon Way RH11 17 E3
Ocean Cl BN12 200 E4
Ocean Dr BN12 200 E4
Ocean Par BN12 200 E4
Ockenden La RH17 84 E6
Ockenden Way BN6 126 E3
Ockley Ct PO21 195 C3
Ockley Hill BN6,RH15 127 B6
Ockley La
Burgess Hill RH15 127 B7
Keymer BN6 127 B4
Ockley Rd PO21 195 C3
Ockley Way BN6 127 A5
Octagon The BN2 188 F3
Offington Ave BN14 182 B6
Offington Cnr BN13 182 A8
Offington Ct BN14 182 C6
Offington Dr BN14 182 B7
Offington Gdns BN14 182 A6
Offington La BN13, BN14 182 A7
Ognells Flats GU29 92 F8
Okehurst La RH14 55 D4
Okehurst Rd RH14 55 A6
Old Arundel Rd PO18 153 F2
Old Bakery Mews PO20 206 E7
Old Barn Cl PO21 194 A2
Old Barn Ct RH16 85 D2
Old Barn Way BN42 186 A7
Old Boat Cnr BN1 168 D8
Old Boat Wlk BN1 168 B7
Old Boundary La RH20 119 B8
Old Bridge Rd PO18 171 C7
Old Bridge St PO18 171 C7
Old Brighton Rd N RH11 39 C7
Old Brighton Rd S
Crawley RH11 39 B6
Pease Pottage RH6,RH11 5 E5
Old Broyle Rd PO19 152 D2
Old Buddington La GU29 70 E3
Old Church Ho The PO21 195 A6
Old Coach Ho The BN11 182 B3
Old Coastguard Cotts PO20 206 C7
Old Coastguards PO22 195 F3
Old Control Rd RH6 5 D6
Old Convent The RH19 9 E2
Old Cottage Cl PO20 154 C1
Old Cotts BN14 161 E7
Old Court Cl BN1 167 F4
Old Courthouse The [3] BN44 143 D3
Old Crawley Rd RH12 37 C7
Old Dairy Workshops PO10 149 D3
Old Denne Gdns RH12 36 C1
Old Farm Cl
Bognor Regis PO21 194 D2
Bracklesham PO20 202 B5
Old Farm Ct BN43 184 C6
Old Farm Dr PO20 175 D7
Old Farm La PO10 149 E3
Old Farm Rd Brighton BN1 167 F5
Selsey PO20 206 C8
Old Fort Rd BN43 185 B6
Old Glebe GU27 49 B6
Old Granary The PO18 154 D4
Old Guildford Rd RH12 35 E4
Old Haslemere Rd GU27 27 C5
Old Holbrook RH12 15 F2
Old Horsham Rd RH11 18 B4
Old Hospital The RH17 84 F8
Old London Rd
Brighton BN1 167 E6
Coldwaltham RH20 117 D6
Washington RH20 141 E8
Old Manor Cl RH11 18 A8
Old Manor Ct RH11 18 A8
Old Manor House Gdns PO22 196 B5
Old Manor Rd BN16 199 B6
Old Market Ave [10] PO19 173 A6
Old Market Sq BN44 143 E3
Old Martyrs RH11 5 D1
Old Mead Rd BN17 178 C5
Old Mill Cl Brighton BN1 167 E5
Southwick BN41 186 A7
Old Mill Dr RH20 119 D1
Old Mill Pl
Pulborough RH20 98 D1
Shottermill GU27 26 F7
Old Mill Sq RH20 119 D1
Old Mill The Arundel BN18 158 B3
Bognor Regis PO22 195 F3
Chichester PO19 173 A7
Old Millmeads RH12 36 C5
Old Moat Cl PO22 175 C1
Old Mus Ct GU27 27 D6
Old Orchards RH10 19 E6
Old Park Cl RH17 85 A6
Old Park La Bosham PO18 171 D2
Fishbourne PO18 171 E5
Old Patcham Mews BN1 167 E6
Old Pl PO21 194 E3
Old Point PO22 196 E4
Old Quarry The GU27 26 F4
Old Rd RH19 9 F1
Old Rectory Cl PO10 149 D3
Old Rectory Dr PO20 175 E7
Old Rectory Flats PO22 196 A4
Old Rectory Gdns
Bognor Regis PO22 196 A4
Southwick BN42 185 D8
Old Rectory The PO22 196 A4
Old Salts Farm Rd BN15 184 A5
Old School Cl PO20 191 E4
Old School Mews PO22 196 A5
Old School Pl
Burgess Hill RH15 106 F2
Woodgate PO20 175 D6
Old School Rd GU33 45 B4
Old School The RH20 97 A2
Old Shoreham Rd
North Lancing BN15 184 A8
Portslade-by-Sea BN3, BN41 186 C8
Shoreham-by-Sea BN43 184 E8
Southwick BN42 165 E1
Old Slipway The BN18 158 B2
Old Stables The PO22 195 F4
Old Station Cl RH10 21 B7
Old Steine BN1, BN2 207 B2
Old Viaduct Ct [10] BN2 188 C8
Old Wickham La RH16 85 E7
Old Wickhurst La RH12 35 D2
Old Worthing Rd BN16 180 B3
Old Yard Cl RH13 103 A3
Oldbury Cl RH12 37 A7
Older Way BN16 179 F6
Oldfield Cl RH6 1 F1
Oldfield Cres BN42 185 E8
Oldfield Rd RH6 1 F1
Oldhouse La
Balls Green RH14,RH13 78 B2
Broadford Bridge RH14, RH20 100 A7
Sidlesham PO20 203 C7
West Marden PO18,PO9 130 A6
Oldlands Ave
Balcombe RH17 41 A1
Keymer BN6 127 A4
Oldlands Way PO22 195 E7
Oldwick Mdws PO18 152 F5
Olive Rd BN3 186 D8
Oliver Cl BN2 188 C5
Oliver Ho [9] BN3 187 B5
Oliver Rd RH12 36 A1
Oliver Whitby Rd PO19 172 E7
Olivers Mdw PO20 175 D7
Olivier Ct PO21 195 A6
Olivier Rd RH10 19 D5
Onslow Ct [9] BN11 183 B3
Onslow Dr BN12 200 E6
Onslow Rd BN3 167 C2
Ontario Cl BN13 181 C6
Ontario Gdns BN13 181 C6
Ontario Way GU30 25 C3
Open Mkt The BN1 207 B4
Ophir Rd BN11 183 A3
Orange Row Brighton BN1 207 B2
Emsworth PO10 169 B8
Orchard Ave
Chichester PO19 172 F7
Hove BN3 167 A1
Lancing BN15 183 E7
Selsey PO20 206 E6
Worthing BN14 182 B5
Orchard Bsns Ctr The RH1 2 A8
Orchard Cl
Camelsdale GU27 26 F5
East Harting GU31 90 A4
Elsted GU29 90 D4
Ferring BN12 180 E3
Haywards Heath RH16 85 D8
Horley RH6 1 F4
Petworth GU28 95 F7
Scaynes Hill RH17 86 F3
Shoreham-by-Sea BN43 184 E8
Small Dole BN5 144 F6
Southwick BN42 185 F8
Worthing BN14 182 B5
Orchard Cl The PO21 195 B3
Orchard Cnr RH16 86 B5
Orchard Cott RH17 84 F6
Orchard Cotts
Charlwood RH6 4 F7
Fishbourne PO18 172 A8
Woodgate PO20 175 D5
Orchard Cres BN18 156 A3
Orchard Ct BN11 182 A3
Orchard Dell RH20 99 E2
Orchard Gdns
Chichester PO19 172 F7
Hove BN3 167 B1
Rustington BN16 199 D6
Woodgate PO20 175 D5
Orchard Hill RH12 33 C7
Orchard Ho BN15 183 E6
Orchard La Ditchling BN6 127 D4
Hassocks BN6 126 F4
Hermitage PO10 169 D8
Orchard Par PO20 206 F8
Orchard Pl BN18 158 B3
Orchard Rd
Burgess Hill RH15 106 E3
East Preston BN16 200 A6
Horsham RH13 36 E2
Hove BN3 167 B1
West Itchenor PO20 191 A7
Orchard Side PO20 193 A8
Orchard St
Chichester PO19 172 F7
Crawley RH10, RH11 18 D6
Orchard The
Bognor Regis PO21 194 C1
Crawley RH11 18 A8
Hassocks BN6 126 F3
Horley RH6 2 A3
Horsham RH13 37 B4
Orchard Way
Barnham PO22 176 B6
Bognor Regis PO22 195 C5
Bolney RH17 83 D8
Burgess Hill RH15 106 F3
East Grinstead RH19 9 E1
Fontwell BN18 156 A3
Haywards Heath RH16 85 D8
Hurstpierpoint BN6 125 F6
Lancing BN15 183 E7
Midhurst GU29 92 F8
Pulborough RH20 98 C3
Orchards Mid Sch The BN12 181 D4
Orchards Sh Ctr [11] RH16 85 E4
Orchards The
Brighton BN2 168 E3
[4] Crawley RH11 17 D5
Horsham RH12 36 F5
Orchid Pk RH16 86 C4
Orchid View BN1 168 C6
Orde Cl RH10 6 D1
Oriel Cl Crawley RH10 6 C1
West Barnham PO22 176 B6
Orient Rd BN15 184 C5
Oriental Pl BN1 187 E5
Orion Ct Crawley RH11 17 D4
Horsham RH12 36 B3
Orion Par BN6 126 F3
Orkney Ct BN13 181 B5
Orltons La RH12 3 F2
Orme Cotts BN16 179 F6
Orme Rd BN11 182 C3
Ormerod Ct RH16 85 E5
Ormesby Cres PO22 196 A5
Ormesby Wlk RH10 19 B4
Ormonde Ave PO19 173 B6
Ormonde Way BN43 184 D6
Orpen Pl PO20 206 F7
Orpen Rd BN3 167 D1
Osborn Cres PO19 153 A1
Osborne Cl BN15 183 C6
Osborne Cres PO19 173 D6
Osborne Ct Crawley RH11 18 B2
[7] Shoreham-by-Sea BN43 185 C8
Osborne Dr BN15 183 C6
Osborne Rd BN1 168 A2
Osborne Villas BN3 187 B6
Osmond Gdns BN3 187 E7
Osmond Rd BN3 187 E7
Osmonde Cl BN14 182 C4
Osmonde Ct [3] BN14 182 C4
Osmund Cl RH10 19 E6
Osmunda Bank RH19 9 E6
Osney Cl RH11 18 C5
Osprey Cl BN17 178 D4
Osprey Gdns PO22 195 C7
Osprey Ho [18] BN1 187 E5
Osprey Quay PO10 169 C7
Ostlers View RH14 77 C7
Otard Cl PO20 206 E7
Otford Cl RH11 39 C8
Ottafield Ct RH16 85 F6
Otter Cl PO19 172 E8
Otterbourne Pl RH19 9 B1
Otway Cl RH11 17 F4
Otway Rd PO19 153 A2
Oulton Wlk RH10 19 B4
Our Lady of Sion Jun Sch BN11 182 D2
Our Lady of Sion Sch BN11 182 C2
Our Lady Queen of Heaven RC Prim Sch RH11 18 B8
Outerwyke Ave PO22 196 A6
Outerwyke Gdns PO22 196 B6
Outerwyke Rd PO22 196 A6
Outram Ho PO22 195 F3
Outram Rd PO22 195 F3
Oval La PO20 206 E5
Oval The Findon BN14 161 E7
Liss GU33 45 B4
Worthing BN13 182 A5
Oval Waye BN12 200 E4
Over St BN1 207 B3
Overdene Dr RH11 18 A6
Overdown Rd PO22 196 B5
Overdown Rise BN41 165 F4
Overhill BN42 165 E1
Overhill Dr BN1 167 E5
Overhill Gdns BN1 167 E5
Overhill Way BN1 167 E6
Overmead BN43 184 E8
Overstrand Ave BN16 199 C4
Overton Rd PO10 150 A1
Overton Shaw RH19 9 E4
Oving Ct PO19 173 C6
Oving Rd Chichester PO19 173 C6
Oving PO20 174 B7
Oving Terr PO19 173 C6
Owen Cl RH15 106 F1
Owers Cl RH13 36 E2
Owers Way PO20 201 E7
Owlbeech Ct RH13 37 B4
Owlbeech Pl RH13 37 B4
Owlbeech Way RH13 37 B4
Owletts RH10 19 D7
Owlscastle Cl RH12 36 D5
Oxen Ave BN43 184 F8
Oxen Ct BN43 184 F8
Oxford Cl PO20 201 F7
Oxford Ct Brighton BN1 207 B4
[7] Midhurst GU29 92 E7
Oxford Dr PO21 194 F3
Oxford Mews BN3 187 C7
Oxford Pl BN1 207 B4
Oxford Rd Crawley RH10 18 F2
Horsham RH13 36 E2
Worthing BN11 182 C3
Oxford St
Bognor Regis PO21 195 B2
Brighton BN1, BN2 207 B4
Oxford Terr [8] BN44 143 D3
Oyster Mews [7] PO10 169 B8

P

Pacific Ct [3] BN43 184 F6
Pacific Way PO20 206 E6
Packer Cl RH19 10 A3
Packham Way RH15 106 F4
Paddock Cl GU27 49 A5
Paddock Ct BN41 165 F3
Paddock Gdns RH19 22 E7
Paddock Gn BN16 199 E6
Paddock La PO20 206 D8
Paddock The
Bognor Regis PO22 195 C5
Crawley RH10 19 D7
Haslemere GU27 27 A8
Hove BN3 167 C1
Littlehampton BN17 178 C6
Shoreham-by-Sea BN43 164 D1
Paddock Way
Findon BN14 161 E6
Liphook GU30 25 C5
Paddockhall Rd RH16 85 D5
Paddockhurst La RH17 41 D3
Paddockhurst Rd
Crawley RH11 18 A5
Turners Hill RH10 20 C2
Paddocks PO22 176 B6
Paddocks The
Lancing BN15 183 F5
Upper Beeding BN44 144 B3
Padstow Wlk RH11 17 F4
Padwick Rd RH13 37 A2
Padwicks Field RH20 97 A3
Page Ct RH13 36 D1
Pages Cnr BN11 183 A3

Pages La BN11 .... 183 A4
Paget Cl RH13 .... 58 E8
Pagewood Cl RH10 .... 19 C4
Pagham Cl PO10 .... 169 C8
Pagham Gdns PO11 ..... 189 B2
Pagham Harbour
Nature Reserve
PO20,PO21 .... 204 C6
Pagham Ho BN17 .... 178 B3
Pagham Rd
Bognor Regis PO20 ...... 194 A3
Runcton PO20 .... 173 D1
Pain's Flat RH15, RH17 ... 106 D8
Palace Pier BN2 .... 207 B1
Palace Pl BN1 .... 207 B2
Palace Yd PO19 .... 172 F6
Palatine Rd BN12 .... 181 D4
Palatine Sch BN12 ...... 181 D5
Palings Way GU27 .... 49 A5
Pallant The BN12 .... 181 B4
Pallingham Dr RH10 ...... 19 C3
Pallingham La RH14 ...... 75 F2
Palm Court Cotts 12
BN16 .... 200 A4
Palm Ct 2 Hove BN3 ..... 187 D6
Worthing BN13 .... 181 E7
Palmeira Ave BN3 ...... 187 D6
Palmeira Ct BN3 .... 187 C6
Palmeira Ho 6 BN3 ..... 187 D7
Palmeira Mans 21 BN3 ... 187 C6
Palmeira Pl BN3 .... 187 D7
Palmeira Sq BN3 .... 187 C6
Palmer Cl Horley RH6 .... 1 F5
Storrington RH20 .... 119 F2
Palmer Pl PO20 .... 173 D1
Palmer Rd
Angmering BN16 .... 179 F7
Crawley RH10 .... 19 C3
Palmer's Rd PO10 .... 149 B1
Palmers Field Ave PO19 .153 B1
Palmers Way BN13 ...... 161 D1
Palmerston Ave BN12 ... 181 C2
Pangdean La BN6, RH15 . 106 C4
Pangdene Cl RH15 ...... 106 E1
Pankhurst Ave BN2 ..... 188 D6
Pankhurst Ct 11 RH11 .... 18 B1
Pannell Cl RH19 .... 9 D1
Pannett RH15 .... 106 E4
Pantiles The BN12 ...... 200 E5
Panton Cl PO10 .... 149 A3
Parade Mans 8 BN16 ... 200 A4
Parade The
Bognor Regis PO21 ...... 205 A7
Brighton BN1 .... 167 B4
Crawley RH10 .... 18 E7
East Grinstead RH19 .... 9 B3
East Wittering PO20 ..... 201 F7
Horsham RH12 .... 36 A3
Hove BN3 .... 166 E2
7 West Kingston BN16 ... 200 A4
Paradise La PO10 .... 149 D4
Parchment St PO19 ..... 172 F7
Parham Cl Brighton BN2 . 188 D5
Littlehampton,
Rustington BN16 .... 199 B4
Littlehampton, Wick BN17 . 198 D6
Worthing BN14 .... 161 F1
Parham Ct 6 BN11 ...... 182 A2
Parham Ho 13 BN3 ...... 187 D7
Parham House
& Gardens RH20 .... 118 D1
Parham Rd Crawley RH11 .. 17 F7
Worthing BN14 .... 161 F1
Parish Ho 6 RH11 .... 18 D5
Parish La RH10, RH11 ..... 39 E6
Park Ave Hove BN3 ...... 186 E7
Keymer BN6 .... 127 A2
Selsey PO20 .... 206 F7
Shoreham-by-Sea BN43 .. 185 A8
Worthing BN11 .... 182 E3
Park Cl Brighton BN1 .... 168 E5
Burgess Hill RH15 .... 106 F4
Hove BN3 .... 166 E3
Hurstpierpoint BN6 ...... 126 A6
Portslade-by-Sea BN41 ... 166 B1
Worthing BN14 .... 182 A7
Park Copse PO20 .... 204 C1
Park Cotts BN6 .... 125 F6
Park Cres Brighton BN2 .. 207 C4
Emsworth PO10 .... 149 A1
Midhurst GU29 .... 92 E8
Portslade-by-Sea BN41 .. 186 A8
Selsey PO20 .... 206 G8
Worthing BN11 .... 182 C2
Park Crescent Pl BN2 ... 207 C4
Park Crescent Rd BN2 .. 207 C4
Park Crescent Terr BN2 . 207 C4
Park Ct
Brighton, Patcham BN1 ... 167 E6
Brighton, Preston BN1 .... 167 F1
Burgess Hill RH15 .... 107 A3
4 Haywards Heath RH16 ... 85 E4
Hove BN3 .... 187 D7
Park Dr Bognor Regis PO22 196 D5
Burndell BN18 .... 177 A2
Ferring BN12 .... 200 F6
Rustington BN16 .... 199 D6
Park Farm Cl RH12 ...... 36 D7
Park Farm Rd RH12 ...... 36 D7
Park Gate Brighton BN1 .. 187 F8
Hove BN3 .... 187 D6
Park Hill BN2 .... 207 C2
Park Ho 5 BN11 .... 183 B3
Park La Aldingbourne PO20 175 B7
Aldsworth PO10, PO18 .... 149 E8
Park La continued
Ashurst Wood RH19 .... 23 D6
East Beach PO20 .... 204 A1
Fernhurst GU27 .... 49 B6
Halnaker PO18 .... 154 D5
Lindfield RH16 .... 64 D2
Maplehurst RH13 .... 81 B6
Slindon BN18 .... 156 C4
Southwick BN42 .... 185 D7
Warminghurst RH20 ..... 120 D5
West Grinstead RH13 .... 102 D8
Park Lodge BN3 .... 187 D8
Park Manor BN1 .... 167 D3
Park Par RH16 .... 85 E4
Park Pl Arundel BN18 ..... 158 A3
Horsham RH12 .... 36 C1
Park Rd Barnham PO22 ... 176 D6
Bognor Regis PO21 ...... 195 B2
Breach PO10 .... 149 F1
Brighton BN1 .... 168 E5
Burgess Hill RH15 .... 107 A3
Burndell BN18 .... 177 A2
Dormans Park RH19 .... 9 F6
East Grinstead RH19 .... 9 D1
Faygate RH12 .... 16 F1
Goodwood Park PO18 ..... 153 F8
Haslemere GU27 .... 27 C5
Haywards Heath RH16 ..... 85 E4
Henfield BN5 .... 123 E4
Petworth GU28 .... 95 F8
Selsey PO20 .... 206 G8
Shoreham-by-Sea BN43 ... 185 A8
Slinfold RH13 .... 34 D3
Worthing BN11 .... 182 E3
Park Rise Horsham RH12 ... 36 B4
Hove BN3 .... 166 E3
Petworth GU28 .... 95 E7
Park Road Terr 4 BN2 ... 207 C2
Park Royal BN1 .... 187 E6
Park St Brighton BN2 .... 207 C2
Horsham RH12 .... 36 D2
Park Street RH13 .... 34 C3
Park Terr
Bognor Regis PO21 ...... 195 B2
Tillington GU28 .... 73 C1
Park Terr E RH13 .... 36 D1
Park Terr W RH12 .... 36 D1
Park View Brighton BN2 .. 188 C6
Brighton, Preston BN1 .... 187 E8
Crawley RH11 .... 18 C5
Haywards Heath RH16 ..... 85 E6
Horley RH6 .... 2 A3
Park View Ct BN16 ...... 199 C6
Park View Rd BN3 ...... 167 B1
Park View Terr BN1 ..... 187 E8
Park Way Crawley RH10 ... 19 C7
Easebourne GU29 .... 71 B2
Horsham RH12 .... 36 C2
Southwick BN42 .... 185 F8
Park Way Cl BN42 ...... 185 F8
Parker Cl RH10 .... 19 D5
Parker Ct BN41 .... 166 B2
Parker's Cotts PO18 ..... 153 A6
Parkers RH13 .... 56 F3
Parkfield RH12 .... 36 C3
Parkfield Ave PO21 ..... 194 D3
Parkfield Cl RH11 .... 17 F6
Parkfield Ct BN13 ...... 182 A4
Parkfield Rd BN13 ...... 182 A4
Parkhaven Ct BN15 ...... 183 E6
Parkhurst Gr RH6 .... 1 F4
Parkhurst Rd RH6 .... 1 E4
Parkland Bsns Ctr BN15 . 183 D4
Parklands BN43 .... 185 C8
Parklands Ave
Bognor Regis PO21 ...... 195 B4
Worthing BN12 .... 181 D1
Parklands Ct BN12 ...... 181 D2
Parklands Cty Prim Sch
PO19 .... 172 E7
Parklands Rd
Chichester PO19 .... 172 F7
Hassocks BN6 .... 126 F3
Parklawn Ave RH6 .... 1 F5
Parkmead BN2 .... 207 C4
Parkmore Terr BN1 ..... 207 A5
Parks The BN41 .... 166 B3
Parkside
10 Bognor Regis PO21 .... 195 D4
Burgess Hill RH15 .... 106 F3
Crawley RH10 .... 18 E6
East Grinstead RH19 .... 9 C1
Keymer BN6 .... 127 A4
Portslade-by-Sea BN43 ... 165 A1
Worthing BN11 .... 182 E3
Parkside Ave BN17 ..... 198 F5
Parkside Ct BN17 .... 198 F5
Parkside Mews RH12 ..... 36 D2
Parkview BN6 .... 126 A5
Parkway
Bognor Regis PO21 ...... 195 A3
Horley RH6 .... 2 A3
Parkway The BN16 ...... 199 D5
Parnell Cl RH10 .... 19 D4
Parnell Ct 3 BN3 .... 187 B6
Parochial Terr BN2 ..... 207 B2
Parry Cl RH13 .... 37 C4
Parry Dr BN16 .... 199 B5
Parson's Hill BN18 ...... 158 B3
Parsonage Bsns Pk RH12 . 36 E4
Parsonage Est GU31 ...... 68 B4
Parsonage Rd
Henfield BN5 .... 123 E6
Horsham RH13 .... 36 E4
Parsonage Way RH12 ..... 36 E4
Parsons Cl Haslemere GU27 27 C8
Horley RH6 .... 1 E4
Parsons Gn GU27 .... 27 C8
Parsons Wlk Horsham RH12 57 F8
Walberton BN18 .... 176 E8
Parthings La RH12, RH13 .. 57 F8
Partridge La
Cudworth RH12, RH5 .... 3 F3
Newdigate RH5, RH12 .... 3 F3
Pascoe Ct 2 PO19 .... 172 F7
Pashley Ct 10 BN43 ..... 184 F7
Passfield Ent Ctr GU30 ... 24 D8
Passfield Rd GU30 .... 24 E8
Paston Ho BN1 .... 187 F8
Paston Pl BN2 .... 188 D4
Pasture Hill Rd RH16 ..... 85 D6
Pasture The RH10 .... 19 C6
Patcham By-Pass BN1 ... 167 E6
Patcham Grange BN1 .... 167 E5
Patcham High Sch BN1 .. 167 F6
Patcham House Sch BN1 167 E6
Patcham Inf Sch BN1 ... 167 E6
Patcham Jun Sch BN1 ... 167 F6
Patcham Place (YH) BN1 167 E6
Patchdean BN1 .... 167 F5
Patching Cl Crawley RH11 .. 17 F7
Worthing BN12 .... 181 B4
Patching Lodge 5 BN2 .. 188 C5
Patchings RH13 .... 36 F3
Paterson Wilson Rd
BN17 .... 198 E6
Path Link RH10 .... 18 E7
Pathfield Cl RH12 .... 33 D7
Pathfield Rd RH12 .... 33 D7
Pathfields Cl GU27 .... 27 D7
Patnore PO18 .... 152 E7
Patricia Ave BN12 ...... 181 D1
Patricia Cl BN12 .... 181 D1
Patrick's Cl GU33 .... 45 C4
Patrick's Copse Rd GU33 .45 C4
Patrington Cl RH11 .... 18 A3
Patterdale Cl RH11 .... 18 C4
Paulus Ct 1 PO19 .... 172 F7
Pavilion Bldgs BN1 ..... 207 B2
Pavilion Cl BN6 .... 126 E5
Pavilion Ct 15 BN1 ..... 187 E7
Pavilion Ho BN14 .... 182 B3
Pavilion Par BN2 .... 207 B2
Pavilion Rd BN14 .... 182 B3
Pavilion Ret Pk BN2 .... 168 C1
Pavilion St BN2 .... 207 B2
Pavilion Way RH19 .... 22 E8
Pavilions The RH11 .... 39 C6
Pax Cl RH11 .... 17 E4
Paxmead Cres BN14 .... 182 F6
Payne Ave BN3 .... 186 F8
Payne Cl
Bognor Regis PO21 ...... 205 A8
Crawley RH10 .... 19 D8
Payne Terr BN1 .... 168 B1
Paynesfield RH17 .... 83 C3
Paythorne Cl BN42 ..... 165 D1
Paythorne Dro BN5 ..... 145 D4
Payton Dr RH15 .... 106 F2
Payton Ho RH15 .... 107 D3
Peace Cl BN1 .... 168 C1
Peace Rd GU29 .... 93 A2
Peacemaker Cl RH11 ..... 17 E4
Peacheries The PO19 .... 173 C5
Peachey Rd PO20 .... 206 D6
Peacock Cl PO19 .... 153 C1
Peacock Ind Est BN3 .... 187 D7
Peacock La BN1 .... 167 E4
Peacock Wlk 8 RH11 ..... 18 A3
Peacock's Hill RH13 ...... 81 D6
Peacocks RH13 .... 103 A3
Peacocks La RH20 ...... 100 C1
Peak La BN16 .... 200 C4
Peak The PO9 .... 128 E2
Pear Tree Hill RH1 .... 2 A8
Pearson Rd Arundel BN18 .157 F2
Crawley RH10 .... 19 C6
Pearsons Retreat 10
BN11 .... 183 B3
Peartree Cl RH15 .... 106 E3
Peartree Cnr RH13 .... 81 C2
Peary Cl RH12 .... 36 D6
Pease Croft GU31 .... 89 D3
Pease Pottage
Service Area RH11 ...... 39 C7
Pebble Cotts PO21 ..... 194 B2
Pebble Ct PO22 .... 195 E5
Pebble Wlk BN17 .... 179 A3
Peckhams Copse La
PO20 .... 173 D3
Peeks Brook La Fernhill RH6 6 E7
Horley RH6 .... 2 F2
Peel Cl BN17 .... 198 C6
Peel Rd BN2 .... 188 F4
Peerley Cl PO20 .... 202 A6
Peerley Rd PO20 .... 202 A6
Pegasus Cl GU27 .... 26 D5
Pegasus Ct Crawley RH11 .. 17 E4
11 Worthing BN11 .... 182 C2
Pegasus Way RH19 .... 10 B3
Pegler Way RH10, RH11 ... 18 D6
Pegwell Cl RH11 .... 17 F4
Pelham Ct
4 Horsham RH12 .... 36 B2
6 Worthing BN13 .... 182 A5
Pelham Ct Bsns Ctr RH11 .18 B2
Pelham Dr RH11 .... 18 A2
Pelham Pl RH11 .... 18 B2
Pelham Place Cotts RH16 .86 A7
Pelham Rd Lindfield RH16 .. 86 A6
Worthing BN13 .... 182 A5
Pelham Sq BN1 .... 207 B3
Pelham St BN1 .... 207 B3
Pelham Terr Brighton BN2 . 168 C1
Lumley PO10 .... 169 C8
Pelleys La PO20 .... 172 F1
Pemberton Cl BN15 ..... 183 E7
Pembley Gn RH10 .... 7 E3
Pembroke Ave Hove BN3 .187 A7
Worthing BN11 .... 181 F2
Pembroke Cres BN3 ..... 187 A7
Pembroke Ct 2 BN3 .... 187 A6
Pembroke Gdns BN3 .... 187 A6
Pembroke Rd RH10 .... 6 C1
Pembroke Way PO21 .... 194 E4
Pembury Cl
Haywards Heath RH16 ..... 86 B3
Worthing BN14 .... 182 D4
Pembury Rd BN14 ...... 182 D4
Pempeys Terr BN44 ..... 143 C4
Penarth Gdns BN17 ..... 178 D5
Pende Cl BN15 .... 183 D8
Pendean RH15 .... 107 C1
Pendine Ave BN11 ...... 183 A3
Pendragon Ct BN3 ...... 187 A8
Penfold La BN16 .... 179 C3
Penfold Rd Crawley RH10 .. 19 B2
Worthing BN14 .... 182 E5
Penfold Way BN44 ...... 143 D2
Penfolds Pl BN18 .... 158 A2
Penhill Ct 4 BN15 ...... 183 F5
Penhill Rd BN15 .... 183 E5
Penhurst Ct
Worthing BN13 .... 181 B5
Worthing,
Broadwater BN14 .... 182 C6
Penhurst Pl BN2 .... 188 F6
Penland Cl RH16 .... 85 D7
Penland Ct BN44 .... 143 D2
Penland Rd RH16 .... 85 D7
Penland's Cl BN44 ..... 143 D2
Penlands Rise BN44 .... 143 C2
Penlands Vale BN44 .... 143 C2
Penlands Way BN44 ..... 143 D2
Penleigh Cl BN15 .... 183 F5
Penn Cl Crawley RH11 ...... 5 D1
Middleton-on-Sea PO22 ... 196 E5
Penn Cres RH16 .... 86 A5
Penn Gdns RH20 .... 120 E5
Pennels Cl GU30 .... 47 B2
Pennett Ho RH16 .... 85 D2
Pennine Cl RH11 .... 18 B6
Pennington Ho RH16 ..... 86 A3
Penns Ct BN44 .... 143 C4
Pennthorpe Sch RH12 ..... 33 C7
Penny La PO10 .... 169 D8
Pennycord Cl PO20 ..... 206 E5
Pennycress Ave BN13 ... 181 A5
Pennyfields PO22 .... 196 C5
Penrith Ct BN14 .... 182 D5
Pensfold La RH12 .... 33 E5
Penshurst Cl RH10 .... 19 D7
Penstone Cl BN15 ...... 183 D6
Penstone Ct 4 BN43 .... 185 C8
Penstone Pk BN15 ...... 183 E6
Pentland Rd BN13 ...... 181 E8
Penwarden Way PO18 ... 171 C7
Penwith Dr GU27 .... 26 E5
Peperham Ho GU27 .... 27 C7
Peperham Rd GU27 .... 27 C8
Peppard Cl RH10 .... 19 D3
Pepper Ct BN17 .... 198 C5
Pepper Dr RH15 .... 106 F1
Pepper's La BN44 ...... 122 C5
Peppering La BN18 ..... 159 A7
Pepperscoombe La BN44 144 B2
Peppersgate RH13 .... 82 A7
Perche Ct GU29 .... 92 D6
Perching Dro BN5 ...... 145 E4
Percival Terr 14 BN2 .... 188 D4
Percy Rd RH12 .... 36 B3
Percy Row GU28 .... 95 F8
Peregrine Rd BN17 ..... 198 F6
Perimeter Rd E RH6 .... 6 B6
Perimeter Rd N RH6 ...... 5 D8
Perimeter Rd S RH6,RH11 .. 5 E5
Perkstead Ct 6 RH11 ..... 18 A3
Perrots La BN44 .... 143 C2
Perry Ave RH19 .... 9 E3
Perryfield Ho 7 RH11 .... 18 D5
Perryfield La RH13 .... 82 C6
Perryfield Rd RH11 .... 18 D5
Perryfields RH15 .... 106 E4
Perrylands RH6 .... 4 F7
Perrylands La RH6 .... 2 F2
Perryman's La RH17 ...... 66 D3
Perrymount Rd RH16 ..... 85 E5
Perth Cl RH11 .... 5 D1
Perth Ho GU29 .... 92 E6
Perth Way RH12 .... 36 F4
Pescott's Cl PO20 ...... 191 E5
Peskett Cl RH13 .... 56 F3
Peter Gladwin
Cty Prim Sch BN41 ..... 166 B2
Peter Rd BN15 .... 183 C4
Peter Weston Pl PO19 ... 173 B6
Peter's La PO20 .... 206 A8
Peter's Pl PO20 .... 206 A8
Peterborough Rd RH10 ... 18 E2
Peterhouse Cl PO21 .... 194 F4
Peterhouse Par RH10 ...... 6 C1
Peterlee Wlk RH11 .... 17 E2
Petersfield Rd GU29 ..... 92 E8
Petland Gdns RH16 ...... 85 F3
Petlands Rd RH16 .... 85 E3
Pett Cl BN2 .... 188 F6
Petworth Ave BN12 ..... 181 C1
Petworth CE Prim Sch
GU28 .... 95 F7
Petworth Cottage Mus
GU28 .... 95 F8
Petworth Ct Crawley RH11 .17 F3
Haslemere GU27 .... 27 D6
5 Rustington BN16 ...... 199 B3
Petworth Dr
Burgess Hill RH15 .... 107 A4
Horsham RH12 .... 36 F7
Petworth Ho 14 BN3 ..... 187 D7
Petworth House & Pk
GU28 .... 95 F7
Petworth Pk GU28 .... 73 D2
Petworth Rd
Ansteadbrook GU27 .... 28 B6
Brighton BN1 .... 168 B6
Pevensey Cl RH10 .... 19 C5
Pevensey Gdn BN11 ..... 182 A1
Pevensey Rd
Bognor Regis PO21 ...... 195 A4
7 Brighton BN2 .... 188 C8
Southwater RH13 .... 58 A2
Worthing BN11 .... 182 A1
Peverel Rd Crawley RH11 .. 17 E5
Worthing BN14 .... 182 A4
Peveril Cl BN15 .... 183 B6
Peveril Dr BN15 .... 183 B6
Pharos Quay BN17 ...... 198 C5
Pheasant Cotts PO18 ... 132 F6
Philip Ct
Bognor Regis PO20 ...... 194 C3
8 Hove BN3 .... 187 C7
Phillips Bsns Ctr PO19 .. 172 E5
Phillips Cl RH10 .... 19 C2
Philliswood La PO18 .... 110 D3
Philpots La RH19 .... 42 D5
Philpots Manor Sch RH19 .42 C5
Phoenix Brewery
Halls BN2 .... 207 C4
Phoenix Cl PO19 .... 173 A5
Phoenix Cres BN42 ..... 185 D8
Phoenix La RH19 .... 23 E6
Phoenix Pl BN2 .... 207 C3
Phoenix Rise BN2 ...... 207 C3
Phoenix Way BN42 ..... 185 D8
Phrosso Rd BN11 .... 181 F1
Pickers Gn RH16 .... 86 A8
Picketts La RH1 .... 2 C8
Pickhurst La RH20 .... 98 B6
Pickhurst Rd GU8 .... 29 D8
Pickwell La RH17 .... 83 F4
Picton St BN2 .... 188 C7
Picts Hill RH13 .... 58 A7
Picts La RH13 .... 82 A4
Pier Four Rd N RH6 .... 5 F8
Pier Rd BN17 .... 198 D4
Pierpoint Cl BN6 .... 125 F6
Piers Secomb Cl RH20 .. 117 D5
Pigbush La RH14 .... 32 A7
Pigeonhouse La BN16 ... 199 E4
Piggery Hall La PO20 ... 190 F1
Piggott Ct RH13 .... 36 E1
Piggott's Bsns Pk 5
BN11 .... 182 C3
Pike The RH20 .... 141 F7
Pilgrim Ct RH16 .... 86 A5
Pilgrims Cl 1 BN14 ..... 182 B3
Pilgrims Terr BN13 ..... 182 A3
Pilgrims Way PO21 ..... 194 B1
Pilgrims Wlk BN13 ..... 182 A3
Pilot Ho 1 BN2 .... 207 C2
Piltdown Rd BN2 .... 188 F6
Pine Cl Billingshurst RH14 .. 55 C1
Crawley RH11 .... 5 C1
Heath Common RH20 ..... 120 B3
Midhurst GU29 .... 92 F5
Pine Cotts GU33 .... 45 C7
Pine Ct PO10 .... 149 B4
Pine Gdns RH6 .... 2 A2
Pine Gr Chichester PO19 .. 152 C1
East Grinstead RH19 .... 9 B3
Pine Shaw RH10 .... 19 D7
Pine Tree Cl BN6 .... 126 B5
Pine Trees BN6 .... 126 D4
Pine Trees Cl BN16 ..... 179 F7
Pine Trees Ct BN6 ...... 126 D4
Pine View Cl GU27 .... 27 C8
Pine Way Cl RH19 .... 22 E7
Pine Wlk
Bognor Regis PO21 ...... 194 D4
Liss Forest GU33 .... 45 C6
Pineham Copse RH16 ..... 85 F4
Pinehurst
Burgess Hill RH15 .... 107 A1
Horsham RH12 .... 36 C4
Pinehurst Pk PO21 ..... 194 D4
Pines Ave BN14 .... 182 D7
Pines Rd GU30 .... 24 E4
Pines The Angmering BN16 179 F4
2 Brighton BN2 .... 207 C4
Haywards Heath RH16 ..... 86 B4
Horsham RH12 .... 37 C5
Hove BN3 .... 187 E6
Yapton BN18 .... 176 F3
Pinetops RH12 .... 37 C4
Pinetrees Cl RH10 .... 7 B3
Pinewood 5 BN1 .... 167 E3
Pinewood Cl
Brighton BN1 .... 167 D2
Broadridge Heath RH12 .... 35 D3
East Preston BN16 ...... 200 A6
Pinewood Ct
Haywards Heath RH16 ..... 85 D2
West Lavington GU29 ..... 93 A6
Pinewood Gdns PO21 ... 195 A3
Pinewood Ho PO19 ..... 153 B1
Pinewood Way
Haywards Heath RH16 ..... 85 D2
Midhurst GU29 .... 92 E5
Pinfold 4 RH16 .... 85 D6
Pinkhurst La RH13 .... 35 A2
Pinks La PO20 .... 191 D3
Pinland Rd RH13 .... 102 F1
Pipers Cl Hove BN3 ..... 166 C3

Pipers Cl *continued*
Southwater RH13 57 F1
Pipers End RH13 34 E3
Pipers La Ebernoe GU28 52 A4
Northchapel GU28 51 A7
Pipers Mead PO20 191 D3
Pirles Pl RH12 36 C2
Pit La BN6 126 A5
Pitcroft La GU31 88 B5
Pitcroft The PO19 173 C8
Pitfold Ave GU27 26 D6
Pitfold Cl GU27 26 E6
Pitsham La GU29 92 D5
Pitsham Wood GU29 92 D6
Plainfields Ave BN1 168 A7
Plainwood Cl PO19 152 F2
Plaistow Cl BN2 188 F6
Plaistow Inf Sch RH14 30 F3
Plaistow Rd Ifold RH14 31 D1
Kirdford RH14 53 B5
Ramsnest Common GU8 29 D6
Plantain Cres RH11 18 A2
Plantation Cl BN13 181 F7
Plantation Rd GU33 45 D2
Plantation Rise BN13 182 A7
Plantation The
East Preston BN16 200 A5
Storrington RH20 119 B1
Worthing BN13 182 A7
Plantation Way
Storrington RH20 119 C1
Worthing BN13 181 F7
Plat The RH12 36 A3
Platt The Dormansland RH7 10 A8
Handcross RH17 61 C8
Haywards Heath RH16 86 B5
Platts Mdw RH14 77 C8
Plaw Hatch La RH18, RH19 43 E5
Playden Cl 1 BN2 188 E4
Playden Ct 3 RH11 18 A3
Pleasant La PO10 169 F1
Plough Cl RH11 17 F8
Plough La RH12 36 E5
Plover Cl
Bognor Regis PO22 195 C7
Bracklesham PO20 202 A6
Crawley RH11 18 C8
Plovers Rd RH13 36 F3
Plovers The BN15 184 A5
Plumb Pudding Cnr GU28 96 D6
Plummerden La RH16 64 F2
Plumpton Rd BN2 188 D6
Plumtree Cross RH13 57 A5
Plumtree Cross La RH13 57 A5
Plymouth Ave BN2 168 F1
Polecat La RH13 80 C8
Poles La RH11 5 C3
Polestub La RH17 84 F7
Policemans La BN6 125 F5
Poling Cl BN12 181 B4
Poling St BN18 179 B7
Pollard Ct BN11 182 A2
Pollard's Hill RH13 80 A6
Pollards RH11 18 A5
Pollards Dr RH13 36 F2
Polperro Cl BN12 200 E5
Pomper La BN6 106 A2
Pond Cl Billingshurst RH14 77 C8
Loxwood RH14 31 F4
Pond Copse La RH14 31 F5
Pond Farm Cl RH13 57 F4
Pond La BN13 181 D7
Pond Mews BN13 181 D7
Pond Rd
Bracklesham PO20 202 B6
Shoreham-by-Sea BN43 184 F7
Pond Rise RH20 99 E1
Pond Way RH19 10 B1
Pond Wood Rd RH10 19 A8
Pondcroft Rd RH16 86 B7
Pondfield Rd RH12 33 D8
Pondtail Cl RH12 36 D6
Pondtail Copse RH12 36 D6
Pondtail Dr RH12 36 D7
Pondtail Rd RH12 36 D6
Pony Farm BN14 161 F6
Pook La PO18 153 A5
Pookbourne La BN6 105 E4
Pool Valley BN2 207 B1
Popes Mead GU27 27 C7
Poplar Ave BN3 166 E3
Poplar Cl Brighton BN1 167 F2
Crawley RH11 5 C1
Hove BN3 166 E3
Poplar Ct Pulborough RH20 98 A2
Worthing BN13 181 C5
Poplar Rd BN13 181 C5
Poplar Way GU29 92 E5
Poplars The
Burndell BN18 177 A3
Ferring BN12 200 E4
Horsham RH12 36 E3
Keymer BN6 127 A3
Poppy Cl Rustington BN17 179 A3
Southwater RH13 58 A3
Porchester Cl RH13 58 A2
Port Hall Ave BN1 187 E8
Port Hall Mews BN1 187 E8
Port Hall Pl BN1 187 E8
Port Hall Rd BN1 187 E8
Port Hall St BN1 187 E8
Portfield Ave BN1 168 A6
Portfield Ret Pk PO19 173 D7
Portfield Trad Ctr PO19 173 D5
Portfield Way PO19, PO20 173 D8
Portland Ave BN3 186 E7
Portland Cl BN17 199 A6
Portland Gate BN3 186 E7
Portland Ho 5 RH19 22 F8
Portland Mews 19 BN2 188 C4
Portland Pl 18 BN2 188 C4
Portland Rd
Burgess Hill RH15 106 F3
East Grinstead RH19 22 F8
Hove BN3 186 E7
Worthing BN11 182 D2
Portland Road Trad Est
BN3 186 D8
Portland Sq Liss GU33 45 B4
Worthing BN11 182 D2
Portland St BN1 207 A2
Portland Villas BN3 186 D7
Portside BN2 188 F3
Portslade Com Coll
Portslade-by-Sea BN41 165 F2
Portslade-by-Sea BN41 166 A1
Portslade Com Coll
(Lower) BN41 166 A3
Portslade Inf Sch BN41 186 B8
Portslade Sta BN3 186 C8
Portsmouth La RH16 85 F8
Portsmouth Rd
Bramshott GU26,GU30 25 E6
Liphook GU30 25 B2
Portsmouth Wood RH16 85 F8
Portsmouth Wood Cl
RH16 85 F8
Portsmouth Wood Dr
RH16 85 F8
Portway BN44 143 C2
Post Office La PO20 173 D1
Post View RH20 140 E8
Posthorses RH20 121 A4
Potters Croft RH13 36 E2
Potters Field GU33 45 C4
Potters Gn RH13 81 E2
Potters La RH15 106 F1
Potters Mead BN17 178 C3
Potters Pl RH12 36 C2
Pottersfield RH10 18 D7
Pottery La PO18 170 D8
Poulner Cl PO22 196 A5
Poulter's Cnr BN14 182 A6
Poulter's La BN14 182 B6
Pound Cl Loxwood RH14 31 F5
Petworth GU28 95 F7
Pound Cnr RH13 101 D7
Pound Farm Rd PO19 173 C6
Pound Gate BN6 126 D3
Pound Hill
Fst & Mid Schs RH10 19 C7
Pound Hill Par RH10 19 C7
Pound Hill Pl RH10 19 C6
Pound La
Little Parkminster RH13 103 D8
Mannings Heath RH13 59 C6
Shipley RH13 79 E2
Upper Beeding BN44 144 B2
Pound Rd Walberton BN18 156 D1
West Wittering PO20 190 B2
Pound St GU28 95 F8
Pound The
Bognor Regis PO21 194 E2
Burgess Hill RH15 106 F4
Poundfield La RH14 31 B3
Povey Cross Rd RH6 1 E1
Poveys Cl RH15 106 D3
Powell Cl RH6 1 E4
Powis Gr BN1 207 A3
Powis Rd BN1 187 E6
Powis Sq BN1 187 E6
Powis Villas BN1 207 A3
Poynes Rd RH6 1 E5
Poynings Crossways BN6 125 B1
Poynings Dr BN3 166 F3
Poynings Rd RH11 17 E5
Poynter Rd BN3 187 A8
Poyntz Cl PO19 172 F3
Pratton Ave BN15 183 D7
Prawn Cl PO20 206 C8
Prebendal Sch The PO19 172 F6
Precinct The PO21 194 F4
Prescott Gdns RH15 107 A3
Preston Ave BN16 199 D5
Preston Cir BN1 207 B4
Preston Dro BN1 167 D2
Preston Grange BN1 167 E1
Preston Manor (Mus)
BN1 167 E1
Preston Paddock BN16 199 E5
Preston Park Ave BN1 167 F1
Preston Park Sta BN1 167 D2
Preston Rd BN1 187 F8
Preston St BN1 187 E5
Preston Village Mews
BN1 167 E1
Prestonville Ct 1 BN1 207 A4
Prestonville Rd BN1, BN3 207 A4
Prestwick Cl RH11 17 D5
Prestwood Cl RH11 5 B1
Prestwood La RH11 4 C3
Pretoria Ave GU29 92 E7
Pretoria Rd 4 GU29 92 E7
Price Way RH17 64 B7
Priceholm RH17 64 B7
Priest Croft Cl RH11 18 A6
Priest House (Mus) The
RH19 42 E6
Priestley Way Crawley RH10 6 A3
Middleton-on-Sea PO22 196 D5
Prime Cl BN18 176 E8
Primrose Ave RH6 2 B1
Primrose Cl
Burgess Hill RH15 106 D4
Crawley RH11 18 B3
Rustington BN17 179 A3
Primrose Copse RH12 36 E7
Primrose Ct BN44 143 D2
Primrose La GU33 45 F4
Prince Albert St BN1 207 B2
Prince Ave BN15 184 B5
Prince Charles Cl
BN41, BN42 166 A1
Prince Of Wales Ct BN41 186 F6
Prince Regent's Cl BN2 188 E4
Prince Regent's Ct 2
BN2 188 E4
Prince William Cl BN14 182 A8
Prince William Ct 4
PO21 195 D3
Prince's Cres BN2 207 C5
Prince's Dr PO18 133 E1
Prince's Pl BN1 207 B2
Prince's Rd BN2 188 B8
Prince's St BN2 207 B2
Prince's Terr BN2 188 E4
Princes Ave BN3 187 A6
Princes Cres BN3 187 A6
Princes Croft PO21 194 A1
Princes Ct 6 BN3 187 A6
Princes Gate BN11 181 F2
Princes Sq BN3 187 A6
Princess Anne Rd RH12 33 D6
Princess Ave
Bognor Regis PO21 195 A2
Worthing BN13 181 F4
Princess Ct BN13 181 F3
Princess Ho 20 PO21 195 D3
Princess Margaret Rd
RH12 33 D7
Princess Rd RH11 18 C6
Prings La RH13 81 C8
Prinsep Rd BN3 187 A8
Prinsted La PO10 169 F7
Priors Acre PO18 154 D3
Priors Cl Breach PO10 150 A1
Upper Beeding BN44 144 A2
Priors Leaze La
PO10,PO18 150 C1
Priors Waye PO21 194 A2
Priors Wlk RH10 18 F6
Priors Wood GU27 26 F6
Priory Cl
Bognor Regis PO21 205 B8
Boxgrove PO18 154 D3
Horley RH6 1 F4
Lancing BN15 183 B7
Worthing BN14 182 A4
Priory Ct
17 Bognor Regis PO21 195 D3
Brighton BN1 187 F8
Priory Field BN44 144 A2
Priory Gate BN15 183 E6
Priory La PO19 173 A7
Priory Rd Arundel BN18 157 F2
Burgess Hill RH15 107 A1
Chichester PO19 173 A7
Forest Row RH18 23 D2
Hassocks BN6 126 E5
Rustington BN16 199 B6
Priory The Brighton BN1 167 D5
5 Hove BN3 187 B5
Priory Way RH16 85 F4
Proctor Cl RH10 19 C4
Promenade The
Emsworth PO10 169 B7
Littlehampton BN17 198 E3
Pronger's Cnr RH13 59 E3
Prospect Pl Crawley RH11 18 C6
3 Worthing BN11 182 D1
Providence Pl
Brighton BN1 207 B4
6 Chichester PO19 172 F7
Providence Terr BN11 182 E2
Providence The 5 PO19 172 F7
Pruetts La GU31, GU33 45 B1
Pryors Gn PO21 194 C2
Pryors La PO21 194 C1
Puckshott Way GU27 27 D8
Pudding La RH6 4 E7
Puffin Rd RH11 17 D5
Pulborough Brooks
Nature Reserve RH20 118 D5
Pulborough Cl BN2 188 F7
Pulborough Rd RH20 119 B2
Pulborough Sta RH20 98 A2
Pulborough Way PO22 196 D6
Pump Ho The BN3 186 D8
Punch Copse Rd RH10 18 F7
Punches La PO20 193 D5
Punnetts Ct RH11 17 F2
Purbeck Pl BN17 198 C5
Purcell Rd RH11 17 F3
Purley Cl RH10 19 D3
Purton Rd RH12 36 B4
Putmans La GU31 89 B7
Puttick Cl RH20 119 E2
Puttock Cl GU27 26 D5
Pyecombe Ct 4 RH11 17 F3
Pyecombe St BN45 147 A6
Pyrford Cl PO21 194 B2

Q

Quadrangle The BN14 161 E4
Quadrant BN1 207 A2
Quadrant The
Keymer BN6 127 A4
Worthing BN12 181 C3
Quail Cl RH12 36 D7
Quakers La RH16 86 A5
Quantock Cl Crawley RH11 18 B6
Worthing BN13 181 F8
Quantock Rd BN13 181 F7
Quantocks 2 BN17 198 D6
Quarries The RH13 59 D6
Quarry Bank Rd BN1 168 B2
Quarry Cl
Burgess hill RH15 107 D3
Horsham RH12 36 F6
Quarry Hill RH16 85 C6
Quarry La PO19 173 C5
Quarry Lane Ind Est
PO19 173 C5
Quarry Rise RH19 10 A3
Quarry Way RH13 57 F2
Quarterbrass Farm Rd
RH12 36 D7
Quashetts The
Worthing BN14 182 D4
Worthing BN14 182 D5
Quay Ct BN43 185 B6
Quay The 5 BN43 185 A6
Quayside BN17 198 B5
Quebec St BN2 207 C3
Queen Alexandra Ave
BN3 167 A3
Queen Caroline Cl BN3 167 A3
Queen Elizabeth Ave
RH15 107 A2
Queen Elizabeth II Silver
Jubilee Sch The RH13 36 F1
Queen Elizabeth Rd RH12 33 D7
Queen Mary Ave BN3 167 A3
Queen Par 2 RH13 36 D1
Queen Sq BN1 207 A2
Queen St Arundel BN18 158 B2
Emsworth PO10 169 C8
Horsham RH13 36 D1
Littlehampton BN17 198 D5
Worthing BN14 182 C4
Queen Victoria Ave BN3 167 A3
Queen Victoria Hospl
The RH19 9 F3
Queen's Ave PO19 172 F4
Queen's Ct RH16 85 F6
Queen's Gdns
Brighton BN1 207 B3
Hove BN3 187 C5
Stockbridge PO19 172 F4
Queen's Par BN3 166 E2
Queen's Park Prim Sch
BN2 188 C5
Queen's Park Rd BN2 188 C6
Queen's Park Rise BN2 188 C6
Queen's Park Terr BN2 188 C6
Queen's Pl Brighton BN1 207 B4
Hove BN3 187 C6
Shoreham-by-Sea BN43 184 F7
Queen's Rd Brighton BN1 207 A3
East Grinstead RH19 9 E1
Horley RH6 2 A3
Worthing BN11 182 C1
Queen's Sq PO21 195 D3
Queen's Wlk RH19 9 E1
Queens Cres RH15 107 A2
Queens Ct 1 RH13 36 D1
Queens Dr BN6 126 F4
Queens Fields E PO21 194 F4
Queens Fields W PO21 194 F4
Queens Fields Wlk PO21 194 F4
Queens Gate RH6 6 A8
Queens La BN18 158 B2
Queens Rd
Haywards Heath RH16 85 E6
Lancing BN15 183 F5
Liphook GU30 24 C3
Southwick BN42 165 E1
Queens Sq RH10 18 D6
Queens St GU29 70 A2
Queensborough Ct 5
BN11 182 A3
Queensbury Mews BN1 187 E5
Queensdown Sch BN1 168 C3
Queensdown School Rd
BN1, BN2 168 D2
Queensmead PO21 204 F8
Queensway
Bognor Regis PO21 195 C3
Bognor Regis, Aldwick PO21 194 E1
Brighton BN2 188 D6
Crawley RH10 18 E6
East Grinstead RH19 9 E1
Horsham RH13 36 C1
Lancing BN15 183 E6
Queensway Ho 7 PO21 195 C3
Quell Farm Ind Est RH20 117 E4
Querneby Cl BN43 185 D7
Quest Cl PO19 173 B6
Quinta Carmen 10 BN11 182 B1

R

Racecourse Rd RH6 6 A8
Racecourse Way RH6 5 F8
Rackfield GU27 26 D7
Rackham Cl Crawley RH11 18 D4
Worthing BN13 181 F5
Rackham Rd
Amberley BN18 138 F7
3 Littlehampton BN16 199 B3
Worthing BN13 181 F5
Rackham St
Amberley BN18,RH20 139 A8
Rackham RH20 139 C8
Racton Rd PO10 149 C3
Radford Rd
Bognor Regis PO21,PO22 195 B5
Tinsley Green RH10 6 C4
Radinden Dr BN3 167 D1
Radinden Manor Rd BN3 187 D8
Radnor Cl BN13 181 F4
Radnor Rd BN13 181 F4
Raglan Ave BN13 181 E5
Raglan Ct Brighton BN1 207 A2
5 Worthing BN11 182 A2
Raglan Terr PO10 149 C1
Railey Rd RH10 18 E7
Railway App
East Grinstead RH19 9 E1
Worthing BN11 182 D3
Railway Cotts
Horsted Keynes RH17 65 A8
Maplehurst RH13 80 E2
Railway St BN1 207 A3
Railway Terr GU29 92 D7
Rainbow Way RH20 119 F3
Rake Bsns Pk GU33 46 B4
Rake CE Fst Inf Sch GU33 46 B5
Rake Rd Liss GU33 45 D4
Milland GU30 47 A2
Rakers Ridge RH12 36 D5
Raleigh Cl BN43 184 F6
Raleigh Cres BN12 181 D3
Raleigh Ct RH10 6 A3
Raleigh Rd PO21 194 C3
Raleigh Way BN12 181 C3
Raleigh Wlk RH10 18 E4
Rambledown La RH20 119 C6
Ramblers Ct RH12 35 E3
Ramblers Way RH11 39 B8
Ramillies Gdns PO22 196 C5
Ramsey Cl Horley RH6 1 F3
Horsham RH12 36 D5
Ramsey Ct 17 RH11 18 B1
Randall Schofield Ct RH10 19 A7
Randiddles Cl BN6 126 B4
Ranelagh Villas BN3 187 B8
Rangers Lodge RH13 36 E2
Ranmore Cl RH11 39 C8
Ransome Cl RH11 17 E3
Ranville Cl GU28 95 E7
Ranworth Cl PO22 195 F5
Rapeland Hill RH12 15 F2
Raphael Rd BN3 186 F7
Rapley Ave RH20 119 B2
Rascals Cl RH13 79 F7
Rastrick Cl RH15 106 F1
Ratham La
Broadbridge PO18 171 C8
West Ashling PO18 151 C1
Rathbone Ho RH11 18 B3
Rathlin Rd RH11 18 B3
Raughmere Ct PO18 152 F4
Raughmere Dr
PO18, PO19 152 F4
Raven Cl RH12 36 E6
Raven La RH11 18 C8
Raven's Rd BN43 184 F7
Ravendene Ct 3 RH11 18 D5
Ravens Croft 7 BN16 199 C4
Ravens Way PO22 195 B6
Ravensbourne Ave BN43 164 F1
Ravensbourne Cl 11
BN43 164 F1
Ravenscroft RH20 140 D8
Ravenscroft Ct RH12 36 C3
Ravenswood BN6 126 E4
Ravenswood Ct BN13 182 A4
Ravenswood Rd RH15 107 B3
Ravenwood Ct PO21 194 E2
Raworth Cl RH10 19 C4
Rawson Ct 10 BN16 199 B4
Rawson Villas BN16 199 C6
Raycroft Cl PO21 194 F2
Rayden Cl BN17 198 E5
Raymede Ho BN11 182 B3
Raymer Wlk RH6 2 C4
Rayner Ct BN5 123 E4
Reading Rd BN2 188 F4
Reapers Cl RH12 36 D5
Record Rd PO10 149 A1
Rectory Cl Ashington RH20 121 A5
Hove BN3 186 D7
Pulborough RH20 98 C2
Shoreham-by-Sea BN43 185 D7
Storrington RH20 119 D1
Rectory Cotts 1 RH20 119 D1
Rectory Ct 15 BN43 185 C8
Rectory Farm Rd BN15 183 B7
Rectory Gdns BN14 182 C5
Rectory La
Angmering BN16 179 F5
Bramshott GU30 25 D7
Charlwood RH6 4 D7
Church Norton PO20 204 B3
Crawley RH11 17 F8
Pulborough RH20 98 C2
Warminghurst RH20 120 E6
Rectory Mews 1 BN14 182 A5
Rectory Rd
Shoreham-by-Sea BN43 185 D7
Storrington RH20 119 D1
Worthing BN13, BN14 182 A5
Rectory Wlk Lancing BN15 183 C7
Storrington RH20 119 D1
Red Acre Ct PO21 195 D4
Red Admiral St RH12 36 E5
Red Deer Cl RH13 37 B4
Red Ho BN13 182 A7
Red House Ct GU31 68 B4
Red La RH13 79 D1
Red Lion St GU29 92 F7
Red Oak Ct GU29 71 A2
Red Ridges PO21 195 A2

Red River Ct RH12 . . . . .36 B5
Redcotts 1 BN11 . . . . .182 B2
Redditch Cl RH11 . . . . .17 E2
Redehall Rd RH6 . . . . .7 C8
Redford Ave RH12 . . . . .36 B4
Redgarth Ct RH19 . . . . .9 B3
Redgrave Dr RH10 . . . . . . .19 D5
Redhill Cl BN1 . . . . .167 C5
Redhill Distribution Ctr
RH1 . . . . .2 A8
Redhill Dr BN1 . . . . .167 C5
Redhill Rd PO9 . . . . .128 D1
Redhouse Mews GU30 . . . .25 C2
Redkiln Cl RH13 . . . . .36 F4
Redkiln Way RH13 . . . . .36 F3
Redlands La
New Brighton PO10 . . . . . . .149 B4
Shipton Green PO20 . . . . . .190 F3
Redmoor PO20 . . . . .191 E4
Redshank Ct 5 RH11 . . . . . .17 D5
Redvers Rd BN2 . . . . .168 D1
Redwing Cl Horsham RH13 . .36 F3
Littlehampton BN17 . . . . . . .178 C4
Redwood Cl Crawley RH10 . .18 E8
Worthing BN13 . . . . .181 C5
Redwood Ct BN17 . . . . .198 F5
Redwood Dr RH16 . . . . . . .85 D3
Redwood Manor GU27 . . . .27 C7
Redwood Pl PO21 . . . . . . .194 E2
Reed Cl RH20 . . . . .119 C1
Reed Pond Wlk RH16 . . . . .86 A4
Reed's La BN6 . . . . .125 B8
Reedings RH11 . . . . .17 D4
Reeds La Liss Forest GU33 . .45 F6
Southwater Street RH13 . . . .58 B3
Reef Cl BN17 . . . . .198 F4
Rees Cl BN13 . . . . .181 B6
Reeves Hill BN1 . . . . .168 D5
Regal Dr 10 RH19 . . . . .22 F8
Regency Ct Brighton BN1 .167 D3
Ferring BN12 . . . . .200 F6
Worthing BN13 . . . . .182 A6
Regency Mews 15 BN1 . . . .187 E5
Regency Rd BN1 . . . . .207 A2
Regency Sq BN1 . . . . .187 E5
Regent Arc BN1 . . . . .207 B2
Regent Bsns Pk RH15 . . .106 E2
Regent Cl BN15 . . . . .184 B6
Regent Hill BN1 . . . . .207 A2
Regent Mews 11 PO21 . . .195 B2
Regent Row BN1 . . . . .207 A2
Regent St BN1 . . . . .207 B2
Regents Cl RH11 . . . . .18 C2
Regents Way PO21 . . . . . .194 F4
Regis Ave PO21 . . . . .205 B8
Regis Ct
Bognor Regis PO21 . . . . . . .195 D3
Worthing BN11 . . . . .182 A1
Regis Ho 17 PO21 . . . . . . .195 C3
Regnum Ct PO19 . . . . .173 A7
Reigate Cl RH10 . . . . .6 D1
Reigate Ct BN11 . . . . .181 F2
Reigate Rd Brighton BN1 .167 D1
Hookwood RH2, RH6 . . . . .1 C4
Worthing BN11 . . . . .181 F3
Renoir Ct PO22 . . . . .195 A6
Renoir Mews PO22 . . . . . .195 A6
Renton Cl RH14 . . . . .77 D8
Rew La PO19 . . . . .152 F3
Rex Ct Shottermill GU27 . . . .26 F6
Shottermill GU27 . . . . .26 F6
Reydon Ho BN11 . . . . .182 F3
Reynard Cl RH12 . . . . .37 B5
Reynolds La BN18 . . . . . . .156 D4
Reynolds Pl RH11 . . . . .18 C7
Reynolds Rd Crawley RH11 .18 C7
Hove BN3 . . . . .186 F7
Rhodes Way RH10 . . . . .18 F3
Ribbetts Cotts BN6 . . . . . .126 A5
Ribbetts Ho BN6 . . . . .126 A5
Rices Hill RH19 . . . . .9 E1
Richard Allen Ct BN2 . . . .168 C1
Richard Ho 6 PO21 . . . . . .195 C2
Richardson Ct
16 Crawley RH11 . . . . .18 B1
5 Hove BN3 . . . . .186 F7
Richardson Rd BN3 . . . . .186 F7
Richmond Ave
Bognor Regis PO21 . . . . . . .195 B2
Chichester PO19 . . . . .153 A1
Richmond Ave W PO21 . .195 A3
Richmond Cl 1 BN16 . . . .199 E6
Richmond Ct
9 Brighton BN3 . . . . .187 E7
Crawley RH10 . . . . .18 E5
3 Rustington BN16 . . . . . . .199 B5
Worthing BN11 . . . . .182 C2
Richmond Gdns 2 BN2 . .207 C3
Richmond Ho 11 PO21 . . .195 C3
Richmond Hts 12 BN2 . . .207 C3
Richmond Par BN2 . . . . . .207 C3
Richmond Pl BN2 . . . . . . .207 B3
Richmond Rd
16 Bognor Regis PO21 . . . .195 C3
Brighton BN2 . . . . .188 B8
Horsham RH12 . . . . .36 D4
Westerton PO18 . . . . .153 F3
Worthing BN11 . . . . .182 D2
Richmond Rd N 6 PO21 .195 D4
Richmond Sq RH19 . . . . .9 D2
Richmond St BN2 . . . . . . .207 C3
Richmond Terr BN2 . . . . .207 C4
Richmond Villas PO22 . . . .195 F3
Richmond Way RH19 . . . . .22 F8
Rickfield RH11 . . . . .18 A5
Rickwood RH6 . . . . .2 B4
Riddens The RH12 . . . . .33 A6
Ride The Brighton BN1 . . . .167 F1
Ifold RH14 . . . . .31 C2
Ridge Cl BN41 . . . . .166 A4
Ridge The RH12 . . . . .33 E8
Ridge View BN1 . . . . .168 E5
Ridge Way RH17 . . . . .86 B2
Ridgedale RH10 . . . . .21 B8
Ridgehurst Dr RH12 . . . . . .35 F1
Ridgeside RH10 . . . . .18 F6
Ridgeside Ave BN1 . . . . . .167 E5
Ridgeway
East Grinstead RH19 . . . . . . .22 E7
Southwick BN41, BN42 . . . .165 F1
Ridgeway Cl BN42 . . . . . . .165 F1
Ridgeway The
Burgess Hill RH15 . . . . .107 B4
Chichester PO19 . . . . .172 E7
Fernhurst GU27 . . . . .49 B6
Horley RH6 . . . . .2 A1
Horsham RH12 . . . . .36 B4
Ridgway The PO22 . . . . . . .196 B4
Ridings The
Bognor Regis PO21 . . . . . . .194 C1
Burgess Hill RH15 . . . . .107 C2
Crawley RH10 . . . . .19 D7
Fontwell BN18 . . . . .156 A2
Liss GU33 . . . . .45 D4
Littlehampton BN16 . . . . . . .199 F4
Steyning BN44 . . . . .143 D1
Ridley's Ct RH10 . . . . .19 D8
Ridleys RH19 . . . . .42 E6
Rife La PO20 . . . . .206 B8
Rife Way
Bognor Regis PO22 . . . . . . .195 F4
Ferring BN12 . . . . .200 E6
Rifeside Gdns BN12 . . . . .180 E3
Rigden Rd BN3 . . . . .167 C1
Rikkyo Sch in England
RH12 . . . . .32 D8
Riley Rd BN2 . . . . .168 C1
Rill Wlk RH19 . . . . .10 B1
Rillside RH10 . . . . .19 A3
Rimmer Cl RH11 . . . . .39 B8
Ring Rd BN15 . . . . .163 F1
Ring Rd N RH6 . . . . .6 C8
Ring Rd S RH6 . . . . .6 C7
Ringley Ave RH6 . . . . .2 A2
Ringley Oak RH12 . . . . .36 F4
Ringley Rd RH12 . . . . .36 E4
Ringmer Cl BN1 . . . . .168 E4
Ringmer Rd Brighton BN1 .168 E4
Brighton BN1 . . . . .168 F4
Worthing BN13 . . . . .181 E5
Ringwood Cl RH10 . . . . . . .18 E4
Ripley Rd BN11 . . . . .181 F3
Ripon Gdns PO21 . . . . . . .194 E3
Rise The Crawley RH10 . . . .19 D6
East Grinstead RH19 . . . . . . .22 F8
Lindfield RH16 . . . . .86 B5
Partridge Green RH13 . . . . .103 A4
Portslade-by-Sea BN41 . . . .165 F2
Rissom Ct BN1 . . . . .167 E2
Ritchie Cl RH10 . . . . .19 C2
River Cl BN43 . . . . .184 E6
River La River GU28 . . . . . . .72 E3
Watersfield RH20 . . . . .117 B4
River Mead Crawley RH11 . . .5 A1
Horsham RH12 . . . . .36 B1
River Rd Arundel BN18 . . . .158 B2
Littlehampton BN17 . . . . . . .198 C5
River St PO10 . . . . .149 D4
River's Rd RH16 . . . . .63 D3
Riverbank Bsns Ctr BN43 184 E7
Riverhill La GU28, RH20 . . .96 E7
Rivermead RH20 . . . . .98 D1
Rivermead Ct PO10 . . . . .149 C3
Riverside Chichester PO19 .173 B7
Forest Row RH18 . . . . .23 E3
Horley RH6 . . . . .2 A1
Horsham RH12 . . . . .36 A2
Littlehampton BN17 . . . . . . .198 C4
Shoreham-by-Sea BN43 . . . .184 F6
Southwick BN42 . . . . .185 E7
Storrington RH20 . . . . .119 D2
Upper Beeding BN44 . . . . . .144 A2
Riverside Bsns Ctr BN43 .185 A7
Riverside Cl GU33 . . . . .45 B4
Riverside Ct RH20 . . . . .98 A1
Riverside Ho BN43 . . . . . .184 E6
Riverside Ind Est BN17 . . .198 B5
Riverside Rd BN43 . . . . . .184 F6
Rixons Cl RH17 . . . . .65 C5
Rixons Orch RH17 . . . . .65 C5
Robell Way RH20 . . . . . . .119 F3
Robert Lodge BN2 . . . . . . .188 F4
Robert St BN1 . . . . .207 B3
Robert Way RH12 . . . . .36 F7
Roberts Cl RH13 . . . . .57 F4
Roberts Marine Mans
BN11 . . . . .181 F1
Roberts Rd BN15 . . . . .183 E4
Robertson Rd BN1 . . . . . .167 D1
Robin Cl Crawley RH11 . . . .18 C8
East Grinstead RH19 . . . . .9 F2
Littlehampton BN17 . . . . . . .178 C4
Southwater RH13 . . . . .58 A2
Robin Davis Cl BN2 . . . . .168 E1
Robin Dene BN2 . . . . .188 E4
Robin Hood La RH12 . . . . . .35 F5
Robin Rd RH15 . . . . .106 D2
Robin's Cl PO20 . . . . .206 E8
Robinia Lodge BN1 . . . . . .167 E2
Robins Dr PO21 . . . . .194 D3
Robins La GU29 . . . . .69 D7
Robins Row BN41 . . . . . . .166 A1
Robinson Cl BN15 . . . . . . .183 E6
Robinson Rd RH11 . . . . . . .18 D5
Robinswood Ct RH12 . . . . .36 F4
Robson Rd BN12 . . . . .181 E2
Rochester Cl
Chichester PO19 . . . . .152 F1
5 Hove BN3 . . . . .187 D6
Worthing BN13 . . . . .181 B5
Rochester Ct 4 BN3 . . . .187 D6
Rochester Gdns BN3 . . . .187 D6
Rochester St BN2 . . . . . . .188 D5
Rochester Way PO21 . . . .194 E3
Rock Cl 12 BN42 . . . . .185 E7
Rock Gdns PO21 . . . . .195 C2
Rock Gr BN2 . . . . .188 E4
Rock La RH20 . . . . .120 E1
Rock Lodge Vineyard
RH17 . . . . .87 A2
Rock Pl BN2 . . . . .207 C1
Rock Rd RH20 . . . . .120 C2
Rock St BN2 . . . . .188 E4
Rockall Cl BN17 . . . . .179 A3
Rockingham Cl BN13 . . . .181 E6
Rockingham Ct BN13 . . . .181 E6
Rockpit Cotts GU33 . . . . . .45 D4
Rocks La RH17 . . . . .40 F1
Rocks The RH19 . . . . .23 D6
Rocksacre Cotts BN15 . . .182 F7
Rocky La RH16 . . . . .85 D1
Rodgate La GU27 . . . . .28 E5
Rodmell Pl BN1 . . . . .168 A6
Rodmell Rd BN13 . . . . . . .181 E5
Rodney Cl PO21 . . . . .194 C3
Rodney Cres BN18 . . . . . .177 D4
Roebuck Cl RH13 . . . . .37 B4
Roedale Rd BN1 . . . . .168 B1
Roedean Rd Brighton BN2 .188 F4
Worthing BN13 . . . . .181 E6
Roedeer Copse GU27 . . . . .26 E6
Roffey Cl RH6 . . . . .1 F3
Roffey Cnr RH12 . . . . .37 B4
Roffey Ct RH13 . . . . .37 A4
Roffey's Cl RH10 . . . . .7 A4
Rogate CE Prim Sch GU31 68 B4
Rogate Cl Lancing BN15 . . .183 B7
Worthing BN13 . . . . .182 A6
Rogate Rd BN13 . . . . .182 A6
Roger's La BN14 . . . . .161 E4
Rolfe Dr RH15 . . . . .107 D3
Rollaston Pk BN18 . . . . . .177 C2
Romaine Cl RH15 . . . . . . .107 D5
Roman Acre BN17 . . . . . . .198 C6
Roman Cres BN42 . . . . . . .185 E8
Roman Fields PO21 . . . . . .195 A4
Roman Landing PO20 . . . .190 B2
Roman Rd Bramber BN44 .143 E3
Hove BN3 . . . . .186 D6
Southwick BN42 . . . . .185 E8
Roman Way
Billingshurst RH14 . . . . .55 D1
Fishbourne PO19 . . . . .172 B6
Southwick BN42 . . . . .185 E8
Roman Wlk BN15 . . . . .183 B7
Romany Cl BN41 . . . . .186 B8
Romany Rd BN13 . . . . . . .181 B5
Romney Broadwalk
PO22 . . . . .195 B6
Romney Ct BN11 . . . . .181 F1
Romney Garth PO20 . . . . .206 F7
Romney Rd BN11 . . . . .181 F1
Romsey Cl BN1 . . . . .168 C2
Rona Cl RH11 . . . . .18 B3
Rook Way RH12 . . . . .36 F6
Rookcross La RH13 . . . . .102 A4
Rookery Cl BN1 . . . . .167 E1
Rookery La PO20 . . . . . . .203 F8
Rookery The Lumley PO10 .149 C1
Selsey PO20 . . . . .206 F8
Rookery Way RH16 . . . . . . .85 E1
Rookwood La PO20 . . . . . .190 D4
Rookwood Pk RH12 . . . . . .35 F3
Rookwood Rd PO20 . . . . .190 C2
Roosthole Forest Walks
RH13 . . . . .59 D8
Rope Wlk
Littlehampton BN17 . . . . . . .198 C4
Shoreham-by-Sea BN43 . . . .184 E7
Ropeland Way RH12 . . . . . .36 E7
Ropes La GU27 . . . . .49 C5
Ropetackle BN43 . . . . . . .184 E7
Rosamund Rd RH10 . . . . . .19 B3
Rosary Ct RH15 . . . . .107 B2
Rose Ave 2 PO22 . . . . . . .196 F5
Rose Cottage La RH17 . . . .62 A5
Rose Cotts RH17 . . . . .66 A4
Rose Ct Bognor Regis PO21 194 D3
Chichester PO19 . . . . .173 A7
Hassocks BN6 . . . . .126 E4
7 Littlehampton BN17 . . . . .198 D5
2 Worthing BN11 . . . . .183 B3
Rose Garden The PO20 . . .172 C3
Rose Green Inf Sch PO21 194 C2
Rose Green Jun Sch
PO21 . . . . .194 C3
Rose Green Rd PO21 . . . . .194 C3
Rose Hill BN2 . . . . .207 C4
Rose Hill Cl BN1, BN2 . . . .207 B4
Rose Hill Ct BN1 . . . . .207 B4
Rose Hill Terr BN1 . . . . . .207 B4
Rose Pl BN17 . . . . .179 B3
Rose Wlk Crawley RH11 . . .18 B4
Worthing BN12 . . . . .181 E1
Rosebarn Cl RH15 . . . . . .107 C1
Rosebery Ave BN12 . . . . .181 E2
Rosecroft Cl BN15 . . . . . .183 E5
Rosedale Cl RH11 . . . . . . .18 A4
Rosehill RH14 . . . . .55 D1
Roseleigh Gdns RH17 . . . . .86 F3
Rosemary Ave BN44 . . . . .143 E3
Rosemary Cl
Bognor Regis PO21 . . . . . . .194 C3
Bramber BN44 . . . . .143 E3
Haywards Heath RH16 . . . . .85 B6
Petworth GU28 . . . . .95 F8
Storrington RH20 . . . . .119 D1
Rosemary Ct
Haslemere GU27 . . . . .27 C7
Horley RH6 . . . . .1 E4
Rosemary Dr BN43 . . . . . .165 C1
Rosemary La Charlwood RH6 .4 E7
Horley RH6 . . . . .2 B3
Petworth GU28 . . . . .95 F8
Rosemead BN17 . . . . .198 E5
Rosewood GU27 . . . . .27 C5
Rosier Commercial Ctr
RH14 . . . . .77 F7
Rosier Way RH14 . . . . .77 E6
Roslan Ct 6 RH6 . . . . .2 B2
Ross Cl Bognor Regis PO21 194 B2
Crawley RH10 . . . . .18 F3
Rossalyn Cl PO21 . . . . . . .194 B3
Rossiter Rd BN15 . . . . . . .183 E8
Rosslyn Ave BN43 . . . . . . .185 A7
Rosslyn Ct BN43 . . . . .184 F7
Rosslyn Rd BN43 . . . . .184 F7
Rossmore Cl RH10 . . . . .6 D2
Rostock Ct PO20 . . . . .202 B6
Rosvara Ave PO20 . . . . . . .175 D7
Rotary Ho BN15 . . . . .183 E4
Rotary Lodge
Brighton BN1 . . . . .168 E6
Worthing BN11 . . . . .182 B3
Rotary Point BN41 . . . . . .166 B1
Rothbury Rd BN3 . . . . . . .186 D7
Rother Cl RH20 . . . . .119 F3
Rother Cres RH11 . . . . .17 F5
Rother Ho GU33 . . . . .45 B3
Rother La GU31 . . . . .69 A1
Rotherbank Farm La GU33 45 C6
Rotherbridge La GU28 . . . .95 E5
Rotherfield Cl BN1 . . . . . .168 B6
Rotherfield Cres BN1 . . . .168 B5
Rothermead GU28 . . . . .95 E7
Rothervale RH6 . . . . .1 F5
Rothesay Cl BN13 . . . . . . .181 E4
Rothley Chase RH16 . . . . . .85 F4
Rotten Row PO20 . . . . . . .192 E3
Rough Field RH19 . . . . .9 D4
Rough Way RH12 . . . . .36 F5
Round Hill Rd 2 BN2 . . . .188 B8
Round Hill St 3 BN2 . . . .188 B8
Round Piece La PO20 . . . .206 B8
Roundabout Copse RH20 119 D5
Roundabout Cotts RH12 . . .33 C5
Roundabout La RH20 . . . .119 D6
Roundabouts The GU33 . . .45 C5
Roundhill Cres BN2 . . . . .188 B8
Roundhouse Mdw PO10 . .169 C7
Roundle Ave PO22 . . . . . .196 C6
Roundle Rd PO22 . . . . . . .196 C5
Roundle Sq PO22 . . . . . . .196 B5
Roundle Square Rd
PO22 . . . . .196 B5
Roundstone By-Pass Rd
BN16 . . . . .180 A3
Roundstone Cres BN16 . .200 A6
Roundstone Dr BN16 . . . .200 A6
Roundstone La BN16 . . . .180 A4
Roundstone Way PO20 . .206 F8
Roundway BN1 . . . . .168 E5
Roundway Ct RH10 . . . . . .18 D8
Roundway The BN16 . . . .199 D4
Roundwood La RH16 . . . . .85 F8
Row Hill La RH17 . . . . .62 E7
Rowan Ave BN3 . . . . .166 E1
Rowan Cl Crawley RH10 . . .18 F6
Haywards Heath RH16 . . . . .86 B4
Horsham RH12 . . . . .37 B5
Portslade-by-Sea BN41 . . . .166 A1
Storrington RH20 . . . . .119 F2
Rowan Ct Billingshurst RH14 55 D1
Brighton BN1 . . . . .167 E1
Rowan Dr RH14 . . . . .55 D1
Rowan Ho
1 Rustington BN16 . . . . . . .199 C5
Worthing BN12 . . . . .181 A4
Rowan Tree Cl GU33 . . . . .45 C4
Rowan Way
Bognor Regis PO22 . . . . . . .195 C7
Horsham RH12 . . . . .37 C5
Rowans The
Burgess hill RH15 . . . . .106 D4
Worthing BN11 . . . . .182 A2
Rowena Ct RH12 . . . . .36 A1
Rowena Ho RH11 . . . . .5 D1
Rowfant Bsns Ctr RH10 . . .20 E6
Rowfant Cl RH10 . . . . .19 E6
Rowhook Hill RH12 . . . . . .34 F8
Rowhook Rd Rowhook RH12 34 F8
Slinfold RH12 . . . . .35 A8
Rowland Cl RH10 . . . . .7 E5
Rowlands Castle Rd PO8 128 B6
Rowlands Castle Sta PO9 128 E2
Rowlands Ct BN11 . . . . . . .182 C1
Rowlands Rd
Horsham RH12 . . . . .37 A6
Worthing BN11 . . . . .182 B1
Rowner Rd RH14 . . . . .55 A2
Rowplatt La RH19 . . . . .8 E4
Roxburgh Cl BN13 . . . . . .181 F7
Royal Alexandra Hospl
for Sick Children The
BN1 . . . . .207 A3
Royal Arc BN11 . . . . .182 D1
Royal Bldgs BN15 . . . . . . .183 C4
Royal Cl PO19 . . . . .173 C5
Royal Cres BN2 . . . . .188 C4
Royal Crescent Mans
BN2 . . . . .188 C4
Royal Crescent Mews
BN2 . . . . .188 C4
Royal Gdns PO9 . . . . .128 C1
Royal George Par BN43 . .165 C1
Royal George Rd RH15 . .106 E3
Royal Oak Cotts BN45 . . .146 C5
Royal Oak Ho RH10 . . . . . .21 B7
Royal Par PO21 . . . . .195 A6
Royal Pavilion BN1 . . . . . .207 B2
Royal Sussex Cty Hospl
(General) BN2 . . . . .188 D4
Royce Cl PO20 . . . . .190 C1
Royce Rd RH10 . . . . .6 A3
Royce Way PO20 . . . . .190 C1
Royston Cl RH10 . . . . .6 A2
Roystons The BN16 . . . . .199 F4
Ruckmans La RH5 . . . . . . .14 B7
Rucrofts Cl PO21 . . . . . . .194 F3
Rudd Ho BN13 . . . . .181 E7
Rudford Ind Est BN18 . . .177 D2
Rudgwick Ave BN12 . . . . .181 A2
Rudgwick Cl BN16 . . . . . .199 B4
Rudgwick Keep RH6 . . . . . . .2 C4
Rudgwick Prim Sch RH12 .33 D7
Rudgwick Rd RH11 . . . . . . .17 F7
Rudwick Way PO22 . . . . . .196 C4
Rudwick's Cl PO22 . . . . . .196 C4
Rufwood RH10 . . . . .21 A8
Rugby Ct 5 Brighton BN2 .188 E4
3 Worthing BN11 . . . . .182 A3
Rugby Pl BN2 . . . . .188 E4
Rugby Rd Brighton BN1 . . .168 A1
Worthing BN11 . . . . .182 A3
Ruislip Gdns PO21 . . . . . .194 C2
Rumbolds Cl PO19 . . . . . .173 C5
Rumbolds Hill GU29 . . . . . .92 F7
Rumbolds La RH16 . . . . . . .85 D2
Rumboldswyke
CE Prim Sch PO19 . . . . .173 C5
Runcorn Cl RH11 . . . . .17 E2
Runcton La PO20 . . . . . . .193 E7
Runnymede Ct PO21 . . . . .194 F5
Runshooke Ct 9 RH11 . . . .18 A3
Rusbridge Cl PO21 . . . . . .194 D4
Rushams Rd RH12 . . . . . . .36 B3
Rushes The RH16 . . . . .86 C4
Rushetts Pl RH11 . . . . .5 C1
Rushetts Rd RH11 . . . . .5 B1
Rushfield Rd GU33 . . . . . . .45 B3
Rushlake Cl BN1 . . . . .168 E5
Rushlake Rd BN1 . . . . .168 E5
Rushwood Cl RH16 . . . . . . .86 B4
Ruskin Cl Crawley RH10 . . . . .6 C1
Selsey PO20 . . . . .206 F7
Ruskin Pl BN3 . . . . .186 F7
Ruskin Rd Hove BN3 . . . . .186 F8
Worthing BN14 . . . . .182 F4
Rusper Prim Sch RH12 . . .16 C7
Rusper Rd Brighton BN1 . .168 D6
Crawley RH11, RH12 . . . . . . .17 D7
Faygate RH12 . . . . .16 A1
Horsham RH12 . . . . .36 F6
Newdigate RH12, RH5 . . . . . .3 C4
Rusper RH5 . . . . .15 E8
Worthing BN13 . . . . .181 E5
Rusper Rd S BN13 . . . . . . .181 F5
Ruspers RH15 . . . . .107 D2
Ruspers Keep RH11 . . . . . . .17 F7
Russ Hill RH6 . . . . .4 C5
Russell Cl BN14 . . . . .182 E5
Russell Cres 2 BN1, BN3 .207 A4
Russell Ct 5 BN15 . . . . . .183 E5
Russell Mews 14 BN1 . . . .187 E5
Russell Pl
7 Bognor Regis PO21 . . . . .195 D3
Brighton BN1 . . . . .207 A2
Russell Rd Brighton BN1 . .207 A2
East Wittering PO20 . . . . . .201 E7
Russell Sq BN1 . . . . .207 A2
Russell St PO19 . . . . .173 C6
Russell Way RH10 . . . . .19 A5
Russell's Cl BN16 . . . . . . .200 B6
Russells Cres RH6 . . . . .2 A2
Russells Dr BN15 . . . . .183 E5
Russet Cl RH6 . . . . .2 C3
Russet Ct Fernhurst GU27 . .49 B5
Horsham RH12 . . . . .37 A4
Russet Gdns PO10 . . . . . .169 D8
Rustington
Com Prim Sch BN16 . . . .199 B6
Rustington Rd BN1 . . . . . .168 A5
Rustington Trad Est
BN16 . . . . .179 F3
Rustlings Cl RH16 . . . . .86 B5
Ruston Ave BN16 . . . . .199 D5
Ruston Cl RH10 . . . . .19 C3
Ruston Pk BN16 . . . . .199 E5
Rutherford Way RH10 . . . . . .6 A3
Rutherwick Cl RH6 . . . . .1 F3
Ruthven Cl RH17 . . . . .84 F7
Rutland Ct BN3 . . . . .186 F6
Rutland Gdns BN3 . . . . . . .186 F7
Rutland Rd BN3 . . . . .187 A7
Rutland Way PO18, PO20 .173 D8
Rycroft Cl BN12 . . . . .181 C1
Rydal Cl Crawley RH11 . . . .17 D4
Littlehampton BN17 . . . . . . .179 A3
Ryde Ct BN3 . . . . .166 D1
Ryde Rd BN2 . . . . .188 D7
Ryders Way RH12 . . . . .36 F7
Rydon Com Coll RH20 . . .120 A2
Rye Ash RH10 . . . . .19 A7
Rye Cl BN11 . . . . .182 A1
Rye Farm La RH13 . . . . . . .57 A2
Ryecroft 12 Brighton BN2 . .188 F5
Haywards Heath RH16 . . . . .85 E3

Ryecroft Ct BN15 183 E5
Ryecroft Dr RH12 36 A3
Ryecroft Gdns BN12 181 C2
Ryecroft La RH20 119 D1
Ryecroft Mdw RH13 59 C6
Ryecroft Rd RH17 83 C3
Ryelands Crawley RH11 18 A5
Horley RH6 2 C4
Ryelands Dr BN2 168 D3

S

Sabey Ct 16 PO21 195 D3
Sabre Rd PO10 169 C3
Sack La PO22 175 E2
Sackville Cl RH19 9 C3
Sackville Coll RH19 9 F1
Sackville Com Coll RH19 23 A8
Sackville Cres BN14 182 E4
Sackville Ct 3 RH19 22 F8
Sackville Gdns
East Grinstead RH19 9 C3
Hove BN3 186 F6
Sackville La RH19 9 C3
Sackville Rd Hove BN3 187 A7
Worthing BN14 182 E4
Sackville Trad Est BN3 187 B8
Sackville Way BN14 182 E4
Saddle La PO20 206 D8
Saddler Row RH10 18 D3
Saddler's Row GU28 95 F8
Saddlers Cl RH15 107 D1
Sadler St PO21 195 C2
Sadler Way BN2 188 F6
Sadlers The PO18 153 D1
Sadlers Wlk
4 Chichester PO19 173 A6
Lumley PO10 169 C8
Saffron Cl Crawley RH11 18 A3
Shoreham-by-Sea BN43 165 C1
Saffron Ct
8 Bognor Regis PO21 195 C4
Worthing BN13 182 A3
Saffron Gate BN3 187 C7
Saffrons The RH15 106 F5
Saint Hill Manor RH19 22 C4
Saint Hill Rd RH19 22 C5
St Agnes Rd RH19 9 E2
St Andrew's
CE Boys High Sch BN14 182 E4
St Andrew's
CE Fst & Mid Sch RH10 19 A4
St Andrew's CE Prim Sch
Hove BN3 187 B6
Nuthurst RH13 59 A1
Steyning BN44 143 D4
St Andrew's Cl
Ferring BN12 200 E6
Oving PO20 174 C6
St Andrew's Gdns BN13 182 A4
St Andrew's Rd
Brighton BN1 168 A1
Portslade-by-Sea BN41 186 C7
Worthing BN13 181 F4
St Andrews 4 RH6 2 B2
St Andrews Ct BN11 182 C2
St Andrews La PO20 154 C1
St Andrews Rd
Burgess Hill RH15 107 C4
Crawley RH11 17 D5
St Ann's Ct BN3 187 D7
St Ann's Hill GU29 92 F7
St Ann's Ho GU29 92 F8
St Anne's Ct
6 Brighton BN1 207 A4
9 Brighton BN2 188 C4
East Wittering PO20 201 F7
St Anne's Gdns BN6 127 A3
St Anne's Ho 7 BN1 207 A4
St Anne's Rd RH10 6 C2
St Annes Well Ho 6
BN3 187 D6
St Anns Mans 5 BN1 187 E7
St Anselm's Rd BN14 182 B4
St Anthony's Sch PO19 172 F8
St Anthony's Way 1
BN16 199 D6
St Anthony's Wlk PO21 194 D3
St Aubin Cl RH11 17 F2
St Aubins Ct 1 BN12 200 F4
St Aubins Rd 3 BN12 200 F4
St Aubyn's Cres BN41 186 B7
St Aubyn's Gdns 13 BN3 187 A6
St Aubyn's Rd
Portslade-by-Sea BN41 186 C7
Southwick BN41 186 A7
St Aubyns BN3 187 B6
St Aubyns Mans BN3 187 A5
St Aubyns S BN3 187 A5
St Augustine Cl RH17 86 F3
St Augustine Rd 12 BN17 198 E4
St Barnabas Ct RH10 19 C7
St Bartholomew
CE Prim Sch GU27 27 C7
St Bartholomew's
CE Prim Sch BN1 207 B4
St Bartholomews Cl
PO19 172 E6
St Bernadette's
RC Prim Sch BN1 167 E2
St Bernards Ct BN15 183 E5
St Blaises Rd PO18 154 C4
St Botolph's Rd BN11 182 B3
St Botolphs Ct 2 BN11 182 B3
St Brelades Rd RH11 17 F2
St Catherine's
RC Prim Sch BN17 198 D6
St Catherine's Rd BN17 198 D4
St Catherine's Terr 6
BN3 187 B5
St Catherines Rd RH10 6 D1
St Cathrinres Ct BN17 198 D4
St Christopher's Cl
Fishbourne PO19 172 C6
Haslemere GU27 27 A6
St Christopher's Gn GU27 27 A6
St Christopher's Rd
Haslemere GU27 27 A6
Hurstpierpoint BN6 126 A6
St Christopher's Sch
BN3 187 A6
St Christophers Cl RH12 36 D4
St Christophers
Day Hospl RH12 36 D3
St Clement Rd RH11 17 F2
St Cuthman's Rd BN44 143 D4
St Cuthman's Sch GU29 70 A6
St Cuthmans Cl BN2 188 F6
St Cyriacs PO19 173 A7
St David's Gate 4 BN15 183 D6
St Dunstan's Rd BN13 182 A3
St Edmund Cl RH11 5 D1
St Edmund's Rd RH16 85 F3
St Edward's Cl RH19 9 C1
St Elmo Rd BN14 182 B4
St Flora's Cl BN17 198 F5
St Flora's Rd BN17 198 F5
St Francis Cl RH16 85 F2
St Francis Gdns RH10 7 C4
St Francis of Assisi
RC Prim Sch RH10 18 E4
St Francis Wlk RH11 17 E4
St Gabriels Rd RH14 77 E8
St George's Cl PO20 206 F8
St George's Dr PO19 172 F3
St George's Gdns
Horsham RH13 36 E4
1 Worthing BN11 182 F2
St George's La BN6 126 B5
St George's Mews BN1 207 B3
St George's Pl
Brighton BN1 207 B3
Hurstpierpoint BN6 126 B5
St George's Rd
Brighton BN2 188 D4
Worthing BN11 182 F2
St George's Terr 5 BN2 188 C4
St Georges 9 RH6 2 B2
St Georges Cl RH6 2 B3
St Georges Ct
Crawley RH10 18 D8
East Grinstead RH19 9 C3
St Georges Rd RH13 103 A3
St Georges Wlk PO20 175 F7
St Giles CE Prim Sch
RH17 65 C6
St Giles Cl BN43 185 B8
St Helen's Cres BN3 166 D3
St Helen's Dr BN3 166 D3
St Helen's Rd BN2 188 D7
St Helier Cl RH11 18 A2
St Helier Ct 2 BN12 200 F4
St Helier Rd BN12 200 F4
St Heliers Ave BN3 186 E7
St Hilda's Cl Crawley RH10 6 C1
Horley RH6 2 B3
Selsey PO20 206 D6
St Hugh's Cl RH10 6 C1
St Itha Cl PO20 206 E7
St Itha Rd PO20 206 E6
St Ives RH10 19 C7
St Ives Sch GU27 27 E8
St James Ave BN15 183 E8
St James CE Prim Sch
PO10 149 B2
St James Cotts RH17 41 A1
St James Ct PO19 173 B7
St James Wlk RH11 18 C2
St James' CE Prim Sch
RH20 117 C6
St James' Ho 13 BN2 207 C2
St James' Ind Est PO19 173 C7
St James' Prim Sch
PO19 173 C7
St James' Rd
Chichester PO19 173 C7
Emsworth PO10 149 B1
St James's Ave BN2 207 C2
St James's Cl PO20 191 E5
St James's Rd RH19 9 D1
St James's Sq PO19 173 C7
St James's St BN2 207 C2
St James's Street Mews
BN2 207 C2
St Joan Cl RH11 5 D1
St John Cl RH13 36 E1
St John The Baptist
CE Prim Sch BN14 161 E6
St John the Baptist
RC Prim Sch BN2 188 D5
St John's Ave
Burgess Hill RH15 106 F4
Worthing BN12 181 D1
St John's Cl
Bognor Regis PO21 194 F4
East Grinstead RH19 9 E2
Midhurst GU29 92 E7
Worthing BN12 181 D1
St John's Cres RH12 35 E3
St John's Ct 5 BN15 183 D6
St John's Mews Cotts
BN43 184 E7
St John's Mount 8 BN2 207 C2
St John's Pl Brighton BN2 207 C2
22 Hove BN3 187 C6
St John's RC Sch RH12 36 A1
St John's Rd Breach PO10 149 F1
Crawley RH11 18 C6
East Grinstead RH19 9 E2
Haywards Heath RH16 85 E2
Hove BN3 187 C5
St John's Res Sch BN2 188 D5
St John's St PO19 173 A6
St Johns Cl PO20 175 D5
St Johns Ct RH15 107 A3
St Johns Rd RH15 107 A3
St Joseph's Cl BN3 187 A8
St Joseph's RC Prim Sch
Brighton BN2 168 C1
Haywards Heath RH16 85 E4
St Joseph's Trad Est
BN3 187 A8
St Josephs Way RH16 85 E4
St Julian's La BN43 185 D7
St Julians Cl BN43 185 C7
St Keyna Ave BN3 186 D6
St Lawrence Ave BN14 182 B4
St Lawrence
CE Prim Sch BN6 126 A6
St Lawrence Ct BN14 182 B4
St Lawrence Way BN6 126 A7
St Leodegar's Way PO20 173 A1
St Leonard"s Park Ho
RH13 37 C3
St Leonard's Ave BN3 186 C7
St Leonard's Gdns BN3 186 D7
St Leonard's Rd
9 Brighton BN2 188 C8
Hove BN3 186 C7
St Leonards RH13 36 F4
St Leonards Com Inf Sch
RH13 36 E2
St Leonards Dr RH10 19 A4
St Leonards Pk RH19 9 E1
St Leonards Rd RH13 37 A1
St Louie Cl BN42 186 A8
St Luke's Cl BN15 183 B4
St Luke's Inf Sch BN2 188 C6
St Luke's Jun Sch BN2 188 C6
St Luke's Rd BN2 188 C6
St Luke's Terr BN2 188 C6
St Lukes Ct RH15 107 A3
St Malo Cl BN12 200 F4
St Malo Ct 4 BN12 200 F4
St Margaret's Ave RH19 9 F6
St Margaret's
CE Fst & Mid Sch RH11 18 B7
St Margaret's
CE Prim Sch BN16 179 F7
St Margaret's Cotts GU27 49 B6
St Margaret's Ct BN16 179 F6
St Margaret's Pl BN1 207 A2
St Margaret's Rd RH19 9 F3
St Margaret's Sch GU29 92 E8
St Margarets Ct RH12 35 F7
St Mark's CE Prim Sch
Brighton BN2 188 E5
Staplefield RH17 61 F5
St Mark's Cres BN15 183 B4
St Mark's La RH12 36 E6
St Mark's St BN2 188 E4
St Martin Cl RH17 61 B7
St Martin's Flats 6 BN2 188 C7
St Martin's La 10 BN17 198 D5
St Martin's Pl BN2 188 C7
St Martin's Sq PO19 173 A7
St Martin's St
Brighton BN2 207 C5
Chichester PO19 173 A6
St Martins CE Prim Sch
BN2 188 C8
St Martins Rd BN17 198 D5
St Mary & St Paul
CE Fst Sch GU31 89 D3
St Mary Magdalen
RC Prim Sch BN1 187 E5
St Mary Magdalene St
BN2 207 C5
St Mary's CE Fst Sch
Washington RH20 141 D6
Worthing BN12 181 C2
St Mary's CE Prim Sch
Horsham RH12 36 C1
Pulborough RH20 98 C3
St Mary's CE Sch
Climping BN17 197 E8
East Grinstead RH19 9 D2
St Mary's Cl
Billingshurst RH14 77 D8
Littlehampton BN17 198 E5
Mid Lavant PO18 152 F7
Pulborough RH20 98 C2
Shoreham-by-Sea BN43 184 F7
St Mary's Ct
Bramber BN44 143 F2
6 Littlehampton BN17 198 E5
Worthing BN13 181 D6
St Mary's Ctyd PO22 195 F4
St Mary's Dr Crawley RH10 19 B8
Rustington BN16 199 F5
St Mary's Gdns
Horsham RH12 36 C1
1 Littlehampton BN17 198 E5
St Mary's Ho RH12 36 C1
St Mary's Ho & Gdns
BN44 143 F2
St Mary's Lodge 1 PO19 173 A6
St Mary's Mews PO22 195 F4
St Mary's Pl BN2 207 C2
St Mary's RC Prim Sch
Bognor regis PO21 195 D3
Portslade-by-Sea BN41 186 B7
Worthing BN11 182 C2
St Mary's Rd
Boxgrove PO18 154 C4
Burgess Hill RH15 106 F4
Liss GU33 45 B4
Shoreham-by-Sea BN43 184 F7
St Mary's Rd W RH15 106 E4
St Mary's Sq 17 BN2 188 D4
St Mary's Terr 6 BN43 184 E7
St Mary's Way BN17 198 E5
St Marys Cl
Bognor Regis PO22 195 D5
Lancing BN15 183 B7
St Marys Meadow BN18 176 F4
St Marys Pl 3 BN43 185 A6
St Matthew's Rd BN11 182 C3
St Matthews Ct BN2 188 C5
St Maur's Rd BN12 200 E6
St Michael's Ct 7 BN15 183 D5
St Michael's Ct BN11 182 B2
St Michael's Pl BN1 187 E6
St Michael's Rd
Portslade-by-Sea BN41 186 B7
Worthing BN11 182 B2
St Michaels Cl GU28 51 A7
St Michaels Rd RH19 9 E2
St Michaels Way RH13 103 A3
St Nicholas Ct
Crawley RH10 19 C7
Lindfield RH16 86 A6
8 Middleton-on-Sea PO22 196 F5
St Nicholas Lodge BN1 207 A2
St Nicholas Pl 2 BN43 185 A6
St Nicholas Rd
Brighton BN1 207 A3
Mid Lavant PO18 152 E6
Portslade-by-Sea BN41 186 B7
St Nicholas' CE Jun Sch
BN41 186 B8
St Nicholas' Ct 3 BN15 183 D6
St Nicholas' La 5 PO22 196 F5
St Nicolas & St Mary CE
Fst & Mid Sch BN43 185 A8
St Nicolas Ct BN43 184 D8
St Nicolas La BN43 184 D8
St Osmund Rd BN12 200 E6
St Pancras PO19 173 B7
St Pancras Ct PO19 173 B6
St Patrick's La GU33 45 F5
St Patrick's Rd BN3 187 A7
St Paul's Ave BN15 183 B4
St Paul's CE Prim Sch
BN1 207 A3
St Paul's Cl RH16 85 F5
St Paul's Gdns PO19 172 F7
St Paul's RC Coll RH16 85 F5
St Paul's Rd PO19 172 F8
St Paul's St BN2 207 C5
St Peter's PO19 173 A7
St Peter's CE Prim Sch
Ardingly RH17 64 A8
Henfield BN5 123 D5
St Peter's Cl Cowfold RH13 81 E1
Hove BN3 166 F2
St Peter's Com Inf Sch
BN41 186 B7
St Peter's Cres PO20 206 E8
St Peter's Gn BN44 144 A2
St Peter's Pl
Brighton BN1, BN2 207 B3
Lancing BN15 183 C4
St Peter's RC Prim Sch
East Grinstead RH19 9 C1
Shoreham-by-Sea BN43 185 A8
St Peter's Rd Crawley RH11 18 C6
Portslade-by-Sea BN41 186 B7
St Peter's Sq 9 PO10 169 B8
St Peter's St BN1 207 B4
St Peters Cl PO21 194 E4
St Peters Ct 1 PO10 169 C8
St Peters Rd RH15 107 A4
St Peters View BN5 123 E6
St Philip's Ct BN17 178 D3
St Philip's RC Prim Sch
BN18 158 A3
St Philips Mews 3 BN3 186 F7
St Raphael's Rd BN11 181 F2
St Richard's Cotts GU31 90 A4
St Richard's Ct BN3 166 D1
St Richard's Dr PO21 194 D3
St Richard's Flats BN41 186 B7
St Richard's Hospl PO19 173 B8
St Richard's Mews RH10 18 F6
St Richard's RC Prim Sch
PO19 173 A5
St Richard's Rd BN41 186 B7
St Richard's Way PO21 194 D3
St Richard's Wlk PO19 172 F6
St Richards Cotts
Codmore Hill RH20 98 D6
Cootham RH20 119 A1
Lower Fittleworth RH20 97 A2
St Richards Flats GU29 92 D8
St Richards Rd PO20 175 E7
St Robert Southwell
RC Prim Sch RH12 37 A6
St Robert's Lodge 1
BN15 183 E5
St Roche's Cl PO18 152 F7
St Sampson Rd RH11 17 F2
St Saviours Ct 1 BN1 188 B8
St Stephen's Cl GU27 26 F6
St Stephens Cl GU27 27 C7
St Swithun's Cl RH19 9 F1
St Thomas Ct PO21 205 A8
St Thomas Dr PO21 204 F8
St Thomas's Ct BN14 182 B4
St Thomas's Rd BN14 182 B4
St Valerie Rd BN11 182 A1
St Vincent Cl RH10 19 D5
St Wilfred's Ct 5 RH16 85 E4
St Wilfred's Rd BN14 182 D4
St Wilfreds Cl PO20 206 G8
St Wilfreds Rd RH15 107 B4
St Wilfrid Rd PO19 172 D7
St Wilfrid's
Catholic Prim Sch BN16 179 F6
St Wilfrid's CE Prim Sch
RH16 85 F3
St Wilfrid's RC Comp Sch
RH11 18 B5
St Wilfrid's RC Prim Sch
RH15 106 F2
St Wilfrid's Way RH16 85 E4
St Wilfrids View PO20 206 C6
St Winefride's Rd BN17 198 E4
St Winifred's Cl PO21 195 B2
Sake Ride La BN5 104 C1
Salbrook Rd RH1 2 A8
Salehurst Rd RH10 19 E6
Salisbury Ct RH13 58 A2
Salisbury Ho BN12 181 A3
Salisbury Rd Crawley RH10 18 F2
Hove BN3 187 C6
Tower Hill RH13 58 A8
Worthing BN11 182 D2
Salisbury Way PO19 152 F1
Salt Box Cl RH13 56 F2
Saltdean Cl RH10 18 D3
Salterns Rd RH10 19 C3
Saltham La PO20 173 E1
Salthill La PO19 172 C8
Salthill Rd PO19 172 B7
Saltings The
Birdham PO20 191 E4
Lancing BN15 183 F5
Littlehampton BN17 199 A6
Shoreham-by-Sea BN43 184 D6
Saltings Way BN44 144 A2
Salvington Cl BN13 181 D7
Salvington Ct BN13 161 F2
Salvington Gdns BN13 181 F6
Salvington Hill BN13 161 E1
Salvington Rd
Crawley RH11 17 F3
Worthing BN13 181 E7
Samaritan Cl RH11 17 E4
Samphire Cl RH11 18 A3
Samphire Dr BN13 181 A5
Sampsons Dr PO20 174 C7
San Feliu Ct RH19 10 B2
Sanctuary La RH20 120 C1
Sandbrook BN6 126 F3
Sandcroft PO20 175 D7
Sandeman Way RH13 58 F8
Sanders Ho BN3 186 E8
Sanderstead 1 BN2 188 F5
Sandfield Ave BN17 178 D4
Sandgate La RH20 120 A2
Sandgate Rd BN1 168 A2
Sandhawes Hill RH19 10 A4
Sandhill La
Crawley Down RH10 21 B7
Washington RH20 141 E7
Sandhills Rd RH13 56 F3
Sandhurst Sch BN11 182 F2
Sandown Ave BN12 181 C1
Sandown Cl BN12 181 C1
Sandown Ct Crawley RH10 19 D6
Hove BN3 166 D1
1 Worthing BN11 182 C1
Sandown Rd Brighton BN2 188 D7
Southwick BN42 185 E8
Sandpiper Cl RH11 17 D4
Sandpiper Ct PO20 202 A6
Sandridge La RH16 63 F1
Sandringham Cl
Bracklesham PO20 202 B5
East Grinstead RH19 23 A8
Hove BN3 167 A3
Sandringham Ct 5 BN15 183 F5
Sandringham Dr BN3 167 A3
Sandringham Lodge 17
BN3 187 C6
Sandringham Mews
Worthing BN14 182 D6
Worthing, Durrington BN13 181 D7
Sandringham Rd
Chichester PO19 173 C6
Crawley RH11 18 B2
Sandringham Way PO21 195 B4
Sandrock Haslemere GU27 27 C6
Midhurst GU29 92 D8
Sandrock Cotts GU28 51 A7
Sandrocks Way RH16 85 E2
Sands La BN5 144 F6
Sands The RH20 121 A5
Sandwich Rd BN11 181 F1
Sandy Beach Est PO11 189 B1
Sandy La
Chelwood Gate RH17 66 C8
Crawley Down RH10 21 A8
East Ashling PO18 151 D4
East Grinstead RH19 9 F1
Fittleworth RH20 97 A2
Haslemere GU26, GU27 26 C7
Heath Common RH20 120 C1
Henfield BN5 123 D4
Midhurst GU29 92 D8
Rake GU33 46 A4
Waterfield RH20 117 A5
West Hoathly RH19 42 E6
Sandy Point Cl PO20 206 B8
Sandy Point La PO20 206 B8

Sandy Point Rd PO11 ... 189 A1
Sandy Rd PO21 ... 205 A7
Sandy Vale RH16 ... 85 E2
Sandygate La RH13 ... 59 F3
Sandymount Ave PO22 ... 195 B5
Sandymount Cl PO22 ... 195 C6
Sangers Cty Jun Sch RH6 ... 1 F3
Sangers Dr RH6 ... 1 F3
Sanyhils Ave BN1 ... 167 F7
Sapex Bldgs PO19 ... 173 B7
Sarel Way RH6 ... 2 B5
Sargent Cl RH10 ... 18 F2
Sarisbury Cl PO22 ... 196 A5
Sark Cl RH11 ... 18 A2
Sark Gdns BN12 ... 200 F4
Satellite Bsns Village The RH10 ... 5 E2
Satinwood Cl PO22 ... 196 E6
Saturn Cl RH11 ... 17 E4
Saucelands Rd RH13 ... 100 E7
Saunders Cl RH10 ... 19 B7
Saunders Hill BN1 ... 168 D7
Saunders Park Ho 2 BN2 ... 188 C8
Saunders Park Rise BN2 ... 168 C1
Saunders Park View BN2 ... 168 C1
Savernake Wlk RH10 ... 18 F3
Savill Rd RH16 ... 86 A8
Saville Ct RH14 ... 77 D7
Saville Gdns RH14 ... 77 D7
Sawyers Cl RH15 ... 107 D1
Saxby Rd RH15 ... 106 D4
Saxifrage Way BN13 ... 181 A5
Saxley RH6 ... 2 C4
Saxon Cl Billingshurst RH14 ... 55 D1
Bognor Regis PO21 ... 204 F8
East Preston BN16 ... 180 B3
Saxon Cres RH12 ... 36 B4
Saxon Ct BN3 ... 186 D6
Saxon Mdw PO20 ... 154 C1
Saxon Rd Bramber BN44 ... 143 F3
Crawley RH10 ... 19 E5
Hove BN3 ... 186 D6
Saxonbury 16 BN2 ... 207 C3
Saxons BN43 ... 164 F1
Saxony Rd BN14 ... 182 C4
Sayers Cl RH13 ... 36 E2
Sayers The 5 RH19 ... 9 C1
Scallows Cl RH10 ... 19 A7
Scallows Rd RH10 ... 19 A7
Scamps Hill RH16 ... 86 C6
Scant Rd E PO18 ... 150 F2
Scant Rd W PO18 ... 150 E2
Scarborough Rd BN1 ... 167 D1
Scaynes Hill St Augustine's CE Prim Sch RH17 ... 86 F3
Sceptre BN1 ... 167 E2
Schaffer Ho RH10 ... 19 C4
Scholars Ct RH10 ... 21 A8
School Cl
Burgess Hill RH15 ... 106 F2
Fittleworth RH20 ... 97 A3
Horsham RH12 ... 37 A6
1 Southwick BN42 ... 185 E7
School Dell PO18 ... 151 A3
School Hill Findon BN14 ... 161 E6
Slindon BN18 ... 156 C5
Storrington RH20 ... 119 E1
Warnham RH12 ... 35 F8
School La Arundel BN18 ... 158 A2
Ashurst BN44 ... 122 D5
Ashurst Wood RH19 ... 23 E6
Bosham PO18 ... 171 C5
Compton PO18 ... 109 B2
Danehill RH17 ... 66 B5
Eastergate PO20 ... 175 F7
Emsworth PO10 ... 169 B8
Fittleworth RH20 ... 97 A3
Forest Row RH18 ... 23 F2
Liss GU33 ... 45 B4
Lodsworth GU28 ... 72 B4
North Mundham PO20 ... 173 D2
Nutbourne PO18 ... 170 B7
Pyecombe BN45 ... 147 C6
Selsey PO20 ... 206 D8
Shipley RH13 ... 79 C1
Stedham GU29 ... 69 F1
Steyning BN44 ... 143 D3
Storrington RH20 ... 119 C1
Sutton RH20 ... 115 F4
Washington RH20 ... 141 E6
Westbourne PO10 ... 149 D5
School Rd Amberley BN18 ... 138 E7
Camelsdale GU27 ... 26 F5
Hove BN3 ... 186 F8
Upper Beeding BN44 ... 144 B2
School Rise BN2 ... 188 E6
Schooner Ct 3 BN17 ... 199 A6
Scolliers Crossways RH13 ... 79 B3
Scory Cl RH11 ... 18 A3
Scotland La GU27 ... 27 C5
Scotland St BN2 ... 207 C3
Scotlands Cl GU27 ... 27 B5
Scotlands Dr GU27 ... 27 C5
Scotney Cl BN13 ... 181 B5
Scott Cl PO21 ... 195 C2
Scott Lodge 1 BN17 ... 198 D5
Scott Rd Crawley RH10 ... 18 F3
Hove BN3 ... 186 F7
Scott St PO21 ... 195 C2
Scrace Hill Terr RH16 ... 107 F8
Scrase Lodge RH15 ... 107 D3
Scratchings La GU28, RH14 ... 52 C6
Sculpture at Goodwood PO18 ... 154 C8
Sea Ave BN16 ... 199 D4
Sea Cl
Middleton-on-Sea PO22 ... 196 E5
Worthing BN12 ... 181 E2
Sea Dr Bognor Regis PO22 ... 196 D4
Ferring BN12 ... 200 F4
Sea Gr PO20 ... 206 C6
Sea Ho 14 BN42 ... 185 E7
Sea La East Preston BN16 ... 199 F4
Bognor Regis PO21 ... 204 F7
Ferring BN12 ... 200 F6
Kingston Gorse BN16 ... 200 D4
Middleton-on-Sea PO22 ... 196 E5
Rustington BN16 ... 199 B4
Worthing BN12 ... 181 C1
Sea Lane Cl
East Preston BN16 ... 199 F5
Ferring BN12 ... 200 F6
Sea Lane Gdns BN12 ... 200 F5
Sea Pl BN12 ... 181 E1
Sea Rd Bognor Regis PO22 ... 195 F3
Littlehampton BN16, BN17 ... 199 A3
West Kingston BN16 ... 200 A4
Sea View Cotts PO10 ... 169 B8
Sea View Rd BN11 ... 182 B1
Sea Way
Bognor Regis PO21 ... 204 F8
Elmer PO22 ... 197 B5
Middleton-on-Sea PO22 ... 196 E4
Seabright 11 BN11 ... 182 B1
Seabrook Cl PO21 ... 194 D3
Seabrook Ct BN15 ... 183 E4
Seacourt Cl PO21 ... 194 D2
Seadown Par BN15 ... 183 C5
Seafarers Wlk PO11 ... 189 B1
Seafield Ave BN12 ... 181 D1
Seafield Cl
East Wittering PO20 ... 202 A6
Littlehampton BN16 ... 199 C4
Seafield Rd Hove BN3 ... 187 B6
Littlehampton BN16 ... 199 C4
West Kingston BN16 ... 200 A4
Seafield Terr 5 PO21 ... 195 B2
Seafield Way PO20 ... 202 A6
Seafields
Bracklesham PO20 ... 202 C5
Emsworth PO10 ... 169 B8
Shoreham-by-Sea BN43 ... 184 F8
Seaford Coll GU28 ... 114 E5
Seaford Rd Crawley RH11 ... 18 A2
Hove BN3 ... 186 C6
Seagate Ct PO20 ... 201 E6
Seagate Wlk BN17 ... 199 A4
Seagull Cl PO20 ... 203 C1
Seagull La PO10 ... 149 B1
Seahaven Gdns BN43 ... 184 D5
Seal Ct PO20 ... 206 D7
Seal Prim Sch PO20 ... 206 E7
Seal Rd PO20 ... 206 D5
Seal Sq PO20 ... 206 D5
Seamill Ct 7 BN11 ... 183 B3
Seamill Park Ave BN11 ... 183 B3
Seamill Park Cres BN11 ... 183 B3
Seamill Way BN11 ... 183 B3
Searle's View RH12 ... 36 E5
Seasaw Way BN2 ... 188 F7
Seaside Ave BN15 ... 183 F5
Seaside Cl BN15 ... 183 F5
Seaside Rd BN15 ... 183 F5
Seaton Cl BN17 ... 178 D4
Seaton La BN17 ... 178 D4
Seaton Park Cotts BN17 ... 178 D4
Seaton Pk BN17 ... 178 D4
Seaton Rd BN17 ... 178 D4
Seaview Ave
Kingston Gorse BN16 ... 200 D4
West Kingston BN16 ... 200 A4
Seaview Ct
2 Bognor Regis PO21 ... 195 C2
Lancing BN15 ... 183 D4
Selsey PO20 ... 206 D6
4 Worthing BN11 ... 182 B1
Seaview Est BN42 ... 185 F7
Seaview Gdns 5 BN16 ... 199 C4
Seaview Rd BN16 ... 200 A4
Seaward Ct 6 PO21 ... 195 C3
Seaward Dr PO20 ... 190 C1
Seawaves Cl BN16 ... 200 A5
Seawood Ho PO20 ... 201 F7
Second Ave
Almodington PO20 ... 191 F1
Bognor Regis PO22 ... 196 B4
Bracklesham PO20 ... 202 B5
Hove BN3 ... 187 C6
Lancing BN15 ... 183 E7
Southbourne PO10 ... 169 F8
Worthing BN14 ... 182 D7
Sedbury Rd BN15 ... 183 C8
Seddon Ct RH11 ... 18 B1
Sedgefield Cl RH10 ... 19 E7
Sedgewick Cl RH10 ... 19 C6
Sedgwick La RH13 ... 58 E4
Sefter Rd PO21 ... 194 B3
Sefton Ave PO21 ... 194 D3
Sefton Cl BN13 ... 181 D6
Sefton Place (YH) BN18 ... 158 E3
Sefton Rd BN41 ... 165 F3
Selba Dr BN2 ... 168 E3
Selborne Pl Hove BN3 ... 187 C7
Littlehampton BN17 ... 198 E4
Selborne Rd Hove BN3 ... 187 C6
Littlehampton BN17 ... 198 E4
Worthing BN11 ... 182 F3
Selborne Way BN16 ... 199 F4
Selbourne Cl RH10 ... 6 D2
Selby Ct RH16 ... 85 E3
Selden La
Hammerpot BN13 ... 160 B1
Worthing BN11 ... 182 F2
Selden Mews 3 BN11 ... 182 F2
Selden Par BN13 ... 181 F7
Selden Rd BN11 ... 182 F2
Selden's Mews BN13 ... 181 F6
Selden's Way BN13 ... 181 F7
Sele Gdns BN44 ... 144 B2
Selham Cl Brighton BN1 ... 168 D6
Chichester PO19 ... 153 A3
Crawley RH11 ... 18 A7
Selham Dr BN1 ... 168 D6
Selham Pl BN1 ... 168 D6
Selham Rd GU29 ... 93 C6
Selhurst Cl BN16 ... 199 F5
Selhurstpark Rd PO18 ... 135 B4
Selkirk Cl BN13 ... 181 E4
Selmeston Pl BN2 ... 188 F6
Selmestone Rd BN2 ... 188 F5
Selsey Ave PO21 ... 195 A2
Selsey Cl Brighton BN1 ... 168 E6
South Hayling PO11 ... 189 B2
Worthing BN13 ... 181 F5
Selsey Ct 3 Crawley RH11 ... 18 B2
7 Rustington BN16 ... 199 B4
Selsey PO20 ... 206 D6
Selsey Rd Crawley RH11 ... 18 A2
Sidlesham PO20 ... 203 F7
Stockbridge PO19 ... 172 E3
Street End PO20,PO19 ... 192 D7
Street End PO20,PO19 ... 192 F6
Selsfield Dr BN2 ... 168 D3
Selsfield Rd
Little London RH17, RH19 ... 42 A4
West Hoathly RH19 ... 42 C7
Selway La BN17 ... 198 F6
Selwyn Ave BN17 ... 178 D3
Selwyn Cl
Bognor Regis PO21 ... 194 F4
Crawley RH10 ... 6 C1
Semley Lodge BN6 ... 126 E4
Semley Rd Brighton BN1 ... 168 A1
Hassocks BN6 ... 126 E4
Senator Gdns PO19 ... 172 B7
Sequoia Pk RH11 ... 18 D4
Sergison Cl RH16 ... 85 C5
Sergison Rd RH16 ... 85 D5
Serrin Way RH12 ... 36 E5
Service Rd RH6 ... 5 F8
Servite Cl PO21 ... 195 B4
Servite Ho PO21 ... 195 B4
Sevelands Cl BN2 ... 188 F7
Seven Dials BN1 ... 207 A4
Sevenfields RH15 ... 106 D4
Seventh Ave BN15 ... 183 E8
Severals Rd GU29 ... 92 C7
Severn Rd RH10 ... 19 C5
Seville St BN2 ... 188 C7
Sewill Cl RH6 ... 4 F7
Sextant Ct 6 BN17 ... 199 A6
Seymore Pl 12 PO21 ... 195 C3
Seymour Ho 5 BN2 ... 188 D4
Seymour Rd RH11 ... 18 B2
Seymour Sq 3 BN2 ... 188 D4
Seymour St 4 BN2 ... 188 D4
Shackleton Rd RH10 ... 18 F3
Shadwells Cl BN15 ... 183 F7
Shadwells Ct BN15 ... 183 F7
Shadwells Rd BN15 ... 183 F7
Shaftesbury Ave
BN12, BN13 ... 181 E3
Shaftesbury Ct 4 BN16 ... 199 C4
Shaftesbury Pl BN1 ... 188 A8
Shaftesbury Rd
Brighton BN1 ... 207 B5
Crawley RH10 ... 19 D4
Littlehampton BN16 ... 199 C4
Shakespeare Rd BN11 ... 182 C2
Shakespeare Ho 12 BN11 ... 182 C2
Shakespeare Rd BN11 ... 182 C3
Shakespeare St BN3 ... 187 A8
Shalbourne Cres PO20 ... 202 C5
Shamrock Cl
Bosham PO18 ... 171 C5
Chichester PO19 ... 173 B8
Shandon Gdns BN14 ... 182 D6
Shandon Rd BN14 ... 182 D6
Shandon Way BN14 ... 182 D6
Shands BN6 ... 126 F3
Shandys Cl RH12 ... 36 A1
Shanklin Ct
11 Brighton BN2 ... 188 C8
Hove BN3 ... 166 D1
Shanklin Rd BN2 ... 188 C8
Shannon Cl BN17 ... 199 A4
Shardeloes Rd BN16 ... 179 F6
Sharon Cl RH10 ... 19 A4
Sharpthorne Cl RH11 ... 17 F6
Sharpthorne Cres BN41 ... 166 C1
Sharrow Cl RH16 ... 85 E5
Shaves Wood La BN6 ... 125 A2
Shaw Cl 1 PO22 ... 196 F5
Shaw's La RH13 ... 57 D1
Shawcross Ho BN1 ... 167 E2
Shaws Rd RH10 ... 18 F7
Shearwater Ct 6 RH11 ... 17 D5
Shearwater Dr PO22 ... 195 C6
Sheddingdean Bsns Ctr RH15 ... 106 F5
Sheddingdean Cl RH15 ... 107 A4
Sheddingdean Com Prim Sch RH15 ... 107 A5
Sheddingdean Ct RH15 ... 106 F4
Sheddingdean Neighbourhood Ctr RH15 ... 107 A5
Sheep Fold Ave BN16 ... 199 E6
Sheep La GU29 ... 92 F8
Sheep Pen La BN44 ... 143 D3
Sheepbell Cl BN41 ... 166 B3
Sheepdown Cl GU28 ... 96 A7
Sheepdown Dr GU28 ... 96 A7
Sheepwash La
East Lavant PO18 ... 152 F5
Shipton Green PO20 ... 190 E4
Sheffield Cl RH10 ... 19 B4
Shelby Rd BN13 ... 181 C6
Sheldon Cl RH10 ... 19 D5
Sheldon Ct BN11 ... 182 B1
Shelhurst Forest Wlk PO18 ... 135 B4
Shell La RH17 ... 41 C1
Shellbridge Rd BN18 ... 156 E3
Shelldale Ave BN41 ... 186 B7
Shelldale Cres BN41 ... 186 B7
Shelldale Rd BN41 ... 186 B8
Shelley Cl RH10 ... 19 C8
Shelley Ct 4 RH16 ... 85 D5
Shelley Dr RH12 ... 35 C3
Shelley Lodge BN17 ... 198 F4
Shelley Prim Sch RH12 ... 35 E3
Shelley Rd
Bognor Regis PO21 ... 195 B3
East Grinstead RH19 ... 9 D1
Horsham RH12 ... 36 B3
Hove BN3 ... 186 F7
Worthing BN11 ... 182 C2
Shelley Wood RH15 ... 106 D4
Shellys Ct RH13 ... 37 A3
Shenfield Way BN1 ... 168 B3
Shenstone RH16 ... 86 B8
Shepherd Cl RH10 ... 18 E3
Shepherd's Hill GU27 ... 27 C6
Shepherd's Hill Bglws GU27 ... 27 C6
Shepherds Cl PO18 ... 150 D2
Shepherds Croft
Brighton BN1 ... 167 C4
Findon BN14 ... 161 E6
Shepherds La GU28 ... 72 B3
Shepherds Mead
Burgess Hill RH15 ... 106 F4
Worthing BN14 ... 162 A2
Shepherds Way
Horsham RH12 ... 37 A5
Liphook GU30 ... 25 D3
Shepherds Wlk BN6 ... 126 F5
Sheppard Way BN41 ... 166 A3
Sheppey Cl RH11 ... 18 C3
Sheppeys RH16 ... 85 D2
Sheraton Ct 12 BN11 ... 182 B1
Sheraton Wlk 12 RH11 ... 18 B1
Sherborne Rd PO19 ... 172 E7
Sherbourne Cl BN3 ... 166 D3
Sherbourne La PO20 ... 206 B8
Sherbourne Rd BN3 ... 166 D3
Sherbourne Way BN3 ... 166 D3
Sherbrooke Cl BN13 ... 181 D6
Sherburne Hospl The PO19 ... 152 F1
Sheridan Cl RH19 ... 9 C1
Sheridan Mans BN3 ... 187 A8
Sheridan Rd BN14 ... 182 E5
Sheridan Terr BN3 ... 187 A8
Sherlock Ave PO19 ... 172 E7
Shermanbury Ct
Horsham RH12 ... 36 D4
Lancing BN15 ... 183 C5
Shermanbury Dr RH20 ... 119 C2
Shermanbury Rd BN14 ... 182 B4
Sherston Cl RH20 ... 119 E2
Sherwood Cl
Bognor Regis PO22 ... 195 B6
Liss Forest GU33 ... 45 C7
Sherwood Dr RH16 ... 85 C5
Sherwood Rd PO22 ... 195 B6
Sherwood Wlk RH10 ... 18 F3
Shetland Cl RH10 ... 19 E7
Shetland Ct BN13 ... 181 B5
Shillinglee Rd RH14 ... 30 B4
Shingle Rd BN43 ... 185 A6
Shingle Wlk PO20 ... 201 F6
Shinwell Wlk 3 RH11 ... 18 B1
Ship St Brighton BN1 ... 207 A2
East Grinstead RH19 ... 22 E8
Shoreham-by-Sea BN43 ... 184 E7
Ship Street Gdns BN1 ... 207 A2
Shipfield PO21 ... 194 F2
Shipley Bridge La RH10 ... 7 A3
Shipley CE Prim Sch RH13 ... 79 B1
Shipley Ct GU30 ... 25 C3
Shipley Rd Crawley RH11 ... 18 A6
Southwater RH13 ... 79 E5
Shipleybridge La RH10, RH6 ... 6 F4
Shipton Green La PO20 ... 191 B4
Shire Par RH10 ... 19 D7
Shire Pl RH10 ... 19 D7
Shirlands Ct 3 BN16 ... 199 D6
Shirley Ave BN3 ... 167 B2
Shirley Cl
Bognor Regis PO21 ... 205 A8
Crawley RH11 ... 17 E2
Littlehampton BN16 ... 199 D4
Shoreham-by-Sea BN43 ... 185 D8
Worthing BN14 ... 182 B7
Shirley Dr
Bognor Regis PO22 ... 196 A6
Hove BN3 ... 167 C2
Worthing BN14 ... 182 B6
Shirley Mews BN3 ... 187 B7
Shirley Rd BN3 ... 187 C8
Shirley St BN3 ... 187 B7
Shirleys BN6 ... 127 E2
Shirleys Gdn PO22 ... 196 B5
Shooting Field BN44 ... 143 D4
Shop La PO18 ... 153 A5
Shopfield Cl BN16 ... 199 C6
Shopsdam Rd BN15 ... 183 F4
Shopwhyke Ind Ctr PO20 ... 173 D7
Shopwhyke Rd
PO19, PO20 ... 173 E7
Shore Rd Bosham PO18 ... 171 B3
East Wittering PO20 ... 201 E7
Shorecroft PO21 ... 194 F1
Shoreham Airport BN15, BN43 ... 184 C8
Shoreham Beach Com Fst Sch BN43 ... 185 A6
Shoreham By-Pass BN41,BN43 ... 165 D2
Shoreham Coll BN43 ... 185 D7
Shoreham Ct BN43 ... 184 F8
Shoreham Fst Sch BN43 ... 184 E7
Shoreham Rd
Crawley RH10 ... 19 C3
Small Dole BN5 ... 144 F8
Upper Beeding BN44 ... 164 B7
Shoreham-by-Sea Sta BN43 ... 184 F7
Shoreside Wlk PO20 ... 201 F7
Short Cl RH11 ... 18 D8
Short Furlong BN17 ... 198 F5
Short Gallop RH10 ... 19 D7
Shortgate Rd BN2 ... 168 F4
Shorts Cl RH16 ... 85 E3
Shortsfield Cl RH12 ... 36 C5
Shotford PO20 ... 203 F8
Shotterfield Terr GU33 ... 45 B4
Shottermill RH12 ... 37 A7
Shottermill Cty Jun Sch GU27 ... 26 F7
Shottermill Inf Sch GU27 ... 26 F7
Shottermill Pk GU27 ... 26 F7
Shottermill Rd GU27 ... 26 E5
Shotters RH15 ... 106 E1
Shovelstrode La RH19 ... 23 D8
Shrewsbury Ct 6 BN11 ... 182 B1
Shripney La PO22 ... 175 C1
Shripney Rd
Bognor Regis PO22 ... 195 D5
Bognor Regis PO22 ... 195 E7
Shrubbs Dr PO22 ... 196 F5
Sickle Mill GU27 ... 26 F6
Sickle Rd GU27 ... 27 A5
Sidehill Dr BN41 ... 165 F2
Sideways La RH6 ... 1 D2
Sidings The RH12 ... 33 D7
Sidlesham Cl PO11 ... 189 B2
Sidlesham La PO20 ... 192 A4
Sidlesham Prim Sch PO20 ... 203 D8
Silchester Dr RH11 ... 18 B4
Silkin Wlk 8 RH11 ... 18 B1
Sillwood Ct 19 BN1 ... 187 E5
Sillwood Hall 2 BN1 ... 187 E5
Sillwood Pl 17 BN1 ... 187 E5
Sillwood Rd BN1 ... 187 E5
Sillwood St BN1 ... 187 E5
Sillwood Terr 22 BN1 ... 187 E5
Silver Birch Cl GU33 ... 45 C4
Silver Birch Dr
Middleton-on-Sea PO22 ... 196 E6
Worthing BN13 ... 181 C5
Silver Birches
Brighton BN1 ... 167 E1
Haywards Heath RH16 ... 86 A4
Small Dole BN5 ... 144 F7
Silver Glade RH20 ... 119 E6
Silver La RH14 ... 77 D8
Silver Way PO20 ... 202 C4
Silverdale
Coldwaltham RH20 ... 117 C5
Keymer BN6 ... 127 B3
Silverdale Ave BN3 ... 187 D7
Silverdale Cl PO21 ... 205 A8
Silverdale Dr BN15 ... 183 C5
Silverdale Ind Est BN11 ... 183 B3
Silverdale Rd
Burgess Hill RH15 ... 107 B2
Hove BN3 ... 187 D7
Silverlea Gdns RH6 ... 2 C2
Silverlock Pl PO10 ... 149 D5
Silverston Ave PO21 ... 195 A2
Silvertrees PO10 ... 149 B2
Silverwood RH20 ... 119 B7
Silverwood Copse RH20 ... 119 B7
Silverwood Ct 10 BN16 ... 199 C5
Simon Ct 13 PO21 ... 195 C3
Sinclair Cl RH10 ... 19 C4
Sincox La RH13 ... 100 D6
Singleton CE Prim Sch PO18 ... 133 D7
Singleton Cl
Bognor Regis PO21 ... 194 C1
Ferring BN12 ... 180 F3
Singleton Cres BN12 ... 200 F6
Singleton Ho BN17 ... 178 B3
Singleton Rd
Brighton BN1 ... 168 A6
Broadridge Heath RH12 ... 35 D3
Singleton Way RH15 ... 107 C1
Sinnocks RH20 ... 99 E1
Sir George's Pl BN44 ... 143 C3
Sir Robert Peel Ct 14 PO21 ... 195 D4
Siskin Cl RH12 ... 36 E5
Sissinghurst Cl RH10 ... 19 D7
Six Acres Cl RH13 ... 56 F2
Skelmersdale Wlk RH11 ... 17 E2
Skeyne Dr 4 RH20 ... 98 C2
Skiff La RH14 ... 53 F5
Skipton Way RH6 ... 2 B5
Skylark View RH12 ... 36 D7

Slade La GU31 67 F5
Slattsfield Cl PO20 206 F7
Slaugham Ct RH11 17 F3
Slaugham La RH17 61 A2
Sleets Rd RH12 35 E3
Slider's La
Furner's Green TN22 66 B1
Sheffield Green TN22 87 F6
Slimbridge Rd RH15 106 F3
Slindon Bottom Rd BN18 156 A4
Slindon CE Prim Sch BN18 156 D4
Slindon Cl BN14 182 D6
Slindon Coll BN18 156 B5
Slindon Rd BN14 182 D6
Slinfold CE Prim Sch RH12 34 D4
Slinfold Wlk RH11 18 A6
Slinford Cl BN2 188 D5
Slipe The BN18 158 B2
Slipper Rd PO10 169 C8
Sloane Ct 4 BN2 188 C5
Sloe Cl PO19 173 C7
Slonk Hill Rd BN43 165 A1
Sloop La RH17 87 D5
Sloughbrook Cl RH12 36 F6
Sloughgreen La RH17 61 E1
Small's La RH11 18 C6
Smallcroft Cl BN17 198 C5
Smallcuts Ave PO10 149 F1
Smallfield Rd RH6 2 D3
Smallmead RH6 2 B3
Smalls Mead RH11 18 C6
Smee La PO18 153 D1
Smith Cl RH10 18 D3
Smith La PO10 169 F1
Smith's Cross RH13 82 C3
Smithbarn RH13 37 A2
Smithbarn Cl RH6 2 B4
Smithers Cotts RH12 33 F7
Smithers Hill La RH13 79 B2
Smithy The RH13 81 E1
Smock Alley RH20 119 E7
Smokejack Hill RH5 13 D7
Smokyhouse La GU28 94 B5
Smolletts RH19 22 C8
Smuggler's La PO18 171 B1
Smugglers End RH17 61 C8
Smugglers La BN44 144 B2
Smugglers Way RH13 56 F2
Smugglers Wlk BN12 181 E1
Smugglers' La
Barns Green RH13 56 D3
Barns Green RH13 56 F3
Paynes Green RH5 14 E7
Snapes Rd RH20 119 F3
Snell Hatch RH11 18 B6
Snipe La GU27 27 A1
Snow Hill RH10 8 A4
Snow Hill Bsns Ctr RH10 8 A4
Snowdrop Cl Crawley RH11 18 A2
Rustington BN17 179 B3
Snowdrop La RH16 86 C4
Snowflakes La RH16 86 D6
Snowhill La RH10 7 F5
Soames Ct RH15 106 F4
Soane Cl RH11 17 E4
Solent Cl BN17 179 A3
Solent Rd PO20 201 F6
Solent Way PO20 206 E5
Solway Ave BN1 167 F7
Solway Cl BN17 199 A5
Somergate RH12 35 F2
Somerhill Ave BN3 187 D7
Somerhill Ct 10 BN3 187 D7
Somerhill Cty Jun Sch BN3 187 D6
Somerhill Lodge BN3 187 D6
Somerhill Rd BN3 187 D6
Somerley La PO20 191 E1
Somersbury La GU6, RH12 12 F7
Somerset Cl BN13 182 A5
Somerset Ct 3 BN3 187 C7
Somerset Gdns PO21 195 C5
Somerset Hospl GU28 95 F8
Somerset Point 1 BN2 188 C4
Somerset Rd
East Preston BN16 200 B6
Ferring BN12 200 F4
Somerset St BN2 188 C5
Somerstown PO19 172 F8
Somerton Gn PO22 195 F5
Somerville Dr RH10 6 C1
Somping Rd BN14 182 E7
Sompting Abbotts Sch BN15 183 A8
Sompting Ave BN14 182 D5
Sompting By-Pass BN14 182 E7
Sompting Cl BN2 188 F7
Sompting Ct 3 BN43 185 B8
Sompting Lodge 5 BN15 183 D5
Sompting Rd
Lancing BN15 183 D5
Worthing BN14 182 E6
Sopers La BN44 163 C7
Sorrel Cl RH11 18 A2
Sorrel Rd RH12 36 E5
South Acre GU31 89 D3
South Ash BN44 143 D4
South Ave
Bognor Regis PO21 194 F3
Brighton BN2 188 C5
Hurstpierpoint BN6 126 A5
Worthing BN12 181 E1
South Bank Hassocks BN6 126 E3
Stockbridge PO19 172 F4
South Bank Ct BN15 184 A4
South Bay PO10 169 C3
South Beach 6 BN43 184 F6
South Bersted CE Prim Sch PO22 195 C5
South Bersted Ind Est PO22 195 D6
South Cl Burgess Hill RH15 106 E3
Crawley RH10 18 F7
South Dr Angmering BN16 179 E3
Bognor Regis PO22 196 C5
Burgess Hill RH15 106 E3
Ferring BN12 200 E4
South Farm Cotts BN14 182 C5
South Farm Inds BN14 182 C5
South Farm Rd BN14 182 C5
South Gr Horsham RH13 36 D1
Petworth GU28 95 F7
South Holmes Rd RH13 37 B4
South La Breach PO10 150 A2
Houghton BN18 138 B3
Tillington GU28 94 F7
Woodmancote PO10 150 A3
South Lodge
Bognor Regis PO21 194 A2
9 Brighton BN2 188 F5
3 Lancing BN15 183 C7
South Lodge Cl RH15 106 F4
South Pallant PO19 173 A6
South Par RH6 1 F4
South Pas BN17 198 F4
South Pier Rd RH6 6 B7
South Point 9 BN43 185 A6
South Rd
Bognor Regis PO22 195 F5
Brighton BN1 167 E1
Haywards Heath RH16 85 E4
Liphook GU30 25 D1
South Rd Mews BN1 167 E1
South St Brighton BN1 207 A2
Chichester PO19 173 A6
Cuckfield RH17 84 E6
Ditchling BN6 127 D3
Emsworth PO10 169 B8
Horsham RH12 36 C2
Lancing BN15 183 E4
Midhurst GU29 92 F7
Partridge Green RH13 103 A3
Portslade-by-Sea BN41 166 A1
Worthing BN11 182 D1
Worthing, West Tarring BN11, BN13, BN14 182 A4
South Strand BN16 200 A4
South Strand Par 6 BN16 200 A4
South Terr
Bognor Regis PO22 195 D5
Littlehampton BN17 198 E4
South View Ditchling BN6 127 E5
West Kingston BN16 200 B4
South View Cl RH10 7 E3
South View Terr BN5 123 E4
South Way PO21 195 A5
South Wlk PO22 196 E5
South Woodlands BN1 167 E5
Southall Ave BN2 168 D2
Southampton St BN2 207 C3
Southbank Ct PO19 172 F4
Southbourne Ave PO10 169 D8
Southbourne Halt PO10 170 A8
Southbourne Jun & Inf Sch PO10 170 A8
Southbrook RH11 18 C1
Southbrook Rd
West Ashling PO18 151 B2
West Ashling PO18 151 C3
Southcote Ave PO20 201 E7
Southcourt Cl BN16 199 E6
Southcourt Rd BN14 182 C3
Southdean Cl 9 PO22 196 F5
Southdean Dr PO22 196 F5
Southdown Ave
Brighton BN1 168 A1
Portslade-by-Sea BN41 186 C8
Southdown Cl
Haywards Heath RH16 85 D2
Horsham RH12 37 A5
Midhurst GU29 92 D6
Southdown Ct PO20 202 A7
Southdown Ho BN12 181 D2
Southdown Mews BN2 188 C5
Southdown Pl BN1 168 A1
Southdown Rd
Bognor Regis PO21 195 C3
Brighton BN1 168 A1
Portslade-by-Sea BN41 166 A2
Shoreham-by-Sea BN43 184 F7
Southwick BN42 185 E7
Southdown Terr BN44 143 E3
Southdown View Cl BN14 182 F5
Southdown View Rd BN14 182 F5
Southdown View Way BN14 182 E6
Southdown Way RH20 119 F3
Southern Cross Ind Est PO22 195 E7
Southern L Ctr PO20 173 D3
Southern Rd PO20 206 E6
Southey Rd BN11 182 C1
Southfield Ind Pk PO18 171 B6
Southfield Rd BN14 182 D5
Southfields Cl PO19 172 F3
Southfields Rd BN17,BN16 198 F5
Southgate PO19 172 F5
Southgate Ave RH10, RH11 18 E4
Southgate Dr RH10, RH11 18 E4
Southgate Fst & Mid Sch RH10 18 D4
Southgate Par RH10 18 D4
Southgate Rd RH10 18 D4
Southgate West Fst & Mid Sch RH11 18 C4
Southlands
East Grinstead RH19 22 E7
Horley RH6 1 F3
Southlands Ave RH6 2 A4
Southlands Ct
14 Littlehampton BN17 198 E4
1 Shoreham-by-Sea BN43 185 B8
Southlands Gen Hospl BN43 165 B1
Southlands La RH20 119 E8
Southlands Pk GU29 92 E5
Southleigh Rd PO10, PO9 149 B3
Southleys GU27 49 A5
Southmount BN1 168 B1
Southon Cl BN41 165 F3
Southon View BN15 183 C3
Southover Pl BN2 207 C4
Southover Rd PO21 195 C3
Southover St BN2 207 C3
Southover Way PO20 173 A1
Southsea Ave BN12 181 E1
Southside RH20 98 D2
Southview
Scaynes Hill RH17 86 F3
Small Dole BN5 144 F6
Southview Cl
Southwick BN42 165 E1
Southwick, Kingston by Sea BN43 185 C7
Southview Dr BN11 182 A2
Southview Gdns BN11 182 A2
Southview Rd
Bognor Regis PO22 196 B4
Findon BN14 161 E6
Southwick BN42 185 E8
Southwark Cl RH11 18 B2
Southwark Wlk PO21 194 E4
Southwater Bsns Pk RH13 57 F1
Southwater Cl
Brighton BN2 188 D6
Crawley RH11 18 A6
Worthing BN12 181 B3
Southwater Inf Sch RH13 57 F2
Southwater Jun Sch RH13 57 F2
Southwater St RH13 58 A4
Southway
Burgess Hill RH15 106 D3
Littlehampton BN17 198 F4
Southway Jun Sch RH15 106 D3
Southways Ave BN14 182 E6
Southways Pk RH10 5 D3
Southwick Cl RH19 9 D2
Southwick Ho 6 RH19 9 D2
Southwick Sq BN42 185 E7
Southwick St BN42 185 E8
Southwick Sta BN42 185 E7
Southwold Cl BN13 161 E1
Southwood Rd PO11 189 A1
Sovereign Ct 21 PO21 195 D3
Sovereign Ctr RH15 106 E2
Spa Ct 4 BN3 187 B5
Spanish Ct RH15 107 B4
Spark's La RH17 62 E2
Sparks Ct BN17 198 D5
Sparrow Way RH15 106 D3
Sparrows La RH20 121 A5
Sparshott Rd PO20 206 E5
Spartan Cl PO10 169 C3
Spatham La BN6 127 F4
Spear Hill RH20 121 A7
Speedwell Cl BN13 181 A5
Speedwell Way RH12 36 E5
Spencer Ave BN3 166 D3
Spencer Rd Lancing BN15 183 D5
New Brighton PO10 149 A4
Spencer St PO21 195 D4
Spencer's Rd RH12 36 B3
Spencers La RH6 1 A2
Spencers Pl RH12 36 B4
Spencers Rd RH11 18 D5
Spey Cl BN13 181 C8
Spicers Cl RH15 106 F5
Spierbridge Rd RH20 119 C2
Spiers Way RH6 2 B1
Spindle Way RH10 18 F5
Spinnaker Cl BN17 199 A5
Spinnals Gr BN42 185 D7
Spinney Cl
Crawley Down RH10 21 C8
Horsham RH12 37 B6
Hurstpierpoint BN6 126 C5
Selsey PO20 206 D8
Spinney La West Chiltington Common RH20 119 D5
West Itchenor PO20 191 A6
Spinney North RH20 98 D2
Spinney The
Bognor Regis PO21 194 E3
Burgess Hill RH15 107 B5
Crawley RH11 18 B4
Haslemere GU27 27 C8
Hassocks BN6 126 F5
Haywards Heath RH16 85 D8
Haywards Heath RH16 85 F3
Horley RH6 2 A5
Hove BN3 167 C3
Pulborough RH20 98 D2
West Itchenor PO20 191 A5
West Kingston BN16 200 A4
Spinney Wlk PO22 176 B6
Spitalfield La PO19 173 B7
Spitfire Ct PO20 154 D2
Spithandle La BN44 122 B3
Spooners Rd RH12 37 A4
Spring Copse
Copthorne RH10 7 C3
East Grinstead RH19 9 D3
Spring Copse Bsns Pk RH13 34 C3
Spring Cotts RH20 119 C1
Spring Gdns Brighton BN1 207 B2
Copthorne RH10 7 C3
Emsworth PO10 169 C8
Heath Common RH20 120 E2
6 Southwick BN42 185 E7
Spring Hill Wildfowl Pk RH18 23 A1
Spring La Clayton BN6 147 E8
Lindfield RH16 64 B1
Slinfold RH13 34 C3
Spring Mdw RH18 23 F1
Spring Mdws GU29 92 E6
Spring Plat RH10 19 C6
Spring Plat Ct RH10 19 C6
Spring St BN1 187 E5
Spring Way RH19 10 A4
Springate Rd BN42 185 F8
Springbank PO19 152 F1
Springfarm Rd GU27 26 E5
Springfield
Bognor Regis PO21 194 A2
East Grinstead RH19 9 D4
Liss GU33 45 B4
Springfield Cl
Birdham PO20 191 F5
Bolney RH17 83 C4
Mid Lavant PO18 152 F7
Rustington BN16 199 E5
Springfield Cotts RH17 83 C4
Springfield Cres RH12 36 B2
Springfield Ct 1 RH12 36 C2
Springfield Fst Sch BN14 182 E4
Springfield Gdns BN13 182 A7
Springfield La RH12, RH13 38 B5
Springfield Park Rd RH12 36 B2
Springfield Pk RH12 36 C3
Springfield Pk Ho RH12 36 C3
Springfield Rd
Brighton BN1 188 A8
Crawley RH11 18 D5
Horsham RH12 36 C2
Springfields Farm Ind Est RH17 107 F5
Springhead Farm Cotts RH20 139 E7
Springhills BN5 123 E4
Springmead Ct GU27 26 D5
Spronkett's La RH17 82 E3
Sproule Cl BN18 177 B2
Sproutes La RH13 100 D8
Sprucefield Ct RH11 18 B6
Spur Rd PO19 173 D5
Spurgeon Cl RH11 18 C7
Spy La RH14 32 A4
Squadron Dr BN13 181 B6
Square Dr Fernhurst GU27 49 B7
Marley Heights GU27 27 B1
Square The Brighton BN1 167 E6
Crawley RH10 18 D6
Findon BN14 161 E6
Prinsted PO10 169 F7
South Harting GU31 89 D4
Storrington RH20 119 D1
Washington RH20 141 C3
West Barnham PO22 176 B5
Westbourne PO10 149 D3
Squire Way BN5 123 E4
Squires Cl RH10 21 A8
Squires Cotts RH20 138 A7
Squirrel Cl RH11 5 B1
Squirrels Copse RH20 120 C3
Stable Cl RH10 19 D3
Stable Cotts Crawley RH11 39 A8
Shopwyke PO20 173 F7
Stable Ctyd The BN18 177 E7
Stable Field PO22 197 B5
Stable Flats RH11 39 A8
Stable La BN14 161 E6
Stace Way RH10 19 E8
Stackfield Rd RH11 17 E5
Stafford House F Ed Ctr BN6 127 A3
Stafford Rd Brighton BN1 187 E8
Crawley RH11 5 B1
Stafford Way BN6 127 A3
Staffords Cl BN16 199 B6
Staffords Pl RH6 2 B2
Stag Cl BN5 123 E6
Stagelands RH11 18 C8
Stagelands Ct RH11 18 C8
Stairbridge La RH17 105 E7
Stakers La RH13 80 A8
Stalham Way PO22 196 A6
Stall House La RH20 99 A8
Stallard Cl PO10 149 A1
Stamford 6 RH16 85 D6
Stamford Lodge 2 BN1 167 E2
Stammerham Bsns Ctr RH12 15 E7
Stammers Hill BN5 145 F3
Stan Hill RH6 4 D8
Stan's Way 7 RH12 36 C2
Stanbridge Cl RH11 17 E6
Stanbridge Way RH17 64 B7
Stanbrok Cl PO21 194 E3
Stanbury Cl PO18 171 C7
Standean Cl BN1 168 D6
Standen (NT) RH19 22 D4
Standen Cl RH19 9 A4
Standen Ct BN44 144 B2
Standen Pl RH12 37 A7
Standgrove Pl RH17 64 A6
Standinghall La RH10 20 A3
Stane St
Billingshurst RH14,RH20 77 B4
Codmore Hill RH20 98 D6
Five Oaks RH14 55 E4
Park Street RH13 34 C4
Strettington PO18 154 B3
Westhampnett PO18 153 E1
Stane Street Cl RH20 98 C4
Stanford (Scout Camp Site) RH11 39 B8
Stanford Ave
Brighton BN1 168 A1
Hassocks BN6 126 E4
Stanford Cl
Bognor Regis PO22 195 E5
Hassocks BN6 126 E4
Hove BN3 167 C1
Stanford Ct BN1 187 F8
Stanford Cty Inf Sch BN1 187 E8
Stanford Cty Jun Sch BN1 187 F8
Stanford Orch RH12 35 F8
Stanford Rd BN1 187 F8
Stanford Sq BN11 182 E2
Stanford Terr BN6 126 E4
Stanford Way RH12 35 D3
Stanhope Rd
Littlehampton BN17 198 E5
Worthing BN11 182 D3
Stanier Cl RH10 19 B5
Stanley Ave BN41 165 F3
Stanley Ave S BN41 165 F3
Stanley Cl
Bognor Regis PO21 195 D4
Crawley RH10 18 E4
Stanley Ct 3 BN2 188 C8
Stanley Ctr RH10 5 F2
Stanley Deason L Ctr BN2 188 F5
Stanley Rd Brighton BN1 207 B4
Emsworth PO10 169 C8
Littlehampton BN17 178 D3
Portslade-by-Sea BN41 186 A8
Worthing BN11 182 D3
Stanley St BN2 207 C3
Stanley Wlk 10 RH13 36 D2
Stanmer BN1 168 F8
Stanmer Ct BN1 168 A2
Stanmer Ho BN1 168 B2
Stanmer Park Rd BN1 168 B2
Stanmer St BN1 168 B2
Stanmer Villas BN1 168 B2
Stanmore Gdns PO21 194 E2
Stanmore Ho 5 RH20 119 E1
Stanover La PO22 196 A7
Stansfield Ct BN16 199 D6
Stanstead Cl PO9 128 E2
Stansted Ho PO9 129 E1
Stanton Dr PO19 153 A3
Stanwater La GU29 69 F3
Staple La PO18 152 F8
Staplecross Ct 1 RH11 18 A3
Staplefield Dr BN2 168 F3
Staplefield Rd
Cuckfield RH17 84 C8
Staplefield RH17 61 E4
Staples Barn BN5 123 D5
Staples Barn La BN5 123 D5
Staples Hill RH13 102 F4
Stapleton Ct PO21 194 D2
Stapley Ct BN3 186 D8
Stapley Rd BN3 166 D1
Star Cl RH13 37 A4
Star Rd RH13 103 A2
Star Rd Trad Est RH13 103 A2
Starboard Ct BN2 188 F3
Starboard Wlk 9 BN17 198 F4
Starborough Cotts RH7 9 F7
Starling Cl RH15 106 C3
Station App
Haslemere GU27 27 B6
Hassocks BN6 126 F4
Horley RH6 2 B2
Horsted Keynes RH17 65 A7
Hove BN3 187 B8
Station App E BN6 126 E4
Station App W BN6 126 E4
Station Approach Rd RH6 6 B7
Station Cl RH13 36 D2
Station Cotts
Hassocks BN6 126 E4
Horsham RH13 57 D7
Station Hill RH10 19 B7
Station Par
2 Lancing BN15 183 E5
6 Rustington BN16 199 E6
1 Worthing BN11 182 A3
Station Rd
Angmering BN16 179 F4
Billingshurst RH14 77 D7
15 Bognor Regis PO21 195 C3
Brighton BN1 167 D3
Broadbridge PO18 171 C7
Burgess Hill RH15 107 B2
Cowfold RH13 81 B2
Cranleigh RH12 12 C3
Crawley RH10 18 D5
Crawley Down RH10 21 B8
Crossbush BN18 158 D1
East Grinstead RH19 9 D1
Ford BN18 177 E4
Forest Row RH18 23 F3

Station Rd *continued*
Henfield BN5 ... 123 D5
Horley RH6 ... 2 B3
Horsham RH13 ... 36 D2
Horsted Keynes RH17 ... 65 C5
Liphook GU30 ... 25 C2
Liss GU33 ... 45 B4
Littlehampton BN16 ... 199 E5
Loxwood RH14 ... 32 A3
Midhurst GU29 ... 92 D7
Petworth GU28 ... 95 E5
Portslade-by-Sea BN3, BN41 ... 186 C7
Pulborough RH20 ... 98 A2
Rudgwick RH12 ... 33 D7
Rustington BN16 ... 199 F6
Sharpthorne RH19 ... 43 A6
Southwater RH13 ... 57 F1
7 Southwick BN42 ... 185 E7
Steyning BN44 ... 143 E3
Tower Hill RH13 ... 57 D7
Warnham RH12 ... 36 B8
Worthing BN11 ... 182 E3
Station St BN1 ... 207 B3
Station Villas RH20 ... 98 A2
Station Way RH10 ... 18 D5
Staunton Ctry Pk PO9 ... 128 A2
Stavely Gdns PO19 ... 152 F3
Stean Furlong BN17 ... 178 C3
Stedham La GU29 ... 70 A3
Stedham Prim Sch GU29 ... 69 F1
Steeds Cnr RH13 ... 80 D6
Steele Cl RH20 ... 99 E1
Steels La PO18 ... 170 E5
Steep Cl BN14 ... 161 E5
Steep La BN14 ... 161 E5
Steepdown Rd BN15 ... 183 C8
Steeple View BN13 ... 182 A5
Steeres Hill RH12 ... 16 C6
Steers La RH10 ... 6 C4
Stein Rd PO10 ... 149 F2
Steine Gdns BN2 ... 207 B2
Steine La BN1, BN2 ... 207 B2
Steine St BN2 ... 207 B1
Stemp Dr RH14 ... 77 C8
Stempswood Way PO22 ... 176 C6
Stennings The RH19 ... 9 C3
Stephen Cl RH11 ... 5 D1
Stephens Rd BN1 ... 168 B2
Stephenson Dr RH19 ... 22 F7
Stephenson Pl RH10 ... 19 B6
Stephenson Way RH10 ... 19 B6
Stepney Cl RH10 ... 19 C4
Sterling Bldgs 3 RH12 ... 36 C2
Sterling Par 3 BN16 ... 199 C5
Sternway BN17 ... 199 A5
Stevenage Rd RH11 ... 17 E3
Stevens Ct BN3 ... 186 E7
Stevenson Rd BN2 ... 188 C5
Stewards Rise BN18 ... 157 F1
Steyne Gdns BN11 ... 182 E2
Steyne Hall 4 PO21 ... 195 C2
Steyne St PO21 ... 195 C3
Steyne The
Bognor Regis PO21 ... 195 C2
Worthing BN11 ... 182 E2
Steyning 2 BN15 ... 183 D5
Steyning Ave BN3 ... 166 F3
Steyning By-Pass BN44 ... 143 E3
Steyning Cl Crawley RH10 ... 18 E8
Lancing BN15 ... 183 D8
Worthing BN12 ... 181 B3
Steyning Cres RH20 ... 119 C2
Steyning Ct 7 BN3 ... 187 B7
Steyning Gram Lower Sch BN44 ... 143 D3
Steyning Gram Upper Sch BN44 ... 143 D4
Steyning Ho 1 BN14 ... 182 D5
Steyning Mus BN44 ... 143 D3
Steyning Rd
Shoreham-by-Sea BN43,BN44 BN43,BN44 ... 164 C4
Shoreham-by-Sea, Mill Hill BN43 ... 164 D1
West Grinstead RH13 ... 102 C7
Steyning Way PO22 ... 195 E7
Stile Gdns GU27 ... 26 F6
Stipenhoks BN5 ... 123 F4
Stirling Cl
Burgess Hill RH15 ... 107 C4
Crawley RH10 ... 19 C5
Stirling Court Rd RH15 ... 107 C4
Stirling Ct 5 BN3 ... 187 C7
Stirling Pl BN3 ... 187 A6
Stirling Rd PO19 ... 173 A5
Stirling Way
Bognor Regis PO21 ... 194 E2
East Grinstead RH19 ... 10 B3
Horsham RH12 ... 36 E3
Stirrup Way RH10 ... 19 D7
Stoatley Hollow GU27 ... 27 A8
Stoatley Rise GU27 ... 27 A8
Stock Ho BN15 ... 183 A7
Stockbridge Gdns PO19 ... 172 E4
Stockbridge Pl PO19 ... 172 F4
Stockbridge Rd PO19 ... 172 F4
Stockcroft Rd RH17 ... 41 A1
Stocker Rd PO21 ... 195 B2
Stockfield RH6 ... 2 B4
Stocklands Cl RH17 ... 84 F8
Stocks Cl RH6 ... 2 B2
Stocks Field BN44 ... 121 D1
Stocks La
Bracklesham PO20 ... 202 A6
Stocks La *continued*
Chichester PO18, PO19 ... 153 C3
Stocks Mead RH20 ... 141 E6
Stockwell Ct
Burgess Hill RH15 ... 106 F3
1 Haywards Heath RH16 ... 85 E3
Stockwell Ctr RH10 ... 19 A6
Stockwell Rd RH19 ... 22 E6
Stodham La Hill Side GU33 ... 45 C2
Prince's Marsh GU33, GU31 ... 45 B1
Stoke Abbott Ct 2 BN11 ... 182 D2
Stoke Abbott Rd BN11 ... 182 D2
Stoke Brunswick Sch RH19 ... 23 E7
Stoke Rd BN18 ... 138 D3
Stokes Cl RH10 ... 19 C3
Stone Cl BN13 ... 181 F6
Stone Cross RH16 ... 64 D3
Stone Ct GU29 ... 92 D8
Stone Hatch GU6 ... 11 A3
Stone La BN13 ... 181 F6
Stone Quarry Rd RH17 ... 66 D7
Stone St BN1 ... 187 E5
Stoneage Cl PO22 ... 195 C7
Stonebridge Ct
Crawley RH11 ... 18 C2
Horsham RH12 ... 36 A2
Stonecourt Cl RH6 ... 2 C3
Stonecourt Cotts RH17 ... 62 A5
Stonecroft BN44 ... 143 D3
Stonecroft Cl BN3 ... 166 E4
Stonecrop Cl RH11 ... 18 B3
Stonecross La RH16 ... 64 E3
Stonecross Rd BN2 ... 168 F4
Stonefield Cl RH10, RH11 ... 18 D5
Stonefield Way RH15 ... 106 F5
Stonefields BN16 ... 199 D5
Stonehall La RH17 ... 63 C6
Stoneham Rd BN3 ... 186 F7
Stonehill Cres PO21 ... 194 B3
Stonehouse La RH13 ... 81 B1
Stonehouse Rd GU30 ... 25 D4
Stonehurst Ct 10 BN2 ... 188 C6
Stonehurst Rd BN13 ... 182 A5
Stoneleigh Ave BN1 ... 167 F6
Stoneleigh Cl
Brighton BN1 ... 167 F6
East Grinstead RH19 ... 9 F1
Stonepit La BN5 ... 123 C5
Stonepound Crossroads BN6 ... 126 D4
Stonepound Rd BN6 ... 126 E4
Stoners Cl RH6 ... 5 E7
Stonery Cl BN41 ... 166 A2
Stonery Rd BN41 ... 166 A2
Stoney La
Balcombe Lane RH17 ... 41 B5
Bracklesham PO20 ... 202 D4
Shoreham-by-Sea BN43 ... 185 C8
Stoney Stile Cl PO21 ... 194 C2
Stoney Stile La PO21 ... 194 C1
Stoneybrook RH12 ... 35 F1
Stoneycroft Wlk 3 RH11 ... 17 D5
Stoneyfield Cotts PO20 ... 156 B1
Stoneywish Ctry Pk BN6 ... 127 E3
Stopham Cl BN14 ... 182 A5
Stopham Rd Crawley RH10 ... 19 C3
Stopham RH20 ... 97 E1
Stor Mdw RH20 ... 119 D2
Storrington Cl
Fishbourne PO19 ... 172 B7
Hove BN3 ... 166 E2
Storrington Ct RH11 ... 18 A7
Storrington Fst Sch RH20 ... 119 C2
Storrington Rd
Heath Common RH20 ... 120 A5
Washington RH20 ... 141 C8
Storrington Rise BN14 ... 161 F4
Story Rd PO19 ... 173 C7
Stour Cl BN13 ... 181 C8
Stour Rd BN13 ... 181 C8
Strachey Ct 1 RH11 ... 18 B1
Strand Cl RH10 ... 19 D4
Strand Ct Rustington BN16 ... 199 B3
11 West Kingston BN16 ... 200 A4
Strand Par BN12 ... 181 E3
Strand The Ferring BN12 ... 200 E4
Worthing BN12 ... 181 C3
Strand Way PO22 ... 196 B4
Strange Gdn PO21 ... 194 E1
Stratford Ct BN11 ... 182 C2
Strathfield Cl RH16 ... 85 F4
Strathmoor Gdns GU29 ... 70 F1
Strathmore Cl BN13 ... 181 E4
Strathmore Rd
Crawley RH11 ... 5 A1
Worthing BN13 ... 181 E4
Stratton Ct
Bognor Regis PO22 ... 195 E5
6 Hove BN3 ... 186 F7
Strawberry La RH20 ... 120 B5
Stream Cl PO18 ... 171 B5
Stream La RH20 ... 99 B1
Stream Pk RH19 ... 9 A3
Streathleigh Ct PO21 ... 195 A2
Streel's La GU28 ... 51 F5
Street End La PO20 ... 192 E3
Street End Rd PO20 ... 192 E3
Street Hill RH10 ... 19 E5
Street La RH17 ... 64 A8
Street The
Albourne Green BN6 ... 125 C6
Boxgrove PO18 ... 154 D4
Bramber BN44 ... 143 F2
Bury RH20 ... 138 A7
Charlwood RH6 ... 4 E7
Clapham BN13 ... 160 E1
Street The *continued*
Cowfold RH13 ... 81 E2
East Preston BN16 ... 199 F6
Lancing BN15 ... 183 F8
Nutbourne RH20 ... 99 A2
Patching BN13 ... 160 D2
Plaistow RH14 ... 30 E2
Rustington BN16 ... 199 C5
Shoreham-by-Sea BN43 ... 164 E1
Slinfold RH13 ... 34 D4
Stedham GU29 ... 70 A1
Thakeham RH20 ... 120 B7
Walberton BN18 ... 156 D1
Walberton BN18 ... 176 E8
Warninglid RH17 ... 82 F8
Washington RH20 ... 141 D6
West Itchenor PO20 ... 190 F7
Westmeston BN6 ... 148 F8
Streete Ct 12 PO21 ... 195 B2
Streetfield Rd RH13 ... 34 E3
Stretch Hill RH20 ... 97 A5
Strettington La PO18 ... 154 A3
Strettons Copse GU30 ... 47 B2
Strickland Cl RH11 ... 17 E5
Stride Cl PO19 ... 173 C6
Stringer Way BN1 ... 167 F3
Strone Ct BN11 ... 181 F1
Strood La RH12 ... 35 C7
Stroud Green Dr PO21 ... 194 F5
Stroudley Cl RH10 ... 19 B5
Stroudley Ct BN16 ... 199 E6
Strouds La PO21 ... 194 F5
Strudgate Cl RH10 ... 19 B4
Strudwick Ho BN11 ... 183 A3
Stuart Cl Crawley RH10 ... 19 D5
Worthing BN11 ... 182 F4
Stuart Ho 2 RH12 ... 36 F3
Stuart Way RH19 ... 22 F7
Stuarts Mdw GU28 ... 114 C8
Stubbermere PO9 ... 149 B8
Stubcroft La PO20 ... 202 B7
Stubfield RH12 ... 36 A3
Stubpond La RH19, RH7 ... 8 D7
Stumblemead RH17 ... 41 A1
Stumblets RH10 ... 19 C7
Stumps End PO18 ... 171 C4
Stumps La PO18 ... 171 C4
Sturges Rd PO21 ... 195 C3
Sturt Ave GU27 ... 26 F5
Sturt Rd GU27 ... 26 F5
Sudbury Cl PO21 ... 194 C1
Sudeley Pl BN2 ... 188 D4
Sudeley St BN2 ... 188 D4
Sudeley Terr 6 BN2 ... 188 D4
Sudley Gdns PO21 ... 195 D3
Sudley Rd PO21 ... 195 D3
Suffolk Cl RH6 ... 2 A2
Suffolk St BN3 ... 186 F8
Sugar La RH17 ... 65 C4
Sugden Rd BN11 ... 182 F3
Sugworth Cl RH16 ... 85 D7
Sullington Cl BN2 ... 168 F4
Sullington Copse RH20 ... 119 F2
Sullington Gdns BN14 ... 161 F3
Sullington Hill RH11 ... 18 D4
Sullington La RH20 ... 140 F7
Sullington Mead RH12 ... 35 E3
Sullington Way BN43 ... 185 A8
Sullivan Dr RH11 ... 17 E3
Sultan Rd PO10 ... 149 B1
Summer Cl BN41 ... 186 A7
Summer La PO21 ... 193 F1
Summerdale Rd BN3 ... 166 D2
Summerdown Cl BN13 ... 181 B5
Summerdown Ct BN13 ... 181 B5
Summerfield Rd PO20 ... 190 C2
Summerfields BN14 ... 161 E6
Summerhill Cl
Bognor Regis PO22 ... 196 D6
Haywards Heath RH16 ... 85 F7
Summerhill Dr
Bognor Regis PO22 ... 196 C6
Lindfield RH16 ... 86 A7
Summerhill Grange RH16 ... 85 F7
Summerhill La RH16 ... 85 F7
Summerlea Cl BN16 ... 179 B4
Summerlea Cty Prim Sch BN16 ... 179 B3
Summerlea Gdns 5 BN17 ... 198 E5
Summerley Cnr PO22 ... 196 B4
Summerley La PO22 ... 196 B5
Summers Ho GU29 ... 92 D6
Summersdale Ct PO19 ... 152 F3
Summersdale Rd PO19 ... 153 A1
Summersdeane BN42 ... 165 F1
Summersfield GU33 ... 45 B4
Summersvere Cl RH10 ... 6 A1
Sumners RH17 ... 64 B7
Sun Brow GU27 ... 27 A5
Sun Ct Chichester PO19 ... 173 A5
10 Worthing BN11 ... 182 A1
Sun Park Cl PO21 ... 195 A6
Sundale La PO22 ... 196 E5
Sunderland Cl PO20 ... 154 D2
Sundew Cl RH11 ... 18 A2
Sunflower Cl BN17 ... 179 B3
Sunneymead Cl PO20 ... 206 E6
Sunningdale 12 RH6 ... 2 B2
Sunningdale Ct
Crawley RH11 ... 18 D4
Worthing BN12 ... 181 C3
Sunningdale Gdns
Bognor Regis PO22 ... 195 B7
East Wittering PO20 ... 201 D7
Sunningdale Rd BN13 ... 181 E6
Sunninghill Ave BN3 ... 166 F2
Sunninghill Cl BN3 ... 166 E2
Sunny Ave RH10 ... 21 A8
Sunny Cl BN12 ... 181 E1
Sunny Way PO18 ... 171 B5
Sunnybox La BN18 ... 156 E4
Sunnycroft Cl RH17 ... 86 E2
Sunnydale Ave BN1 ... 168 A6
Sunnydale Cl BN1 ... 168 A6
Sunnydown Ct BN16 ... 199 A3
Sunnyhill Cl RH10 ... 21 A8
Sunnymead Crawley RH11 ... 18 D6
Crawley Down RH10 ... 21 B8
Sunnymead Cl PO22 ... 197 A6
Sunnymead Dr PO20 ... 206 E6
Sunnyside Cotts RH20 ... 119 D1
Sunnywood Ct RH16 ... 85 D3
Sunnywood Dr RH16 ... 85 D3
Sunset La RH20 ... 119 C5
Sunte Ave RH16 ... 85 F7
Sunte Cl RH16 ... 85 E7
Sunvale Ave GU27 ... 26 D6
Sunvale Cl GU27 ... 26 D6
Surrenden Cl BN1 ... 167 F4
Surrenden Cres BN1 ... 167 E4
Surrenden Holt BN1 ... 167 F3
Surrenden Lodge BN1 ... 167 F2
Surrenden Pk BN1 ... 168 A4
Surrenden Rd BN1 ... 167 F3
Surrenden Rise RH11 ... 39 C8
Surrey Cott 5 BN17 ... 198 F4
Surrey Ct Arundel BN18 ... 158 A2
4 Horsham RH13 ... 36 D2
Surrey Ho 12 BN2 ... 188 D4
Surrey St Arundel BN18 ... 158 A2
Brighton BN1 ... 207 A3
Littlehampton BN17 ... 198 D5
Worthing BN11 ... 182 C1
Surrey Wharf BN18 ... 158 B2
Surry St BN43 ... 184 F7
Sussex Bsns Village The PO22 ... 176 E6
Sussex Ct
7 Bognor Regis PO21 ... 195 B2
Elmer PO22 ... 197 B5
Findon BN14 ... 161 E6
2 Haywards Heath RH16 ... 85 E3
Horsham RH13 ... 36 E1
15 Hove BN3 ... 187 C6
4 Shoreham-by-Sea BN43 ... 185 A6
Sussex Cty Cricket Gd BN3 ... 187 C7
Sussex Dr PO21 ... 194 A1
Sussex Eye Hospl BN2 ... 188 D4
Sussex Falconry Ctr PO20 ... 192 C7
Sussex Gdns
Haywards Heath RH17 ... 86 B3
Rustington BN16 ... 199 C6
Sussex Gr PO20 ... 202 C5
Sussex House Bsns Pk BN3 ... 186 F8
Sussex Hts 18 BN1 ... 187 E5
Sussex Lodge RH12 ... 36 C4
Sussex Manor Bsns Pk RH10 ... 6 A2
Sussex Mews 4 BN2 ... 188 E4
Sussex Pl BN2 ... 207 C3
Sussex Rd
Haywards Heath RH16 ... 85 E3
Hove BN3 ... 187 B5
Nursted GU31 ... 88 D7
Shoreham-by-Sea BN15 ... 184 C5
Worthing BN11 ... 182 D3
Sussex Sq Brighton BN2 ... 188 E4
17 Haywards Heath RH16 ... 85 E4
Sussex St
Bognor Regis PO21 ... 195 D3
Brighton BN2 ... 207 C2
Littlehampton BN17 ... 198 D6
Sussex Terr Brighton BN2 ... 207 C3
3 Midhurst GU29 ... 92 E7
Sussex Toy & Model Mus BN1 ... 207 B3
Sussex Village PO22 ... 197 B5
Sussex Way RH15 ... 106 E5
Sutherland Cl
Bognor Regis PO21 ... 195 C3
Rustington BN16 ... 199 B5
Sutherland Ct 4 PO21 ... 195 C3
Sutherland Rd BN2 ... 188 C5
Sutton Ave BN16 ... 199 C4
Sutton Cl PO22 ... 195 F6
Swainsthorpe Cl RH16 ... 85 F3
Swaledale Cl RH11 ... 18 C3
Swallow Rd RH11 ... 18 C8
Swallow Rest RH15 ... 106 C3
Swallowfield Cl RH13 ... 59 C5
Swallows Cl 3 BN15 ... 184 C5
Swallows Green Dr BN13 ... 181 C5
Swallows La RH13 ... 101 F6
Swallows The BN17 ... 198 D4
Swallowtail Rd RH12 ... 36 E6
Swan Barn Rd GU27 ... 27 D6
Swan Cl Emsworth PO10 ... 169 C8
Southwater RH13 ... 58 A2
Storrington RH20 ... 119 C2
Swan Cnr RH20 ... 98 B2
Swan Ct RH20 ... 98 B2
Swan Dene PO21 ... 204 F7
Swan La RH6 ... 4 F7
Swan Sq RH12 ... 36 C2
Swan View RH20 ... 98 C1
Swan Wlk RH12 ... 36 C2
Swanborough Ct 7 BN43 ... 184 F7
Swanborough Dr BN2 ... 188 F7
Swanborough Pl BN2 ... 188 F7
Swanbourne Cl BN15 ... 183 F8
Swanbourne Rd BN17 ... 178 D3
Swandean Hospl BN13 ... 181 D8
Swanfield Dr
Chichester PO19 ... 173 B8
Chichester PO19 ... 173 C7
Swann Cl RH15 ... 107 D3
Swann Way RH12 ... 35 E3
Swans Ghyll RH18 ... 23 E3
Swansea Gdns PO21 ... 195 B2
Sweda Ct 18 BN2 ... 188 D4
Sweetlands BN6 ... 127 B5
Swift Cl RH15 ... 106 D3
Swift La RH11 ... 18 C8
Swift Rd PO10 ... 169 C3
Swift Way BN17 ... 178 C4
Swillage La BN16,BN13 ... 180 A8
Swindon Rd RH12 ... 36 B4
Swiss Gdns BN43 ... 184 E7
Swissland Hill RH19, RH7 ... 9 E7
Sycamore Ave RH12 ... 37 C6
Sycamore Cl
Angmering BN16 ... 179 F4
Crawley RH11 ... 5 C1
Portslade-by-Sea BN41 ... 166 C3
Sycamore Dr RH19 ... 10 A1
Sycamore Rd PO22 ... 195 C7
Sycamores The
Chichester PO19 ... 173 A7
Sayers Common BN6 ... 105 D1
Sydenham Terr PO10 ... 149 D5
Sydney Rd RH16 ... 85 E6
Sydney St BN1 ... 207 B3
Sydney Tidy Ho 5 BN2 ... 188 C6
Syers Cl GU33 ... 45 B4
Syers Rd GU33 ... 45 B4
Syke Cluan Cl PO22 ... 176 B6
Sylvan Cl RH16 ... 86 B4
Sylvan Rd Crawley RH10 ... 19 A4
Lancing BN15 ... 183 B6
Sylvan Way PO21 ... 195 B3
Sylvester Way BN3 ... 166 C3
Sylvia Cl PO21 ... 194 A1
Symbister Rd BN41 ... 186 C7
Syresham Gdns RH16 ... 85 F4
Syvlan Ct BN15 ... 183 B6

T

Tabard Gate PO21 ... 194 B1
Tack Lee Rd BN18 ... 176 F3
Talbot Cres BN1 ... 168 D6
Talbot La RH12 ... 36 C1
Talbot Rd BN17 ... 198 C5
Tallis Cl RH11 ... 17 F3
Talman Cl RH11 ... 17 E5
Tamar Ave BN13 ... 181 C7
Tamar Cl Crawley RH10 ... 19 C5
Worthing BN13 ... 181 C7
Tamar Way PO20 ... 154 D2
Tamarisk Cl PO22 ... 195 C6
Tamarisk Way
Ferring BN12 ... 200 F5
Littlehampton BN16 ... 199 F4
Tamarisk Wlk PO20 ... 201 F6
Tamplin Terr BN2 ... 207 C3
Tamworth Rd BN3 ... 186 F7
Tanbridge Ho RH12 ... 36 B1
Tanbridge House Sch RH12 ... 35 F2
Tanbridge Pk RH12 ... 36 B1
Tanbridge Pl RH12 ... 36 B1
Tandridge Rd BN3 ... 186 E6
Tanfield Ct 3 RH12 ... 36 B2
Tangle Oak RH19 ... 8 E4
Tangmere Gdns PO21 ... 194 D2
Tangmere Military Aviation Mus PO20 ... 154 D1
Tangmere Prim Sch PO20 ... 154 D2
Tangmere Rd
Brighton BN1 ... 168 A6
Crawley RH11 ... 17 F6
Oving PO20 ... 174 B8
Tankerdale La GU33 ... 45 A1
Tanners Ct GU27 ... 27 C7
Tanners La GU27 ... 27 C7
Tanners Mead RH17 ... 61 E5
Tannery Cl RH13 ... 34 D3
Tansy Mead RH20 ... 119 B2
Tanyard Ave RH19 ... 23 A8
Tanyard Cl Crawley RH10 ... 19 C3
Horsham RH13 ... 36 E1
Tanyard Cotts BN44 ... 143 C3
Tanyard La Chelwood Common RH17,TN22 ... 66 C4
Steyning BN44 ... 143 D3
Tanyard Way RH6 ... 2 B4
Tarham Cl RH6 ... 1 E5
Tarmount La BN43 ... 184 F7
Tarner Rd BN2 ... 207 C3
Tarragon Way BN43 ... 165 C1
Tarrant St BN18 ... 158 B2
Tarrant Wharf BN18 ... 158 B2
Tarring Gate BN14 ... 182 A4
Tarring Rd BN11 ... 182 B3
Tasman Cl BN16 ... 199 D4
Tasman Way BN13 ... 181 C6
Tatchells GU29 ... 92 D6
Tate Cres RH15 ... 106 F5
Tate's Way RH12 ... 33 D7
Tatham Ct RH11 ... 18 B1
Taunton Cl RH10 ... 19 D6
Taunton Rd BN2 ... 168 F1
Tavern Ct GU27 ... 49 B6
Taverner Pl PO19 ... 173 B5
Tavistock & Summerhill Sch RH16 ... 85 F7
Tavistock Down BN1 ... 168 C2

Tavy Cl BN13 181 C6
Tavy Rd BN13 181 C6
Taw Cl BN13 181 D7
Taylor Wlk RH11 18 C6
Taylor's La PO18 171 C4
Taylors Field GU29 92 E6
Taylors Rise GU29 92 E6
Taymor Ct BN11 182 A1
Teachers Terr GU33 45 B4
Teal Cl RH12 36 C5
Teal La PO20 206 C8
Teasel Cl RH11 18 B3
Teesdale RH11 18 C3
Teg Cl BN41 166 C2
Teign Wlk BN13 181 C8
Teknol Ho RH15 106 E2
Telegraph La GU31 90 A3
Telegraph St 12 BN2 188 C4
Telford Pl RH10 18 E5
Telgarth Rd BN12 200 F4
Telham Ct 5 RH11 17 F3
Templars Cl PO22 196 D6
Templars Fst Sch BN15 183 B6
Templars The BN14 182 E7
Temple Cl RH10 19 D5
Temple Ct 2 BN17 198 E5
Temple Gdns BN1, BN3 187 E6
Temple Gr RH15 106 D4
Temple La RH5 3 A4
Temple Rd GU33 45 C6
Temple St BN1 187 E6
Templesheen Rd PO22 197 B5
Ten Acres BN11 183 A3
Tenacre Cl PO19 173 C8
Tenantry Down Rd BN2 188 E8
Tenantry Rd BN2 188 D8
Tennis Rd BN3 186 E6
Tennyson Ave BN16 199 B5
Tennyson Cl Crawley RH10 19 B8
Horsham RH12 36 E6
Tennyson Ct 5 RH16 85 D5
Tennyson Ho 4 BN11 182 C2
Tennyson Rd
Bognor Regis PO21 195 B3
Worthing BN11 182 C2
Tennyson Rise RH19 22 C8
Tennyson's La GU27 27 E4
Tennyson's Ridge GU27 27 E4
Terminus Mill PO19 172 F5
Terminus Pl
9 Brighton BN1 207 A4
Littlehampton BN17 198 D5
Terminus Rd
Brighton BN1 207 A4
Chichester PO19 172 E5
Littlehampton BN17 198 C5
Terminus Road Ind Est
PO19 172 E5
Terminus St BN1 207 A3
Tern Rd RH11 17 D5
Terrace The
Crossbush BN18 158 E1
Lancing BN15 183 E4
Sidlesham PO20 203 F7
Worthing BN12 181 C2
Terringes Ave BN13 181 F5
Terry Rd RH11 18 B1
Terry's Cross BN5 124 C2
Terwick La GU31 91 A8
Terwick Rise GU31 68 D6
Test Rd BN15 183 B6
Testers Cl RH13 80 A7
Teville Gate BN11 182 D3
Teville Inds BN14 182 F5
Teville Pl BN11 182 C3
Teville Rd BN11 182 D3
Thackeray Rd BN14 182 F4
Thakeham Cl
East Preston BN16 180 B3
Worthing BN12 181 A2
Thakeham Copse RH20 120 B3
Thakeham Dr BN12 181 A2
Thakeham Fst Sch RH20 120 B7
Thakeham Rd RH20 119 F2
Thalassa Rd BN11 183 B3
Thames Cl Brighton BN2 207 C2
Littlehampton BN17 199 A4
Thames Way BN13 181 D7
Thatch Ct BN15 183 F8
Thatcher Cl RH10 18 D3
Thatchers Cl
Burgess Hill RH15 107 D1
Horley RH6 2 B5
Horsham RH12 36 E4
Thatchers Lodge 2
BN17 198 D5
Thatchway Cl BN17 198 D6
Thatchway The
Angmering BN16 179 E5
Littlehampton BN16 199 D4
Theatre La PO19 173 A6
Theatre Pl 9 PO19 173 A6
Thelton Ave RH12 35 D3
Theobalds Rd RH15 107 D6
Theobold Ho 1 BN1 207 B3
Thesiger Cl BN11 183 A4
Thesiger Rd BN11 183 A4
Thetford Wlk RH11 17 E2
Theydon Cl RH10 19 A4
Thicket La PO18 155 B5
Third Ave
Almodington PO20 202 E8
Bognor Regis PO22 196 B4
Bracklesham PO21 202 B5
Hove BN3 187 B6
Lancing BN15 183 E7
Worthing BN14 182 D7
Thirlmere Cres BN15 183 B5
Thirlmere Rd RH11 17 D4
Thirlmere Way PO22 196 B6
Thistle Way RH13 58 A3
Thistledown Vale RH14 31 D3
Thistledowne Gdns
PO10 169 D8
Thomas a'Becket
Fst Sch BN13 182 A5
Thomas a'Becket
Mid Sch BN14 182 A5
Thomas Bennett
Com Coll RH10 18 D3
Thomas Bennett
Com Sch RH10 18 E2
Thompson Ct 15 RH11 18 B1
Thompson Rd
Bognor Regis PO22 196 F5
Brighton BN1 168 C1
Thompson's Hospl GU28 73 F1
Thomson Cl BN13 181 B6
Thorgate Rd BN17 178 B3
Thorn Rd BN11 182 C1
Thornberry Mid Sch
BN15 183 F5
Thornbush Cres BN41 166 B3
Thorncroft Rd BN17 198 F6
Thorndean Dr RH17 83 D7
Thorndean Rd BN2 168 D3
Thornden RH13 81 E2
Thorndene Ave PO21 195 B4
Thorndyke Cl RH10 19 D5
Thorney Dr PO20 206 C7
Thorney Island
Com Prim Sch PO10 169 C3
Thorney Old Pk PO10 169 F1
Thorney Rd PO10 169 D6
Thornham La PO10 169 E6
Thornham Marina PO10 169 E6
Thornhill RH11 18 B4
Thornhill Ave BN1 168 A7
Thornhill Cl BN3 166 E2
Thornhill Rise BN41 166 A4
Thornhill Way BN41 166 A3
Thornscroft BN44 143 D4
Thornsdale 5 BN2 207 C3
Thornton Cl RH6 1 E3
Thornton Ct 2 BN16 199 E6
Thornton Mdw RH14 76 B8
Thornton Pl RH6 1 F3
Threal's La RH20 119 E6
Threals Copse RH20 119 E5
Three Acres RH12 36 A1
Three Bridges
Fst & Mid Sch RH10 18 F6
Three Bridges Fst Sch
RH10 19 A7
Three Bridges Rd RH10 19 A6
Three Bridges Sta RH10 19 B6
Three Gates La GU27 27 E8
Threestile Rd RH12 14 F1
Thrusloes PO21 194 F3
Thurlow Rd BN11 182 F3
Thurne Way RH12 33 D7
Thyme Cl BN43 165 C1
Ticehurst Cl RH10 19 E6
Ticehurst Rd BN2 188 F5
Tichborne Cotts RH16 86 C6
Tichborne St BN1 207 B2
Tideway BN17 199 A4
Tidy St BN1 207 B3
Tilbury Pl BN2 207 C2
Tilbury Way BN2 207 C3
Tile Barn Est PO20 191 C1
Tile Barn La PO20 191 C1
Tilebarn Ct RH16 85 E2
Tilers Cl RH15 107 D3
Tilgate Cl BN2 188 D6
Tilgate Dr RH10, RH11 18 E2
Tilgate Forest Bsns Ctr
RH11 18 D1
Tilgate Forest Recn Ctr
RH10 18 D1
Tilgate Forest Row RH11 39 C5
Tilgate Par RH10 18 E3
Tilgate Park Ctry Pk RH10 18 F1
Tilgate Pl RH10 18 E3
Tilgate Way RH10 18 E3
Tilletts La RH12 35 E8
Tillinghurst La RH17 42 A2
Tillington BN2 188 F7
Tillington Cotts BN18 176 F3
Tillotson Cl RH10 19 D5
Tillstone Cl BN2 168 D2
Tillstone St BN2 207 C2
Tiltwood Dr RH10 21 C8
Timber Cl BN13 181 C5
Timber Ct RH12 36 C3
Timber Mill RH13 57 F2
Timberham Farm Rd RH6 5 D8
Timberham Link RH6 5 E8
Timberham Way RH6 5 E7
Timberlaine Ind Est
PO19 173 C5
Timberlaine Trad Est
BN14 182 F5
Timberlands
13 Crawley RH11 18 B1
Storrington RH20 119 E2
Timberlea Cl RH20 121 A5
Timberleys 1 BN17 199 A6
Timbermill Ct GU27 26 F6
Timbers The RH13 59 C6
Tindal Cl RH15 107 D3
Tinghall PO21 194 E3
Tinsley Cl RH10 6 A1
Tinsley Gn RH10 6 B4
Tinsley La RH10 6 A1
Tinsley La N RH10 6 B3
Tinsley La S RH10 19 A8
Tintagel Ct Horsham RH13 36 D1
Hove BN3 187 A8
6 Shoreham-by-Sea BN43 184 F7
Tintern Cl BN1 168 B1
Tintern Rd RH11 18 A4
Tinwood La PO18 154 E5
Tipper La GU31 89 D3
Tiree Path RH11 18 B3
Tisbury Rd BN3 187 C6
Titch Hill BN15 163 A3
Titchfield Cl RH15 107 D1
Tithe Barn BN15 183 E8
Tithe Barn Chalets PO20 206 B8
Tithe Barn Cl PO21 194 C1
Tithe Barn Ct PO21 205 B8
Tithe Barn Way PO21 194 B1
Tithe Gn BN16 199 B5
Tithe Orch RH19 8 E4
Titian Rd BN3 186 F7
Titmus Dr RH10 18 F2
Titnore La BN12, BN13 181 A6
Titnore Way BN12, BN13 181 A6
Tivoli BN1 167 E2
Tivoli Cres BN1 167 D1
Tivoli Cres N BN1 167 D2
Tivoli Pl BN1 167 D2
Tivoli Rd BN1 167 D2
Toat Hill RH13 56 E8
Toat La RH20 98 A8
Tobias Sch of Art RH19 22 E6
Toddington La BN17 178 E4
Toddington Pk BN17 178 E3
Todds Cl RH6 1 E5
Toftwood Cl RH10 19 C5
Tollbridge Ho BN43 184 D8
Tollgate RH16 86 B8
Tollgate Hill RH11 18 C1
Tollgate La RH17 84 E8
Tollhouse Cl PO19 172 F6
Tompset's Bank RH18 23 F1
Tomtits La RH18 23 E1
Tongdean Ave BN3 167 C2
Tongdean Ct BN1 167 D4
Tongdean La
Brighton BN1 167 C4
Brighton BN1 167 D4
Tongdean Rd BN3 167 C3
Tongdean Rise BN1 167 C4
Toomey Rd BN44 143 D5
Top Rd Sharpthorne RH19 43 B5
Slindon BN18 156 C5
Top St RH17 83 C4
Torcross Cl BN2 168 E1
Toronto Cl BN13 181 D6
Toronto Terr BN2 188 C6
Torrance Cl BN3 166 F1
Torridge Cl BN13 181 C7
Torton Hill Rd BN18 157 F2
Tote La GU29 70 A5
Totland Rd BN2 188 D7
Tott Hill BN6 126 B5
Tottington Dr BN5 144 F6
Tottington Way BN43 165 B1
Tower Cl Chichester PO19 172 F7
East Grinstead RH19 9 E2
Horley RH6 1 F3
Liphook GU30 25 B4
Tower Hill RH13 58 A8
Tower Ct RH19 9 E2
Tower Hill RH13 58 A8
Tower Ho Brighton BN1 167 E2
Burgess Hill RH15 107 B2
Tower House Cl RH17 84 E7
Tower Pl PO20 201 F7
Tower Rd Brighton BN2 188 C6
Colgate RH12 38 A7
Lancing BN15 183 D5
Liphook GU30 25 B4
Worthing BN11 182 E3
Tower Rd Flats 6 BN15 183 D5
Tower St Chichester PO19 172 F6
Emsworth PO10 169 C8
Towergate BN1 167 E2
Towers Convent Sch The
BN44 144 B1
Towers Rd BN44 144 B2
Town Barn Rd RH11 18 C7
Town Cross Ave PO21 195 C4
Town La PO18 133 C4
Town Mead RH11 18 D7
Town Place Farm Cotts
RH17 87 C7
Townfield RH14 53 B2
Townsend Cres BN17 198 F6
Tozer Ct BN41 186 B7
Tozer Way PO19 173 B6
Trafalgar Com Inf Sch
RH12 36 B4
Trafalgar Ct
14 Bognor Regis PO21 195 B2
Brighton BN1 207 B3
3 Rustington BN16 199 C6
Trafalgar Gate BN2 188 F3
Trafalgar La BN1 207 B3
Trafalgar Pl BN1 207 B3
Trafalgar Rd
Horsham RH12 36 C4
Portslade-by-Sea BN41 186 B8
Trafalgar St BN1 207 B3
Trafalgar Terr BN1 207 B3
Tramway Cl PO20 192 F8
Treadcroft Dr RH12 36 E5
Treadwheel Rd PO8 128 D6
Tredcroft Rd BN3 167 C2
Tree Ave GU27 26 F8
Treemans Rd RH17 65 B2
Trees Ct PO20 206 E8
Treetops RH13 79 F7
Treeview RH11 18 C1
Trefoil Cl RH12 36 E5
Trefoil Cres RH11 18 A2
Tregarth Rd PO19 153 A2
Tregenna Ho GU30 25 B5
Treharne Cl BN13 181 D7
Treloar Rd PO11 189 B1
Trendle Gn PO21 194 F2
Trenear Cl RH13 36 E2
Trent Cl Crawley RH11 17 F4
Lancing BN15 183 C6
Trent Ho 3 BN14 182 A5
Trent Rd BN12 181 E2
Tretawn Gdns PO20 206 F6
Trevanne Plat RH10 19 D7
Trevelyan Pl RH16 85 E5
Treveor Cl BN11 182 C2
Treyford Cl RH11 17 F6
Triangle Ho 4 RH16 85 F3
Triangle Rd RH16 85 E3
Triangle The BN15 183 C4
Triangle Way RH15 106 D5
Trinity Cl RH10 19 C8
Trinity Ct Horsham RH12 36 C3
Hurstpierpoint BN6 126 B5
Trinity Rd BN6 126 A6
Trinity St BN2 207 C4
Trinity Way
Bognor Regis PO21 194 F4
Littlehampton BN17 198 F4
Tripp Hill RH20 116 F7
Tristar Bsns Ctr RH13 103 A2
Tristram Cl BN15 183 B7
Triton Pl PO22 196 C5
Tritton Pl RH20 119 B2
Troon 7 RH6 2 B2
Troon Cl RH11 17 D5
Troon Ct RH16 85 E4
Trotton Cl RH10 19 C3
Trotton Rd GU29, GU31 91 A7
Trotyn Croft PO21 194 F2
Trout La RH13 79 A7
Trout Rd GU27 26 E6
Troymede RH17 41 A1
True Blue Prec BN17 178 D3
Truggers RH17 61 C8
Truleigh Ct BN44 144 B2
Truleigh Dr BN41 166 A4
Truleigh Hill YH BN43 145 A2
Truleigh Rd BN44 144 B2
Truleigh Way BN43 165 A1
Trumpers La GU28 95 F8
Trundle Cl PO18 152 E6
Trundle Mead RH12 36 C5
Trundle View Cl PO22 176 B6
Truro Cl PO19 152 F1
Truro Cres PO21 194 E3
Trusler's Hill BN6 124 F6
Tryndel Way PO22 196 B4
Tudor Ave PO10 149 A4
Tudor Cl Chichester PO19 152 F2
Crawley RH10 19 D5
East Grinstead RH19 22 F8
Findon BN14 161 E6
Hove BN3 166 F2
Marehill RH20 98 F1
Middleton-on-Sea PO22 196 D5
Shoreham-by-Sea BN15 184 B6
Tudor Ct 11 PO21 195 D4
Tudor Dr
Upper Beeding BN44 144 A3
Westergate PO20 175 D8
Tudor Gdns RH15 106 F4
Tudor Ho 4 RH13 36 F3
Tudor View BN17 198 C4
Tudor Village RH20 120 C3
Tuff's Hard PO18 191 C7
Tufts Field GU29 92 D6
Tufts Mdw GU29 92 E6
Tuggles Plat RH12 35 E7
Tulip Ct RH12 36 C4
Tullett Rd RH10 19 B2
Tunbridge Cres GU30 25 B5
Tunbridge La GU30 25 B6
Tunnel Rd RH6 5 E8
Tunnmeade RH11 17 E5
Tunsgate 5 BN44 143 D3
Tuppenny La PO10 169 E8
Turkey La RH15 107 B3
Turnberry Ct 14 RH16 85 E4
Turnbull Rd PO19 173 B7
Turner Ave RH14 77 C6
Turner Ct RH19 10 A3
Turner Rd BN14 182 E6
Turner Way PO20 206 F7
Turner's Hill Rd RH19 22 B6
Turners Hill CE Prim Sch
RH10 21 A3
Turners Hill Rd RH10 21 A7
Turners Mead RH20 119 B2
Turners Mill Cl RH16 85 D7
Turners Mill Rd RH16 85 D6
Turners Way RH15 106 F4
Turnpike Cl PO19 172 F3
Turnpike Pl RH11 18 D8
Turnpike Rd BN18 138 F6
Turnpike Way RH20 121 A4
Turret Ct RH19 9 C3
Turton Cl BN2 188 D5
Tuscan Ave PO22 196 F5
Tuscany Gdns RH10 18 E8
Tushmore Ave RH10 5 E1
Tushmore Cres RH10 5 E1
Tushmore La RH10 18 E8
Tushmore Rdbt RH11 18 D8
Tussock Cl RH11 18 A4
Tuxford Cl RH10 19 C4
Tweed La RH11 4 F1
Twineham CE Prim Sch
RH17 105 A4
Twineham Cl BN2 188 F7
Twineham La BN6, RH17 105 A3
Twitten Cl 2 BN42 185 E7
Twitten La RH19 8 E4
Twitten The
Albourne Green BN6 125 C6
Burgess Hill RH15 107 B4
Crawley RH11 18 C6
Ditchling BN6 127 D3
Southwick BN42 185 E7
Twitten Way BN14 182 A4
Two Barns La PO18 152 D6
Two Mile Ash Rd RH13 57 D3
Two Ways RH14 32 A4
Twyford Cl BN13 181 E6
Twyford Gdns BN13 181 E6
Twyford Rd Brighton BN1 168 E6
Worthing BN13 181 E6
Twyhurst Ct RH19 9 D3
Twyne Cl RH11 17 F4
Twyner Cl RH6 2 D4
Tye La BN18 156 E1
Tylden Way RH12 36 F6
Tyler Rd RH10 18 D3
Tyler's Gn RH16, RH17 85 B4
Tylston Meadow GU30 25 B5
Tymperley Ct 1 RH12 36 E3
Tyne Cl Crawley RH10 19 C5
Worthing BN13 181 C7
Tyne Way PO21 194 D4
Tynings The BN15 183 E5
Tyson Pl 9 BN2 207 C2
Tythe Barn RH17 83 C3
Tythe Barn Rd PO20 206 E6

U

Uckfield Cl BN2 188 F6
Ullswater Dr BN17 179 A3
Ullswater Gr PO22 196 B6
Ullswater Rd BN15 183 B5
Underdown Rd BN42 185 E8
Underhill La Clayton BN6 147 E8
Westmeston BN6 148 C8
Undermill Rd BN44 144 B2
Underwood Cl RH10 21 B8
Underwood Rd GU27 26 F7
Unicorn Trad Est The
GU27 27 B6
Unifax BN12 181 C3
Union Pl BN11 182 D2
Union Rd BN2 207 C4
Union St BN1 207 B2
Unita Ho 5 BN11 182 B1
Univ Coll Chichester
PO21 195 E4
Univ of Brighton BN1 207 B2
Univ of Brighton
(Belgrave St Annexe)
BN2 207 C3
Univ of Brighton
(Cockcroft/Watts
Annexes) BN2 168 D2
Univ of Brighton
(Finsbury Rd Annexe)
BN2 207 C3
Univ of Brighton
(St Peter's Ho) BN2 207 B3
Upfield RH6 2 A1
Upfield Cl RH6 2 A1
Upfield Villas RH14 54 C2
Uphill Way PO20 193 A8
Uplands Ave BN13 181 F8
Uplands Cl GU27 27 D8
Uplands Rd Brighton BN1 168 C2
Rowland's Castle PO9 128 E2
Uplands Sch BN1 168 C2
Uppark GU31 109 B8
Uppark Gdns RH12 36 F6
Uppark Way PO22 196 D7
Upper Abbey Rd BN2 188 D4
Upper Bedford St BN2 188 C4
Upper Beeding Prim Sch
BN44 144 A2
Upper Bevendean Ave
BN2 168 E1
Upper Bognor Rd
3 Bognor Regis PO21 195 D4
Bognor Regis PO21 195 E4
Upper Boundstone La
Lancing BN15 183 D7
Lancing BN15 183 D8
Upper Brighton Rd
Lancing BN15 183 C8
Worthing BN14 182 D7
Upper Chalvington Pl
BN2 188 E5
Upper Cl RH18 23 F2
Upper Dr BN16 200 B4
Upper Dr The BN3 187 D8
Upper Forecourt RH6 6 B7
Upper Gardner St BN1 207 B3
Upper Gloucester Rd
BN1 207 A3
Upper Hamilton Rd BN1 207 A5
Upper High St BN11 182 E3
Upper Hollingdean Rd
BN1 168 B1
Upper Kingston La
BN42, BN43 165 D1
Upper Lewes Rd BN2 207 C4

Upper Lodges BN1 .....168 D8
Upper Market St 5 BN3 .187 D5
Upper Mount GU33 ......45 A3
Upper North St BN1 .....207 A2
Upper Park Pl 7 BN2 ...207 C2
Upper Rock Gdns BN2 ...207 C2
Upper Roedale Cotts
BN1 ....168 B4
Upper School Dr GU27 ....26 F5
Upper Shoreham Rd
Shoreham-by-Sea
BN42, BN43 ....165 D1
Shoreham-by-Sea BN43 ....165 B1
Upper Sq RH18 ....23 E3
Upper St RH20 ....97 A3
Upper St James's St BN2 207 C1
Upper St Johns Rd RH15 107 A4
Upper Station Rd BN5 ...123 D5
Upper Sudeley St 7
BN2 ....188 D4
Upper Wellington Rd
BN2 ....188 C7
Upper West Dr BN12 ....200 E5
Upper West La BN15 ....183 E8
Upper Winfield Ave BN1 .167 F6
Upperfield GU29 ....70 F2
Upperton Rd GU28 ....73 C1
Upton Ave BN42 ....165 E1
Upton Ct BN13 ....181 F3
Upton Gdns BN13 ....181 F4
Upton Rd
Stockbridge PO19 ....172 F4
Worthing BN13 ....181 F4
Upways Cl PO20 ....203 F1
Ursula Ave PO20 ....206 D6
Ursula Ave N PO20 ......206 D6
Ursula Sq PO20 ....206 D5

V

Vachery La GU6 ....11 E7
Vale Ave Brighton BN1 ....167 F6
Worthing BN14 ....161 F2
Vale Ct BN41 ....186 B7
Vale Cty Fst & Mid Sch
BN14 ....161 F2
Vale Dr Horsham RH12 .....36 B3
Worthing BN14 ....161 F2
Vale Gdns BN41 ....186 B7
Vale Rd
Haywards Heath RH16 .....85 E2
Portslade-by-Sea BN41 ....186 C7
Vale Wlk BN14 ....161 F1
Valebridge Cl RH15 .....107 C6
Valebridge Dr RH15 .....107 C5
Valebridge Rd RH15 .....107 C6
Valencia Rd BN11 ....182 A3
Valentine Cl BN14 ....182 B7
Valentine Ct 14 BN3 .....187 C7
Valentine Dr RH15 ....106 E4
Valentines Gdns PO21 ...194 C2
Valentines Lea GU28 .....51 A8
Valerie Cl BN41 ....166 C2
Valetta Pk PO10 ....169 A8
Valetta Rd PO10 ....169 F1
Valewood Cl RH13 ....56 D1
Valewood La RH13 ....56 D1
Valewood Rd GU27 ....27 C4
Valiant Rd PO10 ....169 F1
Vallance Cl RH15 ....106 E4
Vallance Ct 7 BN3 ....187 A6
Vallance Gdns BN3 ....187 A6
Vallance Rd BN3 ....187 A6
Vallensdean Cotts BN41 .166 C2
Valley Cl BN1 ....167 C4
Valley Dr BN1 ....167 C4
Valley Rd Lancing BN15 ...183 C8
Portslade-by-Sea BN41 ....166 A2
Valley Side GU30 ....25 B5
Valverde Ho 13 BN3 ......187 C7
Van Dyck Pl PO22 ....195 A6
Van Gogh Pl PO22 ....195 B6
Vanbrugh Cl RH11 ....17 E3
Vanbrugh Ct 21 BN3 .....187 C7
Vancouver Cl BN13 ......181 D6
Vancouver Dr RH11 ....5 D1
Vancouver Rd BN13 ......181 D6
Vann Bridge Cl GU27 .....49 A6
Vann Rd GU27 ....49 A6
Vanners RH10 ....18 E7
Vanzell Rd GU29 ....71 A1
Varey Rd BN13 ....181 B6
Varndean Cl BN1 ....167 E3
Varndean Coll BN1 ......167 F3
Varndean Dr BN1 ....167 E3
Varndean Gdns BN1 .....167 E3
Varndean Holt BN1 ......167 F3
Varndean Rd BN1 ....167 E3
Varndean Sch BN1 ....168 A3
Varsity Rd PO10 ....169 F1
Velyn Ave PO19 ....173 B6
Ventnor Villas BN3 ......187 B6
Venus La PO21 ....204 E7
Veras Wlk RH20 ....120 C1
Verbania Way RH19 ......10 B1
Vere Rd BN1, BN2 ....207 B5
Veric 12 BN3 ....187 C7
Verica Ct PO19 ....172 B7
Vermont Dr BN16 ....200 A5
Vermont Way BN16 ......200 A5
Vernon Cl Horsham RH12 ..37 A4
Rustington BN16 ....199 C5
Vernon Ct 3 BN1 ....187 E6
Vernon Gdns 4 BN1 .....187 E6
Vernon Terr BN1 ....187 E7
Veronica Cl BN16 ....200 A4
Veronica Way BN2 ......207 C1
Via Ravenna PO19 ......172 E5
Viaduct Rd BN1, BN2 .....207 B4
Vicarage Fields
BN13 ....181 D7
Vicarage La
Bognor Regis PO22 ....196 A4
East Preston BN16 ....199 F5
Haslemere GU27 ....26 F6
Horley RH6 ....1 F4
Lodsworth GU28 ....72 B2
Scaynes Hill RH17 ....86 F3
Steyning BN44 ....143 D3
Vicarage Rd RH10 ....21 A8
Vicars Cl 8 PO19 ....173 A6
Viceroy Ct BN12 ....200 E5
Viceroy Lodge 10 BN3 ...187 A6
Victor Ct RH10 ....6 D1
Victor Rd PO10 ....169 F1
Victoria Ave
Burgess Hill RH15 ....106 E3
Easebourne GU29 ....71 A1
Victoria Bldgs BN11 .....182 E2
Victoria Cl
Burgess Hill RH15 ....106 E3
Burgess Hill RH15 ....106 F2
Horley RH6 ....2 A3
5 Midhurst GU29 ....92 E7
Victoria Cottage Hospl
PO10 ....169 B8
Victoria Cotts 2 BN3 ....187 B5
Victoria Ct
10 Bognor Regis PO21 .....195 B2
11 Horsham RH13 ....36 D2
6 Hove BN3 ....187 C6
Portslade-by-Sea BN41 ....186 C8
3 Shoreham-by-Sea BN43 .184 E7
10 Worthing BN11 ....182 C3
3 Worthing BN11 ....182 C3
Victoria Dr PO21 ....195 B3
Victoria Gdns
Burgess Hill RH15 ....106 F2
Westergate PO20 ....175 D7
Victoria Gr 7 BN3 ....187 C6
Victoria Ind Est RH15 ....106 E2
Victoria Lodge 7
BN11 ....182 C3
Victoria Park Gdns 2
BN11 ....182 C3
Victoria Pl
6 Brighton BN1 ....187 E6
Liphook GU30 ....47 E8
Victoria Rd
Balcombe RH17 ....41 A1
Bognor Regis PO21 ....195 B2
Brighton BN1 ....187 E6
Burgess Hill RH15 ....106 E2
Chichester PO19 ....173 C7
Crawley RH11 ....18 C6
Emsworth PO10 ....149 A1
Haywards Heath RH16 .....86 A3
Horley RH6 ....2 B2
Portslade-by-Sea BN41 ....186 C8
Shoreham-by-Sea BN43 ...184 E7
Southwick BN42 ....185 D7
Worthing BN11 ....182 C3
Victoria Rd S PO21 ......195 B2
Victoria St
Brighton BN1 ....187 E6
Horsham RH13 ....36 D2
Victoria Terr
Bognor Regis PO22 ....195 F3
1 Hove BN3 ....187 B5
Lumley PO10 ....149 C1
Southbourne PO10 ....169 E8
Westbourne PO10 ....149 D3
Victoria Villas BN18 .....177 A3
Victoria Way
Burgess Hill RH15 ....106 F2
East Grinstead RH19 ....22 F7
Victory Ct 15 PO21 ......195 B2
Victory Rd RH12 ....36 B3
View Terr RH7 ....10 A8
View The PO21 ....205 A8
Views Path RH16 ....86 B4
Villa Plage PO22 ....197 A5
Village Barn The BN1 ....167 E7
Villiers Ct BN1 ....207 B3
Vinall Gdns RH12 ....35 D4
Vincent Cl
Horsham RH13 ....36 F2
Lancing BN15 ....183 D6
Vincent Rd PO20 ....206 C6
Vine Pl BN1 ....207 A3
Vine St BN1 ....207 B3
Vinells Bsns Ctr BN5 ....123 E4
Vineries Cl BN13 ....182 A6
Vineries The
Burgess Hill RH15 ....107 D3
Hove BN3 ....187 E6
Vinery Ct BN13 ....182 A6
Vines Cross Rd BN2 .....188 F7
Viney Cl RH20 ....120 F5
Vinnetrow Rd PO20 .....173 E3
Vinols Cross RH19 ....42 F6
Vinson Rd GU33 ....45 C4
Viscount Dr PO21 ....205 B8
Vivienne Cl RH11 ....5 D1
Volks Electric Rly
BN1, BN2 ....188 C4
Vowells Forest Wlk
RH19 ....21 E3
Vowels La RH19 ....21 E2
Vulcan Cl RH11 ....18 C2
Vulcan Ho 4 RH20 ......119 E1
Vulcan Rd PO10 ....169 F1

W

Wad The PO20 ....190 B1
Waddington Cl RH11 .....18 A3
Wade End PO20 ....206 C8
Wadeway The PO20 .....206 C8
Wadeys The RH14 ....77 C8
Wadham Cl RH10 ....6 C1
Wadhurst Cl PO21 ....195 B4
Wadhurst Ct BN13 ......182 A3
Wadhurst Dr BN12 ......181 B2
Wadhurst Rise BN2 .....188 F5
Wadlands Brook Rd RH19 ..9 D5
Wagg Cl RH19 ....10 A1
Wagtail Cl RH12 ....36 D7
Wain End RH12 ....36 D5
Wainwrights RH10 ....18 D3
Wakefield Rd BN2 ....207 C5
Wakefield Way PO21 ....194 E4
Wakehams Green Dr RH10 .6 D1
Wakehurst Ct BN11 .....182 F3
Wakehurst Dr RH10 ......18 D3
Wakehurst La RH17 ......64 A8
Wakehurst Mews RH12 ...35 F1
Wakehurst Pl BN16 .....199 C6
Wakehurst Place
(Royal Bot Gdn) RH17 ...41 F3
Wakestone La RH20 .....75 A2
Walberton & Binstead
CE Prim Sch BN18 .....156 E1
Walberton Cl PO22 .....196 B5
Walberton Ct BN11 .....181 F1
Walberton Pk BN18 .....176 E8
Waldby Ct RH11 ....18 A3
Waldegrave Rd BN1 .....168 A1
Walders Rd BN16 ....199 B6
Waldron Ave BN1 ....168 D6
Waldron Pl BN1 ....168 D6
Walesbeech RH10 ....19 A5
Walker Rd RH10 ....19 C4
Wall Hill Rd RH18, RH19 ..23 E5
Wallace Ave BN11 ......181 F1
Wallace Ct 11 BN11 .....181 F2
Wallace Par 5 BN11 .....181 F2
Wallace Rd BN16 ....179 C3
Wallage La RH10 ....20 D6
Walled Gdn The RH14 ....31 F7
Wallfield PO21 ....194 F2
Wallis Ct RH10 ....5 F2
Wallis Ho RH19 ....9 E1
Wallis Way
Burgess Hill RH15 ....106 E4
Horsham RH13 ....37 A4
Wallner Cres PO22 ......196 C5
Wallrock Wlk PO10 ......149 B4
Walmer Cl RH13 ....58 A2
Walmsleys Way PO20 ....202 C5
Walnut Ave
Chichester PO19 ....172 F8
Rustington BN16 ....199 B5
Walnut Cl BN1 ....167 E3
Walnut Ct RH13 ....36 E1
Walnut La RH11 ....5 B1
Walnut Lodge BN14 .....182 C4
Walnut Pk RH16 ....86 B4
Walnut Tree Cotts RH14 ..77 A3
Walnut Tree Dr PO10 ....150 A3
Walnut Tree Way BN13 ...181 B5
Walnuts The RH12 ....36 C4
Walpole Ave BN12 ......181 D2
Walpole Rd BN2 ....188 D5
Walpole Terr BN2 ....188 D5
Walsham Cl PO22 ....195 F6
Walsingham Rd BN3 .....186 F6
Walstead Ho 2 RH10 .....18 D5
Walter May Ho 14 BN2 ...188 F5
Waltham Park Rd RH20 ..117 B6
Walton Ave PO21 ....195 E3
Walton Bank BN1 ....168 E5
Walton Cl BN13 ....181 F6
Walton Dr RH13 ....37 B4
Walton Heath RH10 ......19 D8
Walton La PO18 ....171 C5
Walton Lodge BN13 .....181 F6
Walton Rd PO21 ....195 E3
Walwyn Cl PO20 ....191 E5
Wandle Cl RH10 ....19 C5
Wandleys Cl PO20 ......155 F1
Wandleys Dr PO20 ......155 F1
Wandleys La BN18,PO20 .156 A2
Wandleys Lane Cvn Site
PO20 ....155 F1
Wansford Way PO22 .....196 C4
Wantage Cl RH10 ....19 C3
Wantley Hill Est BN5 ....123 F6
Wantley La RH20 ....119 E2
Wantley Rd BN14 ....162 A1
War Meml Hospl PO22 ...195 C5
Warble Heath Cl PO18 ...152 F6
Warblers Way PO22 .....195 B7
Warbleton Cl BN2 ......188 E5
Warbleton Ho 6 RH11 ....17 F3
Warblington Rd PO10 ...169 A8
Warburton Cl RH19 ......23 A8
Ward Cres PO10 ....149 C3
Warden Ct RH17 ....85 A6
Warden Park Sch RH17 ...85 A5
Wardley Cotts GU30 .....47 D4
Ware Ct RH15 ....107 D3
Warelands RH15 ....106 F1
Waremere Ct BN18 ......177 A3
Warenne Rd BN3 ....166 C4
Warleigh Rd BN1, BN2 ...207 B5
Warltersville Way RH6 ....2 C1
Warmdene Ave BN1 ....167 F6
Warmdene Cl BN1 ......167 F5
Warmdene Rd BN1 .....167 F6
Warmdene Way BN1 ....167 F6
Warminghurst Cl RH20 ..120 F5
Warminghurst Ct RH12 ...36 D5
Warner Ct RH15 ....107 A3
Warner Rd Selsey PO20 ..206 C6
Worthing BN14 ....182 F4
Warner's La PO20 ....206 C8
Warnham CE Prim Sch
RH12 ....35 F8
Warnham Cl BN12 ......181 D1
Warnham Ct BN3 ....187 C5
Warnham
Nature Reserve RH12 ....36 D6
Warnham Rd
Broadridge Heath RH12 ...35 D4
Crawley RH10 ....19 B4
Horsham RH12 ....36 B5
Worthing BN12 ....181 D2
Warnham Rise BN1 .....168 A5
Warnham Sta RH12 ......36 C8
Warninglid La RH13,RH17 .60 D2
Warninglid Prim Sch
RH17 ....61 A2
Warren Cl RH19 ....8 E3
Warren Cotts
Handcross RH17 ....61 B8
West Dean PO18 ....132 F6
Warren Cres BN16 ......200 A6
Warren Croft RH20 .....119 B1
Warren Ct Lancing BN15 ..183 D5
Southwick BN42 ....165 E1
Worthing BN14 ....182 B7
Warren Dr Crawley RH11 ..18 A8
Southwater Street RH13 ....58 A3
Warren Farm La PO19 ...152 F2
Warren Gdns BN14 ......182 B7
Warren Rd Liss Forest GU33 45 E7
Worthing BN14 ....182 B7
Warren Side GU31 ....89 D3
Warren The
Burgess Hill RH15 ....107 C1
Ferring BN12 ....200 F4
Handcross RH17 ....60 E6
Warren Way PO22 ....176 B6
Warrington Cl RH11 .....17 E2
Warrior Cl BN41 ....166 B2
Warrs Hill La BN8 ....87 E1
Warwick Cl PO21 ....194 B2
Warwick Ct Arundel BN18 .158 A2
5 Emsworth PO10 ....169 B8
8 Hove BN3 ....187 E7
Warwick Gdns BN11 ....182 E2
Warwick La BN11 ....182 E2
Warwick Mount 2 BN2 ...188 C4
Warwick Pl
Bognor Regis PO22 ....196 D5
Worthing BN11 ....182 E2
Warwick Rd BN11 ......182 E2
Warwick St BN11 ....182 E2
Warwick Wlk 3 BN43 ....164 F1
Washbrooks Farm Park
BN6 ....125 F5
Washington Bostal RH20 141 D5
Washington Cotts RH20 .141 D8
Washington Rd
Buncton BN44 ....142 E8
Crawley RH11 ....17 E3
Emsworth PO10 ....149 B1
Haywards Heath RH16 .....86 A5
Storrington RH20 ....119 E1
Washington RH20 ....141 A8
Washington St
Brighton BN2 ....207 C4
Chichester PO19 ....172 F7
Wassand Cl RH10 ....19 A6
Water La Angmering BN16 .179 F5
Buncton BN44 ....142 C8
Littlehampton BN17 ......198 D6
Selden BN16,BN13 ....180 C7
Storrington RH20 ....119 F2
Water Lane Ind Est RH20 119 E3
Water Lea RH10 ....19 A5
Water View RH6 ....2 C3
Waterbury Hill RH17 .....65 B5
Waterdyke Ave BN42 ....185 E7
Waterfield Cl 5 RH12 ....36 E3
Waterfield Fst Sch RH11 ..17 E4
Waterfield Gdns RH11 ...17 E4
Waterhall Rd BN1 ......167 C6
Waterlands La RH12 .....13 E1
Waterloo Ct 1 PO21 .....195 C2
Waterloo Ho 9 BN3 .....187 D5
Waterloo Pl 1 BN1 .....207 C3
Waterloo Rd PO22 ......196 A4
Waterloo Sq PO21 ......195 C2
Waterloo St BN3 ....187 D5
Waterplat The PO19 .....173 C8
Waters Edge
Bognor Regis PO21 ....194 E1
Pulborough RH20 ....98 A1
13 Shoreham-by-Sea BN43 .185 A6
Waters Edge Gdns PO10 .169 B8
Watersedge Gdns PO20 ..201 E6
Watersfield Rd BN14 ....182 B5
Waterside
East Grinstead RH19 ......10 B1
Horley RH6 ....2 A5
Waterside Cl RH11 ....17 E4
Waterside Dr PO19 .....172 F4
Waterside The BN17 .....198 C5
Waterstone Cl PO20 .....191 A7
Watery La
Chichester PO20 ....173 A4
Funtington PO18 ....151 A4
Watling Cl 5 BN42 ......185 E7
Watling Ct 8 BN42 ......185 E7
Watling Rd BN42 ....185 E7
Watney Cotts RH17 ......42 E1
Watson Cl RH10 ....19 C4
Watson Way PO20 ....175 E7
Watts Lodge RH15 ......107 D3
Waveney Wlk RH10 ......19 B4
Waverley Cres BN1 .....168 C1
Waverley Ct
5 Horsham RH12 ....36 B2
7 Worthing BN11 ....182 B1
Waverley Rd
Bognor Regis PO21 ....195 A4
Rustington BN16 ....199 D5
Wavertree Rd BN12 .....181 D3
Way The BN16 ....200 A4
Wayfield Ave BN3 ....166 F1
Wayfield Cl BN3 ....166 F1
Wayland Ave BN1 ....167 C3
Wayland Hts BN1 ....167 C4
Wayside Brighton BN1 ...167 D6
Crawley RH11 ....17 E4
Lancing BN15 ....183 C5
Wayside Ave BN13 ......181 D7
Weald & Downland
Open Air Mus PO18 ....133 C6
Weald Ave BN3 ....186 F8
Weald Cl Horsham RH13 ...58 E8
Hurstpierpoint BN6 ......125 F6
Weald Ct RH14 ....77 D7
Weald Day Hospl The
RH11 ....18 C6
Weald Dr RH10 ....19 A4
Weald Dyke BN43 ......184 F6
Weald Rd RH15 ....106 E3
Weald Rise RH16 ....85 E1
Weald Sch The RH14 .....77 D7
Weald The RH19 ....9 F4
Wealden Way RH16 ......85 D4
Wealdon Cl RH13 ....79 F7
Wear Cl BN13 ....181 C7
Wear Rd BN13 ....181 C7
Weare St RH5 ....14 D7
Weatherhill Cl RH6 ....2 F3
Weatherhill Rd RH6 ....2 F3
Weaver Cl RH11 ....17 E5
Weavers Cl
Burgess Hill RH15 ....107 D1
Easebourne GU29 ....70 F2
Weavers Hill BN16 ......180 A5
Weavers La BN5 ....123 E4
Weavers Mead Cotts
BN16 ....180 A6
Weavers Ring BN16 .....180 A5
Webb Cl
Bognor Regis PO21 ....205 A7
Crawley RH11 ....18 B1
Weddell Rd RH10 ....18 F3
Wedges The RH13 ....56 D5
Wedglen Ind Est GU29 ....92 D7
Wedgwood Rd PO22 .....196 A4
Weir Wood Resr
(Nature Reserve) RH19 ..22 D1
Weirbrook RH10 ....19 A3
Welbeck Ave BN3 ....186 E6
Welbeck Cl RH15 ....107 D4
Welbeck Dr RH15 ....107 D4
Welkin The RH16 ....86 B8
Well House Rd RH20 ....121 A5
Well La GU27 ....27 D6
Well Lodge PO21 ....194 A2
Well Rd PO21 ....204 F7
Welland Cl BN13 ....181 D8
Welland Rd BN13 ....181 D8
Wellcroft Cotts BN6 .....125 C5
Weller Cl RH10 ....19 D5
Wellesey Ct BN11 ....181 F1
Wellesley Ave BN12 .....181 D2
Wellesley Ct 8 BN17 ....198 E4
Wellfield RH19 ....23 C7
Wellfield Cotts GU31 .....89 D3
Wellhouse La RH15 .....127 C7
Wellingham La BN13 ....161 E1
Wellington Cl RH10 ....6 E1
Wellington Ct 1 BN11 ...182 A2
Wellington Gdns PO20 ...206 E8
Wellington Rd
Bognor Regis PO21 ....195 B3
Brighton BN2 ....207 C4
Chichester PO19 ....153 A1
Horsham RH12 ....36 D2
Portslade-by-Sea BN41 ....186 B6
Wellington St BN2 ......188 C7
Wellington Town Rd RH19 ..9 D2
Wellington Way RH6 ......1 F5
Wellingtonia Cl 8 BN1 ...167 E3
Wells Cl RH12 ....35 F2
Wells Cres
Bognor Regis PO21 ....194 E4
Chichester PO19 ....152 F1
Wells Ho GU29 ....92 E6
Wells Lea RH19 ....9 D3
Wells Mdw RH19 ....9 D4
Wells Rd RH10 ....18 E2
Wells The GU27 ....27 C6
Wellsbourne 8 BN2 .....188 F5
Wellsfield PO20 ....190 C1
Wellswood Gdns PO9 ....128 E3
Wellsworth La PO9 .....128 E3
Wellwood Cl RH13 ....37 B4
Welwyn Cl RH11 ....17 E2
Wembley Ave BN15 .....183 D6
Wembley Gdns BN15 ....183 D6
Wembury Pk RH7 ....8 E8
Wenban Rd BN11 ....182 D3
Wenceling Cotts 4
BN15 ....184 C5
Wendover Grange 3
BN3 ....187 A6
Wendy Ridge BN16 ....199 B6
Wenlock Cl RH11 ....18 A4

Wensley Gdns PO10 149 B3
Wensleydale RH11 18 C3
Wentworth 2 RH6 2 B2
Wentworth Cl
West Barnham PO22 176 B7
Worthing BN13 181 F8
Wentworth Ct 1 BN16 200 A4
Wentworth Dr RH10 19 D7
Wentworth St BN2 207 C1
Weppons 2 BN43 184 F7
Wesley Cl Crawley RH11 17 E6
Horley RH6 2 A5
Wessex Ave
Bognor Regis PO21 195 B2
East Wittering PO20 202 A7
Wessex Ct 2 BN11 182 C2
Wessex Wlk 1 BN43 164 F1
West Ashling Rd PO18 150 E3
West Ave
Bognor Regis PO21 194 F3
Crawley RH10 19 A8
Middleton-on-Sea PO22 196 F6
Shoreham-by-Sea BN15 184 A5
Worthing BN11 182 A2
West Bank BN18 177 A5
West Beach Rd BN43 184 D5
West Blatchington Inf Sch BN3 166 E4
West Blatchington Jun Sch BN3 166 E4
West Blatchington Windmill (dis) BN3 166 F2
West Bldgs BN11 182 D1
West Bracklesham Dr PO20 202 A6
West Brook Cl PO18 171 A5
West Broyle Dr PO19 152 C2
West Burton La RH20 137 E8
West Burton Rd RH20 137 D8
West Chiltington Com Fst Sch RH20 99 E1
West Chiltington La
Balls Green RH14 77 F2
Coneyhurst RH14,RH13 78 C6
West Chiltington Rd
West Chiltington RH20 100 A2
West Chiltington Common RH20 119 D5
West Cl Bognor Regis PO22 196 B4
Fernhurst GU27 49 B6
Middleton-on-Sea PO22 196 D5
West Comm RH16 85 F6
West Common Dr RH16 86 A7
West Dean CE Prim Sch PO18 132 F5
West Dean Coll PO18 133 A6
West Dean Gdns PO18 133 A6
West Dr Angmering BN16 179 D4
Bognor Regis PO21 194 B1
Brighton BN2 188 C6
Ferring BN12 200 E4
Middleton-on-Sea PO22 197 A5
West End La
Ansteadbrook GU27 28 D8
Henfield BN5 123 B5
West End Way BN15 183 D3
West Front Rd PO21 204 F7
West Furlong Ct BN6 126 A5
West Furlong La BN6 126 A5
West Green Dr RH11 18 C6
West Green Fst Sch RH11 18 C7
West Gun Copse Rd RH13 57 D5
West Head BN17 198 F4
West Hill Ardingly RH17 63 E8
Dormans Park RH19 9 E6
East Grinstead RH19 22 D8
Worthing BN13 161 E2
West Hill Cl BN13 161 E2
West Hill Pl BN1 207 A3
West Hill Rd BN1 207 A3
West Hill St BN1 207 A4
West Hoathly CE Prim Sch RH19 42 E6
West Hoathly Rd RH19 22 D4
West Hove Inf Sch BN3 186 F7
West Hove Jun Sch BN3 186 F7
West La
East Grinstead RH19 22 D8
Lancing BN15 183 E7
West Lavington CE First Sch GU29 93 A6
West Leigh RH19 22 E7
West Mallion RH16 85 F3
West Mans BN11 182 B1
West Mare La RH20 98 F1
West Mead Horley RH6 2 C3
Littlehampton BN16 199 E4
West Mead Dr PO21 194 F4
West Meade GU30 47 B2
West Onslow Cl BN12 180 E3
West Pallant PO19 173 A6
West Par Horsham RH12 36 C4
Worthing BN11 182 A1
West Park CE Fst & Mid Sch BN12 181 D2
West Park Cres RH15 106 D4
West Park Rd
Domewood RH7,RH10 8 B7
Handcross RH17 61 B7
West Point 8 BN43 185 A6
West Preston Manor BN16 199 E5
West Preston Mews BN16 199 E5
West Rd Emsworth PO10 169 A8
Portslade-by-Sea BN41 186 A7
Poynings BN45, BN6 146 E7
West Ridings BN16 199 F4
West Sands Cvn Pk PO20 206 B8
West Sands La PO20 206 B7
West Side GU28 95 B8
West St Billingshurst RH14 77 C8
Bognor Regis PO21 195 C2
Brighton BN1 207 A2
Burgess Hill RH15 106 E4
Chichester PO19 172 F6
Crawley RH11 18 D5
Ditchling BN6 127 D3
Dormansland RH7 10 A8
East Grinstead RH19 22 E8
Emsworth PO10 169 B8
Haslemere GU27 27 C6
Horsham RH12 36 C2
Lancing BN15 183 B7
Midhurst GU29 92 F7
Portslade-by-Sea BN41 186 C7
Selsey PO20 206 C7
Shoreham-by-Sea BN43 184 E7
Storrington RH20 119 D1
Worthing BN11 182 C1
West Stoke Rd PO19 152 C3
West Strand PO20 201 B8
West Tyne BN13 181 D5
West View
Fishbourne PO19 172 B6
Hove BN3 187 C8
Lindfield RH16 86 B6
West View Cotts
Breach PO10 150 A2
Lindfield RH16 86 B6
West View Ct 9 BN11 182 B2
West View Dr BN18 176 F2
West View Gdns RH19 22 E8
West Walberton La BN18 156 C2
West Way Chichester PO19 152 C2
Crawley RH10 19 A7
Hove BN3 166 D2
Littlehampton BN17 178 C3
Shoreham-by-Sea BN15 184 B5
Slinfold RH13 34 D3
Worthing BN13 161 D1
West Wittering Parochial CE Sch PO20 190 B2
West Worthing Sta BN13 182 A3
Westbourne Ave
New Brighton PO10 149 C2
Worthing BN14 182 D4
Westbourne Cl PO10 149 C2
Westbourne Gdns BN3 187 A7
Westbourne Gr BN3 187 A7
Westbourne House Sch PO20 173 F7
Westbourne Pl BN3 187 A6
Westbourne Prim Sch PO10 149 D4
Westbourne Rd PO10 149 C3
Westbourne St BN3 187 A7
Westbourne Villas BN3 186 F6
Westbrook RH18 23 E3
Westbrook Field PO18 171 A5
Westbrook Way BN42 185 F7
Westbrooke BN11 182 D2
Westbrooke Ct 12 BN11 182 D2
Westbury Ct 4 BN11 182 B2
Westbury Lodge BN18 158 B2
Westcombe 1 BN1 187 E7
Westcott Cl RH11 39 C8
Westcott Keep RH6 2 C4
Westcourt Pl BN14 182 C3
Westcourt Rd BN14 182 C4
Westdean Rd BN14 182 B5
Westdene Dr BN1 167 C5
Westdene Prim Sch BN1 167 C5
Westdown Ct 2 BN11 182 A3
Westergate Cl BN12 200 F6
Westergate Com Sch PO20 175 E7
Westergate Mews PO20 175 D8
Westergate Rd BN2 168 E4
Westergate St PO20 175 D6
Westerley Gdns PO20 202 B6
Western Ave PO10 169 A8
Western Cl BN15 183 C4
Western Espl BN3, BN41 186 D6
Western Lodge 2 BN15 183 C7
Western Par PO10 169 A7
Western Pl BN11 182 C1
Western Rd
Burgess Hill RH15 106 E3
Haywards Heath RH16 85 F4
Hove BN1, BN3 187 E5
Hurstpierpoint BN6 125 F6
Lancing BN15 183 C4
Liss GU33 45 B4
Littlehampton BN17 198 F4
Selsey PO20 206 E6
Shoreham-by-Sea BN43 184 F7
Western Rd N BN15 183 C6
Western Row BN11 182 C1
Western St BN1 187 D5
Western Terr
21 Brighton BN1 187 E5
Worthing BN15 182 F7
Westfield PO22 195 B7
Westfield Ave BN16 200 A4
Westfield Cl BN1 168 A4
Westfield Cres BN1 168 A5
Westfield Ct 1 BN17 198 F4
Westfield Rd RH11 18 B6
Westgate PO19 172 E6
Westgate Ct BN12 181 B2
Westgate L Ctr PO19 172 F5
Westgrove Gdns 10 PO10 169 B8
Westham 13 BN2 188 F5
Westhampnett Rd PO19 173 C7
Westhill Dr RH15 106 E3
Westingway PO21 195 A3
Westlake Cl BN13 181 E5
Westlake Gdns BN13 181 F5
Westland Ave BN14 182 A4
Westland Ct BN41 186 A7
Westland's Copse La GU28 73 A4
Westlands Ferring BN12 200 E5
2 Horsham RH12 36 E3
Littlehampton BN16 199 A6
Westlands La PO20 191 D5
Westlands Rd
Hunston PO20 193 A8
Lindfield RH16 86 B5
Westleas RH6 1 E5
Westloats Gdns PO21 195 A5
Westloats La PO21 195 B5
Westmead Gdns BN11 181 F2
Westmead Rd PO19 172 C6
Westminster Ct BN11 182 F2
Westminster Dr PO21 194 E3
Westminster Rd RH10 19 C5
Westmorland Ct 16 BN1 187 E7
Westmorland Dr PO22 196 B6
Westmorland Wlk 2 BN43 164 F1
Westmount 3 BN2 188 C6
Westmount Cl BN42 185 D8
Weston La PO18 150 F5
Westons Cl RH12 36 D7
Westons Hill RH13 57 B6
Westout Cotts BN14 182 F7
Westpark La BN12 181 E2
Westup Rd RH17 40 E2
Westview Terr BN14 161 E6
Westward Cl PO18 171 C5
Westward Ho PO19 172 C6
Westward La RH20 119 C6
Westway
Bognor Regis PO22 195 D5
Copthorne RH10 7 A3
Gatwick Airport RH6 6 B7
Westway Cl BN41 165 E4
Westway Gdns BN41 165 E4
Westwood Cl PO10 149 C3
Wey Lodge Cl GU30 25 D4
Weycombe Rd GU27 27 C8
Weydown Ct GU27 27 B7
Weydown Ind Est GU27 27 B7
Weydown Rd GU27 27 B7
Weyhill GU27 27 A6
Weyland Cl GU30 25 C5
Weysprings GU27 27 A6
Whapple The 7 BN17 198 F4
Wharf Rd Hove BN3 186 D6
Littlehampton BN17 198 C5
Wharf The GU29 92 F7
Wheatcroft BN17 178 C3
Wheatfield Rd PO20 206 F8
Wheatfield Way
Brighton BN2 168 F3
Horley RH6 2 C4
Wheatlands Ave PO11 189 A1
Wheatlands Cres PO11 189 A1
Wheatsheaf Cl
Burgess Hill RH15 106 E5
Horsham RH12 36 E5
Wheatsheaf La RH17 85 A6
Wheatstone Cl RH10 6 B3
Wheelbarrow Castle GU29 71 A2
Wheeler Ct RH16 85 F2
Wheeler Rd RH10 19 B4
Wheelers Way RH19 8 E3
Wheelwright La RH15 107 D1
Wheelwrights RH20 99 E1
Wheelwrights Cl BN18 158 A2
Whichelo Pl BN2 188 C6
Whippingham Rd BN2 188 C7
Whippingham St BN2 188 C8
Whistler Ave PO19 153 A1
Whistler Cl RH10 18 F3
Whistler Ct BN1 167 F1
Whitaker Pl PO20 174 B7
White Acre BN17 178 C3
White City GU29 92 E7
White Hart Ct RH12 36 C4
White Horse Cnr PO20 175 A8
White Horse Ct 2 RH20 119 D1
White Horse Sq BN44 143 D3
White Horses Way BN17 199 A5
White Lion Ct 5 BN43 184 E7
White Lodge Hove BN3 187 C8
4 Littlehampton BN17 198 E5
White St BN2 207 C2
White Styles Mid Sch BN15 183 B6
White Styles Rd BN15 183 B7
White Styles Terr BN15 183 B7
White's Cl BN6 126 A7
Whitebeam Rd BN13 181 C5
Whitebeam Way
Middleton-on-Sea PO22 196 E6
Tangmere PO20 154 D1
Whitechimney Row PO10 149 D3
Whitecroft Horley RH6 2 B4
7 Littlehampton BN16 199 C5
Whitecross St BN1 207 B3
Whitehall Dr RH11 17 E6
Whitehall Par 8 RH19 9 E1
Whitehawk Cl BN2 188 E5
Whitehawk Cres BN2 188 E5
Whitehawk Hill Rd BN2 188 D5
Whitehawk Jun Sch BN2 188 E6
Whitehawk Prim Sch BN2 188 E6
Whitehawk Rd
Brighton BN2 188 E6
Whitehawk Rd *continued*
Brighton BN2 188 F5
Whitehawk Way BN2 188 F6
Whitehorse Rd RH12 37 B6
Whitelands PO22 196 A6
Whitelea Rd BN17 198 D6
Whitelot Cl BN42 165 E2
Whitelot Way BN42 165 E2
Whitely Hill RH10 19 F1
Whiteman's Cl RH17 84 E8
Whitemans Gn RH17 84 E8
Whiterock Pl BN42 185 E7
Whites La GU27 48 E3
Whiteside Cl PO19 173 B7
Whitethorn Dr BN1 167 B4
Whitethroat La RH17 62 D6
Whiteways PO22 195 A6
Whiteways Cl
Bognor Regis PO22 195 A6
Littlehampton BN17 198 D6
Whitfield Cl PO22 195 E5
Whitfield Rd GU27 27 C8
Whitgift Wlk RH10 18 D3
Whitley Cl PO10 149 D5
Whitmore Way RH6 1 E3
Whittingehame Gdns BN1 167 F3
Whittington Coll RH19 9 A4
Whittington Ct 1 PO10 169 B8
Whittington Rd RH10 18 E3
Whittle Way RH10 6 A3
Whitwell Hatch GU27 27 D5
Whitworth Ho 3 BN11 182 B3
Whitworth Rd RH11 5 D2
Whyke Cl PO19 173 B4
Whyke Ct PO19 173 B4
Whyke La PO19 173 B5
Whyke Rd PO19, PO20 173 B5
Whylands Ave BN13 181 D8
Whylands Cl BN13 181 D8
Whylands Cres BN13 181 D8
Whytemead Fst Sch BN14 182 E5
Whytings RH13 59 C6
Wick Cl PO22 196 B5
Wick Farm Rd BN17 198 C6
Wick Hall BN3 187 D6
Wick La Bognor Regis PO22 196 B5
Easebourne GU29 71 B4
Wick Par BN17 178 D3
Wick St BN17 178 D3
Wickbourne Cty Inf Sch BN17 198 C6
Wickbourne Ho BN17 198 C6
Wickets The RH15 106 F5
Wickham Cl
Haywards Heath RH16 85 F7
Horley RH6 1 F4
Wickham Dr BN6 126 C5
Wickham Hill BN6 126 C4
Wickham Way RH16 85 E7
Wickhurst Cl BN41 165 F2
Wickhurst Gdns RH12 35 E3
Wickhurst La
Broadbridge Heath RH12 35 E3
Broadbridge Heath RH12 35 E2
Wickhurst Rd BN41 166 A2
Wickhurst Rise BN41 165 F3
Wickland Ct RH10 18 D3
Wickor Cl PO10 149 C2
Wickor Way PO10 149 C2
Wicks Cotts BN18 177 C4
Wicks Rd RH14 77 C8
Widdicombe Way BN2 168 E2
Widewater Cl 1 BN15 184 C5
Widewater Ct 7 BN15 184 C5
Widgeon La PO20 206 B8
Widgeon Way RH12 36 C5
Widworthy Mews 7 PO21 195 B3
Wight Way PO20 206 E5
Wigmore Cl BN1 168 B1
Wigmore Rd BN14 182 D6
Wigmore Trad Est BN14 182 F5
Wilberforce Cl RH11 39 C8
Wilberforce Way RH13 58 A4
Wilbury Ave BN3 187 C8
Wilbury Cres BN3 187 D7
Wilbury Gdns BN3 187 C8
Wilbury Gr BN3 187 C6
Wilbury Grange 9 BN3 187 C6
Wilbury Lodge 13 BN3 187 C6
Wilbury Rd BN3 187 C6
Wilbury Villas BN3 187 C7
Wilby Ave BN42 165 E1
Wild Orchid Way RH13 58 A3
Wild Park Cl BN2 168 E3
Wild Park Nature Trail BN2 168 D5
Wildacre Cl RH14 31 D3
Wilderness Rd BN6 126 A6
Wilderness Rise RH19 10 A6
Wilderness The RH16 86 B8
Wilderwick Rd RH19, RH7 10 A5
Wildfowl & Wetlands Trust Nature Reserve BN18 158 C5
Wildgoose Dr RH12 35 F3
Wildwood La GU6 11 C5
Wilfrid Rd BN3 166 D1
Wiliamson Cott Homes BN3 187 A7
Wilkinson Ct 4 RH11 18 B1
Willard Way RH20 120 F5
Willett Cl GU28 115 B7
William Allen La RH16 86 B6
William Morris Way RH11 39 C8
William Penn Sch RH13 78 E2
William Rd PO19 173 D6
William St
Bognor Regis PO21 195 D3
Brighton BN2 207 B2
Southwick BN41 186 B7
William Sutton Ho BN1 207 B2
Williams Rd
Broadbridge PO18 171 C7
Shoreham-by-Sea BN43 185 C8
Williams Way RH10 19 B5
Willingdon Rd BN2 168 E1
Willmington Ct 2 BN11 182 B1
Willoughby Ho BN12 181 C2
Willow Ave BN16 199 E5
Willow Brean RH6 1 E5
Willow Brook
Littlehampton BN17 178 C3
Middleton-on-Sea PO22 197 A5
Willow Cl Crawley RH10 18 E8
East Grinstead RH19 9 D3
Hurstpierpoint BN6 125 F7
Liphook GU30 25 D3
2 Shoreham-by-Sea BN15 184 C5
Steyning BN44 143 D4
West Chiltington Common RH20 119 E6
Willow Cnr RH6 4 F7
Willow Cres BN13 181 C5
Willow Ct Chichester PO19 172 D6
Horley RH6 2 B6
4 Hove BN3 187 D7
Worthing BN11 182 A3
Willow Dr RH14 77 D8
Willow Gdns
Hurstpierpoint BN6 126 A7
Liphook GU30 25 D3
Westbourne PO10 149 D4
Willow Ho Hassocks BN6 126 E5
Worthing BN12 181 A4
Willow Mead 8 RH19 22 F8
Willow Pk RH16 86 B4
Willow Rd Horsham RH12 37 B5
Liss GU33 45 B4
Willow Ridge RH10 21 A3
Willow Way
Ashington RH20 121 A4
Bognor Regis PO21 194 B1
Hurstpierpoint BN6 125 F8
Willow Wlk GU28 95 E7
Willowbed Ave PO19 173 C4
Willowbed Dr PO19 173 C4
Willowbrook Pk BN15 184 A5
Willowbrook Rd BN14 183 A4
Willowbrook Way BN6 127 A3
Willowfield 4 RH11 18 D5
Willowhale Ave PO21 194 D2
Willowhale Gn PO21 194 C2
Willowhayne Ave BN16 200 A4
Willowhayne Cl 4 BN16 200 A4
Willowhayne Cres 5 BN16 200 A4
Willowhayne Ct 9 BN16 200 A4
Willows Fst Sch The BN15 183 E7
Willows The
5 Bognor Regis PO21 195 C4
2 Brighton BN2 207 C5
Burgess Hill RH15 107 B5
Findon BN14 161 E6
Ford BN18 177 E5
Hassocks BN6 126 E4
Horsham RH12 36 D5
4 Lancing BN15 183 E5
Pulborough RH20 98 A1
Rustington BN16 199 D6
Selsey PO20 206 E8
Storrington RH20 119 C1
Wills Cl BN18 177 B2
Wilman Gdns PO21 194 D2
Wilmington Cl
Brighton BN1 168 A5
Crawley RH11 18 C1
Hassocks BN6 126 F4
Wilmington Par BN1 167 F5
Wilmington Way
Brighton BN1 168 A5
Haywards Heath RH16 86 A5
Wilmot Ct 6 BN43 185 C8
Wilmot Rd BN43 185 C8
Wilson Ave BN2 188 F6
Wilson Cl Chichester PO19 172 D7
Crawley RH10 19 D3
Wilson Ct BN18 177 B2
Wilton 1 RH16 85 D6
Wilton Cl
Bracklesham PO20 202 C5
Partridge Green RH13 103 A3
Rustington BN16 179 B3
Wilton Dr BN16 179 B3
Wilton Villas RH17 41 A1
Wiltshire Croft Ct PO20 206 D7
Wiltshire Ho 10 BN2 207 C2
Wimbledon Ct BN14 182 D5
Wimblehurst Ct RH12 36 C4
Wimblehurst Rd RH12 36 C4
Wimborne Ct BN11 181 F2
Wimbourne Ho RH11 18 C6
Wimland Hill RH12 16 D2
Wimland Rd Faygate RH12 16 D1
Rusper RH12 16 C4
Wimlands La RH12 16 E3
Wimrod Ho 3 RH20 119 E1
Wincanton Cl RH10 19 D6
Winchelsea Ct 8 BN11 182 A1
Winchelsea Gdns BN11 182 A1

Winchester Ct
Southwater RH13 .... 58 A2
Worthing BN11 .... 182 B2
Winchester Dr PO19 .... 172 F8
Winchester Ho BN12 .... 181 A3
Winchester Rd
Crawley RH10 .... 18 E2
Rustington BN16 .... 199 E6
Worthing BN11 .... 182 C2
Winchester St BN1 .... 207 B5
Wincombe Rd BN1 .... 167 D1
Winden Ave PO19 .... 173 B6
Windermere 2 BN16 .... 199 C5
Windermere Cres BN12 .... 181 D5
Windermere Ct
9 Brighton BN2 .... 188 C6
Worthing BN12 .... 181 B2
Windermere Rd RH16 .... 85 F4
Windlesham Ave
BN1, BN3 .... 187 E6
Windlesham Cl BN41 .... 166 A1
Windlesham Ct
14 Brighton BN1 .... 187 E7
Littlehampton BN17 .... 178 D3
5 Worthing BN11 .... 182 A1
Windlesham Gdns
Brighton BN1, BN3 .... 187 E7
East Preston BN16 .... 200 A6
Shoreham-by-Sea BN43 .... 184 F8
Windlesham House Sch
RH20 .... 141 D3
Windlesham Rd
Brighton BN1 .... 187 E6
Shoreham-by-Sea BN43 .... 184 F8
Windlesham Sch BN1 .... 187 E8
Windmill Ave BN6 .... 126 F3
Windmill Cl
Ashington RH20 .... 121 A5
Bognor Regis PO21 .... 194 B1
Horley RH6 .... 2 B3
Horsham RH13 .... 37 A4
Hove BN3 .... 166 F2
Upper Beeding BN44 .... 144 B2
Windmill Copse RH20 .... 119 E2
Windmill Ct Crawley RH10 .... 18 D8
East Wittering PO20 .... 201 F7
Tangmere PO20 .... 154 D1
Windmill Dr Brighton BN1 .... 167 C6
Burgess Hill RH15 .... 107 A4
Rustington BN16 .... 199 D6
Windmill Field PO18 .... 171 A5
Windmill La
Ashurst Wood RH19 .... 23 C7
East Grinstead RH19 .... 9 D3
Nep Town BN5 .... 123 E4
Windmill Par
Rustington BN16 .... 199 C6
Southwick BN42 .... 165 E1
Windmill Platt RH17 .... 61 C8
Windmill Rd
Littlehampton BN17 .... 198 D4
Southwick BN42 .... 165 E1
Windmill St BN2 .... 207 C3
Windmill Terr 20 BN2 .... 207 C3
Windmill View BN1 .... 168 B7
Windmills Jun Sch BN6 .... 127 A3
Windrum Cl RH12 .... 57 F8
Windrush Cl Crawley RH11 .... 17 F4
Worthing BN13 .... 181 C8
Windsor Cl
Bognor Regis PO21 .... 194 E4
Crawley RH11 .... 18 C2
Haywards Heath RH16 .... 85 E2
Hove BN3 .... 167 A3
Rustington BN16 .... 179 B3
Southwater RH13 .... 58 A1
Windsor Ct Brighton BN1 .... 207 A2
Brighton, Withdean BN1 .... 167 D4
5 Horsham RH13 .... 36 F3
Worthing BN11 .... 183 A2
Windsor Dr
East Wittering PO20 .... 201 F7
Rustington BN16 .... 179 B3
Windsor Lodge 5 BN3 .... 187 B6
Windsor Pl RH19 .... 23 A8
Windsor Rd
Chichester PO19 .... 173 D6
Selsey PO20 .... 206 E6
Worthing BN11 .... 182 F3
Windsor St BN1 .... 207 A2
Windsor Way BN15 .... 184 B6
Windward Cl BN17 .... 199 A5
Windyridge RH11 .... 18 A5
Wineham La BN5,RH17 .... 104 D5
Winfield Ave BN1 .... 167 F6
Winfield Cl Brighton BN1 .... 167 F5
Portslade-by-Sea BN41 .... 166 A3
Winfield Gr RH5 .... 3 A8
Winfield Way PO10 .... 149 B4
Wingle Tye Rd RH15 .... 127 A8
Winguard Way PO19 .... 173 A5
Winkfield Ct RH16 .... 85 D5
Winkhurst Way RH15 .... 107 D1
Winnals Pk RH16 .... 85 D5
Winner Way RH6 .... 5 D6
Winnet Way RH13 .... 58 A2
Winnipeg Cl GU30 .... 25 C3
Winston Bsns Ctr BN15 .... 183 C5
Winston Cl PO21 .... 194 F6
Winston Cres PO21 .... 194 F6
Winston Ct PO19 .... 152 F3
Winston Rd BN15 .... 183 D4
Winter Knoll The BN17 .... 198 F5
Winterbourne RH12 .... 36 F7
Winterbourne Cl BN13 .... 181 B5
Winterbourne Ct BN13 .... 181 B5
Winterbourne Rd PO19 .... 153 A2
Winterbourne Way BN13 .... 181 B5
Winterfold RH10 .... 19 A3
Winterpit Cl RH13 .... 59 D6
Winterpit La RH13 .... 59 E6
Winters Cotts 8 GU29 .... 92 E7
Winters La GU29 .... 71 A4
Winterton Ct RH13 .... 36 D2
Winterton Lodge BN17 .... 198 E5
Winterton Way BN43 .... 185 B6
Winton Lodge BN13 .... 181 D7
Winton Pl BN11 .... 182 D3
Wire Mill La RH7 .... 8 F8
Wisborough Ct
Crawley RH11 .... 17 F3
Worthing BN13 .... 181 F6
Wisborough Gdns RH14 .... 76 D8
Wisborough Green
Prim Sch RH14 .... 54 C1
Wisborough La RH20 .... 119 E1
Wisden Ave RH15 .... 106 E5
Wisden Ct BN14 .... 162 A1
Wish Ct BN3 .... 186 E8
Wish Rd BN3 .... 186 E6
Wisley Ct BN11 .... 182 A2
Wiston Ave
Stockbridge PO19 .... 172 E4
Worthing BN14 .... 182 B5
Wiston Bsns Pk RH20 .... 120 E2
Wiston Cl BN14 .... 182 B5
Wiston Ct Crawley RH11 .... 17 F3
12 Shoreham-by-Sea BN43 .... 185 C8
Wiston Rd BN2 .... 188 F6
Wiston Way BN2 .... 188 F7
Withdean Ave
Brighton BN1 .... 167 D2
Worthing BN12 .... 181 B1
Withdean Cl BN1 .... 167 D3
Withdean Court Ave BN1 .... 167 D3
Withdean Cres BN1 .... 167 E3
Withdean Ct 7 BN1 .... 167 E3
Withdean Hall BN1 .... 167 E3
Withdean Rd BN1 .... 167 D3
Withdean Rise BN1 .... 167 D3
Withdene Stad
(Brighton & Hove
Albion FC) BN1 .... 167 D3
Wither Dale RH6 .... 1 E4
Withey Brook RH6 .... 1 D1
Withey Mdws RH6 .... 1 D1
Withy Bush RH15 .... 106 E5
Withypitts RH10 .... 21 A3
Withypitts E RH10 .... 21 A3
Wittering Rd PO11 .... 189 B2
Wivelsfield Cty Prim Sch
RH17 .... 107 F6
Wivelsfield Rd RH16 .... 85 E2
Wivelsfield Sta RH15 .... 107 C4
Woburn Ct BN11 .... 182 C1
Woburn Pl BN1 .... 168 F5
Woburn Rd RH11 .... 18 A4
Woelfs Cl RH20 .... 121 A5
Woking Ct BN16 .... 199 E6
Wold Cl RH11 .... 17 F4
Woldhurstlea Cl RH11 .... 18 A4
Wolseley Rd Brighton BN1 .... 168 D6
Portslade-by-Sea BN41 .... 186 A8
Wolsey Cl PO21 .... 194 B1
Wolstead Lodge 8 RH16 .... 85 F3
Wolstenbury Rd BN16 .... 179 C3
Wolstonbury Cl
Crawley RH11 .... 18 C4
Hurstpierpoint BN6 .... 126 B4
Wolstonbury Ct RH15 .... 107 B2
Wolstonbury Rd BN3 .... 187 E7
Wolstonbury Way RH15 .... 107 B2
Wolstonbury Wlk 7
BN43 .... 164 F1
Wolverstone Dr BN1 .... 168 C2
Wolverton Cl RH6 .... 1 F1
Wolverton Gdns RH6 .... 1 F2
Wood Acre Ct 9 PO21 .... 195 D4
Wood Cl RH1 .... 2 A8
Wood End RH12 .... 37 C5
Wood La BN5 .... 144 F7
Wood Ride RH16 .... 85 D3
Wood St
Bognor Regis PO21 .... 195 B2
East Grinstead RH19 .... 9 D1
Wood View BN18 .... 158 A2
Wood's Mill
Countryside Ctr BN5 .... 144 F8
Woodard Rd BN15 .... 183 F7
Woodards View BN43 .... 184 D5
Woodberry La
Rowland's Castle PO9 .... 128 F1
Stubbermere PO10, PO9 .... 149 B7
Woodbine Ct 8 PO21 .... 195 D4
Woodborough Cl PO20 .... 202 C5
Woodbourne Ave BN1 .... 168 A4
Woodbourne Cl GU33 .... 45 C4
Woodbridge Ct RH12 .... 37 A5
Woodbridge Pk BN16 .... 200 A5
Woodbury Ave RH19 .... 10 B1
Woodbury Cl RH19 .... 23 B8
Woodcock Hill RH19, RH7 .... 8 F6
Woodcote Graffham GU28 .... 114 A8
Horley RH6 .... 2 C4
Woodcote La
Harwoods Green RH20 .... 97 D5
Littlehampton BN17 .... 178 D5
Woodcote Rd RH18 .... 23 F2
Woodcourt RH11 .... 18 C1
Woodcrest Rd RH15 .... 106 F1
Woodcroft RH15 .... 106 F5
Woodcroft Rd RH11 .... 17 D4
Woodcutters RH17 .... 86 F3
Wooddale La RH14 .... 56 A2
Woodend
Bognor Regis PO21 .... 195 A4
West Ashling PO18 .... 151 C5
Woodend Cl RH10 .... 19 A8
Woodfield RH13 .... 57 F1
Woodfield Cl
Bognor Regis PO21 .... 205 A7
Crawley RH10 .... 18 E7
Tangmere PO20 .... 154 D1
Woodfield Park Rd PO10 .... 169 D8
Woodfield Rd
Crawley RH10 .... 18 F7
Rudgwick RH12 .... 33 D7
Woodfield Terr RH13 .... 81 E1
Woodgate Cl PO20 .... 175 D5
Woodgate Pk PO20 .... 175 D6
Woodgate Rd PO20 .... 175 D5
Woodgates Cl RH13 .... 36 F3
Woodhall Cl RH17 .... 84 F7
Woodhatch RH13 .... 57 F2
Woodhayes RH6 .... 2 B4
Woodhorn Cotts PO20 .... 174 E6
Woodhorn La PO20 .... 174 D6
Woodhouse Cl BN3 .... 186 E7
Woodhouse La
Blendworth PO8 .... 128 C6
Rowland's Castle PO8, PO9 .... 128 E4
Woodhouse Rd BN3 .... 186 E7
Wooding Gr 14 RH11 .... 18 B1
Woodland Ave
Burgess Hill RH15 .... 107 C4
Hove BN3 .... 167 B3
Worthing BN13 .... 161 F1
Woodland Cl
Burgess Hill RH15 .... 107 C4
Five Oaks RH14 .... 55 E6
Horsham RH13 .... 37 B4
Hove BN3 .... 167 B2
Woodland Cotts RH20 .... 120 A7
Woodland Cres RH15 .... 107 C4
Woodland Ct
Burgess Hill RH15 .... 107 B3
Hove BN3 .... 167 B4
Woodland Dr
Crawley Down RH10 .... 21 B8
Hove BN3 .... 167 B3
Woodland La RH13 .... 38 C3
Woodland Par BN3 .... 167 B3
Woodland Pl PO19 .... 153 A3
Woodland Rd PO20 .... 206 D6
Woodland Villas PO20 .... 155 F1
Woodland Way
Brighton BN1 .... 167 F4
Horsham RH13 .... 37 B4
Woodlands Crawley RH10 .... 19 D8
Horley RH6 .... 2 D4
Hove BN3 .... 167 C2
Woodlands Ave
New Brighton PO10 .... 149 B3
Rustington BN16 .... 199 C6
Woodlands Cl
Angmering BN16 .... 180 A7
Clapham BN13 .... 160 F1
Crawley Down RH10 .... 21 B7
Rustington BN16 .... 199 C6
Woodlands Cotts BN16 .... 199 C6
Woodlands La
Chichester PO19 .... 172 F8
Haslemere GU27 .... 26 F7
Heath Common RH20 .... 120 C3
Hill Side GU33 .... 45 D3
Walderton PO18 .... 130 B2
Woodlands Pk BN18 .... 176 F3
Woodlands Rd
Bognor Regis PO22 .... 195 B6
East Grinstead RH19 .... 10 A4
Haywards Heath RH16 .... 85 F4
Littlehampton BN17 .... 198 E4
Woodlands The BN1 .... 167 E5
Woodlands Way
Billingshurst RH14 .... 77 E6
Southwater RH13 .... 79 E8
Woodlands Wlk RH13 .... 59 C5
Woodlea Rd BN13 .... 182 A4
Woodleigh Rd RH15 .... 107 C4
Woodmancote Ct RH12 .... 36 D5
Woodmancote La
PO10, PO18 .... 150 B4
Woodmancote Rd BN14 .... 182 B4
Woodmans Hill RH11 .... 18 C2
Woodpecker Cres RH15 .... 106 D3
Woodpecker Ct GU28 .... 95 F7
Woodpecker La RH20 .... 119 E1
Woodpecker Rd GU28 .... 95 E7
Woodpecker Way BN13 .... 181 C5
Woodridge Cl RH16 .... 86 A3
Woodroffe Wlk PO10 .... 149 B4
Woodroyd Ave RH6 .... 1 F2
Woodroyd Gdns RH6 .... 1 F1
Woodruff Ave BN3 .... 167 C2
Woodruff Bsns Ctr The
PO19 .... 172 E5
Woods Hill Cl RH19 .... 23 D6
Woods Hill La RH19 .... 23 D6
Woods Ho BN3 .... 187 A8
Woods Mill Cl BN5 .... 144 E6
Woods Way BN12 .... 181 C3
Woodsdale Ct BN14 .... 182 E5
Woodside Horsham RH13 .... 37 B4
West Barnham PO22 .... 176 B6
Woodside Ave BN1 .... 167 D2
Woodside Cl
Shermanbury RH13 .... 103 D4
Storrington RH20 .... 119 E2
Woodside Ct 6 BN17 .... 198 E4
Woodside Lodge BN1 .... 167 D2
Woodside Rd Crawley RH10 .... 18 F8
Woodside Rd *continued*
Worthing BN14 .... 182 B4
Woodsland Cross RH16 .... 64 E3
Woodslands Cl BN6 .... 126 F4
Woodslands Rd BN6 .... 126 F4
Woodstock RH19 .... 9 C2
Woodstock Cl RH12 .... 36 D5
Woodstock Gdns PO21 .... 194 F2
Woodview BN43 .... 164 F1
Woodview Cl BN1 .... 168 D6
Woodview Ct 13 BN43 .... 164 F1
Woodwards RH11 .... 18 C1
Woodwards Cl RH15 .... 107 B1
Wool La GU29 .... 92 F7
Woolbeding La GU29 .... 70 B4
Woolborough Cl RH10 .... 18 E7
Woolborough La
Crawley RH10 .... 19 A8
Crawley RH10 .... 5 F1
Horley RH1 .... 2 F8
Woolborough Rd RH10 .... 18 E7
Wooldridge Wlk BN17 .... 177 D1
Woolmer Hill Rd
GU26, GU27 .... 26 D7
Woolmer Hill Sch GU27 .... 26 D7
Woolmer La GU30 .... 25 C8
Woolmer St PO10 .... 149 A4
Woolstaplers The PO19 .... 172 F6
Woolven Cl RH15 .... 106 E1
Woolven Row BN5 .... 123 F5
Wophams La PO20 .... 192 D7
Worcester Cl PO21 .... 194 E3
Worcester Ct 1 BN3 .... 187 E6
Worcester Rd
Chichester PO19 .... 152 F2
Crawley RH10 .... 18 E2
Worcester Villas BN3 .... 186 C7
Wordsworth Cl RH10 .... 19 B8
Wordsworth Gdns PO22 .... 196 D6
Wordsworth Pl RH12 .... 36 E7
Wordsworth Rd BN11 .... 182 C1
Wordsworth Rise 6 RH19 .... 9 C1
Wordsworth St BN3 .... 187 A7
Worms La PO22 .... 196 E7
Worsted La RH19 .... 23 B8
Worth Park Ave RH10 .... 19 C7
Worth Rd RH10 .... 19 C6
Worth Sch RH10 .... 20 B1
Worth Way RH10 .... 19 E5
Worthing High Sch BN14 .... 182 C4
Worthing Hospl BN11 .... 182 E3
Worthing Mus
& Art Gallery BN11 .... 182 D2
Worthing Rd
Dial Post RH13 .... 101 E3
East Preston BN16 .... 199 F6
Littlehampton BN17 .... 178 E3
Rustington BN16, BN17 .... 179 B3
Southwater RH13 .... 57 F2
Tower Hill RH12, RH13 .... 58 A7
West Grinstead RH13 .... 102 A6
Worthing
Sixth Form Coll BN13 .... 181 E3
Worthing Sta BN11 .... 182 C3
Wr Twr Bldgs 3 PO21 .... 195 D3
Wray Cl RH19 .... 23 D6
Wraysbury Park Dr PO10 .... 149 B4
Wren Cl Burgess Hill RH15 .... 106 D3
Horsham RH12 .... 36 D7
Pulborough RH20 .... 98 B2
Wren Cres PO22 .... 195 B6
Wren Ct RH10 .... 18 E3
Wren Ctr The PO10 .... 149 C3
Wrenfield Pl 9 PO21 .... 195 C2
Wrentham Ho RH15 .... 107 B3
Wright Cl RH10 .... 19 C2
Wroxham Way PO22 .... 195 F6
Wroxham Wlk RH10 .... 19 B4
Wyatt Cl RH14 .... 54 B1
Wyatt Ct PO20 .... 201 F7
Wyatts La RH17 .... 65 D5
Wyberlye Rd RH15 .... 107 A4
Wyberton Ho PO19 .... 153 A3
Wychcroft 4 BN17 .... 198 D5
Wychperry Rd RH16 .... 85 D5
Wychwood RH14 .... 31 D3
Wychwood Cl PO21 .... 194 E1
Wychwood Gdns BN11 .... 183 B3
Wychwood Wlk PO21 .... 194 E1
Wyck Ct BN41 .... 186 A7
Wycliffe Ct RH11 .... 17 E3
Wyde Feld PO21 .... 194 F2
Wye Cl RH11 .... 39 C8
Wye Ho BN11 .... 182 B2
Wyke Ave BN11 .... 182 E2
Wyke La N PO22 .... 196 C6
Wykeham Cl BN44 .... 143 D3
Wykeham Ct BN11 .... 182 C2
Wykeham Rd BN11 .... 182 C2
Wykeham Terr BN1 .... 207 A2
Wykeham Way RH15 .... 107 C2
Wykwood GU30 .... 25 D4
Wyld Green La GU33 .... 45 D5
Wyncombe Cl RH20 .... 97 B3
Wyndham Bsns Pk
GU29 .... 92 D7
Wyndham Lea RH20 .... 119 D6
Wyndham Rd GU28 .... 95 F7
Wyndham St BN2 .... 207 C1
Wynlea Cl RH10 .... 21 A8
Wynnes Mews BN3 .... 187 A7
Wynnstay RH15 .... 107 B2
Wysemead RH6 .... 2 C4
Wyshe The BN45 .... 147 C6
Wythering Cl PO21 .... 204 F7
Wythwood RH16 .... 85 E1
Wyvern Cl PO20 .... 154 E1
Wyvern Ct 6 BN11 .... 182 C1

Y

Yachtsmens Cotts PO18 .... 171 C5
Yapton CE Prim Sch
BN18 .... 176 F4
Yapton La BN18 .... 176 F7
Yapton Rd
Barnham BN18, PO22 .... 176 D4
Horsemere
Green BN17,BN18 .... 177 C1
Middleton-on-Sea BN18,PO22
BN18,PO22 .... 196 E7
Yarbrook PO18 .... 152 E7
Yardlea Cl PO9 .... 128 D1
Yardley St BN1 .... 207 B5
Yarmouth Cl RH10 .... 19 A4
Yarrow Cl RH12 .... 36 E5
Yattendon Rd RH6 .... 2 B3
Yattendon Sch RH6 .... 2 A4
Yeoman Rd BN13 .... 181 B5
Yeoman Way BN13 .... 181 B4
Yeomans Acre PO21 .... 194 F3
Yeomans Field PO18 .... 150 D1
Yeomans La GU30 .... 25 A4
Yew Ct Crawley RH11 .... 18 D5
1 East Grinstead RH19 .... 9 D2
Yew La RH19 .... 9 B3
Yew Tree Cl
Bognor Regis PO22 .... 195 B6
Horley RH6 .... 2 A4
Lancing BN15 .... 183 E5
Yew Tree Cotts RH15 .... 107 B3
Yew Tree Ct RH17 .... 84 F6
Yew Tree Pl GU33 .... 45 C4
Yew Tree Rd RH6 .... 4 E7
Yewlands Wlk RH11 .... 17 D4
Yewtree Cl RH13 .... 81 E2
York Ave
East Grinstead RH19 .... 23 A8
Hove BN3 .... 187 E6
York Chase PO19 .... 152 F1
York Cl Horsham RH13 .... 36 F3
Southwater RH13 .... 58 A1
York Ct 13 BN3 .... 187 E7
York Gdns BN17 .... 198 D5
York Gr BN1 .... 207 A4
York Hill BN1 .... 207 B4
York Ho
Portslade-by-Sea BN41 .... 186 B8
Worthing BN11 .... 183 A3
York Lodge 11 BN11 .... 182 C3
York Pl Brighton BN1, BN2 .... 207 B3
Hove BN3 .... 187 E6
York Rd
Bognor Regis PO21 .... 195 D3
Burgess Hill RH15 .... 106 D2
Chichester PO19 .... 173 C5
Crawley RH10 .... 18 E2
Hove BN1, BN3 .... 187 E6
Littlehampton BN17 .... 198 D5
Selsey PO20 .... 206 E5
Worthing BN11 .... 182 E2
York Villas BN1 .... 207 A4
Yorkhurst Hill PO18 .... 112 F1
Yorkwood GU33 .... 45 B4
Young St 4 PO19 .... 153 A2
Youngsmere Cl BN1 .... 168 B6

Z

Zachary Merton
Com Hospl BN16 .... 199 D4

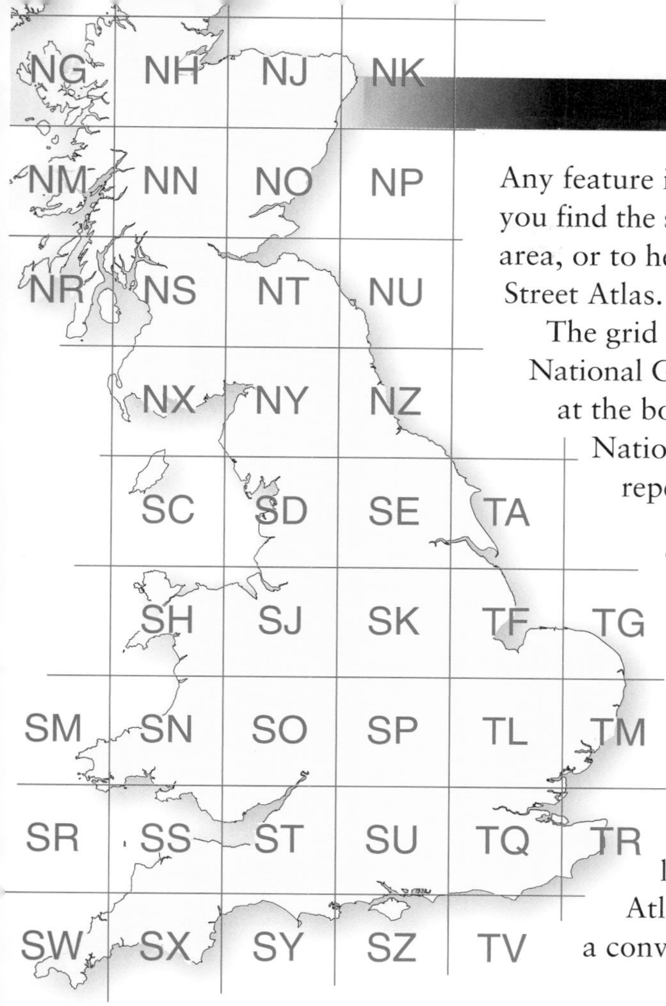

NG
NH
NJ
NK
NM
NN
NO
NP
NR
NS
NT
NU
NX
NY
NZ
SC
SD
SE
TA
SH
SJ
SK
TF
TG
SM
SN
SO
SP
TL
TM
SR
SS
ST
SU
TQ
TR
SW
SX
SY
SZ
TV

Using the Ordnance Survey National Grid

Any feature in this atlas can be given a unique reference to help you find the same feature on other Ordnance Survey maps of the area, or to help someone else locate you if they do not have a Street Atlas.

The grid squares in this atlas match the Ordnance Survey National Grid and are at 500 metre intervals. The small figures at the bottom and sides of every other grid line are the National Grid kilometre values (**00** to **99** km) and are repeated across the country every 100 km (see left).

To give a unique National Grid reference you need to locate where in the country you are. The country is divided into 100 km squares with each square given a unique two-letter reference. Use the administrative map to determine in which 100 km square a particular page of this atlas falls.

The bold letters and numbers between each grid line (**A** to **F**, **1** to **8**) are for use within a specific Street Atlas only, and when used with the page number, are a convenient way of referencing these grid squares.

Example *The railway bridge over DARLEY GREEN RD in grid square B1*

Step 1: Identify the two-letter reference, in this example the page is in **SP**

Step 2: Identify the 1 km square in which the railway bridge falls. Use the figures in the southwest corner of this square: Eastings **17**, Northings **74**. This gives a unique reference: **SP 17 74**, accurate to 1 km.

Step 3: To give a more precise reference accurate to 100 m you need to estimate how many tenths along and how many tenths up this 1 km square the feature is (to help with this the 1 km square is divided into four 500 m squares). This makes the bridge about **8** tenths along and about **1** tenth up from the southwest corner.

This gives a unique reference: **SP 178 741**, accurate to 100 m.

Eastings (read from left to right along the bottom) come before Northings (read from bottom to top). If you have trouble remembering say to yourself "Along the hall, THEN up the stairs"!

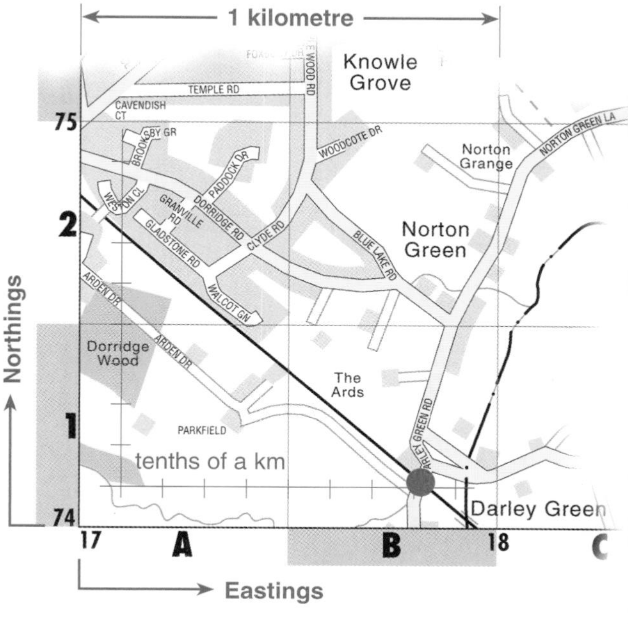

1 kilometre
Knowle Grove
TEMPLE RD
CAVENDISH CT
75
WOODCOTE DR
Norton Grange
NORTON GREEN LA
PADDOCK DR
GRANVILLE RD
DORRIDGE RD
CLYDE RD
GLADSTONE RD
BLUE LAKE RD
Norton Green
2
ARDEN DR
WALCOT GN
Dorridge Wood
The Ards
PARKFIELD
1
tenths of a km
Darley Green
74
17
A
B
18
C
Northings
Eastings

Notes

Addresses

Name and Address	Telephone	Page	Grid reference